International Directory of
COMPANY
HISTORIES

International Directory of
COMPANY HISTORIES

VOLUME 36

Editor
Jay P. Pederson

St. James Press

AN IMPRINT OF THE GALE GROUP

DETROIT • NEW YORK • SAN FRANCISCO
LONDON • BOSTON • WOODBRIDGE, CT

STAFF

Jay P. Pederson, *Editor*

Miranda H. Ferrara, *Project Manager*

Erin Bealmear, Joann Cerrito, Jim Craddock, Steve Cusack,
Kristin Hart, Melissa Hill, Margaret Mazurkiewicz, Carol Schwartz,
Christine Tomassini, Michael J. Tyrkus, *St. James Press Editorial Staff*

Peter M. Gareffa, *Managing Editor, St. James Press*

Library of Congress Catalog Number: 89-190943

British Library Cataloguing in Publication Data

International directory of company histories. Vol. 36
I. Jay P. Pederson
338.7409

ISBN 1-55862-441-4

Printed in the United States of America
Published simultaneously in the United Kingdom

St. James Press is an imprint of The Gale Group

Cover photograph: Royal Exchange, London
(courtesy: Jay P. Pederson)

10 9 8 7 6 5 4 3 2 1

CONTENTS _____

Company Histories

PREFACE

The St. James Press series *The International Directory of Company Histories (IDCH)* is intended for reference use by students, business people, librarians, historians, economists, investors, job candidates, and others who seek to learn more about the historical development of the world's most important companies. To date, *IDCH* has covered over 4,775 companies in 36 volumes.

Inclusion Criteria

Most companies chosen for inclusion in *IDCH* have achieved a minimum of US$50 million in annual sales and are leading influences in their industries or geographical locations. Companies may be publicly held, private, or nonprofit. State-owned companies that are important in their industries and that may operate much like public or private companies also are included. Wholly owned subsidiaries and divisions are profiled if they meet the requirements for inclusion. Entries on companies that have had major changes since they were last profiled may be selected for updating.

The *IDCH* series highlights 10% private and nonprofit companies, and features updated entries on approximately 45 companies per volume.

Entry Format

Each entry begins with the company's legal name, the address of its headquarters, its telephone, toll-free, and fax numbers, and its web site. A statement of public, private, state, or parent ownership follows. A company with a legal name in both English and the language of its headquarters country is listed by the English name, with the native-language name in parentheses.

The company's founding or earliest incorporation date, the number of employees, and the most recent available sales figures follow. Sales figures are given in local currencies with equivalents in U.S. dollars. For some private companies, sales figures are estimates and indicated by the abbreviation *est.* The entry lists the exchanges on which a company's stock is traded and its ticker symbol, as well as the company's NAIC codes.

Entries generally contain a *Company Perspectives* box which provides a short summary of the company's mission, goals, and ideals, a *Key Dates* box highlighting milestones in the company's history, lists of *Principal Subsidiaries, Principal Divisions, Principal Operating Units, Principal Competitors,* and articles for *Further Reading.*

American spelling is used throughout *IDCH*, and the word "billion" is used in its U.S. sense of one thousand million.

Sources

Entries have been compiled from publicly accessible sources both in print and on the Internet such as general and academic periodicals, books, annual reports, and material supplied by the companies themselves.

Cumulative Indexes

IDCH contains two indexes: the **Index to Companies**, which provides an alphabetical index to companies discussed in the text as well as to companies profiled, and the **Index to Industries**, which allows researchers to locate companies by their principal industry. Both indexes are cumulative and specific instructions for using them are found immediately preceding each index.

Suggestions Welcome

Comments and suggestions from users of *IDCH* on any aspect of the product as well as suggestions for companies to be included or updated are cordially invited. Please write:

The Editor
International Directory of Company Histories
St. James Press
27500 Drake Rd.
Farmington Hills, Michigan 48331-3535

ABBREVIATIONS FOR FORMS OF COMPANY INCORPORATION

A.B.	Aktiebolaget (Sweden)
A.G.	Aktiengesellschaft (Germany, Switzerland)
A.S.	Atieselskab (Denmark)
A.S.	Aksjeselskap (Denmark, Norway)
A.Ş.	Anomin Şirket (Turkey)
B.V.	Besloten Vennootschap met beperkte, Aansprakelijkheid (The Netherlands)
Co.	Company (United Kingdom, United States)
Corp.	Corporation (United States)
G.I.E.	Groupement d'Intérêt Economique (France)
GmbH	Gesellschaft mit beschränkter Haftung (Germany)
H.B.	Handelsbolaget (Sweden)
Inc.	Incorporated (United States)
KGaA	Kommanditgesellschaft auf Aktien (Germany)
K.K.	Kabushiki Kaisha (Japan)
LLC	Limited Liability Company (Middle East)
Ltd.	Limited (Canada, Japan, United Kingdom, United States)
N.V.	Naamloze Vennootschap (The Netherlands)
OY	Osakeyhtiöt (Finland)
PLC	Public Limited Company (United Kingdom)
PTY.	Proprietary (Australia, Hong Kong, South Africa)
S.A.	Société Anonyme (Belgium, France, Switzerland)
SpA	Società per Azioni (Italy)

ABBREVIATIONS FOR CURRENCY

DA	Algerian dinar	M$	Malaysian ringgit
A$	Australian dollar	Dfl	Netherlands florin
Sch	Austrian schilling	Nfl	Netherlands florin
BFr	Belgian franc	NZ$	New Zealand dollar
Cr	Brazilian cruzado	N	Nigerian naira
R	Brazilian Real	NKr	Norwegian krone
C$	Canadian dollar	RO	Omani rial
RMB	Chinese renminbi	P	Philippine peso
COL	Colombian Peso	PLN	Polish Zloty
DKr	Danish krone	Esc	Portuguese escudo
E£	Egyptian pound	Ru	Russian ruble
EUR	Euro Dollars	SRls	Saudi Arabian riyal
Fmk	Finnish markka	S$	Singapore dollar
FFr	French franc	R	South African rand
DM	German mark	W	South Korean won
HK$	Hong Kong dollar	Pta	Spanish peseta
HUF	Hungarian forint	SKr	Swedish krona
Rs	Indian rupee	SFr	Swiss franc
Rp	Indonesian rupiah	NT$	Taiwanese dollar
IR£	Irish pound	B	Thai baht
L	Italian lira	£	United Kingdom pound
¥	Japanese yen	$	United States dollar
W	Korean won	B	Venezuelan bolivar
KD	Kuwaiti dinar	K	Zambian kwacha
LuxFr	Luxembourgian franc		

International Directory of

COMPANY
HISTORIES

acuson

Acuson Corporation

1220 Charleston Road
P.O. Box 7393
Mountain View, California 94039-7393
U.S.A.
Telephone: (650) 969-9112
Toll Free: (800) 422-8766
Fax: (650) 961-4726
Web site: http://www.acuson.com

Public Company
Incorporated: 1981
Employees: 1,932
Sales: $475.9 million (1999)
Stock Exchanges: New York
Ticker Symbol: ACN
NAIC: 334510 Electromedical and Electrotherapeutic
   Apparatus Manufacturing

Acuson Corporation is one of the top manufacturers of ultrasound imaging equipment for medical diagnosis. These systems beam low-power, high-frequency sound waves into the body, and the returning echoes are processed as real-time, static, or moving images of internal organs, tissue, and blood flows. Acuson's ultrasound products are used in hospitals and medical centers throughout the world in a variety of applications, including radiology, cardiology, and obstetrics/gynecology.

Company Founding and Rapid Success

Founder Samuel Maslak became interested in ultrasound in the early 1970s, when he was a doctoral student at the Massachusetts Institute of Technology (MIT). At that time, his wife was pregnant with their second child, and doctors ordered an examination of the fetus using ultrasound to test for intrauterine growth retardation. His daughter turned out to be fine, but Maslak noted that the existing technology was relatively crude. Moreover, he recognized that ultrasound had the potential to give doctors a tremendous amount of information, noninvasively, about the body. Maslak thus found a subject for his dissertation, as well as the keystone for what would eventually become a $475 million company.

After graduating from MIT, Maslak moved to California to work on ultrasound for Hewlett-Packard Company. While his achievement in creating and patenting a key subsystem of the company's ultrasound system was recognized, Hewlett-Packard did not want to press ahead with additional improvements. Maslak believed, however, that much greater advances could be made, and he left the company in December 1978, continuing to investigate ultrasound technology and the potential market for innovative products. Over the next nine months, he supported himself through a part-time job as a circuit design consultant, drawing on personal savings and home equity as well.

In September 1979, Maslak formed a general partnership with Robert Younge, a colleague at Hewlett-Packard; another engineer, Amin Hanafy, came on board in 1981. Maslak later asserted that instead of aiming at an immediate market introduction, the three spent much of their time thinking about how they could contribute to the industry's development. During this period, they picked up $100,000 in seed money from entrepreneur Karl Johannsmeier, and, late in 1981, the three partners distributed a business plan among several venture capital firms. While all of the firms expressed interest in the company, the partners decided that, aside from Johannsmeier, they would limit their outside investors to the firm of Kleiner, Perkins, Caufield & Byers of Palo Alto. Kleiner, Perkins initially invested $2.5 million, raising another $22 million over the next three years. The partners filed incorporation papers in 1981, and two years later Acuson introduced its first ultrasound machine. Acuson gained a listing on the New York Stock Exchange in 1986, raising $21 million in an initial public offering.

Describing industry conditions during this time, *Business Week* observed that "the market is nearly saturated, and sales have started to slip," while one of Acuson's competitors characterized the industry as "very difficult . . . to break into, because the mature companies can quickly match any advances that come along." Nevertheless, the fledgling Acuson increased its sales from $3 million in 1983 to $18 million in 1984, while revenues rose 60 percent or more annually, reaching $169 million by 1988. Moreover, following the usual initial losses for a start-up company during this time, Acuson's pretax margins reached 13 percent in 1985, and from 1986 to 1988 they were a superlative 24 to 26 percent. Acuson managed to overcome the odds through the superiority of its products.

Ultrasound was often the physician's imaging technique of choice because it was noninvasive, easy to use, and relatively inexpensive. Although good for soft tissue, the ultrasound could not penetrate bone or air-filled tissue and was, therefore, not used to examine the brain or lungs, for example. In a wide variety of applications, however, ultrasound was the first test that doctors ordered, being both the safest (there was no ionizing radiation or toxic dye) and the cheapest.

Given the strong preference for ultrasound testing, Maslak predicted that hospitals and doctors would be willing to pay more—as much as 30 percent more—for superior equipment that produced a clearer, sharper image. Acuson's first offering, the Acuson 128 ultrasound system, was so named because it was equipped with 128 separate transmit/receive channels for image formation, which enabled it to produce a better picture than existing machines that had only 64 channels.

The Acuson system could utilize more channels because it was based on a hybrid analog/digital computer. Although computer technologies had long been used in ultrasound systems to control ancillary functions, such as measurements and calculations, in Acuson's machines the image itself was formed in an ultrasound computer under software control. As in photography, conventional ultrasound technology produced images that had much sharper resolution in the focal center of their fields than elsewhere. In contrast, Acuson systems could electronically focus at each point of the field of view, optimize the lens aperture at each focal point, and substantially filter out stray reflected sound ordinarily captured by conventional units. The result was superior pictures that doctors widely praised. Indeed, in some cases it allowed them to make diagnoses that would have been unlikely using conventional equipment. In addition, Acuson systems proved extremely reliable, with up-time of better than 99.9 percent.

The emphasis on computer technology was also essential to the second key factor in Acuson's success: field upgradeability. Every unit that Acuson sold could be upgraded, at the customer's site, to the level of the most advanced current model, simply by adding new software. Although complete upgradeability would appear to act as a drag on sales of new machines, sales of new units continued to rise in the 1980s, since doctors continued to find new applications in which Acuson's products outperformed those of competitors.

Late 1980s: Continued Growth and International Expansion

Acuson's string of impressive sales increases reflected its commitment to upgrading its technology. Outlays for product development rose from $2 million in 1983 to $18 million in 1988, representing ten to 12 percent of sales for most of this period. In late 1985, Acuson began to market its Doppler option, which measured the velocity of blood flow in the heart and major arteries. Doppler could instantly alert doctors to constricted blood flow in a vessel, helping them determine the extent of the blockage and the need for further intervention. In September 1987, Acuson shipped its first color Doppler imaging system, an important diagnostic tool for physicians since it allowed them to visualize directly the flow of blood, depicted as a color overlay on the standard black and white ultrasound image.

Early on, Acuson established an international presence, setting up operations in the United Kingdom and Germany. Wholly owned sales and service subsidiaries followed in Sweden and Australia in 1986 and in Canada and France in 1987. The company also began to make significant shipments to China and other Asian markets. By 1989, 18 percent of Acuson's sales, $40 million, came from international operations, up 68 percent from the prior year.

That year, Acuson passed several milestones. Cardiology equipment became its second largest segment, after radiology. Acuson employed more than 1,000 people worldwide, and sales surged beyond the $200 million level for the first time, rising 35 percent from the prior-year total to $227 million. Profitability remained stunning, with gross, pretax, and net margins at 62, 27, and 17 percent. Net income rose to $38 million, up 40 percent from the prior year and more than double the $17 million recorded in 1987.

Early 1990s: Reversal of Fortunes

In July 1990, Acuson introduced its 128XP, its first new system mainframe since it entered the ultrasound market in 1983. The new model featured Vector Array, which provided a wider field of view in many ultrasound applications where anatomical access to the organ of interest was limited, such as when imaging near ribs, wounds, sutures, or bandages. The new machine also provided for higher resolution and higher quality images. The company continued to post record results; sales for the year totaled $282 million (up 24 percent) and net earnings were $48 million (up 26 percent). Strong performance continued in 1991, as sales grew 19 percent and earnings 22 percent. During that year, the company introduced the 128XP Xcelerator, which significantly enhanced the capabilities that the 128XP had introduced. The following year came the debut of the AEGIS digital image and data management system, through which ultrasound images could be captured electronically for storage and viewing at personal computer-based review stations.

Also in 1992, Acuson suffered its first significant reversal. During a period of economic recession worldwide, hospitals became more cost-conscious and, instead of buying new systems, they were making do with older equipment. Moreover, the ultrasound market had been driven by dramatic technological

Key Dates:

1981: Samuel Maslak and partners incorporate Acuson Corporation.
1983: The company's first product, the Acuson 128 ultrasound system, is launched.
1985: Marketing of the Doppler option for cardiology applications begins.
1990: The 128XP hits the market.
1992: The AEGIS digital image and data management system is first marketed.
1996: Company introduces the Sequoia and Aspen ultrasound systems.
1999: Ecton, Inc., developer of a portable ultrasound system, is acquired.
2000: Marketing of the AcuNav diagnostic ultrasound catheter begins.

improvements, and while the company's new products represented significant advances, they were not as revolutionary as those it had introduced in the 1980s. Earnings dropped from $59 million to $37 million on basically flat sales of $343 million. Acuson's decline in net income was also a result of its increased expenses for expanding the field sales organization and for product development. Indeed, while other companies cut research and development when business conditions worsened, Acuson continued to increase product development expenditures, regardless of market conditions; outlays more than doubled to $47 million between 1989 and 1992, representing almost 14 percent of total sales.

Acuson's hopes for a quick turnaround in 1993 were dashed when Bill Clinton assumed the U.S. presidency. Clinton's plans for healthcare reform caused a great deal of uncertainty in the medical sector, and makers of ultrasound equipment—like those of other medical devices—found that hospitals and clinics were postponing significant new purchases until they had a clearer idea of the possible impacts of new healthcare plans. In this tough business climate, the company decided to cut its workforce by 15 percent and took a $12 million charge for restructuring costs. In addition, continuing recessions in Europe and Japan hurt overseas markets, and international sales fell from $88 million to $78 million, or about 26 percent of total revenue. For the year, worldwide sales at Acuson were down 14 percent to $295 million, while earnings tumbled 89 percent to just $4 million.

Acuson also faced the possibility of new competition in the market. By 1993, large medical equipment makers—General Electric Company, Siemens A.G. of Germany, and Philips Electronics N.V. of the Netherlands—had not significantly penetrated the ultrasound sector, each having market shares of less than ten percent. Nevertheless, these firms were beginning to realize that, with hospitals scrambling to cut costs, relatively inexpensive ultrasonic systems would prove more attractive to hard-pressed administrators than their magnetic resonance imaging (MRI) machines and computed topography (CT) scanners. Moreover, ultrasound had already replaced MRI and CT as the preferred imaging method in some applications and was

well positioned to challenge the two competing modes in cardiology and abdominal imaging. Thus the shift of healthcare dollars to ultrasound promised bigger markets for the industry's leaders in the future. Although smaller companies such as Acuson had proved more flexible and quicker to bring new technologies to market, some large firms considered refocusing their operations to compete in the ultrasound market, representing a palpable threat to Acuson.

Nevertheless, Acuson held an advantage as an established and reputable player in the ultrasound industry. Moreover, the company continued to win praise for its steadfast commitment to product development. Despite the contraction in sales and profits in 1993, the company continued to pour funds into research and development, bolstered by its strong, debt-free balance sheet. In fact, its research and development outlays increased to $58 million—up 22 percent from 1992 levels and representing nearly 20 percent of sales. This expenditure proved worthwhile, since Acuson introduced successful new products, such as Acoustic Response Technology, which provided a significant enhancement to image quality.

Late 1990s: Sequoia, Aspen, and Ecton

Although the Clinton healthcare reform agenda went nowhere, the market for ultrasound equipment remained depressed into the late 1990s because of market saturation and the ascendancy of managed care health plans, which emphasized cost containment. As it had with its first ultrasound system, Acuson hoped to deliver new systems that were superior in quality to anything else on the market, and thereby regain its competitive edge. After seven years of development, Acuson began marketing what it considered a revolutionary new ultrasound system, the Sequoia, in 1996. Ultrasound echoes contain two pieces of information: amplitude, the height of the waves, and phase, the distance between each wave. Conventional ultrasound devices measure only amplitude. The Sequoia was able to produce images based on both amplitude and phase, increasing their sharpness and detail. The price tag was steep, however, with models selling for $200,000 to $350,000, about double the cost of conventional systems (the 128XP, for example, sold at this time for between $75,000 and $160,000). Later in 1996, Acuson introduced the Aspen system, which was based on conventional technology but incorporated some of the advances of the Sequoia. The company positioned it between the 128XP and the Sequoia, pricing it at $150,000 to $250,000. The high cost of launching these new models led to a 1996 net loss of $10.6 million. But the new products also fueled the company's first growth spurt since 1991; revenues for 1997 were $437.8 million, an increase of 26 percent over the previous year. The 1997 net income figure of $22.4 million was the largest since 1992. The profit margin of 5.1 percent, however, was a far cry from the double-digit figures of the late 1980s and early 1990s.

In the late 1990s Acuson began to increasingly pursue systems for the cardiology/cardiac sector. In December 1999 the company acquired Ecton, Inc., based in Plymouth Meeting, Pennsylvania. Ecton had developed a portable, all-digital ultrasound system designed particularly for cardiography applications. In addition to its expected high image quality, the Ecton system was noteworthy for its light weight of 20 pounds and its low cost of $40,000 to $60,000. Acuson for the first time would be able to penetrate the $300 million annual market for low- to mid-priced ultrasound equipment. The company planned to market the Ecton system as the Cypress Echocardiography system, with a launch scheduled for the second half of 2000.

In May 2000 Acuson began marketing the AcuNav diagnostic ultrasound catheter, following nearly eight years of development. Aimed at helping in the diagnosis and treatment of heart disease and irregular heart rhythms, the AcuNav catheter was a device inserted into a patient's leg or the jugular vein in the neck and then threaded to the right ventricle of the heart; by bouncing high-frequency sound waves off the surrounding tissue, the catheter was able to generate images and blow flow data throughout the entire heart. The AcuNav could be used only once and was priced at $2,000 to $3,000. It was developed in conjunction with the renowned Mayo Clinic, which shared licensing rights. With revenue growth and earnings having stagnated once again in 1998 and 1999, Acuson was hoping that the introduction of the Cypress system and the AcuNav catheter in 2000 would spark a return to the heady years of the 1980s and early 1990s.

Principal Subsidiaries

Acuson Pty. Ltd. (Australia); Acuson GesmbH (Austria); Acuson Belgium SA/NV (Belgium); Acuson Canada Ltd.; Acuson A/S (Denmark); Acuson OY (Finland); Acuson S.A.R.L. (France); Acuson GmbH (Germany); Acuson Hong Kong Ltd.; Acuson S.p.A. (Italy); Acuson Nippon K.K. (Japan); Acuson BV (Netherlands); Acuson A/S (Norway); Acuson Singapore Ltd.; Acuson Iberica SA (Spain); Acuson AB (Sweden); Acuson Ltd. (U.K.); Acuson Foreign Sales Corporation (Virgin Islands); Acuson International Sales Corporation; Acuson Worldwide Sales Corporation; Sound Technology, Inc.; Ecton, Inc.

Principal Competitors

Agfa Corporation; Agilent Technologies, Inc.; ATL Ultrasound, Inc.; Biosound Esaote, Inc.; Cemax-Icon, Inc.; General Electric Company; Hitachi Corporation; R4 Telemedicine Systems, Inc.; Siemens Medical Systems, Inc.; SonoSite, Inc.; Toshiba Medical Systems, Inc.

Further Reading

"Acuson Gains Low-Cost Portable Ultrasound System via $23 Million Ecton Buy," *Gray Sheet,* September 20, 1999.

Anders, George, "Acuson Plans Heart Catheter Market Entry," *Wall Street Journal,* May 5, 1999, p. B6.

Aragon, Lawrence, "Acuson Probes Human Body for Its Growth," *Business Journal* (San Jose), January 7, 1991, p. 1.

——, "Ultrasound Equipment Makers Hurt by Hospital Spending Cuts," *Business Journal* (San Jose), August 3, 1992, p. 1.

Barlas, Pete, "It All Began in the Womb," *Business Journal* (San Jose), January 29, 1996, p. 12.

Barrier, Michael, "The Ultimate in Ultrasound," *Nation's Business,* September 1991, pp. 53–54.

Brammer, Rhonda, "Ultra-Cheap Ultrasound?," *Barron's,* June 7, 1993, p. 20.

Cone, Edward, "Ultrasound, Ultraprofitable," *Forbes,* October 31, 1988, pp. 142–44.

Hall, Carl T., "The Newest Thing in Ultrasound: Acuson's New Power Tool May Benefit Patients, Company Profits," *San Francisco Chronicle,* August 23, 1996, p. B1.

King, Ralph T., Jr., "Acuson Bets It Has the Breakthrough Device It Needs," *Wall Street Journal,* May 13, 1996, p. B3.

Naj, Amal Kumar, "Big Medical-Equipment Makers Try Ultrasound Market," *Wall Street Journal,* November 30, 1993, p. B4.

Raine, George, "Acuson Clears Up Ultrasound: Company's New Equipment Gives Sharper Image," *San Francisco Examiner,* October 29, 1996, p. C1.

Seligman, Philip, "Acuson Corp.," *Value Line Investment Survey Ratings & Reports,* June 17, 1994, p. 195.

"Ultrasound Is Probing New Markets," *Business Week,* May 2, 1983, pp. 35–37.

—Bob Schneider
—updated by David E. Salamie

Adecco S.A.

Rue de Langallerie 11
Case Postale 16
1000 Lausanne 4
Switzerland
Telephone: (+41) 21 321-66-66
Fax: (+41) 21 321-66-28
Web site: http://www.adecco.com

Public Company
Incorporated: 1957
Employees: 28,000
Sales: SFr 18.47 billion (US$11.64 billion) (1999)
Stock Exchanges: Zürich Paris New York
Ticker Symbols: ADEN; ADO
NAIC: 561310 Employment Placement Agencies

Adecco S.A. is the world's largest temporary employment company. In addition, since its acquisition of Olsten Corporation in 1999, the company is also the leading staffing services group in the United States, outpacing longtime rival Manpower Inc. A product of the 1996 merger between Switzerland's Adia and France's ECCO, Adecco has built a network of more than 5,000 offices in some 60 countries. Each year the company supplies some 200,000 customers with more than three million temporary and permanent employees. On any given day, some 600,000 people find employment through Adecco around the world. The company's largest business comes under its Adecco brand name. Yet Adecco has also ridden the rising demand for technical skills, especially in the booming telecommunications and computer industries, to become the world's leading provider of specialty staffing services, through subsidiaries including TAD Technical, TAD Telecom, and Ajilon. Adecco is also a leading provider of staffing, executive recruitment, training, and career management to the financial services industry, through subsidiaries AOC (Accountants on Call), Alexandre TIC, and Asia-based Templar International Consultants (TIC). While staffing services continue to produce as much as 84 percent of Adecco's annual revenues, its strong range of specialty services has grown to produce more than 16 percent of

sales. The company, listed on the New York, Switzerland, and Paris stock exchanges, has seen strong growth in the late 1990s through acquisitions including those of TAD Resources International, Delphi Group Plc. in the United Kingdom, and Olsten. The company is led by CEO John Bowmer, Chairman and ECCO founder Philippe Foriel-Destezet, and Vice-Chairman Klaus Jacobs. The company's sales neared SFr 18.5 billion (US$11.6 billion) in 1999.

Filling a Gap in the 1950s

Adia was founded in Lausanne, Switzerland, in 1957 by Henri-Ferdinand Lavanchy. An independent accountant, Lavanchy got into the employment business when a client asked him to find a worker to fill in quickly on a job. Lavanchy's enterprise remained simply a domestic employment agency for its first four years in business.

In 1961 the company opened its first international office, in Belgium. Adia expanded further the following year, adding an office in Germany. Denmark came on line in 1965, and in 1972 the company moved overseas, opening an office in Menlo Park, California, its first American outpost. By then, Adia has been joined in Europe by another fast-growing company, ECCO, based in France, and founded in 1964 by Philippe Foriel-Destezet.

In the 1970s Adia became one of the first temporary agencies to offer its workers benefits such as healthcare and paid vacations. In 1974 Lavanchy recruited Swiss executive Martin O. Pestalozzi to help him run the company; Pestalozzi had spent many years working in the United States for a number of consumer services and manufacturing businesses. Pestalozzi later recalled to *International Management* that when he came aboard at Adia, "all the figures were too small. They all needed several more zeros." Pestalozzi and Lavanchy set out to change this situation through a policy of aggressive acquisitions in countries around the world. During the next 12 years Pestalozzi spent more than half of his time shuttling around the globe, propounding the theory that the temporary employment industry needed to increase its efforts to provide high quality workers in order to improve its credibility. In that time Adia purchased

Company Perspectives:

Until fairly recently, employment agencies were primarily called to replace an absent employee, or to satisfy an unexpected, albeit temporary, increase in workload. Today, Adecco clients consider a flexible workforce as a core component of their business strategy. In today's competitive employment market the key concepts are workforce productivity, reactivity and flexibility. As a central constituent of this strategy, staffing companies are increasingly becoming the long-term partners managing this new workforce.

more than 85 companies, tripling its size and operating in more than a dozen countries. This process was aided by the highly fragmented nature of the temporary help industry, which made it easy for a large company to scoop up many small operations.

In the year following Pestalozzi's arrival at the company, Adia entered the French market, and in 1976 the company moved into the British Isles, buying an agency in Ireland. Also in 1976 Adia made an unsuccessful attempt to expand to Brazil. In 1977 the company purchased the Alfred Marks Bureau, Ltd., a venerable British temporary agency, for US$3.4 million from its founder's son, Bernard Marks. Aside from the United States, the United Kingdom was the only other market in which Adia franchised offices, in addition to owning them outright.

Expansion continued at a rapid pace throughout the late 1970s and early 1980s, as the company branched out to Austria in 1978 and to Holland in 1979. In that year founder Lavanchy stepped aside as acting chairman of the company to become honorary chairman. He was replaced at the helm by Pestalozzi, who became president and chief operating officer. At that time Adia also sold shares to the public on the Zurich Stock Exchange for the first time. The company's highly valued stock offerings helped to finance further expansion through acquisitions.

The extent of Adia's growth in the second half of the 1970s became clear at the end of the decade, as the company reported revenues and profits three times higher in 1980 than those in 1975. The company's far-flung operations, however, had not spawned a large, multilayered corporate bureaucracy at their center. Operations remained heavily decentralized, as purchased subsidiaries were allowed to continue doing business in much the same way that they had before, to the extent that each made use of its own financial reporting procedures. Although uniform accounting practices were instituted in the early 1980s, controls in general, at Chairman Pestalozzi's insistence, remained at a minimum. This was signified by the fact that the company's corporate headquarters staff in Lausanne consisted of just 25 people.

Building a Staffing Giant in the 1980s

Adia took its largest leap yet in 1981 with an acquisition in Australia. In 1983 the company expanded its North American operations when it opened offices in Canada. Japan came on board in 1985, one year before the company added New Zealand, Spain, and Hong Kong. "Our aim is for balanced geographical growth," Pestalozzi told *International Management*,

"and we would like to be recognized as the best, rather than the biggest, in all our markets." While Adia continued its international growth, ECCO had focused its development largely on its home market, expanding to become a market leader in France by the mid-1980s, and, by the mid-1990s, the world's second largest staffing services provider, in terms of annual revenues.

Concerned that its steady growth might make Adia the target of an unwanted corporate takeover, Pestalozzi and Adia's other top managers formed Adiainvest S.A., a holding company, in 1985. Adiainvest purchased most of the equity holdings of company founder Lavanchy, giving it effective control of a majority of the company's voting shares. This move guaranteed that the current management could stay in charge of the company it was building.

By the following year, Adia's revenues had increased 12-fold in as many years, and its earnings had grown to 15 times their initial size. This dramatic growth was part of an industry-wide phenomenon, as temporary help agencies became the world's third fastest growing industry in the 1980s. After the economic downturns at the start of the decade, employers trimmed their permanent full-time staffs in an effort to keep their human resources expenditures low. With leaner staffing levels in place across many entire industries, companies looked more and more to temporary workers to augment their regular staffs for large projects or if business simply picked up. This was in marked contrast to the early years of the temporary employment industry, when short-term workers were used only to fill in for regular employees who were ill or on vacation. In later years, although temporary workers were paid higher hourly wages than full-time employees, this cost was offset by savings on fringe benefits and overhead costs, making temporary help cost-effective.

Benefiting from these changes in the workforce of the developed world, Adia in 1986 reported sales topping $1 billion for the first time; the company became the European industry leader, with the largest share of the market in three countries: Switzerland, France, and Germany. In addition, its operation in the Netherlands secured a larger share of that country's temporary help business, and the company moved up to fourth place in the United States. In the United Kingdom, however, the Alfred Marks Bureau, Adia's subsidiary, relinquished its leading position in the British market, slipping to number two.

The growth of Adia's profits was also attributable to the company's strong emphasis on quality. Because it stressed high-value services, the company was able to charge more for its temporary workers than some of its competitors, giving it higher earnings. In its quest for quality workers and the high margins they brought, Adia implemented in-house training programs and niche marketing. In the mid-1980s Adia moved strongly into the specialized accounting and word processing fields, providing highly skilled workers to its clients. As an investment in its workforce, Adia subsidiaries provided specialized training in the latest word processing programs to their employees. Alfred Marks, for instance, trained 10,000 secretaries a year on various computer programs at its London headquarters.

In addition, Adia made a point of allowing subsidiaries with well-known and long-established businesses to retain their

Key Dates:

1957: Henri-Ferdinand Lavanchy founds Adia.
1961: Adia opens office in Belgium.
1962: German office opens.
1964: Philippe Foriel-Destezet founds ECCO in France.
1972: Adia enters U.S. market with Adia Services Inc.
1979: Adia goes public on Swiss stock exchange.
1984: Adia Services goes public.
1991: Klaus Jacobs takes control of Adia.
1996: Adia and ECCO merge to form Adecco; company acquires ICON Recruitment (Australia).
1997: Adecco acquires TAD Resources International and Seagate Associates.
1999: Company acquires Delphi Group Plc., Career Staff Co., and Olsten Corporation.

names, rather than insisting that they switch to the corporate parent's name. "If you acquire a company with a strong brand name, it makes little sense to change it to Adia," Pestalozzi told *International Management.* These policies, in addition to the company's broad geographical base, helped to insulate Adia from the effects of periodic downturns in the economy on the notoriously sensitive temporary employment industry. In addition, the company's extensive American operations acted as a cushion for recessions in the European economy.

Those American operations were run by Walter Macauley, a former executive with the Manpower temporary agency who had been recruited to run American subsidiary Adia Services, Inc., in 1979. In that year the company had sales of $45 million, and it had not yet reached the ranks of the top ten temporary agencies in the country. Adia Services adopted an aggressive two-pronged growth strategy that involved opening company-owned offices in clusters and franchising branches in smaller markets where the company name was little known. As a result of this policy, the company had opened 360 offices by the end of 1987.

In 1984 Adia's American subsidiary went public, offering 1.2 million common shares in conjunction with its Swiss parent company. Also in that year the American subsidiary entered the permanent placement market, following the lead of Adia S.A., which had maintained the activities of a regular permanent employment agency in addition to its temporary business. Adia Services took part in the 1984 Los Angeles Olympics when the company won a contract to hire and coordinate 7,500 transportation workers for the games.

In keeping with Adia's policy of niche marketing, the company's American subsidiary purchased eight companies in 1986 that allowed it to serve various specialized sectors of the employment field. Businesses such as Word Processors Personnel Service and Accountants on Call brought with them higher profit margins on their operations than Adia's general office placement business. The company's $45 million purchase of Nursefinders, a medical staffing concern, launched Adia into the fast-growing healthcare industry at a time when a shortage of nurses was driving up demand and prices for their services. Each new division retained its own president and headquarters

and was allowed to operate independently according to Adia's policy of decentralized control of its acquisitions.

By February 1987 Adia had operations in 16 countries. This figure grew to 17 later that year when the company purchased an agency in Norway. In August 1987 Adia became involved in the attempt by a British firm to take over American temporary services giant Manpower. Adia offered Manpower some form of business combination that would have allowed the American firm to thwart the hostile takeover attempt but, ultimately, Adia bowed out and the deal went through.

In October of that year the value of Adia's 70 percent holdings in American subsidiary Adia Services, Inc. was battered, as the stock dropped dramatically in the sharp plunge suffered by the New York Stock Exchange. Overall, however, 1987 was a good year for Adia Services, as the company reported earnings of $11.4 million, up from $6.2 million the year before. The company purchased another temporary agency at the end of the year, adding Temp World, Inc. to its holdings. It also entered the market for computer professionals with its year-end purchase of Comp-U-Staff.

This move was followed by another string of acquisitions by the American subsidiary in 1988. In April the company bought Lee Hecht Harrison, an "outplacement" firm that helped laid-off employees find work. Two months later Adia Services continued its acquisition of firms serving small but profitable niches of its industry when it purchased the StarMed Staffing Corporation. That fall, the company bought Computer Dynamics, Inc., a second data processing concern.

With these acquisitions, almost half of Adia's American operations were now in highly skilled, specialized fields. The company ended 1988 with record profits of $17.6 million, derived from the activities of 520 offices. All together, Adia had made seven acquisitions during the year. Though fueled by these steady purchases, Adia experienced slower growth in the late 1980s due to the economy-wide shortage of labor. "The younger workers are shrinking in numbers," Macauley told *Personnel Administrator.* "We have to do a better job of getting the elderly worker back into the work force," he added. In an effort to do so, Adia Services introduced its "Renaissance Program" to entice workers over the age of 48 to take temporary assignments. In addition, the company increased its employee training to make use of people with low skills who might previously not have been in demand. In 1989 Adia Services also bought four more temporary agencies.

As its American unit was expanding through the purchase of companies in complementary fields, Adia added to its worldwide operations. In 1988 and 1989 the company opened offices in three more countries, including Italy. Because Italian laws forbid the operation of a permanent or temporary employment agency such as those Adia operated in other countries, Adia entered the only business open to it in Italy, that of intermediary between companies wishing to place an advertisement for a new employee and the newspapers where the ad would run. In this limited fashion the company put itself in contact with the Italian labor market. International expansion continued in 1990 when Brazil, Portugal, Greece, Thailand, and Hungary were added.

Morocco and Czechoslovakia were subsequently brought on board in 1991 and 1992, respectively.

In January 1989 Adia's managers, through their holding company Adiainvest S.A., sold 40 percent of the company to Inspectorate International S.A., a Swiss conglomerate that provided inspection services, security, and computer leasing. The two companies merged, and Inspectorate's owner—and later fugitive—Werner Ray, became a major shareholder in Adia through his stock holding company, Omni Holding AG.

At the end of that year Adia attempted to increase its holdings in the United States market when it made a bid to take over Hestair PLC, a British firm that owned Talent Tree, a large American subsidiary. The attempt was ultimately unsuccessful, despite the generally softening demand for temporary services in the United States and a slowing economy.

Merging into Market Leadership in the 1990s

By the middle of 1990 Adia's American subsidiary was reporting continued economic sluggishness and the implementation of cost-cutting measures. Adia announced that it would increase its holdings in the American company to 80 percent, at an estimated cost of $37 million, a move that would allow the American company to take advantage of a tax loophole to significantly lower its tax payments. Despite this measure, economic conditions were difficult for Adia's American franchise holders. A group of franchisees brought a class-action suit against Adia, charging that the company had defrauded them by distributing a falsely optimistic profit plan for its operations. Twenty-two months later a panel of arbitrators ruled that the company was not liable in the franchisees' claims.

Adia's Swiss owners also suffered financial difficulties. These culminated in February 1991 when Ray, Adia's half-owner, was forced to sell a 53 percent voting interest in the company, held by his Omni Holding company, for $612.4 million. The majority stake in Adia was sold to a German retailer, Asko Deutsche Kaufhaus AG, and to Swiss investor Klaus J. Jacobs. The new owners promptly moved to replace the company's managers. In May it was announced that Adia's current chief executive officer, along with former leader Pestalozzi and another member of the company's governing board, would be replaced by Nico Issenmann. Issenmann had previously been an executive with Jacobs's company. The change in leadership took place on June 12, 1991.

By July of that year, Adia's American subsidiary had reported decreasing revenues. One month later its corporate parent did the same, announcing international revenues down nearly eight percent from the year before, as the economic downturn continued to take its toll. By the second half of the year, Adia's U.S. division had resorted to a wage freeze, layoffs in some areas of operations, and the closing of selected branch offices. The company ended 1991 with profits down 3.6 percent. The change in command of Adia became more complete in March 1992, when Macauley, the longtime president of the key American subsidiary, submitted his resignation.

The lingering economic recession, especially severe in Europe, continued to place pressure on the temporary employment market. Yet the sector as a whole was to benefit from the changing employer-employee relationship. While the workplace in much of Europe remained tightly controlled—with employers finding it exceedingly difficult, if not nearly impossible to fire full-time employees—in the United States and elsewhere, many employers, caught up in a wave of "downsizing" efforts, turned increasingly to temporary staffing services providers. As the idea of permanent and even lifetime employment seemed to fade in the United States, companies also looked to temporary staffing companies to provide recruitment and screening services as well, helping to eliminate the costly expense and guesswork of the hiring procedure.

By the mid-1990s, ECCO's sales had risen to give it the world's number two position, ahead of Adia's number three position, while both trailed industry leader Manpower Inc. Yet ECCO and Adia joined forces in 1996, merging to form Adecco S.A., a company with combined sales of US$6.2 billion. Adecco's headquarters were located in Lausanne, Switzerland. ECCO founder Foriel-Destezet and Adia's Jacobs agreed to share the company's leadership, in a revolving chairmanship. This arrangement was resolved in 1999, however, when Jacobs—whose other business interests ranged from the chocolate industries, through his holdings of Barry Callebaut, Van Houten & Zoon, and Brach, to the sporting goods industry, with surfboard maker Mistral—took the vice-chairmanship. The company recruited John Bowmer as CEO.

Adecco could now claim the world leadership in its industry; however, the company remained number four in the United States, behind Manpower, Kelly Services, and Olsten Corporation. Adecco quickly went on an acquisition drive, boosting its United States position with acquisitions including TAD Resources International based in Massachusetts, and Seagate Associates, based in New Jersey, in 1997. The company was also expanding on the global arena, buying up Australia's ICON Recruitment, giving the company a bigger share of that region's IT market. In 1999, Adecco's acquisition of Delphi Group Plc, in England, made it a leading world provider to the computer industry; the company also boosted its Asian position with the acquisition of Japan's Career Staff Co.

By the end of 1999, Adecco had reached an agreement to acquire Olsten Corporation for nearly US$1.5 billion. The Olsten acquisition not only padded Adecco's world leadership position, it also placed the company in front of Manpower in the United States. The addition of Olsten—which kept only its healthcare division, to be spun off under a new name—also caused Adecco to move its U.S. headquarters to Olsten's hometown, Melville, New York. By the end of 1999, Adecco was able to report sales of nearly SFr 18.5 billion. The company had successfully negotiated the consolidation of its industry to claim the leadership position into the new century.

Principal Subsidiaries

Adecco; Adecco Consulting; Adia (France); Ajilon; AOC (Accountants on Call); Alexandre TIC; Computer People; Delphi Group Plc. (U.K.); ICON Recruitment (Australia); Jonathan Wren; Lee Hecht Harrison; Olsten Corporation (U.S.A.); TAD & ROEVIN; TAD Technical; TAD Telecom; Templar International Consultants.

Principal Competitors

Ackermans & van Haaren; Robert Half International Inc.; Administaff; Sidergie; Employee Solutions, Inc.; Spherion; Kelly Services, Inc.; Staff Leasing; Manpower, Inc.; TAC Worldwide; Modis Professional Services; Vedior; Onet; Volt Information Sciences Inc.; Randstad Holding n.v.; Westaff.

Further Reading

Ammerlaan, Nieck, "Adecco Sees Strong 2000," *Reuters*, April 19, 2000.

Arbose, Jules, "Adia's Quality Route to Being World's No. 2 in Temp Help," *International Management*, February 1987.

Bergheim, Kim, "Sociology Degree Proves Useful for Adia's Macauley," *Business Journal-San Jose*, September 21, 1987.

Bernstein, James, "Olsten Sells Out to Competitor," *Newsday*, August 19, 1999, p. 57.

Greising, David, "Temp Agencies Are Praying the Slump Is Just Temporary," *Business Week*, December 11, 1989.

Larsen, Peter Thal, "Adecco to Form IT Staffing Giant with £167m Buy," *Independent*, February 5, 1999, p. 19.

Paton, Huntley, "Adia Stands Ready for Boom or Bust," *San Francisco Business Times*, April 18, 1988.

—Elizabeth Rourke
—updated by M.L. Cohen

Adolph Coors Company

17735 West 32nd Avenue
Golden, Colorado 80401
U.S.A.
Telephone: (303) 279-6565
Fax: (303) 277-6246
Web site: http://www.coors.com

Public Company
Incorporated: 1913 as Adolph Coors Brewing and
    Manufacturing Company
Employees: 5,800
Sales: $2.06 billion (1999)
Stock Exchanges: New York
Ticker Symbol: RKY
NAIC: 312120 Breweries; 327213 Glass Container
    Manufacturing; 332431 Metal Can Manufacturing;
    422810 Beer and Ale Wholesalers

Adolph Coors Company is the only family-owned brewery in the United States that was able to survive the late 20th-century consolidation of the American beer industry without relinquishing family control. The regional brewer gained national prominence in the 1960s and 1970s, but only officially achieved national distribution in 1986. Prodded from its conservative management tendencies by stagnant sales and meager profits in the late 1980s, a new generation of Coors family (and nonfamily) leaders sought to revitalize the business in the 1990s. Coors entered the 21st century ranked a distant third to market leaders Anheuser-Busch Companies, Inc. and Miller Brewing Company. Coors operates the world's largest brewery at its headquarters in Golden, Colorado, and distributes its 13 branded malt beverages in 30 countries worldwide—although 98 percent of revenues are generated in the United States. In addition to its brewing and distribution activities, which are conducted through a subsidiary, Coors Brewing Company, Adolph Coors Company also owns and/or operates aluminum can and glass manufacturing facilities in Colorado.

The Foundation of the Brewery

Adolph Herman Joseph Coors emigrated to the United States from Germany in 1868 at the age of 21. After purchasing a Denver bottling company in 1872, Coors formed a partnership with Jacob Schueler in 1873. Although Schueler invested the lion's share of the $20,000 necessary to purchase and convert an old tannery in nearby Golden into a brewery, Coors was able to buy out his partner in 1880. His acquisition inaugurated more than a century of Coors family control.

The fledgling brewery's sales increased steadily in the ensuing decades. In 1887 the brewery sold 7,049 barrels of beer (31 gallons per barrel). Three years later that figure more than doubled, reaching 17,600 barrels. Over the years Adolph Coors slowly expanded his market. By the time he officially incorporated his brewery in 1913 as Adolph Coors Brewing and Manufacturing Company, Coors beer was being distributed throughout Colorado.

Even at this early point in the company's history, the distinctive Coors philosophy was emerging. The main tenets of this philosophy adhered to by four successive generations of Coors beermakers, each generation further refining the knowledge inherited from the preceding generation, were the following: Adolph Coors believed in sparing no effort or expense in producing the best beer possible. To this end, he believed that only Colorado spring water was good enough for his beer. He also commissioned farmers to grow the barley and hops that he needed for his brewing process. The second tenet of the philosophy was that his family always came first, without exception; the Coors family brewery remained a tight-knit, protective, almost secretive enterprise. The last tenet was that "a good beer sells itself." Until 1980 Coors spent substantially less on advertising than any other brewer.

Prohibition came early to Colorado. In 1916 the state's legislature passed a law banning the production and consumption of alcoholic beverages within the state. Obviously, Prohibition was detrimental to Adolph Coors's brewery; some business historians assert, however, that the legislation strengthened the burgeoning company. The obvious changes in product offerings—Coors manufactured "near beer" and malted milk dur-

Company Perspectives:

Coors—it's a name that conjures up an image of cool mountain streams, clear blue skies and all that is inspiring about the Rocky Mountain West.

It is a name associated with an uncompromising commitment to quality—a reputation that began more than 100 years ago and thrives to this day.

It is the name of an ambitious 19th-century pioneer whose humble dream grew into the world's largest single-site brewery.

But more than anything else, the name Coors is one held dear in the hearts of beer lovers across the country and, increasingly, around the globe.

ing this period—were reflected in a name change, in 1920, to Adolph Coors Company. Adolph Coors and his son, Adolph, Jr., also used the opportunity to diversify their company, creating what was eventually to become a small-scale vertical monopoly: Coors acquired all that it needed to produce its beer, from the oil wells that created the energy necessary to run the brewery to the farms that grew the ingredients, and from the bottling plant that made the containers to the trucks used for distribution. This expansion was financed entirely with family money.

Astounding Post-Prohibition Growth

The repeal of Prohibition in 1933 did not result in as dramatic a sales increase for Coors as it did for many other producers of alcoholic beverages. Instead, the Adolph Coors Company, under the direction of Adolph, Jr., and his two brothers, expanded its market slowly in the 1930s. Their insistence on the use of all natural ingredients and no preservatives—in accordance with the brewery's founding tenets—made wider distribution prohibitively expensive. The beer had to be brewed, transported, and stored under refrigeration, and its shelf life was limited to one month. But if Coors's growth and development in the decades following the repeal of Prohibition was less dramatic than that of brewing powerhouses such as Anheuser-Busch and Miller, it was no less amazing. For while other regional breweries were squeezed out of the market—the number of independents shrank from 450 in 1947 to 120 in 1967—Coors grew steadily into one of America's leading beer brands. Coors's production increased 20-fold, from 123,000 barrels in 1930 to 3.5 million barrels in 1960, as the brewer expanded its reach into 11 western states. Coors's ranking among the nation's beer companies advanced accordingly, from 14th in 1959 to fourth by 1969.

How did Coors grow 1,500 percent between 1947 and 1967, with only one product, made in a single brewery, and sold in only ten states? A quality product was certainly one reason for Coors's success. The company's technological innovations, including the development of both the first cold-filtered beer and the first aluminum can in 1959, also placed it in the vanguard of the beer industry. Another reason was a unique marketing ploy that Coors perfected during the 1960s. When Coors entered a new market, it would lead with draft beer only. The company would sell kegs to taverns and bars at a price under that of its lowest competition. Then Coors would encourage the barkeepers to sell the beer at a premium price. Once Coors's premium image was established, the company would then introduce the beer in retail stores. Since Coors spent so little on advertising, the company was able to offer a better profit margin to its wholesalers. These profit incentives to both wholesalers and retailers worked well. Through the 1970s Coors was the leading beer in nine of the 11 western states in which it was sold. In California, the second largest beer market in the country (New York was first), Coors at one time held an astonishing 43 percent of the market.

1970s Through Mid-1980s: Cult Status, Controversies, and Declining Fortunes

Marketing, innovation, and product quality, however, could not account for what was later considered one of the strangest phenomena in U.S. business history. Beginning in the late 1960s and culminating in the mid-1970s Coors developed, without any effort by the company, an unusual reputation as a "cult" beer. Limited availability created intense demand on the East Coast. Westerners, keen to flaunt their perceived superiority to Easterners, got caught up in a "we have what you want" syndrome and unwittingly became the company's unpaid advertisers. As a result, Coors virtually eliminated its competition in nine western states. Those nine states provided Coors with all the market it needed to become the fourth largest brewery in the nation.

But all was not well with the company and its enigmatic founding family. The 1960 kidnapping and murder of Adolph III had intensified the clan's already strong tendency toward secrecy. Their cautious, elusive nature produced circumspect hiring practices, including polygraphs and sworn statements of loyalty. Outsiders saw these practices as both unfair and as a means of enforcing racial discrimination: the limited numbers of African Americans and Hispanics employed by the company seemed to support this view. Lawsuits were filed alleging discrimination and, more important, a coalition of minority and labor groups organized a boycott, which intensified the negative publicity surrounding the company. The boycott and lawsuits provoked more public scrutiny of the Coors dynasty. A series of articles appeared in the *Washington Post* in May 1975 documenting Joe Coors's ultraconservative political philosophy. Not only did these revelations exacerbate the boycott, they also influenced the average consumer and generally undermined Coors's market position.

At first, the Coors family's response was retrenchment and litigation. But when sales dropped ten percent in California in 1975 (at the time that state accounted for 49 percent of total sales), the family changed its tactics. They settled the lawsuits, agreed to a minority hiring plan, and launched advertising campaigns aimed at showing the company's "good side." Television advertisements showed that minorities were happily employed in the brewery. Bill Coors took the initiative on environmental issues and proclaimed that the company was well ahead of the industry and the government in keeping the environment clean. The replacement of pull-tabs with "pop-down" tabs and the first aluminum recycling program were cited as proof of Coors's commitment.

Key Dates:

1873: Adolph Herman Joseph Coors forms a partnership with Jacob Schueler to convert a tannery in Golden, Colorado, into a brewery.
1880: Coors buys out Schueler.
1913: Company is incorporated as Adolph Coors Brewing and Manufacturing Company.
1916: Prohibition is enacted into law in Colorado.
1920: Company changes its name to Adolph Coors Company.
1933: Prohibition is repealed.
1959: Company develops the first aluminum can.
1969: Coors becomes the number four brewer in the United States.
1975: Company goes public, offering only nonvoting shares.
1978: Coors Light is introduced.
1981: Coors' distribution area expands across the Mississippi for the first time.
1987: Coors Brewing Company is created as a beer-focused subsidiary of Adolph Coors Company; Peter Coors is named vice-chairman, president, and CEO of Coors Brewing.
1989: Keystone and Keystone Light brands make their debut.
1990: A brewery in Memphis, Tennessee, is purchased from Stroh Brewing.
1991: Coors beer is now available in all 50 states.
1992: Coors introduces Zima, a clear, foam-free malted brew; the company's nonbeer assets are spun off to shareholders as ACX Technologies, Inc.
1993: For the first time, a nonfamily member, W. Leo Kiely, is selected as president of the brewing business.
1995: The SandLot Brewery opens at Denver's Coors Field; the Blue Moon specialty brand is launched.
1997: Coors Non-Alcoholic is introduced.
2000: Peter Coors is named chairman of Coors Brewing and president and CEO of Adolph Coors Company.

After a decrease in sales through the late 1970s, the company appeared to revive in 1980. Sales volume dropped by one million barrels between 1976 and 1978, bottoming out at 12.5 million barrels before rebounding in 1980 to 13.7 million. Bill and Joe Coors, the third generation of the family to take charge, concluded that their sales problem emanated from their image problem and that they had successfully solved both.

Two separate situations, one in 1975 and the other in 1976, should have signaled that the company's problems went beyond that of image. In 1975 the Coors family was forced for the first time to offer shares to the public to raise $50 million to pay inheritance tax for a family member. The original offering was successful, raising more than $130 million. The stock sold was of a nonvoting class, so the family did not relinquish any control over the company. Analysts suggested, however, that the reluctance with which the company undertook the offering disclosed a disdain for modern methods of capitalization. The second situa-

tion involved a Federal Trade Commission ruling, later upheld by the U.S. Supreme Court, striking down Coors's strong-arm distribution tactics. Coors refused to sell its product to distributors that the company regarded as unable to handle the beer properly. Once again, many industry analysts remarked that the company exhibited a disdain for mass marketing techniques.

Indeed, Coors remained committed to its founder's decidedly outdated idea that "a good beer sells itself." In 1975 William Coors claimed, "We don't need marketing. We know we make the best beer in the world." Throughout its entire history, Coors had spent far less than its competitors on advertising. In the 1970s, Coors's ad budget amounted to about $.65 per barrel, compared with the $3.50 per barrel promoting the leading beers. Anheuser-Busch and Miller spent billions of dollars on promotion in a market that they continually expanded with new products. Coors, on the other hand, only reluctantly joined the light beer movement—introducing Coors Light in 1978—and grudgingly increased its meager marketing outlay. As a result, Coors's 1982 sales volume declined to less than 12 million barrels for the first time in ten years, and the company relinquished its third-place ranking to Stroh Brewing Company. This decline came in spite of the expansion of Coors's distribution area across the Mississippi for the first time in 1981, when the company began selling its beer in Louisiana, Mississippi, and Tennessee.

Although Coors's sales increased from $1.1 billion in 1983 to $1.8 billion in 1989, profits declined from $89 million to $13 million, and the company's return on sales dropped from eight percent to less than one percent. Some observers blamed the brewery's entrenched family management, which they characterized as reactionary. But larger industrywide trends also contributed to the low earnings. The beer market's customer base began to stagnate in the mid-1980s, forcing brewers to use margin-lowering tactics to build volume and share. These included brand segmentation, increased advertising, international expansion, and heavy discounting.

Late 1980s into the 21st Century: Changing Times Under Peter Coors

Under the direction of Peter Coors, the brewery eagerly sought to catch up with its larger rivals. In 1987 Peter Coors, a great-grandson of the founder, was named vice-chairman, president, and CEO of Coors Brewing Company, a new beer-focused subsidiary of Adolph Coors Company (Bill Coors remained chairman of the parent company). The new leader was a driving force behind Coors's groundswell of change and continued on that course in the late 1980s into the early 1990s. Under his direction, the brewery completely reversed its advertising course: by the early 1990s, Coors began to spend more—in terms of advertising per barrel of beer sold—than its bigger rivals. Coors Light became the company's best-selling beer, America's third-ranking light beer, and the number one light beer in Canada. The company embraced the concept of brand segmentation and discounting, introducing the "economy" or "popularly priced" Keystone and Keystone Light in 1989. Ostensibly offering "bottled-beer taste in a can," these beers boosted sales volume, raising overall Coors sales to ten percent of the beer market and winning back the number three spot. But at the same time, such new products took market share away from other Coors brands, including the family's original label, which lost one-third of its sales volume from the mid-1980s to the mid-1990s.

While Keystone appealed to the budget-minded beer drinker, other new beverages targeted the higher-margin "specialty" and "boutique" markets. The domestic company craftily entered the fast-growing import market with the introduction of "George Killian's Irish Red," a defunct Irish brand licensed by Coors and produced in the United States. Even without the support of television advertising, the faux import was able to compete with the Boston Beer Company, Inc.'s domestically microbrewed Samuel Adams brand for leadership of the specialty beer segment.

In 1992, Coors launched Zima, one of the beer industry's most creative new beverages. The clear, foam-free malted brew created a whole new beverage category. The drink's novelty won it instant popularity that fizzled even before Coors could introduce its first derivative, Zima Gold, in 1995. Analysts noted the telling fact that neither Anheuser-Busch nor Miller, both savvy marketers, followed Coors's lead into the clearmalt category. Zima Gold was pulled from the market after six weeks of disappointing sales.

Peter Coors was not afraid to buck decades of family tradition, chalking up several firsts that had previously been renounced. With Coors running up against its lone brewery's 20-million-barrel annual capacity, Peter floated the company's first long-term debt offering in 1990. Later in 1990, he tried to negotiate a $425 million acquisition of Stroh Brewing, but ended up buying its three-million-barrel-capacity Memphis, Tennessee brewery for about $50 million. If, as Peter Coors hinted to a reporter in a March 1991 *Forbes* article, the company wanted to mount a challenge to second-ranking Miller Brewing, it would still need to double its U.S. brewing capacity. Meanwhile, in 1991, the company's distribution area covered all 50 states for the first time.

In 1992 Coors spun off the company's nonbeer assets—including the high-tech ceramics division, as well as the aluminum and packaging businesses—as ACX Technologies, Inc. Coors shareholders received one share of ACX for every three shares of the brewing company. The divestment was considered successful: ACX's sales increased from $544 million in 1991 to $732 million in 1994, and profits multiplied from $1.3 million to $20 million over the same period.

In 1993, Peter Coors broke with 121 years of history by hiring the first nonfamily member to the presidency of the brewing business. His choice, W. Leo Kiely, reflected Coors's new emphasis on marketing. Kiely had been a top marketing executive with Frito-Lay Company, a division of PepsiCo, Inc. The new president was given a straightforward, but arduous mandate: increase Coors's return on investment from less than five percent to ten percent by 1997. A significant cost-cutting move came in the form of a 1993 workforce reduction of 700, which was accompanied by a $70 million charge that led to the company's first full-year loss in ten years.

With the Zima brand faltering, Coors looked for growth from overseas markets and from a new specialty brewing venture. In 1994 the company purchased the El Aquila brewery in

Zaragoza, Spain, to manufacture Coors Gold for the Spanish market and Coors Extra Gold and Coors Light for several markets in Europe. That same year Jinro-Coors brewery in Cheong-Won, South Korea—which was one-third owned by Coors—began operation. Coors's partner in the venture, Jinro Limited, ran into financial difficulties later in the decade, leading to the sale of the brewery to another company and ending Coors's involvement. In 1995 Coors entered the microbrewery market with the opening of the SandLot Brewery located at Coors Field in Denver, the home of Major League Baseball's Colorado Rockies. Specialty beers under the Blue Moon label began to be crafted at this 4,000-barrel-capacity facility. In 1997 the company entered into a partnership with Foster's Brewing Group Limited of Australia and the Molson Companies Limited of Canada for the distribution of Coors brands in Canada. The following year Molson gained Foster's stake, giving Molson a 49.9 percent stake and Coors a 50.1 percent stake.

From 1988 to 1997 Coors increased its share of the U.S. market from 8.8 percent to 10.7 percent. Production increased over the same period from 16.5 million barrels to 20.4 million. Coors remained a distant third to Anheuser-Busch and Miller, but it had made strides in improving profitability, in part from an overhaul of what had been a convoluted U.S. distribution system. In 1997 the company reported net income of $82.3 million on sales of $1.82 billion, which translated into a net profit margin of 4.5 percent—a significant increase over the previous year's figure of 2.5 percent.

By 1999 sales had surpassed the $2 billion mark for the first time, and net income reached $92.3 million. Return on average shareholders' equity reached 11.4 percent, a vast improvement over the low single-digit figures of the early 1990s. That year Coors sold 23 million barrels of malt beverages. Surprisingly, a comeback by Zima was a driving force behind the improving results. Zima was repositioning as a refreshing alcoholic beverage, and as an alternative to beer—and its taste was altered to make it less sweet and more tangy. Consequently, sales began rising in 1998 and 1999, although they failed to reattain the peak level of 1994. In 1999 Zima Citrus was introduced, offering a blend of natural citrus flavors. Among other late 1990s new product introductions was Coors Non-Alcoholic, a premium brew with less than 0.5 percent alcohol by volume.

In May 2000, on the heels of the record 1999 performance, Peter Coors was named chairman of Coors Brewing Company and president and CEO of Adolph Coors Company, with Bill Coors remaining chairman of the parent company. Kiely was promoted to president and CEO of Coors Brewing. Under the leadership of Peter Coors and Kiely, the company was likely to continue its increasing focus on profitability and growth. With only two percent of revenues being derived outside the United States, the management team was also likely to pursue overseas opportunities in a prudent manner, keeping a keen eye on the earnings potential of such ventures.

Principal Subsidiaries

Coors Brewing Company; Coors Brewing Company International, Inc.; Coors Brewing Iberica, S.A. (Spain); Coors Distributing Company; Coors Energy Company; Gap Run Pipeline Company; Coors Nova Scotia Co. (Canada); Coors Global, Inc.;

Coors Intercontinental, Inc.; The Rocky Mountain Water Company; The Wannamaker Ditch Company; Coors Japan Company, Ltd.; Coors Brewing Company de Mexico, S. de R.L. de C.V.; Coors Brewing International, Ltd. (U.K.); Coors Export Ltd. (Barbados); Coors Canada, Inc.

Principal Competitors

Anheuser-Busch Companies, Inc.; Bass Brewers; The Boston Beer Company, Inc.; Brauerei Beck & Co.; Canandaigua Brands, Inc.; Carlsberg A/S; Foster's Brewing Group Limited; The Gambrinus Company; Genesee Corporation; Grupo Modelo, S.A. de C.V.; Guinness Ltd.; Heineken N.V.; Interbrew S.A.; Kirin Brewery Company, Limited; Miller Brewing Company; S&P Company; Scottish & Newcastle plc.

Further Reading

"Adolph Coors: Brewing Up Plans for an Invasion of the East Coast," *Business Week,* September 29, 1980, p. 120.

Atchison, Sandra D., and Marc Frons, "Can Pete and Jeff Coors Brew Up a Comeback?," *Business Week,* December 16, 1985, pp. 86+.

Banham, Russ, *Coors: A Rocky Mountain Legend,* Lyme, Conn.: Greenwich Publishing, 1998.

Baum, Dan, *Citizen Coors: An American Dynasty,* New York: Morrow, 1999.

Burgess, Robert J., "Popular Keystone Hurt Other Coors Brands," *Denver Business Journal,* April 30, 1993, p. A1.

——, *Silver Bullets: A Soldier's Story of How Coors Bombed in the Beer Wars,* New York: St. Martin's Press, 1993.

Cloud, John, "Why Coors Went Soft," *Time,* November 2, 1998, p. 70.

Conny, Beth Mende, *Coors, A Catalyst for Change: The Pioneering of the Aluminum Can,* Golden, Colo.: Adolph Coors Company, 1990.

"Coors' Bitter Brew," *Financial World,* April 30, 1983, pp. 31+.

"Coors: The Adolph Coors Story," Golden, Colo.: Adolph Coors Company, 1984.

Dawson, Havis, "Hey. Beer. Plan.," *Beverage World,* August 15, 1998, pp. 37–38, 40, 42.

Fulscher, Todd James, *A Study of Labor Relations at the Adolph Coors Brewery,* M.A. thesis, Denver: University of Denver, 1994.

Hunter, Kris, "Battle of the Beers," *Memphis Business Journal,* March 13, 1995, p. 34.

Lane, Randall, "Splitsville in Coors Country," *Forbes,* April 10, 1995, p. 52.

Lang, Tam, *Coors: A Report on the Company's Environmental Policies and Practices,* New York: Council on Economic Priorities, Corporate Environmental Data Clearinghouse, 1992.

Lubove, Seth, "No Fizz in the Profits," *Forbes,* September 7, 1998, pp. 72–74.

Melcher, Richard A., "Why Zima Faded So Fast," *Business Week,* March 10, 1997, p. 110.

Ortega, Bob, "Zima Goes Cool and Gets Hot, Sells What It Is, Not What It's Not," *Wall Street Journal,* July 2, 1999, p. B6.

Poole, Claire, "Shirtsleeves to Shirtsleeves," *Forbes,* March 4, 1991, p. 52.

The Pre-Prohibition History of Adolph Coors Company, 1873–1933, Golden, Colo.: Adolph Coors Company, 1973.

Sellers, Patricia, "A Whole New Ball Game in Beer," *Fortune,* September 19, 1994, p. 79.

Theodore, Sarah, "Company of the Year: The Nation's Third-Largest Brewer Puts Focus on Results," *Beverage Industry,* January 2000, pp. 21–22.

"Time in a Bottle: Adolph Coors Company," Golden, Colo.: Adolph Coors Company, 1984.

Verespej, Michael A., "This Coors Is Different," *Industry Week,* July 22, 1985, pp. 53+.

—April Dougal Gasbarre
—updated by David E. Salamie

AEP Industries, Inc.

125 Phillips Avenue
South Hackensack, New Jersey 07606
U.S.A.
Telephone: (201) 641-6600
Toll Free: (800) 999-2374
Fax: (201) 807-2490
Web site: http://www.aepinc.com

Public Company
Incorporated: 1970 as A.E.P. Industries, Inc.
Employees: 3,200
Sales: $670.05 million (fiscal 1999)
Stock Exchanges: NASDAQ
Ticker Symbol: AEPI
NAIC: 326112 Unsupported Packaging Film and Sheet
Manufacturing

AEP Industries, Inc. is a leading worldwide manufacturer of multipurpose flexible plastic packaging films, both general and specialty. These more than 15,000 types of films are used in the packaging, transportation, beverage, food, automotive, pharmaceutical, chemical, electronics, construction, agriculture, and textile industries. AEP's manufacturing operations, producing over one billion pounds of film per year, are located in 11 countries in North America, Europe, and the Asia/Pacific region.

Private Startup Firm: 1970–86

AEP was founded in 1970 by Brendan Barba and his uncle, David J. McFarland, with Barba taking the positions of president and chief executive officer. He later also took the post of chairman of the board. McFarland became executive vice-president, secretary, and treasurer in 1974 and retired in 1989. The company, based in Moonachie, New Jersey, originally specialized in film-grade low-density polyethylene. The recessionary, high-inflation 1970s were a difficult decade for business, but AEP introduced Herculon films, which were difficult-to-manufacture products based on its own proprietary compounding, blending, and processing technology. The develop-

ment of these films enabled AEP to save money on the costs of its resin supplies in a fragmented field noted for intense competition and low profit margins.

AEP opened a factory in Moonachie in 1973, a second in Matthews, North Carolina, in 1977, and a third in Los Angeles in 1978, with total capacity in 1980 of 34,000 metric tons. About 40 percent of all its products were Herculon films. The product line included trash bags; construction and agricultural films; clarity sheeting; shrink and stretch films; pallet covers; other low-density polyethylene bags, tubing, and sheeting; high-density polyethylene grease-proof liners; industrial packaging; and merchandise bags and specialties. AEP provided film in widths ranging from one inch to 12 feet and printed bags in up to six colors. All shipping was being done in company-owned trucks, with distribution over a 500-mile radius.

In 1982 AEP Industries initiated a program to penetrate the specialty and premium market, where profit margins were higher. AEP's net sales increased from $36.84 million in fiscal 1982 (the year ended October 31, 1982) to $62.4 million in fiscal 1986. Net income rose from $1.06 million to $2.76 million. With the opening of a 25-million-pound plant in Waxahachie, Texas, in 1985, the company now had total capacity of more than 125 million pounds and claimed to be the largest independent film processor in the United States. In 1986 AEP became a public company, raising $11.18 million in net proceeds by selling about one-third of its outstanding common stock at $11 a share.

At this time AEP's main products included a wide assortment of packaging materials, such as carton and drum liners; bundle film used to package small containers, periodicals, and other products; furniture and mattress covers; shrink pallet covers; textile and carpet wrappers and bags; sheeting materials; and a variety of other packaging films. The company also was producing heavy-duty films used in the construction industry as moisture and insulating barriers and mulch films used to cover crop fields in order to achieve more efficient plant growth. Additional products included nursery film used to cover greenhouses, embossed film lamination-grade and high-clarity film for special applications, and a variety of industrial wrapping materials. Specialty and premium items accounted for about

---

Company Perspectives:

With over a quarter of a century of expertise in flexible packaging films, AEP can offer you the best knowledge, service and delivery schedules in the industry. We have over one hundred sales representatives dedicated exclusively to serving AEP customers in every major market. Our AEP representative will learn your business needs, answer your questions, help you select the most cost-efficient products, and even help you design new films to meet special applications.

At AEP, you get tomorrow's capabilities and products . . . today.

---

11 percent of total sales in fiscal 1986. The company had about 4,800 customers, none of them representing over two percent of sales.

Raising the Bar: 1987–98

AEP Industries' technicians had begun working by this time on a new generation of high-strength stretch films, a recent and fast-growing market used mostly for wrapping pallets of merchandise; that offered cost and other advantages over shrink films or strapping. Production of stretch films began in 1988, with concentration on the ultra-high-performance grade and no production of the standard grade. By now the company had one of the most varied product lines available from a single source as well as national distribution, which distinguished it from more than 90 percent of the 300 or so companies in its field. AEP's net sales passed $100 million in fiscal 1988, when it earned record net income of $4.06 million. New records of $120.96 million and $5.33 million, respectively, were established in fiscal 1989.

In 1989 AEP Industries purchased Design Poly Bag Corp. for stock from its shareholders, who included Barba and McFarland. The company acquired the stretch-film business of Princeton Packaging Inc. in December 1990 for $8.16 million. Production capacity reached 209 million pounds of extruded polyethylene film in fiscal 1990. Film gauge ranged from one to ten mils, with one mil being .001 inch. AEP's proprietary agricultural polyethylene white-on-white films were being used in the South, where sunlight is intense. Plants grew through the film, and the reflective properties of the white-on-white material prevented them from burning. A similar black film was being used in the North to conduct heat. AEP moved its headquarters from Moonachie to South Hackensack, New Jersey, and the Los Angeles plant to Chico, California, about this time.

By the end of 1992 the average annual production capacity of AEP Industries' plants exceeded 290 million pounds. Its extrusion equipment could produce and print film sheets up to 40 feet wide. Specialty products, a category including industrial stretch film, now accounted for about 38 percent of total sales. Foreign sales were becoming significant, although still comprising less than six percent of the total. AEP added a plant in Alsip, Illinois, in 1994 and broke ground on a 300,000-square-foot, $16.4 million facility in Wright Township, Pennsylvania, in 1995. Operations in Moonachie were transferred to this plant in 1996.

Fiscal 1993 through 1995 were banner years for AEP Industries, with net sales rising from $153.31 million to $242.89 million and net income from $6.88 million to $13.49 million over this period. In October 1996 AEP acquired the packaging division of Borden, Inc. from investment firm Kohlberg, Kravis, Roberts & Co. for about $280 million and 2.4 million shares of stock, thereby raising its long-term debt from $81.5 million to $328 million. This purchase established AEP as the largest manufacturer of polyvinyl chloride (PVC) food wrap and polyethylene stretch film in North America. The major Borden lines included PVC stretch films for packaging of seats, poultry, and produce; PVC-based food wrap films in cutter boxes and in perforated rolls for institutions; polyethylene-based stretch wrap films for utilizing pallet loads; oriented polypropylene (OPP) films for flexible packaging of salted snacks, confectionery, and baked goods; polypropylene films for processed cheese products; and rigid containers and trays.

Borden entered the plastics packaging field in 1957, when it began making polyvinyl chloride in two plants. It ranked 14th among North American film and sheet makers in 1995, but its operations were worldwide, with about $300 million of its $625 million in sales in Europe, $250 million in North America, and $75 million in the Asia/Pacific region. Based in North Andover, Massachusetts, the plastics packaging division was operating plants making Resinite PVC-based films there and in Griffin, Georgia; Gainesville, Texas; Edmonton, Alberta; and West Hill, Ontario. It was also making OPP Proponite film at a second plant in North Andover. In Europe, Borden had three plastics packaging plants in France and the Netherlands; two in England; and one each in Belgium, Italy, and Scotland. There were two each in Australia, New Zealand, and South Africa. A Japanese plant was a joint venture with Hitachi Chemical Company Ltd.

Following the acquisition, AEP closed the Borden plant making Resinite PVC films in North Andover. The second Proponite plant was sold in 1999 for $13.3 million, and the South African operation was sold in 1998 for $1.3 million. In 1998 AEP sold all five of Borden's former oriented polypropylene (OPP) film units for producing rigid containers and trays to Applied Extrusion Technologies for net proceeds of $13.9 million. In 1998 AEP was the packaging industry's largest provider of supermarket, processor, and food-service films. The Stretch Film Division ranked first in sales and capacity in North America, with production of more than 255 million pounds.

In North America, AEP was manufacturing Resinite (PVC) food wrap in Griffin for the supermarket, consumer, institutional, and industrial markets, offering a broad range of products with about 45 different formulations. These films were used for packaging of fresh red meats, poultry, fish, fruits and vegetables, and bakery products. This facility was also manufacturing dispenser (cutter) boxes containing PVC food wrap for sales to consumers and institutions. AEP was manufacturing a broad range of industrial films in North America, generally custom-designed, including sheeting, tubing, and bags. It was also manufacturing a family of high-performance stretch wrap for wrapping and securing palletized products for shipping.

AEP's European Resinite Division was manufacturing polyvinyl chloride food wrap in cutter boxes and perforated rolls at three plants. The European Flexibles division was manufacturing

Key Dates:

1970: Company is founded by Brendan Barba and David J. McFarland.
1973: Company opens its first factory in Moonachie, New Jersey.
1986: AEP becomes a public company, selling one-third of its stock.
1988: AEP begins producing ultra-high-performance stretch films.
1992: Specialty products, including stretch film, account for 38 percent of sales.
1995: Net income peaks at $13.49 million in this fiscal year.
1996: AEP greatly expands its scope by acquiring Borden, Inc.'s packaging division.

flexible packaging and converted films used in the food-processing and pharmaceutical industries and polyethylene-based stretch wrap for wrapping and securing pallet loads. The Italian plant, Fabbrica Italiana Articoli Plastici (FIAP), was manufacturing PVC food wrap, unplasticized PVC twist wrap, and converted and printed films. Unplasticized PVC twist wrap was being used to wrap candles, candies, and similar products as a low-cost substitute for cellophane. AEP's Asia/Pacific operations resembled its North American and European operations, with the same variety of films produced in Australia and New Zealand. The 50 percent joint venture, Hitachi Chemical Filtec Inc., was supplying PVC food wrap to the Japanese market.

Entering the New Millennium

In 2000 AEP Industries was making over 15,000 types of multipurpose and flexible packaging films to meet any type of application in almost any combination of tensile strength, thickness, shrinkability, toughness, surface friction, sealability, permeability, transparency, and clarity, in every existing form—sheeting, tubing and cut, rolled or perforated bags. Polyvinyl chloride wrap, industrial films, stretched (pallet) wrap, and other products and specialty films were being produced in North America, Europe, and the Asia/Pacific region. Printed and converted films providing flexible packaging to consumer markets were being produced in Europe and the Asia/Pacific region. During 1999 North America accounted for 61 percent of sales, Europe for 28 percent, and the Asia/Pacific region for 11 percent. There were 22 plants in 11 countries in 1999. In 2000

the number of plants rose to 27: 11 in North America, nine in Western Europe, and seven in Asia and the Pacific.

AEP Industries' net sales peaked at $709.07 million in fiscal 1997 and declined with the sale of the OPP units; the 1999 total was $670.05 million. Net income peaked with the fiscal 1995 figure of $13.49 million. After deducting a $5.51 million charge for discontinued operations, the company had net income of only $263,000 in fiscal 1998, a result it attributed mainly to the Asian financial crisis. AEP took a charge of $18.97 million for the discontinued OPP operations in fiscal 1999 and had a net loss of $14.5 million for the year. The long-term debt was $302 million at the end of fiscal 1999. In January 2000 Borden, Inc. owned 32.4 percent of AEP's common stock. EGS Partners owned 23.9 percent, and Barba owned 17.5 percent.

Principal Subsidiaries

Design Poly Bag Corp.; Rhodes Plastics Corp.

Principal Operating Units

Asia/Pacific Group; FIAP Group; Flexibles Group; Industrial Products Division; Polyvinyl Chloride; PROformance Films Group; Resinite Division; Resinite Group; Stretch Film Division.

Principal Competitors

Bemis Co., Inc.; Bonar Packaging Inc.; Flex Products Inc.; Tekron Corp.

Further Reading

Campanella, Frank W., "Film Highlight," *Barron's* July 20, 1987, pp. 52–53.
Cross, Zeta, "Manufacturer Lured by Rail Service," *Northeast Pennsylvania Business Journal,* June 1995, p. 9.
Ford, Tom, "OPP, Polyester Film Makers Restructuring," *Plastics News,* January 29, 1996, pp. 1, 24.
"How a Film Company More Than Survives," *Modern Plastics,* July 1980, p. 16.
Metz, Robert, "Polyethylene Makers' Bad News Brings at Least One Major Supplier into Focus," *Boston Globe,* February 11, 1990, p. A2.
Schmitt, Bill, "OPP Films: More Consolidation to Come," *Chemical Week,* March 11, 1999, p. 11.
Ziegler, Martin, "AEP Industries, Inc. (AEPI)," *Wall Street Transcript,* July 14, 1986, pp. 82,524–82,525.

—Robert Halasz

Aggregate Industries plc

Bardon Hall, Copt Oak Road
Markfield, Leicestershire LE67 9PJ,
United Kingdom
Telephone: (+44) 1530 816-600
Fax: (+44) 1530 816-666
Web site: http://www.aggregate.com

Public Company
Incorporated: 1999
Employees: 6,910
Sales: £933.7 million (US$1.51 billion) (1999)
Stock Exchanges: London
Ticker Symbol: AGG.L
NAIC: 212312 Crushed and Broken Limestone Mining
and Quarrying

Anglo-American group Aggregate Industries plc is a leading producer of aggregates, stone and paving products and concrete products. In the United Kingdom, the company holds the number five position in its overall market, while in the United States the company has quickly risen to a number six position, and this despite the company's focus on regional rather than national operations. The product of the 1997 merger between the Bardon Group and Camas, Aggregate Industries is itself an aggregate of a long list of acquisitions—since 1998 the company has spent more than US$300 million acquiring more than 23 companies, primarily located in the company's U.S. focus regions of Massachusetts, Minnesota, North Dakota, the Mid-Atlantic region (Maryland, Virginia, Washington, D.C.), Colorado, and Michigan. In the United Kingdom, Aggregate Industries concentrates on the Southwest, Midlands, and northern England regions and Scotland, with a network of more than 20 factories. The company's reserve holdings include sites at the Leicestershire super quarry. Aggregate Industries' aggressive growth drive in the United States coincides with declining infrastructure spending in the United Kingdom and the massive US$200 billion federal budget earmarked for improvements to the U.S. roads, bridges, and highway system. One of the leaders of the consolidation wave in the aggregates industry, the company has built up more than three billion tons of consented stone reserve quarries in the United Kingdom and in the United States, which alone accounted for 1.7 billion tons of consented stone reserves, giving the company more than 20 years' worth of raw materials reserves. After failing in its reverse takeover attempt of rival Tarmac (subsequently merged with Anglo American Ltd.), Aggregate Industries has contented itself with a policy of growth through acquisition, which enabled the company to raise its annual sales to £933 million (US$1.5 billion) in 1999. More than half of the company's sales are generated in the United States; the United Kingdom accounts for most of the remaining sales, although the company does some business in the rest of Europe, particularly in Norway, where Aggregate Industries operates an undersea quarrying business. In January 2000, all of the company's operations—which previously traded under the Bardon, Camas, and other names—were regrouped under two divisions, Aggregate Industries US and Aggregate Industries Europe. Aggregate Industries is led by CEO Peter Tom.

An Aggregates Aggregate in the 1990s

The formation of Aggregate Industries represented the result of a long string of mergers and acquisitions made primarily during the aggregates industry's consolidation wave in the early 1990s. The chief components of the merger were the Bardon Group and Camas, the quarrying, sand, and gravel concern spun off from English China Clays in 1994. Another component of the company was Evered Plc., founded in 1922, one of the early entrants in the United Kingdom's aggregates industries. Evered, however, found itself in trouble at the start of the 1990s, particularly after its £138 million acquisition of subsea quarrying unit Civil & Marine Ltd.

The popularization of the automobile as a transportation means brought on an increasing demand for aggregates and new concrete products needed for building national road, bridge, and highway systems. For much of the 20th century, quarrying and processing of aggregates remained a highly fragmented industry, with many small and mid-sized producers supplying largely local and regional markets. One of these companies was Bardon Hill Quarries Limited, which operated a granite quarry at Charnwood Forest, the Leicestershire super quarry. Joining

Bardon Hill in 1956 was Peter Tom, who later took over leadership of the company and helped build it into one of the United Kingdom's largest in the industry. Despite taking Bardon public with a listing on the London stock exchange in 1988, the Tom family's stake remained at nearly 60 percent of Bardon Hill into the early years of the 1990s.

Another of the Aggregate Industries founding companies was also taking shape by the early 1990s. English China Clay, which specialized for much of the century in the mining of kaolin—the fine white clay used for making porcelain and a variety of other uses—had branched out into more diversified quarrying and aggregate product areas, with operations including sand, gravel, building block, and crushed rock production. In 1994, however, English China Clay, which had been attempting to transform itself into a specialty chemicals company—before being taken over by France's Imetal—spun off its aggregates interests into a new company, Camas, which was led by CEO Alan Shearer. With operations in the United States, Camas also owned a quarry at the Leicestershire super quarry site.

Camas, which joined the market as the United Kingdom's fifth largest aggregates producer, was part of a new wave of aggregates companies amidst an industry hard hit during the protracted economic crisis in the United Kingdom. Helping to lead the consolidation was Bardon Hill, led by Peter Tom. In 1991, Bardon Hill merged with Evered Plc. to form Evered Bardon Plc. The merger created an entity of more than 15 member companies—including quarrying operations in the United States—and took a position as one of the United Kingdom's industry leaders. A year after the merger, the company changed its name to the Bardon Group.

By then, however, the Bardon Group was having its own financial difficulties. In 1992, the company posted some £8 million in losses. The company attempted to sell the Civil & Marine subsidiary inherited from Evered in order to reduce the company's debt level. But, facing a collapsing market, the sale was halted, forcing the company to write off some £63 million and sinking it deeper into the red, to the tune of £28 million. The Civil & Marine sell-off was not completed until 1995.

The aggregates markets in both the United Kingdom and United States began to rebound toward the middle of the 1990s, leading to a new wave of industry consolidations. The Bardon Group showed itself an aggressive mover, particularly in the United States, where its acquisitions included EL Gardner in 1996, and AH Smith, Mid Atlantic Materials, and assets of Solite, boosting the company's Mid-Atlantic regional presence. Bardon had also built a strong presence in the Massachusetts area. The spinoff of Camas from English China Clays in 1994 set the stage for the emergence of a new major player in both the European and North American aggregates markets.

Aggressive Aggregates for the 21st Century

By the mid-1990s, the Bardon Group had grown to sales of more than £317 million. Camas itself had reached sales of more than £338 million. The two companies' operations were largely complementary—which led to merger talks in 1996. After a year of negotiations—held up by disagreements between Peter Tom and Alan Shearer over which CEO was to lead the merged entity—the deal was struck in 1997. Tom had won the battle for the CEO seat in what was described as a reverse takeover—while Shearer, only two years from retirement, agreed to walk away with a £500,000 settlement. The new company was given a new name, Aggregate Industries—suggesting the company's intention to be an aggressive player in the consolidating aggregates industry. The combination of the company's operations already gave it a strong position in both the United Kingdom and the United States, where the company could claim leadership status in four major regions.

By 1998, Aggregate Industries was set to become a powerhouse in the aggregates industry. Already during the year, the company had made a number of acquisitions, including that of Douglas Concrete. Then the company confirmed that it had spent more than a year in talks with rival aggregates group Tarmac plc to merge the two companies. Yet these talks, too, had stumbled on the question of company leadership—as Tom, gambling on shareholder impatience to see the deal through, insisted that Tarmac give up management control of the merged company, despite Tarmac being the larger player.

Tarmac refused, and the deal died at the end of 1998. Instead, Aggregate Industries adopted a new strategy, that of an aggressive campaign of acquisitions of smaller companies, and especially in order to build up leadership positions in its target U.S. regions—which now included Michigan. As such, Aggregate Industries expected to capitalize on the massive US$216 billion infrastructure spending plan announced by Congress in 1998, calling for repairs and new construction for U.S. roads, bridges, and highways.

Aggregate Industries was by then launching its own massive spending plan—in 1998 and 1999 the company spent more than US$300 million on acquisitions. A major acquisition came in 1998 when the company spent US$53 million acquiring Bill Smith Sand & Gravel, giving the company a strong entry into the Michigan market. The following year, however, proved to be the company's most aggressive, as Aggregate Industries spent some US$230 million in ten strategic acquisitions, including Hammer Group of Colorado, for US$18.7 million in February 1999, and Golden's, also in Colorado, in November for US$61.5 million.

By the beginning of 2000, Aggregate Industries' operations in the United States had topped its U.K. operations in terms of sales. The robustness of the U.S. economy and the high level of fragmentation in the industry there made that market a top target for the company's future growth. In order to present a unified presence, the company decided to change all of the names of its U.S. subsidiaries under the single Aggregate Industries name.

Key Dates:

1922:	Evered Plc is founded.
1956:	Peter Tom joins Bardon Hill Quarries Limited.
1988:	Bardon Hill goes public.
1990:	Evered acquires Civil & Marine.
1991:	Evered and Bardon Hill merge to form Evered Bardon.
1993:	Company changes name to Bardon Group.
1994:	Camas is spun off from English China Clay.
1995:	Bardon Group sells Civil & Marine.
1997:	Bardon Group and Camas merge to form Aggregate Industries.
1998:	Company aborts proposed merger with Tarmac plc.
1999:	Aggregate Industries begins acquisition spree.
2000:	Company changes name of all U.S. operations to Aggregate Industries US.

The company also continued its acquisition drive, picking up ten new companies in the first half of the year, including Holst Excavating, Mobilcrete and Sioux Valley Ready Mix, in Minneapolis and Michigan Colprovia Company.

Aggregate Industries looked forward to making more acquisitions, with a promise to spend another £50 million in the second half of 2000. Moreover, the company could even look forward to acquiring parts of Tarmac after all. After the takeover of Tarmac by Anglo-American Inc., the minerals giant was said to be seeking to sell off Tarmac's U.S.-based aggregates operations. That move fit right into Aggregate Industries' plans to build itself into a major aggregates leader through an aggressive acquisition program in the new century.

Principal Subsidiaries

Aggregate Industries US; Aggregate Industries Europe.

Principal Competitors

Boral Limited; Holnam Inc.; Cemex SA de CV; Lafarge SA; CRH; Martin Marietta Materials; Essroc; Southdown, Inc.; Florida Rock Industries; Taiheiyo Cement; Giant Cement Holding, Inc.; Titan Cement Company; Holderbank; Vulcan Materials Company.

Further Reading

"Aggregate Industries Consolidates Division Names," *Rock Products*, February 1, 2000.

Casciato, Paul, "Aggregate Year Profits up 27 pct.," *Reuters*, March 6, 2000.

Doran, James, "Aggregate Set for £50m Spending Spree," *Times*, August 8, 2000.

Guerrera, Francesco, "AI Plans £60m Buying Spree," *Independent*, March 11, 1999, p. 21.

Morrison, Doug, "Clear the Tarmac for Talks," *Sunday Telegraph*, December 20, 1998.

—M. L. Cohen

Alberto-Culver Company

2525 Armitage Avenue
Melrose Park, Illinois 60160
U.S.A.
Telephone: (708) 450-3000
Fax: (708) 450-3354
Web site: http://www.alberto.com

Public Company
Incorporated: 1955
Employees: 13,400
Sales: $1.98 billion (1999)
Stock Exchanges: New York
Ticker Symbols: ACVA; ACV
NAIC: 325620 Toilet Preparation Manufacturing; 311942
    Spice and Extract Manufacturing; 446120 Cosmetics,
    Beauty Supplies, and Perfume Stores; 421850 Service
    Establishment Equipment and Supplies Wholesalers;
    422210 Drugs and Druggists' Sundries Wholesalers

Alberto-Culver Company markets a range of toiletry, grocery, and household brands. Its flagship brand is the Alberto VO5 line of hair care products. Other products include the St. Ives Swiss Formula hair care and skin care line, the TRESemmé hair care line, the FDS feminine hygiene line, Mrs. Dash spices, Molly McButter sprinkle-on butter substitute, Static Guard anti-static spray, and several brands of ethnic-specific personal care products. Generating more than half of the company's revenues is the Sally Beauty Company unit, the largest distributor of professional beauty products in the world, with more than 2,250 outlets and a distribution network catering to salon professionals and beauticians. Alberto-Culver has done well as a moderate-sized, family-run company in an industry of giants primarily through introducing new products and aggressively advertising them, and by making carefully selected acquisitions.

1955–69: From Alberto VO5 to Sally Beauty

The company dates back to the 1950s. Under the harsh, hair-frying lights of Hollywood motion picture studios, word was spreading about a product named after the chemist who invented it: Alberto VO5 Conditioning Hairdressing. With a unique water-free, five-oil formula, VO5 had been developed at the request of studios and had proven successful at rescuing hair from dryness and damage. In 1955 Leonard H. Lavin borrowed $400,000 and bought the small beauty supply firm that manufactured VO5. This regional Los Angeles-based company also made more than 100 other products, but Alberto VO5 made up 85 percent of its sales. After buying the firm, Lavin dropped its other products, relocated to Chicago, and concentrated on VO5. He was just 36 years old at the time and his wife, Bernice, joined the company as secretary-treasurer. The Alberto-Culver Company had five employees on the production line and two employees in sales for its first year of operation.

The first television commercial for VO5 ran in Pennsylvania in 1955. It marked the company's first year of operation and the start of a company mainstay—aggressive marketing. In three years, sales were more than $5 million. By 1958 Alberto VO5 Conditioning Hairdressing had raced to the top of its category, outselling many sizable competitors. In 1956 and 1959 some other products were added to the line, and TRESemmé—a regional line of hair colors—was purchased. TRESemmé later grew to include a best-selling professional mousse. Then in 1961 and 1962, Alberto VO5 Hair Spray and Alberto VO5 Shampoo were introduced and, along with Alberto VO5 Conditioning Hairdressing, became the financial cornerstones of the company.

The 1960s were a time of explosive growth. The company went public in 1961, trading stock over the counter. A new plant and corporate offices were built in Melrose Park, Illinois, in 1960, and a plant opened in Canada in 1961. That same year, an international division was formed to sell products in Mexico, England, Australia, Guatemala, and elsewhere. Company sales surged to $25 million in 1961, then boomed to $61 million in 1962. By 1963 Alberto-Culver was ranked second among advertisers of hair care products. The results were evident: in 1964 sales were still climbing, exceeding more than $100 million. Company stock was listed on the New York Stock Exchange in 1965.

Other products were introduced in the mid-1960s. Consort Hair Spray was the first product of its kind made specifically for men. New Dawn Hair Color was the first shampoo-in permanent hair color on the retail market. The first feminine deodorant spray, FDS, was introduced in 1966 and has been a leader in that product category ever since—despite a dip in sales following the hexachlorophene scare of the early 1970s. Kleen Guard Furniture Polish went on sale in 1966, and new manufacturing operations were initiated in Mexico and Puerto Rico. By 1967 Alberto-Culver Company had more than 2,000 employees and sold products in more than 65 countries.

Alberto-Culver acquired several companies toward the end of the 1960s. The first was SugarTwin, a low-calorie sugar substitute sold regionally as part of Alberto-Culver's Food Service Division. The company slashed SugarTwin's calories in half and released it into national distribution, along with Brown SugarTwin, the first low-calorie granulated brown sugar replacement. These items were credited with much of the growth of the food sector of Alberto-Culver. With the federal ban on cyclamates and the conversion to a saccharin formula, SugarTwin's double-digit growth slowed, but it remained a profitable brand for the company.

In 1969 Alberto-Culver acquired Milani Foods and Sally Beauty Company, Inc. Milani represented a range of food products sold to restaurants, hospitals, and other institutions. Milani was folded into Alberto-Culver's Food Service Division and marketed about 400 items, including food bases, beverages, soups, and dressings. Sally Beauty Company was not unlike Alberto VO5: a concept with a lot of promise. At the time Alberto-Culver purchased it, Sally Beauty consisted of one store and nine independent franchises that sold professional products for hair stylists and barbers. The franchises were closed, and Alberto-Culver developed a new merchandising strategy. This eventually bloomed into more than 1,000 company-owned and -operated outlets. Located mostly in shopping centers, with some 40 outlets in the United Kingdom, Sally Beauty Supply stores offered thousands of salon products and appliances to professionals as well as retail customers.

New Products and Acquisitions in the 1970s and 1980s

Alberto-Culver had another significant first in 1972: it won the fight for 30-second commercials. By buying standard 60-second slots, then dividing them to run two separate commercials for different products, the company caused an uproar. Networks balked and ad agencies scoffed, but before long, the 30-second commercial was an industry standard.

Alberto-Culver's hair care line seemed to reach its peak in the early 1970s. Sales were down in 1974, although company products were being sold in more than 100 countries, and a new food plant had been built in Melrose Park. Earnings were hard hit at this time by the Organization of Petroleum Exporting Countries

(OPEC) price increases that impacted petroleum-based raw material costs. After a decade of dizzying growth, the slump was alarming. As a result, money was redirected into new products.

Meanwhile, Alberto-Culver Company had developed an ethnic hair care line, TCB. It was launched in 1975 with eight products and grew to include 36 products considered leaders in domestic retail and professional markets as well as selling solidly abroad. The first 60-second hot oil deep conditioner, Alberto VO5 Hot Oil Treatment, was introduced in 1976 and became the country's number one selling brand. Static Guard, the first antistatic spray, was presented that same year and became a best-seller. Then in 1977, Alberto VO5 Hair Spray became the first nationally advertised premium brand to introduce an aerosol free of chlorofluorocarbons. According to Lavin, the company preferred to develop original products rather than copy products already on the market, a strategy that would require heavy investment to promote over competitors'. Alberto-Culver thus earned a reputation for innovation and for spending generously to promote the products it developed.

Another aspect of Alberto-Culver's comeback effort was the 1977 acquisition of the John A. Frye Shoe Company. Then a maker of western leather boots, Frye grew to include hand-sewn men's shoes and belts as well as products for women and children. In the 1980s Frye boots were nearly staple items, and by 1981 Frye accounted for 19 percent of Alberto-Culver's revenues. Following its established recipe for success, the company took Frye's regional name recognition and aggressively advertised and distributed its products. In 1980 Phillippe of California was acquired, along with its line of handbags. Phillippe underwent the same transformation as Frye, including the addition of a line of small leather accessories; within a year Phillippe was contributing five percent of the company's total sales. By 1986, however, Frye and Phillippe of California were both sold after accumulating $16 million in losses over three years. Alberto-Culver thereby returned to its core toiletries business.

A high degree of brand loyalty continued to make the Alberto VO5 hair care line a stable one. In 1982 it represented about a third of total Alberto-Culver sales. Research and marketing efforts were paying off in the company's other divisions. In 1983 Mrs. Dash—the first herb and spice alternative to salt—was introduced and went on to dominate sales in its category. This set the tone for a series of new healthful products in the Household/Grocery Products Division, including the first all-natural butter-flavor powder, Molly McButter, released in 1987.

Also performing well in the mid-1980s was Sally Beauty Company, which boasted 145 outlets by 1983, making it the nation's largest wholesaler of barber and beauty supplies. That same year, Alberto-Culver acquired Indola Cosmetics B.V., a prominent Dutch firm well known throughout Europe for products used by professional hairdressers. At first financially unsuccessful, Indola was extensively revamped, and its line was expanded to include all aspects of salon service, such as perms, hair colors, and specialty products. In 1990 it began to perform better and was making a fresh entrance into markets in Spain, Australia, and the Far East.

Alberto-Culver's sales improved in 1984, when they topped $400 million. Compared with such hair industry giants as Proc-

Key Dates:

1955: Leonard H. Lavin buys Alberto VO5 Conditioning Hairdressing and founds Alberto-Culver Company.
1961: Company goes public, introduces Alberto VO5 Hair Spray, and establishes an international sales division.
1962: Alberto VO5 Shampoo debuts.
1965: Company stock is listed on the New York Stock Exchange.
1969: Sally Beauty Company is acquired.
1975: Company launches an ethnic hair care line, TCB.
1977: Company acquires John A. Frye Shoe Company.
1980: Handbag maker Phillippe of California is purchased.
1983: Mrs. Dash is introduced.
1986: Frye and Phillippe of California are sold off.
1987: Molly McButter makes its debut.
1991: Company acquires Swedish firm, Cederroth International AB.
1994: Howard Bernick takes over as CEO.
1995: Molnlycke Toiletries is acquired and merged into Cederroth.
1996: St. Ives Laboratories Inc., with its St. Ives Swiss Formula brand, is acquired.
2000: Pro-Line Corporation is acquired.

ter & Gamble and Bristol-Myers, Alberto-Culver was tiny, but tough. Unable to compete with the industry goliaths in the areas of promotion, advertising, sales force, and recoverable losses, Alberto-Culver had to rely on sharp-wittedness and timing. In addition to its many firsts in products, the company distinguished itself as an innovator in advertising. After championing the 30-second commercial, Alberto-Culver again entered the ring to fight for the 15-second commercial. This battle actually led to a threatened class-action antitrust suit against the larger station group owners in broadcasting who refused to carry the split 30-second commercials. The suit was dropped when the restrictions against the ads were dropped. This was a significant win for companies of Alberto-Culver's size, which were pinched by the high advertising costs that larger firms could more easily afford.

Although still for the most part a family-owned company in 1986—the Lavin family controlled about 45 percent of the stock—Alberto-Culver that year offered a new class of common stock with reduced voting rights. Lavin had his eye on several possible acquisitions. When sales topped $500 million in 1987, Alberto-Culver joined the ranks of the *Fortune* 500. The advance in revenue also led to a 37 percent leap in net income, a sign that the company was on the right track. Sally Beauty was thriving at this time, with 470 stores and successful overseas sales, making it the largest international beauty supply company in the world.

Extending its tradition for niche-building, Alberto-Culver introduced its Bold Hold Styling Line in 1988. Targeted at teens, the products included Scrunch Spritz, Frizz Taming Mousse, and Mega Gel, all helping to achieve the latest in hair-

styling trends. Meanwhile, the company's overseas sales and profits were reaching record levels. That same year, company founder Leonard Lavin relinquished the title of president and chief operating officer to his son-in-law Howard Bernick, then the company's chief financial officer; Lavin remained chairman and chief executive officer. Bernick joined Alberto-Culver in 1977. His wife, Carol Bernick, was Lavin's daughter and head of the company's New Products Division.

1990s Marked by Acquisitions and International Expansion

In 1990 the strongest growth area for Alberto-Culver continued to be international sales and the Sally stores, which grew to nearly 900 outlets that year. The company enjoyed a solid market in Canada and England. As the domestic economy forced retailers to cut back on inventory levels, the marketplace at home was more competitive than ever. Because of the expense of opening new stores, Alberto-Culver slowed the Sally store openings in 1990. In 1989 175 stores that had been owned and operated as Safeway Stores were purchased and converted. In 1990 the company said it would be opening only about 75 stores.

Papa Dash Lite Salt, which was introduced in 1991, was the first to meet the government's low-sodium guidelines. Containing no potassium chloride, Papa Dash used an agglomeration technology to bond real salt molecules onto the surface of tiny carbohydrate particles, thus providing the taste of salt without the excess sodium.

Alberto-Culver was ranked 396th in the *Fortune* 500 in 1991. Also that year, the company agreed to drop the "ozone friendly" label from its aerosol hair products, which, while containing no ozone-depleting chlorofluorocarbons, did feature other propellants such as propane and isobutane, which were harmful to the atmosphere. Without admitting wrongdoing or inaccuracy, the company paid $50,000 in costs as part of a settlement with ten state attorneys general. Alberto-Culver purchased Cederroth International AB, a Swedish producer of health and hygiene goods, in 1991. Among the brands acquired were Salvekvick adhesive bandages, Samarin antacids, Seltin salt substitute, and Latacyd skin soaps and shampoos. Cederroth also provided a vehicle for introducing the Alberto VO5 line into Scandinavia.

When sales rose again in 1992, and profits improved considerably in the toiletries and household/grocery divisions, Alberto-Culver Company attributed its decision to plump up advertising spending that year to a desire to overcome the weak market. Alberto-Culver crossed the billion dollar mark in sales that year.

By 1994 revenues had reached $1.22 billion, and profits were a record $44.1 million. The company's growth and profits continued to be driven by Sally Beauty rather than the personal care and household products. By this time there were nearly 1,400 Sally stores, with plans being made to extend the chain in Japan in 1995. Meanwhile, in October 1994, Bernick was named CEO with Lavin retaining the chairmanship. Bernick initiated a major restructuring that divided the company into three business units: Alberto-Culver USA (later called Alberto-Culver North America), Alberto-Culver International, and Sally

Beauty. Each unit was given its own president with a great deal of autonomy. Sally Beauty had already been operating in this manner quite successfully, and Bernick hoped that the extension of this strategy would help revitalize the other product lines. Carol Bernick was named president of Alberto-Culver USA.

To fuel growth outside of Sally Beauty, Howard Bernick focused on carefully targeted acquisitions. In April 1995 Alberto-Culver acquired another Swedish firm, Molnlycke Toiletries, whose lines of personal care and household products—which generated about $100 million in annual sales—were rolled into Cederroth International. Cederroth was now one of the leading marketers of packaged consumer goods in Scandinavia. In February 1996 Alberto-Culver made its largest acquisition yet when it paid $110 million for St. Ives Laboratories Inc., the Chatsworth, California-based maker of hair care and skin care products under the St. Ives Swiss Formula brand. The addition of Molnlycke and St. Ives quickly provided Alberto-Culver with a significant presence in the skin care market for the first time. The St. Ives acquisition also highlighted the company's move into the burgeoning area of personal care products featuring natural ingredients. Around the time of the purchase, Alberto-Culver was rolling out Alberto VO5 Naturals and TCB Naturals.

Sally Beauty entered the Canadian market in 1998. For 1999, sales at Sally passed the $1 billion mark for the first time. There were now more than 2,150 Sally outlets worldwide, with the international network including Canada, Germany, Japan, and the United Kingdom. The Beauty Systems Group, the distribution arm of Sally Beauty, expanded in late 1999 and early 2000 through the acquisitions of Heil Beauty Supply, based in Paducah, Kentucky, with annual sales of more than $30 million; Macon Beauty Supply, a distributor based in Macon, Georgia, with annual sales of $40 million; and Davidson Supply Company, a Laurel, Maryland-based distributor with sales of $65 million. Annual sales for the Beauty Systems Group approached $400 million following these deals, representing about one-third of overall Sally Beauty revenues.

Acquisitions continued in the international arena as well. In 1999 Alberto-Culver bought La Farmaco Argentina I. y C.S.A., producer of leading lines of deodorant body powders (Veritas) and glycerin soaps (Farmaco). The company planned to use the manufacturing and distribution facilities of this Argentine firm to locally produce such brands as Alberto VO5 and St. Ives for sale across Latin America. A push into the markets of central and Eastern Europe was aided by the March 2000 acquisition of Soraya, S.A., a maker of skin care products in Poland. That same month, Alberto-Culver extended its ethnic personal care lines through the acquisition of Dallas, Texas-based Pro-Line Corporation, a leader in personal care products for the African American market through such brands as Soft & Beautiful and Just for Me. When combined with the existing brands—TCB and recently introduced Motions—Pro-Line propelled Alberto-Culver into the number two position among the world's makers of hair care products for African Americans. In May 2000 Alberto-Culver restructured its North American operations into three product-centered groups: Alberto Personal Care Products, which would include hair and skin care products; Culver Specialty Brands, spices and household products; and Pro-Line International, ethnic personal care products. Alberto-Culver

International was likewise divided into three units. This restructuring signaled a possible slowdown in the firm's steady stream of acquisitions, with integration of the various new units taking precedence.

Principal Subsidiaries

Alberto-Culver (Australia) Pty. Ltd.; Alberto-Culver Canada, Inc.; Alberto-Culver Company (U.K.), Limited; Alberto-Culver International, Inc.; Alberto-Culver de Mexico, S.A. de C.V.; Alberto-Culver (P.R.), Inc.; Alberto-Culver USA, Inc.; BDM Grange, Ltd. (New Zealand); Cederroth International AB (Sweden); CIFCO, Inc.; Indola Cosmetics, B.V. (Netherlands); Indola SpA (Italy); La Farmaco Argentina I. y C.S.A.; Sally Beauty Company, Inc.; Soraya, S.A. (Poland); St. Ives Laboratories, Inc.

Principal Operating Units

Alberto-Culver North America; Alberto-Culver International; Specialty Distribution—Sally.

Principal Competitors

Allou Health & Beauty Care, Inc.; Amway Corporation; Avon Products, Inc.; Bristol-Myers Squibb Company; Burns, Philp and Company Ltd.; Church & Dwight Co., Inc.; Colgate-Palmolive Company; Cumberland Packing Corp.; Del Laboratories, Inc.; The Dial Corporation; The Gillette Company; Helen of Troy Limited; Johnson & Johnson; Johnson Publishing Company, Inc.; L'Oreal SA; Mary Kay Inc.; McCormick & Company, Incorporated; Nu Skin Enterprises, Inc.; Pharmacia Corporation; The Procter & Gamble Company; Regis Corporation; Revlon, Inc.; Schwarzkopf & DEP Inc.; Shiseido Company, Limited; Unilever; Wella Beteiligungen AG.

Further Reading

"Alberto-Culver Co.," *Insiders' Chronicle,* July 22, 1991, p. 3.

"Alberto-Culver Co.," *New York Times,* September 11, 1991, p. D4.

"Alberto-Culver Co.," *Wall Street Journal,* July 23, 1992, p. B4.

"Alberto-Culver Company: Truly Entrepreneurial," *Drug and Cosmetic Industry,* August 1996, pp. 22–26.

"Alberto-Culver Wins Split-30 Battle, Drops Antitrust Suit," *Broadcasting,* March 19, 1984, p. 42.

"Alberto to Modify Labels," *New York Times,* August 7, 1991, p. D19.

Anderson, Veronica, "Its Flagship Business Limp, Alberto Seeks New Style," *Crain's Chicago Business,* February 13, 1995, p. 3.

Appelbaum, Cara, "Alberto VO5, Graying at the Temples, Gets a Younger Look," *Adweek's Marketing Week,* January 28, 1991, p. 12.

Arndorfer, James B., and Deborah L. Cohen, "Alberto Breaks Out Second-Tier Brands," *Crain's Chicago Business,* March 27, 2000, p. 4.

Braham, James, "Leonard Lavin," *Industry Week,* August 18, 1986, p. 48.

Byrne, Harlan S., "Alberto-Culver: Looking Good," *Barron's,* October 20, 1997, pp. 30–31.

Coleman, Calmetta Y., "New Leadership Puts a Fresh Face on Alberto-Culver," *Wall Street Journal,* January 4, 1996, p. B4.

Crown, Judith, "Alberto Clipped by VO5 Pricing Strategy," *Crain's Chicago Business,* August 19, 1991, p. 1.

Feldman, Amy, "When Lenny Met Sally," *Forbes,* February 13, 1995, p. 62.

Freeman, Laurie, "Alberto Gambles on Prestige Haircare Line," *Advertising Age,* April 14, 1986, p. 22.

——, "Knack for Niches," *Advertising Age,* April 18, 1988, pp. 70–74.

Furman, Phyllis, "Ethnic Haircare Marketers Battling for Share," *Advertising Age,* March 2, 1987, p. S2.

"Green Settlement," *Wall Street Journal,* August 6, 1991, p. B6.

Hoggan, Karen, "Alberto Bounces Back," *Marketing,* May 24, 1990, p. 2.

Hoppe, Karen, "Alberto-Culver's Leonard Lavin, An Industry Original," *Drug and Cosmetic Industry,* August 1988, p. 26.

Kentouris, Chris, "Alberto-Culver Sees Gains in Toiletries," *Women's Wear Daily,* October 31, 1989, p. 16.

Kuhn, Susan, "The Hidden Allure of Alberto-Culver," *Fortune,* May 20, 1991, p. 3.

Loeffelholz, Suzanne, "Lavin's Coat of Many Colors," *Financial World,* February 21, 1989, pp. 26–27.

McCarthy, Michael, "Alberto-Culver Continues Its Spending Ways," *Adweek Eastern Edition,* August 3, 1992, p. 4.

Norris, Floyd, "Disparity in Stock of Alberto-Culver," *New York Times,* May 29, 1990, p. D12.

O'Toole, John, "Second Splits: Advertising," *Atlantic,* June 1984, p. 30.

"Papa Dash Lite Salt," *Fortune,* May 6, 1991, p. 81.

Parr, Jan, "How Often Matters, Not How Long," *Forbes,* August 25, 1986, p. 139.

Pitzer, Mary, "An Acid Test for Antitakeover Laws," *Business Week,* September 28, 1987, p. 31.

"The Regrooming of Alberto-Culver," *Financial World,* February 15, 1982, pp. 25–26.

Teitelbaum, Richard, "Carol L. Bernick," *Fortune,* May 21, 1990, p. 158.

Waters, Jennifer, "Things Getting Hairy at Alberto-Culver," *Crain's Chicago Business,* July 8, 1996, p. 3.

Weimer, De'Ann, "Daughter Knows Best," *Business Week,* April 19, 1999, pp. 132, 134.

—Carol Keeley
—updated by David E. Salamie

Alcatel S.A.

54, rue La Boetie
75008 Paris
France
Telephone: (+33) 1 40-76-10-10
Fax: (+33) 1 40-76-14-00
Web site: http://www.alcatel.com

Public Company
Incorporated: 1898 as Compagnie Générale d'Electricité
Employees: 116,000
Sales: EUR 23.02 billion (US$22.02 billion) (1999)
Stock Exchanges: Paris New York
Ticker Symbol: ALA
NAIC: 513322 Cellular and Other Wireless
Telecommunications

France's second largest company in terms of market capitalization (after France Telecom), Alcatel S.A., formerly known as Alcatel Alsthom Compagnie Générale d'Electricité, has transformed itself into a telecommunications solutions provider for the 21st century. Led by Serge Tchuruk, former head of French petroleum powerhouse TotalFina Elf, Alcatel has shed much of its traditional industrial base to make increasing inroads in the worldwide mobile and fixed telephony market, with a focus on ATM equipment and network integration, as well as a mobile telephone manufacturing operation that places it as the number three producer (behind Nokia and Ericsson) of mobile telephone handsets in Europe. Yet it is the North American telecommunications market—worth about 60 percent of the world's market—that is receiving most of Alcatel's attention, as the company rushes to build a position to enable it to compete head-to-head with U.S. industry giants Cisco and Lucent. Toward this end Alcatel took a huge step when it acquired Canada's Newbridge Networks in a deal worth more than US$7 billion in early 2000. That purchase completed a two-year US$16 billion spending spree—begun with the US$4 billion purchase of DSC Communications in 1998—that has allowed Alcatel to build a manufacturer and service network capable of providing turnkey network and telecommunications systems. In addition to its fiber optics capacity, a segment in which the company holds worldwide leadership, Alcatel is also the North American leader in supplying DSL (digital subscriber line, for high-speed Internet access) equipment. In its five-year restructuring drive, Alcatel has trimmed some 30,000 jobs and spun off industrial and other holdings in order to become a telecommunications powerhouse with annual sales worth more than EUR 23 billion.

Late 19th-Century French Industrial Giant

Compagnie Générale d'Electricité (CGE) was created in 1898 through the combination of two electric generating companies and a light bulb manufacturer. The merger, engineered by Pierre Azaria, formed one of Europe's pioneer electric power and manufacturing companies, with interests in electric utilities in France and abroad.

During the first half of the 20th century, CGE expanded its electrical equipment manufacturing through acquisitions. The most important of these were: Société Française des Cables Electriques Bertrand-Borel, merged in 1911; Atelier de Construction Electrique de Delle, acquired in 1912; and Cie Générale d'Electro-Ceramique, purchased in 1921. The growth led CGE into building and equipping electric power plants as well as manufacturing cable used for the distribution of electricity.

In the 1920s CGE entered into a joint venture with its primary French competitor, Thomson-Brandt (an electronics manufacturer later renamed Thomson). The creation of the new concern, a light bulb manufacturer called Cie des Lampes, was encouraged by the French government, which would involve itself in CGE's affairs in varying degrees over the course of the 20th century.

During the 1930s CGE diversified through the acquisition of construction and civil engineering companies and added batteries to its line of electrical products. By World War II, CGE was a diversified manufacturer of electrical equipment, a primary supplier to utilities, and itself an important distributor of electricity. The French government nationalized CGE as part of its effort to coordinate resistance to the German attack. But when the country came under Nazi occupation in 1941, the business was taken over by the invaders and run by collaborators. Unfor-

Company Perspectives:

Alcatel is: The leading architect of Internet communications solutions. Creating end-to-end networks that help people communicate smarter. At the center of the convergence revolution. Integrating communications onto a single broadband network. Making strong investments in people and technology. A company with unique international reach.

tunately, this made CGE's factories regular targets of Allied bombs. After the war, all of France's electric utilities were nationalized, but the remainder of CGE's operations returned to private management. The company's traumatic experience under government control led it to reduce its dependence on government contracts.

A Conglomerate in the 1950s

CGE played a key role in the postwar redevelopment of the French economy. The company diversified into home appliances, telephone equipment, and industrial electronics, and expanded its traditional businesses in the manufacture of electric utility equipment, especially cables. By the end of the 1950s, CGE was a conglomerate with over 200 subsidiaries and the bureaucratic inertia that came with such a far-flung enterprise.

A reorganization in the 1960s formed six primary business groups: power generation, engineering, telecommunications, cable and wire, raw materials, and other products. In 1966 the conglomerate acquired a large construction company, the Société Générale d'Entreprises. In the late 1960s the French government enforced a restructuring of the country's entire electrical engineering industry. The government felt that the industry would run better if Thomson-Brandt's large Alsthom subsidiary, which manufactured power generating equipment and constructed power plants, were transferred to CGE. CGE, in turn, was enjoined to shift its data processing and appliance businesses to Thompson.

The new arrangement seemed to work out well at first: France enjoyed a period of rapid growth during the 1970s. CGE expanded its telecommunications interests with the purchase of Alcatel, a French communications pioneer established in 1879. Alcatel had introduced high-speed, high-capacity digital switching exchanges in 1970. The new division was combined with CGE's existing telecommunications group, CIT, to form CIT Alcatel. The conglomerate's General Contracting group became one of Europe's top construction companies with the acquisition of a controlling interest in Sainrapt et Brice. CGE merged its Alsthom group with Chantiers de l'Atlantique, a top shipbuilding company, to form Alsthom-Atlantique, in 1976.

During the 1980s CGE consolidated its manufacturing and service operations in two broad areas: communications and energy. Communications included: public network switching, transmission, business communications, and cable manufacture. Energy included power generation, transmission and distribution, railway transport, and battery manufacture. Over the course of the decade, several major acquisitions were made, and non-core businesses were divested.

After François Mitterand's administration re-nationalized CGE in 1982, the company acquired the electrical equipment operations of Sprecher & Schub and the railroad business of Jeumont-Schneide. The 1983 transfer of Thomson's telecommunications operations to CGE made the latter company the fifth largest telephone equipment manufacturer in the world.

When conservative Jacques Chirac was elected prime minister of France, the political pendulum swung away from nationalization. In 1986 CGE returned to private control with a US$1.9 billion initial public offering—one of the largest stock offers in French history. Pierre Suard became chairman and CEO. He sought to remake CGE as an international conglomerate run by a cosmopolitan management team. He eschewed France's renowned cultural pride by making English the official working language at CGE's Paris headquarters.

Suard was praised for his skill with acquisitions and divestments, which he began to apply as soon as the company was privatized. CGE increased its energy holdings with the purchase of a 40 percent stake in Framatome—a nuclear power company—and sold unsuccessful operations in markets including televisions and personal computers.

Transitioning to Telecommunications for the New Century

One analyst called the conglomerate's 1986 purchase of a majority interest in the European telephone equipment operations of the United States's ITT Corp. "the most important development in CGE's modern history." ITT's operations were combined with CGE's CIT Alcatel subsidiary to form Alcatel N.V., the world's second largest telecommunications company. CGE owned 55.6 percent of the new multinational operation, which was registered in Holland with headquarters in Brussels. ITT held 37 percent of Alcatel, and the remainder was split between Belgium's Société Générale and Credit Lyonnais, a French bank. Alcatel N.V. became the hub of CGE's strategy as a privatized company. From 1980 to 1990 the group's telecommunications business grew from US$9 billion annually to US$27.6 billion.

A 1987 acquisitions spree diversified CGE into pumping systems, batteries, nuclear boilers, and publishing. CGE also formed joint ventures with the United States' Intermagnetics General Corp., Ferro Corp., and Exide Electronics during the year.

The 1989 merger of CGE's Alsthom power and transportation subsidiary with the United Kingdom's General Electric Company's Powers System Division formed GEC Alsthom N.V., a 50/50 joint venture. CGE increased its ownership to 61.5 percent later that year through an internal consolidation of two major subsidiaries, Compagnie Financière Alcatel and Alsthom. CGE also acquired 15 energy, transportation, and communications companies during that year alone.

Suard was acclaimed for his ability to integrate these new divisions' management, research, and manufacturing into the overall group scheme. He also emphasized research and development, spending about eight percent of total sales, or US$2.3 billion, in 1990 alone.

Key Dates:

1879: Alcatel is founded.
1898: Compagnie Générale d'Electricité (CGE) is created.
1911: CGE acquires Société Française des Cables Electriques Bertrand-Borel.
1912: CGE acquires Atelier de Construction Electrique de Delle.
1921: Company acquires Cie Générale d'Electro-Ceramique.
1966: Company acquires Société Générale d'Entreprises.
1970: CGE acquires Alcatel, forms CIT Alcatel.
1976: Company acquires Chantiers de l'Atlantique.
1982: CGE is nationalized by French government.
1983: Thomson's telecommunications operations are transferred to CGE.
1986: CGE is privatized; acquires ITT's European telecommunications operations.
1989: Company forms GEC Alsthom N.V joint venture with General Electric Company's Powers System Division.
1991: CGE changes name to Alcatel Alsthom Compagnie Générale d'Electricité; acquires Rockwell International Corporation's telephone transmission equipment division.
1995: Company launches major restructuring drive.
1998: Company changes name to Alcatel S.A.; acquires DSC Communications, Assured Access Technology, Internet Devices, Packet Engines, and Xylan Corp.
2000: Company acquires Newbridge Networks.

In the 1990s CGE focused on forging strategic alliances with foreign companies. It was hoped that the joint ventures would maximize the partners' research and development efforts and give CGE entree to local markets. In 1990 the conglomerate formed a joint venture with Fiat S.p.A. that gave CGE control over the telephone transmission business of Fiat's Telettra S.p.A. subsidiary. The two parent companies exchanged shares (Fiat received six percent of Alcatel and Alcatel secured three percent of Fiat), and Telettra was merged with Alcatel's existing Italian operations. The new venture was 75 percent owned by Fiat and 25 percent owned by Alcatel N.V. This complex deal was carefully observed by the European Commission, which used its authority over cross-border business alliances to regulate transactions between the two companies.

From 1985 to 1990 alone, CGE's sales doubled, from FFr 71.94 billion to FFr 143.90 billion. As the company grew, its net income on sales followed suit, increasing from 1.1 percent in 1985 to 2.9 percent in 1990.

During 1990 Suard decided to change CGE's name, which was often mistaken in the global marketplace for the United States' GE (General Electric Corp.) or the United Kingdom's GEC (General Electric Co.). In fact, the French entity was prohibited from using its initials in some markets because of this type of confusion. Although not particularly well known in the United States, the Alcatel division had by this time over-

taken AT&T as the world's largest manufacturer of telecommunications equipment. The Alsthom name was well known in heavy electrical engineering, especially for the development of France's Trains à Grande Vitesse. These two subsidiaries had also grown to become the primary businesses of CGE by 1990. As of January 1, 1991, CGE's name was changed to Alcatel Alsthom Compagnie Générale d'Electricité, and the conglomerate was commonly known as Alcatel Alsthom.

Suard hoped to parlay the company's more cosmopolitan name into an increased global presence: in 1991, 80 percent of Alcatel Alsthom's business was still focused in Europe. Efforts were concentrated on Asia (especially China), the Pacific Rim, and Latin America. The People's Republic of China represented a substantial opportunity for growth, because its 1.16 billion population needed the three services Alcatel Alsthom was prepared to provide: communications, energy, and transportation. Although the country's limited infrastructure and politically inspired five-year plans held up progress, by 1991 GEC Alsthom was China's primary provider of power, and Alcatel had a 40 percent share of the country's public communications equipment market. By 1992, sales to China contributed five percent of Alcatel Alsthom's total sales.

Alcatel also targeted the substantial U.S. telecommunications equipment market, which purchased 40 percent of the world's telephone equipment. Alcatel acquired America's number three supplier, Rockwell International Corporation's telephone transmission equipment division, for US$625 million in 1991. When combined with the company's existing Alcatel Network Systems subsidiary, the purchase brought Alcatel's share of the U.S. market to 15 percent, a distant second to AT&T's 58 percent stake. Alsthom also penetrated the U.S. market when it formed a consortium to build a TGV-type high-speed rail system linking the major cities of Texas in the early 1990s.

The new Alcatel 1000 telecommunication system, developed to provide high-speed data and image transmission and high-density television capability, as well as conventional telephone functions, was launched in 1991. Alcatel also became the first European company to test its cellular phone system that year.

Alcatel Alsthom purchased two more telecommunications and power cable manufacturers, Canada Cable & Wire Company and Germany's AEG Kabel A.G., in 1991 and formed a "Space Alliance" with two European companies, Aerospatiale and Alenia, and the Loral Corporation of New York. The cooperative venture formed the world's second largest supplier of satellite equipment.

Alcatel Alsthom slowed its acquisitions pace in 1992, but bought out ITT's 30 percent stake in Alcatel N.V. for US$3.7 billion in cash and a seven percent share of Alcatel that spring. The transaction made ITT one of Alcatel's primary shareholders.

By the early 1990s, Alcatel Alsthom controlled 80 percent of France's telephone transmission business. The company had also captured 20 percent of Germany's telephone equipment market, second only to the venerable Siemens A.G. In 1993 Alcatel Alsthom commanded 23 percent of the worldwide market for telephone line transmission. Unlike other segments of the telephone equipment business, this highly profitable trade had grown on strong demand for high-capacity fiber-optic cables. Whereas other electronics companies were hard hit by the global recession of the early 1990s, Alcatel Alsthom suffered slower growth, rather than an actual decline. The company hoped to expand into the development of software for telecommunication switching and transmission in the 1990s.

Yet the company faced new tests as the century neared its end. In 1995, Suard was forced to resign after being indicted for fraud—including bribery allegations. Suard was later convicted and sentenced to three years in prison. In the meantime, a series of bad investments made by the company had come back to haunt it—and by the end of the year Alcatel Alsthom showed a loss of more than FFr 25 billion—the largest loss ever by a French company.

The company called in Serge Tchuruk, who, as head of Total (later TotalFina Elf), had mastered the turnaround of that ailing French giant. Tchuruk quickly set to work on a restructuring of Alcatel Alsthom, targeting particularly its telecommunications wing. Tchuruk's timing was fortuitous, as the worldwide telecommunications sector was about to experience an explosion of activity. Yet, as Tchuruk explained to *Institutional Investor:* "I could tell you that I was a visionary and that in 1995 I suspected there would be a tremendous growth explosion in telecommunications. But if I were to say that, I'd be lying. Telecommunications was Alcatel's biggest business but by far not the only one. And it was sick. It was really losing momentum. I realized if we did not correct the telecommunications problems, the whole company would drown. I decided perhaps 12 or 18 months later that the focus on telecommunications had to be exclusive, once we began to understand that the growth potential there would be just enormous."

After trimming its payroll by 12,500 and selling off a number of its non-core assets, Alcatel Alsthom had returned to profits. But Tchuruk's restructuring took on greater steam as the company, renamed simply Alcatel in 1998, transformed itself from a traditional industrial conglomerate into a focused high-technology company. Sales of the company's assets, including its stakes in GEC Alsthom and its Cegelec engineering divisions, helped the company generate some US$12 billion in capital, used to fuel an ambitious US$16 billion acquisition drive designed to establish Alcatel as a major presence in the North American telecommunications market. The company's acquisitions ranged from Texas-based DSC Communications, for US$4 billion, through the purchases of Assured Access Technology, Internet Devices, Packet Engines, and Xylan Corp, which were grouped together under the Xylan name with the 1998 acquisition of Packet Systems. In July 2000 came the culminating US$7 billion purchase of Newbridge Networks.

These acquisitions enabled Alcatel to take up a competitive position as it went head-to-head with industry giants Cisco Systems and Lucent Technologies on their home ground. The company's low debt ratio and other sellable assets—including a 24 percent stake in French nuclear power leader Framatome and the company's energy cables manufacturing division, expected to be spun off as a public company at the end of 2000—gave the company a war chest of more than EUR 10 billion for future acquisitions.

Principal Subsidiaries

Alcatel Space (51%); Alcatel STK ASA (Norway; 81%); Alcatel Telecom Norway A/S (81%); Alcatel USA Inc.; ALSTOM (24%); Compagnie Financière Alcatel; Cie Immobilière Méridionale; Civelec Electro Banque; Générale Occidentale; Genesys Telecommunications Laboratories, Inc.; Lacroix & Kress GmbH (Germany); Saft Groupe; Shanghai Bell Telephone Equipment Manufacturing Co. (China; 32%); SIKL; Société de Coulée Continue de Cuivre; Taiwan International Standard Electronic Ltd. (Taisel) (60%); Teletas (Turkey; 65%); Thomson-CSF (25%); Xylan Corporation.

Principal Competitors

3Com Corporation; Matsushita Communication; Ascom Holding; Motorola, Inc.; AT&T Broadband; NEC Corporation; Nokia Corporation; Cap Gemini; Nortel Networks Corporation; Cisco Systems, Inc.; Oki Electric; Cookson Group; Philips Electronics N.V.; Corning Incorporated; Pirelli S.p.A.; Ericsson; Qualcomm Inc.; Fujikura; Sagem; Harris Corporation; Samsung Electronics Co., Ltd.; Hitachi, Ltd.; SANYO Electric Co., Ltd.; Hughes Electronics Corporation; Siemens AG; Hyundai Group; Sony Corporation; Koor Industries Ltd.; Sumitomo Electric Industries; Lucent Technologies Inc.; Toshiba Corporation; Marconi plc.

Further Reading

"Alcatel Alsthom: Power Play," *Economist,* August 3, 1991, pp. 65–66.

Brown, Heidi, "Laggard," *Forbes,* May 15, 2000.

Harbrecht, Douglas, "Interview with Serge Tchuruk," *Business Week Online,* October 12, 1999.

"ITT Sells Its 30% Alcatel N.V. Stake for $3.7 Billion for $600 Million Gain," *Wall Street Journal,* July 6, 1992, p. 16.

Mason, Joanne, "Giants Ride Out the Crisis," *International Management,* January/February 1993, pp. 26–59.

Neher, Jacques, "A French Giant Stalks U.S. Telephone Market," *New York Times,* November 25, 1991, p. D1.

"Net Income Increased 20% to $1.13 Billion Last Year," *Wall Street Journal,* April 9, 1992, p. A11.

Schack, Justin, "Serge Tchuruk of Alcatel: French Connection," *Institutional Investor,*

Shinal, John, "Here Come the French," *Forbes,* January 20, 2000.

—April S. Dougal
—updated by M.L. Cohen

Alfa Romeo

Fiat S.p.A.
Corso Marconi 10
Turin
Italy
Telephone: (+39) 11 65651
Fax: (+39) 11 6863525
Web site: http://www.alfaromeo.com

Wholly Owned Subsidiary of Fiat S.p.A.
Incorporated: 1910 as Società Anonima Lombarda
   Fabbrica Automobili
Employees: 1,500
NAIC: 33611 Automobile Manufacturing

Alfa Romeo is one of the most famous sports cars in the world, along with Porsche, Ferrari, Maserati, Corvette, Lamborghini, and Jaguar. After experiencing severe economic difficulties during the early 1990s, which resulted in the company's pullout from the U.S. market, Alfa Romeo and its parent company, Fiat, have performed a turnaround of the legendary carmaker—booking international success with the 156 model, introduced in 1998 to universal acclaim, followed by the 166 sedan. In 2000 the company prepared for more success with the October launch of the 147. Alfa Romeo's renewed success has not been enough for Fiat, however, which saw losses totaling more than US$100 million in 1999. In March 2000, Fiat announced a share-swap partnership agreement with General Motors Corporation (GM), giving the U.S. carmaker 20 percent of Fiat and making Italy's dominant automaker the largest single GM shareholder, with 5.1 percent of the Detroit company. The GM-Fiat agreement has already produced a bonus for Alfa Romeo—following the agreement, Fiat announced its intention to reintroduce Alfa Romeo to the U.S. market with a new Spider design.

Founding an Automotive Legend in 1910

Alfa Romeo was founded in Portello, just north of Milan, in 1910. Cav Ugo Stella, managing director of a Portello assembly plant for the Darracq, a French automobile, decided to organize a group to purchase the plant and build a car more suitable for the harsh and mountainous Italian roads. Along with a few Milanese businessmen, he took out a loan to purchase the Darracq plant. The group named itself the Lombardy Car Manufacturing Company (Società Anonima Lombarda Fabbrica Automobili) and soon was known by its initials—ALFA.

Ugo Stella hired Giuseppi Merosi as chief automotive designer of the new company. Merosi had worked previously as a designer for Marchand, Fiat, and Bianchi car companies and was well qualified to design both touring cars and cars for the racing circuit. His first design for ALFA included a monobloc engine, high tension magneto ignition, three-bearing crankshaft, side valves, and pressure lubrication. A radiator badge also was designed for the new firm's cars, including the soon-to-be famous red cross and snake, symbols that were part of the emblems of the city of Milan and the Visconti family. A blue border surrounded the edge of the circular badge, with the word "ALFA" at the top and "MILANO" at the bottom. First inscribed in brass lettering, the lettering was replaced shortly afterward with white enamel. During the first year of business, ALFA manufactured ten cars each of a 12 horsepower and a 24 horsepower model; one year later, production had increased to 40 cars of each model. By the time World War I began in 1914, ALFA was manufacturing 272 chassis a year with a staff of almost 300.

Although revenues from car sales seemed to provide adequate funds for ALFA to continue business, in 1915 the company was acquired, suddenly and surprisingly, by Nicola Romeo. From rather humble beginnings, Romeo had graduated from the University of Liège with a degree in electrical engineering. After working for a short time in Germany and then France, he returned to his native Italy and started a business in Milan in association with the American company Ingersoll-Rand. Romeo's business was so successful that he soon formed his own firm to manufacture mining equipment. This, too, proved successful; the expansion of his company was so rapid, that the number of employees he hired increased from 100 to more than 1,200 in three months during the summer of 1915.

When Romeo purchased ALFA in 1915, there were fears among the remaining management and workers that the company was doomed for extinction. Romeo had purchased not only ALFA, but also numerous other firms in the area. His goal was to create an engineering combine that manufactured compressors, tractors, air brakes, ploughs, railway equipment, and other assorted products for use in heavy industry. Fortunately, Romeo was also a motoring enthusiast and had always dreamed of making a prestigious Italian sports car. As a result, he immediately expanded the production facilities at the ALFA factory in Portello. In February 1918, he changed the name of the firm to Società Anonima Italiana Ing. Nicola Romeo & Company. In addition, he decided to place his own name next to the well-respected ALFA name on the company's radiator badge, and after 1918 all the firm's cars appeared with "Alfa Romeo" on the hood.

During the 1920s Alfa Romeos on the racing circuit established the company as one of the premier sports car manufacturers in the world. Alfa Romeo relied heavily on modified versions of its prewar racing cars, while designer Merosi labored frantically to design more up-to-date models. As Merosi's new designs were introduced on the raceways, the company began to win such prestigious competitions as the Parma-Berceto, the Consuma Hill Climb, the Coppa Florio, the Aosta-Great St. Bernard Hill Climb, the Autumn Grand Prix, the Circuit of Savio race, the Circuit of Mantua race, the European Grand Prix, and many, many more. Nicola Romeo was determined to wrest the European racing crown from Italian competitor and rival Fiat, and he employed the best drivers and mechanics in order to do so. Enzo Ferrari, who was to become famous in his own right as an Italian sports car manufacturer, won the 1927 Circuit of Modena in a six-cylinder 150 Alfa Romeo. As Alfa Romeo continued to win races, the innovations that led to the successes of the racing cars directly affected the design and production of the company's touring cars and roadsters; for example, front wheel brakes, adapted from the Alfa Romeo racing cars, were installed on touring cars for the first time.

Vittorio Jano, who replaced Merosi as head of design at Alfa Romeo in 1926, continued the tradition of improving the company's cars through his creations for the racing circuit. Jano's first design for general production was the NR (Nicola Romeo) touring car, which included a single overhead camshaft, coil ignition, a four-speed gearbox, and rod-operated brakes. Despite the growing success and reputation of the company, Nicola Romeo suddenly and inexplicably retired in 1928, and management of the company was assumed by the board of directors. Unfortunately, the firm began to experience financial difficulties as soon as Romeo retired.

During the early 1930s, management changed the name of the firm from Ing Nicola Romeo and Company to Societe Anonmie Alfa Romeo. Alfa Romeo's revenues continued to diminish, and in 1933 the government-sponsored Istituto Riconstruzione Industriale (IRI) assumed control of the company. Although Alfa Romeo technically retained its status as a private corporation with its own board of directors, the company had essentially been nationalized. Under the auspices of IRI, and with the rise of Benito Mussolini as dictator of Italy, Alfa Romeo's production facilities at Portello were expanded to include airplane engines, armaments, diesel engines, and even light aircraft. Jano continued to design touring cars and racing cars for the company through the mid-1930s, but car production became less and less important as Mussolini prepared Italy for war.

Alfa Romeo's fortunes during World War II slipped even further. In 1936 a Spanish engineer by the name of Wilfredo Ricart was hired to replace Jano as head of the design office at Alfa Romeo. Ricart had extensive experience designing diesel engines and sports and racing cars and also had organized public transportation in the city of Valencia before arriving in Italy. Expectations of his potential for designing Alfa Romeo cars were very high. But Ricart, it was soon discovered, exhibited some very strange habits, including a penchant for wearing enormously thick rubber-soled shoes. When asked by Enzo Ferrari why he affected these shoes, Ricart replied in all seriousness that a genius's brain must be cushioned against the harsh unevenness of the ground lest its delicate mechanics be disrupted. Upon hearing Ricart's response, Ferrari left Alfa Romeo. During the war years, Ricart's designs for the company never went beyond the prototype stage.

Postwar Reconstruction

After the end of World War II, Alfa Romeo's factory at Portello needed rebuilding because of the damage inflicted by American and British bombing raids. At the same time, the company's board of directors decided to release Ricart from his contract and hire Orazio Satta to replace him. Satta was the last of the great Alfa Romeo designers. Educated as an aeronautical engineer, Satta guided the company into an era of racing success and economic prosperity. Satta was responsible for designing the 6C 2500 Super Sport, the 1900 Sprint, the Giulietta Sprint Special, and the famous Spider Veloce. All of these cars sold extremely well abroad, with the Spider Veloce selling especially well in both Britain and the United States. During Satta's tenure, Alfa Romeo also continued to be successful in racing, winning such prestigious races as the 1950 and 1951 Swiss Grand Prix and the 1953 Grand Prix of Supercortmaggiore at Merano.

By the early 1960s, the factory at Portello was unable to produce enough cars to suit the growing demand of Alfa Romeo customers, so the company built a new assembly plant at Arese,

Key Dates:

1910: Società Anonima Lombarda Fabbrica Automobili (Alfa) is founded.
1915: Nicola Romeo acquires Alfa.
1918: Changes name to Società Anonima Italiana Ing. Nicola Romeo & Company; production of first ''Alfa Romeo'' cars.
1930: Company changes name to Société Anonomie Alfa Romeo.
1933: Italian government takes control of Alfa Romeo.
1960: Construction begins on new assembly plant in Arese.
1963: Launch of Giulia Sprint GT model.
1980: State-owned Finmeccanica acquires Alfa Romeo's factories.
1986: Fiat acquires Alfa Romeo.
1989: Establishes Alfa Romeo Distributors of North America joint venture with Chrysler.
1993: Alfa Romeo is pulled out of American market.
1998: Company launches 156 sedan.
1999: Company launches 166 sedan.
2000: Fiat enters partnership with GM, announces return of Alfa Romeo to U.S. market by 2004.

about ten miles from Portello. In 1963 the first Giulia Sprint GT rolled out of the plant at Arese, and by 1970 manufacturing capacity had increased to 150,000 automobiles per year. Still striving for the best performance from its vehicles, the company built a test track at Balocco, west of Milan. Numerous prototypes were tested on this track, and Satta's reputation as a designer continued to grow with each successful production. As sales increased, Alfa Romeo laid the foundation for a new plant just outside Naples, the place of Nicola Romeo's birth.

In 1970 Alfa Romeo sold 109,598 cars worldwide, primarily in Europe and the United States. The company was at the height of its success, with a growing share of the sports car market in every country where it sold cars. When Satta retired, accolades were heaped upon him, both by his peers and by the Italian government. After Satta's retirement, however, Alfa Romeo began to experience managerial and financial problems. Rising production costs and increased competition from Ferrari, Maserati, Jaguar, Porsche, and American car manufacturers led to declining revenues. In addition, the tradition of testing new Alfa Romeo models through the racing circuit was growing less important to the design office, and technical problems began to occur in cars purchased by customers expecting high levels of performance. By the early 1980s, the manufacturer's financial position had deteriorated so rapidly that the state-owned holding company Finmeccanica had taken control of the Alfa Romeo factories.

Under the auspices of Finmeccanica, Alfa Romeo's fortunes fared no better. Management was unable to stop the company's financial hemorrhaging and, as a result, Alfa Romeo became an attractive takeover target. Ford Motor Company expressed interest, but in 1986 Fiat outbid Ford, acquiring Alfa Romeo and all its holdings for US$1.75 billion. Fiat, a well-established

Italian car manufacturer owned by the Agnelli family, regarded Alfa Romeo as the perfect complement to its own line of European sports cars.

Alfa Romeo benefited from Fiat's largesse—Fiat decided to invest more than US$1 billion in rehabilitating and improving the company's manufacturing plants in Portello, Naples, and Arese, while more than US$1.25 billion was earmarked for research and development. Yet Fiat's direct management and supervision of Alfa Romeo car production and distribution was unable to reverse the company's fortunes. In 1989 Fiat formed Alfa Romeo Distributors of North America, a 50–50 joint venture with Chrysler. This arrangement, it was hoped, would enable Alfa Romeo to increase its presence in the American automobile market. Since Alfa Romeo had sold 8,201 cars in 1986 in the United States, it was not an unwarranted prediction that annual sales would increase to 12,000 by 1991. With new designs ready to roll from the company's Italian factories, Chrysler and Fiat were even confident enough to project annual sales figures of US$40,000 to US$50,000 by 1995. Fiat depended on Chrysler's knowledge of the American car market and gave Chrysler management a free hand in advertising and distributing Alfa Romeo cars.

Falling and Rising in the 1990s

From the beginning of the collaboration, however, almost nothing went according to plan. The first Alfa Romeo car produced under Fiat ownership, the 164 sedan, was delayed so that Fiat engineers could improve its quality and add a 2.0-liter turbo engine. The delay lasted months longer than expected, and distributors in the United States were left with nothing to sell except the Milano sedan and the old version of the Spider convertible. Unfortunately, the Alfa Romeo Milano, another design significantly influenced by Fiat engineers, was plagued with mechanical problems and quickly developed a reputation for unreliability. Chrysler, dissatisfied with the results of the joint venture, decided to dissolve the partnership in 1991. Chrysler's withdrawal left Fiat to market Alfa Romeo cars alone in the United States and, as a result, Alfa Romeo's presence in the United States began to decline dramatically. During 1991 only 649 Alfa Romeo cars were sold in the United States.

In an attempt to improve Alfa Romeo's dwindling market share, Fiat engineers conceived the 155, introducing the car in Europe in 1992. The car did not sell well, however, which industry analysts attributed to the lackluster exterior and interior design. With earnings decreasing and debt rising for its U.S. operation, Fiat decided not to export the 155 to the United States. In 1993 Alfa Romeo's car production dropped 24 percent to only 109,598 units, most of which were sold in Europe. A decision by Fiat management not to sell the new Spider convertible, the Spider coupe, or the newly designed 145 hatchback in the United States confirmed the company's decision to pull out of the U.S. market.

Nonetheless, Fiat had far from abandoned the legendary Alfa Romeo name. Throughout the 1990s, the company initiated a retooling of the Alfa Romeo, aimed at winning back customers through an increased commitment to quality in manufacturing as well as a return to the design excellence that had built the Alfa Romeo name. By 1998, Alfa Romeo was officially ''back'': in that year the company's new 156 sedan won the European Car of the Year award, sparking a rush of orders. By the end of 1998, the success of the 156 was confirmed, with orders nearing 200,000 cars from 60 countries.

Alfa Romeo celebrated its 90th anniversary in 1999 with another success, the launch of the 166 sedan, designed to compete in the same class as the Mercedes E series. The 166 proved as successful as the 156, and in Europe, at least, Alfa Romeo had once again become a favorite among car buyers. The return of the Alfa Romeo image was not enough to rescue the failing Fiat, however. After posting losses of more than US$100 million in 1999, Fiat acknowledged that it was seeking a ''partner'' automotive company.

In March 2000, the company reached a partnership agreement with General Motors. In a share-swap agreement, which gave GM 20 percent of Fiat and Fiat 5.1 percent of GM—making the Italian company the largest GM shareholder—the two companies announced their intention to join forces to enhance their positions in the European and Latin American markets. At the same time, Fiat acknowledged its intention to return Alfa Romeo to the U.S. market as early as 2004, with a new Spider model especially designed for the U.S. car market. With the backing of Fiat, Italy's largest industrial concern, and GM, the world's largest automaker, the Alfa Romeo name seemed certain to continue thrilling sports car enthusiasts well into the 21st century.

Principal Competitors

AUDI AG; Bayerische Motoren Werke; DaimlerChrysler AG; Ford Motor Company; Honda Motor Company Limited; Hyundai Group; Isuzu Motors, Ltd.; Kia Motors Corporation; Mazda Motor Corporation; Mitsubishi Motors Corporation; Nissan Motor Company; Peugeot S.A.; Porsche AG; Renault S.A.; Saab Automobile AB; Suzuki Motor Corporation; Toyota Motor Corporation; Volkswagen A.G.

Further Reading

Ciferri, Luca, ''Fiat Performs CPR to Revive Alfa Romeo,'' *Automotive News,* May 16, 1994, p. 26.
Green, Gavin, ''Alfa Romeo Keeps Good Times Rolling,'' *International Herald Tribune,* December 4, 1998.
Henry, Jim, ''Fiat Weighs Alfa's Fate in U.S.,'' *Automotive News,* July 5, 1993, p. 4.
Kiley, David, ''Fiat's Alfa Romeo May Return to USA,'' *USA Today,* June 22, 2000, p. 6B.
Pitt, Barrie, *Alfa Romeo,* New York: Ballantine Books, Inc., 1971.
Wielgat, Andrea, ''Europe's Comeback Kid,'' *Lighting Dimensions,* February 1, 1999.

—Thomas Derdak
—updated by M.L. Cohen

ALZA Corporation

1900 Charleston Road
P.O. Box 7210
Mountain View, California 94039-7210
U.S.A.
Telephone: (650) 564-5000
Fax: (650) 494-5121
Web site: http://www.alza.com

Public Company
Incorporated: 1968
Employees: 2,034
Sales: $795.9 million (1999)
Stock Exchanges: New York
Ticker Symbol: AZA
NAIC: 325412 Pharmaceutical Preparation
    Manufacturing; 541710 Research and Development in
    the Physical, Engineering, and Life Sciences

As one of the world's leading producers of drug delivery systems, ALZA Corporation develops and manufactures a variety of systems that make administration of medication more efficient and effective. The systems ALZA develops are used by other pharmaceutical companies as well as by ALZA itself for its own drug portfolio. A pioneer in the field of transdermal therapy, ALZA developed the Nicoderm patch marketed by Marion Merrell Dow as an aid to help smokers kick the habit. Other well-known products developed by ALZA include Procardia XL for both angina and hypertension, Duragesic for the management of cancer pain, and Glucotrol XL for the treatment of Type II diabetes. The company's sales and marketing efforts focus on urology, oncology, and the central nervous system/pediatrics areas.

Early History: Transdermal Systems

ALZA was founded in 1968 by Alejandro Zaffaroni, a cofounder of the major pharmaceutical company Syntex Corporation, based in Palo Alto, California. ALZA was to be unique in that its research and development activities would be directed not toward creating new drugs, but rather toward developing better delivery systems for existing medications. Specifically, the company's mission was to improve on the longstanding methods of injections and pills taken orally by introducing products and systems that would help to stabilize the amount of drug in a patient's bloodstream.

The fledgling company leased land in Stanford's Research Park for its first facility, and Martin Gerstel, who had recently graduated from Stanford's business school, became the company's second employee after Zaffaroni. In a 1989 interview for *Business Journal-San Jose,* Gerstel recalled that when he asked Zaffaroni about a title, the founder replied ''that I could be anything I wanted except president. He wanted that title.'' So Gerstel became the vice-president in charge of planning, administration, and finances, and his first task was to find an architect to design the building that would become the company's headquarters.

Although the company was small, it pursued its mission diligently, filing a patent application for a transdermal system invented by Zaffaroni in 1969. The transdermal system was innovative because it would allow medicines to be absorbed through the skin for a controlled, continuous dosage. While waiting for Food and Drug Administration (FDA) approval, ALZA became a public company, with Syntex distributing its shares. In 1974, Ocusert Pilo-20/40, used in the treatment of glaucoma, became the first ALZA product to gain FDA approval.

In 1977, Ciba-Geigy Ltd., a pharmaceutical giant, acquired a controlling interest in ALZA. This was the beginning of a difficult five-year period for ALZA and its stockholders, who began losing money. Despite economic challenges, however, the company continued to improve its drug delivery systems, and in August 1981, the FDA approved ALZA's first transdermal product, the Transderm Scop for treatment of motion sickness. Two months later, Transderm-Nitro won FDA approval for use in the treatment of angina. Both transdermal treatments were administered via small patches that resembled adhesive bandages. Once the patches were applied, a steady dosage of the drugs they contained permeated the skin and entered the bloodstream at a regulated rate.

The benefits of transdermal drug therapy were numerous. In addition to providing consistent drug levels in the bloodstream, the transdermal system offered improved absorption. Unlike the medication in orally ingested pills—which was often destroyed or neutralized in the stomach, intestine, or liver before reaching the bloodstream—transdermal delivery allowed more of the medication to be absorbed, making lower dosages possible. The transdermal system also potentially reduced the incidence of side effects.

ALZA was nearly bankrupt when it split from Ciba-Geigy in 1982 and began working with other large players in the pharmaceutical industry. The company had its first profitable year in 1983 and was listed on the American Stock Exchange. The following year, ALZA purchased land in Vacaville, California, to build a 117,000-square-foot commercial manufacturing facility. The Vacaville facility became the center for the manufacture of several transdermal and oral products.

Late 1980s: The OROS System

ALZA flourished during the late 1980s. Transderm-Nitro became the first ALZA product to hit $100 million in combined licensee sales, and company revenues had reached $71 million by 1987, when Gerstel was named CEO and cochairman. The following year, the company opened new facilities in Mountain View, California, to accommodate its growing research and development team. In 1989, the FDA approved ALZA's Procardia XL tablets, and Pfizer Inc. began to market the drug for treatment of angina and hypertension under a royalty license from ALZA.

Procardia XL reflected ALZA's contribution to osmotic technology, which controlled the release rate of medication in capsule or tablet form. This technology, known as OROS, involved the osmotic design of the capsule's core and membrane, which contained both the drug and osmotic agent. When a patient swallowed an OROS tablet, water would be drawn from the membrane to saturate the drug, which would then be released in liquid form drop by drop through laser-drilled holes in the tablet. This permitted a gradual release of the drug and led to reduced side effects and predictable levels of the drug in the bloodstream.

ALZA's Acutrim—an appetite suppressant marketed over the counter by Ciba Consumer Pharmaceuticals—also utilized the OROS osmotic technology. In late 1989, ALZA filed a new drug application with the FDA for a nasal decongestant tablet that would use the OROS controlled-release technology. The product, designed for sufferers of colds and allergies, was a once-a-day tablet that continuously delivered pseudoephedrine

for 24 hours. Called Efidac/24, the cold medication was sold over the counter and was used to relieve nasal congestion from colds, hay fever, and sinusitis.

Early 1990s: Glucotrol, Duragesic, Nicoderm, and More

By 1990, ALZA had about 40 products in development and 650 employees, more than half of whom comprised the research and development team. In January of that year, ALZA announced the development of an osmotic syringe pump for subcutaneous or intravenous delivery of medications. A wearable, disposable system, the pump consisted of two reservoirs—one for water and one for the drug being administered—and an osmotic tablet compartment. The tablet facilitated the workings of the syringe pump, so that a mixture of water and drug could be introduced into the patient's bloodstream. Unlike traditional intravenous devices, the osmotic syringe pump did not rely on gravity and permitted the patient to move about freely.

During this time, ALZA entered into several joint agreements intended to bolster its development of new technologies. A partnership with the Procter & Gamble Company, focusing on the development, manufacture, and marketing of treatments for periodontal disease, resulted in the July 1994 U.S. introduction of Actisite Periodontal Fiber, which delivered the antibiotic tetracycline directly to the affected site. Another joint effort, with Pfizer Inc., led to the development of Glucotrol XL, Pfizer's oral hypoglycemic medicine for non-insulin-dependent (or Type II) diabetics. With Pfizer, ALZA developed a once-daily form of the drug—cleared for marketing by the FDA—incorporating ALZA's OROS controlled-release technology.

Moreover, ALZA established a new company called Bio-Electro Systems Inc. This company, formed independent of ALZA in order to minimize risk to shareholders, explored the concept of electro transport, in which electrical currents propel drugs into the skin. Bio-Electro's mission also included the development of Alzamer, erodible polymers that could be filled with a drug and then injected or inserted into the body.

In 1990, the FDA approved ALZA's Duragesic transdermal system, designed to deliver fentanyl for the relief of chronic pain in cancer patients. Revenues for that year reached $109.4 million, up from $92.7 million in 1989. The considerable increase, due mainly to royalties from the sale of Procardia XL, was nothing new for ALZA; since the early 1980s, the company had enjoyed annual revenue growth of 48 percent and yearly profit growth of 220 percent. Analysts noted that ALZA had no real competition, since no other company concentrated exclusively on the development of a broad range of drug delivery systems covering various technologies.

In 1991, to consolidate its stake in electrotransport systems, the company announced that it would acquire Bio-Electro Systems as well as Medtronic Inc.'s electrotransport business unit. ALZA stock was trading at $80 a share in late 1991, double the price it garnered the year before. There were 11 ALZA products on the market, and a dozen more awaited FDA approval.

During the final months of 1991, ALZA and Marion Merrell Dow faced a patent lawsuit that threatened the introduction of Nicoderm, the first transdermal nicotine delivery system. Al-

Key Dates:

1968: Alejandro Zaffaroni founds ALZA Corporation.
1969: Zaffaroni invents a transdermal drug delivery system.
1974: Ocusert Pilo-20/40 becomes the first ALZA product to gain FDA approval.
1977: Ciba-Geigy gains controlling interest in ALZA.
1981: FDA approves ALZA's first transdermal product, the Transderm Scop.
1982: ALZA splits from Ciba-Geigy.
1983: Company posts first profit and is listed on the American Stock Exchange.
1989: FDA approves Procardia XL tablets, which feature ALZA's OROS technology.
1990: FDA approves Duragesic transdermal system for the management of cancer pain.
1991: FDA approves the Nicoderm nicotine patch.
1992: Stock begins trading on the New York Stock Exchange; Procardia XL becomes the first ALZA-developed product to reach $1 billion in annual sales.
1993: Company forms Therapeutic Discovery Corporation to do research on new products; Dr. Ernest Mario is named CEO of ALZA.
1994: Testoderm hormone replacement therapy system is introduced.
1999: Sequus Pharmaceuticals, Inc. is acquired; ALZA agrees to be acquired by Abbott Laboratories but the deal collapses later in the year.
2000: Viadur, which uses a new implant technology called DUROS, is approved for the palliative treatment of advanced prostate cancer.

though the FDA approved Nicoderm in November, sales of the breakthrough technology were suspended by court order for one month, when an Irish pharmaceutical company, Elan Corp. plc, claimed that ALZA's nicotine patch infringed on one of its patents. Elan's American marketing partner, American Cyanamid, joined in the lawsuit, but by mid-1992 the suit was withdrawn and the parties reached an out-of-court settlement with no financial impact to those involved. Nicotine patch sales were quick to take off, and the product immediately became popular among the thousands of people trying to stop smoking. Due to the companies' inability to supply enough product to meet the extraordinary demand, however, sales dropped and stayed below original launch levels.

ALZA recovered its stride, and the company's stock began trading on the New York Stock Exchange in the summer of 1992. By the end of the year, Procardia XL became the first ALZA-developed product to hit $1 billion in annual sales. Moreover, Efidac/24, a nasal decongestant utilizing OROS technology, received FDA approval. Other ALZA innovations during this time included the development of MOTS (Mucosal Oral Therapeutic System) nystatin, a controlled-release lozenge designed to deliver nystatin for the treatment of oral candidiasis in AIDS patients.

In 1992, ALZA announced the development of two new systems based on its proprietary osmotic technology. One sys-

tem, Chronset, was designed to deliver proteins and peptides orally. The second system was a veterinary implant called VITS. ALZA also continued its research into electrotransport, developing prototypes of small, reusable devices that delivered drug dosages through the skin. The mild electrical currents emitted by the system propelled controlled, consistent dosages into the bloodstream and allowed the patient direct control.

ALZA finished 1992 with $250.5 million in revenues and net income of $72.2 million. More than 50 new products were in development, including an oral form of an anti-epileptic drug, Dilantin. In addition, the company was working with G.D. Searle & Co. to develop a new hypertensive therapy based on the OROS system. The new therapy, Calan OROS, was designed to release medication early in the morning, when dangers from high blood pressure are greatest.

Mid-1990s and Beyond: Transitioning to a Fully Integrated Pharmaceutical Firm

The company celebrated its 25th anniversary in 1993. Fifty-seven patents were granted worldwide, and the company announced the development of its unique Human Implantable Therapeutic Systems (HITS). This new system was designed for long-term, subcutaneous delivery of drugs to patients suffering from such chronic diseases as Alzheimer's, hepatitis, and prostate cancer. That year, the company also formed Therapeutic Discovery Corporation in order to develop new human pharmaceutical products that would combine ALZA's proprietary drug delivery systems with various drug compounds. This move was a key part of the company's effort to shift from being strictly a licenser of drug delivery systems to becoming a fully integrated pharmaceutical firm that developed, manufactured, marketed, and sold its own drug products. Therapeutic Discovery was spun off to shareholders as a separate company in 1993 but ALZA retained all rights to the products it developed (ALZA reacquired Therapeutic in 1997). Another key development came late in 1993 when a new management team was installed to implement the company's new strategy. Hired to lead the team as CEO and cochairman was Dr. Ernest Mario, a former chief executive of Glaxo Holdings P.L.C. Mario became sole chairman at the end of 1997 upon Zaffaroni's retirement.

One of ALZA's first self-developed and self-marketed products was the Testoderm system, which was introduced early in 1994. This transdermal system was designed to deliver testosterone for hormone replacement therapy in hypogonadal males. ALZA had elected to focus its proprietary drug development efforts on two areas—urology and oncology—and Testoderm fell within the latter. Later in the 1990s ALZA developed another urological treatment called Ditropan XL, which was introduced in 1999 for the treatment of overactive bladder.

In the oncology realm, ALZA won FDA approval for Ethyol in 1995. Ethyol was initially approved for patients undergoing chemotherapy to treat kidney-related side effects, then in 1999 was approved to protect the salivary glands of head and neck cancer patients undergoing radiation therapy. Aiding the company's move into cancer-fighting drugs was the March 1999 acquisition of Menlo Park, California-based Sequus Pharmaceuticals, Inc. for approximately $580 million in stock. Sequus had won approval in 1995 for Doxil, which was designed to treat Kaposi's sarcoma, a cancerlike condition associated with AIDS; in 1999 Doxil was approved as a secondary remedy for certain ovarian cancer patients. ALZA also gained Sequus's Stealth drug-delivery system, which improved the effectiveness of cancer-fighting drugs and reduced side effects. It did so by encapsulating the medication in fat globules that were delivered to the body intravenously. The medication remained encapsulated until it reached the areas of disease within the body, thereby delivering higher concentrations of the drug to these areas while bypassing healthy tissue which resulted in reduced side effects. Doxil was the first medication delivered via the Stealth technology.

In June 1999 ALZA agreed to be acquired by Abbott Laboratories for $7.3 billion in stock, with ALZA slated to become a division of Abbott. The agreement was part of a general industry trend in which pharmaceutical giants were snatching up biotech firms; the drug companies desired the biotech firms' research into new drugs, while the biotech firms wanted access to the global sales forces of the drug giants. Being acquired by Abbott thereby appeared to be part of ALZA's move toward becoming a fully integrated drug firm. Nevertheless, ALZA called off the deal in December 1999 after the Federal Trade Commission raised antitrust objections to the merger.

An immediate consequence of the collapse of the merger was that ALZA retained a promising prostate-cancer drug, Viadur, which it would have had to divest because Abbott had its own prostate-cancer treatment, Lupron. In March 2000 the FDA approved Viadur for the palliative treatment of advanced prostate cancer. Viadur utilized a new ALZA technology called DUROS, which was a matchstick-sized pump made from titanium alloy that was implanted under the skin to continuously deliver medication—in this case leuprolide—for up to a year. ALZA entered into an agreement with Bayer Corporation, which would market Viadur in the United States. ALZA was also testing other drugs for delivery through the miniature pump.

ALZA showed remarkable growth in the second half of the 1990s, with revenues increasing from $261 million in 1994 to $795.9 million in 1999. Net income for 1999 was $91 million. Although the company's future was somewhat clouded by speculation that a merger with another drug giant would be pursued, ALZA continued to move new products and new applications of existing products through the pipeline. Approved by the FDA in August 2000 was Concerta, a once-daily treatment of attention deficit/hyperactivity disorder that used the OROS technology. Following its final approval, Concerta was to be copromoted in the United States by ALZA and McNeil Consumer Healthcare, a unit of Johnson & Johnson. Concerta was part of a new area of research for the company, that of central nervous system/pediatrics. Also in advanced development was E-TRANS fentanyl, which was slated to be ALZA's first commercial product to use the E-TRANS electrotransport system, a system using low-level electrical energy to transport drugs through the skin. E-TRANS fentanyl, which contained the same drug as Duragesic, was designed for the management of acute pain in postsurgery and emergency room situations. ALZA was also investigating Doxil for two new indicated uses: the treatment of breast cancer and multiple myeloma, a cancer of the bone marrow.

Principal Subsidiaries

ALZA Development Corporation; ALZA International, Inc.; ALZA Limited (U.K.); Therapeutic Discovery Corporation; ALZA Land Management, Inc.

Principal Operating Units

ALZA Pharmaceuticals; ALZA Technologies.

Principal Competitors

Abbott Laboratories; Amarin Corporation plc; Bausch & Lomb Incorporated; Becton, Dickinson & Company; Bristol-Myers Squibb Company; C.R. Bard, Inc.; Cygnus, Inc.; Elan Corporation, plc; Faulding Oral Pharmaceuticals; Merck & Co., Inc.; Minnesota Mining and Manufacturing Company; Noven Pharmaceuticals, Inc.; R.P. Scherer Corporation; TheraTech, Inc.

Further Reading

Abate, Tom, "ALZA Deals Collapses—Stock Tumbles," *San Francisco Chronicle,* December 17, 1999, p. B1.
——, "ALZA Gets Strong Backing for New Uses of Two Drugs," *San Francisco Chronicle,* June 9, 1999, p. B2.
——, "FDA Approves ALZA's Tiny Drug Dispenser," *San Francisco Chronicle,* March 7, 2000, p. E1.
Abate, Tom, and Carol Emert, "Abbott Labs to Buy Palo Alto Drugmaker ALZA for $7.3 Billion," *San Francisco Chronicle,* June 22, 1999, p. A1.
Adelson, Andrea, "ALZA Has Taken the Wraps Off Its Drug Pipeline, Pleasing Analysts," *New York Times,* February 16, 1996.
Barry, David, and James S. Goldman, "ALZA Opens Throttle on Expansion," *Business Journal-San Jose,* May 6, 1991, p. 1.
"Biotech's Father William," *Economist,* June 26, 1999, p. 78.
Burton, Thomas M., "Abbott Laboratories and ALZA Call Off Their Deal," *Wall Street Journal,* December 17, 1999, p. B10.
Gengo, Lorraine, "Martin Gerstel: Modesty Masks Highly Praised, Innovative Leader," *Business Journal-San Jose,* January 9, 1989, p. 10.
Goldman, James S., "ALZA Buys Back a Firm, Agrees on Marketing Pact," *Business Journal-San Jose,* November 18, 1991, p. 2.
——, "ALZA's Key Product Is Target of Patent Dispute," *Business Journal-San Jose,* December 2, 1991, p. 2.
Grzanka, Len, "Drug Company Patches In to Growing World Market," *San Francisco Business Times,* June 11, 1999, p. S6.
King, Ralph T., Jr., "ALZA Corp. Agrees to Purchase Sequus for $580 Million," *Wall Street Journal,* October 6, 1998, p. B4.
Marcial, Gene G., "ALZA May Get Swallowed Up," *Business Week,* March 13, 1995, p. 86.
Miller, James P., "Abbott Labs Agrees to Purchase ALZA," *Wall Street Journal,* June 22, 1999, p. A3.
Moukheiber, Zina, "Putting a Spin on R&D," *Forbes,* February 8, 1999, p. 111.
Sloan, Allan, "Miracle Drug for Earnings: ALZA Shooting Fish in a Barrel with Merrill Lynch's Arrow," *Newsday,* April 11, 1993, p. 68.
Smith, Rebecca, "ALZA Buying Sequus for $580 Million," *San Francisco Chronicle,* October 6, 1998, p. C1.

—Marinell James
—updated by David E. Salamie

Analysts International Corporation

3601 West 76th Street
Minneapolis, Minnesota 55435
U.S.A.
Telephone: (612) 835-5900
Toll Free: (800) 800-5044
Fax: (612) 897-4555
Web site: http://www.analysts.com

Public Company
Incorporated: 1966
Employees: 4,900
Sales: $558.7 million (2000)
Stock Exchanges: NASDAQ
Ticker Symbol: ANLY
NAIC: 541511 Custom Computer Programming Services;
    541512 Computer Systems Design Services; 561320
    Temporary Help Services; 561330 Employee Leasing
    Services

Analysts International Corporation (AiC) describes itself as "a premier information technology services company serving more than 900 corporate and governmental clients." Established in 1966 to provide contract programming services, AiC has expanded its information technology (IT) services to include electronic commerce and eBusiness solutions, technical staffing, information management, mobile business computing, and digital asset management, among others. Its client base includes a range of old and new economy companies in nearly 20 different industries. Its two biggest clients, US West and IBM Corporation, account for about 40 percent of its revenue. AiC employs more than 4,000 IT professionals—whose services are billable to client organizations—in 45 markets in the United States, Canada, and the United Kingdom.

Focusing on Contract Programming: 1960s–70s

Analysts International was formed by Frederick W. Lang in 1966, with offices in a carriage house behind his home in Minneapolis. In its first year the firm opened offices in Minne-apolis, Los Angeles, and Washington, D.C. Victor C. Benda joined the firm and later became president of the company. The company's stock was initially traded over the counter. By 1969 revenue had reached $1.6 million. In 1969 AiC acquired United Capital Investors Co. and used its office building as corporate headquarters until 1999.

In 1970 AiC negotiated a national agreement with General Motors. For the next several years AiC would be one of the largest suppliers of outside programming services to GM. AiC had more than 100 clients in 1970, and by 1973 had a staff of more than 100. One project involved developing programs for the U.S. Army's anti-ICBM missile systems at Huntsville, Alabama. In 1976 AiC stock began trading on the NASDAQ. At the end of the decade revenues were $12.3 million. The firm had expanded nationally and adopted a regional management structure.

Rapid Growth in the 1980s

In 1981 *Forbes* magazines spotted AiC and named it one of the "Up and Comers." *Inc.* magazine listed AiC as one of the top promising small growth companies. Revenue reached $23 million, and the firm's national staff grew to 560. By 1988 the company's staff exceeded 1,000, and it had more than 400 active clients. Business was being conducted from 17 branches.

Between 1986 and 1989 AiC's revenue grew at a 24 percent compound annual rate, from $46.7 million to $89.9 million. One analyst predicted AiC's revenue would grow by 15 percent a year in the early 1990s. The company's revenue and earnings growth as well as its debt-free balance sheet made it attractive to investors. All of AiC's growth came about internally rather than through acquisitions.

Benefiting from Industry Outsourcing: 1990s

During the early 1990s AiC benefited from increased outsourcing, as many of its clients downsized in tight economic times. For fiscal 1991 ending June 30 AiC had revenue of $116.8 million, up from $107.8 million in fiscal 1990. The company had more than 500 active clients, including many who were with the company since its first five years. AiC was ranked

54th on *Business Week*'s list of the "100 Best Small Companies." The firm had a staff of 1,700 and 22 branch offices.

For fiscal 1992 revenue rose 10.9 percent to $130 million. The number of employees increased from 1,750 to 2,070. For several years the company was able to support the growth in its business with internally generated funds, so it dropped its line of bank credit at the beginning of the year. Capital expenditures were limited to expanding and remodeling some of its 24 branch offices. During fiscal 1992 AiC established a southern regional headquarters in Atlanta.

In the mid-1990s four major lines of business were implemented: Solutions, Professional Consulting, Technical Staffing, and Managed Services. The company's Managed Services Group, established in 1997, was responsible for managing the systems analysts, computer programmers, and other technical personnel who were on assignment with AiC's clients. Starting in 1995, AiC had more than 1,000 programmers and other technical personnel on assignment at US West, the firm's largest customer. US West accounted for about 22 percent of AiC's revenue in the latter half of the 1990s. The company's second largest customer was IBM, for which AiC provided services through 30 branch offices as part of IBM's National Procurement initiative. IBM accounted for 16 to 20 percent of AiC's revenue.

Revenue for fiscal 1997 was $440 million. After 1997 AiC established additional new national practices: eBusiness, Rapid Application Design and Development (RADD), and Lawson Software. Mike LaVelle was promoted from regional vice-president to president and COO.

AiC first partnered with Lawson Software in 1995, when Lawson established its partner program, Global Alliance Integrated Network (GAIN). AiC provided technical support for Lawson and its clients internationally, in Europe, Africa, South America, Canada, and the United States. AiC's Lawson Software Practice was focused on helping customers implement their Lawson enterprise resource planning software. AiC maintained three fully staffed centers in the United States to assist Lawson with its latest product developments.

Between 1997 and 2000 AiC's eBusiness services developed into a wide range of e-commerce solutions, from front-end web development to back-end systems integration. Rapid Application Design and Development (RADD) formed a key component in the company's overall eBusiness strategy. RADD is a rapid prototyping methodology that enables client companies to implement eBusiness solutions quickly and efficiently.

Y2K, Electronic Commerce: 1996–2000

Around 1996 companies anticipated having Y2K problems with their computer systems. During 1997 Wall Street thought that computer services companies would benefit from Y2K concerns, and AiC's stock doubled in price. In 1998 the company's stock was affected by economic uncertainty in Asia and other world markets, as well as by missed earnings targets. Early in the year AiC stock was trading around $37. When its quarterly results for September 1998 failed to meet Wall Street's expectations, the already declining stock fell another 30 percent to around $18 a share. The stocks of computer services companies in general were losing ground, largely because of concerns over global economic conditions.

For fiscal 1998 ending June 30 AiC had revenue of $587.4 million. Revenue had grown 29 percent compounded annually for the past five years. By 1999 Wall Street was looking unfavorably on stocks of computer services companies, because it thought that they would lose a lot of Y2K business once the fixes were put in place. In addition, many companies were delaying the implementation of computer projects until the year 2000 to avoid additional compliance issues.

For fiscal 1999 AiC had revenue of $620.2 million. During the year AiC experienced a temporary but dramatic change in its clients' spending pattern. The company's revenue growth slowed as clients worldwide focused on finalizing their Y2K initiatives, often using inhouse staff for testing. Many companies were also deferring new projects until the year 2000. In 1999 AiC consolidated its three locations in the Minneapolis/St. Paul area into a new headquarters in Edina, Minnesota.

In 2000 AiC acquired Sequoia Diversified Products, which changed its name to SequoiaNet.com in mid-2000, from parent company Panurgy Corp. of Columbia, Maryland, for $43.5 million. For 1999 Sequoia, which was founded in 1990, had revenue of $57 million. Sequoia had more than 500 employees and was based in Auburn Hills, Michigan. AiC acquired about 80 percent of the company, with the remainder retained by Sequoia's founder and president John Bamberger and the firm's management team. Sequoia would continue to operate as a separate subsidiary of AiC and provide web hosting and development services as well as business reengineering and marketing services. Bamberger also became a vice president of AiC and reported to AiC president Mike LaVelle. The acquisition was part of AiC's strategy to strengthen its position in providing e-commerce solutions.

In June 2000 it was revealed that Minnesota entrepreneur Rick Born had bought a 5.8 percent interest in AiC. Born was the founder of Born Information Systems, an information technology consulting firm that *Inc.* magazine ranked as one of the fastest-growing private companies in the mid-1990s. Although Born's purchase spawned rumors of a possible takeover, Born insisted it was simply a good investment and that he had no intentions of mounting a takeover bid for AiC.

For the future, AiC's strategy included strengthening its e-business and e-commerce consulting business, which offered higher margins, and placing less emphasis on low-margin businesses such as technical staffing. The acquisition of SequoiaNet.com added some 420 technical consultants experienced in e-business network infrastructure. In mid-2000 AiC announced the establishment of its Enterprise Consulting eBusiness team, which would be based in Raleigh, North Carolina, and headed by AiC's executive consultant Brad Bradstreet, formerly the chief architect behind IBM's eBusiness infrastructure.

For fiscal 2000 ending June 30, AiC's revenue dropped nearly ten percent to $558.7 million. Net income declined from $22.7 million in fiscal 1999 to $9.8 million in fiscal 2000. Despite the impact of Y2K on AiC's clients' spending, the company remained profitable and was poised to take advantage of anticipated growth in the IT services market over the coming year. AiC had strong customer relationships with more than 900 clients worldwide, including many *Fortune* 500 companies.

Principal Subsidiaries

SequoiaNet.com.

Principal Competitors

Cambridge Technology Partners, Inc.; Computer Task Group; CGA; Keane Inc.; Computer Horizons Corp.; Andersen Consulting; IBM Corporation.

Further Reading

"Analysts International Corp.," *Corporate Report-Minnesota,* July 1990, p. 100.

Arginteanu, Judy, "Analysts International Corp.," *Minneapolis-St. Paul CityBusiness,* January 14, 1991, p. 29.

Beal, Dave, "Saint Paul Pioneer Press, Minn., Dave Beal Column," *Knight-Ridder/Tribune Business News,* January 24, 1999.

Carlson, Scott, "Edina, Minn., Consulting Firm's Stock Takes Hit," *Knight-Ridder/Tribune Business News,* October 13, 1998.

——, "Minnesota Software Firm's Niche Is the Year-2000 Computing Fiasco," *Knight-Ridder/Tribune Business News,* May 21, 1996.

Hoogesteger, John, "Born Acquires 5.8 Percent of Analysts Stock," *Minneapolis-St. Paul CityBusiness,* June 23, 2000, p. 33.

O'Shaughnessy, Maryellen, "Software Firm Makes Big Plans for Growth," *Business First-Columbus,* September 30, 1991, p. 5.

Parsons, Martha, "The Benefactor," *Corporate Report-Minnesota,* October 1998, p. 43.

Rosa, Jerry, "Sequoia Changes Name, Shifts Focus," *Computer Reseller News,* June 5, 2000, p. 22.

Solberg, Carla, "Analysts International Corp.," *Minneapolis-St. Paul CityBusiness,* October 30, 1992, p. 28.

—David P. Bianco

The Anschutz Corporation

555 17th Street, Suite 2400
Denver, Colorado 80202
U.S.A.
Telephone: (303) 298-1000
Fax: (303) 298-8881

Private Company
Incorporated: 1958
NAIC: 551112 Offices of Other Holding Companies

The Anschutz Corporation and its affiliates, including Anschutz Company and Anschutz Investment Company, are the investment vehicles for the diversified interests of Philip F. Anschutz. Originally funded by the oil and gas holdings of his father, Anschutz, who consistently shuns publicity, quietly became a billionaire in the early 1980s as a result of his oil and gas exploration ventures. Consistently ranked as the richest person in Denver, Anschutz became better known nationally in the late 1980s and early 1990s for acquiring railroad lines, including the small Rio Grande Railroad and a railroad giant, Southern Pacific Rail Corporation. In 1996 he engineered the sale of Southern Pacific to rival Union Pacific Corporation, pocketing $1.4 billion in profits from an initial $90 million investment. By that time he had invested about $55 million into a sleepy offshoot of Southern Pacific to develop what would eventually become Qwest Communications International Inc., the number four long-distance company in the United States as well as the owner of U S West Inc., one of the Baby Bells. In addition to maintaining a five percent stake in Union Pacific and being the largest shareholder of Qwest with a 38 percent stake, Anschutz continues his involvement in the energy sector through a 37 percent stake in Forest Oil Corporation, a Denver-based oil and gas exploration and production company; is heavily involved in the Los Angeles sports scene with his ownership of the Los Angeles Kings hockey franchise and a professional soccer team as well as partial ownership of the Los Angeles Lakers basketball team and the state-of-the-art Staples Center; and has extensive real estate holdings. A marathon runner, Anschutz has built his $16-billion-plus fortune through tenacity, savvy dealmaking, strategic timing, and a knack for spotting trends.

From Struggling Wildcatter to Billionaire Dealmaker: 1960s–Early 1980s

Philip Anschutz was born in Russell, Kansas, in 1939 (one source says it was Grand Bend). His father, Fred Anschutz, was a renowned oil field wildcatter who made and lost several fortunes. It was Fred Anschutz who founded the Anschutz Corporation, incorporating it in 1958. At that time, Philip Anschutz was in college at the University of Kansas, where he earned a bachelor's degree in finance, with honors, in 1961. The following year, Anschutz was days away from his first day of classes at the prestigious University of Virginia law school, when his father became ill; he returned home to take over the family businesses, including Anschutz Corporation and the oil wildcatting company, Circle A Drilling.

Success did not come immediately for the young wildcatter. It was not until 1968 that he made his first major strike—and his first million—while contract drilling for Chevron near Gillette, Wyoming. When the huge oil field caught fire soon after its discovery, Anschutz averted disaster by persuading the famed oil-fire fighter Red Adair to take on the blaze despite Anschutz's shaky finances, and by securing $100,000—enough to tide him over until he could get financing from his bankers—from Universal Studios. Universal just happened to be filming *Hellfighters,* which had John Wayne playing Adair, and were pleased to be able to take footage of a real fire and the real Adair in action.

Over the next several years, Anschutz's fortunes waxed and waned, and it was during this period that he began to expand outside of the oil industry while continuing to own oil fields in Montana, Texas, Colorado, and Wyoming. Anschutz purchased cattle ranches, uranium and coal mines, and wheat and vegetable farms, and launched a New York-based commodity trading company specializing in oil and metals. He was nearly ruined by a disastrous coal mining investment before managing to sell the money-losing mines to an electric utility.

Among the real estate Anschutz purchased in the 1970s was a property on the Wyoming-Utah border, known as Anschutz Ranch East. In 1978 Amoco Corporation discovered a huge reservoir of oil and natural gas adjacent to this ranch—what turned out to be one of the largest discoveries since Alaska's

Prudhoe Bay. Amoco attempted to buy Anschutz's mineral rights but he refused. Instead, he expanded his holdings of what became known as the Overthrust Belt, acquiring leases on ten million acres. Then in a prime example of his exquisite timing, Anschutz sold a half-interest in the mineral rights on his ranchlands to Mobil Corporation for $500 million in 1982, not long before the 1980s oil crash. Were it not for this shrewd maneuver that made him a billionaire, Anschutz could have been one of the crash's casualties.

Anschutz parlayed his oil and gas wealth into the stock market, downtown real estate (primarily in Denver), and, ultimately, the railroad industry. Anschutz contemplated and then abandoned takeovers of two publicly traded companies in the 1980s, ITT and Pennwalt; in the process of buying and selling shares in the companies, he pocketed more than $100 million. In the early 1980s, Anschutz spent $61.5 million for a nearly 25 percent stake in troubled Ideal Basic Industries, one of the largest companies in Colorado and one of the country's leading producers of cement and potash. Anschutz ended up clearing a $30 million profit on what had looked like an extremely risky investment.

Anschutz's first major venture into real estate began when he secured a 30 percent interest in all projects developed by the Oxford-AnsCo Development Co.—a subsidiary of a leading Canadian development company, Oxford Properties Inc.—for $1 million and downtown property owned by Anschutz in Denver and Colorado Springs. By the early 1980s, Oxford-AnsCo had developed several major skyscrapers in Denver, including the 56-story Republic Tower and the 39-story Anaconda Tower, worth an estimated $250 million. The relationship with Oxford-AnsCo soured when Anschutz gained the vast real estate holdings of the Denver & Rio Grande Railroad in 1984 and wanted to begin to develop real estate on his own rather than through the Oxford partnership. Late in 1984, the partnership was dissolved and the holdings divided between Anschutz and Oxford, with Anschutz keeping the Anaconda Tower (where the company's offices were still located in the early 21st century), Denver's Fairmont Hotel, and a half-block of undeveloped land in Denver.

Mid- to Late-1980s: Modern-Day Rail Baron

Soon after Ronald Reagan became president in 1980, he deregulated the U.S. railroad industry. Anschutz spotted a huge opportunity here, anticipating that the deregulation would inevitably lead to consolidation and the possibility of profiting from dealmaking. He started modestly, with the 1984 purchase of the Denver & Rio Grande Railroad, commonly known as the Rio Grande, a small railroad that then consisted of more than 3,400 miles of track from Missouri to Utah. Anschutz Corp. purchased the Rio Grande's parent, Rio Grande Industries, Inc., for $500 million, $90 million of which was in cash and the remainder in loans. This heavy debt load, coupled with competition from the Union Pacific line and several lost coal-hauling accounts, led to an approximate revenue loss of 20 percent over the first four years under Anschutz and a net loss of $1.8 million over an 11-month period in 1987 and 1988.

The Rio Grande's small size and its position as a bridge carrier (providing connections between other rail lines) led Anschutz to pursue the acquisition of the railroad giant Southern Pacific (SP) in an attempt to save the much smaller Rio Grande. With 20,000 miles of track thoroughly covering the West Coast and a line through the southern United States to the Mississippi River, the SP was even more attractive to Anschutz for its connections to the Rio Grande lines in Kansas City and Ogden, Utah, making for a synergistic coupling.

Anschutz had to overcome a major hurdle to achieve his objective of solidifying his railroad holdings. Santa Fe Industries Inc. had purchased Southern Pacific in 1983 with the intention of merging SP with the Atchison, Topeka & Santa Fe Railway (known as the Santa Fe), one of SP's main competitors. The proposed merger elicited immediate opposition from government officials and Santa Fe's competition, and with the added impetus of pressure from Anschutz, whom *Forbes* called "politically influential," the Interstate Commerce Commission (ICC) in 1987 blocked the Santa Fe-SP merger as anticompetitive. Robert Krebs, the chairman of Santa Fe Industries, was forced to sell one of his lines and chose SP, which he felt was the weaker of the two.

Anschutz closed the deal for Southern Pacific in the fall of 1988. Similar to many other takeovers of the 1980s, Anschutz engineered a highly leveraged purchase in which Rio Grande Industries paid Santa Fe Industries just over $1 billion in cash, most of it borrowed, for SP, assuming more than $700 million in SP debt. After the deal, Anschutz controlled 71 percent of the Rio Grande, which now controlled SP, while Morgan Stanley as a minority partner controlled the remaining 29 percent through its purchase of $111 million in Rio Grande common stock. As William P. Barrett noted in *Forbes,* ''Beyond the original cash stake in the Rio Grande, Anschutz put not a penny more into the deal,'' thereby making him the first individual to own a major railroad in decades.

Early 1990s: Turning SP Around

In the initial years after the purchase, Rio Grande Industries struggled to overcome its huge debt load, which had led to $100 million-plus interest payments each year, as well as the decline in SP's traditional accounts in auto parts, lumber, and food; increased competition from Union Pacific and Santa Fe; and more rigorous safety inspections in California, where SP trains were involved in two chemical spills in July 1991. Amid speculation that he would be better off breaking up SP and selling it piecemeal (Krebs of the Santa Fe still coveted much of the SP line and approached Anschutz about a deal several times without success), Anschutz told *Forbes:* ''I said in my original ICC filing that we would turn this railroad around; I'm in it for the long haul.'' Anschutz also foresaw that Southern Pacific would be far more valuable intact than in parts, especially after industry consolidation proceeded to its endgame when one of the western railroads, in order to remain competitive, would pay dearly for SP.

To reduce the debt load, Anschutz sold large portions of Southern Pacific's vast real estate holdings, more than $1 billion worth by the end of 1991 and nearly $400 million in 1992 alone. Anschutz also began to improve the quality of its service through heavy expenditures to maintain its track and hiring a quality expert, Kent Sterett, from its competitor Union Pacific. As trade between the United States and Mexico increased in the early 1990s, SP seemed best positioned to profit from it with its six Mexican gateways in California, Texas, and Arizona. Anschutz's strategy appeared to be working as an operating loss of $347.7 million in 1991 had been reduced to $24.6 million in 1992. But in 1993, SP slid back to a loss of $149 million.

In the summer of 1993, Anschutz turned to a railroad company veteran, Edward Moyers, to assist in turning SP around. Moyers had retired after a very successful four-year stint at Illinois Central, where he cut its operating ratio (operating expenses as a percentage of revenues) from 98 percent to 71 percent. Anschutz hired Moyers as chief executive, and Moyers immediately focused on Southern Pacific's operating ratio, which stood at 96.5 percent in 1993. The hiring enabled Anschutz to embark on a new and surprising strategy for a man who preferred to keep his dealings private: taking SP public.

In another effort to reduce the debt load, 30 million shares were offered in August 1993. Although the initial offering price was estimated at $20 per share, the actual price of the shares as issued was $13.50. Still, that the offering was successful at all was attributed by many to the hiring of Moyers. Investor interest in Southern Pacific increased in the several months that

followed, so that by February 1994, when a second stock offering of 25 million shares was initiated, they sold for $19.75 per share. Following these sales, Anschutz owned 41 percent of the shares outstanding. Henry Dubroff of the *Denver Post* estimated that Anschutz had pocketed pretax profits of as much as $500 million from the stock offerings.

Meanwhile, Moyers started a multipronged strategy for revitalizing Southern Pacific. First, he planned to cut costs by reducing the employee ranks through a buyout program and a reorganization. In his first year, he reduced the labor force by more than 3,000 to about 19,000 jobs. Second, Moyers focused on service to SP's customers, putting pressure on his subordinates to improve the operations. This initiative saved a lucrative Georgia-Pacific account by increasing on-time Georgia-Pacific deliveries from zero to 80 percent in three months. Overall, on-time deliveries were up by more than 50 percent in his first year. Moyers also sought to bolster Southern Pacific's equipment through the purchase of new locomotives, the rebuilding of existing locomotives, and better maintenance of both trains and track. Although SP was still in weak financial condition, Moyers had managed to make a number of improvements, and in February 1995 he once again retired. Moyers was succeeded as president and CEO by veteran railroader Jerry R. Davis.

Anschutz was also attempting to leverage the real estate holdings of Southern Pacific by developing some of the land rather than selling it to other developers. Starting around 1994, Anschutz was involved in the planning of a downtown development in his base city of Denver on land along the South Platte River that he had purchased from SP. Anschutz and Comsat (later Ascent Entertainment), then owners of the National Basketball Association's Denver Nuggets and later the owners of the National Hockey League's Colorado Avalanche, developed a proposal for a $130 million sports and entertainment center that would include a new basketball and hockey arena and film and television studios. But the plan fell through when Anschutz insisted that Ascent sell him 50 percent of the Avalanche and Ascent refused. In the end, Anschutz sold the land underneath what would eventually become the Pepsi Center to Ascent for top dollar; he would also turn away from Denver and seek his entrée into the sports world to the west, in Los Angeles.

Mid-1990s and Beyond: Exit Railroads, Enter Qwest and Sports, Reenter Oil

By 1995 railroad industry consolidation was reaching a crescendo, with the number of major railroads having been reduced from 40 in 1980 to ten, and with the completion of the merger of Burlington Northern and the Sante Fe. There were now just three major rail companies in the western United States: Southern Pacific, Union Pacific, and the newly named Burlington Northern Sante Fe, which was about the size of the other two combined. Not surprisingly, then, the Southern Pacific and Union Pacific entered into what turned out to be lengthy discussions about a merger. Finally, in November 1995 Union Pacific filed an application with the ICC to acquire Southern Pacific.

Completion of the merger was by no means certain. The rail systems of Burlington Northern and the Sante Fe scarcely had any overlap, while the merger of SP and UP would eliminate competition on certain runs, most notably in Texas and between Colorado and California. Meanwhile, the U.S. Congress, under full Republican control for the first time in decades, was considering the abolition of the ICC and its replacement by a more industry-friendly Surface Transportation Board (STB). With Anschutz once again wielding political pressure, the Congress passed the legislation that replaced the ICC with the STB in December 1995. In July 1996—despite opposition from the U.S. departments of Justice, Transportation, and Agriculture; from such rival railroads as Kansas City Southern and Consolidated Rail; and from the governor of Texas, George W. Bush—the STB approved the merger in July 1996, with the only major stipulation being that UP grant trackage rights for about 4,000 miles of track to Burlington Northern Sante Fe.

Union Pacific paid $5.4 billion for Southern Pacific, with Anschutz pocketing about $1.4 billion from the sale. Part of this came in the form of stakes of more than five percent each he gained in Union Pacific (a stake initially worth about $700 million) and in Union Pacific Resources Group Inc., a leading independent oil and gas exploration and production company that was spun off from Union Pacific in 1995 and 1996 (the stake in the latter was worth about $300 million). The $1.4 billion figure was an astounding gain on what had essentially been Anschutz's initial cash investment (in the Denver & Rio Grande Railroad) of $90 million.

Anschutz continued to hold his five percent stake in Union Pacific into the 21st century. UP suffered from highly publicized difficulties integrating SP, resulting in massive gridlock in the summer of 1997 and extending into 1998; it was estimated that by March 1998 delays in UP shipments had cost rail customers about $1 billion in curtailed production, reduced sales, and higher shipping costs. The *New York Times* called the takeover "the most spectacular merger fiasco of modern times."

While Anschutz's railroading venture garnered him the most publicity in the early- to mid-1990s, other activities stepped into the spotlight in the late 1990s. Emerging seemingly out of nowhere to replace Southern Pacific as Anschutz's key venture was Qwest, a company whose lineage came straight out of Southern Pacific. Beginning in 1987, the railroad operated a sleepy subsidiary called SP Telecommunications Company, which installed fiber-optic cable along its tracks for the use of the railroad and for telephone companies. In 1991 Anschutz carved SP Telecom out of Southern Pacific, taking full control of it for an investment of $55 million. SP Telecom continued digging trenches along the tracks and laying fiber-optic cable, then leasing the lines to such telecommunications firms as AT&T and MCI. The company began offering its own long distance service to business customers in the Southwest in 1993. Two years later, Anschutz acquired Qwest Communications Inc., a Dallas-based digital microwave company, and merged SP Telecom into it, setting up headquarters in Denver. He also began securing the rights to lay cable along the tracks of other railroads, eventually gaining agreements to lay cable along 40,000 miles of railway.

In the fall of 1996, perhaps not coincidentally soon after Union Pacific's takeover of Southern Pacific was consummated, Qwest announced that it planned to develop a nationwide fiber-

optic network, using the most advanced technology and offering the highest capacity of any U.S. telecommunications network. With the Internet beginning its explosive late 1990s growth, telecommunications companies were clamoring for additional capacity. To fund the cost of constructing the massive network—initially estimated at $1.4 billion—Qwest in 1996 reached an agreement with Frontier Corporation, whereby Frontier, at the time the number five U.S. long distance company, would invest $500 million in Qwest in exchange for the right to 25 percent of the capacity of the Qwest network for the following 50 years. Anschutz next pulled off a coup by hiring Joseph Nacchio, a top AT&T executive, to run Qwest as CEO (Anschutz remained chairman). Following Nacchio's hiring in January 1997, Qwest inked two additional deals with WorldCom and GTE, similar to the one with Frontier, for another $600 million. To pare down the company's $311 million in debt, Anschutz took Qwest public in June 1997 through an IPO that raised $321 million. Anschutz retained an 84 percent stake in Qwest, whose stock soared from $22 per share at offering to more than $50 by the end of 1997. At that point, Anschutz had managed to turn his initial $55 million investment in SP Telecom into $4.9 billion. He had now made billion-dollar fortunes in three separate industries: oil, railroads, and telecommunications.

Over the next few years, Qwest grew rapidly through acquisitions. In 1998 the company became the number four long distance company in the United States through a $4.4 billion stock-swap purchase of LCI International. The following year Qwest battled for control of local telephone provider U S West Inc., one of the original Baby Bells, with another upstart telecommunications company, Global Crossing Ltd. Qwest eventually won the battle, acquiring U S West for about $43.5 billion in stock in 2000. These and other deals diluted Anschutz's stake in Qwest by mid-2000 to about 38 percent, which still translated into about $12 billion.

Meanwhile, Anschutz began his move into the sports world in 1995 when he teamed with Los Angeles developer Edward Roski, Jr., to buy the Los Angeles Kings hockey team for $114 million. Anschutz also bought three professional soccer teams, the Los Angeles Galaxy, the Colorado Rapids, and the Chicago Fire, all part of Major League Soccer, which Anschutz owned a part of as well. In 1997 Anschutz and Roski inked a deal to build a state-of-the-art sports arena in Los Angeles that would become the home ice for the Kings. The following year the partners purchased a 25 percent stake in the Los Angeles Lakers, one of the premier teams of the National Basketball Association. The Lakers, the Kings, and another NBA team, the Los Angeles Clippers, began playing in what became the $400 million, 20,000-seat Staples Center in the fall of 1999. Anschutz also owned 30 acres of land around the arena that he planned to develop into a vast entertainment complex with hotels, restaurants, theaters, and offices. It was also speculated that Anschutz envisioned synergies between Qwest and his sports activities, specifically the possibility of using the high-tech electronics that were installed in the Staples Center to transmit high-definition images of sporting events over the Qwest network to television sets and computers. It was possible that a similar motive was behind a report in the *Wall Street Journal* in June 2000 that Anschutz, along with a partner, was launching a film production company.

While his ventures into telecommunications and sports grabbed most of the headlines in the second half of the 1990s, behind the scenes, Anschutz became increasingly active in the industry in which he made his first fortune, petroleum. In 1995 Anschutz purchased a 40 percent stake in Forest Oil Corporation, a Denver-based oil and gas exploration and production company founded in 1916, for $45 million. Anschutz attempted to build Forest Oil into a major independent oil company through mergers and acquisitions. In 1996 and 1997 Forest Oil acquired two Canadian exploration and production companies, Saxon Petroleum Inc. and ATCOR Resources Ltd. Forest Oil then purchased some of Anschutz's oil and gas properties in 1998 for about $80 million in stock. In 2000 the company agreed to acquire a Miami, Florida-based exploration and production firm called Forcenergy Inc., which Anschutz had gained control of after it went into bankruptcy.

By the early 21st century, Anschutz had an estimated net worth of more than $16 billion. What was next for this seemingly modern-day Midas? As always, Anschutz had several irons in the fire. In addition to his move into film production, Anschutz in 1999 purchased companies that were involved in storing video in digital form on computers and in sending high-quality video over fiber-optics lines. He had also purchased a substantial amount of the debt of the financially troubled United Artists Theatre Corp., one of the largest owners and operators of movie theaters in the country. Through a restructuring, it was possible that Anschutz could wind up as the largest shareholder of United Artists, and would have done so on the cheap. No one could say if any of these ventures would turn into another billion-dollar payoff, but after the naysayers were proved very wrong when they had questioned Anschutz's forays into railroads and telecommunications, few people were willing to bet against him.

Further Reading

Barrett, William P., "Working over the Railroad," *Forbes*, October 31, 1988, pp. 51–54.

Berman, Phyllis, and Roula Khalaf, "I Might Be a Seller, I Might Be a Buyer," *Forbes*, February 3, 1992, pp. 86–87.

Burke, Jack, "With Alameda Corridor Deal in Hand, Southern Pacific Prepares to Sell 25 Million More Shares," *Traffic World*, December 20, 1993, pp. 26–27.

Caulk, Steve, "SP Deal Forges Biggest Railroad," *Rocky Mountain News*, August 4, 1995, p. 62A.

"A Cowboy's Dream," *Financial Executive*, March/April 1993, pp. 32–33.

Curtis, Carol E., "Take a Ride on the Rio Grande," *Forbes*, May 20, 1985, pp. 106–107.

Dubroff, Henry, "Anschutz's Ride on Southern Pacific Has Been a Profitable One," *Denver Post*, November 13, 1994, p. 1H.

Everitt, Lisa Greim, "Anschutz Works Behind Scenes to Secure Deals," *Denver Rocky Mountain News*, July 19, 1999, p. 9B.

Fridson, Martin S., "How Phil Anschutz Made His Fortune," *Denver Rocky Mountain News*, January 16, 2000, p. 2G.

MacAdams, Lewis, "The Invisible Man," *Los Angeles Magazine*, October 1998, pp. 70–78 +.

Machan, Dan, "The Man Who Won't Let Go," *Forbes*, August 1, 1994, pp. 64–65.

Mack, Toni, "The Next Quest," *Forbes*, July 26, 1999, p. 53.

——, "Stark Raving Rich," *Forbes*, February 26, 1996, p. 44.

Mahoney, Michelle, "Southern Pacific Going Public," *Denver Post*, May 14, 1993, p. 1C.

Moore, Paula, "Anschutz Tackles Sports," *Denver Business Journal*, September 13, 1999.

Morris, Kathleen, and Steven V. Brull, "Phil Anschutz: Qwest's $7 Billion Man," *Business Week*, December 8, 1997, pp. 70, 72, 74.

O'Reilly, Brian, "Billionaire Next Door," *Fortune*, September 6, 1999, pp. 139–40 +.

Ortega, Bob, "Southern Pacific's Chairman Turns Attention to Oil and Gas and New Areas," *Wall Street Journal*, August 4, 1995, p. B8.

Sandberg, Jared, "Qwest Is Building the Basics of Better Communications," *Wall Street Journal*, December 24, 1996, p. B3.

Sherer, Paul M., "Anschutz May Be Making Play for United Artists," *Wall Street Journal*, June 1, 2000, pp. C1, C23.

Smith, Jerd, "The Man with the Cash: Phil Anschutz Pours Success into Almost Any Deal," *Rocky Mountain News*, December 21, 1997, p. 5W.

Weaver, Nancy, "Denver's Billionaires: Low-Key Anschutz Built His Empire Quietly," *Denver Post*, October 9, 1983, pp. 1A-17A.

—David E. Salamie

Apple Computer, Inc.

1 Infinite Loop
Cupertino, California 95014
U.S.A.
Telephone: (408) 996-1010
Fax: (408) 974-2113
Web site: http://www.apple.com

Public Company
Incorporated: 1977
Employees: 9,736
Sales: $6.13 billion (1999)
Stock Exchanges: NASDAQ
Ticker Symbol: AAPL
NAIC: 334111 Electronic Computer Manufacturing;
     334119 Other Computer Peripheral Equipment
     Manufacturing (pt); 51121 Software Publishers

Apple Computer, Inc. is largely responsible for the enormous growth of the personal computer industry in the 20th century. The introduction of the Macintosh line of personal computers in 1984 established the company as an innovator in industrial design whose products became renowned for their intuitive ease of use. Though battered by bad decision-making during the 1990s, Apple continues to exude the same enviable characteristics in the 21st century that catapulted the company toward fame during the 1980s. The company designs, manufactures, and markets personal computers, software, and peripherals, concentrating on lower-cost, uniquely designed computers such as iMAC and Power Macintosh models.

Origins

Apple was founded in April 1976 by Steve Wozniak, then 26 years old, and Steve Jobs, 21, both college dropouts. Their partnership began several years earlier when Wozniak, a talented, self-taught electronics engineer, began building boxes that allowed him to make long-distance phone calls for free. The pair sold several hundred such boxes.

In 1976 Wozniak was working on another box—the Apple I computer, without keyboard or power supply—for a computer hobbyist club. Jobs and Wozniak sold their most valuable possessions, a van and two calculators, raising $1,300 with which to start a company. A local retailer ordered 50 of the computers, which were built in Jobs's garage. They eventually sold 200 to computer hobbyists in the San Francisco Bay area for $666 each. Later that summer, Wozniak began work on the Apple II, designed to appeal to a greater market than computer hobbyists. Jobs hired local computer enthusiasts, many of them still in high school, to assemble circuit boards and design software. Early microcomputers had usually been housed in metal boxes. With the general consumer in mind, Jobs planned to house the Apple II in a more attractive modular beige plastic container.

Jobs wanted to create a large company and consulted with Mike Markkula, a retired electronics engineer who had managed marketing for Intel Corporation and Fairchild Semiconductor. Chairman Markkula bought one-third of the company for $250,000, helped Jobs with the business plan, and in 1977 hired Mike Scott as president. Wozniak worked for Apple full time in his engineering capacity.

Jobs recruited Regis McKenna, owner of one of the most successful advertising and public relations firms in Silicon Valley, to devise an advertising strategy for the company. McKenna designed the Apple logo and began advertising personal computers in consumer magazines. Apple's professional marketing team placed the Apple II in retail stores, and by June 1977, annual sales reached $1 million. It was the first microcomputer to use color graphics, with a television set as the screen. In addition, the Apple II expansion slot made it more versatile than competing computers.

The earliest Apple IIs read and stored information on cassette tapes, which were unreliable and slow. By 1978 Wozniak had invented the Apple Disk II, at the time the fastest and cheapest disk drive offered by any computer manufacturer. The Disk II made possible the development of software for the Apple II. The introduction of Apple II, with a user manual, at a consumer electronics show signaled that Apple was expanding beyond the hobbyist market to make its computers consumer items. By the end of 1978, Apple was one of the fastest-growing companies in the United States, with its products carried by over 100 dealers.

Company Perspectives:

Apple ignited the personal computer revolution in the 1970s with the Apple II and reinvented the personal computer in the 1980s with the Macintosh. Apple is committed to bringing the best personal computing experience to students, educators, creative professionals and consumers around the world through its innovative hardware, software and Internet offerings.

In 1979 Apple introduced the Apple II+ with far more memory than the Apple II and an easier startup system, and the Silentype, the company's first printer. VisiCalc, the first spreadsheet for microcomputers, was also released that year. Its popularity helped to sell many Apple IIs. By the end of the year sales were up 400 percent from 1978, at over 35,000 computers. Apple Fortran, introduced in March 1980, led to the further development of software, particularly technical and educational applications.

In December 1980, Apple went public. Its offering of 4.6 million shares at $22 each sold out within minutes. A second offering of 2.6 million shares quickly sold out in May 1981.

Meanwhile Apple was working on the Apple II's successor, which was intended to feature expanded memory and graphics capabilities and run the software already designed for the Apple II. The company, fearful that the Apple II would soon be outdated, put time pressures on the designers of the Apple III, despite the fact that sales of the Apple II more than doubled to 78,000 in 1980. The Apple III was well received when it was released in September 1980 at $3,495, and many predicted it would achieve its goal of breaking into the office market dominated by IBM. However, the Apple III was released without adequate testing, and many units proved to be defective. Production was halted and the problems were fixed, but the Apple III never sold as well as the Apple II. It was discontinued in April 1984.

The problems with the Apple III prompted Mike Scott to lay off employees in February 1981, a move with which Jobs disagreed. As a result, Mike Markkula became president and Jobs chairman. Scott was named vice-chairman shortly before leaving the firm.

Despite the problems with Apple III, the company forged ahead, tripling its 1981 research and development budget to $21 million, releasing 40 new software programs, opening European offices, and putting out its first hard disk. By January 1982, 650,000 Apple computers had been sold worldwide. In December 1982, Apple became the first personal computer company to reach $1 billion in annual sales.

The next year, Apple lost its position as chief supplier of personal computers in Europe to IBM, and tried to challenge IBM in the business market with the Lisa computer. Lisa introduced the mouse, a hand-controlled pointer, and displayed pictures on the computer screen that substituted for keyboard commands. These innovations come out of Jobs's determination to design an unintimidating computer that anyone could use.

Unfortunately, the Lisa did not sell as well as Apple had hoped. Apple was having difficulty designing the elaborate software to link together a number of Lisas and was finding it hard to break IBM's hold on the business market. Apple's earnings went down and its stock plummeted to $35, half of its sale price in 1982. Mike Markkula had viewed his presidency as a temporary position, and in April 1983, Jobs brought in John Sculley, formerly president of Pepsi-Cola, as the new president of Apple. Jobs felt the company needed Sculley's marketing expertise.

1984 Debut of the Macintosh

The production division for Lisa had been vying with Jobs's Macintosh division. The Macintosh personal computer offered Lisa's innovations at a fraction of the price. Jobs saw the Macintosh as the "people's computer"—designed for people with little technical knowledge. With the failure of the Lisa, the Macintosh was seen as the future of the company. Launched with a television commercial in January 1984, the Macintosh was unveiled soon after, with a price tag of $2,495 and a new 3½-inch disk drive that was faster than the 5¼-inch drives used in other machines, including the Apple II.

Apple sold 70,000 Macintosh computers in the first 100 days. In September 1984 a new Macintosh was released with more memory and two disk drives. Jobs was convinced that anyone who tried the Macintosh would buy it. A national advertisement offered people the chance to take a Macintosh home for 24 hours, and over 200,000 people did so. At the same time, Apple sold its two millionth Apple II. Over the next six months Apple released numerous products for the Macintosh, including a laser printer and a hard drive.

Despite these successes, Macintosh sales temporarily fell off after a promising start, and the company was troubled by internal problems. Infighting between divisions continued, and poor inventory tracking led to overproduction. Although Jobs had originally been a strong supporter of Sculley, Jobs eventually decided to oust Sculley; Jobs, however, lost the ensuing showdown. Sculley reorganized Apple in June 1985 to end the infighting caused by the product-line divisions, and Jobs, along with several other Apple executives, left the company in September. They founded a new computer company, NeXT Incorporated, which would later emerge as a rival to Apple in the business computer market.

The Macintosh personal computer finally moved Apple into the business office market. Corporations saw its ease of use as a distinct advantage. It was far cheaper than the Lisa and had the necessary software to link office computers. In 1986 and 1987 Apple produced three new Macintosh personal computers with improved memory and power. By 1988, over one million Macintosh computers had been sold, with 70 percent of sales to corporations. Software was created that allowed the Macintosh to be connected to IBM-based systems. Apple grew rapidly; income for 1988 topped $400 million on sales of $4.07 billion, up from income of $217 million on sales of $1.9 billion in 1986. Apple had 5,500 employees in 1986 and over 14,600 by the early 1990s.

In 1988, Apple management had expected a worldwide shortage of memory chips to worsen. They bought millions

Key Dates:
1976: With $1,300, Steve Jobs and Steve Wozniak found Apple Computer, Inc.
1980: Apple converts to public ownership.
1982: Apple becomes the first personal computer company to reach $1 billion in annual sales.
1985: John Sculley assumes the helm after a management shakeup that causes the departure of Jobs and several other Apple executives.
1991: PowerBook line of notebook computers is released.
1994: Power Macintosh line is released.
1996: Acquisition of NeXT brings Steve Jobs back to Apple as a special advisor.
1997: Steve Jobs is named interim chief executive officer.
1998: The all-in-one iMac is released.
2000: Jobs, now firmly in command as CEO, oversees a leaner, more tightly focused Apple.

when prices were high, only to have the shortage end and prices fall soon after. Apple ordered sharp price increases for the Macintosh line just before the Christmas buying season, and consumers bought the less expensive Apple line or other brands. In early 1989, Apple released significantly enhanced versions of the two upper-end Macintosh computers, the SE and the Macintosh II, primarily to compete for the office market. At the same time IBM marketed a new operating system that mimicked the Macintosh's ease of use. In May 1989 Apple announced plans for its new operating system, System 7, which would be available to users the next year and allow Macintoshes to run tasks on more than one program simultaneously.

Apple was reorganized in August 1988 into four operating divisions: Apple USA, Apple Europe, Apple Pacific, and Apple Products. Dissatisfied with the changes, many longtime Apple executives left. In July 1990, Robert Puette, former head of Hewlett-Packard's personal computer business, became head of the Apple USA division. Sculley saw the reorganization as an attempt to create fewer layers of management within Apple, thus encouraging innovation among staff. Analysts credit Sculley with expanding Apple from a consumer and education computer company to a business computer company, one of the biggest and fastest-growing corporations in the United States.

Competition in the industry of information technology involved Apple in a number of lawsuits. In December 1989 for instance, the Xerox Corporation, in a $150 million lawsuit, charged Apple with unlawfully using Xerox technology for the Macintosh software. Apple did not deny borrowing from Xerox technology but explained that the company had spent millions to refine that technology and had used other sources as well. In 1990 the court found in favor of Apple in the Xerox case. Earlier, in March 1988, Apple had brought suits against Microsoft and Hewlett-Packard, charging copyright infringement. Four years later, in the spring of 1992, Apple's case was dealt a severe blow in a surprise ruling: copyright protection cannot be based on "look and feel" (appearance) alone; rather, "specific" features of an original program must be detailed by developers for protection.

Mismanagement—Crippling an Industry Giant: 1990s

Apple entered the 1990s well aware that the conditions that made the company an industry giant in the previous decade had changed dramatically. Management recognized that for Apple to succeed in the future, corporate strategies would have to be reexamined.

Apple had soared through the 1980s on the backs of its large, expensive computers, which earned the company a committed, yet relatively small following. Sculley and his team saw that competitors were relying increasingly on the user-friendly graphics that had become the Macintosh signature and recognized that Apple needed to introduce smaller, cheaper models, such as the Classic and LC, which were instant hits. At a time when the industry was seeing slow unit sales, the numbers at Apple were skyrocketing. In 1990, desktop Macs accounted for 11 percent of the PCs sold through American computer dealers. In mid-1992, the figure was 19 percent.

But these modestly priced models had a considerably smaller profit margin than their larger cousins. So even if sales took off, as they did, profits were threatened. In a severe austerity move, Apple laid off nearly ten percent of its workforce, consolidated facilities, moved production plants to areas where it was cheaper to operate, and drastically altered its corporate organizational chart. The bill for such forward-looking surgery was great, however, and in 1991 profits were off 35 percent. But analysts said that such pitfalls were expected, indeed necessary, if the company intended to position itself as a leaner, better-conditioned fighter in the years ahead.

Looking ahead is what analysts say saved Apple from foundering. In 1992, after the core of the suit that Apple had brought against Microsoft and Hewlett-Packard was dismissed, industry observers pointed out that although the loss was a disappointment for Apple, the company wisely had not banked on a victory. They credited Apple's ambitious plans for the future with quickly turning the lawsuit into yesterday's news.

In addition to remaining faithful to its central business of computer making—the notebook PowerBook series, released in 1991, garnered a 21 percent market share in less than six months—Apple intended to ride a digital wave into the next century. The company geared itself to participate in a revolution in the consumer electronics industry, in which products that were limited by a slow, restrictive analog system would be replaced by faster, digital gadgets on the cutting edge of telecommunications technology. Apple also experimented with the interweaving of sound and visuals in the operations of its computers.

For Apple, the most pressing issue of the 1990s was not related to technology, but concerned capable and consistent management. The company endured tortuous failures throughout much of the decade, as one chief executive officer after another faltered miserably. Scully was forced out of his leadership position by Apple's board of directors in 1993. His replacement, Michael Spindler, broke tradition by licensing Apple technology to outside firms, paving the way for ill-fated Apple clones that ultimately eroded Apple's profits. Spindler also oversaw the introduction of the Power Macintosh line in 1994, an episode in Apple's history that typified the perception that the company had the right products but not the right people to deliver the products to the market. Power Macintosh computers were highly sought after, but after overestimating demand for the earlier release of its PowerBook laptops, the company grossly underestimated demand for the Power Macintosh line. By 1995, Apple had $1 billion worth of unfilled orders, and investors took note of the embarrassing miscue. In a two-day period, Apple's stock value plunged 15 percent.

After Spindler's much-publicized mistake of 1995, Apple's directors were ready to hand the leadership reins to someone new. Gil Amelio, credited with spearheading the recovery of National Semiconductor, was named chief executive officer in February 1996, beginning another notorious era of leadership for the beleaguered Cupertino company. Amelio cut Apple's payroll by a third and slashed operating costs, but drew a hail of criticism for his compensation package and his inability to relate to Apple's unique corporate culture. Apple's financial losses, meanwhile, mounted, reaching $816 million in 1996 and a staggering $1 billion in 1997. The company' stock, which had traded at more than $70 per share in 1991, fell to $14 per share. Its market share, 16 percent in the late 1980s, stood at less than four percent. *Fortune* magazine offered its analysis, referring to Apple in its March 3, 1997 issue as "Silicon Valley's paragon of dysfunctional management."

Amelio was ousted from the company in July 1997, but before his departure a significant deal was concluded that brought Apple's savior to Cupertino. In December 1996, Apple paid $377 million for NeXT, a small, $50-million-in-sales company founded and led by Steve Jobs. Concurrent with the acquisition, Amelio hired Jobs as his special advisor, marking the return of Apple's visionary 12 years after he had left. In September 1997, two months after Amelio's exit, Apple's board of directors named Jobs interim chief executive officer. Apple's recovery occurred during the ensuing months.

Jobs assumed his responsibilities with the same passion and understanding that had made Apple one of the greatest success stories in business history. He immediately discontinued the licensing agreement that spawned Apple clones. He eliminated 15 of the company's 19 products, withdrawing Apple's involvement in making printers, scanners, portable digital assistants, and other peripherals. From 1997 forward, Apple would focus exclusively on desktop and portable Macintoshes for professional and consumer customers. Jobs closed plants, laid off thousands of workers, and sold stock to rival Microsoft Corporation, receiving a cash infusion of $150 million in exchange. Apple's organizational hierarchy underwent sweeping reorganization as well, but the most visible indication of Jobs's return was unveiled in August 1998. Distressed by his company's lack of popular computers that retailed for less than $2,000, Jobs tapped Apple's resources and, ten months after the project began, unveiled the massively successful iMAC, a sleek and colorful computer that embodied Apple's skill in design and functionality.

Because of Jobs's restorative efforts, Apple exited the 1990s as a pared-down version of its former self, but, importantly, a profitable company once again. Annual sales, which totaled $11.5 billion in 1995, stood at $5.9 billion in 1998, from which the company recorded a profit of $309 million. In 1999, sales grew a modest 3.2 percent, but the newfound health of the company was evident in a 94 percent gain in net income, as Apple's profits swelled to $601 million. Further, Apples' stock mustered a remarkable rebound, climbing 140 percent to $99 per share in 1999. By the decade's end, "interim" was dropped from Jobs's corporate title, signaling Jobs's return on a permanent basis and fueling optimism that Apple could look forward to a decade of vibrant and consistent growth.

Principal Subsidiaries

Apple Computer, Inc. Limited (Ireland); Apple Computer Limited (Ireland); Apple Computer U.K. Limited (U.K.); Apple Computer International (Ireland); FileMaker Inc.; Apple Japan, LLC; Apple Computer B.V. (Netherlands); A C Real Properties, Inc.

Principal Competitors

Compaq Computer Corporation; Dell Computer Corporation; International Business Machines Corporation; Microsoft Corporation; Sun Microsystems, Inc.

Further Reading

"Apple Crumble," *Economist (US),* July 12, 1997, p. 54.

Bartholomew, Doug, "What's Really Driving Apple's Recovery," *Industry Week,* March 15, 1999, p. 34.

Fawcett, Neil, "Can Microsoft Put Apple Together Again?," *Computer Weekly,* August 14, 1997, p. 17.

Frieberger, Paul, and Michael Swaine, *Fire in the Valley: The Making of the Personal Computer,* Berkeley, Calif.: Osborne-McGraw-Hill, 1984.

Hogan, Thom, "Apple: The First Ten Years," *A+: The #1 Apple II Magazine,* September 1987.

Kirkpatrick, David, "The Second Coming of Apple," *Fortune,* November 9, 1998, p. 86.

Kupfer, Andrew, "Apple's Plan to Survive and Grow," *Fortune,* May 4, 1992.

Pollack, Andrew, "Apple Shows Products for Its Macintosh Line," *Time,* March 4, 1992.

Quittner, Joshua, "Apple Turnover?," *Time,* October 2, 1995, p. 56.

Rebello, Kathy, "Apple's Daring Leap into the All-Digital Future," *Business Week,* May 25, 1992.

Rebello, Kathy, Michele Galen, and Evan I. Schwartz, "It Looks and Feels As If Apple Lost," *Business Week,* April 27, 1992.

Rose, Frank, *West of Eden,* New York: Penguin Books, 1989.

Schlender, Brent, "Something's Rotten in Cupertino," *Fortune,* March 3, 1997, p. 100.

Zachary, G. Pascal, and Stephen Kreider Yoder, "Apple Moves Its Microsoft Battle to the Marketplace," *Wall Street Journal,* April 16, 1992.

—Scott Lewis
—updated by Jeffrey L. Covell

Avianca Aerovías Nacionales de Colombia SA

Avenida El Dorado 93-30, Piso 5,
Santafe de Bogota D.C.
Colombia
Telephone: +57 (1) 413 9511
Fax: (1) 413 8716
Web site: http://www.avianca.com

Private Company
Incorporated: 1919 as Sociedad Colombo-Alemana de
    Transportes Aéreos (SCADTA)
Employees: 3,200 (1999)
Sales: COL 932.93 billion (1999)
NAIC: 481111 Scheduled Passenger Air Transportation;
    481112 Scheduled Freight Air Transportation

Considered the world's second oldest operating airline after KLM Royal Dutch Airlines, Avianca Aerovías Nacionales de Colombia SA pioneered civil aviation in South America. Once controlled by Pan American Airways (Pan Am), the company is now 60.7 percent owned by Bavaria SA, a $5 billion a year Colombian conglomerate with interests in beverages, media, and energy. The unique challenges of Colombia's topography have never truly been mastered, and economic and political conditions also have been difficult for the company to navigate.

Germanic Origins

Colombia's first airline, the Compañía Colombiana de Navegación Aérea (CCNA), was founded on September 16, 1919 but suffered a string of fatal accidents and folded three years later. Avianca's predecessor, the Sociedad Colombo-Alemana de Transportes Aéreos or SCADTA, was created on December 5, 1919 by a group of Colombian and expatriate German businessmen. At the time of SCADTA's founding, CCNA had already won the government contract for airmail and passenger service between Bogotá and the more populated provinces.

According to the detailed accounting by R.E.G. Davies in *Airlines of Latin America,* however, experience was a very cruel teacher in CCNA's case. By the time SCADTA's first two all-metal Junkers F-13 floatplanes arrived from Germany in July 1920, CCNA had lost two-thirds of its planes and flight crews in accidents.

Austrian industrialist Dr. Peter Paul von Bauer began investing in SCADTA in 1921 and soon came to manage the enterprise and promote it overseas. After months of preparations and at least one fatal accident, the company began scheduled service between Barranquilla and Girardot on September 19, 1921. Davies calls this probably the most significant date in Latin American civil aviation: the continent finally had a reliable airline.

By this time, SCADTA's fleet had grown to six F-13s. Although not subsidized like U.S. and European airlines, SCADTA was able to issue its own stamps at a premium and eventually operated its own post offices. Passengers also were carried, at the rate of about 250 pesos (US$250) each way (more for those weighing more than 65 kilograms). The journey took about eight hours, many times faster than the fortnight required by riverboats. Barranquilla-Girardot operated twice a week, with one flight a week extending up the Magdalena River to Neiva. Soon Cartagena and Santa Marta were added to the network.

Shortly after scheduled service began, SCADTA created a Sección Científica to handle aerial photography, made possible by cameras smuggled from Germany. One of this unit's first projects was to provide reconnaissance concerning a border dispute between Colombia and Venezuela near Cúcuta.

Von Bauer bought out one of the original partners in July 1922 and became a director, owning four-fifths of the shares. The company won its first airmail contract a couple of months after carrying Colombia President Pedro nel Ospina on a flight that September. The next May, SCADTA flew 3.5 million pesos from Medellín to the State Bank in Bogotá when there was a run on the bank. The year 1924 was especially unlucky, however: one crash killed six people, including chief pilot Hellmuth von Krohn and company President Don Ernesto Cortissoz, and another two planes were lost later.

Key Dates:

1919: SCADTA is formed with backing from German and Colombian businessmen.
1921: After years of preparations and survey flights, SCADTA starts scheduled operations.
1928: International service begins to Ecuador via the Servicio Bolivariano de Transportes Aéreos.
1930: Pan Am secretly acquires control of SCADTA.
1940: All German employees are fired and company is renamed Avianca.
1947: Avianca becomes the second South American airline to connect with the United States.
1950: Avianca's network reaches Europe.
1960: First jets are introduced on international routes.
1970: Brick red color scheme is adopted.
1986: Debts reach US$170 million.
1991: Colombian civil aviation market is liberalized as Avianca struggles to maintain its stature.
1996: Avianca enters a strategic alliance with American Airlines.
2000: Avianca invests US$12 million to upgrade services.

SCADTA bought a couple of twin-engined Dornier Wal flying boats in 1925 and began exploring opportunities for routes in the Caribbean. U.S. politicians blocked access to Miami or New York, however, ostensibly to prevent German interests from gaining a foothold in U.S. trade but also likely due to the fact that the United States had yet to field an international airline of its own. One of the planes was shipped back to Germany and the other crashed the next year. SCADTA then looked south to start its first international passenger and airmail service, to Guayaquil, Ecuador, beginning in June 1928. This was extended to Panama City and Cristóbal in April the next year, tripling the airline's route mileage. During this time, SCADTA began using the name Servicio Bolivariano de Transportes Aéreos in its marketing, referring to the great liberator of South America Simón Bolívar.

Pan Am Takes Control in 1930

The United States signed a bilateral air agreement, its first ever, with Colombia on February 23, 1929. PANAGRA, a partnership of Pan American Airways and the W.R. Grace shipping line, had started its own service from Miami to Panama City on February 3. Charles Lindbergh piloted the inaugural flight in a Sikorsky S-38 flying boat. PANAGRA had stronger finances, more influence, better equipment, and more publicity than SCADTA. Von Bauer signed a secret agreement with Pan Am president Juan Trippe in which SCADTA surrendered its international routes in exchange for an infusion of capital. Pan Am acquired 84.4 percent of the capital after a formal agreement was signed in February 1930 and SCADTA essentially became the Colombian part of the Pan Am network. Von Bauer resigned as president, and two U.S. citizens were added to the SCADTA board. In addition, new American- and British-made planes began appearing in SCADTA's diverse fleet.

At home, SCADTA benefited from the election of a new president of Colombia, Dr. Olaya Herrera, a supporter of von Bauer with progressive views regarding transportation. In January 1932, SCADTA began acting as the official airmail agency of the country, employing 300 letter carriers. The airline did its patriotic duty in return, supporting the Colombian military when Peru attempted to annex the Leticia Trapezium in 1932.

With Pan Am's backing, SCADTA expanded its domestic network in the early 1930s, connecting Medellín with the company's home base of Barranquilla, and with Colombia's other large city, Bogotá. Equipment limitations meant that none of these routes were nonstop, however. Unfortunately, accidents were endemic, including one in Medellín that killed 17 people. A network of grass field airports was developed to accommodate the faster and more powerful aircraft that were replacing SCADTA's floatplanes. The Boeing 247D displaced the Ford Tri-Motor as the flagship of the fleet.

SCADTA merged with the Servicio Aéreo Colombiano, a minor competitor, in 1940. Although von Bauer, alarmed at developments in Nazi Germany, had returned from retirement in Austria to lead the airline once again, the U.S. state department was pressuring Pan Am and the Colombian government to curb the German influence at the airline. On June 8, 1940 all 80 German employees were fired and the company was officially renamed Aerovías Nacionales de Colombia— AVIANCA—on June 14. Pan Am's shareholding was reduced to 64 percent from 80 percent, and the Colombian government held 15 percent.

Postwar Consolidation and Expansion

By the late 1940s, the fleet had been updated with Douglas DC-3s and most of the seaplane bases had been closed. Avianca resumed international services with a route to Ecuador launched on March 21, 1946. Service soon was added to the Panama Canal Zone and by the next year a new Douglas DC-4 was connecting Colombia nonstop with Miami. Avianca thus became only the second airline, after Aerovias Brasil, to connect with the U.S. mainland. The carrier remained part of the Pan Am system, however.

Avianca's network reached to New York in April 1949; Lisbon, Rome, and Paris were added the next year. By 1957, Avianca had leveraged its strategic location with a number of new routes to the north and south and had upgraded its international service with the Lockheed Super Constellation, its new flagship.

A number of independent operators had sprung up in Colombia to capitalize on the availability of war surplus aircraft. Most faltered within a few years; Avianca absorbed two of them, Sociedad Aérea de Tolima (SAETA) and Líneas Aéreas Nacionales, S.A. (LANSA), in the early 1950s. The LANSA merger in 1951 reduced Pan Am's shareholding to less than 40 percent. In 1963, Avianca bought the failed Sociedad Aeronáutica de Medellín, S.A. (SAM), founded by a retired U.S. Air Force captain, through its Aerotaxi subsidiary. Another generation of airlines started in the mid-1950s, including Lloyd Aéreo Colombiano (LAC), Taxi Aéreo de Santander

(TAXADER), Líneas Aéreas La Urraca, and Aerovías Condor de Colombia, Ltda (Aerocondor). Of these, Aerocondor proved the most effective competitor and mishap-laden Urraca survived until 1979. The Colombian Air Force also operated an air service to remote provinces known as the Servicio Aeronavegación a Territorios Nacionales (SATENA).

Avianca began flying to New York by jet in October 1960 via a leased Boeing 707. By 1962, it operated Boeing 720 jets on all its international routes. It began flying the three-engined Boeing 727 on domestic routes in January 1966. A couple of years later, Pan Am's shareholding was reduced to 25 percent; it fell to 11 percent by 1975 as Avianca regained its independence, as displayed in a bold brick red color scheme adopted in 1970.

International services were expanded in the 1970s and the airline began operating Boeing 747 jumbo jets in December 1976. Bogotá-Frankfurt became the most important route. A number of air taxi services and tiny airlines sprang up in the 1960s and 1970s, but Avianca remained the dominant carrier by far.

The Troubling 1980s

Avianca's influence waned in the 1980s, however. The company ran up debts reaching US$170 million in 1986, when its terms were renegotiated. As *Air Transport World* reported, Avianca's public image at home deteriorated as its on-time performance fell from 66 percent in 1986 to 32 percent in 1988. The carrier was tremendously overstaffed at 11,000 employees and suffered poor labor relations. SAM, which concentrated on tourist traffic to resorts, maintained a good reputation, unlike its sister airline.

To improve the bottom line, Avianca sold off its massive Boeing 747s and began ordering 767s in 1988 to renew its fleet. It also began to update its computer reservation system, contracting with IBM and acquiring Maxipars CRS from British Airways. The number of employees was reduced to 5,000 by 1990.

U.S. efforts against drug smuggling in the 1980s eventually prompted Avianca to retreat from the Colombia-U.S. cargo market. Penalties totaled US$14 million by 1988; 450 kilos of drugs had been found aboard the company's planes the previous year. Avianca subsequently invested a huge amount of resources in drug detection. Although it was privately owned, terrorists targeted the carrier after a government crackdown on drug dealers, downing a Boeing 727 in 1989.

Liberalized in 1991

Spurred by customer complaints, the Colombian government deregulated the country's civil aviation industry in 1991, opening the skies to 25 foreign airlines and a number of domestic start-ups. Local competitors Aces and Intercontinental hit Avianca hard. Aces even won the right to fly the Bogotá-Miami route, also eyed by United Airlines and Iberia. Mexicana, Alitalia, KLM, and British Airways also were flying to Bogotá by then. Avianca was again allowed to carry cargo to the United States aboard its Boeing 767s; however, it faced competition

from ARCA, Aerosucre, and Aces (Aerolineas Centrales de Colombia) and U.S.-based Challenge and Arrow Air on the freight side.

Alvaro Jamarillo Buitagro became CEO in December 1991. He sought to instill a "corporate mystique" centering on customer service. The company launched a major restructuring in 1994, taking aim at productivity problems and reducing management levels from 13 to five. Catering and ground handling were outsourced. Avianca gained management control over SAM and the helicopter service Helicol in 1994. Its major stockholder was Grupo Empresarial Bavaria, the massive Colombian conglomerate.

Revenues were COL 933 billion (US$470 million) in 1997. Avianca's market share, 61 percent at the beginning of the decade, had fallen to 41 percent. Company officials blamed much of the damage on the suddenness with which the markets were opened to competition and claimed the country's bilateral agreements did not value its own market adequately against those of other countries. Another source of irritation was a lack of administrative scrutiny regarding safety procedures among low-cost operators, as well as the country's grossly inadequate aviation infrastructure. The carrier also paid a price for Colombia's political instability.

According to *Flight International,* although traffic in the region was booming, there was need for consolidation for the airline sector to become profitable again, since capacity was growing even faster than demand. Avianca's latest president and CEO, Dr. Gustavo Alberto Lenis Steffens, compared the situation in South America with that of the United States and Europe at the beginning of deregulation. Several prominent carriers in neighboring states were either in bankruptcy (Viasa Venezuelan International Airlines, Ladeco Chilean Airlines) or had ceased operations (Ecuatoriana). Avianca looked for strategic alliances to ensure its share of traffic, but as of 1997 had a couple of code-share partners within Latin America, SAETA of Ecuador and the TACA group. The carrier had entered an alliance with American Airlines in December 1996.

Although Avianca maintained a relatively young fleet of 30 planes and continued to fly to Europe and North America, Lenis said the company had become conservative in its growth. Its SAM subsidiary had by then merged its operations with Avianca itself. Employment had been reduced to just 3,000.

Avianca and SAM launched a new marketing effort in November 1997. New concepts tried included a frequent flier program for children and a mobile check-in unit. The popular Night Express program kept the carrier's regional planes full on red-eye trips between major cities. Priced to compete with buses, the service connected with a unique niche of business travelers.

In spite of these refinements and rising international traffic, Avianca lost COL 124 billion in 1999. The company was investing US$12 million in 2000 to upgrade services. Avianca and SAM both were planning to renew their fleets in 2003, when leasing agreements expired.

Principal Competitors

Aces; AeroRepública; AMR Corporation; Continental Airlines, Inc.; Intercontinental de Aviación.

Further Reading

"Avianca se fortalece en el mercado Andino," *Portafolio,* April 4, 2000, p. 17.

Davies, R.E.G., *Airlines of Latin America,* Washington, D.C.: Smithsonian Institution, 1984.

Learmount, David, "Struggle for Success," *Flight International,* March 19, 1997, pp. 36–37.

Lima, Edvaldo Pereira, "Avianca: Adalante!," *Air Transport World,* June 1992, pp. 49–52.

——, "Reshaping Avianca," *Air Transport World,* May 1998, pp. 81–83.

—Frederick C. Ingram

Balfour Beatty

Balfour Beatty plc

Devonshire House
Mayfair Place
London W1X 5FH
United Kingdom
Telephone: (020) 7629-6622
Fax: (020) 7409-0070
Web site: http://www.balfourbeatty.com

Public Company
Incorporated: 1945 as British Insulated Callender's
    Cables Limited
Employees: 24,344
Sales: £2.9 billion (US$4.26 billion) (1999)
Stock Exchanges: London
Ticker Symbol: BBY
NAIC: 233310 Manufacturing and Industrial Building
    Construction; 233320 Commercial and Institutional
    Building Construction; 234110 Highway and Street
    Construction; 234930 Industrial Nonbuilding Structure
    Construction; 234990 All Other Heavy Construction;
    235310 Electrical Contractors; 334512 Automatic
    Environmental Control Manufacturing for Regulating
    Residential, Commercial, and Appliance Use; 488210
    Support Activities for Rail Transportation; 541330
    Engineering Services; 561210 Facilities Support
    Services

Balfour Beatty plc is a leading worldwide engineering, construction, and services company, with three main business segments: building, engineering, and rail. The building segment, which generates about 40 percent of overall revenues, is involved in the design, construction, equipping, maintenance, and management of buildings. The engineering segment, responsible for 39 percent of revenues, provides civil and other specialized engineering, design, and management services in such areas as hydroelectric dams, tunnels, roads and bridges, and overhead transmission lines and towers. The rail segment, generating 15 percent of revenues, specializes in the design, construction, equipping, maintenance, management, and overhauling of rail systems and equipment. The remaining revenues come from Balfour Beatty's promotion of and investment in privately funded infrastructure projects, such as roadways, hospitals, power stations, and educational facilities.

The history of Balfour Beatty is intertwined with that of BICC PLC. This firm was the outgrowth of the 1945 merger of Great Britain's two largest cable manufacturers, British Insulated Cables and Callender's Cable and Construction Company, to create British Insulated Callender's Cables Limited, which changed its name to BICC PLC in 1975. The two antecedents of BICC both traced their origins to the late 19th century and pioneered in the nascent electrical cable industry; in the early 20th century, Balfour Beatty & Company Limited was formed with initial interests in the design, construction, and operation of electric streetcars and railways, which were then just being developed in Britain. In 1969 BICC acquired Balfour Beatty, which operated as a subsidiary and eventually accounted for more than half of BICC's revenues and profits. In 1999 BICC reached a strategic decision to exit from its founding cable business. Following the company's divestment of its last cable activities in early 2000, it was effectively reduced to the operations of Balfour Beatty. BICC, therefore, changed its name to Balfour Beatty plc in May 2000.

The Predecessors of BICC

The predecessors of BICC were both outgrowths of the late 19th-century scramble to devise the safest and most economical means to distribute electricity across the length and breadth of the United Kingdom. In 1882, when the Edison Company demonstrated the feasibility of incandescent lighting by illuminating its London offices at Holborn Viaduct, William Ormiston Callender realized that he was in the wrong business. Callender and his five sons ran a profitable construction company, importing for the purpose of road surfacing large amounts of the petroleum compound bitumen. Spurred by the recent developments in electricity, William M. Callender, one of the sons, invented a process for insulating electric wire using vulcanized bitumen, a tarlike, elastic substance that could be used as a coating for copper wire that was flexible, strong, waterproof, and non-

Company Perspectives:

Our aim is to create shareholder value by providing value-added engineering, construction and service skills to customers for whom infrastructure quality, efficiency and reliability are critical.

conducting. First used in an installation at the Marquis of Salisbury's home, vulcanized bitumen-insulated wire proved to be excellent for the transmission of low voltage electricity and was soon adopted for a wide variety of such applications.

The Callender family built a plant in Kent, and Callender's Cable and Construction Co. Ltd. quickly became a leader in the rapidly proliferating electrical business. Among many other innovations, the Callenders devised a method of laying cable beneath city streets, running the lines through shallow iron troughs that were then filled with more bitumen. Callender's also began making a second type of low voltage cable using oil-filled jute as insulation, thus acquiring expertise in both of the methods favored for the distribution of low voltage electricity.

About the time that Callender realized the value of his bitumen supply, James B. Atherton heard a lecture in New York on the remarkable electrical properties of paper—specifically, that it was a poor conductor. Atherton was in the fur business, but he too was caught up in the excitement over electricity. Arming himself with the British rights to certain U.S. patents, he returned to London and founded the British Insulated Wire Company (BI) in 1890. Joining him on the board of directors was famed Italian inventor Sebastian de Ferranti, through whose influence the company was asked to manufacture new high-voltage cables for the main London generators at Deptford. Carrying 11,000 volts, the paper-insulated cables passed every test, proving the viability of paper insulation and giving BI a strong debut in the marketplace. The company refined its manufacturing techniques, eliminating production problems while bettering the flexibility and other properties of its insulation, and by 1903 had joined forces with the Telegraph Manufacturing Company of Helsby and Anchor Cable of Leigh. The new company was British Insulated and Helsby Cables Limited. It quickly became the leading supplier of high-voltage cable in the nation.

Both BI and Callender's were involved in virtually every important cable project in the United Kingdom after 1900, including telegraph, telephone, electrical, and petroleum networks operating below ground, in the air, and across the ocean. In 1904, for example, the two competed for and collaborated on the electrification of the London Underground, together laying about 250 miles of high-voltage wire. Along with a third company, W.T. Henley's Telegraph Works, BI and Callender's early established themselves as the dominant power cable manufacturers in the country, vying with one another for business in all sectors of the vast electrical industry. Though the companies tended originally to pursue opposite ends of the high-low-voltage spectrum, by World War II both of them were well equipped for any type of power-distribution assignment.

During the early part of the war, British shipping suffered severe losses caused by German magnetic mines hidden in the English Channel and ocean traffic lanes. P.V. Hunter of Callender's designed a magnetized cable strong enough to push through ocean swells yet light enough to float, and Callender's produced about 2,000 such "minesweeps," each one approximately 500 yards long and capable of detonating submerged mines at a safe distance from the sweeper ship. The entire cable industry subsequently worked on practical methods of degaussing, or demagnetizing, the British fleet, eventually manufacturing many thousands of miles of cable for installation in the hulls of seagoing vessels. The combination of sweeping and degaussing succeeded in substantially reducing the damage inflicted by magnetic mines. Later still, BI and Callender's contributed to the construction of a gasoline pipeline across the English Channel to supply the World War II D-Day forces with fuel.

Pre-Balfour Beatty BICC: 1945–69

By war's end the two companies, already the largest U.K. cable manufacturers, merged their forces to become British Insulated Callender's Cables Limited (BICC). The company's formidable assets and technical expertise provided sustained growth during the decades following. BICC's experience with cable installation led the company into the allied fields of civil engineering and large-scale construction work. BICC as a whole was active around the globe, establishing an especially strong Australian presence in both cables and construction and later expanding there into the retail electrical and electronics businesses. At home, the company dominated the U.K. cable market, making the most of its powerful position to win contracts on the nation's most important electrical and civil engineering projects.

BICC carved for itself a secure place in the heavy construction industry, but the company's profits failed to dazzle the stock market. By the 1960s the firm was generally recognized as a rather stolid blue chip: safe, slowly growing, and modestly profitable. Between 1966 and 1970, for example, sales increased from £300 to £400 million but profit remained around £20 million. Investors were sometimes made uneasy by BICC's heavy dependence on the price of copper, which it needed to make its power cables. Importing some 300,000 tons a year, the company's profitability was directly tied to the fluctuating copper market. In addition, BICC's product mix was not calculated to excite the interest of stock watchers. Contracts for the electrification of a London subway extension or the widening of highways do not provide the cachet of a so-called glamour stock. With or without the market's enthusiasm, BICC ended the 1960s with an important acquisition, the 1969 purchase of Balfour Beatty.

The Creation and Construction of Balfour Beatty: 1909–69

Balfour Beatty & Company Limited was founded in 1909 in London by George Balfour and Andrew Beatty, two former employees of the London branch of J.G. White & Company, a New York-based engineering concern. Balfour had an engineering background and had worked on the construction of a number of electric streetcar lines while working at J.G. White, while Beatty was a trained accountant. The new company soon had its first contract, for £141,450, which involved laying new track and cables and upgrading a power plant for a streetcar line in

Key Dates:

Late 19th century: Callender's Cable and Construction Co. Ltd. becomes a leader in electric wiring.

1890: British Insulated Wire Company is founded.

1903: British Insulated merges with Telegraph Manufacturing Company of Helsby and Anchor Cable of Leigh to form British Insulated and Helsby Cables Limited.

1909: Balfour Beatty & Company Limited is formed by George Balfour and Andrew Beatty.

1922: Power Securities Corporation Limited is founded and becomes the parent of Balfour Beatty.

1924: Balfour Beatty undertakes its first major overseas venture.

1945: British Insulated and Callender's Cable merge to form British Insulated Callender's Cables Limited (BICC).

1969: BICC acquires Balfour Beatty, which becomes a wholly owned subsidiary.

1975: British Insulated and Callender's Cables changes its name to BICC PLC.

1999: Company divests its optical and energy cable businesses.

2000: Company divests its data-communication and specialty cable unit, and is now focused solely on engineering, construction, and related services; BICC changes its name to Balfour Beatty plc.

Dumfermline, Scotland. Other contracts followed, but in the initial years Balfour Beatty mainly concerned itself with investing in and managing the finances of existing and new streetcar companies. During World War I, streetcar construction in Great Britain came to a halt. The war, however, provided an impetus for Balfour Beatty's expansion into civil engineering as the company took on commissioned construction work, such as a five-mile-long aqueduct in Scotland that was needed to supply water to an important aluminum manufacturing operation.

The war also made clear the need for a nationwide system of transmission lines, an electrical ''Grid'' that would be flexible yet economical. George Balfour, as a member of Parliament starting in 1918, played a key role in the passage of legislation in the 1920s that would eventually lead to the completion of the Grid by the early 1930s, with Balfour Beatty heavily involved in its construction. Balfour Beatty managed several expanding power companies in the 1920s, including the Scottish Power Company and Midland Counties Electric Supply Company. By the early 1930s, these firms were the two largest power companies in Great Britain in terms of area served. Meantime, in 1922 Balfour Beatty, and their colleagues established a new company called Power Securities Corporation Limited so that they could fund larger projects than they previously could, projects that would then be carried out by Balfour Beatty, which became wholly owned by the new corporation. Under this new arrangement, Balfour Beatty secured its first major construction contract in 1926, a £2.5 million hydroelectric power project in Scotland which was most noteworthy for involving a 15-mile-long tunnel.

The 1920s also saw Balfour Beatty venture overseas for the first time, mainly through the management—but not ownership—of power utilities in the British Commonwealth. The first major such venture came in 1924, when Balfour Beatty took over management of the East African Power & Lighting Company in Kenya. After constructing a power station on the Tana River near Fort Hall (later known as Murang'a), Balfour Beatty helped expand the power system throughout Kenya and into Tanganyika and Uganda as well. In 1926 Balfour Beatty took over a commission to supply electricity and water to the Palestine cities of Jerusalem and Bethlehem. Other early overseas ventures were undertaken in India, Italy, Bermuda, Argentina, Uruguay, Nigeria, and Malaya.

In the 1930s Balfour Beatty began taking on overseas projects outside the power industry. The largest of these was the four-year, £1.25 million construction of the Kut Barrage, a dam that was built across the Tigris River in Iraq to divert floodwaters via irrigation channels into vast areas of desert. Meanwhile, cofounder Beatty died in 1934.

During World War II, Balfour Beatty's overseas activities were largely curtailed. By the end of 1939 half of the company's staff were serving in the army while the other half began concentrating on construction activities that proved vital to the war effort. The largest project undertaken was a massive four-year project to close the channels around the Royal Navy's chief base, which was located at Scapa Flow in the Orkney Islands. The project had been ordered by Winston Churchill following the torpedoing and destruction of the battleship *Royal Oak* by a German U-boat in October 1939. It involved the construction of 9,150 feet of causeway, up to 70 feet deep, using half a million cubic yards of quarried rock and 300,000 tons of concrete blocks. Balfour Beatty undertook numerous other wartime projects, including the expansion of power stations, the repair of electrical installations and underground railway stations that had suffered bomb damage, and the building of underground bomb shelters. In January 1941 George Balfour was appointed to chair a committee charged with assessing the organization of cement production. Balfour died in September of that year, however. Succeeding Balfour as chairman of both Balfour Beatty and Power Securities Corporation was William Shearer, who had been with Balfour Beatty since its founding, first serving as secretary.

With the end of the war and the victory by the Labour Party in the general election of 1945 came the nationalization of the British electricity industry. A New British Electrical Authority took over the financing, operation, and management of all the power companies. Balfour Beatty and Power Securities were thus pushed into the decision to build up the construction side of their operations and to diversify into other areas of construction. An example of the latter was the 1949 acquisition by Power Securities of James Kilpatrick & Son, an electrical contracting firm. Balfour Beatty completed a number of major construction projects in the immediate postwar years, including: a second large irrigation project in Iraq that involved diverting floodwaters of the Euphrates River into Lake Habbaniyah, finished in 1948; the 160-foot-high Loch Sloy dam in Scotland, completed in 1950; and a third large flood control/irrigation project in Iraq, the Wadi Tharthar project, which was built to protect Baghdad from the floods of the River Tigris and was completed in 1956. In the 1960s Balfour Beatty took on an increasingly wider array of engineering and construction work both at home and overseas, including electric transmission lines, power stations (including nuclear power stations), dams and reservoirs, tunnels, railway stations, and roads. In 1969 British Insulated Callender's Cables acquired Power Securities, and with it Balfour Beatty, which became a subsidiary of BICC. The construction side of BICC was merged into Balfour Beatty, thus enlarging the company. Balfour Beatty also took over the electrical contracting activities of Power Securities, which were reorganized in 1973 as Balfour Kilpatrick.

The BICC/Balfour Beatty Era: 1970–2000

The newly enlarged British Insulated Callender's Cables, which changed its name to BICC PLC in 1975, enjoyed steady growth throughout the 1970s. Its Australian division became easily the largest of BICC's many overseas operations, while Balfour Beatty quickly became the company's most reliably profitable subsidiary. Balfour Beatty continued to diversify during the 1970s, taking on five major road construction projects in Scotland; expanding into the building of factories and commercial buildings, such as a £2 million shopping and office development in Kilmarnock, Scotland, and a £3 million terminal at an airport in Aberdeen; and participating in the North Sea oil boom through the construction of concrete offshore oil platforms. In the late 1970s, the company expanded further by delving into residential property development and construction. Overseas, Balfour Beatty took on a massive £16 million expansion of the Chambishi mine in Zambia. The firm then entered into a joint venture that in 1976 won a £350 million contract to build the Mina Jebel Ali port in Dubai, a four-year project that included not only the port but also a 300-house village complete with clubs, sports facilities, a power station, roads, and other services.

In 1979 BICC began diversifying into the rapidly growing electronics field, for a more balanced and, hopefully, recession-proof portfolio. The firm bought Vero, a U.K. manufacturer of printed circuit boards, and the U.S. companies Boschert and Sealectro, makers of switching equipment and high-frequency connectors, respectively. Chairman Sir Raymond Pennock predicted that by 1990 a quarter of BICC's revenue would be generated by electronics. Of equal interest was the 1981 agreement with Corning, the U.S. glass maker, to build a plant in Wales for the purpose of manufacturing fiber-optic cables. These hair-thin fibers of glass were capable of transmitting many more telephone and data messages than comparable copper wires and quickly became the new standard for long-distance trunk lines. The Corning-BICC plant was finished in 1983 at a cost of £17.5 million and was an immediate success.

In 1981 BICC sales hit £1.36 billion and its profits, £102 million, both healthy figures, and the company looked forward to the new decade with much confidence. The worldwide recession of the early 1980s soon took its toll, however, with profit levels slipping into a trough from which they did not fully emerge until 1987. Halfway through these doldrums, in 1984, the BICC board of directors named Sir William Barlow as its new chairman. Barlow, the former head of Britain's postal service, soon brought in Robin Biggam as president and CEO, and the two men designed a program of sharp labor cuts and further acquisitions to prod their sleepy giant. Upper-level management was also shaken up, the much-heralded electronics

division pared down to a handful of companies in fields directly allied to BICC's main interests, and the Australian division, Metal Manufacturers, restructured to provide greater control. Most significantly, BICC closed out the decade with several major purchases of foreign cable companies. Its acquisition of Cablec and BRIntec in the United States made BICC the leading high-power cable maker in North America, with combined sales of around US$750 million. For the first time, BICC expanded into continental Europe, with the purchase of Ceat Cavi Industrie, Italy's second largest cable concern, and of 20 percent of Grupo Español General Cable (GEGC), Spain's cable leader. The expansion onto the continent came in anticipation of the ending of European trade barriers in the early 1990s. BICC also acquired U.S.-based Andover Controls Corporation, a leading manufacturer of building automation systems, in 1989.

The combination of stringent staff reductions and international expansion showed excellent results. In 1987 profits finally passed the 1981 level, with the company recording earnings of £128 million on sales of £2.49 billion. The following year showed further gains, as did 1989 over 1988. Earnings in 1989 were £201 million on sales of £3.79 billion.

In the early 1990s Balfour Beatty felt the effects of the worldwide economic recession but not as deeply as other construction companies that were more heavily involved in residential development. BICC, meanwhile, continued to build its cable operations, increasing its stake in GEGC to 67 percent and taking over the U.K. cable maker Sterling Greengate, both in 1990; doubling its share of the U.S. cable market with the 1993 acquisition of the electrical division of Reynolds Metals Co.; and, also in 1993, purchasing KWO Kabel, the third largest cable maker in Germany and prior to German reunification the largest cable maker in East Germany.

A markedly rapid decline in BICC's fortunes began in the mid-1990s. The construction activities of Balfour Beatty were hurt first by a prolonged slump in the housing market, and then by sluggish demand for infrastructure projects at home and in Europe. New CEO Alan Jones, who joined the company in early 1995, took the immediate step of selling the housebuilding unit to Westbury plc. Balfour Beatty barely eked out a profit in 1996. BICC's cables business was at the same time hit hard by fierce price competition and high raw material prices, particularly of copper. Deregulation of the European utilities market also cut demand for cable as the utilities cut their spending. Jones determined that the company should concentrate on higher margin optical, data communication, and high-voltage cables. Several cable-making plants were closed in Europe and North America as part of a resultant restructuring of the cable operations. In 1997 BICC merged its troubled German cable business with those of NKF of the Netherlands to form a joint venture called Kaiser Kwo Kabel. In early 1998 the company announced that it would lay off 2,000 workers across Europe in its cable operations, and it also swapped its remaining low-voltage building wire operations to Delta for that firm's heavy power cable business. A further thinning of the company's portfolio came later in 1998 when BICC parted ways with its majority owned Australian subsidiary, Metal Manufacturers, retaining that company's cabling operations.

By late 1998 BICC seemed to be teetering on the brink. The company had seen its market value fall from £1.65 billion in

1993 to £165 million. It was becoming readily apparent that the company's cable business was simply unable to compete anymore with the giants of the industry—Alcatel, Siemens AG, and Pirelli S.p.A. By contrast, Balfour Beatty was showing the beginnings of a strong recovery, aided by tighter management control, large overseas contracts, and a growing rail unit which gained business from the 1996 privatization of British Rail. In 1998 Balfour Beatty made profits of £69 million compared to only £25 million from cables. Jones then took his most drastic action yet; in early 1999 he began the divestment of all of BICC's cable units in order to focus the company entirely on Balfour Beatty. In April 1999 BICC sold its optical cable unit to Corning, then one month later sold its energy cable business to General Cable Corporation. While making these deals, the company fended off takeover overtures from Wassall, a venture capital group. In March 2000 BICC sold its data-communication and specialty cable unit, Brand-Rex, to Caradon plc. Two months later, BICC fittingly changed its name to Balfour Beatty plc, embarking on a new era focused on engineering, construction, and related services.

Principal Subsidiaries

Andover Controls Corporation (U.S.A.); Balfour Beatty Capital Projects Ltd.; Balfour Beatty Construction Ltd.; Balfour Beatty Construction (Scotland) Ltd.; Balfour Beatty Inc. (U.S.A.); Balfour Beatty Construction Inc. (U.S.A.); Balfour Beatty Ltd.; Balfour Beatty Rail Ltd.; Balfour Beatty Rail Engineering Ltd.; Balfour Beatty Rail Maintenance Ltd.; Balfour Beatty Rail Projects Ltd.; Balfour Beatty Rail Renewals Ltd.; Balfour Beatty Refurbishment Ltd.; Balfour Kilpatrick Ltd.; Balfour Kilpatrick International Ltd.; Balvac Whitley Moran Ltd.; BICC Developments Ltd.; Cruickshanks Ltd.; Emform Ltd.; Haden Building Management Ltd.; Haden Building Services Ltd.; Haden Young Ltd.; Heery International Ltd.; Heery International Inc. (U.S.A.); Lounsdale Electric Ltd.; Painter Brothers Ltd.; Raynesway Construction Services Ltd.; Raynesway Construction Southern Ltd.; Stent Foundations Ltd.

Principal Operating Units

Building, Building Management and Services; Civil and Specialist Engineering and Services; Rail Engineering and Services; Investments and Developments.

Principal Competitors

ABB Ltd.; Acciona, S.A.; ACS, Actividades de Construccion y Servicios, S.A.; AMEC p.l.c.; Bechtel Group, Inc.; Bouygues S.A.; Grupo Dragados; Grupo Ferrovial, S.A.; Fomento de Construcciones y Contratas, S.A.; Fluor Corporation; Groupe GTM; Peter Kiewit Sons, Inc.; Serco Group plc; Skanska AB.

Further Reading

Balfour Beatty: Fifty Years, London: Balfour Beatty, 1959, 78 p.

Balfour Beatty, 1909–1984, London: Balfour Beatty, 1984, 83 p.

Barker, Thorold, ''BICC to Sell Cables Arm for £275m: Engineering Group to Focus on Construction,'' *Financial Times,* April 8, 1999, p. 29.

Barker, Thorold, and Charles Pretzlik, ''Industrial Logician Who Aims to Conjure Rabbit from Hat,'' *Financial Times,* April 10, 1999, p. 20.

Batchelor, Charles, ''An End of the Line but It's Not the End of the Road,'' *Financial Times,* May 10, 2000, p. 29.

Baxter, Andrew, ''Building from a Local Base: A Look at BICC's Strategy for Winning Work in Asia,'' *Financial Times,* October 7, 1994, p. 23.

''BICC Plugs into the 1990's,'' *Management Today,* February 1989.

Burt, Tim, ''Jones' Setting to Rights at BICC: The Cable Group's New Chief Is Keen on Change,'' *Financial Times,* September 20, 1996, p. 25.

——, ''Taking Up Slack from the Cable Business,'' *Financial Times,* November 16, 1995, p. 30.

Byatt, Ian C., *The British Electrical Industry, 1875–1914: The Economic Returns to a New Technology,* New York: Oxford University Press, 1979, 228 p.

Crisp, Jason, ''Tuning in to a Wire-less Future,'' *Financial Times,* April 22, 1981.

Edgecliffe-Johnson, Andrew, ''BICC Stumbles Off the Ropes into Another Left Hook,'' *Financial Times,* October 21, 1998, p. 26.

——, ''Can BICC Sink Any Further?,'' *Financial Times,* October 24, 1998, p. 4.

Garnett, Nick, ''Limbering up for the Acquisition Trail,'' *Financial Times,* May 11, 1987.

Hill, Roy, ''Cable Superpower,'' *International Management,* March 1993, pp. 46+.

Morgan, R.M., *Callender's, 1882–1945,* Prescot, Merseyside, England: BICC, 1982, 256 p.

Waller, David, ''Radical Changes in a Quiet Revolution,'' *Financial Times,* July 6, 1989.

—updated by David E. Salamie

Banco Santander Central Hispano S.A.

Plaza de Canalejas, 1
28014 Madrid
Spain
Telephone: (+34) 91 558-10-31
Fax: (+34) 91-552-66-70
Web site: http://www.bancosantander.com

Public Company
Incorporated: 1999
Employees: 106,000
Total Assets: EUR 330 billion (US$337 billion) (1999)
Stock Exchanges: Mercado Continuo New York
Ticker Symbol: STD (ADRs)
NAIC: 522110 Commercial Banking; 522120 Savings
    Institutions; 522293 International Trade Financing

Banco Santander Central Hispano S.A. (BSCH) was created from the merger of Spain's number one bank, Banco Santander, with its number three rival, Banco Central Hispanoamericano, in 1999. The new entity represents Europe's leading bank in terms of market capitalization, and one of the region's largest asset-holders, with more than EUR 330 billion. Apart from being the dominant banker in its native Spain, BSCH has also inherited extensive assets in the Latin American region, particularly in the boom states of Brazil, Chile, and Argentina, as well as in Mexico, where BSCH has acquired Grupo Financiero Serfin. The company is also active in Venezuela, Colombia, Paraguay, and Peru. BSCH has also formed partnership deals with France's Société Générale, Scotland's Royal Bank of Scotland, and Germany's Commerzbank. With more than 106,000 employees across more than 6,200 branches at the time of the merger, BSCH, under new management led by Angel Corcostegui, is expected to streamline its operations beginning in 2000, cutting payroll back as much as 30 percent.

Spanish Banking in the 20th Century

Banco Santander Central Hispano S.A. was the product of the merger of two of Spain's oldest and most powerful banking empires—Banco Central and Banco Santander. The Santander bank was formed in 1857, in Spain's Cantabria region, with a particular focus on financing trade between Spain and the Latin American countries. Santander's location was to prove fortuitous, as the Cantabria region grew to become one of Spain's most important financial centers. By World War I, Santander had already gained a position among Spain's leading banks. In the early 1920s, the Botin family first entered Santander's leadership; the Botins later took over majority control of Santander, building it into Spain's leading bank by the late 1990s.

Banco Central was founded in Madrid on December 6, 1919 by the Marquis of Aldama, the Count of Los Gaitanes, and Juan Nùnez Anchustegui. These businessmen realized that the economic growth of the post-World War I era would require financing—and could lead to profits. Banco Central quickly became a major actor in emerging industries, especially coal, iron and steel, shipping, and papermaking. In 1921, the bank made its first major acquisition, of Banco de Albacete, and by 1922, it had established 18 branches. Banco Central was on its way to meeting its goals of promoting industrial development and establishing a presence throughout the country.

Postwar economic nationalism led to similar expansion throughout the banking industry during the 1920s, but not all the expansion could be supported by Spain's underdeveloped industrial base. When the U.S. stock market crash in 1929 led to a worldwide depression, Spanish banks were hard hit. Banco Central's investments in heavy industry gave it a strong position, however, and it was able to continue its policy of growth through merger and acquisition by taking over some of its ailing peers.

Government measures passed in 1931 to meet the crisis in Spanish banking consolidated Banco Central's position. Under the new laws, the Bank of Spain was made responsible for centralized banking functions and would no longer serve the public. This opened a new share of the market for other banks, and Banco Central moved aggressively to fill it.

Following the Depression came a new crisis for Spain. The Spanish Civil War pitted Loyalists faithful to the liberal constitution of the republic (which had replaced the monarchy in

1931) against Nationalists, who stood for Spain's traditional identification as an autocratic Catholic country. The conflict devastated nascent industrial development and set back Spaniards' hopes for a better standard of living. When Francisco Franco came to power in 1939, he faced a neglected land that could no longer feed the people and severe shortages of raw materials, including fuel.

Banking Under Franco in the 1940s

Many of Banco Central's branches were located in the republican zone, subject to nationalist blockade. However, under the bank's new chairman of the board, Ignacio Villalonga, the bank consolidated its position to become one of the Big Five of Spanish banking after the war.

One reason for Banco Central's growth was that its policy of acquiring or merging with other banking institutions was compatible with the tight new regulations on banking that Franco instituted in an attempt to put Spain back on its feet. In May 1940, Franco passed restrictions preventing banks from entering new areas of business. The only way for banks to grow under these restrictions was to acquire the existing operations of other banks, and Banco Central's business investment gave it the ready money to do so.

The devastation left by the war presented the bank with many opportunities. Like other major Spanish banks, Banco Central created industries from the ground up, providing not only capital but also managerial expertise to run the new firms. The bank often gained seats on the boards of directors of the companies it financed. This close relationship between banks and industry led to a high rate of postwar industrialization, although Spain remained underdeveloped compared to the rest of Europe. It also solidified Banco Central's position in the business world.

In 1958 and 1959 the Franco government took steps to improve the country's depressed economic condition, joining the International Monetary Fund, the International Bank for Reconstruction and Development, and the Organization for European Economic Cooperation (OEEC). In 1959, with the help of these international organizations, the government set up a

financial stabilization plan. The plan's provisions included devaluing the peseta; limiting government spending; limiting both government and private credit, which had fueled inflation; improving tax collection; abolishing price controls; freezing wages; establishing higher bank rates; and encouraging foreign investment. In addition, the International Monetary Fund, the OEEC, the U.S. government, and a group of U.S. banks came up with $5.75 million in assistance.

In 1962 the reforms continued with the establishment of a new government department to plan and coordinate economic development, and laws reforming Spanish banking were passed in April and June that year. These laws nationalized and reorganized the Bank of Spain and gave all authority over currency and credit to the government. In effect, the reforms institutionalized the positions of the major Spanish banks.

In the new financial environment, Banco Central continued to concentrate on developing industries that could meet rising consumer expectations. During the 1960s, Banco Central created Saltos del Sil, a hydroelectric development in Galicia; Compania Espanola de Petroleos S.A., the first privately owned petroleum company in the country, and Dragados y Construcciones S.A., a leader in the construction industry. To comply with the new banking regulations, Banco Central also formed Banco de Fomento in 1963 to compete in the newly established industrial bank category.

By the end of the 1960s, analysts abroad referred to a Spanish "economic miracle." A rising standard of living and increased opportunities for middle-class business ventures led Banco Central to offer more consumer services, such as credit and checking accounts.

Even so, by the beginning of the 1970s, Spanish banks were known for their conservative approach to doing business, the legacy of Franco's restrictive measures. In comparison to other European banking systems, there were too many Spanish banks in proportion to the population. Spanish banks also had too many branches and their staffs were too large. Those weaknesses were demonstrated all too well when rising oil prices in the 1970s led to raging inflation and the collapse of many firms—along with the banks that had lent them money. To combat inflation, the government raised the bank rate to make it comparable to international rates, extended business access to credit, and eliminated legal restrictions between industrial and commercial banks.

Banco Central concentrated on "saving" other financial entities during this period by buying them up as they failed and making them part of the Banco Central chain. The bank doubled its number of operating offices between 1970 and 1975, bringing its total to over 1,000 offices. Banco Central also followed a strategy of financially supporting Spanish industrial capacity, which increased the bank's influence in industry.

By the 1980s, Banco Central was the largest Spanish bank, but it was not considered flexible enough to compete effectively in the liberalized and internationalized Spanish economy of the post-Franco era since its longtime chairman, Alfonso Escamez (known as "the dean of Spanish banking"), refused to reduce his operating costs to become more competitive.

Consolidation in the 1990s

If Escamez refused to modernize, the Spanish banking community was not immune to the forces of change. As the gentlemanly traditions of the financial world crumbled in the face of the new need to compete effectively, cousins Alberto Alcocer and Alberto Cortina (los Albertos to the popular press) put their business acumen to work to challenge Escamez. From their base as operators of their wives' construction company Construcciones y Contratas (Conycon) and executors of family money, the cousins began to buy Banco Central stock in 1988, eventually joining forces with the Kuwait Investment office (KIO) for about a 12 percent stake. The cousins then demanded a managerial role in the bank and received five of the 24 seats on the bank's board. They were determined to streamline operations and make it an international player. "We knew that the management of Banco Central was antiquated but we trusted our instincts, our people and management capabilities to improve it," Cortina told the *Financial Times.*

Escamez, however, was furious, and determined not to allow control to be wrested from him by young businessmen with foreign money. He offered to buy them out. Failing that, he turned to another tactic, merger with Banco Espanol de Credito (Banesto) and its friendly chairman, the young Mario Conde, to offset the influence of his challengers. The new unit was to be named Banco Espanol Central de Credito, and with consolidated assets of over Pta 7 trillion (about US$60 billion) it would have become one of the top 25 banks in Europe.

Forty-year-old Conde was new to his position (he became chairman in December 1987). *Newsweek* had described his appointment as "a changing of the guard . . . in Spain's financial community." But Banesto, Spain's second largest bank, still represented old-line financial conservatism and family-oriented elite control, just as Banco Central did. Conde had taken over from 78-year-old Pablo Granica, who had followed his father in controlling Banesto. Both banks were seen as cumbersome and old-fashioned, without the flexibility to compete effectively in the new market that EEC membership would mean. The planned merger also failed to stop the original impetus for it: the Albertos began to buy up Banesto stock so they would continue to have a voice in management of the new merged unit.

When the Albertos assured Conde that they would sell out of Banesto if the merger were called off, the nine-month-old plan came to an inglorious end. The Kuwait Investment office sold its Spanish banking interests (and then invested in other Spanish industries). Cortina resigned from his seat on the board of Conycon in the wake of a scandal about an extramarital affair and was replaced by his wife. Conde was left to bring Banesto back to financial viability on his own, and Escamez was left back in control at Banco Central, with no successor in sight.

Banco Central did not brood long over the loss of Banesto: in 1991, the company agreed to merge with Banco Hispano Americano (BHA). While BHA had long been a leading Spanish bank, founded in 1900, it had stumbled from a series of costly acquisitions during the 1980s that left its profit margins weakened just as Spain looked forward to entry into the European Market. In order to boost both banks' positions, BHA agreed to be merged into Banco Central, forming Banco Central Hispanoamericano (BCH). The merger took place just as Europe slipped into an extended recession. Struggling to merge the two banking entities, BCH called in Angel Corcostegui, then just 40 years old, to restructure its operations. Under Corcostegui, BCH underwent a streamlining, cutting back on some 10,000 jobs—at a time when Spain's unemployment rate had soared to 20 percent—and closing about one-fifth of its combined branches. The restructuring brought BCH back to healthy profits.

Meanwhile, Santander, which itself had attempted to buy up Banco Hispano Americano, began to acquire a position in Banesto, building up a controlling stake of 60 percent during the first half of the 1990s before taking full control in 1998. That year, however, proved disastrous for a bank with extensive Latin American holdings. As much of the South and Central American economies reeled from an economic crisis—with Brazil in particular hard-hit by the slump in the stock market—Santander saw its profits slip. Finally, Banco Santander, seeing its position further threatened by the coming transition to the Euro, looked to its smaller rival, Banco Central Hispanoamericano, to secure its future position.

The announcement of the merger agreement between Banco Santander and Banco Central Hispanoamericano at the beginning of 1999 caught the financial community by surprise. Yet the new bank, with more than US$330 billion in assets, was welcomed as one of Europe's most powerful. Leadership to the company was given to Angel Corcostegui—as Santander heir Ana Botin agreed to take a step back—in order to preserve the appearance of a merger, rather than takeover. Corcostegui's history in guiding the BCH merger gave industry analysts comfort, as the new entity, dubbed Banco Santander Central Hispano (BSCH), was deemed overly large—some analysts suggested that BSCH might cut away as much as one-third of its more than 106,000-strong workforce and over 6,200 branch offices. Since the merger, BSCH moved to step up its holdings, winning a bid to buy Mexico's Grupo Financiero Serfin, acquiring Champalimaud of Portugal (a move disputed by the Portuguese government), and buying up Patagon.com, in order to boost its online services offerings.

Principal Subsidiaries

Banco Santander de Negocios; Banco Santander-Portugal; Banesto; Banif; BCH Benelux; CC-Bank A.G.; Hispamer; Hispano Commerzbank Gibraltar; Open Bank; Santander Direkt Bank; Santander Investment; Banco de Rio de la Plata; Banco Noroeste, S.A.; Banco Santa Cruz; Banco Santander Brasil; Banco Santander de Venezuela; Banco Santander Internacional Miami; Banco Santander Mexicano; Banco Santander Miami; Banco Santander-Chile; Banco Santander-Colombia; Banco Santander-Peru; Banco Santander-Uruguay; Banco Santiago; Banco Tornquist; Grupo Financiero Bital; Santander BanCorp (Puerto Rico).

Principal Competitors

Banco Bilbao Vizcaya, S.A.; Banco Popular Espanol; Banco Comercial Portugues; BBV Banco BHIF; Banco de Galicia y

Buenos Aires; The Chase Manhattan Corporation; Banco de la Nacion Argentina; Deutsche Bank A.G.; Banco do Brasil S.A.; Espirito Santo; Banco Ganadero; Itausa.

Further Reading

"Banco Central History," Madrid: Banco Central S.A., 1988.
Kaihla, Paul, "Riding the Iberian Tiger," *Canadian Business*, October 29, 1999, p. 21.
Nash, Elizabeth, "Spanish Banks in £20bn Merger," *Independent*, January 16, 1999, p. 20.
Popper, Margaret, "Spanish Banks: First Mover," *Economist*, January 23, 1999.
——, "A Titan Looks Way Past the Pyrenees," *Business Week International*, February 1, 1999, p. 27.

—updated by M.L. Cohen

Banfi Products Corp.

1111 Cedar Swamp Road
Glen Head, New York 11545
U.S.A.
Telephone: (516) 626-9200
Toll Free: (800) 645-6511
Fax: (516) 626-9218
Web site: http://www.banfivintners.com

Private Company
Founded: 1919
Employees: 150
Sales: $251 million (1998)
NAIC: 31213 Wineries; 42282 Wine & Distilled
Alcoholic Beverage Wholesalers

Banfi Products Corp. is a family-owned and -operated firm whose Banfi Vintners division is the leading wine importer in the United States. Its top-selling brand—and the leading imported wine label in the nation—is Riunite, a fizzy, sweetish Italian wine which Banfi introduced in the 1970s and marketed by convincing Americans it was all right to ignore wine snobs and drink it on the rocks. Hard on Riunite's heels is Concha y Toro, a Chilean brand distributed by Banfi that ranks second among wine imports to the United States. Banfi is the exclusive importer of both labels.

In another class entirely are the products of the company's Italian vineyards and wineries, especially the fine wines produced at Castello Banfi, a Tuscan estate.

Banfi to 1980: Striking Gold on Italian Red

Giovanni (John) Mariani and a brother founded the House of Banfi in 1919 to import medicinal bitters and Italian food products, naming it for Teodolinda Banfi, an aunt who was head of the household staff of the Milanese archbishop who later became Pope Pius XI. Located in the Little Italy area of Manhattan just below Greenwich Village, the firm began importing classic Italian wines after the end of Prohibition. World War II interrupted this trade, and after the war the firm turned to Bordeaux wines from France. Mariani's sons made annual visits

to the vineyards and cellars of the Bordeaux region and also to other renowned wine-growing areas, such as France's Burgundy and Germany's Rhineland.

Over the objections of their father, John Mariani, Jr. and his brother Harry went to Italy in 1967 to search for a low-alcohol, semisweet wine that could be chilled. While in the Emilia Romagna region of north central Italy, they were introduced to a fruity, fizzy Lambrusco grown from the grapes of a growers' cooperative federation named Cantine Cooperative Riunite. Over the next year John Mariani spent much of his time speaking to the cooperative managers and oenologists about making changes for the U.S. market. "We tried several blends based on different proportions of the grapes they used, and experimented with ways to bring out the fruit and body," he later told Charles G. Bruck of *Fortune*. Mariani not only wanted Riunite Lambrusco to be sweeter, he wanted its natural effervescence to be reduced so that the wine would not be subject to a U.S. tax aimed at imported champagne. Riunite's technicians solved the problem by stopping fermentation early, keeping sugar content high, alcohol low, and bubbly carbon dioxide below the tax level.

Banfi, which moved from New York City to Long Island in 1970, began test marketing Riunite in New York, Los Angeles, Chicago, and Miami in 1968, sponsoring tastings for consumer groups and pressing distributors for orders. The initial consignment of 100 cases grew to 20,000 cases in 1969 and 50,000 in 1970. The drink—packaged with a twist-off top rather than corked—caught on with young people and showed great potential as an entry-level wine, but Banfi restricted it to the test areas until 1974. After going into nationwide distribution, Riunite reached second place among imported wine brands in 1975, with 1.2 million cases sold. The following year Banfi invested $4 million in promotion and advertising, and sales reached two million cases, putting Riunite into first place, displacing Portugal's Mateus.

During the 1970s Riunite rode the crest of a wave that saw table-wine imports grow by 500 percent in the United States and Lambrusco-type wines by an eye-popping 40-fold. "Somehow or other, in the 1970s, it became fashionable to drink wine," a Banfi executive explained to Warren Thayer for a 1984 *Marketing & Media Decisions* article. At the same time, he added, "wine became accessible to a broader group of people. The

65

wine business went from being a specialty business to one that is on the cusp of being a mass appeal business.''

Banfi's first advertisements were low-budget radio spots featuring Buffalo Bob Smith of the early TV show *Howdy Doody*, backed by a chorus, which included Harry Mariani, singing ''It's Ri-u-ni-te time!'' to the tune of the show's theme song. In 1974 the company switched its account to a firm that introduced award-winning television commercials typically suggesting a dose of Riunite to settle lovers' quarrels. Banfi switched to more upscale commercials in 1978, although still with a hint of romance. At the same time the Marianis were encouraging the public to quaff Riunite casually, with ads that matched the words ''nice'' and ''ice.'' By 1981 one ad showed a bottle of wine being tossed from hand to hand at a picnic, like a soft drink. In addition, like beer or soda, Riunite was as light on the pocketbook as on the palette, averaging just $3 a bottle.

Branching Out in the 1980s

By 1980 Banfi alone was importing more wine from Italy—some nine million cases a year—than France and Germany combined were exporting to the United States. Its Riunite imports now included a white (Bianco) and a rosé (Rosato) wine as well as Lambrusco red. The distributor, now known as Villa Banfi, moved its headquarters in 1983 from Farmingdale, Long Island, to an estate, complete with a 60-room mansion, in Old Brookville. Adjacent to the 52-acre grounds, Banfi purchased 75 acres of rolling farmland for eventual planting of grapevines. It also took a half-interest in Villa Armando, a California winery.

Beyond these acquisitions, John Mariani sought to bring to fruition a longstanding dream—to produce internationally acknowledged fine wines. Between 1978 and 1981 his company invested $40 million in Italian vineyards or acreage suitable for planting grapevines. By 1984—when company sales reached an estimated $225 million—Villa Banfi had not only purchased two wineries in the Piedmont region of northern Italy but 7,100 acres of prime wine-producing land just outside the medieval walled town of Montalcino, perched on a hilltop south of Siena. Here workers planted vines of cabernet sauvignon, chardonnay, pinot grigio, and brunello, the ancient grape of Tuscany, very similar to sangiovese. The company restored a 1,000-year-old fortress on the property (renamed Castello Banfi) and established one of the most technologically advanced wineries in western Europe, including computer-monitored pressing and temperature-control systems and vats made of stainless steel rather than concrete.

Aided by $17 million worth of advertising—90 percent on television—Villa Banfi sold about 11 million cases of Riunite in 1983, more than the next six imported brands combined. The following year the company topped even this total with 11.2 million cases, but the boom ended in 1985 when Banfi had to recall 1.4 million cases of Riunite after the federal government found trace amounts in samples of a chemical normally used in antifreeze. This debacle not only cost the company $34 million to recall and destroy the wine but left Riunite with a stigma that could not be erased, even though the Food and Drug Administration later acknowledged that the wine was safe to drink. Ironically, John Mariani had told Jeanne Toomey of *Advertising Age* four years earlier that, after traces of asbestos had been found in his father during a postmortem examination, ''I then became engrossed in the pure and natural aspect of our products . . . I . . . made every effort to see that there were no additives.'' In 1986, in addition, sales of all Italian wines were rocked by a scandal arising from the addition of toxic wood alcohol to cheap bulk wines.

Villa Banfi had already taken a step to broaden its line by introducing D'Oro, a product of its Strevi winery in Piedmont fermented from the same muscat grape from which sparkling Asti Spumante is produced. To compensate for the drop in sales of its standard Riunite table wines, the company, in 1986, introduced fruit-flavored Riunite Peach and Riunite Raspberry as competitors in the wine-cooler category, adding a third—Sunny Apple—soon after. D'Oro and the standard Riunite red, rosé, and white wines were positioned against popular California table wines, while the company's own fine wines began to appear in the United States at prices ranging from $5 to $28 a bottle.

The switch to fruit-flavored Riunite came just in time for Villa Banfi—now renamed Banfi Vintners—as sales of the company's standard table wines continued to drop in 1986 and 1987. Some 8.1 million cases of Riunite were sold in 1987, with the fruit-flavored brands accounting for more than 30 percent of sales. With wine-cooler sales stagnating the following year, however, Banfi introduced its fourth Riunite table wine, Blush Bianco. Also in 1988, the company purchased Excelsior, a small company that was importing Concha y Toro, the leading wine brand in Chile. To exploit foreign markets, Banfi had signed agreements with companies as large and diverse as Mitsubishi in Japan, Hiram Walker in Canada, and Allied Breweries in Great Britain to act as its agents.

Harvesting Its Own Wine in the 1990s

In 1991 the Excelsior operation became Excelsior Wines & Spirits, in order to emphasize that it was distributing a wide variety of alcoholic beverages other than the traditional Banfi products. Excelsior was carrying more than 100 wine lines in the New York metropolitan area and also had signed an agreement to distribute M.S. Walker's liquor brands. Excelsior, a subsidiary, grew in sales from $12 million in 1990 to $26 million in 1996 but sold its wholesale line the following year to Charmer Industries Inc., a larger wine and liquor wholesaler. Harry Mariani explained to Alan J. Wax of *Newsday* that it would have been ''economically difficult'' for Excelsior to compete with major national distributors.

By 1994 Banfi was producing a wide range of wines at its estate in Tuscany, where 2,700 of the 7,100 acres now had been given to plantings. Brunello di Montalcino was selling for $50

Key Dates:

1919: Company is founded to import Italian foods and medicinal bitters.
1969: Now a wine distributor, Banfi imports 20,000 cases of Riunite.
1975: Riunite becomes top U.S. wine import, with two million cases sold.
1978: Banfi begins buying Italian vineyards and wineries.
1984: Riunite's U.S. sales peak at 11.2 million cases.
1988: Banfi inherits distribution of the Chilean brand Concha y Toro.
1999: The Tuscan operation is voted Italy's best wine estate.

a bottle. Another Brunello, Poggio all'Oro, was named best of show that year in a competition of 741 wines from 16 countries. Besides Castello Banfi's Brunellos, the estate was producing blends of sangiovese, cabernet sauvignon, syrah, pinot grigio, and chardonnay, and the Strevi winery operation was continuing to produce a sparkling red wine named Barchetto d'Acqui.

The company also had planted chardonnay grapes on about 47 acres of its Old Brookville property but sold the grapes to other vintners instead of making its own wine. North Shore Old Wealth, a chardonnay made at Chateau Frank from these grapes, was selling for about $12 a bottle in 1998. Banfi also had owned, since the 1980s, Jumby Bay, a 312-acre resort and vacation-home community on a private island north of Antigua in the West Indies. In 1997 the company brought suit against developer Homer G. Williams after reportedly losing in excess of $20 million of its $50 million investment on a failed business venture there.

By 1999 Banfi Vintners had spent $200 million—none of it borrowed—on its Tuscan operation, which was producing 400,000 cases of wine per year, plus olive oil and balsamic vinegar. About one-tenth of the wine yield was Brunello di Montalcino, selling for between $25 and $250 a bottle. A British wine writer was quoted by Phyllis Berman of *Forbes* in these words, "The great wine estates of France have nothing to compare with it. In all of Europe, Castello Banfi is unique." The 16,000-member Association of Italian Sommeliers voted Castello Banfi Italy's "Best Wine Estate" in 1999, and in 2000 the VinItaly Wine Competition voted Castello Banfi "International Winery of the Year" for an unprecedented fourth time. Vini Banfi of Strevi was continuing to produce premium sparkling wines, and Principessa Gavia of Gavi, also in Piedmont, was producing Principessa Gavia from the Cortese di Gavi grape. On Long Island, Banfi continued to maintain the only commercial vineyard in Long Island's Nassau County and the closest one to New York City, growing grapes for about 2,000 gallons a year of Old Brookville Chardonnay.

Riunite continued to be the leading imported wine brand in the United States in 1998, with 2.1 million cases sold at $5 a bottle. Some 60 percent of this volume consisted of Lambrusco. In second place was Concha y Toro, with two million cases

sold, compared to only 90,000 in 1988, when Banfi purchased Excelsior. Created by Banfi, another Chilean brand, Walnut Crest, was in ninth place. In 1999 Banfi introduced to the United States BRL Hardy's Stonehaven brand, produced from a $13 million new winery on Australia's Limestone Coast. Other wines being carried by Banfi were those from the Borgogno, Cecchi, Florio, Placido, and Sartrori wineries of Italy and the TriVento label from Argentina's Vina Patagonia winery.

Banfi was still being run in 2000 by John Mariani, chairman and chief executive officer, and Harry Mariani, president and chief operating officer. Both of them had children actively involved in the business, with John's daughter, Cristina, and Harry's son, James, slated to lead the company into the next millennium. In addition to its other holdings, the company had a warehouse in Farmingdale, Long Island, and 22 undeveloped acres in Melville, Long Island.

Principal Divisions

Banfi Vintners.

Principal Competitors

Austin Nichols and Company Inc.; Peerless Importers Inc.; Southern Wine & Spirits Inc.; United Liquors Ltd.

Further Reading

Berman, Phyllis, "Up from Buffalo Bob," *Forbes,* April 19, 1999, pp. 120, 124.
Boyd, Gerald D., "Italy's Beloved Brunello," *San Francisco Chronicle,* July 22, 1998, Food section, p. 4.
Burck, Charles G., "The Toyota of the Wine Trade," *Fortune,* November 30, 1981, pp. 154–56, 160, 162, 166.
Durie, Elspeth, "Riunite Lambrusco: A Natural Sparkler Bubbling in Success," *Advertising Age,* September 26, 1977, p. 96.
Eskenazi, Gerald, "Investing in Success," *New York Times Magazine,* February 16, 1986, p. 66.
Khermouch, Gerry, "Banfi's Beer Guy Rethinks Riunite," *Brandweek,* July 5, 1999, p. 12.
Miller, Brian K., "Hoyt Street's Williams Sued Over Failed Venture," *Business Journal-Portland,* July 2, 1999, p. 5.
Thayer, Warren, "Riunite's Bubbly Rise to the Top of the Wine Market," *Marketing & Media Decisions,* Spring 1984, pp. 85–87.
Toomey, Jeanne, "A Citadel of Success," *Advertising Age,* July 27, 1981, pp. S42–S43.
"Villa Banfi: Aspiring to World-Class Wines," *Business Week,* October 15, 1984, pp. 93–95.
Wax, Alan J., "Banfi Vintners to Close Wholesale Operation," *Newsday,* January 21, 1997, p. A41.
——, "The House That Riunite Built," *Newsday,* June 27, 1994, pp. C1, C6–C7.
——, "Spirit-Filled Competition," *Newsday,* August 28, 1997, p. 47.
——, "Wine Importer Ends Suit," *Newsday,* June 23, 1998, p. A41.
Winters, Patricia, "Banfi Backs Chilean Wine," *Advertising Age,* July 24, 1989, p. 72.
——, "Banfi Casts Riunite as Award-Winner," *Advertising Age,* October 13, 1986, p. 36.
——, "Riunite Blushes," *Advertising Age,* February 15, 1988, p. 4.
——, "Riunite's New Twist," *Advertising Age,* August 3, 1987, p. 12.

—Robert Halasz

Bank One Corporation

1 Bank One Plaza
Chicago, Illinois 60670
U.S.A.
Telephone: (312) 732-4000
Fax: (312) 732-3366
Web site: http://www.bankone.com

Public Company
Incorporated: 1998
Employees: 91,310
Sales: $25.98 billion (1999)
Stock Exchanges: New York Chicago
Ticker Symbol: ONE
NAIC: 551111 Offices of Bank Holding Companies;
    52211 Commercial Banking (pt); 52221 Credit Card
    Issuing (pt); 52232 Financial Transactions Processing;
    52239 Other Activities Related to Credit
    Intermediation (pt)

Chicago-based Bank One Corporation formed in 1998 through the merger of Banc One Corporation, headquartered in Columbus, Ohio, and First Chicago NBD Corp. The fourth largest bank in the United States in the late 1990s, Bank One is also the number two issuer of credit cards. The company offers such services as commercial and corporate banking, loan and leasing, insurance, and investment and brokerage services. With branches primarily located in the Midwest and Southwest, Bank One has more than 1,800 branches spread across 14 states.

History of Banc One Corporation

While the corporation was created in 1968 as First Banc Group of Ohio, Inc., a holding company of The City National Bank & Trust Company of Columbus, the organization's origins may be traced to the Great Depression and the McCoy family. John H. McCoy began his career in banking when he left the eighth grade to work in a bank in Marietta, Ohio. By 1930, he was successful in the field and began serving on the Ohio state bank advisory board, soon thereafter becoming the

Ohio representative to President Herbert Hoover's Reconstruction Finance Corp. (RFC). In 1935, the RFC appointed McCoy president of Columbus' City National Bank & Trust (CNB).

CNB, formed from the consolidation of two small Columbus banks, had an infamous anniversary: October 29, 1929, Black Friday. The bank had struggled through the Depression, surviving only with the help of the RFC, and when John H. McCoy took control, the two banks were still operating semi-autonomously. During this time, two families dominated banking in the state capitol: the Huntingtons, with their namesake Huntington National Bank, and the Wolfes, who owned Ohio National Bank and several major media outlets. While the Huntingtons controlled the lucrative trust business, Ohio National, by far the biggest bank in town, had the majority of the commercial lending.

Moreover, during this time Ohio state regulations prohibited banks from expanding across county lines, limiting growth possibilities and creating interdependence among banks in most of Ohio's 88 predominantly rural counties. When large transactions were required, smaller banks established affiliations with bigger banks like Huntington National in Columbus or Fifth Third in Cincinnati, which in turn established ties to money center banks in New York or Chicago. These cooperative banking relationships in Ohio formed a "pyramid" in which small banks were, out of necessity, dependent on larger ones. As a result, there was little competition among local banks, and none at all among banks in different counties.

John H. McCoy made a fortuitous decision when he opted to focus CNB's operations on retail banking, a field virtually untapped by his primary Columbus competitors. John H. was an impressive figure and established an enduring corporate culture at CNB. He is said to have worked so hard that he fainted several times at CNB, and, despite enduring four heart attacks between 1943 and his death in 1958, the patriarch never quit the bank. He established strictures against drinking coffee in the office and alcohol at lunch, and he earned the nickname "five percent McCoy" due to his insistence on charging customers five percent interest on loans, when most bankers were charging much less. John H. maintained that the valuable added services CNB offered its customers were worth these higher rates. McCoy's progeny carried on that legacy: net interest margins still ranked among the highest in the business in 1992. Moreover, CNB's corporate culture came to reflect John H.'s often paradoxical principles: autonomy, control, individuality, and uniformity; over the years, CNB entered many new ventures, as long as the stakes were low and the potential fallout from failure was limited.

In 1937, John G. McCoy finished his studies at Stanford and joined his father at the bank. One of the keys to CNB's local success during this time was its transformation of branch banks from smaller replicas of cold, imposing bank buildings to friendlier neighborhood centers. During World War II, John G. served in the Navy and a younger McCoy, Chuck, ran the bank when a heart attack briefly put John H. out of commission. John G. returned to find that Columbus in general, and his father's bank, in particular, were enjoying a boom in retail. Moreover, Chuck had introduced several innovations at the branches, including carpeting, modern lighting, community rooms with kitchens for local meetings, and continuous counters to replace the traditional teller cages. In the postwar period, CNB built the first drive-in branch bank; a few other banks were providing window service, but CNB built a specially designed, freestanding, drive-in bank.

When John H. McCoy suffered a fifth heart attack and died in November 1958, CNB was still ranked third among the banks in Columbus. John G., an operations specialist, was quickly named president, and one year later he was asked to take over as chairperson. The 46-year-old countered the board's offer with demands of his own, including the creation of a research fund consisting of three percent of the bank's profits. The board agreed, and John G. went to work. The research fund provided financial support for the technological innovations CNB would pioneer in the years to come, including a computer center for check-reading and other data processing functions.

By the late 1950s, the increasingly profitable CNB was gaining on local competitors Huntington and Ohio National, and John G. brought on an innovative advertiser, John Fisher, to promote new retail products like checking accounts. Over the course of his 30-year career at CNB, John Fisher combined marketing and computing intuition to revolutionize CNB and the banking industry as a whole. Moreover, Fisher, a former disc jockey, cultivated a unique image for the bank when he hired comedienne Phyllis Diller as CNB's spokesperson in 1962. Board members worried that Diller would not convey the dignified image typically cultivated by banking institutions, and they voiced their concerns to John G. at subsequent board meetings. As Fisher told *Institutional Investor* in 1991, the CEO defended his visionary marketing director to the board by saying, "Gentlemen, it's very simple: You can have either dignity or dividends. I vote for dividends."

While Fisher's outlandish campaign gave CNB a higher profile among competitors as well as customers, his unconventional ideas were not limited to advertising. At his and McCoy's instigation, CNB became the first bank outside of California to market Bankamericard (which later became Visa) in 1966, beginning a very profitable credit card processing sideline. Handling all the data processing duties associated with the credit card, CNB helped to make Bankamericard the first nationally accepted credit card. This innovation not only poured revenue and credibility into CNB but helped transform Americans' buying and spending habits, ushering in the "age of plastic." In 1968, CNB helped issue more than one million credit cards through 50 banks. Two years later, on Columbus Day, Fisher activated the country's first automated teller machine (ATM). Fisher also led unprecedented, and ultimately failed, efforts into videotex-based home banking, with which customers could view their accounts and pay their bills using their television screens.

During this time, John G. devised a plan to sidestep state banking regulations prohibiting interstate mergers and acquire other Ohio banks in the process. He decided to develop a holding company—a corporate body that, technically, was not a bank and thus could lawfully expand across county and state lines. The holding company, formed in October 1967, was called First Banc; its unusual spelling was the result of Ohio laws forbidding holding companies from calling themselves "banks." John G. first approached the directors of Farmers Savings & Trust, a county-seat bank in Mansfield, Ohio. The directors of Farmers Savings, nearing retirement and looking to sell the company, agreed to the merger proposition, becoming CNB's first acquisition through a stock swap.

Strict guidelines for acquisition soon developed. Proposed acquisitions were required to have assets amounting to no more than one-third of those of the buyer, a policy that ensured manageable deals and allowed the buyer to survive a bad acquisition. In addition, acquisitions were forbidden from diluting earnings, even during the first year of the merger. First Banc usually avoided such turnaround situations by focusing on acquiring banks that were strongest in its own retail and small business markets, which would generate economies of scale in areas such as processing. Under First Banc's merger policy, salaries, hiring and firing, staff allocation, and even the pricing of products and services remained the responsibility of the affiliate bank, which maintained its own president, board of directors, and business plan.

First Banc soon proved especially proficient at consolidating management information systems. Each new affiliate was required to submit detailed monthly reports, which were then compiled on First Banc's powerful computer system for comparative purposes. The surveys induced competition among the branches and provided an incentive to match the best. Virtually all new affiliates met the challenge and improved their return on assets and profitability after merging with First Banc.

From 1968 to 1978, First Banc acquired at least 15 Ohio banks, raising its profits to over $25 million annually, and formed First Banc Group Financial Services Corporation to offer personal property leasing and mortgage servicing. The company's growth was also fueled by the liberalization of Ohio banking laws during this time, which were amended to allow statewide branching and

Key Dates:

1863: First Chicago (the First) opens for business.
1903: The First opens the First Trust and Savings Bank to serve non-commercial customers.
1928: First Trust merges with Union Trust Company to form the First Union Trust and Savings Bank.
1935: John H. McCoy becomes president of City National Bank & Trust (CNB) of Columbus, Ohio.
1966: CNB becomes the first bank outside of California to market Bankamericard (later Visa).
1967: First Banc Group of Ohio, Inc., a holding company of CNB, is formed.
1969: First Chicago Corporation is established.
1979: First Banc Group is renamed Banc One, and its affiliated banks adopt the name Bank One.
1985: Banc One expands beyond state boundaries through an agreement with Purdue National Corporation in Indiana.
1989: Banc One enters Texas through the acquisition of MCorp and its family of failed banks.
1995: First Chicago and NBD Bancorp, Inc. merge to form First Chicago NBD Corp.
1997: Banc One acquires First USA Inc., a fast-growing credit card company.
1998: Bank One Corporation is formed through the merger of Banc One and First Chicago NBD.
1999: Bank One launches an Internet-only bank called WingspanBank.com.

mergers between banks located in any county. The holding company's name was changed to Banc One in 1979, and by 1980 the corporation was one of only seven banking organizations among the 100 largest in the United States to have recorded ten consecutive years of increases in both earnings and dividends. In 1981, *Time* magazine called Banc One "perhaps the most advanced financial institution in the United States."

The corporation's assets passed the $5 billion mark in 1982, as barriers to interstate branching continued to deteriorate. Federal and state banking regulations changed dramatically in September 1985, enabling Banc One to enter its first agreement with a banking organization outside of Ohio. Purdue National Corporation in Lafayette, Indiana, became the first out-of-state bank to affiliate itself with Banc One. After a relative lull in acquisitions from 1983 to 1986, Banc One's merger activity picked up. In 1987, for example, the company purchased the $4.4 billion American Fletcher of Indianapolis, and the next year it acquired $4.3 billion Marine Corp. of Milwaukee. Banc One took advantage of nationwide reciprocal banking soon after it was legitimized in Ohio in 1988. By the end of the following year, the corporation had added affiliates in Kentucky, Michigan, and Wisconsin. Nevertheless, the corporation focused on regional operations until the early 1990s, when it began to extend its presence west and south as virtually every barrier to interstate banking was removed.

John B. McCoy, son of John G., also entered the banking business. Like his father, John B. graduated from Stanford.

After three years in the U.S. Air Force, he took a position at Citicorp in New York, where he stayed for less than a year before returning home to Columbus in 1970. The younger McCoy worked his way through six different sections of the bank—including the credit card division, which he built into one of the nation's largest—and, in 1984, he was named CEO of the corporation. John B.'s efforts to keep Banc One focused on consumer banking allowed the corporation to avoid the real estate loans, Third World debt, and leveraged buyout problems that troubled many banks during the 1980s. The bank lent more to consumers than to businesses and rarely offered loans at all to large companies. From 1984 to 1990, John B. engineered 54 acquisitions, thereby tripling Banc One's assets to $27 billion. These acquisitions helped Banc One to thrive during an early 1990s recession.

Banc One continued to refine the branch banking experience in the 1980s by decreasing its number of tellers, adding new drive-in lanes and ATMs, giving the platform officers separate offices, adding travel agencies and a discount securities broker, and leasing space to insurance agents and real estate brokers. The corporation also introduced such innovative concepts as Sunday hours in Ohio, "weekly specials," and credit card tie-ins with groups such as the American Association of Retired Persons and airline frequent flyer programs.

However, by the beginning of the 1990s, Banc One's five-state Midwestern market, in which the population had remained stagnant for years, was becoming saturated. In order to maintain the corporation's customary 15 percent annual profit growth, John B. decided on a course of expansion. Focusing on Texas, the nation's third largest bank state with $175 billion in deposits in 1990, McCoy found a retail void in the banking market that could be filled by his bank's successful formula. First, he agreed to the government-assisted purchase of 20 failed Texas banks, known as MCorp, for $500 million, which brought Banc One's assets to approximately $36 billion. Just two days after taking control of those former MCorp banks, he bought Dallas-based Bright Banc Savings Association and its 48 branches for $45 million from the Resolution Trust Corporation, making Banc One the country's 16th largest bank, with $37 billion in assets. MCorp was Banc One's first turnaround situation, and observers wondered whether the corporation was up to the challenge, especially given the competitive banking environment in Texas. Led by John B., the corporation achieved that and more, acquiring banks in Colorado, Arizona, California, Utah, West Virginia, Kentucky, and Oklahoma in 1992 and 1993.

For fiscal 1993, Banc One earned a return on assets of 1.53 percent, marking the first time in history that an American banking institution with over $50 billion in assets crossed the 1.5 percent mark. The company sustained its annual earnings per share increase, becoming one of only 14 nationally traded U.S. companies to do so in 25 years. *American Banker* named John B. McCoy "Banker of the Year" for 1993.

In the mid-1990s, the inadequacy and inefficiency of Banc One's decentralized management strategy rose to the surface, and the company reorganized operations, which by 1994 included a network of 57 banks, along five core business lines: commercial banking, retail banking, specialty finance, investments, and credit cards. Banc One also sought to streamline operations and cut costs, and thus the company eliminated about 4,300 jobs and sold or closed about 100 bank branches. The bank planned to devote time and energy to restructuring and strengthening the company. Plans to develop national, profitable businesses and to enhance marketing efforts were put in place.

By 1997 Banc One was the tenth largest bank in the nation, with more than $90 billion in assets and more than 1,500 offices spread across 13 states, mostly in the Midwest and Southwest. The bank's focus on strengthening operations culminated in its largest acquisition to date when the company bought First USA Inc., one of the fastest-growing credit card businesses in the nation, for an estimated $6.75 billion. The acquisition effectively created the third largest U.S. credit card company, with about 32 million cardholders, and boosted Banc One's presence in the rapidly growing credit card industry. The company indicated interest in further growth through acquisitions and in working toward the building of a national presence.

History of First Chicago Corporation

In the summer of 1863, Edmund Aiken headed a group of ten investors who wanted to take advantage of the National Banking Act that President Abraham Lincoln had signed into law earlier that year. This act allowed national banks for the first time to exist along with state-chartered institutions. Aiken, a 51-year-old private banker, realized that the demands of financing war-related businesses, together with the industrial and commercial growth of Chicago and the development of Illinois, created a need for a national bank in the Midwest. Aiken's group invested $100,000 to start First Chicago (the First). The bank opened its doors for business on July 1, 1863, the day the Battle of Gettysburg began.

The First was an immediate success. After only 18 months, the board of directors voted to increase its capital stock to $1 million, which was the limit in the bank's Articles of Association. The First moved twice during its first five years, as increasing business forced it into larger quarters. Although the First was housed in a fireproof structure when the Chicago Fire struck in 1871, its building was seriously damaged. Fortunately, the bank's safes and vaults withstood the flames and nothing of importance was lost. The job of collecting records and monies buried in the ashes fell to Lyman Gage, a young cashier who eventually became president of the bank and then secretary of the treasury in President William McKinley's cabinet. Gage was one of a long line of employees who used his training and experience at the First to serve the federal government. Three months after the Great Fire, the First reoccupied its charred quarters and began helping Chicagoans rebuild their city. Out of the ruins, the First emerged as one of the most prominent and respected business leaders in the community.

As Chicago prospered, the First expanded and changed with its growing customer base. To motivate employees the First began awarding bonuses for "able and meritorious" effort; in 1881 the bank distributed $20,000 as incentives to employees. The bank began declaring quarterly dividends to customers at mid-year in 1882. That same year, it became the first bank to open a women's banking department, to make ladies more comfortable when conducting business in the male-dominated bank. During the Panic of 1893, the First found an original solution for the currency shortage: it imported gold from its London correspondent bank, a practice that quickly spread to other banks. In 1899 the bank was the first American bank to establish a formal pension plan, a clear indication of its employee-oriented management style.

At the turn of the century, the industrial revolution created an unprecedented demand for credit. The First met this need through mergers. When it joined with the Union National Bank in 1900, the First's assets climbed from $56 million to $76 million. It combined with the Metropolitan National Bank in 1902 and raised its assets to $100 million. In this way the First acquired the resources to serve both the needs of its regular customers, whose businesses were flourishing, and the needs of new customers, who were trying to capitalize on the opportunities of the era.

In 1903 the First opened the First Trust and Savings Bank, a separate corporation to serve the non-commercial members of the community. During its first seven days of operation this bank tallied more than 1,000 savings accounts totaling in excess of $3 million. In two years the First Trust and Savings Bank had more than 10,000 depositors whose balances totaled nearly $18 million.

The First celebrated its 50th anniversary in 1913 by becoming a charter member of the Federal Reserve system. By 1915 the bank was one of the three most active banks in foreign exchange in the country.

During World War I, the First played a major role in helping the country finance the war effort. When local support for Liberty Bonds and government securities weakened, the First and the First Trust and Savings Bank purchased $10 million for their own accounts. This patriotic act, coupled with the First's President James B. Forgan's active promotion, helped inspire Americans to purchase another $12 million worth of government bonds and securities.

During the 1920s the bank grew steadily. A new addition to its headquarters, designed by Daniel Burnham, was completed in 1928 just as the number of depositors reached 20,000. When the Union Trust Company merged with the First Trust and Savings Bank in 1928 to become the First Union Trust and Savings Bank, the First looked optimistically toward the future. But as 1929 passed, this optimism turned into a painful pessimism. As the great crash neared, the First witnessed a stream of large customer withdrawals to cover speculative securities purchases.

During the Depression that followed the 1929 stock market crash, the First's sound financial base kept it from failing as 11,000 weaker banks did. Even in the depths of the Depression, the First never skipped an interest payment on savings deposits. Its strength allowed the First to merge with the Foreman State Banks in early 1931 and accept all of their deposit liabilities. Moreover, during a frenzy to acquire liquidity in early 1933, depositors were able to withdraw $50 million in just three days from the First without severely hampering the bank's operations.

When President Franklin Roosevelt proclaimed a national bank holiday in 1933 to give banks a chance to stabilize, the First was one of the few banks able to open its doors without regulatory delays. Part of the reason for the First's quick reopening was its status as a Federal Reserve member bank, which meant that it accrued advantages that non-member banks did not. Because the First Union Trust and Savings Bank was not a member, the First decided to absorb all of the savings bank's business in order to retain its customers' loyalty.

The establishment of the National Recovery Administration by Congress and the passage of the Banking Act of 1933 (better known as the Glass-Steagall Act), which created the Federal Deposit Insurance Corporation and separated commercial banking from investment banking, strengthened confidence in the First. When the Securities and Exchange Commission was established in 1934, fears of a second crash dissipated.

The First weathered the Depression and continued to grow as Roosevelt's recovery policies took hold. In 1938, on its 75th birthday, the First's assets reached the $1 billion mark, just as the American economy began to accelerate in anticipation of war. Remembering that capital costs skyrocketed during World War I, the First advised businessmen to avoid high prices by borrowing money for investment before any outbreak of fighting.

During World War II a quarter of the First's staff served on active duty. Women were hired to fill wartime vacancies and to staff new positions as business increased rapidly. In the six years after the start of World War II, women helped the First double the value of its assets to $2 billion.

In 1944 President Roosevelt chose the First's president, Edward Eagle Brown, to be the only American banker to serve at the United Nations Monetary and Finance Conference that met at Bretton Woods, New Hampshire, to sketch plans for the World Bank and the International Monetary Fund. Brown pioneered the development of highly specialized lending divisions to respond quickly and innovatively to corporate customers' financial needs.

During the 1950s and 1960s the First enjoyed a period of sustained growth as it continued to build on its reputation as both a specialist and an innovator in business loans. As a result, the First's assets more than doubled and the number of its loans quadrupled during this period. In 1959 the First opened a London office to improve its service to foreign correspondent banks and customers engaged in international trade. Three years later, the First started a Far East office in Tokyo. In 1980 the bank opened a representative office in Beijing, the first American bank to open such an office in China.

As the First approached the end of the 1960s, the bank prepared to expand, as fast as it could, throughout the Midwest and the world. When Homer Livingston passed leadership of the bank to Gaylord Freeman in 1969, an attitude of unrestrained optimism pervaded at the First.

That year the bank was reorganized as the major subsidiary of the new First Chicago Corporation to allow it to broaden the scope of its activities worldwide. This reorganization gave the First a way around restrictive banking laws. From the beginning of his tenure, Freeman followed an aggressive program to increase its assets through the acquisition of more loans. Freeman doubled First Chicago's size in just five years. He accomplished this by recruiting top business-school graduates and quickly promoting them to positions of considerable lending

authority. Unfortunately, this program produced one of the worst loan portfolios in the industry: in 1976 the bank's percentage of non-performing loans reached a high of 11 percent—twice the national average.

A. Robert Abboud replaced Freeman in 1975 and immediately began dealing with First Chicago's bad loans. Unlike Freeman, who was warm and supportive, Abboud's methods were described as tyrannical and intimidating. Where Freeman favored a decentralized managerial style that bestowed maximum freedom on loan officers to make decisions, Abboud favored a centralized style to check and double-check every loan. In one 18-month period 118 officers left, reducing the bank's executive ranks by 12 percent. Even after promoting 84 employees from within, Abboud was still 149 officers short of his budget, but he refused to hire recent business school graduates because he feared their lack of experience.

Abboud also drove away established clients with his highly conservative loan policy. His new controls doubled the time it took to approve loans and also left old customers uncertain as to whether their loans would be approved. Abboud raised interest rates on loans and required corporate customers to maintain compensating balances of 15 percent on an unexercised credit line when his competition required ten percent. Abboud justified his actions by pointing proudly to First Chicago's balance sheet, which showed a 22-to-1 ratio of assets to equity; only one other bank in the country had a better ratio. By 1980 Abboud had brought non-performing loans down six percent. First Chicago's five percent rate was still double the national average, however.

After three years, Abboud realized that First Chicago was not prospering. Clients were not returning and new customers were repelled by First Chicago's reputation for insensitivity to its customers' needs. In 1975 Continental Illinois, First Chicago's chief rival, was strikingly similar to First Chicago in size and makeup; they both depended heavily on commercial loans for volume and on money markets for funding. Five years later, Continental's loan volume had grown to $23 billion, 50 percent larger than First Chicago's, and its earnings grew 73 percent while First Chicago's grew four percent. Abboud decided that First Chicago had to become a risk-taker to catch up.

Abboud chose to gamble in two speculative areas: fixed-rate loans and arbitrage in the Eurodollar market. By mid-1979, with interest rates on the verge of a historic climb, First Chicago found itself with $1 billion in fixed-rate loans that were being funded by short-term money whose cost was quickly rising above the yields of the loans. In 1978 Abboud more than doubled the bank's Eurodollar commitment, to $6.7 billion, from $3.1 billion the year before. He was hoping for interest rates to fall, but, following the bank's own forecast, they rose in late 1979 and early 1980. The Federal Reserve made the bank's Eurodollar situation worse by tightening up regulations. Thus, First Chicago found itself funding its Eurodollar placements with higher-cost deposits. Although consumer banking doubled in five years under Abboud, his speculative decisions cost the bank dearly.

Barry F. Sullivan, an executive vice-president of Chase Manhattan Corporation, succeeded Abboud as chairman and chief executive of First Chicago in July 1980. He had the "people skills" the autocratic Abboud lacked, as well as the experience of putting a floundering bank back on its feet. Once in office, Sullivan zeroed in on building a new management team. He recruited 300 officers for product development and corporate accounts, expanded the corporate-planning staff from three to 44, and reshuffled the talent he already had.

At the same time, Sullivan created a new organizational structure for First Chicago based on strategic business units (SBUs). Sullivan partitioned operations into 145 SBUs in an attempt to decentralize and place responsibility for strategic planning and marketing on middle management. Sullivan's philosophy and efforts got results: in the first nine months of 1983, earnings jumped 43 percent and return on assets, which were 0.23 percent in 1980, reached 0.53 percent, close to the 0.57 percent average return on assets at the ten largest money-center banks in the country. First Chicago caught the attention of Wall Street; at the end of 1983, three and a half years after Sullivan became chairman, First Chicago's stock reached $24 a share, double its price when Sullivan took over.

Sullivan's success can be attributed to more than just his managerial style. He instituted a more competitive pricing schedule for corporate loans and marketed it, and the bank's new organization, aggressively. He eliminated a costly mismatch of maturities and rates in funding the bank's loan portfolio. He abandoned the bank's Brussels office and a Visa traveler's check operation because of poor performance. He developed the industrial specializations that First Chicago had once been known for but that had been neglected by Abboud: energy and commercial real estate. Finally, he drew small- and medium-sized companies to First Chicago, a feat he accomplished by purchasing American National Bank and Trust Company, Chicago's fifth largest bank and an expert in dealing with mid-size and smaller companies.

In October 1984, the comptroller of the currency examined First Chicago's loan portfolio. Surprisingly, the comptroller judged that First Chicago had failed to acknowledge some bad loans. As a result, First Chicago was pressured to write off $279 million in its third quarter, six times the amount taken in the second quarter. In addition, the comptroller forced Sullivan to recategorize as nonperforming another $125 million in loans, bringing the total of nonperforming assets for the third quarter to $840 million.

First Chicago had to report a $71.8 million loss for the third quarter. Outsiders expected that these bad loans came from the bank's foreign-debt portfolio, but most came from First Chicago's domestic-lending group of energy and agriculture businesses. The oil glut had depressed energy prices far below the break-even point for local drillers, and the strong U.S. dollar had cut American farm exports. A few months later, First Chicago had to establish a $115 million reserve fund to cover losses stemming from a recent investment in a Brazilian bank. By the end of 1985, First Chicago had written off $131.1 million on its Brazilian fiasco.

Nonetheless, earnings increased in 1985 because Sullivan had made some astute decisions. His purchase of American National Corporation added record profits of $42 million to First Chicago's bottom line. The promotion of First Chicago's credit cards produced consumer loan profits that totaled $65 million. A third decision that paid off was First Chicago's venture-capital stock portfolio, which added $121 million in pretax profits in 1985.

The bank's net income in 1986 climbed to $276 million, which represented the strongest financial results in First Chicago's history to date. In the wake of these profits, Moody's Investor Service gave the bank a vote of confidence by raising the rating of First Chicago's securities. More significantly, the office of the comptroller of the currency acknowledged that First Chicago had met all of its requirements for reducing risk on loans well ahead of the targeted dates.

What the banking industry feared most, happened in 1987: Third World countries suspended interest payments on their loans. This situation compelled First Chicago to raise its reserves on troubled-country debtors (mostly Brazil) by $1 billion. At the end of the year, First Chicago reported a loss of $571 million, in dramatic contrast with its historic earnings of 1986.

In 1987 First Chicago acquired First United Financial Services Inc., a five-bank holding company with a solid base of business in the growing western and northwestern suburbs. The bank also purchased Beneficial National Bank USA, Wilmington, Delaware, and renamed it FCC National Bank. With this addition, First Chicago became the third largest issuer of bank credit cards in the United States. As profits rebounded in 1988, First Chicago took another giant step in developing its customer-banking base through the acquisition of Gary-Wheaton Corporation, a four-bank holding company.

The early 1990s were not kind to First Chicago, however, and the bank suffered from problem loans in commercial real estate as well as highly leveraged companies. Sullivan left the company at the end of 1991, and new Chairman and CEO Richard L. Thomas assumed the task of turning the around the ailing bank. Thomas began by cutting the dividend 40 percent—in 1991, when the company was still under Sullivan's command, First Chicago paid out more dividends than it earned. First Chicago posted a $15.1 million loss during the fourth quarter of 1991 for problem loans and expense-cutting costs. In order to streamline operations, the bank downsized its staff by about 1,000 workers in 1991, and additional personnel cuts were expected.

The changes implemented at First Chicago met with success, and earnings for the first quarter of 1993 rose more than 51 percent compared to the same period in 1992. The bank was also able to take some control of its problem loans by selling off $1 billion of its nonperforming real estate loans to GE Capital in February 1993 for about $500 million. The company's first-quarter results were also helped by gains in First Chicago's venture-capital portfolio and its rapidly growing credit card operations.

In 1995 First Chicago made a big move when it merged with NBD Bancorp Inc., based in Detroit, Michigan, to form First Chicago NBD Corp., the seventh largest bank in the United States and a leader in the Midwest. Prior to the $5 billion merger, First Chicago had $72.4 billion in assets and was ranked tenth in the nation. The bank was also one of the nation's largest issuers of credit cards and was the market leader among corporate banking operations in the Midwest. NBD Bancorp ranked 18th and had assets of $47.8 billion. Thomas retired in May 1996, leaving command of the new bank to NBD Bancorp's chairman and CEO, Verne G. Istock. Istock planned to make First Chicago NBD an even more powerful presence in the Midwest and to generate revenue growth by stimulating the slightly ailing credit card business and increasing marketing. Istock also hoped to make some strategic acquisitions to fight competition, as well as takeover attempts, and intended to turn around corporate bank operations by decreasing capital and shedding unprofitable product lines.

The Merger of Banc One and First Chicago NBD: Late 1990s

In April 1998 Banc One and First Chicago NBD announced plans to merge their operations in an estimated $30 billion deal. The newly formed company took the name Bank One Corporation and consolidated its headquarters in Chicago. Banc One's McCoy became president and CEO of Bank One, while First Chicago NBD's Istock assumed the role of chairman. The new company formed a powerhouse in the Midwest, and the bank expected the merger to generate $930 million in savings and $1.2 billion in additional revenue over the following two years.

Bank One placed hopes of expansion on the relatively new area of online banking and online services. Growth through the Internet, the bank believed, would be less costly than acquiring companies, a practice the bank planned to put on hold while it integrated the operations of Banc One and First Chicago NBD. In October 1998 Bank One's First USA division made an agreement with Microsoft to pay about $90 million for advertising on the MSN Network, Microsoft's online service, for five years. A month later Bank One inked a deal with Excite Inc., an Internet media company, to develop an online financial services area for Excite's home page. Clients would be able to access personalized banking information, and Bank One would have access to potential new customers. In early 1999 First USA made another online deal when it signed a five-year agreement with America Online Inc. to market its credit cards to America Online members. It was estimated that the deal could generate nearly $500 million in revenues for America Online.

Bank One took a significant leap of faith in the Internet in mid-1999 when it launched an exclusively online bank, known as WingspanBank.com. By creating a new brand separate from the Bank One image, the company hoped to lure new, Internet-savvy customers who traditionally shunned the conventional banking system. The new venture was expected to add as much as $150 million to Bank One's annual operating expenses.

As part of the new company's consolidation efforts, Bank One reduced its workforce by about five percent, or 4,500 jobs, in 1999. Bank One also sold the mortgage servicing portfolio and transaction processing services of First Chicago NBD. For the second quarter of 1999, Bank One reported net income of $992 million, an increase over the year-earlier net income of $895 million. First USA continued to contribute significantly to revenues, with $920 million in sales during the second quarter, but increased competition and slowing growth in the credit card industry led industry observers to view Bank One's results with a hint of skepticism.

In the summer of 1999 Bank One announced that 1999 profits would not meet with Wall Street expectations. Problems with First USA and the slowing credit card industry were blamed. Indeed, First USA had grown at 20 percent a year in the mid- to late 1990s, but growth for the remainder of 1999 was projected to remain stagnant. First USA's attempts to stave off competition and falling profits included stiffer penalties for submitting late payments and jumps in interest rates. Cardholders retaliated by canceling their First USA cards, and First USA's attrition rate climbed as high as 17 percent in 1999. The credit card division was unable to sign up enough new members to balance out its losses.

Reaction to Bank One's announcement included a 23 percent drop in its stock price. McCoy and Istock traded positions, and though McCoy remained CEO, he lost a large portion of his operating responsibilities. By the end of 1999 the climate at Bank One was so bleak, and the former Banc One and First Chicago NBD factions so opposed, that in December McCoy was in essence forced to resign from the company he had worked so hard to build. Istock took over as interim CEO and had the task of announcing that earnings for 2000 would also be less than favorable—First USA's profits were projected to fall 30 to 35 percent. Istock also announced a restructuring strategy designed to raise profitability and said the company would take a $725 million charge against fourth-quarter 1999 earnings.

Problems continued to plague Bank One in early 2000 as it struggled to turn around its underperforming operations. Though Bank One blamed the majority of its problems on First USA, the company faced some challenges in other areas. For instance, Bank One used $80 million to cover losses in auto leases, and the company struggled to integrate the computer systems of First Chicago, NBD, and Bank One. For the first quarter of 2000, First USA's net income was $70 million, down considerably from the year-earlier amount of $303 million. Bank One's overall earnings for the first quarter reached $689 million, compared to $1.15 billion in 1999. Bank One remained confident, however, of its ability to return the ailing First USA division to profitability by 2001.

In March Bank One announced it would reduce its workforce again in order to cut costs. About six percent, or some 5,100 jobs, would be eliminated, mostly from the credit card, consumer lending, and staff services operations. Also that month Bank One gained a new CEO and chairman, Jamie Dimon, formerly a president with Citigroup Inc. Dimon quickly got started on his challenging task of turning around the floundering company. Bank One's retail credit card business in Canada was sold to Royal Bank of Canada, and its retail credit card business in the United Kingdom was sold to Halifax Group plc. Both the Canadian and U.K. divisions had been launched in late 1998. The sales reflected Bank One's attempt to refocus on strengthening domestic businesses. Bank One also sold its subprime real estate loan portfolio to Household International Inc. The division, which included 97 Bank One Financial Services branches in 29 states, was not considered to be a core operation. Another division that faced changes was WingspanBank.com. The online bank's launch was accompanied by intensive marketing efforts and in its early stages gained 50,000 customers, but the bank soon lost steam—though analysts expected the bank to attract about 500,000 customers in its initial year, the bank only had about 107,000 accounts after its first six months. Bank One considered selling off the division but in July chose to integrate it into its retail division and planned to combine WingspanBank.com and Bank One into one Internet platform.

With the legacies of Banc One and First Chicago NBD providing strength and support, and a new CEO with an effective track record in the financial services sector, supporters of Bank One remained positive and hopeful. As Bank One looked forward, its future was unpredictable, but the company planned to put its problems behind and to live up to its promise of great savings and unprecedented revenue growth.

Principal Subsidiaries

First USA Bank, National Association; Paymentech, Inc.; Banc One Loan Services Corporation; Banc One Insurance Company; First Chicago NBD Insurance Company; Banc One Management Corporation; Banc One Texas Corporation; Bank One, National Association; Bank One International Holdings Corporation; Banc One Capital Holdings Corporation; BOCP Holdings Corporation; Finance One Corporation; Banc One Financial Corporation; Banc One Capital Corporation; First Chicago Leasing Corporation; Banc One Capital Markets, Inc.

Principal Competitors

Bank of America Corporation; The Chase Manhattan Corporation; MBNA Corporation; Citigroup Inc.; Wells Fargo & Company.

Further Reading

''Banc One: Costly Hedging,'' *Economist,* December 25, 1993, pp. 100–01.

''Banc One: Mightier Than Its Parts,'' *Economist,* December 19, 1992, p. 76.

Cahill, Joseph B., ''Acquisitive Bank One Turns Its Back on Takeovers, Pins Hopes on Internet,'' *Wall Street Journal,* May 10, 1999, p. A4.

——, ''Bank One Shares Drop 23% on Forecast—Doubt Is Cast on Strategy of Consumer Lending As Profit Margins Shrink,'' *Wall Street Journal,* August 26, 1999, p. A2.

——, ''Bank One to Take $725 Million Charge, Plans to Overhaul Its Credit-Card Lines,'' *Wall Street Journal,* January 12, 2000, p. A3.

First Chicagoan: 125th Anniversary Issue, Chicago: First Chicago Corporation, March 1988.

Lipin, Steven, and Matt Murray, ''Banc One Is Expected to Buy First USA—Tax-Free Stock Exchange for Credit Card Firm Seen As $7 Billion Deal,'' *Wall Street Journal,* January 20, 1997, p. A3.

Melcher, Richard A., ''Is 'Nice, Big, Dull' Good Enough? NBD Is Bringing Its Conservative Style to First Chicago,'' *Business Week,* May 12, 1997, p. 84.

Morris, Henry C., *The History of the First National Bank of Chicago,* Chicago: R.R. Donnelley & Sons Company, 1902.

O'Brien, Timothy L., ''First Chicago, NBD Agree to a $5.14 Billion Merger,'' *Wall Street Journal,* July 13, 1995, p. A3.

Phillips, Stephen, ''Just Your Friendly Hometown Banker—With a Megabank,'' *Business Week,* April 9, 1990, pp. 64–6.

Raghavan, Anita, and Jathon Sapsford, ''Deals & Deal Makers: Bank One Names Dimon Chairman, CEO,'' *Wall Street Journal,* March 28, 2000, p. C1.

Rifkin, Glenn, ''He Changed the Rules in Banking,'' *Computerworld,* April 25, 1988, pp. 1, 84–5.

Svare, J. Christopher, ''Acquiring for Growth and Profit: The Banc One Experience,'' *Bank Management,* November 1990, pp. 18–24.

Taylor, John H., ''A Tale of Two Strategies,'' *Forbes,* August 31, 1992, pp. 40–1.

Teitelman, Robert, ''The Magnificent McCoys: Running America's Best Bank,'' *Institutional Investor,* July 1991, pp. 47–56.

Vanac, Mary, ''Merger Changes Bank One's Local Operations in Ohio,'' *Akron Beacon Journal, Ohio,* November 5, 1998.

Weber, Joseph, ''The Mess at Bank One: Ex-CEO McCoy Shared Power Too Much,'' *Business Week,* May 1, 2000, p. 162.

—April Dougal Gasbarre
—updated by Mariko Fujinaka

Bath Iron Works

700 Washington Street
Bath, Maine 04530
U.S.A.
Telephone: (207) 443-3311
Fax: (207) 442-1567
Web site: http://www.gdbiw.com

Wholly Owned Subsidiary of General Dynamics
* Corporation*
Incorporated: 1884 as Bath Iron Works, Ltd.
Employees: 7,700
Sales: $936 million (1998)
NAIC: 336611 Ship Building and Repairing; 54133
  Engineering Services

For more than a century, Bath Iron Works (BIW) has been building ships, chiefly for the U.S. Navy. From its mile-long stretch of waterfront along the Kennebec River have come more oceangoing vessels than from any area of similar size in the world. In its busiest period, BIW built a quarter of the Navy's destroyers launched during World War II. The fourth largest shipyard in the United States and the largest private employer in Maine, BIW has not built a commercial vessel since 1984 and, with the end of the Cold War and diminishing naval contracts, has sought to supplement its business, investigating, for example, the prospect of building large carriers to transport automobiles and trucks. Its 1995 acquisition by General Dynamics Corp., however, has allowed the company to focus on Navy vessels.

Origins

The history of Bath Iron Works is a vital chapter in Maine's seafaring history. Not more than a dozen miles away from the town of Bath, settlers established the first colony in New England—13 years before the landing of the *Mayflower*—and built the first oceangoing vessel made by Englishmen in America in order to take themselves home. But curiously, the company owes its origin to a soldier rather than a sailor. The scion of

a prosperous Bath merchant family, Thomas Worcester Hyde was a Civil War army officer who rose to the rank of brigadier general in the Union Army at the age of 23. Hyde leased a local iron foundry after returning home and opened Bath Iron Works, Ltd. in 1884 as a family enterprise.

Starting with capital of just a little more than $40,000, Hyde raised another $60,000, purchased a defunct iron works along the Bath riverfront, and equipped it to make steel ships, which were rarities at the time. Producing a wooden steamer in 1890, before obtaining his first naval contract, Hyde delivered to the Navy the first steel vessels built in Maine—two gunboats with auxiliary sails—in 1893. Two years later the Navy ordered two more such gunboats. During this time, BIW built other wooden steamers, lightships for the United States Bureau of Lighthouses, and private yachts as well. In 1894 Bath built the largest and most luxurious American-built yacht of its time, the *Eleanor*, for William A. Slater, at a cost of $300,000. The ship immediately embarked on a two-year, around-the-world voyage with a crew of 30. The company also built the 302-foot-long *Aphrodite* in 1898 for Colonel Oliver Payne.

But the Navy remained Bath's primary customer. Between 1899 and 1901 the company delivered five very light and high-speed torpedo boats to the Navy. These pioneering craft were the Navy's first of this type until World War II's PT boats. A cruiser, the *Cleveland*, was built in 1904, and BIW's only battleship, the *Georgia*, was completed the same year.

The hull of the *Georgia*, however, was barely able to clear the riverbed in Bath, and as battleships graduated into the larger Dreadnought class, it became clear that Bath would have to confine itself to building smaller ships. BIW's scout cruiser *Chester*, completed in 1908, was the first turbine-propelled ship in the Navy and its fastest vessel, except for torpedo boats. In a race against two other ships of this type, it averaged 25.8 knots over 24 hours.

In 1909 BIW built its first two torpedo boat destroyers. This new type of craft was designed to counter the smaller torpedo boat, yet carry its basic weapon. The name was soon shortened to simply "destroyer," and by 1912 BIW was the Navy's chief specialist for this kind of light, fast warship, which would

Company Perspectives:

BIW employees are premier designers and builders of complex, technologically advanced naval ships. Since the 1950s, BIW has served as lead shipyard for 10 non-nuclear surface ship classes produced by the U.S. Navy, more than any other U.S. shipyard. In 1995, BIW was purchased by General Dynamics, further enhancing the company's technological expertise and capabilities through key investments and access to the complementary capabilities of other General Dynamics companies.

Bath Iron Works today is the lead designer and builder of the ARLEIGH BURKE Class AEGIS guided missile destroyer, the most technologically advanced surface combatant in the world.

become the most versatile of modern naval vessels. The destroyer has served as an escort ship on convoy duty and performed many other essential functions, but its chief mandate—especially since World War II—has been to detect, hunt down, and destroy submarines.

BIW briefly came under the control of Charles Schwab's U.S. Shipbuilding Trust between 1902 and 1905, and when this enterprise failed it was sold to John S. Hyde, the late general's younger son, for $275,000. Hyde died in 1917 while the shipyard was awash in World War I orders, and his heirs promptly sold out to a banking syndicate for $3 million. The investors awarded themselves big dividends during the fat war years, however, leaving BIW no margin for coping with the inevitable postwar bust. The naval disarmament treaty of 1921 sealed the company's doom. BIW went into receivership in 1924 and shut down operations the following year. In 1927 the idle facilities were slated for conversion—to the task of turning out paper pie plates.

Renewed Under Newell in 1928

Nevertheless, the shipyard was saved from this fate by its former works manager, William S. "Pete" Newell. He leased it for $17,000 a year, established the Bath Iron Works Corp. with $125,000 in borrowed capital, successfully bid on three fishing trawlers, and won an order for a 240-foot yacht. Between 1928 and 1937 BIW built and delivered 18 trawlers. The company also constructed seven Coast Guard cutters designated for combating rumrunners during the Prohibition years. In 1931 BIW won the contract for the *Dewey* and *Farragut,* the first destroyers authorized by the Navy since 1918.

Building yachts for captains of industry proved a profitable sideline. For J.P. Morgan II, BIW built the 343-foot-long *Corsair IV,* which was launched in 1930. Although the Great Depression ended, in large part, Bath's yachtbuilding operations, in 1936 Harold S. Vanderbilt commissioned the company to build a racer to defend the America's Cup. The resulting *Ranger* was the last of the J class sloops to defend the Cup, defeating the *Endeavor II* in four straight 1937 races.

In 1936 BIW offered stock to the public, for the first time, on the New York Curb Exchange (later the American Stock Exchange). This action placed the company on a sounder financial

basis, enabling Newell to pay off the company's outstanding first mortgage bonds and to augment its working capital. By the time BIW was registered on the New York Stock Exchange in 1940, it had paid off all its bank loans.

During World War II, BIW employment peaked at 12,000 (1,600 of whom were women) in 1943, compared with 300 a decade earlier. Between Pearl Harbor and the war's end, BIW built 82 destroyers—one-fourth of the total ordered by the Navy—launching one on an average of every 17 days. Only eight of the ships were sunk during the war. Bath also established, jointly with Todd Shipyard Corp., a facility in South Portland to build 30 British cargo ships. This yard, which turned out Liberty ships for the U.S. Maritime Commission, was closed after the war.

Following a familiar pattern, employment sank to 350 in 1947. But BIW had already begun work on the first of 32 trawlers commissioned by the French government. Moreover, the company soon received new orders for destroyers from the Navy as well as contracts for frigates, ocean escorts, and LSTs (landing ship-tanks). Yachtbuilding also resumed. John R. Newell succeeded his father as the company's president in 1950.

Part of a Conglomerate: 1968

By 1968, however, the company was beset by managerial and economic problems. That year the parent holding company, Bath Industries Inc., merged with Congoleum-Nairn Inc., a manufacturer of flooring materials. Troubles continued, with BIW losing out on major naval contracts and incurring losses on others because its fixed prices did not allow for the rapidly rising inflation of the early 1970s. In 1974 the shipyard lost $10 million.

The following year the parent company (now called Congoleum Corp.) brought in John R. Sullivan, Jr., a chemical engineer, to run the yard. Although Sullivan had never seen a shipyard, he set about putting Bath on a sounder basis. Sullivan made the yard's modular construction system, which had been adopted from Japanese practice, effective at BIW for the first time. Bath was the first U.S. shipyard to employ this technique, which involved building a hull out of modules constructed indoors and fitted there with electrical wiring, plumbing, ventilation, and hydraulic equipment. These modules were then hauled outdoors by crane and welded together. By 1981, Bath's safety record, once one of the worst in the industry, had become one of the best.

By this time BIW had built 13 of 24 FFG 7-class guided-missile frigates for the Navy, completing each in less than two years. The project was 99 weeks ahead of schedule and $44 million under budget. Bath's operations were comfortably profitable, and there was a backlog of $800 million in military orders.

Leveraged in the 1980s

In early 1980 Congoleum went private in a leveraged buyout. Several insurance companies joined the company's management in borrowing heavily to buy all the outstanding publicly held stock for about $450 million. Prudential secured 29

Key Dates:

1884: Thomas Worcester Hyde starts Bath Iron Works in Bath, Maine.

1893: BIW delivers the U.S. Navy its first steel ships.

1899: High-speed torpedo boats launched.

1908: The *Chester* becomes the first turbine-propelled ship in the Navy.

1909: BIW builds its first destroyers.

1928: Former manager William Newell resuscitates BIW after post-World War I failure.

1936: An initial public offering is launched.

1943: Employment peaks at 12,000 during World War II.

1968: BIW merges with flooring producer Congoleum-Nairn Inc.

1986: New York investment firm acquires BIW in a leveraged buyout.

1995: General Dynamics acquires BIW.

---

percent of the company, with Aetna, Travelers, and Connecticut General investing as well.

A *Forbes* article published in September 1984 indicated that this move was paying off. BIW's frigates were still coming in ahead of schedule and under budget, and the company's earnings for the past five years were estimated at about 15 percent on sales of about $400 million annually. In 1982 Bath won a contract to build the *Thomas S. Gates,* the first of eight Ticonderoga-class Aegis cruisers it was to build through 1991. More good news came on April 2, 1985, when Bath won an order worth about $322 million to build the *Arleigh Burke,* first of the DDG 51 Aegis destroyer class. By mid-1986, BIW had a $1.4 billion backlog in naval orders, including these Aegis-class cruisers and destroyers.

On this prosperous note, Congoleum's investors were ready to cash in, but before doing so management determined to make BIW even more attractive by putting a lid on labor costs. This initiative met with protest, however, as BIW workers walked out for 14 weeks in 1985. Labor and management eventually agreed to a wage freeze, with bonuses equivalent to an increase of three percent over three years.

In another leveraged buyout, announced August 21, 1986, the closely held New York investment firm of Gibbons, Green, Van Amerongen Ltd. bought BIW for an estimated $500 million. BIW then became a subsidiary of the new Bath Holding Corp., which itself became a subsidiary of the Fulcrum II Limited Partnership, the managing partners of which were Edward Gibbons, Todd Goodwin, and Louis van Amerongen.

New Markets After the Cold War

By late 1992 BIW had a backlog of $2 billion worth of orders carried through 1997; in 1994, the backlog of 14 Burke-class destroyers extended through the year 2000. Aware, however, of impending defense cuts in the wake of the Cold War, company managers began looking for ways to solicit civilian work. Bath had not built a civilian craft since 1985 and had "no contingency plan whatsoever," according to its president,

Duane D. "Buzz" Fitzgerald, who sent a four-man team to Holland to "benchmark" ten shipyards there.

Fitzgerald replaced William Haggett as BIW's chief executive officer in September 1991, when Haggett opted to resign his posts as CEO and chairperson. A BIW official for 23 years, Haggett announced at a news conference that year that he had violated business ethics, admitting that he had ordered the photocopying of a government document, inadvertently left behind at the BIW shipyard by Navy officials. Although the document, which had included cost reviews of work performed by Bath and its chief competitor, Ingalls Shipbuilding of Pascagoula, Mississippi, had reportedly not been used to BIW's advantage, Haggett and two BIW vice-presidents involved in the photocopying resigned in 1991.

Under the leadership of Buzz Fitzgerald, BIW continued to be a major supplier to the Pentagon. The company was asked to build three $850 million Burke-class Aegis destroyers for the Navy in June 1994. Moreover, in an effort to diversify, BIW joined with American Automar Inc. and Great American Lines Inc. in 1993 to develop carriers of automobiles and other vehicles that could also meet military needs. Also participating in the $14 million project were a giant Japanese shipbuilder and the Canadian ship-designing subsidiary of a Finnish group. This program received a $5 million federal grant and was being coordinated by a special Pentagon agency intended to foster ties between shipyards, carriers, university research centers, and the federal government. According to a 1994 Bath press release, the company was "on course to be competitive in the world commercial shipbuilding market by 1997."

A New Dynamic in 1995

Employment at BIW fell from 12,000 in 1989 to 8,300 in 1995 as military procurement slowed in the wake of the Cold War and consolidation spread throughout the defense sector. Prudential Insurance Co., BIW's largest shareholder, began looking for a buyer in April 1995 and specifically targeted General Dynamics Corp. (GD), the $3 billion defense conglomerate based in Falls Church, Virginia. In August, GD announced plans to buy BIW for $300 million.

GD's purchase, considered a bargain, allowed BIW to remain focused on military ships, said Duane "Buzz" Fitzgerald, BIW president. The commercial market had been saturated anyway. The previous owners, laden with debt, had not invested much in modernization, while GD invested $200 million in updating BIW's facilities between 1997 and 2000.

GD already supplied the Navy through its Electric Boat division, which built nuclear submarines. It had sold off its computer, missile, aircraft, and rocket divisions over the previous four years but was attracted to BIW for its $2 billion backlog (orders for 11 Arleigh Burke-class DDG-51 destroyers). In spite of a recent labor accord aimed at raising productivity, GD planned to cut costs at BIW even further to become more competitive.

The BIW acquisition helped GD raise profits 35 percent in 1995, even as business declined at its other divisions. Operating profits at BIW were $50 million on revenues of $830 million. The unit's performance was sluggish in 1996, however, leading

GD to reorganize steel fabrication and materials handling operations there.

BIW had won, though, a $217 million contract to build an amphibious assault vehicle (AAV) for the Marine Corps that had the potential of bringing in $4 billion through 2014. It also won a $9.6 billion contract to build 12 LPD-17 transport ships for the U.S. Navy. BIW won that bid over a consortium including Lockheed Martin, Litton Industries, and Newport News Shipbuilding & Drydock Co. BIW was part of a consortium led by Avondale Industries of New Orleans that won the LPD-17 contract in December 1996. Senate Majority Leader Trent Lott, hoping to secure work for his constituents in Mississippi (home of Ingalls), vigorously protested the Navy's selection.

In October 1998, General Dynamics announced that it was buying its third shipyard (after BIW and Electric Boat). It paid $370 million in cash and assumed $45 million in debt to acquire Nassco Holdings Inc., parent of National Steel & Shipbuilding Co. in San Diego. Nassco repaired combat ships and built smaller Navy vessels and commercial ships.

BIW teamed with Energy Research Corporation in 1999 to develop new fuel cells to bring electric power to military ships. The Direct FuelCell Ship Service Power Plant promised to be efficient, quiet, and clean to run. Another high-tech joint venture launched in 2000 tested HyperSonic Sound Technology (HSS) aboard an Aegis destroyer under construction. American Technology Corp.'s proprietary HSS system could focus sound in a tight beam, like light through a lens. Still another project announced in June 2000 teamed BIW with Kronos Air Technologies in studying electronic wind generation for use in bunk installations. The Kronos device used no moving parts yet could circulate and clean air silently.

In December 1999, BIW won a $324 million contract modification to build an additional Arleigh Burke Aegis Class guided missile destroyer in 2000. Nine DDG 51 class destroyers remained in BIW's backlog, with 16 having been delivered. BIW joined Ingalls in the two-member DD-21 Shipbuilder Alliance, charged with designing the next generation of surface combatants.

Principal Divisions

Engineering; Purchasing; Shipbuilding.

Principal Competitors

Ingalls Shipbuilding (Litton); Newport News Shipbuilding & Drydock Co.

Further Reading

Alpert, Bruce, ''Billion-Dollar Contracts Ignite Heated Struggles; Avondale Victory Pits Lott Vs. Livingston,'' *Times-Picayune,* June 2, 1997, p. A1.

Biesada, Alexandra, ''Strategic Benchmarking,'' *Financial World,* September 29, 1992, pp. 30–31.

Buell, Barbara, ''Bath: A Tight Ship That Could Spring a Leak,'' *Business Week,* May 20, 1985, pp. 88–90.

''City of Ships,'' *American Heritage,* September 1991, pp. 28–30.

DeMott, John S., ''Bath's Fighting Company,'' *Time,* October 12, 1981, p. 82.

Eskew, Garrett Laidlaw, *Cradle of Ships,* New York: G.P. Putnam's Sons, 1958.

Frank, Allen Dodds, ''The Bath Money Works,'' *Forbes,* September 10, 1984, pp. 58–62.

Lewis, Diane, ''Bath Shipyard Accord Reflects Fight to Remain Competitive,'' *Boston Globe,* September 5, 1994, pp. 1, 5.

Mintz, John, ''General Dynamics to Buy Shipyard for $300 Million; Deal for Bath Iron Works Called Shrewd Bargain for Defense Firm,'' *Washington Post,* August 18, 1995, p. D1.

Payne, Seth, ''A Yard Sale Worth $600 Million?,'' *Business Week,* June 23, 1986, p. 47.

Ricks, Thomas E., ''Navy Allocates Ship Contracts in Policy Shift,'' *Wall Street Journal,* June 9, 1994, p. A16.

Rosenberg, Ronald, ''Company Buys Bath Iron Works; General Dynamics to Spend $300 Million,'' *Boston Globe,* Economy Sec., August 18, 1995, p. 35.

Shorrock, Tim, ''Maine Yard Gets US Aid in Designing Cargo Vessels,'' *Journal of Commerce,* December 16, 1993, pp. 1A, 10A.

Stevens, David Weld, ''Floating the Navy the Bath Way,'' *Fortune,* October 6, 1981, pp. 160–63.

''Vote of Merger Plan,'' *Wall Street Journal,* September 9, 1968, p. 22.

Williams, John D., and Jan Wong, ''Congoleum Sells Bath Iron Works Unit in Buyout Valued at About $500 Million,'' *Wall Street Journal,* August 22, 1986, p. 4.

—Robert Halasz
—updated by Frederick C. Ingram

BEA Systems, Inc.

2315 North 1st Street
San Jose, California 95131
U.S.A.
Telephone: (408) 570-8000
Fax: (408) 570-8091
Web site: http://www.beasys.com

Public Company
Incorporated: 1995
Employees: 1,900
Sales: $464.4 million (2000)
Stock Exchanges: NASDAQ
Ticker Symbol: BEAS
NAIC: 511210 Software Publishers; 541511 Custom
   Computer Programming Services; 541512 Computer
   Systems Design Services

BEA Systems, Inc. is a company that is right in the middle of the burgeoning electronic commerce (e-commerce) marketplace. Originally established in 1995 to provide "middleware," a type of platform software, to corporate clients who were switching from mainframe computing to distributed client-server systems, BEA developed a family of software and servers to support high-volume e-commerce transactions in real time. Toward the end of 1999 the company repositioned itself as "The E-Commerce Transactions Company."

Supplier of Middleware to
Corporate Clients: 1995–96

BEA Systems, Inc. was founded in 1995 by Bill Coleman, Ed Scott, and Alfred Chuang. All three held management or executive positions with Sun Microsystems Inc. before founding BEA Systems, which was named using the first letter of the first name of each of the three founders. Coleman became BEA's chairman and CEO. Scott was in charge of BEA's sales and marketing and served as president and, later, counselor for the company. Chuang would hold a variety of positions at BEA, including chief technology officer, chief operations officer, and president. The New York-based venture capital firm E.M.

Warburg, Pincus & Co. invested $50 million for a half-interest in the company.

BEA was established to fill a niche called "middleware." Middleware is a form of platform software. At the time BEA came into being, mainframe computing was giving way to a client-server environment. In the client-server environment, each client and each server have an operating system, typically Windows for the client and Unix for the server. Middleware was a solution to the problem of how to have applications run on multiple machines. Middleware acts as an operating system in the client-server environment, so that applications can run on the middleware platform.

Rather than inventing platform software from scratch, BEA was interested in a product known as Tuxedo, an online transaction processing monitor. The original program for Tuxedo was developed by Bell Labs in 1983 to enable large numbers of users to simultaneously access and manipulate a database on a mainframe computer. It was then sold to Novell Inc., with variations developed by other smaller companies. In 1996 BEA bought the rights to Tuxedo from Novell, along with much of its independent distribution network. Novell retained ownership of Tuxedo, but BEA would take over development and distribution of the product. Also included in the deal were the core of Novell's Tuxedo business team, including engineers and programmers who developed Tuxedo, and existing contracts and agreements.

By all accounts Tuxedo had been languishing under Novell, but BEA quickly announced a new suite of products for the fall of 1996. Transaction processing (TP) monitors were beginning to attract the attention of corporate information system buyers as a key component of electronic commerce. BEA also produced a Java interface called BEA Jolt, which extended Tuxedo transaction processing to the Internet. By translating between Tuxedo and Java applets, BEA Jolt would permit any Java-enabled browser or Java program to access the Tuxedo middleware. With Jolt, Tuxedo users could perform transactions with any Java-enabled browser or stand-alone Java application.

By maintaining a continuous transaction state, Jolt would enable electronic commerce to be conducted in real time. In 1996 electronic commerce was limited to placing orders that

Company Perspectives:

The vision of BEA's founders has always been bigger than middleware. Their goal from the beginning was to provide a comprehensive infrastructure for development and deployment of reliable, salable business applications for e-commerce. As the Internet Economy has profoundly transformed the business landscape, BEA too has transformed itself to better serve its business customers by offering the E-commerce Transaction Platform.

were processed offline. Jolt also enabled financial applications to be extended to the Internet. The introduction of Jolt gave BEA an edge over competitors such as NCR Corp. and IBM. Significant Jolt partners included Hewlett-Packard Co., Digital Equipment Corp., and Sun Microsystems Inc.

BEA began to expand its sales efforts internationally in 1996. It launched its European operations by opening offices in London, Munich, Paris, and Brussels. It also established subsidiaries in Japan, Sweden, and South Africa, and before the end of the year opened its Latin American regional headquarters in Sao Paulo, Brazil.

Deepening the Product Line: 1997–98

In early 1997 BEA acquired object and messaging technology from Digital Equipment Corporation. ObjectBroker and DECmessageQ, along with Tuxedo, were soon available as part of the BEA Enterprise Middleware Suite. The combined technology allowed BEA to focus on creating an infrastructure for running applications.

BEA completed its initial public offering (IPO), which raised $150 million, in April 1997. Shares were initially offered at $6. By July 1 they were trading at $18. A secondary stock offering in July raised another $150 million. At the time BEA was one of the few companies aside from IBM that was offering platform software. For the rest of 1997 and 1998 BEA's stock went through a period of ups and downs following the IPO.

In mid-1998 BEA acquired the Top End transaction processing monitor from NCR Corp. for the purpose of combining its technology with Tuxedo, which had become the market leader in TP monitors. Top End had been Tuxedo's largest competitor. According to one source, Tuxedo accounted for 41 percent of all installed TP monitors in 1998, with Top End holding 13 percent of the market. BEA also planned to proceed with an upgrade to Top End, which was being used by such customers as Wal-Mart, Amazon.com, and Reuters.

By mid-1998 BEA was a major supplier of message-queuing and transaction-oriented middleware. The company launched the M3 Object Transaction Manager, an object-oriented successor to its Tuxedo TP monitor. Such object-oriented TP software allowed servers to process heavy transaction loads generated by Internet traffic. M3 combined ObjectBroker and DECmessageQ, which BEA acquired from Digital Equipment, with Tuxedo. BEA's goal was to quickly assemble a broad portfolio of middleware products for mission-critical applications.

In September 1998 BEA acquired WebLogic Inc., which made a well-regarded Java-based web-application server, for $192 million in stock. BEA planned to combine WebLogic with Tuxedo to create a reliable method for processing transactions over the Internet. WebLogic had been perfecting its Java-based technology for about three years. The acquisition put BEA in direct competition with Sun Microsystems.

BEA management regarded the acquisition of WebLogic as the company's most important strategic move since acquiring Tuxedo. WebLogic would be the core of a new BEA division, WebXpress, with BEA cofounder and Chief Technology Officer Alfred Chuang in charge. It was the beginning of a transformation at BEA, from a middleware company to one that produced an e-commerce transaction platform.

"The E-Commerce Transactions Company": 1999–2000

For its fiscal year ending January 31, 1999, BEA reported sales of $289 million and a net loss of $51.6 million. The company had more than 1,200 employees in 24 countries. In February 1999 BEA introduced eLink, a group of enterprise application integration (EAI) products that integrated new web applications in real time with existing legacy applications. ELink, together with Tuxedo and WebLogic, would become the key components of BEA's "End-to-End E-Commerce Transaction Solution."

In April 1999 BEA and Hewlett-Packard (HP) entered into a cooperative agreement, with HP committing $100 million to BEA over three years to develop software and technology to support both companies' e-commerce strategies. As part of the agreement BEA would put up $50 million over three years and commit 200 employees to the joint effort. The goal of the agreement was to build applications that would provide as much as 80 percent of what would be needed for a company to build an e-commerce site, either for business-to-business or business-to-consumer transactions. As envisioned by HP and BEA, the e-commerce software would be based on the Enterprise JavaBean (EJB) model and run on the BEA WebLogic application server. BEA Tuxedo and BEA eLink would also be part of the applications package. Like BEA, HP was in the process of reinventing itself as an Internet company that offered solutions for electronic commerce. BEA expected that its new partnership with HP would add $100 million in revenues over the next three years.

The year 1999 saw a growing demand for transaction processing software. According to an article in *InternetWeek,* one bank recorded 15.8 billion transactions through three data processing centers, or 3,300 transactions per minute. Banks were experiencing a rise in the number of transactions because of more online banking traffic and growth through mergers and acquisitions.

Transaction processing included any request that required an automated response, from updating customer records to electronic funds transfers and issuing payroll checks. For many companies, transactions were becoming more distributed, requiring systems that ran transactions across multiple network protocols and server operating systems. These systems also

Key Dates:

1995: BEA Systems, Inc. is founded by Bill Coleman, Ed Scott, and Alfred Chuang.
1996: BEA acquires Tuxedo, a transaction processing system, from Novell Inc.
1997: BEA completes its initial public offering.
1998: BEA acquires WebLogic Inc., which makes a Java-based web-application server.
1999: BEA redefines itself as ''The E-Commerce Transactions Company.''

would integrate back-office applications and older legacy systems. They also supported Java and object-oriented programming. Whereas IBM was considered the leader in the mainframe market, BEA's Tuxedo was the leader in distributed computing with an estimated 60 percent of the market.

The newest transaction processing software incorporated OTM, or object transaction monitors. Newer companies such as Iona Technologies and Inprise Corp. were developing OTMs, and BEA was building OTMs into its Tuxedo and WebLogic systems. OTMs enabled companies to support multiple resources and different environments at the database level through a distributed transaction server.

For companies that wanted to build mission-critical applications over Linux, BEA added Linux support to both Tuxedo and WebLogic. After BEA put up a trial version of Tuxedo for visitors to download, there were more than 1,600 downloads within a couple of weeks, reflecting pent-up demand among companies for Linux support.

Internet-based transaction processing was having the biggest impact on the field, making the client-server model obsolete. In August BEA introduced a new version of the enterprise edition of its WebLogic application server with added multiple-language support for Java as well as C or C++. The WebLogic enterprise edition would offer EJB support by the end of the year.

In mid-1999 BEA acquired Avitek Inc., a Java software developed in Boulder, Colorado, with 42 employees, and folded it into the company's eSolutions division. Other mid-1999 acquisitions included Component Systems LLC, a consulting firm based in Pleasanton, California, which specialized in designing and developing large-scale e-commerce applications. BEA also acquired Technology Resource Group Inc., an educational company focused on Java technology, based in Maynard, Massachusetts.

Following these acquisitions BEA began to reposition itself from a middleware company to an e-commerce company. It committed $20 million to rebrand as ''The E-Commerce Transactions Company'' and planned to advertise heavily in major business and trade publications as well as on news web sites and portals. It also took billboard signs in technology centers such as Silicon Valley, Boston, Chicago, Dallas, and New York.

From August 23, 1999 to February 18, 2000, BEA's stock rose more than 1,200 percent. Revenue for the quarter ending

October 31, 1999 was up 56 percent to $126.5 million, and net income, excluding acquisition-related charges, rose 84 percent to $14.4 million. BEA reported that more than half of its licensing revenue for the quarter was tied to Internet projects. BEA also announced a two-for-one stock split and appointed cofounder Alfred Chuang as chief operating officer. Chuang had been devoting his time to sales efforts and the integration of WebLogic. Following the better-than-expected third quarter report, BEA's stock rose to around $82 a share, compared with less than $9 a share the previous November. The company had reported record revenues for 16 consecutive quarters.

BEA's longstanding business strategy was to develop leading component technology and tools to enable customers to quickly create and implement business applications. Its 120 engineers and support personnel gave it strong technical capability. At the end of 1999 BEA hosted a technology conference in San Francisco, attended by more than 1,000 executives. Testimonials of BEA's e-commerce platform were delivered by clients such as Hewlett-Packard Co. and Charles Schwab Corporation.

Before the year was over BEA announced a major restructuring into four e-commerce divisions: e-commerce software, e-commerce integration, e-commerce component applications, and e-commerce services. Each division head would hold the title of president and report to Chuang.

Toward the end of 1999 BEA acquired The Theory Center Inc., a Boston-based maker of Enterprise JavaBeans (EJB) components, for about $100 million in stock and cash. Its product JumpStart provided 75 percent of an Internet retail application, including order, shopping, and customer management. BEA, together with investment partner Warburg, Pincus Ventures, acquired Symantec Corp.'s Internet Tools Business Unit for $75 million. The acquisition gave BEA more Java technology and tools, including Visual Café for Java, and formed the basis of a new company BEA spun off in January 2000 called WebGain Inc. The new company was focused on developing and marketing a Java-based tool set for e-commerce applications.

BEA continued to add to its Java holdings with the acquisition of The Workflow Automation Corporation in March 2000. The company produced a Java workflow-management system that could integrate applications across the Internet. BEA planned to incorporate the technology into its business-to-business collaboration architecture and relaunch it as the BEA E-Process Integrator later in 2000.

Other acquisitions during the first half of 2000 included Softport Systems Inc., a systems integration firm based in New York City. BEA integrated Softport's 20 employees, who were highly skilled in Java-based e-commerce application development, into its e-commerce services division. BEA added another 70 consultants to its e-commerce services division with the acquisition of the consulting and education group of The Object People, which was based in Ottawa, Ontario, Canada. BEA also announced an alliance with Nokia Corporation to integrate WebLogic and the Nokia WAP Server to accelerate the development of wireless e-commerce solutions.

For the fiscal year ending January 31, 2000, BEA reported a 61 percent increase in revenue to $464.4 million. Operating income more than doubled to $51.4 million, and net income, excluding acquisition-related charges, doubled from $4 million to $8 million. One-time acquisition-related charges and other extraordinary items resulted in a net loss of $13.7 million for the year.

By redefining itself late in 1999 as "The E-Commerce Transactions Company," BEA achieved a high profile in the emerging e-business integration software category. BEA was proving itself a tough competitor in this evolving market, which analysts predicted would grow from $470 million into a multibillion-dollar sector over the next five years. With its eLink, Tuxedo, and WebLogic product lines and a strong service organization, BEA was capable of emerging as the top e-business integrator for companies racing to build web infrastructures.

Principal Subsidiaries

WebGain, Inc.; BEA Systems Europe Ltd. (England); BEA Systems Japan Ltd.

Principal Divisions

E-Commerce Software; E-Commerce Integration; E-Commerce Component Applications; E-Commerce Services.

Principal Competitors

IBM; Microsoft Corp.; Oracle Corp.; Iona Technologies PLC; Inprise Corp.; Bluestone Software Inc.; Secant Technologies Inc.; TSI Software Inc.; Lutris Technologies Inc.; Sun Microsystems Inc.; SilverStream Software Inc.

Further Reading

"BEA Buys Avitek to Bolster EJB Offerings," *InfoWorld,* August 16, 1999, p. 5.

"BEA Grabs Workflow," *Information Week,* March 27, 2000, p. 215.

"BEA Systems Gets Spiffy with Digital's Tuxedo," *PC Week,* March 3, 1997, p. 62.

"BEA to Spin Off Unit," *PC Week,* March 20, 2000, p. 33.

"BEA's Revenue Rises," *InformationWeek,* May 24, 1999, p. 173.

Carr, David F., "Market Narrows with BEA Purchase of WebLogic," *Internet World,* October 5, 1998, p. 1.

Copeland, Lee, "E-Commerce Strategy Pays Off for BEA," *Computerworld,* November 22, 1999, p. 25.

Cornetto, Jon, "BEA Buys Web App-Server Vendor," *InfoWorld,* October 5, 1998, p. 31.

"E-Commerce Growth Boosts Revenue for BEA Systems," *InformationWeek,* February 28, 2000, p. 129.

Gonsalves, Antone, "Acquisitions Bolster E-Com Apps," *PC Week,* December 20, 1999, p. 12.

——, "BEA Adds Java Flexibility to WebLogic Enterprise Server," *PC Week,* August 9, 1999, p. 29.

——, "BEA Continues E-Com Buying Spree," *PC Week,* August 16, 1999, p. 20.

——, "BEA Reorgs Around Web," *PC Week,* December 6, 1999, p. 1.

——, "BEA Takes Wing to New Course," *PC Week,* October 4, 1999, p. 31.

——, "HP Gets Busy with Web Plan," *PC Week,* April 19, 1999, p. 39.

Hoffman, Richard, "Java Application Servers Pass Real-World Test," *InformationWeek,* November 1, 1999, p. 62.

Howle, Amber, "BEA Continues Acquisition Streak, Forms Tool Company," *Computer Reseller News,* January 3, 2000, p. 31.

"HP in Pact with BEA Systems," *Computer Reseller News,* April 12, 1999, p. 6.

Karpinski, Richard, "BEA Systems Adds Java Layer to Transactions," *InternetWeek,* October 5, 1998, p. 8.

Krill, Paul, "Novell Rents Out Tuxedo Development," *InfoWorld,* February 5, 1996, p. 12.

LaMonica, Martin, "Giving Tuxedo Another Chance," *InfoWorld,* May 20, 1996, p. 35.

——, "Tuxedo to Get Facelift from New Owner," *InfoWorld,* April 8, 1996, p. 12.

Lattig, Michael, "Application Server Vendors Grow by Acquisition," *InfoWorld,* December 20, 1999, p. 24.

Leon, Mark, "BEA Will Deliver a Jolt to Tuxedo," *InfoWorld,* August 12, 1996, p. 41.

Liebmann, Lenny, "Web Development—App Servers Branch Out," *InternetWeek,* October 4, 1999, p. 57.

McHugh, Josh, "Old Software, New Money," *Forbes,* December 15, 1997, p. 248.

"The Middleware Zone," *Software Magazine,* April 1997, p. 22.

Montalbano, Elizabeth, "Java Evolution Spurs Wireless Web Apps," *Computer Reseller News,* May 1, 2000, p. 127.

Murphy, Chris, "Demand for E-Commerce Software Fuels BEA Systems," *InformationWeek,* November 22, 1999, p. 125.

"A New Home for Tuxedo," *Software Magazine,* April 1996, p. 12.

Ploskina, Brian, "BEA Systems Realigns to Focus on E-Commerce Transactions," *ENT,* January 12, 2000, p. 21.

——, "BEA to Acquire Theory Center's Beans," *ENT,* December 8, 1999, p. 30.

——, "Visual Café Acquired by Company to Be Named Later," *ENT,* January 12, 2000, p. 14.

Robbins, Mike, "How BEA Systems Broke the Momentum Barrier," *Money Central Investor,* July 10, 2000, http://moneycentral.msn.com/articles/invest/strat/5264.asp?ID=5264.

Robinson, Teri, "Think Big Picture," *InternetWeek,* July 5, 1999, p. 37.

Rodriguez, Karen, "BEA Set to Dominate E-Commerce Framework Business," *Business Journal,* December 3, 1999, p. 5.

Rooney, Paula, "BEA Systems: Ready for Its Close-Up," *Computer Reseller News,* June 12, 2000, p. 70.

Schaff, William, "The BEA-All of Middleware?," *InformationWeek,* August 24, 1998, p. 98.

——, "BEA Shifts Gears, Not Results," *InformationWeek,* November 29, 1999, p. 166.

Schulaka, Carly, "California Company Buys Boulder, Colo.-Based Software Firm," *Knight-Ridder/Tribune Business News,* August 11, 1999.

Schwartz, Jeffrey, "Tuxedo to Get Top End," *InternetWeek,* June 1, 1998, p. 11.

"A Successful Move to Middleware—William Coleman, BEA Systems Chairman and CEO," *InternetWeek,* June 29, 1998, p. 27.

Taylor, Dennis, and Lorna Fernandes, "BEA Systems Sees Its Stock Price Take Off," *Business Journal,* July 7, 1997, p. 3.

Turek, Norbert, "High-End Strategy Pays Off for BEA—Middleware Vendor Uses Acquisitions, Partnerships to Fuel Growth," *InformationWeek,* May 17, 1999, p. 94.

Vijayan, Jaikumar, "HP Drives Hard, Soft at Users," *Computerworld,* April 19, 1999, p. 20.

Vizard, Michael, and Jon Cornetto, "BEA Founders Bill Coleman, Ed Scott, and Alfred Chuang," *InfoWorld,* August 17, 1998, p. 25.

Wirthman, Lisa, "Electronic Commerce Jolted into Real Time," *PC Week,* August 12, 1996, p. 15.

—David P. Bianco

Becton, Dickinson & Company

One Becton Road
Franklin Lakes, New Jersey 07417-1880
U.S.A.
Telephone: (201) 847-6800
Toll Free: (800) 284-6845
Fax: (201) 847-6475
Web site: http://www.bd.com

Public Company
Incorporated: 1906
Employees: 24,000
Sales: $3.42 billion (1999)
Stock Exchanges: New York
Ticker Symbol: BDX
NAIC: 339112 Surgical and Medical Instrument
   Manufacturing; 339113 Surgical Appliance and
   Supplies Manufacturing; 334516 Analytical
   Laboratory Instrument Manufacturing; 326199 All
   Other Plastics Product Manufacturing; 541710
   Research and Development in the Physical,
   Engineering, and Life Sciences

Becton, Dickinson & Company manufactures and markets medical supplies and devices and diagnostic systems for use by healthcare professionals, medical research institutions, and the general public. The company's operations are arranged into three business segments: Medical Systems, Biosciences, and Preanalytical Solutions. The Medical Systems unit holds the number one market positions worldwide in hypodermic needles and syringes, insulin delivery syringes, I.V. catheters, and prefillable drug delivery systems. Products produced by the Biosciences unit include cellular analysis systems, infectious disease diagnostic kits and tests, and automated blood culturing systems. The Preanalytical Solutions unit focuses on products and services for the collection and management of specimens. With operations in the United States and numerous countries around the world, Becton, Dickinson derives nearly half of its revenue from its international business activities.

First 50 Years: Steady, Conservative Growth

The company was founded in 1897 by two salesmen, Maxwell W. Becton and Fairleigh S. Dickinson, as a partnership first to sell medical thermometers and syringes (imported from Europe) and then to manufacture them. Expansion into new product lines in the early years came via acquisitions. In 1904 the partnership acquired Philadelphia Surgical Company and Wigmore Company, both of which were makers of surgical, dental, and veterinary instruments. The manufacture of medical bags was added the following year through the purchase of Comstock Bag Company. One year later, Becton, Dickinson & Company was incorporated in the state of New Jersey and built a manufacturing plant in East Rutherford, New Jersey, for the production of thermometers, syringes, and hypodermic needles.

Even with the company's new plant, Becton, Dickinson continued to rely on European suppliers for some of the products it sold, mainly because of the higher quality of the imports versus those made domestically. Along these lines, the acquisition of New York-based Surgical Supply Import Company in 1913 was completed to gain the company's network of high-quality foreign suppliers. The purchase also helped broaden Becton, Dickinson's product line through such Surgical Supply products as the Asepto bulb syringe.

During World War I, Becton, Dickinson's import supplies were, in large part, cut off, propelling the company deeper into manufacturing its own products. In the midst of the war, the president of Surgical Supply, Oscar O.R. Schwidetzky, who stayed with Becton, Dickinson following the acquisition, developed a new American-made cotton elastic bandage. In 1918 the company conducted a contest among physicians to name the new bandage, out of which emerged the ACE bandage, "ACE" being an acronym for "All Cotton Elastic." Meantime, the slow but steady growth of Becton, Dickinson was evidenced by the company reaching the milestone of $1 million in sales in 1917, two decades after the founding.

Throughout the early decades, the family-run business built a reputation as a maker and marketer of products superior to those of its competitors. Through its product development—and acquisitions—the company kept pace with the latest advances in medical technology and standards. Such was the case with the 1921 purchase of Physicians Specialty Company, which was headed by Andrew W. "Doc" Fleischer, who like Schwidetzky took a position with Becton, Dickinson following the merger. Fleischer had developed the mercurial sphygmomanometer (an instrument for measuring blood pressure) as well as the binaural stethoscope. In 1924 Becton, Dickinson began making syringes designed specifically for insulin injection, marking the company's first foray into the diabetes care sector. The following year Fairleigh Dickinson received a patent for the Luer-Lok tip, a locking collar that more securely attached a hypodermic needle to a syringe, thereby making injections safer, less painful, and more accurate.

Through the difficult years of the Great Depression, the company's workers retained their jobs by agreeing to a series of voluntary pay cuts. A key development in the World War II years came in 1943 with the acquisition of Multifit, which had been founded by Joseph J. Kleiner eight years earlier. Kleiner had developed a syringe system with interchangeable barrels and plungers. Kleiner's product had a number of advantages, including reduced labor costs, reduced breakage because it was made from a very strong kind of glass, and enhanced convenience for its users. Kleiner also brought to Becton, Dickinson another key concept he was developing called the Evacutainer. Patented in 1949, the Evacutainer used a vacuum system, a needle, and a test tube to draw blood from patients. The device was later renamed the Vacutainer tube, and marked Becton, Dickinson's entry into the burgeoning field of diagnostic medicine. Also in 1949 the company's first manufacturing facility located outside New Jersey was established in Columbus, Nebraska. Overall revenues reached $16 million by 1950.

Postwar Expansion into a Fortune 500 Company

Throughout its first 50 years Becton, Dickinson was a conservatively managed, family-run business. The enterprise entered the affluent postwar years with a solid market share in medical supplies and was well prepared for a major expansion. The company recognized that its traditional approach to business would not be appropriate for the future. Therefore, in 1948, the sons of the founders, Henry P. Becton and Fairleigh Dickinson, Jr.—both astute businessmen—assumed managerial control of the company.

With Dickinson as chief executive officer and Becton serving in a variety of other capacities during the 1950s, Becton, Dickinson gradually expanded its product line. By 1964, more

than 8,000 products were being manufactured by Becton, Dickinson, including a broad line of medical supplies of superior diagnostic accuracy. The company divided its business into four operating divisions—medical health, laboratory, animal research and testing, and overseas sales. In the course of an acquisition program, Becton, Dickinson purchased Carworth Inc., the leading producer of laboratory mice; Canton, Ohio-based Wilson Rubber Company, maker of rubber gloves for surgical, industrial, and household use (acquired in 1954); the Bard-Parker Company, manufacturer of surgical blades and scalpels (1956); and several specialized research laboratories. Increasingly, Becton, Dickinson's strongest growth was experienced in the market for disposable items, with the company becoming a leader in this burgeoning area. The 1955 acquisition of Baltimore Biological Laboratories (BBL) was particularly important in this regard as BBL was already making sterile, one-use blood donor kits for the American Red Cross (with Becton, Dickinson acting as distributor). By 1964, such products as disposable syringes and needles accounted for 60 percent of the company's $70 million in sales.

The new management team also was noted for its attention to international expansion. The first such move came in 1951 with the acquisition of the company's Canadian distributor to create Becton Dickinson Canada, Ltd., its first wholly owned subsidiary and foreign operation. The following year Becton, Dickinson acquired the Mexican firm MAPAD S.A. de C.V., maker of syringes, needles, and clinical thermometers, and established a manufacturing plant in Le Pont-de-Claix, France. The Brazilian market was next on the expansion list and Becton, Dickinson began supplying syringes in that country in 1956 and eventually became the number one medical supply company there. In 1963 Becton, Dickinson constructed a disposable syringe plant in Drogheda, Ireland.

The company's need for massive amounts of funding to pay for the conversion from reusable products to sterile disposable products led to a 1962 initial public offering of stock at $25 per share. The following year Becton, Dickinson stock began trading on the New York Stock Exchange. By 1966 the company's rapid rate of growth had landed it on the *Fortune* 500 list for the first time.

Early 1970s: New FDA Regulation and New Management

During the 1970s, Becton, Dickinson continued to make gains in the medical supplies business, despite increasingly difficult market conditions. The world oil crisis of 1973–74 caused a reduction in petrochemical feedstocks, which, in turn, made medical raw materials difficult to obtain. In addition, the Food and Drug Administration (FDA) planned to adopt the same strict certification standards for diagnostic equipment as it had applied to pharmaceuticals. This would delay the commercial introduction of new products and, with technological advances, expose them to higher rates of obsolescence. Although these conditions lessened Wall Street's interest in companies in the medical industry, Becton, Dickinson remained highly optimistic. With sales figures doubling every five years and with 19 percent of all sales derived overseas, Dickinson declared to shareholders that the company did not fear the impending

Key Dates:

1897: Maxwell W. Becton and Fairleigh S. Dickinson form partnership.

1904: Philadelphia Surgical Company and Wigmore Company are acquired.

1906: Partnership is incorporated as Becton, Dickinson & Company; factory is built in East Rutherford, New Jersey.

1913: Surgical Supply Import Company is acquired.

1917: Sales reach $1 million.

1918: Company introduces the ACE bandage.

1921: Company acquires Physicians Specialty Company.

1924: Company begins making syringes designed specifically for insulin injection.

1925: Fairleigh Dickinson receives a patent for the Luer-Lok tip.

1943: Multifit, maker of a syringe with interchangeable parts, is acquired.

1948: Henry P. Becton and Fairleigh Dickinson, Jr., sons of the founders, assume managerial control of the company.

1949: Entry into diagnostic medicine with the patenting of the Evacutainer blood collection device.

1951: International expansion begins with the formation of a Canadian subsidiary.

1955: Baltimore Biological Laboratories is acquired, enlarging the firm's presence in the burgeoning market for disposable medical products.

1962: Company goes public.

1974: Wesley J. Howe is named president and CEO.

1978: Sun Oil Company acquires a 34 percent stake in the company.

1979: Becton, Dickinson and Sun reach agreement on the eventual disposal of Sun's stake.

1980s: Restructuring and disposal of noncore operations.

1989: Raymond V. Gilmartin is named CEO.

1994: Clateo Castellini is named chairman, CEO, and president.

1997: PharMingen Inc. and Difco Laboratories Incorporated are acquired.

1998: The Medical Devices Division of the BOC Group is acquired.

1999: Company reorganizes its operations into three business segments: BD Medical Systems, BD Biosciences, and BD Preanalytical Solutions; company launches a global brand strategy focusing on the "BD" name.

device regulation, but instead was helping the FDA to formulate its new regulations.

When the FDA's Medical Device Act was enacted, Becton, Dickinson found, to some dismay, that 85 percent of its products were subject to the new regulation. Wesley J. Howe, who succeeded Dickinson as president and chief executive officer in 1974, was confident that the company's products would be able to meet all the new FDA requirements; to be sure, he hired a team of legal and technical experts to guarantee standardization.

Despite growing regulation, the early years of Howe's direction were marked by a continuity of policies; Howe was hand-picked by Dickinson and dedicated to the same conservative style of management. To increase efficiency, Howe automated and integrated more of the company's facilities and reduced his staff by 13 percent. To increase his influence, he also replaced 14 of the company's 17 division presidents.

Howe's leadership was proving highly effective. In one area, Becton, Dickinson's marketing approach was particularly effective: targeting insulin users through doctors, diabetes associations, camps, pharmacies, and pharmacy schools. With control of almost 100 percent of the insulin syringe market, Becton, Dickinson saw its sales increase to $456 million in 1975.

Late 1970s: Boardroom Intrigue and Takeover Bids

This success, however, was greatly compromised in the boardroom by Fairleigh Dickinson, who, despite having relinquished his posts voluntarily, continued to demand managerial control. At the heart of the matter was a conflict between family members determined to maintain control and board members who favored control by a more professional corporate elite. Although Howe remained above this conflict, several other important managers did not; ultimately, Dickinson would order Howe to fire them. In 1977, four board members resigned. With morale an increasingly serious problem, Howe asserted his position. Four new, "unprejudiced" board members were named to the board and Dickinson was relegated to the ceremonial post of chairman. But the power struggle was not over.

Dickinson was asked to approach the Salomon Brothers investment banking firm and initiate a study on a company Howe wanted Becton, Dickinson to acquire. When completed, the study warned of numerous problems with the takeover. Howe maintained that Dickinson had sabotaged the study and, when the situation proved unresolvable, ordered Dickinson removed from the payroll.

Dickinson then resorted to another strategy. With 4.5 percent of the company's stock, Dickinson authorized Salomon Brothers to line up additional investors to lead a takeover of Becton, Dickinson. A Salomon agent named Kenneth Lipper approached several companies, including Avon, American Home Products, Monsanto, and Squibb, in an effort to set up a takeover. Becton, Dickinson's attorneys warned Lipper that his action was illegal. Rather than call off the search for buyers, Lipper challenged the attorneys to stop him in court—cognizant that a well-publicized court battle would only gain more attention for his cause.

On January 16, 1978, before Lipper could be stopped, Becton, Dickinson learned that the Philadelphia-based Sun Oil Company had acquired 34 percent of its stock. The transaction lasted only 15 minutes and involved 6.5 million shares at a purchase price of $45 each—well above the trading price of $33. Sun created a special subsidiary called LHIW (for "Let's Hope It Works") to manage the shares until a controlling majority of shares could be acquired.

The takeover had severe consequences. Like Becton, Dickinson, Sun had just emerged from an important battle against founding family interests. H. Robert Sharbaugh, CEO of Sun, came into strong disagreement over the takeover with the founding Pew family and was eventually forced out of the company. Becton, Dickinson, in the meantime, learned that Sun's purchase had been conducted off the trading floor, in violation of numerous laws. Finally, three Becton, Dickinson shareholders sued Fairleigh Dickinson, complaining that they had been excluded from Sun's tender offer.

The New York Stock Exchange refused to file charges against Salomon and instead turned the matter over to the Securities and Exchange Commission (SEC). At this point, Sun decided to dispose of its interest in Becton, Dickinson and offered to indemnify Salomon against any liabilities resulting from court action. The legality of the takeover was no longer in question. Instead, the question concerned the manner in which Sun should dispose of its Becton, Dickinson shares. With Sun no longer in pursuit of Becton, Dickinson, the only clear beneficiaries of the takeover were the lawyers left to pick up the pieces.

Ironically, Sun and Becton, Dickinson had a common interest in the divestiture. If the 34 percent share were placed on the market in one parcel, share prices would plummet and Sun would lose millions. Becton, Dickinson, on the other hand, opposed summary disposal because large blocks of its shares could fall under the control of still other hostile acquisitors. An agreement was finally reached in December 1979, under which Sun would distribute a 25-year debenture convertible into Becton, Dickinson shares. The unprecedented agreement ensured both a gradual spinoff of Becton, Dickinson shares and the maintenance of stable share prices. Although the agreement was said to have cost Sun extremely large sums of money, Sun was satisfied with the arrangement.

Fairleigh Dickinson continued to seek injunctive relief from the SEC and remained under attack from Becton, Dickinson shareholders demanding the return of the $15 million profit from the original Sun tender offer. Sun's board at this time was nervously awaiting the response of its shareholders to the costly defense of Salomon Brothers. Around this time, American Home Products made a brief and uncharacteristic hostile bid for 2.5 percent of Becton, Dickinson—by comparison with Sun, a minor incident. Ironically, Sun's debenture scheme prevented any company from gaining greater control of Becton, Dickinson.

1980s: Restructuring and a Refocusing on the Core

The first order of business after this debacle, according to Howe, was to position Becton, Dickinson for future growth. With company profits rising, Howe arranged to reinvest cash on hand into new projects. He reorganized the company into 42 units so that each division's performance could be more accurately scrutinized. Unprofitable operations, such as a computer parts manufacturer, were either sold or closed down. Older products were reassessed and, in some cases, improved; for instance, insulin syringes were redesigned for more accurate dosages. Foreign sales were stepped up, and, despite a negative effect on earnings, an expansion of the product line was carried out. Whereas some new products were added by takeovers, others, such as the balloon catheter, were developed internally.

The expansion had been justified to ensure future viability, but by 1983 bad investments had cost the company $75 mil-

lion—$23 million alone from a failed immunoassay instrument division. Bad planning caused production stoppages and cost overruns. Howe then came under criticism for failing to invest heavily enough in research and development. With remedial measures in place, the company's financial condition had improved greatly by 1985. That year the company declared an $88 million profit on sales of $1.44 billion. Much of this turnaround, however, came from nonoperating profits resulting from the sale of unprofitable divisions and a reduction in overhead. Howe instituted a new strategy involving slower growth rates and raised productivity. To balance this more modest business plan, Howe allocated a 5.1 percent share of revenue to research and development, particularly for more cost-effective new products, and purchased a 12 percent share of a company that manufactured equipment for synthesizing DNA.

In the late 1980s, Becton faced increased competition on the domestic front, but continued to maintain its estimated 70 percent to 80 percent share of the needle and syringe market. This period also was marked by the company's move into a new corporate headquarters in Franklin Lakes, New Jersey, and a transition in leadership. In 1987 Raymond V. Gilmartin was named president of the company, then added the CEO title in 1989, with Howe remaining chairman. Gilmartin had joined Becton, Dickinson in 1976 as vice-president of corporate planning.

1990s: International Expansion and Acquisitions

Sales increased from $1.71 billion in 1988 to $2.47 billion in 1993 as Becton, Dickinson moved into many new global markets and accelerated new proprietary product introductions. The firm focused expansion efforts on Latin America, the Asia-Pacific region, and Europe. By 1993, international sales contributed 44 percent of annual sales. Howe, who was credited by Robert Teitelman of *Financial World* with reenergizing Becton, Dickinson, retired that year and was supplanted as chairman by Gilmartin.

Becton, Dickinson introduced new drug delivery and blood handling products in the early 1990s that helped reduce healthcare workers' exposure to acquired immune deficiency syndrome (AIDS) and hepatitis. Some of the company's newest diagnostic tests helped researchers and physicians determine when to begin drug therapy for cancer and AIDS patients. In 1993 the firm moved its PRECISE brand pregnancy test from the professional to the over-the-counter market. Becton, Dickinson's investment of 5.6 percent of its 1993 revenues represented a continuing accent on new product introductions.

As criticism of high healthcare costs accelerated in the early 1990s, the wisdom of Howe's shift to more cost-effective new product introductions became evident. Becton, Dickinson positioned its diagnostic tests as accurate, fast ways to reduce healthcare costs by speeding diagnosis and treatment.

In mid-1994 Gilmartin left the company to take the top position at pharmaceutical giant Merck & Co., Inc. Tapped as his successor was Clateo Castellini, who was head of the company's medical unit and had joined Becton, Dickinson in 1978.

Under Castellini, who was born in Italy and had extensive international experience, the company actively expanded its overseas operations in the middle to late 1990s. Despite the economic turmoil in the region during much of this period, the Asia-Pacific region was the object of much of this growth. In 1995 the company entered into a joint venture in China to produce medical products for the Chinese and other markets. That same year Becton, Dickinson set up a subsidiary in India to construct a manufacturing plant. When it finally opened in 1999, it boasted an annual capacity of more than one billion disposable needles and syringes, making it one of the largest facilities of its kind in Asia. In 1998 Becton Dickinson acquired Boin Medica Co., Ltd., the largest medical supply company in South Korea. The company also began expanding in Latin America, outside of its two strongholds, Mexico and Brazil.

Flush with annual free cash flow of $350 million, Becton, Dickinson earmarked some of the money to buy back shares of its stock to improve earnings per share. The company also made a number of acquisitions, particularly in the late 1990s—a period of consolidation in healthcare across the board, from hospitals to insurance providers to pharmaceutical firms to medical product makers. In 1997 Becton, Dickinson spent $217.4 million on two major acquisitions: PharMingen Inc., a privately held maker of reagents for biomedical research with annual revenues of $30 million; and Difco Laboratories Incorporated, a manufacturer of media and supplies for microbiology labs with sales of $82 million. Six more acquisitions were completed in 1998, the most significant of which was the purchase of the Medical Devices Division of the BOC Group for about $457 million. Among the ten purchases completed in 1999 were Clontech Laboratories, Inc., maker of genetic tests; Biometric Imaging Inc., producer of cell analysis systems for clinical applications; and Transduction Laboratories, manufacturer of reagents for cell biology research.

In the late 1990s Becton, Dickinson was troubled by a spate of lawsuits arising from healthcare workers who had contracted blood-borne diseases using the company's conventional, unguarded needles and syringes. The suits alleged that safer needles had been available for years but Becton, Dickinson had not been promoting their use. For its part, the company said that it had invested more than $100 million into development of safer products, which were available for its customers to purchase, but it was up to the hospitals and medical centers to make the conversion. By decade's end, a shift to safer needles was clearly underway, in part due to government mandates at the state level.

During 1999 Edward J. Ludwig became president and CEO of Becton, Dickinson, with Castellini remaining chairman. The financial results for that year were a disappointment, stemming from weaker-than-expected sales in Europe and emerging markets and from an ailing home healthcare unit, which made such items as ear thermometers and blood pressure monitors. A restructuring was launched in the second half of the year that included the company's exit from the home healthcare sector. In addition, the company reorganized its remaining operations into three business segments: BD Medical Systems, BD Biosciences, and BD Preanalytical Solutions. Becton, Dickinson also began implementing a global brand strategy in which the "BD" name would appear on all of the company's products, either alone or alongside such well-known brands as ACE, Vacutainer, and Tru-Fit. Becton, Dickinson ambitiously aimed to have its new "BD" logo "become as universally recognized

worldwide as the Red Cross." Becton, Dickinson thus headed into the new century with a new identity, a new structure, and a commitment to achieving a quick turnaround during what was certain to be an even more competitive period for medical device companies.

Principal Subsidiaries

BDX INO LLC; Becton Dickinson AcuteCare Holdings, Inc.; Becton Dickinson Asia Pacific Limited (British Virgin Islands); Becton Dickinson B.V. (Netherlands); Becton Dickinson Caribe, Ltd. (Cayman Islands); Becton Dickinson Infusion Therapy Holdings Inc.; Becton Dickinson Infusion Therapy Systems Inc.; Becton Dickinson Korea, Inc.; Becton Dickinson Korea Holding, Inc.; Becton Dickinson Malaysia, Inc.; Becton Dickinson (Mauritius) Limited; Becton Dickinson Medical Devices Co. Ltd., Suzhou (China; 99%); Becton Dickinson Medical Products Pte. Ltd. (Singapore); Becton Dickinson Monoclonal Center, Inc.; Becton Dickinson Overseas Services Ltd.; Becton Dickinson Pen Limited (Ireland); Becton Dickinson Service (Pvt.) Ltd. (Pakistan; 51%); Becton Dickinson Venture LLC; Becton, Dickinson and Company, Ltd. (Ireland); Becton, Dickinson B.V. (Netherlands); Becton Dickinson France, S.A.; Benex Ltd. (Ireland); Biometric Imaging, Inc.; Clontech Laboratories, Inc.; Critical Device Corporation; Collaborative Biomedical Products, Inc.; Difco Laboratories Incorporated; Franklin Lakes Enterprises, L.L.C.; IBD Holdings LLC (50%); Johnston Laboratories, Inc.; MDI Instruments, Inc.; Med-Safe Systems, Inc.; PharMingen; Saf-T-Med Inc.; Staged Diabetes Management L.L.C. (50%).

Principal Operating Units

BD Medical Systems; BD Biosciences; BD Preanalytical Solutions.

Principal Competitors

Abbott Laboratories; ALZA Corporation; American Home Products Corporation; Ballard Medical Products; Baxter International Inc.; Boston Scientific Corporation; Bristol-Myers Squibb Company; C.R. Bard, Inc.; Diagnostic Products Corporation; Isolyser Company, Inc.; Johnson & Johnson; Mallinckrodt Inc.; Maxxim Medical, Inc.; McKesson General Medical; Medical Action Industries Inc.; Medline Industries, Inc.; Novo Nordisk A/S; Pfizer Inc; Teleflex Corporation; Trinity Biotech Plc; United States Surgical Corporation; Vital Signs, Inc.

Further Reading

"Becton Dickinson Buys PharMingen," *Newark (N.J.) Star-Ledger,* April 13, 1997.

"Becton Dickinson Facelift Unveils New Direction, New Logo," *Health Industry Today,* October 1999, pp. 1, 12.

"Clateo Catellini on Growing a 100-Year-Old Medical-Products Firm in the 1990s," *Business News New Jersey,* March 17, 1997, p. 13.

Middleton, Timothy, "A Shot in the Arm," *Chief Executive,* June 1997, p. 22.

Mosk, Matthew, "Fear of Needles: Care-Givers Demand Safer Hypodermics," *Northern New Jersey Record,* December 10, 1998, p. A1.

Osterland, Andrew, "Becton Dickinson: Time to Check Out," *Financial World,* February 14, 1995, pp. 20+.

Phalon, Richard, *The Takeover Barons of Wall Street: Inside the Billion-Dollar Merger Game,* New York: Putnam, 1981.

——, "Time of Troubles," *Forbes,* September 26, 1983, pp. 80+.

Shook, David, "Becton, Dickinson, Rival in Sharp Exchange," *Northern New Jersey Record,* February 13, 2000, p. B1.

——, "Booster for Becton, Dickinson: Future Looking Sharp," *Northern New Jersey Record,* December 16, 1999, p. B1.

Taylor, Iris, "Becton, Dickinson Chief to Take Merck Helm," *Newark (N.J.) Star-Ledger,* June 10, 1994.

Teitelman, Robert, "The Devil and the Deep Blue Sea," *Financial World,* June 14, 1988, pp. 30–31.

Tergesen, Anne E., "Team Player: Merck's Gilmartin Is a Regular Guy," *Northern New Jersey Record,* August 14, 1994, p. B1.

Troxell, Thomas N., Jr., "Fighting Back: Clobbered Last Year, Becton, Dickinson Comes Off the Mat," *Barron's,* September 24, 1984, pp. 53+.

——, "Staying Healthy: Becton, Dickinson Bucks the Trend in Health Care, Sees Profits Grow," *Barron's,* December 9, 1985, pp. 60+.

—April Dougal Gasbarre
—updated by David E. Salamie

Biogen Inc.

14 Cambridge Center
Cambridge, Massachusetts 02142
U.S.A.
Telephone: (617) 679-9200
Fax: (617) 679-2617
Web site: http://www.biogen.com

Public Company
Incorporated: 1978
Employees: 1,351
Sales: $794.4 million (1999)
Stock Exchanges: NASDAQ
Ticker Symbol: BGEN
NAIC: 325412 Pharmaceutical Preparation Manufacturing;
    325413 In-Vitro Diagnostic Substance Manufacturing;
    541710 Research and Development in the Physical,
    Engineering, and Life Sciences

Biogen Inc. develops, manufactures, and markets drugs for human healthcare through genetic engineering. Its top product is Avonex, which is used in the treatment of multiple sclerosis. A pioneer and key player in the dynamic and volatile biotechnology industry, Biogen has distinguished itself as one of the few biotech companies to remain independent and to achieve profitability. With annual research and development expenditures of $300 million as it entered the 21st century, Biogen had a number of drugs in its development pipeline.

Birth of a Biotech Pioneer

Biogen is considered one of the pioneers of the biotechnology industry. It got its start in 1978 when Walter H. Gilbert, a Nobel prize-winning biologist who was teaching at Harvard at the time, decided to try developing his research into marketable products. Biotechnology, as it was known in the mid-1970s, was still in its infancy. The discovery of the structure of DNA, which led to the understanding of the process by which proteins are produced by cells, had occurred in 1953. But it was not until the early 1970s that more rapid progress ensued. Significantly, in 1973 two U.S. scientists discovered the process of recombi-

nant DNA, whereby a piece of DNA is snipped from one gene and spliced into another gene. The significance of that discovery was that it proved that scientists could genetically alter microorganisms and, particularly important, produce mass amounts of proteins that naturally occurred only in small quantities.

Walter Gilbert had been a major contributor to the development of recombinant DNA technology during the 1970s, and he had earned his Nobel prize as a result of his research in that area. Subsequent related breakthroughs during the middle and late 1970s indicated that scientists would eventually be able to use gene-splicing and cloning techniques to create various "wonder" drugs and products that could, among other benefits, cure cancer and many other diseases or create perfect produce and livestock with fantastic characteristics. Despite the promise of the technology, a recognizable industry that could develop such drugs and take them to market was slow to form. Before 1980, in fact, only a few significant biotech start-ups had appeared: Cetus (founded in 1971); Genentech (1976); Genex (1977); Biogen (1978); Centocor (1979); and Amgen (1980).

Biogen, like its biotech peers, was able to capitalize on the belief of some investors during the late 1970s that biotechnology was going to radically impact many areas of industry, medicine, food, energy, and agriculture. Although Biogen and some other companies made significant contributions to the burgeoning field of biotech, it was not until the 1980s that the industry boomed. The growth was in large part the result of a U.S. Supreme Court ruling that genetically engineered bacterium could be patented. For many, that ruling suggested the possibility of unimaginable wealth for biotech innovators. As a result, millions of dollars poured into the industry, primarily through venture capital but also through the sale of publicly traded stock. Companies that showed promise, such as Biogen, benefited the most.

Biogen launched a number of research initiatives during the late 1970s and early 1980s related to a variety of healthcare drugs. Some efforts fizzled, but, unlike many other biotech start-ups, Biogen eventually succeeded in generating some marketable products. The two biggest winners were a hepatitis B vaccine and alpha interferon. The hepatitis B vaccine was, as its name implies, a vaccine for hepatitis B, a blood-borne disease that causes a serious infection of the liver and substantially increases the risk of liver cancer; more than 250 million people worldwide still suffered from chronic hepatitis B virus infections in the early 1990s. Biogen eventually obtained patents in several countries related to its hepatitis B antigens produced by genetic engineering techniques, and the drug—marketed by SmithKline Beecham plc and Merck & Co., Inc.—became a big seller. In many countries, in fact, infants were commonly vaccinated against hepatitis B using Biogen's drug.

Alpha interferon was an even bigger source of revenue for Biogen. Alpha interferon is a naturally occurring protein produced by normal white blood cells. Biogen developed and patented a process of producing vast amounts of the protein using recombinant DNA techniques. Its alpha interferon compound became the first genetically engineered drug to receive market approval in the United States. Biogen's alpha interferon, also known as Intron A, was eventually being sold by licensee Schering-Plough Corporation in more than 60 countries to treat a variety of conditions including hepatitis B, hepatitis C, genital warts, Kaposi's sarcoma (an AIDS-related cancer), and hairy-cell leukemia.

1980s: Near Bankruptcy, Then Recovery

Biogen racked up major points in the research and development game during the early 1980s, and positive press brought tens of millions of dollars into its coffers. Like most biotechnology companies, though, Biogen was burning through the cash as fast, or faster, than it poured in (the company went public in 1983). CEO Gilbert, in his quest for new genetically engineered drugs, established a global research and development network during the early 1980s that sported operations in Zurich, Geneva, Belgium, Germany, and the United States. Although impressive and sometimes effective, the organization eventually became unwieldy and lacked focus. Some critics charged that despite his scientific prowess, Gilbert lacked business skills. The company was a great place to do research, but it had yet to show a profit. By 1984, in fact, Biogen had racked up a stunning $100 million in losses and was teetering on the edge of bankruptcy.

Gilbert managed to keep Biogen afloat during the early 1980s by licensing other companies to manufacture, market, and distribute its drugs. To make ends meet, he also started selling Biogen's patents. Some criticized the move as representing a sellout of the company's technological achievements; Biogen's original goal, in fact, had been both to develop and manufacture its inventions. Instead, the company had essentially become a research boutique that supplied drug companies

in Europe, Japan, and the United States with technology. In the end, however, Gilbert's licensing and selling was credited with saving the company from total bankruptcy. Indeed, many of Biogen's scientifically savvy biotech start-up peers were effectively forced out of business—often through merger or acquisition—because of financial difficulties.

By 1985 Biogen was using an estimated $100,000 each day in research costs. Furthermore, royalty revenues had slid to less than $20 million annually because the company had sold some of its patents. Biogen investors were fed up; the company's directors had already, in fact, pulled Gilbert from the chief executive slot and had been searching for a replacement for more than a year. Finally, in 1985, they hired James L. Vincent. Vincent graduated from Duke University, where he had been recruited to play football but did not because of a neck injury. He earned his M.B.A. at Wharton before joining Bell Telephone Company of Pennsylvania. From there he served in various positions including president of Texas Instruments-Asia, chief operating officer at Abbott Laboratories, and president of Allied Health and Scientific Products Company. He was known as a hard-charging, imposing, and capable manager.

Biogen began a radical restructuring and turnaround under Vincent's command. Soon after arriving at Biogen, Vincent sold or closed the European operations and brought in some new managers. Significantly, he also began working to recover some of the patents that the company had sold off during the early 1980s. By the time Vincent arrived, in fact, Biogen had sold off nearly 90 percent of its patents. Vincent succeeded in negotiating with companies to get or buy back most of those patents. By 1989 Biogen had regained control of 90 percent of all of its original patents. As Vincent got back the rights to the company's technology, he started licensing them to other manufacturers. The result was that the company's royalty revenues increased and Biogen's balance sheet gradually began to move back toward solvency.

The impact of Vincent's efforts was slow to materialize. Biogen lost more than $70 million between 1985 and 1988, and gross revenues actually plummeted to a low of about $8.5 million in 1987 after net income dipped to a $28 million deficit in 1986. But Biogen started to spring back in the late 1980s. Sales reached $28.5 million in 1989, and the company posted its first-ever profit—a $3.2 million surplus. Revenues surpassed $50 million in 1990 and then hit $61 million in 1991, by which time the company was generating net income of more than $7 million annually. That growth was in part attributable to new additions to Biogen's product line. By 1991 the company was selling through licensees several different drugs that were generating global sales of about $600 million annually: Intron A Alpha Interferon, Hepatitis B vaccine, Hepatitis B diagnostics, and Gamma Interferon (used to treat renal cell carcinoma).

1990s and Beyond: Moving from Licensor to Manufacturer and Marketer

Biogen benefited in 1992 from heady gains in sales of several of its drugs, particularly alpha interferon. The company stunned analysts, in fact, by reporting revenues of $123.8 million for the year and an increase of more than 500 percent in its net income to $38.3 million. The company expected those gains to continue in the near future. Furthermore, Biogen had several new products in its research and development pipeline that had the potential to add big sums to its bottom line. The most promising of its drugs going into the mid-1990s was Hirulog, a blood thinner derived from leeches. Hirulog, which acted as a direct inhibitor of Thrombin (the main enzyme that coagulates blood), was designed to provide immediate relief to people with severe and sudden chest pains, and to prevent clotting complications after veins were opened up through balloon angioplasty or coronary bypass surgery. Biogen had invested heavily in Hirulog and was trying to gain Food and Drug Administration (FDA) approval to market it.

The Hirulog project represented Biogen's drive to become a manufacturer and marketer, rather than just a developer and licensor, of drugs. Simultaneously, Biogen was seeking approval for a drug that it had developed and wanted to manufacture called interferon beta-1a (the trade name of which was Avonex), designed as a treatment for relapsing multiple sclerosis. Both drugs were in the final stages of clinical testing in mid-1994. If approved, they would usher Biogen into a new era as a full-fledged pharmaceutical company that developed and sold its own drugs and products. Moreover, Vincent had been beefing up Biogen's management and sales force to prepare for their approval. To that end, in January 1994 he had conducted a major coup by recruiting James R. Tobin to Biogen's management ranks to serve in the newly created position of president and chief operating officer.

The 49-year-old Tobin had previously spent 21 years at pharmaceutical giant Baxter International Inc., where he rose from a financial analyst to president of the company. Tobin received his master's degree from Harvard Business School before joining Baxter. He was apparently being groomed to assume the chief executive position at Baxter when he decided that he was looking for a different kind of challenge. Tobin was considered a heavy hitter in the pharmaceutical industry, and his move to Biogen

gave that company a new respect in the industry. Tobin's job at Biogen would be to shepherd the company from a licensor to a manufacturer and marketer of drugs. Shortly before he arrived, Biogen posted record revenues of $136.5 million for the year and net income of about $32.5 million.

Biogen entered 1994 with high hopes. Its dreams were temporarily stalled, however, by a string of setbacks. In the fall of 1994, Biogen announced that it was discontinuing its efforts to bring Hirulog to market because of disappointing test results. That news was greeted by shareholder lawsuits alleging securities violations for stopping work on the drug. Then, early in January 1995, news came that German pharmaceutical giant Schering AG (since World War II, not affiliated with Schering-Plough) announced plans to produce interferon beta-1a, Biogen's other breakthrough drug, using the same method as Biogen. Biogen, however, maintained that it had access to all patents necessary to market Avonex interferon beta-1a. Nevertheless, the news sent Biogen's stock price tumbling $7 to $35.37, which was down from a high of $55.75 before the Hirulog setback.

In large part because of writeoffs related to Hirulog, Biogen posted a net loss of $4.9 million from revenues of $156.34 million. The company's problems were exacerbated early in 1995 when pricing changes in Japan of the alpha interferon that Biogen developed and licensed to Schering-Plough Corp. contributed to a significant reduction in first-quarter profits. However, that news only marginally affected the company's stock price, as Biogen's balance sheet easily withstood the hit. Indeed, Biogen's gains during the early 1990s had put it in excellent financial shape. The company entered the mid-1990s cash-rich and among the healthiest biotechnology companies in the country. It was still generating revenues from licensing its marketable drugs, and some of those products were positioned well to benefit from market changes. It also had a number of promising products in development, although they had not yet progressed past the clinical, or final, stage of premarket testing.

In May 1996, in a key event in the company's history, Biogen announced that the FDA had unanimously approved Biogen's Avonex interferon beta-1a drug for treating relapsing forms of multiple sclerosis. Studies had found that Avonex was, in the words of Biogen CEO Vincent, "the first and only drug to show in a blinded clinical trial that it slows the progression of [MS] disability as well as reduces the frequency of exacerbations." Thanks to 18 months of planning following the preliminary FDA approval, Biogen began marketing Avonex in the United States within 35 hours of final FDA approval. A successful launch was jeopardized, however, by a lawsuit filed by Schering AG, which had begun selling its beta interferon drug in the United States in 1995 under the name Betaseron. When approving it in 1993, the FDA had given Schering rights to exclusivity vis-à-vis Betaseron under the federal Orphan Drug Act (so-called "orphan drug status"); in an unprecedented move three years later, however, the agency gave parallel orphan drug status to Avonex because of the latter's method of injection, which reduced skin side effects. Schering sued the FDA, but in October 1996 a federal judge dismissed the suit, agreeing with the FDA that Avonex was "clinically superior" to Betaseron and, therefore, deserving of parallel protection, as stipulated in the Orphan Drug Act. By late 1996 Avonex was outselling Betaseron in the United States, with more than 60 percent of new prescriptions being written for the Biogen treatment.

The launch of Avonex helped increase sales at Biogen from $134.7 million in 1995 to $259.7 million in 1996, an increase of nearly 93 percent. Net income was a record $40.5 million. In early 1997 Tobin was promoted to president and CEO, with Vincent remaining chairman. That year, the company began marketing Avonex in the European Union, despite its loss in a patent battle with Schering in Europe. Litigation between Biogen and Schering over their beta interferon products continued into the early 21st century, clouding Biogen's future. Also hanging over Biogen was a lack of new products in the pipeline for introduction by 1998 and 1999 as well as the potential for falling income from royalties starting in 2000. Partly in response, Biogen entered into an agreement with Merck to develop small molecule inhibitors for the treatment of asthma and other diseases. As part of the deal, Merck agreed to pay Biogen as much as $145 million over several years, representing a significant cash infusion.

Biogen was a 1998 recipient of the National Medal of Technology, so honored for developing pharmaceuticals "designed to treat large, previously underserved patient populations throughout the world"—and particularly for its development of hepatitis B vaccines, which were the first vaccines using recombinant DNA technology. Soon after the announcement of this prestigious award, however, the company was rocked by the sudden departure of Tobin. The president and CEO had clashed with Vincent and had demanded a freer hand from the company board. The board refused, leading to Tobin's resignation. Vincent was named interim CEO, and James C. Mullen, a ten-year company veteran who had been in charge of European operations, was promoted to president and COO in February 1999. Meantime, Biogen recorded record net income of $138.7 million on record revenues of $557.6 million. Sales of Avonex were $394 million, or more than 70 percent of the total.

With Avonex's orphan drug status set to expire in 2003, Biogen needed to bring additional products to market. The company suffered a setback in late 1999 when it halted trials of Antova, an immune system regulator, after some patients participating in the trials developed blood clots. Proceeding more smoothly through the approval process, however, was Amevive, a drug to treat the skin disease psoriasis. Biogen hoped to get FDA approval by early 2002. Also in the pipeline was a congestive heart failure treatment called Adentri. The company was investigating other potential uses of its blockbuster Avonex drug, the sales of which reached $621 million in 1999 in part because of geographic market expansion. In early 2000 Biogen announced that Avonex had proven effective in delaying the development of multiple sclerosis in people showing early signs of the disease. The company immediately moved to gain approval from the FDA and other regulatory agencies worldwide to expand the drug's prescription labeling to include these potential new patients. In June 2000 Mullen was promoted to president and CEO, with Vincent continuing as chairman. Mullen, therefore, assumed the important responsibility for shepherding the follow-up to Avonex through the pipeline.

Principal Subsidiaries

Biogen Canada, Inc.; Bio Holding I, Inc.; Bio Holding II, Inc.; Biogen Realty Corporation; Biogen Realty Limited Partnership; Biogen Technologies, Inc.; Biogen Belgium S.A./NV; Biogen B.V. (Netherlands); Biogen France S.A.; Biogen GmbH (Austria); Biogen GmbH (Germany); Biogen International B.V. (Netherlands); Biogen Limited (U.K.); Biotech Manufacturing CV (Netherlands); Biotech Manufacturing Limited (Channel Islands); Biogen Norway AS; Biogen Sweden AB; Biogen (Denmark) A/S; Biogen Finland Oy; Biogen Foreign Sales Company, Ltd. (Barbados).

Principal Competitors

Amgen Inc.; Serono S.A.; Cephalon, Inc.; Genentech, Inc.; Glaxo Wellcome plc; Interferon Sciences, Inc.; Merck & Co., Inc.; Novartis AG; Schering AG; Teva Pharmaceuticals Industries Limited; Vertex Pharmaceuticals Incorporated.

Further Reading

Ackerman, Jerry, "Biogen Veteran Mullen Is Named President," *Boston Globe,* January 7, 1999, p. C5.

Bovet, David, and Joseph Martha, "Biogen Unchained," *Harvard Business Review,* May/June 2000, p. 28.

Brandel, William, "Businessperson of the Year: How Biogen's Jim Vincent Got Biotech to Turn a Profit," *New England Business,* January 1991, p. 16.

Carton, Barbara, "Biogen Scores Win As Judge Dismisses Avonex Challenge," *Wall Street Journal,* October 9, 1996, p. B4.

"CEO Interview: Biogen, Inc.," *Wall Street Transcript,* November 1, 1999.

Gendron, Marie, "Biogen Pushes Ahead to Develop New Multiple-Sclerosis Treatment," *Boston Herald,* January 25, 1994.

Hower, Wendy, "Antsy Investors Eye Biogen's Drug Trials," *Boston Business Journal,* July 20, 1992, p. 6.

Johannes, Laura, "Biogen Chief Executive Resigns," *Wall Street Journal,* December 24, 1998, p. B2.

——, "Biogen Searches for Another Blockbuster Medication," *Wall Street Journal,* August 13, 1999, p. B4.

Moore, Stephen D., "Drug Makers Battle Over MS Treatment," *Wall Street Journal,* November 9, 1998, p. B13A.

Pollack, Andrew, "An Air of Mystery Surrounds the Abrupt Resignation of Biogen Chief," *New York Times,* December 24, 1998, p. C1.

Prince, Cathryn J., "Patent Deal Rocks Biogen," *Boston Business Journal,* January 13, 1995, p. 1.

——, "Tobin: The Direct Approach," *Boston Business Journal,* January 13, 1995, p. 20.

Rosenberg, Ronald, "Biogen Bets on the Leach: Biotech Company Seeks Approval of Drug Expected to Capture a Chunk of $500 Million Market for Blood Thinners," *Boston Globe,* November 17, 1992, p. 39.

——, "Biogen Cuts $145m Deal with Merck Firm to Get Cash to Develop and Market Asthma Drug," *Boston Globe,* December 4, 1997, p. C1.

——, "Deal Tempers Fears Over Gap in Drug Development," *Boston Globe,* December 7, 1997, p. F1.

——, "Royalty Drop Slashes Biogen Profits," *Boston Globe,* April 28, 1995, p. 69.

——, "Tobin Hired by Biogen a 'Coup,' " *Boston Globe,* January 20, 1994, p. 33.

Shao, Maria, "Growth—The Globe 100; Biogen Inc.," *Boston Globe,* May 17, 1994, p. 56.

Syre, Steven, "Biogen Faces Patent Hurdles," *Boston Herald,* January 21, 1995, p. 17.

—Dave Mote
—updated by David E. Salamie

BNP Paribas Group

16, boulevard des Italiens
75009 Paris Cedex 09
France
Telephone: (+33) 1 40-14-45-46
Fax: (+33) 1 40-14-75-46
Web site: http://www.bnpgroup.com

Public Company
Incorporated: 1966 as Banque Nationale de Paris
Employees: 77,500
Sales: EUR 32.6 billion (US$31.05 billion) (1999)
Stock Exchanges: Paris
NAIC: 522110 Commercial Banking; 522120 Savings
　　Institutions; 522293 International Trade Financing

BNP Paribas Group is the fruit of the 1999 merger between two of France's most influential banking groups, the retail-oriented Banque Nationale de Paris and Banque Paribas, traditionally focused on the institutional sector. The newly merged group is France's largest bank and among the top five European banks (and number two among euro-based banks). Apart from its retail and institutional banking services and operations in France, BNP Paribas also trades internationally in more than 85 countries, including in the United States through its control of BancWest. The banking group is also active on the Internet, through its retail brands Banque Directe, Cortal, and BNP Net, and its corporate brands BNP Net Entreprises, Issue Master, and Bond Click. Led by Chairman Michel Pebereau and President Baudouin Prot, BNP narrowly lost a bitter battle to take over rival French retail bank Société Générale at the same time as gaining control of Paribas, which would have created the world's largest bank and the first to achieve assets over US$1 trillion. Despite the backing of the French government, the takeover plan failed—for the time being, at least. Given the widespread chauvinism of the European banking community, eager to maintain national control over their leading banks, a future merger between the two French banking giants could not be ruled out as a possibility.

Rise of a Banking Leader in the 19th Century

Banque Nationale de Paris (BNP) was formed in 1966 by a merger between two long-established French banks, the Comptoir National d'Escompte de Paris (CNEP) and the Banque Nationale Pour le Commerce et l'Industrie (BNCI). In the 1980s, it was one of the largest financial institutions in France.

The Comptoir d'Escompte was founded in 1848, primarily to rescue Paris businesses from difficulties in obtaining financing. In 1854, after the crisis had passed and the bank no longer had a special mission, it became a commercial institution, greatly increasing its capital and range of activities. Although it continued to concentrate on commerce in Paris instead of expanding by forming local branches, the Comptoir d'Escompte did establish itself in French colonies and foreign countries, becoming seriously involved in copper speculation. The bank was very active in the wool trade, and for many years was the only foreign bank in Australia. It was also one of the leading banks in India, and had a significant business presence in London and Brussels. Unfortunately, the bank soon spread itself too thin and, by the late 1880s, its liabilities were of such gigantic proportions that the president, Denfert Rochereau, chose to commit suicide. The Bank of France and others in the banking community came to Comptoir d'Escompte's aid, meeting its liabilities and repaying its loans. Out of these ruins, a new deposit bank called Comptoir National d'Escompte de Paris arose in 1889.

Only a short time passed before the bank had recovered its health. Although it kept its interests abroad, its growth now focused on the French provinces. By 1920, it had opened 223 branches, and had twice that many by the end of the decade. During the Depression, expansion slowed, and things improved little during World War II. In 1946, along with the Bank of France and three other major deposit banks (including BNCI, with which it would later merge), CNEP was nationalized as part of the government's postwar recovery plan. This plan also included legislation requiring banks to identify themselves as investment or deposit (commercial) banks. Altogether the plan created a more specialized and concentrated banking system and gave the government better control over the distribution of credit. The nationalized banks kept the same personnel, charac-

Company Perspectives:

BNP Paribas, powerful growth potential and value creation. With its EUR 20 billion in reserves, and its large international presence, the new Group has the means to achieve its ambitions: to become a European leader in each of its markets by seizing the opportunities linked to the euro and to be a major player on the global scale, while continuing to improve shareholder value.

ters, and administrative autonomy that they possessed before nationalization, but representatives of state agencies joined their boards of directors. With nationalization, CNEP was assured a central position in the French financial system, and this helped it grow at a strong pace, especially during France's boom years in the 1960s. Nonetheless, throughout the 1950s and 1960s, CNEP remained smaller than the other nationalized banks.

BNCI began as the Banque Nationale de Crédit in 1913, founded by a deposit bank, the Comptoir d'Escompte de Mulhouse (which was founded at the same time as CNEP and for the same reason) and an investment bank, the Banque Française pour le Commerce et l'Industrie. By absorbing several smaller banks and opening new branches, it grew geographically at a rapid pace. At the end of World War I, it was the fourth largest French bank. In the 1920s, Banque Nationale de Crédit merged with the Banque Française pour le Commerce et l'Industrie. But the connection was badly timed, since the investment bank was heavily involved in long-term lending to industry, and the economic chaos of 1930 precipitated its ruin. Eventually the minister of finance guaranteed the bank's deposits through the state in order to prevent a panic. In April 1932, with the help of several larger banks, the Banque Nationale de Crédit was resurrected as the Banque Nationale pour le Commerce et l'Industrie, strictly a deposit bank.

Because the economic chaos of the early 1930s hit local and regional banks especially severely, BNCI was able to grow quickly by absorbing them. In 1940, BNCI established an affiliate, the Banque Nationale pour le Commerce et l'Industrie (Afrique).

Postwar Consolidation

In 1946, under the same postwar recovery plan that nationalized CNEP, BNCI came under state control. The bank continued to grow internationally and, by the 1950s, it had branches in London, Madagascar, the West Indies, and Latin America. After World War II, London was an especially important financial center, and England and France were eager to help each other recover economically. In 1947, BNCI transformed its London branch into a separate subsidiary called the British and French Bank, with shares held by BNCI and two British investment firms, S.G. Warburg and Company and Robert Benson and Company. The British and French Bank continued to grow in international territory and assets, and BNCI itself grew much faster than the other three nationalized banks.

In the mid-1960s, along with an imposition of strict lending ceilings to shrink the money supply, the government began to

talk about rationalizing banks and insurance companies in an effort to better concentrate the financial sector. In 1966, this led to the merger of CNEP and BNCI and the formation of Banque Nationale de Paris. Henry Bizot was president of the new bank. Since CNEP had retained its strength in Paris and BNCI its strength overseas (it had the widest foreign territory of any French bank), the two banks complemented each other neatly. As a result of the merger, the British and French Bank subsidiary took in the operations of CNEP's London branch.

BNP's first year was a productive one. The new bank offered customers several new account options and also lent a large amount of money for equipment and operations in foreign countries. In addition, the bank established the Société de garantie des Crédits à court terme to provide financing for small- and medium-sized firms. BNP's subsidiary, Intercomi, helped back the plan for the construction of an underground system in Mexico City that year also, and BNP formed, along with four other major European banks, a new financial organization called Société Financière Européenne to promote international business through material and strategic support.

In 1968, BNP was one of the first institutions to become involved with Eurocurrency, and its international operations continued to strengthen and grow. By 1970, the bank had reentered the investment-banking business with the creation of its capital arm, Banexi.

From the time of the imposition of frugal credit limits on the French financial system in the mid-1960s, many French banks had been seeking financial expansion outside the country, where the limits did not apply. Since BNP was already heavily involved in international operations, the credit ceilings hurt it less than they did other banks. Throughout the 1970s, BNP continued to be a leader in international dealings, and France's export strength in the 1960s and 1970s helped the overseas market even more.

In 1972, BNP was one of the first foreign banks allowed to open a branch in Tokyo. In the United States, the Federal Reserve Board gave BNP permission to establish itself in San Francisco with a new institution, the French Bank of California. By then, BNP was the second largest bank in Europe, controlling $9.2 billion in deposits.

In 1974, BNP opened a branch in Chicago, and in 1975 and 1976, it opened branches in Seoul, Manila, Cairo, Los Angeles, Newport Beach, Houston, Toronto, Vancouver, Moscow, and Teheran. In 1977, it opened branches in Düsseldorf, Stockholm, and Amsterdam.

In 1977, BNP followed several other French banks when it opened a trading company in a joint venture with Inchcape and Company, a British trading firm. The new organization was called Compex, and its founders hoped to attract clients from BNP's branches in 65 countries and from Inchcape's 450 subsidiaries and affiliates.

In 1979, Jacques Calvet, who had been BNP's general manager since 1975, was named president of the bank. He had been a member of Cour des Comptes, a distinguished part of the financial bureaucracy that had been in existence since before the French Revolution. Because of the government's stance on credit ceilings, Calvet continued to fortify BNP's status as the most internationally oriented of the nationalized banks. The next year, BNP opened banks in Yugoslavia and Niger and planned to open more branches in South America. Soon after that, BNP gained approval to acquire the Bank of the West, based in San Jose, California.

By the 1980s, the nationalized deposit banks were creeping back into investment banking, since government regulations had limited the growth potential of domestic commercial banking. They had been criticized in the 1970s for practicing so much caution that it hindered their growth. By international standards, the state-owned banks were low in capital and high in loans, and investment banking was one way to remedy this. Again, BNP was a leader among the nationalized banks, with its Banexi capital arm for investment already in operation for more than ten years. In 1985, BNP focused on acquiring stakes in small companies, making mergers and acquisitions, and providing advice to business managers. Banexi examined around 150 entrepreneurs' dossiers that year, and by September it had made 15 investment decisions. In November, BNP introduced a new approach to acquiring a "backup" line of credit. In selling $600 million in notes, the bank offered backup lenders a listed security that they could sell if desired. Before, the backup credit that banks offered each other was non-transferable and did not appear on balance sheets until drawn upon.

Privatized for the Future

In 1986, BNP's profits rose 52 percent. The new conservative government that came to power that year implemented a privatization program, selling several state-owned companies. One of the first slated for denationalization was Société Générale, one of BNP's main competitors. Although now the privatization of BNP was also possible, as the largest bank in France it was expected to be the last one sold. In the meantime, the privatization of some 65 companies in 1987 required FFr 300 billion, making it a busy time for banks.

By 1987, Socialists were loudly contesting the government's sale of nationalized companies, claiming the businesses were sold too cheaply and that the sales favored the government's political allies. Edouard Balladur, the finance minister, reacted to these attacks by rushing ahead with his denationalization program to be sure to complete several sales before the next presidential election. BNP's privatization began to look more likely.

In July 1987, in anticipation of a law expected to be passed shortly to allow banks to buy into investment firms, BNP acquired a 54 percent controlling interest in the Du Bouzet stockbrokerage firm in Paris. BNP also organized its own investment company, which appeared on the Paris stock exchange as Compagnie d'Investissements de Paris.

In October, BNP acquired Ark Securities Company, of London, to gain entry into the European equity market. Ark had already gained a secure foothold in European stock markets and was beginning to do business in the Far East. This was the first of several moves BNP made over the next two years to strengthen its ties with England.

Despite its active expansion in 1987, the bank's profits fell because of a rise in general operating costs together with the dollar's decline and the stock market crash. The crash also slowed the government's privatization program and BNP's turn was pushed further back.

In 1988, the Socialists regained power in the government, and BNP's chances for privatization were wiped out. The bank faced the problem of finding new ways to increase its capital under the restrictions of the state. To this end, the bank announced plans to issue $400 million in perpetual capital notes and non-voting certificates of investment. The plans were later dropped when it seemed that such an issue would not meet international criteria for increasing its capital-adequacy ratio.

In 1989, BNP opened an office in Budapest in an effort to help joint projects between Hungary and France as well as the businesses of Hungarian state trading companies. That year BNP also took measures to improve its international base in areas other than deposits, focusing mainly on England. It moved its capital markets operations from Paris to London and bought Chemical Bank Home Loans Ltd., a British mortgage operation. BNP increased its involvement in insurance as it had been planning since 1988. Its Natiovie life insurance subsidiary had been a major insurer since the 1970s, and in 1989 BNP forged an alliance with the largest insurer in France, Union des Assurance de Paris, also a nationalized company. The agreement would make the two companies one of France's strongest financial groups.

Throughout its history, BNP had worked on developing its international range. In the 1980s, that strategy was modified to build the bank into a forceful competitor in global finance as the European Economic Community achieved its unified internal market in 1992. The return of a right-wing government under Jacques Chirac in 1993, meanwhile, once again revived BNP's privatization hopes—and this time the measure passed.

The newly private bank stepped up its international expansion in the 1990s, entering such markets as New Zealand, the

Bahamas, and Brazil, and gaining full control of Banque du Caire, in Egypt. In 1998, BNP bought control of troubled Peregrine Investment's business in China, then moved into Algeria, Uzbekistan, Peru, and India. BNP's acquisition of the Australian stock brokerage arm of Prudential Insurance Company brought BNP into Australia before the end of that year.

The launch of the euro in 1999 had engendered a wave of consolidation activity within Europe's financial community, sparking a series of mergers and acquisitions across the continent as banks—largely within a national context—sought to achieve sufficient size in the increasingly global market. BNP's answer to the consolidation had been to enter secret merger talks with rival Société Générale, in which BNP already held a substantial stock position. Yet in January 1999, Société Générale abruptly broke off talks—and announced that it had reached an agreement to merge with the institutional lender Banque Paribas instead.

BNP immediately countered with its own bid—a hostile takeover of both Société Générale and Paribas that would create the world's largest banking enterprise, and the first bank to achieve assets of more than US$1 trillion dollars. The resulting battle rocked the French business community—where hostile takeovers were exceedingly rare—and, with a bid of more than EUR 30 billion represented the largest takeover bid in French history. BNP received backing from the French government, eager to keep France's financial power in French hands. Banque Paribas's shareholders reluctantly agreed to the takeover bid. Yet, after a six-month battle, in which both sides waged a highly visible media war, BNP had failed to achieve the needed shareholder position in Société Générale to complete the double-takeover.

BNP was forced to withdraw the takeover bid—and then return the 37 percent it had gained to Société Générale—and content itself with its successful bid for Paribas. Merging the two entities began with a name change, to BNP Paribas Group. The new financial services company was faced with the task of combining the retail banking experience of BNP with the institutional investment leadership of Paribas—with many analysts suggesting the key to a successful merger involved allowing Paribas's 3000-strong team of investors to retain a dominant position in the institutional side of the company's operations.

While both BNP and Société Générale claimed victory after the takeover battle, most observers remained skeptical that the story would end there. Instead, with the rapid consolidation of the worldwide banking industry, and with both BNP and Société Générale remaining attractive—and even vulnerable—to possible mergers with foreign institutions, the French penchant for retaining control of their most vital industries suggested that a future marriage between BNP Paribas and Société Générale could not be ruled out altogether.

Principal Subsidiaries

Antin Gerance; Arval; BancWest (U.S.A.); Banque de Bretagne; Banque Directe; BNP Factor; BNP Gestions; BNP Lease; Cardif; Cetelem; Cobepa; Cortal; Credit Universel; Europcar Lease; Klepierre; Meunier Promotion; Natio Assurances; Natiovie; Segece; Sinvin; UCB; UFB Locabail.

Principal Competitors

ABN AMRO; Citigroup Inc.; Banco Bilbao; Credit Lyonnais; Banco Comercial Portugues; Dai-Ichi Kangyo; Banco Popular Espanol; Deutsche Bank A.G.; Generale de Belgique; Barclays PLC; HSBC Holdings plc; Caisse d'Epargne; Natexis; Caisse Nationale de Credit Agricole; Société Générale; The Chase Manhattan Corporation; Wells Fargo & Company.

Further Reading

''BNP Wants to Be the World's Biggest Bank,'' *United Press International*, March 10, 1999.

Clarke, David, ''French Bank War Only Just Beginning,'' *Reuters*, August 29, 1999.

Edmondson, Gail, ''The Man Who May Be King,'' *Business Week International*, July 5, 1999, p. 20.

''French Banks Weak As Bid-Battle Dust Settles,'' *Reuters*, August 30, 1999.

Lichfield, John, ''New French Super-Bank Scuppered,'' *Independent on Sunday*, August 29, 1999, p. 1.

Rankine, Kate, ''The French Revolutionary,'' *Daily Telegraph*, April 17, 1999, p. 31.

''Yes, but Who Won?,'' *Economist*, August 21, 1999.

—updated by M.L. Cohen

Bose Corporation

The Mountain
Framingham, Massachusetts 01701-9168
U.S.A.
Telephone: (508) 879-7330
Toll Free: (800) 444-2673
Fax: (508) 872-6541
Web site: http://www.bose.com

Private Company
Founded: 1964
Employees: 4,000
Sales: $1.1 billion (2000 est.)
NAIC: 334310 Audio and Video Equipment
  Manufacturing

Ranking 220th on *Fortune*'s Private 500 list, Bose Corporation is engaged in the development, manufacture, and marketing of loudspeakers, consumer and professional audio systems, automobile sound systems, noise cancellation technology for the aviation industry, and computer simulation software to analyze auditorium acoustics. Initially producing amplifiers for the U.S. Defense Department, Bose later introduced the Bose 901 Direct/Reflecting speaker, which, with modifications, would remain the company's flagship speaker into the early 21st century. Known for its industry innovations and the high quality of its products, Bose markets a wide variety of sound equipment popular among consumers and corporate clients, most notably automobile manufacturers General Motors Corporation, DaimlerChrysler AG, Honda Motor Co., Ltd., Nissan Motor Co., Ltd., and Audi AG. The company maintains production facilities in the United States, Canada, Mexico, and Ireland. Its products are sold through retailers, via 60 company-owned Bose outlets in the United States, and directly to consumers through the company web site, direct mail, and newspaper and magazine advertisements.

Early History

The Bose Corporation's founder, Dr. Amar G. Bose, was born in 1929 to a political refugee from India and his wife, a Philadelphia school teacher. Bose would later suggest, in an interview in *USA Today,* that defending himself as a young boy in a racially prejudiced America equipped him with the fighting spirit important to his success. When his father's import business suffered during World War II, the teenaged Amar Bose convinced his father to begin a radio repair facility in the family business. There, the self-taught Amar did the repair work. Following this early experience in the electronics field, Bose attended the Massachusetts Institute of Technology (MIT), where he earned a doctoral degree in electrical engineering in 1956.

Bose Corporation arose in part from Dr. Bose's dissatisfaction when he attempted to buy speakers for his home stereo system in 1956. As an engineer, he had expected that laboratory measurements would indicate sound quality. To his dismay, however, he realized that measured sound and perceived sound differed. Dr. Bose directed his research efforts into psychoacoustics, the study of sound as humans perceive it, and psychophysics, the study of the relationship between measurement and perception. His research led to numerous patents and the creation of Bose Corporation in 1964 to develop and market products using those patents. Despite the later financial success of his company, Dr. Bose, professor of electrical engineering and computer science, remained on the staff at MIT, teaching acoustics and mentoring undergraduate and graduate thesis students.

Bose started his company at the suggestion of MIT professor Y.W. Lee, who provided Bose with $10,000 in start-up capital. That investment would later be worth an estimated $250,000, when the company repurchased Lee's stock in 1972. So that he could continue his teaching career, Bose hired one of his students, Sherwin Greenblatt, to help develop and market a product. During their first year of business, according to a company publication, Greenblatt was the company's only employee, and "Bose, who was [still] teaching, was paying Greenblatt more than he, himself, was earning as a professor at MIT." Greenblatt would later become president of the company.

Bose produced its first 901 direct/reflecting loudspeaker in 1968, and its first customers were secured through contracts with the military and NASA. The 901 was based on Bose's earlier research, which indicated that in excess of 80 percent of what audiences heard at a concert, for example, was reflected sound; sound bouncing off walls, floors, and ceilings apparently contributed to the quality of the listening experience. Bose determined that his disappointment in speakers then on the market resulted from the fact that speakers only directed sound straight forward. To achieve a better spatial distribution of sound, therefore, Bose developed the 901, which aimed eight of the nine transducers in the speaker to the rear of the speaker where the sound could bounce before it reached the listener. The 901 employed an active equalizer to allow the speaker to reproduce the audio spectrum.

Bose's 901 series was not an immediate success. In fact, *Consumer Reports* dismissed the product in 1970, alleging that "individual instruments heard through the 901 ... tended to wander about the room." Wounded by such criticism, Dr. Bose filed a lawsuit against the magazine, claiming that it had unfairly disparaged his speaker system. Litigation continued for nearly 13 years, and although Dr. Bose ultimately lost his case at the U.S. Supreme Court level in 1983, the 901 series had long since gained a reputation as one of the finer products on the market.

Critical to Bose's success was the company philosophy, itself a reflection of its founder. Company literature stated: "Bose believes that audio products exist to provide music for everyone, everywhere—that music, not equipment, is the ultimate benefit. The Bose goal is to create products that combine high technology with simplicity and small size, to create the best possible sound systems that are easy to use and accessible to all consumers." From the beginning, Bose directed all profits back into research and development, avowing a greater interest in producing excellent speakers than in money, and keeping his company privately held, and therefore not responsible to stockholders. Dr. Bose and company officials also stressed the importance of creativity at the company. In *Operations* magazine, for example, Greenblatt stated "Our challenge is to prod people into being innovative and using their creativity to do something that's better. In the long run, this is the source of sustainable advantage over our competition."

Since its introduction in 1968, the 901 speaker series underwent several revisions in which sound quality was improved and the speakers were made suitable for the digital age. Bose also applied the direct/reflecting concept to lower priced speakers in the company line and began marketing speakers to the general public for use in home stereo systems.

1970s: Car Stereos and Japanese Expansion

In 1972 Bose Corporation began selling loudspeakers for professional musicians. Later in the decade, Dr. Bose became interested in developing sound reproduction systems for auto-mobiles, having noted that consumers, dissatisfied with the stereo equipment then standard in American cars, were purchasing Japanese systems for installation. The project seemed to present particular challenges given the glass, upholstery, and plastic surfaces in a car's interior. Bose, however, was optimistic, later recalling in a 1990 *Electronic Business* article: "I thought I could actually create better sound in a car than in a room, [since] we can control where the sound goes in a car."

Bose's auto sound system ideas were presented to General Motors Corporation in 1979, and a verbal agreement was reached between Dr. Bose and Edward Czapor, GM's Delco Electronics president, which resulted in four years of Bose research at an estimated $13 million to adapt car audio systems to the acoustic environment of the automobile. At the conclusion of the successful research, Bose formed a joint venture with GM to design and manufacture car audio systems for certain Cadillac, Buick, and Oldsmobile models.

Although initially slow to realize profits, Bose's car stereos and the Original Equipment Manufacturer (OEM) division they necessitated at the company, eventually became highly successful, leading to Bose partnerships with Honda, Acura, Nissan, Infiniti, Audi, Mercedes Benz, and Mazda. In many cases, Bose was able to design products not only for a specific model of car but also for specific options packages offered by the automakers. Bose was even able to meet Honda's requirement that product failure rate not exceed 30 parts per million, an exacting standard. By 1995, Bose's car audio systems represented about one-fourth of its total sales.

Also in the 1970s, Bose began efforts to introduce its products to the Japanese consumer audio market, an effort begun with much frustration. Bose's initial efforts in the Japanese market were failures; in fact, the company lost money its first eight years in Japan. Then, Dr. Bose recognized the problem as one in which Bose market representatives had neglected to establish close personal relationships with Japanese distributors. Bose decided to hire a native Japanese to head the company's sales efforts in Japan. After interviewing several unsuitable American candidates, Bose made a few trips to Japan, during which he established social and business contacts. Eventually he hired someone who would have great success introducing Bose products to Japan and would later become a vice-president in the corporation.

1980s: Acoustic Waveguide and Other Innovations

Further Bose innovations involved acoustic waveguide technology, through which Bose engineers eventually developed smaller, portable speakers and sound systems capable of producing "big sound." Specifically, acoustic waveguide technology showed that bass notes could be reproduced through a small tube or pipe, similar to that employed in a pipe organ, instead of the much larger "moving cones" used by traditional stereo manufacturers. Amplifying the bass notes via an 80-inch tube folded into less than one cubic foot of space, Bose's Acoustic Wave Music System was introduced in 1984. The stereo system won praise for its compact, simple design as well as sound that many reviewers found rivaled that of larger and more costly stereo speakers and components.

Key Dates:

1964: Amar G. Bose founds Bose Corporation.
1968: Company introduces the 901 direct/reflecting loud-speaker.
1970s: Research into car stereos begins.
1972: Bose begins selling loudspeakers for professional musicians.
1983: Company loses libel lawsuit against *Consumer Reports* magazine, at the U.S. Supreme Court level.
1984: Acoustic Wave Music System is introduced.
1990: Lifestyle speaker systems are introduced.
1993: The Bose Wave radio makes its debut.
1997: New corporate headquarters building is dedicated at ''The Mountain.''
1999: Company launches online sales from its web site.

In 1985 Bose began investigating the market for its products in television. As he had with General Motors, Dr. Bose approached a major television manufacturer, Zenith Electronics Corporation, and proposed that his engineers design a sound system, incorporating their acoustic waveguide technology to produce high fidelity sound in Zenith televisions. Zenith agreed, and the two companies entered into a joint venture that resulted in the deluxe Zenith/Bose television, a set that featured rich sound, and that, since its tube was folded inside, was only about an inch larger than Zenith's earlier 27-inch screen model.

Company innovation continued in 1986 with the introduction of Acoustimass speaker technology. Proving that bigger is not always better, the line featured compact yet high-quality speakers, some of which were so small they could fit in the palm of one's hand.

During the late 1980s, Bose introduced its Acoustic Noise Canceling headset, a sealed headset designed to cancel out unwanted sound. Remarking on the need for the headset, one writer for *New Scientist* magazine quoted Dr. Bose: ''The US government pays out $200 million a year in compensation for hearing loss caused by military service. . . . Hearing loss is a common reason for early retirement of pilots, second only to psychological stress.'' Indeed, the headset proved valuable in military use, particularly among pilots and tank drivers. The headset also had civilian applications and could be used by small aircraft and helicopter pilots. Bose donated two of these headsets to Dick Rutan and Jeanna Yeager, who piloted their light plane the *Voyager* on a nonstop around the world flight in 1986. Moreover, the technology Bose developed could be tailored to cancel out noise in several environments, such as airline passenger compartments or city streets.

By 1989 Bose's sales were estimated at $300 million, a figure that some analysts suggested was conservative. Also at this time, nearly half of Bose's sales were derived from foreign markets; indeed, Bose speakers were outselling all other brands in Japan, including those of the Japanese manufacturers. The early 1990s saw steady gains for Bose, with net revenues increasing to $424 million by 1992.

The 1990s and Beyond

The acoustiwave technology in Bose speakers and stereo systems made Bose products popular in the 1990s at concerts, theaters, and nightclubs. A Bose loudspeaker was even used at the 1992 Winter Olympics in Albertville, France. On the consumer front, the decade began with the introduction of a new line of speaker systems called Lifestyle. Featuring an integrated design, the Lifestyle system was designed to provide high quality sound while offering ease of use for both home music systems and the burgeoning market for home theater systems.

In 1993 consumers were introduced to the Bose Wave radio, a small remote-controlled clock radio suited for use in the home. The Wave boasted rich, full sound not found in other portable radios and could also be hooked up to a television or CD player, enhancing the sound capabilities of the user's existing stereo components. Expensive for a radio and featuring an unusual design, the Wave befuddled retailers, leading the company to sell the product directly to consumers via direct mail and newspaper and magazine advertisements. It went on to be a huge success; by 1998 the company was able to boast sales of 200,000 Waves in a single year.

At its manufacturing facilities, Bose became a subscriber to the total quality management concept (TQM) introduced by W. Edwards Deming. Toward that end, Bose assembly line workers were cross-trained and promoted based on performance. Moreover, Bose sought to build teams based upon mutual trust and respect, operating according to principles of responsibility and quality consciousness. Describing the company's management style in a 1993 *Production* article, Bose's vice-president of manufacturing, Tom Beeson, asserted: ''Communicate. Spend a lot of time on the factory floor. Micromanage every aspect. Involve all of the people. Foolproof the system so mistakes can't be made. Find the root cause of problems. Operate manufacturing with the fundamental principle: Do it right the first time.''

In 1994 Bose unveiled the Auditioner audio demonstrator, a computer system that enabled builders, architects, and facility managers to hear the acoustics of a building's proposed sound system, working from as little input as the building's blueprints. This technology was under development for ten years, and became reality only after computer technology caught up with the imagination of Bose engineers.

The mid-1990s also saw Bose undertake a $150 million expansion of its corporate headquarters in Framingham, Massachusetts, known as The Mountain for its commanding view of the countryside. The expansion included construction of a new six-story, all-glass-facade, ultramodern headquarters building, which had room for 800 employees and was completed in 1997. At the same time, the company phased out its factory in nearby Westboro, Massachusetts, citing the high cost of manufacturing in that state. (The company did continue to maintain a small manufacturing operation at the Framingham campus.) The production at Westboro was transferred to facilities in Hillsdale, Michigan, and Columbia, South Carolina. By the late 1990s, Bose had eight manufacturing sites, including the three aforementioned along with sites in Yuma, Arizona; Sainte Marie, Quebec, Canada; San Luis Río Colorado and Tijuana, Mexico; and Carrickmacross, Ireland.

Starting with the company's long legal battle with *Consumer Reports,* Bose gained a reputation for litigiousness. In the mid-to late-1990s the company was involved in a number of lawsuits with Cambridge SoundWorks, Inc. (CSW), which was based in nearby Newton, Massachusetts. In 1994 Bose sued CSW after the latter claimed that its speakers were "better than Bose at half the price." After that suit was settled, Bose soon filed another lawsuit against CSW, this time alleging patent violations. In early 1999 CSW filed a countersuit alleging that Bose had made false advertising claims when it stated that its Wave radio was the best reviewed product of its kind on the market.

Other developments in the late 1990s included the expansion of the company's car audio business in 1998 to include more popular and lower priced vehicles, such as the Chevrolet Blazer and the Oldsmobile Intrigue; the launch of online sales of Bose products at the company web site the following year; and the introduction of a new version of the Wave radio that included a built-in CD player. According to research firm NPD, the Bose brand at decade's end was the number one speaker brand in the United States, with a market share of 20 percent, while the company's closest rival, Harman International Industries, Inc., claimed only 13 percent with its two top brands, JBL and Infinity, combined. Bose also held the number one position worldwide in speakers, with a 25 percent share of that market. For the fiscal year ending in March 1999, Bose had estimated operating profits of $170 million on sales of nearly $1 billion. The company reported its sales for the following year at more than $1.1 billion. With its innovative product development, streamlined manufacturing and delivery, and wide array of marketing channels, Bose was likely positioned to retain its top rank well into the 21st century.

Principal Subsidiaries

Bose AG (Switzerland); Bose A/S (Denmark); Bose Australia; Bose B.V. (Netherlands); Bose Canada, Inc.; Bose GmbH (Germany); Bose K.K. (Japan); Bose Ltd. (Canada); Bose N.V. (Belgium); Bose S.A. de C.V. (Mexico); Bose S.A.R.L. (France); Bose S.p.A. (Italy); Bose U.K., Ltd.

Principal Competitors

Harman International Industries, Inc.; Kenwood Corporation; Koss Corporation; Bang & Olufsen Holding a/s; Boston Acoustics, Inc.; Cambridge SoundWorks, Inc.; Carver Corporation; Cerwin-Vega Inc.; Jamo A/S; Matsushita Electric Industrial Co., Ltd.; Koninklijke Philips Electronics N.V.; Pioneer Electronic Corporation; Polk Audio, Inc.; Recoton Corporation; Snell Acoustics Inc.; Sony Corporation; Telex Communications, Inc.

Further Reading

Amemeson, Jane, "Sound Is Golden for Dr. Bose," *Compass Readings,* February 1991.

Beam, Alex, "Bose's High-Decibel Litigation," *Boston Globe,* May 14, 1999, p. C1.

Bradley, Peter, "Global Sourcing Takes Split-Second," *Purchasing,* July 20, 1989, pp. 53–58.

Bulkeley, William M., "Sound Program Lets User Mimic Site's Acoustics," *Wall Street Journal,* October 19, 1994, p. B1.

DeJong, Jennifer, "Redesigning Design," *Computerworld,* November 22, 1993, pp. 87–90.

Donker, Peter P., "Bose Corp. Unveils Its Latest Wave: New Corporate Center Dedicated," *Worcester (Mass.) Telegram and Gazette,* September 13, 1997, p. B8.

Esposito, Andi, "Shift of Base Business Fuels Manufacturing Move," *Worcester (Mass.) Sunday Telegram,* September 1, 1996, p. E1.

Fox, Barry, "Antisound Makes It All Quiet on the Western Front," *New Scientist,* December 5, 1992, p. 20.

Greenblatt, Sherwin, "Continuous Improvement in Supply Chain Management," *Chief Executive,* June 1993, pp. 40–43.

Hirsch, Julian, "Bose Lifestyle 12 Home Theater System," *Stereo Review,* March 1995, pp. 34–38.

"Hotels Move to a New Beat" *Lodging Hospitality,* April 1994, p. 84.

La Franco, Robert, "Loudspeaker Envy," *Forbes,* August 9, 1999, p. 68.

Lander, Kathleen, " *HPR* Interview: Amar Bose," *HPR: High Performance Review,* June 2, 1994, pp. 51–53.

McClenahen, John S., "So Long, Salespeople," *Industry Week,* February 18, 1991, pp. 48–51.

O'Connor, Leo, "Putting a Lid on Noise Pollution," *Mechanical Engineering,* June 1991, pp. 46–51.

Radding, Alan, "Quality Is Job #1," *Datamation,* October 1, 1992, pp. 98–100.

Reed, J.D., "Beating Japan Loud and Clear," *Fortune,* October 26, 1987, pp. 65–72.

Rosenbloom, Bert, "Motivating Your International Channel Partners," *Business Horizons,* March/April 1990, pp. 53–57.

"Taking Control of Noise," *Occupational Hazards,* July 1993, p. 34.

Vannan, Thomas, "Of Science and Stereos," *New England Business,* January 1990, p. 80.

Vasilash, Gary, "Bose Manufacturing Audiophiles Extraordinaire," *Production,* September 1993, pp. 64–67.

"Vox Populi," *Economist,* January 15, 2000, p. 71.

Wallack, Todd, "It's a Sound Strategy: Bose Knows Investment in Research Pays Off," *Boston Herald,* June 21, 1999, p. 27.

—Terry W. Hughes
—updated by David E. Salamie

Calpine Corporation

50 West San Fernando Street
San Jose, California 95113
U.S.A.
Telephone: (408) 995-5115
Fax: (408) 294-1740
Web site: http://www.calpine.com

Public Company
Incorporated: 1984
Employees: 865
Sales: $847.7 million (1999)
Stock Exchanges: New York
Ticker Symbol: CPN
NAIC: 221112 Fossil Fuel Electric Power Generation (pt)

Calpine Corporation is a leading independent power company with 90 percent of its capacity derived from gas-fired power plants and ten percent derived from geothermal facilities. Calpine is a vertically integrated organization capable of handling each stage of a power plant's development, including the design, financing, and construction of the facility, as well as each aspect of its operation, such as fuel management, maintenance, and power marketing. The company owns interests in 44 plants with an aggregate capacity of 4,273 megawatts, but construction underway in 2000 is slated to increase Calpine's capacity to 10,208 megawatts. Calpine sells its electricity and steam to utilities and other third-party end users. California-based Pacific Gas and Electric Company and Texas Utilities Electric Company account for nearly 50 percent of the company's annual sales.

Origins

Calpine was founded by three executives from the San Jose, California, office of New York-based Gibbs & Hill, Inc., an environmental engineering firm specializing in power engineering projects. Peter Cartwright, the senior member of the small group, had spent five years at Gibbs & Hill, serving as the vice-president and general manager of the company's western regional office. His career, however, included far more than his five-year stint at Gibbs & Hill. Cartwright earned his Bachelor of Science degree in geological engineering from Princeton University in 1952 and his Master of Science degree in civil engineering from Columbia University in 1953. His academic training eventually provided entry into General Electric Co.'s nuclear energy division, where he spent 19 years working on plant construction, project management, and new business development.

When Cartwright left Gibbs & Hill in 1984 to start Calpine, he was joined by Ann Curtis and John Rocchio, two Gibbs & Hill executives who became vice-presidents of the newly formed Calpine. The company received financial backing from Guy F. Atkinson Co., which later sold its 50 percent stake in the firm, and from Electrowatt Ltd., a Switzerland-based utility, industrial products, and engineering services company. (An oversized Swiss cowbell on display at corporate headquarters in San Jose, as well as the "alpine" in the company's name were testaments to Calpine's Swiss lineage). Initially, Calpine provided engineering, management, finance, and maintenance services to the then emerging independent power production industry, which was entering a new era of competition as regulatory constraints loosened. Calpine built turnkey power plants—facilities ready for immediate use—for its clients, registering its first annual profit two years after its founding.

Calpine went on to record a string of profitable years, but much of the company's consistent success was achieved while pursuing a substantially different corporate objective than it had proclaimed at its outset. Cartwright was inspired by the impressive gains of his clients, the operators of Calpine's turnkey power plants, who were registering tantalizing financial growth. He became convinced that the greatest prospects for financial growth were to be found as a power plant operator, rather than serving the operators. Accordingly, in 1989, Cartwright altered Calpine's business focus by concentrating the company's energies on the acquisition, development, ownership, operation, and maintenance of gas-fired and geothermal power generation facilities.

As Calpine set out to fulfill its new role as a power plant developer and operator, the company's growth was measured not only by its financial totals, but also by the number of plants it owned and by the amount of electricity it produced, expressed by the megawatt (one megawatt is sufficient to light 1,000 households). Based on these criteria, Calpine achieved only moderate progress during its first years as a power plant developer and operator. By 1992, the company produced approximately 297 megawatts of electricity at four plants, enabling it to collect nearly $40 million in revenue for the year. Although Calpine's production capacity represented sufficient electricity to power more than a quarter million homes, the total was unimpressive. Relative to its stature at the end of the decade and relative to the more than $200-billion-a-year power generation industry, the company was a diminutive national force during the early 1990s, its anonymity not helped by its standing as a privately held, wholly owned subsidiary of a foreign parent company.

Despite its lack of status, Calpine was beginning to distinguish itself during the early 1990s. The company was most widely recognized for its geothermal plants, ranking "as one of the top four or five in the business," according to Tsvi Meidav, president of a geothermal engineering company, in the July 20, 1992 issue of *Business Journal—San Jose*. "They [Calpine] are most outstanding in the area of engineering and very strong in operations maintenance," Meidav added. Calpine would add substantially to its list of admirers once it pursued expansion more aggressively. Toward that end, the company announced plans in 1992 to complete an initial public offering of stock in three to five years and to triple its capacity by 1994.

Calpine's commitment to aggressive expansion occurred at an opportune time. As the company grew, more than tripling its annual revenue volume by collecting $132 million in 1995, the dynamics of the U.S. electric industry were about to be dramatically changed. In what would spark a national movement, the California legislature announced in 1996 that it would deregulate the state's electric industry and allow customers to choose their electricity supplier. The state legislation, scheduled to be enacted in 1998, touched off a wave of similar resolutions across the country as deregulation spread state by state. Within a year of California's announcement, nearly a dozen states had announced they would deregulate their electric industries as well, with 24 other states taking the action under consideration. As the movement toward deregulation intensified, members of the U.S. Congress tried to accelerate the national trend by introducing a bill that would bypass state legislatures and promulgate nationwide electric deregulation.

As an independent power company, Calpine stood to benefit enormously from the fervor for deregulation that swept across the country during the late 1990s. The company's foundation as a service provider to power plant operators and its subsequent development into a power plant operator itself engendered a vertically integrated enterprise primed for the new competitive era. Calpine presided over every stage of a plant's development, handling each phase from conceptual design, financing, and construction, to operation, fuel management, and power marketing. With this synergistic approach to the business of producing electricity, the company was capable of offering highly competitive rates that did not sacrifice profitability. Accordingly, Cartwright and his senior executives welcomed the changes that were transforming their industry, particularly because they had anticipated the changes and, unlike many of their competitors, had moved aggressively to take advantage of the changes. The effect of their anticipatory actions was most evident in one pivotal transaction completed in 1996.

Accelerating Expansion: Mid-1990s

Although Cartwright and his team completed scores of deals during the 1990s, their shrewdness reached unprecedented acuity in a purchase from Siemens Westinghouse Power Corp. In 1996, Calpine placed an order with Siemens Westinghouse for 46 gas-fired turbines. The acquisition represented a gamble considering that many of the turbines involved in the deal were purchased before the company had commitments to build new power plants, but Cartwright pressed ahead despite the risk. He had launched an ambitious plan at the beginning of 1996 to develop 6,300 megawatts of new capacity before the end of the decade, expansion that required new equipment to actualize. Although the purchase of 46 turbines shocked outside observers, the timing of the deal later justified Cartwright's gamble. The purchase was made before the tidal wave of support for deregulation reached its acme and before the majority of utilities realized more industry capacity was needed. Consequently, at the time of the Calpine-Siemen Westinghouse deal, power generation equipment was cheaper and easier to obtain than it would be once the movement toward deregulation took hold.

The combination of Calpine management's intuitive powers in foreseeing a growing demand for capacity and its willingness to gamble heavily paid handsome dividends. Commitments for new power plants arrived, thereby necessitating the acquisition of the turbines and prompting industry pundits to hail the turbine purchase as the primary cause for Calpine's glowing success at the turn of the century. Less than three years after the deal, companies were clamoring for turbines, with demand exceeding supply to the point that some companies were selling their turbine delivery slots, essentially exchanging their place in line for cash.

The decisive Siemens Westinghouse purchase coincided with another important corporate event in 1996, one that saw the Swiss cowbell at company headquarters lose its relevance. Electrowatt Ltd. informed Cartwright that it was narrowing its strategic focus on its industrial business, a decision that paved the way for Calpine's independence. In response to the news from Switzerland, Cartwright prepared Calpine for its debut as a publicly traded company, completing an initial public offering of stock in September 1996. The stock sale netted the company

$82 million and gave management an 11 percent ownership stake in Calpine.

Calpine evolved from a relative unknown in the power industry to a recognizable, burgeoning national force during the mid-1990s. Between the end of 1992 and the end of 1997, the company completed transactions involving 13 gas-fired cogeneration facilities and two steam fields, more than quadrupling its total power generating capacity and substantially diversifying its fuel mix. Calpine achieved its growth by taking on the posture of an aggressive acquirer, resulting in $855 million of total indebtedness by the end of 1997. For Cartwright, the debt taken on was the price to pay for rapidly expanding in the promising business climate of the late 1990s, a sacrifice that greatly elevated his company's stature. Between 1992 and 1997, Calpine's net interest in power generation facilities increased from 297 megawatts to 1,981 megawatts, fueling a 48 percent compound annual growth rate in revenue that enabled the company to announce $276.3 million in revenue in 1997. Equally impressive, the value of Calpine's assets increased from $55 million in 1992 to $1.4 billion in 1997. The company's greatest surge in growth, however, was yet to come.

Ambitious Plans for the Future

Calpine entered the 1990s endeavoring to slip past $40 million in sales. The company ended the decade flirting with the $1-billion-in-sales mark. Much of this growth was achieved between 1997 and 1999, when the company's revenue volume swelled from $276 million to $847 million as the number of plants in which it held interests increased from 23 to 44. Deregulation was in full swing during the last years of the 1990s, prompting Cartwright to develop expansion plans that promised to exponentially increase the size of his company within the coming five years. With a flurry of acquisitions and development projects that nearly doubled the size of the company's power plant portfolio, Cartwright fleshed out Calpine's presence in California, New England, New York, and Texas. By the end of the decade, he had targeted the Southeast, Florida in particular, as the company's next major growth area for gas-fired generation.

Cartwright's short-term plans for the first years of the 21st century were of staggering proportions. Building on a total capacity of 4,273 megawatts in 1999, Cartwright hoped to increase the company's capacity to 25,000 megawatts by 2004. To help finance such expansion, the company secured a $1 billion revolving loan backed by a syndication of more than 20 banks in late 1999. The line of credit provided the means for the construction of approximately six plants, but Cartwright's plans called for far more than six additional plants. As the company entered the 21st century, ten new power plants were under construction, representing nearly 6,000 megawatts of additional capacity. In addition, the company announced plans for developing 12 more plants in the near future, which represented another 7,990 megawatts of capacity. Based on these projections, Calpine figured to be a major force in the power industry during the 21st century.

Principal Subsidiaries

Gas Energy Inc.; Calpine Natural Gas Company; Cogeneration Corporation of America (80%).

Principal Competitors

The AES Corporation; MidAmerican Energy Holdings Company; Sithe Energies Inc.

Further Reading

Anderson, Mark, "Cogen Plant's Under Way," *Sacramento Business Journal,* December 10, 1999, p. 11.

Gosmano, Jeff, "Calpine's Eye-Popping Streak Set Off by Canny Turbine Buys," *Natural Gas Week,* August 30, 1999, p. 1.

Keegan, Jeffrey, "Building Calpine's Financing Future," *Investment Dealers' Digest,* December 13, 1999, p. 99347019.

McLane, Tegan M., "Calpine Execs Steamed Up to Power Up," *Business Journal—San Jose,* July 20, 1992, p. 1.

Speaker, Scott C., "Calpine Eyes the Sunshine State," *Natural Gas Week,* September 13, 1999, p. 10.

—Jeffrey L. Covell

Cambridge Technology Partners, Inc.

8 Cambridge Center
Cambridge, Massachusetts 02142
U.S.A.
Telephone: (617) 374-9800
Fax: (617) 914-8300
Web site: http://www.ctp.com

Public Company
Incorporated: 1991
Employees: 4,200
Sales: $628.1 million (1999)
Stock Exchanges: NASDAQ
Ticker Symbol: CATP
NAIC: 541511 Custom Computer Programming Services;
541512 Computer Systems Design Services; 541611
Administrative Management and General Management
Consulting Services; 541613 Marketing Consulting
Services

Founded in 1991, Cambridge Technology Partners, Inc. (CTP) is a new economy business that has enjoyed rapid growth for much of its history. It specializes in client/server systems integration and promises customers fixed prices and guaranteed completion dates. With the evolution of electronic commerce in the latter part of the decade, CTP faced a host of start-up consulting firms that were more focused on web solutions and e-commerce. As CTP's traditional businesses involving enterprise resource planning (ERP) and legacy systems began to slow, the company sought to increase its revenue from e-business projects. At the end of the 1990s the company experienced high employee turnover and brought in new management to negotiate the change to an emphasis on electronic commerce solutions for its clients.

Enjoying Rapid Growth As Systems Integrator: 1991–96

CTP was formed from the consulting business of the Cambridge Technology Group in Cambridge, Massachusetts, in mid-1991. Information technology (IT) investor Safeguard Scientifics Inc. and its affiliated venture capital fund Radnor Venture Partners LP invested $5 million in CTP for a majority interest. James Sims was CTP's first CEO.

In its first year of operation, CTP completed 20 projects averaging $1.2 million each and had another 25 projects underway. Using its own suite of rapid application development tools and methodologies, CTP was able to reduce the amount of time it took for a customer to have a new computer system from two years to six months. CTP's CEO James Sims told *Systems Integration Business,* ''The purpose of our company is to listen carefully to the client, and to offer open systems, fixed-price contracts and realistic deadlines that put our clients ahead of the competition.'' CTP would prepare a report for clients within a week and have a working prototype that cost the client $100,000 ready a few days later. The prototype was used to demonstrate the economic benefits of system implementation for the client. After the client's new system was installed, CTP would provide training for the client's employees, teaching them how to maintain the CTP-built system.

CTP's clients had large sums invested in their mainframe computer systems. In some cases clients would scrap their mainframe systems for an open-systems environment with application servers. In other cases, CTP would provide a three-tier architecture that allowed clients to keep their current system, which would continue to host existing databases and run software too costly to move. The three tiers involved PCs on each user's desk, the client's existing system, and Unix servers connecting the two.

At the end of 1992 Jack Messman joined the CTP board. He was president of Union Pacific Resources Co. and former president of Novell Inc. Messman would later succeed Sims as CEO in 1999. In 1993 CTP went public; annual revenue was around $56 million. By 1995 CTP's revenues had grown to about $100 million. During its first five years revenue grew an average of 76 percent annually. The firm was hiring about 400 new employees a year. The fast-growing company specialized in client/server systems integration. Its fixed-price, fixed-time strategy, which guaranteed clients the cost of a project and the time it would take to complete, gave it a strong competitive advantage. In 1995 it formed a new unit, CTP West, by joining its regional offices in Palo Alto, California, Los Angeles, Dallas, and Seattle. In 1995 CTP acquired Systems Consulting Group, Inc. of

Company Perspectives:

Cambridge Technology Partners provides management consulting and systems integration services to transform its clients into e-businesses. Working in collaboration with Global 1000, high-velocity middle market companies, and .com start-ups, Cambridge combines a deep understanding of New Economy issues with integrated, end-to-end services and a proven track record of shared risk and rapid, guaranteed delivery.

Miami, and Axiom Management Consulting, Inc. of San Francisco. Axiom would continue as a wholly owned subsidiary of CTP and contribute about ten percent of CTP's revenue, or about $14 million, in 1996. Under CTP, Axiom would specialize in business reengineering consulting.

At the beginning of 1996 CTP introduced KnowledgeShare, an Internet application that bundled software, training, and consulting. Priced between $150,000 and $200,000, KnowledgeShare enabled companies to harness their internal knowledge and allow employees access through the World Wide Web. The service included software, training seminars, and consulting from CTP. With Internet firewalls and other security measures built in, KnowledgeShare could be used for limited or open internal access or as a public web site.

Between 1995 and 1996 CTP moved from doing custom projects exclusively to earning about half of its revenue from packaged products. Customers were demanding prepackaged client/server applications in areas such as sales force automation, financial management, and manufacturing management. With customers wanting their new client/server systems running in the shortest amount of time possible, it was thought that business process reengineering projects took too long.

In 1996 CTP introduced the Cambridge Information Network (CiN), a free Internet service that provided chief information officers (CIOs) and other senior information officers with a forum to discuss business and technology issues. The service gave CTP greater exposure to potential clients. By the end of 1996 more than 100 IT executives had registered at the site. They were from companies such as Federal Express, Microsoft, and Cisco Systems.

At the end of 1996 CTP acquired California-based Ramos & Associates, Inc., a strategic information solutions consultancy specializing in enterprise resource planning (ERP), for $39 million in stock. Ramos was considered the leading implementor of PeopleSoft ERP systems, and the acquisition launched CTP into the fast-growing ERP market. CTP had grown to 27 global offices and had about 1,800 employees. Another 1996 acquisition involved NatSoft S.A. of Geneva, Switzerland.

Rise of Electronic Commerce: 1997–2000

By mid-1997 CTP had completed nearly 100 electronic commerce projects since its first one was finished in 1994. Some 70 percent of these projects involved ''interactive space.'' In mid-1997 CTP introduced a new integrated electronic commerce service called Consumer Oriented Rapid Application Develop-

ment (Co-RAD). Combining technical and creative issues for its clients, the new service included four phases: an electronic commerce strategy workshop, product design, a product definition workshop, and product development. For each stage, CTP guaranteed a time of three months and a fixed price. In addition to Internet projects, the service included developing wireless solutions and kiosks for electronic commerce.

Toward the end of 1997 CTP formed a venture capital company to invest in developers of enterprise software applications that would be of interest to CTP's current customers. The Cambridge Technology Capital Fund began with $24 million in equity, of which CTP contributed $10 million and outside investors the rest. At the end of 1997 CTP had 41 offices and more than 2,600 employees worldwide. Sales were $406.7 million, and net income was $37.7 million.

In early 1998 CTP opened the Worldwide Center for ERP Excellence in San Ramon, California. Its director would be Tim Ramos, formerly of Ramos & Associates, which CTP acquired in 1996. The Enterprise Resource Solutions business unit would offer clients the same fixed-price, rapid implementation service characteristic of all CTP projects. Target companies would have sales in the $50 million to $500 million range. The company planned a special initiative for manufacturers to serve the needs of industrial companies that wanted software implementation at a fixed price. Later in the year the Enterprise Resource Solutions business unit, headed by Ramos, was merged with CTP's North American Rapid Application Deployment business unit into a new North American business unit to be headed by Ramos.

During 1998 CTP established its Enterprise Security Services unit to focus on computer security issues. It put Yobie Benjamin, a well-known hacker who was once a political prisoner in the Philippines under military dictator Ferdinand Marcos, in charge. It was estimated that U.S. companies lost $300 billion per year in costs associated with hacker attacks and network security violations.

In August 1998 CTP acquired Excell Data Corp., a systems integrator based in Bellevue, Washington. While most of CTP's business had involved Unix systems, Excell was highly regarded for its expertise with Windows NT. In 1997 Excell was named Microsoft PacWest Solution Provider Partner of the Year. The acquisition of Excell would enable CTP to provide more custom applications for Windows NT, an area that was expected to grow dramatically over the next few years. Following the acquisition, which added about 500 employees in Bellevue, Portland, and Denver, CTP had about 4,200 employees in 50 offices.

Later in the year Microsoft Corporation announced that it had chosen CTP to develop enterprise business applications based on the Windows NT operating system and other Microsoft technology. Under the agreement Microsoft and CTP would jointly market and sell the frameworks and integration services, which would then be executed by CTP under its fixed-time, fixed-price contracts. CTP planned to hire 1,000 Microsoft certified systems engineers over the next three years. The company also planned to standardize its 4,300-plus internal desktops on Microsoft enterprise products.

After reporting disappointing revenues for the quarter ending September 30, 1998, CTP blamed the results on a shift among clients toward Y2K projects. CTP did not provide services for Y2K remediation. Still, CTP enjoyed a 50 percent increase in revenue for the first half of 1998 and a 31 percent increase in the third quarter, somewhat below an expected 40 percent gain. Spending on Y2K projects for the rest of 1998 and 1999 was expected to negatively affect CTP's revenue. The company's stock dropped from a high of $58 early in 1998 to around $21 toward the end of the year. CTP issued an advisory that its annual revenue growth would decline from around 40 percent to 20–25 percent.

For 1998 more than 60 percent of CTP's projects were Internet-related. The company's CoRAD initiative had proven popular with customers who wanted to build an online business in three or four months. For fiscal 1998, revenue rose 40 percent to $612 million, up from $438.3 million. Net income increased nearly 50 percent to $57.7 million, up from $38.5 million in 1997. Those figures excluded costs associated with the Excell acquisition in 1998 and the acquisition of Peter Chadwick Holdings Ltd. in 1997. At the end of 1998 a group of former employees and shareholders of Excell Data Corp. filed a lawsuit against CTP in connection with CTP's acquisition of Excell. The suit was subsequently dismissed in March 2000.

Year of High Employee Turnover, Executive Changes: 1999

At the beginning of 1999 CTP had 53 offices and more than 4,400 employees worldwide. The firm restructured its services and organization, switching from a geographical focus to one that targeted specific industry segments. As a softening in the enterprise resource planning (ERP) market became more pronounced in the first quarter of 1999, CTP's business was affected. Its stock dropped to around $11 a share, down from its 52-week high of more than $58. CTP announced that it expected its sales and profits would not meet analysts' expectations.

In mid-1999 CTP hired Bruce Culbert as vice-president of interactive solutions. He was previously involved in the start-up of IBM Interactive Media and led an 1,100-person consulting practice at IBM Global Services. Shortly thereafter CEO James Sims announced he would be retiring from CTP, effective July 30. Succeeding Sims was Jack Messman, a one-time president and CEO of Novell Inc. and former chairman and CEO of Pacific Resources Group Inc. Messman was also a director of Safeguard Scientifics and had been a member of CTP's board since 1992.

Before the year was over, other key executives began to leave CTP. Senior vice-president Malcolm Frank left to head a new business-to-business e-commerce consulting firm called NerveWire. He took five key employees with him, including CTP's web division head, its chief technology officer, and the director of digital strategy. In January 2000 Bruce Culbert, the head of CTP's e-business unit, left the firm because he did not want to relocate from Atlanta to Massachusetts. Also leaving the firm was CFO Arthur Toscanini.

Executive turnover and other factors such as employee bonus payments of nearly $17 million negatively affected CTP's financial performance for 1999. Projects affected by year 2000 problems and fewer PeopleSoft implementations also reduced revenue and income. For the year overall revenue grew just 2.6 percent to $628 million, and net income was $2 million. Revenue associated with e-business projects rose 27 percent to $243 million.

CTP was facing new competition from a rash of start-up consulting firms that were focused entirely on the Internet and providing e-commerce solutions. In the Boston and Cambridge area alone they included NerveWire Inc., Zefer Corp., Viant Corp., and Breakaway Solutions Inc. In the fourth quarter of 1999 e-commerce revenue accounted for 39 percent of CTP's revenue, up from 31 percent for the same quarter of 1998. Enterprise resource planning and other enterprise application integration businesses were slowing.

In an effort to increase shareholder value, CTP began selling off some of its niche businesses. It divested its Cambridge Information Network to EarthWeb Inc. for $8 million. The company also announced it would invest in dot-com start-ups under a program called Newco for "New Economy Companies." The ventures would be funded through the Cambridge Technology Capital Fund and partnerships with other venture capital firms. The announcement served to boost CTP's stock 33 percent in one day.

Meanwhile, CTP brought a lawsuit against its former CEO, James Sims, who had started a new consulting firm called Gen3 Partners after leaving CTP. The lawsuit charged that Sims had begun creating Gen3 while being paid as a consultant to CTP after his departure. He was also charged with luring dozens of CTP employees to his new firm. CTP's former CFO, Arthur Toscanini, who had followed Sims to Gen3, was also named in the suit. Sims and Toscanini responded by filing a countersuit against CTP in May 2000. Another suit brought by CTP against Semtor Inc., a Florida-based consulting firm founded by another former CTP executive, was settled in August 2000 when the company agreed not to hire any more employees from CTP.

For the quarter ending March 31, 2000, CTP reported a loss of $4.3 million, following a loss of $17.3 million in the fourth quarter of 1999. The loss in 2000 was attributed to CTP's failure to move quickly into web consulting and e-business projects. One analyst estimated that CTP was suffering from a 48 percent employee turnover rate, the highest in the information technology sector, involving some 1,000 employees. Although CTP would aggressively pursue e-business projects in 2000, its depressed stock price made it a possible takeover target, according to some analysts.

Principal Subsidiaries

Cambridge Technology Capital Fund LP; Cambridge Educational Services; Excell Data Corporation; Cambridge Management Consulting (U.K.); Cambridge Enterprise Resource.

Principal Competitors

American Management Systems; Andersen Consulting; AnswerThink; Aztec Technology Partners Inc.; Breakaway Solutions Inc.; Cap Gemini America; Electronic Data Systems Corporation; International Business Machines Corporation; Keane, Inc.; marchFIRST; McKinsey & Co.; Sapient Corporation; Viant Corporation; Zefer Corporation.

Further Reading

Bartholomew, Doug, "ERP Center Opens," *Industry Week,* February 2, 1998, p. 16.

Blanton, Kimberly, "Cambridge, Mass., Internet Consulting Firm Sues Former CEO," *Knight-Ridder/Tribune Business News,* April 6, 2000.

——, "Massachusetts' Cambridge Technology Partners Helps Firms Integrate Systems," *Knight-Ridder/Tribune Business News,* May 19, 1999.

"The Boston Globe Boston Capital Column," *Knight-Ridder/Tribune Business News,* November 9, 1999.

Burke, Steven, "Cambridge Charts New Course," *Computer Reseller News,* June 3, 1996, p. 187.

"Cambridge Tech Partners (CATP)," *First Call/Thomson Financial Insiders' Chronicle,* January 17, 2000, p. 1.

"Cambridge Technology Partners," *Oil Daily,* December 15, 1992, p. 7.

Caminiti, Susan, "Adding a Twist to the Hot Server Market," *Fortune,* December 11, 1995, p. 209.

"Consultants Expand," *Software Magazine,* October 15, 1995, p. 14.

Dash, Julekha, "IT News That's Fit to Download," *Software Magazine,* March 1997, p. 26.

——, "Peer-to-Peer Communications," *Software Magazine,* December 1996, p. 31.

——, "Y2K, Turnover Blamed for Red Ink," *Computerworld,* November 1, 1999, p. 8.

"Goodbye, Mr. Sims," *Business Week,* August 2, 1999, p. 45.

Gordon, Joanne, "Feeding the Monster," *Forbes,* September 4, 2000, p. 70.

——, "True Colors," *Forbes,* November 1, 1999, p. 53.

Harrar, George, "Welcome to IS Boot Camp," *Forbes,* October 25, 1993, p. S112.

Hersch, Warren S., "Cambridge to Invest in Developers," *Computer Reseller News,* November 10, 1997, p. 53.

Kenney, Kathleen, and Mark Schlack, "Rapid Prototyping Yields Quick Growth," *Systems Integration Business,* July 1992, p. 44.

King, Julia, "Big Integrators Face Backlash," *Computerworld,* July 6, 1998, p. 35.

——, "CIOs Swap Tips on Web Forum," *Computerworld,* October 28, 1996, p. 69.

——, "Microsoft Targets Enterprise Apps," *Computerworld,* December 21, 1998, p. 21.

"Lawsuit Filed Against Cambridge," *Computer Reseller News,* December 7, 1998, p. 300.

Madden, John, "CTP Looks to Excell in NT Apps," *PC Week,* September 14, 1998, p. 72.

——, "Extended Alliance Focuses on NT in the Enterprise," *PC Week,* January 25, 1999, p. 74.

Mateyaschuk, Jennifer, "E-Biz Chief Decides to Stay Home," *InformationWeek,* January 24, 2000, p. 18.

——, "Services Companies See E-Business Benefit—Rivals Rise and Fall on E-Commerce Work," *InformationWeek,* July 19, 1999, p. 117.

——, "Y2K Affects Outsourcers—Keane Tops Estimate, Cambridge Lags," *InformationWeek,* October 19, 1998, p. 192.

McGee, Marianne Kolbasuk, "Cambridge Reports Strong First Quarter," *InformationWeek,* April 20, 1998, p. 38.

——, "E-Commerce Applications in Three Months," *InformationWeek,* August 11, 1997, p. 121.

Mehling, Herman, "James Sims: Cambridge—He Is Selling the Fixed-Price Contract and Riding the Internet Boom to the Top," *Computer Reseller News,* November 9, 1998, p. 127.

Merrill, Kevin, "CTP Creates Tool for Knowledge Sharing on Net," *Computer Reseller News,* January 1, 1996, p. 39.

——, "CTP Puts Shine on Service Offerings," *Computer Reseller News,* October 30, 1995, p. 59.

Moltzen, Edward F., and Christina Torode, "The Clock Is Ticking: Service Companies Feel Pinch As Projects Shift," *Computer Reseller News,* October 19, 1998, p. 5.

Piller, Dan, "Union Pacific Resources Chairman to Take Over at Massachusetts Tech Firm," *Knight-Ridder/Tribune Business News,* July 20, 1999.

Radcliff, Deborah, "Rebel Rebel," *Computerworld,* April 6, 1998, p. 81.

Rosa, Jerry, and David Jastrow, "A Flat World—Declining Channel Stocks Force Tough Choices," *Computer Reseller News,* November 2, 1998, p. 53.

Rosenberg, Ronald, "First CEO to Leave Cambridge, Mass.-Based Consultant," *Knight-Ridder/Tribune Business News,* July 19, 1999.

Scannel, Tim, "Arm in Arm: Seven-Year Relationship Gets Stronger," *Computer Reseller News,* December 21, 1998, p. 51.

——, "Putting Service into High Gear," *Computer Reseller News,* February 15, 1999, p. 47.

Scannel, Tim, and David Jastrow, "Enterprise Implementation Slowdown Takes Toll," *Computer Reseller News,* March 29, 1999, p. 7.

Schaff, William, "Cambridge: Down, Not Out," *InformationWeek,* February 21, 2000, p. 182.

——, "Cambridge Technology Partners Offers Solutions," *InformationWeek,* October 14, 1996, p. 120.

Smith, Tom, "Prepackaged Apps Fuel Explosion," *Computer Reseller News,* January 15, 1996, p. 61.

Stoughton, Stephanie, "Boston Start-Up Founder Countersues Former Employer, Ups Ante in Tech Feud," *Knight-Ridder/Tribune Business News,* May 4, 2000.

——, "Cambridge, Mass.,-Based Computer Services Firm Settles Suit over Rival Start-Up," *Knight-Ridder/Tribune Business News,* August 15, 2000.

——, "Cambridge, Mass., Internet-Consulting Company Struggles to Stay on Top," *Knight-Ridder/Tribune Business News,* May 30, 2000.

——, "Former CEO Allowed to Retain Position at Cambridge, Mass., Technology Firm," *Knight-Ridder/Tribune Business News,* August 16, 2000.

——, "Massachusetts' Cambridge Technology Partners Reports Quarterly Loss," *Knight-Ridder/Tribune Business News,* April 28, 2000.

"Tech Bytes: Mass. Tech Firm Hires a Former IBM Exec," *American Banker,* July 15, 1999, p. 9.

Torode, Christina, "Building from the Ground Up," *Computer Reseller News,* October 4, 1999, p. 39.

——, "Cambridge Cashing in on E-Commerce," *Computer Reseller News,* July 21, 1997, p. 57.

——, "A Winning Integrator's How-To Ability Delivers Know-How to Win Customers," *Computer Reseller News,* July 20, 1998, p. 59.

Torode, Christina, and David Jastrow, "Greenhouse Effect: Nurturing Start-Up Firms," *Computer Reseller News,* December 13, 1999, p. 5.

Whitmore, Sam, "Making Them Squirm and Other Secrets," *PC Week,* July 3, 1995, p. E8.

—David P. Bianco

Chadbourne & Parke

30 Rockefeller Plaza, 31st Floor
New York, New York 10112
U.S.A.
Telephone: (212) 408-5100
Fax: (212) 541-5406
Web site: http://www.chadbourne.com

Partnership
Founded: 1902
Employees: 700
Sales: $187 million (1999 est.)
NAIC: 54111 Offices of Lawyers

Chadbourne & Parke is a major international law firm. Based in New York City, it operates branch offices in Hong Kong, Moscow, London, Tokyo, Los Angeles, and Washington, D.C. The firm represents numerous corporations, foundations, financial institutions, and individuals in most areas of modern law, from mergers and acquisitions and financing options to antitrust, environmental, and intellectual property. Numbering among its long-term clients are Brown and Williamson Tobacco Corporation and The American Forest and Paper Association, formerly known as The American Paper Institute.

Origins, Career of the Founder

Thomas L. Chadbourne, Jr., founded Chadbourne & Parke in 1902, but he had gained considerable experience before starting that firm in New York City. In Chicago he began as a clerk for Judge Russell M. Wing. After studying the law on his own, he was admitted to the bar in Milwaukee, where he worked with a few partners.

In his autobiography Chadbourne described his decision to focus on corporate law. "The panic of 1893 . . . worked a tremendous change in the legal profession. Up to that time, criminal and civil trial practice had received the emphasis. . . . It was a change that I saw plainly, and one which suited me admirably. Criminal and trial practice, so loved by Wing, had failed to arouse my deeper enthusiasms, but the very first contact with business made me feel that I had struck my medium."

On January 1, 1896 the Chicago law firm of Wing, Chadbourne & Leach opened for business. Clients included the natural gas firm Crane Company, the financial and railroad businesses of Arthur B. Stilwell, and the Pullman Company, which made railroad cars. In spite of Chadbourne's successful early career, in 1902 he decided to leave Chicago for New York City, the nation's center for finance and the legal profession.

In 1909 Chadbourne was joined by Arthur Shores. After Shores left the partnership in 1918, the firm became known as Chadbourne, Babbitt, & Wallace with the addition of New York lawyer Kurnal Babbit and William Wallace, Jr., a formerly prominent Montana lawyer. In 1924 the Chadbourne firm took over the practice of John Stanchfield and Louis Levy and was renamed Chadbourne, Stanchfield & Levy. William M. Parke, later a name partner, came into the firm as part of the 1924 acquisition.

In New York, many of Chadbourne's main early clients were railroad companies. Thomas Chadbourne in his autobiography wrote about aiding George Jay Gould's many companies, including the Pacific Express Company, the Missouri Pacific Railway, the Texas and Pacific Railway, the International and Great Northern Railway, and the Wabash Railroad. George Gould (1864–1923), the son of financier Jay Gould, took over his father's corporate empire after he died in 1892, but by 1918 the last of the Gould railroads had declared bankruptcy, in part from increased ship transportation after the Panama Canal opened in 1914.

When Thomas Chadbourne wrote his autobiography in 1928, he claimed his law firm of 38 lawyers brought in more than $2 million in annual receipts. He said that when he began practicing law, "all was personal. Yet today I see only one or two clients of the hundreds that come into the office, and I do not even know some of my assistants by name or sight."

In 1928 the Chadbourne partnership represented over 150 major corporations, and Thomas Chadbourne was one of New York City's top corporate lawyers and businessmen. He served

Company Perspectives:

Although we have grown substantially in recent years, we have continued to maintain an informal, friendly working environment while delivering legal services at the highest level of the profession. The standard we set for our firm is to maintain professional excellence in an environment that is hospitable and welcoming to all people, regardless of gender, race or other classifications. We respect and value each other's differences. The people who work at Chadbourne & Parke—lawyers and non-lawyers alike—are our greatest assets.

as chairman or director of the Wright Aeronautical Corporation, Mack Truck Incorporated, International Mining Corporation, New York Rapid Transit Corporation, Brooklyn-Manhattan Transit Corporation, Adams Express Company, Otis Elevator Company, Vertientes Sugar Company, Manufacturers Trust Company, and the Marlin Rockwell Corporation.

In the last phase of his distinguished career, Thomas Chadbourne represented some of the nation's largest sugar producers in negotiations with several other nations that stabilized the international sugar market. Chadbourne's plan was adopted in Brussels in 1931. *Fortune* called Chadbourne's work "one of the greatest ventures ever undertaken in business diplomacy."

The Chadbourne law firm in its early decades represented some prominent individuals, such as Eddie Rickenbacker, World War I flying ace and later president of Eastern Airlines; actress Maxine Elliot; novelist Fannie Hurst; and writer James Joyce in sensational litigation concerning his famous book *Ulysses*.

Cherovsky said that during the depression years of the 1930s, the Chadbourne law firm had a "high-powered aviation law practice," with Eastern Airlines, TWA, and North American Aviation (later renamed Rockwell International after a merger) as clients. In 1942 the firm was involved in much publicized litigation concerning a Nevada plane crash that killed 22 passengers, including Carole Lombard, Clark Gable's wife.

Unfortunately, the firm lost a name partner in 1936 with the departure of Louis S. Levy. At that time Levy was being investigated for earlier helping Judge Martin T. Manton's business partner gain a $250,000 loan that never was repaid at the same time Judge Manton presided over a case in which he ruled in favor of a firm client. In 1939 Levy was disbarred and Judge Manton was convicted of judicial corruption.

Post-World War II Developments

In its February 1958 issue, *Fortune* wrote about how the big Wall Street law firms operated. The article ranked the firm of Chadbourne, Parke, Whiteside & Wolff as Wall Street's tenth largest law firm, with 21 partners and 49 associates as of December 1957. The article estimated that the 20 largest Wall Street firms employed about 1,700 lawyers. Although the article estimated the revenues and earnings of an average Wall Street law firm, much information about the internal workings of the

nation's large firms remained unavailable until the late 1970s when legal journalism was revolutionized by the start of the *National Law Review* and the *American Lawyer*.

In the late 1960s and 1970s Chadbourne, Parke, Whiteside & Wolff represented the Piper family in extended litigation. Chris-Craft Industries, Inc. tried to take over the family's Piper Aircraft Company, but the Piper family and First Boston Corporation opposed that deal. After the Pipers sold their business to Bangor-Punta Corporation, Chris-Craft sued Bangor-Punta, First Boston, and the Piper family for committing fraud. Although Chris-Craft won a $36 million damage award in the lower courts, in 1977 the U.S. Supreme Court reversed that decision. Chadbourne Parke and other law firms on both sides of the case earned a total of almost $5 million in what Justice John Paul Stevens called "monumental litigation."

According to author Erwin Cherovsky, Chadbourne & Parke "was in disarray by the mid-1980s." Based on its 1986 gross revenues of $39 million, the firm was ranked as number 96 in the nation's top 100 law firms by the *American Lawyer*. However, the firm's finances improved with gross revenues increasing to $75 million in 1989, making it the nation's 57th largest law firm. Its 1989 gross revenues were $95 million. Cherovsky listed American Brands, TWA, American Hoechst, Belgian Airlines, Renault, American Paper Institute, and Unysis as some of Chadbourne & Parke's representative clients.

Like other law firms, Chadbourne & Parke in the 1980s increased its initial salaries for new associates just out of law school. From $65,000 in 1986 and 1987, its starting associates were offered $83,000 in 1990. The big law firms increased those salaries in the 1990s to beyond $150,000 as they competed for the best graduates from elite law schools.

By the 1980s Chadbourne & Parke had added a significant number of women attorneys but few minorities. From four women partners and 27 associates in 1986, the firm in 1990 included seven women partners and 64 associates. In 1990, a total of 60 partners and 143 associates worked at Chadbourne & Parke, but that included only 13 minority associates and no minority partners.

A significant part of Chadbourne & Parke's growth came from lateral hires from the Manhattan law firm Barrett Smith Schapiro Simon & Armstrong. After merger talks failed in November 1987, some of Barrett Smith's top tax attorneys decided to move as a group to Chadbourne & Parke. By early 1998 Chadbourne had hired seven partners and one senior associate from the smaller firm that had about 85 lawyers before these defections. Several other Barrett Smith lawyers later joined Chadbourne.

Practice in the 1990s and Beyond

Chadbourne & Parke in the late 20th century continued its longtime representation of tobacco industry clients. For example, in 1981 the Tobacco Institute's Committee of Counsel met in Chadbourne's New York office. The committee's 13 lawyers, including two from Chadbourne, represented the industry's major companies (Brown & Williamson Tobacco, Philip Morris, and R.J. Reynolds, Lorillard Tobacco, and Liggett Group). Although those corporations competed for market share, in

Key Dates:

1902: Thomas L. Chadbourne, Jr., starts his solo practice in New York City.

1909: The partnership of Chadbourne & Shores is organized.

1918: Chadbourne, Babbitt & Wallace is started.

1924: The firm takes over the law practice of Stanchfield & Levy.

1935: Firm opens its Washington, D.C. office.

1936: Firm is renamed Chadbourne, Wallace, Parke & Whiteside.

1979: Offices are started in the United Arab Emirates of Dubai, Abu Dhabi, and Sharjah.

1984: Partnership is renamed Chadbourne & Parke; Los Angeles branch office is established.

1993: Firm opens its Hong Kong office.

1958 they had formed the Tobacco Institute to coordinate efforts to defend themselves against early legal attacks.

Critics accused the Committee of Counsel of playing a key role in keeping secret any information indicating tobacco-caused health problems and also preventing scientists from developing safer cigarettes because that might lead to lawsuits against the tobacco companies. The *Wall Street Journal* on April 23, 1998 said the allegation was that the tobacco ''firms participated in a conspiracy to deceive the public.'' Industry lawyers replied that they were just doing their job in defending their clients.

In the late 1980s Chadbourne & Parke's client American Tobacco Company had been sued by the family survivors of Nathan Horton, a longtime smoker who died in 1987. The TV show *60 Minutes* covered Horton v. American Tobacco on the eve of the trial in Lexington, Mississippi. After the jury deadlocked 7-5 against Horton, the judge declared a mistrial. Author John A. Jenkins wrote in his 1989 book that this ''was the first case in which the verdict wasn't simply, 'not guilty.' ''

In 1996 a Florida jury issued a guilty verdict against Brown & Williamson, defended by Chadbourne & Parke. The plaintiff originally had sued American Tobacco Company, which was acquired by Brown & Williamson in 1995. In 1998 the First District Court of Appeal in Tallahassee overturned the guilty verdict, a big victory for the tobacco industry and Chadbourne & Parke.

However, in 1998 the tobacco industry reached an agreement with several state attorneys general who had sued the big tobacco firms, including Brown & Williamson, for extensive damages. The tobacco companies were required to make periodic payments totaling $206 billion through 2025, to be divided among the various states. The tobacco settlement ended or changed many of the industry's common practices. No more advertising to minors. No more outdoor advertising of any kind. No more ''Joe Camel'' cartoon characters to promote cigarettes. Many other restrictions applied, including no more secret documents kept from the public by the tobacco companies and their lawyers. Although some critics claimed the tobacco com-

panies got off easy, many saw it as a victory. The National Association of Attorneys General detailed this historic 1998 agreement on its web site at www.naag.com.

Chadbourne & Parke attorneys represented some major clients in patent disputes and other areas of intellectual property law. For example, the firm represented Symbol Technologies, Inc. in patent cases involving bar code technology. Other IP clients included United States Surgical Corporation, Walt Disney Corporation, Acushnet, Rockwell International Corporation, SAP AG, Siemens Corporation, and Digital Equipment Corporation.

In the late 1990s several Asian nations suffered an economic downturn that hurt some American law firms with Asian offices. For example, by May 1998 Chadbourne & Parke's Singapore office declined to just one partner and two associates and later in the year was closed, leaving just the Hong Kong office as its sole Asian location.

Chadbourne & Parke in 1998 was one of three major U.S. law firms that were involved in the financing of $567 million to construct the new Meizhouwan power plant in the People's Republic of China's Fujian province. *Corporate Finance* in December 1998 rated this as one of the largest project finance deals of the year and also pointed out that it ''was exceptional for its entirely foreign ownership—the second time ever in China—and the lack of implied central government support.''

The firm's project finance work had begun in the early 1980s when it started to represent various clients in the U.S. private power sector. That practice grew to include many overseas project finance deals in the Middle East, Africa, and Asia. The firm represented the African Plantations Corporation in Malawi, Tanzania, Zambia, and Zimbabwe; the Carthage Power Company in Tunisia; and Colgate-Palmolive in Nigeria.

In Israel Chadbourne & Parke represented Newcourt Capital Inc., Energy Investors Funds, and the government of Israel in various energy and road financing projects. Other clients involved in Middle Eastern deals included EQUATE Petrochemical Company, the International Finance Corporation, and Panda Energy International.

After the collapse of the Soviet Union in 1991, several large law firms, including Chadbourne & Parke, established Moscow offices to help companies invest in Russia and the other former Soviet countries. Chadbourne also created relationships with affiliated local law firms to expand its international practice.

The point was that Chadbourne & Parke, like other large law firms, played an important role in the globalized economy in which money and corporate influence flowed in what some called the borderless economy. Chadbourne hired its own attorneys with foreign language skills, worked with affiliated law firms, and used modern telecommunications and computer technology to link its overseas lawyers with its main offices in the United States.

In its July 5, 2000 issue, the *American Lawyer* ranked Chadbourne & Parke as the nation's 67th largest law firm, based on its 1999 gross revenues of $187 million. That marked a decline from its 1998 ranking as the nation's 50th largest firm.

At the dawn of the new millennium, Chadbourne & Parke faced some tough challenges, not only from competing law firms and the big accounting firms that hired thousands of attorneys but also from the rapid pace of technological, socioeconomic, and political change. New multinational agreements, such as the North American Free Trade Agreement (NAFTA), expanded international trade. Many people all over the world demanded stricter environmental standards, thus creating new legal issues for attorneys. New nations emerged, such as the Slovak and Czech republics. Moreover, the so-called New Economy based on Internet transactions posed multiple challenges to attorneys and their clients. Built on the legacy left by Thomas Chadbourne and other early partners who served American clients, the much larger firm of Chadbourne & Parke in 2000 served not only American but global clients, often in legal specialties that did not even exist years ago.

Principal Subsidiaries

Chadbourne & Parke Gaikokuho Jimu Bengoshi Jimusho (Chadbourne & Parke Japan LLC).

Principal Competitors

King & Spalding; Kirkland & Ellis; Milbank, Tweed, Hadley & McCloy.

Further Reading

Barrett, Paul M., "As Economies Dip, a Global Law Firm Parties On," *Wall Street Journal*, October 28, 1998, p. B1.

Chadbourne, Thomas L., *The Autobiography of Thomas L. Chadbourne*, ed. Charles C. Goetsch and Margaret L. Shivers, New York: Oceana Publications, Inc., 1985.

"Chadbourne & Parke Project Team in Crisis," *International Financial Law Review*, May 1998, p. 5.

Cherovsky, Erwin, "Chadbourne & Parke," *The Guide to New York Law Firms*, New York: St. Martin's Press, 1991, pp. 49–52.

France, Mike, "Inside Big Tobacco's Secret War Room," *Business Week*, June 15, 1998, p. 134.

Geyelin, Milo and Ann Davis, "Tobacco: A Vast Trove of Tobacco Documents Opens Up—Tobacco's Foes Target Role of Lawyers," *Wall Street Journal*, April 23, 1998, p. B1.

——, "Verdict Against Tobacco Firm Is Reversed—Florida Appellate Ruling in Smoker's Case Favors Brown & Williamson," *Wall Street Journal*, June 23, 1998, p. A3.

Goulden, Joseph C., *The Million Dollar Lawyers,* New York: G.P. Putnam's Sons, 1977, p. 324.

Hoffman, Paul, *Lions of the Eighties: The Inside Story of the Powerhouse Law Firms,* Garden City, N.Y.: Doubleday & Company, 1982, pp. 123–124, 132, 202.

Jenkins, John A., *The Litigators: Inside the Powerful World of America's High-Stakes Trial Lawyers,* New York: Doubleday, 1989, pp. 184–192.

Klaw, Spencer, "The Wall Street Lawyers," *Fortune*, February 1958, pp. 140–44.

Lundberg, Ferdinand, "The Law Factories: Brains of the Status Quo," *Harper's Magazine*, July 1939, pp. 180–92.

Sebastian, Pamela, "Chadbourne Parke Hires Attorneys from Barrett Smith," *Wall Street Journal*, February 1, 1988, p. 1.

Wright, Chris, "Fired Up: Tri Energy Closes Thai Deal," *Corporate Finance*, December 1998, pp. 64–66.

—David M. Walden

The Chalone Wine Group, Ltd.

621 Airpark Road
Napa, California 94558
U.S.A.
Telephone: (707) 254-4200
Fax: (707) 254-4201
Web site: http://www.chalonewinegroup.com

Public Company
Incorporated: 1969 as Chalone Inc.
Employees: 156
Sales: $51.45 million (2000)
Stock Exchanges: NASDAQ
Ticker Symbol: CHLN
NAIC: 31213 Wineries (pt); 11132 Grape Vineyards

The Chalone Wine Group, Ltd. produces and markets premium-priced red and white wines under the labels Chalone, Acacia, Sagelands, Carmenet, Edna Valley, Canoe Ridge, and Echelon. Chalone's wines, which include Pinot Blanc, Pinot Noir, Merlot, Chardonnay, Sauvignon Blanc, and Cabernet Sauvignon, are produced at six wineries, four in California and two in Washington. Instead of expanding by increasing production capacity at one facility, the company increases production volume by developing or acquiring additional wineries, each managed and operated as autonomous entities. All of the wineries share sales, marketing, financial, and administrative support provided by Chalone's main corporate offices. The vintner's prices range between $12 and $45 per bottle. Chalone also operates an import business, distributing premium wine from Mexico, Chile, and France. World-renowned French winemaker Domaines Barons de Rothschild owns approximately 45 percent of the company.

Origins

Chalone was founded by Richard Graff, whose career was determined by a fateful discovery in 1964. At the time, Graff, a Harvard graduate with a degree in music, was reacquainting himself with civilian life, having finished a stint with the U.S. Navy. He took a trip to Windsor Vineyard in Sonoma County, where he tasted the 1960 vintage of a Chalone Vineyard Pinot Blanc. The wine made a strong impression on the 27-year-old Graff, who had previously taken a wine appreciation class and was just beginning to develop a lifelong passion for wine. Few others, experts and novices alike, could have shared in Graff's high appraisal of the 1960 Chalone Vineyard Pinot Blanc. Graff had tasted the first vintage adorned with the Chalone Vineyard label, and, as he would later discover, perhaps the last wine bearing the Chalone Vineyard label.

Despite the infancy of the Chalone Vineyard label, the Chalone Vineyard itself was the oldest commercial vineyard in Monterey County. The vineyard, located in a remote location near the town of Soledad, took its name from Chalone Peak, so named by the native Ohlone tribe who once occupied part of the land. The first ten acres of grapevine had been planted in 1919 by a French vintner named Curtis Tamm, but the first wine bearing the Chalone Vineyard label was not produced until 1960.

After his introduction to Chalone wine, Graff visited the vineyard and, not long after, pointed his life in a new direction. The vineyard, comprising 160 acres of land and a weathered cabin, was insolvent, a financial condition that provided Graff with the opportunity he needed to begin his career as a vintner. In 1965, Graff, with the financial help of his mother, purchased the bankrupt Chalone Vineyard and produced his first vintage the following year. Graff's grape harvests were pilfered by birds the next two seasons, making for a painful introduction to the caprices of winemaking, but the winery reached full production again in 1969, a vintage, like 1960's, that had a profound influence on the history of the secluded and virtually anonymous Chalone Vineyard. Graff's company incorporated as Chalone, Inc. the same year and also gained the corporate strategist who would promote the vineyard's ascension toward recognition.

Philip Woodward, raised on a farm in Illinois, became the financial and marketing muscle underpinning Chalone's success. After earning an M.B.A. degree from the Kellogg School of Business at Northwestern University, Woodward spent much of the 1960s working in Detroit for the international accounting firm Touche Ross & Co. While working for Touche Ross, Woodward enrolled in a three-week wine appreciation course offered by the company. The effect of the course on Woodward was profound. "Out went the gin, out went the scotch," he remarked in an October 12, 1987 interview with *San Francisco Business Times,* "and in came the wine. I even started a wine club." His passion for wine taking a firm hold, Woodward left Detroit in 1970 for San Francisco, but the pursuit of the nearby wine country was not foremost in his mind. As a business consultant, Woodward preferred advising small companies; in Detroit, most of his clients were large industrial concerns. San Francisco, where Touche Ross maintained a thriving small business consulting practice, was the solution.

In San Francisco, Woodward set his sights on small businesses, which included winery and vineyard commercial concerns. He assisted Robert Mondavi in the buyout of Rainier Brewing's interest in his winery, helped a small winery with its start-up, and provided advice to Inglenook. Woodward, finding himself in the epicenter of wine production in the United States, devoted his spare time to experimenting with new wines and to exploring the region's wineries, a practice that further intertwined Woodward's professional career and his personal interests. When wine-sellers learned of Woodward's occupation— he had become a regular customer at many of the region's smaller shops—they often asked for his professional help. Woodward's billing price, however, was beyond the means of many of those who solicited his advice, prompting him to offer his services in exchange for wine. It was through such a barter arrangement that Woodward came into possession of a bottle of Graff's 1969 Chalone Vineyard Pinot Blanc.

He soon arranged a meeting with Graff—not an easy task considering that Chalone Vineyard, sheltered by the Gavilan Mountains, had not yet received telephone service (nor would it until the late 1980s). Shortly after the meeting, Woodward resigned from Touche Ross and joined Chalone in 1972 as vice-president of finance, a post that would see the new arrival take over the financial and marketing responsibilities of running the winery. Significantly, Woodward brought with him much-needed capital by forming a partnership that included some of his Touche Ross clients. He also espoused a corporate vision that complemented Graff's insistence on quality over volume. "The strategy I had from the beginning," Woodward revealed in a January 1987 interview with *Inc.* magazine, "was to grow by staying small, to keep the production facilities separate and limited, and to build a different winery in each of the four premium wine-growing areas of California."

1980s Expansion, Public Stock Offering

Graff and Woodward envisioned creating a number of autonomous wineries, managed and operated separately from each other and from the company's flagship Chalone Vineyard. Rather than expand the capacity of the company's existing facility, the company would grow by establishing or acquiring additional wineries, thereby keeping quality—and prices— high, ideally, according to Graff, limiting production to 50,000 cases per year at any given facility. Such was the reasoning behind the company's joint venture with Paragon Vineyard Company in 1980. Wishing to expand, Graff and Woodward chose to create a new winery rather than greatly expand Chalone Vineyard. Under the terms of the arrangement, Paragon Vineyard, located near San Luis Obispo, California, grew the grapes and Chalone produced the wine at a separate facility christened Edna Valley Vineyard.

Edna Valley became the second wine-producing property for Chalone. Its debut was quickly followed by the addition of another winery. The company was more ambitious with its second attempt at expansion, forgoing a partnership arrangement and creating its third winery on its own. After buying a vineyard near Sonoma, California, the company founded Carmenet Vineyard in 1981, burrowing a series of tunnels into the Mayacamas Mountains to build a winery modeled on the concept of a Bordeaux estate. The cost of developing the winery ran high, however, more than doubling projected costs to reach $3.1 million. Chalone's interest expenses doubled because of the cost overruns, saddling the company with debt. To pay off the debt, Woodward and Graff made an unprecedented move, completing an initial public offering (IPO) of stock in May 1984. Chalone, with only $1.7 million in annual sales, raised $5 million from the IPO and became the first publicly traded premium wine producer in the United States.

The IPO relieved Chalone of some of its debt, but expansion plans soon lifted the total again. In 1986, the company added a fourth winery to its portfolio, paying $8.5 million for Napa Valley, California-based Acacia Winery, a producer of Chardonnay and Pinot Noir that had been founded in 1978. Although long-term debt remained substantial, it was the price the company paid for operating its wineries separately and projecting itself as a premium wine producer. The prestige associated with the company's labels helped sales, but, according to Woodward's estimate, operating costs were 25 percent higher than they would have been if the company produced the same amount of wine at one winery.

By the end of 1986, thanks in large part to the previous six years of expansion, the company's annual sales approached $7.4 million, having doubled every year since the addition of Edna Valley Vineyard in 1980. Chalone produced approximately 125,000 cases of wine each year from its four wineries,

Key Dates:

1960: First wine bearing the Chalone Vineyard label is released.

1965: Richard Graff, impressed by the 1960 Chalone Vineyard vintage, buys the vineyard; four years later he incorporates the business as Chalone Inc.

1972: Graff is joined by Philip Woodward, who takes charge of marketing and financial matters.

1980: Chalone forms a partnership with Paragon Vineyard Co., creating Edna Valley Vineyard.

1981: Company develops Carmenet Vineyard.

1984: Chalone completes its initial public offering of stock, becoming the first company of its kind to go public.

1986: Company acquires Acacia Winery.

1990: Canoe Ridge Vineyard is established in Washington.

1996: Carmenet Vineyard is ravaged by a wildfire.

1998: Echelon Vineyard is formed.

1999: Washington-based Staton Hills Winery is acquired and renamed Sagelands Vineyard.

2000: Jade Mountain is acquired.

each with a chief winemaker responsible for monitoring production and hiring and firing employees. Roughly 60 percent of the company's Chardonnay, Pinot Blanc, Pinot Noir, and Cabernet Sauvignon wines were sold in restaurants, 25 percent in retail stores, and 15 percent by mail order. Prices ranged between $10 and $20 per bottle, with distribution handled by a network of independent agents who sold the company's wines in 40 states and six foreign countries.

Following the addition of the Acacia Winery, Chalone prepared for what promised to be a highly competitive decade ahead. Before entering the 1990s, the company forged a bond with the famous Rothschild family, headed by Baron Eric de Rothschild. In 1989, Chalone and Domaines de Barons de Rothschild (DBR), one of the most prestigious winemakers in the world, agreed to exchange purchases of approximately six percent of the stock of each company. The investment by the Rothschild family, which totaled more than $5 million over the ensuing two years, marked the beginning of a distribution and production partnership between Chalone and DBR that would grow stronger in the coming years.

Growth in the 1990s

The 1990s began as the 1980s did, with Chalone adding a winery through a joint venture agreement. For the first time, the company extended its operating territory beyond California's borders, choosing to expand in Washington where land prices were substantially less expensive than in California. In June 1990, the company announced a 50 percent purchase of Canoe Ridge Vineyard, located in eastern Washington, which paved the way for a proposed $2.5 million winery. At the time, property ranged between $5,000 and $6,000 per acre in eastern Washington, compared with as much as $30,000 per acre in Napa Valley.

After changing its name from Chalone Inc. to The Chalone Wine Group in 1991, the company moved its headquarters from San Francisco to Napa, completing the relocation in 1993. Two years later the company acquired 24 percent of Bordeaux-based Chateau Duhart-Milon, an investment facilitated by Chalone's relationship with DBR. In the same year, in 1995, the company's annual sales eclipsed $25 million, capping a period of strident growth during the first half of the decade. The latter half of the 1990s brought equally impressive growth, but the period was marred by two tragic events.

In 1996, Chalone fell victim to a wildfire. The blaze occurred at the company's Carmenet Vineyard, where terraced vineyards rose more than 1,000 feet up the Mayacamas Mountains. On July 31, the grasses and mulch put in place to prevent soil erosion on the steep slopes caught fire. The winery's winemaker quickly hosed down the roof of the winery, saving it from the flames, but the blaze destroyed 75 percent of Carmenet Vineyard's crop. The local utility company later admitted blame for the incident and agreed to pay a settlement fee, but the winery was not expected to reach full production until 2004. Replanting of the vineyards was completed in 1998, the same year the company suffered another loss. Richard Graff was killed in January when the single-engine Cessna he was flying crashed near Salinas, California. His death marked the loss of one of the leading American vintners and, for the small, tightly knit Chalone workforce, left a leadership void not easily replaced. Woodward, who had been serving as president of the company since 1974, was named chairman. Thomas Selfridge, recruited by Woodward from Kendall-Jackson Winery, was named president and chief executive officer.

During the last years of the 1990s, Chalone enjoyed decidedly more positive events, as the company set a tone toward expansion for the beginning of the 21st century. In 1998, the company established another California facility, Echelon Vineyards, which began producing Chardonnay, Pinot Noir, Merlot, and its signature Syrah. In 1999, the company established a second wine-producing property in Washington through the acquisition of Staton Hills Winery. The winery was subsequently renamed, creating a new brand named Sagelands.

As Woodward guided Chalone into the 21st century, there were no indications of the company's expansion slowing down. In April 2000, the company acquired Jade Mountain, a transaction that gave Chalone its first Rhône varietal brand. The company also acquired the 62-acre Hewitt Ranch in Rutherford, California, and the 160-acre Suscol Ranch in northeastern Napa, with plans to develop both properties into wine-producing facilities. Sales for the year edged past the $50 million mark, a total that was sure to grow as the stable of wineries operated by Chalone increased.

Principal Subsidiaries

Acacia Winery; Carmenet Vineyard; Chalone Vineyard; Echelon Vineyards; Canoe Ridge Vineyards; Staton Hills Winery.

Principal Competitors

The Robert Mondavi Corporation; E. & J. Gallo Company; Beringer Wine Estates Holdings, Inc.

Further Reading

Brown, Katie, "Wine Woos Woodward's Palate," *San Francisco Business Times,* October 12, 1987, p. 14.

"Chalone to Benefit from Winery Buy Out by French Partner," *San Francisco Business Times,* May 21, 1990, p. 15.

Denne, Lorianne, "Outside Investors Acquire a Taste of State's Wine," *Puget Sound Business Journal,* September 24, 1990, p. 5.

Elson, John, "A Golden Age for Grapes," *Time,* December 10, 1990, p. 88.

Heuslein, William, "Family Ties," *Forbes,* February 18, 1991, p. 124.

Koselka, Rita, "For Whom the Bell Tolls," *Forbes,* December 2, 1996, p. 127.

Paris, Ellen, "Wine—$6.50 a Glass," *Forbes,* June 13, 1988, p. 34.

Rosenbloom, Joe, "Sour Grapes," *Inc.,* January 1987, p. 66.

Shaw, Jan, "Chalone, Paragon Extend Pact on Edna Valley Wine," *San Francisco Business Times,* June 14, 1991, p. 5.

Slovak, Julianne, "Chalone Inc.," *Fortune,* October 10, 1988, p. 104.

Smith, Geoffrey N., "Drink the Dividends," *Financial World,* February 28, 1995, p. 12.

—Jeffrey L. Covell

CHIRON

Chiron Corporation

4560 Horton Street
Emeryville, California 94608-2916
U.S.A.
Telephone: (510) 655-8730
Fax: (510) 655-9910
Web site: http://www.chiron.com

Public Company
Incorporated: 1981
Employees: 3,110
Sales: $762.6 million (1999)
Stock Exchanges: NASDAQ
Ticker Symbol: CHIR
NAIC: 325412 Pharmaceutical Preparation Manufacturing;
325413 In-Vitro Diagnostic Substance Manufacturing;
325414 Biological Product (Except Diagnostic)
Manufacturing; 541710 Research and Development in
the Physical, Engineering, and Life Sciences

Chiron Corporation is a leading biotechnology company focusing on cancer, infectious diseases, and cardiovascular diseases. In the area of biopharmaceuticals, Chiron's therapeutic drugs include Proleukin, used to treat metastatic kidney cancer and metastatic melanoma, and Betaseron, a treatment for a specific form of multiple sclerosis. The company is a leading provider of blood testing products used by the blood banking industry to screen donated blood, including widely used tests for hepatitis and HIV. Chiron has a strong presence as well, particularly in Europe, in the vaccines market, making and marketing a wide range of pediatric and adult vaccines. Among Chiron's innovations in the pharmaceutical industry are the first genetically engineered vaccine, the first blood screening test for hepatitis C, the first drugs to treat multiple sclerosis and metastatic kidney cancer, and the first cloning and sequencing of the HIV genome. Chiron was also one of the first biotechnology companies to post a profit, making $6.8 million in 1990. The company has an alliance with Swiss life sciences company Novartis AG, which holds about 44 percent of Chiron's common stock.

1980s Start-Up

Chiron was founded by Dr. William Rutter, a biotechnology researcher at the University of California in San Francisco. In the late 1970s, Rutter led a team of researchers that made an important breakthrough in the relatively new science of genetic engineering: equipping bacteria with the ability to produce limitless quantities of insulin. Advances in the field rapidly ensued, and several companies sprang up in the early 1980s with the intent of developing these discoveries into marketable healthcare products. As the industry took off, new companies began recruiting the best scientists from university laboratories, including the one led by Rutter. Rather than see his best researchers work for other companies, Rutter chose to found his own biotechnology firm. As he told *Fortune* magazine, "It became obvious that I had to either get in or lose out."

In 1981, Rutter, Edward Penhoet, and Pablo Valenzuela founded Chiron Corporation, which they named after the centaur in Greek mythology who taught medicine to Asclepias, the first physician. Soon after its founding, Chiron produced the first genetically engineered vaccine, another milestone in the burgeoning biotechnology industry. Chiron licensed this new vaccine, created for the prevention of hepatitis B, to the pharmaceutical giant Merck & Co., Inc. Pending Food and Drug Administration (FDA) approval, Merck would market the vaccine and pay royalties to Chiron.

Unlike many start-up biotech firms at that time, Chiron did not intend to become a fully integrated pharmaceutical company. Its marketing agreement with Merck became the first in a series of partnerships through which Chiron would bring new products to the marketplace while focusing primarily on biotechnological research into infectious diseases and viruses. In 1983, Chiron made another breakthrough when it became the first to clone epidermal growth factors—a genetically engineered protein that controls the way a wound heals. Funding for the project was provided by Ethicon, Inc. which, in return, gained the right to market the proteins once they received FDA approval. Also that year, although it had no products on the market, Chiron went public at $12 a share.

In 1984, Chiron became the first to clone a genome (genetic skeleton) of an AIDS virus called HTLV-3, the second step in

117

developing a method of detecting and some day preventing infection by HIV. Two years later, Chiron won FDA approval to sell its hepatitis B vaccine through Merck. Chiron also formed a division called the Biocine Company, a joint-venture with Ciba-Geigy, Ltd., focusing on the development and marketing of other new vaccines. In 1988, Chiron's Biocine division filed with the FDA for approval of an AIDS screening test and began research into an AIDS vaccine. The following year, the Biocine Company purchased Canada's Connaught BioSciences, a vaccine manufacturer to be owned 50 percent by Chiron and 50 percent by Ciba-Geigy.

Chiron researchers also continued to study hepatitis, and, in 1988, they discovered the hepatitis C virus. Previously undetected, the hepatitis C virus had caused approximately 150,000 people each year to become ill through infected blood transfusions. To market hepatitis C screening tests, Chiron joined forces with Johnson & Johnson's Ortho Diagnostics Systems. Under the name Chiron Diagnostics, the division developed several blood tests to screen for various forms of hepatitis, and these tests were sold to blood banks and hospitals worldwide.

Primarily due to heavy outlays in research and development, Chiron posted losses for eight straight years. In the spring of 1989, Chiron raised $52 million through an equity offering and sold an eight percent share to Ciba-Geigy. While this move greatly increased the company's cash reserve, Chiron finished this year with a loss of $21.6 million on revenues of $35.4 million. In 1990, however, Chiron posted its first profit: $6.8 million on revenues of $78.5 million. Its products, including the hepatitis B vaccine (marketed through Merck), its blood testing systems, and recombinant human insulin marketed through Novo/Nordisk brought in over $600 million in sales.

Steady Growth in the Early 1990s

Chiron entered 1991 with a strong balance sheet. In July of that year, the company purchased a rival biotechnology firm, Cetus Corporation, for $650 million in stock. Cetus's major product was a highly touted cancer treatment called Proleukin or interleukin-2, which its EuroCetus division had been selling in Europe for several years. The FDA had refused to approve use of the drug in the United States, however, and Cetus's chairperson resigned his post, leaving the company without direction and with a product whose image had been greatly tarnished. Chiron stepped in, continued testing Proleukin as the FDA had requested, and merged Cetus's projects with its own. With the purchase, Chiron also acquired a state-of-the art research facility, not far from its own headquarters in Emeryville, California.

By 1991, Chiron's operations had grown to include a complex network of joint ventures and marketing agreements with several pharmaceutical companies. Chiron thus reorganized its business into five units. Its cancer research department was merged with Cetus's oncology business under the umbrella of Chiron Therapeutics. Chiron Diagnostics, the joint venture with Ortho, absorbed Chiron's research on the HIV virus and began developing various forms of testing for that and other viruses. Chiron's burgeoning ophthalmic business merged with IntraOptics, Inc. to form Chiron IntraOptics, which manufactured a comprehensive line of surgical instruments used to correct cataracts and other vision problems. The Biocine Company purchased the children's vaccine division of Italy's Sclavo SpA, and renamed it Biocine Sclavo. A fifth business, Chiron Technologies, was created to absorb the company's Ethicon-funded research into growth factors, the development of a drug to treat multiple sclerosis (Betaseron), and also to develop and acquire new products and business.

Chiron posted a loss of $425 million in 1991, primarily due to its merger with Cetus, which had also been posting heavy losses. The next two years, however, proved promising for the company. Biocine began the first phase of testing its AIDS vaccine under the sponsorship of the AIDS Vaccine Evaluation Group and the National Institute for Allergies and Infectious Disease. In 1992, Chiron Therapeutics finally obtained FDA approval to market Cetus's Proleukin, and, in 1993, Chiron Technologies received approval to market Betaseron, its first genetically engineered drug to treat multiple sclerosis, and an agreement was reached with Schering AG's Berlex Laboratories to market the new treatment, giving Chiron 25 percent of sales revenue. Buoyed by the successes of Proleukin, as well as strong sales of its blood-testing products, vaccines, and insulin, Chiron posted a 1993 profit of $18.4 million on revenue of $317.5 million.

In late 1994 Ciba-Geigy increased its stake in Chiron to 49.9 percent as part of an alliance agreement whereby the two companies would remain independent but would collaborate in certain areas of research, manufacturing, and marketing. In addition to an infusion of cash, Chiron also gained full control of the Biocine vaccine joint venture and took over Ciba-Geigy's Corning Diagnostics unit.

Searching for the Right Formula in the Late 1990s

Chiron further bolstered its operations in 1995 through two acquisitions. In March the company purchased for $95 million Johnson & Johnson's Iolab division, maker of eye-surgery equipment, thus expanding its ophthalmic business. Then in September Chiron completed a $120 million cash-and-stock buyout of Viagene Inc., a San Diego-based biotechnology firm that had been collaborating with Chiron on gene therapy research since November 1993. In 1996 Chiron purchased 49 percent of Hoechst AG's vaccine business, then purchased the remainder in early 1998. This acquisition vaulted Chiron into the top five among the world's vaccine makers, with a particularly strong presence in the European market.

In 1996 and 1997 Chiron suffered a series of setbacks. In November 1996 the company dropped development of a potential vaccine against genital herpes upon finding, after 14 years of research, that the product simply did not work. A few months

---

Key Dates:

1981: William Rutter, Edward Penhoet, and Pablo Valenzuela found Chiron Corporation.

1983: Company goes public.

1990: Company posts first profit.

1991: Company acquires Cetus Corporation and its cancer treatment, Proleukin.

1992: FDA approves Proleukin for the treatment of metastatic kidney cancer.

1994: Ciba-Geigy and Chiron form alliance, with Ciba-Geigy gaining a 49.9 percent stake in the company (Ciba-Geigy later became Novartis AG and the alliance continued, with a 44 percent stake).

1995: Chiron acquires the Iolab division of Johnson & Johnson and Viagene.

1997: Company sells its ophthalmic business to Bausch & Lomb.

1998: Seán P. Lance is named CEO; the company sells the bulk of Chiron Diagnostics to Bayer.

2000: Company announces that it will acquire PathoGenesis Corporation.

---

later, the FDA refused to grant approval to a treatment for Lou Gehrig's disease that Chiron had developed in partnership with Cephalon Inc. The FDA said that the companies, who had spent $130 million on the drug, had failed to prove its effectiveness. By this time, Betaseron had proven to be less than the blockbuster anticipated due to troubling side effects and the 1996 FDA approval of the competing drug Avonex, which had been developed by Biogen, Inc. Chiron had also encountered difficulty manufacturing its whooping cough vaccine that had emerged from final testing in mid-1995; as a result, competing vaccines reached the market first.

In the midst of these travails, Penhoet, who had served as president and CEO since the company's founding, announced in January 1997 that he planned to step down from his operational posts to become vice-chairman. While a lengthy search for a successor dragged on, Chiron sold its ophthalmic business to Bausch & Lomb Inc. in December 1997 for about $300 million. That same month, the FDA granted approval for a second use of Proleukin, that of treating metastatic melanoma.

A 14-month CEO search finally ended in March 1998 with the hiring of Seán P. Lance, a 30-year pharmaceutical industry veteran who had most recently served as the head of international operations at Glaxo Wellcome plc. Under Lance's leadership, Chiron began restructuring, closing facilities in St. Louis and Puerto Rico, integrating others, and selling off another unit. In November 1998 the bulk of Chiron Diagnostics was sold to Bayer AG for about $1 billion in cash. Chiron retained its highly profitable HIV and hepatitis C blood testing businesses. Lance also more tightly focused the company's research efforts, emphasizing blood-screening applications and a handful of the most promising new drugs, as well as attempting to find new uses for current drugs, including Proleukin and Betaseron.

In May 1999 Lance took on the additional post of chairman, as Rutter stayed on the board as chairman emeritus. Lance's

new direction for the company appeared to be paying off by the turn of the millennium. In the first half of 1999 Chiron launched a new blood testing system for both HIV and hepatitis C that used a new nucleic acid testing process and was an improvement over previous systems. In October 1999 Menjugate was approved in the United Kingdom as a vaccine against meningococcal C disease, a deadly form of meningitis. In August 2000 Chiron agreed to pay $700 million in cash for Seattle-based PathoGenesis Corporation, best known as the manufacturer of Tobi, an inhalable antibiotic used to treat chronic lung infections arising from cystic fibrosis. PathoGenesis had a number of other antibiotics in its pipeline, with its specialty being drugs that could be inhaled, and that were therefore targeted to treat pulmonary conditions.

The addition of Tobi to its major commercial products and the bolstering of its product pipeline would provide a significant boost to Chiron. A major question hanging over the company, however, was whether it would continue in its quasi-independent state. Novartis AG, the Swiss company that resulted from the December 1996 merger of Ciba-Geigy and Sandoz Limited, held about 44 percent of Chiron's common stock and could, after January 5, 2001, raise its stake or initiate an outright buyout.

Principal Subsidiaries

Cetus Generic Corporation; Chiron B.V. (Netherlands); Cephalon Chiron B.V. (Netherlands); Chiron Blood Testing B.V. (Netherlands); Chiron Blood Testing S.a.r.l. (France); Chiron Blood Testing (Bermuda) Ltd.; Chiron Blood Testing Distributor (Bermuda) Ltd.; Chiron Blood Testing Pty Ltd (Australia); Chiron IL-2 Technology (Bermuda) Ltd.; Chiron GmbH (Germany); Chiron France S.a.r.l.; Chiron Italia S.r.l (Italy); Chiron U.K. Ltd.; Chiron Iberia S.L. (Spain); Chiron Limited (Hong Kong); Chiron Partners, Inc.; Chiron Alpha Corporation; Chiron/Cephalon JV; Chiron Properties, Inc.; Chiron Delta Corporation; Chiron Investment Corporation; Chiron (Bermuda) Ltd.; Chiron Redevelopment Corp. & Co. KG (Germany); 31. Corsa Verwaltungsgesellschaft GmbH (Germany); Chiron Behring GmbH & Co (Germany); Chiron Behring Verwaltungsgesellschaft GmbH (Germany); Chiron S.p.A. (Italy); Instituto Vaccinogen Pozzi S.p.A. (Italy); Biocine S.A.R.L. (France); Chiron Technologies Pty. Ltd. (Australia); Chiron Mimotopes U.S.; Chiron Redevelopment Corporation; Chiron Foreign Sales Corporation (U.S. Virgin Islands); Chiron Funding LLC; Chiron Funding Corporation; Biocent Insurance Company, Inc.; Chiron AB (Sweden); Chiron Vision Canada, Inc.; Chiron Behring Vaccines Limited (India; 51%).

Principal Competitors

Abbott Laboratories; American Home Products Corporation; Amgen Inc.; Aventis Pasteur; Bayer Corporation; Biogen, Inc.; Genentech, Inc.; Genzyme Corporation; Immunex Corporation; Johnson & Johnson; Merck & Co., Inc.; Roche Holding Ltd.; Schering Plough Corporation; SmithKline Beecham plc; Teva Pharmaceutical Industries, Ltd.

Further Reading

Abate, Tom, ''Biotech Giants' Court Fight over Credit Could Be Worth Millions: Chiron Says Its Patent Proves It Deserves Slice of

Genentech Drug Sales,'' *San Francisco Chronicle,* June 19, 2000, p. G1.

——, ''Chiron Corp. Believes a Slow and Steady Pace Will Win the Race: Biotech Firm's Leader Sees No Need for Speed to Realize Its Potential,'' *San Francisco Chronicle,* August 2, 1999, p. B1.

——, ''Genetic Bloodhound: New Test from Rival Bay Area Biotech Firms Can Sniff Out Viral Infection in Donations,'' *San Francisco Chronicle,* May 31, 1999, p. E1.

——, ''Investors Yawn at Chiron's $700 Million Deal,'' *San Francisco Chronicle,* August 15, 2000, p. C1.

Barnum, Alex, ''Chiron Takes a New Turn: Merger with Cetus May Speed Rebirth of Biotech Firm,'' *San Francisco Chronicle,* December 10, 1991, p. C1.

——, ''U.S. Biotech Is Thriving in Japan: Chiron Got Start by Using Blood Test on Emperor Hirohito,'' *San Francisco Chronicle,* May 12, 1992, p. C1.

Bronson, Gail, ''Beyond the Band-Aid,'' *Forbes,* June 1, 1987, p. 160.

DeBare, Ilana, ''Chiron Finally Names Its New Chief Executive,'' *San Francisco Chronicle,* March 24, 1998, p. C1.

Emert, Carol, ''Chiron's Lab Kit Unit Sold: $1.1 Billion Agreement Will Help Firm Refocus,'' *San Francisco Chronicle,* September 18, 1998, p. B1.

Fisher, Lawrence M., ''Market Place: Chiron Investors Pay a Price for the Biotech Company's Success,'' *New York Times,* March 25, 1994, pp. C6, D6.

Gannes, Stuart, ''Striking It Rich in Biotech,'' *Fortune,* November 9, 1987, p. 131.

Hall, Carl T., ''Chiron Drops Its Herpes Vaccine,'' *San Francisco Chronicle,* November 26, 1996, p. C1.

——, ''Chiron Leads the Rebound in Biotechnology: Complicated Company Surprises Wall Street,'' *San Francisco Chronicle,* August 14, 1995, p. D1.

Hamilton, Joan, O'C., ''Revenge of the Nerds in Biotech Land,'' *Business Week,* August 5, 1991, p. 26.

Hill, G. Christian, ''Chiron Agrees to Buy Viagene for Cash, Stock,'' *Wall Street Journal,* April 25, 1995, p. B7.

Kazakoff, Lois, ''Chiron Seeks New Blood: A Year Later, Biotech Firm Is Still in Search of Chief Executive,'' *San Francisco Chronicle,* January 13, 1998, p. C1.

King, Ralph T., Jr., ''Chiron Names Industry Veteran Lance As Its CEO,'' *Wall Street Journal,* March 24, 1998, p. B10.

——, ''Chiron Will Pay About $120 Million for 49% of Hoechst's Vaccine Business,'' *Wall Street Journal,* February 21, 1996, p. B6.

——, ''Troubles at Chiron Tarnish Chairman's Reputation,'' *Wall Street Journal,* October 27, 1997, p. B1.

Moore, Stephen D., and Martin du Bois, ''Bayer Is Buying Chiron's Diagnostics Unit,'' *Wall Street Journal,* September 18, 1998, p. B5.

Savitz, Eric J., and Edward A. Wyatt, ''Fulfilling Their Promise: Wondrous Products and Even Profits Are in Sight for Biotech Firms,'' *Barron's,* September 25, 1989, p. 6.

Sinton, Peter, ''Chiron President Quits Post,'' *San Francisco Chronicle,* January 30, 1997, p. E1.

Tanaka, Wendy, ''A Swiss Pill for Chiron: Basel Drug Giant Ciba-Geigy Gets 49.9% Stake in Biotech Company,'' *San Francisco Examiner,* November 22, 1994, p. C1.

Tran, Khanh T.L., ''Chiron to Acquire PathoGenesis for $700 Million,'' *Wall Street Journal,* August 15, 2000, p. B9.

Zipser, Andy, ''Hit or Myth? Mutual Choice,'' *Barron's,* May 25, 1992, p. 30.

—Maura Troester
—updated by David E. Salamie

Conexant Systems, Inc.

4311 Jamboree Road
Newport Beach, California 92660-3095
U.S.A.
Telephone: (949) 483-4600
Fax: (949) 483-4078
Web site: http://www.conexant.com

Public Company
Incorporated: 1999
Employees: 7,200
Sales: $1.44 billion (1999)
Stock Exchanges: NASDAQ
Ticker Symbol: CNXT
NAIC: 334413 Semiconductor and Related Device
Manufacturing

As a unit of Rockwell International, the predecessor of Conexant Systems, Inc. has made semiconductors, or chips, since the 1960s. Although not its largest division, Rockwell Semiconductor Systems (RSS) was Rockwell International's fastest growing business in the 1990s, until demand for chips fell off in 1996 and the industry went through a period of excess supplies. In 1998 parent company Rockwell International decided to spin off RSS to its shareholders in a tax-free stock exchange in an effort to improve its profits and make its semiconductor business more competitive. The new company, Conexant Systems, Inc., began business in January 1999 with $1.2 billion in revenues and a workforce of about 6,300. Conexant quickly returned to profitability by focusing exclusively on developing semiconductors for the communications market.

Innovative Products from
Rockwell's Semiconductor Division: 1960s–90s

The business unit of Rockwell International that later became its Microelectronics Division developed 4800bps/9600bps IC modems in the 1960s. In 1968 the company entered the commercial modem business, when the first modem market was fax machines. In 1971 it developed the first 4800bps LST

modems. The Rockwell International Microelectronics Division was created in 1971 to fuel the development of microprocessor technology and computer products. In 1977 it was renamed the Electronic Devices Division and became the largest producer of the R6502 microprocessor. In 1978 it began shipping high-speed OEM (original equipment manufacturer) modems (4800bps and 9600bps) to facsimile (fax) manufacturers.

The division was renamed Semiconductor Products Division in 1982. During the 1980s it introduced a series of OEM fax, data, and VLSI modems and in 1985 began its fax-modem chipset business that it would subsequently dominate. It also helped create the analog modem market for desktop computers. In 1988 it opened its European Design Center in Sophia Antipolis, France.

In 1990 the division was again renamed, this time as the Digital Communications Division, with headquarters in Newport Beach, California, as part of Rockwell International's reorganization of its semiconductor and communications business. It opened its Japanese Design Center in Tokyo, Japan, and introduced the world's first integrated, low-speed data and fax modem as well as the first high-speed, single-device fax modem operating at 14,400bps transmission.

The division continued to introduce innovative data and fax modem products throughout the decade. In 1993 the division became Rockwell International's Telecommunications business unit as part of the firm's reorganization of its digital communications and switching systems business. In 1994 it completed a $200 million expansion of its wafer fabrication facility in Newport Beach.

Rockwell, Focusing on Multimedia and
Wireless Communications: 1995–98

In 1995 the division was renamed Rockwell Semiconductor Systems (RSS) and focused on multimedia and wireless communications. Another $200 million expansion of the Newport Beach fabrication facility was begun. During the year RSS introduced several new products, including the industry's first single-package 28.8Kbps modem-chip family integrating speakerphone/data/fax/telephone answering machine functions. RSS was not Rockwell International's largest business, but it

Company Perspectives:

Conexant is the world's largest independent company focused exclusively on providing semiconductor system solutions for communications electronics. With revenues of approximately $1.5 billion, Conexant has aligned its business to target the fastest-growing markets of the worldwide communications marketplace. The company's solutions are found in the wireline voice and data products that power the Internet, cordless and cellular wireless telephony systems, personal imaging communications equipment, and emerging cable and wireless broadband networks.

was the fastest growing. It dominated the fax modem market, selling 80 percent of the chips used in fax machines. From 1992 through 1995 RSS enjoyed a compound annual growth rate of about 35 percent.

In 1996 RSS opened a semiconductor systems design center in Israel. Early in the year it broke ground for a new wafer fabrication facility in Colorado Springs on land that it had acquired from United Technologies. The plant was scheduled to open in mid-1997. In addition to its plant in Newport Beach, Rockwell had another chipmaking plant in Newbury Park, California. Later in the year Rockwell announced that it would delay the opening of the Colorado Springs plant until early 1998. The delay reflected a change in the overall semiconductor industry, which was experiencing a slump in demand that made it cheaper for Rockwell to purchase wafers rather than make its own. Chip manufacturers with excess capacity were selling wafers at significant discounts in the face of a falloff in demand.

Later in 1996 parent company Rockwell International sold its military and aerospace business to Boeing Co. in a deal valued at $3.2 billion. Boeing assumed $2.17 billion in debt and other Rockwell liabilities and gave Rockwell shareholders about $860 million in Boeing stock. The deal would leave Rockwell virtually debt-free and in a position to expand through acquisitions. Rockwell International would keep its four commercial electronics and automation businesses. At the time of the sale, semiconductors accounted for about 16 percent of Rockwell's revenues. The semiconductor division planned to focus on higher margin products and not concentrate on commodity semiconductors. These products included personal communications chipsets for sale to OEMs, global positioning system (GPS) receivers, and wireless systems devices.

Around this same time Rockwell acquired chipmaker Brooktree Corp. for $275 million in stock. The acquisition of Brooktree, a San Diego-based firm with 575 employees and operations in Colorado and Texas as well as San Diego, gave RSS the technology to expand its high-speed digital communications and multimedia product lines.

Also in 1996 RSS and Lucent Technologies agreed to make their 56Kbps modem chipsets interoperable, even though industry standards had not yet been determined. RSS introduced several new products, including new modem technology enabling Internet connections at rates up to 56Kbps across standard phone lines. RSS also introduced the first in a family of

56Kbps digital modem devices for central-site equipment at the fall 1996 Comdex industry trade show and exhibition. At the time Rockwell was proposing 56Kbps as the new industry standard for Internet modems, almost twice as fast as the then current rate of 28.8Kbps of most high-end modems.

RSS planned to begin volume production of the 56Kbps chipsets in the first quarter of 1997, but a problem discovered by Motorola in field tests delayed full production until April. By May Rockwell was shipping a million units per month. Rockwell's primary competitor was U.S. Robotics, which had signed major Internet service providers (ISP) America Online and Compuserve (later merged into AOL), while Rockwell had received commitments from hundreds of smaller ISPs. U.S. Robotics was subsequently acquired by 3Com Corp. Rockwell and 3Com used different standards, and their modems could only talk to each other at speeds up to 33.6Kbps.

Toward the end of 1997 inventor Brent Townshend, a consulting electrical engineering professor at Stanford University, claimed that RSS had illegally acquired the technology and fundamental concepts behind its 56Kbps modems. Townshend claimed he disclosed his ideas to Rockwell in a series of 1995 meetings aimed at reaching a licensing agreement. When no agreement was reached, Townshend later granted an exclusive, worldwide license to U.S. Robotics.

In December 1996 RSS acquired Pacific Communications Sciences, Inc., a subsidiary of Cirrus Logic that specialized in wireless semiconductor products, for $18.1 million. The acquisition added about 125 employees and enabled RSS to produce a line of chips for pagers and cellular and cordless telephones.

In 1997 RSS reorganized into five divisions based on strategic product platforms: Personal Computing, Personal Imaging, Digital Infotainment, Wireless Communications, and Network Access. It acquired the Hi-Media broadband communications chipset business of ComStream Corporation. It also licensed microprocessor technology from Advanced Risc Machines Inc.

Toward the end of 1997 RSS introduced a new high-speed modem technology called consumer digital subscriber line (CDSL). CDSL was designed to ease the transition for consumers from analog modems to higher speed digital formats. CDSL technology would enable modem manufacturers to combine DSL and traditional modem technology in a single device. The CDSL chips were expected to be ready for shipment to OEMs in the spring of 1998. As part of its CDSL initiative, RSS entered into a joint development agreement with Orckit Communications for high bit rate DSL products (HDSL) and with Northern Telecom (Nortel) to make Rockwell's CDSL format interoperable with Nortel's similar one-megabyte modem system. At the same time RSS announced its first chipset to support high-speed cable modems, which were considered the primary competition for xDSL lines in the consumer market. The company also reached a tentative agreement with 3Com Corp. to produce 56Kbps modems using a common standard before the end of 1997.

Continuing Business As
Conexant Systems, Inc.: 1998–2000

In mid-1998 Rockwell International Corp. announced that it would spin off Rockwell Semiconductor Systems as a separate company, which would subsequently be called Conexant Systems, Inc., by the end of 1998. For fiscal 1998 RSS was expected to show an operating loss, due in part to a weak PC modem market and a work stoppage at its Newport Beach facility. Parent company Rockwell International's quarterly results were also well below analysts' expectations, and the company planned to cut 3,800 jobs from its workforce after spinning off RSS to its shareholders. RSS had about 7,000 employees and would have about $1.3 billion in revenues for fiscal 1998.

Before the spinoff was completed, RSS laid off 700 employees, about ten percent of its workforce, and closed its wafer fabrication plant in Colorado Springs. For fiscal 1998 ending September 30, RSS posted a loss of $275 million, including charges of about $90 million to close its Colorado Springs facility and reduce its workforce. The semiconductor industry was going through a period of weak demand and faced a worldwide glut of semiconductors.

In its first formal filing regarding the spinoff, RSS estimated that it had 70 percent of the worldwide market for fax chips and was the largest single maker of modem chips. Approximately 45 percent of its revenues came from Asia, which was going through a financial crisis. The company had experienced 18 months of declining sales as weak demand and excess inventories buffeted the semiconductor sector.

In January 1999 Conexant Systems, Inc. was launched as an independent entity after Rockwell International Corp. completed the spinoff of Rockwell Semiconductor Systems to shareholders. The new name was announced at the fall Comdex show in Las Vegas in November 1998. Dwight Decker, president of RSS, would continue as chairman and CEO of Conexant. Conexant's stock began trading on the NASDAQ stock exchange on January 4 at $17 to $18 a share. Conexant

began operations with nearly 6,300 employees and annual revenues of about $1.2 billion.

Conexant would continue to share some resources with Rockwell International, including the Rockwell Science Center, where technologies such as gallium arsenide chips and CMOS imaging technology were invented. Conexant would provide some funding for the lab, which employed 280 researchers, and share in technology research focused on the communications market. Rockwell International also would remain a customer for Conexant's avionics and automotive products.

In March 1999 Conexant announced that it had developed a single chip for cable modems that could handle digital data, audio, and video signals—functions that were currently being performed by four to six chips. The same month Conexant also unveiled its interactive digital television (DTV) set-top box (STB) platform.

With its strategy firmly focused on semiconductors for the communications market, Conexant returned to profitability ahead of schedule in its second quarter ending March 30, 1999, with net income of $7.6 million on revenue of $316.9 million. Its third quarter results exceeded analysts' expectations. Conexant was the largest semiconductor company in the world focused exclusively on communications semiconductors, and it had the broadest product portfolio of communications products of any similar company. It had achieved twice the market share of its nearest competitor in 56K modems. The company's wireless communications and network access divisions were growing faster than expected. In addition, the personal computing division was experiencing a reversal of declining demand for PC modems. In July 1999 Conexant became part of the NASDAQ 100 Index. Later in the year Conexant announced a two-for-one stock split.

Acquisition of New Technologies: 1999–2000

Before the end of 1999 Conexant announced plans to acquire smaller technology firms over the next several months. Rival chip makers Intel Corp. and Broadcom Corp. had recently acquired communication-technology companies as demand fueled by Internet communications exploded. In August Conexant invested $10 million in Entridia Corp., a 1997 privately held start-up that designed chips that route voice, video, and data transmissions from a server to a workplace computer. In December it acquired Maker Communications Inc. of Framingham, Massachusetts, for $942.8 million in stock. The company developed software that enabled engineers to create semiconductors for Internet communications. Conexant also opened a design center in Portland, Oregon, to attract talent in the area known as Silicon Forest.

At the end of 1999 Broadcom and Conexant both announced competing versions of a tuner chip to replace the bulky channel-switching device in cable boxes and televisions. An inexpensive tuner chip would make multiple functions like Internet access over a television screen and features like picture-in-picture more commonplace. Conexant also was seeking industry certification for its cable modem, which failed the first test. Broadcom was considered the industry leader in cable modems.

At the start of 2000 Conexant acquired British chip maker Microcosm Communications Ltd. for about $128 million in stock. The acquisition of the high-volume chip producer was expected to boost revenue in Conexant's fiber-optic networking business. In acquiring smaller firms, Conexant was focusing on companies that already had products and were generating revenue.

In January 2000 Conexant was chosen to replace Consolidated Natural Gas Co. in the Standard & Poor's 500 Index. The company's stock rose 18 percent in one day. At the end of February, though, it dropped about 16 percent in one day when an investment banker downgraded the stock from "strong buy" to "buy." In early March analysts were concerned about one of Conexant's major customers, Lucent Technologies, and the possibility Conexant had been designed out of some of Lucent's next-generation products. One analyst estimated Lucent accounted for six percent of Conexant's revenues and as much as ten percent of its profits. Conexant was also facing new competition from companies such as RF Micro Devices in the power amplifier business for cell phones, which accounted for 12 percent of Conexant's revenues. On the positive side, analysts noted that Conexant seemed to be making a successful transition from its older analog modem business to digital technology and cable. After initial problems getting its cable modem design certified, Conexant received industry certification in July 2000 for a single-chip cable modem that would allow consumers to purchase PCs with always-on, high-speed cable modems.

In April 2000 Conexant acquired Philsar Semiconductor Inc. of Ottawa, Canada, for stock worth from $166.5 million to $186 million. Philsar designed chips that enabled wireless devices to connect to one another and change functions quickly. Another acquisition involved Illinois-based Applied Telecom Inc., a supplier of telecommunications software and hardware. In May Conexant bought Sierra Imaging Inc. for about $43.6 million in stock. Sierra made software and semiconductors for digital cameras.

In June 2000 Conexant acquired high-speed network chip maker HotRail Inc. for about $394 million in stock. The acquisition strengthened Conexant's network offerings. The acquired technology would enable the company to deliver complete systems for next-generation Internet infrastructure, including high-speed routers, Internet protocol and Ethernet switches, and optical networking equipment.

Conexant continued its acquisitions in July with the purchase of two companies. One was NetPlane Systems of Dedham, Massachusetts, which developed software for network control and other functions. The technology would facilitate Conexant's entry into network switching and complemented the HotRail acquisition. Conexant acquired NetPlane for 2.4 million shares of stock valued at about $120 million. The second company was Novanet Semiconductor, a designer of high-speed physical layer networking solutions based in Israel. Conexant acquired Novanet for 2.7 million shares of stock valued at about $140 million. Both companies became part of Conexant's Network Access division.

Facing an inevitable decline in its core dial-up PC modem business, Conexant's acquisition strategy was designed to strengthen its Network Access and Wireless divisions. For its third quarter ending June 30, 2000, Conexant's record revenues of $530.5 million broke down as follows: $155.3 million (30 percent) from Network Access; $92.6 million (17 percent) from Wireless Communications; $71.0 million (13 percent) from Digital Infotainment; $27.6 million (five percent) from Personal Imaging; and $184.0 million (35 percent) from Personal Computing. In the newer wireless and broadband technologies, Conexant was facing a host of new competitors that were focused on specific sectors of the market. The company's goal, however, was to be the number one communications semiconductor company.

Principal Divisions

Network Access; Personal Computing; Personal Imaging; Wireless Communications; Digital Infotainment.

Principal Competitors

C-Cube Microsystems Corporation; uniView Technologies Corporation; Broadcom Corporation; Intel Corporation; International Business Machines Corporation; Lucent Technologies Inc.; Texas Instruments Inc.; STMicroelectronics Inc.; Anadigics Inc.; RF Micro Devices; Triquint Semiconductor Inc.; Alpha Industries Inc.; Network Device Inc.; Analog Devices Inc.

Further Reading

Bean, Joanna, "Rockwell Delays Start-Up of Colorado Springs Computer Chip Plant," *Knight-Ridder/Tribune Business News,* July 17, 1996.

——, "Rockwell Semiconductor Systems to Leave Colorado Springs, Colo.," *Knight-Ridder/Tribune Business News,* September 16, 1998.

——, "Rockwell Semiconductor to Build Computer Chip Factory in Colorado," *Knight-Ridder/Tribune Business News,* February 9, 1996.

Berry, Kate, "Newport Beach, Calif., Communications-Chip Maker Buys British Firm," *Knight-Ridder/Tribune Business News,* January 7, 2000.

Bradley, Gale, "Done Deal! It's Now Boeing North American," *Electronic News (1991),* December 9, 1996, p. 56.

Bradley, Gary, "Rockwell Handing Boeing Defense and Aerospace," *Electronic News (1991),* August 5, 1996, p. 1.

Brinton, James B., "Reborn Rockwell Rolls Toward 2000," *Electronic Business Today,* December 1996, p. 45.

Brown, Peter, "The Race for STB Dominance," *Electronic News (1991),* March 22, 1999, p. 20.

Campbell, Ronald, "Rockwell Picks Up Speed, Saying Bug in Its Modems Has Been Fixed," *Knight-Ridder/Tribune Business News,* April 10, 1997.

——, "Rockwell Semiconductor Expects $275 Million Loss for Fiscal Year," *Knight-Ridder/Tribune Business News,* September 30, 1998.

——, "Rockwell Semiconductor Faces Restructuring Pains," *Knight-Ridder/Tribune Business News,* September 15, 1998.

——, "War of Two Modem Technologies Rages at 56,000 Bits Per Second," *Knight-Ridder/Tribune Business News,* August 13, 1997.

Cassell, Jonathan, "CEO Maps Conexant's Course," *Electronic News (1991),* April 5, 1999, p. 10.

Chaney, Lindsay, "Rockwell Bows Out of Aerospace," *Knight-Ridder/Tribune Business News,* December 6, 1996.

Chmielewski, Dawn C., "California's Broadcom and Conexant Make Separate Buyout Deals," *Knight-Ridder/Tribune Business News,* May 23, 2000.

Cohen, Sarah, "Rockwell: 56-Kbit Modems Just Around the Corner," *Electronic News (1991),* February 10, 1997, p. 20.

Colman, Price, "Conexant Risks Dip into Cable Modem Chips," *Broadcasting & Cable,* March 1, 1999, p. 40.

"Conexant a Nasdaq Choice," *Electronic News (1991),* July 19, 1999, p. 6.

"Conexant Buys Sierra Imaging," *Electronic News (1991),* May 29, 2000, p. 4.

"Conexant Stock Split," *Electronic News (1991),* September 20, 1999, p. 6.

"Conexant Systems, Inc.," *Business Journal-Portland,* November 5, 1999, p. 4.

"Conexant Takes Its First Steps," *Electronic News (1991),* January 11, 1999, p. 14.

"Conexant to Beat Analysts," *Electronic News (1991),* June 14, 1999, p. 6.

DeTar, Jim, "Rockwell Spins Semi Unit," *Electronic News (1991),* July 6, 1998, p. 1.

Doan, Amy, "56Kbps Modems Arrive Without Standards," *InfoWorld,* November 25, 1996, p. 47.

Farnsworth, Chris, "California's Broadcom, Conexant Brace for Cable-TV Computer-Chip Battle," *Knight-Ridder/Tribune Business News,* December 7, 1999.

——, "Chip Manufacturer Expands into New Irvine, Calif., Office," *Knight-Ridder/Tribune Business News,* December 2, 1999.

——, "Newport Beach, Calif.-Based Cable Firm Gets Rejected for Modem Bid," *Knight-Ridder/Tribune Business News,* December 9, 1999.

——, "Newport Beach, Calif.-Based Firm's Cable Modem Fails Again," *Knight-Ridder/Tribune Business News,* March 9, 2000.

——, "New Products Intensify Rivalry Between California Tuner-Chip Makers," *Knight-Ridder/Tribune Business News,* December 6, 1999.

——, "Orange County, Calif.-Based Communications-Chip Maker Buys Canadian Firm," *Knight-Ridder/Tribune Business News,* April 12, 2000.

——, "Orange County, Calif., Chip Maker Spends $394 Million for Network Firm," *Knight-Ridder/Tribune Business News,* June 27, 2000.

Haber, Carol, "Conexant Challenge: Modem, Wireless," *Electronic News (1991),* May 1, 2000, p. 56.

——, "Conexant Shares Socked," *Electronic News (1991),* March 6, 2000, p. 42.

——, "Spin-Offs Proliferate, Setting Stage for New IPOs," *Electronic News (1991),* June 7, 1999, p. 46.

——, "Wireless Winners in Acquisition Mode," *Electronic News (1991),* February 21, 2000, p. 36.

Hardie, Crista, "Rockwell to Buy Cirrus Wireless Unit," *Electronic News (1991),* December 23, 1996, p. 8.

Humphry, Sara, "56K bps Across Regular Phone Lines?," *PC Week,* September 23, 1996, p. N14.

Lavilla, Stacy, "Rockwell Nabs Brooktree to Bolster Chip Holdings," *PC Week,* July 8, 1996, p. 10.

MacLellan, Andrew, "Rockwell Proposes New Internet Modem Standard," *Electronic News (1991),* September 16, 1996, p. 18.

——, "Rockwell to Buy Brooktree," *Electronic News (1991),* July 8, 1996, p. 1.

Mateyaschuk, Jennifer, "Rockwell to Spin Off Semiconductor Unit," *InformationWeek,* July 6, 1998, p. 12.

Morrison, Gale, "Binge on Optical Gear," *Electronic News (1991),* January 10, 2000, p. 4.

Murphy, Tom, "Conexant Adds PHY Filly," *Electronic News (1991),* April 17, 2000, p. 18.

——, "Conexant Rolls STB Chipsets," *Electronic News (1991),* May 22, 2000, p. 50.

Niccolai, James, "Modem Companies Rush to Get on 56Kbps Uplink Bandwagon," *InfoWorld,* September 23, 1996, p. 49.

Presti, Ken, "Glitch Found in Rockwell 56-Kbps Modem Chipsets," *Computer Reseller News,* March 24, 1997, p. 14.

Roberts, Bill, "Spinning-off to Profits," *Electronic Business,* August 1999, p. 50.

"Rockwell Starts First Phase of $1.2B Colorado 'Megafab,' " *Electronic News (1991),* February 12, 1996, p. 60.

"Rockwell, 3Com Make a Pact," *Computerworld,* December 8, 1997, p. 8.

Rosenberg, Ronald, "Newport Beach, Calif.-Based Communications Supplier Buys Software Maker," *Knight-Ridder/Tribune Business News,* December 20, 1999.

Salamone, Salvatore, "New Flavors of DSL Just Keep Coming," *InternetWeek,* November 10, 1997, p. 41.

Schaff, William, "Conexant Is Worth a Premium," *InformationWeek,* July 3, 2000, p. 146.

Wade, Will, "Inventor Claims Rockwell Used His 56K Technology," *Electronic News (1991),* October 27, 1997, p. 62.

——, "Rockwell Launches High-Speed Modem Technology for Home User," *Electronic News (1991),* November 3, 1997, p. 14.

——, "Rockwell Pushes into DSL Development," *Electronic News (1991),* December 1, 1997, p. 6.

Wallace, Bob, "56K Modems on Deck," *Computerworld,* September 16, 1996, p. 1.

"Week in Review: Top Business Stories for Week of 12/28," *Electronic News (1991),* January 4, 1999, p. 55.

—David P. Bianco

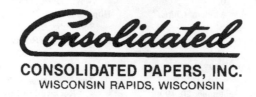

CONSOLIDATED PAPERS, INC.
WISCONSIN RAPIDS, WISCONSIN

Consolidated Papers, Inc.

P.O. Box 8050
Wisconsin Rapids, Wisconsin 54495-8050
U.S.A.
Telephone: (715) 422-3111
Fax: (715) 422-3882
Web site: http://www.consolidatedpapers.com

Wholly Owned Subsidiary of Stora Enso Oyj
Incorporated: 1894 as Consolidated Water Power
    Company
Employees: 6,792
Sales: $1.84 billion (1999)
NAIC: 113110 Timber Tract Operations; 113310
    Logging; 322110 Pulp Mills; 322121 Paper (Except
    Newsprint) Mills; 322130 Paperboard Mills; 322222
    Coated and Laminated Paper Manufacturing

Consolidated Papers, Inc., which was acquired by Finnish-Swedish paper giant Stora Enso Oyj in August 2000, is the leading North American producer of coated and supercalendered printing papers. These are specially finished, glazed papers used for such things as magazines, brochures, and corporate annual reports, as well as catalogs, newspaper inserts, and direct mailings. More than 85 percent of company revenues are derived from these specialty papers. Consolidated also makes specialty papers used in the packaging and labeling of food and consumer products, paperboard and paperboard products, and pulp. The company owns and manages about 700,000 acres of forestland located in Wisconsin, Michigan, Minnesota, and the Canadian province of Ontario.

Early Years

In 1894, several small water power concerns on the Wisconsin River organized to form the Consolidated Water Power Company. Eight years later, the company expanded its operations to include the manufacturing of paper, changing its name to Consolidated Water Power & Paper Company. Consolidated started up the world's first electrically powered paper machines

in 1904. Over the next decade, the company manufactured newsprint and wallpaper, as well as power. Expansions included the 1911 acquisition of Grand Rapids Pulp and Paper Company and its mill at Biron, Wisconsin, which became Consolidated's Biron Division; and the 1916 purchase of a pulp mill in Appleton, Wisconsin, which became the Interlake Division. By 1919, the company had constructed a hydroelectric plant and paper mill in Stevens Point, Wisconsin, in order to manufacture tissue, waxing, and specialty papers.

With the acquisition of Newaygo Timber Company, Limited in 1920, Consolidated grew to include timberland acreage in Ontario, Canada. The previously acquired Biron division was converted in 1929—along with the Wisconsin Rapids division—to produce book and writing papers.

1930s Through 1970s: Pioneering and Innovating in Coated Paper

Emmett Hurst launched the company's forestry program in 1930. Five years later, Consolidated developed and introduced the Consolidated Massey coater. This revolutionized the industry by producing the first coated paper manufactured by a single high-speed operation. Over the next seven years, Consolidated converted five paper machines to the high-speed coating process and began to focus on the production of coated papers.

In addition to the coating technology, Consolidated developed an exceptionally strong plastics material in 1943. During World War II, in order to produce aircraft materials, the company formed a Plastic Division, which later became Consoweld Corporation. In 1945, the company acquired Wisconsin River Paper and Pulp Company, which operated a paper mill and dam in Whiting, Wisconsin; the mill became Consolidated's Wisconsin River Division and was converted to produce coated printing papers. The merger with Ahdawagam Paper Products Company in 1948 expanded Consolidated's product line to include paperboard containers and cartons (Ahdawagam eventually became the Paperboard Products Division).

Throughout the 1950s, Consolidated concentrated on the sale and production of its coated papers, introducing a new line of coated papers and launching a major national advertising program. In 1959, a new research and development center was completed. Another groundbreaking invention in paper-coating technology came in 1961, with the Dip Roll Blade coater. At this point, the company was undergoing conversion from roll to blade coating. This same year marked the one millionth ton of enamel papers sold by Consolidated's merchants. In 1962 the company changed its name to Consolidated Papers, Inc.

Toward the end of the 1960s, construction began on a $37 million kraft pulp mill and power complex that launched the new Kraft Division. Kraft paper is a stronger grade of pulp that replaced sulfate. Consolidated purchased Castle Rock Container Company, a corrugated container plant, in 1970. The next decade reflected increased environmental as well as market considerations as the company began pouring its capital into modifications and expansions. In 1970 and 1971, the company put more than $1 million into primary wastewater treatment plants, and in 1972 announced plans for an $8.6 million treatment plant to serve the Wisconsin Rapids, Biron, and Kraft Divisions. A pollution abatement program was completed that same year. In 1973 ground was broken for a $2.7 million sheet converting plant in Wisconsin and a $5.6 million lumber/chip complex in Ontario, Canada, which closed in 1984. The following year, Consolidated began a $12.8 million modification program at its Kraft Division to increase pulp capacity by 26,000 tons a year. In 1975, the company launched a $6 million boiler plant to burn coal and bark. Consolidated then broke ground for a $4 million secondary treatment plant.

Two years later, a $64.6 million papermaking expansion project was underway at the Wisconsin River Division to increase enamel paper capacity by 95,000 tons per year and a new thermomechanical pulp system was begun at the Biron Division. Also in 1977, Consolidated introduced another frontrunner in paper-coating technology: the short-dwell-time applicator. This applicator was considered the progenitor of later state-of-the-art technology in lightweight coating. Greater automation was introduced into various production aspects in 1978, such as high-speed computerized presses and an automatic splicer.

1980s: Expanding in Volatile Times

The 1980s were volatile years in the paper industry. The explosion in the use of computers and copying machines cre-

ated a boom in the paper industry early in the decade. Consolidated's earnings benefited particularly with the increase in direct-mail advertising and color inserts in newspapers, which made use of the company's specialized lightweight coated papers. The company at this point had enjoyed steady, above-average profit margins and had become a solid leader in specialized papers. Consolidated started the 1980s with the construction of a new office building in Wisconsin Rapids and the celebration of its forestry program's 50th year. The company also acquired sole ownership of Consoweld Corporation that year and began a $1.5 million expansion program for that company. Consoweld was sold to LOF Plastics, Inc. in 1986.

In order to catch up with demand, Consolidated began a multimillion-dollar expansion program in 1981, seeking to increase capacity of specialty coated papers by 24 percent. The following year, it began a $17 million Wisconsin Rapids Division expansion. In 1985, Consolidated celebrated its 50th year of manufacturing coated printing and specialty papers. At this point, the Wisconsin-based company was considered the world's largest producer of enamel papers. The company was also producing lightweight, coated specialty papers for packaging and labeling, in addition to more conventional corrugated containers—used for shipping large items such as refrigerators and televisions—and paperboard products.

While the company's manufacturing base was centralized in Wisconsin, Consolidated's timberland base spread across 670,000 acres of Wisconsin, Michigan, Minnesota, and Ontario. By 1985, the company was generating about 23 percent of its raw material requirements, a goal it had set for itself some six years prior, when management analyzed long-term fiber requirements against softwood availability. At that point, a softwood shortage was forecast for the upper Midwest by the year 2030—about the same time demand was expected to have doubled. To circumvent this shortage, Consolidated's timberlands division intensified all aspects of reforestation, including harvesting, site preparation, planting, seedling research, and production. A program was laid out that included the replanting of 2,000 acres annually for the first five years. By 1983, 3,500 acres were planted. The following year, 3,300 acres were planted. Most of the acreage was being converted from low-quality hardwoods to red pine—chosen for its preferred fiber and rapid growth—and the goal was to plant 50,000 acres by the year 2000. In 1985, however, some 7,000 acres were being harvested annually and that was still not meeting the growth rate.

In addition to these incentives to the timberlands division, the company was instituting a program to recycle sludge material from its Water Quality Center. Made up of natural materials used in the papermaking process, sludge was spread on commercial farmland as a combination fertilizer/soil amendment. This saved on landfill costs while improving soil fertility. The sludge—called ConsoGro—and its application was the result of a six-year research program conducted by Consolidated. Another environmentally sound breakthrough about this time was the addition of peroxide to the high-density storage stage of production in order to increase pulp brightness and output. This proved an innovative solution with the added benefit that hydrogen peroxide is environmentally safe.

In 1986, Consolidated's Biron mill won *Newsweek*'s "Mill of the Year" award for the second time in four years. The Biron

Key Dates:

1894: Several small water power companies on the Wisconsin River merge to form Consolidated Water Power Company.

1902: Company expands into the manufacture of paper and changes its name to Consolidated Water Power & Paper Company.

1911: Company acquires Grand Rapids Pulp and Paper Company, which becomes the Biron Division.

1919: Stevens Point Division is launched with the opening of a paper mill and hydroelectric plant.

1935: Company produces the first coated paper made in a single, high-speed operation.

1945: Wisconsin River Paper and Pulp Company is acquired and becomes the Wisconsin River Division.

1948: Acquisition of Ahdawagam Paper Products Company expands Consolidated into paperboard containers and cartons.

1962: The company changes its name to Consolidated Papers, Inc.

1984: $215 million expansion of the Biron mill is launched.

1995: $166 million expansion of the Stevens Point mill begins; company acquires Niagara of Wisconsin Paper Corporation (which becomes the Niagara Division), Lake Superior Paper Industries, and Superior Recycled Fiber Industries.

1997: Company acquires Repap USA, Inc., which is renamed Inter Lake Papers, Inc.

2000: Consolidated is acquired by Stora Enso Oyj of Finland.

Division had been the focal point of Consolidated's largest capital project, an expansion investment of $215 million of internal cash flow launched in late 1984. The result was a state-of-the-art coating plant. Company Chairman and CEO George Mead told *Pulp and Paper* magazine in 1987, "When I joined this industry, the general feeling was that companies our size did not have the muscle to keep up. They were thought to be inadequate in financing and in depth of skilled personnel. Many companies felt they had to become part of larger, more powerful organizations in order to survive. We have shown that this is not necessarily true."

The following year, Consolidated announced a $96.7 million capital expense program. This included a further $46 million expansion of pulp production at the Kraft Division. Another $22 million was slated for improvements of the production of heavier coated free-sheet papers. Some of this money was also earmarked for further computerization of inventory.

Additional expansion plans were announced in 1989 to produce top quality coated paper for annual reports and high-grade brochures. That same year the Paperboard Products Division added a seven-color press to its equipment, allowing it to produce high-quality, multicolor folding cartons. Diversifications such as these helped protect Consolidated from the rumblings in the industry caused by the recession as well as the fact that paper mills everywhere had been running near capacity and fear of a shortage was setting in. Coated paper had proven to be a more profitable and steady business than commodity paper. The company's operating margin remained more than 20 percent in eight out of ten years between 1979 and 1989.

1990s: The Final Decade of Independence

Being a largely family-run company had kept Consolidated small and disciplined. In 1992, nearly 30 percent of Consolidated's employees had been with the company for more than 20 years—a remarkable record of loyalty. In 1989, 41 percent of company stock was in the hands of one of its founder's descendants, including then Chairman George Mead. In the manner of a conservative, family-run company, Consolidated had generally avoided accumulating debt, opting instead to finance capital spending out of its own cash flow. Its growth, furthermore, was always on par with industry demands and internal manageability. All of the intensive expansion projects around this time, however, resulted in a considerable long-term debt for the first time in Consolidated's history. In the early 1990s Consolidated generated sufficient cash to subtract from its debts, while still spending enough to keep its plants current and competitive. Nevertheless, the company did feel the effects of the recession. The early 1990s were a rough time for the entire coated paper industry as advertising in magazines—among the largest consumers of lightweight coated papers—plunged with the sustained economic downturn. Consolidated's sales were punished. The economy also affected the company's heavyweight coated paper profits as well as its overall profits, although Consolidated generally outperformed its industry competitors.

Consolidated was ahead of the landfill problems that plagued many industries in the late 1980s and early 1990s. The company's solid waste management program worked closely with consultants, regulatory agencies, and the community to develop a plan that included landfills on company-owned land as near to treatment plants as possible. Water quality and water renewal center landfills were also located on land near the treatment plants, which allowed Consolidated to keep a close watch on the operations. Such environmental requirements significantly affected Consolidated's profits in the early 1990s. Between 1991 and 1993, the company spent $34.4 million in its Kraft Division alone for environmental improvements that brought it up to regulatory codes. Also, the increased demand for recycled fiber content in Consolidated's papers introduced costly variables, as contamination of recycled fiber was a problem, and producing specialty papers of different weights with recycled pulp was a technological challenge.

In 1990, the development and expansion of wetland mitigation sites around these water quality and water renewal centers began. Consolidated also joined with the Wisconsin Department of Natural Resources to enhance wildlife management and habitat development on company-owned land adjacent to the Mead Wildlife Area. Company forestlands were managed as a source of pulpwood for papermaking, as well as a source of enjoyment to the public through hiking, hunting, and other recreation.

In October 1993 Mead stepped down from the position of CEO while remaining chairperson. President Patrick F. Brennan succeeded Mead as CEO. Brennan had joined the company in 1963 and had moved up the corporate ladder, gaining the position of president and chief operating officer in 1988. He was the first Consolidated chief executive to come from outside the Mead family.

As the paper industry recovered strongly in the robust economy of the mid-1990s, Consolidated began expanding again. The company's mill at Stevens Point was the subject of a $166 million expansion. Started in 1995 and completed two years later, the project involved the addition of a paper machine capable of producing, on an annual basis, 64,000 tons of lightweight coated specialty paper used in food and consumer product packaging and labeling, gift wrap, bar-code labels, and pressure-sensitive release papers. In addition to making capital expenditures, Consolidated also returned to the growth-through-acquisition method. In July 1995 the company acquired Niagara of Wisconsin Paper Corporation, maker of coated groundwood publication papers (which became the Niagara Division); and two Duluth, Minnesota-based companies: Lake Superior Paper Industries, maker of supercalendered paper, and Superior Recycled Fiber Industries, producer of pulp made from deinked waste office paper. In addition to transforming Consolidated into the largest maker of coated printing papers in the country, these acquisitions also expanded the company geographically. All the company's mills had been located within 35 miles of the company's headquarters in Wisconsin Rapids.

Brennan retired at the end of 1995, a year in which the company set records in earnings ($229.2 million) and sales ($1.58 billion). During his tenure, Consolidated had surpassed the $1 billion revenue mark for the first time in 1994. Taking over as president and CEO was Gorton M. Evans, who had joined the company in 1973 and had most recently served as an executive vice-president. Evans led Consolidated through an even larger acquisition, that of Repap USA, Inc., which was purchased in October 1997 from Montreal-based Repap Enterprises Inc. for $258 million in cash and $419 million in assumed debt. The Repap USA operations included a mill in Kimberly, Wisconsin, located about 100 miles east of Wisconsin Rapids, with three machines that produced coated printing papers. The addition of what became known as Inter Lake Papers, Inc. increased Consolidated's share of the U.S. coated printing paper market from 15 to 20 percent.

In the last years of the 1990s, Consolidated saw its earnings fall thanks to rising pulp costs, global overcapacity, and increased competition from foreign players able to make inroads into the U.S. market because of a strong U.S. dollar. In response, Consolidated launched a two-year cost-cutting drive in early 1999 aimed at reducing annual operating expenses by $100 million. In addition to the implementation of various operating efficiency initiatives, the company also announced the layoff of 700 workers in mid-2000. Consolidated also disposed of one of its non-coated-paper operations, namely the corrugated packaging subsidiary Castle Rock Container, which was sold to St. Laurent Paperboard Inc. in May 1999.

By early 2000, with global consolidation creating ever more intense pressure on Consolidated and other smaller industry players, the company agreed to be acquired by one of the leading forest products companies in the world, Helsinki-based Stora Enso Oyj. The $4.8 billion cash-and-stock deal, which was completed in August 2000, pushed Stora Enso into the top spot worldwide in coated paper and provided the Finnish-Swedish company with its first significant presence in the North American market, the largest paper market in the world. Although the merger ended 100-plus-years of independence for Consolidated, by partnering with an internationally focused concern, Consolidated could itself gain a more global position. With the Mead family's stake in Consolidated translating into a post-acquisition interest in Stora Enso of 5.7 percent, George Mead was granted a seat on the Stora Enso board.

Principal Subsidiaries

Consolidated Water Power Company; Newaygo Forest Products Limited (Canada); Consolidated Papers Foreign Sales Corporation (U.S. Virgin Islands); Inter Lake Papers, Inc.; LSPI Paper Corporation; Superior Recycled Fiber Corporation; Consolidated Papers International Leasing, L.L.C.; CONDEPCO, Inc.; Consolidated Papers (Canada), Inc. (U.S.A.).

Principal Divisions

Biron Division; Converting Division; Kraft Division; Niagara Division; Paperboard Products Division; Stevens Point Division; Wisconsin Rapids Division; Wisconsin River Division.

Principal Competitors

Bowater Incorporated; Crown Vantage Inc.; Georgia-Pacific Corporation; International Paper Company; The Mead Corporation; Potlatch Corporation; Sappi Fine Paper North America; Westvaco Corporation.

Further Reading

Barrett, Rick, "Consolidated Papers to Be Sold: Finnish Firm to Make $4.8 Billion Purchase," *Wisconsin State Journal*, February 23, 2000, p. 1E.

Bartocci, Stephen, "Consolidated Mill Adds Peroxide to Boost Brightness, Maintain Stability," *Pulp and Paper*, November 1985, pp.147–49.

Bergquist, Lee, "Consolidated Papers Makes Deal: Planned Acquisition of Repap USA to Boost Coated Paper Business," *Milwaukee Journal Sentinel*, July 10, 1997, p. 1.

Coleman, Matthew, "Primary/Secondary Sludge Recycled," *Pulp and Paper*, April 1985, pp. 130–31.

"Consolidated Papers Expands Pulp Capacity," *Pulp and Paper*, January 1988, p. 23.

"Consolidated to Buy Pentair Assets," *Pulp and Paper*, July 1995, p. 17.

Dresang, Joel, "Consolidated Papers to Lay Off 700 As Part of Cost-Cutting Plan," *Milwaukee Journal Sentinel*, July 20, 2000, p. 15A.

Engel, Larry, "Consolidated Giving Boost to Production: Paper Machine Being Added," *Milwaukee Sentinel*, February 11, 1995, p. D1.

Ferguson, Kelly H., "Consolidated Keys on Coated Specialties with Startup of Stevens Point Machine," *Pulp and Paper*, July 1997, pp. 63–64, 67–68.

Flanders, Lou, "Screening Processes Introduced at MOTG-North Winter Meeting," *Pulp and Paper*, March 1991, pp. 114–15.

"Four Major Mergers: Two Trans-Atlantic Blockbusters," *Pulp and Paper*, April 2000, pp. 13–15.

Griffin, Griff, "Mechanized Site Prep Crews Lead Intensified Program," *Forest Industries,* April 1985, pp. 38–40.

Harrison, Andy, "New Technology Solves Permitting Problems for Landfill Expansion," *Pulp and Paper,* September 1989, pp. 213–18.

Jewitt, Caroline, "Stora Enso Sets Off on a Global Crusade," *Pulp and Paper International,* June 2000, pp. 29–31.

Koncel, Jerome, "Quality Emphasized in All Aspects of Pulping Operations," *Paper Trade Journal,* January 1986, p. 28.

Lurie, Sidney, "It's the Time to Think Big," *Financial World,* March 7-20, 1984, p. 6.

McGough, Robert, "Consolidated Papers: Family Knows Best," *Financial World,* May 16, 1989, p. 15.

Smith, Kenneth, "Consolidated Paper's Biron 26 LWC Paper Machine Starts Up Smoothly," *Pulp and Paper,* July 1987, pp. 113–15.

Starkman, Dean, "Stora Enso to Buy Consolidated Papers," *Wall Street Journal,* February 23, 2000, p. A3.

Stowall, Robert, "A World Turned Upside Down," *Financial World,* February 7, 1989, p. 99.

Verespej, Michael A., "Who Owns Whose Trees?," *Industry Week,* March 20, 2000, pp. 58 + .

—Carol I. Keeley
—updated by David E. Salamie

Consorcio G Grupo Dina, S.A. de C.V.

Tlacoquemecatl 41
Mexico, D.F. 03100
Mexico
Telephone: (525) 420-3900
Fax: (525) 420-3981
Web site: http://www.dina.com.mx

Public Company
Incorporated: 1951 as Diesel Nacional, S.A.
Employees: 4,934
Sales: 5.91 billion pesos (US$596.97 million) (1999)
Stock Exchanges: Mexico City New York
Ticker Symbols: DINA; DIN (ADRs)
NAIC: 325211 Plastics Material and Resin
  Manufacturing; 33612 Heavy Duty Truck
  Manufacturing; 336212 Truck Trailer Manufacturing;
  Offices of Other Holding Companies

Consorcio G Grupo Dina, S.A. de C.V. is a holding company that, through a subsidiary, is one of the leading producers of medium- and heavy-duty trucks and tractor-trailers in Mexico. It also has a 39 percent stake in MCII Holdings (USA), Inc., a leading manufacturer of intercity bus coaches and automotive replacement parts. In addition, Dina manufactures plastic components for internal use and external sale.

Government-Owned Automotive Company: 1951–89

The company was founded in 1951 as Diesel Nacional, S.A.—popularly shortened to Dina—with the Mexican government as the majority shareholder and Italian private interests forming the minority. Its mandate was to produce, assemble, and distribute motor vehicles—including automobiles, trucks, and trailers—as well as diesel engines for industrial and agricultural use, plus accessories and replacement parts and molds. A manufacturing plant was established at Ciudad Sahagun in the state of Hidalgo.

Dina signed a pact with Fiat, S.p.A. in 1952 to assemble and distribute heavy diesel trucks in Mexico for the Italian manufac-

turer. Between 1955 and 1959 it assembled Fiat's 682, 682T, and 682RN models. Production ended in 1959. The company assembled and distributed Fiat 500, 1100, and 1400 automobiles from 1957 to 1960. Dina signed a contract with Regie Nationale des Usines Renault in 1962 to provide parts and assembly in Mexico for the French manufacturer. It began assembly of Renault's D-500, D-680, and D-700 buses in 1963, production of NT and NH engines in 1968, and Delfine buses in 1971. A Dina subsidiary also assembled Renault automobiles, which held about ten percent of the Mexico new-car market in 1976. In 1978 Renault established its own assembly operation in Mexico, with Dina taking a 60 percent share. This stake was sold to Renault in 1983. In 1973 Dina took a 60 percent stake in Motores Perkins, S.A., a diesel-engine manufacturer formerly in the hands of Chrysler Corporation's Mexican subsidiary.

Dina, in 1980, opened a plant in Monterrey for the assembly of 1000-, 3000-, and 3200-model trucks. It was then providing the Mexican market with over 20 percent of its medium trucks and about 18 percent of its heavy trucks, a total of about 15,000 units annually. The following year Dina signed a ten-year pact with International Harvester Corp., by which the latter licensed Dina to manufacture three of its truck models, using its parts and components produced in the United States and sold to Dina.

The sharp fall in world oil prices of 1981–82 led to a financial crisis in Mexico that resulted in production cuts. The number of units assembled by Dina in 1982 fell from the planned 15,400 to 10,500; the number of integrated buses from 1,800 to 700; and the number of city-passenger buses from 4,000 to 2,000. By early 1983 Dina was operating at only a little more than 25 percent capacity. The company lost about 20 billion pesos (perhaps US$150 million) that year and adopted a reorganization program that involved laying off 2,500 of its 7,570 workers. It was helped, however, by a 1983 government decree requiring trucks over 11 tons to be diesel-powered and made only by companies with majority Mexican shareholding. By 1987 Dina had 75 percent of the Mexican market for semiheavy-duty and heavy-duty trucks, plus 25 percent of the trailer market.

In 1985 Dina established a US$100-million joint venture with General Motors Corporation to produce some 50,000 diesel-powered trucks a year, mostly for export to the U.S. market,

Key Dates:

1951: Mexican government founds Diesel Nacional, S.A. (Dina).
1963: Dina begins assembling buses in Mexico for Renault; it later assembles and distributes automobiles for Renault as well.
1980: Dina is turning out 15,000 trucks a year.
1989: Dina is sold to Raymundo Gomez Flores, a Guadalajara entrepreneur.
1994: Dina becomes the largest bus manufacturer in North America after acquiring Motor Coaches Industries International (MCII).
1999: Dina sells 61 percent of MCII in order to pay down its debt.

by 1987. GM received 40 percent of the equity and was charged with marketing the vehicles abroad, but this agreement never went into effect. In 1987 Navistar International Corp. (the former International Harvester) purchased a five percent stake in Dina Camiones for US$1.5 million. Dina was producing Navistar's new S-series of trucks and trailers, which had been specially designed for use on Mexico's roads and highways. Chrysler's Mexican subsidiary followed suit later in the year by acquiring eight percent of this subsidiary for US$2.4 million. Dina also had a connection with Ford Motor Company, supplying plastic bumpers for the Mercury Tracer.

Financial Ups and Downs: 1989–99

Dina, which became a holding company in 1982, now consisted of seven manufacturing companies. It lost US$25 million in 1988 and was sold in 1989, apparently for US$84 million in cash plus the assumption of US$148 million in debt, to Raymundo Gomez Flores, a Guadalajara businessman who renamed it Consorcio G, S.A. de C.V. Gomez Flores extended US$30 million of his own money and received financing from Union Bank of Switzerland, which provided a 15-year, US$150 million loan that Gomez Flores paid off in three years. Chrysler and Navistar retained their shares in Dina Camiones, and the Mexican government also kept a 5.7 percent stake in this subsidiary. Navistar raised its stake in 1991 to 17.5 percent and negotiated a deal to supply Dina Camiones with diesel engines produced at Navistar's plant in Melrose Park, Illinois.

The new management, in return for flexible work rules, promised the union there would be no layoffs, established bonuses based on productivity gains, and placed union floor managers and quality-control personnel in management positions. The company became more of an assembler and less of a manufacturer by purchasing more components abroad. It licensed a bus body design from Brazil that was mounted on a chassis made from U.S. parts and more than tripled its truck production. "Dina was an uncut diamond," its chief executive told Ted Bardacke of *Euromoney* in 1993. "But the state is simply not a good administration and the company was being used for political purposes. Now all anyone here, including the union, thinks about is making money and giving a good return on investment to the shareholder."

Consorcio G became Consorcio G Grupo Dina, S.A. de C.V. in 1991, when a public offering of shares on the Mexican stock market and American Depositary Shares (ADRs) on the New York Stock Exchange yielded about US$342 million and represented about 30 percent of the outstanding shares. The company had sales of more than US$900 million that year and—for the first and only time—declared a dividend, following a US$91 million profit in 1992.

Dina's bus manufacturing subsidiary was now the largest facility of its kind in North America. After the Mexican government eliminated regulations on bus fares in 1990, the company raised its production of buses to about 2,000 a year. These included the Paradiso, a superluxury coach intended for Mexico's growing system of new highways, and the Viaggio, a smaller version of the Paradiso. In 1993 Dina held a 46 percent market share of the Mexican intercity bus market, which was significant in size since the vast majority of Mexicans traveling between cities were doing so by bus, because air fares were high and not many people could afford an automobile. Dina also held 40 percent of the Mexican truck market.

In 1994 Dina purchased Motor Coaches Industries International Inc. (MCII), the largest manufacturer of intercity bus coaches in the United States, for US$311.6 million in stock and debt securities. This acquisition made Dina the largest bus manufacturer in North America, with annual revenues of US$1.4 billion. However, Mexico's highway-construction program came to a grinding halt with the capital flight of late 1994 that resulted in the devaluation of the peso and a severe economic recession. Net sales plummeted to 5.25 billion pesos (about US$687 million) in 1995. Bus sales fell from 2,040 to 169 and truck sales from 30,644 to 5,219. This catastrophic drop was not only due to the Mexican recession but also to the effect of the North American Free Trade Agreement (NAFTA), which opened wider the Mexican market to U.S. competitors.

NAFTA, however, also had positive aspects for Dina, because it could now buy U.S. components at lower cost. In addition, it could more easily penetrate the U.S. and Canadian markets through its alliance with Navistar and its acquisition of MCII, which became MCII Holdings (USA) Inc. in 1996 and absorbed Dina Autobuses, S.A. de C.V. in 1997. In 1998 only 23 percent of Dina's revenues came from Mexico, and 83 percent of its profits were in dollars. MCII had an installed base of about 75 percent of the bus coaches operating in the United States and Canada. More than half of Dina's trucks were being exported. In 1998 Dina severed its alliance with Navistar and unveiled a new lineup of medium- and heavy-duty trucks.

Nevertheless, although Dina made money in 1996 and 1997, it remained in serious financial difficulty. Although sales reached about US$1.14 billion in 1998—the first time it had topped the billion-dollar mark since 1994—the company incurred a net loss of about US$85.14 million because of large interest payments on its debt, which was about US$700 million at the end of 1998. By June 1999 Dina's ADRs had fallen from their January 1994 high of US$31 a share on the NYSE to US$1.25. In order to reduce company debt, Dina sold 61 percent of MCII to the New York-based buyout firm Joseph Littlejohn & Levy Inc. for US$175 million in June 1999. The sale included Universal Coach Parts, Inc., which was producing and distributing replacement parts, and Mexicana de Manufactures Especiales, which was manufacturing automotive parts for MCII. MCII had accounted for more than 90 percent of Dina's operating profits between 1995 and 1998.

Consorcio G Grupo Dina: 1998–99

MCII Holdings constituted 68 percent of Dina's net sales in 1998. Based in Des Plaines, Illinois, this company was operating bus plants in Pembina, North Dakota, and Winnipeg, Manitoba, as well as at Ciudad Sahagun. Its customers included Greyhound Lines, Inc. and Coach USA, Inc. Its Dina Autobuses, S.A. de C.V. subsidiary had an installed base of about 65 percent of the estimated 34,000 industry-wide fleet of coaches operating in Mexico and a 25 percent market share in 1998. MCII was also providing used-coach and dealership services.

Trucks represented 14 percent of Dina's revenues in 1998, with 2,304 units sold, of which 1,166 were for export. Its share of the Mexican market was ten percent. Dina Camiones continued to maintain its assembly plant in Ciudad Sahagun, while a new subsidiary, Dina Internacional, was manufacturing trucks in Mercedes, Argentina, for the South American market. The truck segment of Dina's business was not profitable in 1998.

Seventeen percent of Grupo Dina's 1998 revenues came from Universal Coach Parts, MCII's replacement parts subsidiary. It was making over 160,000 replacement parts, including diesel-engine parts for trucks and coaches, and chassis for buses, in Guadalajara. Less than one percent of Dina's revenues were generated from the manufacture of plastic components.

The sale of 61 percent of MCII Holdings reduced Dina's net sales to 5.91 billion pesos (US$596.97 million) in 1999. The company had net income of 498.29 million pesos (US$50.33 million). Of this total, its 39 percent stake in MCII accounted for about 30 percent of its sales and about 95 percent of its net income. Of Dina's 1999 sales, Mexico accounted for 26 percent and other countries 74 percent. A Gomez Flores family corporation, Grupo Empresarial G, S.A. de C.V., owned 62.5 percent of the Class B shares of common stock in Dina at the end of 1999.

Principal Subsidiaries

Desarollo Integral de Nuevas Actividades, S.A. de C.V.; Dina Camiones, S.A. de C.V. (92.59%); Dina Comercializadora, S.A. de C.V.; Dina Internacional, S.A. de C.V. (Argentina).

Principal Competitors

DaimlerChrysler Corporation; Ford Motor Company; General Motors Corporation; Kenworth Truck Co.; Navistar International Transportation Co.; PACCAR Inc.; Prevost; Van Hool.

Further Reading

Bardacke, Ted, ''Mexico's Dina Shows How Privatization Works,'' *Euromoney*, November 1993, pp. 63–64.

Blears, James, ''Getting Down to Business,'' *Business Mexico*, October 1993, p. 26.

''Boards Approve Grupo Dina Motor Coach Merger,'' *New York Times*, May 19, 1994, p. D4.

Castellanos, Camila, ''15 Minutes with . . . Gamaliel Garcia,'' *Business Mexico*, May 1999, pp. 10–11.

Cullen, David, ''Dina Takes to World Stage,'' *Fleet Owner*, November 1998, p. 18.

DePalma, Anthony, ''Mexican Truck Maker Heads to New Destinations,'' *New York Times*, December 27, 1993, pp. D1–D2.

Downer, Stephen, ''Chrysler, Navistar Eye Big Stakes in Mexico's Dina,'' *Automotive News*, March 21, 1988, p. D4.

''GM's Truck Project Expected to Shift U.S. Jobs to Mexico,'' *Journal of Commerce*, February 22, 1986, p. 23B.

''Harvester Announces 2nd Mexican Venture,'' *Automotive News*, June 8, 1981, p. 20.

''Mexican Workers Cut Hours to Keep DINA Plant Running,'' *Automotive News*, September 20, 1982, p. 31.

''Mexico Sells DINA; U.S. Equity Intact,'' *Automotive News*, November 20, 1989, p. 20.

Millman, Joel, ''Bus Empire Fades for Mexican Entrepreneur,'' *Wall Street Journal*, June 7, 1999, p. A18.

——, ''Shares in Mexican Bus Maker and Tortilla Firm Attract Interest Again, but Caution Is Advised,'' *Wall Street Journal*, April 1, 1998, p. C2.

Moffett, Matt, ''Mexican Industrialist Rolls Up His Sleeves to Win TV Stations,'' *Wall Street Journal*, April 5, 1993, p. A12.

''Navistar, the Sleeping Truck Giant, May Be Set to Awake, Analysts Say,'' *Journal of Commerce*, March 19, 1991, p. 2B.

—Robert Halasz

The Container Store

200 Valwood Parkway
Dallas, Texas 75234-8800
U.S.A.
Telephone: (214) 654-2000
Fax: (214) 654-2003
Web site: http://www.containerstore.com

Private Company
Founded: 1978
Employees: 1,400
Sales: $160 million (1999 est.)
NAIC: 442299 All Other Home Furnishings Stores

The Container Store is a leading retail chain specializing in home organization products, such as wire shelving, plastic shower totes, shoe bags, food packaging, knife and peg racks, and bins. Based in Dallas, Texas, the company has 21 stores—nine in Texas, four in Illinois, two in Georgia, two in the Washington, D.C. area, two in California, one in Colorado, and one in Florida. The company planned to open its 22nd store in White Plains, New York, in the fall of 2000. In addition to its retail outlets, The Container Store also sells merchandise through several catalogs. In 1999 it purchased Elfa International, a European-based wire shelving company. The Container Store attributes much of its success to its employees, who are specially trained to offer customers superior service. The company pays its employees above-average wages and has an employee turnover far below the industry average. The Container Store placed first in *Fortune* magazine's "100 Best Companies to Work for in America" survey in 1999. The company is owned by its founders: CEO Garrett Boone and President Kip Tindell. Since inception, The Container Store's sales have increased about 20 to 25 percent a year.

A New Concept in 1978

Garrett Boone and Kip Tindell decided to go into business together while working in a paint department at Montgomery Ward. The entrepreneurs initially hoped to open a custom-made furniture store. But when they tried to get a lease at Olla Podrida, a craft mall in northern Dallas, their business plan was rejected; management believed their furniture store was too similar to a woodworking store already in the mall. Shortly after, Boone and Tindell noticed stackable Akro Bins at a trade show. According to the *Fort Worth Star-Telegram* the two men looked at the bins and thought, "There's a need for storage pieces. There might be business in this." Boone and Tindell knew that busy people needed more time—and that having a place to keep things saved time. According to the article, "Boone firmly believes a chunk of lifetime is wasted looking for car keys." The men decided to open a home organization product store—an idea that was easier said than done. At that time organizational products were sold only for commercial use. Boone and Tindell had to persuade each manufacturer to sell their products to them, so they could in turn sell them to the general public. Eventually they succeeded. The duo opened their first store in northern Dallas in 1978.

Expansion in the 1980s

The first Container Store was a big hit. Boone and Tindell coupled a unique strategy of offering a wide selection of products with outstanding customer service. They offered many different products—so many that its customers were amazed. Employees at The Container Store were trained to problem-solve, so they could better help customers with organizational problems. "We are best known for our highly trained experts that we have on staff. We provide customers with exceptional customer service like no other retailer. What is even more outstanding about our staff is that they will develop effective storage solutions," said Casey Priest, marketing manager in a company press release. "They will take the time out to sit down with each and every customer."

When it came to organization, Boone and Tindell practiced what they preached. Boone, who has been described as being "quite tidy," lived in a house full of elfa shelves and had a Skandia, the company's modular wood shelf product, in every room. According to the *Fort Worth Star-Telegram:* "Enter Boone's house by the kitchen door, the entryway the family uses, and find a row of white plastic shower caddies with handles, lined up and labeled, one for each member of the

Company Perspectives:

The Container Store is the nation's leading retailer of storage and organization products. Through its legendary customer service, The Container Store's mission is to offer its customers multifunctional and innovative storage and organizational solutions designed to save them space and ultimately, save them time.

family. 'It saves time,' explained Boone. 'When you're psychologically organized, you save time.' ''

The Container Store succeeded in boosting sales during the holiday season, typically a slow time for home organizational product sales. The company offered a host of packaging products in addition to ribbons and wrapping. ''We can package everything from a diamond ring to a bicycle,'' said buyer Mona Williams in an article in *HFN*.

Rapid Growth in the 1980s and 1990s

After carefully evaluating locations, the company opened other stores in Texas—it had seven by 1989. In 1990 The Container Store opened its first out-of-state store in Atlanta, Georgia. During the same year it opened another in Texas. In time the company expanded into California, Illinois, and Colorado.

Although the company expanded quickly, it thoroughly researched an area before opening a store. It makes sure that the demographics match its typical customer profile. In general, the company opened stores in areas where the average household income is about $50,000 or more. Boone and Tindell believed that the company's careful selection of location was one of the reasons its stores were so successful. ''We looked for nine years in Houston and it took that long to find our location,'' Tindell said in the *Dallas Business Journal*.

In 1999 the company opened its first store in Florida. Located in Miami, the store was 25,000 square feet and stocked with typical Container Store offerings. ''Miami is an ideal place for one of our stores as it offers a hot and happening venue,'' said marketing manager Casey Priest. The Container Store planned to open its 22nd store in White Plains, New York, in the fall of 2000.

Recognition and Elfa in 1999

In 1999 The Container Store entered *Fortune* magazine's survey for ''100 Best Companies to Work for in America'' and placed first. *Fortune* acknowledged the company's in-depth employee training program of more than 180 hours, above average wages, and the sabbaticals it offered employees who had been with the company for ten or more years. The Container Store also was praised for having exceptional communication between managers and employees. Managers typically shared daily sales reports with employees, so everyone was aware of how and what the company was doing. ''Since the very beginning, The Container Store has always seen its employees as its single most important element,'' said Boone in a company press release. Management noted that its philosophy regarding em-

ployees was simple: it promised to treat its staff like human beings. In return, managers asked the staff to focus on ''being Gumby.'' In other words, employees were asked to be flexible and go outside of their regular job to help other workers and customers. Management followed this practice, too; even Boone and Tindell were occasionally seen unloading trucks and helping customers.

The company's fair management practices created an incredibly loyal staff. In 1999 The Container Store had an employee turnover of only 25 percent, far below the industry average of 73.6 percent. The company's turnover for managers was only 5.3 percent, compared with the industry average of 33.6 percent. Also in 1999 The Container Store received the Retail Innovations Award from the National Retail Federation.

Dr. Leonard Berry, an expert on customer service, included The Container Store in his book *Discovering the Soul of Service*. Dr. Berry's book profiled 14 companies with exceptional customer service.

In May 1999, The Container Store purchased Elfa International, a European manufacturer of wire drawer and shelving systems. The acquisition included Elfa International in Sweden, Denmark, Finland, Norway, Holland, Germany, and France, along with working capital and brand names. Prior to the acquisition, The Container Store was the North American distributor for Elfa, which had been its best-selling product since the company's inception in 1978. ''There is a closeness between Elfa and The Container Store, a synergy. Our philosophies and cultures are aligned,'' Tindell explained in *HFN*. As of 2000 the two companies continued to operate as separate entities.

In August 1999 the company launched its first television advertising campaign in more than a decade. ''Garage'' took a humorous look at over-organization. It showed an impeccably organized garage—even the family dog was placed neatly on a shelf. A mother and son tried to balance the car on one wall as if they were hanging a picture. A voiceover asked, ''How will we inspire you?''

Clustering in 2000

The Container Store believed that malls were declining in popularity around the turn of the century and that people would rather shop at a cluster of specialty stores. The company began ''clustering'' its stores with other stores in the same category. It announced plans to open stores near Crate & Barrel stores in Chicago, Dallas, and, possibly, Washington D.C. Crate & Barrel was a popular home furnishings store that sold quality-made casual furniture, bakeware, and cookware. Crate & Barrel products complemented The Container Store's products, and the two companies believed they could attract more customers if their freestanding stores were located next to each other.

The idea struck fear in some employees, who worried that Crate & Barrel would steal the company's business. ''At first, maybe people said, 'They'll take business away from us or they'll compete for employees.' But we've convinced everyone that, long-term, this will be great for us,'' Tindell explained in *Inc.*

As of 2000 The Container Store continued to thrive. In 1999 it had sales of $160 million. The company faced growing

"Consumers Choose the New Clustered Stores Over the Malls," *Inc.,* June 2000, p. 106.

Gill, Penny, "Home Org's Hot Retail Niche," *HFN The Weekly Newspaper for the Home Furnishings Network,* December 9, 1996, p. 51.

Hill, Dawn, "The Container Store Can't Contain Itself," *HFN The Weekly Newspaper for the Home Furnishing Network,* November 27, 1996, p. 47.

——, "Container Store: Category Creator," *HFN The Weekly Newspaper for the Home Furnishings Network,* June 17, 1996, p. 42.

——, "The Container Store Finds This Is the Time to Clean Up," *HFN The Weekly Newspaper for the Home Furnishings Network,* December 18, 1995, p. 114.

——, "Container Store Girds for Growth," *HFN The Weekly Newspaper for the Home Furnishing Network,* November 13, 1995, p. 67.

Hill, Dee, "The Container Store Gets Elfa Exclusive," *HFN The Weekly Newspaper for the Home Furnishings Network,* December 9, 1996, p. 52.

Hill, J. Dee, "TV Obsessions for Super Organizer," *Adweek Southeast,* August 2, 1999, p. 5.

Meyer, Nancy, "Container Store Bursting Seams," *HFN The Weekly Home Furnishings Newspaper,* June 13, 1994, p. 60.

"The 100 Best Companies to Work For: With Labor in Short Supply, These Companies Are Pulling Out All the Stops for Employees," *Fortune,* January 10, 2000, p. 82.

Porter, Thyra, "Food Gift Storage Prospers, Container Store Wraps Up Sales for the Holidays," *HFN The Weekly Newspaper for the Home Furnishing Network,* November 2, 1998, p. 32.

Roth, Daniel, "My Job at The Container Store," *Fortune,* January 10, 2000, p. 74.

Staton, Tracy, "Container Store Move Signals Stepped-Up Expansion Plans," *Dallas Business Journal,* October 2, 1989, p. 4.

—Tracey Vasil Biscontini

Key Dates:

1978: Entrepreneurs Garrett Boone and Kip Tindell open their first store in northern Dallas.

1990: The company opens its first out-of-state store in Atlanta, Georgia.

1999: The Container Store purchases Elfa International; company places first in *Fortune* magazine's survey of "100 Best Companies to Work for in America."

---

competition, however, from home improvement stores, discount stores, and even grocery stores selling organizational products. Tindell asserted that the company's main line of defense against its competition was its depth of selection. "We don't just have a handful of paper towel holders, we have 20 different kinds in wood, metal, and plastic in a wide range of price points," he said in *HFN.*

Principal Competitors

Lechters, Inc.; Linens 'n Things, Inc.; Organized Living; Totally Organized.

Further Reading

Berry, Dr. Leonard L., *Discovering the Soul of Service: The Nine Drivers of Sustainable Business Service,* New York: The Free Press, 1999.

Bryceland, Kristen, "The Container Store Acquires Elfa International; Retailer Considers European Expansion," *HFN The Weekly Newspaper for the Home Furnishing Network,* May 3, 1999, p. 1.

Controladora Comercial Mexicana, S.A. de C.V.

Avenida Revolucion 780
Mexico City, D.F. 03730
Mexico
Telephone: (525) 371-7312
Fax: (525) 371-7302
Web site: http://comerci.com.mx

Public Company
Incorporated: 1957 as Comercial Mexicana, S.A.
Employees: 32,007
Sales: 27.16 billion pesos (US$2.86 billion) (1999)
Stock Exchanges: Mexico City New York
Ticker Symbols: COMERCI; MCM (GDRs)
NAIC: 44511 Supermarkets and Other Grocery Stores;
45299 All Other General Merchandise Stores; 551112
Offices of Other Holding Companies; 72211 Full-
Service Restaurants

Controladora Comercial Mexicana, S.A. de C.V. (CCM or Comerci) is the parent company of a group of Mexican hypermarkets, self-service stores, and discount warehouses offering both food and nonfood products; supermarkets that sell high-quality food products; and family-style restaurants. It ranks second in sales volume to Cifra, S.A. de C.V. among Mexican retailers.

Comercial Mexicana to 1995

Antonio Gonzalez Abascul was a Spanish immigrant to Mexico who sold fabrics and notions from a small stall in Mexico City. Carlos Gonzalez Nova, the second of his 12 children, left school in 1932 at the age of 15 to join his father. During World War II, when he became the main factor in the business, he bought raw cloth from textile firms and sold it in such countries as the United States and China. He also began to export goods to Central America. In 1946 father and son began to produce cloth of their own in Puebla, Queretaro, and Veracruz.

Comercial Mexicana, S.A. was incorporated in 1957. The self-service concept was beginning to take root in Mexico about this time, and in 1962 the company opened its first such store, in the southern part of Mexico City, with 12,000 square meters (about 130,000 square feet) of space. Comercial Mexicana opened three more Mexico City self-service stores in 1964 and later expanded not only in the metropolitan area but also into some of Mexico's 31 states. During the 1970s 20 Comercial Mexicana self-service stores were established. In 1977, among Mexican companies reporting their sales volume, Comerci ranked 21st, at 2.4 billion pesos (US$105 million).

In 1981 Comercial Mexicana acquired the Sumesa supermarket chain, and the following year it opened the first unit of its California restaurant chain. The company was renamed Controladora Comercial Mexicana (CCM) in 1988, when there were 103 units, of which more than 70 were Comercial Mexicana stores. CCM , in 1989, began operation of a Bodega chain of discount warehouses. Also that year, the company began leasing chattels and real estate, as well as investing in companies engaged in the purchase, sale, and distribution of groceries and general merchandise. CCM made its initial public offering of stock in 1991 and also issued its first company credit card that year. Its net sales came to 4.87 billion (new) pesos that year, or about US$1.61 billion.

CCM joined with Price Co. in 1991 to form Price Club de Mexico, a 50–50 joint venture that began establishing members-only warehouse stores in Mexico the following year, when it opened its first such store in Mexico City. These stores offered low prices on volume purchases of a limited selection of branded and private-label products. In 1993 Price Co. merged to become Price Costco Inc., and the following year split into two companies—Price Costco Inc. and Price Enterprises Inc.—which divided the 50 percent stake in this venture. Also in 1993, CCM initiated the first of its Mega hypermarket stores, in Guadalajara. The 1.4-million-square-foot store, in addition to offering a full line of groceries, clothing, and household items, housed a bank, pharmacy, optical center, and shoe-repair store. In 1995 CCM established a joint venture agreement with the French hypermarket chain Auchon. The partners opened a hypermarket the following year in Mexico City but terminated their pact at the end of the year, with the store continuing as part of the Mega chain.

CCM, in 1994, opened 19 stores: four Comercial Mexicana units, seven Bodegas, six Price Clubs, and two Mega stores. It also opened nine new California restaurants, including units in Acapulco, Guadalajara, Puebla, and Puerto Vallerta, plus two in Mexico City. The company now passed Grupo Gigante, S.A. de C.V. to take second place among Mexican self-service retailers. It was operating 142 stores and 29 restaurants, with a total of 154.79 million customers that year.

Still Growing Despite Recession: 1995–97

The good times came to an end with the capital flight of late 1994, followed by the devaluation of the peso and the consequent severe recession of 1995. CCM's sales dropped by 18 percent in 1995 and another five percent in 1996, Moreover, because of the devalued peso, the company's dollar-denominated debt of US$300 million now took on critical proportions. In order to make payments on the debt, Comerci had to lay off staff and scale back expansion plans. In order to cut costs, the Price Costco stores shifted their stock from about half domestic, half foreign goods, to 70 percent domestic, 30 percent foreign. Nevertheless, the company continued to add more stores and restaurants and in late 1996 was planning to spend US$260 million over the next two years to open 34 new stores. In 1997 Comerci purchased Kmart Mexico, S.A. de C.V. for US$148.5 million. This money-losing subsidiary of the giant U.S. retailer, in collaboration with the department store chain El Puerto de Liverpool, S.A. de C.V., had opened three large stores in Mexico City, one in Cuernavaca, and one in Puebla. The acquisition also included commercial sites near the stores, land reserves of more than 600,000 square feet, and an office building with 84,000 square feet.

In spite of the still-sour Mexican economy, Comerci remained profitable in every year following 1994. The 79 Comercial Mexicana stores in 1997 carried an extensive line of food and nonfood items, with the former including fresh, frozen, baked, and canned goods; prepared foods; delicatessen; and wines and liquors; and the latter, clothing and shoes; paper products and office supplies; books and magazines; health and beauty products; garden, automotive, and photographic supplies; electric appliances; sporting goods; toys and gifts; and numerous household items. Almost all units had one or more specialty departments, such as a bakery, tortilla press, or video rental shop. They averaged 69,000 square feet of selling space and were generally in neighborhood shopping centers with large parking lots.

The 23 Bodega warehouse stores offered mainly food items, pharmaceutical items, and general merchandise of the type sold in Comercial Mexicana stores, at discount prices and with less selection of brands and sizes of items. These stores also offered fewer amenities and product introductions. Because their customers generally did not have cars, they were within walking distance of residential areas or accessible by public transportation. They averaged 50,600 square feet of selling area. The 17 Sumesa stores were all in Mexico City. Developed as neighborhood stand-alone supermarkets, they averaged 8,600 square feet of selling area and emphasized sales of quality groceries and perishables.

Each of the 11 Mega units contained a bakery, pharmacy, video rental club, and separate specialty retail facilities leased to and operated by third-party tenants, such as banks, key makers, jewelry shops, shoe-repair stores, photo developers, and optical centers. They carried about 60,000 items and averaged 120,000 square feet of selling area. The five Kmart Mexico stores were given the Mega Supercenter name. They had an average selling area of 130,000 square feet.

The 14 Price Costco stores offered members low prices on volume purchases of a limited selection of some 3,000 branded and private-label products in a wide range of merchandise categories, including baked goods and a selection of high-quality perishables and meats. Membership was limited to businesses and professionals and members of their families, with a primary membership, including one affiliate membership, costing 177 pesos (US$21.95) a year. Price Costco stores averaged 100,000 square feet of selling area and were designed with minimal amenities and decorations.

Comerci owned about 70 percent of the land on which its store operations were located and the sites of 26 of its 32 California Restaurants, which were usually located in commercial areas near a Comercial Mexicana. Two-thirds of the company's net sales in 1997 came from food. In all, perishable goods accounted for 37.6 percent of sales; groceries, 29.7 percent; general merchandise, 26.7 percent; and clothing, 11 percent. Comerci offered 585 private-label products that year, primarily groceries.

CCM in 1998–99

CCM continued to make modest gains in 1998 and in 1999 had net income of 1.26 billion pesos (US$131.8 million) on net sales of 27.16 billion pesos (US$2.84 billion). The long-term debt was still 1.7 billion pesos (US$177.82 million) at the end of 1998, but the company reduced the dollar amount by 23 percent in 1999, to 1.31 billion pesos (US$137.03 million). It opened six new stores and three new restaurants in 1999 and remodeled nine stores and one restaurant.

Of Comerci's 158 stores at the end of 1999, Comercial Mexicana accounted for 80, with 53 percent of the company's net sales for that year. These stores were aimed at the middle and upper-middle class of Mexico and carried an average of 55,000 products. The 28 Bodega CM discount warehouse stores were aimed at the middle- and lower-middle income brackets and averaged about 30,000 products in stock. They accounted for 13 percent of sales. The 16 Mega hypermarket stores, catering to all income groups and carrying an average of 60,000 products each, accounted for 19 percent of sales. The 17 Sumesa supermarkets stocked about 8,000 high-quality food products each and were aimed at the middle-upper and upper income brackets. They accounted for two percent of Comerci's sales.

The 17 Costco membership warehouses were aimed at the middle and upper classes and carried about 3,000 branded and private-label products—including the chain's own Kirkland brand—each in high volume. They accounted for 12 percent of CCM's sales. Membership grew by 32 percent in 1998, after increasing by 38 percent in 1997. The name of the chain was scheduled to change from Price Costco to simply Costco in 1999.

The 39 California Restaurants chain offered Mexican and international cuisine in an informal family atmosphere. Comerci considered the main features of this chain, which was oriented toward the middle and upper-middle class, to be its all-included Superbuffet service, its gourmet-quality coffee, and innovative promotions. The restaurants had a total of 8,654 seats. The chain's sales—of which the Superbuffet accounted for 48 percent—came to one percent of the company total.

CCM's business was largely confined to the Mexico City metropolitan area and the central Mexican states, which (in 1998) accounted for 47 and 34 percent of the stores, respectively. Twelve stores were in the northwest of the country, eight in the southeast, seven in the southwest, and two in the north-

east. Of the 35 California Restaurants, 22 were in the Mexico City metropolitan area, 11 in other parts of central Mexico, one in the northeast, and one in the southwest. Of CCM's 1999 sales, groceries accounted for 38 percent, perishables for 26 percent, general merchandise for 24 percent, and clothing for 12 percent. Private-label goods accounted for 11 percent. The company owned 91 of its 158 stores and leased 67; it owned 28 of its restaurants and leased 11.

Carlos Gonzalez Nova's brothers Guillermo and Jaime were chairman and vice-chairman, respectively, of Comerci in the late 1990s. His son Carlos Gonzalez Zabalegui was chief executive officer of the company. At the end of 1997 Carlo, Guillermo, and Jaime Nova owned two-thirds of the company's Class B common stock.

Principal Subsidiaries

Comerci, S.A. de C.V.; Comercial Mexicana, S.A. de C.V.; Contraladora Price Club de Mexico, S.A. de C.V. (50%); Hipertiendas Mexico, S.A. de C.V.; Price Club de Mexico, S.A. de C.V. (50%); Super Mercados, S.A. de C.V.

Principal Competitors

Cifra, S.A. de C.V.; Grupo Gigante, S.A. de C.V.; Organizacion Soriana, S.A. de C.V.

Further Reading

Fuentes, Rossana, "CCM's Mexican Survival Kit," *Institutional Investor,* May 1995, pp. 80–81.

Hernandez, Ulises, "Carlos Gonzalez Nova," *Expansion,* May 20, 1999, pp. 45–47.

"Retail Dueling: Mexican Chain Gets Drop on Wal-Mart," *St. Louis Post-Dispatch,* September 24, 1993, p. C1.

Torres, Craig, "Mexican Grocery Store Chain Comes to Market As Analysts Fret About Cash-Starved Shoppers," *Wall Street Journal,* October 18, 1996, p. C2.

"Vamos: Kmart Exits Mexico; Canada in Question," *Discount Store News,* March 3, 1997, pp. 3, 94.

—Robert Halasz

Coty, Inc.

1325 Avenue of the Americas
New York, New York 10019
U.S.A.
Telephone: (212) 479-4300
Fax: (212) 479-4399
Web site: http://www.coty.com

Wholly Owned Subsidiary of Joh. A. Benckiser GmbH
Incorporated: 1922
Employees: 8,000
Sales: $1.78 billion (fiscal 1999)
NAIC: 32562 Toilet Preparation Manufacturing; 42221
  Drug and Druggists' Sundries Wholesalers

Coty, Inc. is a century-old fragrance manufacturer that also produces cosmetics and other health and beauty aids. Founded by a Corsican who exploited his marketing knack to become, reputedly, the richest man in France, the company has experienced numerous changes in ownership and management over the years. Coty is now a subsidiary of Joh. A. Benckiser GmbH, a family-controlled German holding company. It is the world's leading manufacturer of mass-market fragrances and occasionally markets products of other manufacturers. Although New York-based, Coty registers the bulk of its sales in Western Europe.

Perfume and Cosmetics Pioneer: 1904–62

Born on the island of Corsica in 1875, François Spoturno was orphaned at an early age and reared by a grandmother. After leaving school he drifted to Marseille and then—in 1900—to Paris, where he worked as a haberdashery salesman. Following a year's training in Grasse—birthplace of the perfume industry—he borrowed 10,000 francs from his grandmother in order to establish a makeshift laboratory in his small flat. Taking the name Coty from his mother's family name (Coti), he created his first perfume, La Rose Jacqueminot, in 1904 from concentrated flower oils rejected by others because of their novelty. By 1908 he was successful enough to establish a factory on the outskirts of Paris. Then he introduced face powder, packaging it with a powder puff in a round box.

Maison Coty owed its success to much more than its founder's training in and sensitivity to the materials from which commercial fragrances are derived. Coty catered to the rich and well-born—even the Russian czar and czarina, who commissioned fragrances for their daughters—yet sold small bottles within the price range of even the Paris shopgirl. He was the first to create a range of cosmetics in the same fragrance. Above all, Coty was a pioneer in every aspect of product design, including perfume bottles and cosmetics boxes. His close collaborator, René Lalique, created Art Nouveau crystal bottles that were works of art in themselves. Using red, black, and gold papers, Leon Bakst, set designer for the acclaimed Ballets Russes, designed the powder box which still serves for Coty's Air-Spun face powder. Coty was also quick to exploit foreign markets, opening a Moscow store and establishing a London subsidiary in 1910. Two years later he founded a New York branch in a Fifth Avenue building furnished with stained glass windows by Lalique. Other agencies of what later became Coty, S.A., were established in Buenos Aires, Johannesburg, Madrid, and Rio de Janeiro.

After American soldiers returning from World War I brought home Coty perfumes and face powder, the U.S. market was recognized as of paramount importance. In 1922 Coty, Inc. was formed, with laboratories and a large assembly plant established on Manhattan's West Side to avoid the heavy tariff on luxury goods. By 1929 the American company was assembling and selling 23 perfumes, plus powders, toilet soaps and waters, bath salts, brilliantines, hair and hand lotions, rouges, vanishing cream, shaving soap, and powder and rouge compacts. The firm was vigilant in forestalling pricecutting by retailers and achieved a 60 percent profit margin. Net income rose from $1.07 million in 1923 to $4.05 million in 1928. In that year Coty, S.A. had earnings of $1.64 million.

Coty, Inc. became a publicly traded company in 1925 and acquired a majority interest in the five European Coty companies in 1929. After Coty's death in 1934, his divorced wife, now Mme. Yvonne Cotnareanu, received a controlling interest in Coty, Inc. in lieu of the unpaid balance of an alimony settlement. Administration of the company remained in the hands of Benjamin E. Levy, who had become chairman of the board on its inception.

Key Dates:

1904: François Coty creates his first perfume.
1922: Coty, Inc. is founded in New York City.
1939: The five foreign Coty companies are reorganized in Coty International Corp.
1963: Coty and Coty International are sold to Chas. Pfizer & Co.
1992: Coty is sold to Joh. A. Benckiser GmbH, a German company.
1996: Addition of Benckiser's Lancaster Group makes Coty the global leader in production and sales of mass-market fragrances.

With the advent of the Great Depression, Coty, like other companies dependent on luxury goods, fell into difficulties. According to a later *New York Times* article, sales in the United States fell from $50 million in 1929 to $3.5 million in 1933. The author, Richard Rutter, wrote that management "compounded its mounting problems by slashing prices in a desperate effort to gain a mass market ... a near-fatal move in a field in which prestige and the luxury symbol were vital." Even so, Coty lost money on its American operations only in 1935. With World War II imminent, the foreign companies were folded into the newly created Panama-based Coty International Corp. in 1939. The ownership remained the same, however, and the two corporations had interlocking directorships.

Levy retired in 1940 and was succeeded as chairman by Grover Whalen, a civic booster and promoter who was finishing his stint as president of the body that organized and ran the New York World's Fair of 1939–40. In his role as the company's public face, Whalen established the Coty American Fashion Critics' Award, an annual presentation that kept its name before the public for 40 years. Administration was in the hands of Coty's president, Herman L. Brooks, from 1938 to 1946, when Mme. Cotnareanu, who spent the war years in the United States before returning to Paris, replaced him with her brother-in-law Philippe Cotnareanu.

Cotnareanu, who changed his name to Philip Cortney, secured bank financing to keep Coty going and, in one of his first decisions, raised prices for the entire line. In spite of a long-range program to double the company's retail business, he cut off drugstores carrying Coty products if they would not agree to provide display space of at least 16 feet in length for exclusive stocking of these goods. Production lines were automated, packaging restyled, and new lines of goods added periodically, including, in 1955, a new toilet-goods line for men named "Preferred Stock." Research laboratories were established in Morris Plains, New Jersey, and overseas.

In 1946, Coty's first postwar year, sales nearly doubled from the 1941 total, to $19.1 million, and net profit reached $1.24 million. The company lost money in 1947, however, and although it returned to profitability, sales stagnated. Fiscal 1955 (the year ended June 30, 1955) was Coty's best postwar year, with net income of $1.61 million on sales of $22.76 million. The firm lost money in fiscal 1957 and 1958, with management

blaming the results on the high cost of advertising, which rose from seven to 16 percent of sales in this period. Moreover, firms like Revlon, Inc., which reaped huge publicity from its sponsorship of television's *The $64,000 Question*, seemed to be getting better results for the money. In fiscal 1962, Coty had net income of only $386,985 on sales of $25.46 million. Coty International had a profit of $319,331 on sales of $7.38 million.

Pfizer Subsidiary: 1963–92

Coty and Coty International were sold in 1963 to Chas. Pfizer & Co. for about $26 million and became divisions in the pharmaceuticals company's consumer products group. In 1965 Coty introduced Imprevu, its first new perfume in 25 years. This became the leading Coty fragrance by the end of 1968. Introduced in 1967, Coty Originals offered a comprehensive collection of newly designed makeup products at popular prices. Coty then added a high-priced, prestigious Dina Merrill line. In 1969 the division introduced the Bacchus line, a full collection of men's grooming aids, including aftershave lotion and cologne.

Coty and Coty International were united in 1973. Among the new products introduced in the early 1970s were the Styx, Sweet Earth, and Wild Musk fragrances and the Equatone beauty-treatment line. The production facility was moved from New York City to Sanford, North Carolina, at this time. Coty products were being marketed to franchised accounts, including distributors, independent drugstores, mass merchandisers, and department stores. Results were not meeting expectations, however, for the subsidiary was reported to be on the block in 1974 for possibly as little as $20 million—less than Pfizer had paid a decade earlier.

The battle for display space remained intense, but in 1984 Coty won a promotional award for its point-of-purchase Image Awareness campaign in 11,000 drug and mass-merchandise stores. Departing from tradition, the campaign included posters, buttons, and aprons involving a whole store as well as a selection of traditional point-of-purchase materials, such as booklets, fragrance testers, and test cards within the cosmetics department. In 1985 Coty followed up with a similar Ingenious Solutions campaign. A specially designed consumer "colorkit" was provided for each of four fragrances—Nuance, Emeraude, Wild Musk, and Sophia. Each was graphically associated with an exotic locale.

Stetson, a highly successful men's scent, was introduced in 1981, and Lady Stetson was added in 1986. With more than $100 million a year in women's fragrance sales, Coty, in 1988, ranked second only to Revlon in this $3-billion-plus category. Besides the preceding, Coty's brands included L'Aimant, Lady Stetson, and Sand & Sable. Its cosmetics and treatment products included Air Spun face powder, Coty "24," Overnight Success, and Sheer To Stay lipsticks, Sweet Earth face-care-treatment products, and Thick 'N Healthy mascara. The men's fragrance line included Stetson, Iron, and Musk for Men. Coty ranked first in mass-market men's fragrance sales in 1991, with a 22.6 percent share, and first in women's, with 16.4 percent.

Benckiser's Coty: 1992–99

Coty was purchased in 1992 by Benckiser Consumer Products, the U.S. arm of a family-owned German household-products giant named Joh. A. Benckiser GmbH. That fall Coty introduced Gravity, a new upscale men's fragrance, and Truly Lace, a new bath-and-body-fragrance collection. Vanilla Fields, a women's fragrance that proved hugely successful, was introduced soon after. In 1993 Benckiser merged into Coty its Quintessence Inc. unit, which it had acquired the previous year. Founded in Chicago by Bernard Mitchell in 1968 as Jovan, Inc., this company had struck it big in 1972 with Jovan Musk Oil. The company was sold to the Beecham Group in 1979 and, in 1988, to its managers in a leveraged buyout, when it became Quintessence.

Coty, Inc. grew into a $1.5-billion-a-year company in 1996, when Benckiser made its Lancaster Group a Coty division. (The existing Coty, renamed Coty Beauty, became the other division.) Lancaster, founded in Monaco in 1946 and acquired from SmithKline Beecham plc in 1990, consisted of the cosmetics brand of that name and an Isabella Rossellini line, and a number of designer and prestige fragrances, including Davidoff, Jil Sander, and VivienneWestwood.

The consolidated Coty was now the global leader in mass-market fragrance sales. Lancaster also introduced to Europe, in 1996, the leading Chinese cosmetics brand, named Yue-Sai for its developer, Yue-Sai Kan. In addition, it acquired a hip London-based cosmetics line, Rimmel. Coty Beauty's own line of color cosmetics was Margaret Astor.

The hot new introductions of 1997 were The Healing Garden, a line of four herbal-based "aromatherapy" fragrances that quickly developed into a collection of 34 stockkeeping units, and its first fragrance bath-and-body line, Calgon Body Mists. Like the company's traditional fragrance brands, these products were merchandised as mini-departments within a store. Calgon quickly moved into first place and Healing Garden third among mass-market women's fragrances in the United States.

In 1998 Coty added a five-item Minitherapy for Feet line as an extension of the aromatherapy concept, and Isabella Rossellini launched a new cosmetics collection called Manifesto. During the year 45 percent of the company's sales were in mass fragrances, 24 percent in mass cosmetics, and 31 percent in prestige-market beauty products. Fifty-five percent of sales volume came from Western Europe and 30 percent from North America. Lancaster represented 75 percent of the company's European sales. In North America, Calgon, Healing Garden, and Vanilla Fields ranked second, third, and fourth, respectively, among women's fragrances. Stetson, Aspen, and Preferred Stock ranked first, fourth, and fifth among men's fragrances.

In 1999 Coty introduced adidas Moves, a men's fragrance, to the United States and was planning to add its line of soaps as well.

It also introduced Jovan Body Splash and a Dulce Vanilla fragrance, and it brought the Rimmel makeup line to the United States. The Lancaster Group's U.S. division introduced an Aromatopia line of 37 bath and body products in collaboration with May Department Stores Co., which took a one-year exclusive on the collection, to be sold in all 410 of its stores. For 2000, Coty was planning to introduce a new mass-market perfume, Esprit, in 44 countries under a licensing agreement with apparel marketer Esprit de Corp. Also planned for 2000 were line extensions of Aspen and adidas. In all, Coty was marketing 44 scents.

Principal Divisions

Coty Beauty; Lancaster Group.

Principal Competitors

L'Oreal S.A.; Procter & Gamble Co.; Revlon, Inc.; Unilever N.V.

Further Reading

Barille, Elisabeth, *Coty: Perfumeur and Visionary.* Paris: Editions Assouline, 1996.

Bender, Marylin, "Jovan, Inc., Chicago's Fragrance Purveyor," *New York Times*, August 10, 1975, Sec. 3, p. 3.

Berman, Phyllis, "Getting Hip," *Forbes,* August 23, 1999, pp. 50–52.

Bertrand, Kate, "Point-of-Purchase, Media Make Up Coty Solution," *Advertising Age*, August 15, 1985, pp. 30–31.

Born, Peter, "Coty Outlines Plans to Construct Network of Worldwide Brands," *WWD*, May 7, 1999, pp. 1, 10.

Brookman, Faye, "Coty's Aromatherapy From Head to Toe," *WWD,* March 13, 1998, p. 9.

"Chosen Outlets," *Business Week,* April 27, 1946, p. 85.

Coty, Inc., New York: Lehman Brothers, 1929.

"Coty's Ex-Wife Wins Point in Stock Suit," *New York Times,* October 12, 1934, p. 7.

Day, Julia, "Benckiser Gears Up for Brand Dominance," *Marketing Week,* August 5, 1999, p. 19.

Hellman, Geoffrey T., "Profiles: For City and for Coty—II," *The New Yorker,* July 21, 1951, pp. 28–29.

"It's a New Ball Game at Coty," *American Druggist,* April 20, 1970, p. 65.

Parks, Liz, "Coty Eyes Growth in New Fragrance Experiences," *Drug Store News,* December 8, 1997, p. 101.

"Pfizer Acquires Control of Coty, Coty International," *Wall Street Journal,* September 26, 1963, p. 12.

Rutter, Richard, "Personality: He Has Young Ideas in Old Line," *New York Times,* September 2, 1962, Sec. 3, p. 3.

Sloan, Pat, "Coty's New Scent Gets Its Point Across," *Advertising Age,* July 11, 1988, p. 10.

Sloan, Pat, and Kate Fitzgerald, "Coty Targets Scent Invaders," *Advertising Age,* May 4, 1992, p. 4.

—Robert Halasz

Crompton

Crompton Corporation

One American Lane
Greenwich, Connecticut 06831-2559
U.S.A.
Telephone: (203) 552-2000
Fax: (203) 552-2870
Web site: http://www.cromptoncorp.com

Public Company
Incorporated: 1999 as CK Witco Corporation
Employees: 8,612
Sales: $3.1 billion (1999)
Stock Exchanges: New York
Ticker Symbol: CK
NAIC: 325132 Synthetic Organic Dye and Pigment
    Manufacturing; 325199 All Other Basic Organic
    Chemical Manufacturing; 325212 Synthetic Rubber
    Manufacturing; 325320 Pesticide and Other
    Agricultural Chemical Manufacturing; 325998 All
    Other Miscellaneous Chemical Product and
    Preparation Manufacturing; 333298 All Other
    Industrial Machinery Manufacturing

Crompton Corporation is a specialty chemical manufacturer whose main operations involve the creation of additives, ingredients, and intermediates that are incorporated into the end products of the company's customers. Formed in 1999 from the merger of Crompton & Knowles Corporation and Witco Corporation, and briefly known as CK Witco Corporation, Crompton has three main business segments: polymer products, which include additives for plastics and rubber, urethane chemicals, polymers, and polymer processing equipment; organosilicones, which include intermediates used in such applications as fiberglass, polyurethane foam, textiles, coatings, adhesives, and sealants; and crop protection products, which include fungicides, insecticides, herbicides, seed treatments, and other agricultural chemicals. The company operates more than 50 manufacturing facilities in 20 countries and offers its product lines in 120 countries, with 43 percent of revenues originating outside the United States—28 percent from Europe alone.

C&K: Origins in Loom Manufacturing

Crompton & Knowles's roots lie in the cotton weaving industry, one of the first enterprises to be mechanized in western Europe in the late 18th century. William Crompton was a New England businessman who originated an improved loom, which he began manufacturing and marketing in the town of Worcester, Massachusetts, in 1837. For the next four decades, Crompton Loom Works was practically without competitors, and it steadily prospered. Toward the end of this exclusive reign, Lucius J. Knowles, another New England businessman, developed an improved version of the textile loom in 1862, whereupon he, too, established his own company, L.J. Knowles & Bros., in the town of Warren, Massachusetts.

There was no bad blood between the two competitors until 1879, when Knowles decided to move his manufacturing establishment to Crompton's hometown of Worcester. The next 18 years witnessed fierce rivalry between the two firms, both of which meanwhile developed many improvements in their respective looms, perhaps because of the intense pressure of competition. Finally, in 1897, the two companies took the surprising but sensible step of merging into Crompton & Knowles Loom Works, which was incorporated in 1900. The new company prospered and expanded; by 1907 it had opened offices and warehouses in Philadelphia and in Charlotte, North Carolina. In time, Crompton & Knowles, whose mainstay was the manufacture and marketing of the textile loom, became renowned for the production of multicolor weaving machines, which were exported all over the world. By World War II, the company was one of the largest textile machinery manufacturers in the world.

Meanwhile, the Neversink Dyeing Company, a business that would add an important dimension to the Crompton & Knowles firm in future decades, operated in Reading, Pennsylvania. Founded by Nathan Althouse, this company became one of the biggest textile dyeing facilities in the nation by World War I. Unfortunately, as the war in Europe progressed, the company increasingly was deprived of dyestuffs. To relieve this crisis, the firm began manufacturing its own dyes. By the end of the war, the company had changed so much that it adopted a new name, the Althouse Chemical Company, and thereafter it emphasized research into new and improved dye products for natural textiles as well as for the increasingly popular synthetic fabrics.

Crompton & Knowles Loom Works continued to produce and sell its famous textile machines until the advent of World War II, when traditional production gave way to fulfilling military needs. With the return to civilian production in 1945, Crompton & Knowles's workforce stood at 3,000. The company continued to manufacture its textile machines well into the early 1950s.

1950s Through Early 1980s: The Diversifying of C&K

While there was still strong demand for the textile machinery in the early 1950s, it became apparent that the company's future success depended on diversification rather than reliance on only one major commercial product. In 1954 the firm branched off into the dye and chemical business with the purchase of the Althouse Chemical Company. The purchase laid the foundations for the manufacture of dyestuffs, which eventually would become the company's most important enterprise.

Crompton & Knowles continued to manufacture textile weaving machines, and through most of the 1960s the textile machinery division was the company's biggest in terms of sales revenues. Diversification continued, however, and other enterprises gradually dwarfed the textile machinery business. The process drastically altered the company's identity and size. In 1956 stockholders changed the name of the company from Crompton & Knowles Loom Works to Crompton & Knowles Corporation; the company ceased manufacturing textile looms altogether by 1981.

Further expansion took place in 1969, when Crompton & Knowles established its first European subsidiary, Crompton & Knowles Tertre, a dye and chemical company in Belgium; this was followed in 1971 with the acquisition from Ciba Chemical & Dyestuff Company of Intracolor, another dye and chemical enterprise that further strengthened Crompton & Knowles's dye manufacturing base. Seven years later, the company bought the dye business of Harshaw Chemical Company, based in Lowell, North Carolina.

When the Du Pont Company exited the dye business in 1979, Crompton & Knowles was waiting eagerly in the wings to purchase its holdings, which included the high-quality Sevron dye products. The range of Crompton & Knowles's dyestuffs expanded significantly. Two years later, the company bought the rights from the Du Pont Company to manufacture Dybln dyes for polyester and cotton textiles. Crompton & Knowles acquired and absorbed other dye and chemical businesses, becoming in the process a leader in the domestic dye business. The company's dye and chemical business had expanded so much that, by the early 1980s, Crompton & Knowles supplied dyes and chemicals to a variety of industries including paper, leather, printing ink, and heat transfer printing establishments, in addition to the textile and garment industry.

Over the years, dye and chemical operations became the company's biggest division and its mainstay. In 1960, the company diversified further into the manufacture of flavors, food colorings, and fragrances for the food processing and drug industries, the company's second major operation. In that year, Crompton & Knowles acquired the Bates Chemical Company, founded in 1923 when the federal government first certified food colorings. Crompton & Knowles expanded even further in this direction when it acquired the American Flavor & Fragrance Company in 1980.

A third significant operation was added to the company in 1961 with the purchase of the Davis-Standard Company, a major manufacturer of plastic processing, or extrusion, machinery and systems, marking the origins of Crompton & Knowles's extrusion machinery business. This purchase added a great variety of products to Crompton & Knowles's inventory. Within two decades, the company had not only survived but altered its identity significantly, expanding from the production of only one major commercial product, to hundreds of diverse products and three principal operations.

Mid-1980s Through Mid-1990s: Further Expansion and International Growth at C&K

By the mid-1980s, Crompton & Knowles was one of the last remaining U.S. dye producers and marketers, and one of the largest, marketing its products to Europe, Latin America, and Asia. It was also a leading provider of dyes to the clothing and hosiery businesses in North America. How and why this company succeeded—increasing sales revenues 15 percent during the worst year of the recession in the early 1990s—had much to do with the dynamic leadership of President and CEO Vincent Calarco. When he came on board in 1985, having previously headed the specialty chemical division of Uniroyal Inc., the company had not fully recovered from the economic downturn of the early 1980s. Calarco expanded the company's business by buying up dye operations that large companies, such as Du Pont and Allied Chemical, were unloading. By the early 1990s, Crompton & Knowles had a healthy eight percent share of the worldwide market in dye products and had strengthened its own dye business, especially in carpeting and clothing. Moreover, Crompton & Knowles became the sole producer of at least 40 percent of its own dye products, making it the most influential dyestuff producer and marketer in North America. Under Calarco's management, the firm also became a major player in the flavor/fragrance market, following the 1988 acquisition of the Ingredients Technology Corp. of Pelhem, New York. At the same time, the company's specialty process equipment and

Key Dates:

1897: Two loom manufacturers merge to form Crompton & Knowles Loom Works.

1900: Crompton & Knowles Loom Works is incorporated.

1920: Wishnick-Tumpeer Chemical Company is founded as a chemical distributing concern.

1926: Wishnick is renamed Wishnick-Tumpeer Incorporated.

1935: Wishnick acquires its first overseas operation.

1939: Wishnick builds its first manufacturing plant, in Chicago.

1944: Wishnick is renamed Witco Chemical Incorporated.

1954: Crompton & Knowles acquires Althouse Chemical Company, expanding into the dye and chemical business.

1956: Crompton & Knowles Loom Works is renamed Crompton & Knowles Corporation (C&K).

1958: Witco goes public.

1960: C&K acquires Bates Chemical Company, maker of flavors, food colorings, and fragrances; Witco acquires Sonneborn Chemical and Refining Corporation.

1961: C&K acquires Davis-Standard Company, maker of plastic processing machinery.

1966: Witco purchases Argus Chemical Corporation, maker of polyvinyl chloride additives.

1969: C&K establishes its first European subsidiary, in Belgium.

1971: C&K purchases Ciba Chemical & Dyestuff Company.

1979: C&K acquires dye business of Du Pont.

1980: C&K acquires American Flavor & Fragrance Company.

1981: C&K exits loom manufacturing.

1985: Witco drops "Chemical" from its name.

1992: Witco acquires Industrial Chemicals and Natural Substances divisions of Schering AG.

1996: C&K acquires Uniroyal Chemical Corporation; Witco initiates a major restructuring.

1999: C&K and Witco merge to form CK Witco Corporation.

2000: Company changes its name to Crompton Corporation.

controls division gradually moved out of the cable business and into the far more lucrative medical tubing, food packaging, and blow molding equipment fields, which were ignored or underestimated by bigger competitors. Calarco also led Crompton & Knowles further into international business endeavors.

By the early 1990s, 75 percent of Crompton & Knowles's sales came from its specialty chemicals division. The company had become the leading manufacturer of dyestuffs in North America, and it produced a variety of chemical intermediates (essential to the making of dyes) for the textile industry as well as a steady stream of artificial flavor, color, and fragrance ingredients to the food and drug industries. Approximately one quarter of Crompton & Knowles's sales derived from the specialty process equipment and controls division. Overseas ex-

pansion continued in the early 1990s, including the 1991 purchase of ICI Colours in Oissel, France, from a major British chemical firm. In one stroke, this acquisition doubled Crompton & Knowles's productive capacity in Europe, making the company a major player in the European dye and chemical markets. Worldwide sales of Crompton & Knowles's products in Latin America, Europe, and Asia soon reached record levels, constituting approximately one-third of sales revenues.

By 1995, sales at Crompton & Knowles had reached $665.5 million. The company surprised many industry observers the following year with a blockbuster acquisition. In August Crompton & Knowles spent about $365 million in stock and agreed to assume $1 billion in debt to take over Uniroyal Chemical Corporation, the former specialty chemical division of Uniroyal. Uniroyal Chemical, which had 1995 revenues of $1.1 billion, had been having difficulty servicing its large debt load, enabling Crompton & Knowles to acquire the much larger company. Aside from the rarity of a smaller company swallowing a larger one, the deal also was unexpected because the two firms had little in common in terms of their product portfolios, with few opportunities for synergistic savings. Uniroyal Chemical's largest area of operation was in polymer products and rubber chemicals and additives; it also produced crop protection products, including fungicides, insecticides, and herbicides, as well as other specialty chemicals, such as lubricant additives. In one of the few synergies, Uniroyal's polymer product business served the same customers as Crompton & Knowles's polymer processing equipment operation. Calarco remained chairman and CEO of Crompton & Knowles following the purchase of the company he formerly headed.

In the immediate aftermath of the Uniroyal takeover, Crompton & Knowles concentrated on debt reduction; by the end of 1998, $400 million had been removed from the debt load. The company also expanded into new international markets, set up a joint venture in Mexico in 1998 to build a rubber plant, and made selective acquisitions, including the 1998 purchase of Betol Machinery, a U.K. maker of polymer processing equipment. In November 1998 the company sold a 50 percent interest in Gustafson, its North American seed treatment business, to Bayer Corporation for $180 million, thereby turning Gustafson into a joint venture of the two firms. Crompton & Knowles continued its full ownership of crop protection operations in international markets. In January 1999 the company exited from the specialty ingredients sector through the sale of that business to Chr. Hansen Holding A/S of Denmark for $103 million. Five months later Crompton & Knowles agreed to merge with Witco Corporation.

Witco's Roots and Early History

Witco was founded as Wishnick-Tumpeer Chemical Company by Robert I. Wishnick in association with brothers Julius and David Tumpeer. Wishnick was president, owning 51 percent of the company's shares, and was chairman emeritus of Witco until his death in 1980. It was Wishnick who shaped the company's growth and direction for over half its life. His two original partners, who together owned only 20 percent of the company's shares, sold their interest shortly after World War II.

Born in Koltchina, Russia, in 1892, Robert Wishnick came to the United States to join his father and oldest brother in 1896. At age seven he lost his right arm at the elbow after breaking it badly in a fall. This childhood accident seems only to have hardened Wishnick's determination to succeed in life. He put himself through school, earning one of the first degrees in chemical engineering from the Armour Institute of Technology, now the Illinois Institute of Technology. Then, employed days as a chemist, he worked toward a law degree, which he received in 1917 from Kent College of Law.

His first job with the American Magnesium Products Company brought near disaster to his employers, but ironically foretold the successful business strategy Wishnick would follow to bring Witco to its position in the chemical industry in the late 20th century. His company sold a floor wax that complemented its product line of magnasite floor materials. Wishnick, however, thought that the company should produce its own floor wax, rather than reselling floor wax originally purchased elsewhere. He had his own mixture of wax and turpentine on a burner when the telephone rang and drew him away. In his absence, the mixture boiled over and set the entire factory on fire, burning it to the ground. This may not have been the most auspicious of beginnings, but it demonstrated clearly Wishnick's drive for independence. From that time Wishnick continually strived to push Witco to self-sufficiency through manufacturing its own products.

In 1920, after working as a sales representative with A. Dager & Company for two years, Wishnick, with Julius Tumpeer, incorporated Wishnick-Tumpeer Chemical Company as a chemical distributing concern on East Illinois Street in Chicago. The company's largest market was in carbon black and various other coloring agents needed by Chicago's vigorous printing industry. Before the company was a year old, however, a recession set in and sales declined considerably. Wishnick responded by cutting costs wherever possible. He reduced his own salary, cut the company's profit margin, then worked to increase volume. These measures were successful and were used later to great effect whenever Witco suffered from changes in the market. Cost-cutting also helped the company record a profit during its first year, despite the recession.

In 1922 the company was able to buy a 20 percent interest in a carbon black plant in Swartz, Louisiana. Witco then marketed the product on a commission basis in its own area. In 1923 Wishnick felt it was time to expand further and asked Julius Tumpeer to head the company's first New York office, though Wishnick later replaced him.

Also in 1924, Wishnick-Tumpeer purchased its first manufacturing concern, Pioneer Asphalt Company in Lawrenceville, Illinois. By 1926 so much of the company's business was in asphalt products that the board elected to drop Chemical from the company name, making the new name simply Wishnick-Tumpeer Incorporated. The steady growth that had marked the company from its beginnings continued through the 1920s until the crash of 1929.

Once again, Wishnick and his company implemented cost-cutting measures. Wishnick reduced wages, salaries, and, of course, margins. This strategy worked again and the company

managed to turn a profit in each year of the 1930s. During this time, cash flow was a severe problem, but Wishnick had a unique solution. Most of the company's cash flow problems were caused by its customers' late bill payments. Each month Wishnick made a special trip to the accounts payable departments of the company's major accounts. There he left a small gift of candy or flowers with the secretaries and politely suggested that his bill be moved from the bottom of the pile to the top where it could be paid as soon as possible.

In 1933 the company acquired another carbon black plant, which, after additional negotiations, led to Wishnick's formation of Continental Carbon Company in association with Continental Oil Company and Shamrock Oil and Gas Company. These two other concerns supplied the needed natural gas for carbon black production and Wishnick-Tumpeer became the exclusive sales agents for the new company.

In 1935 Wishnick's first overseas operation was created in Britain: the company acquired an interest in Harold A. Wilson & Company, a supplier of pigments to the United States. Eventually, the entire company was bought by Wishnick.

The company's last important move before World War II came in 1939, when it built its first chemical plant in Chicago to produce industrial chemicals and asphalt products. The war brought large amounts of business for Wishnick-Tumpeer, but it also led to problems of shortages and rationing. Most of the company's business was still in distribution, and at times Wishnick's suppliers were unable to deliver what was needed.

Witco's Postwar Transition to Manufacturing

As the war was ending, annual sales were at approximately $7.8 million. The company was larger than ever before, but its future was uncertain. Many of the larger chemical companies from which Wishnick was accustomed to buying were developing their own competing sales forces. In 1944 Wishnick changed the name of his company to Witco Chemical Incorporated, "Witco" having been used as a brand name for several years. Then, in 1945, the board of the new company made official its plans to move as quickly as possible into manufacturing and to leave the distributing business.

Soon thereafter, the Chicago plant was expanded to include the production of metallic stearates, and then a number of new companies were acquired. Franks Chemical Products Inc. was purchased and then moved to less expensive quarters in Perth Amboy, New Jersey. A Los Angeles plant was bought from the India Paint and Varnish division of American Marietta, and new equipment was ordered for the plant to begin production of stearates. In 1954, by the time sales had grown to nearly $20 million, a British stearate plant also was purchased. This steady and extended expansion was not without difficulties, however. There were recurring operating problems in the Perth Amboy plant, some of which William Wishnick, the president's son, was asked to help solve. There was also a major fire in the Chicago plant, and then in 1953 the first strike in Witco's history took place in the Lawrenceville plant.

None of this weakened William Wishnick's resolve, however. In 1955 the decision was announced to end the company's distributing business altogether and to begin moving toward complete self-sufficiency. Witco sales were as high as $30 million, but over a ten-year period only 35 percent of that was from its own manufacturing operations. Some major acquisitions were on the horizon, but not until after a management reorganization. The Tumpeer brothers were no longer with the company (Julius had retired in 1947 and David had died in 1951). It was then, in 1955, that Robert Wishnick became chairman of the board, and Max Minnig, a longtime senior employee, became president. At that time, William Wishnick rose to the executive vice-presidency from his position as vice-president and treasurer.

In keeping with its new corporate strategy, Witco spent the next two years making acquisitions and expanding operations. Sales rose to $40 million, 40 percent of which came from Witco manufacturing facilities. Then, in 1958 Witco went public and sold 150,000 shares of common stock. This expansion continued unabated through the mid-1960s. In 1960 the Sonneborn Chemical and Refining Corporation was acquired, bringing sales up to the $100 million mark. International expansion accelerated as well, with new acquisitions in Belgium, France, and Canada.

Witco's Expansion in the 1960s and 1970s

In 1964 further administrative changes led the way for even greater expansion. Robert Wishnick became chairman of the finance committee as well as managing director of international activities. Robert's son, William, succeeded him as chairman of the board, and Max Minnig became chief executive officer while maintaining his position as president. As chairman, William initiated the greatest growth period in Witco's history. He began with the 1966 acquisition of Argus Chemical Corporation at a price of $22 million. This provided Witco with a new plastics operation, specializing in polyvinyl chloride (PVC) additives, and one of its senior managers, William Setzler. Later in 1966 Witco acquired Kendall Refining Company, a maker of lubricants. The younger Wishnick also spent considerable sums on plant modernization and research and development. This tendency toward reinvestment of generated capital was to characterize the next two decades of Witco growth. In the period from 1966 to 1975 William Wishnick increased the company's sales by 250 percent. During this period he also assumed the duties of president and chief executive officer after Max Minnig's retirement in 1971.

In fulfillment of Robert Wishnick's dream, Witco became a firm devoted exclusively to manufacturing chemical products when its 1933 agreement with Continental Carbon Company expired in 1970. Witco kept its 20 percent interest in the company, but did not renew its licensing contract with the company. Witco now sold only Witco-manufactured products.

The recession in 1974 led to the traditional cost-cutting measures at Witco. The recession also brought a fourth-quarter drop of 50 percent in sales compared with the previous quarter. In addition, there was a sharp earnings drop in early 1975. By the end of 1975 matters had returned to normal, but there was still an overall drop in operating earnings of 23 percent. Despite this, Witco continued to expand, albeit more slowly. The Waverly Oil Works was purchased and a new $10 million hydrogenation plant was built in Pennsylvania.

The year 1975 witnessed additional administrative changes as highly talented managers from acquired companies rose to executive levels. Henry Sonneborn, brought in when his company was purchased in 1960, assumed the presidency and also became chief executive officer while William Setzler of the Argus division was appointed to the board of directors. William Wishnick returned to the position of chairman and his father Robert was appointed chairman emeritus, a position he held until his death in 1980.

Witco's 1980s Acquisitions and Divestments

The period from 1975 to 1986, half of it spent without the founder's presence, was characterized by a somewhat haphazard approach to acquisitions. Under William Wishnick's guidance, the new administration made several purchases, such as the $38 million deal with Kraft in 1980 for Humko Chemical, a manufacturer of oleochemicals that are used in a variety of industries. But other acquisitions made during the period diversified Witco away from its core specialty chemicals and petroleum businesses. This was particularly true of the 1982 purchase of the Richardson Company for $62.6 million. Although the company was a market leader, Richardson's variety of products—including battery casings, conveyor belts, and offset plates for printing—had little in common with Witco's product lines.

At this same time, Witco, along with the U.S. chemical industry in general, was hit hard by the "double-dip" recession of the early 1980s, which had been brought on by the oil shock of 1979. The company's numerous acquisitions of the 1970s and 1980s had created not only a much larger company but also a more unwieldy one with 18 operating divisions. Wishnick was forced to launch a divestment program to improve earnings. From 1981 through 1985, a variety of operations were sold, including a detergent business, urethane systems operations, Richardson's offset plates business, and Pioneer Asphalt's Lawrenceville plant (which had been Witco's first manufacturing facility). Witco also sold off some of its oil reserves since petroleum prices were falling rapidly. Coupled with the divestments, Wishnick began to invest more heavily in the company's existing operations, in particular upgrading aging facilities; by 1985, 75 percent of the $70 million used for reinvestment went to plant modernization.

Although the company's growth was slowed during this retrenchment—sales increased only to $1.35 billion in 1986 from the $1.2 billion posted in 1980—net income of $65.2 million was a company record. Further, Witco's 1986 profit margin of 4.8 percent was the best in 18 years.

In October 1985 "Chemical" was again dropped from the company name, making the new company title Witco Corporation. At that time lubricants and specialty petroleum products made up 53 percent of the company's business, and specialty chemical products accounted for only 41 percent. The remaining six percent consisted of a variety of engineered materials for special applications.

In 1986 Thomas J. Bickett took over as president and CEO from the retiring William J. Ashe, who had occupied the job since Henry Sonneborn retired. In 1978 Bickett had been asked to join Witco while working for an accounting firm contracted by Witco. His appointment to the position came after he had been with the company for 12 years, serving for much of that time on the board of directors. Although Bickett was considered a possible heir apparent to Wishnick, who was nearing retirement, Bickett left the company in 1989, reportedly because his and Wishnick's operational styles clashed. Although Denis Andreuzzi was named president and chief operating officer following Bickett's departure, it was William R. Toller whom Wishnick recommended be elected chairman upon his retirement in October 1990. Toller had joined Witco in 1984 when the company acquired Continental Carbon from Conoco.

Witco's 1990s Restructuring

Toller inherited a company that had struggled during the latter half of the 1980s. Net sales reached only $1.59 billion by 1989, an increase of just 9.7 percent over a five-year period. The company stayed away from major acquisitions during the period, while organic growth was difficult given Witco's mature markets.

Toller knew that major changes were needed to get the company growing again. Just two months after gaining the chairmanship, he asserted that the company had to globalize its operations. He also set a goal of reaching $2 billion in sales and a 16 percent return on equity by 1995. In 1991, Toller's first major undertaking was to commit the company to developing a state-of-the-art information system that would help the divisions' managers run their operations more efficiently as well as provide upper management a better handle on the overall operations. The new system began operation in 1994.

Meanwhile, the future shape of Witco began to take form as Toller slowly began to win over the other senior managers to his vision of a company dedicated to the specialty chemicals business. Although some managers recommended that the company remain diversified, Witco's largest acquisition to date propelled it into a new era. In 1992, Witco acquired the Industrial Chemicals and Natural Substances divisions of Germany's Schering AG for $440 million. The deal not only solidified the company's future in specialty chemicals (in 1993 chemicals accounted for 58 percent of Witco's sales), it also significantly enhanced the firm's global presence. A key symbol of the company's newfound international strength came in 1994 when Witco stock began to be traded on the Frankfurt Stock Exchange. Also in 1994, Witco moved its corporate headquarters from New York to Greenwich, Connecticut.

A major reorganization in 1993 did away with the divisional structure, replacing it with a structure that revolved around market-focused operating units. Initially, the groups included Oleo/Surfactants, Polymer Additives, and Resins within the chemicals area; Petroleum Specialties and Lubricants within the petroleum area; and the Diversified Products Group, which consisted of noncore businesses to be divested. During the mid-1990s, Witco divested itself of numerous nonchemical units and announced in 1995 that it intended to divest its Lubricants Group as well, after which it would be almost exclusively in the specialty chemicals business (with a relatively small Petroleum Specialties Group).

Toller's goal of international expansion led to another major acquisition in 1995, which improved Witco's position in Europe but, more important, expanded the company's presence in the Pacific Rim and South America. Witco acquired OSi Specialties, Inc. in October 1995 in a $486 million deal. OSi was the global leader in silicone specialty chemicals and had significant operations in Asia, a region in which Witco was eager to expand. Under Witco, OSi became one of the company's operating groups, the OSi Specialties Group. Also in 1995 Witco took a $33.8 million charge related to the closure of five facilities.

In a few short years, Toller and his team had overseen a major transformation at Witco, one at least as important as the shift from distribution to manufacturing that occurred earlier in the century. Witco was now a major player in the international specialty chemicals industry and was more focused than ever before. In 1993, the company had already passed the $2 billion sales goal Toller had set when he took over the chairmanship, and even when the company began in 1995 to report its Lubricants Group as a discontinued operation, Witco fell just barely short of the $2 billion mark that year, thanks to its acquisition of OSi. In mid-1996 Toller retired. Hired as chairman, president, and CEO was E. Gary Cook, who had been president of Albemarle Corporation.

Under Cook's leadership, the restructuring pace quickened. In late 1996 Witco announced that it would close an additional 15 manufacturing plants over a three-year period, with a concomitant workforce reduction of 1,800. This restructuring, which involved a 1996 charge of $345.1 million, aimed to reduce operating costs by more than $200 million per year by the end of the decade. During the same period, Witco planned to invest more than $600 million in plant modernizations, capacity upgrades, environmental and safety enhancements, and information systems upgrades. During 1997 the company finally completed its long anticipated exit from the lubricants sector and divested a number of other noncore businesses. Witco's remaining operations were reorganized into four units: oleochemicals and derivatives, polymer chemicals, performance chemicals, and organosilicones. In May 1998 Witco swapped its epoxy and adhesives business for Ciba Specialty Chemical's PVC heat stabilizer business, thereby bolstering its vinyl additives business. In January 1999 the company announced that it was seeking a buyer for its oleochemicals and derivatives unit. In May came a similar announcement regarding the firm's petroleum additives business. The following month, Witco agreed to a merger with Crompton & Knowles Corporation, leading to a decision to retain the petroleum additives unit, in order to combine it with Crompton's plastics and lubricant additives business. Then in August, immediately prior to the consummation of the Witco-Crompton union, Witco completed the sale of its oleochemicals and derivatives unit to Goldschmidt AG, a unit of Viag AG, for around $249 million.

Late 20th-Century Creation of Crompton Corporation

The specialty chemicals sector was marked by a consolidation trend in the late 1990s fueled by intensifying global competition, cutthroat pricing, and the concomitant need for greater economies of scale. Joining in on the merger wave, Witco and Crompton & Knowles announced in June 1999 that they would combine forces. The two companies were near equals in size (Witco posted 1998 revenues of $1.94 billion, while Crompton & Knowles brought in $1.8 billion in sales that year), but

Crompton was operating at a higher profit level. The two firms' product lines were complementary, with 84 percent of the combined operations situated in overlapping end-use markets—most notably, rubber and polymer processing, elastomers, crop protection chemicals, and lubricant/petroleum additives. Through the merger, which was completed in September 1999 with the creation of the newly formed CK Witco Corporation, the companies aimed to achieve pretax operating savings of about $60 million per year by the second full year of combined operations. Cook retired soon after the merger was finalized, leaving Calarco fully in charge of CK Witco as chairman, president, and CEO.

In addition to integration efforts, CK Witco concentrated on divesting a number of noncore businesses. In December 1999 the company sold its entire textile dyes operation and most of its non-U.S. industrial colors business—both of which had come from the Crompton & Knowles side—to Yorkshire Group PLC for $86.5 million. Then in April and May 2000, CK Witco announced that it was seeking to sell two units that had been part of Witco's performance chemicals unit: refined products and industrial specialties. Also in April, the company changed its name to Crompton Corporation—in part because the Crompton name had a better reputation with the financial community than that of the tarnished Witco; it planned, however, to continue to market products under other established brand names, including Witco, Uniroyal Chemical, OSi, and Davis-Standard. With the expected completion of the latest divestments, Crompton would derive nearly 60 percent of its revenues from polymer products, including additives, polymers, and polymer equipment. The OSi organosilicones unit would contribute 17 percent; crop protection, ten percent; the remaining industrial colors business, six percent; lubricant additives, five percent; and glycerine and fatty acids, three percent. Other initiatives for the early 21st century included winning back customers who had been lost when the firm was concentrating on restructuring—at the expense of customer service—in the late 1990s. Crompton also aimed to reduce its debt load and increase its operating margin from ten percent to 15 percent.

Principal Subsidiaries

9056-0921 Quebec Inc. (Canada); Agro ST Inc.; Assured Insurance Company; Baxenden Chemicals Limited (U.K.; 53.5%); Baxenden Scandinavia AS (Denmark; 53.5%); CNK Disposition Corporation; CNK One B.V. (Netherlands); CNK Two B.V. (Netherlands); CNK Italiana SRL (Italy); CK Holding Corporation; CK Witco Asia Pacific PTE Ltd. (Singapore); CK Witco China Limited; CK Witco Europe Financial Services Co.; CK Witco Financial Services Co. (Ireland); CK Witco Funding Corporation; CK Witco Hong Kong Limited; CK Witco International Corporation; CK Witco International Services Corporation; CK Witco Singapore Private Limited; Crompton & Knowles Acceptance Corporation; Crompton & Knowles Canada Ltd.; Crompton & Knowles Chemische Produckte GmbH & Co. K.G. (Germany); Crompton & Knowles Colors Incorporated; Crompton & Knowles Europe S.P.R.L (Belgium); Crompton & Knowles International, Inc. (U.S. Virgin Islands); Crompton & Knowles International SARL (France); Crompton & Knowles I.P.R. Corporation (Delaware); Crompton & Knowles Overseas Corporation; Crompton &

Knowles Realty Corporation; Crompton & Knowles Receivables Corporation; Crompton & Knowles Services S.P.R.L. (Belgium); Crompton & Knowles Specialties Holdings B.V. (Netherlands); Davis-Standard Corporation; Davis-Standard (France) SARL; Davis-Standard (Deutschland) GmbH (Germany); Davis-Standard Limited (U.K.); Enenco, Incorporated (50%); ER-WE-PA Davis-Standard GmbH (Germany); Ecart, Inc; Firma W/K Witco EPA (Netherlands; 50%); GT Seed Treatment, Inc.; Gustafson International Company; Gustafson LLC (50%); Gustafson Partnership (Canada; 50%); Hannaford Seedmaster Services (Australia) Pty. Ltd.; Australia Industrias Gustafson S.A. de C.V. (Mexico); Immobiliaria Huilquimex, S.A. de C.V. (Mexico); Interbel Trading, Inc.; Jonk BV (Netherlands); Kem Manufacturing Corporation; Kem International Corporation; Lokar Enterprises, Inc.; Naugatuck Treatment Company; Nerap Expeditie BV (Netherlands); ParaTec S.A. de C.V. (Mexico; 49%); OSi Specialties Inc. (Chile) Limitada; ParaTec Elastomers LLC (51%); PT Witco Indonesia; Quebec, Inc. (Canada); Rubicon Inc. (50%); TOA Uni Chemicals Ltd. (Thailand; 48.98%); TOA Uni Chemical Manufacturing Ltd (Thailand; 48.94%); Trace Chemicals LLC; Unicorb Limited (U.K.); Uniroyal Chemica Srl (Italy); Uniroyal Chemical Asia, Ltd.; Uniroyal Chemical Asia Pte. Ltd. (Singapore); Uniroyal Chemical B.V. (Netherlands); Uniroyal Chemical Brazil Holding, Inc.; Uniroyal Chemical Co./Cie. (Canada); Uniroyal Chemical Company, Inc.; Uniroyal Chemical Company Limited (Bahamas/U.S.A.); Uniroyal Chemical (Europe) B.V. (Netherlands); Uniroyal Chemical European Holdings B.V. (Netherlands); Uniroyal Chemical Export Limited; Uniroyal Chemical Holding S.A. de C.V. (Mexico); Uniroyal Chemical Holdings B.V. (Netherlands); Uniroyal Chemical International Company; Uniroyal Chemical International Sales Corp. (Barbados); Uniroyal Chemical Investments Ltd. (Canada); Uniroyal Chemical Korea Inc.; Uniroyal Chemical Leasing Company, Inc.; Uniroyal Chemical Limited (U.K.); Uniroyal Chemical Netherlands B.V. (Netherlands); Uniroyal Chemical Overseas B.V. (Netherlands); Uniroyal Chemical Partipacoes Ltda (Brazil); Uniroyal Chemical (Proprietary) Limited (South Africa); Uniroyal Chemical Pty. Ltd. (Australia); Uniroyal Chemical S.A (Spain); Uniroyal Chemical S.A. de C.V. (Mexico); Uniroyal Chemical S.A.R.L. (Switzerland); Uniroyal Chemical Specialties, Inc.; Uniroyal Chemical Taiwan Ltd. (80%); Uniroyal Chemical Technology B.V. (Netherlands); Uniroyal Quimica S.A. (Brazil); Uniroyal Quimica Sociedad Anonima Comerciale Industrial (Argentina); Witco (Europe) S.A. (Switzerland); Witco Australia Pty Limited; Witco Benelux N.V (Belgium); Witco BV (Netherlands); Witco Canada Inc.; Witco Corporation (Malaysia) Sdn Bhd.; Witco Corporation UK Osil Group Limited; Witco Corporation UK Limited; Witco Deutschland GmbH (Germany); Witco do Brasil Ltda (Brazil); Witco Dominion Financial Services Company, Ltd. (Canada); Witco Ecuador S.A.; Witco Espana, S.L. (Spain); Witco Europe Investment Partners; Witco Foreign Sales Corporation (Barbados); Witco GmbH (Germany); Witco Grand Banks, Inc. (Canada); Witco Handels GmbH (Austria); Witco Investment Holdings BV (Netherlands); Witco Investments BV (Netherlands); Witco Investments SNC (France); Witco Ireland Investment Company Limited; Witco Italiana SrL (Italy); Witco Korea Ltd.; Witco Mexico S.A. de C.V.; Witco Polymers and Resins BV (Netherlands); Witco S.A. (France); Witco Solvay Duromer GmbH (Germany; 50%); Witco Specialties (Thailand) Ltd.;

Witco Specialties Italia S.p.A. (Italy); Witco Specialties PTE Ltd. (Singapore); Witco Surfactants GmbH (Germany); Witco Taiwan Ltd.; Witco Warmtekracht BV (Netherlands).

Principal Competitors

American Vanguard Corporation; BASF Corporation; Ciba Specialty Chemicals Corporation; Holliday Chemical Holdings PLC; Jilin Chemical Industrial Company Limited; Milliken & Company Inc.; PMC Global, Inc.; Struthers Industries Inc.; Terra Industries Inc.; Terra Nitrogen Company L.P.; United-Guardian, Inc.

Further Reading

"An Acquiring Lifestyle," *Forbes,* July 19, 1993, p. 230.

"Bright Acid Dyes," *Textile World,* March, 1992, p. 64.

Brown, Alan S., *The Witco Story: Hard Work and Integrity,* Lyme, Conn.: Greenwich Publishing, 1995.

Brown, Robert, "Executive Q&A: Gary Cook," *Chemical Market Reporter,* March 8, 1999, p. 20.

"C & K Operation Net Up 21% in Quarter," *Daily News Record,* January 29, 1993, p. 10.

Chang, Joseph, "C&K and Witco Combination to Create $3.2 Billion Entity," *Chemical Market Reporter,* June 7, 1999, pp. 1, 19.

"Crompton & Knowles Corp.," *Wall Street Journal,* December 16, 1992, p. C11.

"Crompton & Knowles Corp. to Purchase a Unit of Imperial Chemical Industries PLC," *Wall Street Journal,* May 11, 1992, p. B3.

Fink, Ronald, "Pass the Rolaids: The Chemical Businesses Witco Has Acquired Will Sharpen Its Focus and Broaden Its Reach—If They Aren't Too Much to Digest," *Financial World,* June 22, 1993, pp. 54–55.

Freedman, William, "Witco Absorbs OSi," *Chemical Week,* September 20, 1995, p. 8.

Gain, Bruce, "Cook's Recipe for a Trimmer Witco," *Chemical Week,* December 10, 1997, p. 34.

Henry, Brian, "C&K and Uniroyal Sign Merger Deal," *Chemical Marketing Reporter,* May 6, 1996, pp. 3, 40.

Hunter, David, "Witco's $5-Billion Ambitions," *Chemical Week,* June 26, 1996, p. 12.

Labate, John, "Crompton & Knowles," *Fortune,* July 12, 1993, p. 100.

Lerner, Ivan, "Crompton Moves to Sell Off Its Industrial Specialties Unit," *Chemical Market Reporter,* May 29, 2000, pp. 1, 21.

Lipin, Steven, "Crompton to Purchase Uniroyal for Stock Valued at $363 Million," *Wall Street Journal,* May 2, 1996, p. B4.

Lipin, Steven, and Susan Warren, "Crompton & Knowles and Witco to Merge in $1 Billion Stock Deal," *Wall Street Journal,* June 1, 1999, p. A4.

McCarthy, Joseph L., "Better Living Through Chemistry," *Chief Executive,* April 1996, p. 25.

Mitchell, Gordon, "The Right Chemistry: It's Now the Main Line for Crompton & Knowles," *Barron's,* January 30, 194, pp. 43 +.

Morris, Kathleen, "Crompton & Knowles: Playing the Niches in Slumping Markets," *Financial World,* November 12, 1991, p. 16.

Plishner, Emily S., "Crompton & Knowles: The Pessimism Could Also Fade," *Financial World,* November 7, 1995, p. 20.

——, "Passing the Baton: Bill Toller Has Transformed Witco into a Growing Specialty Chemical Company. Who's Next?," *Financial World,* November 21, 1995, pp. 52–53.

Protzman, Ferdinand, "Witco's Move in Europe Grows into Better-Than-Expected Fit," *New York Times,* November 16, 1993, p. C6.

Reingold, Jennifer, "Niche Rich: Crompton & Knowles Hunts for Treasure in Staid Markets—and Strikes Gold," *Financial World,* June 22, 1993, p. 56.

Scheraga, Dan, "Witco and C&K Merger Draws Industry Praise," *Chemical Market Reporter,* June 7, 1999, pp. 1, 23.

Stringer, Judy, "Managing Change at Witco," *Chemical Week,* June 7, 1995, pp. 44–45.

Tinsley, John F., *Looms for the World: Crompton & Knowles in Textile Machinery Manufacture, Since 1837,* New York: Newcomen Society in North America, 1949.

Walsh, Kerri, "Yorkshire Takes Textile Dyes Off CK Witco's Hands," *Chemical Week,* December 8, 1999, p. 18.

Warren, J. Robert, "Witco Has Bold Asian Goals," *Chemical Marketing Reporter,* April 17, 1995, pp. 7, 20.

Wishnick, William, *The Witco Story,* New York: Newcomen Society in North America, 1976.

"Witco Opts for Asset Focus to Carry Out Streamlining Plan," *Chemical Marketing Reporter,* February 24, 1997, pp. 8, 27.

Wood, Andrew, "Trimming Down into One Witco," *Chemical Week,* March 5, 1997, p. 45.

Wood, Andrew, and Kerri Walsh, "Crompton Cleans Up: Winning Back Witco Customers," *Chemical Week,* June 14, 2000, pp. 24–26.

—Sina Dubovoj
—updated by David E. Salamie

Davis Polk & Wardwell

450 Lexington Avenue
New York, New York 10017
U.S.A.
Telephone: (212) 450-4000
Fax: (212) 450-3800
Web site: http://www.dpw.com

Partnership
Founded: 1849
Employees: 515
Sales: $460 million (1999 est.)
NAIC: 54111 Offices of Lawyers

Davis Polk & Wardwell is one of the largest U.S. law firms, ranked by its annual gross revenues. It represents some of the world's largest corporations, including J.P. Morgan and Morgan Stanley Dean Witter, the modern companies founded by J. Pierpont Morgan, who first became a Davis Polk client in the late 1800s. The law firm's other clients are found all over the world, including EMI Group in the United Kingdom, Telefonica in Spain, and Korea Electric Power. It consistently ranks as one of the top law firms involved in corporate and financial transactions, with expertise in securities, banking, taxation, antitrust, government regulation, and most areas of modern business law. Its litigation practice includes defending RJR Nabisco in much publicized lawsuits filed by smokers. In addition to its New York City headquarters, the firm maintains offices in Menlo Park, California, to serve Silicon Valley clients; offices in Washington, D.C., to help clients deal with government laws and regulations; and five overseas offices (London, Paris, Frankfurt, Hong Kong, and Tokyo) in response to the increasingly globalized economy. The firm's legacy includes participation in major American court cases, probably the most famous being the 1954 case of *Brown v. the Board of Education of Topeka, Kansas.* That was also the last of 140 U.S. Supreme Court cases argued by John W. Davis, the most of any 20th-century lawyer at that time.

Origins and Expansion in the Early 20th Century

Davis Polk & Wardwell's roots began in 1849 when Francis N. Bangs started a law practice in the days when relatively few businesses incorporated. Francis L. Stetson graduated from Columbia, fought against the corruption of New York City's Democratic Party Boss Tweed, and then served New York City as its assistant corporation counsel before he joined Bangs as a partner in 1880.

Stetson brought the young partnership some of its most important early clients, most notably J.P. Morgan & Company, named for J. Pierpont Morgan, the famous banker and big businessman. In 1895, for example, Stetson went with Morgan to the White House to buy $65 million worth of bonds to help the federal government survive the depression that had started in 1893. In 1901 he helped Morgan create the United States Steel Corporation, the nation's first billion-dollar corporation, which survived in the late 20th century as USX. Stetson in 1901 also served Morgan when he set up the Northern Securities Company, a railroad trust that later was split up because it violated the 1890 Sherman Antitrust Act. Stetson helped J.P. Morgan & Company on various mergers.

In addition, Stetson after 1900 reorganized the United States Rubber Company and helped establish the International Harvester Company. Thus "Stetson became one of the most prominent corporation lawyers in the nation," reported author William H. Harbaugh. "He pioneered in transforming the corporate mortgage from a simple real estate lien into a complex agreement running to as many as 200 pages, and he eventually became the country's foremost specialist in corporate reorganization."

Although Stetson had partners and associates at his firm, called Stetson, Jennings & Russell, he was not interested in expanding his partnership. The firm from 1896 to the start of World War I in 1914 had no more than seven partners. Its average annual income between 1911 and 1914 was just $287,197.

Younger attorneys became frustrated since they did the bulk of the routine legal work without receiving adequate compensa-

Company Perspectives:

Davis Polk & Wardwell serves U.S. and non-U.S. clients who look to us for advice, representation, and transactional assistance in a broad range of practices. We regularly work on matters that, because of their intricacy and magnitude, raise novel questions of law and practice. Davis Polk lawyers are known for their ability both to create practical, innovative solutions to intractable problems and to manage the many facets of complex transactions and cases.

tion. The time was ripe for a major change, which happened in 1919, after Stetson had become senile and Jennings and Russell partially retired. The younger generation created the first "true partnership," according to Harbaugh, under such leaders as Allen Wardwell, who had joined the firm as a clerk after graduating from Harvard Law School in 1898.

Acting as the de facto head of the law firm, Wardwell recruited two key men in 1920. First he negotiated with Frank Polk, who in turn wrote to his friend John W. Davis about the advantages of joining the New York law firm. Davis was in the process of leaving public service as the U.S. ambassador to Great Britain. Polk told Davis that the Stetson law firm represented Morgan and was general counsel to New York's Guaranty Trust Company. It also represented the Associated Press, the International Paper Company, the Erie Railroad, and various others in trial and estates work. Admiralty and patent law were the only two areas it ignored.

John W. Davis, the law firm's most prominent attorney for several decades, was born in 1873 in West Virginia. When he became the head of the firm in 1921, it was renamed Davis Polk Wardwell Gardiner & Reed, the last two name partners being George H. Gardiner and Lansing P. Reed. According to the 1932 *Martindale-Hubbell Law Directory,* the partnership at 15 Broad Street in New York City had 17 partners and one "of counsel" member. It consistently received an "av" rating, the highest available from the directory.

During the Great Depression, John Davis represented name partner Louis Levy of the New York City law firm of Chadbourne, Stanchfield & Levy, later named Chadbourne & Parke. In spite of Davis's vigorous defense, Levy was disbarred after helping get Judge Martin Manton a $250,000 loan, which was never repaid, from American Tobacco's ad agency at the same time American Tobacco faced a lawsuit before Judge Manton.

In a 1939 article, Ferdinand Lundberg described Davis Polk as one of the nation's top "law factories," meaning it was "organized on factory principles and [grinded] out standardized legal advice, documents, and services . . ." Lundberg mentioned how the nation's top corporations tended to rely on the major law firms, thus concentrating wealth in just a few institutions. With 20 partners in 1939, Davis Polk Wardwell Gardiner & Reed for years had represented J.P. Morgan & Company and the Guaranty Trust Company. The law firm's attorneys also served as 22 corporate directors.

Post-World War II Law Practice

After being delayed by World War II, the federal government finally brought a major antitrust lawsuit against the nation's major investment banks, including Morgan Stanley and Harriman Ripley, who were represented by Davis Polk. The government accused the banks of price fixing, stifling competition from smaller investment banks, and several related charges. Whereas most banks and their lawyers wanted to settle the case, the New York law firm of Sullivan & Cromwell took the lead in fighting the government. The trial ran from 1950 to 1953, when the judge accepted the defense motion to dismiss *United States of America v. Henry S. Morgan, Harold Stanley, et al. doing business as Morgan Stanley & Co., et al.,* described by authors Nancy Lisagor and Frank Lipsius as "the granddaddy of modern antitrust cases."

During the Korean War, President Harry Truman in April 1952 announced that he had seized control of the nation's steel industry to prevent a threatened work slowdown or complete shutdown because of an industry-union dispute. John Davis represented Republic Steel in the steel industry's fight to reverse the seizure. After many calls for President Truman's impeachment, the U.S. Supreme Court in 1952 heard arguments from Davis and others before ruling in a 6–3 decision that Truman had no constitutional or congressional authority to take control of the steel industry.

Although John Davis won in the steel case, he lost just two years later in one of the nation's most famous court rulings, *Brown v. Board of Education of Topeka, Kansas.* Davis represented South Carolina in *Briggs v. Elliott,* which along with others was lumped together with the Brown case. Davis and other attorneys argued that the 1896 *Plessey v. Ferguson* ruling in favor of separate but equal schools should be upheld. Led by attorneys such as Thurgood Marshall, the NAACP won this court battle that led to school desegregation and was a major development in the postwar civil rights movement.

That was the last time John Davis argued a case before the U.S. Supreme Court. Starting in 1913, Davis made oral arguments before the nation's highest tribunal in 140 cases, the most of any 20th-century lawyer. Only two 19th-century lawyers exceeded that number: Walter Jones with 317 cases and Daniel Webster with at least 185 cases. Davis's distinguished career brought him many honors before he died in 1955, including the United Kingdom's highest award for a non-British citizen.

In 1954 the law firm included 26 members or partners, according to the *Martindale-Hubbell Directory.* It then was called Davis Polk Wardwell Sunderland & Kiendl. The last two name partners were Edwin Sunderland and Theodore Kiendl.

Four years later the firm had 30 partners and 67 associates when Spencer Klaw published his *Fortune* article on the large Wall Street law firms. Klaw mentioned that Davis Polk, "sometimes known as the Tiffany of law firms," was one of the so-called "white-shoe" law firms where its lawyers wore "buckskin shoes that used to be part of the accepted uniform at certain eastern prep schools and colleges." Part of that law firm tradition involved hiring mostly prominent young associates listed in the *Social Register.*

Key Dates:

1849: Francis N. Bangs starts his law practice.
1880: Francis L. Stetson joins firm and becomes its main partner in the late 1800s.
1921: John W. Davis becomes head of firm renamed Davis, Polk, Wardwell, Gardiner & Reed.
1962: The Paris office is started.
1973: Firm opens its London office.
1987: Firm opens its new Tokyo office.
1991: The Frankfurt office is opened.
1993: The Hong Kong office is established.
1999: Davis Polk ranks as eighth largest U.S. law firm, based on revenues.

By 1964 the law firm of 37 partners had added a Paris office and moved to its new headquarters at One Chase Manhattan Plaza in New York City. The firm, renamed Davis Polk & Wardwell, had overseas branches in both Paris and London in 1974 and included 43 partners and nine "of counsel" lawyers.

In the 1970s some of Davis Polk's major clients included Morgan Stanley & Company, Morgan Guaranty Trust Company, International Telephone & Telegraph, International Paper, Johns-Manville, LTV Corporation, R.J. Reynolds, and McDermott, Inc.

During the Carter Administration, the United States suffered from its seeming inability to resolve the Iranian hostage crisis after Moslem fundamentalists captured Americans in Tehran. Carter froze Iranian assets in American banks, while millions in U.S. money was loaned to various Iranian institutions. The crisis finally was resolved in early 1981 when a group of lawyers from New York law firms representing the nation's largest banks negotiated with attorneys representing Iranian interests. Davis Polk & Wardwell, on behalf of its historic client Morgan Guaranty, thus helped end one of the nation's more humiliating episodes during the Cold War. Unfortunately, few history books mentioned such behind-the-scenes roles of law firms.

Practice in the Late 20th Century

Starting in the late 1970s and early 1980s the nation's largest law firms began a major transformation. Part of the change came from a 1977 U.S. Supreme Court ruling that said restrictions on professional advertising violated the First Amendment's guarantee of free speech. At about the same time two new periodicals, the *National Law Journal* and the *American Lawyer,* began publishing articles on law firm management and finances. From that point on, law firms began to be more open about their operations, ending much of the secrecy of the past. In addition, lawyers gained competitive data about law firm profits, thus fueling more lateral hiring of experienced lawyers. The bottom line was that most big law firms became much larger in the 1980s, a time of rapid expansion in the American economy. They became more business-oriented as well, adding public relations personnel and hiring consultants for advice on better management practices.

As attorney salaries increased rapidly, law firms competed not only with each other for the top talents but also with corporations, including some of their clients. That happened relatively rarely in the 1980s, but by the mid-1990s more senior partners left for top corporate positions. Ellen Joan Pollock, in the September 11, 1996 *Wall Street Journal,* wrote, "What makes this recent spate of legal defectors noteworthy is the sheer number making the switch, and that they are moving into top corporate posts."

A good example was Steven Goldstone, a senior partner at Davis Polk & Wardwell. In 1994 he earned about $1 million at the law firm. He had represented RJR Nabisco for several years, including a 1994 tobacco lawsuit. As the company's outside general counsel, Goldstone said he spent more than half his time on business strategy, not legal issues per se. Then in late 1995 Goldstone accepted an offer to become the CEO of RJR Nabisco Holdings Inc.

In the so-called New Economy, high-technology firms required all kinds of legal support, so the nation's largest law firms opened new offices to meet the demands of their clients. For example, in 1999 Davis Polk & Wardwell, along with two other New York firms, Shearman & Sterling and Simpson Thacher & Bartlett, started branch offices in Silicon Valley. Davis Polk's high-tech clients included Comcast, Compaq Computer, and Texas Instruments.

In March 2000 Davis Polk & Wardwell represented its long-term client Morgan Stanley & Company Incorporated and other underwriters of Crayfish Company, Ltd. in its initial public offering (IPO). Crayfish was a "Japanese e-mail hosting services provider," according to the Davis Polk web site.

Although Davis Polk & Wardwell continued to serve both Morgan Stanley and J.P. Morgan, the two firms formerly united as the House of Morgan, their relationships had changed. For decades Wall Street law firms had very close institutional ties to investment banks. "When I started 30 years ago, [these relationships] were virtually monogamous," said Francis J. Morison, Davis Polk's managing partner in the *Investment Dealers' Digest* of November 3, 1997. But as laws became more complex and law firms specialized, such long-term ties dwindled as clients turned to the firms that possessed the expertise they needed for specific situations.

In the 1990s Davis Polk & Wardwell advised clients in more than 700 mergers, acquisitions, and joint ventures valued at more than $1 trillion. Some of its corporate clients in 2000 were Banco Santander Central Hispano; Comcast Corporation; Network Solutions, Inc.; ImClone Systems Incorporated; Quintus Corporation; Bass PLC; Mission Critical Software Inc.; Emerson Electric Company; Salomon Smith Barney; Merrill Lynch International; Warburg Dillon Read; Credit Suisse First Boston; Canadian National Railway; and Pharmacia & Upjohn.

Davis Polk & Wardwell continued to be one of the major law firms in the late 1990s. The *American Lawyer* in July/August 1998 ranked Davis Polk as the United States' sixth largest law firm, based on its 1997 gross revenue of $390 million. At that point it had 447 lawyers.

In November 1998 the same magazine, in cooperation with London's *Legal Business*, published its first ranking of the world's largest law firms. Davis Polk ranked number eight based on its 1997 gross revenue, but it did not rank in the top 50 based on the number of lawyers. Its revenue per lawyer of $870,000 was the third highest in the world.

Based on its 1998 gross revenues of $435 million, Davis Polk & Wardwell ranked number five in the United States, according to the *American Lawyer* in July 1999. In 1999 the firm slipped to number eight based on its gross revenues of $460 million. Its profits per partner in 1999 were $1.61 million, a 63 percent increase since 1990 that made Davis Polk one of the ten most successful American law firms in the 1990s.

At the dawn of the new millennium, Davis Polk & Wardwell faced numerous challenges. Law firms were getting larger and larger, whether from mergers or internal recruiting, thus making management issues more crucial. Law firms faced competition from accounting firms that hired many lawyers, raising the possibility of the American bar allowing multidisciplinary practices involving lawyers, accountants, and other professionals. Rapid technological change, involving such issues as intellectual property conflicts and computer security for Internet transactions, also gave Davis Polk & Wardwell and other large law firms plenty to deal with in the Information Age.

Principal Operating Units

Corporate; Tax; Litigation; Trusts Real Estate.

Principal Competitors

Baker & McKenzie; Skadden, Arps, Slate, Meagher & Flom; Debevoise & Plimpton.

Further Reading

Davis Polk Wardwell Gardiner & Reed: Some of the Antecedents, New York: Davis Polk Wardwell Gardiner & Reed, 1935.

Harbaugh, William H., *Lawyer's Lawyer: The Life of John W. Davis,* New York: Oxford University Press, 1973.

Hoffman, Paul, *Lions of the Eighties: The Inside Story of the Powerhouse Law Firms,* Garden City, N.Y.: Doubleday & Company, 1982, pp. 51–53.

Huntley, Theodore A., *The Life of John W. Davis,* New York: privately printed, 1924.

Klaw, Spencer, "The Wall Street Lawyers," *Fortune,* February 1958, pp. 140–144 + .

McMenamin, Brigid, "The Trophy Lawyers," *Forbes,* November 6, 1995, p. 132.

Lundberg, Ferdinand, "The Law Factories: Brains of the Status Quo," *Harper's Magazine,* July 1939, pp. 180–192.

Mannix, Rob, "Redrawing the Map of the US Legal Market," *International Financial Law Review,* December 1999, pp. 31–33.

Pollock, Ellen Joan, "Order in the Boardroom: Lawyers Rise to CEO," *Wall Street Journal,* September 11, 1996, p. B1.

Rogers, James Grafton, "John William Davis," in *American Bar Leaders: Biographies of the Presidents of the American Bar Association, 1878–1928,* Chicago: American Bar Association, 1932, pp. 217–21.

Rosenberg, Geanne, "Bring in the Lawyers," *Investment Dealers' Digest,* November 3, 1997, pp. 18–24.

Stewart, James B., "Iran: Shearman & Sterling; Davis Polk & Wardwell," in *The Partners: Inside America's Most Powerful Law Firms,* New York: Simon and Schuster, 1983, pp. 19–52.

Thompson, Sydnor, "John W. Davis and His Role in the Public School Segregation Cases—A Personal Memoir," *Washington and Lee Law Review,* 1996, p. 5 + .

—David M. Walden

DEAN & DELUCA

Dean & DeLuca, Inc.

560 Broadway
New York, New York 10012
U.S.A.
Telephone: (212) 226-6800
Toll Free: (800) 221-7714
Fax: (212) 334-6183
Web site: http://www.dean-deluca.com

Private Company
Incorporated: 1977
Employees: 795
Sales: $59.6 million (2000)
NAIC: 44511 Supermarkets and Other Grocery (Except Convenience) Stores; 722211 Limited-Service Restaurants

For the ultimate American gastronome, there is just one place: Dean & DeLuca, Inc. Whether shoppers seek leek pie and candied flowers, white truffle oil or black truffle cream, Scottish salmon or Sevruga caviar, they can find it at Dean & DeLuca's large emporiums in New York, Washington, D.C., and North Carolina, or sample smaller selections at three Charlotte, North Carolina restaurants or seven Manhattan espresso bars. From spices to chocolate, stainless steel to mother of pearl, Dean & DeLuca's high-end stores carry everything necessary to create and eat gourmet meals. On the verge of going public in late summer 2000, Dean & DeLuca hoped to expand its presence both nationally and internationally, through additional locations and increased electronic business with its online catalogue and gift services.

Gastronomic Dreams: 1970s–88

The story of Dean & DeLuca begins in a Greenwich Village brownstone where Giorgio DeLuca lived in the basement apartment and Joel B. Dean lived on the top floor. The two became friends—more of a mentor (Dean) and student (DeLuca) relationship in actuality—and shared a love of the finer things in life: excellent food, wine, and the arts. Along with other friends of Dean, they had long discussions on quality—quality in its most esoteric terms, whether in literature, performance, or business, and how many had forsaken quality in their busy lives. The discourses altered DeLuca's life; he soon gave up his job as a history teacher in New York's public school system and pursued his passion for cheese by opening a small shop on Prince Street in SoHo (the region south of Houston Street) in 1973.

DeLuca, whose father was a food importer, was an expert on cheese and wanted not only to bring exotic cheeses to the neighborhood, but to educate his customers on the proliferation of cheeses available from around the world. Freshness and quality were his mainstays and soon the little store was a success. Dean, who worked as a business manager at Simon & Schuster, was buoyed by DeLuca's accomplishment and wanted to open his own retail store selling cookbooks and kitchenware. They considered collaborating, and when a 2,500-square-foot storefront across from the cheese shop became available, a partnership was born. This store would be a haven of taste, an emporium of excellence—where customers found unusual cookbooks, stylish housewares, exotic fruits and vegetables, dozens of cheese varieties, savory vinegars and oils, freshly baked breads, and aromatic coffees.

DeLuca, Dean, and the latter's friends, chef Felipe Rojas-Lombardi and artist Jack Ceglic, selected the decor and products for the upscale market and "Dean & DeLuca" opened its doors on the lower west side of Manhattan in the fall of 1977. Among its wondrous fare was the little-known radicchio, sun-dried tomatoes, 175 varieties of cheese, balsamic vinegar, and DeLuca's cherished gastronomic *raison d'être*—extra virgin olive oil. As DeLuca told Jesse Kornbluth in a 1981 *Metropolitan Home* article, "Olive oil is *pivotal*! The Greeks prized it, the Romans prized it—today, in France and Italy, cooks still examine oil with the same care they bring to wine." Decades before such items were in vogue on the East and West Coasts, Dean & DeLuca spawned trend after culinary trend, and the store became the "in" place in not only SoHo, but in Manhattan as a whole. Locals and visitors alike flocked to the market with the funny name, and its purveyors introduced New Yorkers to a growing array of enchanting victuals by insisting customers sample their wares.

Company Perspectives:

Our Reason for Being: Dean & DeLuca's mission is to lead the marketplace in the exploration, discovery, and celebration of food from around the globe. Through intelligent and tasteful merchandising, we offer a wide selection of food and kitchenwear from the commonplace to the extraordinary. Our Vision: Dean & DeLuca will become the preeminent purveyor of food and kitchenwear worldwide. With international brand recognition and a reputation for excellence in retailing, we will set the standard for culinary taste and quality in the marketplace.

Food As Fad and Fashion: 1980s

Customers who delighted in Dean & DeLuca's edibles, however, paid a premium for their habit; the store's prices were high-end, though patrons did not seem to care. By the early 1980s Dean & DeLuca's retail flow had helped revitalize the SoHo area, and it became an arts-related oasis filled with galleries, boutiques, eateries, and lofts. To capitalize on their growing brand recognition and reputation, Joel and Giorgio decided to increase sales through a mail-order catalogue. The first catalogue was produced in late 1981 and a fulfillment center in Wichita, Kansas, was later added to process the orders. Eugenio Pozzolini, a former Rizzoli Bookstore clerk who happened to speak three languages, was a native Italian, and had tastes similar to DeLuca's in specialty foods, came aboard as a partner.

Ever increasing demand soon forced the gourmands to search for additional space, and in 1986 Dean & DeLuca found nearly 10,000 square feet of retail space after an army/navy surplus store and a manufacturer were persuaded to move elsewhere. The corner of Broadway and Prince Street became the new epicurean hot spot when Dean & DeLuca opened its doors on October 6, 1988.

By the end of the 1980s Dean & DeLuca parlayed its success into smaller cafés around Manhattan and were followed by seven Dean & DeLuca Espresso Bars. With Starbucks coffee bars the rage on the West Coast, Dean & DeLuca rode the crest of the wave with its own brands of coffee served with exotic breads and pastries. Coffee craze naysayers, who refused to believe Americans would pay premium prices for a cup of coffee, were effectively silenced by the phenomenal success of Starbucks, Dean & DeLuca, and a slew of imitators.

Bigger and Better: 1990s

By 1993 Joel and Giorgio were ready to take another step, to open another large market like their flagship store in SoHo—this one in the Georgetown neighborhood of Washington, D.C. Like its iconic sibling, the D.C. hybrid flourished and plans for additional Dean & DeLuca satellites were under way. These newer outlets were not large emporiums like the SoHo or Georgetown markets, nor small espresso bars, but medium-sized cafés. The first cafés, in Philadelphia, were built at prime locations within the city, with hopes of opening as many as ten additional cafés over the next few years. This marketing strat-

egy, however, did not pan out and the Philadelphia cafés were closed. Speculation was rife as to why the cafés closed, and Dean & DeLuca management remained mum, though analysts argued whether sales, quality, and/or timing were issues. A former employee told the *Philadelphia Inquirer* in October 1995 the company was restructuring, and the closures were part of a new plan to keep cafés in areas where Dean & DeLuca emporiums already existed and were thriving.

Despite problems in Philadelphia, Dean & DeLuca had grown to 450 employees and brought in sales of $30 million in 1995. At this time company founders Joel Dean and Giorgio DeLuca had decided to retire from the daily grind (though each held substantial stock and remained on the board of directors). The founders sold a controlling interest in their company to Midwestern entrepreneur Leslie Rudd, who was well known in the restaurant industry for his successful expansion of the Lone Star Steakhouse chain, which then went public. Both Dean and DeLuca had high hopes Rudd could transform their company into a national powerhouse. Part of the new regime included Dane Neller, who joined Dean & DeLuca, Inc. as president and CEO, to spearhead expansion plans.

Dean & DeLuca celebrated its 20th anniversary in 1997 with its two large emporiums in New York and Washington, D.C., and new gourmet stores in North Carolina (Charlotte), Kansas (Kansas City), and California (St. Helena). The occasion was touted in the media, including a backhanded tribute in *Washington Monthly* by Pilar Guzman, who had actually gone to work in the Manhattan flagship. Guzman called Dean & DeLuca one of "New York's most flavorful institutions—the Vatican of Vichyssoise, the Pantheon of Porcini, the Alhambra of Arugula." Guzman's article covered everything from the correct way to preserve cheese in Saran Wrap to the emporium's exorbitant prices. Yet taste and image were a perfect blend, as reiterated by Guzman: "With its signature medley of marble slabs and crusty breads, stainless steel and Moroccan trout, wooden crates and runny Stiltons, Dean & Deluca has pioneered an overall aesthetic that is more lifestyle museum than mere food Mecca." Or as Kornbluth said in his *Metropolitan Home* article, "Somehow your basket is full, your bill astronomical. You don't care: you have bought the best-quality foodstuffs available in America."

Two new Dean & DeLuca satellites were opened in Charlotte, North Carolina, while its original 9,000-square-foot emporium was still going strong. The new 4,000-square-foot outlets represented a format change, from store to restaurant, with salad and sandwich bars, bakery, wines and beer, and prepackaged "fresh" meals for takeout. These particular locations were even baking their own bread (nearly 30 different kinds), a departure from the larger markets who bought from scores of local bakeries. By 1998 annual revenues had slowly climbed to $33 million, but the company had yet to show a profit. Customers were buying and product was selling, but the costs of maintaining fresh and exceptional food items was high.

In 1999 Dean & DeLuca had a total of five gourmet emporiums (a few with wine selections), eight cafés, and burgeoning exposure on the Internet. Not only were Dean & DeLuca products offered through sites such as the San Francisco-based BravoGifts.com, but the company had its own online shopping

Key Dates:

1977: Company is founded by Giorgio DeLuca and Joel B. Dean.
1988: Business outgrows original store; new market at Broadway and Prince Streets opens.
1993: Georgetown emporium opens; Dean & DeLuca Espresso Bars pop up around Manhattan.
1995: Owners Dean and DeLuca sell a controlling interest to restauranteur Leslie Rudd; Dane Neller is appointed president and CEO.
1997: Company celebrates 20th anniversary.
1999: Sales reach $51 million.
2000: John Richards is named president; company prepares to go public.

service for corporations and individuals. This was also the year the specialty marketer began selling only California wines in the few stores selling wine, at the request of majority owner Leslie Rudd. Yet despite a healthy jump in sales to $51 million for the year, the company experienced its fifth straight loss since 1994. To remedy the situation and staunch the flow of red ink, John Richards, who had run Starbucks Coffee Inc.'s North American operations for two years, was offered a top slot at Dean & DeLuca to work alongside Dane Neller.

Morsels and Millions: 2000 and Beyond

In a January 24, 2000 press release, John Richards commented on his appointment as president: ''Joining Dean & DeLuca provides me with a rare opportunity to directly oversee a sterling consumer brand at a particularly exciting point in its growth cycle.'' Having doubled the number of Starbucks stores during his stint, Richards knew more than a little about national expansion. Part of his incentive to jump ship was a six-figure salary and reportedly 450,000 shares of Dean & DeLuca stock in the company's planned IPO sometime later in the year. In addition to hiring Richards, a $20 million infusion of venture capital came from Silicon Valley's Hummer, Winblad Venture Partners for a 25 percent stake in the company. Founding partner Ann Winblad gained a seat on the Dean & DeLuca board and told Michele Leder of *Crain's New York Business,* ''When we find a company that makes sense, we want to give it a lot of fuel.''

Hummer, Winblad had been approached by other specialty food start-ups but turned them down in favor of Dean & DeLuca. Hummer, Winblad Venture Partners, primarily known for its interests in Internet and software companies, seemed like an odd fit for Dean & DeLuca, but in addition to opening new gourmet food stores, the foodsmith intended to expand its online catalogue (especially wine) and electronic business services. ''Dean & Deluca offers the kind of opportunity we prize because of its innovative integration of the Internet into its strategy,'' Winblad commented to Clifford Carlsen of the *San Francisco Business Times.*

With a $20 million investment, a dynamic new president, and an upcoming IPO, Dean & DeLuca aimed to go where no

gourmet foods marketer had successfully gone before. Dean & DeLuca was not only going large, but going public. Rudd, Neller, Richards, Dean, and DeLuca hoped the bold move would give the company the financial stability and cash to expand into ripe markets in California, Florida, Georgia, Illinois, and possibly overseas. Dean & DeLuca was not just looking to survive—but to thrive. Yet despite the more than $35 billion spent annually on gourmet and specialty foods at the end of the 1990s, analysts doubted even a company with the brand recognition of Dean & DeLuca could maintain the high quality necessary to sustain national, much less international, stores.

The management at Dean & DeLuca begged to differ and were determined to prove it. Not only were there plans for two or three stores during the year, but several more each year for the foreseeable future. Sales for 2000 were barely less than $60 million from its 12 locations, and overall employees had leapt to nearly 800. Pilar Guzman, in her 1997 *Washington Monthly* feature, summed up the attraction of Dean & DeLuca for its many patrons: ''The genius of Dean & DeLuca is that it strikes a balance of the bountiful and the minimal. . . . It is reminiscent of the French or Italian central market but done in pure Soho style—epic loft ceilings and all the right stainless steel touches. The store achieves a paradoxical industrial rusticity, at once both inviting like a country-kitchen table and Euro-aloof like the double-cheek kiss of a Soho gallery keeper.''

Chic, inviting, expensive, unique: the 23-year-old Dean & DeLuca was still among things bright and beautiful in the year 2000. Its incredible edibles and café lattes were still so trendy they were featured in the WB television network's series *Felicity,* where the lead character worked part-time at a Dean & DeLuca while attending college. With an IPO on the horizon to raise $69 million for expansion, the sky appeared bright indeed.

Principal Competitors

Bloomingdale's Inc.; Crate and Barrel; R.H. Macy & Co., Inc.; Starbucks Corporation; Sutton Place Gourmet; Williams-Sonoma Inc.; Zabar's & Company, Inc.

Further Reading

Carlson, Clifford, ''Hummer Winblad Adds $20M Zip to Gourmet Venture,'' *San Francisco Business Times,* February 4, 2000, p. 5.
Chapman, Francesca, ''Dean & DeLuca Plans to Open Cafes Around Philadelphia in 1994,'' *Knight-Ridder/Tribune Business News,* October 20, 1993, p. 10200013.
Conan, Kerri, ''Urban and Outward,'' *Baking Buyer,* April 1998.
''Grounds for a New Job,'' *Puget Sound Business Journal,* June 2, 2000, p. 2.
Guzman, Pilar, ''Edible Complex,'' *Washington Monthly,* December 1997, p. 38.
Kornbluth, Jesse, ''Dean & DeLuca: Curators of the New Cuisine,'' *Metropolitan Home,* August 1981, p. 89.
Leder, Michele, ''Dean & Deluca Aims to Fatten Up . . . ,'' *Crain's New York Business,* January 31, 2000, p. 1.
Murray, Barbara, ''Store Owner: Only Wines from California Sold Here,'' *Supermarket News,* August 2, 1999 p. 33.
Robertiello, Jack, ''Upscale Spread: Dean & Deluca Is Moving South and West and Bringing Its Pricey Movable Feasts with It,'' *Supermarket News,* August 18, 1997, p. 21.

—Nelson Rhodes

DeCrane Aircraft Holdings Inc.

2361 Rosecrans Avenue, Suite 180
El Segundo, California 90245
U.S.A.
Telephone: (310) 725-9123
Fax: (310) 643-0746
Web site: http://www.decraneaircraft.com

Wholly Owned Subsidiary of Decrane Holdings Co.
Incorporated: 1989
Employees: 2,500
Sales: $244.05 million (1999)
NAIC: 336413 Other Aircraft Parts and Auxiliary
Equipment Manufacturing

DeCrane Aircraft Holdings Inc. (DAH) has grown aggressively through focused acquisitions. Originally a supplier to commercial airliners, DeCrane bought its first business jet supplier in 1997 and has since become a dominant player in that field. Clients include virtually all commercial and business jet manufacturers, including Boeing, Airbus, Dassault, Bombardier, and Cessna. New York-based DLJ Merchant Banking Partners II, L.P. owns DAH parent DeCrane Holdings Co.

Origins

R. Jack DeCrane was an executive at B.F. Goodrich from 1986 to 1989. He left to form a new holding company, DeCrane Aircraft Holdings, Inc. (DAH), in December 1989. The first acquisition was Hollingsead, a maker of avionics support structures, which was bought in October 1990 for $9.1 million.

In 1991, DAH purchased the Tri-Star Companies (i.e., Tri-Star including Tri-Star Europe and TST). Tri-Star made contacts and connectors, and TST made wire marking equipment. The purchase cost $10.4 million. That same year, DAH also bought a 75 percent share of Cory Components, which made connectors and harness assemblies, for $2 million. The remaining shareholding was acquired a few years later.

Revenues at Hollingsead increased almost 75 percent from 1992 through 1995. By this time, virtually all airliners in production carried components made by one of the DAH companies. DeCrane's strategy was to buy complementary businesses, working up from component manufacture to that of complete systems. The company still managed to grow by a third as annual aircraft production fell from 800 to 400 from 1992 to 1995. Profits were hard to come by, though—DAH lost $2.4 million on revenues of $47.1 million in 1994 and $3.4 million on revenues of $55.8 million in 1995.

Two factors weighed significantly in DeCrane's favor in the mid-1990s. As the recovering commercial airline industry began to replace its aging planes, producers began reducing their vendor lists to better control quality and speed production. Every commercial aircraft had between one million and five million parts, and the industry had supported thousands of suppliers.

As consolidation among suppliers accelerated in 1996, DAH made three more acquisitions: Aerospace Display Systems (ADS), Elsinore L.P.'s Aerospace Services and Engineering Services divisions, and a $7 million facility owned by electronic connector giant AMP. The company paid $13.3 million for ADS, the market leader in dichroic LCD devices and a division of Allard Industries Inc. This promised to raise DAH's share of original equipment manufacturer (OEM) contracts. Engineering firm Elsinore cost $2.6 million and fortified the company's systems integration business and brought an important new client: Daimler Benz Aerospace. The AMP plant allowed for the more efficient production of contact blanks. DAH also paid $5.7 million for the remaining 25 percent share of Cory Components. With these purchases, DAH developed Hollingsead into a provider of complete systems, focusing primarily on the retrofit market. Losses for the year were reduced to $817,000 on revenues of $65 million.

Public in 1997

DAH aimed to raise around $40 million to pay off debt in its April 1997 initial public offering on the NASDAQ stock exchange. Four investment firms had held shares in DAH before the offering: Nassau Capital Partners L.P. (29.3 percent), DSV Partners IV (19.6 percent), Brantley Venture Partners (19.6 percent), and London-based Electra Investment Trust PLC (18 percent).

In August 1997, The Network Connection Inc. (TNCI) contracted with DeCrane's Hollingsead International unit to integrate in-flight entertainment and information management systems at French start-up carrier Fairlines, which operated McDonnell Douglas MD-80s. Sales of commercial aircraft continued to increase as carriers restored their aging fleets. DAH enjoyed a strong relationship with Boeing as that manufacturer merged with McDonnell Douglas.

Nevertheless, DAH decided to expand its acquisition strategy and enter the business jet market at a time of growth. Deliveries of new business jets were projected to total 2,300 between 1997 and 2001, an increase of 60 percent over the previous five years, spurred by a decline in available used aircraft, an increase in the number of charter operators, and the growing fractional ownership trend led by Executive Jet, Inc. The company bought Audio International Inc., a private, Arkansas-based market leader producing aircraft entertainment and cabin management products for business jets.

Revenues increased by two-thirds to $109 million in 1997 as operating profit nearly doubled to 12 million. The company had about 1,000 employees. Chuck Becker, president of Tri-Star Electronics, was named DAH president and COO in April 1998.

DAH completed a secondary offering by April 1998, leaving the company about $70 million in capital to spend. As Jack DeCrane told CNNfn, DAH typically sought out companies that were not for sale and secretly and quickly developed the deals they felt would enhance both sides' futures. DAH bought Seattle-based Avtech Corp. in June 1998. The innovative company had been founded in 1963 and produced electronics systems for the civil aerospace industry. The purchase of Dettmers Industries Inc. followed within a month. Dettmers was a fast-growing Florida-based company that built motorized seating for corpo-

rate jets. DAH believed the products of its Audio International and Avtech subsidiaries would complement those of Dettmers.

Private in 1998

DeCrane itself agreed to be acquired by DLJ Merchant Banking Partners II, an affiliate of New York investment bank Donaldson, Lufkin & Jenrette, Inc., in July 1998. DLJ agreed to pay $23 per share at a time when the DAH stock was trading for $17 a share; the total price was about $182 million. DLJ also promised to bankroll the company's ambitious acquisition strategy. Management received a minority share and the company became a private company again. DeCrane shareholder Taam Associates, Inc. had sued, saying the board should have shopped the company around more. Company officials agreed to release more information about the deal before it closed, and the suit was dropped. DLJ organized DeCrane Holdings Co. as a holding company for DeCrane Aircraft Holdings (DAH).

DAH continued to grow its corporate jet business by acquiring PATS Inc., a leading producer of auxiliary fuel tanks. PATS, founded in 1976, also had developed a line of auxiliary power units. It had recently won a seven-year, $180 million contract to install them on the new Boeing Business Jet (BBJ), a derivative of the Boeing 737 airliner.

The buying spree continued with the April 1999 purchase of Precision Pattern Inc. (PPI), based in Wichita, Kansas. The company, founded in 1952, supplied custom furniture for business jets (including the two Air Force One Boeing 747s). PPI had 350 employees and was planning to add 50 a year to keep pace with the business jet industry. Annual sales averaged $24 million. Like other DAH acquisitions, Precision Pattern was not for sale when DeCrane executives approached it. Combined with Audio International and Dettmers, the purchase made DeCrane the largest supplier of interior products to the corporate market.

DAH augmented these purchases that August by buying Custom Woodwork & Plastics Inc. (CWP). CWP made interior furniture components for corporate aircraft. Based in Savannah, Georgia, the 54-person company had been supplying Gulfstream Aerospace for a dozen years.

Another Wichita company, PCI NewCo Inc., was added in October 1999. PCI made sidewalls and headliners for corporate jet interiors. DAH added the business to its Cabin Management Group. The company, founded in 1978, also made ducting, doors, and flight surfaces. It had been bought by local businessman Russell Bomhoff in 1995 while it was in bankruptcy. Customers included most business jet manufacturers, including Boeing.

Regrouped in 1999

In September 1999, DAH reorganized its ten subsidiaries into three business groups: the Cabin Management Group, the Specialty Avionics Group, and the Systems Integration Group. Jack DeCrane said the new groups would help aircraft manufacturers speed completion times by weeks or months without compromising quality. The Cabin Management Group offered "cabins in a box"—pre-engineered, pre-fitted interior kits. The

Key Dates:

1989: Former B.F. Goodrich executive Jack DeCrane starts his own holding company.
1990: DAH makes its first acquisition, Hollingsead.
1997: DAH goes public; enters business jet market.
1998: DLJ buys DAH.

Specialty Avionics Group supplied components for electronics equipment. Systems Integration provided auxiliary fuel tanks and auxiliary power units as well as engineering and other services.

The Infinity Partners, a maker of pre-engineered interior kits and cabin components for corporate jets, was acquired in December 1999. Bombardier was Infinity's main customer. Infinity, based in Denton, Texas, had been founded just three years prior to its acquisition by DeCrane. Completing its line of interior products remained a priority for DeCrane entering the new millennium. DAH bought Carl F. Booth & Co. of New Albany, Indiana, in May 2000. Booth supplied wood veneer products for business aircraft.

Soon after came the acquisition of ERDA Inc., a business aircraft seating maker based in Peshtigo, Wisconsin. DeCrane officials announced plans to double production there, potentially adding 100 new jobs in Wisconsin. Employment had already risen by 100 to 250 in the previous year. ERDA, which also operated a plant in Monterrey, Mexico, had recently won a contract with Dassault Falcon Jet. It had been founded in 1979 and itself acquired rival Derlan Industries of Santa Ana, California. DAH also picked up ERDA's medical imaging division in the deal, but not its interest in San Marcos, California-based Trident Inc., which went to ERDA shareholders. ERDA joined DeCrane's newly formed Seating Division with Dettmers Industries. The manufacturing operations of the Aviart Group, based in San Antonio, Texas, were also acquired in the spring of 2000. Aviart employed 115 people and produced upholstery, cabinetry, and finishes. It was renamed DeCrane Aircraft Furniture Co., L.P.

DeCrane forecast total sales of $370 million for the year 2000. It was consolidating its Hollingsead International operations in a new facility near Santa Barbara, California. The Teal Group Corp. predicted a 50 percent increase in the corporate jet deliveries over the next ten years. As this segment accounted for more than 40 percent of DAH's business, the company seemed assured of another successful decade.

Principal Subsidiaries

Audio International; Carl F. Booth & Co., Inc.; Custom Woodwork & Plastics, Inc.; Dettmers Industries, Inc.; Infinity Partners; International Custom Interiors, Inc.; PCI NewCo; Precision Pattern, Inc.; Aerospace Display Systems, Inc.; Avtech Corporation; Cory Components; ERDA Inc.; Tri-Star Electronics International, Inc.; Hollingsead International, Inc.; PATS, Inc.

Principal Divisions

Cabin Management Group; Specialty Avionics Group; Systems Integration Group.

Principal Competitors

AAR Corp.; Aerospace Lighting; Air Show/Pacific Systems; AlliedSignal Inc.; AMP, Inc.; Amphenol; Baker Electronics; B/E Aerospace, Inc.; Becker Avionics; Burnham; Crane ELDEC; Cristalloid; Custom Aircraft Cabinets; Deutsch Engineered Connecting Devices; Diehl GmbH; DPI Labs; Electronic Cable Specialists; Fibre Art; Gables Engineering; Grimes Aerospace; Hiller; ITT Cannon; Marshall Engineering; Plastic Fab; Nellcor Puritan Bennett; The Nordam Group; Page Aerospace; Radiall S.A.; Sealed Composites Works.

Further Reading

"DeCrane Aircraft Hopes to Launch Public Offering," *Going Public: The IPO Reporter,* February 3, 1997, p. 8.

Defterios, John, "Trading Places" (interview of Jack DeCrane), CNNfn, May 22, 1998.

Moriarty, George, "DLJ Merchant Banking Acquires DeCrane Aircraft," *Private Equity Week,* July 27, 1998.

Pearce, Dennis, "DeCrane Aircraft Buys Precision Pattern, of Wichita, Kan.," *Wichita Eagle,* April 27, 1999.

Prizinsky, David, "DeCrane Aircraft Looking to Soar with IPO Assist," *Crain's Cleveland Business,* Finance Sec., April 7, 1997, p. 3.

Savage, Mark, "California Avionics Company to Buy Peshtigo, Wis. Airplane Seat Maker," *Milwaukee Journal Sentinel,* May 31, 2000.

Snow, David, "DLJ Flies Higher with DeCrane Add-On," *BuyOuts,* May 31, 1999.

Stickel, Amy I., "Booming Aircraft Market Sends Suppliers Soaring," *Mergers & Acquisitions Report,* Industry Focus Sec., May 5, 1997, p. 1.

—Frederick C. Ingram

The Earthgrains Company

8400 Maryland Avenue
St. Louis, Missouri 63105-3668
U.S.A.
Telephone: (314) 259-7000
Fax: (314) 259-7036
Web site: http://www.earthgrains.com

Public Company
Incorporated: 1927 as Win M. Campbell Corporation
Employees: 26,300
Sales: $2.6 billion (2000)
Stock Exchanges: New York
Ticker Symbol: EGR
NAIC: 311812 Commercial Bakeries; 311821 Cookie and
    Cracker Manufacturers

The Earthgrains Company is the second largest bakery in the United States, supplying a variety of breads, buns, rolls, and sweet baked goods to markets in the South, Midwest, Southwest, and California. The company's major brands include Rainbo, Grant's Farm, Colonial, Old Home, Master, Break Cake (sweet goods), IronKids, and San Luis Sourdough, as well as the company's Earth Grains brand. The company also holds franchise licenses to produce bread products under the Holsum, Roman Meal, Sunbeam, Taystee, Country Hearth, and other brand names. Earthgrains sells bread and baked goods in Spain and Portugal under Bimbo, Martinez, Silueta, Semilla de Oro, Madame Brioche, and other brand names.

Earthgrains also sells refrigerated dough products in the United States and Europe. Products include cinnamon rolls, biscuits, cookie dough, pie crusts, puff pastry, and rolled dough. Most products are sold under private label retailer brands; Earthgrains offers the Merico, Sun Maid, and other brands in the United States and the Raulet and CroustiPate brands throughout Europe. Earthgrains is the largest manufacturer of refrigerated dough products in France.

Founding of Cooperative Association of Bakeries

For most of its existence The Earthgrains Company operated under the name Campbell Taggart, after Winfield Campbell, the founder of the company, and A.L. Taggart, an early investor. Campbell, former president of Continental Baking, started the company in 1925 with the idea to develop a national association of local bakeries that produced a large selection of quality baked goods. The Win M. Campbell Corporation began with one bakery in Kansas City, The Manor Baking Company, which sold bread door-to-door from 15 horse-drawn carriages. The company grew to six bakeries within three years. Taggart became a partner in the company in 1928, then renamed Campbell Taggart Associated Bakeries. Taggart's investment made it possible to expand the company to 19 bakeries with operations in nine states within a year. The bakeries produced bread under several brands, including Colonial, Rainbo, Holsum, Kilpatrick, and Betsy Ross.

As an association of bakeries, Campbell Taggart's local bakeries made decisions about productivity, labor, and delivery, while the company's executive committee of subsidiary presidents concerned itself with procuring supplies at volume rates, thus enabling small bakeries to compete with large corporations. This form of consolidation occurred during the 1930s, when Campbell Taggart acquired 25 bakeries, and during the 1950s, when grocery store chains, such as Kroger and Safeway, introduced their own brands of bread products. Independent bakeries either went out of business or affiliated with larger companies.

When Bill O. Mead sold his family's bakery to Campbell Taggart in 1960, he took successive positions with the parent company through which he redirected its course. Mead initiated the purchase of American Foods, Inc., renamed Merico, Inc., which produced refrigerated bread dough, cookie dough, and canned biscuit dough. In 1970 Mead became CEO and chairman and Connie B. Lane, a cost-control analyst who started with the company in 1947, became president. At that time Campbell Taggart operated bakeries in 74 cities in the south, southwest, and west.

Company Perspectives:

In four years, we have gone from a turnaround company to a proven industry leader. So, what do we do to improve further? We're sticking with our game plan: We'll continue to get bigger and better in the United States and Europe by taking advantage of acquisitions to drive profitable growth, by serving customers better, by controlling costs, and by delivering quality, value and variety to consumers. We have created the best growth and improvement model in the industry, and we have the best people and products to execute our plans. We believe records are made to be broken.

Mead and Lane sought to improve operations through a more centralized organizational structure that replaced the executive committee. Mead and Lane fired ten subsidiary presidents, consolidated certain bakery operations to improve efficiency, and closed several plants. Spending more than $40 million annually on capital investments in baking facilities, Campbell Taggart became among the most efficient commercial bakeries in the industry. Lane developed a system for cost control that allowed him to monitor the profitability of each bakery on a weekly basis. Using computer printouts of sales and expenses, Lane analyzed 60 bread products by a number of criteria, such as pounds of waste per employee and number of unsold loaves of bread. Mead implemented a manager training program and revised the company's incentive programs to include everyone in the company, from route salesmen to executives.

Mead and Lane sought growth through international markets. In 1971 Campbell Taggart formed a joint venture with the Mexican bakery, Grupo Bimbo, to introduce American-style sandwich bread in Spain. Bimbo, S.A. produced the bread with a slightly saltier flavor for Spanish tastes. The product became popular quickly and the venture built five plants in less than ten years. Campbell Taggart formed a similar venture, Plus Vita, to sell American-style bread in Brazil. In addition, under the subsidiary Europate, S.A., located in France, Campbell Taggart expanded Merico's market for refrigerated dough products.

As public nutritional concerns generated a demand for whole grain breads, Campbell Taggart introduced a superpremium line of whole grain bread and bakery products under the Earth Grains brand. Launched in 1975, the new brand included 40 products, such as Yogurt Bran, 100% Whole Wheat, and other pan-baked breads. Campbell Taggart produced the branded products at three large plants in Oakland, California; Paris, Texas; and Fort Payne, Alabama. At Paris and Fort Payne the bread was flash-frozen for long distance distribution. Wholesale bakeries kept the bread frozen until they needed it, then thawed it through a special process. Sales of Earth Grains products offset the decline in sales for white bread. In addition, the premium bread products sold at $1.00 per loaf retail, compared with $0.66 per loaf of enriched white bread.

As sales of Earth Grains brand products grew steadily, Campbell Taggart introduced a line of sweet baked goods to compete with the popular Entenmann's brand. The company overdid its initial production with 55 new products in six

months. Executives found it difficult to compete with a company that took several years to establish a loyal customer base and many of the products sold poorly. Campbell Taggart cut the line to 12 baked sweet products that sold well, such as walnut sticky buns and French-style puff pastries.

Campbell Taggart expanded its capacity for producing snacks and baked goods with the acquisitions of the Coosa Baking Company in Rome, Georgia, and the Penn Dutch Cookie Corporation in Fleetwood, Pennsylvania. Coosa produced cookies and wafers, while Penn Dutch produced cookies and snack crackers. In addition to marketing existing company brands and private label brands, the two bakeries began to produce products under Campbell Taggart brand names.

New products under Campbell Taggart's existing facilities included new refrigerated dough products, such as Merico Hot 'n Fresh Quick Breads and large, flaky biscuits under the new Mountain Man brand. Merico also produced Earth Grains new frozen garlic bread and French bread pizza.

Late 1970s Diversification, Capitalizing on Distribution Channels

The company decided to capitalize on its distribution network to diversify the kinds of food products that it sold. In 1977 Campbell Taggart bought the El Chico chain of more than 90 Mexican restaurants in 11 states and the El Chico line of canned and frozen foods. Campbell Taggart intended to sell the prepared foods along the same distribution channels as its refrigerated dough products and bread line. Campbell Taggart executives discovered a number of problems at El Chico, however, including a great deal of waste and outdated production methods at the commissary. Lane established portion and cost control measures and installed new automated equipment, such as a tortilla maker, which produced 800 corn tortillas per minute. With improved efficiency Campbell Taggart doubled the number of frozen food entrees, under the brand name El Charrito, to 27.

After an evaluation of every El Chico restaurant, Lane found extreme variations in the quality of food and service at each restaurant, leading to the closure of 18 restaurants. Campbell Taggart revised the menu, introduced measures to create uniformity in the food, and created a management training program. The company upgraded the interiors of many restaurants and opened 26 new restaurants in 1978 and 1979.

Campbell Taggart's international subsidiaries continued to do well. Installation of a high-speed production line in 1978 allowed Plus Vita to keep pace with increased demand for its bread products from McDonald's and other fast-food restaurants in Brazil. When a competitor closed its doors, Europate, S.A. became the only European supplier of canned refrigerator products in Europe. Campbell Taggart obtained complete ownership of Bimbo, S.A. and began construction on a sixth plant in southern Spain in 1978.

A decade after Mead and Lane took the lead at Campbell Taggart, the company became one of the top bakeries in the country. Sales increased from $31 million in 1969 to $1.1 billion in 1980, and net earnings increased from $8.1 million to $36.2 million. Dividends tripled and the company's stock split three times. In addition, the company surpassed its main com-

Key Dates:

1925: Company is founded by Winfield Campbell; incorporates two years later as Win M. Campbell Corporation.

1928: A.L. Taggart joins company, renamed Campbell Taggart Associated Bakeries.

1960: Company begins production of refrigerated dough products.

1971: International joint venture, Bimbo, S.A., introduces American-style sandwich bread in Spain.

1975: Company launches Earth Grains brand of premium breads.

1977: Diversification begins with acquisition of El Chico restaurants and frozen foods.

1982: Company is acquired by Anheuser-Busch Brewing Company.

1989: Company introduces IronKids bread.

1994: Company is restructured to focus on bread and baked goods.

1996: Spinoff as independent public company; company is renamed The Earthgrains Company.

1998: Acquisitions spur national, international growth.

2000: Company acquires Metz Baking Company.

petitors—ITT Continental Baking, Interstate Brands, and American Bakeries—in terms of operating income, at $75 million in 1980. Campbell Taggart weathered a recession and the higher cost of energy, labor, and commodities in 1979 and 1980 as Lane's cost controls allowed the company to maintain stable profit margins.

Campbell Taggart continued to diversify in the area of food production with the 1981 acquisitions of Larry's Food Products, Rod's Food Products, Herby's Foods, and Royal Food Products. Larry's prepared precooked meals served in schools, hospitals, nursing homes, restaurants, and corporate cafeterias. Products included sausage, beef, and chicken patties packaged in individual portions. With customers in 39 states, Larry's operated a state-of-the-art plant in Gardenia, California.

Campbell Taggart merged Rod's Food Products and Royal Food Products into Merico. Both companies produced refrigerated salad dressings, sandwich spreads, snack dips, and dairy and nondairy toppings. Rod's customers included food brokers for retail distribution and the foodservice industry. Its sales territory encompassed ten western states served by a modern plant located in City of Industry, California. Royal served customers in the Midwest and East through a plant in Indianapolis.

Herby's Foods of the Dallas-Ft. Worth area prepared and distributed fresh sandwiches, burritos, and desserts to convenience stores in Texas, Oklahoma, New Mexico, Arkansas, and Kansas. The company operated similar to a bakery, with daily delivery directly to the store. The company also produced the Mrs. Vees line of frozen sandwiches, distributed wholesale in 23 states.

Within its line of bakery products, Campbell Taggart expanded with the acquisition of Janin, S.A., which merged with Campbell Taggart's French subsidiary, Europate, S.A. Like Europate, Janin produced refrigerated and frozen dough products to retail stores and the foodservice industry.

1982 Acquisition by Anheuser-Busch Brewing Company

In 1982 Campbell Taggart began negotiations to be purchased by Anheuser-Busch Brewing Company. In order for the acquisition to go through, Campbell Taggart sold the El Chico restaurant chain, because Texas law would not allow Anheuser-Busch to own restaurants that held liquor licenses. Once that transaction was complete, Anheuser-Busch bought Campbell Taggart for $560 million, almost 20 times 1981 profits of $41.7 million.

Under Anheuser-Busch ownership Campbell Taggart continued to build on its previous success with new products, new markets, and product improvements. For Eagle Snacks, another subsidiary of Anheuser-Busch, Campbell Taggart produced cheese crackers and pretzels, which the company also distributed to 40 markets. In 1982 the company launched the Grant's Farm brand of premium, soft wheat breads; within two years Grant's Farm products sold in 18 markets. Merico formulated a croissant recipe for Burger King's new breakfast sandwiches, becoming the number one croissant supplier to the fast-food chain from the start.

Campbell Taggart restaged its line of frozen Mexican foods in 1985 and its line of Pattycake snack foods in 1987. The company reformulated its El Charrito recipes for a more distinctive taste, added new products, and repackaged the products with new graphics. Campbell Taggart renamed the Pattycake brand of snack cakes, including doughnuts, cupcakes, and other baked sweets, Break Cake, and repositioned promotion of the products to children.

Campbell Taggart continued to update baking facilities, close older plants, and build new ones. The company modernized the Kilpatrick Baking Company plant in Oakland, California, spending $11.5 million for state-of-the art technology and enabling the company to close an outmoded facility in San Francisco. Other modernized bakeries included the St. Louis, Sacramento, Charlotte, and Denver facilities, as well as several Merico facilities. In 1989 the company started construction on a new, 162,000-square-foot bakery under the Colonial Baking Company name in Atlanta. The capacity of the $25 million facility allowed for the production of 167 loaves and 1,200 buns per minute.

Public concern for nutritional health again played a role in new product development. In 1990 Campbell Taggart introduced the IronKids brand of bread, formulated for children's taste, texture, and color preferences, while providing children with a high-fiber bread enriched with iron and other nutrients. In addition to television advertisements, in-store displays, and promotional coupons, Campbell Taggart promoted the bread in conjunction with the IronKids Health and Fitness Program. Started in 1985, Rainbo and Colonial bakeries sponsored the program, which involved local triathalons for children, from seven to 14 years old. Campbell Taggart introduced the IronKids bread in five markets in the South, with systemwide implementation in 1991. Campbell Taggart appealed to adult tastes and health concerns with a line of low-calorie and low-fat products, such as an Earth Grains bread at 35 calories per slice. Earthgrains advertising capitalized on the new Food Pyramid, which recommended six to ten servings of carbohydrates daily with the tagline, ''Bread is Best.''

Restructuring, Spinoff in 1996 of The Earthgrains Company

After some product lines did not garner the returns expected, Anheuser-Busch decided to focus the company's business on bread and bakery products. With Barry Beracha as CEO, restructuring in 1994 involved the sale of Larry's Food Products, Rod's Food Products, and Royal Food Products, as well as the El Charrito line of frozen foods. Campbell Taggart learned that ethnic foods did not serve the same customer base as its bread line; although 99 percent of American households purchased bread on a regular basis, Mexican foods had a much narrower range of buyers. Management operations consolidated and relocated from Dallas to St. Louis, resulting in an almost completely new management and research staff. The company's new facilities included a new 44,000-square-foot technical center for ingredient testing and the development of new products. Campbell Taggart introduced new products through its Merico subsidiary, but later decided to sell Merico; the company continued to market refrigerated dough through Merico. In 1996 Anheuser-Busch decided to spin off Campbell Taggart as an independent public company, renamed The Earthgrains Company.

The focus of the new company became product development, improvements to existing products, operational efficiency, and new merchandising methods. Earthgrains withdrew from markets where established bread companies were difficult competition, closed eight inefficient, outmoded plants, and directed production toward premium breads and baked goods with higher profit margins. Earthgrains used a strategy of acquisition to maximize its production and distribution capacity, allowing for the introduction of the company's products into new territories. The $193 million acquisition of Atlanta-based Coopersmith included a 163,000-square-foot facility in Decatur, Georgia, with the capacity to produce 800 rolls of dough and 152 loaves of bread per minute. The acquisition gave Earthgrains new markets in the South and Southeast, which allowed the company to maximize production at existing facilities. Coopersmith also had a bakery in New Bedford, Massachusetts, outside of Earthgrains' territory, which the company traded for cash and an Interstate Bakeries plant in Grand Junction, Colorado, to supplement production at Earthgrains plants in Denver and Pueblo. The 1998 acquisition of San Luis Sourdough in San Luis Obispo and the 1999 acquisition of Redding French Bakery of Redding, California, positioned Earthgrains in the burgeoning market for artisan round breads.

International growth involved acquisitions, new markets, and new products. Purchases included refrigerated dough manufacturers Chevalier Servant, S.A. in 1998 and Patrick Raulet, S.A. in 1999. Patrick Raulet produced brand name and private label brands of refrigerated rolled dough for home-baked quiches, tarts, and pies. EuroDough expanded Raulet's product line with new refrigerated dough products, such as the CroustiPate brand pizza kit, which provided refrigerated dough

and all of the ingredients for making pizza. With the 1999 acquisition of Reposteria Martinez Group, Bimbo, S.A. gained a new line of fresh baked sweet goods for distribution with Bimbo bread products. Bimbo used the facilities at Reposteria Martinez to support expansion of its premium products, including the new Madame Brioche brand of French sweet rolls.

Earthgrains combined new information technology and existing production capacity to improve customer service. In August 1998 Earthgrains reached an agreement with Kroger to produce and distribute that company's private label bread and rolls. While Kroger closed its Texas Bakery, Earthgrains utilized bakeries in Dallas and Houston to supply 174 Kroger stores in Texas and Louisiana. Earthgrains route drivers delivered Kroger brand breads with Earthgrains' branded products. Using the company's Vendor-Managed Inventory (VMI) system, delivery personnel accessed sales data and category management data from hand-held computers to determine the right mix of products and appropriate product display in accordance with each store's demographics. Earthgrains made a similar arrangement with Albertson's, producing and distributing bread to Super Saver and Lucky grocery stores in northern California.

VMI integrated the hand-held inventory management computers and scan-based trading (SBT), an electronic data interchange that tracked sales directly from scanners at the cashier's stand. The paperless transactions increased sales and profit margins, reduced waste, and provided accurate invoice management. Through its Efficient Customer Response partnerships, Earthgrains provided efficient inventory tracking and restocking to Wal-Mart, Schnuck Markets, H.E. Butt grocery stores, and Jitney Jungle Stores of America in Mississippi. In conjunction with the system, Earthgrains consolidated accounting functions of local bakeries into the new Financial Share Services Center in St. Louis. Local bakeries downloaded data from the hand-held computers to the computer network for financial management and analysis in St. Louis.

In November 1999 Earthgrains announced that it planned to acquire Metz Baking Company, one of the largest regional commercial bakers in the country, for $625 million. Assets of the company included 21 bakeries that served customers in 18 states. Metz held the major market for bread products in Chicago, Minneapolis, and Milwaukee, producing Old Home and Master brands, and holding the license for the Roman Meal, Country Hearth, Pillsbury, and Healthy Choice brands. The acquisition would give Earthgrains market coverage for 50 percent of the U.S. population.

New products launched in 2000 focused on premium bread products with high profit margins and higher retail prices. New artisan breads included Earth Grains superpremium International Hearth Rosemary and Olive French Bread and San Luis Sourdough Garlic Round. Premium products included Grant's Farm Cornflour bread and Merico Hearty Layers Flaky Biscuits (a refrigerated dough product). Patrick Raulet introduced rolled dough pie kits with lemon, apple, French cream custard, or salmon filling.

In March 2000 the Metz acquisition was finalized and Earthgrains appeared well positioned to rise above the competition.

Within the territory it controlled, the company now ranked as the largest producing bakery for bread, buns, rolls, and bagels. Earthgrains had come a long way indeed from its humble beginnings back in 1925.

Principal Subsidiaries

Bimbo, S.A.; Earthgrains Baking Companies, Inc.; Earthgrains Refrigerated Dough Products, L.P.; EuroDough, S.A.S.

Principal Competitors

Flowers Industries, Inc.; ITT Continental Baking Company; Interstate Bakeries Corporation.

Further Reading

"Alex Foods Purchases Campbell Taggart Lines," *Supermarket News,* January 31, 1994, p. 3A.

"Anheuser-Busch Divests Merico," *Supermarket News,* August 14, 1995, p. 24.

"Anheuser-Busch to Spin Off Campbell Taggart Subsidiary," *Nation's Restaurant News,* August 14, 1995, p. 66.

Barrett, Rick, "St. Louis-Based Earthgrains Buys Madison, Wis.-Area Bakery," *Knight-Ridder/Tribune Business News,* November 15, 1999, p. OKRB9931915F.

"Building ECR Partnerships with Information Technology," *Progressive Grocer,* December 1998, p. 28.

"Campbell Taggart Will Sell Product Lines, Refocus on Baking Business," *Nation's Restaurant News,* August 7, 1995, p. 154.

Demertrakakes, Pan, "Making Dough from Bread," *Food Processing,* February 1998, p. 7.

Desloge, Rick, "Earthgrains Heats Up Hunt for Acquisitions; Philly Bakery Fits Analysts Say," *St. Louis Business Journal,* March 8, 1999, p. 5.

Dornblaser, Lynn, "Pyramid Power Lures Bakers," *Prepared Foods,* April 15, 1993, p. 48.

Dziuk O'Donnell, Claudia, "Earthgrains R&D: Designed for Speed, Anchored in Business," *Prepared Foods,* March 1997, p. 33.

"Earthgrains Creates Spanish Holding," *Eurofood,* June 3, 1999, p. 18.

"Growth Spurt at Earthgrains," *Supermarket News,* May 3, 1999, p. 129.

Hill, J. Dee, "Earthgrains Breaks Bread Spots," *ADWEEK,* September 20, 1999, p. 5.

Jennison, Stewart, "Colonial Baking in Owensboro, Ky., Changes Name to The Earthgrains Co.," *Knight-Ridder/Tribune Business News,* March 1, 1996, p. 3010299.

"Kicking in Dough," *St. Louis Business Journal,* February 7, 2000, p. 2.

Kroskey, Carol, "Kroger Signs New Bakery Pact with Earthgrains," *Supermarket News,* August 3, 1998, p. 29.

Krumrei, Doug, "A Whole New Box," *Bakery Production and Marketing,* April 15, 1996, p. 24.

Lerner, Howard, "Campbell Taggart: Baker to Buy Brown Group Buildings," *St. Louis Business Journal,* January 31, 1994, p. 1A.

Morrison, Ann M., "A Big Baker That Won't Live by Bread Alone," *Fortune,* September 7, 1981, p. 70.

Poole, Clair, and Jeffrey A. Trachtenberg, "Bear Hug," *Forbes,* November 16, 1987, p. 186.

"R&D Director's Viewpoint: Metrics and Motivation," *Prepared Foods,* March 1997, p. 34.

"St. Louis-Based Food Firm Testing New Breakfasts, Snacks," *Knight-Ridder/Tribune Business News,* May 18, 1999, p. OKRB991384F.

Steyer, Robert, "Clayton, Mo.-Based Earthgrains Co. Buys Two Bakeries," *Knight-Ridder/Tribune Business News,* June 29, 1998, p. OKRB981800DF.

Stroud, Jerri, "Bakery to Add Jobs in St. Louis Area," *Knight-Ridder/Tribune Business News,* October 4, 1998, p. OKRB982770F5.

——, "Earthgrains to Close Bakeries in Macon, Ga, and Montgomery, Ala," *Knight-Ridder/Tribune Business News,* August 20, 1998, p. OKRB98232110.

——, "Earthgrains Trades Bakeries with Kansas City's Interstate Bakeries," *Knight-Ridder/Tribune Business News,* June 12, 1998, p. OKRB981630FB.

——, "St. Louis-Based Earthgrains Warms Up to French Dough Company," *Knight-Ridder/Tribune Business News,* June 30, 1999, p. OKRB9918130.

——, "St. Louis-Based Firm Offers Incentive to Executives," *Knight-Ridder/Tribune Business News,* May 21, 1999, p. OKRB99141160.

Tucci, Linda, "Beracha Brings in the Dough at Earthgrains," *St. Louis Business Journal,* November 8, 1999, p. 1.

—Mary Tradii

EarthLink, Inc.

1430 West Peachtree Street Northwest, Suite 4
Atlanta, Georgia
U.S.A.
Telephone: (404) 815-0770
Toll Free: (800) 395-8425
Fax: (404) 815-8805
Web site: http://www.EarthLink.net

Public Company
Incorporated: 1994 as EarthLink Network, Inc.
Employees: 1,343
Sales: $670.43 million (1999)
Stock Exchanges: NASDAQ
Ticker Symbol: ELNK
NAIC: 51331 Wired Telecommunications Carriers (pt)

EarthLink, Inc. is the second largest Internet service provider (ISP) in the United States, trailing 25-million-member America Online, Inc. EarthLink provides dial-up Internet access, high-speed broadband access using digital subscriber line (DSL), single ISDN, and cable modem technology to 4.2 million consumer and business customers. The company uses a nationwide telecommunications network of leased, high-speed, dedicated data lines and more than 1,700 dial-up access sites.

Background

EarthLink attained its phenomenal rise in the world of Internet-related business through the ambition and timing of its founder, Sky Dylan Dayton. Dayton was born in New York City in 1971, but he was raised in the Los Angeles area, where his parents moved while he was still an infant. For someone who gained national prominence as a teenager, it was not surprising that Dayton's drive and ambition were exhibited at an early age. He set a goal at age 12 to become a millionaire by the time he was 24, an objective he intended to fulfill by embarking on his professional career as soon as possible. Deeply interested in computers, Dayton, at age 13, convinced his parents to send him to Delphian Academy, a progressive, private school near Portland, Oregon, that encouraged students to supplement their academic studies with experience in the workplace. Through the assistance of Delphian Academy, Dayton spent his high school years working for a Portland-area advertising agency, helping to create computer-generated music videos for artists such as Michael Jackson. By the time he was 16, Dayton was working full-time.

Dayton graduated from Delphian Academy in 1988, marking the end of his academic career. He never seriously considered attending college; instead, he returned home and began working at Wallen Green Design, an advertising agency in Burbank. His first position at Wallen Green was in the mailroom, but before long his employers noticed his computer skills and put him in charge of running the company's computer system. Less than a year after joining Wallen Green, Dayton left and joined another advertising agency, Mednick & Associates, where he created computer-generated print advertisements. Dayton was 17 years old and earning $35,000 a year.

After a year at Mednick & Associates, Dayton moved in a completely different direction. Along with a friend, he opened a coffeehouse on Melrose Avenue called Care Mocha. Care Mocha, frequented by celebrities such as Julia Roberts, quickly blossomed into a trendy success, but after a year-and-a-half Dayton's interests returned to computers. He sold his stake in Care Mocha and was hired by Executive Software as the company's director of marketing.

Dayton's executive position at Executive Software was the last job he held before founding EarthLink. The inspiration for his second entrepreneurial creation came from his own frustration in trying to connect to the Internet. In late 1993, Dayton became intrigued with the Internet, but the troublesome process of getting his computer online tempered his initial zeal. It took him a week to find a service provider and, he claimed, another 80 hours to get his computer connected and working properly. Dayton envisioned the Internet as a new medium for mass communication, but in order for the Internet to realize its potential the difficulty and cost of getting connected had to be reduced. EarthLink was his solution.

Launch of EarthLink: May 1994

Dayton spent the early months of 1994 mustering financial support for his business venture. He invested his personal

Company Perspectives:

What's important at EarthLink? We are convinced that the key to creating a truly great organization is an intense focus on the values that guide its people's actions. These are Earth-Link's "Core Values and Beliefs." If we don't seem to be living up to them, call us on it! We respect the individual, and believe that individuals who are treated with respect and given responsibility respond by giving their best. We require complete honesty and integrity in everything we do. We make commitments with care, and then live up to them. In all things, we do what we say we are going to do. Work is an important part of life, and it should be fun. Being a good businessperson does not mean being stuffy and boring. We love to compete, and we believe that competition brings out the best in us. We are frugal. We guard and conserve the company's resources with at least the same vigilance that we would use to guard and conserve our own personal resources. We insist on giving our best effort in everything we undertake. Furthermore, we see a huge difference between "good mistakes" (best effort, bad result) and "bad mistakes" (sloppiness or lack of effort). Clarity in understanding our mission, our goals, and what we expect from each other is critical to our success. We are believers in the Golden Rule. In all our dealings we will strive to be friendly and courteous, as well as fair and compassionate. We feel a sense of urgency on any matters related to our customers. We own problems and we are always responsive. We are customer-driven.

savings, borrowed money from friends and family, and, after writing a business plan, secured a sizable investment from a professional venture capitalist. By May 1994, the 23-year-old Dayton had the money he needed to lease the modems and communications wiring to serve as EarthLink's Internet backbone. In July, the company's first member logged onto the Internet through one of the company's ten modems, and Dayton was on his way toward becoming a multimillionaire.

By the end of 1994, EarthLink had collected $100,000 in revenue, a total the company would exceed on a daily basis by 1996. Part of the reason for the enormous growth achieved by EarthLink during its formative years was the release of Earth-Link's TotalAccess software, the first open and direct Internet software ever released. Debuting on the company's first anniversary in May 1995, the software was distributed in two versions, TotalAccess USA 800, which enabled subscribers to connect through a toll free telephone number, and TotalAccess Southern California, designed for southern California residents. Dayton hoped to distribute 500,000 copies of the regional version by the end of 1995.

Although TotalAccess USA 800 allowed residents outside of southern California to join EarthLink, Dayton at this point was concentrating almost exclusively on building his business regionally. By August 1995, however, the geographic scope of his objective had widened considerably. An alliance with UUNET Technologies enabled Dayton to roll out nationwide service. Within two weeks of signing the contract with UUNET, EarthLink was able to offer local dial-up access in 98 cities scattered across the country. Two months later, EarthLink be-

came the first ISP to charge a flat rate, offering unlimited usage on the Internet for $19.95 a month.

The growth of EarthLink, measured by the number of the company's subscribers, began to pick up speed in 1996, as the popularity of the Internet increased. The company eclipsed the 100,000-member mark on its second anniversary in May 1996, prompting Dayton to relocate headquarters from Los Angeles to Pasadena. After starting business with two employees, Dayton's workforce had grown to 60, a number that was expected to increase by 300 in the coming months as waves of subscribers joined the EarthLink network. Strategic alliances played a crucial role in fueling the company's growth during this period, including a partnership with PSINet in July 1996 that gave EarthLink hundreds of points of presence (POPs), or local access points, in the United States and Canada. After extending his service territory to include North America, Dayton signed an agreement with Microsoft Corporation in September 1996 that put EarthLink on the Windows 95 desktop. By October 1996, the company's membership passed 200,000 subscribers thanks in large part to the mass distribution of its software. In the last three months of 1996, a record six million copies of EarthLink's software were distributed through marketing partnerships with United Airlines, CompUSA, Simon & Schuster, CNN, and Warner Brothers, among others. By the end of the year, Earth-Link maintained a presence in 313 cities and towns in the United States and Canada.

In January 1997, EarthLink debuted as a publicly traded company, completing an initial public offering of stock that raised $26 million. With a fresh supply of capital, Dayton pressed ahead with expansion. By the end of 1997, EarthLink ranked as the third-largest ISP in the country, having increased its membership ranks tenfold during the previous three years. Dayton offered a simple explanation for the company's prolific growth. "We keep our eye on the customer," he told *Entrepreneur* magazine in a January 1998 interview. "That's where our focus is, and it's the key to our success." The company employed 800 people by this point in its development, the majority of whom worked as customer service representatives. By providing comprehensive assistance to its customers, EarthLink, as evinced by its ever-expanding customer base, was attracting Internet users from other ISPs (there were roughly 4,500 ISPs in existence by the end of 1997) and luring the uninitiated consumers who wanted to access the Internet for the first time.

In February 1998, EarthLink announced a massive deal with Sprint Corporation that closed the ground separating Dayton's company with Microsoft's MSN. In exchange for a 30 percent ownership stake in EarthLink, Sprint gave the Pasadena-based company 130,000 of its Internet-access customers, a $100 million line of credit, and $24 million in cash. With the customers gained through the Sprint deal, EarthLink's membership eclipsed 500,000 by April 1998, at which time Dayton's interest in the company was worth an estimated $89 million.

After finalizing the strategic alliance with Sprint, EarthLink officials projected the company would overtake MSN within 12 months and become the second largest ISP in the country. Toward this end, the company achieved meaningful strides in 1998, doubling its number of subscribers before the end of the year to reach the milestone of one million members. Helping to drive such expansion were two marketing alliances that made

Key Dates:

1994:   Sky Dayton forms EarthLink.
1995:   After establishing a partnership with UUNET Technologies, EarthLink launches nationwide service.
1996:   EarthLink icon appears on the Windows 95 desktop; membership eclipses 200,000.
1997:   Company completes its initial public offering of stock and begins trading on the NASDAQ.
1998:   EarthLink and Sprint forge strategic alliance.
1999:   EarthLink and Mindspring announce $4 billion merger agreement.
2000:   EarthLink announces acquisition of rurally oriented OneMain.com.

the selection of EarthLink a default option for many new computer buyers. Beginning in August 1998, EarthLink software was pre-loaded on all iMacs, a popular personal computer made by Apple Computer Inc. In November 1998, EarthLink became the official ISP for CompUSA, one of the nation's largest computer retailers.

Merger with Mindspring in 2000

EarthLink continued to broker partnerships with original equipment manufacturers (OEMs) as it entered its sixth year of business. In April 1999, the company was named as the exclusive ISP on all Micron Millennia computers. In June 1999, a ''Join EarthLink'' icon was placed on approximately one million computers made by Phoenix Technologies. The following month, EarthLink was announced as the default ISP for all new Apple iBooks, the notebook computers manufactured by Apple Computer. In August 1999, EarthLink and USAA, a massive insurance and financial services concern, entered a three-year agreement that appointed EarthLink as the official service provider for USAA's 3.3 million members. As they had in the past, the marketing partnerships of 1999 greatly increased the exposure of EarthLink's Internet-access services, but, however important, the partnership agreements were overshadowed by one landmark deal announced in 1999. In September, EarthLink and Mindspring Enterprises, Inc., a leading national ISP, announced a merger agreement, a deal that created the second largest ISP in the country.

The EarthLink-Mindspring merger, valued at $4 billion, was concluded in February 2000, creating a newly formed company that used the EarthLink name and combined the senior executives of the two companies. Dayton, who had served as chairman of EarthLink, became a director of the new EarthLink. Mindspring's founder and chairman, Charles Brewer, was named chairman of the new EarthLink, while the posts of chief executive officer and president were filled by the individuals who held identical posts at EarthLink and Mindspring, respectively. The new company occupied Mindspring's headquarters in Atlanta, Georgia.

The combination of the old EarthLink's 1,500 local Internet-service locations and Mindspring's 890 local Internet-service locations created an ISP with more than three million subscribers and $650 million in annual revenues. Although the company lagged far behind the more than 20 million sub-

scribers comprising America Online, the new EarthLink had overtaken MSN in the frenetic race to sign up Internet users. Considering the overwhelming lead maintained by America Online, the short-term prospects of eclipsing the industry's behemoth seemed bleak, but EarthLink's management was undaunted by the ambitious task at hand. At the time of the merger, more than 70 percent of U.S. households had yet to connect to the Internet, prompting the senior executives in Atlanta to boldly proclaim that their goal was to make EarthLink the world's largest ISP.

In the wake of the merger, EarthLink secured some of the financial resources it would need to wage the enormous battle that lay ahead. Because of the merger and a $200 million investment in EarthLink by Apple Computer in January 2000, Sprint's ownership interest in EarthLink had been halved. In May 2000, Sprint recommitted itself to taking part in EarthLink's future by increasing its investment in the company by $431 million. The money invested by Sprint increased EarthLink's cash reserves 64 percent, giving the company $1.1 billion to spend on increasing its customer base. The following month, in June 2000, EarthLink announced a definitive agreement to acquire OneMain.com, one of the country's ten largest ISPs, with more than 750,000 subscribers. OneMain.com, based in Reston, Virginia, provided Internet access to individuals and businesses predominantly located in small cities and rural communities. Once completed, the $308 million deal was expected to increase EarthLink's membership to 4.2 million subscribers, a total that was sure to increase as the company pressed ahead with its plans to overtake America Online.

Principal Subsidiaries

EarthLink Operations Inc.

Principal Competitors

America Online, Inc.; AT&T Corp.; Microsoft Corporation.

Further Reading

Armstrong, Larry, ''The Mac of Internet Providers,'' *Business Week,* December 15, 1997, p. 138.
Brown, Eryn, ''Could Earthlink Possibly Be the Next America Online,'' *Fortune,* April 27, 1998, p. 424.
Dawson, Angela, ''Earthlink Taking Spots National,'' *ADWEEK Western Advertising News,* January 10, 2000, p. 8.
Deady, Tim, ''Earthlink Opens Gates to Infonet,'' *Los Angeles Business Journal,* July 31, 1995, p. 1.
——, ''Southland Firm Blazes Trail into Cyberspace,'' *Los Angeles Business Journal,* June 12, 1995, p. 23.
''Earthlink to AOL: Watch Your Rearview Mirror,'' *Business Week,* October 11, 1999, p. 130
Hesseldahl, Arik, ''Earthlink to Offer Nationwide DSL,'' *Electronic News,* July 19, 1999, p. 28.
Katz, Frances, ''Sprint to Increase Stake in Atlanta-Based Internet Service Provider,'' *Knight-Ridder/Tribune Business News,* May 10, 2000, p. ITEM0013200C.
McGarvey, Robert, ''Sky's the Limit,'' *Entrepreneur,* January 1998, p. 127.
Nee, Eric, ''Surf's Up,'' *Forbes,* July 27, 1998, p. 106.
Sullivan, Ben, ''Glowing Sky,'' *Los Angeles Business Journal,* October 28, 1996, p. 19.

—Jeffrey L. Covell

Eastman Kodak Company

343 State Street
Rochester, New York 14650
U.S.A.
Telephone: (716) 724-4000
Fax: (716) 724-1089
Web site: http://www.kodak.com

Public Company
Incorporated: 1901
Employees: 80,650
Sales: $14.09 billion (1999)
Stock Exchanges: New York Pacific Boston Cincinnati
   Detroit Midwest Philadelphia
Ticker Symbol: EK
NAIC: 325992 Photographic Film, Paper, Plate, and
   Chemical Manufacturing; 333315 Photographic and
   Photocopying Equipment Manufacturing; 325411 Medi-
   cinal and Botanical Manufacturing; 325414 Biological
   Product (Except Diagnostic) Manufacturing; 334119
   Other Computer Peripheral Equipment Manufacturing;
   334510 Electromedical and Electrotherapeutic
   Apparatus Manufacturing; 511210 Software Publishers

A multinational corporation whose name and film products are familiar to photographers around the world, Eastman Kodak Company is a diversified manufacturer of equipment, supplies, and systems in consumer and professional imaging, including films, photographic papers, one-time-use and digital cameras, printers and scanners, photoprocessing services, photofinishing equipment, and photographic chemicals. The company's health imaging unit specializes in products and services for radiography, cardiology, dental, mammography, oncology, and ultrasound imaging. Other Kodak products include motion picture films, audiovisual equipment, microfilm products, and optics and optical systems.

Late 19th-Century Origins:
Photography for the Masses

The company bears the name of its founder, George Eastman, who became interested in photography during the late 1870s while planning a vacation from his job as a bank clerk in Rochester, New York. Taking a coworker's suggestion to make a photographic record of his intended trip to Santo Domingo, the 24-year-old Eastman soon found that the camera, film, and wet-plate-developing chemicals and equipment he had purchased were far too bulky. Instead of following through with his original vacation plans, Eastman spent the time studying how to make photography more convenient. He discovered a description of a dry-plate process that was being used by British photographers. He tried to replicate this process in his mother's kitchen at night after work.

After three years Eastman produced a dry glass plate with which he was satisfied. In 1880 he obtained a U.S. patent for the dry plate and for a machine for preparing many plates at one time, and he started manufacturing dry plates for sale to photographers. Henry A. Strong, a local businessman impressed by Eastman's work, joined him on January 1, 1881, to form the Eastman Dry Plate Company. Eastman left his position at the bank later that year to give his complete attention to the new company.

The new venture almost collapsed several times during its early years because the quality of the dry plates was inconsistent and Eastman insisted that the defective plates be replaced at no charge to the customer. Despite these setbacks, he was determined to make the camera ''as convenient as the pencil.''

As his business grew, Eastman experimented to find a lighter and more flexible substitute for the glass plate. In 1884 he introduced a new film system using gelatin-coated paper packed in a roll holder that could be used in almost every plate camera available at that time. Also that year, the company was reorganized as Eastman Dry Plate and Film Company. Strong was president and Eastman treasurer and general manager of the 14-shareholder corporation. The company also opened a sales office in London in 1885 to take advantage of the growing European photography market.

In 1888 Eastman's company introduced its first portable camera. Priced at $25, it included enough film for 100 pictures. After shooting the roll of film, the owner sent both the film and the camera to Rochester for processing. For $10, the company sent back the developed prints and the camera loaded with a

Company Perspectives:

On February 2, 2000, exactly 100 years from the day George Eastman introduced the Brownie camera, a group of Kodak researchers, inventors and business strategists met at the company's Rochester headquarters to speculate on what the next 100 years might bring to their industry. All agreed that the true power of imaging has barely been tapped—and that the advances of this century will vindicate Eastman's dream of making communicating with pictures as easy as "using a pencil."

new roll of film. This breakthrough is considered to be the birth of snapshot photography. It was also at this time that Eastman trademarked "Kodak," which he invented by experimenting with words that began and ended with his favorite letter, "K." The company advertised its new camera extensively using the slogan, "You push the button, we do the rest."

The following year, the Eastman Photographic Materials Company was incorporated in the United Kingdom to distribute Kodak products outside the United States from its headquarters in London. The company built a manufacturing plant in 1891 outside London to accommodate the growing product demand overseas and set up additional distribution sites in France, Germany, and Italy by 1900. In 1889 the firm's name was changed to Eastman Company and in 1892 to Eastman Kodak Company of New York.

Eastman was committed to bringing photography to the greatest number of people at the lowest possible price. As his company grew and production of both the camera and film increased, manufacturing costs decreased significantly. This allowed the firm to introduce a number of new cameras, including the Folding Pocket Kodak Camera, the precursor of all modern roll-film cameras, in 1898. It also brought out the first of a complete line of Brownie cameras, an easy-to-operate model that sold for $1 and used film that sold at 15 cents per roll, in 1900. The following year, the company was reorganized and incorporated in New Jersey as Eastman Kodak Company.

1900s Through 1960s: Continuing New Product Success

Over the next 20 years, the company continued to introduce photographic innovations. In 1902 Kodak brought to market a new developing machine that allowed film processing without benefit of a darkroom. The 1913 introduction of Eastman Portrait Film provided professional photographers with a sheet film alternative to glass plates.

In 1912 George Eastman hired Dr. C.E. Kenneth Mees, a British scientist, to head one of the first U.S. industrial research centers. Based in Rochester, New York, this lab was where various tools and manufacturing processes that provided the company with a continuing stream of new products in the 1920s were invented. These new products—which included 16-millimeter Kodacolor motion picture film, the 16-millimeter Cine-Kodak motion picture camera, and the Kodascope projector (all of which debuted in 1923)—were targeted at the mass market and priced appropriately.

Kodak developed other new products to support the country's involvement in World War I. In 1917 the company developed aerial cameras and trained U.S. Signal Corps photographers in their use. It also supplied the U.S. Navy with cellulose acetate, a film product, for coating airplane wings, and produced the unbreakable lenses used on gas masks. Following the war, Eastman became president of the company upon Strong's death in 1919.

George Eastman had always been civic-minded; even as a struggling bank clerk he donated money to the Mechanics Institute of Rochester. As Kodak grew, his philanthropy extended to such institutions as the Massachusetts Institute of Technology, the Hampton and Tuskegee Institutes, and the University of Rochester. He was instrumental in starting numerous dental clinics around the world, and he enjoyed a reputation as a paternalistic employer because of his profit-sharing programs and insurance benefits for workers. In 1932 George Eastman committed suicide at the age of 77, leaving a note that read, "To my friends. My work is done. Why wait? G.E."

That same year, the company introduced the first eight-millimeter motion picture system for the amateur photographer, consisting of film, cameras, and projectors. Three years later, it made available 16-millimeter Kodachrome film, the first amateur color film to gain commercial success. Similar film products for 35-millimeter slides and eight-millimeter home movies were introduced in 1936.

New photographic products continued to be introduced over the next decade, even as the company devoted a portion of its manufacturing capability to the production of equipment and film for the military during World War II. Following the war, Kodak focused its total attention once again on amateur photography with the introduction of a low-priced Brownie eight-millimeter movie camera in 1951 and the accompanying projector one year later.

In 1953 the company formed Eastman Chemical Products, Inc. to market alcohols, plastics, and fibers for industrial use. These substances were manufactured by Tennessee Eastman Company and Texas Eastman Company, two subsidiaries that had been formed in 1920 and 1952, respectively. The company had begun to manufacture these items because of its own use of chemicals in film manufacturing and processing.

Until this point, the company had always included the cost of film processing in the cost of film. A consent decree filed in 1954 forced Eastman Kodak to abandon this practice, but it also provided an opportunity for the company to serve a new market, independent photofinishers, with its film developing products. Kodak acquired several photofinishing laboratories, including Fox Photo and American Photographic Group, to form an independent joint venture known as Qualex with Colorcraft Corp., owned by Fuqua Industries.

By 1958 the company had made significant advances in 35-millimeter color slide technology and introduced the first completely automatic projector, called the Kodak Cavalcade. A line of Kodak Carousel projectors introduced three years later became highly successful.

In 1963, one year after astronaut John Glenn had used Kodak film to record his orbit of the earth, the company

Key Dates:

1880: George Eastman begins manufacturing dry plates for sale to photographers.

1881: Eastman and Henry A. Strong form partnership, Eastman Dry Plate Company.

1884: Company is reorganized as a corporation under the name Eastman Dry Plate and Film Company.

1888: Snapshot photography is born through the introduction of the Kodak portable camera.

1889: Name changes to Eastman Company.

1892: Name changes to Eastman Kodak Company of New York.

1898: The Folding Pocket Kodak Camera is introduced.

1900: The Brownie camera makes its debut.

1901: Company is reorganized and incorporated in New Jersey as Eastman Kodak Company.

1912: One of the first U.S. industrial research centers is set up in Rochester, New York.

1920: Tennessee Eastman Company, forerunner of Eastman Chemical, is created.

1923: Company introduces motion picture camera, film, and projector for the consumer market.

1932: George Eastman commits suicide at the age of 77.

1935: Kodachrome film, the first commercially successful color film for amateurs, debuts.

1951: Low-priced Brownie eight-millimeter movie camera is introduced.

1953: Eastman Chemical Products, Inc. is created as a new subsidiary.

1961: Highly successful line of Kodak Carousel slide projectors is introduced.

1963: The revolutionary Instamatic camera makes its debut.

1965: Company introduces the super-eight format Instamatic movie camera.

1972: The pocket Instamatic camera is launched.

1975: Company enters the copier market with the debut of the Kodak Ektaprint 100 Copier-Duplicator.

1976: Kodak enters the market for instant cameras; Polaroid files patent-infringement suit against Kodak.

1980: Company expands its health imaging operations with the launch of the Ektachem 400 blood analyzer.

1982: Company launches "disc photography," an ultimately unsuccessful innovation.

1984: Lines of videotapes and floppy discs are introduced.

1985: Floppy disc maker Verbatim Corporation is acquired.

1986: A federal appeals court orders Kodak's exit from the instant camera market; a line of alkaline batteries under the Supralife brand is launched; Eastman Pharmaceuticals Division is established.

1988: Sterling Drug Inc., maker of prescription and OTC drugs, is acquired.

1990: Verbatim is sold to Mitsubishi Kasei Corporation.

1991: Polaroid's suit against Kodak is settled, with the latter paying the former $925 million.

1992: The Kodak Photo CD player hits the market.

1993: George Fisher becomes the first outsider to head the company; Eastman Chemical is spun off to shareholders.

1994: The company's pharmaceutical arm, Sterling Winthrop, its diagnostics products division, and several other nonimaging units are divested.

1997: The WTO rules against Kodak in its dispute with Fuji Photo Film over access to the Japanese market; major restructuring is initiated.

1998: Kodak Picture Maker debuts; company acquires the DryView laser imaging system from Imation.

1999: The office imaging unit is sold.

introduced the Instamatic camera. Using a film cartridge instead of film roll, the Instamatic revolutionized amateur photography and became a commercial success because it was easy to use. Two years later, Kodak brought out a similar cartridge system for super-eight format Instamatic movie cameras and projectors. In 1972 five different models of a pocket version of the Instamatic camera were launched and proved immediately popular. The following year, the company acquired Spin Physics, a San Diego, California-based producer of magnetic heads used in recording equipment.

1970s Through Early 1990s: Diversifying and Losing Ground Amid Increasing Competition

In the early 1970s, Eastman Kodak became the defendant in a series of antitrust suits filed by several smaller film, camera, and processing companies. These legal actions alleged that Kodak illegally monopolized the photographic market. The most widely publicized suit, filed by Berkey Photo, charged that Kodak had violated the Sherman Anti-Trust Act by conspiring with two other companies, Sylvania Companies, a subsidiary of GTE Products Corporation, and General Electric Company, to develop two photographic flash devices. Berkey requested that

Eastman Kodak be divided into ten separate companies and asked for $300 million in damages. The case was settled in 1981 for $6.8 million.

In 1975 Kodak introduced the Ektaprint 100 Copier-Duplicator, putting itself into direct competition with two firmly entrenched rivals, Xerox Corporation and International Business Machines Corporation. Kodak considered this market to be a good fit with its existing microfilm business. In addition, the company had already established a foothold with a similar product, the Verifax machine, which had been introduced in 1953. This copier used a wet process like that used in photography, but it had become obsolete when Xerox introduced a technological advancement called xerography, which was less messy and produced better quality copies than previous systems. After careful research and planning, the Ektaprint copier was developed to serve businesses with large-scale duplicating needs. Not only could the Ektaprint produce numerous copies at high speed, but it could also collate them while duplicating, a unique feature at the time.

In 1976 Kodak took on another well-established firm when it challenged Polaroid Corporation's 30-year lock on instant photography with a new line of instant cameras and film that developed pictures outside the camera within a few minutes. Kodak had missed an opportunity to get in on the ground floor of this technology in the 1940s when it declined an offer to market an instant camera invented by Polaroid founder Edwin Land. The general feeling among Kodak's management at the time had been that Land's camera was a toy and the quality of its pictures not up to the company's accepted standards. Kodak had, however, also gained from Polaroid's success. It had become the exclusive supplier of negatives for Polaroid's instant, pull-apart color film in 1963. In 1969 Polaroid elected to take over this part of its film manufacturing itself. At the same time Polaroid cut prices drastically to bring its instant cameras more in line with the Kodak Instamatics. Kodak was convinced that Polaroid's instant photography products posed a threat to the company's market leadership. But the company's methodical product-development process, which emphasized long-term product quality over quick market entry, as well as Polaroid's ownership of hundreds of related patents, proved to be major obstacles to an immediate competitive response. When Kodak finally introduced its own instant camera four years after the decision was made to develop it, the company was plagued by production problems and a near-instant Polaroid lawsuit alleging patent infringement. Although the company captured about 25 percent of the U.S. instant camera market within its first year, reports of quality flaws with the camera's instant photographs and Polaroid's response with another new instant camera stifled sales. Polaroid successfully exploited the business applications of instant photography—identity cards, for example—and retained its strong position in the market.

During this period, Kodak's president and CEO, Walter A. Fallon, and chairman, Gerald B. Zomow, oversaw product development. When Zomow retired in 1977, Fallon assumed the chairmanship and was succeeded as president by Colby H. Chandler. Employed with Kodak since 1941, Fallon had worked his way up from production to direct the U.S. and Canadian photographic division. He had been responsible for the launch of the pocket Instamatic camera line. Chandler had joined the company in 1951 and, as Fallon's successor in the U.S. and Canadian photographic division, he was directly responsible for both the instant camera and the Ektaprint copier.

Upon becoming president, Chandler faced a challenge to Eastman Kodak's dominance in the photographic paper market from several Japanese competitors and U.S. suppliers, including Fuji Photo Film Co., Ltd. and 3M Company. These firms undercut Kodak's prices for a paper product of similar quality. Fuji also had the advantage of competing against a strong U.S. dollar, a factor that conversely reduced Kodak's profits significantly in foreign markets. The company responded with price reductions of its own, but suffered lower earnings and a decreasing level of investor confidence. Losing the title of official film of the 1984 Summer Olympics to Fuji added further insult to injury.

As the U.S. economy entered a recession in the late 1970s and sales growth in the company's consumer photographic products slowed, higher sales in other areas such as chemicals, business systems, and professional photofinishing pushed profits upward once again. Several prior years of flat earnings across product areas were attributed in large part to a lack of strategic planning. At the end of 1978 company operations were reorganized to consolidate the U.S., Canadian, and international photographic areas into one division. The company's first director of corporate planning also was hired to speed the product development process and institute the controls needed to enable new products to become profitable more quickly.

The year 1980 marked the company's 100th anniversary. That year Kodak introduced the Ektachem 400 blood analyzer. This entry into the health sciences field represented a natural application of the company's film manufacturing technology and reinforced its already strong presence as a supplier of X-ray film to hospitals and other healthcare facilities.

During the 1980s the company faced intensifying Japanese competition in photography and a continuing decline in product demand. Rapid technological breakthroughs by other firms threatened to replace Kodak's core product line with more advanced equipment. The company instituted several measures to improve its performance. These included a stronger emphasis on nonphotographic products with high profit potential, a more aggressive approach to protecting its chemical imaging capabilities, a broader international marketing strategy, and a sharper focus on making acquisitions to bring the company up to speed technologically, particularly in electronics.

In 1981 the company purchased Atex, Inc., a major supplier of electronic text editing systems used by publishers. Formed as an entrepreneurial venture in 1972 and the leader in its field at the time of the acquisition, Atex later lost ground to fast-changing computer technology as Kodak's traditionally slow-moving product development process was unable to keep pace with the industry.

Despite its shift in priorities to other areas, Kodak continued to support its bread-and-butter line of photographic products. In 1982 it introduced a line of small cameras that used film discs instead of cartridges and was considered a replacement for the pocket Instamatic camera.

Since the company's founding, Kodak had maintained a policy of treating its employees fairly and with respect, earning the nickname of the "Great Yellow Father." It was George Eastman's belief that an organization's prosperity was not necessarily due to its technological achievements, but more to its workers' goodwill and loyalty. As a result, company benefits were well above average, morale had always remained high, and employees never felt the need to unionize. This protective culture came to an end in 1983, however, when the company was forced to reduce its workforce by five percent to cut costs. Competitive pressures from the Japanese and domestic and international economic problems had slowed product demand. Even the widely publicized disc camera failed to sustain its initial "hot" sales rate.

Upon Fallon's retirement in 1983, Colby Chandler took over as chairman and, in an attempt to keep up with the pace of change, pointed Kodak toward the electronics and video areas in earnest. During the 1970s the company had brought out products that either lacked quality or important features, or arrived too late on the scene to capitalize on new opportunities. Of all the products introduced during Fallon's tenure, only the Ektaprint copier was considered a success, although it gradually lost its marketing advantage to competitive offerings with greater speed and more features. Neither the instant nor the disc cameras had met original expectations. The company's X-ray film business also took a beating as hospital admissions dropped and attempts by medical institutions to control costs increased.

The company's new electronics division consisted of its Spin Physics subsidiary, a solid-state research laboratory, and another facility dedicated to the production of integrated circuits. Many of the products later introduced by the division, however, resulted from acquisitions or joint ventures with other companies. For example, in 1984 Kodak launched its first electronic product, a camcorder that combined an eight-millimeter video camera and recorder, in conjunction with Matsushita Electric Industrial Co., Ltd. of Japan. This represented a major departure for Kodak, which historically had been self-reliant in everything from manufacturing cardboard boxes to maintaining its own fire department.

Also in 1984 Kodak introduced complete lines of videotape cassettes for all video formats and floppy discs for use in personal computers. It bolstered the latter area in 1985 with the purchase of Verbatim Corporation, a floppy disc manufacturer. After five years of disappointing sales, Verbatim was sold to Mitsubishi Kasei Corporation of Japan.

Kodak underwent another major reorganization at the beginning of 1985 to capitalize more quickly on growth opportunities. Seventeen business units and a new Life Sciences Group were formed, the latter division to be involved in developing biomedical technology. Each of the 17 operating units, which had previously existed as a centralized group under the photographic division, were given more autonomy and flexibility to run their businesses as independent profit centers.

The company reentered the 35-millimeter camera market in 1985 with a product made by Chinon Industries of Japan. Fifteen years earlier, it had withdrawn from the market because of doubts about the 35-millimeter camera's mass appeal.

In 1986, ten years after Polaroid filed its patent-infringement suit over Kodak's instant camera, a federal appeals court upheld a lower court ruling and ordered Kodak to leave the instant camera business. Kodak voluntarily offered its customers trade-in options for their obsolete cameras but was forced to make a somewhat different offer as a result of a class-action lawsuit. The financial implications of this development and the continuing struggle to boost earnings led the company to institute another workforce reduction in 1986, this time by ten percent. Although the domestic picture was somewhat grim, the fact that nearly 40 percent of the company's sales came from overseas helped produce strong bottom-line gains over the previous year. A weakening U.S. dollar blunted the impact of foreign competition and allowed Kodak to reclaim lost ground in its core businesses while also entering new ones. An employee's suggestion to apply the company's manufacturing capabilities to the production of lithium batteries resulted in the successful introduction of a complete line of alkaline battery products under the Supralife brand in 1986.

That same year, Kodak also formed the Eastman Pharmaceuticals Division to establish an even stronger presence in healthcare. Joint venture agreements and licensing arrangements with existing pharmaceutical companies initially occupied division management's attention. In 1988 Kodak acquired Sterling Drug Inc., a manufacturer of prescription drugs and such consumer products as Bayer aspirin and Lysol cleaner, to make the company more competitive in the pharmaceutical industry. The $5.1 billion acquisition, however, was viewed unfavorably by the company's shareholders, in part because Sterling had a second-rate reputation as a pharmaceutical manufacturer. One year later, this negative perception seemed correct. Intense competition had reduced the sales of Sterling's existing pharmaceuticals while new products under development showed questionable effectiveness during testing.

In 1988 evidence came to light indicating that toxic chemicals from the company's Rochester plant had leaked into the area's groundwater, posing a possible health hazard to local residents. In April 1990 the company admitted that it had violated New York's environmental regulations and was fined $1 million. It also agreed to clean up the site of its Kodak Park manufacturing facility and reduce chemical emissions from the plant.

Under the direction of Mr. Kay Whitmore, who became chairman and CEO in 1990, profits of the goliath company grew steadily. The positive results that emerged from the company's restructuring of 1985, however, were eroded by the recession of the early 1990s. Coupled with the recession came the Persian Gulf War, which seriously dampened the tourist and travel industry and hurt sales of photographic equipment. The year 1991 also finally saw the culmination of the Polaroid suit against Kodak, with the latter agreeing to pay the former a settlement of $925 million.

Once again, Kodak embarked on a path of restructuring and cost cutting. As a cost-cutting incentive, management in 1990 devised an early retirement plan that would trim approximately 5,800 people from the workforce. One year later, however, the plan backfired somewhat when 6,600 decided to retire early. With a shortfall of employees, the company was forced to hire 1,600 new workers. Management also was trimmed. Only three managers were replaced out of the 12 who retired in 1991.

Of the four business segments that had been in place since the previous restructuring—photographic, information, health, and chemicals—management merged photographic and information into a single group named Imaging. Three group presidents were appointed to head the three divisions. Downsizing, cost cutting, restructuring, and a "suspicion of red tape," as one market analyst described it, injected new growth into Kodak and returned the company slowly to profitability.

The Imaging Division, the largest unit, focused on Kodak's core business of photography and photofinishing, as well as copying machines, computer printers, and software. As part of its exploration of various new technologies, including digital photography, the division in 1992 developed a camera able to store photographic shots on a compact disc that could be displayed on a CD player. Such advances, including Kodak's introduction in the fall of 1992 of a writable compact disc publishing system (enabling the consumer to write, store, and retrieve information on a CD), enabled Kodak to retain its position as the world leader in electronic imaging. To maintain this lead, the company established a small Center for Creative Imaging in Camden, Maine, an artistic haven, to encourage imaging innovations in a creative atmosphere. Meantime, one piece of the former information business segment, Atex, was sold off in 1992 following the dwindling away of its market position because of its outmoded technology.

Kodak's Health Product Division also was restructured with the 1991 merger of two pharmaceutical companies into one entity, Sterling Winthrop, which manufactured both pharmaceuticals and nonpharmaceutical consumer products. Sterling Winthrop in turn formed a joint venture with the French firm Sanofi in 1991, enabling it to penetrate the European pharmaceutical market more easily than before. The joint venture placed Kodak's Health Division among the top 20 pharmaceutical concerns in the world. Included within Kodak's Health Division was the Clinical Products Division, which originated in 1980 when Kodak introduced its Ektachem blood analyzer. Other businesses within the health group included X-ray machines and electronic health imaging products.

The third division of Kodak, the Chemical Product Division, manufactured and marketed chemicals, fibers, and plastics. As of the early 1990s Eastman Chemical Company was the 15th largest chemical firm in the United States. The focus of the Chemical Division was on expansion and overseas sales. As a result, the Chemical Division became a global enterprise, with joint ventures in many foreign countries. In 1991 Eastman Chemical entered the propylene business with the purchase of propylene interests as well as the urethane polyols business of ARCO Chemical Company. In the early 1990s, the Tenite Plastics division of Eastman Chemical was the largest plastic bottle and container supplier in the world.

1993 into the 21st Century: Refocusing on Imaging, with an Emphasis on Digital

Despite the restructuring efforts, Kodak remained, according to Peter Nulty writing in *Fortune* magazine in early 1994, "one of the most bureaucratic, wasteful, paternalistic, slow-moving, isolated, and beloved companies in America." The company continued to lose market share in its core film and photographic paper operations; not only was Kodak reluctant to fully embrace the digital future out of fear of undermining its chemical photography business, it also had been slow to recognize huge opportunities in that chemical core, such as the explosive growth of 35-millimeter film sales following the debut of "point-and-shoot" 35-millimeter cameras. The moves to diversify outside imaging, most notably the move into pharmaceuticals, proved ill-advised and saddled the company with more than $7 billion in debt. With earnings stagnating and no turnaround in sight, the board of directors, under pressure from outside investors, fired Whitmore in late 1993. Replacing him as chairman and CEO was George Fisher, who left the top spot at Motorola, Inc. to join Kodak, thereby becoming the first outsider to head the company.

Fisher almost immediately moved to refocus the company on its imaging core. Fisher and a newly installed top financial team went ahead with the spinoff to shareholders of Eastman Chemical at year-end 1993; this divestment had already been in the works under Whitmore. The following year, Kodak sold Sterling Winthrop to SmithKline Beecham plc for $4.6 billion, its diagnostics products division to Johnson & Johnson for $1

billion, and several other nonimaging units for about another $2.4 billion. These businesses had together accounted for $7.4 billion in revenues in 1993 but only $46 million in pretax profit. The asset sales reduced the debt load to a manageable $1.5 billion and returned the company to its roots.

Next, Fisher moved to transform Kodak into a digital company for the 21st century. Rather than viewing the digital future as a threat to the chemical photography past, Fisher saw digital photography as a great opportunity to revitalize Kodak's core, as he related to *Forbes* in early 1997: "I think there was a fear of what digital was all about, whereas I was coming here because I believed digital imaging and the core photography business had a symbiotic relationship, which was, in fact, exciting." During 1994 Fisher created a new division called Digital and Applied Imaging, and hired Carl Gustin, a marketing executive who had previously worked at Digital Equipment Corporation and Apple Computer, Inc., as its head. Among the early developments of the new division was the 1995 relaunch of the Kodak Photo CD with a new design aimed at desktop personal computer users and the introduction that year of a full-featured digital camera priced at less than $1,000.

Back on the chemical photography front, Kodak under Fisher's leadership took a more aggressive approach to trade disputes with its archrival Fuji Photo Film. In 1995 Kodak accused the Japanese government and Fuji of illegally restricting access to the Japanese market for film and photographic paper. The U.S. government took the case to the newly formed World Trade Organization (WTO) in 1996, with the European Union soon joining the Kodak side. Fuji contended that Kodak's policies in pricing and marketing its products in Japan were to blame for the company's low market share, and that Kodak faced an environment in Japan similar to what Fuji faced in the United States. In fact, both companies held about 70 percent of their respective home markets, while Kodak held about 12 percent of the Japanese market and Fuji still only ten percent of the U.S. market. In 1997 the WTO rejected Kodak's claims, ruling in Fuji's favor.

Ironically in the midst of this legal battle, a Kodak-led consortium that included Fuji (as well as Canon Inc., Minolta Co., Ltd., and Nikon Corporation) developed the Advanced Photo System (APS), an effort to revitalize the stagnant still photography market. APS, which was a hybrid between conventional and digital photography technology, offered drop-in film loading and the ability to select from three photo sizes (four by six-inch, four by seven-inch, and a panoramic four by ten-inch) as photos were taken. In February 1996 Kodak unveiled the Advantix brand, which it used for its APS film, cameras, and related equipment and services. APS proved to be an instant success, and Kodak quickly captured 85 percent of the U.S. market for APS film.

In December 1996 Daniel A. Carp was named president and chief operating officer of Eastman Kodak. One month later Kodak completed the sale to Danka Business Systems PLC of its loss-making imaging services unit, which sold and serviced copiers and provided document management services. Later in 1997 Kodak acquired Wang Laboratories' software business unit, which focused on imaging and work management software. The following year Kodak beefed up its health imaging division through the $530 million purchase of the bulk of Imation Corporation's medical imaging business, including the DryView laser imaging system. Divestments in 1998 included the Fox Photo, Inc. photofinishing chain, which was sold to Wolf Camera. Also in 1998 the company introduced the Kodak Picture Maker, a digital imaging kiosk through which consumers could manipulate, enlarge, and/or crop and then reprint an existing photograph.

Despite all of Fisher's maneuvering, Kodak was still vulnerable. In the summer of 1997 the seeming turnaround turned sour when Fuji Photo initiated a brutal price war in the U.S. market at the same time that a strong U.S. dollar and the emerging Asian economic crisis wreaked additional havoc overseas. The nascent digital division, for all its innovative new products, was on its way to losing $440 million for the year. In late 1997 Fisher announced a major restructuring, involving a workforce reduction of 20,000, a shakeup of top management, and a goal to cut more than $1 billion from annual costs. After having nearly all of its profits wiped out by a $1.46 billion restructuring charge in 1997, Kodak returned to post net income of $1.39 billion in both 1998 and 1999, on revenues of $13.41 billion and $14.09 billion, respectively.

During 1999 Kodak continued its drive to divest underperforming units through the sale of its office imaging unit—which included digital printers, copiers, and roller assemblies—to Heidelberger Druckmaschinen AG of Germany. In January 2000 Fisher stepped down as CEO, remaining chairman until the end of that year; Carp was named his successor. Although Kodak had managed to make a profit of $20 million from its digital businesses in 1999, it was far from clear whether Kodak would be a major player in the digital world of the new millennium. For his part, Carp announced in mid-2000 that the company expected 45 percent of revenue to be generated from digital imaging in 2005, which would be a huge increase from the 17 percent of 1999. Eastman Kodak's progress toward this predicted level, or lack thereof, was likely to be highly indicative of the overall direction of the company in the early 21st century.

Principal Subsidiaries

Eastman Kodak International Sales Corporation (Barbados); Torrey Pines Realty Company, Inc.; Cinesite, Inc.; FPC Inc.; Qualex Inc.; Qualex Canada Photofinishing Inc.; Eastman Software Inc.; PictureVision Inc.; Eastman Gelatine Corporation; Eastman Canada Inc.; Kodak Canada Inc.; Kodak (Export Sales) Ltd. (Hong Kong); Kodak Argentina S.A.I.C.; Kodak Chilena S.A.F. (Chile); Kodak Caceo Ltd.; Kodak Panama, Ltd.; Kodak Americas, Ltd.; Kodak Venezuela, S.A.; Kodak (Near East), Inc.; Kodak (Singapore) Pte. Limited; Kodak Philippines, Ltd.; Kodak Limited (U.K.); Cinesite (Europe) Limited (U.K.); Kodak India Limited; Kodak International Finance Ltd. (U.K.); Kodak Polska Sp.zo.o (Poland); Kodak AO (Russia); Kodak (Ireland) Manufacturing Limited; Kodak Ireland Limited; Kodak-Pathe SA (France); Kodak A.G. (Germany); E.K. Holdings, B.V. (Netherlands); Kodak Brasileira C.I.L. (Brazil); Kodak Korea Limited; Kodak Far East Purchasing, Inc.; Kodak New Zealand Limited; Kodak (Australasia) Pty. Ltd. (Australia); Kodak (Kenya) Limited; Kodak (Egypt) S.A.E.; Kodak (Malaysia) S.B.; Kodak Taiwan Limited; Eastman Kodak International Capital Company, Inc.; Kodak de Mexico S.A. de C.V.; Kodak Export de Mexico, S. de R.L. de C.V.; Kodak Mexicana S.A. de C.V. (Mexico); N.V. Kodak S.A. (Belgium); Kodak a.s. (Denmark); Kodak Norge A/S (Norway); Kodak SA (Switzerland); Kodak (Far East) Limited (Hong Kong); Kodak (Thailand) Limited; Kodak G.m.b.H. (Austria); Kodak Kft. (Hungary); Kodak Oy (Finland); Kodak Nederland B.V. (Netherlands); Kodak S.p.A. (Italy); Kodak Portuguesa Limited; Kodak S.A. (Spain); Kodak AB (Sweden); Eastman Kodak (Japan) Ltd.; Kodak Japan Ltd.; Kodak Imagex K.K. (Japan); K.K. Kodak Information Systems (Japan); Kodak Japan Industries Ltd.; Kodak (China) Limited (Hong Kong); Kodak Electronic Products (Shanghai) Co., Ltd. (China); BASO Precision Optics, Ltd. (Taiwan); K.H. Optical Company Limited (Hong Kong); Kodak Photographic Equipment (Shanghai) Co., Ltd. (China); Kodak (China) Co. Ltd.; Kodak (WUXI) Co. Ltd. (China).

Principal Operating Units

Document Imaging; Eastman Software; Consumer Imaging; Commercial and Government Systems; Global Customer Service and Support; Digital and Applied Imaging; Health Imaging; Entertainment Imaging; KODAK Professional.

Principal Competitors

Agfa-Gevaert Group; Canon Inc.; Casio Computer Co., Ltd.; Fuji Photo Film Co., Ltd.; Hewlett-Packard Company; Leica Camera AG; Matsushita Electric Industrial Co., Ltd.; Minnesota Mining and Manufacturing Company; Minolta Co., Ltd.; Nikon Corporation; Olympus Optical Co., Ltd.; Koninklijke Philips Electronics N.V.; PhotoWorks, Inc.; Polaroid Corporation; Ricoh Company, Ltd.; Sharp Corporation; Sony Corporation; Xerox Corporation.

Further Reading

Astor, Will, "Huge Pioneer-Kodak Project Marks Progress," *Rochester Business Journal,* September 25, 1992.

Bounds, Wendy, "George Fisher Pushes Kodak into Digital Era," *Wall Street Journal,* June 9, 1995, p. B1.

Brayer, Elizabeth, *George Eastman: A Biography,* Baltimore: Johns Hopkins University Press, 1996.

Buell, Barbara, and Rebecca Aikman, "Kodak Is Trying to Break Out of Its Shell," *Business Week,* June 10, 1985, pp. 92+.

Burgess, John, "Firms Plan Multimedia Consortium," *Washington Post,* October 1, 1992.

Chakravarty, Subrata N., "How an Outsider's Vision Saved Kodak," *Forbes,* January 13, 1997, pp. 45–47.

Chakravarty, Subrata N., and Ruth Simon, "Has the World Passed Kodak By?," *Forbes,* November 5, 1984.

Collins, Douglas, *The Story of Kodak,* New York: Abrams, 1990.

Desmond, Edward W., "What's Ailing Kodak? Fuji," *Fortune,* October 27, 1997, pp. 185+.

Deutsch, Claudia H., "More Paths to Profits: Kodak Hopes Demand for Digital Images Will Sell Film," *New York Times,* December 2, 1996, p. D1.

Dvorak, John C., "Razors with No Blades," *Forbes,* October 18, 1999, p. 168.

Grant, Linda, "Can Fisher Focus Kodak?," *Fortune,* January 13, 1997, pp. 76+.

——, "A New Picture at Kodak," *U.S. News and World Report,* September 19, 1994, pp. 58–60.

——, "Why Kodak Still Isn't Fixed," *Fortune,* May 11, 1998, pp. 179–81.

Hammonds, Keith H., "Kodak May Wish It Never Went to the Drugstore," *Business Week,* December 4, 1989, pp. 72+.

Helm, Leslie, "Has Kodak Set Itself Up for a Fall?," *Business Week,* February 22, 1988, pp. 134+.

——, "Why Kodak Is Starting to Click Again," *Business Week,* February 23, 1987, pp. 134+.

Johnson, Greg, "Kodak Device Places Images of Film on Disc," *Los Angeles Times,* July 31, 1992.

Journey into Imagination: The Kodak Story, Rochester, N.Y.: Eastman Kodak Company, 1988.

Klein, Alec, "Kodak Expects Digital Imaging to Be 45% of Revenue by 2005," *Wall Street Journal,* June 15, 2000, p. B14.

——, "Kodak Losing U.S. Market Share to Fuji," *Wall Street Journal,* May 28, 1999, p. A3.

——, "Shutter Snaps on Fisher's Leadership at Kodak," *Wall Street Journal,* June 10, 1999, p. B1.

"Kodak Fights Back: Everybody Wants a Piece of Its Markets," *Business Week,* February 1, 1982, pp. 48+.

Leib, Jeffrey, "Kodak Colorado Peddles Injection-Molding Expertise," *Denver Post,* March 6, 1992.

Maremont, Mark, "Kodak's New Focus: An Inside Look at George Fisher's Strategy," *Business Week,* January 30, 1995, pp. 62–68.

Maremont, Mark, and Elizabeth Lesly, "Getting the Picture: Kodak Finally Heeds the Shareholders," *Business Week,* February 1, 1993, pp. 24–26.

——, "The Revolution That Wasn't at Eastman Kodak," *Business Week,* May 10, 1993, pp. 24–25.

Maremont, Mark, and Gary McWilliams, "Kodak: Shoot the Works," *Business Week,* November 15, 1993, pp. 30–32.

McGinn, Daniel, "A Star Image Blurs," *Newsweek,* April 6, 1998, pp. 36–38.

Moore, Thomas, and Lee Smith, "Embattled Kodak Enters the Electronic Age," *Fortune,* August 22, 1983, pp. 120+.

Nulty, Peter, "Digital Imaging Had Better Boom Before Kodak Film Busts," *Fortune,* May 1, 1995, pp. 80–83.

——, "Kodak Grabs for Growth Again," *Fortune,* May 16, 1994, pp. 76–78.

Perdue, Wes, "Eastman Kodak and BioScan Inc. Form Alliance," *Business Wire,* August 10, 1992.

Santoli, Michael, "Kodak's New Colors," *Barron's,* August 24, 1998, pp. 25–26, 28–29.

Smith, Emily T., "Picture This: Kodak Wants to Be a Biotech Giant, Too," *Business Week,* May 26, 1986, pp. 88+.

Smith, Geoffrey, "Film Vs. Digital: Can Kodak Build a Bridge?," *Business Week,* August 2, 1999, p. 66.

Smith, Geoffrey, et al., "Can George Fisher Fix Kodak?," *Business Week,* October 20, 1997, pp. 116–20, 124, 128.

Smith, Geoffrey, Brad Wolverton, and Ann Therese Palmer, "A Dark Kodak Moment," *Business Week,* August 4, 1997, pp. 30–31.

Swasy, Alecia, *Changing Focus: Kodak and the Battle to Save a Great American Company,* New York: Times Business, 1997.

Taylor, Alex, III, "Kodak Scrambles to Refocus," *Fortune,* March 3, 1986, pp. 113+.

Treece, James B., Barbara Buell, and Jane Sasseen, "How Kodak Is Trying to Move Mount Fuji," *Business Week,* December 2, 1985, pp. 62+.

Webb, Chanoine, "The Picture Just Keeps Getting Darker at Kodak," *Fortune,* June 21, 1999, p. 206.

Weber, Jonathan, "Top High-Tech Firms Team Up on 'Multimedia,'" *Los Angeles Times,* October 7, 1992.

—Sandy Schusteff and Sina Dubovoj
—updated by David E. Salamie

Eddie Bauer

Eddie Bauer, Inc.

Post Office Box 97000
Redmond, Washington 98073-9700
U.S.A.
Telephone: (425) 882-6100
Fax: (425) 882-6127
Web site: http://www.eddiebauer.com

Wholly Owned Subsidiary of Spiegel, Inc.
Incorporated: 1968
Employees: 10,000
Sales: $1.79 billion (1999)
NAIC: 442299 All Other Home Furnishings Stores;
    454110 Electronic Shopping and Mail-Order Houses;
    448140 Family Clothing Stores

Eddie Bauer, Inc. is a catalog, storefront, and e-commerce retailer through two concepts: Eddie Bauer Sportswear, which offers outdoor apparel, sportswear, and accessories; and Eddie Bauer Home, which features bedding, home furnishings, and decor. The company mails out 110 million catalogs per year, with about a quarter of revenues stemming from catalog and web site orders. On the storefront side, there are 430 Eddie Bauer sportswear stores in North America and 38 Eddie Bauer Home units in the United States. To clear excess merchandise, the company runs an additional 52 Eddie Bauer Outlet stores in the United States, as well as the eddiebaueroutlet.com web site. The company is a wholly owned subsidiary of catalog retailer Spiegel, Inc., which in turn is controlled by Germany's Otto family, majority owners and operators of Otto Versand GmbII & Co., the world's largest mail-order firm. Through joint ventures with units of Otto Versand, Eddie Bauer operates retail outlets and distributes catalogs in Japan and Germany and has a cataloging only venture in the United Kingdom. The company also licenses the Eddie Bauer brand to several other companies, including Ford Motor Company, which has made Eddie Bauer edition sport-utility vehicles since 1984; the Lane Company, for a line of Eddie Bauer furniture; and Cosco, Inc., which sells Eddie Bauer car seats.

Early History

Created by the son of Russian immigrants, Eddie Bauer, Inc. began as a tennis racquet stringing business in Seattle, Washington. While his parents would eventually play a significant role in the development of Eddie Bauer, Inc., Eddie Bauer initially drew upon his childhood years on Orcas Island, a sparsely populated island near Seattle, as the inspiration for what eventually would become a billion-dollar retail business.

Those early years were spent fishing, hunting, and trapping on the wooded island, imbuing Bauer with a love of the outdoors. When his family moved to Seattle in 1912, Bauer was 13 years old and looking for work. He immediately gravitated toward the only full-line sporting goods store in the city, Piper & Taft, and landed a job as a stock boy. Over the years, Bauer watched and learned, eventually becoming adept at making guns, fly rods, and golf clubs. In addition to these talents, Bauer also developed considerable skill in stringing tennis racquets, winning the world speed championship, while in a display window at Piper & Taft, by stringing 12 racquets in slightly more than three and a half hours. Still in his teens, Bauer already had gained the attention of Seattle's sporting community. He often was referred to in local newspapers for killing the biggest elk, or catching the most fish, or for winning rifle- and pistol-shooting competitions. This local recognition would serve Bauer well when, in 1919, with $25 in his pocket and $500 borrowed on a 120-day loan, he rented 15 feet of wall space in a gun shop for $15 a month and began stringing racquets on his own. In this venture, Bauer enjoyed immediate success, stringing enough racquets to accumulate $10,000 within his first year. Encouraged by his initial success, Bauer arranged for credit from a bank and opened his own shop, Eddie Bauer's Sport Shop, in 1920, the predecessor of Eddie Bauer, Inc.

In addition to his renowned racquet-stringing abilities, Bauer also offered golf equipment and trout fishing flies during his first year of business, and the 20-foot storefront quickly became a haven for sporting enthusiasts throughout the Pacific Northwest. Bauer's success during these nascent years was in large part due to his reputation as an experienced outdoorsman and his active participation in the sporting community. He worked at his store from February through August each year, then hunted and fished throughout the winter. During these sojourns in the wild, he field tested all of the equipment he sold in his stores, which, after the first year, included an array of outdoor equipment and clothing. Two years after he opened for business, this firsthand knowledge of his stock enabled him to offer an unconditional guarantee of satisfaction on all of the products sold in his store, a rarity for retail businesses during the 1920s; he also established a company creed. Bauer promoted sporting activities in his spare time, increasing the public's awareness of such sports as skiing by importing Norwegian hickory skis and persuading Norwegian skiers to come to the Pacific Northwest to help foster growth in the sport.

By 1924, Bauer had added a complete selection of fishing tackle, firearms, and skeet and trap equipment to his store and renamed it Eddie Bauer's Sporting Goods. Customers continued to flock to Bauer's store, lured by his unconditional guarantee and his knowledge of the outdoors. Eddie Bauer's Sporting Goods had quickly become a favorite place for outdoorsmen to outfit themselves for a wide variety of sporting endeavors. With a large and loyal clientele, Bauer's future success appeared as guaranteed as the products he sold, but, in the coming years, Bauer's position as a successful operator of a local sporting goods store would be elevated to a height not imagined even during the optimistic 1920s.

1930s: From Shuttlecocks to Goose Down Jackets

Bauer's success had been predicated on his experience and interest in sporting equipment, so it was fitting that the innovation that would eventually launch his company into the upper echelon of the outdoor apparel industry came as a result, at least in part, of his desire to improve sporting equipment. In the late 1920s, Bauer attempted to improve the consistency of flight in badminton shuttlecocks. He imported premium feathers from Europe and developed a method utilizing buckshot that achieved the desired results. In 1934, his design was patented and eventually adopted for use in the badminton world championships.

While investigating which type of feather would improve the flight of shuttlecocks, Bauer came across goose down, reminding him of an uncle who had once extolled the virtues of goose down's insulating quality. Years earlier, Bauer's uncle, a Cossack fighting in Manchuria during the Russo-Japanese war, had worn a coat lined with goose down to stave off the 50 degrees below zero winter weather. Bauer, who had suffered through many cold winters fishing and hunting in the mountains near Seattle, decided to use goose down to make a coat for himself. After designing and sewing a quilted goose down jacket for himself, Bauer discovered the truth of his uncle's story and soon was making down jackets for a few of his friends. The popularity of these jackets led Bauer to patent his design and begin production of America's first quilted, goose down insulated jacket in 1936. Called the "Skyliner" and selling for $34.50, the jacket was an immediate success, particularly with Alaska bush pilots, and led to the production of a wide assortment of garments with different quilting styles. Starting with ten seamstresses in 1936, Bauer needed 125 by 1940 to meet the voracious demand for his quilted jackets. By this time, Bauer had secured a virtual monopoly on the insulated jacket market, employing as many seamstresses as his rapidly expanding business required and purchasing all the European and North American goose down he wanted.

World War II Contributions

This supply of goose down, however, ended just as Bauer's quilted down garments began to attract orders through the mail. When the United States entered World War II in 1941, the war production board requisitioned all of the goose down supply on the market and froze Bauer's existing supply. No longer able to purchase or use goose down, he was relegated to using eiderdown as a replacement, a substitution that negatively affected his sales. It appeared as if his flourishing retail trade had been swept away from him, but whatever losses Bauer incurred as a result of the government's seizure, he more than made up for them by providing goose down products to the U.S. Army Air Corps, beginning in 1942. At first, Bauer provided the military with sleeping bags and snowshoes and binders, which he sold at retail prices, and eventually his business with the government increased considerably. Using the war production board's goose down, Bauer manufactured 25,000 flight suits and nearly 250,000 sleeping bags for Air Corps flight crews and those fighting in the frigid Aleutian campaign. To satisfy the military's needs, Bauer constructed a production factory, invested roughly $200,000 in specially built machinery, and hired 400 power sewing machine operators to work in three shifts, seven days a week. This prodigious wartime production salvaged what otherwise could have been a recessive period for Bauer's company and, more importantly, it also carried the Eddie Bauer name across the nation. All of the garments Bauer manufactured for the military had the Eddie Bauer label stitched on them, the only garments during the war that carried the manufacturer's private label.

Although Bauer's civilian business slackened during the war, he continued to advertise to create a demand for his products when the war ended. Once it did, he steeled himself for an immediate return to the prosperous days of the late 1930s. Expectations now ran higher, however, considering the tremendous strides in name recognition the company had made as a result of the war, so Bauer introduced a new way to bring his products to the public. In 1945, just as many of those who had worn Eddie Bauer products during the war were returning home, Bauer issued the company's first mail-order catalogs, through a division that had been formed in 1942 to sell the goose down products, Eddie Bauer Expedition Outfitters. Although the introduction of the catalogs represented a significant landmark in the company's history, a more pressing concern during these immediate postwar years overshadowed their import. Bauer's company seemed in danger of failing.

1950s Through Mid-1960s: Concentrating on Mail-Order Cataloging

To fill the demands of his contract with the Air Corps, Bauer had invested in equipment that could serve only his production needs during the war. Both the profits and the machinery were

Key Dates:

1920: Eddie Bauer opens Eddie Bauer's Sport Shop in Seattle.

1922: Bauer begins offering his customers an unconditional guarantee of satisfaction.

1924: Store is renamed Eddie Bauer's Sporting Goods.

1936: Bauer patents and introduces the first goose down insulated jacket, marking the company's entrance into outdoor apparel.

1942: Bauer begins providing goose down products to the U.S. Army Air Corps.

1945: Company sends out its first mail-order catalogs.

1953: Company is reorganized as a 50–50 partnership between Eddie Bauer and William F. Niemi, Sr., under the name William F. Niemi Co., doing business as Eddie Bauer Expedition Outfitters.

1968: Bauer retires, selling his interest in the company to Niemi; the company is incorporated as Eddie Bauer, Inc.

1971: General Mills, Inc. acquires Eddie Bauer for $10 million.

1984: Through a licensing deal with Ford, the first Eddie Bauer edition SUV makes its debut.

1988: Spiegel, Inc. acquires the company for $260 million.

1991: Eddie Bauer Home makes its debut.

1993: Company enters into joint venture to open stores and start catalog operations in Japan.

1995: Joint venture is created to form retailing and cataloging operations in Germany.

1996: Company moves into e-commerce with the launch of eddiebauer.com.

2000: With expansion into Hawaii, there are now Eddie Bauer stores in all 50 states.

temporary, so, once the war ended, Bauer was left with the machinery and nowhere to sell it, leaving him in a precarious situation. As he would later recall, ''We were stuck with the machinery and I lost practically everything I owned, down to where I had to start all over again.'' To assist with this rebuilding process, Bauer entered into a partnership in 1953 with William F. Niemi, Sr., a friend with whom Bauer hunted and fished, and together they strengthened the company by placing an emphasis on the mail-order side of the business and concentrating on producing a larger selection of products (the company was now officially called William F. Niemi Co. but was doing business as Eddie Bauer Expedition Outfitters). From this point forward, until the 1970s, Bauer's company would be primarily a mail-order business. Before the end of the decade, Bauer would close his stores in Seattle and rely almost exclusively on purchases made through the mail, with the only retail sales being generated by a factory store in Seattle. In the late 1950s Bauer and Niemi also brought their sons into the partnership.

The changes made by Bauer and Niemi worked. By mailing catalogs to potential customers and outfitting those outdoorsmen who came to the factory in Seattle, the company generated $1 million in sales in 1960. Although Bauer's financial position had seemed bleak 15 years earlier, the widespread recognition of the Eddie Bauer name had always remained secure. Now a new generation of potential customers were being introduced to the Eddie Bauer line of products through the catalogs arriving in the mail. By this time, Bauer's company used nearly half of the world's supply of northern goose down and had outfitted every American expedition to the Himalayas over the previous ten years. When mountain climbers needed to train for assaults on the towering peaks in the Himalayan range, they often selected the mountains in proximity to Seattle as suitable sites. By the 1960s, a visit to Bauer's factory store became a natural stop for climbers needing clothing and equipment, which further bolstered the nation's recognition of the Eddie Bauer name. When James W. Whittaker became the first American to reach the top of Mount Everest in 1963, he wore an Eddie Bauer parka, slept in an Eddie Bauer sleeping bag, and used Eddie Bauer gear, as did the entire expedition. Three years later, Bauer's company outfitted the American Antarctic Mountaineering Expedition, and it continued to produce the preferred gear for expeditions to follow in later years.

1968–71: Brief Stab at Independent Expansion

By 1968, annual sales at the company were approaching $5 million and professional management and financial planning was clearly needed at the rapidly growing firm. Eddie Bauer and his son decided to sell their half of the company to Niemi and his son, Bill Niemi, Jr., for $1.5 million; a group of investors who had helped finance the buyout gained stock in the company, which was incorporated as Eddie Bauer, Inc. The completion of the sale in June 1968 marked Eddie Bauer's retirement from the firm he had launched nearly 50 years earlier.

The new management team, headed by Niemi as chairman and Niemi, Jr., as president, made some initial moves back into retailing, opening the first store outside Seattle, in San Francisco, in 1968, and a new store in downtown Seattle, the company's first large store, in early 1970. The company also consolidated its scattered Seattle operations in a building on Airport Way in South Seattle that included administration, customer service, manufacturing, warehousing, and distribution at one location. By 1970 sales had surged to $9.1 million, with earnings exceeding $500,000. Needing capital to fund a more ambitious expansion, Eddie Bauer, Inc. made plans for a public offering in the spring of 1970, but the underwriter of the IPO recommended a postponement following a stock market dip. It was at this point that the management concluded that the best course of action would be a sale of the undercapitalized company.

1971–88: The General Mills Era

In March 1971 food conglomerate General Mills, Inc. purchased Eddie Bauer for about 311,000 shares of General Mills common stock, or about $10 million. The acquisition of Eddie Bauer was part of General Mills' aggressive move into specialty retailing. What General Mills received was still essentially a mail-order business, with a small retail side. It was the latter segment of Eddie Bauer that General Mills wanted to fortify.

Several years passed, however, before the disparate merchandising philosophies of the two companies would effectively join together and even longer until Eddie Bauer obtained consistent leadership. From 1975 to 1978 the company went through four presidents, until finally settling on James J. Casey, who had joined Eddie Bauer three years earlier. At this time, the state of Eddie Bauer's product line was still in flux, as General Mills attempted to reshape its subsidiary's market appeal. Six months after Casey assumed leadership of the company, he maneuvered it away from a merchandising failure that had added golf and tennis apparel to the company's product line. For customers inured to a product line whose reputation had been built on manufacturing down parkas and outfitting expeditions to the Antarctic, the shift was a difficult one to make, and potential customers went elsewhere when purchasing items for warmer climes. Although General Mills continued to struggle with the specialty outdoor market niche, it had increased the number of Eddie Bauer retail locations. By the end of the decade, there were 16 retail stores and plans in place to double that figure. In General Mills' first year of ownership, Eddie Bauer posted $11 million in sales, and, with the boost in sales provided by the additional stores, sales climbed to $80 million, ranking the company second only to L.L. Bean, Inc. in the specialty outdoor market. The disparity between retail and catalog sales disappeared, with half of the total revenues generated by the stores, and 14 million catalog customers accounting for the remainder. In the meantime, the company moved its headquarters once again in 1973, settling into a 14-acre campus in Redmond, Washington.

By 1984, the changes initiated by General Mills had substantially altered the image Eddie Bauer projected to its customers. Apparel now generated approximately 70 percent of the retail store revenues, and much of it did not resemble the clothing worn by members of a Mount Everest expedition, or even the clothing worn by weekend adventurers camping in the woods. Tents, backpacks, and fishing rods had slowly begun to disappear from the shelves of the company's stores and were replaced with oxford cloth shirts, lamb's wool sweaters, and other items uncharacteristic of the rugged, expedition outfitter. With 41 stores located in Canada and the United States, the company broadened its appeal—enough for Ford Motor Company to begin production of the Eddie Bauer Bronco II in 1984—and attracted a more diverse clientele. The expansion of the retail side of the business represented a move toward greater growth for the mail-order segment as well. In 1983, Eddie Bauer mailed 14 million catalogs, and, by the following year, 30 million catalogs were sent to potential customers, two million of which were printed in French to accommodate the company's burgeoning clientele in Canada. Plans called for further expansion of the company's retail business, some 60 stores over the next five years. To lead the company toward this goal, a switch in leadership was made. In 1984, Michael Rayden replaced Casey and began separating retail, mail-order, and manufacturing into three distinct divisions.

By 1988, Eddie Bauer had 57 retail stores located in the United States and Canada. But just as General Mills was announcing further plans to augment Eddie Bauer's retail holdings, the corporation put Eddie Bauer up for sale along with another specialty clothing chain it owned, Talbots, in a bid to divest itself of all nonfood-related businesses.

1988 into the 21st Century: The Spiegel Era

In 1988 Spiegel, Inc., a catalog marketer of apparel, home furnishings, and other merchandise, bought Eddie Bauer for $260 million, roughly equal to the sales the company generated at the time of its purchase. Wayne Badovinus was selected to lead Eddie Bauer and, over the next two years, 100 stores were added to the retail chain, bringing total sales up to $448 million. In 1991, Eddie Bauer's first "Premier" store was opened in Chicago, which housed all of the company's recently introduced specialty product lines. "All Week Long," Eddie Bauer's collection of women's sportswear and casual attire, first introduced as a catalog business in 1987, had evolved into a retail business by 1991 with the opening of its first store in Portland, Oregon, and now was part of the Premier store concept. Also included in the Premier stores were "The Sport Shop at Eddie Bauer," featuring custom-built fishing rods, reels, and fishing flies, and "The Eddie Bauer Home Collection," which sold a wide assortment of indoor and outdoor furnishings. The addition of these specialty retail concepts, each first introduced in 1991, marked another dramatic leap in revenues. In the three years since Spiegel had purchased Eddie Bauer, the parent company had witnessed an increase in revenues from roughly $260 million, to nearly $750 million, occasioned primarily by the dramatic increase in Eddie Bauer's retail business. This expansion continued after 1991, giving the company 265 retail stores by the end of 1992. Eddie Bauer Home became the longest lasting of the new concepts, and by 1994 there were 15 such outlets in 11 states, and the company was mailing out separate Home catalogs six times per year. Revenues surpassed the $1 billion mark for the first time in 1993.

The mid-1990s were marked by continued expansion in North America as well as the company's first forays into overseas territory. The international expansion was pursued through joint ventures with units of Otto Versand (GmbH & Co.), a German mail-order giant controlled by the Otto family, which also controlled Spiegel. In 1993 Eddie Bauer entered into a venture with Otto-Sumisho, Inc. to open retail stores and sell through catalogs in Japan. Two years later the company joined with Otto Versand unit's Heinrich Heine GmbH and Sport-Scheck GmbH in another venture created to launch retail and catalog sales in Germany. By the end of the decade there were 35 Eddie Bauer stores in Japan and nine in Germany. A similar venture for the U.K. market was created in 1996 but was discontinued three years later, with catalog sales continuing through Eddie Bauer's German joint venture.

During 1995, when the company celebrated its 75th anniversary, Eddie Bauer launched a new retail and catalog concept, called AKA Eddie Bauer, selling upscale dress clothing for men and women—a new line aimed at the burgeoning market for more casual work clothes. The company's All Week Long concept was discontinued, with those stores converted into AKA Eddie Bauer units. Even amidst a slump in the entire retailing industry, Eddie Bauer continued to expand in other ways as well. In 1996 came the debut of the EBTEK line of high performance outerwear and casual activewear featuring such fabrics as Goretex and Polartec 200. That same year, the company established a third distribution channel with the launching of its Internet web site. Bucking the early trend in e-commerce, eddiebauer.com was generating a profit within two years of its debut. During 1997 Eddie Bauer opened its 500th U.S. store.

With its Ford partnership continuing, Eddie Bauer entered into several more licensing deals in the late 1990s to further leverage its increasingly well-known name. In 1997 the company inked a deal with the Lane Company for the development of a line of Eddie Bauer furniture. The following year Eddie Bauer mountain bikes were launched with Giant Bicycle, Inc.; Eddie Bauer eyewear debuted through an agreement with Signature Eyewear, Inc.; and Eddie Bauer infant and juvenile car seats were introduced in conjunction with Cosco, Inc.

After adding a net 39 stores in 1998, and suffering from declining sales because of increased competition and a slow reaction to hot new fashion trends such as cargo pants, Eddie Bauer reined in its North American expansion the following year, when the chain's net gain was just nine stores. The company also made some alterations to its store concepts that year. Eddie Bauer Home was revamped to include less in the way of upholstered furniture and tabletop items and more of the domestic items for bed and bath, such as bedding and towels. The 40 home stores also began featuring the Eddie Bauer Juvenile line of bedding and beds and increased its "baby by Eddie Bauer" line of infant bedding and furniture. The AKA Eddie Bauer concept was discontinued in the form of separate stores, and the AKA merchandise was integrated into adjacent Eddie Bauer sportswear stores.

With a revamp of its sportswear lines, Eddie Bauer managed to post a six percent increase in comparable store sales in 1999, compared with a nine percent decrease the previous year. Overall revenues increased slightly that year, reaching $1.79 billion. During 2000, when Eddie Bauer planned to increase its North American retail units to 565 and to expand or remodel 40 existing stores, a milestone was reached when the first Eddie Bauer store opened in Hawaii, completing the chain's entrance into all 50 states.

Since 1920, the Eddie Bauer name has evoked several images. What once represented fishing tackle, guns, and mountaineering equipment now, in the early 21st century, stood for durable, comfortable apparel As Eddie Bauer planned for the future, supported by its multiple channels of distribution, its product lines appeared to remain as strong as the legendary Eddie Bauer name.

Principal Subsidiaries

Eddie Bauer of Canada, Inc.; Eddie Bauer International, Inc.

Principal Competitors

Abercrombie & Fitch Co.; American Eagle Outfitters, Inc.; Coldwater Creek Inc.; Cornerstone Brands, Inc.; Dillard's Inc.; Euromarket Designs Inc.; Federated Department Stores, Inc.; The Gap, Inc.; Hanover Direct, Inc.; J.C. Penney Company, Inc.; J. Crew Group, Inc.; The J. Jill Group, Inc.; L.L. Bean, Inc.; Lands' End, Inc.; The Limited, Inc.; The May Department Stores Company; Montgomery Ward, LLC; The Neiman Marcus Group, Inc.; Nordstrom, Inc.; Pier 1 Imports, Inc.; Saks Incorporated; Sears, Roebuck and Co.; The Talbots, Inc.; Target Corporation; Wal-Mart Stores, Inc.; Williams-Sonoma, Inc.

Further Reading

Chandler, Susan, "New Fashion Focus Helps Eddie Bauer Rebound," *Seattle Times,* August 29, 1999, p. F1.
"Eddie Bauer: A Name You Can Trust," *Catalog Age,* September 1993, pp. 135–36.
"Eddie Bauer Catalog Sidesteps Recession Doldrums," *Direct Marketing,* November 1983, p. 72.
"Eddie Bauer: The Man Behind the Name," *Pacific Northwest Magazine,* May 1983, pp. 61–64.
Enbysk, Monte, "Snug Fit: Eddie Bauer Inc. Has Profited Handsomely from Acquisition by Spiegel," *Tacoma News Tribune,* February 27, 1994, p. F4.
"Evolution of a Down-Wear Retailer," *New York Times,* March 12, 1981, p. D4.
George, Melissa, "Why Eddie Bauer Is Lost in the Woods," *Crain's Chicago Business,* August 10, 1998, p. 1.
Green, Jeff, "Bauer Power," *Brandweek,* July 5, 1999, pp. 16–17.
Hanover, Dan, "EddieBauer.com Gets It Done," *Chain Store Age,* October 1998, pp. 197–98.
Lim, Paul J., "Eddie Bauer Plans Aggressive Expansion," *Seattle Times,* January 18, 1996, p. C1.
Moriwaki, Lee, "It Takes More Than Flannel," *Seattle Times,* October 19, 1997, p. E1.
Nogaki, Sylvia Wieland, "Out of the Woods: Eddie Bauer Hikes Trail Leading to Higher Profits," *Seattle Times,* July 26, 1993, p. E1.
Palmeri, Christopher, "Indoor Sportsman," *Forbes,* March 29, 1993, p. 43.
Pasternack, Edward D., "Eddie Bauer Expanding in Japan and Germany," *Direct Marketing,* March 1996, pp. 36, 38–39.
"REI, Eddie Bauer Expand," *Chain Store Age Executive,* August 1987, pp. 46–47.
"Retreat, Hell: Four Contrarians Who Hear Opportunity Knocking," *Business Week,* January 14, 1991, p. 64.
Ricketts, Chip, "Eddie Bauer's Southern Expansion Push Includes Metroplex," *Dallas Business Journal,* February 26, 1990, p. 3.
Schwadel, Francine, "Waters Resigns from General Mills, Pursues Purchase of Units He Managed," *Wall Street Journal,* January 11, 1988, p. 32.
Schwadel, Francine, and Richard Gibson, "General Mills Is Putting Up for Sale Talbots, Eddie Bauer Clothing Chain," *Wall Street Journal,* January 8, 1988, p. 4.
——, "General Mills to Sell Last Retail Units, Talbots and Bauer, for $585 Million," *Wall Street Journal,* May 19, 1988, p. 4.
Spector, Robert, "Eddie Bauer's New Look," *The Weekly,* January 2, 1985, pp. 20–22.
——, *The Legend of Eddie Bauer,* Lyme, Conn.: Greenwich Publishing, 1994.
Warren, James R., "Eddie Bauer's Guarantee Was Key to Firm's Success," *Seattle Business Journal,* June 13, 1983, pp. 6–7.

—Jeffrey L. Covell
—updated by David E. Salamie

Empresa Brasileira de Aeronáutica S.A. (Embraer)

Av. Brig. Faria Lima, 2170
12227-901 Sao José dos Campos
Sao Paulo
Brazil
Telephone: (55 12) 345-1000
Fax: (55 12) 345-2411
Web site: http://www.embraer.com

Public Company
Incorporated: 1969
Employees: 9,000
Sales: R 3.36 billion (US$1.89 billion) (1999)
Stock Exchanges: New York Sao Paulo
Ticker Symbols: ERJ; EMBR3; EMBR4
NAIC: 336411 Aircraft Manufacturing

Empresa Brasileira de Aeronáutica S.A. (Embraer) is one of Brazil's most successful high tech companies. In the 1990s, Embraer became the world's fourth largest civil aircraft manufacturer by riding the regional jet trend pioneered by arch-rival Bombardier of Canada. Half the planes in the Brazilian Air Force are Embraer products and military aircraft continue to account for ten percent of revenues.

Military Origins

Three military cabinet leaders (army, navy, and air force) took over Brazil in 1968 after elected president General Artur Costa e Silva was incapacitated by strokes. General Emílio Médici was installed as the new head of state. The military wanted Brazil to have its own aircraft-manufacturing capacity and created Empresa Brasileira de Aeronáutica S.A. (Embraer) the next year.

The Brazilian government held 51 percent of the voting shares while private investors held the rest. Embraer was based in the provincial town of Sao José dos Campos in Sao Paulo State. Operations started in 1970 and the company broke even the next year.

Embraer's first design, the EMB-110 Bandeirante ("Pioneer"), was the first aircraft produced in Brazil. Powered by two turboprop engines, the plane could carry up to 21 passengers and was quite popular with U.S. commuter airlines. Embraer also developed military versions of this versatile plane. Another early design was the Xingu, which carried six to nine passengers. Embraer's Neiva subsidiary built the Ipanema crop duster and various Piper light planes under license.

Embraer built a version of the Italian Aermacchi MB-326BG military jet trainer under license for the Brazilian air force. The company then teamed with Aermacchi and Aeritalia in developing the AM-X subsonic fighter aircraft to replace Fiat G-91 and Lockheed F-104 fighters in the Italian air force. The program was valued at US$600 million. Embraer also developed its own basic trainer, the EMB-312 Tucano. The Brazilian air force ordered 168 of them in the early 1980s.

A Variety of Projects in the 1980s

Embraer had been profitable from its second year in operation, but posted an annual loss in 1981. By 1982, Embraer had 6,000 workers and had produced 2,500 aircraft. The company was developing a maritime surveillance version of the Bandeirante in the early 1980s. Work had also begun on the EMB-120 Brasilia, a 30-seat turboprop with similar applications to its smaller predecessor. Embraer held more than 130 orders and options for the Brasilia before it entered production in 1985. However, airlines were slow to convert options into firm orders.

Sales were between US$170 and US$180 million in 1984. The company garnered 40 percent of its revenues abroad. Although Brazil was suffering an economic depression, trade barriers protected the company's home market.

In the *London Financial Times,* company President Colonel Ozires Silva predicted the extinction of purely civilian aircraft manufacturers. (Silva went on to lead Varig, Brazil's largest airline.) The first prototype AMX crashed in May 1983, but the program continued. Embraer began filling a large order from Egypt for the Tucano trainer in 1985. Meanwhile, Short Brothers of Belfast, Northern Ireland, was bidding to produce the

Tucano under license for the Royal Air Force. Production continued on military variants of the Bandeirante.

Embraer also developed missiles, and was part of a consortium that in 1988 agreed to help Iraq develop satellite and missile technology. According to the *New York Times,* at the time of the invasion of Kuwait, a few of Embraer's engineers (possibly former employees) were in Iraq helping to increase the range of the country's notorious Scud missiles.

Embraer remained dependent on imported avionics and communications equipment. When it tried to buy a Model 3090 computer from IBM in 1990, the sale was blocked after Brazil would not guarantee that the computer would not be used for military purposes or transferred to other countries.

Privatized in 1994

The recession that followed the Gulf War affected the whole aviation industry, and Embraer suffered with everyone else. By 1994, the company was bankrupt, on its way to losing US$337 million for the year. The Brazilian government sought a world-class aerospace company to help rescue it during its privatization in May 1994. However, other makers of regional aircraft were blocked from participating.

Ultimately, a group led by Banco Bozano, Simonsen SA acquired 60 percent of the company's voting shares. Two large pension funds joined the Rio de Janeiro-based holding company: Caixa de Previdência dos Funcionários do Banco do Brasil S.A. (PREVI) and Fundaçao SISTEL de Seguridade Social (SISTEL). Seeking to create a leaner, more efficient manufacturer, after a six-month ban on layoffs, the new owners cut a third of the company's 5,500 jobs. Mauricio Botelho, an engineer and executive at Bozano Simonsen, became company president in September 1995.

By the mid-1990s, the Brasilia had become the most widely used turboprop in the United States, according to the *New York Times.* However, since the introduction of Bombardier Aerospace's Canadair Regional Jet (RJ) in 1993, the whole category was being displaced by regional jets—small airliners that were less noisy, more spacious, and faster, yet still economical to operate on short routes.

Embraer's entrant, the EMB-145 (also called the ERJ-145), took its first test flight in August 1995. The planes sold for US$14.5 million each—somewhat less than the Canadair—its only direct competitor—but twice as much as the Brasilia. Embraer's own regional jet had originally been conceived in 1989, according to the *Financial Times,* but was slower to market due to organizational sluggishness. (Fairchild Aerospace, formed when U.S.-based Fairchild Aircraft took over the

German Dornier Luftfahrt in 1996, also made airliners with fewer than 100 seats.)

Continental Express ordered 25 of the EMB-145s for US$375 million in the fall of 1996, and reserved options for 175 more. Within a year, American Eagle had ordered 42. (A number of smaller foreign operators had been the first to sign up for the jet.) At the time the 50-seat EMB-145 was launched, plans for 35-seat and 70-seat jets were already in the works.

The regional jet would help save the company, but it would take time. Embraer, which still carried US$600 million in debt, posted a loss of US$40 million (R 42 million) in 1996 and a loss of US$30 million (R 33 million) in 1997.

Competition between Embraer and Bombardier—and between Brazil and Canada—was intense. Bombardier ran want ads for engineers in Brazil, luring them to Canada with superior pay and quality-of-life benefits. Embraer alleged that in 1997 Bombardier dropped the company from a US$100 million NATO contract to supply Tucano trainers due to the success of Embraer's EMB-145.

Embraer and Bombardier each accused the other of thriving because of government subsidies. Bombardier criticized the special financing the Brazilian government offered through its Proex export promotion program. However, Brazil countered that as a developing country it was not required to follow World Trade Organization (WTO) rules until 2002. The country did agree to modify its Proex program to comply with a WTO ruling in 1999, however the WTO ruled that Proex still kept financing rates below international levels, and ordered Brazil to stop this subsidy. (Brazil had not complied as of April 2000.)

Embraer had become Brazil's second largest exporter, with foreign sales of US$1.2 billion in 1998. It was the fourth largest aircraft manufacturer in the world.

The Brazilian Real lost 40 percent of its value in the first few weeks of 1999. Although most of Embraer's revenues came in hard currency, rising interest rates accompanied the Real's devaluation, making money to finance sales and develop new designs harder to find. Ultimately, though, Embraer benefited from lowered manufacturing costs.

Embraer pressed on with plans to develop larger versions of the EMB-145, dubbed the EMB-170 and EMB-190. The project was expected to cost US$750 million; Embraer expected to contribute US$250 million itself, and to raise another third each from a strategic partner and the international financial markets.

In June 1999, Embraer announced a record US$4.9 billion order from Crossair, a Swiss regional airline. Crossair placed firm orders for 15 ERJ-145s, 30 ERJ-170s, and 30 ERJ-190s. The latter two had delivery dates of 2002 and 2004. Crossair also placed options on another 125 aircraft.

New Capital for the New Millennium

A consortium of four French aerospace companies—Aerospatiale-Matra, Dassault Aviation, Snecma, and Thomson-CSF—acquired 20 percent of Embraer's voting shares in 1999. The Brazilian government retained 20 percent under a ''golden

Key Dates:

1969: Embraer is founded by Brazil's military dictatorship.
1981: Embraer posts only the second annual loss in its history.
1994: Nearly bankrupt, Embraer is privatized.
1995: Embraer begins testing its ERJ-145 regional jet.
1999: French aerospace consortium buys 20 percent of company's voting shares.
2000: Embraer attains listing on the New York Stock Exchange.

share'' provision. Brazilian air force officials were wary of letting a foreign aerospace company own part of Embraer. However, Embraer seemed more likely to benefit from applying French technology in its military jets. At the time, the company was only devoting ten percent of its production to jet fighters. In the same year, Embraer created a landing gear and hydraulics joint venture with a German company, Liebherr International.

Embraer realized record earnings of R 412 million (US$240 million) in 1999 due to strong sales in Europe as well as the United States. According to the *New York Times,* the company sold 100 jets during the year, and sales were expected to rise by 50 percent in 2000. Revenues and profits doubled for the first half of 2000. Embraer was listed on the New York Stock Exchange in July 2000. The company had a US$20 billion backlog and was developing its Legacy business jet.

Principal Subsidiaries

Embraer Aircraft Corporation (U.S.A.); Embraer Australia Pty. Ltd.; Embraer Aviation International (France); Embraer-Liebherr Equipamentos do Brasil S.A. (60%); Indústria Aeronáutica Neiva SA.

Principal Competitors

Bombardier Aerospace; Fairchild Aircraft, Inc.; Gulfstream Aerospace Corporation.

Further Reading

Alden, Edward, and Jonathan Wheatley, "Noise Levels Rise As Canada and Brazil Seek Aircraft Peace," *Financial Times,* World Trade Sec., May 29, 1998, p. 7.

Barham, John, "Brazil to Amend Subsidy Scheme," *Financial Times,* World Trade Sec., March 16, 1999, p. 8.

——, "Embraer Planning New Large Regional Airliners," *Financial Times,* World Trade Sec., April 9, 1999, p. 8.

Barham, John, and Richard Lapper, "Aircraft Maker Is Rocked by Currency Turbulence," *Financial Times,* p. 31.

Done, Kevin, "Smaller Airliners Flying High," *Financial Times,* Aerospace 2000, July 24, 2000, p. 9.

Donne, Michael, "One of the Most Vigorous Industries in the Developing World," *Financial Times,* August 23, 1982.

Dyer, Geoff, and Frances Williams, "Brazil Loses WTO Ruling on Aircraft Subsidies," *Financial Times,* World News, April 29, 2000, p. 6.

Farnsworth, Clyde H., "A Standoff with Brazil Over Sale of a Computer," *New York Times,* April 12, 1991, p. D2.

Johnston, David Cay, "Relief for the Turboprop Blues; Small Is Suddenly Beautiful for Short-Hop Travelers," *New York Times,* Bus. Sec., August 19, 1995, p. 31.

Moffett, Matt, "Bombardier's Brazilian Rival: Embraer Muscles Its Way into the Market for Fifty-Seat Jets," *Gazette* (Montreal), March 24, 1997, p. C3.

Morrison, Scott, "Canada and Brazil Near Aircraft Subsidies Deal," *Financial Times,* July 20, 2000, p. 14.

Rich, Jennifer L., "A Real Aircraft Man Running Brazil's Top Airline," *New York Times,* July 12, 2000, p. C4.

Romero, Simon, "Brazilian Aircraft Maker Reports Strong Earnings," *New York Times,* March 30, 2000, p. C4.

Silva, Ozires, *A decolagem de um sonho: a história da criaçao da EMBRAER,* Sao Paulo: Lemos Editorial, 1998.

U.S. Dept. of Commerce, International Trade Commission, *Brazilian Government Support for the Aerospace Industry,* by Ronald D. Green, Washington, D.C.: 1987.

Wheatley, Jonathan, "Embraer Gets Back on Course," *Financial Times,* Bus. Sec., July 29, 1997, p. 22.

Whitley, Andrew, "Embraer Steps Up Sales Drive," *Financial Times,* August 28, 1984.

—Frederick C. Ingram

Eridania Béghin-Say S.A.

14, blvd. du General Leclerc
F 92572 Neuilly-sur-Seine Cedex
France
Telephone: (+33) 1 41 43 14 50
Fax: (+33) 1 41 43 11 51
Web site: http://www.eridania-béghin-say.com

Public Company (51% Owned by Montedison S.p.A.)
Founded: 1821
Employees: 21,693
Sales: EUR 9.01 billion (US$8 billion) (1999)
Stock Exchanges: Paris
NAIC: 311225 Fats and Oils Refining and Blending;
    311312 Cane Sugar Refining; 311119 Other Animal
    Food Manufacturing; 311111 Dog and Cat Food
    Manufacturing

Eridania Béghin-Say S.A. is one of the world's leading agro-industrial concerns with operations centered around raw foods and ingredients processing and interests ranging from sugar refining to pet foods. Eridania Béghin-Say's activities are divided into five major divisions: Ceresucre; Cerestar; Central Soya; Cereol; and Provimi. The company's sugar division, Ceresucre, which combines the company's France-based Béghin-Say subsidiary and Italy-based Eridania subsidiary, is the world's number three sugar refiner, operating 26 refineries and processing more than 20 million tons of sugar (primarily beetroot-based), worth some 15 percent of the total European Community sugar quota. Cerestar, the company's starch and derivatives division, produces more than 3.5 million tons of starch products from corn, wheat, and potatoes, as well as 1.9 million tons of starch byproducts. Cerestar, which operates 15 factories, leads the European market in its category and is the fifth largest starches producer in the United States. Central Soya processes nearly 6.5 million tons of oilseeds annually and produces proteins and lecithins for the North American market; through subsidiary CanAmera, this division holds the number three position in its market. In Europe, Cereol is a diversified division offering oilseed processing, seed and olive oil marketing (including sunflower, rapeseed, soya, and other food oils under brands Lesieur, Koipe, Carapelli, and other brand names), and other products, including rice, margarines, and condiments such as ketchup, mustard, and vinegar. This division also contained the Ducros herb and spices subsidiary, which was sold to McCormick in 2000. With 40 production facilities, annual processing of more than 7.2 million tons of oilseeds, 195 million liters of olive oil, and 880 million liters of seed oils, Cereol also represents Eridania Béghin-Say's largest division. The last division, Provimi, is the Rotterdam-based holding company for the company's worldwide pet foods subsidiaries, with 66 production facilities producing nearly two million tons of animal feed products—from raw ingredients to packaged pet foods—each year. Provimi holds seven percent of the world market in this category, making it the international leader. Led by Stefano Meloni, approximately 51 percent (and more than 68 percent of voting rights) of Eridania Béghin is owned by Italian agro-industrial-energy conglomerate Montedison. The company has been hard hit by the economic crises in the Russian and Asian markets and, especially, by the collapse in market prices for much of its key products. As such, Eridania Béghin-Say, which launched a downsizing of its sugar division at the beginning of 2000, has seen its annual sales slip back to barely more than EUR 9 billion, while net profits have slid to less than EUR 93 million—a drop of more than 60 percent over the previous year.

Rise of a Sugar Giant in the 19th Century

War with England had closed off France's access to its cane sugar-producing island colonies in the early years of the 19th century; French-imposed blockades also closed off imports of British sugar to the continent. By then, per capita consumption of sugar in France had risen to some three kilograms per person and already had become important not only as a flavoring ingredient, but also as a preservative for fruits and other foods. The search for an alternative sugar source, especially for a plant that could be grown on the European continent, was stepped up under orders from Napoleon.

France was to play a leading role in developing the first viable non-cane sugar source. French agriculturists initially turned to the grape, but the resulting sugar was not satisfactory. Beets were long known to contain sugar—but their sugar con-

Company Perspectives:

Our mission will be achieved by: Focusing our innovative efforts on higher value-added products that enhance our earnings and reduce risk and volatility. Giving priority to investments that increase our cost effectiveness and competitiveness, as well as the value of our products and brands. Making products that are totally safe to consume or use, in factories that provide quality-assurance through good manufacturing practice and respect for the environment. Providing world-class technical and marketing support to those of our products that need it in order to be successful. Understanding consumer trends as well as customer needs with respect to the sources and types of raw materials used in our processes. Leveraging our core competencies—process knowledge, product innovation and development, sales and logistics—to achieve synergies across our entire business spectrum. Key to achieving these objectives will be a policy of developing and rewarding our employees commensurately.

tent was low and extracting and crystallizing the sugar was not technically possible. The first sugar beet refinery was built in Germany at the end of the 18th century, but failed because of the beet's low sugar content.

Under Napoleon, French agriculturists began developing a variety of beet with a higher sugar content, successfully raising content to nearly 20 percent by the end of the first decade of the 19th century. Napoleon ordered the wide-scale planting of the new beet variety—more than 32,000 hectares were planted in 1811. The following year proved decisive for the sugar industry, when Benjamin Délectait successfully crystallized the sugar from the new beet. Among the earliest of the new refineries was that of Etablissements Say, one of the predecessor companies to Eridania Béghin-Say.

French sugar beet production was launched on a large scale; by 1813, France counted some 300 sugar refineries, with total sugar production reaching 3,500 tons. This level remained small compared with the country's colonial sugar cane production, which had reached 150,000 tons per year before the turn of the century, and prices remained high during the war, reaching 2.5 francs per kilogram. Nonetheless, it enabled France—and the rest of Northern Europe—to achieve a degree of self-sufficiency in its sugar production.

The collapse of Napoleon's regime in 1814 was to send the sugar beet industry into disarray. The stocks of colonial sugar—warehoused during the British blockade—arrived in the ports of Europe and brought on the collapse of sugar prices. Many of the country's sugar beet refineries were forced to close, and the sugar beet industry, unable to compete against the larger, more mature sugar cane industry—which not only used slaves for its labor force, but also held a great deal of political clout in the French government—entered a downswing.

Nevertheless, the appeal of the sugar beet crop for France's farmers—particularly in the country's northern regions—remained high. By the late 1830s, the country counted nearly 600 sugar producers. Among them was the sugar beet farm of

the Béghin family, founded in 1821, at Thumeries near the Belgian border.

In the 1840s, Béghin, Say, and the rest of France's domestic sugar producers faced a major threat from a coalition between the country's colonial cane sugar producers and its shipping industry, which convinced the French government to propose legislation barring the production of beet sugar. The political power of the colonial sugar masters meant that the legislation nearly passed. Defeated in the house of deputies (equivalent to the French congress), the colonial sugar industry faced a new setback with the abolition of slavery in the French colonies.

The resulting rise in cane sugar prices made beet sugar a competitive commodity and paved the way for the maturation of the French sugar industry. By the 1880s, France had become the top European producer of sugar. The Béghin family, represented by Ferdinand Béghin, and Etablissements Say began their rise to dominance of the French sugar industry. For the Béghin family, growth came especially after sons Joseph and Henri Béghin inherited Ferdinand Béghin's business, renaming the company Société F. Béghin in 1898. The two Béghin brothers went on to build the company into one of France's major sugar refineries, transforming the family farm into a true industrial complex. Etablissements Say, meanwhile, also was expanding, with refineries, warehouses, and other facilities located in Paris and elsewhere.

The outbreak of World War I spelled the beginning of a crisis period for the French sugar beet industry—with much of the country's sugar production and refineries located in the North, much of the domestic industry's production facilities were destroyed. Cane sugar once again dominated the market; beet sugar slowly rebuilt its position, only to face a new crisis when, at the beginning of the 1920s, world sugar prices collapsed. Despite production quotas established in the mid-1930s, agreed upon among the various producer-nations, the entry into World War II marked a new period of crisis for the sugar industry. By then, however, beet sugar had captured more than one-third of worldwide sugar production.

France's sugar industry was marked by consolidation, which reached its peak in 1973 when F. Béghin and Etablissements Say merged to create the country's leading sugar manufacturer, Béghin-Say. The company went on to diversify, taking a leading position in the paper and cardboard industry as well, through its holdings in Kaysersberg and Corbehem.

Agribusiness Giant for the 21st Century

By the late 1970s, Béghin-Say had attracted the interests of Italy's Serafino Ferruzzi. Nicknamed ''the Farmer,'' Ferruzzi had built an agricultural empire that included a minority share of Eridania, Italy's top sugar producer, itself founded in 1899. Ferruzzi, through the family-run Ferruzzi Finanziaria, boosted its share of Eridania to nearly 65 percent in 1978. Eridania was added to Ferruzzi's growing portfolio of agricultural, industrial, and other interests, forming Montedison. Montedison also included the holding of the Edison electric power utility, Italy's largest private electricity supplier.

Ferruzzi's agro-industrial ambitions quickly crossed the border. In 1980, the Ferruzzi family attempted a surprise takeover

Key Dates:

1812: Etablissements Say is founded.

1821: Béghin family sugar beet farm is founded.

1898: Henry and Joseph Béghin found F. Béghin sugar refinery operation.

1899: Eridania is founded.

1973: Merger forms Béghin-Say.

1978: Ferruzzi Finanziaria gains control of Eridania.

1980: Ferruzzi Finanziaria attempts takeover of Béghin Say.

1981: Agreement with French government limits Ferruzzi Finanziaria to 50 percent of Béghin Say.

1987: Sell-off of Béghin-Say's paper holdings; joint acquisition of the European starch and derivatives arm of Corn Products International, renamed Cerestar; joint acquisition of Central Soya.

1989–91: Acquisitions of Olii e Risi; Lesieur; Carapelli.

1991: Following relaxation of restrictions, Ferruzzi increases its ownership of Béghin-Say to 60 percent.

1992: Formation of Eridania Béghin-Say; acquisition of Ducros.

1995: Acquisition of American Maize Products.

1997: Acquisition of ZT Kruszwica (Poland).

1998: Acquisition of Top Number Feeds and Happidog Pet Foods (U.K.); acquires Vigortone (U.S.A.) and Alimental (Argentina).

1999: Downsizing of Béghin-Say is undertaken; launch of Health and Nutrition division.

2000: Company completes sale of Ducros to McCormick & Co.

of Béghin-Say, building up a more than 24 percent share in the French sugar leader. Intervention from the French government helped prevent the takeover, and the following year, in an agreement made between Ferruzzi and the government, Ferruzzi agreed to leave Béghin-Say's French management in place and not to exceed a shareholding of 50 percent in the French sugar producer. Ferruzzi reached that limit by 1986, though the restriction was later lifted.

Despite the limits imposed by the 1981 agreement, Ferruzzi's control of Béghin-Say enabled him to begin transforming the company from a primarily French-focused company into a diversified agro-industry concern. In 1986, Béghin-Say sold off its interests in the paper industry—including selling 50 percent of its Kaysersberg subsidiary to Montedison (and the other 50 percent to James River). Next, Ferruzzi led Béghin-Say and Eridania on a combined buying spree, branching out from sugar refineries and products into the wide agro-industrial field. The first of the combined acquisitions was made in 1987, with the purchase of the European starch and derivatives arm of Corn Products International. Held 50–50 by Eridania and Béghin-Say, the new operations were regrouped under the name Cerestar.

In that same year, the Eridania Béghin-Say partnership acquired Central Soya, based in Decatur, Indiana, and founded in 1934. The Eridania Béghin-Say buying spree continued into the early 1990s, adding Italy's leading soybean processor Olii e Risi, then French fats and oil leader Lesieur, which also brought control of Spanish edible oil leader Koipe. These acquisitions were joined by a 90 percent share in Carapelli, Italy's olive oil leader, founded in 1893, as well as the oilseed crushing and refinery facility of Unilever at Mannheim, Germany, boosting Eridania Béghin-Say's growing interest in that sector by 1.2 million tons.

In 1991, Eridania increased its holding in Béghin-Say to 60 percent. That year, the partners expanded their sugar production operations into eastern Europe, acquiring shares in three Hungarian sugar companies and gaining control of some 40 percent of that country's total sugar production. The following year, the companies added Ducros, founded in 1963, which in less than 30 years had risen to take the market leadership in France, Italy, Spain, and Portugal for its Ducros range of herbs and spices and its Vahine brand of baking ingredients.

In 1992 Eridania and Béghin-Say formalized what had by then become a single operation. Transferring shares of Eridania into those of Béghin-Say, the company adopted the single name of Eridania Béghin-Say, maintaining headquarters in France but becoming a subsidiary of Montedison. By then, Montedison—and its parent Ferruzzi Finanziaria—had risen to become Italy's second largest industrial conglomerate. Yet the Ferruzzi empire—led, after Serafino Ferruzzi's accidental death, by his son-in-law Raul Gardino—was about to collapse. Following his father-in-law's lead, Gardino had gone on a diversification buying spree, financing the conglomerate's growth through debt. By the early 1990s, the company's debt had reached L 31 trillion, or nearly US$16 billion. Then Gardino came under scrutiny during a government corruption investigation that was to bring down the Italian government and see the ruin of two of its major political parties. Gardino himself committed suicide, rather than face bribery and corruption charges.

Montedison fell into the hands of its creditor banks. Reorganized into two major components, the Eridania Béghin-Say agro-industrial unit and the Edison energy utility, Montedison appointed a new chairman and CEO for Eridania Béghin-Say, Stefano Meloni. Under Meloni, the company continued its expansion, adding an animal and pet foods component, and then purchasing American Maize Products in 1995 to establish the Cerestar USA subsidiary. The company also began an international marketing campaign for its Carapelli olive oil brand, introducing it first in Europe and then moving into the North American market.

Eridania Béghin-Say continued its expansion in the late 1990s, entering the Polish market with the acquisition of a majority stake in ZT Kruszwica, that market's leading oilseed and bottled oil concern, then adding the Ukraine-based sunflower oil producer DOEP. The company also entered South Africa, China, and Brazil, while continuing to expand its holdings in Spain, Italy, and France. In 1998, the company boosted its animal feeds section with the acquisitions of the United Kingdom's Top Number Feeds and Happidog Pet Foods, the United States' Vigortone, and Alimental, the Argentine-based maker of animal feed products.

Despite its expansion moves, Eridania Béghin-Say was rocked by the economic crises in Asia and Russia. The collapse of prices for many of the company's core products, including worldwide sugar prices, caused the company to see its annual sales slip and its net profits fall. In response, the company took a two-pronged approach, announcing at the beginning of 1999 its intention to downsize its Béghin-Say operations, while introducing new sugar-based products, including its Zefiro and Actisucre. The latter was the product of the company's new Health and Nutrition division, launched in March 2000, and devoted to creating so-called "functional foods" with health-benefit properties. The company also disposed of a number of other nonstrategic operations, among them a majority share of its seeds operations, sold to Novartis in mid-1999.

By then, the company had reached an agreement to sell its Ducros subsidiary to McCormick & Co. for US$394 million. This disposal represented a major step in the company's restructuring around a core range of strategic activities—sugar, starch, oilseeds and food oils, and animal nutrition—meant to return the company to sales and profits growth in the early years of the new century. Meanwhile, the Ferruzzi company, reorganized as Compart, moved to regain full control of Montedison in 2000, building a position to 92 percent in that company and its 51 percent share of Eridania Béghin-Say.

Principal Subsidiaries

Ceresucre; Agronomica (Italy); Béghin-Say; Béghin-Say Espana; Béghin-Meiji Industries; Eridania Béghin-Say Budapest; Eridania—Divisione Zucchero (Italy); Isi—Industria Saccarifera Italiana Agroindustriale (Italy); Cerestar; Blattman Cerestar Ag (Germany); Cerestar Product Development (Belgium); Cerestar Austria; Cerestar Benelux; Cerestar Deutschland; Cerestar Finland Oy; Cerestar France; Cerestar Iberica; Cerestar Italia; Cerestar Jifa Maize Industry Co., Ltd. (China); Cerestar Scandinavia (Sweden); Pendik Nisasta Sanayi A.S. (Turkey); Central Soya Company (U.S.A.); Canamera (Canada); Central Soya European Proteins (Denmark); Carapelli S.A. (Italy); Eridania Béghin-Say Do Brasil (Cereol Division); Koipe Group S.A. (Spain); Lesieur S.A.; Moyresa; Novaol (Italy); Riso Eurico Italia; Unirea S.A. Iasi (Roumania); Provimi Holding B.V. (Netherlands); Alimental (Argentina); Nutec Southern Africa Ltd (South Africa); Nutron Alimentos Ltda (Brazil); Proaqua Nutricion Sa (Spain); Protector (Switzerland); Provimi Beijing (China); Sca Iberica SA; Sca Nutrition Limited (U.K.); Top Number (U.K.); Vigortone (U.S.A.).

Principal Competitors

Archer-Daniels-Midland Co.; Ag Processing; Agribrands International, Inc.; Ajinomoto Co., Inc.; American Crystal Sugar Company; Associated British Foods PLC; Bestfoods; Bunge International; Cargill, Inc.; Cenex Harvest States; Ceval; Corn Products International; CSR Limited; Goodman Fielder; Goya Foods Inc.; Honen; Imperial Sugar Company; Nisshin Oil Mills; Riceland Foods; Südzucker AG; Tate & Lyle plc; US Sugar.

Further Reading

Hancock, Julia, "Italy's Compart Bids to Absorb Montedison," *Reuters,* February 4, 2000.
Helffer, Jérôme, "Interview: Stefano Meloni, président d'Eridania Béghin-Say," *Journal des Finances,* March 20, 1999.
Sullivan, Ruth, "How Ferruzzi Came Back from the Dead," *European,* January 13, 1995, p. 28.
——, "Novartis Buys Majority of Eridania Seed," *European Report,* July 21, 1999.

—M. L. Cohen

Executive Jet, Inc.

85 Chestnut Ridge Road
Woodbridge, New Jersey 07095
U.S.A.
Telephone: (732) 326-3700
Toll Free: (800) 821-2299
Fax: (732) 326-3737
Web site: http://www.netjets.com

Wholly Owned Subsidiary of Berkshire Hathaway
Incorporated: 1964 as Executive Jet Aviation, Inc.
Employees: 1,000
Sales: $1 billion (1999 est.)
NAIC: 481211 Nonscheduled Chartered Passenger Air
    Transportation; 532411 Commercial Air, Rail, and
    Water Transportation Equipment Rental and Leasing;
    48819 Other Support Activities for Air Transportation

Executive Jet, Inc. has made multimillion-dollar business jets viable for executives and wealthy individuals by selling fractional ownership in the planes. Similar to timeshares in real estate, the company's NetJets program allows participants to buy as little as a sixteenth share in a new aircraft, then pay fixed fees for maintenance and hourly flight usage. More than 1,600 owners, including such entertainers and sports stars as Arnold Schwarzenegger, David Letterman, Pete Sampras, and Tiger Woods, turn to NetJets for an escape from the increasingly crowded airports and unruly passengers of commercial airlines. Executive Jet bought more than a third of all business jets produced worldwide in the late 1990s.

Calculated Origins

Executive Jet Aviation, Inc. (EJA) was started in Columbus, Ohio, in 1964 by a group of retired Air Force generals. Its president, Paul W. Tibbets, Jr., had piloted the plane that dropped the A-bomb on Hiroshima; its board included entertainers Jimmy Stewart and Arthur Godfrey. The company focused on chartering business jets until it was bought by a former mathematics professor in 1986.

Richard T. Santulli was born in Brooklyn, New York, circa 1944. The son of a civil servant, he developed a love for horses early, riding rented mounts in Prospect Park. According to *Business Week,* Santulli studied applied mathematics at the Polytechnic University of New York, earning two M.S. degrees before the arrival of his son in 1967 prompted him to pursue more lucrative work. After a two-year stint with Shell Oil Co., he landed a job at Goldman, Sachs & Co. writing computer-based modeling programs.

Santulli thrived there but left in 1979 after becoming head of the leasing unit and at the verge of being named partner. He was concerned that the high compensation at that level would limit his creative freedom. Santulli then started RTS Capital Services, Inc., which would become the leader in helicopter leasing. In 1982, Santulli cofounded Jayeff Stables, a commercial race horse breeder in Kentucky. He bought Executive Jet in 1984. It was losing money but still had a sterling reputation for service.

As *Business Week* recounted in 1997, the military mindset had produced records of EJA's every trip—a motherlode of data for the mathematician to mine. Santulli spent months bringing the ''time-share'' concept of fractional ownership so often seen in resort properties to business jets. He then made a $4 million down payment on eight Cessna Citation IIs and spent heavily to staff the new enterprise. Thus started the NetJets program in 1986.

Private jets offered much more convenient transportation than scheduled airlines—they could fly on demand to more than 5,000 airports in the United States. They were extremely expensive to operate, however, with high maintenance and fuel costs. The average business jet only made economic sense if flown 400 hours a year—most were flown less than 300. Chartering was best suited for individuals flying 50 hours a year.

NetJets sold the shares, while EJA managed the operations. Although the program initially met with heavy doses of skepticism and resentment from corporate flyers and aircraft manufacturers, the premise was infallible. Cessna became the company's first believer among aircraft makers. By the end of 1987, NetJets was operating 14 planes.

Company Perspectives:

At Executive Jet, our focus is on safety and customer satis-faction. Today we provide more individuals with safe and cost-efficient aviation solutions than anyone else in the world.

With more than 30 years of aviation innovation, experi-ence and success, Executive Jet combines a pioneering leg-acy with an unparalleled record of innovation. A pioneer then and the undisputed leader now, we are #1 in our field . . . and in the air.

During the past five years alone, we've introduced more people and companies to business aviation than the top five business aircraft manufacturers combined.

We pioneered fractional jet ownership with our NetJets program, offering a highly efficient and cost-effective way for companies of nearly any size to meet the demanding travel requirements of their executives. When we introduced NetJets in 1986, Executive Jet implemented our corporate vision: fractional ownership of jet aircraft—first in the United States, then networked around the globe.

NetJets sold one-eighth shares equivalent to about 500 flight hours a year—on a Cessna Citation S2, this cost $330,000 in 1994. Fixed costs added about $60,000 per year, and passenger-carrying flight time cost an additional $1,000 an hour. With fractional ownership, there was also no down time for mainte-nance—this usually amounted to 45 days a year for planes owned outright. Quarter-share owners even had access to more than one plane at a time. Like full owners, fractional owners could deduct for depreciation on their taxes.

Santulli maintained a "core fleet" to deal with the problem of simultaneous requests and guaranteed a plane anywhere in the United States within a four-hour notice (later increased to six hours for one-eighth shareholders). The *Economist* noted that the jets could even be customized at the last minute with magnetic logos and monogrammed seat cushions.

A Positive Rate of Climb in the 1990s

When Santulli bought EJA in 1986, Wall Street was flooded with wealth and private planes were the favorite perk of many well-paid executives. The recession of the early 1990s, how-ever, brought boardroom scrutiny to high-visibility expendi-tures such as business jets. EJA benefited from the resulting wave of corporate cost-cutting. Still, the company nearly went bankrupt during this time; Santulli had personally signed for $125 million in bank loans. EJA posted $65 million in revenues in 1992; business lifted in 1993 when the company began offering larger aircraft. The company broke even the next year. The list of clientele reached 220 in 1994. Revenues reportedly tripled in the mid-1990s, although the privately owned com-pany did not release specific figures.

By this time, competition had surfaced in Europe, in theory at least. Air London International began timeshares through its JetCo service before actually buying any planes. Bombardier Aerospace Group and AMR Combs Inc., the charter sibling of American Airlines, introduced the Business JetSolutions pro-gram in May 1994. For its part, EJA entered a partnership with Gulfstream, letting that maker handle the marketing through its Gulfstream Shares program.

NetJets accounted for 85 percent of EJA's business; the company continued to offer charter services. Most of the 290 customers lived in the triangle marked by Chicago, New York, and Miami. Company headquarters were located in Montvale, New Jersey, while operations were based in Columbus, Ohio, where EJA had 340 employees.

Goldman, Sachs & Co. took a 25 percent shareholding in the company in the autumn of 1995. EJA operated more than 40 jets and had become the biggest customer of Gulfstream Aerospace, Cessna Aircraft Co., and Raytheon Co. The company had about 400 employees overall at the beginning of 1996. Vincent Santulli joined his younger brother at Executive Jet later in the year. He had previously developed his own electronics com-pany, PortsSystems.

Entering 1997, EJ employed more than 500 and fielded 80 airplanes. It planned to spend $375 million to expand its fleet to 100—more planes (though much smaller ones) than Air Can-ada, the *Columbus Observer* noted. EJA had revenues of more than $500 million in fiscal year 1996–97. Its customer base had grown to 700, mostly through referrals, according to *Business Week*. Tennis star Pete Sampras gave NetJets one of its most glowing testimonials, crediting the program with extending his playing career by one or two years through sheer convenience.

Although GE was its largest customer, most of EJA's clients had never owned business planes before; they were "concept buyers." About 800 companies and individuals were fractional owners in the United States, according to the National Business Aviation Association figures reported in the *New York Times*. Most of the 11,500 business jets and turboprops were owned by 8,000 companies.

At the time, a one-eighth share in a Cessna Citation S2 cost $305,000 and allowed for 100 occupied flight hours for five years. The plane sold for $2.3 million outright. NetJets also had begun offering sixteenth shares. The price was $389,000 for a sixteenth of a Citation 5 Ultra, a plane that sold for $6 million whole in 1997. A quarter share of a top-of-the-line, 13-seat Gulfstream IV cost $6.8 million.

EJA ordered more than $2 billion worth of aircraft in 1997. Even as Raytheon Aircraft was preparing to launch its own fractional ownership service, in May 1997 EJA gave the com-pany its largest order ever—20 Hawker 800XPs worth $210 million. Raytheon's CEO, Arthur Wegner, praised Santulli as a pioneer who "demonstrated tremendous vision," uplifting the entire business jet industry. A few months later, EJA ordered $400 million worth of Cessna Citations Excels (to be delivered over five years)—the largest order for business jets ever.

A joint venture with Boeing Business Jets and GE was announced in October 1997. The Boeing Business Jet (BBJ) in development was based on the successful Boeing 737 medium-haul airliner, modified to seat fewer people (12 to 50) and have the range for intercontinental trips. Costing a bit more than

Key Dates:

1964: Executive Jet Aviation, Inc. charter service started by retired Air Force generals.
1986: Richard T. Santulli introduces NetJets after buying EJA.
1994: EJA begins to break even.
1995: Goldman Sachs takes a minority shareholding.
1996: NetJets Europe is launched.
1998: Berkshire Hathaway buys EJA.

other top-end corporate jets such as the Gulfstream V, the BBJ offered three times the interior space (807 square feet).

EJA hired 240 pilots in 1997 and planned to add 260 employees in 1998, 200 of them pilots, giving the company 930 employees in Ohio. The number of employees exceeded 1,000; half were pilots. Commercial airlines also were expanding, making flight personnel scarce. The company also was investing $16 million to set up new facilities at a former McDonnell Douglas plant in Columbus.

New Horizons in the Late 1990s

In the spring of 1998, a group of Middle East investors bought a dozen Gulfstream IVs, to enter service in early 1999. Gulfstream Shares also was pitching the 6,500 nautical mile range of the Gulfstream V for the region. The Cessna Citation 10 was another model slated for use within the region. EJA signed contracts for more than $1 billion worth of new aircraft and maintenance from Gulfstream in October 1998, expanding their relationship significantly.

Minority shareholder Goldman, Sachs was urging Santulli to take the company public to raise money for expansion. In July 1998, however, Warren Buffett's Berkshire Hathaway Inc. announced that it was buying EJA for $725 million in stock and cash. Called "the most astute investor of the 20th century," and the world's second richest man after Bill Gates, Buffett had been an avid EJA customer since 1995. Berkshire Hathaway's superior credit rating lowered EJA's interest rates, and the company joined an esteemed portfolio including Coca-Cola Co., Gillette, and Walt Disney.

After buying the company, Buffett, who had appeared in Executive Jet advertising before, spoke at high profile gatherings in expensive hotels to pitch the concept to celebrities. At the time, an eighth share in a Cessna Citation V Ultra cost $835,000 plus $7,608 a month for maintenance. The owner could fly 100 hours a year at $1,242 an hour.

Executive Jets was on its way to billing $900 million in revenues for the year. Santulli continued to run the company after the acquisition. He applied his math acumen to breeding horses as well, and developed a stable said to be worth $60 million.

Executive Jet had entered the European theater in 1996 but found it much more complex. Airport operations were much less flexible there. Buffett stated that only 1,100 of 9,000 business jets around the world were based in Europe, making the market there seem fertile for the fractional ownership concept. NetJets Europe had 40 customers and ten planes in April 1999; by the end of the year, it had 70 customers and 17 planes. Virtually all of the European owners also took advantage of the ability to use their shares in the U.S. NetJets program as well.

Executive Jet gave Raytheon another record-setting order in June 1999, for 50 Hawker Horizon business jets worth $2 billion. Bombardier's FlexJet fleet reached 100 planes in 1999 and was gaining rapidly. Still, Executive Jet remained the king of the sky. Its total fleet was 265 planes in early 2000, with more than 500 on order. A planned expansion into Asia glowed on the company's horizon.

Principal Divisions

Executive Jet Charter; Executive Jet International; Executive Jet Management; NetJets Europe; NetJets Middle East.

Principal Competitors

FlexJet; TravelAir.

Further Reading

Bianco, Anthony, "What's Better Than a Private Plane? A Semiprivate Plane," *Business Week,* July 21, 1997, p. 52.
"Buffett Makes Push for Jets in Europe," *Omaha World-Herald,* April 14, 1999, p. 22.
Carter, Ron, "Aiming for the Clouds, Executive Jet Stakes Future on Business Flights," *Columbus Dispatch,* January 2, 1997, p. 1B.
——, "Executive Jet, Boeing Flying in Formation," *Columbus Dispatch,* October 22, 1997, p. 1C.
——, "Executive Jet Future Soars on New Order," *Columbus Dispatch,* June 17, 1997, p. 1F.
——, "Executive Jet Has High Hopes," *Columbus Dispatch,* May 21, 1996, p. 1D.
——, "High-Flying Venture," *Columbus Dispatch,* October 2, 1995, p. 1.
——, "Hiring Flies High in Plan at Executive Jet," *Columbus Dispatch,* October 2, 1997, p. 1B.
——, "Stars in the Sky: Executive Jet Becoming Transportation of Choice of the Rich and Famous," *Columbus Dispatch,* December 12, 1999, p. 1F.
Gerena-Morales, Rafael, "Warren Buffett to Buy Montvale, N.J. Executive Jet Inc.," *Record,* July 24, 1998.
Minard, Lawrence, "The Great Santullis," *Forbes Global,* November 1, 1999.
Moskal, Brian S., "Up, Up, and Away," *Industry Week,* June 19, 1995, p. 17.
Nussbaum, Debra, "Spending It: Owning a Fraction of a Jet," *New York Times,* July 27, 1997, p. 10.
"The Other Mile-High Club," *Economist,* September 24, 1994, p. 72.
Phillips, Edward H., "Low Cost Key to Fractional Ownership," *Aviation Week & Space Technology,* September 22, 1997, p. 63.
Rasmussen, Jim, "Omaha, Neb.-Based Berkshire Hathaway to Buy New Jersey Jet Firm," *Omaha World-Herald,* July 23, 1998.
Velocci, Anthony L., Jr., "Fractional Ownership Apt to Validate BBJ Market," *Aviation Week & Space Technology,* p. 71.
Zuckerman, Laurence, "Private Jets for (More of) the People," *New York Times,* June 27, 1999, p. 2.

—Frederick C. Ingram

Fairfield Communities, Inc.

8669 Commodity Circle
Orlando, Florida 32819
U.S.A.
Telephone: (407) 370-5200
Fax: (407) 370-5143
Web site: http://www.efairfield.com

Public Company
Incorporated: 1969
Employees: 5,500
Sales: $491.73 million (1999)
Stock Exchanges: New York
Ticker Symbol: FFD
NAIC: 23311 Land Subdividers and Land Development

Fairfield Communities, Inc. is the third largest vacation ownership company in the United States, selling time-share ownership interests through its point-based vacation system, FairShare Plus. Fairfield operates 33 resorts in 12 states and the Bahamas, which are frequented by the company's approximately 280,000 members. The company's vacation ownership interests are generally in resort locations featuring fully furnished accommodations and near such amenities as golf courses, swimming pools, beaches, marinas, tennis courts, and other recreational facilities. Through affiliations with several worldwide vacation exchange companies, Fairfield also offers access to approximately 2,500 additional domestic and international resorts, including Hawaii, the Caribbean, Mexico, Europe, Asia, and Africa.

Origins

C. Randolph Warner triggered the events that led to Fairfield's formation when he purchased 4,000 acres in 1966 in his native Arkansas. A former editor of the *Harvard Law Review* and an attorney by training, Warner developed a resort site on the property, located near Greers Ferry Lake. The business proved promising, prompting Warner to solicit the help of George Donovan, who ran a successful computer-leasing firm. Fairfield, incorporated in 1969, would help pioneer the vacation ownership industry in the United States.

Additional resort locations were added to Fairfield's portfolio during the ensuing years, but Warner did not begin selling ownership interests in his resorts until more than a decade after buying the property on Greers Ferry Lake. Fairfield's signature and pioneering time-share concept, FairShare, was introduced in 1978 at Fairfield Mountains in Lake Lure, North Carolina. Under the guidelines of FairShare, Fairfield members purchased an ownership stake in a particular resort property. Ownership of each property was divided into 52 one-week fixed intervals, allowing Fairfield members to spend a week at the particular resort in which they owned an ownership stake. The price of each ownership interest was determined by the value of the particular resort and by the season. The purchase of high-demand vacation time cost more than less popular times of the year. The FairShare plan was simple yet novel, drawing its inspiration from the European concept of fractional ownership that debuted during the 1950s.

The novelty of FairShare in the United States helped Warner build a bustling business that produced steadily rising profits during the late 1970s and early 1980s. With financing partly provided by junk bonds, Warner established a stable of resorts whose brochures attracted scores of new Fairfield members. By 1984, the company controlled 70,000 acres at more than a dozen locations in ten states and the Virgin Islands, which produced a record-setting $16 million in profits. Warner, who had seen his business grow tremendously during a short period, had already decided to retire by the time 1984's record results were announced. In June 1983, he appointed his longtime associate Donovan as president of Fairfield, who assumed control midway through the company's most ambitious expansion phase in its history. Between 1981 and 1986, Fairfield increased the number of its resort properties from seven to 29, adding retirement communities, time-share resorts, and a ski lodge to a stable of locations stretching from South Carolina to southern California.

Company Perspectives:

Today, over 260,000 families enjoy the Fairfield lifestyle. From the excitement of Myrtle Beach, South Carolina to the shores of California. From the star-filled stages of Branson, Missouri, to the snow-powdered slopes of Pagosa, Colorado. Fairfield has resorts in America's most scenic locations. Golf. Tennis. Fishing. Boating. Swimming indoors and out. Hiking. Dining. Sightseeing. Horseback riding. Activities and entertainment for every age and interest. Fairfield members can even vacation at more than 2,500 additional resorts around the world through our international exchange affiliations. Or they can make themselves at home at one of the several Fairfield resorts that offers homesites. Whatever our members choose, Fairfield offers a Personal Vacation System.

Financial Problems Emerge in the Mid-1980s

As Fairfield exponentially increased its stature, however, serious problems were beginning to surface. Some industry pundits and Fairfield insiders cast part of the blame on Donovan who, prior to his appointment as president, had proven himself a tireless worker but subsequently demonstrated a penchant for corporate extravagances. He persuaded company officials to purchase a corporate Citation Jet, which he would board from his Jaguar. Donovan also refused to move to Little Rock, Arkansas, where Fairfield was based, ignoring a previously agreed upon plan to relocate from his office in Knoxville, Tennessee, once appointed president. Instead, Donovan abruptly moved to Atlanta, Georgia, and within a year, steered Fairfield headlong into the Florida resort home-building market. Within two years of Donovan's presidential appointment, corporate expenses reeled out of control. Selling costs and corporate overhead rose to $85 million in 1985, or 25 percent of sales, a percentage that Warner deemed excessive. Further, the company was saddled with $370 million of debt, a total that exceeded Fairfield's annual sales of $320 million. By December 1985, Donovan was forced to leave and Warner, who shelved his plans for retirement, returned to rescue a floundering company.

Warner faced the daunting task of trying to immediately cure profound problems. In an interview with *Forbes* magazine in September 19, 1988, he offered some insight into Fairfield's miscue during the first half of the 1980s. "We were trying to build a national resort community that would get us within 500 miles of all the major metropolitan centers of the United States," he said. "But we didn't have the trained management to take on that many projects that quickly. We thought we were invincible." Warner had yet to appreciate how vulnerable his company was as he began implementing sweeping turnaround measures in 1986. Among the changes, the salaries of senior management were reduced by ten percent, 20 percent of the company's 2,600-person workforce was laid off, commercial properties in Colorado and Arizona were sold, and corporate offices in Atlanta and Jacksonville, Florida, were closed. Warner also hired a new chief financial officer known for being a corporate turnaround specialist, but little progress was

achieved during the first year. By the end of 1986, the company had set a new record by losing $17.6 million.

Warner redoubled his efforts in 1987. He decided to liquidate Fairfield's home building operations that included ten properties in Florida, Arizona, and Colorado. In May 1988, he reached an agreement to sell five of the company's six remaining Florida housing projects. After the massive restructuring effort, however, the telltale signs of a company nearing insolvency remained. Selling costs and corporate overhead in 1988 totaled $84 million, distressingly close to the total registered three years earlier. Debt stood at $400 million. In 1989, the company set another alarming record, registering the worst financial year in its history by posting a $24.8 million loss. As grave as it was, Fairfield's condition was about to become much worse. Warner had yet to contend with the aftershock of the $500 billion collapse of the savings and loan industry. For Fairfield, the result was disastrous.

Part of Fairfield's rapid growth during the late 1970s and early 1980s was fueled by junk bond financing provided by the infamous Michael Milken and Drexel Burnham Lambert. The company's first junk bonds were issued in 1977, inaugurating a practice that would continue for the next 13 years, ultimately totaling $93 million between 1977 and 1990. When Milken and Drexel captured national newspaper headlines in 1989 because of their financial collapse, Fairfield found it decidedly more difficult to refinance its junk bonds when, as *Arkansas Business* reported on November 12, 1990, "Mike Milken was no longer a phone call away." To make matters worse, one of the company's principal lenders, First National Bank of Boston, was mired in its own financial problems. The bank was plagued by more than $400 million in troubled real estate loans, prompting its directors to reform the company's lending practices. As a result, First National severed Fairfield's $45 million line of credit in August 1990, causing Fairfield's liquidity to evaporate. Roughly a month later, Fairfield, stripped of cash, missed a $3.8 million junk bond payment. Warner was left with few options. On October 3, 1990, Fairfield declared bankruptcy, seeking Chapter 11 protection from a 226-page list of more than 2,000 creditors. It was the largest filing in the state's history.

Fairfield Starts Anew in 1992

Nearly two years after shrouding itself in the veil of bankruptcy, Fairfield emerged from Chapter 11 protection after exchanging much of its bondholder debt for equity. The new era in Fairfield's history began in September 1992. By the end of its first full year after the 1990 debacle, annual sales reached $91 million—a fraction of the annual total collected during the 1980s—but the company was profitable, registering $7.1 million in earnings. The new version of Fairfield comprised 14 resorts frequented by more than 130,000 members and a new time-share plan called FairShare Plus. Unlike its predecessor, FairShare Plus offered Fairfield members considerable flexibility in arranging their vacation time through the adoption of a point-based system. Members' ownership stakes were assigned symbolic points that could be used for vacation stays of a few days, a week, or longer, in any season members chose. The points, or credits, were renewed annually and, in some cases, could be borrowed from the next year's allotment. Fairfield's new marketing plan, like others implemented by other time-share companies, no longer restricted members' choices to a fixed week in fixed seasons.

By 1995, Fairfield, having fully recovered from the travesty of the 1980s, had 15 resort locations in operation. Among the properties were resorts in Orlando, Florida; Branson, Missouri; Myrtle Beach, South Carolina; Williamsburg, Virginia; Nashville, Tennessee; and Pagosa Springs, Colorado, but aside from these resorts and the company's nine other properties, Fairfield members had thousands of other locations to choose from. Through affiliations with several worldwide vacation exchange companies, Fairfield offered access to approximately 2,500 additional domestic and international resorts, including Hawaii, the Caribbean, Mexico, Europe, Asia, and Africa.

The number of vacation destinations available to Fairfield members grew dramatically during the latter half of the 1990s, when the company expanded as aggressively as it had during the early 1980s. Based on the total properties in operation in 1995, the number of Fairfield-operated resorts more than doubled by the end of the decade, with a handful of the new resorts added through a major acquisition in 1997. In a transaction valued at $240 million, Fairfield acquired Fort Lauderdale-based Vacation Break U.S.A. Vacation Break owned and operated four developments in southern Florida, a time-share in Orlando, and a hotel in the Bahamas, giving Fairfield 20 time-share properties comprising 3,000 units. Aside from providing Fairfield with a heavy presence in southern Florida—an area estimated to be worth $100 million in sales—the acquisition of Vacation Break placed Fairfield among the four largest publicly held, time-share companies in the United States. Although there were major costs associated with the acquisition, Fairfield's stock value soared during the year, increasing an impressive 175 percent.

The acquisition of Vacation Break was credited with Fairfield's surge into the small pack of the country's elite time-share companies. After moving its headquarters from Little Rock to Orlando in 1999, the company became the third largest time-share organization in the country, trailing only Marriott Vacation Club and Sunterra Corp., both of which were also based in Orlando. By the end of the 1990s, there were 33 Fairfield resorts

located in 12 states and the Bahamas, with additional properties under development. In 1999, the company began sales operations on a start-up basis at six resorts still under development. The resorts, which were expected to be completed by late 2000 and early 2001 were located in Sedona, Arizona; Durango, Colorado; Daytona Beach, Florida; Las Vegas, Nevada; Gatlinburg, Tennessee; and Destin, Florida.

As Fairfield entered the 21st century, an announcement in January 2000 suggested the beginning of a new era for the company. Late in the month, Miami, Florida-based Carnival Corporation announced it was going to purchase Fairfield in a $775 million deal. Carnival, an operator of 45 cruise ships under the names Carnival Cruise Line, Holland America Line, Windstar Cruises, and Cunard Line Limited, had been a partner with Fairfield since 1996, offering its cruises to Fairfield members. Fairfield members were able to purchase cruises through FairShare Plus, but Carnival wanted to establish a reciprocal relationship with Fairfield. Under the terms of the proposed merger, Fairfield would become a wholly owned subsidiary of Carnival, allowing Carnival to market its cruises to Fairfield while Fairfield marketed its resorts to Carnival customers. Within a month, however, the deal collapsed. After watching his company's shares plunge nearly 35 percent in value during the four weeks after the merger was announced, Carnival's chairman withdrew from the transaction. His decision, as quoted by *Knight-Ridder/Tribune Business News* on February 25, 2000, ''was based on recent disruptions within the stock market that have resulted in a negative impact on Carnival's shares.''

In the wake of the scuttled merger, Fairfield pressed ahead with the development of its resorts. The company, after years of struggling with profound financial problems, faced its future with justifiable optimism. Its leading position within the industry rested on a solid financial foundation, one capable of supporting expansion in the decade ahead and underpinning the company's bid to make Fairfield resorts the choice of vacationers throughout the country.

Principal Subsidiaries

Fairfield Communities, Inc.; Apex Marketing, Inc.; Fairfield Acceptance Corporation-Nevada; Fairfield Capital Corporation; Fairfield Funding Corporation, II; Fairfield Receivables Corporation; Fairfield Bay, Inc.; Fairfield Flagstaff Realty, Inc.; Fairfield Glade, Inc.; Fairfield Homes Construction Company; Fairfield Management Services, Inc.; Fairfield Mortgage Acceptance Corporation; Fairfield Mortgage Corporation; Fairfield Mountains, Inc.; Fairfield Myrtle Beach, Inc.; Fairfield Pagosa Realty, Inc.; Fairfield Sapphire Valley, Inc.; Fairfield Vacations Resorts, Inc.; Fairfield Virgin Islands, Inc.; Imperial Life Insurance Company; Ocean Ranch Development, Inc.; Palm Resort Group, Inc.; Shirley Realty Company; Suntree Development Company; The Florida Companies; Vacation Break, U.S.A., Inc.; Atlantic Marketing Realty, Inc.; Resorts Title, Inc.; Sea Gardens Beach and Tennis Resort, Inc.; Serenity Yacht Club, Inc.; Vacation Break at Ocean Ranch, Inc.; Vacation Break Management, Inc.; Vacation Break Resorts at Palm Aire, Inc.; Vacation Break Resorts at Star Island, Inc.; Vacation Break Resorts, Inc.; Vacation Break Welcome Centers, Inc.;

Vacation Break International Limited (Bahamas); Vacation Break Marketing Company Limited (Bahamas).

Principal Competitors

Sunterra Corp.; Marriott International, Inc.; Cendant Corporation.

Further Reading

Barker, Time, "Orlando, Fla., Solidifies Time-Share Lead," *Knight-Ridder/Tribune Business News,* May 17, 1999, p. OKRB991370ED.

Corzo, Cynthia, "Carnival Abandons Plan to Acquire Orlando, Fla., Time-Share Resort," *Knight-Ridder/Tribune Business News,* February 25, 2000, p. ITEM00057082.

Schifrin, Matthew, "Fairfield the Fair," *Forbes,* June 20, 1994, p. 272.

Taylor, John H., " 'We Thought We Were Invincible,' " *Forbes,* September 19, 1988, p. 72.

"Thank Goodness for Time-Sharing," *Financial World,* February 15, 1983, p. 30.

Waldon, George, "Real Estate Stocks Soar, Apartment Projects Mushroom," *Arkansas Business,* December 29, 1997, p. 20.

Walker, Wythe, Jr., "Fairfield Fights for Its Life," *Arkansas Business,* November 12, 1990, p. 20.

—Jeffrey L. Covell

Ferrari S.p.A.

Via Emilia Est, 1163
41100 Modena
Italy
Telephone: (0536) 949-111
Fax: (0536) 949-259
Web site: http://www.ferrari.it

90 Percent Owned Subsidiary of Fiat S.p.A.
Incorporated: 1960 as Società Esercizio Fabbriche
   Automobili e Corse Ferrari—SEFAC S.p.A
Employees: 1,900
Sales: L 758 million (US$760.8 million) (1999)
NAIC: 336111 Automobile Manufacturing

Ferrari S.p.A. designs and manufactures sports cars that are synonymous with speed and performance. Ferrari sports cars are among the most prestigious automobiles in the world, along with Porsche, Maserati, Alfa Romeo, Jaguar, and Lamborghini. The name Ferrari is still venerated on the international racing circuit, and many automotive experts regard the Ferrari GTO as one of the most exotic sports cars ever made. Only 35 Ferrari GTOs were built, and some of them have been sold as collectors' items for more than $10 million. About 3,800 Ferraris are sold each year, at prices starting at $120,000 apiece. Ferrari S.p.A., which has been affiliated with Fiat S.p.A. since 1969, also owns the Maserati brand. About 20 percent of Ferraris and Maseratis are sold in North America, with the second largest market being Germany, at around 18 percent.

Early 20th Century: Enzo Ferrari, Test Driver and Racer

The company's founder, Enzo Ferrari, was born in 1898 in Modena, Italy, to a lower-middle-class family. Lacking a formal education, he was given the job of shoeing horses for the Italian Army during World War I. After the war, he traveled to Turin and applied for work at Fiat, already one of the most prominent automobile manufacturers in Europe. Unceremoniously rejected, Ferrari nurtured a grudge against Fiat that developed into a driving ambition. Determined to break into the automotive industry, Ferrari began to frequent the bars and cafes around Turin where famous race car drivers sought their entertainment. In one of these bars Ferrari met Ugo Sivocci, a test driver for a new automobile manufacturer named Costruzioni Meccaniche Nazionalia (CMN). Sivocci hired Ferrari as his assistant and the young man competed in his first race in October 1919.

Ferrari did not remain with CMN for very long, and soon joined Alfa Romeo, located in Portello on the outskirts of Milan. Founded in 1909 by Cavaliere Ugo Stella, Alfa manufactured a line of automobiles and sponsored cars for the racing circuit. Ferrari was hired by Alfa Romeo as a test driver and also was contracted by the company to sell its cars. During the early 1920s Ferrari crisscrossed the Italian roads between Milan and Turin selling automobiles, buying parts, delivering new cars to wealthy customers, spying on Fiat, and racing Alfas.

During these years Ferrari earned his laurels as a race car driver. In 1923 he won the Chilometro Lanciato at Geneva, the Circuito del Polesine at Robigo, and the annual race at Ravenna. In 1924 he won the Pescara, run on the Adriatic coast. The death in 1925 of popular Antonio Ascari, Alfa Romeo's premier driver, led the company to cancel all racing competition out of respect for the fallen employee. Disappointed that his own racing career was interrupted, Ferrari redirected his energy and focused on developing his distributorship for Alfa Romeo. By the end of 1925, Ferrari had expanded his holdings into a large dealership and service center. By 1927 he was behind the wheel of a racing car once again, and he won the Modena race and the Circuito di Alessandria that year. In 1928 Ferrari repeated as champion in both of these races.

1929 Through World War II: Early Years of the Ferrari Company

As Alfa Romeo's fortunes declined during the late 1920s and early 1930s, it was taken over by the Istituto di Ricostruzione Industriale (IRI), a government organization formed to assist companies experiencing financial difficulties. As a consequence of this takeover, Alfa Romeo withdrew its direct involvement from the racing car circuit, except for the international Grand Prix races. Ferrari, however, was not to be denied,

Key Dates:

1929: Enzo Ferrari founds Società Anonima Scuderia Ferrari to buy and race cars.

1940: Enzo Ferrari ends his association with Scuderia Ferrari and establishes Auto Avio Costruzione, which was initially involved in making aircraft engines.

1947: The design and manufacture of Ferrari sports cars begins.

1960: Company is restructured as a public company and incorporated under the name Società Esercizio Fabbriche Automobili e Corse Ferrari—SEFAC S.p.A.

Early 1960s: Ford agrees to purchase the company but the deal falls apart.

1965: Company is renamed Ferrari S.p.A. Esercizio Fabbriche Automobili e Corse.

1969: Fiat purchases 50 percent interest in Ferrari and takes control of passenger car operation; Enzo Ferrari retains other 50 percent and maintains control of motor racing operation.

1988: Enzo Ferrari dies; Fiat increases its stake in Ferrari to 90 percent.

1989: Company is renamed Ferrari S.p.A.

1992: Luca Cordero di Montezemolo is hired to head Ferrari, and launches massive overhaul.

1997: Fiat sells 50 percent stake in Maserati to Ferrari, which gains management control over Maserati.

1999: Ferrari gains full ownership of Maserati.

and, parlaying his contacts with the Americans at Shell Oil, the Germans at Bosch ignition systems, and his fellow Italians at Pirelli tires, he formed the Società Anonima Scuderia Ferrari, a stable of racing cars and drivers dedicated to furthering the sport of competitive racing, in 1929. Ferrari promised his fellow investors that his operation would not only buy and race cars, but also build high-performance automobiles for the sports car enthusiast some time in the future. Alfa Romeo contracted the new Scuderia to act as its official representative in some races.

With the increasing strength of the Fascist Party under the leadership of Benito Mussolini during the 1930s, Ferrari decided to become a member of the Fascist Party. His association with the Fascists dovetailed with his ambition to run Alfa Romeo's racing program, which, of course, was operating under the auspices of the government-controlled IRI. Ferrari's ambitions were frustrated, however, with the arrival of Wifredo Ricart, a Spanish engineer hired by IRI to revitalize Alfa Romeo and return the company to the winner's circle on the competitive race car circuit. Ferrari's personal dislike of Ricart was evident from the beginning, but increased dramatically when he discovered that Ricart was behind Alfa Romeo's decision to buy 80 percent of the Scuderia Ferrari and return administration of the racing program to the company's office in Portello. With acrimony and bitterness compounded during every meeting between the two men, and after a particularly unpleasant exchange in which Ricart likened himself to a genius, Ferrari decided it was best to end his association with the Spanish engineer and Alfa Romeo.

Ferrari's parting agreement with Alfa Romeo stipulated that he could neither use the name of Scuderia Ferrari nor engage in racing for four years. For this, he received a generous severance package, and he wasted no time in establishing Auto Avio Costruzione, a custom machine shop that initially manufactured small aircraft engines for planes, in 1940. The famous Ferrari symbol of the prancing horse first appeared during this time on company letterhead and marketing brochures. With Italy's entry into World War II in 1940, Ferrari's factory soon was producing machine tools for the Axis armies, including sophisticated hydraulic grinders. Although his company profited from its association with the Axis Powers, Ferrari was impatient because the war years interrupted international motor racing.

Postwar Entry into Car Design and Manufacturing

After the war, Ferrari was approached by a group of car enthusiasts who convinced him to manufacture the 125, a new car for the racing circuit. In March 1947, the prototype 125 took its initial test drive, and later in the year entered and won the Circuito del Valentino in Turin before the wealthy and elite of Italian society. Soon after the race, such dignitaries as Count Bruno Sterzi and Count Soave Besana of Milan and the Russian Prince Igor Troubetzkoy (husband of Barbara Hutton, the heiress to the Woolworth fortune) were knocking on Ferrari's door in Modena to purchase his cars. By December, Enzo Ferrari was manufacturing a limited number of high-performance sports cars. Ferrari's first cars, such as the Tipo 166 Spider Corsa, were triple-purpose vehicles. They could be used as sports cars on the public road, as competitive sports cars in races such as the Mille Miglia, and as entries in Formula Two racing events (with fenders and other equipment removed).

By the summer of 1948, Ferrari's automobile designers had completed work on a nonracing car. This *gran turismo* automobile would be made with windows, heaters, a top, and leather upholstery. Each car body was to be hand-made by artisans with traditionally exquisite Italian styling and craftsmanship and delivered to distributors in batches of less than ten automobiles at a time. When the car was finally delivered, the customer would have the final decision regarding paint color, upholstery, and external trim. Until Ferrari was taken over by Fiat in 1969, all cars made by the company were manufactured by this method and, hence, no two cars were identical.

During the early 1950s, Ferrari cars were ordered by the international elite, including the Aga Khan, King Leopold of Belgium, the Shah of Iran, Juan Perón, Crown Prince Faisal of Saudi Arabia, and members of both the Dulles and Du Pont families. The company listed dealer franchises in London, Rome, Zurich, Algiers, Casablanca, Melbourne, Florence, Brussels, Montevideo, Sao Paulo, Paris, and New York. Although Ferrari engines were temperamental and frequently overheated, the combination of their nastiness with their brilliant bodywork and designs created an unparalleled mystique. Alfa Romeos, Maseratis, and Jaguars seemed to pale in comparison.

Despite the growing success of his commercial enterprise, Ferrari remained obsessed with racing, with most of the money he earned from selling sports cars in Europe and America used to fund the annual Grand Prix and Formula One races. The fortunes of race car sponsors were volatile, however: in 1952 cars designed and manufactured by Ferrari won 16 of the 17 races the company had entered; in 1957, Ferrari won only a few of the numerous races on the international circuit. Nevertheless, by the end of the 1950s Enzo Ferrari had become a national institution in motor racing, a kind of quasi-official representative of the Italian nation in every race. Ferrari began to believe the press reports about his responsibility in carrying Italy's banner in international racing, and he devoted more and more time to his racing team. While most Italians celebrated Christmas and Easter Sunday, Ferrari was conducting business to improve his chances of winning the next race.

In 1960 the firm was restructured as a public corporation under the name Società Esercizio Fabbriche Automobili e Corse—SEFAC S.p.A. Approximately 40 percent of all Ferrari cars were exported to North America, primarily for the American market. The cars were stripped down and detuned versions of the company's racers, and even though the money made from selling these automobiles to wealthy Americans allowed Ferrari to pursue his motor racing dreams, Ferrari was indifferent to almost every aspect of the manufacturing process.

Ferrari made it known in the industry that he wanted a large firm to take over the administration and management of his factories so he could devote all his energy to racing, and in the early 1960s, Ford Motor Company made overtures to the Italian carmaker. In return for rights to the Ferrari name, trademark, patents, future technical developments, and 90 percent of the company's stock, Ford agreed to purchase the sports car manufacturer for $18 million. The acquisition of Ferrari by Ford developed into a national issue, with the Italian press leading the opposition to the deal as a matter of national honor. Negotiations proceeded smoothly until Ferrari insisted on maintaining complete control over the racing operation. Ford executives balked and could not accept a completely independent operation working within the organization. The deal between Ford and Ferrari, which appeared so promising, was suddenly canceled. In 1965, meanwhile, the company changed its name to Ferrari S.p.A. Esercizio Fabbriche Automobili e Corse.

Sports car manufacturers such as Porsche, Jaguar, and the brand new Lamborghini began to chip away at Ferrari's market in both Europe and the United States, and the grand master's continued indifference to passenger car production at his own firm finally took its toll: the designs of 330GTs, 275GTBs, and other models were downright ugly, and production was shoddy. Car bodies were inclined to rust easily and component parts were badly or cheaply tooled. U.S. distributors soon discovered that the Ferrari sports cars of the late 1960s were almost impossible to sell. Between 1968 and 1969, car sales dropped from 729 to 619 units. Lacking funds for expansion, and with Ferrari's insistence on competing in many races at once rather than concentrating his limited resources on, for example, the Formula One competition, the company began to suffer financially. Yet Ferrari himself was a prisoner of his own public image—he was the focal point, the icon, of a nation hungry for respect in the international community. Ferrari realized that massive amounts of money were required for the company to survive, so he turned to Fiat for help. Since Ferrari had harbored such a lifelong dislike of Fiat, it was an ironic turn of events.

Late 1960s Through Late 1980s: Enter Fiat, Exit Enzo

On June 21, 1969, Fiat purchased Ferrari for $11 million. According to the terms of the agreement, Fiat gained 50 percent of Ferrari stock and would manage the passenger car operation, while Ferrari himself retained the other 50 percent and complete control over the motor racing operation. Fiat immediately took over the daily administration of designing, manufacturing, marketing, and selling Ferrari's road cars, and invested millions in modernizing the company's factory and expanding its production. By 1970, under the new Fiat management, production of Ferrari passenger cars had increased to more than 1,000, and by the end of the decade production had reached 2,000. Fiat doubled the size of the Ferrari factory and was committed to making Ferrari cars the focus of its international marketing.

During the 1970s and 1980s, the collection of Ferrari automobiles by car enthusiasts reached the intensity of a quasi-religious experience. Americans and Europeans alike paid enormous sums of money for the older Ferrari racing machines, and one Frenchman even converted his entire 375-acre estate outside Paris into a shrine for Ferrari automobiles. Enzo Ferrari was not the slightest bit interested in the deification of his cars and, more often than not, displayed contempt for the individuals who bought Ferrari cars as a status symbol. After selling the passenger car operation to Fiat, for nearly two decades the old man remained engrossed by the fortunes of his racing team. When Enzo Ferrari died on August 15, 1988, the Italian population went into mourning. The last of the automotive giants had passed away. Shortly after his death, Fiat management announced that the Ferrari factory works would increase production and that the last remnants of handcrafted car production would be gradually phased out. Fiat increased its stake in the nearly bankrupt Ferrari to 90 percent in 1988 (Enzo's son Piero Ferrari retained the other ten percent), injecting some much needed capital, and the following year the company was renamed Ferrari S.p.A.

1990s: Reviving a Legend

The early 1990s were particularly difficult years for the world auto industry, with recessions plaguing both the U.S. and European economies. Ferrari felt the effects as well, with sales plunging to 2,289 cars by 1993, half the number sold in the 1980s. Fiat hired Luca Cordero di Montezemolo as chairman and managing director of Ferrari in 1992. Di Montezemolo, a marketing whiz with previous stints at both Fiat and Ferrari (he managed Ferrari's Formula One racing team in the 1970s) as well as at liquor company Cinzano, had most recently been in charge of organizing the World Cup Soccer championship held in Italy in 1990. The championship was a huge financial and public relations success, with much of the credit going to di Montezemolo.

Di Montezemolo quickly overhauled nearly every area of the company's operation. He spent $80 million modernizing its factories. The production and design processes were revamped with the help of engineers and designers hired from Fiat. Labor concessions were won that improved factory productivity. The company's product line was completely turned over. At the beginning of the decade the firm was making only two models, "with two seats, very uncomfortable, very extreme," according to di Montezemolo. In the mid-1990s, nine new models replaced the two outdated ones. Customers had a wider range of Ferraris from which to select, including a lower-end Ferrari 355, which started at US$160,000 and sold particularly well. The 456M bucked tradition by including a back seat. Another model was made roomier by moving the engine from the rear to the front, violating another Ferrari tradition. Customers also could now select from a dozen or more colors, rather than being obliged to accept the standard Ferrari red. Di Montezemolo's transformation of Ferrari had clearly paid off by 1997, when the company posted pretax profits of US$22 million on record sales of US$594 million, a vast improvement over the US$2 million in pretax profits and US$399 million in sales of 1995.

As the rebounding company celebrated 50 years of carmaking in 1997, Ferrari faced a new challenge in 1997 when its parent, Fiat, sold a 50 percent stake in Maserati S.p.A., another troubled Italian maker of sports cars, to Ferrari, giving the latter management control over the former. Fiat hoped that di Montezemolo could complete another turnaround; another reason for the move was to provide Ferrari access to Maserati car designs, which included four-door models—Ferrari was making only two-door cars. Maserati had a checkered history noteworthy for its succession of owners and its rare profitable years. Fiat had bought 49 percent of Maserati in 1989, then took full control in 1993.

Under Ferrari management, Maserati was thoroughly overhauled, with US$120 million invested by the late 1990s in an attempt to revive the brand. The Maserati factory in Modena was refurbished, all the assembly line workers were either replaced or retrained, and a new model, the 3200 GT coupe, was introduced in November 1998 to critical acclaim. Maserati sales exceeded 1,500 units in 1999, tripling the figure of the previous year. In November 1999 Ferrari acquired the 50 percent of Maserati stock it did not own already, gaining full ownership.

As befitting a marketing maven, Di Montezemolo also worked to leverage the cachet of the Ferrari brand. He developed a sideline business whereby the Ferrari name and logo were licensed to other companies, which then sold Ferrari-branded goods. Among the licensed Ferrari products in the late 1990s were watches (in partnership with Girard Perregaux), perfumes (Satinine), clothing (TSS&P), video games (Electronics Arts and Sega), and miniature cars and toys (Mattel). In 1999 Ferrari created a wholly owned subsidiary called Ferrari Idea S.A., which was based in Lugano, Switzerland, and which took over responsibility for developing and maintaining these licensing partnerships. About ten percent of Ferrari's profits were attributable to Ferrari Idea in 1999.

Ferrari enjoyed its sixth straight year of sales growth in 1999, with revenues increasing 22.8 percent over 1998, reaching US$760.8 million. During the year, the company completed another successful launch of a new model, the 360 Modena, which replaced the F355—the best-selling Ferrari of all time. Some good news also came from the sporting world, where the Ferrari team won the 1999 Formula One Constructors' Championship for the first time since 1983, although Eddie Irvine narrowly lost the Drivers' Championship in the final race that year (the last individual Ferrari championship dated back to

1979). Nearly 3,800 Ferraris were sold in 1999, edging the brand closer to its goal of 4,000. With its newfound success, Ferrari was under pressure to increase production. The company felt that doing so could undermine the brand. Therefore, Ferrari's strategy for the early 21st century was for Maserati to become the company's volume brand. Production of 2,000 cars was projected to increase to 10,000 per year by 2005. A key to this growth was the planned reintroduction of the Maserati into the U.S. market, with a new two-seat convertible called the Spyder slated to debut in 2001. The following year another new model, a four-door executive car, was scheduled for introduction. To meet these production goals, new assembly options were being explored, including the assembly of cars outside Italy, perhaps in the United States, the largest potential Maserati market. In the meantime, Ferrari followed up its move into licensing with another nonautomotive venture. In April 2000 the company announced that it had entered into alliances with Marsh & McLennan, a U.S. insurance and consulting firm, to offer insurance to new car buyers, and with Fidis, the financial arm of Fiat, to launch retail financial services. As with the company's plans for Maserati brand, these initiatives were seen as alternatives to sharply increasing production of Ferrari vehicles in order to increase sales and profits.

Principal Subsidiaries

Ferrari Deutschland GmbH (Germany); Ferrari Idea S.A. (Switzerland); Maserati S.p.A.

Principal Competitors

Bayerische Motoren Werke AG; DaimlerChrysler AG; Dr. Ing. h.c.F. Porsche AG; Volkswagen AG.

Further Reading

Betts, Paul, "Enthusiast Numero Uno: Interview with Luca di Montezemolo," *Financial Times,* June 8, 1998, p. 17.

——, "Maserati Costs to Put Brake on Ferrari Growth," *Financial Times,* May 16, 1998, p. 19.

Borgomeo, Vincenzo, *L'angelo rosso: storia, leggende e passioni di Enzo Ferrari,* Rome: Edizioni lavoro, 1997.

Burt, Tim, "Ferrari Plans Move into Financial Services," *Financial Times,* April 14, 2000, p. 33.

——, "Maserati Tunes Up for US Tour," *Financial Times,* April 15, 2000, p. 18.

Cancellieri, Gianni, and Karl Ludvigsen, eds., *Ferrari, 1947–1997,* Vimodrone, Italy: Giorgio Nada Editore, 1997.

Casucci, Piero, *Enzo Ferrari: 50 Years of Motoring,* New York: Greenwich House, 1982.

Ciferri, Luca, "After Years of Secrecy, Ferrari Offers Peek into Future," *Automotive News,* January 17, 2000, pp. 41JJ-41KK.

Done, Kevin, "A Look at the Cultural Revolution at a Legendary Italian Carmaker," *Financial Times,* May 28, 1994, p. 9.

Griffiths, John, "Ferrari Learns to Steer a Strategic Course," *Financial Times,* March 30, 1987, p. 24.

——, "Ferrari: The Heritage and the Dream," *Financial Times,* July 19, 1997, Motoring Sec., p. 18.

——, "Rebirth in the Fast Lane: Management Maserati's Modernisation," *Financial Times,* June 8, 1998, p. 17.

Henry, Alan, *Ferrari: The Battle for Revival,* Somerset, England: Patrick Stephens, 1996.

Henry, Jim, "Car Sales Are the Big Prize in Ferrari Race Series," *Automotive News,* July 11, 1994, p. 34.

——, "Fiat Gives U.S. More Attention," *Automotive News,* March 15, 1993, p. 6.

Larner, Monica, "Those High-End Italians Are Revving Up Again," *Business Week,* October 19, 1998, p. 138.

Larner, Monica, and Karen Lowry Miller, "The Man Who Saved Ferrari," *Business Week,* March 8, 1999, p. 74.

Robinson, Aaron, "Ferraris: Expensive to Buy, Expensive to Build," *Automotive News,* April 24, 2000, p. 16.

Rogliatti, Gianni, Sergio Pininfarina, and Valerio Moretti, *Ferrari: Design of a Legend, the Official History and Catalog,* New York: Abbeville Press, 1990.

Yates, Brock, *Enzo Ferrari: The Man, the Cars, the Races, the Machine,* New York: Doubleday, 1991.

—Thomas Derdak
—updated by David E. Salamie

FINGERHUT

Fingerhut Companies, Inc.

4400 Baker Road
Minnetonka, Minnesota 55343
U.S.A.
Telephone: (952) 932-3100
Fax: (952) 932-3292
Web site: http://www.fingerhut.com

*Wholly Owned Subsidiary of Federated Department
Stores, Inc.*
Incorporated: 1978
Employees: 12,000
Sales: $1.61 billion (1998)
NAIC: 454110 Electronic Shopping and Mail-Order
Houses

With an active customer base of 31 million people, Fingerhut Companies, Inc. is a leading database marketer selling via catalogs, direct marketing, telemarketing, and the Internet. The company is the number two catalog retailer in the country, trailing only J.C. Penney Company, Inc. In addition to its core Fingerhut direct marketing business, the company also operates several specialty catalogs: Figi's, gourmet food and gift baskets; Popular Club Plan, a membership-based, general merchandise catalog; women's apparel marketers Arizona Mail Order, Bedford Fair, Brownstone, and Lew Magram; and Macy's By Mail, a consumer catalog with products from Macy's department store (Macy's and Fingerhut are both owned by Federated Department Stores, Inc.). In the e-commerce arena, Fingerhut owns and operates eight retail sites: Fingerhut.com (specializing in general merchandise), AtomicLiving.com (general merchandise for young adults), AndysGarage.com (closeout merchandise), AndysAuction.com (company-to-consumer online auctions), Figis.com (gourmet food and gifts), OutdoorSpirit.com (outdoor merchandise), MyJewelry.com (jewelry), and BirthdayHut.com (an "e-mail reminder and gift recommendation service"). The company also holds equity stakes in a number of other Internet retailers and services. Fingerhut ships an average of more than 330,000 packages per day from four distribution centers, which are located in St. Cloud, Minnesota; Piney Flats, Tennessee; Spanish Forks, Utah; and Cheshire, Connecticut. These centers comprise a total of more than four million square feet of space.

Early History: From Seat Covers to Direct-Marketing Powerhouse

Fingerhut originated in 1948 as a small concern far removed from the world of sophisticated multimedia marketing and high finance. At that time William Fingerhut, the son of Jewish immigrants, was producing and selling automobile seat covers out of his Minneapolis garage to augment the family-run sewing business. William's new enterprise held enough promise—much factory upholstery was then notoriously susceptible to tears and stains—to accommodate his brother, Manny, an exasperated manager of a used-car lot. Aided by four other employees, the Fingerhut brothers saw gross sales during their initial years together that approached $100,000 annually. The "brainstorm that ultimately transformed the company into a big-time operation," wrote Arthur M. Louis, belonged to Manny, who handled sales and bookkeeping.

In 1949, after receiving a mail-order solicitation to purchase neckties, Manny envisioned expanding the seat business far beyond the local car dealer and car buyer market. Fingerhut's new market would be car owners across the United States, all of whom could be reached by mail. Before fully implementing his plan, the younger Fingerhut hired an advertiser to produce an eye-catching circular, which the entrepreneur then mailed to 100 new car owners spread throughout Minnesota. From this first test market, Fingerhut received eight orders, many times more than the necessary response for a successful mailing. Within three years, Manny had reoriented the entire business (now grossing nearly a million a year) to mail-order marketing, acquiring lists of new-car buyers, state-by-state, as he went. Unfortunately, Louis noted, "William Fingerhut had been wary of Manny's bold experiment from the start, and when it worked so well he became resentful. . . . The relationship between the brothers became tense, and in 1954 William angrily withdrew from active participation in the business." (The elder Fingerhut eventually sold his share of the company in 1969 for $12.5 million.)

Company Perspectives:

Fingerhut's vision is to build a world-class, information-based direct marketing company leveraging Fingerhut's core competencies: its proprietary database; its direct marketing expertise; and its state-of-the-art infrastructure.

During the mid-1950s the company faced its first crisis when Detroit automakers introduced vinyl and nylon, fabrics far more durable than previous ones, in their new car models. Fingerhut responded by switching entirely to the production of transparent plastic seat covers, which allowed the car owner both to preserve and display the modern upholstery beneath. The 1950s also saw the company expand its offerings to include towels, dishes, electric drills, and car coats. This last item was so successful that it launched the company firmly into manufacturing as well as merchandising. By the mid-1970s Fingerhut Corporation's product list encompassed some 40 items, a select dozen of which were manufactured internally and responsible for nearly 50 percent of overall sales.

Although a good product mix was certainly crucial to the company's years of continuing growth, even more so was Fingerhut's *modus operandi* of targeting and maintaining its core market of lower-middle-income consumers. Market research showed that this buying group was most likely to shop by mail and, by logical extension, most likely to buy the many low-cost goods offered by Fingerhut. Coupled with Fingerhut's enticement of free gifts with every purchase and installment credit at department store rates, this made for a powerful sales and marketing formula. Crowning everything was Fingerhut's development and maintenance of a large and dependable customer list, a strategy that would ensure long-term corporate health.

1974–79: Surviving Recessionary Times

Following the watershed year of 1969, when the company went public in an immensely successful initial offering, Fingerhut was at the top of its game—the biggest complete mail-order marketer in the country. Then came fiscal 1974, when rising mailing, manufacturing, and interest costs; declining real incomes; mounting inventories; and price controls seriously threatened the company's future. In a management shakeup, newly installed president Ted Deikel, son-in-law of Manny Fingerhut, took charge of domestic operations and focused on a number of key areas, including cost-cutting, boosting company morale, and rethinking product mailings. Two of the most important steps Deikel took were phasing the company out of manufacturing and calling for pinpoint marketing, in which customers would be segmented by their buying preferences. (By the 1980s Fingerhut's database and corresponding mailings had become so advanced that virtually every customer represented a specialized market, thus earning the company the title of perhaps "the ultimate niche company" from *In Search of Excellence* author Thomas J. Peters).

Another positive outcome of the 1974 recession was Fingerhut's development of a multistep contingency plan to deal with future recessions. The plan involved tracking declines in

orders from "solo" product mailings and rises in preshipment cancellations (if certain percentages were reached, a recession was at hand); responding to such key declines and rises by raising credit standards, reducing sales to marginal customers, and increasing sales to core customers; and changing its product mix. By the last months of 1979, a new recession was in sight and Fingerhut was able to implement its plan. The company's ability to reap a profit increase of ten percent in the second quarter of 1980, while other retailers and mail-order houses suffered profit declines ranging from 18 percent to 43 percent during the same period, immediately placed Fingerhut in the limelight. In a November 1980 article for *Fortune,* Herbert Meyer reported: "As word of Fingerhut's triumph has spread, Deikel and his colleagues have begun to receive inquiries from executives throughout U.S. industry and from economists about what Fingerhut's data are saying now. Understandably, the Fingerhut crew is rather enjoying the attention."

1979–89: Subsidiary Status

Ironically, it was Deikel's retailing genius that caused nonretailing conglomerate American Can Company (later renamed Primerica) to acquire Fingerhut in 1979. After the purchase, Deikel assumed the additional responsibility of overseeing other American Can properties, including music merchandiser Pickwick International (then owner of Minnesota retail powerhouse Musicland). By 1983, however, Deikel was ready to build his own marketing organization from scratch and he left Fingerhut and Primerica.

Despite difficulties related to Primerica's later plans to divest Fingerhut, the cataloger managed to flourish through much of the 1980s. As of 1986 the company ranked alongside Spiegel, Inc. and behind retailing giants Sears, Roebuck and Co. and J.C. Penney Company, Inc. in catalog sales and was growing at a rate of 20 percent annually.

Meanwhile, Deikel had founded Plymouth, Minnesota-based CVN Companies, an enormously successful pioneer of the cable home shopping industry. From $63.7 million in sales in 1984, CVN expanded to $683 million in sales in 1989. In October of that year, CVN merged with Pennsylvania-based competitor QVC Network. Deikel, $42 million richer from the deal, was searching for a way to continue his partnership with top CVN managers, who together possessed a wealth of experience in merchandising and general operations. A singularly golden opportunity presented itself virtually next door, at Deikel's former employer, Fingerhut.

Since at least 1986, according to Lee Schafer, Deikel had been discussing the possibility of acquiring Fingerhut with his fellow managers. By that time American Can—now renamed Primerica—was beginning to redefine itself as a diversified financial services company and simultaneously considering selling off some of its interests, including Fingerhut. The situation intensified from late 1986 into 1987, when Deikel was in direct contact with his friend Gerald Tsai, Jr., then chairman of Primerica, about possible business alliances as well as the sale of Fingerhut. Tsai's price of more than $1 billion for the mail-order subsidiary was deemed excessive by Deikel and there the matter rested. Schafer postulated that "Tsai's determination of Fingerhut's price was based less on an analysis of its value than on

Key Dates:

1948: William Fingerhut and his brother Manny begin producing and selling automobile seat covers.

1952: The Fingerhut business is now entirely reoriented to mail-order marketing; offerings are eventually expanded to include towels, dishes, and electric drills.

1969: Company goes public.

1974: Economic recession leads to management shakeup and the installation of Ted Deikel, son-in-law of Manny Fingerhut, as president.

1979: American Can Company (later known as Primerica) acquires Fingerhut.

1983: Deikel leaves the company.

1989: A Deikel-led management group gains leadership of Fingerhut.

1990: Primerica sells 28 percent of Fingerhut to the public.

1993: Primerica divests its remaining Fingerhut stake.

1994: Through financial services arm, company begins marketing cobranded credit cards.

1995: Two e-commerce sites, fingerhut.com and AndysGarage.com, are launched.

1999: Fingerhut is acquired by Federated Department Stores.

Primerica's own pressing financial need.'' Then came Primerica's acquisition of Smith Barney, the October 1987 stock market crash, and Sanford I. Weill's purchase of Primerica. Fingerhut was once again for sale and, as its revenues stalled in 1988 and 1989, it became more and more of a bargain for the right investor under the right circumstances. Just weeks before the CVN-QVC merger, senior management at Fingerhut had resigned. This paved the way for a deal between Deikel and Weill in which a Deikel-led management group would be installed before the end of 1989, and 28 percent of the Primerica subsidiary was spun off to the public the following year.

1990–98: Independent Again

Following Primerica's 1990 offering—part of a full divestiture plan that was completed in January 1993—Sears departed the catalog industry and Fingerhut showed especially strong growth in both sales and net income. Under Deikel, the company also demonstrated that it was a business true to its origins, capable of doing year-in and year-out what it did best—servicing the customer—while remaining open to change as new possibilities and challenges arose. In addition to expanding its product offerings to attract a wealthier customer group (both through Fingerhut Corporation and Montgomery Ward Direct L.P., a joint venture catalog marketer formed in late 1991 with general merchandise mainstay Montgomery Ward & Co., Inc.), Fingerhut placed considerable emphasis on growth opportunities within USA Direct Incorporated, an infomercial subsidiary launched in 1991. As the company's 1992 annual report pointed out, the infomercial business was intimately tied to Fingerhut's direct-mail marketing. Those products that had the best chance of selling via TV (food dehydrators, juicers, exercise equipment, and floor cleaners) were marketed there first, then through

follow-up advertisements in company catalogs and circulars, and finally through retail stores under royalty contract. Two of the most popular of Fingerhut's infomercial-to-retail market products were the Body By Jake exercise machine and the Bissell Big Green carpet-cleaning machine. Telemarketing and television revenues for 1992 accounted for nine percent of all corporate sales, double the amount achieved in 1991.

Also in 1992 Fingerhut opened a new distribution center in Piney Flats, Tennessee. Two years later the company expanded its St. Cloud, Minnesota, distribution facility by 547,000 square feet. Soon thereafter, a new one million square foot facility was opened in Spanish Fork, Utah. By the late 1990s Fingerhut operated four distribution centers with a total of more than four million square feet of operating space.

At the same time, Fingerhut was leveraging its vast proprietary database through an expansion into financial services, including extended product warranties, third-party insurance, and a cobranded Fingerhut/MasterCard credit card. The credit card initiative, launched in 1994, was particularly successful as Fingerhut was able, through its database, to find good credit card prospects who had been largely overlooked by bank and other credit card issuers, most of whom focused on higher-end customers. By 1996 Fingerhut was one of the 25 largest credit card issuers in the United States. In October of that year, Fingerhut took its financial services arm, dubbed Metris Companies, public through an initial offering that raised an estimated $45 million. Two years later, Fingerhut divested its remaining stake in Metris. Meanwhile, Fingerhut in 1997 began a major credit-related transition when it started converting its customers from close-ended installment plans to open-ended revolving credit.

The second half of the 1990s was also notable for Fingerhut's moves into e-commerce, a key move for a direct marketer. In 1995 the company launched fingerhut.com and AndysGarage.com. The latter, named after e-commerce president Andy Johnson, was positioned as a huge ''garage sale'' for overstock and closeout household merchandise, such as electronics and gas grills. The move into cyberspace accelerated following the hiring of Will Lansing as president in May 1998. (Deikel remained chairman and CEO.) Lansing had previously spent nine years at consulting firm McKinsey & Co., where he worked on a number of high-tech projects, including an attempted turnaround of online service provider Prodigy; as well as two years at General Electric Company working directly for legendary CEO Jack Welch. Deikel hired Lansing specifically to bolster Fingerhut's Internet presence and to spearhead an acquisitions drive in a rapidly consolidating catalog sector. Lansing moved quickly on both fronts.

In his first ten months as president, Lansing shepherded through eight acquisitions—five e-commerce sites and three catalogs. The latter included Arizona Mail Order, a women's apparel catalog purchased for $120 million in September 1998; Popular Club Plan, a membership-based, general merchandise catalog purchased from J. Crew Group, Inc. for $42 million in November 1998; and Bedford Fair, another women's apparel catalog, which was purchased out of Chapter 11 bankruptcy for $39 million in December 1998. Fingerhut purchased equity stakes in a number of e-commerce sites in 1998, including

PCFlowers.com, a leading online florist service; Mountainzone.com, which offered climbing and skiing products and information; and Freeshop.com, which offered free samples and trial offers of merchandise and magazine subscriptions. In early 1999 Fingerhut invested in Roxy.com, a marketer of Internet equipment; and Handtech.com, a seller of computers and technology products. By this time, Fingerhut had also launched a number of additional e-commerce sites, including Figis.com, an offshoot of the Figi's gourmet food and gift catalog; and thehut.com, a site offering general merchandise for young adults that was later renamed AtomicLiving.com.

1999 and Beyond

In March 1999 Federated Department Stores, Inc. acquired Fingerhut for $1.7 billion. Many analysts considered this an odd pairing of the downscale direct marketing of Fingerhut and the upmarket retailing of Federated, which owned Macy's and Bloomingdale's department stores. However, Federated wished to bolster its fairly small presence in cataloging and e-commerce and could leverage Fingerhut's catalog and Internet order fulfillment infrastructure. Federated also gained access to Fingerhut's coveted proprietary database. For Fingerhut the acquisition deal included the assumption of the company's $205 million in debt by Federated, a move that improved Fingerhut's financial state and provided it with greater flexibility to continue its own acquisition spree of cataloging and e-commerce firms. As far as the seemingly mismatched customer bases were concerned, officials from the companies saw this as an advantage in that Fingerhut customers could be "graduated" into Federated customers as they moved into higher income brackets.

Management changes soon followed the acquisition. In May 1999 Lansing took over as CEO of Fingerhut, with Deikel remaining chairman. Then in January of the following year Deikel retired, and Lansing took on the chairman's role as well. Just a couple of months later, however, Lansing also left the company. Leadership of Fingerhut was eventually passed to the team of Michael Sherman and John Buck, who together comprised the Office of the Principals, each serving as a president of Fingerhut and reporting directly to Jeffrey Sherman, chairman of Federated Direct, the parent's catalog and e-commerce division. Michael Sherman oversaw marketing operations, while Buck was responsible for financial and administrative functions. Meanwhile, Fingerhut continued to make deals based on its sophisticated distribution and fulfillment systems, including June 1999 deals to handle orders and merchandise shipping for the web sites of Wal-Mart Stores, Inc. and eToys Inc. In March 2000 Fingerhut purchased a 28 percent stake in Empire Direct, a seller of jewelry, electronics, and other goods to Hispanic Americans through its Empire Club catalog. That same month, Fingerhut acquired two more women's apparel catalogs, Brownstone Studio and Lew Magram. Backed by the deep pockets of Federated, Fingerhut was likely to be a major and expanding force in 21st-century direct marketing and e-commerce.

Principal Subsidiaries

Arizona Mail Order Company, Inc.; Axsys National Bank; Bedford Fair Apparel, Inc.; Fingerhut Business Services Inc.; Fingerhut Corporation; Figi's Inc.; Popular Club Plan, Inc.

Principal Competitors

Avon Products, Inc.; Best Buy Co., Inc.; Brylane Inc.; Circuit City Stores, Inc.; Concepts Direct, Inc.; DAMARK International, Inc.; Egghead.com, Inc.; Hanover Direct, Inc.; J.C. Penney Company, Inc.; Kmart Corporation; Lands' End, Inc.; Lillian Vernon Corporation; QVC, Inc.; RadioShack Corporation; Sears, Roebuck and Co.; Spiegel, Inc.; Target Corporation; USA Networks, Inc.; Wal-Mart Stores, Inc.

Further Reading

Andrews, Edmund L., "New Realities, New Rules," *New York Times,* October 27, 1991, p. F12.

Apgar, Sally, "Fingerhut's Profit Soars; Spinoff Planned," *Minneapolis Star Tribune,* January 26, 1996, p. 1D.

——, "Fingerhut Will Try to Sell Figi's; Fourth-Period Earnings up 31%," *Minneapolis Star Tribune,* January 15, 1993, p. 1D.

Bounds, Wendy, and Calmetta Y. Coleman, "A Retail Marriage of Mass and Class," *Wall Street Journal,* February 12, 1999, p. B1.

Byrne, Harlan S., "Shopping Made Easy," *Barron's* July 25, 1994, p. 20.

Chandler, Susan, "Data Is Power. Just Ask Fingerhut," *Business Week,* June 3, 1996, p. 69.

Cyr, Diane, "The New Fingerhut: To Become an 'Infomediary' and Consolidator," *Catalog Age,* July 1999, pp. 1, 14, 16.

"Damark International Inc.," *Wall Street Journal,* June 23, 1993, p. C14.

"Fingerhut Lays Off 200 in St. Cloud," *Minneapolis Star Tribune,* January 1, 1993, p. 3D.

"Fingerhut Stock Sold by Primerica," *Minneapolis Star Tribune,* January 8, 1993, p. 3D.

Gelbach, Deborah L., "Fingerhut Corporation," *From This Land: A History of Minnesota's Empires, Enterprises, and Entrepreneurs,* Northridge, Calif.: Windsor Publications, 1988, p. 303.

Girard, Peter, "Fingerhut Buy Popular Plan," *Catalog Age,* December 1998, p. 6.

"Herman (Sonny) Schwartz, Former Fingerhut President, Dies," *Minneapolis Star Tribune,* December 12, 1993, p. 4B.

Jaffe, Thomas, "Thumbs up on Fingerhut?," *Forbes,* January 21, 1991, p. 124.

Kennedy, Tony, "TV Unit of Fingerhut Companies Is Pursuing Possibility of Being a 24-Hour Shopping Channel," *Minneapolis Star Tribune,* December 1, 1993, pp. 1D, 8D.

Kiley, Kathleen, "Fingerhut Unit Goes Public," *Catalog Age,* December 1996, p. 7.

Louis, Arthur M., "Dead-Letter Days for Fingerhut," *Fortune,* November 1974, pp. 184–90.

Meyer, Herbert E., "How Fingerhut Beat the Recession," *Fortune,* November 17, 1980, pp. 102–04.

Miller, Paul, "Fingerhut, to the Bone," *Catalog Age,* December 1997, p. 5.

"Minority Stake in Fingerhut to Be Offered, Firm Says," *Wall Street Journal,* March 20, 1990, p. A20.

Moore, Janet, "Fingerhut Chairman Lansing Leaving As Part of a Corporate Reshuffling," *Minneapolis Star Tribune,* March 24, 2000, p. 3D.

——, "Fingerhut Continues Acquisition Spree with Deal for Catalog Firm Bedford Fair," *Minneapolis Star Tribune,* December 16, 1998, p. 3D.

——, "Fingerhut Sold for About $1.7 Billion," *Minneapolis Star Tribune,* February 12, 1999, p. 1A.

——, "The Man Behind All Those Deals," *Minneapolis Star Tribune,* March 24, 1999, p. 1D.

Neal, Mollie, "Fingerhut Movin' Ahead," *Direct Marketing,* September 1994, pp. 30–32, 72.

Norris, Eileen, "Fingerhut Gives Customers Credit," *Advertising Age,* March 6, 1986, p. 19.

Peterson, Susan E., "Fingerhut's Deikel Turns Over CEO Reins," *Minneapolis Star Tribune,* May 5, 1999, p. 1D.

Phelps, David, "Pointing a Finger at Fingerhut," *Minneapolis Star Tribune,* January 10, 1999, p. 1D.

"Primerica's Fingerhut Initiates an Offering of Six Million Shares," *Wall Street Journal,* April 26, 1990, p. C19.

Rosenthal, Thomas M., "The Last Straw for Fingerhut Corporation," *Global Trade,* October 1988, pp. 16, 18.

St. Anthony, Neal, "Ted Deikel's Legacy at Fingerhut Includes Controversy," *Minneapolis Star Tribune,* June 4, 1999, p. 1D.

Schafer, Lee, "Why Ted Deikel Returned to Fingerhut," *Corporate Report Minnesota,* August 1990, pp. 49–52; "Fingerhut Companies, Inc.," *Corporate Report Minnesota,* November 1990, p. 101.

Wieffering, Eric J., "I Can't Afford to Fail," *Corporate Report Minnesota,* January 1994, pp. 52–60.

—Jay P. Pederson
—updated by David E. Salamie

FleetBoston Financial Corporation

One Federal Street
Boston, Massachusetts 02110-2010
U.S.A.
Telephone: (617) 346-4000
Fax: (617) 434-6943
Web site: http://www.fleetbankbostonmerger.com

Public Company
Incorporated: 1791 as Providence Bank
Employees: 59,200
Total Assets: $190.69 billion (1999)
Stock Exchanges: New York
Ticker Symbol: FLT
NAIC: 551111 Offices of Bank Holding Companies;
  522110 Commercial Banking; 522210 Credit Card
  Issuing; 522291 Consumer Lending; 522292 Real
  Estate Credit; 522293 International Trade Financing;
  523110 Investment Banking and Securities Dealing;
  523120 Securities Brokerage; 523910 Miscellaneous
  Intermediation; 523920 Portfolio Management;
  523930 Investment Advice; 524113 Direct Life
  Insurance Carriers

FleetBoston Financial Corporation is the eighth largest bank in the United States and the largest in New England, with more than 1,250 branches and 3,500 ATM machines stretching from Maine to Pennsylvania. In addition to serving households and small businesses through its retail banking operations, the company offers a wide variety of financial services to both individuals and institutions throughout the United States and in Latin America. FleetBoston ranks as the number three commercial and industrial lender in the United States, is one of the top five providers of cash management services, and is a leading middle market lender. Other holdings include FleetBoston Robertson Stephens, a full-service investment bank, and Quick & Reilly, a leading discount brokerage firm. Other services and product offerings include mutual funds, insurance and annuities, credit cards, leasing, retirement planning, estate settlement, asset management, and venture capital. In Latin America, operating as

BankBoston, the company has strong positions in Argentina, Brazil, and Chile, serving top companies and high-net-worth consumers. This financial powerhouse is the result of the 1999 merger of two of the oldest banks in the United States, Fleet Financial Group, Inc., whose earliest predecessor was the 1791-founded Providence Bank, and BankBoston Corporation, which traced its roots to the 1784 founding of Massachusetts Bank.

The Development of Fleet's Predecessors

Fleet Financial Group was formed over a period of more than 200 years through the amalgamation of dozens of smaller local banks and savings institutions. As a result, the company has an extremely complex but rich heritage. The earliest predecessor of the Fleet companies was Providence Bank, which was established in Rhode Island in 1791 by a shipping merchant and former Congressional representative named John Brown. He had tried to found a bank seven years before, in the waning years of the Revolutionary War, but failed to inspire the trust of investors. As it was, Providence Bank was only the fifth bank to be established in the newly created United States of America.

In 1803, Elkanah Watson, who had been an apprentice in the shipping business under Brown, established his own financial institution, the State Bank of Albany. Watson had served as a soldier under George Washington and as an emissary to Benjamin Franklin in France. Rather than pursue politics, Watson built on his experience with Brown's shipping company and moved to Holland, where he studied the Dutch canal system. In 1792, after having returned to America, Watson organized a number of inland water transportation systems, including the Western Inland Lock Navigation Company. He continued in these ventures for another 11 years, at which time he reported having a dream about opening a bank. The next morning Watson immediately began drawing up papers to establish the State Bank of Albany. Watson headed the bank until his death in 1842. Throughout its history, the State Bank of Albany financed transportation projects, including the formation of the New York Central Railroad Company, the construction of the Great Western Turnpike (now U.S. Route 20), and a portion of the Erie Canal.

A third predecessor of Fleet Financial was established in 1886 by Samuel Pomeroy Colt, a young man who had been raised by his uncle and namesake, Samuel Colt, inventor of the Colt revolver. After earning his law degree, the younger Colt began a successful career in Rhode Island state politics. He founded the Industrial Trust Company in 1886 as a vehicle for his commercial activities, which included an interest in the National India Rubber Company. While in Europe some years later, Colt noted the European system of branch banking, a system that enabled a bank to conduct business in several areas of a city or county. He brought this idea back to Rhode Island and between 1900 and 1908 purchased 29 smaller banks throughout Providence, with the aim of converting them into branches of his Industrial Trust Company.

Thus, by the early 20th century, the Providence National Bank, the State Bank of Albany, and the Industrial Trust Company had been established and were prospering. All three institutions survived the Panic of 1907, a disastrous run on banks that virtually collapsed the American banking system. Colt's Industrial Trust was the first of the three, and the first bank in Rhode Island, to join the new Federal Reserve system. The Providence Bank, which became a national bank in 1865, recorded its first acquisition in 1926, when it took over the operations of the Merchants National Bank, then the largest financial institution in Rhode Island.

The banks plunged into dire straits in 1929, after the stock market crashed. The sequence of bankruptcies destroyed companies and banks alike and continued despite federal seizure of bank assets. Fortunately, the economies of Rhode Island and upstate New York were primarily—and robustly—maritime and agrarian, enabling the banks to remain solvent. In fact, the State Bank of Albany succeeded in growing during this difficult period by taking over a number of troubled competitors.

The banks remained stable throughout the 1930s, but were quickly drawn into a war mobilization economy in 1941. When war broke out later that year, the banks became essential sources for government investment in new factories. At the end of the war in 1945, there was tremendous demand for housing, food, and other goods, and a ready supply of workers returning from combat. The growing volume and velocity of money flowing through the economy fueled the growth of the banks.

New demands were put on banks, however, when the areas they served became saturated. Unless they could expand geographically, the banks' growth would be tied only to local average income growth. Providence National boosted its geographical coverage in 1951 by merging with another major

Providence bank, the Union Trust Company. A year later, the company changed its name to Providence Union National Bank and Trust. In 1954, this company completed another merger, this time with the company founded by Samuel Colt, the Industrial Trust Company. The new institution took the name Industrial National Bank, but continued to operate under the original Providence Bank's 1791 charter. The company remained strongly involved in lending operations to the local jewelry industry, an area in which it specialized.

Industrial National formed its own holding company, Industrial Bancorp, in 1968 (thereby launching the modern fashion of spelling bank with a "c"). The creation of this holding company permitted the institution to skirt regulatory restrictions in the 1956 Bank Holding Company Act that would have precluded the Industrial National Bank from conducting a range of nonbank financial services. The company gained a listing on the New York Stock Exchange on September 18, 1968. Industrial Bancorp changed its name to the Industrial National Corporation in 1970, and began its diversification in 1972, when it purchased New York-based Ambassador Factors. A year later it took over the Southern Discount Company of Atlanta. In 1974 the company acquired Mortgage Associates, a mortgage banking group headquartered in Milwaukee. The man behind Industrial National's diversification strategy was John J. Cummings, Jr., who believed that there was no justification for perpetuating the distinction between banking and traditionally nonbank financial services.

The State Bank of Albany began a similar transformation in 1972, when it took over the Liberty Bank of Buffalo. Liberty had been established in 1882 as the German-American Bank, but adopted the new name in 1918 amid public opposition to anything "German" during World War I. In fact, the bank was a wholly American-owned institution and had nothing to do with Germany or the war. With this transaction, the State Bank of Albany created a holding company called the Union Bank of New York.

Emergence of Fleet in the 1980s

In 1975 a former insurance executive named Peter D. Kiernan assumed leadership of Union Bank, emphasizing the need for better service. Like Cummings, Kiernan hoped to expand the Union Bank's scope of operations through acquisition. In 1982 he changed the company's name to Norstar Bancorp. He engineered Norstar's acquisition of the Utica-based Oneida Bank & Trust Company and carried out the first interstate bank merger in nearly 30 years by acquiring the Northeast Bankshare Association of Maine. In 1983 the company formed the Norstar Bank of the Hudson Valley by acquiring and merging the Sullivan County National Bank, Rondout National Bank, and Highland National Bank. The Norstar Bank of Long Island was formed by the merger of the Hempstead Bank, Peninsula National Bank, and Island State Bank. Later that year the Oneida National Bank and the State Bank of Albany were merged to form the Norstar Upstate Bank Group.

Cummings also branded his company with a new name, adopting the moniker Fleet Financial Group, Inc. in 1982. He considered the company's various divisions to be like a fleet of ships, all working in support of one another. The maritime name was popular in Rhode Island, where the local economy de-

---

Key Dates:

1784: Massachusetts Bank is founded in Boston.

1791: Providence Bank is founded in Rhode Island.

1803: The State Bank of Albany is formed in upstate New York.

1836: The Warren Bank, predecessor of Shawmut National Corporation, is founded in Boston.

1859: Safety Fund Bank is founded in Boston.

1864: Massachusetts Bank becomes a national bank, as Massachusetts National Bank of Boston; Safety Fund becomes a national bank, as First National Bank of Boston.

1865: Providence Bank becomes a national bank, under the name Providence National Bank.

1886: The Industrial Trust Company is established in Rhode Island.

1903: Massachusetts National and First National Bank of Boston merge, taking the latter's name.

1926: Providence National makes first acquisition, Merchants National Bank.

1944: Baystate Corporation, predecessor of BayBanks, Inc., is founded in Boston.

1951: Providence National acquires Union Trust Company.

1952: Providence National changes its name to Providence Union National Bank and Trust.

1954: Providence Union merges with Industrial Trust, forming Industrial National Bank.

1968: Industrial National forms holding company, Industrial Bancorp.

1970: Industrial Bancorp is renamed Industrial National Corporation; Bank of Boston reorganizes under a new holding company, First National Boston Corporation.

1972: Industrial National begins diversifying into nonbank financial services; State Bank of Albany takes over Liberty Bank of Buffalo, creating a holding company called Union Bank of New York.

1982: Union Bank is renamed Norstar Bancorp; Industrial National is renamed Fleet Financial Group, Inc.

1983: First National Boston changes its name to Bank of Boston Corporation.

1985: Fleet makes its first bank acquisition outside Rhode Island, First Connecticut Bancorp of Hartford.

1988: Fleet acquires Norstar, forming Fleet/Norstar Financial Group.

1991: Fleet/Norstar takes over the failed Bank of New England.

1992: Fleet/Norstar readopts the name Fleet Financial Group, Inc.

1995: Fleet acquires Shawmut National and moves its headquarters to Boston.

1996: Fleet acquires New Jersey-based NatWest Bancorp; Bank of Boston acquires BayBanks.

1997: Fleet acquires Columbia Management Company, an asset management firm; Bank of Boston changes its name to BankBoston Corporation.

1998: Fleet acquires discount broker Quick & Reilly, the consumer credit card operations of Advanta Corpora-tion, and Merrill Lynch Specialists; BankBoston acquires Robertson Stephens, an investment banking firm.

1999: Fleet acquires Sanwa Business Credit, a leasing and asset-based lending firm; Fleet acquires BankBoston and renames itself Fleet Boston Corporation.

2000: Company is renamed FleetBoston Financial Corporation.

---

pended on fishing and shipping. Cummings retired later that year and was succeeded by the decidedly gruff J. Terrence Murray. As chairman and CEO, Murray continued Fleet's rapid expansion in order to build the "critical mass" it would need to compete with bigger banks in New York and California (at the time of Murray's ascension, Fleet had total assets of only $4.5 billion). By 1985 the company had 322 offices in 33 states and four foreign countries. That year, after fighting regulatory and legal battles, Fleet established *de novo* banks in Boston and Hartford. It also acquired First Connecticut Bancorp of Hartford in 1985, the company's first bank acquisition outside Rhode Island, and Merrill Bankshares, a major Maine bank that had been established in Bangor in 1903, the following year.

Meanwhile, Norstar acquired the 102-year-old Security Trust Company in 1984 and the Bank of Maine a year later. In 1986 the company established Norstar Trust. After nearly 200 years of operation, Fleet and Norstar began crowding each other's territory. Murray and Kiernan began informal discussions about merging the two companies.

Murray was distracted, however, by a painful investigation of his company's mortgage lending operation, in which regulators charged that Fleet had taken unfair advantage of the state-

run Rhode Island Housing & Mortgage Finance Corporation. The agency had become a major Fleet customer, and, it was charged, Fleet's relationship with the bank had become so cozy that Fleet's loan officers were allowed to use agency loans to enrich themselves. More than 250 loans were granted to Fleet employees, and one even went to Murray's in-laws. But an investigation exonerated Murray and concluded that only 11 of the loans were improper. Still, the debacle exposed Fleet's capacity for corruption and, more importantly, its lack of effective senior management oversight.

Murray was also suffering from his growing reputation as a ruthless "downsizer." Indeed, many of the institutions acquired by Fleet were inefficiently run companies with poorly administered data systems. One way in which Fleet was able to derive greater productivity from its acquisitions was to consolidate their administrative positions into Fleet's existing staff and fold their diverse computer operations into Fleet's own system. This necessitated firing hundreds of redundant employees, but dramatically increased the profitability of the company's operations.

Driven by increasing competition from the Bank of Boston and the Bank of New England, Murray and Kiernan finally engaged in serious merger talks in 1987. The merger of Fleet and Norstar was announced January 1, 1988. Although Fleet acquired Norstar for $1.3 billion, Norstar's Kiernan was named chairman and CEO of the new company, which was called the Fleet/Norstar Financial Group. The merger mania continued in 1988 as Fleet/Norstar acquired the New Hampshire-based Indian Head Banks and began consolidating banking operations in Maine. Kiernan died suddenly on September 14, and, six days later, Murray was appointed to succeed him.

Early in 1989 it was revealed that the widespread slump in property values and poor federal oversight of the real estate industry had caused a serious banking crisis. Hundreds of financial institutions were saddled with billions of dollars in bad debt. One of these was Fleet/Norstar's chief competitor, the Bank of New England. BNE's crisis began in 1986 when it outbid Fleet for the Conifer Group, a Massachusetts real estate lender. Conifer's portfolio was a shambles, riddled with failed or shaky deals. Ironically, in losing its bid for Conifer, Fleet avoided a ruinous liability that, in the end, caused BNE to be seized by the Federal Deposit Insurance Corporation.

Fleet's Acquisitive and Diversifying 1990s

By 1990, the FDIC was eager to dump BNE and offered exceedingly generous guarantees against its liabilities. Fleet/Norstar badly wanted to bid for BNE, but lacked the capital of leading contenders such as BankAmerica and the Bank of Boston. The leveraged buyout firm Kohlberg Kravis Roberts also wanted to bid for BNE, but regulators soured on the idea of turning New England's second largest bank over to a group of corporate raiders. It became apparent that Murray and KKR's Henry Kravis needed each other, KKR for its money and Fleet/Norstar for its banking expertise. The two groups battled over the terms of their $625 million bid until just five minutes before the FDIC's deadline. To everyone's surprise, the Fleet/Norstar-KKR bid won.

Following the completion of the takeover in 1991, Murray immediately launched into BNE's cost centers, consolidating its data centers with those of Fleet/Norstar and firing nearly half of BNE's 11,000 employees. What remained was a bank with $15 billion in assets, the most extensive retail branch network in the region, and a large number of stable business loans. Within a year, Fleet/Norstar had rehabilitated BNE and turned a number of nonperforming loans back to the FDIC. The failed bank, which *Business Week* said had the allure of a toxic waste dump, was profitable sooner than anyone would have imagined. The BNE takeover enabled Fleet to surpass the Bank of Boston as the largest bank in New England; it also made KKR the company's biggest shareholder.

The company reverted to its old name, Fleet Financial Group, in 1992, the same year it suffered a public relations blow from a *60 Minutes* report alleging that the company had discriminated against low-income minority customers in Georgia by charging them excessively high interest rates and fees in connection with their home equity loans. In 1993 Fleet agreed to pay $30 million to the affected customers and to inject $70 million into low-income housing programs. Also in 1993 came the launch of a massive cost-cutting campaign, which was designed to increase profits, bolster the stock price, and position Fleet to be a survivor of the banking industry's rapid consolida-

tion rather than one of the casualties. After acquiring 49 banks in the 1980s, not to mention the takeover of Bank of New England, Fleet was a somewhat bloated organization. A months-long, top-to-bottom review of the entire operation resulted in the cutting of all kinds of expenses, as well as the March 1994 announcement that the company would lay off ten percent of its workforce, about 3,000 employees. The result would be a reduction in annual expenses of $300 million.

With its expenses pared down, Fleet went on a buying spree over the next few years that rapidly bolstered its position as the leading retail banking firm in New England and diversified it further into nonbank financial services. After entering into merger discussions with Bank of Boston in 1994, Fleet acquired another of the region's longtime banking institutions, Shawmut National Corporation, which traced its history back to the 1836 founding in Boston of the Warren Bank. Bank of Boston had been attempting to merge with Shawmut for several years, meaning that Fleet had once again bested its arch-rival. After completion of the $4.5 billion acquisition of Shawmut in November 1995, Fleet relocated its headquarters to Boston, where the arena that replaced the historic Boston Garden was soon named the FleetCenter. Fleet was now the leading bank in every New England state except Vermont, and its assets had grown from $48.76 billion in 1994 to $84.43 billion in 1995, the latter being nearly double that of Bank of Boston. The consolidation of Shawmut was a difficult one and involved the elimination of about 4,500 jobs. Nonetheless, Fleet pressed ahead with another acquisition in May 1996, acquiring New Jersey-based NatWest Bancorp from National Westminster Plc for $2.7 billion. The addition of NatWest extended Fleet's branch network south to New Jersey as well as bolstering its presence in upstate New York. At the end of 1996, Fleet stood as the 11th largest bank in the United States, and was emerging as one of the leading superregional banks.

Murray held off on making any more bank acquisitions while integrating NatWest, but made a number of moves outside of banking. In December 1997 Fleet acquired Columbia Management Company, a Portland, Oregon-based money management firm with about $21 billion of assets under management. In February 1998 two acquisitions were completed: a $1.6 billion deal for Florida-based Quick & Reilly Group, Inc., the number three discount brokerage in the country; and a $500 million deal for the consumer credit card operations of Advanta Corporation. Fleet also bought Merrill Lynch Specialists, Inc. in December 1998 and merged it into Fleet Specialists, Inc., and then two months later picked up Sanwa Bank, Ltd.'s Sanwa Business Credit unit, which was involved in leasing and asset-based lending. The Sanwa unit became part of the fast-growing commercial finance unit, Fleet Capital Corporation. After swallowing up this series of financial services firms, Fleet then rejoined the realm of retail banking consolidation with the announcement in March 1999 of its biggest acquisition ever, that of crosstown rival BankBoston Corporation (the name adopted by Bank of Boston in 1997).

Early History of BankBoston's Predecessors

BankBoston Corporation was older than that of the Constitution of the United States, and its story was a long and distinctive one. It traced its roots back to the Massachusetts Bank, which was founded in 1784. Its progenitors were Boston import-export merchants who were tired of having to deal with British banks when sending money to distant places. The bank was the first bank in the city of Boston and, indeed, the only one until 1792, when the Union Bank was founded and Alexander Hamilton's Bank of the United States opened a branch in Boston.

From the start, the Massachusetts Bank's strict lending policies and conservative ways made it no friends among consumers, who had few alternatives in seeking credit. It not only did not pay interest on customer deposits, but it even charged a fee for keeping them at one point. But times were uncertain at best during the early years of the Republic; a complete overhaul of the federal government, Shay's Rebellion, the War of 1812, and the ensuing two-year depression all happened within 30 years of the bank's founding. The Massachusetts Bank weathered each of these crises, however, and in 1838 its assets amounted to more than $1 million.

When the Civil War broke out in 1861, the Massachusetts Bank was part of a consortium of Boston banks that extended nearly $35 million in credit to the Union government. It also supported the Union war effort by buying $50,000 worth of treasury bonds. A more important development that occurred during the war was the advent of a national banking system, which Congress created in 1864 to make war financing easier through the establishment and circulation of a national currency. True to the Massachusetts Bank's conservative tradition, President John James Dixwell expressed suspicion about the new system, but saw that if his bank did not join, it would fall behind its competition. In 1864 the bank renamed itself the Massachusetts National Bank of Boston.

By 1884, there were 59 banks in Boston besides Massachusetts National, and the competition was so fierce that it could not afford to maintain its cautious ways and expect to survive. Yet, the bank did just that. As a result, however, its annual profit declined from a record $250,038 in 1873 to $70,000 by the end of the century.

Emergence of First National Bank of Boston in the 20th Century

Near the end of the 19th century, Boston's banking industry also underwent a wave of mergers, the most important of them engineered by the Shawmut National Bank and the investment banker Kidder, Peabody & Company. In reaction to this development, Massachusetts National decided to merge with the First National Bank of Boston, which had openly defied Shawmut National's power play, in 1903. First National had been founded in 1859 as Safety Fund Bank, changing its name in 1864 when it joined the national bank system. The new institution bore the First National name, and although Massachusetts National President Daniel Wing stayed on as president, First National President John Carr became chairman of the board.

The First National Bank of Boston prospered under the guidance of Daniel Wing. When World War I broke out in 1914, the bank took little notice—the United States was still a nonbelligerent and Europe seemed far away. The big event of 1914 for the bank was its participation in the new Federal Reserve system; it purchased 6,000 shares of the Federal Re-

serve bank's capital stock and purged its own board of directors of members involved in securities dealing and investment banking, in compliance with the Federal Reserve Act. In 1915 the bank extended $1 million worth of credit to the British government and made a $5 million loan to Russia the next year. Early in 1917, despite the fact that the distant clash of war was getting closer, the Bank of Boston opened its first overseas office, in Buenos Aires, following New England wool traders there. Once the United States formally entered the war later that year, the bank did its part by purchasing a large quantity of war bonds from the U.S. Treasury.

To say that the Bank of Boston grew and prospered during the boom years of the 1920s would be an understatement. The bank made its first substantial plunge into retail banking in 1923, when it acquired the International Trust Company. By 1924, the bank had grown to many times the size it had been before World War I. It employed 1,657 people, compared to 152 in 1908; its capital stood at $15 million, compared to $2 million; and its loan volume had grown to $222 million, from $28 million.

Despite the October stock market crash that threw the financial community into a panic, 1929 was a prosperous year for the Bank of Boston. Either the directors did not recognize the severity of the crisis right away or they were confident that the bank would withstand it, because they authorized the acquisition of Old Colony Trust Company late that year. In addition, in 1931 the bank bought out the Jamaica Plain Trust Company. Bank of Boston survived the Great Depression in relatively strong condition, although it cut its dividend continually until 1937. It was also forced to divest its investment-banking arm, the First Boston Corporation, after the passage of the Glass-Steagall Act in 1933, which prohibited commercial banks from engaging in investment banking and securities dealing.

Rumors of war once again emanated from Europe at the end of the 1930s. As in 1914, the Bank of Boston took little notice except regarding the matter of outstanding loans to German interests. As the Nazi government in Germany prepared for hostilities, concerns arose that the bank would not be able to collect from its German borrowers. W. Latimer Gray, head of Bank of Boston's foreign operations, went to Germany himself in the summer of 1939 to secure repayment. Gray had met many prominent Germans in the course of his business dealings, but found himself trailed by Gestapo agents during his trip. He and his wife left the country just before the invasion of Poland, carrying with them a draft on Britain's Midland Bank for $500,000, enough to cover the Bank of Boston's loans.

During World War II employees left to join the military and the bank extended emergency credit to the federal government to help finance military orders, but these things were a matter of course for every major American bank during the war. In 1945, with the end of the war in sight, the Bank of Boston acquired the First National Bank in Revere, Massachusetts. Once the war ended the bank went about expanding as before, opening a branch office in Rio de Janeiro in 1947.

By 1950, Bank of Boston's assets totaled more than $1.5 billion. The bank continued to prosper during the decade and its foreign business expanded. Factoring—the practice of buying accounts payable from merchants and assuming responsibility for their collection—also became a substantial part of the Bank of Boston's business during this time. In 1959 the bank posted record revenues of $20.4 million. It was also one of the few American banks to withdraw its assets from Cuba before Fidel Castro nationalized that nation's banks.

In the early 1960s, the Bank of Boston internationalized its factoring operations. In 1961 the bank's newly formed subsidiary, Boston Overseas Financial Corporation, joined with British merchant bankers M. Samuel & Company and Tozer, Kemsley & Millbourn to form International Factors, Limited. The next year, Boston Overseas Financial expanded its factoring business to the Netherlands, Switzerland, Australia, and South Africa. The Bank of Boston increased its international presence even further in 1964 when it opened a branch office in London.

The First National Bank of Boston continued to prosper through the 1960s, although its financial performance suffered somewhat late in the decade when high interest rates, due to inflation and increased demand for credit, caused it to take losses on its bond holdings. By 1970, it had acquired a reputation as a creative lender that was always willing to find unconventional solutions to problems of finance. Serge Semenenko, the flamboyant Russian-born head of the semiautonomous special industries department, contributed substantially to this image. Hilton Hotels, International Paper, the *Saturday Evening Post,* and Warner Brothers Studios were among his many clients.

Bank of Boston's Difficulties in the 1970s and 1980s

In 1970 the Bank of Boston reorganized under a new holding company, First National Boston Corporation. From there, the bank embarked on a string of acquisitions of Massachusetts banks in an effort to become a regional powerhouse. In 1982, reflecting the new prominence that large regional banks would soon have in the national banking arena, the bank renamed itself Bank of Boston National Association. The bank's holding company was renamed Bank of Boston Corporation the following year. In 1985 Bank of Boston moved to solidify its grip on New England with the acquisition of Waterbury, Connecticut-based Colonial Bancorp, and followed in 1987 with the purchase of BankVermont Corporation. Its aggressive lending policies also helped spark Massachusetts' much-heralded economic revival in the 1980s, when the bank made substantial loans to high-technology concerns, including Wang Laboratories and Data General Corporation. Moreover, it did a good job of dodging the Third World debt crisis in 1987 by writing off nearly two-thirds of its loans at the first sign of trouble.

At the same time, however, Bank of Boston developed a reputation for aloofness, even arrogance, during the 1970s and 1980s. One incident that contributed to this perception occurred in the mid-1970s, when the city of Boston underwent its worst fiscal crisis since the Great Depression and turned to the bank for help. Although the Bank of Boston eventually bought the city's notes as requested, many city officials bristled at the bank's demands, including an unsuccessful insistence that the state guarantee certain city debts. For several years thereafter, Boston City Hall pointedly chose Morgan Guaranty Trust, a New York investment bank, as its underwriter. The Bank of

Boston was also known for its unwillingness to discuss its lending practices and local affairs with community activists. "They just project an elitist, uncaring attitude," a spokesman for a rival bank told *Business Week* in 1985.

But the worst public relations disaster of all for the bank came in 1985, when the Justice Department charged that the Bank of Boston had processed more than $1.2 billion worth of cash transactions between 1980 and 1984 without reporting them to the Treasury Department as required by a federal law designed to prevent money laundering. The accusations stemmed from an investigation of Gennaro J. Angiulo, the alleged head of New England's largest organized-crime family. Federal investigators found that Angiulo and his associates had made a habit of walking into a Bank of Boston branch in Boston's North End with paper bags full of cash and exchanging them for cashier's checks. They also found that the bank had not reported large shipments of American currency to and from Swiss banks. At first, Bank of Boston denied any wrongdoing in the Angiulo affair and CEO William Brown charged that it was the victim of misrepresentation in the press. Later, once the evidence came out, Brown was forced to admit to "poor judgment" on the part of lower-level employees; the bank pleaded guilty to the Justice Department's charges and paid a $500,000 fine.

By the late 1980s Bank of Boston seemed to have recovered from the Angiulo affair, but the fiasco raised serious questions about the way the bank was run under William Brown and his predecessor, Richard Hill. Ira Stepanian succeeded Brown as chairman and CEO in 1989, a year in which the company posted a $300 million loss in the last quarter, due in large part to bad property loans. Income for the year fell 79 percent as Bank of Boston felt the effects of the collapse in the New England real estate market and the resulting wave of loan defaults.

String of Setbacks and Takeover of BayBanks in the 1990s

Bank of Boston's troubles continued in the early 1990s with the real estate collapse as well as the recession leading to a record net loss of $395 million in 1990, another loss in 1991, the fall of its stock from $30 a share to as low as $3 in 1991, and whispers of impending insolvency. Another blow came in 1991 when Fleet Financial beat out Bank of Boston in the bidding to take over the failed Bank of New England, and in the process surpassed Bank of Boston as the top bank in New England. Bank of Boston then attempted to leapfrog back over Fleet through a merger with another Boston-based bank, Shawmut National Corporation, but the deal fell apart in January 1992 over the roles of the firms' top executives.

Despite this latest setback, Bank of Boston rebounded during 1992 as it began to focus on community lending—focusing on small businesses, home mortgages, and personal loans; this was a remarkable change for a bank with a reputation for its snootiness. It returned to profitability the year after. The company expanded its financial services offerings in 1993 through the launch of a family of mutual funds called the 1784 Funds. It also expanded its retail banking system through the acquisitions of two small New England banks, Dedham, Massachusetts-based Multibank Financial Corporation and Hartford-based Society for Savings Hancorp for a total of about $400 million. Each of the banks had assets of about $2.5 billion and operated more than 75 branches. Late in 1993 Bank of Boston, seeking to flatten its organizational chart and become more responsive to its customers, eliminated an entire layer of top management.

As bank consolidation proceeded in the mid-1990s, Bank of Boston became increasingly desperate to engineer a merger, lest it be swallowed up by a much larger bank. The company entered into merger discussions with Fleet in 1994, but Fleet decided instead to acquire Shawmut, striking Bank of Boston a double blow. With the completion of Fleet's acquisition of Shawmut in 1995, Fleet's assets of $84.43 billion would be nearly double those of Bank of Boston. While Fleet was finalizing its purchase (and adding insult to injury by relocating its headquarters to Boston), Bank of Boston was seeking another merger partner. But a string of possible mergers—with New Jersey's First Fidelity Bancorp, Pittsburgh-based Mellon Bank Corporation, Philadelphia-based CoreStates Financial Corporation, and Banc One Corporation of Columbus, Ohio—all fell through during the first several months of 1995. Many analysts and shareholders blamed Stepanian for being too inflexible in merger talks, leading to the string of failures. Under increasing pressure from investors, Stepanian resigned in July 1995, and the company's president, Charles Gifford, took over as chairman and CEO.

Under Gifford's leadership, Bank of Boston finally completed a major merger in July 1996, when it took over crosstown rival BayBanks, Inc. in a $2 billion stock swap. BayBanks had been founded in 1944 as Baystate Corporation and had a strong retail banking emphasis, with 205 branches and a superior network of 1,000 ATMs. BayBanks' strong presence in Boston enabled Bank of Boston to regain from Fleet its leadership position in its home city. The addition of BayBanks' $11.5 billion in assets pushed Bank of Boston's assets to $62.31 billion by the end of 1996. The head of BayBanks, William Crozier, was named chairman of Bank of Boston following completion of the deal, with Gifford remaining CEO (he regained the chairmanship the following year). A new president was named as well, Henrique de Campos Meirelles, who had headed up Bank of Boston's Brazilian operations.

Bank of Boston changed its name to BankBoston Corporation in 1997 and began beefing up its international and nonbank financial services operations. That year, the company began expanding its retail banking network in Argentina, opening 17 new branches. Then in January 1998 BankBoston spent about $255 million to purchase Deutsche Bank Argentina, S.A. from Deutsche Bank AG of Germany. Gained through this transaction were 48 branches in Argentina, which were added to the 44 BankBoston already had in that country; by the end of 1998 the opening of additional branches brought the total to 139. In August 1998 BankBoston acquired Robertson Stephens & Co. from BankAmerica Corporation for about $800 million, the second largest acquisition in company history, after the purchase of BayBanks. A San Francisco-based investment banking firm that was one of the leading players in the hot high-tech capital raising sector, Robertson Stephens was combined with BankBoston's existing investment banking unit to form BancBoston Robertson Stephens.

Meantime, in March 1998, the head of BankBoston's private bank in New York, Ricardo S. Carrasco, turned fugitive after he was charged with falsifying records and embezzlement in connection with a fraudulent loan scheme involving an Argentine businessman that totaled more than $62 million—the largest case of fraud in the bank's 214-year history.

The global economic crisis that started in Asia in 1997, then spread to Latin America and other regions in 1998, hurt the company's Boston-based global capital markets business, leading to trading losses of about $100 million in 1998. In October 1998 BankBoston announced that it would close its branches in India, Japan, the Philippines, and Taiwan, reducing its Asian operation to a headquarters in Singapore and branches in Hong Kong and South Korea. BankBoston ended 1998, what would be the last full year of its long history, with assets of $73.51 billion and net income of $783 million.

FleetBoston Financial Corporation Emerges at the Turn of the Millennium

In March 1999 Fleet Financial Group announced that it had reached an agreement to acquire BankBoston in a $16 billion stock swap, ending the long and sometimes bitter rivalry between New England's two largest banks. Upon completion of the acquisition in October 1999, Fleet became the eighth largest bank in the country, with assets of $190.69 billion. With this culmination of a decade of hyperacquisitiveness, Fleet had taken over, directly or indirectly, eight of the ten biggest banks in New England. To gain regulatory approval, Fleet agreed to divest 306 branches and $13. 2 billion in deposits in what was the largest divestiture in U.S. banking history, a divestiture that aimed at enabling another major bank to compete with Fleet in New England. Most of the branches were sold to Philadelphia-based Sovereign Bancorp Inc. during 2000.

After the acquisition was finalized, Fleet changed its name to Fleet Boston Corporation and, ultimately, to FleetBoston Financial Corporation in early 2000. The inclusion of "Boston" in the name was at the insistence of Gifford, who initially served as president of FleetBoston, while Terrence Murray, the head of Fleet, served as chairman and CEO. The "BankBoston" name would largely disappear, with the bank branches all adopting the geography-free "Fleet" moniker, and BancBoston Robertson Stephens was renamed FleetBoston Robertson Stephens Inc. The exception were the Latin American operations, which continued to operate as "BankBoston." As was typical in mergers of this magnitude, FleetBoston announced in 2000 that the consolidation of operations would result in the layoff of about 4,000 workers. The company projected that merger-related efficiencies would eventually lead to annual cost savings of about $600 million.

In addition to focusing on integration issues, FleetBoston was pursuing a number of other strategies for the early 21st century. Already armed with a strong presence in Internet banking and online trading, the company began offering an integrated online service, whereby its customers could check balances, pay bills, and execute securities trades through Quick & Reilly, all through one account and one sign-on. With little room to grow in its core retail banking market of New England, FleetBoston was targeting New York City as its next big growth market, aiming to rapidly expand its existing 18-branch operation. In addition, in July 2000 the company announced that it would pay $200 million to acquire M.J. Meehan & Co., LLC, a specialist firm that it intended to merge into its existing specialist unit to form Fleet Meehan Specialists (specialists are floor-trading firms that execute the trades of specific assigned stock, helping to maintain order on the exchange and aiming to make a profit in the process). Fleet Meehan Specialists would be the largest specialist operator on the floor of the New York Stock Exchange.

Principal Subsidiaries

Fleet National Bank; Fleet Bank (RI), National Association; Fleet Credit Card Holdings, Inc.; Fleet Credit Card Services, L.P. (98.73%); Fleet Mortgage Group, Inc.; Fleet Holding Corp.; Fleet Capital Corporation; Fleet Leasing Partners I, L.P.; Fleet Business Credit Corporation; Fleet RI Holding Corp.; Fleet Investment Advisors Inc.; Fleet Investment Services, Inc.; Boston World Holding Corporation; Boston Overseas Financial Corporation (Argentina); Fleet Bank, National Association; Fleet Private Equity Co., Inc.; Quick & Reilly/Fleet Securities, Inc.; FleetBoston Robertson Stephens Inc.; BancBoston Investments Inc.; BancBoston Capital, Inc.

Principal Competitors

Bank of America Corporation; The Bank of New York Company, Inc.; Bank One Corporation; The Charles Schwab Corporation; The Chase Manhattan Corporation; Citigroup Inc.; Countrywide Credit Industries, Inc.; Deutsche Bank AG; FMR Corp.; First Union Corporation; J.P. Morgan & Co. Incorporated; KeyCorp; Mellon Financial Corporation; Merrill Lynch & Co., Inc.; National Discount Brokers Group, Inc.; Olde Discount Corporation; The PNC Financial Services Group, Inc.; The Royal Bank of Scotland Group plc; SLM Holding Corporation; State Street Corporation.

Further Reading

Babson, Jennifer, "A Stunning Decade Caps 200 Years of Sleepy Growth: Fleet Cements Place as New England's Premier Bank," *Boston Globe,* March 15, 1999, p. A12.

Beam, Alex, "Bank of Boston: A Public Relations Nightmare," *Business Week,* March 4, 1985, p. 38.

Blanton, Kimberly, "Giant Fleet-Shawmut Deal Will Boost Region, Take Toll," *Boston Globe,* February 22, 1995.

Blanton, Kimberly, and Doug Bailey, "Behind the Bank of Boston Bloodbath: Risky New Emphasis on Retail Banking Helped Prompt Axing of Top Executives," *Boston Globe,* November 9, 1993.

Bradford, Stacey L., "All Dressed Up?," *Financial World,* February 18, 1997, pp. 39–41.

Browning, Lynnley, "A Nod to History, Heritage in Bank's Renaming," *Boston Globe,* October 26, 1999, p. D1.

Chacon, Richard, "Managing the Crisis: BankBoston Sticks to Latin Expansion Strategy," *Boston Globe,* September 30, 1998, p. E1.

Chipello, Christopher J., "Lend and Learn: Bank of Boston Faces the Perils That Await Eager 'Superregionals,' " *Wall Street Journal,* November 17, 1989.

Crozier, William M., Jr., *BayBanks,* New York: Newcomen Society of the United States, 1989, 19 p.

"Fleet Financial, to Lessen Realty Woes, May Sell Third of Non-Performing Assets," *Wall Street Journal,* September 17, 1992, p. A3.

"Fleet/Norstar Financial Group, Inc.," *Barron's,* September 11, 1989, p. 20.

"Fleet's Ship Comes In," *Business Week,* November 9, 1992, p. 104.

Grant, John F., and William C. Bullock, Jr., *Merrill Bankshares Company,* New York: Newcomen Society in North America, 1977, 22 p.

Hechinger, John, "Fleet Boston Executives Make Big Bet on Online Strategy," *Wall Street Journal,* October 29, 1999, p. B4.

——, "FleetBoston, Flexing Its Muscles, Focuses on New York," *Wall Street Journal,* April 10, 2000, p. B4.

——, "Fleet Financial to Acquire BankBoston," *Wall Street Journal,* March 15, 1999, p. A3.

——, "Fleet Touts Benefits of BankBoston Deal," *Wall Street Journal,* March 16, 1999, p. A3.

Henderson, Barry, "Siren Song: With Lust in Its Heart, Fleet Grabs Columbia," *Barron's* August 18, 1997, p. 34.

Hirsch, James S., "Bank of Boston's Gifford Attacks Its Hidebound Image," *Wall Street Journal,* December 14, 1995, p. B4.

——, "Once-Stodgy Bank of Boston Is Adding a Brazilian Beat," *Wall Street Journal,* July 26, 1996, p. B4.

Hirsch, James S., and Steven Lipin, "Bank of Boston to Acquire BayBanks for $2 Billion," *Wall Street Journal,* December 13, 1995, p. A3.

Ip, Greg, and John Hechinger, "FleetBoston Is Set to Buy M.J. Meehan & Co., Creating Largest Specialist Firm on NYSE Floor," *Wall Street Journal,* July 25, 2000, p. C18.

Kerber, Ross, "Fleet, BankBoston at E-Crossroads," *Boston Globe,* August 3, 1999, p. D1.

——, "Fleet Financial Faces a Choice: To Buy or Be Bought?," *Wall Street Journal,* December 2, 1997, p. B4.

——, "Robertson Stephens May Not Alter BankBoston's Status: Purchase for $800 Million Still Leaves Firm Vulnerable to Takeovers," *Wall Street Journal,* June 1, 1998, p. B4.

Knecht, G. Bruce, and Suzanne Alexander Ryan, "Grim Procedure: Fleet Financial's Plan to Reduce Its Payroll Involved Long Process," *Wall Street Journal,* March 10, 1994, p. A1.

Knowles, Asa S., *Shawmut: 150 Years of Banking, 1836–1986,* Boston: Houghton Mifflin, 1986, 517 p.

Koselka, Rita, "Repentance," *Forbes,* October 26, 1992, p. 144.

Lipin, Steven, Patrick McGeehan, and James S. Hirsch, "Fleet Financial to Acquire Quick & Reilly," *Wall Street Journal,* September 17, 1997, p. A3.

O'Brien, Timothy L., and Steven Lipin, "Bank of Boston's Ira Stepanian Resigns After Failed Quests for a Merger Partner," *Wall Street Journal,* July 28, 1995, p. A3.

O'Donnell, Thomas, "A Slightly Improper Bostonian," *Forbes,* August 3, 1981, pp. 35+.

Oliveri, David, "Bank of Boston Joins Mutual Fund Parade," *Boston Business Journal,* March 19, 1993, p. 1.

Rebello, Joseph, "Bank of Boston Reaps Rewards of Its Latin Investment," *Wall Street Journal,* November 3, 1994, p. B4.

Rebello, Joseph, and Steven Lipin, "Bank of Boston's CEO Is Odd Man Out in New England," *Wall Street Journal,* February 24, 1995, p. B4.

"Right Time, Right Place, Right Price," *Business Week,* May 6, 1991, pp. 26–29.

Ryan, Suzanne Alexander, "Bank of Boston Ties Fortunes to Loans for Small Firms," *Wall Street Journal,* February 3, 1994, p. B4.

——, "Bank of Boston Top Managers Knew of Weak Loans Ahead of '89 Disclosure," *Wall Street Journal,* April 25, 1994, p. A4.

Smith, Geoffrey, "Fleet's Can-Do Spirit: We Can Do Without," *Business Week,* March 21, 1994, p. 106.

——, "These Brahmins Are Learning to Hustle: Bank of Boston Is Shedding Its Stuffiness to Better Its Bottom Line," *Business Week,* July 26, 1993, p. 69.

Smith, Geoffrey, Phillip L. Zweig, and Alison Rea, "Time to Put Away the Checkbook: Now, Fleet Needs to Bring Order to Its Furious Expansion," *Business Week,* June 10, 1996, p. 97.

Stein, Charles, ''Region's Giant Banks Battle On: BankBoston, Fleet Vie for Funds, Attention,'' *Boston Globe,* July 28, 1997, p. A1.

''Terry Murray's Regional View,'' *Industry Week,* November 11, 1985, p. 66.

Therrien, Lois, ''Bank of Boston Anchors Closer to Home,'' *Business Week,* December 3, 1984, p. 149.

Torres, Craig, and Ross Kerber, ''Argentine Judge Says He Warned BankBoston on Loan-Case Figure,'' *Wall Street Journal,* May 7, 1998, p. B18.

''Unbankerish Banker,'' *Forbes,* July 16, 1984, pp. 123–27.

Wessel, Davis, and Bob Davis, ''Under a Cloud: Bank of Boston Faces Image Problem Likely to Linger for Years,'' *Wall Street Journal,* March 7, 1985.

''Who Was Minding the Shop?,'' *Forbes,* March 10, 1986, p 135.

Wilke, John R., ''Bank of Boston Forces Out Entire Layer of Senior Management in Surprise Move,'' *Wall Street Journal,* November 1, 1993, p. B5.

Williams, Ben Ames, Jr., *Bank of Boston 200: A History of New England's Leading Bank, 1784–1984,* Boston: Houghton, 1984, 480 p.

Zuckoff, Mitchell, ''Bank of Boston Bounces Back,'' *Boston Globe,* December 29, 1992.

—John Simley
—updated by David E. Salamie

Ford Motor Company

The American Road
Dearborn, Michigan 48121-1899
U.S.A.
Telephone: (313) 845-8540
Toll Free: (800) 555-5259
Fax: (313) 845-6073
Web site: http://www.ford.com

Public Company
Incorporated: 1919
Employees: 364,550
Sales: $162.55 billion (1999)
Stock Exchanges: New York Boston Pacific Midwest
    Toronto Montreal London
Ticker Symbol: F
NAIC: 336111 Automobile Manufacturing; 336112 Light
    Truck and Utility Vehicle Manufacturing; 33612
    Heavy Duty Truck Manufacturing; 33621 Motor
    Vehicle Body Manufacturing (pt); 532112 Passenger
    Car Leasing; 524126 Direct Property and Casualty
    Insurance Carriers (pt)

One of a handful of companies that contributes significantly to the growth of the United States, Ford Motor Company represents a more than $150 billion multinational business empire. Known primarily as a manufacturer of automobiles, Ford also holds a considerable stake in financial services, which generate more than $1 billion in income, and owns 81 percent of The Hertz Corporation, the largest automobile rental company in the world. The company manufactures vehicles under the names Ford, Lincoln, Mercury, Jaguar, Volvo, and Aston Martin. Ford also maintains controlling interest in Mazda Motor Corporation.

Origins of an American Legend

Henry Ford, the founder of the Ford Motor Company, was born on a farm near Dearborn, Michigan, in 1863. He had a talent for engineering, which he pursued as a hobby from boyhood, but it was not until 1890 that he commenced his engineering career as an employee of the Detroit Edison Company. In his spare time, Ford constructed experimental gasoline engines and in 1892 completed his first "gasoline buggy." Dissatisfied with the buggy's weight, he sold it in 1896 to help fund the construction of a new car. Ford's superiors at the electric company felt his hobby distracted him from his regular occupation and, despite his promotion to chief engineer, he was forced to quit in 1899.

Shortly afterwards, with financial backing from private investors, Ford established the Detroit Automobile Company. He later withdrew from the venture after a disagreement with business associates over the numbers and prices of cars to be produced. Ford advocated a business strategy which combined a lower profit margin on each car with greater production volumes. In this way, he hoped to gain a larger market share and maintain profitability.

Independently in a small shed in Detroit, Henry Ford developed two four-cylinder, 80-horsepower race cars, called the "999" and the "Arrow." These cars won several races and helped to create a new market for Ford automobiles. With $28,000 of capital raised from friends and neighbors, Henry Ford established a new shop on June 16, 1903. In this facility, a converted wagon factory on Mack Avenue in Detroit, the Ford Motor Company began production of a two-cylinder, eight-horsepower design called the Model A. The company produced 1,708 of these models in the first year of operation.

The Ford Motor Company was sued by the Licensed Association of Automobile Manufacturers, an industrial syndicate which held patent rights for "road locomotives" with internal combustion engines. Ford responded by taking the matter to the courts, arguing that the patent, granted to George B. Selden in 1895, was invalid. During the long process of adjudication, Ford continued to manufacture cars and relocated to a larger plant on Piquette and Beaubien Streets. A Canadian plant was established in Walkerville, Ontario, on August 17, 1904.

Henry Ford and his engineers designed several automobiles, each one designated by a letter of the alphabet; these included the small, four-cylinder Model N (which sold for $500), and the

Company Perspectives:

Ford Motor Company is committed to fully utilizing the rich diversity of its human resources. Company leadership believes that diversity will be the engine that powers the creative energy of corporations of the 21st century. Successful companies will be those that are able to draw on the diverse talents of their people to stay on the innovative and competitive edges of their fields. Ford Motor Company started this century with a single man envisioning products that would meet the needs of people in a world on the verge of high-gear industrialization. The company is ending the century with a worldwide organization that retains and expands Henry Ford's heritage by developing products that serve the varying and ever-changing needs of people in the global community.

more luxurious six-cylinder Model K (which sold poorly for $2,500). The failure of the Model K, coupled with Henry Ford's persistence in developing inexpensive cars for mass production, caused a dispute between Ford and his associate Alexander Malcolmson. The latter, who helped to establish the company in 1903, resigned and his share of the company was acquired by Henry Ford. Ford's holdings then amounted to 58.5 percent. In a further consolidation of his control, Ford replaced John S. Gray, a Detroit banker, as president of the company in 1906.

In October 1908, despite the continuing litigation with the Selden syndicate, Ford introduced the durable and practical Model T. Demand for this car was so great that Ford was forced to enlarge its production facilities. Over 10,000 Model Ts were produced in 1909. Able to vote down business associates who favored more conventional methods of production, Henry Ford applied his ''assembly line'' concept of manufacturing to the Model T.

In developing the assembly line, Ford noted that the average worker performed several tasks in the production of each component, and used a variety of tools in the process. He improved efficiency by having each worker specialize in one task with one tool. The component on which the employee worked was conveyed to him on a moving belt, and after allowing a set time for the task to be performed, the component was moved on to the next operation. Slower workers thus needed to increase their work rate in order to maintain production at the rate determined by the speed of the belts.

Ford's battle with the Selden group led to a decision by the Supreme Court in 1911, eight years after the initial suit. The Court ruled that the Selden patent was invalid. The decision freed many automobile manufacturers from costly licensing obligations; it also enabled others to enter the business.

When the United States became involved in World War I (April 1917), the Ford Motor Company placed its resources at the disposal of the government. For the duration of the war, Ford Motor produced large quantities of automobiles, trucks, and ambulances, as well as Liberty airplane motors, Whippet tanks, Eagle ''submarine chasers,'' and munitions.

In 1918, Henry Ford officially retired from the company, naming his son Edsel president and ceding to him a controlling interest. But, in fact, Henry continued to direct company strategy and spent much of his time developing a farm tractor called the Fordson. He also published a conservative weekly journal, the *Dearborn Independent*. Edsel, who was more reserved and pragmatic than his father, concerned himself with routine operations.

At the end of the war Henry and Edsel Ford disagreed with fellow stockholders over the planned expenditure of several million dollars for a large new manufacturing complex at River Rouge, near Detroit. The Fords eventually resolved the conflict by buying out all the other shareholders. Their company was re-registered as a Delaware corporation in July 1919. The River Rouge facility, built shortly afterward, was a large integrated manufacturing and assembly complex which included a steel mill of substantial capacity.

Cash-Strapped in the 1920s

Between January 1 and April 19, 1921, the Ford Motor Company had $58 million in financial obligations due, and only $20 million available to meet them. Convinced that Ford Motor would be forced into bankruptcy, representatives of several large financial houses offered to extend loans to the company, on the condition that the Fords yield financial control. When the offer was refused, the bankers retreated, certain that they would soon be called upon to repossess the company.

With little time available, Henry Ford transferred as many automobiles as possible to his dealerships, who were instructed to pay in cash. Almost immediately, this generated $25 million. Next, Ford purchased the Detroit, Toledo & Ironton railroad, the primary medium of transportation for his company's supplies. By rearranging the railroad's schedules, Ford was able to reduce by one-third the time that automotive components spent in transit. This allowed him to reduce inventories by one-third, thereby releasing $28 million. With additional income from other sources, and reduction in production costs, Ford had $87 million in cash by April 1, $27 million more than he needed to pay off the company debts.

The Ford Motor Company's only relationship with banks after this crisis was as a depositor. Moreover, despite poor financial management, Ford maintained such strong profitability that it offered to lend money on the New York markets, in competition with banks. With large quantities of cash still available, Ford acquired the financially troubled Lincoln Motor Company in 1922.

Edsel Ford was more enthusiastic about the development of the aircraft industry than his father, and in 1925 persuaded his fellow shareholders (all family members) to purchase the Stout Metal Airplane Company. His close friend William Stout, who was retained as vice-president and general manager of the company, developed a popular three-engine passenger aircraft known as the Ford Trimotor. Nearly 200 of these aircraft were built during its production run.

After 18 years producing the Model T, the Ford Motor Company faced its first serious threat from a competitor. In 1926, General Motors Corporation introduced its Chevrolet automobile, a more stylish and powerful car. Sales of the Model

Key Dates:

1903: Henry Ford sets up shop in a converted wagon factory.
1908: Ford's Model T is introduced.
1922: Lincoln Motor Company is acquired.
1945: Henry Ford II is appointed company president.
1963: Ford Mustang is released.
1985: Ford Taurus is introduced.
1989: Jaguar Cars Ltd. is acquired.
1999: Swedish automaker Volvo is acquired in a $6.45 billion deal.

T dropped sharply. After months of experimenting with a six-cylinder model, Ford decided to discontinue the Model T in favor of the new Model A. On May 31, 1926, Ford plants across the country were closed for six months while assembly lines were retooled.

That year Ford voluntarily reduced its work week to five days, declaring that workers should also benefit from the success of the company. Ford was also one of the first companies to limit the work day to eight hours, and to establish a minimum wage of $5 per day. At Henry Ford's own admission, these policies were instituted more to improve productivity than to appease dissatisfied (and unrepresented) workers.

The British Ford Company was formed in 1928 and shortly thereafter the German Ford Company was founded. Henry Ford recognized the Soviet Union as a market with great potential, and like a number of other American industrialists, he fostered a relationship with officials in the Soviet government. Later, Ford participated in the construction of an automobile factory at Nishni-Novgogrod.

The economic crisis of October 1929, which led to the Great Depression, forced many companies to close. Ford Motor managed to remain in business, despite losses of as much as $68 million per year. By 1932, economic conditions became so difficult that the Ford minimum wage was reduced to $4 per day. But for its Model A, which sold 4.5 million units between 1927 and 1931, Ford's situation would have been much worse.

The economy of Detroit was heavily dependent on large, locally based industrial manufacturers and when companies less successful than Ford were forced to suspend operations, a banking crisis developed. The Ford Motor Company, and Edsel Ford personally, extended about $12 million in loans to these banks in an effort to maintain their solvency. But these efforts failed and the banks were forced to close in February 1933. Ford lost over $32 million in deposits and several million more in bank securities. The principal Ford bank, Guardian National, was subsequently reorganized by Ford interests as the Manufacturers National Bank of Detroit. Ford's largest business rival, General Motors, having suffered a similar crisis, emerged with control over the National Bank of Detroit.

The implementation of President Roosevelt's "New Deal" made conditions more favorable to the organization of labor unions. But Henry Ford, who had supported President Hoover in the election, advised his workers to resist union organization, and in 1935 raised the company's minimum wage to $6 per day.

In 1937, the United Automobile Workers union began a campaign to organize Ford workers by sponsoring the employee occupation of a Ford plant in Kansas City. The conflict was resolved when Ford officials agreed to meet with union representatives. That same year, there was trouble at the River Rouge complex. Several men distributing UAW pamphlets at the gates were severely beaten by unidentified assailants, believed to have been agents of the Ford security office. Following an investigation by the National Labor Relations Board, Ford was cited for numerous unfair labor practices. The finding was contested, but eventually upheld when the Supreme Court refused to hear the case.

In 1940, Henry Ford, who opposed American involvement in World War II, canceled a contract (arranged by Edsel) to build 6,000 Rolls-Royce Merlin aircraft engines for the British Royal Air Force, and 3,000 more for the U.S. Army. In time, however, public opinion led Ford to change his mind. Plans were made for the construction of a large new government-sponsored facility to manufacture aircraft at Willow Run, west of Dearborn.

Unionization activities climaxed in April 1941 when Ford employees went on strike. The NLRB called an employee election, under the terms of the Wagner Act, to establish a union representation for Ford workers. When the ballots were tabulated in June, the UAW drew 70 percent of the votes. Henry Ford, an avowed opponent of labor unions, suddenly altered his stand. He agreed to a contract with union representatives which met all worker demands.

The company devoted its resources to the construction of the Willow Run Aircraft plant. Eight months later, in December 1941, the Japanese bombing of Pearl Harbor resulted in a declaration of war by the United States against Japan, Germany, and Italy. Willow Run was completed the following May. It was the largest manufacturing facility in the world, occupying 2.5 million square feet of floor space, with an assembly line three miles long. Adjacent to the plant were hangars, covering 1.2 million square feet, and a large airfield. The airplanes produced at this facility were four-engine B-24E Liberator bombers, the Consolidated Aircraft version of the Boeing B-24. Production of aircraft got off to a slow start, but after adjustments the rate of production was raised to one plane per hour, 24 hours a day. During the war, other Ford Motor plants produced a variety of engines, as well as trucks, jeeps, M-4 tanks, M-10 tank destroyers, and transport gliders. The company also manufactured large quantities of tires, despite the removal of its tire plant to the Soviet Union.

Edsel Ford died unexpectedly in May 1943 at the age of 49. At the time of his death, Edsel was recognized as a far better manager than his father. Indeed, Henry Ford was often criticized for repeatedly undermining his son's efforts to improve the company, and the managerial crisis which occurred after Edsel's death is directly attributable to Henry Ford's persistent failure to prepare capable managers for future leadership of the company.

Edsel had been responsible for much of the company's wartime mobilization and his absence was deeply felt by his aging father, who was forced to resume the company presidency. In need of assistance, Henry Ford sought a special discharge from the Navy for Edsel's son Henry II. The navy complied, citing the special needs of Ford management during wartime. Henry Ford vigorously prepared his grandson to succeed him. By the end of the war, when the Willow Run plant was turned over to the government, Ford had produced 8,600 B-24E bombers and over 57,000 aircraft engines.

In September 1945, Henry Ford II, aged 28, was named president of the Ford Motor Company. The inexperienced man could not have started at a worse time. No longer supported by government contracts, the company began to lose money at a rate of $10 million per month. The source of the problem was Henry Ford I's financial management policy, specifically designed to perplex the Internal Revenue Service and discourage audits. The severe economic conditions after the war made Ford's finances an albatross.

Unable to bring the company's finances under control, Henry II hired Ernest R. Breech, a General Motors executive and past chairperson of Bendix, in 1946. Breech was placed in charge of two groups—a managerial group and a financial one. The first one was comprised of several managers hired away from General Motors, and the second group was made up of ten talented financial experts who had served with the Air Force Office of Statistical Control. The Air Force group included Robert S. McNamara, J. Edward Lundy, Arjay Miller, and Charles "Tex" Thornton; they spent several years reconstructing the company's system of financial management.

Henry Ford I, who had retained the title of chairperson since 1945, died in April 1947 at the age of 83. Henry II and Ernest Breech were then able to implement their own strategies for recovery, and these included the adoption of the proven General Motors management structure, and the decision to establish the Ford Motor Company in foreign markets. In its first year under Breech, the company registered a profit and it continued to gain strength in the late 1940s and early 1950s. Breech's top priority was strict adherence to a financial plan with strong profit margins; unfortunately, this proved to be at the expense of developing automobiles for an increasingly complex market.

Over the previous two decades, the Ford Motor Company had been a notable pioneer and achiever in the industry, and it was the first company to cast a V-8 engine block (1932). Ford had produced its 25 millionth automobile in 1937 and the following year its Lincoln Division introduced the Mercury line, which proved highly successful in the growing market for medium-priced automobiles. Ford's good image had been further enhanced by its contributions to the Allied effort in World War II; even Josef Stalin had kind words for the enterprising American company.

Before he died, Henry Ford I had created two classes of Ford stock. The B Class was reserved for family members and constituted the controlling 40 percent voting interest. The ordinary common shares were to be retained by the company until January 1956, when they were to be offered to the public for the first time.

Two years after Henry I's death, in 1949, the company unveiled a number of new automatic styles. But while the cars were practical, and to a degree fashionable, the company no longer appeared to be a pioneer; indeed it gained a reputation, not wholly justified, as being an imitator of General Motors.

Regaining its initiative, the Ford Motor Company decided to introduce a new model to fill a gap in the market between the Ford and Lincoln-Mercury lines. In 1958, the much heralded 410 horsepower Edsel made its debut. It was a terrible flop. Ford's market researchers had been very wrong; there was no gap in the market for the Edsel to fill. After just two years, production of the ill-fated car ceased—110,847 units had been produced, at a loss of some $250 million.

The 1960s and 1970s

The 1960s saw many changes at Ford: dissatisfied with his secondary role in the company decision-making, Henry Ford stripped Breech of his power, replacing him with Robert McNamara. But McNamara left the Ford Motor Company in 1961 to serve as Secretary of Defense in the Kennedy administration. Many of McNamara's duties were taken over by Arjay Miller, who succeeded the interim president, John Dykstra, in 1963.

The Ford Motor Company purchased the Philco Corporation in 1961 and established a tractor division in 1962. The following year, Ford introduced its highly successful Mustang; more than 500,000 of these cars were sold in 18 months. The man most responsible for developing the Mustang was a protege of Robert McNamara named Lee Iacocca.

In another move intended to assert his authority over management, Henry Ford II dismissed Arjay Miller in 1968 and named Semon E. Knudsen as president. Knudsen, a former executive vice-president at General Motors known for his aggressive personality, found himself in constant conflict with Henry Ford, and after 19 months he was replaced by Lee Iacocca. Iacocca was a popular figure, highly talented in marketing and sales, but like Knudsen, he frequently disagreed with Henry Ford.

Ford Motor Company subsidiaries in Europe entered a period of strong growth and high profitability in the early 1970s, and these subsidiaries produced components for the Pinto, a sub-compact introduced in the United States in 1971. Pinto models from 1971 to 1976 and similarly configured Bobcats from 1975 to 1976 drew a great deal of attention after several incidents in which the car's gas tank exploded in rear-end collisions. The unfavorable publicity from news reports damaged Ford's public image, as did wrongful death litigation.

In April 1977, Henry Ford II reduced Iacocca's power by creating a new executive triumvirate. Iacocca was a member of this, along with Ford himself and Philip Caldwell. But a year later, Ford added his brother William Clay Ford to the group and relegated Iacocca to a subordinate position; then within a few months, Ford suddenly fired Iacocca and installed Caldwell as president. Henry Ford was battling stockholder allegations of financial misconduct and bribery at the time and his dismissal of Iacocca made him more unpopular than ever (Iacocca, of course, went on to head Chrysler Corporation).

Henry Ford made a critical decision and a very misguided one. He cancelled development of a small car which had been proposed by Iacocca and which was intended to succeed the aging Pinto. Thus, as the Japanese compacts became increasingly popular in the United States, Ford found itself quite unable to compete. Adding to its woes, Ford, along with other U.S. car manufacturers, was obligated by Congressional legislation (particularly the Clean Air Act) to develop automobiles which would emit less pollutants. Henry Ford relinquished his position as chief executive officer to Philip Caldwell in October 1979. The following March, Ford retired and gave the chair to Caldwell, while retaining his seat on the board of directors.

The Ford Motor Company encountered severe economic losses as a result of a reduction in market share, as well as the high costs incurred by labor contracts and the development of automobiles that met the new federal standards. In 1980, the company lost $1.54 billion, despite strong profits from the truck division and European operations. Ford lost a further $1.06 billion in 1981 and $658 million in 1982 while trying to effect a recovery; its market share fell from 23.6 percent in 1978 to 16.6 percent in 1981.

Company officials studied Japanese methods of industrial management, and worked more closely with Toyo Kogyo, the Japanese manufacturer of Mazda automobiles (Ford gained a 25 percent share of Toyo Kogyo in November 1979, when a Ford subsidiary merged with the company). Ford imported Mazda cars and trucks, and in many ways treated Toyo Kogyo as a small car division until the Escort, its successor to the Pinto, reached the showrooms. This new compact was modeled after the Ford (Europe) Erika; another version of it, the Lynx, was produced by Ford's Lincoln-Mercury division.

Caldwell transferred the talented manager Harold Poling from the European division to the United States in an attempt to apply successful European formulas to the American operation. In the restructuring that followed, several plants were closed and more than 100,000 workers were dismissed. Ford's weakness in the market was a major concern of the unions; consequently, the company inaugurated a policy of employee involvement in plant operations and was able to secure more favorable labor contracts. Productivity improved dramatically.

In 1984, with costs reduced, Ford started to repurchase 30 million shares (about ten percent of the company's stock). Its production of cars in Mexico was increased, and through its interest in Kia Motors, output was stepped up in South Korea. The following year, Ford introduced the Taurus (another version, the Sable, was produced by its Mercury division), a modern full-size automobile which had taken five years to develop at a cost of $3 billion. The Taurus proved highly successful and won several design and safety awards.

Sales and profits reached record levels in 1984, and in 1986 Ford surpassed General Motors in income for the first time since 1924. In addition, Ford's market share increased to just under 20 percent. Ford Motor purchased several companies in the mid-1980s, including the First Nationwide Financial Corporation and the New Holland tractor division of Sperry, which was later merged with Ford Tractor. Ford also purchased a 30 percent share of Otosan, the automotive subsidiary of the Turkish Koç Group. The attempted acquisition of the Italian car maker Alfa Romeo in 1986 failed, due to a rival bid from Fiat.

Torturous Early 1990s

The diversification into financial services that began in the mid-1980s continued in earnest throughout the rest of the decade, as each of the major U.S. car manufacturers sought to insulate themselves against the cyclical nature of their business. Ford spent $5.5 billion acquiring assets for its financial services group during the latter half of the decade, including a $3.4 billion purchase in 1989 of the Associates, a Dallas-based finance company. That acquisition, completed the same year Ford purchased the venerable British car manufacturer Jaguar Cars Ltd. for $2.5 billion, made Ford the country's second largest provider of diversified financial services, ranking only behind Citicorp. With plans to eventually derive 30 percent of the company's profits from financial service-related business, Ford entered the 1990s with $115 billion worth of banking-related assets, a portfolio that provided the company's only bright moments during the otherwise deleterious early 1990s.

An economic recession crippled U.S. car manufacturers during the early 1990s, and Ford bore the brunt of the financial malaise that stretched around the globe. Domestically, car sales faltered abroad, particularly in Great Britain and Australia, Ford's sales plummeted. In 1991, Ford's worldwide automotive operations lost an enormous $3.2 billion after recording a $99 million profit the year before. In the United States, automotive losses reached an equally staggering $2.2 billion on the heels of a $17 million loss in 1990. The losses struck a serious blow to Ford, which as recently as 1989 had generated $3.3 billion in net income; however, the financial results of 1991 would have been worse without the company's strategic diversification into financial services. For the year, Ford's financial services group registered a record $927 million in earnings, up from the previous year's total of $761 million, which left the company with a $2.25 billion loss for the year, an inauspicious record in Ford's nearly 90-year history.

The financial disaster of 1991, however, was just a prelude to more pernicious losses the following year, as the global recession reached its greatest intensity. In 1992, with revenue swelling to slightly more than $100 billion, Ford posted a crushing $7.38 billion loss. Although 1992 represented one of the bleakest years in Ford's history, the worst was over, and as the economic climate improved, the company emerged with renewed vitality. Against the backdrop of successive financial losses, Ford had increased its presence in the truck and minivan market niche, which represented the fastest-growing segment of the broadly defined automotive market. Roughly 200,000 minivans and sports utility vehicles were sold in the United States a decade earlier and now, as consumers once again returned to car dealers' showrooms, more than 2.3 million opted for minivans and light trucks, a trend that bolstered Ford's financial position and predicated its return to a profitable future.

In 1993, Ford generated $2.52 billion in net income from $108.5 billion in revenue during a year in which the company actually lost money on passenger car sales, yet recouped the losses through minivan and truck sales. By 1994, such vehicles accounted for 50 percent of Ford's automotive sales, a prodigious increase from the preceding decade and the primary engine driving the company's growth.

Despite the losses suffered several years earlier, there was justifiable hope for further growth as Ford entered the mid-1990s. The gap separating Japanese and American car manufacturers' production standards had narrowed considerably, with the U.S. manufacturers emerging from the early 1990s in a more enviable position—Ford included. As the technological and managerial race between U.S. car manufacturers and their Japanese counterparts tightened, the importance of prudent product development and effective distribution networks increased. Toward this end, Ford reorganized its production and distribution operations in mid-1994 to better respond to the changing economic structure of the numerous countries in which Ford operated facilities. Regional trading areas, rather than nation states, would represent the primary focus of Ford's future efforts, a direction the company moved toward with its worldwide reorganization in 1994.

Ford's notable achievements during the latter half of the 1990s were philosophical in nature, as the company attempted to replace the corporate culture of its past with a new way of thinking for the future. The proponent of Ford's new vision was Lebanese-born, Melbourne, Australia-raised Jacques Nasser, who was named president and chief executive officer in January 1998, concurrent with the appointment of William Clay Ford, Jr., great-grandson of the founder, as chairman. Two years before his historic promotion—at age 51, Nasser became the youngest, non-family chief executive in the company's history—Nasser was named president of Ford's worldwide automotive operations. He did not like what he saw. The company had the lowest profits from total vehicle sales of any U.S. automaker, an alarming statistic that Nasser began to improve by slashing costs. His cost-cutting efforts earned Nasser the nickname "Jac the Knife," but once he was named Ford's chief executive in 1998, the characterization of his influence took on an added dimension.

At a gathering of Ford's top 300 executives shortly after his promotion, Nasser delivered the essence of the new spirit he hoped to inculcate. "We are all bureaucrats," he informed his management team, as quoted in the February 1999 issue of *Automotive Industries*. "I hope that offends you. I want you to be lousy bureaucrats, not sit there with your tie buttoned up, polishing your shoes." Nasser's aim was to replace the corporate culture of decades past with an entrepreneurial style that placed a much more intense emphasis on the customer. He continued making his trademark cuts in costs, realizing $5 billion in savings between 1997 and 1999, but he also worked toward instilling a new ethos at Ford, one in which the retirement of one executive did not automatically trigger the promotion of the next executive in line.

As part of the new movement espoused by Nasser, the company's Lincoln-Mercury division was relocated from Detroit to Irvine, California, an unprecedented move for a major U.S. automaker. Nasser wanted the division to attract younger customers—Lincoln's typical customer was 63 years old, Mercury's was 56 years old—and to be closer to suppliers and to emerging auto trends. Nasser wanted the division to breathe new life into itself away from the scrutiny of company headquarters, to benefit from a more entrepreneurial-driven perspective.

The changes at Lincoln-Mercury typified the profound currents of change sweeping through Ford at the century's end. Much remained to be done to achieve Nasser's vision of a fundamentally revamped Ford, but by the end of the 1990s there were impressive signs of progress. The company ended the decade as the most profitable automaker in the world. Its stock price increased 130 percent between 1996 and 1999, outpacing the increases recorded by its rivals. Further, some analysts projected Ford would eclipse General Motors in worldwide sales by 2001, thanks in large part to the company's increased ownership stake in Mazda Motor Corporation (from 25 percent to 33.4 percent in 1996) and its $6.45 billion acquisition of Swedish auto maker Volvo in 1999. The ultimate success or failure of the Nasser-led era, however, was to be determined in the first decade of the 21st century, as Ford concluded its first 100 years of business and redefined its style of operation for the future.

Principal Subsidiaries

Ford Electronics and Refrigeration Corp.; Ford Export Corp.; Ford International Capital Corp.; Ford International Finance Corp.; Ford Holdings, Inc.; Ford Motor Credit Co.; Ford Leasing Development Co.; Ford Motor Land Development Corp.; First Nationwide Financial Corp.; First Nationwide Savings; Ford Motor Company Ltd. (U.K.); Ford Motor Credit Company Ltd. (U.K.); Ford-Werke A.G. (Germany); Ford Credit Bank A.G. (Germany); Ford Motor Company of Canada Ltd.; Ensite Ltd. (Canada); Ford Glass Ltd. (Canada); Ford Motor Company of Australia Ltd.; Ford Motor Company of New Zealand Ltd.; Ford Brasil S.A. (Brazil); Ford Motor de Venezuela; Ford France S.A.; Ford Motor Company (Belgium) N.V.; Ford Credit N.V. (Belgium); Ford Italiana S.p.A. (Italy); Ford Credit S.p.A. (Italy); Ford Leasing S.p.A. (Italy); Ford Motor Argentina S.A.; Ford Motor Company AS (Denmark); Ford Motor Company S.A. (Mexico); Ford Nederland B.V. (Netherlands); Ford Espana S.A. (Spain); Ford Credit S.A. (Spain); Ford Leasing S.A. (Spain); Ford Credit A.B. (Sweden); Ford Credit S.A. (Switzerland); Transcom Insurance Ltd. (Bermuda); Mazda Motor Corporation (Japan; 33.4%); Ford Motor Company (Japan) Ltd.; Ford Lio Ho Motor Company Ltd. (Taiwan); Jaguar Ltd.

Principal Competitors

DaimlerChrysler AG; General Motors Corporation; Toyota Motor Corporation.

Further Reading

Beynon, Huw, *Working for Ford,* London: Penguin, 1984.
"Carload of Trouble," *Business Week,* March 27, 2000, p. 56.
Connelly, Mary, "Ford's Biggest Job: Lift Lincoln," *Automotive News,* July 31, 2000, p. 23.
Dubashi, Jagannath, "Ford: Looking Beyond the Shadows," *FW,* February 6, 1990, p. 23.
Gelderman, Barbara, *Henry Ford, the Wayward Capitalist,* New York: Dial Press, 1981.
Gross, Ken, "Ford: Big, Bigger, Biggest," *Automotive Industries,* July 2000, p. 64.
Keatley, Robert, "Ford Reorganizes to Stay Competitive and Reach New Markets in the World," *Wall Street Journal,* July 22, 1994, p. A4.

Lewis, David L., *The Public Image of Henry Ford: An American Folk Hero and His Company,* Detroit: Wayne State University Press, 1976.

Meyer, Stephen, *The Five Dollar Day: Labor Management and Social Control in the Ford Motor Company 1908–1921,* Albany: State University of New York Press, 1981.

Moreau, Dan, "Instant Prosperity: Behind Ford's Fast Turnaround," *Kiplinger's Personal Finance Magazine,* July 1993, p. 28.

"Nasser: Ford Be Nimble," *Business Week,* September 27, 1999, p. 42.

Nye, David E., *Henry Ford: "Ignorant Idealist,"* Port Washington: Kennikat Press, 1979.

Reiff, Rick, "Slowing Traffic Ahead," *Forbes,* April 30, 1990, p. 82.

"Remaking Ford," *Business Week,* October 11, 1999, p. 132.

Sorge, Marjorie, "1999 Executive of the Year," *Automotive Industries,* February 1999, p. 54.

Thomas, Charles M., "Ford Loses a Record $2.3 Billion," *Automotive News,* February 17, 1992, p. 4.

Zesiger, Sue, "Ford's Hip Transplant," *Fortune,* May 10, 1999, p. 82.

——, "Mr. Ford and Mr. Nasser Learn to Share: The Lords of Ford," *Fortune,* October 12, 1998, p. 34.

—updated by Jeffrey L. Covell

Freedom Communications, Inc.

17666 Fitch Avenue
Irvine, California 92614
U.S.A.
Telephone: (949) 553-9292
Fax: (949) 474-7675
Web site: http://www.freedom.com

Private Company
Incorporated: 1950 as Freedom Newspapers, Inc.
Employees: 6,500
Sales: $737.5 million (1999)
NAIC: 511110 Newspaper Publishers; 511120 Periodical
   Publishers; 513120 Television Broadcasting

Freedom Communications, Inc. is a privately held media company that owns some 27 daily newspapers, 35 weekly newspapers, more than 20 specialized magazines, and eight broadcast television stations. The Hoiles family, which owns Freedom, began in newspaper publishing in the late 19th century in Ohio, then moved to California and acquired the *Santa Ana Register* in the 1930s. The newspaper later became the *Orange County Register,* the third largest daily newspaper in California. In the 1990s, the company diversified its revenue base by acquiring television stations and starting a magazine division, in addition to acquiring more newspapers. In 1999 it launched an interactive division devoted to developing web sites and Internet-related ventures.

Origins in 19th-Century Ohio

The Freedom Communications story begins in Ohio in the late 19th century. Raymond Cyrus (R.C.) Hoiles was born into a prosperous farm family on November 24, 1878, in Alliance, Ohio. As a young adult he studied electrical engineering at Mt. Union College in Ohio. However, he also took an early interest in the newspaper business, first by selling subscriptions for the *Alliance Review,* a daily newspaper owned by his brother Frank Hoiles.

After Hoiles graduated from college, he worked full-time for the newspaper as a printer's devil, or apprentice. By 1905 he had served as the newspaper's bookkeeper and business manager and had acquired a one-third financial interest in the endeavor. Hoiles and his brother expanded their newspaper business by purchasing the *Lorain Times Herald* in 1919 and the *Mansfield News* in 1921. Hoiles served first as publisher of the *Lorain Times Herald,* and then held that title for the *Mansfield News.*

As publisher of the *Mansfield News,* Hoiles wanted to speak out against what he perceived as the oppressive influence of labor unions. His brother Frank refused to print such criticisms, and the disagreement caused the two brothers to dissolve their partnership. Hoiles bought out his brother and became sole owner of the two newspapers; in return, Frank received R.C.'s one-third interest in the *Alliance Review.*

In 1927 Hoiles acquired the *Bucyrus Telegraph-Forum* and began allowing his 22-year-old son, Clarence (C. H.), to manage the newspaper under his direction. It was the beginning of a long and productive partnership between R.C. and C.H. Hoiles. During this time, a bitter rivalry with another local newspaper reportedly resulted in several attempts on R.C.'s life, and he sold the Lorain and Mansfield newspapers in 1932. For the next three years he stayed away from publishing and read extensively. It was during this period that he began to identify himself as a libertarian.

From Ohio to California: 1935–70

In 1935 R.C. Hoiles moved his family to Santa Ana, California, in the heart of Orange County, and purchased the *Santa Ana Register.* Through that paper, he was able to fully express his political interests; he contributed personal columns and editorials that encouraged his readers to engage in a political and philosophical dialogue. Hoiles strongly objected to the government's power of taxation and to government-run programs. According to Freedom Communications' company history: "Many criticized his views. He was labeled and attacked on several fronts. But the same steadfast convictions that drew him criticism also won him praise when he applied them to the unfair treatment of Japanese-Americans during World War II. Nearly a lone voice among American journalists, R.C. Hoiles publicly protested the internment, an act that would earn him commendation from some of his staunchest critics and recognition by the Japanese-American Citizens League more than 20 years later.''

R.C. and C.H. Hoiles ran the *Register* together. The family publishing business flourished, as they acquired the *Clovis News Journal* (New Mexico) in 1935 and the *Pampa Daily News* (Texas) in 1936. In 1946 the firm acquired the *Gazette-Telegraph* in Colorado Springs and the *Appeal Democrat* of Marysville, California. In 1948 the *Odessa American* (Texas) was added to the group. In 1950 the family's newspaper holdings were incorporated as Freedom Newspapers, Inc. By 1970, the year that R.C. Hoiles died, Freedom Newspapers owned 16 daily newspapers in seven states.

A New Generation of Leadership in the 1970s

When R.C. Hoiles died in 1970, his son Harry moved from Colorado Springs, where he had served as publisher of the company's *Gazette-Telegraph* since 1946, to Santa Ana to become co-publisher of the *Register* with his brother C.H. Hoiles, who was Freedom's CEO. The newspaper was still known as the *Santa Ana Register* at that time.

When C.H. Hoiles died in 1981, Harry expected to succeed him as CEO of Freedom Newspapers. However, in the year before C.H.'s death, both he and his sister, Mary Jane, had decided to eliminate the CEO position and replace it with a three-person committee that would be elected by family representatives and one outsider, D. Robert Segal, who had worked with the company since 1942. Segal was president of Freedom, and Mary Jane Hoiles Hardie's husband, Robert C. Hardie, was company chairman. Thus, Harry's bid to become CEO of the company was opposed by his brother and other family members. A bitter lawsuit ensued, with Harry attempting to dissolve the company and claim his one-third interest. He resigned from the company's board of directors in 1990 and was replaced by his son, Tim. A hard-line libertarian all his life, Harry Hoiles died in Colorado Springs on April 18, 1998, at the age of 82, the last surviving child of founder R.C. Hoiles.

Diversification in the 1980s–90s

By the mid-1980s Freedom owned 29 newspapers, including the *Orange County Register,* which was California's third largest daily newspaper. It also owned four television stations in minor markets. Annual revenues overall were estimated to be $322 million. In 1986 Freedom acquired CBS affiliate WRGB-TV serving Schenectady and Albany, New York, for $56 million. Veteran television executive Alan J. Bell became president of Freedom's Broadcast Division in February 1989. At the time the company owned five network-affiliated television stations, four of them with CBS. The widely scattered stations were located in Providence, Rhode Island; Albany, New York; Chattanooga, Tennessee; Beaumont-Port Arthur, Texas; and Medford, Oregon. By 1994 the Broadcast Division also included a local cable network and the Orange County NewsChannel, which began broadcasting in 1990. Also in 1990 Freedom acquired Golden West Publishing from Media General of Richmond, Virginia. The acquisition included 14 weekly newspapers in Los Angeles and Orange Counties that were operated by Golden West's subsidiary Highlander Publications.

In 1992 James N. Rosse, a former Stanford University economics professor and provost, joined Freedom as president and CEO. Under his leadership, the company adopted an acquisition strategy that continued through the end of the decade. The acquisitions were designed to help balance the company's portfolio, which by the end of the decade consisted of about 25 daily newspapers and 34 weekly newspapers and several business magazines in addition to its five television stations. Under Rosse the company changed its name from Freedom Newspapers to Freedom Communications, Inc. Rosse also launched the company's Magazine Division in 1993 with the acquisition of *World Trade* and *USA Exports.*

In 1994 the *Register* began developing an online interactive classified advertising service to be launched in 1995. Called the American Classified Network, it would be based on cable television and allow viewers to search a database of the *Register*'s classified ads. The service would also sell products from retailers, including J.C. Penney, Hallmark, WaldenBooks, and 800-Flowers, among others.

Facing an uncertain future that included declining revenues from traditional print advertising, Freedom entered into a consortium with other newspaper publishers to explore new opportunities emerging from technology. Called PAFET (Partners Affiliated for Exploring Technology), the consortium included A.H. Belo Co., Central Newspapers, Cowles Media Co., McClatchy Newspapers Inc., and the Pulitzer Publishing Co. The alliance was managed by the CEOs of the participating companies and had its own executive director.

In 1995 Sam Wolgemuth was hired as the first president of Freedom's Magazine Division, which was created in 1993 to help diversify the company's revenue base. The division included two magazines, *World Trade* and *U.S./Latin Trade,* as well as two related directory publications, *USA Exports* and *FashionSource USA.* Wolgemuth was formerly president of Simon & Schuster's Business Technical Publications Group and COO of the Reed Travel Group.

Key Dates:

1935: R.C. Hoiles moves his family from Ohio to Santa Ana, California, and purchases the *Santa Ana Register.*

1950: Hoiles's newspaper holdings are incorporated as Freedom Newspapers, Inc.

1970s: The *Santa Ana Register* changes its name to the *Orange Country Register.*

1989: Alan J. Bell becomes president of Freedom's Broadcast Division, comprising five network-affiliated television stations.

1992: James N. Rosse is named president and CEO of Freedom Newspapers, Inc.

1993: The company's Magazine Division is launched.

1994: Company changes its name to Freedom Communications, Inc.

1999: Freedom's interactive division, Freedom Interactive Media, is introduced.

In 1995 Freedom acquired WPEC-TV, a CBS affiliate serving West Palm Beach and Fort Pierce, Florida. It was the company's first television acquisition in nearly a decade and the largest single transaction in the history of the company. While terms were not disclosed, analysts estimated that Freedom had paid $120 million or more for the station. The next year Freedom agreed to sell its Orange County NewsChannel to Century Communications Corp. The cable news channel had failed to generate any profits since it began operating in 1990. During this time, Freedom also acquired ABC affiliate WLAJ-TV of Lansing, Michigan, and WWMT-TV of Grand Rapids, Michigan.

New Challenges and New Management: 1999–2000

Freedom began 1999 by selling its *Home Theater* and *Mobile Office* magazines. In May 1999 it launched its interactive division, known as Freedom Interactive Media. Its mission was to launch and manage community-specific and customer-interest web businesses and to invest in new media companies. Freedom's management perceived the Internet as a natural and important extension of its core information and entertainment business of serving customers and advertisers. The first community web businesses would be developed in Orange County, to be followed by community sites in other markets served by Freedom's newspapers, including Colorado Springs and eastern North Carolina. Customer-interest web sites were also planned as spinoffs of selected magazines, such as *Mode,* the company's fashion magazine for average-sized women. During the year Freedom Interactive Media launched web sites LatinTrade.com, ModeStyle.com, SmallOffice.com, and MDNetGuide.com. The company also made strategic Internet venture investments in DrDrew.com, eHow.com, WebOrder, Intraspect, TalkCity, and DigitalWork. Before the end of 1999 Freedom established MyOrangeCounty.com as an interactive media company that would form the basis for Freedom's new Orange County Internet portal.

During the year Freedom announced it was looking for a successor to retiring CEO James Rosse. Under Rosse's leader-

ship Freedom had grown from an estimated $500 million in annual revenue to more than $700 million in 1998. In an interview with the *Los Angeles Business Journal,* Rosse maintained that Freedom ought to remain a private company, given the founding Hoiles family's unique Libertarian beliefs. Rosse was credited with improving the company's management and bringing in independent directors.

In August Samuel Wolgemuth, who was president of the Freedom Magazine Division, was named president and CEO of the company to succeed Rosse. Under Wolgemuth's leadership, the magazine division had grown to about 20 titles and annual revenue of $80 million. Among the titles he launched or acquired were *Mode, Girl,* and *P.O.V.* Colin Ungaro succeeded Wolgemuth as president of Freedom's Magazine Division in November 1999. The division was focused on four primary groups: business and consumer technology, healthcare, international trade and business, and women's fashion and beauty.

Also in 1999 the Magazine Division acquired full ownership of the Curtco Freedom Group, which had been a 50–50 partnership with the group's CEO William J. Curtis since 1995. Curtco consisted of two divisions. The SOHO Division published the magazines *Small Business Computing, Home Office Computing, Networked Home,* and *Small Business Solutions Provider.* The CRM Division published *Sales Automation, Field Force Automation, Knowledge Management, eCRM,* and operated a live events group. The group was renamed Freedom Technology Media Group. Freedom was also negotiating to sell its World Trade Media Group and its flagship magazine, *World Trade,* to Business News Publishing of Troy, Michigan.

In mid-2000 the Freedom Technology Media Group launched an Internet gateway devoted to customer relationship management (CRM). It was called destinationCRM.com and would include content from FTMG publications as well as real-time coverage from its own editorial staff.

The previously announced closure of *P.O.V.* magazine, an award-winning lifestyle magazine for young professional men, took place with the February 2000 issue. Freedom had acquired *P.O.V.* in April 1996. Although the magazine boasted more than 100 leading advertisers, Freedom wanted to exit the men's category of magazines and focus on other areas. The company planned to launch a related online venture for young professionals, LiveLarge.com, later in 2000.

In its Community Newspaper Division, Freedom added to its cluster of North Carolina weeklies by acquiring the *Hickory News* and three niche newspapers. In Florida the company traded its daily *Tribune* in Fort Pierce to E.W. Scripps Co. for the twice-weekly *Destin Log,* its sister paper the *Walton Log,* and an undisclosed amount of cash. The acquisition added to Freedom's holdings in northern Florida, where it already published three community newspapers in Fort Walton Beach, Panama City, and Santa Rosa Beach.

In mid-2000 Freedom agreed to purchase several Arizona newspapers from The Thomson Corporation, which was in the process of divesting all of its newspaper operations in the United States and Canada, with the exception of Canada's *Globe and Mail.* The acquisition included the *Tribune* in suburban Phoenix, the *Daily News-Sun* in Sun City, the *Yuma Daily Sun,* and a portfolio of non-daily publications.

Around the same time Freedom formed a new company called Freedom Publicaciones with Mexus Publishing to print and distribute a monthly entertainment and general interest Spanish-language tabloid. The core product would be the Mexus publication *La Onda,* which was a general interest monthly tabloid with the largest circulation (51,000 copies) in the state of Sonora, Mexico. *La Onda* was printed in Tucson and distributed to Mexican communities near the Arizona-Mexico border. Freedom Publicaciones planned to expand the *La Onda* concept to other markets along the U.S.-Mexico border, beginning in 2001 with a Monterrey edition.

For 2000 and beyond, Freedom's challenges included expanding its online activities and an ongoing advertising and circulation battle between the *Orange County Register* and the *Los Angeles Times.* About half of the company's revenues came from the *Orange County Register.* Future growth was expected to come from improving its existing properties, exploiting online opportunities, and developing new Internet and magazine partnerships. According to the company's 1999 annual report, it planned a thorough strategic review during the year 2000 to set long-range goals and challenge current assumptions. Although planning to innovate in times of rapid change, Freedom Communications remained committed to the libertarian values and ideals of its founder, R.C. Hoiles.

Principal Subsidiaries

Freedom Technology Media Group; Lewit & LeWinter/Freedom LLC; Freedom Magazines International; MultiMedia HealthCare/Freedom LLC; Freedom Publicaciones.

Principal Divisions

Orange County Newspapers; Community Newspapers; Broadcast Television; Magazines; Interactive Media.

Principal Competitors

Tribune Company; The Hearst Corporation; The E.W. Scripps Company; Gannett Co., Inc.; Knight-Ridder, Inc.

Further Reading

Beauchamp, Marc, "Cut the Baby in Half?," *Forbes,* October 7, 1985, p. 43.

Berry, Kate, "Freedom Communications' Next CEO Says Publications 'Uphold Human Liberty' " *Knight-Ridder/Tribune Business News,* August 11, 1999.

——, "Newspaper, Magazine Publisher Names New President," *Knight-Ridder/Tribune Business News,* August 10, 1999.

"California-Based Freedom Magazines Buys Out Partner," *Knight-Ridder/Tribune Business News,* June 14, 1999.

Case, Tony, "Scripps Swapping Sunshine Papers," *Mediaweek,* February 21, 2000, p. 14.

Consol, Mike, "Highlander Kills Eight Southland Weeklies; Freedom Newspapers to Buy Parent Firm," *Los Angeles Business Journal,* March 12, 1990, p. 4.

Deemer, Susan, "Freedom's Outgoing CEO Reflects on Firm's Future," *Los Angeles Business Journal,* July 19, 1999, p. 10.

Foisie, Geoffrey, "Alan J. Bell," *Broadcasting & Cable,* August 15, 1994, p. 57.

"Freedom Newspapers," *Mediaweek,* August 30, 1993, p. 20.

"Freedom Rings in N.C.," *Editor & Publisher,* February 14, 2000, p. 18.

"Freedom Sets out on Acquisition Trail," *Folio: The Magazine for Magazine Management,* June 15, 1995, p. 14.

Giobbe, Dorothy, "California Daily Developing Cable Classified Service," *Editor & Publisher,* June 18, 1994, p. 26.

Moses, Lucia, "New CEO at Freedom Comm.," *Editor & Publisher,* August 14, 1999, p. 12.

Rathbun, Elizabeth, "Freedom Rings for West Palm Beach TV," *Broadcasting & Cable,* October 2, 1995, p. 36.

Stein, M.L., "Coping with Threats and Opportunities in New Technology," *Editor & Publisher,* November 26, 1994, p. 15.

——, "From Provost to Newspaper CEO," *Editor & Publisher,* January 30, 1993, p. 12.

——, "Harry Hoiles, Libertarian, Former Freedom Exec.," *Editor & Publisher,* May 2, 1998, p. 21.

——, "Out of the TV News Business," *Editor & Publisher,* March 23, 1996, p. 15.

Trigoboff, Dan, "Tower of Freedom," *Broadcasting & Cable,* August 31, 1998, p. 39.

—David P. Bianco

Gaylord Entertainment Company

1 Gaylord Drive
Nashville, Tennessee 37214
U.S.A.
Telephone: (615) 316-6000
Fax: (615) 316-6555
Web site: http://www.gaylordentertainment.com

Public Company
Incorporated: 1925 as the Oklahoma Publishing
    Company
Employees: 5,820
Sales: $510.8 million (1999)
Stock Exchanges: New York
Ticker Symbol: GET
NAIC: 72111 Hotels (Except Casino Hotels) and Motels
    (pt); 51312 Television Broadcasting; 51322 Cable and
    Other Program Distribution

Gaylord Entertainment Company is a diversified entertainment and communications company whose holdings include the Grand Ole Opry, the Opryland Hotel, and Opry Mills, a massive retail and entertainment center in Nashville, Tennessee. Gaylord Entertainment also owns three Nashville radio stations and controls Christian web sites Musicforce.com and Lightsource.com.

Origins

The Gaylord and Dickinson families began what would become the Gaylord Entertainment Company in the Oklahoma Territory in 1903—Oklahoma would not become a part of the Union until 1907. The company was created as a newspaper publishing business to capitalize on the increasing demand for news in the burgeoning region. The two families incorporated the business in 1925 as the Oklahoma Publishing Company.

Realizing the future potential of radio, which was still in its infancy during the early 1920s, the Gaylords and Dickinsons branched out into the broadcasting industry in 1928 with the purchase of WKY-AM, a station in Oklahoma City. WKY, which started broadcasting in 1920, was the first radio station to operate west of the Mississippi and is the second oldest station in the United States. Shortly after Oklahoma Publishing bought it, WKY gained stature as a "beacon of hope" in the Oklahoma Dust Bowl during the Great Depression. Interestingly, another radio station of import to Oklahoma Publishing's future was getting its start in the mid-1920s: WSM-AM, of Nashville, began broadcasting in 1925. It was WSM's announcer, George D. Hay, that gave birth to the renowned Grand Ole Opry with his country music radio show.

Under the direction of cofounder Edward King Gaylord, Oklahoma Publishing Company prospered during the early and mid-1900s with its radio and publishing operations. Beginning in the late 1940s, the company made a seemingly natural progression into the television broadcasting industry. In fact, television became a primary focus of the company during the 1950s and 1960s. Gaylord snapped up several stations, including KTVT in Dallas, WVTV in Milwaukee, Houston's KHTV, and KSTW in Seattle; at one point, the company was operating seven stations. Oklahoma Publishing Company's television and radio operations were organized under its wholly owned Gaylord Broadcasting subsidiary.

By the early 1970s, Oklahoma Publishing Company was a multimillion-dollar mini-conglomerate primarily comprising radio, television, and newspaper companies. Because the company was privately owned by the Gaylord family, financial and operating data was generally not made available to the public. Furthermore, the Gaylords led relatively private lives and had a reputation for keeping a firm grip on the company. Amazingly, Edward King Gaylord, who had helped start the company in 1903 at the age of 32, was still actively managing the company in the early 1970s. Edward King died in 1974 at the age of 101. His son, Edward L., became chief executive. An Oklahoma billionaire, Edward was described in the media as rich, ultra-conservative, and reclusive.

Acquisition of the Grand Ole Opry in 1983

Gaylord continued to successfully oversee the publishing and broadcasting business founded by his father. The company still owned its original radio station and newspapers and had added another television station the year of Edward King's death. But Gaylord also tried branching out into several new ventures. In the mid-1980s, for example, he made an unsuccessful bid to purchase the Texas Rangers baseball organization—because of his disdain for reporters, Gaylord had his Oklahoma newspapers carry stories (about the failed acquisition) from a Dallas newspaper. The business foray that would bring Gaylord the greatest amount of success and would thrust his company into the national spotlight was his 1983 purchase of Nashville-based Grand Ole Opry and the Opryland Hotel.

Opryland was the culmination of over 50 years of the Grand Ole Opry, which began in WSM-AM radio. Although the Opry was dealt a nearly lethal blow by the popularity of television and rock music during the 1950s, by the mid-1960s the show was regaining its appeal to a mainstream audience. By the late 1960s, in fact, interest in the Opry was surging to such an extent that WSM Inc., its owner, elected to build a new complex to replace the decaying Ryman Auditorium. It also wanted to capitalize on the Opry's popularity by offering related tourist attractions. WSM purchased a 406-acre site and broke ground on an Opry theme park in 1970. The theme park, a musical show park that emphasized live country music, opened in 1972. Two years later, the Grand Ole Opry moved into its new home not far from the theme park. In 1977, moreover, WSM opened the Opryland Hotel to accommodate a growing supply of tourists.

Opryland's vigorous expansion during the late 1970s and early 1980s caught the eye of Gaylord, who viewed the Opry's broadcasting and entertainment operations as a comfortable fit with Gaylord Broadcasting. When WSM's parent corporation went hunting for a buyer for the Opry complex, Gaylord made himself available. In September 1983, Gaylord purchased the Opry properties for $250 million; the transaction would later be called one of the entertainment industry's better bargains. Gaylord renamed the complex Opryland USA. He also maintained the savvy management team that directs the enterprise and develops a strategy designed to help the Opry exploit the rising popularity of country music. Although Nashville locals feared that Dallas-based Gaylord Broadcasting might start selling off Opry properties, Gaylord soon allayed their worries.

Gaylord assumed a minimal role in the management of Opryland, choosing to leave E.W. "Bud" Wendell in charge of the complex. Wendell had started out selling insurance for WSM's parent corporation. After a series of transfers and promotions, the 56-year-old Wendell found himself in charge of WSM's Grand Ole Opry in the late 1960s. Wendell served as general manager of the complex during its development and was promoted to president of WSM in 1978. He began reporting to Gaylord after the 1983 acquisition. In addition to Wendell, several other executives that had helped build the enterprise were retained by Gaylord. For example, Tom Griscom, who had been with WSM since 1950, remained as head of the Opry's broadcast operations. Hal Durham, a 20-year Opry veteran, retained his role as manager of the Grand Ole Opry, and Julio Pierpaili remained manager of the Opryland theme park.

Two figures instrumental in the early success of the important Opryland Hotel also stayed with Opryland. Mike Dimond and Jack Vaughn had left coveted positions in the mid-1970s to join the Opryland team and to try to position the complex as a heavyweight convention and tourism center. Vaughn abandoned his leadership spot at the Century Plaza in Los Angeles and Dimond left a good job at Hyatt. Those two, like many of their co-managers at the Opry complex, had put their reputations on the line in an effort to build what they viewed as an innovative and promising venture. "Most people thought [Dimond] was crazy to leave such a stable background with Hyatt to come to Nashville and build a hotel in a cow pasture," said Jerry Wayne, vice-president of marketing at the hotel in an October 1993 issue of *Nashville Business Journal*.

The Opryland Hotel achieved a healthy 78 percent occupancy rate during its first year of operation and grew at a rapid pace during the 1980s. One of Vaughn's and Dimond's savviest moves after the Gaylord acquisition was the creation of the Country Christmas, which brought country music stars in for a special, seasonal event. That program boosted December hotel occupancy, which had historically lagged at 30 percent, to more than 90 percent. As a result of growth, the hotel continued to add new rooms and expand related facilities. Indeed, although it was originally planned to be a 250-room complex, the Opryland Hotel ballooned in size during the 1980s and early 1990s to almost 2,000 rooms, making it one of the largest and most successful hotels in the world.

The success of the Opryland Hotel was as much a reflection of the overall growth of Opryland USA as it was the ability of its managers. Indeed, as Gaylord beefed up the Opryland complex and stepped up promotional activities, attendance at the Grand Ole Opry and the theme park mushroomed. In addition, Gaylord began extending Opryland's reach in several other directions in an effort to build an entire Opryland enterprise founded on country music. In 1983, Gaylord started beaming The Nashville Network (TNN), an advertiser-supported cable television network featuring country lifestyles and entertainment. By 1993, TNN was reaching a whopping 59.2 million American households and generating sales of nearly $200 million. In 1985, moreover, Gaylord opened the 1,200 passenger General Jackson riverboat, the largest paddlewheel showboat in the world.

Gaylord's success in Nashville prompted him to focus his organization's efforts on Opryland during the late 1980s. Nevertheless, his television operations boosted income during that period. In fact, Gaylord was able to unload one of his television stations in 1987 for a high $365 million. He even saved $100 million in taxes on the deal by selling it to a minority-owned company. An unfortunate corollary of that tax break was that he had to roll the proceeds over into a media-related purchase within two years. Gaylord beat the deadline by acquiring a California cable television company for a pricey $418 million.

Key Dates:

1903:   The Gaylord and Dickinson families enter the newspaper publishing business.
1925:   The two families incorporate their venture as Oklahoma Publishing Company; WSM radio begins broadcasting the "WSM Barn Dance."
1928:   "Barn Dance" is renamed Grand Ole Opry.
1972:   Opryland Themepark opens.
1977:   Opryland Hotel opens.
1983:   Gaylord purchases Grand Ole Opry and the Opryland Hotel for $250 million; the Nashville Network is launched.
1985:   Acuff-Rose Music Publishing is acquired.
1991:   Country Music Television is acquired.
1997:   Opryland Theme Park closes and The Nashville Network and Country Music Television are merged with CBS.
2000:   Opry Mills celebrates grand opening.

Expansion in the 1990s

In 1990, Gaylord Broadcasting and its subsidiaries garnered $512 million in sales. However, only $6.5 million of that amount was netted as income, largely because of the heavy debt load incurred by Gaylord when he purchased the lagging cable division. The debt was burdening his balance sheet and eating away at his profits. Lowering Gaylord's $550 million in debt, among other objectives, prompted the media mogul to take his company public in October 1991. Although he sold 22 percent of the equity in his company, he kept more than 60 percent and structured the offering in such a way that he retained voting control of the company. Oklahoma Publishing Company remained a separate company, but all of its broadcasting and entertainment holdings were folded into a new holding company, Gaylord Entertainment Company. The entity's headquarters were moved closer to its base of profits, Nashville.

Gaylord's stock offering in 1991 drew skepticism from some stock brokers who viewed the company as a large, marginally profitable concern dominated by an aging, out-of-step executive. "This company does a lot of revenues and doesn't make much money," exclaimed a Nashville stock broker in the October 14, 1991, issue of *Nashville Business Journal,* "I will not spend a lot of time cruising through that prospectus." Other analysts predicted that the move signaled the likely exit of Gaylord and his family from ownership of the company.

Despite some negative speculation about Gaylord Entertainment's stock sale, Gaylord continued to focus on bolstering the company's strength in country-related enterprises. In 1991 the company purchased a controlling interest in Country Music Television (CMT), a cable television station similar to TNN but geared toward country music videos. In 1992, Gaylord went international with CMT Europe, which offered the network's videos to viewers primarily in the United Kingdom and Scandinavia. By 1993, CMT Europe was also reaching viewers in Czechoslovakia, Poland, and Slovenia, among other nations. The company also initiated several major expansion projects related to its hotel and theme park and announced plans to renovate the old Ryman Auditorium.

To the dismay of Gaylord's detractors, Opryland management's aggressive, long-term growth efforts during the 1980s and early 1990s began to bear fruit. Gaylord's sales rose to $524 million in 1991 before jumping eight percent in 1992 to $564 million. Furthermore, 1992 net income gushed to nearly $30 million and Gaylord's total long-term debt tumbled to a manageable $300 million. Gaylord's performance in 1993 accelerated—sales bolted to $622 million and net income topped $27 million. By the end of 1993, Gaylord Entertainment had become a diversified media and entertainment conglomerate that was on the road to becoming virtually dominant in the country music industry.

As he prepared to lead his company into the mid-1990s, the 72-year-old Gaylord showed no signs of slowing down. Gaylord maintained an active management and ownership role going into 1994. Wendell restructured the company in 1993 to prepare it for more aggressive expansion, separating the company into four divisions: attraction, communications, music, and production. In addition, the company embarked on a number of new ventures that complemented its country music core. In 1994, Gaylord opened Wildhorse Saloon, a nightclub, restaurant, and television production studio. Gaylord hoped to expand the club internationally. It also initiated several other undertakings, including golf courses, river taxis, new convention facilities, and sports programming.

The latter half of the 1990s saw Gaylord Entertainment continue to pursue new business opportunities and development projects. The last years of the decade also saw Gaylord Entertainment abandon some existing businesses, including the closure of one of the company's signature properties. A $175 million expansion of the Opryland Hotel—the third major expansion in the hotel's 18-year history—was completed in mid-1996. The addition, a skylighted area covering 4.5 acres known as The Delta, made the Opryland Hotel the seventh largest hotel in the country and the largest, in term of number of rooms, outside Las Vegas. In 1997—a busy year for the company—Gaylord Entertainment appointed a new chief executive officer, company veteran Terry London, who had previously served as chief financial officer. The change in leadership marked the end of Wendell's 19-year tenure as the company's leader and the beginning of strategic changes that altered the composition of Gaylord's holdings.

Before Wendell's retirement, Gaylord Entertainment began to carve a niche for itself in Christian-related businesses. In January 1997, the company acquired Word Entertainment, a Christian music label. Two years later, the company pursued the same angle under London's leadership, purchasing 51 percent of the Christian music web site Musicforce.com. Concurrently, Musicforce.com acquired 100 percent of Lightsource.com, a Christian-content provider for the spiritual channel of broadcast.com. Gaylord Entertainment's online activities were subsequently organized into a new division called GETdigitalmedia, a venture that was expected to generate $20 million in revenue in 2000.

As the company developed its presence as an online Christian content provider, it severed its ties to several other businesses. Cable networks TNN and CMT were sold to Westinghouse Corp.'s CBS Cable unit in October 1997, but the biggest news of the year was the announcement that Gaylord Entertainment had decided to close the Opryland Themepark. Citing declining revenues and attendance, the company closed the park on the last day of 1997, deciding to invest its resources instead in a massive retail complex called Opry Mills. After teaming up with Arlington, Virginia-based The Mills Corp., Gaylord Entertainment broke ground on the Opry Mills project in October 1998, a $200 million, 1.2-million-square-foot retail and entertainment complex. On the site where the park once stood, Opry Mills opened in May 2000. The sprawling mall was expected to draw 17 million visitors annually to Nashville, compared to the two million visitors the theme park attracted in 1997.

As Gaylord Entertainment geared itself for the first years of the 21st century, construction crews were busy erecting vital components of the company's future. In late 1998, Gaylord Entertainment announced two new hotel-development projects, a 1,500-room Opryland Hotel in Grapevine, Texas, and a 1,400-room Opryland Hotel in Osceola County, near Orlando, Florida. The Texas and Florida Opryland Hotels, scheduled to open in 2003 and 2002, respectively, were the first of between five and seven hotels the company planned to establish in the future. While construction was underway at the two sites, the company announced plans for the $500 million Opryland Hotel Potomac, a 2,000-room hotel and convention center slated to be a prominent feature of National Harbor, a 543-acre site in Maryland's Prince George's Country. Construction was scheduled to begin in 2002 for a grand opening in 2004.

Principal Subsidiaries

Opryland USA; Acuff-Rose Music Inc.; Blanton Harrell Entertainment; General Jackson Showboat; New Gaylord Entertainment Co.; Opryland Productions Inc.; WSM Inc.; Opry Mills.

Principal Divisions

Gaylord Broadcasting Division; Gaylord Cable Networks Division; Gaylord Digital Division (GETdigitalmedia); Gaylord Entertainment Division; Syndicom Entertainment Group.

Principal Competitors

Integrity Incorporated; Viacom Inc.; The Walt Disney Company.

Further Reading

Chappel, Lindsay, "An Interview with E.W. Wendell," *Advantage,* January 1985, Sec. 1, p. 34.

"Gaylord Entertainment Co. Names Chief Operating Officer," *Business Wire,* February 19, 1993.

"Gaylord Execs Quieted Second-Guessing," *Nashville Business Journal,* October 4, 1993, Sec. 1, p. 6.

Hall, Alan, "Gaylord Entertainment Co. Announces Reorganization," *Business Wire,* September 23, 1993.

Hall, Joe, "Gaylord Eyes Global Chain of Saloons," *Nashville Business Journal,* November 1, 1993, Sec. 1, p. 1.

Hawkins, Chuck, "If Ed Gaylord Is So Private, Why Is He Going Public?," *Business Week,* September 30, 1991, pp. 85–86.

London, Terry, "Gaylord Entertainment Co. Announces 1991 Results," *Business Wire,* February 11, 1992.

"Mills Joins Opryland Complex," *Chain Store Age Executive with Shopping Center Age,* May 2000, p. 124.

Nelson, Carrington, "In Nashville, Tenn., Gaylord Entertainment Trades Tradition for Future," *Knight-Ridder/Tribune Business News,* November 6, 1997, p. 1106B1152.

Oertley, Karen, "What's Your Park Worth?," *Amusement Business,* November 2, 1998, p. 4.

Oliver, Valeri, "Analysts Unexcited by Gaylord Stock Offer," *Nashville Business Journal,* October 14, 1991, Sec. 1, p. 1.

Price, Deborah Evans, "Higher Ground," *Billboard,* August 14, 1999, p. 45.

Serwer, Alan E., "Stand by Your Core Franchise," *Fortune,* January 25, 1993, p. 104.

—Dave Mote
—updated by Jeffrey L. Covell

GE Capital Aviation Services

201 High Ridge Road
Stamford, Connecticut 06927
U.S.A.
Telephone: (203) 357-3776
Fax: (203) 316-7865
Web site: http://www.gecas.com

Wholly Owned Subsidiary of GE Capital Services
Incorporated: 1975 as Guinness Peat Aviation
Employees: 200
Sales: $655 million (1999 est.)
NAIC: 532411 Commercial Air, Rail, and Water
   Transportation Equipment Rental and Leasing

Although it claims to have written its first aircraft lease in 1965, GE Capital Aviation Services (GECAS) did not become a global market leader until its takeover/rescue of Guinness Peat Aviation (GPA) in 1993. The brainchild of longtime Aer Lingus employee Tony Ryan, GPA mastered the air finance game and grew phenomenally during the 1970s and 1980s until its progress was stopped by a failed global flotation.

Origins

T.A. "Tony" Ryan was born in 1936, the son of a train driver and grandson of a stationmaster. He left school at 15 and by age 19 was working for Irish state carrier Aer Lingus as a dispatcher at the Shannon Airport. Ryan progressed smoothly through the ranks. When assigned to Chicago, he earned a business administration degree at night school. He then became manager of the New York station and finally was given responsibility for the airline's leasing of aircraft in the early 1970s. In 1972, when Aer Lingus found itself with an excess Boeing 747 jumbo jet, after the "Troubles" in Northern Ireland, Ryan persuaded Air Siam to lease it complete with Aer Lingus staff— a deal that produced winners on all sides.

Having seen the large profits possible in the field, in January 1975 Ryan proposed an aircraft leasing venture between Aer Lingus, merchant bank Guinness Mahon (in which Aer Lingus

had invested in 1972), and himself, after having borrowed IR £30,000 (US$50,000). Originally called Guinair, the new company was soon renamed Guinness Peat Aviation (GPA).

In writing to Aer Lingus CEO David Kennedy, Ryan outlined four key factors critical to the success of the venture: "high calibre personnel; introductions and high level contacts; access to back-up technical resources; ability to provide or organize financing." Headquartered at a tax-free base in Shannon, the initial staff consisted of six people, including a secretary. They worked hard under the very demanding Ryan and were compensated extremely well. Ryan's righthand man Maurice Foley joined GPA in 1976 as a nonexecutive director on behalf of Aer Lingus. He subsequently became chief executive. Foley's strategic thinking was highly regarded.

GPA started out as an aircraft broker. At the time, many European and American airlines were attempting to trim their fleets due to the global recession. GPA matched these extra planes with needs in the southern hemisphere. As Ryan recalled in 1979, the market changed with the end of the recession in 1977 and GPA was required to purchase its own, new planes for lease. An independent airline, Air Tara, was formed to operate a fleet of fully staffed aircraft for hire. By 1979, GPA was one of Ireland's main sources of hard currency. It had found great success among financially struggling countries (despite its proximity to England, Ireland was considered one of Europe's poorer countries) eager to start airlines of their own. GPA's "wet" leases of fueled and staffed jets allowed governments to set up their own airliners overnight.

Soaring in the 1980s

Air Canada bought a 22.7 percent holding in GPA in 1980 and General Electric Credit Corp., sought by Foley, acquired a similar holding in 1983 for $18 million. The Air Canada link allowed GPA to cull from among Air Canada's diverse fleet to offer a greater variety of aircraft to its clients.

In the mid-1980s, GPA adopted an aggressive new policy of acquiring options for new aircraft before the company had customers in hand. By the end of the decade, GPA dominated aircraft futures and could command premium prices for its operating leases, as well as garnish steep discounts (up to 20 percent) from the aircraft manufacturers. In 1989, GPA had more than $300 million in nonrefundable deposit payments outstanding for aircraft due for delivery as late as 1996.

Leasing accounted for more than 50 percent of GPA's revenue in 1986 and the company formed its own financial services division in 1987. That year, Ryan began to stock GPA's boardroom with business and political luminaries including former Irish Prime Minister Garrett FitzGerald, *Economist* Chairman Sir John Harvey Jones, Mitsubishi Corporation President Shinroku Morohashi, Allied Irish Bank Group Chairman and former Irish attorney general Peter Sutherland, Air Canada Chairman Claude Taylor, and former Rolls-Royce Chairman Lord Keith. Many were also investors.

GPA was seeking to double its credit line to $1.5 billion, but had difficulty convincing banks to invest in the new and complicated world of aircraft finance. Ultimately, it did arrange for what was called the biggest financing ever for a private company. Most of the money went toward acquiring new Boeing 737s. Pretax profits were $71 million in 1987.

GPA ended 1988 with an implied market value of more than $1.5 billion. A group of Irish institutional investors had bought a 14 percent share in the company for IR £145 million. GPA was then controlled about one-third each by European, North American, and Japanese interests. Employees owned six percent of shares and Tony Ryan owned another eight percent. He was reported to be earning IR £9 million (US$13 million) a year.

GPA bought ten percent of Braniff Airlines in 1988, and Braniff agreed to buy a dozen new Fokker 100 aircraft from GPA. This transaction was executed through a joint venture owned half by GPA and 25 percent each by Braniff and Japanese interests. GPA also arranged for Braniff to buy 50 Airbus A320s that Pan American World Airways had on order, half of them via GPA leases. Braniff also acquired Pan Am's 50 options.

In January 1989, GPA had a US$3 billion dollar fleet of 164 aircraft leased to 62 airlines in 29 countries, according to a Salomon Brothers analyst. The average lease length was more than six years. Most were not provided complete with aircrew. The Guinness Mahon merchant bank sold its shares later in the year after the collapse of its parent company, Equiticorp.

GPA had 170 employees and pretax profits of $150 million in 1989. It had ordered $850 million worth of advanced turboprop aircraft for delivery in the early to mid-1990s. By 1996,

however, the industry was demanding small, regional jets for short commuter flights.

A Change of Direction in the 1990s

Only three or four firms were involved in aircraft leasing when GPA started; there were 30 competitors by 1999, including divisions of multinational corporations and aircraft manufacturers themselves. GPA's largest rival was International Lease Finance Corporation (ILFC), of Beverly Hills, California, which had just 18 employees. Some observers felt ILFC's smaller, less complex operation would fare better in a recession.

In 1990 a recession, it turned out, was just over the horizon. U.S. airlines together lost $5 billion that year. At this time, GPA had orders or options on 700 aircraft over the next decade. Further, GPA lost its tax-free status at its Shannon base in April 1990. It was not perhaps the most auspicious moment to launch a share offering, but Aer Lingus and Air Canada were reportedly eager to amortize their holdings to ease their own financial burdens. Still, the firm continued posting respectable numbers. Lease revenues for the 1990–91 fiscal year rose 66 percent to US$8.3 billion. Profits reached nearly $300 million when the company had about 300 employees—an employee-to-revenue ratio unheard of in most industries.

GPA announced plans for a stock flotation in the spring of 1991, but it was delayed for a year. Foley, then president, became CEO in March 1992, and Ryan remained chairman. Ryan took the CEO position back that September, however, as the company was scrambling to find financing. Ryan himself soon was ousted and replaced by Dennis Stevenson, director of the Tate Gallery. By this time the company was referring to itself as GPA Group.

Failed Flotation in 1992

After a year of haggling with advisers over the share price, the company launched its US$1.1 billion (IR £603 million) share sale in June 1992 in London, New York, and Tokyo. Ryan had hoped originally to value the company at $3 billion. Even at the lower price, GPA received applications for only 50 million of 85 million shares on offer, and the company abandoned the offering on June 18, 1992. Institutions avoided the offering, which was most popular with private investors in Japan. Likely factors in the offering's failure included the general poor health of the aviation industry, a lack of understanding of the aircraft leasing business on the part of banks, and GPA's own "icy" relationship with the financial press.

Had the offering succeeded, GPA would have emerged as the largest Irish public company, worth 20 percent of the entire Irish stock market. Instead, the news lowered all types of aviation stocks. As a result of the failed offering, GPA had its credit rating downgraded, forcing it into higher payments on its very substantial borrowings—its aircraft orders through 2000 were worth $12 billion. GPA was able to sell or cancel 66 percent of these, although not without penalty.

GPA lost $993 million in 1992–93. By May 1993, the shares offered at $20 each were worth less than $1 apiece. With bankruptcy imminent, in September 1993, GE Capital announced plans to create a new subsidiary, GE Capital Aviation Services (GECAS), to manage GPA's assets. It also bought 44 of GPA's 464 aircraft outright for US$1.4 billion (IR £920 million). GECAS had the option to buy a nearly two-thirds stake in GPA by March 1998. GPA agreed not to use the names GPA or Guinness Peat Aviation after 2001.

GECAS was staffed by 160 GPA employees (25 remained with GPA) and based at Shannon. The virtual merger was complex and difficult, its structure devised to prevent GE Capital from assuming GPA's liabilities. GPA essentially was divided into two companies, only the namesake being responsible for the $5 billion debt. GECAS was formally established in November 1993. GE Capital's own San Francisco-based Polaris Aircraft Leasing, based in California, was incorporated into it.

Many of GPA's high-profile board members resigned as part of the restructuring. Several GPA executives left during the transition period, uncomfortable with the change to a more hierarchical corporate style. Herb D. Depp, former president of Polaris Aircraft, was appointed GECAS president and CEO in March 1994 as former head Colm Barrington resigned to start his own aircraft management company in Dublin. In December, Depp moved to a vice-president job at GE Aircraft Engines to be replaced at GECAS by James T. Johnson, formerly head of the Large Commercial Engine unit of Pratt & Whitney. Johnson previously had been a vice-president at Boeing, giving him a unique insight into negotiating aircraft purchases.

GECAS owned or managed more than 900 planes at the beginning of 1995. After a lull in new aircraft purchases, in February 1996 the company placed an order worth potentially $4 billion with Boeing for five or six 777s and up to 178 737s. It followed that a few months later with a $2.5 billion Airbus order. GECAS earned an estimated $200 million in profits in 1996, compared with $368 million posted by ILFC, its smaller competitor. GECAS owned 424 aircraft and managed another 435 for other investors. ILFC owned 317 planes. Meanwhile, GPA finally secured a $4 billion bond issue in March 1996 after negotiating with 138 banks.

GECAS accounted for six to seven percent of the business of GE Capital Corp., which had 26 other subsidiaries. The corporate association seemed like good news for GE's engine division, which consistently won GECAS orders over rival Rolls-Royce. Johnson planned to expand the unit's business to include

aircraft upgrades. He left, however, in the summer of 1997 to become COO and president of business jet maker Gulfstream Aerospace. Henry Hubschman became president after Johnson's departure.

GPA found another investor, Texas Pacific, in October 1998 after GE Capital dropped its option to buy its remaining shares. Texas Pacific agreed to pay $115 million for a 47.7 percent stake in the company, for which GPA had logged a $63 million profit in 1997–98, up 15 percent for the year.

In May 1999, GECAS sold the equity interest in 36 aircraft worth $1.3 billion to Miami-based UniCapital Corporation. Rival ILFC increased its portfolio by $2.8 billion between May 1998 and May 1999, closing within $700 million of GECAS. It also showed no signs of slowing. A half dozen smaller competitors, led by Ansett Worldwide Aviation Services, competed even more closely at the next tier.

In the late 1990s, GECAS helped its clients in Asia shuffle $500 million worth of aircraft away from the depressed region to Europe and the Americas. Operating leases remained popular in Asia, since they allowed for such risk mitigation as well as for flexibility in capacity.

Catching the regional jet trend pioneered by Bombardier Inc. in the decade prior, GECAS ordered 50 of that company's Canadair regional jets for $1.3 billion in June 2000. The purchase followed similar ones from Empresa Brasileira de Aeronautica SA (Embraer) and Fairchild Dornier Corp. Even that order was dwarfed by one in July 2000 for 74 Boeing 737 and 777 airliners worth US$5.5 billion.

Principal Competitors

International Lease Finance Corporation; Ansett Worldwide Aviation Services; Boullioun Aviation Services; Singapore Aircraft Leasing Enterprise.

Further Reading

Ashworth, Jon, "Aerobatic Manoeuvres That Pulled GPA Back from Brink," *Times,* Bus. Sec., October 2, 1998.
"Breidenbach Resigns at Gulfstream—to Be Replaced by Boeing Veteran," *Weekly of Business Aviation,* August 4, 1997.
Bryant, Adam, "General Electric Spreads Its Wings," *New York Times,* Bus. Sec., May 16, 1996, p. D1.
Cameron, Douglas, "A Leviathan of World Leasing," *Financial Times,* August 30, 1996, p. 12.
Canniffe, Mary, "GPA: New Deal Vital," *Irish Times,* Bus. Sec., p. 16.
"Champagne Comes to the Country Fair," *Euromoney,* April 1989, p. 39.
Chipello, Christopher J., "Unit of GE Orders 50 Bombardier Jets for $1.3 Billion, Acquires Options on 100," *Wall Street Journal,* June 12, 2000, p. B4.
Cooper, Ron, "Is Ryan of GPA Flying Too High?," *Euromoney,* April 1989, pp. 35–40.
Cope, Nigel, "GPA Comes Down to Earth," *Business,* May 1991, pp. 58ff.
Cullen, Brenda, "GPA: The Global Flotation That Failed," in *The Search for Corporate Strategic Credibility: Concepts and Cases in Global Strategy Communications,* edited by Richard B. Higgins, Westport, Conn.; London: Quorum Books, 1996, pp. 95–108.
Dobie, Clare, "Share Flop Leaves GPA in Crisis," *Independent,* June 19, 1992, p. 22.

Dwyer, Rob, "ILFC Surge Brings It Closer to GECAS," *Airfinance Journal,* July/August 1999, pp. 28–30.

Farrell, David, "A Total Fleet Solutions Approach to Strategic Planning," *Airfinance Journal,* Aircraft Finance in Asia supplement, September 1999, pp. 8–10.

"GECAS Kicks Off Order Chase," *Airfinance Journal,* February 1996, p. 12.

Harrison, Michael, "GPA Flotation May Be Delayed," *Independent,* February 12, 1992, p. 23.

Kjelgaard, Chris, "The New Broom," *Airfinance Journal,* February 1995, p. 26.

Mackay, Angela, "Ryan Takes Back Both Controls at GPA," *Times,* Bus. Sec., September 7, 1992.

Maher, John, "GPA Shareholders Set to Approve GE Deal," *Irish Times,* Bus. Sec., October 18, 1993, p. 16.

Narbrough, Colin, "Luck of the Irish Finally Runs Out for Tony Ryan," *Times,* Bus. Sec., May 14, 1993.

Nisse, Jason, "Sea Change in the Air," *Banker,* December 1987, pp. 90ff.

O'Connor, Anthony, "GE Force," *Airfinance Journal,* May 1997, pp. 20–23.

O'Donnell, Thomas, "Never Too Late," *Forbes,* April 23, 1984, pp. 54, 58.

Olins, Rufus, "GPA Takes Flotation Route," *Sunday Times,* Bus. Sec., May 5, 1991.

Proctor, Paul, "GE Places $4-Billion Boeing Order," *Aviation Week & Space Technology,* January 29, 1996, pp. 50ff.

Rudd, Roland, "GPA Rejects Advice Over Flotation Price," *Financial Times,* Sec. I, February 3, 1992, p. 15.

Shanahan, Ella, "Fortunes Diminished As Issue Fails to Fly," *Irish Times,* Bus. Sec., June 19, 1992, p. 14.

Share, Bernard, *The Flight of the Iolar: The Aer Lingus Experience 1936–1986,* Dublin: Gill and Macmillan, 1986.

Urry, Maggie, "How GPA Will Restructure," *Financial Times,* International Company News, September 24, 1993, p. 23.

Velocci, Anthony L., Jr., "GECAS Study Reveals Leasing Paramount to Aircraft Acquisition," *Aviation Week & Space Technology,* November 25, 1996, p. 44.

Woulfe, Jimmy, "Former GPA Chief Still in Full Flight," interview of Niall Greene, *Limerick Leader,* October 23, 1999.

—Frederick C. Ingram

General Mills

General Mills, Inc.

Number One General Mills Boulevard
Post Office Box 1113
Minneapolis, Minnesota 55440
U.S.A.
Telephone: (612) 764-2311
Fax: (612) 764-2445
Web site: http://www.generalmills.com

Public Company
Incorporated: 1928
Employees: 10,660
Sales: $6.25 billion (1999)
Stock Exchanges: New York Midwest
Ticker Symbol: GIS
NAIC: 311211 Flour Milling; 311230 Breakfast Cereal
    Manufacturing; 311340 Nonchocolate Confectionery
    Manufacturing; 311423 Dried and Dehydrated Food
    Manufacturing; 311511 Fluid Milk Manufacturing;
    311822 Flour Mixes and Dough Manufacturing from
    Purchased Flour; 311919 Other Snack Food
    Manufacturing; 311999 All Other Miscellaneous Food
    Manufacturing

General Mills, Inc. is one of the leading breakfast cereal companies in the world, with such well-known brands as Cheerios, Chex, Cocoa Puffs, Kix, Total, Trix, and Wheaties stocking the shelves of supermarkets everywhere. In addition to its breakfast cereal products, the company includes some of the best names in other food lines such as Gold Medal flour, Bisquick baking mixes, Betty Crocker dessert mixes, Hamburger Helper dinner mixes, Yoplait yogurt, Pop Secret microwave popcorn, and Nature Valley granola bars. General Mills markets its products in more than 90 countries worldwide, with much of this activity stemming from two joint ventures: a 50–50 enterprise with Nestlé S.A. called Cereal Partners Worldwide, which makes and sells ready-to-eat cereals outside North America; and Snack Ventures Europe, a venture with PepsiCo, Inc. 40.5 percent owned by General Mills, which makes and markets snack foods in continental Europe. General Mills is also active outside the grocery sector through its foodservice unit, which markets products under the company's various brands to educational, hospitality, and healthcare institutions, convenience stores, and vending machine operators.

Early History

General Mills was incorporated in 1928, but its origins go back to 1866, when Cadwallader Washburn opened the first flour mill in Minneapolis, Minnesota. His business, originally called the Minneapolis Milling Company, competed with local miller C.A. Pillsbury. In 1869 they joined forces to form the Minneapolis Millers Association. Pillsbury and Washburn both wanted to find a way to make Midwestern winter wheat into a higher grade of flour. Eventually, with the help of a French engineer, Washburn not only improved the method but also made his product the best flour available in the United States. When Pillsbury adopted the same technique, Minneapolis became the country's flour milling center.

When John Crosby entered into partnership with Washburn in 1877, the Minneapolis Milling Company was renamed Washburn Crosby Company. The following year the Minneapolis Millers Association was reorganized to appease farmers who found its business practices unfair. In 1880 Washburn Crosby flours were awarded the gold, silver, and bronze medals at the first International Miller's Exhibition in Cincinnati, Ohio; the company soon changed the name of its best flour to Gold Medal. In 1888, James S. Bell succeeded Washburn as head of the Washburn Crosby Company, ousting Washburn's heirs. The mill prospered through the turn of the century. In 1928, the year General Mills was formed, the company had 5,800 employees and annual sales of $123 million. Its strongest products were Gold Medal flour, Softasilk cake flour (introduced in 1923), and Wheaties, a ready-to-eat cereal that had debuted in 1924.

Bell's son, James Ford, was responsible for creating General Mills, Inc. in 1928 by consolidating the Washburn mill with several other major flour-milling companies around the country, including Red Star Milling Co., Sperry Milling Co., and Larrowe Milling Co. Within five months Ford had collected 27 companies, making General Mills the largest flour-milling company in the world. As a part of General Mills, these mills kept their operational independence but left advertising and product development to General Mills headquarters. This consolidation was well timed, as it gave the company the strength to survive and even prosper through the Great Depression, when earnings grew steadily and stock in the company was stable.

Bell's research emphasis put General Mills in a strong position for the changing demands of increasingly urban consumers. The company soon introduced Bisquick, the first baking mix, which debuted in 1931; the company's first ready-to-eat puffed cereal, Kix, in 1937; and another ready-to-eat cereal, Cheerioats, in 1941. Cheerioats was renamed Cheerios five years after its introduction; under its new name it eventually would become the number one cereal in the United States.

Bell's early interest in diversification and technology made mobilization for World War II easier. General Mills' factories were restructured to produce equipment for the navy, medicinal alcohol, and bags to make into sandbags, as well as the expected dehydrated food. In 1942 Donald D. Davis, president of General Mills since Bell moved to chairman in 1934, resigned to head the U.S. War Production Board.

Henry Bullis, who began at General Mills as a mill hand after World War I, replaced Davis. Following Bell's industrial lead, Bullis immediately entered the animal feed industry by processing soybeans, a venture that ultimately became General Mills' chemical division.

Postwar demand for consumer foods allowed the company to deemphasize industrial activity and to concentrate on the success of its cereals and Betty Crocker cake mixes—the latter having been launched in 1947. Consumers demanded less time in the kitchen and continued to buy foods that required less preparation. Ready-to-eat cereals, now the company's staple, grew dramatically, and more brands were introduced, including Trix, a presweetened cereal that hit the market in 1954.

Throughout the 1920s Bell and his associates had invested heavily in advertising, which was becoming a significant force in selling products to a national market. Betty Crocker, created in 1921, was a legacy from Washburn Crosby. By 1928 Betty Crocker's name, signature, and radio voice had been introduced in connection with General Mills' consumer goods. General Mills also sponsored radio programs and pioneered the use of athlete endorsements on its own radio station, WCCO. In 1933 the advertising slogan "Wheaties. The Breakfast of Champions" was used for the first time. The Wheaties brand sponsored the first commercial sports broadcast on television, a game between the Brooklyn Dodgers and the Cincinnati Reds

on August 29, 1939, which was presented by NBC and featured the sportscasting of the famed Red Barber.

The postwar consumer's interest in convenience complemented General Mills' growing advertising efforts. The company continued to refine its advertising methods after World War II, and such promotions as the *Betty Crocker Cookbook* and advertisements on TV, an exciting new medium at the time, helped to increase sales and consumer recognition of the company. Capitalizing on its research and media prominence, the company soon held the second position in breakfast food sales.

Another career General Mills man, Charles H. Bell, rose to the presidency in 1952. Since advertising had become the main force in marketing its various brands, centralization had crept into the organization. Bell found it necessary to reassign management decisions closer to operations. In 1958 he moved headquarters out of downtown Minneapolis and into suburban Golden Valley. Still stronger changes were needed, but the company was hesitant. General Mills' 1940s ventures into electronics and appliances had failed, and the company had recently begun to post losses in animal feeds and flour milling. Consumer foods remained the main moneymaker, but General Mills' stock value dropped to $1.25 a share in 1962, its lowest point in 12 years.

Diversifying Widely in the 1960s

Bell recruited an outsider, Edwin W. Rawlings, in 1959, and two years later Rawlings was appointed president. Rawlings reevaluated company output and shook up management positions. The family flour market was declining three percent a year, and Rawlings decided consumer preferences had shifted once again. Although the company was then the largest flour miller in the world and flour made up the greatest volume of output, Rawlings closed half of General Mills' mills and renewed the company's commitment to packaged foods by introducing foodservice products for restaurants and hotels. He also divested its interests in electronics, appliances, formula feeds, and other smaller operations. These actions caused a short-term, five-year sales decline for the company.

Next Rawlings began a series of acquisitions that would alter corporate structure for the next 20 years and provide two decades of continual earnings growth. Snack foods entered the company's portfolio with the purchase of Morton Foods, Inc. in 1964. In 1966 came the Tom Huston Peanut Co., and in 1968 General Mills went abroad with the purchase of Smiths Food Group, Ltd. of England and Belgium. The French Biscuiterie Nantaise soon followed, as did snack food companies in Latin America and Japan.

Other major acquisitions were Gorton's, a frozen fish company, and an aggressive move into the toy and game industry with Rainbow Crafts (Play-Doh), Kenner, and Parker Bros., all in 1968. In ten years international toy operations would comprise one-third of the company's sales, at $482.3 million. General Mills was no longer the world's largest miller, but it was now the world's largest toy manufacturer.

Early in 1969 the Federal Trade Commission (FTC) issued a consent order blocking General Mills from further acquisitions within the snack food industry. At the time of purchase, both

Key Dates:

1866: Cadwallader Washburn, owner of Minneapolis Milling Company, opens the first flour mill in Minneapolis.

1877: John Crosby enters into partnership with Washburn, whose company is then renamed Washburn Crosby Company.

1880: Company wins gold medal at the first International Millers' Exhibition, leading to the later creation of the Gold Medal brand.

1888: James S. Bell takes over leadership of Washburn Crosby.

1921: The fictional Betty Crocker is created by Washburn Crosby.

1924: Wheaties ready-to-eat cereal debuts.

1928: Bell's son, James Ford, leads the creation of General Mills through the merger of Washburn Crosby with several other regional millers.

1931: Bisquick, the first baking mix, is introduced.

1941: Cheerioats ready-to-eat cereal debuts.

1946: Cheerioats is renamed Cheerios.

1947: The first Betty Crocker cake mix is introduced.

1954: Trix, a presweetened cereal, hits the market.

1961: Edwin W. Rawlings is appointed president and ushers in a period of wide diversification.

1964: Company enters the snack food sector with the purchase of Morton Foods.

1968: Company acquires Gorton's frozen seafood and several toy and game outfits—Rainbow Crafts, Kenner, and Parker Bros.

1969: Company moves into specialty retailing with purchases of Lacoste clothing and Monet Jewelry.

1970: Red Lobster restaurant chain is acquired; Hamburger Helper makes its debut.

1971: Eddie Bauer is purchased.

1973: Talbot's is acquired.

1977: Company purchases the U.S. rights to the Yoplait yogurt brand.

1983: The Olive Garden Italian restaurant chain is launched.

1985: Company divests its toy, fashion, and nonapparel retailing operations; Pop Secret microwave popcorn is introduced.

1989: Eddie Bauer and Talbot's are sold; Cereal Partners Worldwide, a joint venture with Nestlé, S.A., is formed.

1992: Company establishes Snack Ventures Europe in partnership with PepsiCo, Inc.

1995: The Gorton's brand is sold to Unilever; the restaurant division is spun off to shareholders as a separate public company, Darden Restaurants, Inc.

1997: The branded ready-to-eat cereal and snack mix businesses of Ralcorp Holdings, Inc. are acquired, including the Chex brand.

1999: Lloyd's Barbecue Company, Farmhouse Foods Company, and Gardetto's Bakery, Inc. are acquired.

Morton and Tom Huston were among the top ten producers of potato and corn chips.

During his seven years as General Mills chief, Rawlings managed to double the company's earnings and bring consumer foods to 80 percent of total sales, up from 45 percent. Although Rawlings wanted another outsider to succeed him, the board of directors chose James P. McFarland in 1969. General Mills was the only company for which McFarland had ever worked, and in choosing him the corporation renewed its commitment to balance and stability.

Adding Specialty Retailing and Restaurants in the 1970s

Seeking controlled growth, McFarland slowed, but did not stop, acquisitions. The first of many clothing company purchases was David Crystal, Inc. (Lacoste clothing) in 1969. Along with the purchase of Monet Jewelry in the same year, the purchase introduced General Mills to specialty retailing; the company later bought Eddie Bauer, Inc. (in 1971) and Talbot's (1973). Although the company missed the growth of fast food, purchasing and developing the Red Lobster restaurant chain (in 1970) would eventually make the new restaurant group General Mills' second largest division. Meantime, Hamburger Helper was introduced in 1970.

McFarland, an experienced salesman, involved himself with day-to-day operations and left long-term planning to COO James A. Summer. In his first two years as CEO, McFarland saw sales rise from $885 million to $1.1 billion and operating profits from $37.5 million to $44 million. His goal was to reach $2 billion in sales by 1976. Sales that year were actually $2.6 billion, four times the 1969 level, with earnings of more than $100 million. He then announced E. Robert Kinney as his successor.

Like most quickly expanding companies of this period, however, not all of General Mills' forays were successful. Between 1950 and 1986, General Mills made 86 acquisitions in new industries; 73 percent of those made by 1975 had been divested within five years. A profitable core business in consumer foods eased the burden of these failed efforts.

In the early 1970s the FTC attempted to dismiss General Mills' 1968 acquisition of Gorton's. The block was lifted in 1973. Later, by allying itself with General Foods Corp., the firm succeeded in blocking a 1977 FTC proposal to forbid advertisements aimed at children. Late in 1980, the FTC again filed a complaint against cereal companies, this time an antitrust suit following a ten-year investigation. It charged that between 1958 and 1972 cereal manufacturers had an average after-tax profit of 19.8 percent, compared with a general manufacturing average of 8.9 percent, and suggested that Kellogg Company, General Mills, and General Foods shared a monopoly over the cereal industry. The charges were dismissed in 1981 after the companies had lobbied for and won congressional favor.

By heavily promoting its brands, the company did well in the 1970s, reporting gains in the toy division and the tripling of sales for consumer foods. Between 1973 and 1978, sales increased $1.7 billion. Of this growth, 41 percent came from new products developed internally, 15 percent from acquisitions, and 18 percent from expansion of restaurant and retail centers. General Mills' management system, in which one manager directed the production, marketing, and sales of each brand, also got credit for some of the increase. After the 1977 sale of the chemical division, General Mills divided its business into food processing, restaurants, games and toys, fashion, and specialty retailing. The food sector was bolstered in 1977 when the company purchased the U.S. rights to the Yoplait yogurt brand.

Refocusing on Food in the 1980s

In 1981 H. Brewster Atwater, Jr., became president of General Mills. The following year was a solid one for the company, as consumer foods, restaurants, toys, fashion, and retailing reported sales increases of between 12 percent and 24 percent. Retailing profit was half that of its previous year, however, and although the toy and game division had grown, the toy industry worldwide had decreased 2.9 percent.

Izod Lacoste also performed well. With $400 million in sales, General Mills intended to develop more items under the label. But by 1985 sales had dropped to $225 million, and the company hoped to cut overhead to break even at $180 million by 1986. In 1985 the largest toymaker in the world divested items representing more than 25 percent of its sales, including toys, fashion, and nonapparel retailing. Former president Kinney became head of the spun-off Kenner Parker Toys Inc. The other spinoff, called the Fashion Co., consisted of Monet Jewelry, Izod Lacoste, and Ship 'n Shore. The company kept its furniture group (Pennsylvania House, Kittinger) for future sale. Also kept was Eddie Bauer, despite its reported loss because of excess inventory. General Mills reported a net loss of $72 million due to the restructuring and a 21 percent increase in advertising expenses.

As expected by analysts, General Mills quickly recovered. Earnings were up to $222 million by 1987. Its core businesses were the Big G cereals, Red Lobster, and Talbot's in its consumer foods, restaurants, and specialty retailing divisions. The food division had expanded in 1985 with the introduction of Pop Secret, a microwave popcorn product.

The consolidation process begun in 1985 continued in the latter half of the 1980s. Pared down somewhat, the company originally planned to expand its remaining retailing operations. But the takeover climate of the late 1980s and a disappointing Christmas in 1987 forced the company to exit retailing altogether by selling Eddie Bauer and Talbot's in 1989.

General Mills had divested itself of many of its holdings since 1976, but its surviving businesses had a firm footing in their markets. More than 90 percent of the company's food sales came from products with a first or second place market share position. Streamlining also had allowed the company to keep up with the rapid pace of new product development. From 1985 to 1988, 24 percent to 29 percent of the food division's growth came from new products.

General Mills also increased its share in the fast-growing cereal market, boosted by the oat bran craze of the late 1980s (Cheerios' market share alone climbed 3.1 percent in one year) and the accompanying breakfast food boom. General Mills was the only top cereal producer prepared to respond to these trends.

1990s: Venturing Overseas, Exiting from Restaurateuring, Adding Chex

In 1989 General Mills began to expand into international markets, a sector that archrival Kellogg had been exploiting for years. By forming Cereal Partners Worldwide with Nestlé S.A., the Swiss-based food products giant, General Mills planned to cut into the European cereal market long dominated by Kellogg. By 1991 the partnership was doing so well in Europe that it ventured into the Mexican market. In 1992 General Mills established Snack Ventures Europe, a $600 million partnership with PepsiCo, Inc., to take advantage of the growing market for snack foods in Europe.

After the growth in market share during the late 1980s and early 1990s, by 1993 General Mills experienced a slowdown in its core business of brand name cereal and food products. Nevertheless, in an unprecedented move, the company hired approximately 10,000 new employees during the same year. The reason for this was the growth of the restaurant division. Having already acquired the Red Lobster seafood chain in 1970, General Mills attempted other formats that did not work, including steakhouses and Mexican and health food eateries. In 1983 the company came up with its own Italian restaurant chain called Olive Garden Italian Restaurants and in 1991 launched China Coast, an attempt to fill the void in Chinese food restaurant chains. At the end of 1993, there were 657 Red Lobster and 429 Olive Garden restaurants located throughout the United States, and nine China Coast units in Orlando, Indianapolis, and Fort Worth. With restaurant profits increasing rapidly, General Mills planned to open 100 new locations annually for the next two or three years.

During 1993, in a widely publicized decision amid growing consumer complaints, General Mills decided not to increase its cereal prices to keep pace with Kellogg. Kellogg implemented a 2.1 percent increase on all of its brand name cereals, but General Mills had previously hiked prices nearly 28 percent between 1988 and 1992. As a result, General Mills actually cut prices from 11 to 16 percent on three of its most well-known brands. This discounting strategy increased volume sales on all three of the cereal brands.

General Mills reaped more than $8 billion in sales during 1993, with the company's packaged goods accounting for two-thirds of its revenues and the restaurant division making up the remaining amount. With the highest return on equity of any company in the entire industry for the previous five years—an impressive 42.8 percent compared with the industry median of 17 percent—management was confident enough to predict an average growth in profits of 14 percent annually through 2000.

In 1995 General Mills completed its transformation back into a strictly packaged foods company. In May of that year the company sold the Gorton's brand to Unilever and spun off its restaurant division to its shareholders as a separate public company, Darden Restaurants, Inc. As a result, General Mills saw its 1995 revenues reduced by more than $3.5 billion, compared with 1994, but the company emerged with an increased focus and greater profitability. Upon the completion of these moves, Atwater retired, having led the dismantling of a conglomerate. Taking over as chairman and CEO was Stephen W. Sanger, a 21-year company veteran with a marketing background.

In September 1995 General Mills launched Frosted Cheerios, a sugar-frosted version of the company's flagship cereal. Frosted Cheerios went on to become one of the most successful new cereals in history, capturing 1.5 percent of the market in its first year. In addition to developing successful new products, General Mills also returned to the acquisition arena, but in a core area rather than a new one. In January 1997 the company made its largest purchase in history when it spent $570 million for the branded ready-to-eat cereal and snack mix businesses of Ralcorp Holdings, Inc. The brands gained included Chex and Cookie Crisp cereals and Chex Mix snacks. General Mills thereby solidified its number two position in the U.S. ready-to-eat cereal market (behind Kellogg), increasing its share to about 26 percent. Meanwhile, to mark the 75th anniversary of Betty Crocker, a new portrait of the icon was created based on a computer composite.

By 1999 General Mills was neck-and-neck with Kellogg in the U.S. cereal sector, claiming 31.6 percent of U.S. cereal sales, to Kellogg's 31.7 percent. General Mills had gained on the industry leader through its consistent rollout of successful new products, its ability to maintain the highest price per box average among the leading cereal makers ($3.30, compared with Kellogg's $2.91), and the more distinctive nature of its cereals, such as Cinnamon Toast Crunch, which were less likely to be successfully challenged by generic cereals than such easier-to-copy Kellogg brands as Corn Flakes and Raisin Bran. At the same time, General Mills was moving forward on other fronts. Focusing on convenience foods, the company in 1999 introduced a 12-item line of Betty Crocker rice and pasta mixes, a new Chicken Helper dinner mix line, and Yoplait Go-Gurt, a line of yogurt packaged in a squeeze-and-eat tube that eliminated the need for a spoon. Also debuting was a new Colombo yogurt package that featured a spoon built right into the lid. General Mills added to its product lines in 1999 through several modest acquisitions. In January the company acquired St. Paul, Minnesota-based Lloyd's Barbeque Company, a maker of refrigerated, microwave-ready entrees. The following month saw the purchase of Union City, California-based Farmhouse Foods Company, seller of rice and pasta side dish mixes. In August General Mills bought Milwaukee-based Gardetto's Bakery, Inc., maker of baked snack mixes and flavored pretzels. Early in 2000 the company acquired Small Planet Foods, a maker of organic food products under the Cascadian Farm and Muir Glen brands. This move was part of General Mills' entry into the burgeoning natural foods sector and came around the same time that the company introduced Sunrise organic cereal.

In early 2000 Sanger announced a series of long-term goals for the first decade of the 21st century. The company aimed to achieve seven to eight percent compound annual sales growth, to generate $500 million in pretax cost savings through productivity enhancements, and to sustain double-digit earnings per share growth. By meeting or exceeding these goals, General Mills

would likely be able to remain independent in a food industry that was coming under increasing pressure to consolidate.

Principal Subsidiaries

Colombo, Inc.; C.P.A. Cereal Partners Handelsgesellschaft m.b.H. (Austria; 50%); C.P.D. Cereal Partners Deutschland Verwaltungsgesellschaft m.b.H (Germany; 50%); CPW Mexico S.A. de C.V. (50%); CPW S.A. (Switzerland; 50%); CPW-CI Limited (Cayman Islands; 50%); FYL Corp.; General Mills (BVI) Ltd. (British Virgin Islands); General Mills Continental, Inc.; General Mills Direct Marketing, Inc.; General Mills Europe Limited (U.K.); General Mills Finance, Inc.; General Mills France S.A.; General Mills Holding B.V. (Netherlands); General Mills International Limited; General Mills Maarssen B.V. (Netherlands); General Mills Mauritius, Inc.; General Mills Missouri, Inc.; General Mills Operations, Inc.; General Mills Products Corp.; General Mills Services, Inc.; Gold Medal Insurance Co.; Lloyd's Food Products, Inc.; Mills Media, Inc.; Nestlé Asean Philippines, Inc. (30%); Popcorn Distributors, Inc.; Torun-Pacific Sp. Z o.o. (Poland; 50%); Yoplait USA, Inc.

Principal Competitors

Aurora Foods Inc.; Bestfoods; Borden, Inc.; Campbell Soup Company; ConAgra, Inc.; Groupe Danone; Diageo plc; Gilster-Mary Lee Corporation; H.J. Heinz Company; International Home Foods, Inc.; Kellogg Company; Malt-O-Meal Company; Mars, Inc.; McKee Foods Corporation; Nabisco Holdings Corp.; PepsiCo, Inc.; Philip Morris Companies Inc.; The Pillsbury Company; The Procter & Gamble Company; The Quaker Oats Company; Ralcorp Holdings, Inc.; Unilever.

Further Reading

Beam, Alex, and Judith H. Dobrzynski, ''General Mills: Toys Just Aren't Us,'' *Business Week,* September 16, 1985, pp. 106+.

Burns, Greg, ''Has General Mills Had Its Wheaties?,'' *Business Week,* May 8, 1995, pp. 68–69.

Dubashi, Jugannath, ''Bon Appetit: General Mills Wants to Change the Breakfast Habits of Continentals,'' *Financial World,* July 23, 1991, pp. 40+.

Gibson, Richard, ''For General Mills, Cereal Will Be Main Course Again,'' *Wall Street Journal,* December 16, 1994, p. B3.

——, ''General Mills Gets in Shape for Turnaround,'' *Wall Street Journal,* September 26, 1995, p. B1.

——, ''General Mills to Buy Ralcorp's Chex, Other Branded Cereals for $570 Million,'' *Wall Street Journal,* August 15, 1996, p. B8.

——, ''General Mills to Spin Off Restaurants in Effort to Focus on Its Core Business,'' *Wall Street Journal,* December 15, 1994, p. A3.

Gray, James, *Business Without Boundary: The Story of General Mills,* Minneapolis: University of Minnesota Press, 1954.

Helliker, Kevin, ''A New Mix: Old-Fashioned PR Gives General Mills Advertising Bargains,'' *Wall Street Journal,* March 20, 1997, p. A1.

Houston, Patrick, and Rebecca Aikman, ''General Mills Still Needs Its Wheaties,'' *Business Week,* December 23, 1985, pp. 77+.

Kennedy, Tony, ''The General Mills Spinoff,'' *Minneapolis Star Tribune,* May 15, 1995, p. 1D.

Knowlton, Christopher, ''Europe Cooks Up a Cereal Brawl,'' *Fortune,* June 3, 1991, pp. 175–78.

''Long-Term Vision,'' *Forbes,* January 3, 1994.

Merrill, Ann, ''Hungry for Productivity: At a Time of Slow Growth in the Cereal Industry, General Mills Has Promised Double-Digit

Earnings Increases,'' *Minneapolis Star Tribune,* May 7, 2000, p. 1D.

——, ''Is the Cereal Bowl Half Full or . . . Half Empty?,'' *Minneapolis Star Tribune,* August 16, 1998, p. 1D.

——, ''A New Kind of Energy: Chairman, CEO of General Mills Earning Himself a Gold Medal,'' *Minneapolis Star Tribune,* July 22, 1996, p. 1D.

Mehler, Mark, ''Nagging Problems for the Other GM,'' *Financial World,* January 9–22, 1985, pp. 84+.

Mitchell, Russell, ''Big G Is Growing Fat on Oat Cuisine,'' *Business Week,* September 18, 1989, p. 29.

''The Other GM,'' *Financial World,* June 15, 1981, pp. 28+.

Rawlings, Edwin W., *Born to Fly,* Minneapolis: Great Way Publishing, 1987.

Rublin, Lauren R., ''Crunch Time: General Mills Hopes to Put the Fiber Back into Its Sales Growth,'' *Barron's,* February 22, 1999, pp. 17–19.

Sellers, Patricia, ''A Boring Brand Can Be Beautiful,'' *Fortune,* November 18, 1991, pp. 169+.

Weiner, Steve, and Janis Bultman, ''Calling Betty Crocker,'' *Forbes,* August 8, 1988, pp. 88+.

Wojahn, Ellen, *Playing by Different Rules,* New York: AMACOM, 1988.

Zehnpfennig, Gladys, *Harry A. Bullis, Champion American: A Biography of a Business Leader Who Was a Champion of Human Rights,* Minneapolis: T.S. Denison, 1964.

—Thomas Derdak
—updated by David E. Salamie

General Motors Corporation

300 Renaissance Center
Detroit, Michigan 48265-3000
U.S.A.
Telephone: (313) 556-5000
Fax: (313) 556-5108
Web site: http://www.gm.com

Public Company
Incorporated: 1916
Employees: 693,000
Sales: $176.56 billion (1999)
Stock Exchanges: New York Chicago Pacific
  Philadelphia Montreal Toronto Frankfurt Düsseldorf
  Brussels Paris London
Ticker Symbol: GM
NAIC: 336111 Automobile Manufacturing; 336112 Light
  Truck and Utility Vehicle Manufacturing; 336211
  Motor Vehicle Body Manufacturing; 336350 Motor
  Vehicle Transmission and Power Train Parts Manufac-
  turing; 336510 Railroad Rolling Stock Manufacturing;
  421110 Automobile and Other Motor Vehicle
  Wholesalers; 441110 New Car Dealers; 522220 Sales
  Financing; 522291 Consumer Lending; 522292 Real
  Estate Credit; 524126 Direct Property and Casualty
  Insurance Carriers; 532112 Passenger Cars Leasing;
  334220 Radio and Television Broadcasting and
  Wireless Communications Equipment Manufacturing;
  334290 Other Communications Equipment
  Manufacturing; 513220 Cable and Other Program
  Distribution; 513340 Satellite Telecommunications

General Motors Corporation (GM) is the world's largest full-line vehicle manufacturer and marketer. Its North American nameplates include Chevrolet, Pontiac, GMC, Oldsmobile, Buick, Cadillac, and Saturn. Opel, Vauxhall, Holden, Isuzu, Saab, Buick, Chevrolet, GMC, and Cadillac comprise General Motors' international nameplates. Through its system of global alliances, GM holds a 49 percent stake in Isuzu Motors Limited, 20 percent each of Fuji Heavy Industries Ltd. and Fiat S.p.A.'s Fiat Auto S.p.A. unit, and ten percent of Suzuki Motor Corporation. Other principal businesses include Hughes Electronics Corporation, a provider of digital entertainment, information, and communications services; and General Motors Acceptance Corporation and its subsidiaries, providers of financing and insurance to GM customers and dealers.

19th-Century Origins

The beginning of General Motors can be traced back to 1892, when R.E. Olds collected all of his savings to convert his father's naval and industrial engine factory into the Olds Motor Vehicle Company to build horseless carriages. For a number of years, however, the Oldsmobile (as the product came to be known) did not get beyond the experimental stage. In 1895 the first model, a four-seater with a petrol engine that could produce five horsepower and reach 18.6 mph, went for its trial run.

Olds proved himself not only an innovative engineer but also a good businessman and was very successful with his first model, of which relatively few were built. As a result of his success, he founded the first American factory in Detroit devoted exclusively to the production of automobiles. The first car was a luxury model costing $1,200, but the second model was introduced at a list price of $650 and was very successful. Two years later, at the turn of the century, Olds had sold more than 1,400 cars.

That same year, an engineer named David Buick founded a factory under his own name in Detroit. A third factory for the Cadillac Automobile Company also was built in Detroit. This company was founded by Henry Leland, who was already building car engines with experience gained in the Oldsmobile factory, where he worked until 1901. By the end of 1902 the first Cadillac had been produced—a car distinguished by its luxurious finish. In the following year, tiller steering was replaced by the steering wheel, the reduction gearbox was introduced, and some cars were fitted with celluloid windscreens. Oldsmobile also reached its projected target of manufacturing 4,000 cars in one year.

By 1903, a time of market instability, so many different manufacturers were operating that the financially weakest disappeared and some of the remaining companies were forced to form a consortium. William Durant, a director of the Buick Motor Company, was the man behind the merger. The nephew of a Michigan governor, and a self-made millionaire, Durant believed that the only way for the automobile companies to operate at a profit was to avoid the duplication that occurred when many firms manufactured the same product. General Motors Corporation was thus formed, bringing together Oldsmobile and Buick in 1903, and joined in 1909 by Cadillac and Oakland (renamed Pontiac). Positive financial results were immediately seen from the union, although the establishment of the company drew little attention.

Other early members of the General Motors family were Ewing, Marquette, Welch, Scripps-Booth, Sheridan, and Elmore, together with Rapid and Reliance trucks. General Motors' other U.S. automotive division, Chevrolet, became part of the corporation in 1918. Only Buick, Oldsmobile, Cadillac, and Oakland continued making cars for more than a short time after their acquisition by GM. By 1920 more than 30 companies had been acquired through the purchase of all or part of their stock. Two were forerunners of major GM subsidiaries, the McLaughlin Motor Company of Canada (which later became General Motors of Canada Limited) and the Fisher Body Company, in which GM initially acquired a 60 percent interest.

By 1911 the company set up a central staff of specialists to coordinate work in the various units and factories. An experimental or "testing" laboratory also was established to serve as an additional protection against costly factory mistakes. General Motors' system of administration, research, and development became one of the largest and most complex in private industry.

About the same time that General Motors was establishing itself in Detroit, an engineering breakthrough was taking place in Dayton, Ohio: the electric self-starter, designed by Charles F. Kettering. General Motors introduced Kettering's invention in its 1912 Cadillacs, and with the phasing out of the dangerous and unpredictable hand crank, motoring became much more popular. Kettering's Dayton Engineering Laboratories were merged into General Motors during 1920 and the laboratories were relocated in Detroit in 1925. Kettering later became the scientific director of General Motors, in charge of its research and engineering programs.

During World War I General Motors turned its facilities to the production of war materials. With no previous experience in manufacturing military hardware, the U.S. automobile industry completed a retooling from civilian to war production within 18 months. Between 1917 and 1919, 90 percent of General Motors' truck production was for the war effort. Cadillac supplied army staff cars, V-8 engines for artillery tractors, and trench

mortar shells, while Buick built Liberty airplane motors, tanks, trucks, ambulances, and automotive parts.

It was at this time that Alfred Sloan, Jr., who went on to guide General Motors as president and chairman until 1956, first became associated with the company. In 24 years, Sloan had built a $50,000 investment in the Hyatt Roller Bearing Company to assets of about $3.5 million. When Hyatt became part of General Motors, Sloan joined the corporate management, becoming president in 1923. Overseas expansion soon commenced, with the 1925 purchase of U.K. automaker Vauxhall Motors and the 1931 acquisition of Germany's Adam Opel.

Mid-Century: Surviving the Depression and Contributing to the War Effort

General Motors suffered greatly under the effects of the Great Depression, but it emerged with a new, aggressive management. Coordinated policy control replaced the undirected efforts of the prior years. As its principal architect, Sloan was credited with creating not only an organization that saved General Motors, but a new management policy that was adopted by countless other businesses. Fundamentally, the policy involved coordination of the enterprise under top management, direction of policy through top-level committees, and delegation of operational responsibility throughout the organization. Within this framework management staffs conducted analysis of market trends, advised policy committees, and coordinated administration. For a company comprised of many varied divisions, such a system of organization was crucial to its success.

By 1941 General Motors accounted for 44 percent of the total U.S. automotive sales, compared with 12 percent in 1921. In preparation for America's entry into World War II, General Motors retooled its factories. After Japan struck at Pearl Harbor in 1941, the industrial skills that General Motors had developed were applied with great effectiveness. From 1940 to 1945 General Motors produced defense materiel valued at a total of $12.3 billion. Decentralized and highly flexible local managerial responsibility made possible the almost overnight conversion from civilian production to wartime production. General Motors' contribution included the manufacture of every conceivable product from the smallest ball bearing to large tanks, naval ships, fighting planes, bombers, guns, cannons, and projectiles. The company manufactured 1,300 airplanes and one-fourth of all U.S. aircraft engines.

Postwar Expansion

Car manufacturing resumed after the war, and postwar expansion resulted in increased production. The decade of the 1950s was characterized by automotive sales records and innovations in styling and engineering. The public interest in automatic gears convinced General Motors to concentrate their research in this field; by 1950, all of the models built in the United States were available with an automatic gearbox. Car body developments proceeded at the same time and resulted in better sight lines and improved aerodynamics.

During the Korean war, part of the company's production capacity was diverted into providing supplies for the United Nations forces (although to a smaller extent than during World

Key Dates:

1892: R.E. Olds founds the Olds Motor Vehicle Company.

1895: The first Oldsmobile model is taken on its trial run.

1900: David Buick founds a factory in Detroit.

1902: Henry Leland produces the first Cadillac.

1903: William Durant forms General Motors Corporation, bringing together Oldsmobile and Buick.

1909: Cadillac and Oakland (renamed Pontiac) join GM.

1912: GM introduces the electric self-starter in its Cadillacs.

1918: Chevrolet becomes part of GM.

1923: Alfred Sloan, Jr., is named president.

1925: U.K. automaker Vauxhall Motors is acquired.

1931: Germany's Adam Opel is acquired.

1940–45: GM produces defense materiel valued at $12.3 billion.

1950: All U.S. models are available with an automatic gearbox.

1971: GM acquires a 34 percent stake in Isuzu Motors.

1981: Company purchases a three percent stake in Suzuki Motor Corporation.

1984: GM acquires Electronic Data Systems.

1986: Hughes Aircraft is acquired.

1990: Company acquires a 50 percent stake in Swedish carmaker Saab Automobile AB; Saturn Corporation is created as a subsidiary.

1994: Hughes Electronics introduces Direct TV.

1996: EDS is spun off.

1997: Hughes sells its defense electronics operations to Raytheon and merges its Delco Electronics unit into GM's auto parts subsidiary, Delphi Automotive Systems.

1998: Stake in Suzuki is increased to ten percent.

1999: Stake in Isuzu is increased to 49 percent; GM acquires a 20 percent stake in Fuji Heavy Industries, maker of Subaru cars; Delphi is spun off to shareholders.

2000: GM gains a 20 percent stake in Fiat S.p.A.'s Fiat Auto S.p.A. unit and takes full control of Saab; Hughes sells satellite manufacturing unit to Boeing.

War II). The reallocation reached 19 percent and then leveled off at about five percent from 1956 onward. Between 1951 and 1955 the five divisions of General Motors—Buick, Chevrolet, Pontiac, Oldsmobile, and Cadillac—all began to feature a new V-8 engine with a higher compression ratio. Furthermore, the electrical supply was changed from six to the more reliable 12 volts. Power-assisted steering and brakes appeared on all car models and the window dimensions were increased to further enhance visibility. Interior comfort was improved by the installation of the first air conditioning systems. Also during this period General Motors completely redesigned its classic sedans and introduced front seat safety belts.

The period between 1950 and 1956 was particularly prosperous in the United States, with a rise in demand for a second car in the family. Americans, however, were beginning to show real interest in smaller European cars. By 1956, a year of decreasing sales, Ford Motor Company, Chrysler Corporation,

and General Motors had lost some 15 percent in sales while imports were virtually doubling their market penetration. The longer Detroit's automobiles grew, the more popular imports became. In 1957 the United States imported more cars than it exported, and despite a recession, imports accounted for more than eight percent of U.S. car sales. Although General Motors promised that help was on its way in the form of smaller compact cars, the new models failed to generate much excitement; the company's market share slipped to just 42 percent of 1959's new car sales.

The 1960s were difficult years in Detroit. The 1967 riot in the ghettos surrounding General Motors' facilities forced management to recognize the urban poverty that had for so long been in their midst and they began to employ more workers from minority groups. Much of the new hiring was made possible by the expansionist policies of the Kennedy and Johnson administrations. General Motors prospered and diversified; its interests now included home appliances, insurance, locomotives, electronics, ball bearings, banking, and financing. By the late 1960s after-tax profits for the industry in general reached a 13 percent return on investment, and General Motors' return increased from 16.5 percent to 25.8 percent.   .

Declining Fortunes from the 1970s Through the Early 1990s

Like the rest of the industry, General Motors had ignored, in large part, the importance of air pollution control, but new, costly federal regulations were mandated. By the early 1970s, however, the high cost of developing devices to control pollution was overshadowed by the impact of the oil embargo. General Motors' luxury, gas-guzzling car sales were down by 35 percent in 1974, but the company's compacts and subcompacts rose steadily to attain a 40 percent market share. Ford, Chrysler, and General Motors had been caught unaware by a vast shift in consumer demand, and General Motors suffered the greatest losses. The company spent $2.25 billion in 1974 and 1975 to meet local, state, and federal regulations on pollution control. By the end of 1977 that figure had doubled.

Under the leadership of President F. James McDonald and Chairman Roger Smith, General Motors reported earnings declines from 1985 to 1992. The only respite came from an accounting change in 1987, which effected an earnings increase. McDonald and Smith attempted to place these losses in perspective by arguing that they were necessary if General Motors was to develop a strong and secure position on the worldwide market. Since the start of the 1980s, General Motors had spent more than $60 billion redesigning most of its cars and modernizing the plants that produce them. The company also acquired two major corporations, Hughes Aircraft, in 1986, and Electronic Data Systems (EDS), in 1984. Though expensive, the EDS purchase provided General Motors with better, more centralized communications and backup systems, as well as a vital profit center. GM also purchased a 50 percent stake in Saab Automobile AB, a Sweden-based maker of premium cars, in 1990. That same year Saturn Corporation was created as a subsidiary to produce compact cars in a Japanese-influenced factory in Tennessee; Saturns became popular because of their quality and the no-haggle method employed to sell them.

General Motors' market share dropped steadily from 1982 to 1992. In 1987 Ford's profits exceeded GM's for the first time in 60 years. From 1990 to 1992, the corporation suffered successive and devastating annual losses totaling almost $30 billion. Problems were myriad. Manufacturing costs exceeded competitors' due to high labor costs, overcapacity, and complicated production procedures. GM faced competition from 25 companies, and its market share fell from almost 50 percent to about 35 percent.

Mid-1990s and Beyond: Profits Despite U.S. Market Share Erosion

In 1992 Jack Smith, Jr. advanced to General Motors' chief executive office. He had earned respect as the engineer of GM Europe's late 1980s turnaround, and he quickly applied those strategies to the parent, focusing on North American Operations (NAO). During 1993, Smith simplified the NAO, cut the corporate staff, pared product offerings, and began to divest GM's parts operations. He was hailed for his negotiations with the United Auto Workers. In 1993 he pledged $3.9 billion in jobless benefits, which raised the blue-collar payroll costs about 16 percent over three years. But at the same time the contract gave Smith the ability to cut 65,000 blue-collar jobs by 1996 in conjunction with the closure of nearly 24 plants. Salaried positions were not exempted from Smith's job-cutting scalpel: staffing at the corporate central office was slashed from 13,500 to 2,300 in 1992.

In the early 1990s GM began to recapture the automotive vanguard from Japanese carmakers, with entries in the van, truck, and utility vehicle markets and the launch of Saturn. GM also gained an advantage in the domestic market because the weak dollar caused the price of imported cars to increase much faster than domestics. Market conditions along with Smith's strategies effected a stunning reversal in 1993, when GM recorded net income of $2.47 billion on sales of $138.22 billion. Riding the booming economy, the company recorded record profits of $6.88 billion on record sales of $163.86 billion in 1995. Despite the improved financial performance, General Motors' share of the U.S. car market continued its steady decline, falling to slightly more than 31 percent by 1995. The company's North American operations continued to be criticized by observers for its inability to produce innovative models, the glacial speed of its new product development, and the inefficiencies inherent in running six separate car divisions and a GMC truck division.

The mid-to-late 1990s saw a number of important initiatives in GM's non-automaking operations. In 1994 the renamed Hughes Electronics unit introduced Direct TV, a satellite-based direct-to-home broadcast service. The 1995 sale of the company's National Car Rental business was followed by the spinoff of EDS the following year. One year later, Hughes Electronics was revamped through the sale of its defense electronics operations to Raytheon Company and the merging of its automotive electronics activities (Delco Electronics) into GM's auto parts subsidiary, Delphi Automotive Systems. Hughes began concentrating on digital entertainment, information, and communications services and made a key acquisition in 1999 when it paid $1.3 billion for the direct-to-home satellite business of Primestar. In early 2000 Hughes made a further divestment of a now noncore unit when it sold its satellite manufacturing operations to the Boeing Company for about $3.75 billion. Delphi, meanwhile, was completely separated from GM through a May 1999 spinoff to shareholders.

General Motors remained profitable through the end of the decade, but its U.S. market share dipped below 30 percent by 1999—at times GM's share was less than that of the combined share of all Asian automakers, an unprecedented development. While continuing to attempt to reverse the now three-decades-long fall, GM began looking for future growth from Asia, where early 21st-century growth in car sales was expected to surpass both North America and Europe. Instead of attempting to directly sell its own models, GM began assembling a network of alliances with key Asian automakers for its push into that emerging continent, aiming to increase its market share across Asia from its late 1990s level of four percent to ten percent by 2005. The company already had a 34 percent stake in Isuzu Motors Limited, which it had bought in 1971, and a three percent stake in Suzuki Motor Corporation, obtained in 1981. In 1998 GM increased its stake in Suzuki to ten percent and agreed to build cars with the Japanese automaker. The following year General Motors increased its stake in Isuzu to 49 percent; acquired a 20 percent stake in Fuji Heavy Industries Ltd., maker of Subaru all-wheel-drive vehicles; and entered into an alliance with Honda Motor Co., Ltd. involving Honda producing low-emissions gasoline engines for GM and Isuzu producing diesel engines for Honda. In May 2000 GM, Fuji, and Suzuki agreed to develop compact cars for the European market. Another deal involving Europe was reached in early 2000, when GM agreed to acquire a 20 percent stake in the Fiat Auto S.p.A. unit of Fiat S.p.A., the number six automaker in the world, in exchange for Fiat taking a 5.1 percent stake in GM. Through this deal, General Motors aimed to grab a larger share of the market for the small vehicles that are popular in Europe and Latin America but shunned in the United States. In mid-2000 GM and Fiat jointly bid to acquire troubled South Korean carmaker Daewoo Motor Co., but were outbid by Ford. Also in 2000, General Motors acquired the 50 percent of Saab Automobile that it did not already own.

In another key early 2000 development, General Motors agreed to join with DaimlerChrysler AG and Ford to create an Internet-based global business-to-business supplier exchange, Covisint, that would be open to all suppliers and automakers. This would potentially create the world's largest virtual marketplace, although the Federal Trade Commission quickly opened a preliminary antitrust inquiry into the plan. The company also began building a factory in Lansing, Michigan, its first new plant in 15 years. In June 2000 G. Richard Wagoner was promoted from president to CEO, with Smith remaining chairman. At the age of 47, Wagoner became the youngest CEO in GM history and faced the daunting task of running what was still considered by many observers to be an excessively bureaucratic and overly complex organization, which was extremely resistant to change and seemingly unable to anticipate most market trends.

Principal Subsidiaries

General Motors Acceptance Corporation; General Motors Investment Management Corporation; Hughes Electronics Corporation; Saturn Corporation; Holden, Ltd. (Australia); General Motors do Brasil Ltda. (Brazil); General Motors of Canada, Ltd.; Adam Opel Aktiengesellschaft (Germany); General Motors de Mexico, S.A. de C.V.; Saab Automobile AB (Sweden); Vauxhall Motors Limited (U.K.).

Principal Divisions

Allison Transmission Division; Buick Motor Division; Cadillac Motor Car Division; Chevrolet Motor Division; Electro-Motive Division; Oldsmobile Division; Pontiac-GMC Division; Pontiac-GMC Truck Division.

Principal Operating Units

e-GM Group; GM Asia Pacific; GM Europe; GM Latin America, Africa and Mid-East; GM Locomotive Group; GM North America; GM Powertrain Group; GM Truck Group.

Principal Competitors

AmeriCredit Corp.; Bayerische Motoren Werke AG; Credit Acceptance Corporation; DaimlerChrysler AG; Ford Motor Company; Ford Motor Credit Company; General Electric Capital Corporation; General Electric Company; Honda Motor Co., Ltd.; Hyundai Motor Company; Mazda Motor Corporation; Mitsubishi Motors Corporation; Nissan Motor Co., Ltd.; PSA Peugeot Citroën S.A.; Renault S.A.; Suzuki Motor Corporation; Toyota Motor Corporation; Volkswagen AG.

Further Reading

Bary, Andrew, "How to Fix GM," *Barron's*, July 5, 1999, pp. 18–19.

Cray, Ed, *Chrome Colossus: General Motors and Its Time*, New York: McGraw-Hill, 1980.

Dassbach, Carl H.A., *Global Enterprises and the World Economy: Ford, General Motors, and IBM, the Emergence of the Transnational Enterprise*, New York: Garland, 1989.

De Lorean, John Z., *On a Clear Day You Can See General Motors*, London: Sidgwick and Jackson, 1980.

Geyelin, Milo, "Lasting Impact: How an Internal Memo Written 26 Years Ago Is Costing GM Dearly," *Wall Street Journal*, September 29, 1999, pp. A1+.

Hamper, Ben, *Rivethead: Tales from the Assembly Line*, New York: Warner Books, 1992.

Jacobs, Timothy, *A History of General Motors*, New York: Smithmark, 1992.

Keller, Maryann, *Collision: GM, Toyota, Volkswagen, and the Race to Own the 21st Century*, New York: Currency Doubleday, 1993.

——, *Rude Awakening: General Motors in the 1980s*, New York: Morrow, 1989.

——, *Rude Awakening: The Rise, Fall and Struggle for Recovery of General Motors*, New York: HarperCollins, 1990.

Kerwin, Kathleen, "For GM, Once Again, Little Ventured, Little Gained," *Business Week*, March 27, 2000, pp. 42–43.

Kerwin, Kathleen, and Joann Muller, "Reviving GM," *Business Week*, February 1, 1999, pp. 114+.

Kuhn, Arthur J., *GM Passes Ford, 1918–1938: Designing the General Motors Performance-Control System*, University Park: Pennsylvania State University Press, 1986.

Madsen, Axel, *The Deal Maker: How William C. Durant Made General Motors*, New York: Wiley, 1999.

May, George S., *R.E. Olds, Auto Industry Pioneer*, Grand Rapids, Mich.: Eerdmans, 1977.

Meredith, Robyn, "Can GM Return to the Passing Lane?," *New York Times*, November 7, 1999, Sec. 3, p. 1.

Miller, Scott, "Open No Quick Fix for GM's 'Mr. Fix It,'" *Wall Street Journal*, June 13, 2000, p. A22.

Osterland, Andrew, "Al and Me: Why General Motors Will Finally Get Serious About Downsizing," *Financial World*, December 16, 1996, pp. 39–41.

Palmer, Jay, "Reviving GM," *Barron's*, June 22, 1998, pp. 31–35.

Pollack, Andrew, "Paper Trail GM After It Loses Injury Suit," *New York Times*, July 12, 1999, Sec. A, p. 12.

Ramsey, Douglas K., *The Corporate Warriors: Six Classic Cases in American Business*, Boston: Houghton Mifflin, 1987.

Rothschild, Emma, *Paradise Lost: The Decline of the Auto-Industrial Age*, New York: Random House, 1973.

Shirouzu, Norihiko, "GM Cracks Japan's Market with Its Wallet, Not Its Cars: Network of Alliances Aids Asia Expansion by Filling Gaps in Product Line," *Wall Street Journal*, January 26, 2000, p. A17.

Simison, Robert L., Fara Warner, and Gregory L. White, "Big Three Car Makers Plan Net Exchange," *Wall Street Journal*, February 28, 2000, pp. A3, A16.

Simison, Robert L., Gregory L. White, and Deborah Ball, "GM's Linkup with Fiat Opens Final Act of Consolidation Drama for Industry," *Wall Street Journal*, March 14, 2000, pp. A3, A8.

Sloan, Alfred, Jr., *My Years with General Motors*, New York: Doubleday, 1964.

Smith, Roger B., *Building on 75 Years of Excellence: The General Motors Story*, New York: Newcomen Society of the United States, 1984.

Taylor, Alex, III, "GM's $11 Billion Turnaround," *Fortune*, October 17, 1994, pp. 54–56+.

——, "GM: Some Gain, Much Pain," *Fortune*, May 29, 1995, pp. 78–80, 84.

——, "GM: Time to Get in Gear," *Fortune*, April 28, 1997, pp. 94–96+.

——, "GM: Why They Might Break Up America's Biggest Company," *Fortune*, April 29, 1996, pp. 78–82, 84.

——, "Is Jack Smith the Man to Fix GM?," *Fortune*, August 3, 1998, pp. 86+.

Weisberger, Bernard A., *The Dream Maker: William C. Durant, Founder of General Motors*, Boston: Little Brown, 1979.

White, Gregory L., "As GM Courts the Net, Struggling Saturn Line Exposes Rusty Spots," *Wall Street Journal*, July 11, 2000, pp. A1, A10.

Zachary, Katherine, "Shopping Spree: GM Plunks Down Hard Cash to Add Strength in Asia," *Ward's Auto World*, February 29, 2000.

Zesiger, Sue, "GM's Big Decision: Status Quo," *Fortune*, February 21, 2000, pp. 101–02, 104.

—April Dougal Gasbarre
—updated by David E. Salamie

George Weston Limited

22 St. Clair Avenue East
Toronto, Ontario M4T 2S7
Canada
Telephone: (416) 922-2500
Fax: (416) 922-4395
Web site: http://www.weston.ca

Public Company
Incorporated: 1928
Employees: 119,000
Sales: C$20.85 billion (US$14.35 billion) (1999)
Stock Exchanges: Toronto
Ticker Symbol: WN
NAIC: 112511 Finfish Farming and Fish Hatcheries;
    311511 Fluid Milk Manufacturing; 311711 Seafood
    Canning; 311712 Fresh and Frozen Seafood
    Processing; 311812 Commercial Bakeries; 311821
    Cookie and Cracker Manufacturing; 422410 General
    Line Grocery Wholesalers; 445110 Supermarkets and
    Other Grocery (Except Convenience) Stores

George Weston Limited is a major Canadian food processor and distributor, with a number of operations in the United States as well. Weston Foods Inc., the wholly owned holding company for George Weston's processing operations, manufactures and distributes fresh and frozen bakery products, cookies, and dairy products and also farms and processes fish. George Weston also holds a controlling 63.1 percent stake in Loblaw Companies Limited, the number one operator of supermarkets in Canada with a 40 percent market share, twice the share of its biggest competitor. Among the many grocery chains owned by Loblaw are Atlantic Superstore, Fortinos, Loblaws, No Frills, Provigo, The Real Canadian Superstore, Valu-mart, Your Independent Grocer, and Zehrs. Galen Weston, company chairman and grandson of the founder, owns more than 60 percent of George Weston Limited.

Early History Under George Weston

George Weston, a baker's apprentice, started this family-run business in 1882 with two Toronto bread routes. His early success selling bread led to a rapid increase in the number of routes he managed, and soon encouraged him to establish a bread and cake bakery in Toronto, the Model Bakery, in 1896. The bakery expanded into the production of cookies in 1908, and by 1911 had 30 delivery wagons; its products were sold in more than 500 stores.

In 1910, however, Weston agreed to a merger with other major Toronto bakers to form the Canada Bread Company. As a condition of the deal, Weston had to stay out of the bread business for a ten-year period. Despite having pocketed C$1 million from the sale of his business, Weston continued to make cakes and cookies, establishing a new plant to do so. In 1921, with the ten-year noncompete period over, Weston reentered the bread business through the purchase of the H.C. Tomlin bread bakery, which was located across the street from the Canada Bread Company. At George Weston's death in 1924 his son Garfield Weston took over a business with a thriving biscuit operation and a less well-developed bread operation. In 1928 he incorporated George Weston Limited and took it public.

Expanding Through Acquisitions
Under Garfield Weston: 1930s–60s

Under Garfield's leadership, the firm built its bread and biscuit businesses in Canada and the United States. Weathering the Great Depression without major problems, the company was able to take advantage of its position as a low-cost producer to overtake other competitors in the baking industry. Its 1937 acquisition of McCormick's Limited and its 1938 purchase of Inter-City Western Bakeries, Ltd., for example, provided Weston with the facilities and resources to produce 370 varieties of candy and 100 types of biscuits, in addition to its breads and cakes. Also during the 1930s, the company established operations in the United Kingdom, where it made available the first low-cost, high-quality biscuits. These British bakeries were amalgamated in 1935 into a separate company, Allied Bakeries, which eventually became Associated British Foods PLC. Mean-

---

Company Perspectives:

George Weston Limited is committed to creating value for its shareholders and to the belief that it should participate along with its more than 119,000 employees throughout its businesses in supporting the communities in which it operates.

---

while, George Weston Limited also expanded into the United States through the 1939 purchase of the Associated Biscuit Company.

Despite World War II, expansion continued smoothly throughout the 1940s. The company diversified into the paper industry through the 1943 acquisition of E.B. Eddy, a firm dating back to the 1851 opening in Hull, Quebec, of a mill to make matches. In 1944 the company bought the Southern Biscuit Company, and the acquisition of Western Grocers marked the firm's initial entry into food distribution. This growth was strengthened by purchases of the Edmonton City Bakery in 1945 and Dietrich's Bakeries in 1946. In 1947 the company acquired William Neilson, a major Canadian producer of chocolate, cocoa, milk, and dairy specialty products.

During the 1940s and early 1950s, Weston began buying shares of Loblaw Groceterias, a food distributor, as part of a strategy designed to reach consumers directly with its products. By 1953, the firm had acquired a majority interest in Loblaw, a position that made possible Loblaw's subsequent acquisitions of other food distributors across Canada and the Midwestern United States, including National Grocers of Ontario in 1955; National Tea, a U.S.-based retailer, in 1956; Kelly, Douglas and Company, a British Columbia wholesaler, in 1958; the Maritime-based Atlantic Wholesalers in 1960; and the Zehrmart supermarket chain in 1963.

During the 1960s the company pursued further diversification in an attempt to improve its value to shareholders by expanding into fish processing. Weston bought B.C. Packers, a salmon processor, in 1962, and five years later, Connors Bros., the largest herring and sardine processor in Canada.

1970s: Retrenching Under Galen Weston

Growth was temporarily curtailed in the 1970s as management focused on reorganizing the company's activities and operations to achieve greater control and efficiency. W. Galen Weston, one of Garfield's sons, had become president in 1970, and the firm began to refocus on food as its primary area of emphasis. The various grocery operations were consolidated under Loblaw Companies Limited and new management was installed. Underperforming stores were closed and many others were remodeled.

The most troubled distribution operation was National Tea, which lost $36 million on $1.06 billion in sales in 1973. The decline of National Tea was traced to the company's continued reliance on small stores located at downtown sites while the clear industry trend was to larger stores located in the suburbs. After attempting to turn around the chain's fortunes through

drastic cost-cutting and major repositioning efforts, Weston leadership determined that National Tea's competitors had been given too much of a head start. In 1976, therefore, National Tea sold off 75 percent of its supermarkets, including all of its Chicago operations; the company continued to operate the remaining stores, making limited attempts to improve their operations, with the idea of eventually divesting them.

Meantime, Galen Weston took over as chairman in 1974, four years before the death of Garfield Weston. Also in 1978, Loblaws joined the burgeoning market for private label grocery items by launching the No Name label. The new brand enjoyed immediate success based on its low prices, clean and simple packaging, and high quality. In 1984 Loblaws introduced a new premium private label called President's Choice, so named because the president of Loblaws at the time, David Nichol, chose the products. Offering premium value at low prices, President's Choice was able to compete directly with name-brand goods.

1980s: Returning to Acquisitions

In his initial years as chairman of the company, Galen Weston focused on improving financial results by bolstering management and making capital expenditures to enhance various systems. After posting a net loss in 1976, the changing fortunes of the company were evident by 1979, when record earnings of C$76.5 million on sales of C$5.9 billion were reported. With the outlook for the company looking brighter, Weston began seeking acquisitions once again. After being outbid by the Thomson family in a 1979 battle for control of Hudson's Bay Company, the oldest Canadian company and its leading department store chain, Weston acquired Stroehmann Brothers Company, a major baker of fresh bread based in Pennsylvania, in 1980. The acquired company was later renamed Stroehmann Bakeries Inc. In 1983 Galen Weston was the subject of a foiled kidnap attempt by the Irish Republican Army; following this incident, he and his family began maintaining very private lifestyles.

Also in the early 1980s, George Weston faced major labor problems involving the unionized employees of its Super Valu stores in Manitoba. These difficulties resulted from Weston's aggressive penetration of the Winnipeg retail food market. In order to convert its existing Loblaws stores in the area to larger-scale supermarkets and hire away experienced employees from other retailers, Weston offered to recognize the Manitoba Food and Commercial Workers Union and to match its current contract with Safeway Foods in return for a six-year, no-strike, no-lockout agreement that effectively eliminated the union's contract negotiation rights. Shortly after consummating this arrangement, Super Valu was accused by its employees of violating a number of contract provisions related to seniority, scheduling, and full-time employment, but a compromise was eventually worked out.

In 1986 the food processing operations of Weston were consolidated within an umbrella subsidiary called Weston Foods Ltd. At the time, its operations included baking and milling, biscuits, chocolate, dairy, and specialty products, providing food and ingredients both to intermediate processors and directly to consumers all over North America. Weston Bakeries stood as Canada's largest baker of fresh bread, buns, and cake products (distributed under a variety of brands and private

1990s: Tightening the Company Focus

Key Dates:

1882: George Weston starts in business with two Toronto bread routes.

1896: Weston establishes a bread and cake bakery in Toronto, the Model Bakery.

1908: The bakery begins producing cookies.

1910: Weston merges his bread operations into the Canada Bread Company, while continuing to produce cake and cookies.

1921: Weston reenters the bread business with the purchase of the H.C. Tomlin bread bakery.

1924: George Weston dies and is succeeded by his son, Garfield.

1928: Garfield Weston incorporates the company as George Weston Limited and takes it public.

1943: Papermaker E.B. Eddy is acquired.

1944: The purchase of Western Grocers marks the first foray into food distribution.

1947: William Neilson, confectioner and dairy product producer, is acquired.

1953: Company gains majority control of Loblaw, a food distributor.

1956: National Tea, a U.S.-based food retailer, is acquired.

1970: Galen Weston, son of Garfield, is named president.

1976: 75 percent of the supermarkets of National Tea are sold.

1978: Garfield Weston dies and is succeeded as chairman by Galen Weston; Loblaws launches the No Name private label.

1980: Stroehmann Brothers, a major Pennsylvania-based bread baker, is acquired.

1984: Loblaws introduces a premium private label called President's Choice.

1987: The confectionery operations of Cadbury Schweppes Canada Inc. are acquired.

1995: National Tea is divested, completing the company's exit from U.S. food retailing.

1996: Neilson Cadbury, Weston's chocolate unit, is sold to Cadbury Schweppes PLC.

1998: E.B. Eddy is sold to Domtar Inc.; Loblaws acquires Provigo, thereby gaining a Canada-wide food retail network.

1990s: Tightening the Company Focus

The worldwide recession of the early 1990s coupled with the unfolding consequences of the North American Free Trade Agreement (NAFTA) of 1989 wreaked havoc on both the Canadian economy and George Weston Limited. Sales fell each year through 1993, dropping from US$9.35 billion in 1990 to US$9 billion in 1993. Net income fell during the same period from US$107.7 million to US$43 million. The operations of Weston Foods were hit the hardest, particularly as they increasingly had to compete with such U.S. food giants as RJR Nabisco Inc. and the Pillsbury Company. Anticipating the effects of the expected passage of NAFTA, Weston had in fact begun to overhaul its food processing operations as early as 1988, when it sold its Canadian biscuit operations for C$120 million. Then in early 1991 the company exited from the flour milling business, having determined that it no longer made economic sense to mill wheat in-house when it could instead seek out the best supplier of this raw material from anywhere in North America. The ice cream operations of William Neilson were also under competitive pressure from John Labatt Ltd., Beatrice Foods Inc., and the Pillsbury Company, so Weston decided to sell the operations to Labatt and concentrate on William Neilson's stronger businesses, fresh milk and yogurt. At the same that it was pruning its portfolio of underperforming units, Weston also launched capital improvement programs to bolster its remaining core. For example, the company spent C$55 million to build a new, state-of-the-art bakery in Montreal from which it began distributing fresh bread throughout Quebec and New England. In 1993 E.B. Eddy bought Island Paper Mills Co. Ltd., which operated a coated paper mill located on an island near Vancouver.

In the mid-1990s George Weston continued to unload unprofitable or noncore units. In 1995 Loblaw finally rid itself of its National Tea albatross, selling the company to St. Louis-based Schnuck Markets Inc. for US$368 million. This completed Loblaw's exit from the U.S. market. Another significant divestment occurred the following year when Weston sold Neilson Cadbury, the only domestically owned chocolate company left in Canada, back to Cadbury Schweppes for C$225 million. Weston continued to own dairy food processor William Neilson. Seeking to focus even more strongly on its core food operations, Weston next looked to offload E.B. Eddy. In September 1997 Weston announced that it planned to spin off the paper company through an initial public offering, but two months later shelved that plan because of turmoil in the stock market. It then began shopping E.B. Eddy around, leading to the July 1998 sale of E.B. Eddy to Montreal-based Domtar Inc. for C$803 million. These divestments reduced George Weston to its majority ownership of Loblaw and food processing businesses focusing on bakery products, cookies, milk, and fish.

With revenues and profits growing, a tighter assemblage of operations, and its cash reserves swelled from the divestments, George Weston began looking for acquisition opportunities to bolster its core areas. In 1998 one of the company's U.S. bakery units, Maplehurst Bakeries Inc., purchased the frozen bagel business of the Quaker Oats Company, which included the Arnie's Bagelicious and Petrofsky's brands. That same year, Stroehmann Bakeries acquired Maier's Bakery, a family-owned Reading, Pennsylvania-based bakery that had sales of about US$100 million per year. Loblaw expanded as well, as super-

labels). Stroehmann was one of the largest wholesale baked goods producers in the northeastern United States. Other members of the food processing group included Interbake Foods specialty biscuit division, which consisted of the cookie and cracker businesses acquired between 1928 and 1960, including the Southern Biscuit Company, the focus of operations in the United States; and the Canadian flour milling operations of Soo Line Mills and McCarthy Milling. The chocolate activities of William Neilson were bolstered in 1987 with the acquisition of the confectionery operations of Cadbury Schweppes Canada Inc., a unit of the U.K. firm Cadbury Schweppes PLC. The newly created Neilson Cadbury unit commanded a one-third share of the Canadian chocolate bar market and was Canada's largest chocolate manufacturer.

market consolidation spread from the United States to Canada. In November 1998 Loblaw acquired the 80-store Agora Foods, which had been the Atlantic Canada division of Oshawa Foods, for C$81 million. Then the following month, Loblaw spent C$890 million to acquire Provigo Inc. To this point Loblaw had only a minuscule presence in Quebec, where it operated four stores. With the addition of Provigo, it gained the number one supermarket chain in Quebec and for the first time had truly a Canada-wide retail network, not to mention a dominating 40 percent nationwide market share. Following completion of the acquisition, Loblaw retained the Provigo banner on the more than 250 stores it had acquired in Quebec; but of the 90 or so Provigo stores in Ontario, which were mainly operated under the Loeb name, about half were converted to Loblaws and half were sold off.

George Weston continued to fine-tune its operational portfolio in 1999. Early that year, the dairy operations were bolstered through the purchase of Fieldfresh Farms, the Ontario dairy operation of Oshawa Foods. The fisheries operations were scaled back through the sale of the branded tuna and wild salmon processing businesses of B.C. Packers. This divestment largely exited Weston from the volatile wild fish processing industry, allowing it to focus on its more stable canned sardine and farmed Atlantic salmon operations, which also had greater potential for growth. Weston also earmarked about C$800 million for capital expenditures in 1999, most of which was spent on expanding or remodeling grocery outlets in eastern Canada, particularly the Provigo stores. The addition of Provigo in particular led to a 41 percent jump in sales for George Weston in 1999 to C$20.85 billion. Looking to the future, Weston planned to spend an additional C$900 million to open, expand, and refurbish more than 100 of Loblaw's stores throughout Canada. Loblaw also began expanding the nonfood offerings of its stores, with plans for selling more general merchandise, such as children's clothes, and for marketing financial services, such as no-fee bank accounts.

Principal Subsidiaries

FOOD PROCESSING: Weston Foods Inc.; Boulangeries Weston Québec Limitée; Weston Bakeries Limited; Ready Bake Foods Inc.; Sarsfield Foods Limited; Maplehurst Bakeries (Canada) Inc.; La Baguetterie Inc.; Western Pre-Bake Ltd.; Connors Bros., Limited; Heritage Salmon Company Limited; William Neilson Ltd.; Weston Foods, Inc. (U.S.A.); Stroehmann Bakeries Inc.; Interbake Foods Inc. (U.S.A.); Weston Mills Inc. (U.S.A.); Maplehurst Bakeries Inc. (U.S.A.); Connors Bros., Inc. (U.S.A.); Heritage Salmon, Inc. (U.S.A.); Connors Brunswick Inc. (U.S.A.). FOOD DISTRIBUTION:

Weston Food Distribution Inc.; Loblaw Companies Limited (63.1%); Loblaws Inc. (63.1%); Atlantic Wholesalers Ltd. (63.1%); Loblaws Supermarkets Ltd. (63.1%); National Grocers Co. Ltd. (63.1%); Zehrmart Inc. (63.1%); Loblaw Properties Limited (63.1%); Fortino's Supermarket Ltd. (63.1%); Kelly, Douglas & Company, Limited (63.1%); Westfair Foods Ltd. (63.1%); Loblaw Brands Limited (63.1%); Loblaw Financial Holdings Inc. (63.1%); Provigo Inc. (63.1%); Provigo Distribution Inc. (63.1%).

Principal Competitors

Campbell Soup Company; Canada Safeway Limited; Empire Company Limited; Great Atlantic & Pacific Company of Canada Ltd.; Metro Inc.; Nabisco Holdings Corp.; Overwaitea Food Group; The Pillsbury Company; Sobeys Inc.; Unilever.

Further Reading

Bertin, Oliver, "Investors Lap Up Weston Shares," *Globe and Mail,* June 23, 2000, p. B14.

——, "Weston Adjusts to 'Cruel World': Free Trade Gives Food Firm Big Rivals," *Globe and Mail,* August 19, 1991, p. B1.

Bourette, Susan, and Dave Ebner, "Weston to Bolster Existing Operations: Much of $800 Million to Be Spent on Eastern Businesses and Small U.S. Acquisitions," *Globe and Mail,* May 11, 1999, p. B11.

Davies, Charles, *Bread Men: How the Westons Built an International Empire,* Toronto: Key Porter, 1987, 211 p.

Greenberg, Larry M., and Christopher J. Chipello, *Wall Street Journal,* November 2, 1998, p. B2.

Mahood, Casey, "Weston Sells Two B.C. Packers Seafood Brands to U.S. Company," *Globe and Mail,* January 5, 1999, p. B5.

McFarland, Janet, "Grocers Brace for a Food Fight," *Globe and Mail,* October 31, 1998, p. B1.

Strauss, Marina, "Cadbury to Swallow Neilson: U.K. Giant Grabs Canadian Candy Bar Leader for $225 Million," *Globe and Mail,* December 19, 1995, p. B1.

——, "Loblaw Sells U.S. Operations: Deal for National Tea Holdings Worth an Estimated $300 Million," *Globe and Mail,* January 17, 1995, p. B1.

——, "Loblaw to Boost Non-Food Items," *Globe and Mail,* May 11, 2000, p. B6.

Waldie, Paul, "Domtar Buys E.B. Eddy," *Globe and Mail,* June 17, 1998, p. B1.

——, "E.B. Eddy IPO Shelved," *Globe and Mail,* November 14, 1997, p. B1.

——, "Weston to Spin Off E.B. Eddy in IPO," *Globe and Mail,* September 12, 1997, p. B1.

Yakabuski, Konrad, "New Provigo Bid Wins Over Caisse," *Globe and Mail,* December 1, 1998, p. B1.

—Sandy Schusteff
—updated by David E. Salamie

Gibson, Dunn & Crutcher LLP

---

333 South Grand Avenue
Los Angeles, California 90071-3197
U.S.A.
Telephone: (213) 229-7000
Fax: (213) 229-7520
Web site: http://www.gdclaw.com

Partnership
Founded: 1890 as Bicknell & Trask
Employees: 1,527
Sales: $418 million (1999)
NAIC: 54111 Offices of Lawyers

Gibson, Dunn & Crutcher LLP (Gibson Dunn) is one of the world's largest law firms. From its origins in the late 19th century when it helped Los Angeles and southern California grow, the firm has expanded to serve both national and international clients. Unlike its early years when it relied mainly on work from the railroad, utility, and land companies of Henry Huntington in southern California, Gibson, Dunn & Crutcher at the start of the new millennium has numerous clients, none of which accounts for more than one percent of its annual sales. In addition to its headquarters in Los Angeles, the firm operates branch offices in Denver, Dallas, London, Paris, New York, Palo Alto, San Francisco, Century City, Orange County, and Washington, D.C. The firm's attorneys represent both *Fortune* 500 and small startup companies, industry associations, and other clients in virtually all legal specialties.

Origins and Practice in the Early 20th Century

The 1890 partnership that became Gibson, Dunn & Crutcher began when California's industrialization and economic development were increasing the need for more lawyers, primarily in San Francisco and Los Angeles. In fact, Gordon Bakken's study of the late 19th-century California bar relied on a sample of 1,168 bar members admitted through 1900; half of those practiced in San Francisco or Los Angeles. Almost two-thirds of the Los Angeles lawyers in Bakken's sample joined the bar from 1889 to 1900, good evidence of the rapidly growing profession there.

According to Bakken, ''nineteenth-century California attorneys most often handled land title litigation,'' due in large part to the frenzy of land speculation and poor record-keeping during the real estate boom in Los Angeles in the 1880s.

When John Dustin Bicknell arrived in Los Angeles from Missouri in 1872, the 34-year-old lawyer soon set up his solo law practice. He participated in the real estate boom of the coming years both as an attorney and through his own investments. Then in 1887 the Southern Pacific Railway chose Bicknell as its counsel because of his reputation as a real estate expert. The railway needed additional assistance, for 1887 was the same year Congress created the Interstate Commerce Commission to regulate the nation's railroads.

In 1890 Walter Jones Trask arrived in Los Angeles and became John Bicknell's law associate, thus marking the founding of what became Gibson, Dunn & Crutcher. In 1897 James Alexander Gibson joined the firm as a partner. Like many others, Gibson and Bicknell both had moved to southern California because of its reputation for helping people improve their health.

Meanwhile, William Ellsworth Dunn and Albert Hodges Crutcher from 1888 to 1898 served Los Angeles in the city attorney's office. The two seasoned lawyers formed their own partnership that in 1903 merged with Bicknell, Gibson & Trask. Both law firms had represented the group of railroad and land companies headed by Henry Huntington.

Following the merger, the law firm added new clients. Utility companies such as the Los Angeles Gas & Electric Company provided considerable work. After Bicknell retired in 1907, the firm continued to serve his oil clients, including the Amalgamated, Union, and Akron oil companies. Other clients at that time were the California Mutual Livestock Insurance Corporation and Aetna.

In 1911 New York City's Cravath law firm engaged the Los Angeles law firm to certify Union Oil's ownership of thousands of West Coast properties from Oregon to Mexico. About the same time, the Gibson law firm had to deal with new progressive legislation, such as the state's first Workmen's Compensation Act and its Employers Liability Act.

Los Angeles and other cities were growing, so new water resources were essential. Attorneys Dunn and Crutcher, already directors for Huntington's Pacific Light & Power Company, in 1912 filed the incorporation papers when Huntington started the San Joaquin and Eastern Railroad. The new line took men and equipment to Huntington's Big Creek Power Plant under construction in the Kaiser Mountains.

The practice of law changed significantly in the early 20th century. In the days when John Bicknell began his practice, only a few records of court cases were available, so lawyers simply relied on legal principles. By the early 20th century more records were available, making library research and the case method of referring to previous decisions more important.

When Gibson, Dunn & Crutcher hired Henry Prince in 1914, it marked the firm's transition to the new methods pioneered in the Eastern law schools. The firm's first attorney to be recruited from the Harvard Law School, Prince became "the first member of the firm to send to Washington and New York for advance sheets of recently decided eastern cases as yet unavailable in California," according to Jane Wilson's firm history.

A 1926 map found in Wilson's book showed the extent of the Pacific Electric Railway that Henry Huntington had built with legal advice from Gibson, Dunn & Crutcher. The map said it was the "world's greatest electric railway system," with "1000 Miles of Standard Trolley Lines to All Points of Greatest Interest in the Heart of SOUTHERN CALIFORNIA and Traversed by 2700 Scheduled Trains Daily." Its single-, double-, and four-track lines stretched from San Fernando in the north along most of the coastline to Balboa in the south and also reached Santa Ana, Orange, Corona, Riverside, and San Bernardino. Although the Big Red Cars of the Pacific Electric Railway ran until 1961, the interurban rail system in Los Angeles and other cities was gradually replaced by cars and buses.

Gibson, Dunn & Crutcher in the 1932 *Martindale-Hubbell Law Directory* listed seven partners and 14 associates. By that time its three name attorneys were deceased. Gibson had died in 1922, Dunn in 1925, and Crutcher in 1931.

In 1932 the firm counseled San Marino City, Foster & Kleiser, Griffith Company, Huntington Land & Improvement Company, Janss Investment Corporation, Logan & Bryan, Los Angeles Biltmore Hotel, Los Angeles Junction Railway, Los Angeles Railway Corporation, Los Angeles Shipbuilding & Dry Dock Company, Pacific States Savings & Loan Association, and the Richfield Oil Company. Other clients included Rodeo Land & Water Company, Santa Catalina Island Company, Southern California Edison Company, Southern Surety Company, and Western Dairy Products Company. In addition, the partnership served as local counsel for Aetna Casualty & Surety Company, L.K. Liggett Company, Swift & Company, Westinghouse Electric Company, and William Wrigley, Jr.

Wrigley, the famous chewing gum capitalist from Chicago, and others helped turn Catalina Island into a popular resort area, with assistance from Gibson, Dunn & Crutcher. The law firm also played a crucial role in developing southern California's agriculture, which provided fruit and vegetables for the rest of the nation. Starting in World War I, the firm provided counsel to companies in the Los Angeles area that made tuna fish a popular canned food. At that time, about 80 percent of the nation's tuna came from that area. In the prewar years, Gibson, Dunn & Crutcher also assisted some of the area's major banks, securities firms, and others who provided the financial resources and expertise needed to develop the area.

With the torrent of New Deal legislation in the 1930s, the law firm gained new corporate clients that needed help with the new rules. For example, its labor practice picked up after the Wagner Act greatly stimulated the growth of the nation's unions. Although the firm grew, it and other Los Angeles law firms remained smaller than the large Wall Street law firms that served the banks, brokerage houses, media companies, and other corporations based in the nation's financial and commercial capital.

Developments After World War II

Gibson, Dunn & Crutcher continued to grow after World War II. From a total of 25 lawyers in 1943, it increased to 39 in 1954 and 63 in 1964, according to the *Martindale-Hubbell Law Directory*.

Starting in December 1968, several companies and the federal government filed antitrust lawsuits against IBM that would take over a decade to finally resolve. New York's Cravath, Swaine & Moore represented IBM. Memorex Corporation, represented by Gibson, Dunn & Crutcher, was one of the plaintiffs that sued IBM. In that case, a hung jury led to the trial judge ruling in IBM's favor. In the end, IBM survived these legal challenges that had threatened to break it up.

In 1977 the law firm opened its Washington, D.C. office as the nation's capital became the base for more and more attorneys. Author Joseph C. Goulden in his 1972 book said the number of lawyers in Washington, D.C. was increasing rapidly. At that time the city had only about one half of one percent of the nation's population but almost five percent of its lawyers.

Law firms expanded or started new offices in Washington to help their clients understand and comply with the increasing number of federal laws and regulations, such as the 1964 Civil Rights Act and new environmental protection laws.

Key Dates:

1890: Walter Trask joins John Bicknell's law practice.

1897: James Gibson becomes a partner of Bicknell, Gibson & Trask.

1903: Merger of two law firms creates Bicknell, Gibson, Trask, Dunn & Crutcher.

1907: Firm is renamed Gibson, Trask, Dunn & Crutcher.

1911: Firm becomes Gibson, Dunn & Crutcher.

1964: Firm starts an office in Irvine, Orange County.

1966: Century City, California office is organized.

1967: Firm establishes a Paris office, its first outside the United States.

1976: San Diego office is started, closed later.

1977: Partnership opens its Washington, D.C. office.

1979: Firm opens its San Jose office, its first in the San Francisco bay area.

1980: London branch office is established.

1981: Partnership opens its new branch in Denver.

1984: Dallas office is opened.

1987: Firm's San Francisco office is opened with six attorneys.

1999: Gibson, Dunn ranks as second largest law firm in Los Angeles.

Like many law firms, Gibson, Dunn & Crutcher expanded rapidly in the 1980s, going from about 200 lawyers in 1980 to about 700 lawyers in 1991. During this period, the U.S. Department of Commerce estimated that the amount of money Americans spent on legal services more than doubled, from $40 billion in 1983 to $83 billion in 1989.

The economic boom of most of the 1980s, which included numerous corporate mergers and acquisitions, helped explain the growing number of lawyers at Gibson, Dunn & Crutcher and other law firms. However, the legal profession itself had changed after the U.S. Supreme Court in its 1977 Bates decision said that professional associations could not restrict advertising because it violated First Amendment rights to free speech. Legal journalism in the late 1970s changed with the start of two new periodicals, the *National Law Journal* and the *American Lawyer*. For the first time there was comparative information about law firm finances and management styles, which facilitated lateral hiring of experienced attorneys. Some law firms also started hiring public relations experts and outside consultants to help them survive and prosper in this new era.

Gibson Dunn strengthened its international practice about the same time. Its Paris office was opened in 1977 and others followed after that. To prepare for an undivided European market in which goods and services flowed unimpeded, Gibson Dunn in 1989 agreed to associate with the 25-lawyer Brussels law firm of Van Bael & Bellis.

Practice in the 1990s and Beyond

After the 1980s expansion, many law firms, including Gibson Dunn, declined in the early 1990s as the economy weakened. Almost half the nation's largest law firms cut their lawyer

ranks in 1991, 1992, and 1993. For example, Gibson Dunn went from 724 lawyers in 1992 to 666 lawyers in 1993, according to the *National Law Journal*'s annual surveys. Gibson Dunn also reduced the number of its branch offices. From a total of 19 offices worldwide in 1992, the firm had downsized to 11 offices in 2000. However, a strong economy during most of the 1990s helped Gibson Dunn's sales increase from about $290 million in 1990 to $418 million in 1999.

In the 1990s Gibson Dunn defended Lucky Stores when it and other stores were sued for selling tobacco products to minors. By 1998 some defendants, including Albertson's and Safeway, had settled with the plaintiffs represented by attorney Donald Driscoll, but Lucky Stores continued to fight the charges.

As product liability lawsuits increased along with higher and higher punitive awards, some thought legislation limiting those cases would be appropriate. For example, the Civil Justice Reform Group, a business coalition supporting tort reform, chose Gibson Dunn for its legal counsel to try to rein in punitive damages.

Gibson, Dunn & Crutcher also represented the U.S. Chamber of Commerce, the National Association of Manufacturers, the American Trucking Association, and the Food Marketing Institute. These business groups in early 1998 persuaded the U.S. Court of Appeals for the District of Columbia Circuit to order OSHA to temporarily halt its Cooperative Compliance Program.

In 1999 the U.S. Supreme Court made an important ruling concerning the 1990 Americans with Disabilities Act. It reviewed three lawsuits, including *Murphy v. United Parcel Service Inc.*, in which Gibson Dunn defended UPS. In what the *Wall Street Journal* on June 23, 1999 called "a sweeping win for business," the court restricted the definition of a disability by concluding that it did not include most conditions that could be corrected or treated, for example with eyeglasses or medications. Disability advocates naturally criticized the high court's ruling.

In the rapidly changing Information Age, Gibson Dunn represented a variety of high-tech clients. For example, Intel chose Gibson Dunn's Joseph Kattan to deal with the Federal Trade Commission's investigation of its dominance of the microprocessor industry. The law firm also represented Broadcast.com when it was acquired in 1999 by Yahoo!

During the Clinton Administration, many were concerned that American firms had given the People's Republic of China valuable military secrets. When the House of Representatives held hearings on this problem, Hughes Electronics Corporation in 1998 chose Gibson Dunn as its lobbyist in Washington, D.C. In 1995 the Pentagon had concluded that Hughes without government authority had provided China with valuable data concerning both commercial satellites and ballistic missiles.

Former and current Gibson, Dunn & Crutcher attorneys played important roles in the Clinton scandals of the 1990s. For example, Kenneth Starr, at one time a member of the law firm, was appointed as the special prosecutor to investigate Clinton's misdeeds.

At the end of 1999, Gibson, Dunn & Crutcher's gross revenues were about $418 million, which made it the second largest law firm in Los Angeles behind Latham & Watkins, with $580 million in 1999 gross revenues. According to *The Recorder/Cal Law* of January 11, 2000, Gibson Dunn in 1999 "did well across all practice areas."

However, all law firms faced numerous challenges, including a rapidly changing economy in which some lawyers left their firms for executive positions in technology firms that offered both high salaries and stock options. Gaining and keeping bright new associates was also a major task, since many left after a couple years with their initial law firm. Competition from other large firms that were consolidating also was a factor. With over a century of experience behind it, Gibson, Dunn & Crutcher encountered a future filled with both great obstacles and opportunities.

Principal Divisions

Business and Commercial; Labor and Employment; Litigation; Real Estate; Tax and Estate.

Principal Competitors

Latham & Watkins.

Further Reading

Aragon, Lawrence, "Gibson Dunn May Close Its San Jose Office: Recession, Cost Cutting Force Law Firms to Pare Back Number of Offices," *Business Journal-San Jose*, March 30, 1992, p. 1.

Bakken, Gordon Morris, "Industrialization and the Nineteenth-Century California Bar," in *The New High Priests: Lawyers in Post-Civil War America*, ed. Gerald W. Gawalt, Westport, Conn.: Greenwood Press, 1984, pp. 125–49.

Carter, Terry, "Tort by Tort Reform," *American Bar Association Journal*, September 1998, p. 26.

Ferguson, Tim W., "The Lawsuit Business," *Forbes*, May 18, 1998, pp. 110–12.

Finnegan, Lisa, "Court Forces OSHA to Stop CCP . . . for Now," *Occupational Hazards*, April 1998, p. 11.

Goulden, Joseph C., *The Superlawyers: The Small and Powerful World of the Great Washington Law Firms*, New York: Weybright and Talley, 1972.

Greenberger, Robert S., "Supreme Court Narrows Scope of Disability Act," *Wall Street Journal*, June 23, 1999, p. B1.

Kramer, Farrell, "Soft Economy, Fresh Competition Bring Trying Times to Lawyers," *The Salt Lake Tribune*, October 10, 1993, pp. F1–F2.

Segal, David, and Elizabeth Corcoran, "Unlike Microsoft, Intel Uses Light Touch in D.C. Dealings," *Washington Post*, June 4, 1998, p. E1.

Stewart, James B., "IBM: Cravath, Swaine & Moore," Chapter 2 in *The Partners: Inside America's Most Powerful Law Firms*, New York: Simon and Schuster, 1983, pp. 53–113.

Stone, Peter H., "High-Tech's High Anxiety," *National Journal*, December 12, 1998, pp. 2926–2931.

Wilson, Jane, *Gibson, Dunn & Crutcher, Lawyers, An Early History*, Los Angeles: Gibson, Dunn & Crutcher, 1990.

"Yahoo! Buys Broadcast.com," *International Financial Law Review*, May 1999, p. 8.

—David M. Walden

H.J. Heinz Company

600 Grant Street
P.O. Box 57
Pittsburgh, Pennsylvania 15230-0057
U.S.A.
Telephone: (412) 456-5700
Fax: (412) 456-6128
Web site: http://www.heinz.com

Public Company
Incorporated: 1900
Employees: 46,900
Sales: $9.41 billion (2000)
Stock Exchanges: New York Pacific
Ticker Symbol: HNZ
NAIC: 311111 Dog and Cat Food Manufacturing; 311230
    Breakfast Cereal Manufacturing; 311412 Frozen
    Specialty Food Manufacturing; 311421 Fruit and
    Vegetable Canning; 311422 Canned Specialties;
    311711 Seafood Canning; 311941 Mayonnaise,
    Dressing, and Other Prepared Sauce Manufacturing

Perhaps best known for its ketchup, the H.J. Heinz Company manufactures thousands of food products in plants on six continents and markets these products in more than 200 countries and territories. Heinz ranked first in ketchup in the United States with a market share in excess of 50 percent. Moreover, the company's StarKist brand tuna led its market with a 45 percent share, and its Ore-Ida label held more than 50 percent of the frozen-potato sector. Overall, the company claims to have 150 number one or number two brands worldwide. Breaking the company's sales down by sector, ketchup, condiments, and sauces account for about 24 percent of overall sales; frozen foods (including Ore-Ida, Budget Gourmet, and Weight Watchers), 15 percent; pet products (9-Lives, Gravy Train, and Ken-L-Ration), 14 percent; soups, beans, and pasta meals, 12 percent; tuna, 12 percent; infant foods, 11 percent; and other, 12 percent. Geographically, about 55 percent of revenues are generated in North America, 26 percent in Europe, 11 percent in the Asia-Pacific region, and eight percent elsewhere.

Henry J. Heinz and the Founding of His Company

The origins of this vast food empire may be traced to Pennsylvania, where eight-year-old Henry John Heinz began selling produce from his family's plot to nearby neighbors. At ten he used a wheelbarrow, and, by the time he was 16, Heinz had several employees and was making three deliveries a week to Pittsburgh grocers. Born in 1844 to German immigrant parents, Heinz was the oldest of nine children. He grew up in Sharpsburg, Pennsylvania, near Pittsburgh, and, after graduating from Duff's Business College, he became the bookkeeper at his father's brickyard. At age 21, he became a partner. (Heinz retained an interest in bricks all his life—he personally supervised the buying and laying of brick for his company's buildings, and his office desk was often piled with brick samples acquired on his travels.) In 1869, Heinz and L.C. Noble formed a partnership called Heinz, Noble & Company in Sharpsburg to sell bottled horseradish. Their product line soon expanded to include sauerkraut, vinegar, and pickles.

Following the panic of 1873 and subsequent economic chaos, the business failed in 1875, but Heinz quickly regrouped, and the following year started afresh with the determination to repay his creditors. With his brother John and cousin Frederick as partners and himself as manager, Heinz formed the partnership of F&J Heinz to manufacture condiments, pickles, and other prepared food. Ketchup was added to the product line in 1876. The business prospered, and Heinz made good on his obligations. In 1888, the partnership was reorganized as the H.J. Heinz Company after Heinz gained financial control of the firm. Soon Heinz was known throughout the country as the "pickle king."

Small, energetic, and ambitious, Heinz was a cheerful man with courtly, old-fashioned manners. He exuded enthusiasm, whether for work, family, travel, religious activities, or good horses, and had a passion for involving others in his interests. According to his biographer, Robert C. Alberts, Heinz once installed an 800-pound, 14½-foot, 150-year-old live alligator in a glass tank atop one of his factory buildings so that his employees might enjoy the sight as much as he had in Florida.

In the late 1800s, the typical American diet was bland and monotonous, and the Heinz Company set out to spice it up with a multitude of products. The phrase "57 Varieties" was coined in 1892. Tomato soup and beans in tomato sauce were quickly added to the product line. Even as "57 Varieties" became a household slogan, the company already had more than 60 products. At the World's Columbian Exposition in Chicago in 1893, Heinz had the largest exhibit of any U.S. food company.

By 1900, the year the company was incorporated, the H.J. Heinz Company occupied a major niche in U.S. business. It was first in the production of ketchup, pickles, mustard, and vinegar and fourth in the packing of olives. Overall the company made more than 200 products. Still, Heinz liked the lilt of his original slogan and in 1900 put it up in lights in New York City's first large electric sign, at Fifth Avenue and 23rd Street. A total of 1,200 lights illuminated a 40-foot-long green pickle and its advertising message.

Heinz's clever merchandising won him a reputation as an advertising genius, but he did not allow his ambitions to overshadow his religious convictions; during his lifetime, in deference to the Sabbath, Heinz's advertisements never ran on Sundays. Heinz Company factories were considered models in the industry, both in their facilities and their treatment of workers. The company received many awards, and Harry W. Sherman, grand secretary of the National Brotherhood of Electrical Workers of America, remarked after visiting a Heinz plant that it was "a utopia for working men."

In 1886, Henry Heinz went to England carrying a sample case, and came home with orders for seven products. By 1905, the company had opened its first factory in England. The following year, the Pure Food and Drug Act was vigorously opposed by most food manufacturers, but Heinz, who understood the importance of consumer confidence in the purity of processed foods, was all for it, and even sent his son to Washington, D.C., to campaign for its passage.

Transition from Family Firm to Public Company: 1920s–60s

Henry Heinz died at age 75 in 1919. At that time, the company had a workforce of 6,500 employees and maintained 25 branch factories. Heinz was succeeded as president of the company by his son, Howard, who began his career with H.J. Heinz as advertising manager in 1905 and became sales manager in 1907. In 1931, at the height of the Great Depression, Howard Heinz saved the company by branching into two new

areas: ready-to-eat soups and baby food. He remained president until his death in 1941. In 1939, *Fortune* estimated total sales for the still privately owned company at $105 million.

By the time Howard's son H.J. Heinz II (known as Jack) became president of the company at his father's death, he had worked in all the company's divisions, from the canning factories to the administrative offices. He chose to launch his career as a pickle-salter for $1 a day in the Plymouth, Indiana plant. Later he became part of the cleanup staff, then a salesperson for H.J. Heinz Company, Ltd. in England. In 1935, fresh out of Cambridge University, Jack Heinz was sent by his father to establish a plant in Australia. Heinz-Australia later became that country's biggest food processing plant.

From 1941, when Jack took over, to 1946, H.J. Heinz's sales nearly doubled. That year, Heinz made its first public stock offering and revealed that its net profit was more than $4 million. Foreign sales of baked beans and ketchup, particularly in England, contributed substantially to the company's success. During World War II, Jack Heinz was active in food relief and personally made four war-time trips to England to examine food problems there. The company insignia went to war, too; the 57th Squadron of the 446th Army Air Force chose for its emblem a winged pickle marked "57."

Jack Heinz's tenure was distinguished by expansion of the company, both internationally and at home. Subsidiaries were launched in the Netherlands, Venezuela, Japan, Italy, and Portugal. In 1960 and 1961, the H.J. Heinz Company acquired the assets of Reymer & Bros., Inc. and Hachmeister, Inc. StarKist Foods was acquired in 1963 and Ore-Ida Foods, Inc. in 1965.

During the 25 years that H.J. Heinz II was chief executive, the food industry changed greatly. The era was marked by the rise of supermarket chains and the development of new distribution and marketing systems. In 1966, H.J. Heinz II stepped down as president and CEO, though he retained his position as chairperson until his death in February 1987.

1970s and 1980s: The O'Reilly Revolution

In 1969, R. Burt Gookin, then CEO of Heinz, made Anthony (Tony) J.F. O'Reilly president of the company's profitable British subsidiary. O'Reilly, who was managing director of the Irish Sugar Company at the time, shook up the company by working 14-hour days and stressing a policy of winning through effort. O'Reilly was an uncommon executive; he was, among other things, a world-class rugby player. In 1973, O'Reilly was named president of the parent company, and in 1979 he became CEO. Shortly after the death of H.J. Heinz II, he was also made chairperson. From the beginning, O'Reilly stressed the importance of strong financial results. Some critics claimed that this emphasis created too stressful an atmosphere; in 1979, it was learned that managers of several subsidiaries had for years been misstating quarterly earnings in order to meet their target goals and impress top management.

Overall, O'Reilly's achievements were impressive, however. The timely acquisition of Hubinger Company in 1975 put Heinz in a position to cash in on the demand for high-fructose corn syrup when the price of sugar soared. In 1978, O'Reilly

Key Dates:

1869: Henry J. Heinz and L.C. Noble form partnership, Heinz, Noble & Company, to sell bottled horse-radish.

1875: Business fails following the panic of 1873.

1876: Business is reorganized in a new partnership, F&J Heinz; ketchup is added to the product line.

1888: Henry Heinz gains financial control of F&J Heinz and changes its name to H.J. Heinz Company.

1892: The slogan ''57 Varieties'' is first used.

1900: Company is incorporated.

1905: The first foreign factory is opened in England.

1919: Henry Heinz dies and is succeeded by his son, Howard.

1931: Company branches into ready-to-eat soups and baby food.

1946: Company goes public.

1963: StarKist Foods is acquired.

1965: Ore-Ida Foods, Inc. is acquired.

1978: Weight Watchers International is acquired.

1979: Anthony J.F. O'Reilly is named CEO.

1988: StarKist Foods is reorganized into StarKist Seafood and Heinz Pet Products.

1994: Company acquires the Budget Gourmet line of frozen meals.

1995: The North American pet food businesses of Quaker Oats Company are acquired, including such brands as Kibbles'n Bits, Gravy Train, and Ken-L Ration.

1997: Company initiates a major restructuring.

1999: An even larger, multiyear restructuring is launched; the Weight Watchers diet class business is divested.

acquired Weight Watchers International, just ahead of the fitness craze that swept the nation.

At the same time that the company was branching out into new products, O'Reilly was cutting back on traditional businesses. By 1980, Heinz had increased volume, while cutting its number of plants from 14 to seven and reducing employment by 18 percent. O'Reilly also gave up the battle with Campbell Soup Company for the retail soup market. When generic products hit the supermarket shelves, Heinz countered not by producing for the generics industry but by ''nickel and diming it,'' as he said. For example, Heinz switched to thinner glass bottles that cut the cost not only of packaging but also of transportation. When imports began to undersell StarKist tuna, StarKist decreased the size of the tuna can, just as Hershey had downsized its chocolate bar when cocoa prices soared. This ploy netted StarKist $7 million in savings. Other nickel-and-dime cost savings came from eliminating back labels from bottles, reclaiming heat, and reusing water.

O'Reilly's strategy in the 1980s was to pare costs to the bone and to use the savings to beef up marketing, primarily advertising, in an effort to increase market share. At the same time, Heinz pursued a cautious acquisition policy. By the mid-1980s, the company had spent $416 million to acquire more than 20 companies. Return on equity increased from nine percent in 1972 to 23.3 percent in 1986.

O'Reilly's cost-cutting war included a threat to go to contract manufacturers rather than his own plants if the same products could be purchased elsewhere for less. Such tough talk elicited substantial concessions from labor unions in 1986. O'Reilly's hard-nosed, bottom-line strategies won Heinz recognition as one of the country's five best-managed companies in 1986. When H.J. Heinz died the following year, O'Reilly became the first non-family member to advance to Heinz's chair.

In 1988, Heinz bid $200 million for Bumble Bee Seafoods, the third largest tuna company in the country. The purchase would have given Heinz, whose StarKist brand already ranked number one, more than 50 percent of the domestic tuna market. Accordingly, the U.S. Justice Department prevented the purchase on antitrust grounds. Also in 1988, Heinz reorganized StarKist Foods into StarKist Seafood and Heinz Pet Products in order to strengthen seafood operations for a push abroad. In pet foods, Heinz, already a leading canned cat food producer, strengthened its dog food position through the acquisition of several regional brands.

In overseas markets, Heinz began to expand into the Third World. It became the first foreign investor in Zimbabwe when it acquired a controlling interest in Olivine Industries, Inc. in 1982. Heinz also formed joint ventures in Korea and China, and in 1987 the company bought a controlling interest in Win-Chance Foods of Thailand. Win-Chance produced baby food and milk products, and, of course, Heinz planned to add ketchup to the line.

1990s and Beyond: Slower Growth and Restructurings

O'Reilly's strategies succeeded in the 1980s. Heinz's sales doubled from $2.9 billion in 1980 to $6.1 billion in 1990, and net profits quadrupled to $504 million during the period. The CEO had hoped to increase Heinz's annual revenues to $10 billion by 1994, then retire at the close of his contract in 1995. Recession and competition from private-label products in the early 1990s, however, thwarted that plan and held the company's sales to $7 billion in 1993 and 1994. As Heinz's growth slowed from its double-digit pace of the previous decade, the company's stock declined as well—30 percent from 1992 to 1994—in spite of continuously rising dividends. As a result, O'Reilly postponed his retirement and embarked on a reorganization.

Divestments (most significantly, of the Hubinger subsidiary) in 1993 totaled $700 million. Internal cost-cutting measures included workforce and management staff reductions as well as achievement of manufacturing efficiencies. In America, O'Reilly cut brand advertising by 40 percent from 1990 levels and resorted to discounting to reverse 1991's market share losses to private labels. He shifted the company's domestic sales focus to the high-margin foodservice sector, acquiring J.L. Foods from Borden Inc. in 1994 for $500 million.

But domestic operations were little more than half of Heinz's operations in the 1990s. O'Reilly pinned his expectations for future growth on overseas markets, targeting baby food, in particular, for expansion. Heinz controlled 29 percent of the global infant food market in 1994 and completed the acquisition of Farley's baby food of Great Britain (from the Boots Company PLC) and Glaxo Holdings plc's baby food interests in India that year. Previously unchallenged in international baby food sales, Heinz faced a serious threat from the U.S. leader, Gerber, which was acquired by Swiss pharmaceutical giant Sandoz Ltd. and groomed for international expansion that year as well. Heinz also buttressed its interests in the Asia/Pacific region with the 1992 purchase of New Zealand's Wattie's Limited for $300 million. O'Reilly characterized the new addition as a "mini-Heinz" in a 1994 address to the New York Society of Securities Analysts. Heinz marked its 125th year in business with flat sales that O'Reilly himself characterized as disappointing.

The next two years, however, seemed to indicate that O'Reilly's restructuring efforts were paying off. Sales surged ahead by more than $1 billion in each of those years, culminating in 1996 revenues of $9.11 billion. Further acquisitions played a role as well. In December 1994 Heinz paid $200 million to Kraft General Foods, Inc. for the All American Gourmet Company, maker of the Budget Gourmet line of frozen meals. Heinz nearly doubled the size of its pet food operation through the March 1995 purchase of the North American pet food businesses of the Quaker Oats Company for $725 million. Thereby added to the company's existing brands, which included 9-Lives and Amore, were Kibbles'n Bits, Cycle, Gravy Train, and Ken-L Ration, among others. In March 1996 Heinz acquired Boulder, Colorado-based Earth's Best, Inc., a maker of organic baby food. In June of that year William R. Johnson was named president and COO, positioning him as the likely successor of O'Reilly. Johnson, who had joined Heinz in 1982, was previously head of the tuna and pet food divisions, where he was noted for slashing costs and squeezing out profits from mature brands.

In March 1997 Heinz launched a major restructuring that involved the closure or sale of 25 plants and a workforce reduction of 2,500, as well as a plan to divest the foodservice operations of the Ore-Ida unit. The latter came to fruition in June 1997 with the sale of said operations to McCain Foods Limited of New Brunswick, Canada, for about $500 million (Heinz retained the Ore-Ida retail business). In connection with the restructuring, Heinz took pretax charges of $647.2 million in fiscal 1997, resulting in a reduction in net income to $301.9 million (compared with $659.3 million for 1996). Heinz also continued to make selective acquisitions, with one of the more important ones being the June 1997 purchase of John West Foods Limited from Unilever. John West was the leading brand of canned tuna and fish in the firm's home country, the United Kingdom. In May 1998 Johnson was named president and CEO of Heinz, with O'Reilly becoming nonexecutive chairman.

Restructuring efforts continued into the early 21st century. In late 1998 the company took a $150 million charge to combine the operations of its Ore-Ida Foods and Weight Watchers Gourmet Foods units into a new unit called Heinz Frozen Food Company. Early the following year, Heinz announced its largest restructuring yet. In the first phase of a projected four-year program, the company planned to close 20 of its remaining 100 factories, reduce the workforce by an additional 4,000, and divest the diet class business of Weight Watchers. A key component of the program was the realigning of the company along global category lines, a major shift from the previous geographic arrangement. The six main categories, generating 80 percent of global revenues, were ketchup, tuna, frozen foods, infant foods, pet foods, and convenience meals. Heinz also planned to concentrate on the six countries that generated 80 percent of the company's revenues: the United States, the United Kingdom, Italy, Canada, Australia, and New Zealand. While the company hoped eventually to reap $200 million in annual savings from these efforts, it also planned to spend an additional $100 million during fiscal 2000 to increase its spending on marketing its flagship brands. Pretax restructuring charges for fiscal 1999 totaled $552.8 million.

In late 1999 Heinz completed the sale of the Weight Watchers diet class unit to Artal Luxembourg, S.A., a European venture capital firm, for about $735 million. Around this same time, with pressure for global consolidation among food companies growing, Heinz entered into merger talks with Bestfoods, maker of soups, sauces, bouillons, dressings, and other products. The talks collapsed, however, and Unilever soon stepped in to acquire Bestfoods. In the wake of this failed merger, Heinz continued its acquisitive ways. The company gained a foothold in the fast-growing natural and organic foods sector through the purchase of a 19.5 percent stake in Hain Food Group Inc. for $100 million. The Hain product line included Health Valley cereal and other products, Terra Chip snacks, and Westsoy soy beverages. Through the alliance with Heinz, Hain also acquired the Earth's Best line of organic baby foods. In May 2000 Hain acquired Celestial Seasonings, best known for its herbal teas, in a stock swap, leading Heinz to invest an additional $80 million in Hain to keep its stake at 19.5 percent. Other developments included the acquisition of the frozen food business of U.K.-based United Biscuits PLC for $317 million. Sales for the unit in 1998 were $360 million, with the product line including frozen desserts, pizzas, potato products, and vegetarian/meat-free items. In February 2000 Heinz announced that it had signed an agreement to acquire Milnot Holding Corporation, maker of the Beech-Nut brand of baby food, for $185 million. Beech-Nut was the number two baby food brand in the United States, with 13 percent of the market, while Heinz was number three with 11 percent. The commanding leader was Gerber, with 73 percent. Despite what Heinz officials called Gerber's virtual monopoly position, the Federal Trade Commission moved to block the deal in July 2000 under antitrust laws. In June 2000 Heinz began selling StarKist tuna in vacuum-sealed pouches, claiming that the tuna was fresher-tasting and firmer than the traditional canned variety.

The restructuring efforts launched under Johnson's leadership appeared to be paying off for Heinz. Although overall revenues remained flat—the $9.41 billion for 2000 was only marginally larger than the 1996 total of $9.11 billion—profits were growing. For fiscal 2000, a pretax restructuring charge of $392.7 million was more than offset by a pretax gain of $464.6 million on the sale of the Weight Watchers unit, resulting in overall net income for the year of $890.6 million. The company's future remained uncertain, despite such improvements, as speculation about further food industry consolidation remained rife. Should Heinz not join in the merger wave, Johnson was prepared to pick up some of the brands that were certain to be discarded following the mergers of other food companies.

Principal Subsidiaries

Alimentos Heinz, C.A. (Venezuela); Alimentos Pilar S.A. (Argentina); AIAL S.r.l. (Arimpex Industrie Alimentari S.r.l.) (Italy); The All American Gourmet Company; Boulder, Inc.; Ets. Paul Paulet (France); Heinz Europe Ltd. (U.K.); Heinz Frozen Food Company; Heinz Iberica S.A. (Spain); Heinz India Private Ltd.; Heinz Italia S.r.l. (Italy); Heinz Japan Ltd.; Heinz Polska Sp. Z.o.o. (Poland); Heinz South Africa (Pty) Limited; Heinz-UFE Ltd. (China); Heinz-Wattie Holdings Ltd. (New Zealand); Heinz Win Chance Ltd. (Thailand); H.J. Heinz (Botswana Proprietary) Ltd.; H.J. Heinz B.V. (Netherlands); H.J. Heinz Company Australia Limited; H.J. Heinz Company of Canada Ltd.; H.J. Heinz Company Limited (U.K.); H.J. Heinz Credit Company; H.J. Heinz European Frozen & Chilled Foods, Ltd. (Ireland); Indian Ocean Tuna Ltd. (Seychelles); Industrias de Alimentacao, Lda. (Portugal); Mareblu S.r.l. (Italy); Olivine Industries (Private) Limited (Zimbabwe); Portion Pac, Inc.; Pudliszki S.A. (Poland); PT Heinz ABC Indonesia; Seoul-Heinz Ltd. (South Korea); StarKist Foods, Inc.; Thompson & Hills Limited (New Zealand).

Principal Competitors

Aurora Foods Inc.; Bestfoods; Borden, Inc.; Campbell Soup Company; Chicken of the Sea International; Colgate-Palmolive Company; ConAgra, Inc.; Groupe Danone; Del Monte Foods Company; Hibernia Foods plc; Hormel Foods Corporation; International Home Foods, Inc.; Jenny Craig; Kraft Foods, Inc.; Mars, Inc.; McIlhenny Company; Nabisco Holdings Corp.; Nestlé S.A.; Novartis AG; Pillsbury Company; The Procter & Gamble Company; Ralston Purina Company; Sara Lee Corporation; Slim-Fast Foods Company; Tyson Foods, Inc.; Vlasic Foods International Inc.

Further Reading

Alberts, Robert C., *The Good Provider: H.J. Heinz and His 57 Varieties,* Boston: Houghton Mifflin, 1973.

Alexander, Keith L., and Stephen Baker, "The New Life of O'Reilly," *Business Week,* June 13, 1994, pp. 64–66.

Baker, Stephen, "The Odd Couple at Heinz," *Business Week,* November 4, 1996, p. 176.

Berner, Robert, "Ketchuping Up, or a Classic Condiment Returns As Top Dog," *Wall Street Journal,* November 5, 1999, p. A1.

Berner, Robert, and Kevin Helliker, "Heinz's Worry: 4,000 Products, Only One Star Winner," *Wall Street Journal,* September 17, 1999, p. B1.

Byrne, John A., "The CEO and the Board," *Business Week,* September 15, 1997, pp. 106+.

Campanella, Frank W., "Tomatoes, and More: H.J. Heinz, with $4 Billion in Yearly Sales, Lifts Profits in Stateside Business," *Barron's,* May 20, 1985, pp. 73+.

Dienstag, Eleanor Foa, *In Good Company: 125 Years at the Heinz Table, 1869–1994,* New York: Warner, 1994.

Eig, Jonathan, "Heinz's CEO Unveils Plans to Stimulate Growth," *Wall Street Journal,* June 16, 2000, p. B6.

Fallon, Ivan, *The Luck of O'Reilly: A Biography of Tony O'Reilly,* New York: Warner, 1994.

Hannon, Kerry, "The King of Ketchup," *Forbes,* March 21, 1988, pp. 58+.

"Heinz: Lucky or Good?," *Financial World,* February 15, 1981, p. 38.

Machan, Dyan, "Tony Who?," *Forbes,* June 15, 1998, pp. 98–102.

Mallory, Maria, "Heinz's New Recipe: Take a Dollop of Dollars," *Business Week,* September 30, 1991, pp. 86+.

Miles, Gregory L., "Heinz Ain't Broke, But It's Doing a Lot of Fixing," *Business Week,* December 11, 1989, pp. 84+.

Murray, Matt, "Heinz Unwraps Details of Restructuring," *Wall Street Journal,* March 17, 1997, p. A3.

——, "H.J. Heinz Chairman's Growth Prediction Comes True: Acquisitions and Volume Gains Boost Sales 12 Percent, But Weight Watchers Sags," *Wall Street Journal,* April 10, 1996, p. B4.

Murray, Matt, and Rekha Balu, "Corporate Icons Are a Hard Act to Follow, As Successors Discover: Heinz Chief Copes with Style and Expectations Born of a Very Different Era," *Wall Street Journal,* April 29, 1999, pp. A1+.

Saporito, Bill, "Heinz Pushes to Be the Low-Cost Producer," *Fortune,* June 24, 1985, pp. 44+.

Siklos, Richard, "I Want More of Everything," *Business Week,* December 20, 1999, pp. 158–62.

Symonds, William C., Andrew B. Wilson, and Marc Frons, "Tony O'Reilly of Heinz: His Day Has 57 Varieties," *Business Week,* December 17, 1984, pp. 72+.

Troxell, Thomas N., Jr., "Spicy Results: Heinz Earnings Are Likely to Set Another All-Time Peak," *Barron's,* July 13, 1981, pp. 37+.

—April Dougal Gasbarre
—updated by David E. Salamie

Habitat for Humanity International

121 Habitat Street
Americus, Georgia 31709-3498
U.S.A.
Telephone: (912) 924-6935
Fax: (912) 928-4157
Web site: http://www.hfhi.org

Nonprofit Company
Founded: 1976
Employees: 700
Contributions: $121.1 million (1999)
NAIC: 233210 Single Family Housing Construction;
   813219 Other Grantmaking and Giving Services

Habitat for Humanity International (HFHI) is a world service organization providing affordable homes with interest-free mortgages to families in need. Founded by Millard and Linda Fuller, Habitat's long-term dream is to eradicate housing projects around the world, and to replace them with solid, single-family homes built by HFHI volunteers and the future owners themselves. For the shorter term, however, Habitat will settle for their 200,000th home built by the year 2005, and having housed over 475,000 people internationally. Using their faith and homebuilding skills, the Fullers and a growing list of sponsors and volunteers (including such luminaries as Jimmy Carter, Jerry Falwell, Louis Gossett, Jr., Jack Kemp, Newt Gingrich, and Oprah Winfrey) have transformed the lives of many homeless families into proud homeowners and lifelong Habitat volunteers.

From Less to More: 1920s–50s

Millard Fuller was born in Chambers County in eastern Alabama, the son of poor sharecroppers. His mother died when he was three years old, and he was raised by his father. Religion was a big part of Fuller family life, with Fuller, Sr., working as the deacon of the local church on top of his duties as farmer, grocer, and full-time parent. From a very young age, Millard worked alongside his father in their country store, contributing to the family's income. He raised pigs, trapped minnows, and as he grew older, sought varied ways to earn money, from trading used cars to selling fireworks. He put himself through college at Auburn University, where he was the youngest director of the Junior Achievement program in the nation. He then attended the University of Alabama Law School at Tuscaloosa, Alabama.

As a rising young businessman, Fuller allied himself with another like-minded law student, Morris Dees, who also wanted to become a successful entrepreneur. Through hard work and an acuity beyond their years, the two young men dove into a number of business enterprises, eventually buying real estate and renovating apartments (with help from Millard's father, who mortgaged the family farm to give his son funds). In his senior year of law school, Fuller married his sweetheart, Linda (who earned her B.S. degree from nearby Huntingdon College). They dreamed of living happily ever after.

After passing the bar, Fuller and Dees set out to make serious money. Among their endeavors was publishing regional and specialty cookbooks (*Favorite Recipes of American Home Economics Teachers, Favorite Recipes of New England, Favorite Recipes of the Deep South, Favorite Recipes of the Lions Clubs: A Lion in the Kitchen,* and many more), in which they had discovered a very lucrative market. The two had also founded a law firm in Montgomery, Alabama, and quickly earned a good reputation and growing client base. Before his 30th birthday, Millard Fuller was not only a successful attorney but a self-made millionaire.

Cold Comfort to Warm Hearts: Late 1960s–70s

As many before him had learned, Fuller found money could not buy happiness. More dollars meant more work and he was obsessed with making more and more money. This left little time for Linda and the children, who had all the trappings wealth could buy but virtually no husband or father. Fuller was so busy he and Linda eventually conducted church services in their own living room, because it was more convenient and less time consuming. But Millard's constant absenteeism put his marriage on the rocks and Linda soon had enough; she took the kids and flew to New York City for marriage counseling. Fuller, in deteriorating health, was not ready to give up on his family and hopped a plane. "I could visualize myself as a lonely person with no family and a pile of money. That's cold comfort,'' Fuller later told Kelly Starling of *Ebony* magazine in 1997.

In a cab ride after a counseling session, Millard realized the root of his family and marital problems was money, and decided to get rid of it all. Linda was in complete agreement, though some family members and friends tried to dissuade them. Undeterred, Millard sold his half of the Montgomery law firm as well as his stake in the publishing company. The Fullers sold their belongings and then gave upwards of $1 million to various Christian charities and educational funds, and prepared to live out their faith by doing God's work.

On a trip to Atlanta, Fuller met Clarence Jordan, who ran a controversial (at the time) interracial Christian commune called Koinonia Farm near Americus, Georgia. Though many in Sumpter County, Georgia, considered Koinonia Farm to be a radical cult-like movement, the Fullers found the community comforting and moved in with their four children. There near the end of the 1960s, Millard, Linda, Clarence, and others decided to build affordable housing in the area for lower income families. One of the earliest recipients of their homebuilding plan was Joseph ''Bo'' Johnson, who had saved his money to buy a parcel of land with hopes of building a home for his family. He achieved the first part of his dream and became a property owner, but had nothing left over to build even the simplest house. Fuller met Johnson and wanted to help; he was also a firm believer in the Biblical tenet (Exodus 22:25) of not charging interest or making a profit off the less fortunate. ''You know it's interesting that the world's three great monotheistic religions—Islam, Judaism and Christianity—all teach in their Scriptures not to charge interest to the poor. But in the Western world we've largely taken that Scriptural idea and turned it upside down,'' Fuller explained to William Olcott of *Fund Raising Management* in October 1994. ''We give the prime lending rate to the richest people and charge the highest interest to the poorest.''

After completing Johnson's house and several others in Sumpter County, the Fuller family moved to Zaire (now the Republic of Congo) in 1973 with volunteers from the Disciples of Christ Christian Church to construct housing. The homebuilding project was a success, just as it had been in Georgia, and the Fullers returned to the United States after three years with a more formalized plan to provide housing for those in need. By instituting a ''biblical'' finance plan or ''the economics of Jesus,'' the Fullers and a group of dedicated volunteers would build low-cost houses with interest-free financing everywhere, eradicating substandard housing and the ever present projects. The organization formed in 1976 to oversee and carry out these aspirations was called Habitat for Humanity.

The Economics of Jesus: 1980s

After Habitat had been in the business of building homes with love and faith for a few years, Millard sat down and wrote about his vision—past, present, and future—in a book. The 192-page *Love in the Mortar Joints: The Story of Habitat for Humanity* was the result, published by New Win Publishing in August 1980. The well-received history brought notice to the growing ecumenical organization, yet much wider acknowledgment came in Habitat's eighth year when Millard lassoed a fellow Baptist church member into helping out. The man and his wife were rather well known in Georgia, and in fact, all over the world. HFHI's recognition soared when former president and avid carpenter Jimmy Carter and his wife Rosalynn Carter began devoting their time and effort to building homes for Habitat in 1984. They soon set up the Jimmy Carter Work Project, in which they traveled to a new location every year to construct housing. The Carters' involvement was a tremendous boon for the organization, raising awareness of HFHI's mission and methods. Carter called Millard ''an inspiration'' and the feeling was mutual.

Fuller's second book, *No More Shacks! The Daring Vision of Habitat for Humanity,* a 220-page coffee table-type book filled with photographs, was published in July 1986, followed in 1990 by a treatise called *Restrictive Housing Regulation Increases Problems* and a collaboration with Linda entitled *The Excitement Is Building: How Habitat for Humanity Is Putting Roofs Over Heads and Hope in Hearts.* Writing not only served as a means to spread the word about Habitat and its members, but had become a valuable source of funds. Millard Fuller was well versed in the power of publishing, since his early college days, and the first of a proposed series of gift books was published by the Georgia-based Peachtree Publishers. The 206-page *A Christmas Housewarming,* edited by Gene Stelton, with a foreword written by Jimmy Carter, was published in 1992.

In the early 1990s Habitat-built homes generally cost from $35,000 to $42,000 to construct in the United States (or as little as $500 in Third World countries), usually on donated or bargain-priced land parcels. Local businesses often provided basic building materials free of charge, materials in sync with the other homes in the area. Fuller's army of God, composed of persons of all religious backgrounds, worked tirelessly towards the same goal. As Fuller explained to D'Arcy Jenish of *Maclean's* magazine (August 1993), ''We use the philosophy of the hammer. We may disagree with one another theologically or philosophically, but we can all wield the hammer as an expression of love.'' Although Habitat was clearly a Christian organization, Fuller stressed, ''We are non-denominational and non-doctrinal. We welcome support from whoever wants to give it and we do in fact have support from a broad segment of this country.''

For their part, potential homeowners were required to lend a hand in the construction of their own homes as well as those of others, from 200 to 500 hours of what Habitat referred to as ''sweat equity.'' Additionally, future owners provided a small down payment which HFHI pooled in a revolving fund and put toward the building of other homes.

Onward Christian Soldiers: 1993–97

By 1993 HFHI was constructing an average of two dozen homes per day, a figure Fuller believed would climb to 30 a day by the following year. The fact that Habitat had already built 20,000 homes in 40 countries simply was not enough. Fuller had bigger and brighter plans for HFHI, similar to his earlier entrepreneurial drive, the very drive which nearly cost him his life and his family. Yet his acumen was no longer focused on increasing his personal wealth, but on how far every donated dollar could go in his battle against poverty and homelessness. The same obsessive urges that had made him a millionaire were now harnessed by faith. As the 17th largest home builder in the United States in 1993, according to *Builder* magazine, Fuller wanted Habitat to rise to the top slot within three years. Further, in his five-year plan, he hoped HFHI would construct more than 45,000 houses annually, which came to more than 123 homes every day.

Accolades for Habitat came in 1994 when the Direct Marketing Association (DMA) named the organization as the Non-Profit Organization of the Year. The Fullers later received the Harry S. Truman Public Service Award. By the end of the year, HFHI had constructed more than 40,000 homes in all 50 states and 41 countries worldwide, and the organization and its affiliates had brought in more than $145 million in support and contributions. Habitat also managed a one-million-plus mailing list, which grew with increased exposure, such as when Fuller was named Builder of the Year by *Professional Builder* magazine in 1995. Peachtree Publishers issued its second gift book later that year, *Home for the Holidays: Stories and Art Created for the Benefit of Habitat for Humanity,* again edited by Stelton.

Linda Fuller, meanwhile, in addition to building homes and getting women around the world involved in Habitat with WATCH (Women Accepting the Challenge of Housing), had begun a publishing project of her own. In 1993 she debuted the first in a series of cookbooks called *Partners in the Kitchen,* with *From Our House to Yours,* followed by *Home Sweet Habitat* (1995) and *Simple, Decent Cooking* (1997). Again harking back to Millard's early years in publishing, the cookbooks were a successful fundraising tool for the organization, selling more than 100,000 copies. Millard too had continued to write, publishing *The Theology of the Hammer* (1994), *A Simple, Decent Place to Live: The Building Realization of Habitat for Humanity* (1995), and *Bokotola* (1997).

By 1997 Habitat had become the fourth largest homebuilder in the world and the nation's number one nonprofit home-

builder. There were 60,000 HFHI homes in 54 countries, with two-fifths of the total construction taking place outside the United States. Yet Habitat, long known for its strident volunteers, earned another badge of honor that year in Tucson. Working with the Tucson Urban League and a grant from the National Urban Consortium, HFHI began constructing homes of the future using straw bales, replacing up to 13 percent of traditional wood building materials. Straw, it turned out, had incredible insulating powers and cost homeowners up to 75 percent less to heat and cool their abodes. While Habitat did accept grants from a number of groups, including the federal government (like the previous year's $25 million grant from the Department of Housing and Urban Development), as a rule HFHI did not receive governmental funds, wishing to remain autonomous and also maintain the separation of church and state. Yet the 1996 federal grant marked 20 years of good deeds for Habitat, and Millard was recognized by President Clinton with the Presidential Medal of Freedom (the highest civilian award in the country), who called HFHI "the most successful continuous community service project in the history of the United States."

Housing, Help, and Hope: 1998–2000

Habitat, though not a disaster relief organization like the Red Cross, became involved in such operations in the late 1990s. After a tornado in Alabama and devastation caused by two hurricanes (Georges in September and Mitch in October 1998), HFHI sought donations to help victims of the calamities. Hoping to raise some $2 million in funds after Hurricane Mitch hit Central America, HFHI was buoyed by donations totaling $6 million and immediately began building homes for the many left homeless by the deadly storm. To better respond to natural disasters and coordinate volunteer efforts, Habitat created its Disaster Response Office. Habitat workers lent a hand after the Alabama tornado and a subsequent touchdown in Oklahoma the following year.

Amazingly, Habitat-built homes had withstood other natural disasters such as Hurricane Andrew, the Los Angeles earthquake, and flooding in southern Georgia. When asked about miracles or why these houses had survived, Fuller believed God was indeed keeping an eye on these homes because they were built from love and a firm foundation of faith. While he was quick to point out, "I don't believe that only bad things happen to bad people and only good things happen to good people," his pride in Habitat's work was evident. "But I was down there right after the hurricane and it did look like our houses were built after the hurricane," he told *Fund Raising Management*'s Olcott. "It was amazing."

By the last year in the 20th century, Habitat had built or renovated nearly 80,000 homes around the globe, and made a profound difference in the lives of the more than 400,000 people who lived in these safe, solid homes. Millard was the recipient of the Jefferson Award from the American Institute of Public Service for his work on behalf of the disadvantaged, while *Builder* magazine deemed him one of the 20th century's most influential homebuilders. With nearly 1.3 million worldwide donors in 1999, and funds raised from its publishing ventures (including Millard's new tome, *More Than Houses: How Habitat for Humanity Is Transforming Lives and Neigh-*

borhoods), Habitat brought in over $121.1 million in support for 1999. The next year, Jerome P. Baggett's exhaustive study of the ecumenical organization, *Habitat for Humanity: Building Private Homes, Building Public Religion,* was published by Temple University Press.

The Fullers had big plans for the new century: to construct an additional 100,000 houses by 2005. This, in and of itself, would be a tremendous accomplishment, since it took nearly a quarter-century to build Habitat's first 100,000 homes. With corporate alliances as well as high profile celebrities lending a hand, HFHI was well positioned to meet its goals and, perhaps, would one day eliminate dilapidated housing projects from the planet.

Further Reading

Baggett, Jerome P., *Habitat for Humanity: Building Private Homes, Building Public Religion,* Chicago: Temple University Press, 2000, 360 p.

Fuller, Millard, *Bokotola,* Clinton, N.J.: New Win Publishing, 1997, 176 p.

——, *Love in the Mortar Joints: The Story of Habitat for Humanity,* Clinton, N.J.: New Win Publishing, 1980, 192 p.

——, *More Than Houses: How Habitat for Humanity Is Transforming Lives and Neighborhoods,* Nashville: Word Books, 1999.

——, *No More Shacks! The Daring Vision of Habitat for Humanity,* Nashville: Word Books, 1986, 220 p.

——, *Restrictive Housing Regulation Increases Problems,* Chicago: Heartland Institute, 1990.

——, *A Simple, Decent Place to Live: The Building Realization of Habitat for Humanity,* Nashville: Word Books, 1995.

——, *The Theology of the Hammer,* Macon, Ga.: Smyth & Helwys Publishing, 1994.

Fuller, Millard, and Linda Fuller, *The Excitement Is Building: How Habitat for Humanity Is Putting Roofs Over Heads and Hope in Hearts,* Nashville: Word Books, 1990.

Gaillard, Frye, *If I Were a Carpenter: Twenty Years of Habitat for Humanity,* Winston-Salem, N.C.: John F. Blair Publishers, 1996, 182 p.

Horne, Laura, "Building Straw Houses on a Firm Foundation: Habitat for Humanity Goes Low-Tech with Big Results," *Christianity Today,* February 3, 1997, p. 56.

Jenish, D'Arcy, "Carter the Carpenter," *Maclean's,* August 2, 1993, p. 38.

Maudlin, Michael G., "God's Contractor (Habitat for Humanity's Millard Fuller)," *Christianity Today,* June 14, 1999, p. 44.

Olcott, William, "The Theology of the Hammer," *Fund Raising Management,* October 1994, p. 6.

O'Sullivan, Orla, "Blessed Are the Poor; Habitat Considers Its Homebuilding a Higher Calling," *ABA Banking Journal,* August 1997, p. 57.

Purks, James, *Habitat for Humanity: Building Around the World,* Americus, Ga.: Habitat for Humanity International, 1991.

Rogers, Patrick, "Fire Fighters: Their Dream House Destroyed by Arson, a Family Gets Help from Determined Volunteer Builders," *People Weekly,* September 16, 1996, p. 191.

Starling, Kelly, "Habitat for Humanity: Interracial Organization Builds Houses and Dreams," *Ebony,* November 1997, p. 200.

Stelton, Gene, ed., *A Christmas Housewarming,* Atlanta: Peachtree Publishers, 1992, 206 p.

——, *Home for the Holidays: Stories and Art Created for the Benefit of Habitat for Humanity,* Atlanta: Peachtree Publishers Ltd., 1995.

——, *Thanks, Mom! A Collection of Stories and Artwork to Benefit Habitat for Humanity,* Atlanta: Peachtree Publishers Ltd., 1999, 148 p.

—Nelson Rhodes

HanoverDirect

Hanover Direct, Inc.

1500 Harbor Boulevard
Weehawken, New Jersey 07087
U.S.A.
Telephone: (201) 863-7300
Fax: (201) 392-5009
Web site: http://www.hanoverdirect.com

Public Company
Incorporated: 1898 as Horn & Hardart Baking Co.
Employees: 3,000
Sales: $549.85 million (1999)
Stock Exchanges: American
Ticker Symbol: HNV
NAIC: 45411 Electronic Shopping and Mail-Order
    Houses

Hanover Direct, Inc. is a leading catalog and online retailer. It operates a fleet of catalogs offering consumers clothing, home fashions, and gift items. Some of its best-known catalogs include *The Company Store, Domestications, Kitchen & Home, Silhouettes, International Male, Improvements,* and *Gump's By Mail.* The company moved quickly into web-based retailing in the late 1990s, and many of its catalogs exist online, in tandem with traditional direct mail approaches. With its growing expertise in online retailing, the company established a division named erizon to provide order fulfillment, logistics, and consultation to other e-businesses. Its consumer products division operates under the name Hanover Brands. Until the early 1990s, the company had a substantial stake in various restaurant businesses, running franchises of Burger King, Arby's, the chicken chain Bojangles, and many others. The company originally made its mark as the operator of the famed Automat restaurant chain on the East Coast.

19th-Century Beginnings and Birth of the Automat

Hanover Direct, Inc. operated until 1993 under the name Horn & Hardart. Horn & Hardart was one of the biggest restaurant businesses in the nation from the 1920s into the 1950s. It

was founded by two men in Philadelphia, Joseph V. Horn and Frank Hardart. In 1888 Horn had managed to squeeze $1,000 from his family to help him open a small lunchroom, and he advertised in a local paper for an experienced partner. Legend has it that he received only a single reply to his ad, a line scribbled on a torn sugar sack, reading, ''I'm your man! F. Hardart.'' Horn took up the confident Hardart, who had grown up in New Orleans and brought with him a precious French-influenced coffee recipe. Horn and Hardart's first lunchroom did very well, with its fine coffee a key selling point. The pair opened several more lunchrooms around town and incorporated in 1898 as the Horn & Hardart Baking Co.

In 1900, Hardart took some time off from the business to travel to Europe. It seems to have been a working vacation, however. He announced on his return to Philadelphia that he had invested $30,000 in Berlin to buy equipment for a ''waiterless restaurant.'' Hardart's equipment sank in a shipping accident off Britain in 1901, but by 1902 he had gotten the goods replaced, and the company opened its first Automat restaurant that year. The Automat concept was that customers would deposit nickels into gleaming machines, and hot or cold food would be dispensed automatically. The Automat served not only fine coffee, but staples of American cooking including roast beef, meat loaf, creamed corn, and blueberry pie. Horn & Hardart's chief engineer refined the original German machinery, so that the food popped out of its slots easily. The Automat's staff was located in a central kitchen and did not interact directly with the customers. The décor at first emphasized cleanliness and modernity, striving for a vivid contrast with the often questionable sanitation of neighborhood greasy spoons. The food was cheap but good, with the nickel coffee all but legendary.

Horn & Hardart soon spread its Automats from Philadelphia to New York, in 1912 opening what became a fabled restaurant on Manhattan's Times Square. With stained glass windows conceived by the same artist who designed the windows for the city's Cathedral of St. John the Divine, the Times Square Automat was a bold building, attracting not only poor boardinghouse dwellers but movie stars and Broadway singers. In 1924, Horn & Hardart opened stores to retail prepackaged

Automat food. The chain eventually expanded to include 84 stores in New York and Philadelphia.

Good Times in the Depression, Bad Times After

The Automats were enormously popular in the two cities in which they existed. The food quality was consistently good, something personally assured by founder Horn. Every day he and his top management team tasted the foods the Automat's central kitchens had prepared, and whole batches were thrown out for such sins as the lack of a little oregano. The quick efficiency of the Automat concept appealed to busy workers as well as night-owl theater patrons, and the chain was an East Coast institution. Horn & Hardart was a prosperous business, but its profits really began to rise as the United States entered the Great Depression after the 1929 stock market crash. With millions of people poor and out of work, the Automats had a huge new customer base of people who could afford nothing better. At the peak of the Depression, the Automats in New York and Philadelphia boomed, employing more than 10,000 people. Workers were offered free meals per three hours worked, plus a Christmas bonus. Efforts to unionize Automat's workers failed, as its employees seemed to consider that they already had one of the best deals around. The restaurants were often satirized in cartoons and publicized in films such as *Easy Living* in 1937 and the Irving Berlin musical *Face the Music* from 1932.

Joseph Horn died in 1941, leaving Horn & Hardart to his hand-picked successor, E.K. Daly. While the restaurants continued to be something of a cultural institution, the chain's heyday was past. Other restaurants such as drive-ins and McDonald's carved out new niches for fast food. The quality of the food declined, and the low prices made the Automats gathering places for only the destitute. When Daly died in 1960, he left no clear successor, and the chain drifted, its restaurants becoming steadily dingier and more out of touch with the times. As old employees retired, they were given a token pension, some as low as $10 a month. Automat workers unionized in 1966, and the cost of paying increased benefits to workers drove the company into the red. One by one, the Automats closed, and in 1971, with only a few outlets left, Horn & Hardart filed for bankruptcy.

Transformation in the 1970s and 1980s

Once one of the largest restaurant businesses in the nation, Horn & Hardart was in poor shape in the early 1970s. But it persisted under new management, and it still had various valuable assets. Although it closed nearly all of its Automats, the company still controlled the valuable Manhattan real estate on which its restaurants stood. Some lots were sold, and other Automats were converted into Burger King restaurants. In 1972, in an attempt to diversify into a different line of business, Horn & Hardart acquired a mail-order company headquartered in Hanover, Pennsylvania, called Hanover House Industries. Both the mail-order business and the restaurant business stumbled along, losing a total of $6 million between 1973 and 1977, on sales of $235 million. The firm was being run by Chairman Fred Guterman since 1973. In 1977, a young Burger King franchisee from Florida abruptly acquired roughly four percent of Horn & Hardart and announced that he would be running the company. Barry Florescue ran six Burger Kings in southern Florida and on Long Island, and he wanted to open more in Manhattan. Horn & Hardart had exclusive rights to the Burger King franchise there, so Florescue decided to take over the company. His initial investment in the company cost him only about $400,000. He won a proxy fight, and Guterman resigned. Then Florescue raised $2 million in a public stock sale, settled the lawsuits over cancelled pensions that had dogged the company for a long time, and shut down most of Horn & Hardart's food operations. What Florescue left in place were the mail-order business and the company's 12 Manhattan Burger King franchises. In 1978, the beleaguered Horn & Hardart was making money again.

Both the catalog and food divisions of the company grew under Florescue's direction. Hanover House expanded from six catalogs in 1977 to a line of 21 by 1983. Up to 60 percent of the company's sales came from its catalog division in the early 1980s. Hanover's catalogs were aimed at middle-market consumers and sold gifts, electronics, clothing, and home furnishings. It was one of the nation's largest catalog operations, and in the early 1980s, sales increased in double digits. The division also spent money, investing in a huge, centralized distribution center in 1984.

Florescue also invested in other restaurant chains. Some were not successful, such as a pizza chain called Mark Twain Riverboat Playhouse. The company moved its headquarters to Las Vegas in 1979 when Florescue bought a casino there, and that business also faltered. The company's move into franchising Arby's restaurants did not go as well as expected and had to be scaled back, while also causing dismay at Burger King. Friction between Burger King and Horn & Hardart lasted for years. On the other hand, Florescue picked up a thriving, privately held chicken restaurant chain in 1982 for $12 million. Bojangles was centered around Charlotte, North Carolina, and it had approximately 50 stores in the South and Northeast. Under Florescue's management, Horn & Hardart built up Bojangles, adding stores rapidly. Florescue hoped to take Bojangles from the fourth largest chicken chain to number two behind Kentucky Fried Chicken. Within two years of its purchase, Horn & Hardart had added more than 200 stores to the Bojangles chain.

Neither Bojangles nor Barry Florescue's career at Horn & Hardart survived for long, however. Bojangles was supposed to be an upscale chicken chain, costing more to run but bringing in more per store than the market leader Kentucky Fried Chicken. The chain grew extremely rapidly and was run by hundreds of franchisees. The Bojangles image was hard to sustain outside the South, where it originated, and by 1987, many stores were failing. The entire chain brought in revenues of $90 million in

Key Dates:

1888: Partnership between Horn and Hardart begins.
1898: Horn & Hardart Baking Co. incorporates.
1902: First Automat restaurant opens.
1941: Joseph Horn dies.
1960: Horn's successor dies.
1971: Firm files for bankruptcy.
1972: Horn & Hardart acquires Hanover House Industries.
1991: Last Automat closes.
1993: Name is changed to Hanover Direct.

1986, but lost more than $47 million. Horn & Hardart had sales of $405 million from its catalog and restaurant divisions combined, but the parent company ended 1986 in the red some $28 million. In July 1988, Horn & Hardart announced that it would sell Bojangles. This left the restaurant division with a small number of Burger King franchises, some Arby's, and other lesser known chains including Tony Roma's and International King's Table Buffet. By the late 1980s, it was Hanover House, the company's catalog division, that was bringing in nearly two-thirds of the revenue. Barry Florescue had left the catalog division to others to manage, and it had been at times a highly profitable business. But in 1988 the catalog division also lost money. Horn & Hardart's board decided it was time for a change, and Florescue was let go. After fending off a takeover threat in 1989, the company's management decided in 1990 to get out of the restaurant business altogether.

As a Catalog Company in the 1990s and Beyond

After Florescue's departure, Horn & Hardart was run by CEO Donald Schupak. Schupak first put the company's East Coast restaurant business up for sale. The company initially intended to hang on to a West Coast franchise, International King's Table. Then in October 1991, the company was taken over by an international investment group called North American Resources, which included members of the Quasha family and a Swiss financial firm. Horn & Hardart closed its one remaining Automat in 1991, and by 1993 it had shed the last of its restaurant division. That year Horn & Hardart changed its name to Hanover Direct, and its sole business focus became catalog retailing. Headquarters moved to Weehawken, New Jersey. Management worked to shape up the catalog division, dropping unprofitable lines and adding new ones. In the early 1990s, the company had 15 catalogs, including *Hanover House* and *Domestications*. By 1993 Hanover Direct had acquired two leading catalog businesses, a housewares line called *The Company Store* and the Asian imports and gifts line *Gump's*. Hanover also bought *Gump's* San Francisco retail store and acquired a leading catalog marketer of women's clothing, *Tweed's*.

In 1994 Hanover announced a joint venture with the nation's largest catalog company, Sears, Roebuck, to launch three new catalogs. Sales for 1994 were around $769 million, and the company's stock, which had slouched for a long time, began to perk up. But the company was still plagued by debt and had to make major changes to improve productivity. From 1993 to 1996 the company was managed by Jack Rosenfeld. Rosenfeld

was replaced in 1996 by Rakesh Kaul, a former chief operating officer of the large Fingerhut catalog company. Hanover continued to rebuild in the mid-1990s, adding new catalog lines such as the golf equipment and clothing company Austad.

By the late 1990s, Hanover was a company quite different from what it had been ten years earlier. It was unburdened of its restaurant division, and it had made major structural changes to focus on efficient, up-to-date catalog merchandising. With the rise of the Internet, Hanover made a quick transition to online selling. Its web-based sales were only $700,000 in 1997, but had leapt to $8.3 million the next year. This represented only a small percentage of total sales, but the company was happy to do all it could to encourage online shopping, as it already had the order fulfillment capabilities, and Internet selling was cheaper than mailing out catalogs. In 1999 Hanover announced it would again form itself into two divisions. This time, one was to encompass its catalog and Internet-based consumer retailing, and the other would be a business-to-business service, offering order processing and fulfillment services to other companies selling on the web. Nationwide, the move to the web boomed, including not only catalog and direct-mail marketers like Hanover, but many start-up companies that thought they could sell anything through a web site. Many of these newcomers needed the kind of business service Hanover offered. Hanover named its business-to-business service erizon, and it developed software and systems for customers entering web-based businesses, offering order fulfillment services as well. One key customer for its order fulfillment services was Kbkids.com, an online version of a successful toy company.

As Hanover Direct entered the 21st century, profitability was still spotty. The company lost money in 1998 and again in 1999. Management was sure, however, that Hanover was on the right track. It discontinued two unprofitable catalogs, *Tweed's* and *Austad's*, and continued to focus on the relatively new business of offering its database and electronic commerce expertise to other businesses. Its catalog division, Hanover Brands, focused on the several areas the company expected would grow, including home improvement and kids' clothing and furniture, and also aimed to improve sales in the growing markets of Western Europe and the Asian Pacific countries. The company had gone through many changes since its inception as a chain of diners. Despite its often rocky financial picture, its management by the year 2000 believed the company was in a good position to take advantage of growing online and catalog opportunities.

Principal Divisions

erizon; Hanover Brands.

Principal Competitors

Williams Sonoma, Inc.; Otto Versand Gmbh & Co.

Further Reading

Chaudry, Rajan, "Florescue's Exit Marks End of Era at H&H," *Nation's Restaurant News,* October 17, 1988, p. 1.

Cohen, Daniel, "For Food Both Cold and Hot, Put Your Nickel in the Slot," *Smithsonian,* January 1986, pp. 50–61.

Gordon, Mitchell, "Chicken and Catalogs," *Barron's,* August 6, 1984, pp. 38–39.

"Horn & Hardart Takes the Fast Lane in Fast Food," *Business Week,* August 27, 1984, pp. 95–97.

"In Wake of Red Ink, Kaul Takes Helm at Hanover," *HFN,* February 19, 1996, p. 6.

Leonard, Burr, "Why Didn't They Pay Him to Stay Home?," *Forbes,* June 15, 1987, p. 120.

Marcial, Gene G., "Hanover: A Mail-Order Bargain?," *Business Week,* June 13, 1994, p. 74.

——, "Horn & Hardart: In a Hurry to Get Out of Fast Food," *Business Week,* July 23, 1990, p. 60.

——, "The Net May Make Hanover Bounce," *Business Week,* February 1, 1999, p. 112.

Kletter, Melanie, "Hanover Weighs Sale or Shutdown of Tweeds Book," *WWD,* March 10, 1999, p. 13.

McManus, Kevin, "Florescue's Rescue," *Forbes,* December 19, 1983, pp. 58–62.

"New President for Bojangles," *Nation's Restaurant News,* April 1, 1985, p. 1.

Prewitt, Milford, "Horn & Hardart to Sell East Coast Restaurant Empire," *Nation's Restaurant News,* April 16, 1990, p. 14.

Silberg, Laurie, "Hanover Direct Back in the Black," *HFN,* March 16, 1998, p. 8.

Simon, Ellen, "Weehawken, N.J., Catalog Company Moves to Personalize Web Sales," *Knight-Ridder/Tribune Business News,* April 30, 1999, p. OKRB991200D4.

Sivy, Michael, "How to Double Your Money in a Rebounding Direct-Mail Retailer," *Money,* November 1993, p. 58.

Thau, Barbara, "Hanover Pushes Direct Commerce," *HFN,* May 22, 2000, p. 5.

Valeriano, Lourdes Lee, "Horn & Hardart Set to Focus on Catalog Unit," *Wall Street Journal,* September 25, 1992, p. A5C.

Vincenti, Lisa, "Hanover Direct Puts on Kid Gloves," *HFN,* April 17, 2000, p. 24.

Young, Vicki M., "Hanover Shops for Strategic Alliances," *HFN,* July 12, 1999, p. 8.

—A. Woodward

Holberg Industries, Inc.

545 Steamboat Road
Greenwich, Connecticut 06830
U.S.A.
Telephone: (203) 422-3000
Fax: (203) 661-5756
Web site: http://www.holberg.com

Private Company
Incorporated: 1986
Employees: 20,225
Sales: $9.3 billion (1998 est.)
NAIC: 42241 General Line Grocery Wholesalers; 81293
    Parking Lots and Garages

Holberg Industries, Inc., a holding company, was one of the largest privately held companies in the United States. The company is the majority shareholder in two operating companies which, through acquisitions, became leaders in their respective fields: parking management and foodservice distribution. Holberg owns 77 percent of APCOA/Standard Parking, which, in 2000, managed more than 1,800 paid parking facilities containing over one million parking spaces in over 200 cities in the United States and Canada. Holberg also owned 93 percent of AmeriServe Food Distribution, which filed for bankruptcy in 2000 and was sold by the end of the year. Cofounder John Holten owned 66 percent of Holberg Industries and Orkla A/S, a Norwegian consumer products company, owned the rest.

Starting a Company: 1986–89

During the first half of the 1980s, Norwegian-born, Harvard-educated John Holten worked in New York City at DnC Capital, a merchant bank, where he met managing partner Gunnar Klintberg. In 1986, the pair founded Holberg, Inc. as a merchant bank and opened for business in Greenwich, Connecticut. Orkla ASA, a big Norwegian consumer brands company, supplied one third of the capital for Holberg.

Later in 1986, Holberg bought NEBCO Distribution, an Omaha-based company that distributed candies and snacks to theaters and concession stands, with $60 million in sales and 100 employees. Three years later, in 1989, Holberg bought APCOA, a national company managing parking facilities. Soon afterwards, Holberg, Inc. became Holberg Industries, Inc. The two subsidiaries grew through acquisitions to become AmeriServe Food Distribution, Inc. and APCOA/Standard Parking, which by 1999 were national leaders in their industries. In 2000, however, AmeriServe declared bankruptcy, and by August it had agreed to sell its U.S. distribution system to McLane Co., a unit of Wal-Mart Stores, Inc. AmeriServe's Canadian and food equipment divisions were sold to other purchasers.

The AmeriServe bankruptcy and sale ended John Holten's vision of a national distribution system serving fast-food and casual dining restaurant chains. Holberg Industries' investment in the creation of a nationwide parking management firm appeared more solid, but the future makeup of Holberg was unclear at the end of August 2000.

APCOA/Standard Parking, Inc., First 25 Years: 1949–74

In 1949, future U.S. Senator Howard Metzenbaum and Alva T. "Ted" Bonda founded Airport Parking Company of America (APCOA) in Cleveland, Ohio. For several years the two had done well with Metzenbaum's car rental business, which became one of the largest Avis franchises. Figuring that air travel might be the coming thing, but sticking with what they knew, they leased space from airport authorities, to give travelers a place to park their cars. Thus began APCOA. Then, in 1951, they won a contract to manage paid parking at Cleveland's airport. The company made parking lots more secure by hiring guards and adding lighting, and quickly built its business by taking over lots from municipalities and developers and running them more efficiently. But they did not buy or own parking lots, thus avoiding the risks of real estate ownership. The company continued to diversify, adding franchises for airport hotels and more Avis rental car operations to its parking leases.

Harold Geneen, head of International Telephone and Telegraph Corporation (ITT), liked APCOA's car rental franchises and in 1966 bought the company for $25 million. Edwin Roth, who had worked for Metzenbaum, was named president. As part of ITT, the company added building management services, bus and taxicab operations, and management of parking operations in Europe.

New Owners: 1975–88

In 1975, Roth offered Geneen $10 million for the company's parking operations and took the company private. In the United States, the company managed parking at 403 locations, with nearly two-thirds of its $110 million in 1976 revenue coming from its 100 airport lots, including Miami, La Guardia and Dallas-Fort Worth. In the next five years, revenues doubled and profits quadrupled.

Six years later, in 1981, Roth sold APCOA's North American parking operations to Buffalo-based Delaware North Companies, a private holding company, for an estimated $25 million. Roth kept APCOA's European parking operations. At that time, APCOA owned, leased, or managed some 600 parking properties in 167 cities in 44 states and the District of Columbia. The company had 5,000 employees, parked more than 300 million cars, and had sales of $278 million, making it the largest parking firm in the world and twice the size of its nearest competitor.

APCOA had prospered even as the highly fragmented $2.5 billion U.S. parking industry ran into problems with high mortgage interest rates and land costs. A 1982 *Business Week* article listed several factors contributing to APCOA's success: the company's shift from airports to central city sites to serve the many office complexes being built; concentrating in fast-growing Sunbelt cities; and becoming a leader in raising prices. Perhaps most importantly, according to the article, APCOA helped some developers finance their parking garages (lending credit or cash) in exchange for ''lenient long-term leases'' on them. APCOA was so big it had the money to lend, and the terms of the leases helped the company maintain higher than average profits on sales in a business known for thin margins.

Roth remained as CEO under Delaware North, and APCOA brought in about $150 million a year, approximately 20 percent of the parent's annual revenues of some $750 million. In 1987, G. Walter Stuelpe, Jr., was named chief executive of APCOA, having been appointed president and COO the year before.

A Part of Holberg: 1989–97

In 1989, Delaware North sold APCOA to company managers and other investors, who formed AP Holdings Inc. Holberg, Inc. was the majority investor, owning 77 percent. Two years later, in 1991, APCOA and Holberg formed a joint venture with John Hancock Properties, creating an investment fund for acquiring freestanding garages in the downtown business districts of cities where APCOA was managing parking facilities. This would become a pattern for the parent and subsidiary, with APCOA responsible for managing and operating, but not owning, the facilities.

Parking lots were managed one of two ways: a low-risk, fixed-fee management contract that ran for two to three years and required no capital investment, or a lease contract for four to ten years under which the managing company paid to expand or improve the property and received a set percentage (ten percent) of the revenues. Into the early 1990s, APCOA continued to explore lease options.

For example, APCOA had moved into the management of hospital parking facilities, and in 1993, initiated a first-of-its-kind development project with a public hospital. APCOA financed, designed, and built a parking garage at the Westchester County (NY) Medical Center, all at its own expense. It would operate and maintain the garage for 30 years (along with 19 surface lots at the hospital), at which point the county would own the facility debt free. During that period, the county would receive a guaranteed $10 million, half of the projected net profits of $20 million.

APCOA prided itself in implementing technological improvements at the lots it managed. For example, in 1994, it installed an automated credit card reader at the entrance and exit gates at the lot at Cleveland's airport. Believed to be the first of its kind, the technology quickly became popular with parkers, because it was faster than waiting for a cashier. Other technologies included proprietary software such as ParkStat, to calculate rate alternatives, and Client View, which allowed clients to access financial and operating information about their facilities.

The company also began buying other parking management companies, focusing on companies in the cities where APCOA already operated or on larger, regional companies. In 1997, APCOA made four acquisitions, including one that strengthened its presence in downtown garages in the Northeast. By the end of that year, the company was managing and operating some 700 urban, airport, and hospital parking facilities nationwide.

Standard Parking Merger: 1998

Then, in January 1998, APCOA announced it was buying Standard Parking for 65 million in cash plus assumption of certain liabilities and outstanding shares. In an industry that had been consolidating for several years, the merger resulted in a company that not only increased its size and geographical coverage but also had complementary expertise. APCOA was known for its back-office technology, and Standard Parking, for its innovative customer service.

Standard's most famous innovation was theme parking garages to help people find their cars. Standard President Myron Warshauer introduced the concept in 1984, saying he was tired of hearing people say they hated garages. The first theme was a ''city and song'' garage in Chicago where each floor represented a different city, and speakers beside the elevators played music associated with that city, such as Frank Sinatra singing ''New York, New York.'' Warshauer followed this with a theater-theme garage and one featuring colleges and school fight songs. In Los Angeles, he developed a movie theme (with levels marked ''Gone With the Wind,'' ''The Wizard of Oz,'' ''Singing in the Rain,'' and ''Star Wars'').

Then, in 1994, the company began offering car care services at its garage and lots at O'Hare International Airport. Customers could leave their cars in special spaces and sign up for a muffler

Key Dates:

1986:   John Holberg and Gunnar Klintberg found Holberg, Inc.; Holberg buys NEBCO Distribution.

1989:   Holberg buys controlling interest in parking lot management firm APCOA.

1990:   NEBCO creates NEBCO EVANS with the acquisition of Evans Brothers of Wisconsin.

1996:   NEBCO EVANS buys AmeriServ and creates NEBCO-AmeriServ.

1997:   NEBCO-AmeriServ consolidates as AmeriServe Food Distribution, acquires PepsiCo Food Systems and becomes nation's largest systems distributor.

1998:   AmeriServe acquires ProSource; APCOA buys Standard Parking Inc. to form APCOA/Standard.

2000:   AmeriServe files for Chapter 11 bankruptcy protection and is sold to McLane, a subsidiary of Wal-Mart.

replacement, wheel alignment or brake work to be done while they were gone. The work was performed by Midas International and customers did not have to pay anything above regular parking and service costs. The services, called CarCare, were soon offered at other facilities managed by Standard. In 1997, Standard introduced Books-To-Go, followed by Tapes-To-Go, offering monthly customers audiotape and videotape libraries free of charge.

With the merger, Stuelpe became president of the new company, APCOA/Standard Parking, and Myron Warshauer became CEO. APCOA was the bigger company, with $475 million in 1997 revenues and more than 700 operations in 30 cities. Standard Parking had $450 million in revenues and managed 380 properties in 29 cities. The company continued to grow by acquisition. Before 1998 ended, the company bought Century Parking and Executive Parking, both of Los Angeles.

APCOA/Standard integrated its companies and other acquisitions under its Ambiance in Parking program and continued to buy other companies, including three more in the first half of 1999. Revenues for 1999 were $248 million, with a $9.5 million loss. The company continued to reduce its proportion of its leases, which it had been doing since 1994, and by mid-2000, operated nearly 80 percent of its facilities under management contracts. In February 2000, Myron Warshauer was named president as well as CEO, while Walter Stuelpe remained as a board member.

AmeriServe Food Distribution, Inc., NEBCO to NEBCO Evans: 1986–90

Holberg's first acquisition was in 1986, with the purchase of NEBCO Distribution of Omaha, Inc. The 40-year-old, Nebraska company served theaters and concessions, had 100 employees, and rang up annual sales of $60 million. According to Carol Perkins in a 1997 *ID* article, Holten and Klintberg saw the fragmented foodservice distribution industry as ripe for consolidation and "realized how technology and systems could produce a competitive edge." They decided to concentrate on customers with limited menus, and began with the purchase of NEBCO.

Customers with limited menus (generally fast-food restaurant chains) were served by companies called systems distributors which tailored their services and product mix to those menu lists. The distributors stocked only the specific items used by their customers, working on a low-margin, cost-plus basis. The niche, which was created in the early 1970s, supported about 120 systems distributors (compared to over 3,000 more general companies). The largest ten of these specialists represented more than seven percent of the $96 billion distributor business in 1989.

At the beginning of 1990, NEBCO, with 1989 sales of $86 million, bought Evans Brothers of Wisconsin, creating NEBCO Evans Distribution. Evans, a privately held company formed in 1934, made its money ($116.5 million in 1989) delivering fountain products and salted nuts to drugstores. The new company served 14 north-central states and had combined sales of $210 million for 1990, up 3.7 percent from combined 1989 figures. Longstanding customers included A&W, Carousel Snack Bars, Kmart, Burger King, Wendy's, KFC, Church's, and International Dairy Queen. In December, the regional specialist continued to grow, acquiring L.L. Distribution Systems, a $60 million company out of Minneapolis.

From NEBCO Evans to NEBCO AmeriServ: 1991–96

Holberg invested heavily in new technology for NEBCO Evans. This included on-board truck computers and automated routing and scheduling software as well as an order entry and inventory replenishment system for its 2,500 chain customers. In 1991, NEBCO Evans added Godfather's units to its customer list and bought Condon Supply Co., another Minnesota systems distributor. Sales for that year jumped to $298 million, aided by the acquisitions. By 1995, that revenue had grown to $400 million and NEBCO Evans had 500 employees, with three distribution centers in the Midwest.

Then, in 1996, Nebco Evans bought AmeriServ, a systems distribution company more than twice its size. AmeriServ was the result of a 1989 consolidation of several regional chain distributors into a single division of John Lewis Associates LP. The regionals that became AmeriServ included two of the country's biggest systems distributors, Sonneveldt Co. in Michigan and Interstate Distributors, Inc. (IDI) in Atlanta, along with Post Food Service in Denver, First Choice Food Distributors in Fort Worth, and Alpha Distributors in Wisconsin. The year before it was bought by NEBCO Evans, AmeriServ was distributing to customers in 38 states, had sales of $950 million, and employed over 1,200 people.

John Holten became chairman and CEO of the new company, which was called NEBCO-AmeriServ. He began constructing new distribution centers while closing and consolidating others. The combined company had 1996 revenues of $1.5 billion.

AmeriServe Keeps Buying: 1997–98

Early in 1997, the distribution company announced a new name, AmeriServe, with an "e" added for excellence according to an article in *ID*, and the goal of becoming the number one standardized systems distributor.

In July 1997, AmeriServe agreed to acquire PepsiCo Food Systems Worldwide (PFS) for $830 million. PFS, with sales of $3.4 billion, served some 18,000 restaurants in the United States and Canada. Most of these had been owned by PepsiCo, including KFC, Pizza Hut, and Taco Bell, and had just been spun off into Tricon Global Restaurants. AmeriServe, which now served 28,000 restaurants, had a sales potential of $5.4 billion for 1997.

Within a year (May 1998), AmeriServe completed the purchase of ProSource, Inc., the second largest systems distributor in the United States. AmeriServe refinanced all the Florida-based ProSource's outstanding debt and paid $343 million ($15 cash per share). According to a 2000 *Forbes* article, ProSource stock had been trading at $7 the day before the purchase was announced. AmeriServe was now the largest systems distributor and the second largest foodservice distributor in the country. It served 38,000 restaurants in the United States, Canada, and Mexico, employed 8,500 people, and had sales in 1998 of $7.4 billion. But that year, which was its best sales year, AmeriServe lost $147 million.

AmeriServe Problems: 1999–2000

John Holten's attempt to offset the industry's low margins through volume resulted in "indigestion," a 2000 *Forbes* article put it. Going in two years from a $400 million business to one bringing in over $7 billion proved to be too much. The melding of delivery schedules and accounting systems, installation of software, insuring Y2K compliance, and consolidation of distribution centers were not the only problems. AmeriServe was $2 billion in debt. During 1999, deliveries started to slip or were incomplete.

After three quarters, AmeriServe announced losses of $178 million on sales of $6 billion, laid off 1,500 employees, and dropped its casual dining business. In February 2000, AmeriServe filed for bankruptcy protection and Holten resigned as CEO, although he retained the position of chairman. Burger King pulled out in the spring, taking one-third of AmeriServe's business. In May, the company filed suit against Holten, charging him with wrongfully diverting funds from AmeriServe into other companies. It also charged its largest customer, Tricon Global Restaurants, with refusing to turn over $103 million owed for past sales.

By August 2000, AmeriServe announced it was selling its Canadian division to Prizm Brandz LP for just over $1 million and its entire equipment division to PrimeSource FoodService Equipment, Inc., a company formed by North Texas Opportunity Fund of Dallas. Then it announced it was selling the U.S. distribution division to McLane Company, Inc. McLane, a subsidiary of Wal-Mart Stores with $8.8 billion in revenues, was the largest distributor to convenience stores and the biggest distributor of cigarettes, next to the tobacco companies themselves.

Principal Subsidiaries

AP Holdings, Inc. (APCOA/Standard Parking, Inc.); Nebco Evans Distributors, Inc. (AmeriServe Food Distribution, Inc.).

Principal Competitors

ABM Industries Incorporated; Ace Parking; Central Parking Corporation; Republic Parking; SYSCO Corporation; Alliant Foodservice; U.S. Foodservice.

Further Reading

"AmeriServe Agrees to Sell Canadian Division," *PR Newswire*, August 15, 2000.

"AmeriServe Food Distribution, Inc.," *FoodService Distributor*, August 1997, p. 8.

"AmeriServe Says It's in Talks with Wal-Mart Subsidiary," *Associated Press*, June 30, 2000.

"AmeriServe Signs Definitive Agreement for Acquisition by McLane," *PR Newswire*, August 18, 2000.

"AmeriServe to Acquire PFS," *ID: The Voice of Foodservice Distribution*, July 1997, p. 18.

"APCOA: A Parking Lot Operator Uses Its Big Size to Advantage," *Business Week*, March 22, 1982, p. 107.

"APCOA Deal Boosts Presence in Northeast," *Crain's Cleveland Business*, October 13, 1997, p. 3.

"APCOA Inc. Names G. Walter Stuelpe to Top Post," *Business Wire*, October 20, 1987.

"APCOA Installs Credit-Card Reader at Hopkins Car Lot," *Crain's Cleveland Business*, May 16, 1994, p. 28.

Barron, Kelly, "Indigestion," *Forbes*, April 3, 2000, p. 66.

——, "Smoking Gun," *Forbes*, August 21, 2000, p. 54.

Bentayou, Frank, "Parking Problems," *Corporate Cleveland*, January 1992, p. 24.

Breisch, Sandra Lee, "A Lot More: Midas Brings Car Repair to O'Hare Parking Patrons," *Chicago Tribune*, December 26, 1993, p. 6.

Conway, John, "Garages with Glamour," *Forbes*, June 16, 1986, p. 10.

"Firm's Specialty: Parking Profits," *Modern Healthcare*, June 28, 1993, p. 100.

Koenig, David, "Wal-Mart Buys Food Distributor," *AP Online*, August 18, 2000

Lubinger, Bill, "APCOA Parks Its Lots with Chicago Firm," *Cleveland Plain Dealer*, January 28, 1998, p. 1C.

Mathews, Jay, "Parking in a Multi-Level Memory Lane," *Washington Post*, November 26, 1986, p. A3.

McQuaid, Kevin L., "Constellation Sells Downtown Garage," *Baltimore Business Journal*, March 4, 1991, p. 3.

"North Texas Opportunity Fund Acquires AmeriServe Worldwide Equipment Group," *PR Newswire*, August 15, 2000.

"Nebco Evans Distribution: Two Minnesota Acquisitions Help Push Sales Up 41.9 Percent," *Institutional Distributor*, February 1992, p. 87.

"Parking-Lot King," *Forbes*, April 1, 1977, p. 78.

Perkins, Carol, "AmeriServe: Poised for the Future with 20/20 Hindsight," *ID: The Voice of Foodservice Distribution*, February 1997, p. 51.

Rudnitsky, Howard, "Take-Away Game," *Forbes*, July 29, 1996, p. 50.

Salkin, Stephanie, "Systems Distributors: A Special Breed," *Institutional Distributor*, September 15, 1990, p. 184.

"The Special Breed," *Institutional Distribution*, February 1991, p. 65.

Zimberoff, Aleen, "Creativity's Finding a Spot in Theme Parking Garages," *Crain's Chicago Business*, April 28, 1986, p. 36.

—Ellen D. Wernick

Houghton Mifflin Company

222 Berkeley Street
Boston, Massachusetts 02116
U.S.A.
Telephone: (617) 351-5000
Fax: (617) 227-5409
Web site: http://www.hmco.com

Public Company
Incorporated: 1908
Employees: 3,296
Sales: $920.1 million (1999)
Stock Exchanges: New York
Ticker Symbol: HTN
NAIC: 51113 Book Publishers; 51121 Software Publishers

Houghton Mifflin Company is an established leader in text-book publishing, providing indispensable materials for the elementary, secondary, and college markets. The company also produces testing materials, reference books, children's literature, and a growing line of award-winning trade books of interest to the general public. Formed in the 1800s as a printing house, the company grew and diversified, playing an important role in the intellectual development of generations of Americans. In time Houghton's focus shifted to scholastic publications, and the company has become a major presence in the burgeoning educational market, both in traditional materials as well interactive and electronic products.

From Printer to Publisher: 1820s–60s

Henry Oscar Houghton was born into poverty in Vermont in 1823. At age 13, he was apprenticed to a printer in Burlington. In 1842, he entered the University of Vermont, earning his way through college by working in various printers' offices. In an effort to pay off the debts he had amassed while in school, Houghton moved to Boston after his college graduation in 1846, where he held a series of jobs in journalism and printing. Houghton paid off his debts within two years and bought out one of the partners in one of Boston's premier printing businesses for $3,100 (paid in installments); thus Bolles & Hough-

ton was formed. The business had changed its name by 1851 to Houghton & Haywood, when Houghton exchanged his former partner for one of his cousins. The company moved the following year to an expanded printing plant on the banks of the Charles River and began to call itself the Riverside Press. In 1852 the business changed hands again and took the name H.O. Houghton & Company.

Five years later, in 1857, Houghton was shaken by a widespread economic panic, the lingering effects of which wore on for the next four years. As banks and other businesses closed and paper money lost its value, Houghton found itself in possession of the stereotype plates, used to print off new copies, for a number of books. These assets were given to the printer in lieu of payment by insolvent publishers. Soon after, Houghton purchased the stereotype plates for a 39-volume book on English law from the Boston publisher Little, Brown & Company. With these moves, Houghton took the first step in the process of changing from a printer into a publisher. To exploit the value of the stereotype printing plates he owned, it was necessary for Henry Houghton to print the books, which then needed to be distributed.

By 1863 Houghton had amassed enough plates to flesh out a basic publisher's list: law books, general classics, and a lucrative arithmetic textbook. When one of his primary clients, Little, Brown & Company, terminated their contract, Houghton was forced to diversify to ensure his company's continued financial health. Accordingly, in 1864 Houghton entered into a partnership with Melancthon M. Hurd, a wealthy New Yorker with whose firm Houghton had previously produced a series of books by Charles Dickens. Houghton planned to handle the printing, advertising, and distribution aspects of the business, leaving authors, manuscripts, and editors in the hands of his partner, Hurd. The new New York-based company was called Hurd & Houghton, and a shield with two interlocked Hs became its colophon.

The first catalogue of books published by the new firm included the texts for which Houghton owned the stereotype printing plates, works by Englishmen, and several books written by Americans. In January 1865, the company purchased an additional 20 titles, including works by James Fenimore Cooper. Later the same year, the fledgling enterprise found itself the object of a lawsuit by Hurd's former partners over the rights to publish the Dickens books. Eventually, this was resolved to Houghton's satisfaction.

In 1866, Hurd & Houghton was reorganized when one of Houghton's brothers contributed additional capital. With this money, the company moved to newer, more stylish offices in New York and expanded its Cambridge printing facilities. After purchasing the Riverside Press site, the company added a new four-story building and ten new presses. These new facilities, inaugurated at the end of 1867, allowed the press to keep up with demand for its most popular product, the *Merriam Webster Unabridged Dictionary,* as well as to print newspapers, periodicals, and the books of the Hurd & Houghton line (which included law books, school books, Bibles, prayer books, theological works, and children's literature). Although Houghton's Massachusetts-based printing operations were turning a profit, its New York publishing arm languished. Hurd & Houghton's periodicals, such as the *Riverside Magazine for Young People,* suffered from stiff competition and were expensive to produce. Nonetheless, by the end of the firm's second year in operation it remained profitable overall.

Becoming Houghton Mifflin: 1870s–90s

In 1872, Hurd & Houghton took on several additional business partners, among them Horace Elisha Scudder, who worked on the children's magazine, and George Harrison Mifflin, a rich young man who had joined the firm in 1868. In the 1870s, Houghton & Hurd expanded steadily, acquiring publications in a number of fields, including the *Atlantic Monthly,* and garnered a number of lucrative government contracts. Gradually, it was becoming the predominant Boston publishing house.

Boston suffered a devastating fire in 1872, worsened by the fact that all of the fire department's horses had an equine illness. Many paper manufacturers and printing businesses were destroyed in the catastrophe, which ushered in a prolonged economic slump. The events had forced one of New England's oldest and most illustrious publishing houses, Ticknor & Fields (at the time known as James R. Osgood & Company), into dire economic straits. The 50-year-old publisher had published such leading intellectuals as Ralph Waldo Emerson, Henry David Thoreau, Nathaniel Hawthorne, Mark Twain, Henry Wadsworth Longfellow, Harriet Beecher Stowe, John Greenleaf Whittier, and others. In 1878 Houghton bought out the older firm and formed Houghton, Osgood & Company, moving the company more firmly into the realm of literary publishing, away

from the lucrative printing and textbook publishing with which it had begun.

By the start of the 1880s Houghton, Osgood was operating under the burden of heavy debts assumed under the Osgood takeover. To ameliorate this dangerous situation, the company was reorganized in 1880, to become Houghton, Mifflin & Company. The company spent the next decade reducing its debt, helped by the publications of books by authors such as Henry James and Kate Douglas Wiggins (*Rebecca of Sunnybrook Farm*). During this time Houghton also established an educational department, which worked to update the company's academic offerings. Chief among the company's schoolbooks was the Riverside Literature Series, also inaugurated in 1882, comprised of unabridged American classics annotated with study guides, available to schools as cheaply as possible. One version of the project was printed on opaque paper, with inexpensive paper covers, and sold for 15 cents a volume.

In 1895 company founder Henry Oscar Houghton died and control of the firm passed to his younger partner, George Harrison Mifflin. Houghton left the firm in strong, if not invincible, economic shape, as it faced slowing profits in response to another general economic depression. In the late 1890s, in addition to the firm's standard list of children's works and educational tomes, Houghton added a number of novels designed to attract public attention. Several of these books sold well, moving significantly more than 10,000 copies. In addition to its fiction, Houghton also offered newly updated schoolbooks and the popular *Atlantic Monthly.*

A New Era: 1900s–30s

In 1901 Houghton Mifflin opened a book shop in downtown Boston. In the windows, the company mounted displays promoting its best-selling novels, and inside, samples of the fine printing and binding of the Riverside Press were available. Seven years later, in 1908, after a series of deaths among the firm's original partners, Houghton, Mifflin & Company restructured itself, changing from a partnership into a corporation, under the name Houghton Mifflin Company. At this time, the firm sold its journal, the *Atlantic Monthly,* to a group of investors who planned to install new editors while maintaining some ties with Houghton.

By 1914 George Mifflin's desire to publish novels that would win widespread popularity had brought about a decline in the overall literary quality of the company's offerings. One of the publisher's most prominent poets, Amy Lowell, quit the house for another charging that the company had suffered a decline in prestige through its practice of publishing second-rate fiction. Houghton lost further literary currency when World War I broke out in Europe in 1914. Under the leadership of its Anglophilic editor-in-chief, the company avidly supported the Allied war effort, working with Wellington House, the propaganda division of the British Foreign Office, a policy that later earned Houghton the suspicion of many scholars.

Between 1914 and 1918, Houghton published more than 100 books related to the war effort. Many of Houghton's books concerning the war proved profitable. An additional, unexpected side effect of World War I was an increase in the size of the

Key Dates:

1840s: Henry Oscar Houghton enters printing business.
1850s: Houghton begins transformation from printer to publisher.
1864: Hurd & Houghton is formed.
1870s: Company expands, acquires the *Atlantic Monthly*.
1878: Company purchases Ticknor & Fields and renames itself Houghton, Osgood & Company.
1882: Houghton launches Riverside Literature Series.
1908: Partnership becomes a corporation and is renamed Houghton Mifflin Company.
1910s–50s: Company focuses less on literary and more on educational offerings.
1967: Company sells stock to the public for the first time.
1969: *American Heritage Dictionary* is introduced.
1979: Houghton establishes Riverside Publishing Company subsidiary to produce reading textbooks.
1980: Company acquires Rand McNally for $11.6 million.
1994: Company acquires McDougal, Littell for $138 million.
1995: Houghton acquires D.C. Heath and Company.
1999: Houghton sells remainder of its stake in Inso Corporation (originally spun off in 1993).

reading public, and consequently, the market for books. Programs to put inexpensive books in the hands of servicemen during the war had introduced the habit of reading to a vast number of men. In the years following the war, American letters underwent a renaissance, as new authors introduced fresh literary movements. Despite its heritage of having published many of the leading literary lights of the 19th century, Houghton was, in large part, left out of the contemporary movements.

The company had a strong reputation for conservatism, a product of the archaic tastes of several of its key editors, who sought uplifting works with pleasant themes and found the new stark realism unpalatable. In addition, Houghton's editors perceived themselves to be handicapped in the publication of radical material by their location in Boston, where local authorities frequently banned books found objectionable or dangerous. The company feared the Boston police could seize the entire print run of an offending work as it came off the presses in Cambridge, preventing a book from even entering circulation. Although the literary tumult of the 1920s passed by Houghton, the company did show more success with its nonfiction offerings, and its educational books division thrived. It had begun publishing intelligence quota, or ''I.Q.'' tests back in 1916, and continued to update these best-sellers for decades.

Rebound of Educational Publishing: 1940s–60s

Houghton relied on its perennial sellers and its solid educational lists throughout the economic depression of the 1930s. A key part of this approach was the development of the market for standardized tests. Working with educators at the University of Iowa, the company developed the *Iowa Tests of Basic Skills*. Also during this time, Houghton Mifflin added Adolf Hitler's *Mein Kampf* to its nonfiction list. All royalties from this work

were paid to the Office of Foreign Litigation of the U.S. government. After publishing Hitler, the company went on to publish the works of his adversaries in the wake of World War II. In the late 1940s, Houghton paid its largest advance ever for Winston Churchill's six-volume account of World War II, for which he was later awarded the Nobel Prize in Literature. In addition, the company published the works of General George Patton and Field Marshall Bernard Montgomery.

Following World War II, the U.S. government passed the G.I. Bill, promising a free college education to all who had fought in the war. This move dramatically increased the market for college textbooks, and Houghton's operations in this area expanded greatly. In 1949 the company also introduced the McKee readers, which taught young children how to read, and were purchased by school systems expanding to accommodate the baby boom of the 1950s. Houghton also increased its participation in the standardized testing field.

The company grew in size throughout the 1950s and 1960s, adding such works as Rachel Carson's controversial *Silent Spring* to its nonfiction list. In 1967 Houghton sold stock to the public for the first time, listing its shares on the New York Stock Exchange. Two years later, Houghton introduced the best-selling *American Heritage Dictionary,* one of the first such works to be created using a computerized word base.

Modernization of Houghton: 1970s–80s

The company moved further into the field of computer publishing in 1971 when it began working with a small New Hampshire-based firm called Time-Sharing Information to develop computer programs for use in schools. Four years later, in 1975, Houghton purchased the company, to better integrate its operations with its textbook division. This year also was noteworthy because the company was sued by three women and charged by the Massachusetts attorney general with discrimination against women in hiring and promotions. Two years later, Houghton agreed to pay $750,000 to its female employees and increase its Affirmative Action program. In a separate later settlement, Houghton paid an additional $325,000.

By the late 1970s, as the number of school-age children dwindled, Houghton began to shift its emphasis in educational publishing. The company started to move away from primary and secondary school texts toward college texts, particularly business course and professional offerings. In 1977, it purchased the Pinecliff Publishing Company, a California-based medical publisher, and its textbook sales gained steadily. These gains attracted the attention of Western Pacific Industries, a railroad conglomerate, which had acquired 6.7 percent of the company's stock by March 1978. Concerned about a possible corporate takeover, Houghton authors such as John Kenneth Galbraith and Arthur Schlesinger organized an Author's Guild inquiry into the matter, wrote letters of protest to the buyer, and announced that they might quit the publisher if it was not able to remain independent. The campaign worked, and Houghton bought back its shares.

Houghton established a Chicago subsidiary in 1979, calling it the Riverside Publishing Company, to produce reading textbooks with a new approach. To sell this line, the subsidiary was given its own separate sales force. Further, in its trade books division, Houghton reintroduced the Ticknor & Fields imprint belonging to the venerated Boston publisher the company had purchased long ago. The division was set up to publish a small list of distinguished authors on politics, biography, and historical fiction. Another imprint, J.P. Tarcher, Inc., was added for science books, and all of Houghton's trade activities were consolidated into one division, in the hope of increasing profits.

In 1980, Houghton moved to secure its dominance of the textbook market by purchasing the educational publishing operations of Rand McNally & Company for $11.6 million, though these activities remained separate from Houghton's other businesses. Throughout the 1980s, textbooks reigned supreme in Houghton's publishing empire, growing at a rate of more than ten percent annually.

New Leadership, New Directions: The 1990s

In the early 1990s Houghton was revamped under the leadership of a new chief executive officer, Nader F. Darehshori. Darehshori, who had joined the company as a sales representative in 1966, trimmed Houghton's workforce and gave more autonomy to its publishing divisions. He was also keenly aware of the technological changes in publishing and sought not only to keep up, but to lead the industry. Such titles as 1992's *International Electronic Thesaurus* and the latest edition of the *American Heritage Electronic Dictionary* were major sellers. To bolster the educational divisions, Darehshori spearheaded efforts to buy a 17.5 percent stake in Cassell for $4.4 million, spent $17 million for the testing assets of DLM, and acquired the publishing arm of College Survival Inc. for $10 million. The company also reorganized its foreign publishing operation by shedding a few units.

A major acquisition came in January 1994 when Houghton bought textbook publisher McDougal, Littell & Company for $138 million in an effort to enhance its secondary school market product line. At the same time, the company announced that it would fold its prestigious Ticknor & Fields imprint and merge its 20 or so trade books into the company's general line, in an effort to stem losses. In further restructuring, Houghton spun off its computer software division into a separate company, InfoSoft Corporation (later renamed Inso Corporation), of which it retained a 40 percent stake. Sales for the year had climbed to $483 million, but Houghton was soon on the move, announcing its acquisition of D.C. Heath and Company. To cover some of the debt incurred in the Heath purchase, Houghton sold off a portion of its Inso shares in 1995. Darehshori believed the D.C. Heath purchase would play a significant role in the company's future and would help Houghton reach sales of $1 billion by the year 2000.

In general, Houghton, the country's ninth largest publisher, weathered the cyclical nature of educational publishing well. Most educational publishers experienced losses in the first and fourth quarters annually, since the lion's share of textbook sales always fell in the second and third quarters; but, in addition, the adoption of new textbooks and programs occurred only every five to seven years, and sometimes for longer periods of time. Expenses incurred in developing new elementary and secondary programs were absorbed until the texts were sold and tested in

schools. Fortunately for Houghton, several new curriculum projects were well received in 1996 and, along with further sales by D.C. Heath, revenues were up by 91 percent in the second quarter. Houghton Mifflin Interactive (later renamed Sunburst Technology Corporation), meanwhile, was also steadily gaining in both products and sales. Houghton finished the year strong, with net sales of $717.9 million, up 36 percent from the previous year's $529 million.

Houghton stockholders had reason to cheer in July 1997 when a two-for-one stock split was announced. Each of Houghton's seven divisions, even the traditionally stolid Trade & Reference unit, had strong showings for the first two quarters that followed through to the end of the year. Net sales for 1997 reached $797.3 million, an increase of 11 percent and on track to reach Darehshori's projections for the new century. The following year Houghton was back on the acquisition trail; one bid failed (for a unit of Simon & Schuster) while another succeeded (the purchase of Computer Adaptive Technologies, Inc. [CAT], a firm that designed and developed computerized testing services and products). Year-end results were still on an upswing, topping $861 million, though the 8.1 percent boost was not as sharp as in previous years (1997's increase of 11 percent or the 36 percent net sales leap in 1996).

In 1999 Houghton continued to buy companies with technologically based product lines, including the assets of the Little Planet Literacy Series, a literary program for preschool- to third grade students, followed by the purchase of Sunburst Communications, Inc., an instructional software and video developer. To help finance its new acquisitions, Houghton sold the remainder of its equity in Inso Corporation and continued to climb closer to its year 2000 goal: net sales hit $920.1 million and net income rose to $76.3 million.

Houghton Mifflin in the New Century: 2000 and Beyond

As it approached the new millennium Houghton Mifflin was healthy, wealthy, and wise; sustained sales and profits in its divisions earned the 136-year-old publisher a solid reputation and a foothold in every educational market sector, from elementary to secondary to college. Throughout its long and colorful history, Houghton not only adapted to change but generally embraced it long before many of its competitors. Its forays into interactive and electronic capabilities, including web pages and online services (which averaged nearly half a million visits per month), reflected Houghton's growing appreciation of and commitment to cutting-edge technology in both educational and general publishing services. This was demonstrated further by its latest acquisition, in May 2000, of Virtual Learning Technologies, Inc., another electronic educational testing services company. Houghton Mifflin Company, with net sales approaching the billion dollar mark, had proven itself as a necessary component to education—whether in schools or at home.

Principal Subsidiaries

Great Source Education Group, Inc.; McDougal Littell Inc.; Riverside Publishing Company; Sunburst Technology Corporation; CAT (Computer Adaptive Technologies, Inc.).

Principal Divisions

School Division; College Publishing; Trade Division & Reference Division.

Principal Competitors

Dorling Kindersley Holdings plc; McGraw-Hill Publishers; Harcourt General, Inc.; Follett Educational Publishing; Random House, Inc.

Further Reading

Ballou, Ellen B., *The Building of the House: Houghton Mifflin's Formative Years,* Boston: Houghton Mifflin, 1970.

Gallese, Liz Roman, "Houghton Mifflin's New Trade Book Boss Expands Lines, Cuts Costs, Manages 'Ideas,' " *Wall Street Journal,* December 5, 1980.

Jereski, Laura, "Making Book," *Forbes,* March 7, 1988.

Milliot, Jim, "General Publishing Sales Increase 8% at Houghton," *Publishers Weekly,* April 19, 1993, p. 8.

——, "Houghton Mifflin Sets Sales Goal of $1 Billion," *Publishers Weekly,* April 24, 1995, p. 11.

Sherman, Steve, "HM's Chief Urges Futurist Outlook," *Publishers Weekly,* October 31, 1994, p. 11.

——, "Houghton Mifflin's CEO Hopes to Globalize His Company's Outlook," *Publishers Weekly,* July 12, 1991, p. 19.

"Textbook Case," *Forbes,* July 9, 1979.

—Elizabeth Rourke
—updated by Nelson Rhodes

Hy-Vee, Inc.

5820 Westown Parkway
West Des Moines, Iowa 50266
U.S.A.
Telephone: (515) 267-2800
Fax: (515) 267-2817
Web site: http://www.hy-vee.com

Private Company
Incorporated: 1938 as Hyde & Vredenburg
Employees: 42,000
Sales: $3.5 billion (1999 est.)
NAIC: 44511 Supermarkets and Other (Except Convenience) Stores; 44611 Pharmacies and Drug Stores

One of the 15 largest supermarket chains in the United States, Hy-Vee, Inc. operates over 200 retail stores in Iowa, Illinois, Missouri, Kansas, Nebraska, South Dakota, and Minnesota. That number also includes Drug Town drugstores in Nebraska and Iowa. Like other large supermarket chains, Hy-Vee sells mostly groceries but also offers a wide variety of other goods and services, from photo developing, flowers, banking, and postal services to food for takeout or in-store consumption. It operates huge stores designed for busy customers who can save time with one-stop shopping. As an additional convenience, Hy-Vee also provides online shopping options. With over 42,000 employees, Hy-Vee is Iowa's largest employer, and it has remained an employee-owned business since its incorporation. To highlight its years of service to the Midwest, Hy-Vee operates a $1 million History Center in West Des Moines.

Origins During the Great Depression

In 1930 two Iowa businessmen formed a grocery store partnership. Charles Hyde and David Vredenburg already had separately owned or managed several stores in Iowa and Missouri before starting their partnership's first store, a general retail store in Beaconsfield, Iowa, that sold groceries and dry goods such as clothing.

For a few years both founders continued to run separate stores and stores with other partners, while also running some stores together. However, in 1934 these general stores with such names as The Supply Stores, Hyde Service Store, and Vredenburg Grocery began selling only groceries.

In 1938 the original partnership was dissolved when Hyde & Vredenburg was incorporated. The new operation, with 15 stores in Iowa and Missouri, was owned by 16 store managers who traded ownership in local stores for corporate stock. Thus began the company's heritage of being an employee-owned organization. The new corporation headquartered in Lamoni, Iowa, chose Dwight Vredenburg, a son of the cofounder, as its president. Its 1938 annual sales were about $1.5 million.

In 1940 Hy-Vee found its customers were reluctant to start using "baskets on wheels," or grocery carts, said Dwight Vredenburg in the February 20, 2000 *Des Moines Register*. First introduced in its Centerville, Iowa store, the carts reminded women of baby buggies, and men felt the carts were "for sissies whose arms weren't strong enough to carry a few groceries." But free candy bars in each new cart soon persuaded customers to try the new contraptions.

Early Expansion in the Post-World War II Era

After World War II ended, many in the military returned to civilian life, and the postwar economy saw increased demands for housing and food as a large segment of younger families began having children. To help meet these demands, Hy-Vee expanded mainly in Iowa for several years. In 1945 it moved from Lamoni to Chariton, Iowa, after purchasing the Chariton Wholesale Grocery Company. In 1948 it built its first warehouse/office complex, a 72,000-square-foot facility in Chariton. At the end of 1949 the growing company owned 29 stores that brought in $9.2 million in annual sales.

In the 1950s the company added new warehouse facilities, retail stores, and a new name. In 1952 an employee contest resulted in three employees suggesting that the stores be renamed "Hy-Vee" by combining the last names of the two founders. Although the company's name remained Hyde &

275

Vredenburg, in 1953 the Fairfield, Iowa store was the first to bear the new name of Hy-Vee. Ten years later, in 1963, the corporate name became Hy-Vee Food Stores, Inc.

Company "firsts" in the 1950s included the 1956 introduction of Hy-Vee's first private label brand and the 1959 opening of a store in the Des Moines suburb of Johnson, the first Hy-Vee in a major urban area. The company in the 1950s also started its data processing department and added 28,000 feet to its Chariton warehouse for storing produce and frozen foods. At the end of fiscal year 1959 the company's annual sales stood at almost $36 million from its chain of 37 stores that employed 1,186.

The 1960s brought even more rapid growth in Hy-Vee's operations. The firm built up its headquarters in Chariton, including a 107,000-square-foot addition to its grocery warehouse in 1960; a new corporate headquarters finished in 1963; a 1965 addition of 93,000 square feet to the warehouse; a 12,000-square-foot addition to the warehouse for its Regal Stamp program started in 1956; and a new addition to its warehouse for truck maintenance and cleaning.

The Hy-Vee Employees Trust Fund in 1963 purchased the locally based National Bank & Trust Company of Chariton, and the same year the company broadcast its first television commercial. It opened its first Minnesota store in 1969, one of the 12 gained from a merger with Swanson Stores based in Cherokee, Iowa.

Hy-Vee owned 66 stores, including its Drug Town stores acquired in the 1960s, at the end of fiscal 1969, when annual sales stood at $130 million. With the company doing so well, it decided to start the Hy-Vee Foundation in 1968 to provide college scholarships.

Developments in the 1970s and 1980s

In the 1970s Hy-Vee continued to grow by opening new stores, building more warehouse space, and adding new technology. A 1971 addition of 78,000 square feet brought the total capacity of the Chariton warehouse up to 430,000 square feet. In addition, in 1976 the company built a secondary warehouse/office complex in Cherokee, Iowa. Hy-Vee started stores in three additional states during the decade: South Dakota in 1975, Nebraska in 1977, and Illinois in 1979. Other company landmarks for the decade included the opening of the 100th store, in Keokuk, Iowa (also the first store in the chain to use electronic cash registers), and surpassing the $500 million annual sales mark, in 1978, for the first time.

Hy-Vee in the 1980s added acquisitions, new stores, and new leadership. In 1982 it purchased 12 former Safeway stores in western Iowa and eastern Nebraska. That included seven stores in Omaha and two in the state capital of Lincoln. In 1988 Hy-Vee opened its Overland Park, Kansas Number 1 store, the company's first store in Kansas. To meet the needs of its growing chain, Hy-Vee in 1982 organized Perishable Distributors of Iowa (PDI), an affiliated firm that later became a subsidiary.

In 1983 Ron Pearson replaced Dwight Vredenburg as Hy-Vee's president, while Vredenburg remained the chairman and CEO. However, in 1989 Pearson became the CEO and chairman when Vredenburg finally retired.

At the end of fiscal 1989, Hy-Vee employed 22,778 individuals at 172 stores, up from its 9,591 employees at 124 stores in fiscal 1979. Its annual sales increased from $680.3 million in 1979 to $1.823 billion in 1989. Even greater growth was coming in the decade ahead.

The 1990s and Beyond

The decade began with several acquisitions. Hy-Vee purchased Lomar Distributing in 1990, Sunrise Dairy in 1991, D&D Salads and Florist Distributing in 1992, and the Meyocks & Priebe advertising firm in 1994. In 1995 the firm moved its corporate headquarters to West Des Moines and changed its name to Hy-Vee, Inc.

When Hy-Vee celebrated its 65th anniversary in 1995, President/CEO/Chairman Ron Pearson realized the company should do something to preserve and use its history. Inspired by the Coca-Cola History Center in Atlanta, Pearson persuaded the board of directors to spend $1 million on a 4,000-square-foot History Center located next to the company's headquarters in West Des Moines. Marilyn C. Gahm, a professional librarian with about 20 years experience in corporate libraries, served as the History Center Coordinator.

Meanwhile, the trend of larger grocery stores replacing smaller ones continued. For example, Tait's Foods in Des Moines, a former Safeway supermarket, in 2000 sold its store to Hy-Vee, which planned to convert it to a Drug Town with an attached Regal liquor store. Owner Bob Tait said his sales had been hurt by larger stores with more resources. In the April 1, 2000 *Des Moines Register* Tait said supermarkets had to remodel every seven to ten years to remain competitive, so he decided to sell his business. Thus more Mom and Pop grocery stores died as the supermarket industry consolidated. Of course, this centralization, at least in production, had started about 200 years ago when the first textile factories began replacing home and small shop production.

With a low unemployment rate in a booming economy, most stores, including Hy-Vee, scrambled to gain and keep good employees. Hy-Vee was a good example of a business that made a concerted effort to hire senior citizens. Vice-President Steve Meyer in the April 13, 2000 *Journal Star* said at Hy-Vee, "recruitment and retention of older workers becomes an imperative as well as a desire and goal." Hy-Vee used flexible scheduling to attract older workers, offering jobs for three seasons so seniors could spend winters in warmer climates. This kind of flexibility and other experimental practices were used to

Key Dates:

1930: Charles Hyde and David Vredenburg open a small store in Beaconsfield, Iowa.
1938: Hyde & Vredenburg, Inc. is incorporated.
1945: Company moves from Lamoni to Chariton, Iowa.
1948: Company builds its first office/warehouse complex in Chariton.
1963: Company changes its name to Hy-Vee Food Stores, Inc.
1969: Firm merges with Swanson Stores of Cherokee, Iowa.
1975: First South Dakota store is opened at Brookings.
1977: First Nebraska store is opened in Norfolk.
1979: First Illinois store is opened in Macomb.
1982: Twelve former Safeway stores in Iowa and Nebraska are acquired.
1986: Hy-Vee purchases Midwest Heritage Bank.
1988: First Kansas store is opened in Overland Park.
1989: Ron Pearson becomes Hy-Vee's chairman and CEO.
1991: Hy-Vee becomes Iowa's largest private employer.
1995: Firm moves its corporate headquarters to West Des Moines, Iowa; Hy-Vee, Inc. becomes the new corporate name.
1999: Hy-Vee, Inc. sells Heartland Pantry convenience stores to Kraus Gentle Corporation.
2000: Subsidiary electricfood.com starts offering Internet shopping for specialty foods.

attract older workers by 16 percent of 500 large companies surveyed in 1999.

Hy-Vee, like numerous other supermarkets, began offering more vitamins and natural foods as more consumers tried to improve their health through supplements and organic foods. Hy-Vee called its in-store sections with such products Health Marts, which competed with such huge natural food stores as Wild Oats and numerous multilevel marketing companies that sold supplements.

In the 1990s Hy-Vee began offering more ethnic foods. Chinese Express was introduced in the Independence, Missouri store in 1992, and in 1994 the Des Moines Store Number 3 became the first one in the chain to offer Mexican Express takeout items.

Meanwhile, Hy-Vee ended some of its operations. On January 22, 1999 it sold Heartland Pantry, its chain of 42 Iowa convenience stores, to Kraus Gentle Corporation, which by April 1999 converted all those stores to the Kum & Go name. In February 1999 Hy-Vee sold its partnership in Iowa Beverage Manufacturers, Inc.

Another challenge for all retail industries was the booming electronic commerce trend, sometimes called the New Economy. Shoppers in the 1990s gained the option to buy thousands of items, including food, on the Internet by using a credit card. Although still in its early stages, Internet shopping offered cus-

tomers a way to save time as they ordered from the convenience of their home.

Hy-Vee's Rochester Number 3 store in 1998 was the first in the chain to offer optional telephone or Internet shopping. In June 2000 Hy-Vee organized its newest subsidiary called electricfood.com, which began offering gourmet foods for purchase. In a related move, Hy-Vee in 2000 responded to customer requests by adding two new ways to get discount coupons from its web site at www.hy-vee.com. Hy-Vee also was part of ICS Food One, run by Internet Commerce Systems of Norcross, Georgia, which focused on exchanging information on brands and promotions among farmers, food manufacturers and distributors, and retailers.

In the late 1990s several entities recognized or honored Hy-Vee's achievements and growth. In 1997 *Consumer Reports* ranked the Iowa-based company as the fifth best U.S. supermarket chain. The Better Business Bureau in 1998 honored Hy-Vee with its "Integrity Award." Finally, in 1999, *Forbes* ranked Hy-Vee as the nation's 32nd largest private company. Hy-Vee's annual sales reached an all-time high of $3.5 billion at the end of fiscal 1999. At that time it employed 42,776 persons at 208 stores.

At the start of the new millennium, Hy-Vee and other supermarkets faced competition from the growing strength of Wal-Mart and such warehouse clubs as Sam's Club and Costco. However, strong regional chains including Hy-Vee were praised by retail analysts in the April 15, 2000 *Supermarket Business,* which ranked the nation's leading supermarkets. Consolidation of the grocery industry was expected to continue, and one expert predicted that only two Internet grocers would survive by combining online operations with actual stores. In any case, tough competition, along with changing technology and consumer expectations, gave Hy-Vee plenty of challenges to meet in the future.

Principal Subsidiaries

Perishable Distributors of Iowa; Lomar Distributing, Inc.; D&D Salads, Inc.; Florist Distributing, Inc.; Midwest Heritage Bank, FSB; Hy-Vee/Weitz Construction; Drug Town; Meyocks & Priebe Advertising; electricfood.com.

Principal Competitors

Wal-Mart Stores, Inc.; Albertson's Inc.; Fareway; Dahl's.

Further Reading

Challender, Mary, "Become a Coupon Clicker Hy-Vee Adds Two Online Programs to Its Web Site," *Des Moines Register*, April 20, 2000, p. 3.

Fritz, E. Mae, *The Family of Hy-Vee: A History of Hy-Vee Food Stores*, West Des Moines, Ia.: Hy-Vee Food Stores, Inc., 1989.

"Hy-Vee Center Aisles Stocked with Memories Hy-Vee Center Features Memories in Every Aisle," *Des Moines Register*, February 20, 2000, p. 1.

Lightly, Jeanne, "As Giants Grow, Ma and Pa Die," *Business Record* (Des Moines), April 3, 2000, p. 9.

"Longtime Grocer Tait Ready to Check Out . . . ," *Des Moines Register*, April 1, 2000, p. 1.

Love, Alice Ann, ''Congress' Goal: Help Workers Keep Working— Lawmakers Look for More Ways for Older Employees to Stay on the Job Longer,'' *Journal Star* (Peoria), April 13, 2000, p. A09.

''More Iowans Fork Over More for Organic Foods,'' *Omaha World-Herald*, March 24, 2000, p. 16.

Ryberg, William, ''Ron Pearson Brings High Energy to Hy-Vee,'' *Des Moines Register*, April 23, 2000, p. 1.

Sahm, Phil, ''Grocery Co-op Goes Online with Shopping,'' *Salt Lake Tribune*, June 21, 2000, pp. B7, B12.

Urbanski, Al, ''The Super 50,'' *Supermarket Business*, April 15, 2000, pp. 1, 10+.

Weinstein, Steve, ''Death of a Salesman?'' *Progressive Grocer*, June 2000, p. 33.

—David M. Walden

Iberia Líneas Aéreas de España S.A.

Velázquez, 130
28006 Madrid
Spain
Telephone: +43-91-587-8787
Fax: +34-91-587-74-69
Web site: http://www.iberia.com

Private Company
Incorporated: 1927 as Iberia, Compañia Aérea de
    Transportes, S.A.
Employees: 22,000
Sales: Pta 647 billion (US$3.91 billion) (1999)
NAIC: 481111 Scheduled Passenger Air Transportation;
    481112 Scheduled Freight Air Transportation; 481212
    Nonscheduled Chartered Freight Air Transportation;
    488119 Other Airport Operations; 48819 Other
    Support Activities for Air Transportation

Iberia Líneas Aéreas de España S.A. is Spain's national airline and one of the world's oldest. It carries 26 million people a year to a hundred destinations in 42 countries. Iberia also hauls 220,000 tons of freight a year. The company is also engaged in a wide array of aviation and travel support services. After receiving two substantial government bailouts in the 1990s, Iberia has become partially privatized, trimmed its payrolls, and rediscovered profitability.

Origins

The company was established in 1927 as Iberia, Compañia Aérea de Transportes, S.A. Crucial to the founding of Iberia was support from the German Deutsche Luft Hansa A.G. (Lufthansa) which, in addition to investing 24 percent of the capital, contributed materials and technical support. The majority share of the company was held by Horacio Echevarrieta, a businessman who became chairman of the board. Iberia's objective was to provide peninsular and transatlantic air services. The company immediately applied for, and obtained from the authorities, concession to establish regular flights between Madrid and Barcelona.

The fleet comprised three Rohrbach Roland monoplanes brought in by Luft Hansa. The inaugural flight, Barcelona to Madrid, was launched in December 1927. The three-and-a-half-hour trip was a daily service—except for Sundays—operating in both directions. In February 1928, the company received a permit to carry mail between these two cities and with their entry the whole of Europe was now covered by an airmail network.

In July 1928 a twin-engined Dornier Wal seaplane was chartered and took off from the southern town of Cádiz for the Canary Islands. The object of the flight was to test the viability of setting up a base for seaplanes in the Canaries for a service from Seville, with an eventual extension to the Cape Verde Islands. These would be used as a staging point for a postal route to South America.

In 1929 Iberia, along with Unión Aérea Española, was merged into Compañia de Líneas Aéreas Subvencionadas S.A. (CLASSA) and the new enterprise was granted a monopoly. CLASSA, which initially ran flights between Madrid and Seville, began regular operations in May of that year. Though Iberia as an independent entity disappeared from the air transport scene until 1937, the company's director, Daniel de Araoz, maintained its registration in the Companies Register of Madrid.

CLASSA, unlike its predecessors, indicated no intention of establishing flights across the South Atlantic. Soon after Spain was declared a republic in 1931, CLASSA was replaced by a new public entity known as Líneas Aéreas Postales Españolas (LAPE), which inherited CLASSA's fleet.

World War II Era

LAPE operated only until the outbreak of the Civil War in 1936. Iberia again came on the scene in 1937 when it began making flights in nationalist-held territory under the guidance of Araoz. The fleet consisted of seven Junkers JU-52. Support was once again provided by Luft Hansa to which all of Iberia's capital was transferred, and whose Spanish representative Araoz virtually became. The airline carried 21,000 passengers in 1938 and earned profits of Pta 500,000 on an income of Pta 5.7 million.

At the end of the Civil War, with Barajas airport in Madrid as its base, Iberia began flights between Madrid and Barcelona, Burgos, Seville, and Valencia, as well as Lisbon, in Portugal; between Seville and the Canary Islands via stopovers in Spanish Sahara; and between Palma de Mallorca and Vitoria via Barcelona and Zaragoza.

Nationalized in 1940 when outstanding debt to Luft Hansa was paid off, Iberia was granted a monopoly over regular domestic flights and in colonies and protected territories. The company's capital was sold to the state for a nominal value of Pta 1.1 million.

During World War II, close ties with Luft Hansa continued, though shortages prevented the Germans from supplying Iberia with materials and fuel. As fuel supplier to Spain, the United States refused to undertake deliveries until connections with Germany were severed. With this in view, in 1943 the company was integrated into Instituto Nacional de Industria (INI), the state holding conglomerate created in 1941 to promote Spanish industrial self-sufficiency. Representatives from INI, answerable to the prime minister's office, sat on the airline's board.

In 1945 Iberia received a state subsidy of Pta 10 million. By this year in addition to the Junkers, the company had also added to the fleet 17 DC-3 planes, converted from military to civilian use. In 1946 London, Rome, Montevideo, and Buenos Aires were added to Iberia's list of destinations. The service to South America was a commercial success because it met demand from those cut off from Spain since before the Civil War. However, there was soon stiff competition for this market from such rivals as Air France and the British South American Corporation.

Postwar Expansion

Though the supply of spare parts was interrupted due to the postwar diplomatic isolation imposed on Spain, Iberia continued its international expansion, becoming the flagship company for INI. On the grounds that the company was unable to meet all domestic freight and passenger demand, a second airline, Aviacion y Comercio (AVIACO), was granted authority to operate in 1948. Initially, AVIACO's destinations were to be those not served by Iberia, especially Bilbao and the northwest. In 1954 AVIACO was taken over by INI.

The signing of the Spanish-American defense treaty in 1953, elimination of visa requirements for U.S. visitors to Spain, and the introduction of tourist class on airline trips motivated Iberia to start transatlantic flights in 1954. The 1954 International Convention on Civil Aviation was applied very liberally by Spain and saw the development of mass tourism using charter flights. Over two million people now traveled to the country annually.

While Iberia was under pressure to keep up with rivals acquiring new aircraft from Boeing and Douglas, the company and its parent, INI, could not agree on the need for transatlantic jetliners. INI often imposed restrictive purchasing policies in what it saw as prudent corporate strategy. However, the purchase of three DC-8 jets was eventually approved and these were delivered in 1961. Unlike other INI enterprises, Iberia, a major contributor to the national coffers, was greatly influenced by external factors. However, INI, having control over Iberia's financial and investment decisions, did not allow the company to react to these outside forces.

By 1965 profits rose to Pta 165 million, more DC-8s had been acquired, and a joint AVIACO-Iberia board was set up to coordinate policies. A collaboration agreement with Aerolíneas Argentinas was signed in 1967; Madrid to Buenos Aires was becoming Iberia's busiest route and Aerolíneas Argentinas could now acquire aircraft with the Spaniards acting as financial intermediaries. Similar agreements were entered into with carriers in Uruguay and the Dominican Republic.

The Turbulent 1970s and 1980s

In the 1970s, Douglas DC-9 and Boeing 747 airplanes were added to Iberia's fleet; Madrid's Barajas airport had a new mechanized cargo terminal; services were started to Johannesburg, South Africa, and to cities in Mexico and Central America; and other routes were extended from Munich to Warsaw, Rome to Athens and then Istanbul. During this period a radical change in INI-Iberia relations, never very cordial, occurred when Emilio Gonzalez became head of aviation in the parent company. INI took over all major decision-making regarding Iberia and Gonzalez's power included veto rights over proposals made by the carrier. There was a fierce internal debate over the acquisition of Boeing B-727 planes versus Douglas DC-9s and the risk of duplicating maintenance costs implied by the proposed purchase of DC-9 planes. It culminated in Spanish orders that effectively revived the sagging fortunes of the B-727 production line.

In 1977, while celebrating its 50th anniversary, the airline carried ten million passengers for the first time. However, a three-month strike by Spanish air traffic controllers contributed to a loss of Pta 729 million, as did a three-day work stoppage by all ground staff. A three-year program for the development of organizational reform and a more polished image was launched. Among the issues to be addressed were improved efficiency, lowered costs, and depoliticized management and decision-making. The latter was in response to the political changes in the country leading to the separation of the Air and Defence Ministry from all matters of civil aviation. In addition Iberia entered the Atlas group—comprised of Air France, Lufthansa, Sabena, and Alitalia—for cooperation in the servicing of a number of its planes.

Key Dates:

1927: Iberia is founded with help from Luft Hansa (later Lufthansa).
1929: Iberia merges with Compañia de Líneas Aéreas Subvencionadas S.A. (CLASSA).
1931: CLASSA is replaced by Líneas Aéreas Postales Españolas (LAPE) after Spain becomes a republic.
1937: Iberia displaces LAPE during the Civil War.
1940: Iberia nationalizes with payment of debt to Luft Hansa.
1943: State holding company INI takes over Iberia.
1967: Three Latin American airlines sign agreements with Iberia.
1977: Passenger count exceeds ten million in Iberia's 50th year.
1984: Pilots and maintenance personnel strike.
1987: Amadeus booking system is launched with three other airlines.
1991: Historic bilateral agreement clears way for a Miami hub.
1992: Iberia receives US$1 billion subsidy after expanding in South America.
1996: Restructuring plan is accepted by unions; European Community Commission allows US$711 million subsidy.
1999: Iberia is partially privatized.

In 1980 a dispute arose with Boeing over commissions paid by Iberia for a B-727 aircraft order, which was ultimately canceled by INI. The matter was finally settled the following year when Boeing agreed to give Iberia a letter of credit for US$3.4 million, the amount of the commission. Also, the American company had to declare it had not paid any Spanish official in order to induce the purchase.

In 1982 Iberia entered into cooperation agreements on technology transfer, maintenance, and flight operations with Mexican and Peruvian airlines, though neither agreement involved financial participation. When electronic reservations operations were introduced into those countries' airports, Iberia had sufficient expertise in computer technology to act as adviser.

Two major events for Spain in 1982 were the World Soccer Championship and the visit of Pope John Paul II, both of which were expected to bring large numbers of tourists. The results were disappointing for Iberia, however—only 23 of the 231 charter flights were booked. For the fourth year running there were losses. In 1983 the company lost Pta 9.2 million. This was blamed on a combination of factors: an increase in fuel prices, decline in the Latin American markets, appreciation of the dollar—currency in which many payments were made—as well as the devaluation of the peseta and the consequent increase in costs. The airline also had a policy, from then on abandoned, of subsidizing fares of families with many children between the islands and the mainland. Furthermore, Spanish internal flights were 30 percent cheaper than those in the rest of Western Europe.

As a result of a viability plan introduced for the years 1983 and 1984, some 700 persons were laid off in an effort to reduce costs. Among those laid off were a number of pilots, and in June 1984 a strike was called. The pilots' work stoppage lasted one month and cost Iberia Pta 3 billion. Upon the company's refusal to recognize ASETMA as the maintenance personnel's union and sole representative in negotiations, maintenance technicians also went on strike. For days operations were virtually halted. Nevertheless, a total of 12.5 million passengers were carried that year and the company took delivery of its first Lockheed Superconstellation. Iberia's losses for the year totaled Pta 16 billion.

By 1987 Iberia had expanded to include flights to Tel Aviv, Khartoum, Moscow, and Tokyo, as well as to several Canadian and U.S. cities. In that year the Iberswiss Catering joint venture was established with Swissair, and a cargo subsidiary, CARGOSUR, was started for the company. In addition, Iberia, in conjunction with Air France, Lufthansa, and SAS, created a computerized communications and reservations distribution system called AMADEUS. By 1992 AMADEUS had served over 17,000 travel agencies and 16,000 ticket offices worldwide.

An internal report reviewed the issues that continued to trouble the airline during the 1980s: an unproductive network; low returns per passenger/kilometer carried; lack of motivation among employees; high financial costs; and poor public image. A new strategic plan proposed that these be handled and improved with studied solutions for each, accompanied by the creation of complementary companies that would have a different cost structure and operate specifically for regional traffic. This proposal was implemented in 1988 with the establishment of Binter Canarias, which would shuttle passengers back and forth from the Canary Islands. In the wake of improvements in the company's finances, management started a fleet modernization program in 1988, with US$1 billion in orders for Douglas MD-87, A-320, and A-340 aircraft as well as Boeing B-757 planes. The fleet was scheduled to be completely new by 1994.

New World Expansion in the Early 1990s

As part of its strategy to penetrate the South American market, Iberia acquired a 35 percent share in LADECO, the Chilean national carrier, in 1989. This was followed by an agreement in 1990 to acquire a stake in Aerolíneas Argentinas, Latin America's second largest airline, which was then being privatized by the Argentine government. The agreement gave Iberia a 30 percent holding in the airline, in addition to rights of management, while Argentina retained only a five percent share. Iberia paid US$260 million in cash for its part of the contract.

Iberia was, yet again, beset by strikes in the late 1980s and early 1990s, including a stoppage in May 1991, when a 24-hour strike by both ground and air crews necessitated the cancellation of most international flights. The workers' stoppage was called in response to wage freezes imposed by management following losses of Pta 22.5 billion in 1990. The Gulf crisis and subsequent recession also contributed to the 1991 pre-tax loss of Pta 51.3 billion.

A transaction finalized in 1991 and worth US$145 million enabled Iberia to buy into Venezuela's main airline, VIASA. With this takeover Iberia acquired a 45 percent holding, while the company's partner in the agreement, the local bank Banco Popular, received a 15 percent share in the airline. Iberia thereby further raised its share in the Latin American market and came nearer its aim of being the leading carrier between Europe and that region. Iberia claimed it was defending natural markets, that these ventures had no speculative element.

In the liberalized aviation climate of the 1990s, Iberia saw its major competitive challenge from American rather than European or charter companies. The company's main priorities in meeting this challenge were set out in the strategy announced in April 1992: reorganized corporate management, trimmed company workforce, and strengthened ties to the Latin American market. This Pta 760 billion strategy, with a goal of Pta 56 billion in profits by 1996, was based on several assumptions about the future. One, in particular, was an expected 7.1 percent increase in the rate of air traffic.

Other seemingly optimistic assumptions upon which company forecasts were based included an average annual increase of 13.7 percent in revenue in the years 1992 to 1996 with a 9.5 percent average increase in costs over the same period; profits were anticipated at Pta 4.9 billion in 1992 and at Pta 55.9 billion by 1996. Of the total Pta 7.6 billion, medium-term investment, 51 percent would be from internal cash flow, 33 percent from bank debt—including loans from the European Investment Bank— and the balance from authorized company capital increase.

In an effort to help guarantee the success of Iberia's plan to become profitable again, in 1992 the European Community Commission approved the Spanish government infusion of Pta 120 billion (US$923 million) into the company. Though Iberia chairman Miguel Aguilo tried to convince the Commission's executive committee that the money should not be considered a subsidy, the panel ruled otherwise and stipulated that no further bailouts would be approved.

Another setback occurred in 1992 when it became necessary for the Argentine government to renationalize a portion of Aerolíneas Argentinas. Local minority investors could not provide funds for the loss-making enterprise, forcing the government to increase its share to 33 percent, though Iberia's stake remained at 30 percent. In spite of such problems with its Latin America investments, two major points in Iberia's favor were its 35 percent share of the market for flights between Europe and Latin America and the low break-even point on such flights—65 percent capacity, as compared to 75 percent capacity on North American trips. In addition, to further its stake in the region, Iberia was considering taking over a major Bolivian airline, Lloyd Aereo de Bolivia (LAB), which was in the process of being privatized.

To add to the list of concerns for Iberia's management, in 1992 the company also faced potential competition from such surface transportation systems as the national highway network and railways, both of which were scheduled for improvements in that year. Of particular concern was the high speed train AVE, operating between Madrid and Seville, whose inauguration was timed to coincide with the opening of Expo '92 in the latter city. This major event did, however, provide a welcome bonus for the airline—while 20 daily flights had been anticipated to serve the Andalusian capital, the Iberia Group had to supply ten percent more passenger seats in order to meet the demand. Nevertheless, Iberia lost Pta 35 billion (US$268 million) in 1992.

A new bilateral agreement allowed Iberia to become the first foreign carrier to ever establish a hub in the United States. In return, U.S. carriers were allowed to fly to Spain from several U.S. cities. The hub opened at Miami International Airport in May 1992. In spite of the strategic potential of the Spain-South America connection, cargo and passenger traffic was slow, and new chief executive Juan Saez was soon openly contemplating closing the Miami hub altogether. Iberia faced fierce competition in Miami from American Airlines, which was aggressively developing a South American network through marketing agreements with local airlines. To increase its feeder traffic from the United States, Iberia partnered with Carnival Airlines in April 1993, adding a Miami-Los Angeles code-sharing flight. All other U.S. carriers were either competitors or partners of other European airlines.

Industry observers felt that while Iberia made some reasonable yet ambitious expansion plans in South America, it did not integrate them properly with its own operations. The disastrous relationship with Aerolineas Argentinas was credited with consuming most of the cash given Iberia in the 1992 bailout. Some saw the airline's strategic focus more based on neo-imperial ambition than sound marketing logic.

Restructuring in the Mid-1990s

The airline had yet to post a profit in the 1990s, and in late 1994, with bankruptcy likely within a year, it proposed a rescue plan. Iberia suggested cutting salaries by an average of 15 percent over the next two years and dropping 3,000 of its 24,500 workers from the payroll. Iberia had already renegotiated the terms of an earlier Airbus order.

Iberia also asked the Spanish government for another capital infusion of Pta 125 billion (nearly US$1 billion). However, the European Commission had only allowed the 1992 subsidy on the grounds that no more public money be used until 1996.

Iberia's pilots perceived a failure in the company's management of its restructuring plan needed to gain the billion-dollar subsidy, and the airline suffered several strikes in November 1995. The company posted a loss of Pta 45 billion for the year. In February 1996, the pilots' union accepted the restructuring plan, which safeguarded pilot jobs in return for productivity increases and a two-year pay freeze. The airline had some of the highest paid pilots in the world.

The European Commission authorized Pta 87 billion (US$711 million) in state aid, less than requested. Iberia's domestic competitors complained about the subsidy when Iberia cut airfares at home. (Spain's domestic market had been deregulated in 1993.)

Iberia agreed to sell most of its stake in Aerolineas Argentinas for Pta 67 billion in April 1996. The buyer, Andes Holding BV, was comprised of Iberia parent company Teneo SA and units of Merrill Lynch and Bankers Trust. Xavier de Irala was appointed chairman in July 1996, replacing Javier Salas.

Iberia gave Airbus its single largest European order in February 1998, ordering 76 aircraft worth Pta 400 billion (US$2.6 billion). Iberia already operated Airbus planes, and hoped to reduce its maintenance costs by standardizing its fleet. The year's record results seemed to justify the optimistic purchase: a pre-tax group profit of Pta 65.97 billion on revenues of Pta 664 billion.

Pre-tax group profit fell to Pta 31.2 billion (EUR 187.95 billion or US$182.2 million) in 1999 on revenues of Pta 647 billion. Charter subsidiary Viva Air had ceased operations during the year. Iberia held a one-quarter share in the airline ticketing company Amadeus, whose initial public offering in October 1999 realized EUR 848 million. Iberia later reduced its interest to just over 18 percent.

In December 1999, an agreement was finally reached to sell 40 percent of Iberia to a group of shareholders. British Airways would acquire nine percent of the company for EUR 245 million (£150 million) while American Airlines took one percent. Spanish investors took the other 30 percent. Iberia had two years earlier formed code-sharing arrangements with the two airlines.

A New Outlook in 2000

Iberia foresaw continued profits in its future as it increased capacity and raised productivity. It announced a new cost-cutting plan in March 2000. An often-postponed initial public offering for the carrier was scheduled for October 2000.

An alliance with Air France surfaced in June 2000. The deal would put Iberia passengers on Air France flights to the Far East, while those of Air France would connect with Iberia's Latin American flights. Although Air France had also partnered with Delta Airlines in the United States, Iberia remained in the "oneworld" alliance led by American Airlines and British Airways.

Principal Subsidiaries

Amadeus Global Travel Distribution SA/Amadeus Data Processing GmbH & Co (18.28%); Aviacion Y Comercio SA (AVIACO)(99.9%); Binter Canarias; Binter Mediterráneo; Campos Velazquez SA (99.99%); Compania Auxiliar al Cargo Express SA (CACESA) (74.5%); Iberswiss Catering, SA (70%); SAVIA (66%); ARSA (10%); Mundicolor (18%).

Principal Competitors

Air Europa; Alitalia-Linee Aeree Italiana, S.p.A.; Deutsche Lufthansa Aktiengesellschaft; Spanair; UAL Corporation.

Further Reading

Aceña, P.M., and F. Comín, *INI 50 años de industrialización en España*, Madrid: Espasa Calpe SA, 1991.

"Aerolíneas Sell-Off Collapses," *Financial Times*, July 24, 1992.

Armbruster, William, "Iberia Air's New Chief May Close Miami Hub," *Journal of Commerce*, September 23, 1993, p. 3B.

Barnard, Bruce, "British Airways, Iberia Air at Extremes of EU Airlines," *Journal of Commerce*, November 7, 1995, p. 2B.

——, "Capital Injection Lets Iberia Airlines Get Back to Its Search for Partners," *Journal of Commerce*, December 12, 1996, p. 2B.

Burns, Tom, "Iberia Accused of Price Fixing in Ticket War," *Financial Times*, Europe Section, September 18, 1998, p. 3.

——, "Iberia Eyes Airlines in UK and US As Allies," *Financial Times*, October 18, 1996, p. 27.

——, "Iberia Tries to Avert Strikes As Financial Crisis Grows," *Financial Times*, October 27, 1994, p. 2.

Burns, Tom, and Michael Skapinker, "Spain Rejects British Airways Bid to Buy 25 Percent Stake in Iberia," *Financial Times*, February 18, 1998, p. 28.

Colitt, Raymond, "Iberia Agrees to Deal on Viasa Debt," *Financial Times*, January 29, 1997, p. 31.

"El Gobierno argentino advierte a Iberia que sera inflexible en el contencioso de Aerolíneas," *El País*, June 6, 1992.

Hill, Leonard, "The Strain in Spain," *Air Transport World*, June 1, 1999, pp. 58ff.

Iberia Líneas Aéreas de España Informe Anual 1991, Madrid, Iberia Líneas Aéreas de España, 1992.

"Iberia perdió 25.000 millones en el primer semestre de este año," *El País*, July 14, 1992.

"Iberia propone sacar del balance de Aerolíneas la deuda del Estado argentino," *El País*, June 17, 1992.

Nash, Nathaniel, "The Struggle to Keep Iberia Aloft," *New York Times*, Bus. Sec., January 14, 1995, p. 39.

Reed, Ted, "Iberia's American Hub Is Ailing," *Journal of Commerce*, AirCommerce Supplement, August 30, 1993, p. 7.

Skapinker, Michael, "BA to Take Nine Percent of Iberia for £200 Million," *Financial Times*, February 13, 1999, p. 23.

Velasco, Juan B. Viniegra, *Iberia: Cronología de Seis Décadas*, Madrid, Iberia Líneas Aéreas de España, 1987.

White, David, "Iberia Completes Tie-Up with American Airlines," *Financial Times*, September 16, 1997, p. 30.

——, "Iberia Hit by Strikes and Traffic Chaos," *Financial Times*, February 26, 2000, p. 10.

——, "Iberia Set for Air France Link: Long-Haul Agreement Marks Change in Partnership Strategy," *Financial Times*, June 2, 2000, p. 23.

——, "Iberia Signs $2.6 Billion Deal with Airbus," *Financial Times*, February 4, 1998, p. 8.

——, "Winning Bidders Named in Iberia Sale," *Financial Times*, April 29, 1999, p. 20.

—Edward Pincheson

—updated by Frederick C. Ingram

Intel Corporation

2200 Mission College Boulevard
Santa Clara, California 95052-8119
U.S.A.
Telephone: (408) 765-8080
Toll Free: (800) 628-8686
Fax: (408) 765-6284
Web site: http://www.intel.com

Public Company
Incorporated: 1968 as N M Electronics
Employees: 70,200
Sales: $29.39 billion (1999)
Stock Exchanges: NASDAQ
Ticker Symbol: INTC
NAIC: 334413 Semiconductor and Related Device
   Manufacturing; 334210 Telephone Apparatus
   Manufacturing; 511210 Software Publishers; 541512
   Computer Systems Design Services

Intel Corporation is the largest semiconductor manufacturer in the world, with major facilities in the United States, Europe, and Asia. Intel has changed the world dramatically since it was founded in 1968; the company invented the microprocessor, the ''computer on a chip'' that made possible the first handheld calculators and personal computers (PCs). By the early 21st century, Intel's microprocessors were found in more than 80 percent of PCs worldwide. The company's product line also includes chipsets and motherboards; flash memory used in wireless communications and other applications; hubs, switches, routers, and other products for Ethernet networks; and embedded control chips used in networking products, laser printers, imaging devices, storage media, and other applications. Intel remained competitive through a combination of clever marketing, well-supported research and development, superior manufacturing proficiency, a vital corporate culture, legal proficiency, and an ongoing alliance with software giant Microsoft Corporation often referred to as ''Wintel.''

1968–79: From DRAM to the 8086

Intel's founders, Robert Noyce and Gordon Moore, were among the eight founders of Fairchild Semiconductor, established in 1957. While at Fairchild, Noyce and Moore invented the integrated circuit, and, in 1968, they decided to form their own company. They were soon joined by Andrew Grove, a Hungarian refugee who had arrived in the United States in 1956 and joined Fairchild in 1963. Grove would remain president and CEO of Intel into the 1990s.

To obtain start-up capital, Noyce and Moore approached Arthur Rock, a venture capitalist, with a one-page business plan simply stating their intention of developing large-scale integrated circuits. Rock, who had helped start Fairchild Semiconductor, as well as Teledyne and Scientific Data Systems, had confidence in Noyce and Moore and provided $3 million in capital. The company was incorporated on July 18, 1968, as N M Electronics (the letters standing for Noyce Moore), but quickly changed its name to Intel, formed from the first syllables of ''integrated electronics.'' Intel gathered another $2 million in capital before going public in 1971.

Noyce and Moore's scanty business proposal belied a clear plan to produce large-scale integrated (LSI) semiconductor memories. At that time, semiconductor memories were ten times more expensive than standard magnetic core memories. Costs were falling, however, and Intel's founders felt that with the greater speed and efficiency of LSI technology, semiconductors would soon replace magnetic cores. Within a few months of its startup, Intel produced the 3101 Schottky bipolar memory, a high-speed random access memory (RAM) chip. The 3101 proved popular enough to sustain the company until the 1101, a metal oxide semiconductor (MOS) chip, was perfected and introduced in 1969. The following year, Intel introduced the 1103, a one Kilobyte (K) dynamic RAM, or DRAM, which was the first chip large enough to store a significant amount of information. With the 1103, Intel finally had a chip that really did begin to replace magnetic cores; DRAMs eventually proved indispensable to the personal computer.

The company's most dramatic impact on the computer industry involved its 1971 introduction of the 4004, the world's first microprocessor. Like many of Intel's innovations, the microprocessor was a byproduct of efforts to develop another technology. When a Japanese calculator manufacturer, Busicom, asked Intel to design cost-effective chips for a series of calculators, Intel engineer Ted Hoff was assigned to the project; during his search for such a design, Hoff conceived a plan for a central processing unit (CPU) on one chip. The 4004, which crammed 2,300 transistors onto a one-eighth- by one-sixth-inch chip, had the power of the old 3,000-cubic-foot ENIAC computer, which depended on 38,000 vacuum tubes.

Although Intel initially focused on the microprocessor as a computer enhancement that would allow users to add more memory to their units, the microprocessor's great potential—for everything from calculators to cash registers and traffic lights—soon became clear. The applications were facilitated by Intel's introduction of the 8008, an 8-bit microprocessor developed along with the 4004 but oriented toward data and character (rather than arithmetic) manipulation. The 8080, introduced in 1974, was the first truly general purpose microprocessor. For $360, Intel sold a whole computer on one chip, while conventional computers sold for thousands of dollars. The response was overwhelming. The 8080 soon became the industry standard and Intel the industry leader in the 8-bit market.

In response to ensuing competition in the manufacture of 8-bit microprocessors, Intel introduced the 8085, a faster chip with more functions. The company was also developing two more advanced projects, the 32-bit 432 and the 16-bit 8086. The 8086 was introduced in 1978 but took two years to achieve wide use, and, during this time, Motorola produced a competing chip (the 68000) that seemed to be selling faster. Intel responded with a massive sales effort to establish its architecture as the standard. When International Business Machines Corporation (IBM) chose the 8008, the 8086's 8-bit cousin, for its personal computer in 1980, Intel seemed to have beat out the competition.

During the 1970s, Intel had also developed the erasable programmable read-only memory (EPROM), another revolutionary but unintended research byproduct. Intel physicist Dov Frohman was working on the reliability problems of the silicon gate used in the MOS process when he realized that the disconnected, or ''floating,'' gates that were causing malfunctions could be used to create a chip that was erasable and reprogrammable. Since conventional ROM chips had to be permanently programmed during manufacture, any change required the manufacture of a whole new chip. With EPROM, however, Intel could offer customers chips that could be erased and repro-

grammed with ultraviolet light and electricity. At its introduction in 1971, EPROM was a novelty without much of a market. But the microprocessor, invented at the same time, created a demand for memory; the EPROM offered memory that could be conveniently used to test microprocessors.

Another major development at Intel during this time was that of peripheral controller chips. Streamlined for specific tasks and stripped of unneeded functions, peripheral chips could greatly increase a computer's abilities without raising software development costs. One of Intel's most important developments in peripherals was the coprocessor, first introduced in 1980. Coprocessor chips were an extension of the CPU that could handle specific computer-intensive tasks more efficiently than the CPU itself. Once again, innovation kept Intel ahead of its competition.

Intel's rapid growth, from the 12 employees at its founding in 1968 to 15,000 in 1980, demanded a careful approach to corporate culture. Noyce, Moore, and Grove, who remembered their frustration with Fairchild's bureaucratic bottlenecks, found that defining a workable management style was important. Informal weekly lunches with employees kept communication lines open while the company was small, but that system had become unwieldy. Thus, the founders installed a carefully outlined program emphasizing openness, decision making on the lowest levels, discipline, and problem solving rather than paper shuffling. Moreover, the company's top executives eschewed such luxuries as limousines, expense account lunches, and private parking spaces to establish a sense of teamwork with their subordinates.

In an interview with the *Harvard Business Review* in 1980, Noyce remarked on the company's hiring policy, stating, ''we expect people to work hard. We expect them to be here when they are committed to be here; we measure absolutely everything that we can in terms of performance.'' Employee incentives included options on Intel stock, and technological breakthroughs were celebrated with custom-bottled champagne—''Vintage Intel'' marked the first $250 million quarter, in 1983—the year sales reached $1 billion for the first time.

1980s: From 286 to 486

During the 1974 recession, Intel was forced to lay off 30 percent of its employees, and morale declined substantially as a result. Thus, in 1981, when economic struggles again surfaced, instead of laying off more employees, Intel accelerated new product development with the ''125 Percent Solution,'' which asked exempt employees to work two extra hours per day, without pay, for six months. A brief surge in sales the following year did not last, and, again, instead of more layoffs, Intel imposed pay cuts of up to ten percent. Such measures were not popular among all its workforce, but, by June 1983, all cuts had been restored and retroactive raises had been made. Moreover, in December 1982, IBM paid $250 million for a 12 percent share of Intel, giving the company not only a strong capital boost, but also strong ties to the undisputed industry leader. IBM would eventually increase its stake to 20 percent before selling its Intel stock in 1987.

During the early 1980s, Intel began to slip in some of its markets. Fierce competition in DRAMs, static RAMs, and

Key Dates:

1968: Robert Noyce and Gordon Moore incorporate N M Electronics, which is soon renamed Intel Corporation.
1970: Company develops DRAM, dynamic RAM.
1971: Intel introduces the world's first microprocessor and goes public.
1974: Company introduces the first general purpose microprocessor.
1980: IBM chooses the Intel microprocessor for the first personal computer.
1983: Revenues exceed $1 billion for the first time.
1992: Net income tops $1 billion for the first time.
1993: The fifth generation chip, the Pentium, debuts.
1996: Revenues surpass $20 billion, net income exceeds $5 billion.
1997: Company introduces the Pentium II microprocessor.
1999: Intel debuts the Pentium III and is added to the Dow Jones Industrial Average.
2000: The first Intel 1-gigahertz processor hits the market.

EPROMs left Intel concentrating on microprocessors. While competitors claimed that Intel simply gave away its DRAM market, Moore told *Business Week* in 1988 that the company deliberately focused on microprocessors as the least cyclical field in which to operate. Customer service, an area Intel had been able to overlook for years as it dominated its markets, became more important as highly efficient Japanese and other increasingly innovative competitors challenged Intel's position. In addition, Intel's manufacturing record, strained in years past by undercapacity, needed fixing. Fab 7, Intel's seventh wafer-fabrication plant, opened in 1983 only to face two years of troubled operations before reaching full capacity. Between 1984 and 1988, Intel closed eight old plants, and in 1988 it spent some $450 million on new technology to bring its manufacturing capacity into line with its developmental prowess.

Despite these retrenchments, the company continued to excel in the microprocessor market. In 1982 Intel introduced its 80286 microprocessor, the chip that quickly came to dominate the upper-end PC market, when IBM came out with the 286-powered PC/AT. The 286 was followed in 1985 by Intel's 80386 chip, popularized in 1987 by the Compaq DESKPRO 386, which, despite bugs when it first came out, became one of the most popular chips on the market. While the 286 brought to the personal computer a speed and power that gave larger computers their first real challenge, the 386 offered even greater speed and power together with the ability to run more than one program at a time. The 386 featured 32-bit architecture and 275,000 transistors—more than twice the number of the 286.

In 1989 Intel introduced the 80486, a chip *Business Week* heralded as "a veritable mainframe-on-a-chip." The 486 included 1.2 million transistors and the first built-in math coprocessor, and was 50 times faster than the 4004, the first microprocessor. In designing the i486, Intel resisted an industry trend toward RISC (reduced instruction-set computing), a chip design that eliminated rarely used instructions in order to gain speed. Intel argued that what RISC chips gained in speed they lost in flexibility and that, moreover, RISC chips were not compatible with software already on the market, which Intel felt would secure the 486's position. A new chip, the 64-bit i860 announced in early 1989, however, did make use of RISC technology to offer what Intel claimed would be a "supercomputer on a chip."

Also in 1989, a major lawsuit that Intel had filed against NEC Corporation five years before was decided. Intel had claimed that NEC violated its copyright on the microcode, or embedded software instructions, of Intel's 8086 and 8088 chips. Although Intel had licensed NEC to produce the microcode, NEC had subsequently designed a similar chip of its own. At issue was whether microcode could be copyrighted. The court ruled that it could but that NEC had not violated any copyright in the case at hand. The suit made public some issues surrounding Intel's reputation. Some rivals and consumers, for example, claimed that Intel used its size and power to repress competition through such tactics as filing "meritless" lawsuits and tying microprocessor sales to other chips. Other observers, however, praised Intel's protection of its intellectual property and, subsequently, its profits. The Federal Trade Commission conducted a two-year investigation of Intel's practices and did not recommend criminal charges against the company, but two rival companies—Advanced Micro Devices Inc. and Cyrix Corp.—filed antitrust lawsuits against Intel in 1993.

1990s: The Pentium Decade

Intel's annual net income topped $1 billion for the first time in 1992, following a very successful, brand-building marketing campaign. Intel ads aggressively sought to bolster consumer interest in and demand for computers that featured "Intel Inside." By late 1993, the company's brand equity totaled $17.8 billion—more than three times its 1992 sales. Also during this time, Intel began to branch out from chipmaking. In 1992, the company's Intel Products Group introduced network, communications, and personal conferencing products for retail sale directly to PC users.

In 1993 Intel released its fifth-generation Pentium processor, a trademarked chip capable of executing over 100 million instructions per second (MIPS) and supporting, for example, real-time video communication. The Pentium processor, with its 3.1 million transistors, was up to five times more powerful than the 33-megahertz Intel 486 DX microprocessor (and 1,500 times the speed of the 4004), but, in an unusual marketing maneuver, the company suggested that "all but the most demanding users" would seek out PCs powered by the previous chip. The Pentium's reputation was initially sullied by the revelation of an embedded mathematical flaw, but Intel moved quickly to fix the problem.

The company enjoyed a dramatic 50 percent revenue increase in 1993, reaching $8.78 billion from $5.84 billion in 1992. Moreover, Intel's net income leapt 115 percent to $2.3 billion, repudiating Wall Street's worries that competition had squeezed profit margins. While Intel faced strong competition both from chip makers such as giant Motorola, Inc.'s PowerPC and former partner IBM, its place at the leading edge of technology was undisputed.

A key initiative that kept Intel ahead of its competitors was the company's move beyond chip design into computer design. With the advent of the Pentium, Intel began designing chipsets and motherboards—the latter being the PC circuit board that combined a microprocessor and a chipset into the basic subsystem of a PC. With the company now selling the guts of a PC, dozens of computer manufacturers began making and selling Pentium-based machines.

In the mid-1990s, as sales of PCs accelerated and multimedia and the Internet were beginning to emerge, Intel continued developing ever more powerful microprocessors. In 1995 the Pentium Pro hit the market sporting 5.5 million transistors and capable of performing up to 300 MIPS. Intel next added MMX technology to its existing line of Pentium processors. MMX consisted of a new set of instructions that was designed specifically to improve the multimedia performance of personal computers. Fueled by exploding demand, revenues hit $20.85 billion by 1996, while net income soared to $5.16 billion.

At this point Intel was continuing its longtime strategy of designing new, more powerful chips for the top end of the market while allowing previous-generation microprocessors to migrate down to the lower segments of the market. With the introduction of the Pentium II in May 1997, however, the company adopted a new strategy of developing a range of microprocessors for every segment of the computing market. The Pentium II, with 7.5 transistors, debuted with a top-end model that clocked at 300 MHZ. Originally designed for high-end desktop PCs, the Pentium II was soon adapted for use in notebook and laptop computers. With the following year came the launch of the Celeron processor, which was designed specifically for the value PC desktop sector, a rapidly growing segment of the market ever since the early 1997 debut of a sub-$1,000 PC from Compaq. Also in 1998 Intel for the first time designed a microprocessor—the Pentium II Xeon—especially for midrange and higher-end servers and workstations. At the same time Intel was moving into another burgeoning sector, that of embedded control chips for networking and other applications, such as digital set-top boxes.

Meanwhile Intel settled a dispute with Digital Equipment Corporation (DEC) over the development of the Pentium chip by acquiring DEC's semiconductor operations. In May 1997 Craig R. Barrett was named president of Intel, having joined the company in 1974, serving as head of manufacturing starting in 1985, and being named chief operating officer in 1993. Grove remained chairman and CEO for one year, whereupon Barrett was named president and CEO, with Grove retaining the chairmanship. In early 1999 Intel reached a settlement with the Federal Trade Commission on an antitrust suit, thereby avoiding the protracted litigation and negative publicity that beset its Wintel partner, Microsoft, in the late 1990s. Reflecting the increasing importance of technology to the U.S. economy, Intel was added to the Dow Jones Industrial Average in November 1999.

During the late 1990s Intel made several strategic acquisitions that rapidly gave the company a significant presence in areas outside its microprocessor core: wireless communications products, such as flash memory for mobile phones and two-way pagers; networking building blocks, such as hubs, switches, and routers; and embedded control chips for laser printers, storage media, and automotive systems. Intel also entered the market for e-commerce services, rapidly building up the largest business-to-business e-commerce site in the world, with $1 billion per month in online sales by mid-1999. The company was not neglecting its core, however; in 1999 Intel had its largest microprocessor launch ever with the simultaneous introduction of 15 Pentium III and Pentium III Xeon processors. In early 2000 a one-gigahertz Pentium III chip hit the market. Later in 2000 came the debut of the next generation processor for the early 21st century, the Itanium, the company's first 64-bit processor, which was initially designed to meet the needs of powerful Internet servers. With its continuing development of ever more powerful processors and its aggressive expansion into other key technology areas, Intel appeared certain to remain one of the linchpins of the information economy in the new millennium.

Principal Subsidiaries

Componentes Intel de Costa Rica, S.A.; DSP Communications, Inc.; Dialogic Corporation; Intel Commodities Limited (Cayman); Intel Corporation (UK) Limited; Intel Electronics Limited (Israel); Intel International BV (Netherlands); Intel Ireland Limited (Cayman); Intel Kabushiki Kaisha (Japan); Intel Massachusetts, Inc.; Intel Overseas Corporation; Intel Products (M) Sdn. Bhd. (Malaysia); Intel Puerto Rico, Inc; Intel Semiconductor Limited; Intel Technology Phils, Inc. (Philippines); Intel Technology Sdn. Berhad (Malaysia); IPivot, Inc.; Level One Communications, Inc.; Mission College Investments Limited (Cayman).

Principal Operating Units

Intel Architecture Business Group; Wireless Communications and Computing Group; Communications Products Group; Network Communications Group; New Business Group.

Principal Competitors

Acer Inc.; Advanced Micro Devices, Inc.; Atmel Corporation; Cisco Systems, Inc.; Electronic Data Systems Corporation; Exodus Communications, Inc.; Fujitsu Limited; Harris Corporation; Hitachi, Ltd.; International Business Machines Corporation; Integrated Device Technology, Inc.; Lucent Technologies Inc.; Macronix International Co., Ltd.; Microchip Technology Incorporated; Mitsubishi Electric Industrial Co., Ltd.; Motorola, Inc.; National Semiconductor Corporation; NEC Corporation; Nortel Networks Corporation; Koninklijke Philips Electronics N.V.; Samsung Electronics Co., Ltd.; Sharp Corporation; STMicroelectronics N.V.; Sun Microsystems, Inc.; Texas Instruments Incorporated; 3Com Corporation; Toshiba Corporation; Transmeta Corporation; VIA Technologies, Inc.

Further Reading

Brandt, Richard, Otis Port, and Robert D. Hof, ''Intel: The Next Revolution,'' *Business Week,* September 26, 1988, p. 74.

Bylinsky, Gene, ''Intel's Biggest Shrinking Job Yet,'' *Fortune,* May 3, 1982, pp. 250+.

Clark, Tim, ''Inside Intel's Marketing Machine,'' *Business Marketing,* October 1992, pp. 14–19.

Corcoran, Elizabeth, "Reinventing Intel," *Forbes,* May 3, 1999, pp. 154–59.

Defining Intel: 25 Years/25 Events, Santa Clara: Intel Corporation, 1993.

Garland, Susan B., and Andy Reinhardt, "Making Antitrust Fit High Tech," *Business Week,* March 22, 1999, p. 34.

Gottlieb, Carrie, "Intel's Plan for Staying on Top," *Fortune,* March 27, 1989, pp. 98 +.

Hof, Robert D., Larry Armstrong, and Gary McWilliams, "Intel Unbound," *Business Week,* October 9, 1995, pp. 148 +.

"Is the Semiconductor Boom Too Much of a Good Thing for Intel?," *Business Week,* April 23, 1984, pp. 114 +.

Jackson, Tim, *Inside Intel: Andy Grove and the Rise of the World's Most Powerful Chip Company,* New York: Dutton, 1997, 424 p.

Kirkpatrick, David, "Intel Goes for Broke," *Fortune,* May 16, 1994, pp. 62–66, 68.

——, "Intel's Amazing Profit Machine," *Fortune,* February 17, 1997, pp. 60 +.

——, "Mr. Grove Goes to China," *Fortune,* August 17, 1998, pp. 154–61.

Palmer, Jay, "Zero Hour," *Barron's* October 4, 1999, pp. 33–34, 36.

A Revolution in Progress: A History of Intel to Date, Santa Clara, Calif.: Intel Corporation, 1984.

Reinhardt, Andy, "The New Intel: Craig Barrett Is Leading the Chip Giant into Riskier Terrain," *Business Week,* March 13, 2000, pp. 110 +.

——, "Who Says Intel's Chips Are Down?," *Business Week,* December 7, 1998, p. 103.

Reinhardt, Andy, Ira Sager, and Peter Burrows, "Intel: Can Andy Grove Keep Profits Up in an Era of Cheap PCs?," *Business Week,* December 22, 1997, pp. 71–74, 76–77.

Ristelhueber, Robert, "Intel: The Company People Love to Hate," *Electronic Business Buyer,* September 1993, pp. 58–67.

Wilson, John W., "Intel Wakes Up to a Whole New Marketplace in Chips," *Business Week,* September 2, 1985, pp. 73 +.

Yu, Albert, *Creating the Digital Future: The Secrets of Consistent Innovation at Intel,* New York: Free Press, 1998, 214 p.

—April Dougal Gasbarre
—updated by David E. Salamie

Isetan Company Limited

3-14-1, Shinjuku
Shinjuku-ku
Tokyo 160-8011
Japan
Telephone: (03) 3352-1111
Fax: (03) 5273-5321
Web site: http://www.isetan.co.jp

Public Company
Incorporated: 1930
Employees: 5,115
Sales: ¥578.44 billion (US$5.39 billion) (1999)
Stock Exchanges: Tokyo Niigata
NAIC: 452110 Department Stores

Isetan Company Limited is one of Japan's leading department store companies, particularly noted for its merchandising strength in the area of high-fashion apparel for women in their 20s and 30s. It has compensated for its comparatively late entry into the field by innovation and niche-building, establishing itself as a fashion leader through sophisticated consumer research and extensive introduction of merchandise from abroad, both well-known designer labels and brands developed exclusively for Isetan. The company operates seven department stores in Tokyo as well as two other stores in Shizuoka and Niigata. Isetan is also active outside of Japan, having established overseas presences in China, Malaysia, Singapore, Thailand, Europe, and the United States.

Kimono Shop Origins

In common with other top Japanese department stores, Isetan traces its origins back to a kimono shop. Whereas Mitsukoshi, Daimaru, and Takashimaya have histories going back hundreds of years, Isetan's story begins in 1886, with the opening of the Iseya Tanji Drapery in Tokyo's Kanda district, then a bustling center of commerce located near the Kanda river. Its founder, Tanji Kosuge, was born Tanji Nowatari in 1859. At the age of 12 he was apprenticed to the Isesho Drapery in Kanda. By the age of 20 Tanji had risen to the position of *banto,* or head clerk. In 1881

he married Hanako Kosuge, the daughter of one of Isesho's best customers, a local rice merchant, and took the surname Kosuge. Five years later, with the blessing of his employer, Tanji Kosuge went into business for himself.

Kanda was one of the most densely populated areas of the city, and the new shop's location near a busy intersection guaranteed it a steady stream of business. Because of the shop's proximity to several well-known geisha districts, Kosuge's customers included many geisha who needed to maintain a well-stocked wardrobe of fine kimonos. He created his own range of original products, and the Iseya Tanji Drapery came to be associated with exquisite obi—the belt used to tie the kimono—and quality design.

Tanji Kosuge began expanding the business in various ways. He experimented with staying open at night, he sent out salesmen with samples of the stores' original designs to visit the homes of customers, he introduced seasonal bargain sales, he began buying out other kimono stores, and in 1899, as business prospered, he enlarged the Kanda store. So successful had he been that by the turn of the century, the Iseya Tanji Drapery had entered the ranks of Tokyo's top five dry goods stores.

Nevertheless, there was still a big gap between Kosuge's store and those of its long-established rivals. While the older stores were already thinking of moving to a department store format, complete with display cabinets for their products and a wider variety of merchandise, Kosuge was still concentrating on building up the kimono business.

In an effort to bring the store's image more in line with those of its rivals, in 1907 he simplified the store's name to Isetan Drapery, combining the first two syllables of Iseya with the first syllable of Tanji. Three years later he considered building a department store in Tokyo's Hibiya district but shelved the idea as premature. At his death in 1916, Isetan was well-established as a kimono store, but had yet to make the switch to a department store.

Kosuge was succeeded by his son-in-law, Gihei Takahashi. Takahashi had married Tanji Kosuge's eldest daughter in 1908, taking the family name of Kosuge. Upon his father-in-law's death, he took the name Tanji as well.

Key Dates:

1886: Tanji Kosuge opens a kimono shop called Iseya Tanji Drapery in Tokyo's Kanda district.
1907: The shop's name is changed to Isetan Drapery.
1916: Kosuge dies and is succeeded by his son-in-law, who is known as Tanji Kosuge II.
1923: The Great Kanto Earthquake destroys the Isetan store.
1924: Isetan reopens as a department store.
1930: Firm is incorporated as a limited company, Isetan Company Limited.
1933: Company opens new flagship department store in Tokyo's Shinjuku district. The Kanda store closes.
1945: Allied occupation authorities requisition much of the Isetan store for Allied use.
1952: With the end of the occupation, Isetan regains full control of its building.
1956: Postwar expansion begins with the opening of three new stores.
1961: Company goes public.
1968: First overseas representative office opens in Paris.
1972: First overseas store opens in Singapore.
1988: First European store opens in London.
1989: Company enters into a joint venture with New York-based Barney's, Inc.
1990: Barney's joint venture opens first Barney's store in Japan, in Tokyo.
1992: Sales decline for the first time in company history.
1996: Barney's files for Chapter 11 bankruptcy protection; Isetan and Barney's sue each other.
1999: Barney's emerges from Chapter 11—Isetan holds seven percent stake and control of several stores in Japan and the United States.

Takahashi had been working for another kimono store when he first came to the attention of Isetan in 1908. One day he bought 20 obi for his store at a ten percent discount from an Isetan salesman, who assured him that the obi were not being sold at the Isetan store. Walking past Isetan some days later, he discovered that the same obi were being sold, and for a 20 percent discount. Going in to complain, he handled himself so well that he got a further discount. He impressed the man he dealt with—Tanji Kosuge's younger brother—as both a good businessman and a potential husband for Tanji's eldest daughter. Takahashi joined Isetan shortly afterward and was married within six months.

A man who read widely, Takahashi had many ideas about retailing. As Tanji Kosuge II, he began to lay the groundwork for Isetan's transformation from a kimono shop to a department store. His first move was to place Isetan on a more businesslike footing by creating the Isetan Partnership to run the store in 1917. It was, however, a catastrophic event six years later that would really move Isetan's plans forward.

Shifting to Department Store Format: 1920s–30s

The Great Kanto Earthquake of September 1, 1923, killed some 130,000 people. The Kanda store burned to the ground, along with much of the rest of Kanda. The necessity of rebuilding the Kanda store provided Kosuge with the opportunity to introduce a department store format. When Isetan reopened in 1924 it was selling not only kimonos but also children's clothes, toys, umbrellas, cosmetics, stationery, household goods, and food. If the store had changed, so had Kanda, and it gradually became apparent that Kanda was no longer the prime site it once had been.

There were three reasons for this. First, within Kanda, the devastation caused by the earthquake and subsequent conflagration resulted in a changed street configuration, and Isetan no longer was situated near the corner of a busy intersection. Second, transportation was improving steadily, making the public more mobile. As the subway system was extended, Ginza and Nihonbashi, where Tokyo's leading department stores were located, became more accessible. With the completion of the Yamanote Line, a surface railway that circled Tokyo, new shopping and recreational areas grew up around stations such as Shibuya, Shinjuku, and Ikebukuro. Third, and in many ways most far-reaching, as a result of the Great Kanto Earthquake the center of the population moved away from the devastated areas in central and eastern Tokyo to the suburbs in the west.

By 1928 it was clear that there was no future for Isetan in Kanda. It abandoned a project to build a new eight-story department store there, although four stories of the building had been completed, and began looking for an alternative site. Hibiya, in downtown Tokyo, was considered once more, but after Tanji Kosuge had spent three days looking at the proposed site, he decided that there would not be enough customers and continued the search elsewhere. His eventual choice was Shinjuku, in the west of Tokyo, an area that had begun to develop after the opening of Shinjuku Station in 1875, but which had really taken off after the Great Kanto Earthquake. It was a decision that was to be as important for Shinjuku as it was for Isetan, and the two have grown in tandem ever since.

In 1930, in preparation for its move into the department store business proper, Isetan formed itself into a limited company, Isetan Company Limited, capitalized at ¥500,000. In 1931 it purchased the land on which its new flagship store would stand, adjacent to an existing department store called Hoteiya. Work began on the Isetan building in 1932, and the main building was completed in 1933. It consisted of two floors below ground and seven above, including an auditorium. On its first day of business, it attracted 130,000 customers. Three months later, the old store in Kanda closed.

In 1935 Isetan bought the ailing Hoteiya department store for ¥2 million. This included the building, the land it stood on, and the entire contents of the store. It borrowed ¥3.3 million from the Bank of Japan to pay for the purchase and redevelopment of the store as part of Isetan. A year later, this new addition to Isetan was open for business.

Shinjuku was by then established as one of Tokyo's new city subcenters. It was frequented by middle-class salaried workers and their families, attracted to its shops, cafes, and cinemas. As a new, up-and-coming department store, Isetan blended in perfectly. A play on a popular catch phrase of the day captures the mood of those times. "Today the Imperial Theatre, tomorrow

Mitsukoshi'' went the original, linking together these bastions of tradition in the heart of downtown Tokyo. "Today the Moulin Rouge [a new Shinjuku theater that opened in 1931], tomorrow Isetan," went the other, clearly identifying Isetan as something of a trendsetter, appealing to those who preferred black comedy to traditional Kabuki.

Surviving World War II and the Allied Occupation

During World War II, Isetan remained open for business almost until the end of the war, although its displays grew barer and its sales area gradually shrank to 50 percent of prewar levels. Escalators and elevators were removed and melted down for the war effort in 1943. That year, Isetan was asked by the Imperial Japanese Army to manage a hotel and store taken over by the Japanese in Sumatra, which it did until the end of the war. The Allied fire bomb raids on the night of March 10, 1945, devastated large areas of Tokyo, reducing the old Kanda store to ashes, but Isetan's flagship store remained standing. Quick action that night on the part of employees put out a fire that threatened to rage out of control; neighboring buildings, however, were not so lucky.

According to one of his sons, Tanji Kosuge shrugged off the despondent comments of his employees on August 15, 1945, the day the Japanese emperor announced Japan's surrender. "What are you saying? The store's still standing, isn't it? You've got nothing to worry about. I'm going back to work tomorrow." Kosuge's wish for a quick return to business as usual was not fulfilled for several years, however. Apart from the problem of the lack of merchandise, the Allied occupation authorities had taken a liking to the building, and in 1945 requisitioned it for Allied use from the third floor up. Not until the end of the occupation, in 1952, would Isetan have the building to itself again.

The department store business after World War II saw a much greater emphasis on Western-style clothing. In the years immediately following the war, women made do with what they had—blouses and Japanese-style pantaloons called *monpei*—but from the late 1940s there was a growing fashion-consciousness, initially inspired by the "military look" sported by women in the Allied occupation forces. In 1951 Isetan sponsored Tokyo's first postwar fashion show—Tokyo Fashion 51—which presaged a boom in fashion shows, modeling, and modeling schools.

Launching a Postwar Expansion

In 1956 Isetan underwent its first major postwar extension. Three new buildings were added, increasing the sales area by 25 percent. The purpose was not simply to increase Isetan's size; it was to reaffirm Isetan's image as a fashion leader. From this period Isetan introduced modern merchandising techniques, dividing up customers very specifically on the basis of age, sex, taste, and spending power. The new-look Isetan—it also changed its logo—celebrated the completion of its refurbishment with a grand opening in October 1957.

In 1960 Tanji Kosuge II stepped down as president and was succeeded by his eldest son, Toshio, who took the name Tanji upon his father's death two years later. The new president

was a graduate of Keio University who had joined Mitsui Trading Company in 1941, before being drafted into the Imperial Japanese Army in 1942. After the war he had spent three years at Showa Textile Company before joining Isetan as a director in 1948.

Under Tanji Kosuge III, Isetan maintained its reputation for innovation during the 1960s. Anticipating the growth in private car ownership, it opened a parking garage adjacent to the store in 1960, becoming the first Japanese department store to have its own car park. In 1963 it introduced designer brands to the store with a Pierre Balmain haute couture salon, and in 1964 took the initiative in rationalizing women's clothing sizes, developing a system that has since been utilized by all Japanese department stores. In 1968 it opened a new annex devoted entirely to menswear. Many were opposed to the move, but Kosuge believed that by removing all men's clothes from the main building he could both create space for more women's and children's clothing and target the different categories of male shoppers more effectively in a building designed for that purpose. "Bring him along, too," said the publicity as Isetan sought to reach out to male shoppers through wives, girlfriends, sisters, and daughters who already shopped regularly at Isetan. Meantime, Isetan had become a publicly traded company in 1961.

By the late 1960s Isetan had established itself as the number one fashion merchandiser in Japan and recorded Japan's highest sales per month for a single store. In a move to strengthen its fashion merchandising capability further, in 1967 it established the Isetan Research Institute Company, Ltd., a think tank for collecting and analyzing information about the latest fashion, industrial, and consumer trends. The institute was an important source of ideas for Isetan's new product development. A year later, it opened its first overseas representative office, in Paris, which, along with other offices opened subsequently, also acted as a source of information on fashion trends.

Expanding Overseas and Diversifying: 1970s–80s

From the 1970s Isetan began a period of expansion, opening new stores both at home and overseas. Isetan's first overseas store opened in Singapore in 1972, followed by a store in Hong Kong a year later. The increase in stores continued in the 1980s, accompanied by the growing diversification of Isetan's business activities in the areas of fashion, food, leisure, and finance.

Subsidiaries set up in these areas in the 1980s included J.F. Corporation, which supplied Isetan with originally developed brands and also created brands for specialty stores around the country; Prio Company, Ltd., an importer-wholesaler of quality women's wear; Queen's Isetan Co., Ltd., a gourmet foods store; Isetan Travel Service Company, Ltd., which arranged package tours to domestic and overseas destinations; and Isetan Finance Company, Ltd., which was responsible for a wide range of nonbanking financial operations including the credit management of Isetan's charge card, the I-Card, the use of which was extended in 1988 to all shoppers at Isetan, as well as cashing, leasing, and loan services.

Isetan also ran a chain of supermarkets through Queen's Isetan Co., Ltd.; operated a nationwide restaurant chain of approximately 100 outlets through Isetan Petit Monde Company,

Ltd., started in 1957; and imported and sold cars through Isetan Motors Company, Ltd., started in 1970.

Under Kuniyasu Kosuge, who succeeded his father, Tanji Kosuge III, in 1984, the company continued to grow. A graduate of Keio University who subsequently studied in the United States, Kosuge worked for Mitsubishi Bank for seven years, including a stint in London, before joining Isetan as a director in 1979. His overseas experience was useful as he presided over a growing international network of companies.

In Europe, Isetan operated stores in London, established in 1988, and Vienna, opened in 1990, which together with the company's representative offices in Paris, Milan, and Barcelona strengthened their business capabilities, including the procurement of merchandise through licensing agreements, product development projects, and information gathering. In 1988 Isetan established an international finance company in Amsterdam to support its overseas business activities. It opened a store in Barcelona in October 1991.

Active in the United States since the opening of a representative office in New York in 1979, Isetan moved into the U.S. market with more purpose when it entered into a joint venture with New York-based Barney's, Inc., an upscale retailer of clothing and sundry goods, in 1989. Isetan looked to strengthen its merchandising and increase its expertise in specialty-store management through the joint venture, while helping Barney's to open new stores across the United States. The tie-up also resulted in the opening of a branch of Barney's in Tokyo in November 1990. The Shinjuku store became the largest joint venture between a Japanese and a U.S. retailer, and Isetan had plans to open Barney's outlets in other Japanese cities.

Struggling Through the 1990s

In the mid-1990s Isetan suffered from the aftermath of the rapid decline of the Japanese economy and the souring of the Barney's joint venture. When the Japanese economic bubble burst in 1991, the economy was thrown into a lengthy downturn featuring a precipitous drop in consumer spending. In 1992 overall department store sales fell 3.3 percent, the first such decline in 27 years. Isetan's sales began to decline as well—they fell for the first time in company history in 1992—and at a particularly inopportune time, given the company's far-ranging expansion in the heady days of the late 1980s that left it with a mountain of debt. In the depressed climate of the mid-1990s, Isetan also faced increased competition from the burgeoning ranks of discount stores such as Ito-Yokado Co., Ltd. In fact, Isetan in 1993 was threatened with a takeover by Ito-Yokado after Isetan's largest shareholder, Shuwa Corporation, a financially troubled real estate firm, sought to unload its 29 percent stake. But Mitsubishi Bank, Isetan's main bank, intervened, forcing Kuniyasu Kosuge to step down as president in favor of 30-plus-year company veteran Kazumasa Koshiba, and arranging the sale of the Shuwa shares to 41 of Isetan's major existing shareholders and business partners. The pushing of Kosuge into the honorary chairman's seat marked the end of the Kosuge family's reign over Isetan. Meanwhile, the culminating moves of Kuniyasu Kosuge's overseas expansion also came in 1993 when new stores opened in Bangkok, Thailand—Isetan's largest unit in southeast Asia—and in Shanghai, China.

The company's new president put a halt to any more store building and concentrated on improving profits. He closed underperforming affiliates, including the company's stores in Hong Kong, a fitness club in Tokyo, and Isetan Motors. In the short term, however, Isetan was haunted by the overexpansion of the 1980s. The Amsterdam-based finance company formed in 1988 suffered large losses from secret derivatives trading during the 1994 fiscal year, leading Isetan to post an extraordinary loss of ¥9.7 billion (US$89 million). The relationship with Barney's turned south in 1994 when the U.S. retailer requested more money from Isetan to fund its newly expanded operations but Koshiba refused to do so, his company having already poured more than US$600 million into the joint venture. This led Barney's, unable to make the rent payments on its stores, to file for Chapter 11 bankruptcy protection in early 1996. For the fiscal year ending in March 1996 Isetan posted its first net loss since 1961 as a result of the writing off of billions of yen in loans to Barney's. Legal action ensued as well, with both sides suing each other over the original terms of their joint venture agreement. Kuniyasu Kosuge, the architect of the Barney's venture, voluntarily resigned from the Isetan board in mid-1996, leaving a 0.43 percent stake as the only connection between the founding family and the company.

The dispute with Barney's was not resolved until early 1999 when the company emerged from bankruptcy under a reorganization plan in which the company's creditors received more than 90 percent of the equity. Isetan came away with a stake of about seven percent as well as various concessions that settled the lawsuits. Isetan gained ownership of Barney's stores in New York, Chicago, and Beverly Hills, California, the exclusive right to license the Barney's name in Japan, and a 30 percent stake in a joint venture with Barney's to license the name elsewhere in Asia. Isetan also continued to operate two Barney's units in Japan, located in Tokyo and Yokohama.

With the resolution of the Barney's debacle settled on terms that seemed to favor Isetan, the Japanese retailer was finally in a position to concentrate fully on turning its fortunes around. Isetan, however, continued to face the extremely difficult Japanese retail environment at the dawn of the new millennium, a time in which some prominent Japanese retailers were themselves declaring bankruptcy.

Principal Subsidiaries

Barneys Japan Co. Ltd.; Century Trading Co. Ltd.; Cerruti Japan Corporation; Isetan Clean System Co. Ltd.; Isetan Data Center Co. Ltd.; Isetan Finance Co. Ltd.; Isetan Petit Monde Co. Ltd.; Mamina Co. Ltd.; Musashino Kaihatsu Kanri K.K.; Niigata Isetan Co. Ltd.; Queen's Isetan Co. Ltd.; Shizuoka Isetan K.K.; Isetan (Singapore) Limited; Isetan (U K) Ltd.; Isetan Co. Ltd. (U.K.); Isetan Department Store & Co. (U.K.); Isetan Italia S.p.A. (Italy); Isetan of Japan Ltd. (Hong Kong); Isetan of Japan Sdn. Bhd. (Malaysia); Isetan S.p.A. (Italy).

Principal Competitors

The Daimaru, Inc.; Mitsukoshi, Ltd.; Mycal Corporation; Seibu Department Stores, Ltd.; The Seiyu, Ltd.; Takashimaya Company, Limited; Tokyu Department Store Co., Ltd.

Further Reading

Agins, Teri, "Barney's Style Gets Translated into Japanese," *Wall Street Journal,* May 29, 1990, p. B1.

Agins, Teri, Laura Bird, and Laura Jereski, "Overdoing It: A Thirst for Glitter and a Pliant Partner Got Barney's in a Bind," *Wall Street Journal,* January 19, 1996, pp. A1+.

Bird, Laura, and Laura Jereski, "Isetan Contends Barney's Withheld Data," *Wall Street Journal,* January 18, 1996, p. A10.

Bird, Laura, and Teri Agins, "Bruised Barney's Seeks Shelter from Creditors," *Wall Street Journal,* January 12, 1996, p. B1.

Isetan hyakunenshi, Tokyo: Isetan, 1990.

"Japanese Retailing: The Recovery Department," *Economist,* December 2, 1995, p. 64.

Katayama, Mataichiro, *Isetan 100 nen no shoho,* Tokyo: Hyogensha, 1983.

Kong, Wong Wei, "Isetan's Rebound Damped by Singapore Sales Slump," *Asian Wall Street Journal,* February 14, 1997, p. 13.

Ono, Yumiko, "Japanese Department Stores Fall from 1980s Heyday," *Wall Street Journal,* February 9, 1993, p. B4.

——, "Japanese Stores May Be Hiding Some Bargains: Shares May Offer Value As Department Chains Start to Restructure," *Asian Wall Street Journal,* March 30, 2000, p. 15.

"Reorganization Plan for Barney's Is Cleared by Bankruptcy Judge," *Wall Street Journal,* December 22, 1998, p. B7.

Shirouzu, Norihiko, "Cooperation Sparks Interest in Two Retailers," *Asian Wall Street Journal,* February 7, 1996, p. 15.

——, "Isetan Doesn't Want to Divorce Barney's," *Wall Street Journal,* January 22, 1996, p. A9.

Terazono, Emiko, "Isetan Hangs On to Heritage by Thread," *Financial Times,* June 20, 1996, p. 27.

Yatsko, Pamela, "Wanted: Shoppers: Shanghai's Retail Glut Cramps Japanese Store," *Far Eastern Economic Review,* December 4, 1997, pp. 85–86.

—Jonathan Lloyd-Owen
—updated by David E. Salamie

ITM Entreprises SA

24 rue Auguste Chadrieres
65737 Paris Cedex 5
France
Telephone: (+33) 1 45 33 74 17
Fax: (+33) 1 45 33 39 13
Web site: http://www.itmentreprises.fr

Wholly Owned Subsidiary of Société Civil des Mousquetaires
Incorporated: 1969
Employees: 80,000
Sales: FFr 248 billion (US$41.3 billion) (1999)
NAIC: 445110 Supermarkets and Other Grocery (Except Convenience) Stores

ITM Entreprises SA is France's largest supermarket group, with more than 2,700 stores under some 11 formats throughout the country. The company, led by its "Groupement des Mousquetaires" (Musketeers group) through the Société Civil des Mousquetaires, is also one of Europe's largest retailers, with more than 200 additional stores in Spain, Belgium, Germany, Portugal, Italy, and Poland. ITM Entreprises also holds 51 percent of Intercontessa, the 75 percent holder of Germany's SPAR supermarket chain, adding another 2,000 stores to the group's operations. Not including SPAR, the company's operations generate roughly FFr 250 billion in revenues each year. ITM Entreprises and Groupement des Mousquetaires represent Europe's largest consortium of independent merchants. Each of the company's retail stores are owned by more than 2,400 managers, who benefit from the group's buying power and highly developed distribution network, while "donating" some one-third of their time to performing administrative tasks for the group. The company's flagship Intermarché supermarket format, launched in 1969, has been joined by a variety of other formats, including the do-it-yourself (DIY) concepts Bricomarché and Logimarché; the restaurant group Restaumarché; automotive parts and service network Stationmarché; the ultradiscount chain CDM; clothing merchants Vetimarché; and two formats targeting especially France's rural consumers, Ecomarché and the Relais des Mousquetaires, the latter located exclusively in isolated villages with no other local source of retail food services. A private cooperative, ITM Entreprises is led by Pierre Gourgeon, hand-picked successor to founder Jean-Pierre Le Roch.

Founding a Supermarket Giant in the 1960s

Intermarché, the Société Civil des Mousquetaires, and ITM Entreprises were founded by Breton Jean-Pierre Le Roch in 1969. Le Roch had formerly owned and operated a supermarket as part of the E. Leclerc supermarket cooperative. A scission between Le Roch, together with some 95 other Leclerc supermarket owner-operators, and the rest of the Leclerc group led Le Roch to quit that group and found his own supermarket empire. Initially known as the "Ex-Entreprise," the new company quickly adopted a new name—Intermarché—and a new group identity, borrowed from the Three Musketeers.

In less than 30 years, the company counted more than 2,400 Musketeers. Le Roch set out to build a company with a difference. The Intermarché chain was to be an independent grouping of owner-operators. Each store owner agreed to make all of his stores purchases through the Intermarché chain, which also directed the group's signage, store format, advertising, and other administrative details. At the same time, the store owners—who remained solely responsible for their own businesses, including incurring all financial risk—agreed to "donate" one-third of their professional time to performing administrative duties for the entire group. In this way, Le Roch hoped to form what the company called a "Society of Trust," building a group identity among businesspeople who retained a spirit of independence.

The purchasing power of the new company quickly enabled Intermarché to make a mark on the French consumer. The Intermarché format featured mid-sized stores of some 1,600 square meters, devoted primarily to grocery items. Despite the rising success of the newer "hypermarket" format promoted by E. Leclerc, Carrefour, and others, which added a department store concept to the traditional grocery store, the smaller Intermarché gained a strong share of the French consumer market.

The success of the Intermarché concept led the group to develop other retail store formats based on the same "Society of Trust" concept. In 1979, ITM Entreprises debuted the first of its new formats, Bricomarché. This new format added hardware supplies for the growing French DIY market. Bricomarché became one of the generators for the growth of the DIY market in France—which grew from less than one quarter of the population at the beginning of the 1970s to more than 70 percent by the late 1990s, including some 40 percent of the female population. Like the Intermarché chain, Bricomarché went on to dominate the French DIY scene, building up a network of more than 430 retail stores in France by the end of the century, becoming the largest network of independent DIY store operators.

By sharing the Musketeers logo, as well as an extensive logistics network, which grew to include a fleet of more than 1,800 semi-trailers, as well as a company-owned fleet of fishing vessels, Intermarché and Bricomarché enabled their growing networks of owner-operators to offer competitive prices to counter the rising market shares of the hypermarket groups. ITM Entreprises also continued to expand the "-marché" concept, adding the first Restaumarché in 1980. As opposed to the growing numbers of cafeterias attached to the hypermarkets, the Restaumarché concept offered a traditional restaurant ambiance, complete with table service, while also emphasizing speed of service. At the same time, the restaurants' food purchases, made through ITM Entreprises' distribution and logistics networks, enabled each Restaumarché to offer menus at prices significantly lower than other traditional restaurants.

Two years later saw the opening of another store format, Stationmarché, devoted to the market for automotive services. Offering a selection of parts and accessories, the Stationmarché concept also offered a wide range of repairs and services, including car inspections. The Stationmarché concept grew to more than 150 centers through the 1990s, and continued to represent one of ITM Entreprises' fastest-growing markets. The diversification of the company had already led ITM Entreprises to begin grouping its different formats in close proximity to each other, encouraging consumers to remain within the Musketeers Group for most of their purchases. In 1979, the company launched the "Marché des Mousquetaires" concept, in which a minimum of two separate and distinct stores—of which one was an Intermarché—shared a common terrain. The Marché concept was expanded to include each of the company's new formats in turn, building up a network of more than 400 Marchés by the end of the 1990s.

French Retail Leader in the 1990s

The continued growth of the Intermarché network helped boost ITM Entreprises to the leading ranks of French retailers. In 1986, the company added to its diversified operations with the launch of two new store formats: Vetimarché and Ecomarché. The Vetimarché store format was devoted to clothing, yet benefited by being located next to existing Intermarchés. Ecomarché was a supermarket format developed specifically for the rural consumer market, with stores of just 400 square meters receiving daily deliveries from the ITM Entreprises distribution network, while maintaining the same prices as the larger Intermarché stores.

In 1988, ITM Entreprises launched another store format, Procomarché, a cash and carry concept designed to compete with the rising tide of convenience store sales in France. This new format, however, proved a rare failure for the group, as the company found itself unable to compete with such market heavyweights as Metro. The Procomarché concept was abandoned in 2000. More successful for the group was its first moves onto the international market, with the opening of its first Spanish Intermarché in 1988.

At the beginning of the 1990s, ITM Entreprises responded to another growing retail threat—the downturn in the French and European economies had led to the creation and rapid success of a new form of retail store, the deep discounter. As French consumers rushed to this new breed of retailer, including Aldi, Lidl, Norma, and Leader Price, traditional supermarkets and hypermarkets quickly saw their sales decline. ITM Entreprises' response was to create its own chain of deep discount stores, CDM, acronym for "Comment Depenser Moins" (How to Spend Less). ITM Entreprises deep discount formula included a relatively large range of product categories, but with limited depth, with most products represented by a single ultra-low-priced brand. The CDM format gained quick acceptance from the French consumer, boosting its numbers to more than 200 stores by the end of the decade.

The CDM launch was accompanied by further international growth, as ITM Entreprises moved into the Belgian and Portuguese markets in 1991. The latter country proved particularly receptive to the Musketeer concept, becoming the company's most important foreign market by mid-decade. The group's Belgian, Spanish, and Portuguese members were joined by another European market, Italy, in 1993.

Back in France, ITM Entreprises continued to seek out new retail niches. In 1991, the company launched a new format, the Relais des Mousquetaires. The success of the hypermarché and the growth of large-scale retail parks had forced many small merchants—especially merchants serving France's smallest villages—out of business. By the beginning of the 1990s, it was not uncommon for many of these villages, with populations as little as 500 people, to have lost all of their local retailers. The

Relais format was launched to fill this gap—the tiny Relais stores were joined to the distribution and logistics networks serving the closest Intermarché and Ecomarché stores, thereby allowing the Relais owner-operators to offer their local customers competitive prices. The Relais formula proved so successful that the company counted nearly 700 by the beginning of the new century.

Laws governing the retail market in France—regulations designed to protect the country's smaller merchants against their more powerful competitors—made the opening of new supermarkets in the country more and more difficult. The tightening conditions forced Intermarché, which by the mid-1990s had gained a firm lead as the country's dominant supermarket group, to look toward boosting its international operations. As such the company strengthened its operations in Portugal through the opening of a distribution base in Alcanena. This new center served to support as well the launch of the Ecomarché concept in Portugal. Another foreign distribution and logistics base was opened in Villers Le Bouillet, in order to support the company's growing Belgian operations. The company's also opened a distribution center in Poznan to support its entry into the Polish market.

Support for the euro currency, and tightening building restrictions in many of the European Union's markets saw the beginnings of a wave of consolidations among European supermarket and department store groups. The impending entry of U.S. retailing giant Wal-Mart into the European market added further impetus to the round of mergers and acquisitions sweeping through the industry. ITM Entreprises reacted by joining the bandwagon—in 1996 the company bought 51 percent of Intercontessa, a holding company based in Switzerland set up by ITM Entreprises and its partners in order to acquire a 75 percent stake in Germany's giant SPAR Handels AG. The purchase of SPAR, which boosted the company to the number two position in Germany, gave ITM boardroom control of SPAR's more than 525 supermarkets, 3,250 small groceries, and 775 deep discount stores, and added SPAR's FFr 75 billion in annual revenues.

ITM Entreprises next began to eye the vast North American market. In 1997, the company acquired a 17 percent share in Quebec's Rona Inc. and its chain of DIY stores. Meanwhile, the company continued to eye expansion in Europe, exporting the Bricomarché format for the first time, with the first store opening in Belgium. At the same time, the company opened the first of its Intermarché stores in Poland. That market proved a welcoming one for the company, and by the end of the decade more than 28 Intermarchés had opened across Poland.

Jean-Pierre Le Roch retired at the age of 65, picking Pierre Gourgeon as his successor. Gourgeon himself came from the ranks of the company's Musketeers, retaining ownership of his own two Intermarché stores while taking over the leadership of the group. In 1998, the company celebrated the opening of its 400th Bricomarché, while the group of Intermarché stores neared 1,650. The company also launched its first new store format in nearly a decade, that of Logimarché. A small-store format of just 449 square meters, the Logimarché combined DIY goods with gardening supplies, targeting specifically the rural and semi-rural markets.

By 1999, ITM Entreprises presided over France's dominant retail group, with sales exceeding FFr 240 billion, which also earned it a position as one of the world's largest privately owned companies. That year, however, saw the emergence of a new French retailing powerhouse, when the Carrefour group acquired Promodes, challenging ITM Entreprises in most of its market segments. Yet the Intermarché format was viewed as aging by the French consumer, and the company found itself hard-pressed to retain its more than 15 percent market share in its home market.

In response, the company set to work rejuvenating its image, and especially subjecting the Intermarché store format to a thorough revision. The new Intermarché store, unveiled in 1999, placed a larger emphasis on fresh food items. The company expected to roll out the new store concept to the majority of the Intermarché group with the start of the new century. At the same time, ITM Entreprises stepped up its foreign expansion, seeking to establish itself as one of Europe's major retail groups, including entry into the new market of Sarajevo, in former Yugoslavia, where the company launched the new cash-and-carry format InterEx. Meanwhile, the company's SPAR acquisition seemed to turn sour, as that group posted its first-ever losses in 1999.

Despite the failure of the Procomarché format, which was abandoned in mid-2000, ITM Entreprises entered the new century celebrating more than 30 years of retail success. As the company forecast its interest in entering the U.S. market, it also remained committed to maintaining its status as one of the world's leading independent retailing groups. Yet ITM Entreprises also suggested it would be interested in a future merger with another large French group—with potential partners including the E. Leclerc hypermarket chain.

Principal Subsidiaries

Intercontessa AG (Germany; 51%); Spar Handel AG (Germany; 75%).

Principal Competitors

Auchan; Carrefour SA; Casino Guichard; Castorama; Delhaize; E. Leclerc; Guyenne et Gascogne; Koninklijke Ahold N.V.; Lidl & Schwarz Stiftung; METRO AG; Pinault-Printemps-Redoute SA.

Further Reading

Boileau, Nicolas, "Interview: Pierre Bourgeon, président du Groupe Intermarché," *Nouvel Ouest*, December 26, 1999, p. 64.

Gay, Pierre-Angel, "Pour ses trente ans, Intermarché se voit rattrapé par la concurrence," *Les Echos*, September 21, 1999, p. 22.

Legrand, Constance, "Intermarché se singularise pour refraichir une image jugée vieillotte," *Les Echos*, April 11, 1999, p. 66.

——, "French-Led Group Buys Germany's SPAR Retail Chain," *European Report*, January 5, 1996.

Secher, Raynal, *De l'exil aux mousquetaires*, Paris: ERS, 1996.

—M. L. Cohen

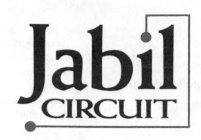

Jabil Circuit, Inc.

10560 Ninth Street North
St. Petersburg, Florida 33716
U.S.A.
Telephone: (727) 577-9749
Fax: (727) 579-8529
Web site: http://www.jabil.com

Public Company
Incorporated: 1966
Employees: 18,000
Sales: $2.0 billion (1999)
Stock Exchanges: New York
Ticker Symbol: JBL
NAIC: 334210 Telephone Apparatus Manufacturing;
    334418 Printed Circuit Assembly (Electronic
    Assembly) Manufacturing

Jabil Circuit, Inc. has benefited from the rapid growth of the electronic manufacturing services (EMS) industry. During the 1990s Jabil's revenues grew from slightly more than $200 million to $2 billion. The company designs and manufactures electronic circuit board assemblies and systems for major original equipment manufacturers (OEMs). It serves customers in communications, computer peripherals, personal computer, automotive, and consumer products industries. The company's strategy has been to serve a small number of major customers. Its customer list includes industry leaders such as Cisco Systems, Inc., Gateway 2000 Inc., Hewlett-Packard Co., Johnson Controls, Inc., and Quantum Corporation. During the 1990s these and other customers outsourced much of their electronic manufacturing to EMS companies such as Jabil.

Jabil was founded in 1966 in suburban Detroit as a producer and repairer of circuit board assemblies for Control Data Systems, a major mainframe computer manufacturer. Jabil (pronounced JAY-bill) took its name from the first names of its cofounders, James Golden and Bill Morean. Golden soon sold his stake to Morean, whose son William Morean joined the firm in 1977. The younger Morean obtained contracts with Burroughs Business Systems and a few other customers to assemble circuit boards. At the time Jabil was taking in less than $50,000 a year, but the younger Morean offered to buy 51 percent of the company from his father for $100,000, to be paid over five years.

More Automated Production: 1980s

In a major strategic shift, Jabil established a high-volume manufacturing relationship with General Motors (GM) in 1979. Under its arrangement with GM, Jabil would purchase all necessary parts and provide the necessary engineering to complete the high-volume production work, thus offering GM a turnkey service. The nature of the work forced Jabil to make a strategic commitment to advanced assembly technology and highly automated manufacturing. Up to this time Jabil had been manually assembling circuit boards.

Over the years Jabil would continue to provide complete turnkey services to manufacturing partners, maintaining its commitment to advanced manufacturing technology and highly automated operations. In 1982 the company moved to St. Petersburg, Florida, after obtaining a contract to make add-on circuit boards for the IBM Personal Computer unit in Boca Raton. Within a year Jabil's sales doubled to $100 million. During the 1980s Jabil took advantage of the trend for original equipment manufacturers (OEMs) to seek a broader range of external manufacturing services to more fully leverage their own internal operations. As an external manufacturer, Jabil would procure components, provide automated assembly services, and design and perform electronic testing.

Also during the 1980s, surface mount technology (SMT) replaced pin-through-hole (PTH) technology as the preferred method for circuit board assembly. SMT greatly reduced the size of the circuit board, reducing system costs while enhancing potential signal speed. To keep up with these developments, contract manufacturers such as Jabil were required to maintain more sophisticated automated assembly equipment and engineering expertise.

Along with these advances in the 1980s, there was a proliferation of smaller, more complex products, with product life

Company Perspectives:

The foundation of Jabil's strategy is the development and support of long-term manufacturing partnerships with leading electronic companies. Jabil offers its customers a complete turnkey solution, including circuit and production design; component selection, sourcing and procurement; automated assembly; design and implementation of product test; and shipment to points of end-user distribution. The Jabil turnkey approach enables a customer to transfer virtually all internal manufacturing responsibilities. This approach, coupled with advanced manufacturing technologies, enables customers to improve cost, manufacturing performance and time-to-volume production. Jabil's production design process is performed concurrently with resolution of manufacturing issues to enhance the manufacturability of products and improve the production benefits achieved.

cycles shrinking dramatically. These factors also contributed to the growth of external manufacturing as a strategy to manage product life cycles and increase product complexity.

In 1981 Jabil began providing independent test engineering and development. In 1982 it initiated volume production of circuit boards using manual SMT processes. Computer-aided production design services were introduced in 1984, and highly automated volume production of circuit boards using SMT processes began in 1985. By the end of the 1980s Jabil was using the automated TAB process for volume production of circuit boards. Toward the end of the decade Jabil had uneven sales and earnings. For fiscal 1988 the company reported net income of $3.8 million on sales of $96 million. In 1989 sales rose to $135 million, while net income declined to $694,000.

Uneven Sales and Earnings: 1990–95

The uneven sales and earnings continued in the 1990s. For 1990 revenues dropped to $124 million, and net income was $1 million. In 1991 revenues were reported at nearly $233 million, with net income of $10.3 million. For 1992 revenues declined to $173.1 million, while earnings fell to nearly $3.2 million. Sales for 1992 were negatively impacted by a $64 million decline in sales to Zenith Data Systems, one of the company's largest clients, and a loss of $32 million in sales to Dell Computer, which temporarily ended its relationship with Jabil.

Jabil went public in April 1993 with shares trading on the New York Stock Exchange. About 20 to 30 percent of the company's shares were offered to the public, depending on whether the underwriters' over-allotment was exercised in full. Jabil was led by Chairman and CEO William D. Morean, who directly and indirectly owned about 72 percent of Jabil's shares before the initial public offering (IPO). Thomas A. Sansone was Jabil's president. The firm's three largest customers—NEC Technologies, Quantum Corp., and Zenith Data Systems— accounted for about two-thirds of its revenues, with NEC accounting for 38 percent. Some ten additional customers accounted for Jabil's remaining revenues. Jabil expected to be dependent on sales to a small number of customers, and it was

competing against such well-known circuit board makers as IBM, Texas Instruments, Intel Corporation, and Digital Equipment.

Growth and Diversification: 1995–2000

For fiscal 1995 ending August 31 Jabil reported sales of $559.5 million, with net income of $7.3 million. During the first half of 1995 Jabil's workforce increased by 30 percent to more than 2,000 employees. The company was working three shifts a day to keep up with demand for printed circuit board assemblies, fueled by growing consumer demand for personal computers and other electronic products. With demand for integrated circuits (ICs) outstripping supply, Jabil claimed it could do 20 percent more business if it could find more of the components.

For fiscal 1996 sales increased 54 percent to $863.3 million. Net income more than tripled to $24.3 million. Jabil was benefiting from a trend among high-tech companies toward external manufacturing. It was supplying computer manufacturer Hewlett-Packard (HP) with 130,000 Pentium-based PC units a month, accounting for 25 percent of Jabil's business. HP was now Jabil's largest customer. Jabil also was targeting data communications companies involved in networking and the Internet as an area of future growth. Some 20 percent of Jabil's revenues came from Internet suppliers such as Chipcom and Compression Labs, up from eight percent in 1995.

In January 1996 one of Jabil's top three customers, Quantum Corporation, canceled orders worth $60 million a quarter, or about 25 percent of Jabil's revenues. Jabil had been supplying Quantum with parts for its hard disc drive products, which Quantum decided to stop producing and turn over to another business partner in an effort to regain profitability. To service Quantum, Jabil had built a high-volume factory in Penang, Malaysia, next to a Quantum site that would now be closed. Jabil planned to continue producing parts for Quantum's tape drive assemblies at the Malaysian factory. Partially offsetting the loss of business from Quantum were announcements of production plans for Cascade Communications, CellNet Data Systems, Cisco Systems, PairGain Technologies, and 3Com. For much of 1996 Jabil's stock price was depressed because of the lost business, trading at around $6 a share.

In May 1996 Jabil announced a five-year contract with PairGain Technologies to produce PG2s, gear that could double the capacity of a single telephone line, as well as a corporate version that could split a single line into 64 lines, or the equivalent of a T1 line. PG2 technology was developed by PairGain in the early 1990s, and the company had about two-thirds of the telecommunications market for the device. Jabil would manufacture the PG2s using plans provided by PairGain, then inventory and sell them. Jabil also planned to make other products for PairGain.

By December 1996 Jabil's stock had risen to more than $30. At the end of the year the company was looking to double its local workforce in St. Petersburg over the next several months. In spite of losing a significant share of Quantum's business, Jabil was able to remain profitable for fiscal 1996. The company also had diversified, from mainly producing circuit boards for personal computers to providing them for laptop computers

---

Key Dates:

1966: Jabil Circuit, Inc. is founded in suburban Detroit to repair and produce circuit board assemblies.
1979: Jabil enters into a high-volume production relationship with General Motors Corporation.
1982: Jabil moves from Detroit to St. Petersburg, Florida.
1993: Jabil goes public with shares trading on the New York Stock Exchange.
1998: Revenues exceed $1 billion for the first time.
1999: Jabil acquires GET Manufacturing Inc. of Hong Kong for $250 million; revenues exceed $2 billion.

---

and, more significant, for data communications hardware to access and maintain the Internet. A new 120,000-square-foot building was completed in January 1997 and doubled Jabil's manufacturing space in St. Petersburg. By February 1997 the company had to lease another 91,000-square-foot building in St. Petersburg to keep up with near-term customer demand. The company's other plants were located in Scotland, Malaysia, and California. Jabil also built a new 150,000-square-foot facility in Guadalajara, Mexico, which opened in November 1997. By early 1997 Jabil's global workforce had grown to about 3,000.

Growing demand, combined with a better-than-expected earnings report for the quarter ending May 31, 1997, resulted in a nearly 20 percent boost in Jabil's stock in one day. In June the stock rose more than $13 a share to close at $82.25, nearly ten times its price of July 1996. *Fortune* magazine ranked Jabil as the number one performing stock among its 100 fastest-growing U.S. companies. When the stock price passed $100 a share, the company declared a two-for-one stock split, which took place in July 1997.

For fiscal 1997 ending August 31, Jabil's net income more than doubled to $52.5 million, while sales rose a modest 13 percent to $978.1 million. Data network products, such as switchers and routers, were accounting for more of Jabil's revenue as the company shifted away from personal computer components. The company's largest customers were 3Com and Cisco Systems, which accounted for about 40 percent of Jabil's revenues. Hewlett-Packard, NEC, and Quantum together accounted for another 30 percent.

For fiscal 1998, sales passed the $1 billion mark, reaching $1.28 billion, while net income rose to $56.9 million. During the year Jabil strengthened its association with Hewlett-Packard and hired 600 former HP employees when it purchased the manufacturing assets of the Hewlett-Packard LaserJet Solutions Formatter Manufacturing Organization (FMO) for $80 million. The assets included two manufacturing facilities in Boise, Idaho, and Bergamo, Italy. They would be used to produce the printed circuit board assemblies for all laser printers sold by HP.

In October 1998 Jabil announced a new manufacturing relationship with Nortel Networks Inc., formerly known as Bay Networks, with production to be increased throughout fiscal 1999. The company also gained new business from Network Applicance, Inc., which made computer servers for the Internet and corporate networks. To expand its North American capac-

ity, Jabil began constructing a 120,000-square-foot addition to its plant in Guadalajara, Mexico, in December. It also broke ground on a 60,000-square-foot corporate headquarters building in St. Petersburg to be completed by the fall of 1999. Between September and December 1998, Jabil's stock tripled from $23 to $69.50. At the end of 1998 the company had more than 5,300 full-time employees worldwide.

In January 1999 Jabil registered to sell 10.5 million shares of stock, including six million shares by the company and 4.5 million by shareholders; they were sold to the public in a secondary offering in March for about $30 a share, following a two-for-one stock split in February. The proceeds would be used to repay debt as well as for capital expenditures and general corporate purposes. The company also made a number of executive changes, promoting Thomas Sansone from president to vice-chairman, and Timothy L. Main from senior vice-president of business development to president. At the beginning of 1999 Jabil had manufacturing facilities in California, Michigan, Idaho, Scotland, Italy, Mexico, and Malaysia.

For 1999 Jabil's revenue of $2 billion was more than double revenue of 1997. For the first six months, Jabil performed ahead of expectations, with sales increasing 45 percent over the same period in 1998. Net income for fiscal 1999 was $91.5 million, an increase of nearly 61 percent over the previous year. The company added four new customers, including Lucent Technologies Inc.

In July 1999 Jabil acquired Denver-based EFTC Corp.'s electronics warranty service business for $30 million. The purchase added 500 employees, increasing Jabil's workforce to 7,500 people. After the acquisition, Jabil renamed the operation Jabil Global Services, Inc. and would offer repair and warranty services from operations in Memphis, Tennessee; Louisville, Kentucky; and Tampa, Florida.

In September 1999 Jabil completed a merger with GET Manufacturing Inc. of Hong Kong. The $250 million acquisition added about 5,000 employees and made Jabil a leading supplier of electronic manufacturing services in China. GET had six manufacturing facilities totaling one million square feet, four of which were located in China, with two smaller operations in Mexico and California. The acquisition of GET was expected to add about $300 million in annual revenue.

To keep up with increased demand, Jabil continued to expand its manufacturing capacity through plant expansions and building and leasing new facilities. In 2000, for example, after receiving a 20-year, $14.5 million tax credit from Michigan, it began a $40 million expansion of its Auburn Hills manufacturing operations to 200,000 square feet. Its southeastern Michigan customers included General Motors, Ford Motor Company, and Johnson Controls.

With more and more OEMs closing or selling off their manufacturing facilities and outsourcing their electronics manufacturing, the electronic manufacturing services sector was expected to grow by about 50 percent a year between 2000 and 2003. Jabil continued to expand its production facilities in mid-2000 to keep up with demand. It also raised $543 million through a secondary stock offering to reduce debt and finance a corporate building program that included plant expansions in

California, Michigan, Massachusetts, Florida, and Idaho. Internationally the company announced plans to build a plant in Hungary, purchase manufacturing capacity in Brazil, and expand its facilities in Malaysia and Mexico. It also acquired a European repair and services operation from Telenor Technology Services of Norway. As one of the leading companies in the electronic manufacturing services sector, which also included Flextronics International, Solectron Corp., SCI Systems, Sanmina Corp., and Toronto-based Celestica, Jabil could look forward to continued revenue and earnings growth.

Principal Subsidiaries

Jabil Circuit Ltd. (U.K.); Jabil Circuit Sdn. Bhd. (Malaysia); Jabil Circuit of Michigan, Inc.; Jabil Circuit Foreign Sales Corporation (Barbados); Jabil Circuit de Mexico, S.A. de C.V.; Jabil Partners (Scotland); Jabil Circuit Luxembourg, SARL; Jabil Circuit Srl (Italy); Jabil MPC, LLC; Jabil Circuit of Texas, LP; Jabil Texas Holdings LLC; Jabil Global Services, Inc.; GET Manufacturing, Inc. (British Virgin Islands); General Electronics (HK) Ltd. (Hong Kong); General Electronics Services, Ltd. (Hong Kong); General Electronics (China) Ltd. (Guernsey); General Electronics Telecommunication (Panyu) Ltd. (China; 85%); Digitek Electronics Ltd. (Hong Kong); Link Win (Far East) Ltd. (Hong Kong); GET Manufacturing USA, Inc.; GETM Mexico S.A. de C.V. (Mexico); GET Manufacturing Services GbmH (Germany); GET Manufacturing Europe (Belgium); General Electronic Development (Hong Kong); Skytop International Ltd. (Hong Kong); CGE International Ltd. (Hong Kong).

Principal Competitors

Flextronics International Ltd. (Singapore); Solectron Corp.; SCI Systems, Inc.; Celestica, Inc. (Canada); Sanmina Corp.

Further Reading

Abercrombie, Paul, "Contract Gives Jabil Shot in Arm," *Tampa Bay Business Journal,* May 3, 1996, p. 1.
Albright, Mark, "St. Petersburg, Fla.-Based Circuit Board Maker Acquires Repair Business," *Knight-Ridder/Tribune Business News,* July 7, 1999.
——, "St. Petersburg, Fla., Circuit Board Maker to Sell Stock, Pay Down Debt," *Knight-Ridder/Tribune Business News,* January 24, 1999.
Burney, Teresa, "Florida-Based Jabil Circuit Inc. Puts Out 'Help Wanted Signs,'" *Knight-Ridder/Tribune Business News,* December 12, 1996.
"Contracting Growth Clear in Latest Financials," *Electronic News (1991),* March 22, 1999, p. 40.
"Detroit Free Press Michigan Memo Column," *Knight-Ridder/Tribune Business News,* May 18, 2000.
Diba, Ahmad, "Blessed Are the Piece Makers," *Fortune,* May 1, 2000, p. 293.
Donsky, Martin, "Borrowings to Continue After Jabil IPO Deal," *Tampa Bay Business Journal,* March 12, 1993, p. 11.
Greengard, Samuel, "Design to Go," *Industry Week,* May 15, 2000, p. 89.
Harrington, Jeff, "St. Petersburg, Fla., Circuit Board Maker to Acquire Hong Kong Firm," *Knight-Ridder/Tribune Business News,* August 8, 1999.
"Here's a Tech Play That Still Looks Solid," *Business Week,* May 1, 2000, p. 210.
Holland, Bill, "Jabil Raises $543 Million 'Overnight,'" *dbusiness.com,* June 7, 2000, http://www.dbusiness.com/Story/0,1118,NOCITY_169326,00.html.
Huntley, Helen, "Jabil Circuit Inc. Profits Leap; Investors Do, Too," *Knight-Ridder/Tribune Business News,* October 11, 1997.
"Jabil Circuit Diversifies and Expands," *Electronic News (1991),* February 22, 1999, p. 36.
"Jabil Expands in Mexico," *Electronic News (1991),* December 14, 1998, p. 42.
"Jabil 2Q Revs Up, Profit Posted," *Electronic News (1991),* March 25, 1996, p. 16.
Johnson, Corey, "Built to Last," *Standard,* May 29, 2000, http://www.thestandard.com/article/display/0,1151,15477,00.html.
Lachinsky, Adam, "San Jose Mercury News, Calif., Silicon Street Column," *Knight-Ridder/Tribune Business News,* March 7, 1999.
"Laser Printer PCB Gear in Idaho, Italy," *Electronic News (1991),* August 10, 1998, p. 44.
Levine, Bernard, "Jabil Circuit," *Electronic News (1991),* October 12, 1998, p. 50.
——, "Jabil Looks to China," *Electronic News (1991),* August 9, 1999, p. 4.
Parker, Jocelyn, "Florida-Based Technology Firm Expands Oakland County, Mich., Operations," *Knight-Ridder/Tribune Business News,* November 9, 1999.
Poppe, David, "Electrifying Comeback: Shares in St. Petersburg, Fla.-Based Jabil Rebound," *Knight-Ridder/Tribune Business News,* October 5, 1997.
"Rejuvenated St. Petersburg, Fla.-Based Jabil Sets Earnings Record," *Knight-Ridder/Tribune Business News,* December 18, 1996.
Sachdev, Ameet, "St. Petersburg, Fla.-Based Electronics Maker Warns of Slower Growth," *Knight-Ridder/Tribune Business News,* June 17, 1999.
——, "St. Petersburg, Fla.-Based Jabil Circuit Beats Analysts' Estimates," *Knight-Ridder/Tribune Business News,* December 16, 1998.
——, "Stock Rises 19 Percent at Florida Electronics Firm Jabil Circuit Inc.," *Knight-Ridder/Tribune Business News,* June 19, 1997.
Sherefkin, Robert, "Supply Line," *Automotive News,* May 22, 2000, p. 32B.
Torbenson, Eric, "Earnings Beat Expectations at Florida-Based Jabil Circuit," *Knight-Ridder/Tribune Business News,* October 8, 1998.
Trigaux, Robert, "Demand for Electronics Forces Florida Firms to Join Hunt for Components," *Knight-Ridder/Tribune Business News,* July 2, 1995.
——, "Florida Electronics Maker Jabil Loses Order Totaling 25 Percent of Revenues," *Knight-Ridder/Tribune Business News,* January 31, 1996.
——, "Jabil Circuit Executives' Outlook Is Bullish," *Knight-Ridder/Tribune Business News,* January 26, 1996.
——, "St. Petersburg-Based Jabil Circuit Adds Space to Keep Up the Pace," *Knight-Ridder/Tribune Business News,* February 26, 1997.
Weinberg, Neil, "Bill Morean's $1.2 Billion Haircut," *Forbes,* June 14, 1999, p. 142.

—David P. Bianco

Johnson & Johnson

Johnson & Johnson

One Johnson & Johnson Plaza
New Brunswick, New Jersey 08933
U.S.A.
Telephone: (732) 524-0400
Fax: (732) 524-3300
Web site: http://www.jnj.com

Public Company
Incorporated: 1887
Employees: 97,800
Sales: $27.47 billion (1999)
Stock Exchanges: New York Toronto
Ticker Symbol: JNJ
NAIC: 322291 Sanitary Paper Product Manufacturing;
325412 Pharmaceutical Preparation Manufacturing;
325413 In-Vitro Diagnostic Substance Manufacturing;
325414 Biological Product (Except Diagnostic)
Manufacturing; 325611 Soap and Other Detergent
Manufacturing; 325620 Toilet Preparation Manufac-
turing; 339112 Surgical and Medical Instrument
Manufacturing; 339113 Surgical Appliance and
Supplies Manufacturing; 339115 Ophthalmic Goods
Manufacturing; 541710 Research and Development in
the Physical, Engineering, and Life Sciences

One of America's most admired companies, Johnson & Johnson (J&J) is one of the largest healthcare firms in the world and one of the most diversified. Its operations are organized into three business segments: pharmaceutical, which generates 39 percent of revenues and 61 percent of operating income; professional, which accounts for 36 percent of revenues and 27 percent of operating income; and consumer, which contributes 25 percent of revenues and 12 percent of operating income. J&J's pharmaceutical products—which are sold under such brands as Janssen Pharmaceutica, Ortho-McNeil Pharmaceutical, and Centocor—include drugs for family planning, mental illness, gastroenterology, oncology, pain management, and other areas. The professional segment includes surgical and patient care equipment and devices, diagnostic products, joint replacements, and disposable contact lenses. The company's well-known line of consumer products includes the Johnson's baby care line, the Neutrogena skin and hair care line, Tylenol and Motrin pain relievers, o.b. and Stayfree feminine hygiene products, the Reach oral care line, Band-Aid brand adhesive bandages, Imodium A-D diarrhea treatment, Mylanta gastrointestinal products, and Pepcid AC acid controller. J&J generates about half of its revenues outside the United States, through its network of 190 operating companies in 51 countries and its marketing organization that sells in more than 175 countries.

Early History: From Surgical Dressings to Baby Cream

J&J traces its beginnings to the late 1800s, when Joseph Lister's discovery that airborne germs were a source of infection in operating rooms sparked the imagination of Robert Wood Johnson, a New England druggist. Johnson joined forces with his brothers, James Wood Johnson and Edward Mead Johnson, and the three began producing dressings in 1886 in New Brunswick, New Jersey, with 14 employees in a former wallpaper factory.

Because Lister's recommended method for sterilization—spraying the operating room with carbolic acid—was found to be impractical and cumbersome, Johnson & Johnson (which was incorporated in 1887) found a ready market for its product. The percentage of deaths due to infections following surgery was quite high and hospitals were eager to find a solution.

J&J's first product was an improved medicinal plaster that used medical compounds mixed in an adhesive. Soon afterward, the company designed a soft, absorbent cotton-and-gauze dressing, and Robert Wood Johnson's dream was realized. Mass production began and the dressings were shipped in large quantities throughout the United States. By 1890 J&J was using dry heat to sterilize the bandages.

The establishment of a bacteriological laboratory in 1891 gave research a boost, and by the following year the company had met accepted requirements for a sterile product. By introducing dry heat, steam, and pressure throughout the manufac-

Company Perspectives:

Our Credo: We believe our first responsibility is to the doctors, nurses and patients, to mothers and fathers and all others who use our products and services. In meeting their needs everything we do must be of high quality. We must constantly strive to reduce our costs in order to maintain reasonable prices. Customers' orders must be serviced promptly and accurately. Our suppliers and distributors must have an opportunity to make a fair profit. We are responsible to our employees, the men and women who work with us throughout the world. Everyone must be considered as an individual. We must respect their dignity and recognize their merit. They must have a sense of security in their jobs. Compensation must be fair and adequate, and working conditions clean, orderly and safe. We must be mindful of ways to help our employees fulfill their family responsibilities. Employees must feel free to make suggestions and complaints. There must be equal opportunity for employment, development and advancement for those qualified. We must provide competent management, and their actions must be just and ethical. We are responsible to the communities in which we live and work and to the world community as well. We must be good citizens—support good works and charities and bear our fair share of taxes. We must encourage civic improvements and better health and education. We must maintain in good order the property we are privileged to use, protecting the environment and natural resources. Our final responsibility is to our stockholders. Business must make a sound profit. We must experiment with new ideas. Research must be carried on, innovative programs developed and mistakes paid for. New equipment must be purchased, new facilities provided and new products launched. Reserves must be created to provide for adverse times. When we operate according to these principles, the stockholders should realize a fair return.

turing process, J&J was able to guarantee the sterility of its bandages. The adhesive bandage was further improved in 1899 when, with the cooperation of surgeons, J&J introduced a zinc oxide-based adhesive plaster that was stronger and overcame much of the problem of the skin irritation that plagued many patients. J&J's fourth original design was an improved method for sterilizing catgut sutures.

From the beginning, J&J was an advocate of antiseptic surgical procedures. In 1888 the company published *Modern Methods of Antiseptic Wound Treatment,* a text used by physicians for many years. That same year, Fred B. Kilmer began his 45-year stint as scientific director at J&J. A well-known science and medicine writer, and father of poet Joyce Kilmer, Fred Kilmer wrote influential articles for J&J's publications, including *Red Cross Notes* and the *Red Cross Messenger.* Physicians, pharmacists, and the general public were encouraged to use antiseptic methods, and J&J products were promoted.

R.W. Johnson died in 1910 and was succeeded as chairman by his brother James. It was then that the company began to grow quickly. To guarantee a source for the company's increasing need for textile materials, J&J purchased Chicopee Manufacturing

Corporation in 1916. The first international affiliate was founded in Canada in 1919. A few years later, in 1923, Robert W. Johnson's sons, Robert Johnson and J. Seward Johnson, took an around-the-world tour that convinced them that J&J should expand overseas, and Johnson & Johnson Limited was established in Great Britain a year later. Diversification continued with the introduction in 1921 of Band-Aid brand adhesive bandages and Johnson's Baby Cream (Johnson's Baby Powder had debuted in 1893) and the debut of the company's first feminine hygiene product, Modess sanitary napkins, in 1927.

1932–63: The General at the Helm

The younger Robert Johnson, who came to be known as "the General," had joined the company as a mill hand while still in his teens. By the age of 25 he had become a vice-president, and he was elected president in 1932. Described as dynamic and restless with a keen sense of duty, Johnson had attained the rank of brigadier general in World War II and served as vice-chairman of the War Production Board.

The General firmly believed in decentralization in business; he was the driving force behind J&J's organizational structure, in which divisions and affiliates were given autonomy to direct their own operations. This policy coincided with a move into pharmaceuticals, hygiene products, and textiles. During Robert Johnson's tenure, the division for the manufacture of surgical packs and gowns became Surgikos, Inc.; the department for sanitary napkin production was initially called the Modess division and then became the Personal Products Company; birth control products were under the supervision of the Ortho Pharmaceutical Corporation; and the separate division for suture business became Ethicon, Inc. Under the General's leadership, annual sales grew from $11 million to $700 million at the time of his death in 1968.

Following his father's lead as a champion of social issues, Johnson spoke out in favor of raising the minimum wage, improving conditions in factories, and emphasizing business's responsibility to society. Johnson called for management to treat workers with respect and to create programs that would improve workers' skills and better prepare them for success in a modern industrial society. In 1943 Johnson wrote a credo outlining the company's four areas of social responsibility: first to its customers; second to its employees; third to the community and environment; and fourth to the stockholders. On the heels of the credo came the company's change from family-owned firm to public company, as J&J was listed on the New York Stock Exchange in 1944.

In 1959 J&J acquired McNeil Laboratories, Inc., maker of a non-aspirin (acetaminophen) pain reliever called Tylenol—which was at that time available only by prescription. Just one year after the acquisition, McNeil launched Tylenol as an over-the-counter (OTC) medication. Also in 1959, Cilag-Chemie, a Swiss pharmaceutical firm, was purchased, followed in two years by the purchase of Janssen Pharmaceutica, maker of the major antipsychotic drug Haldol, which had been introduced in 1958.

In 1963 Johnson retired. Although he remained active in the business, chairmanship of the company went outside the family for the first time. Johnson's immediate successor was Philip

Key Dates:

1886: Johnson brothers begin producing dressings in New Brunswick, New Jersey.

1887: Company is incorporated as Johnson & Johnson.

1893: Johnson's Baby Powder is introduced.

1921: Band-Aid brand adhesive bandages make their debut.

1924: Overseas expansion begins with the establishment of Johnson & Johnson Limited in the United Kingdom.

1932: Robert Johnson, known as "the General," takes over leadership as president.

1943: Johnson writes the company credo.

1944: Company goes public on the New York Stock Exchange.

1959: McNeil Laboratories, Inc. (McNeil Labs) is acquired.

1960: McNeil Labs introduces Tylenol as an over-the-counter (OTC) pain reliever.

1961: Janssen Pharmaceutica is acquired.

1975: Through a significant price decrease, Tylenol is transformed into a mass-marketed product.

1982: Tylenol tampering tragedy occurs.

1988: Acuvue disposable contact lenses are introduced.

1989: J&J and Merck form joint venture to develop OTC versions of Merck's prescription medications.

1994: Neutrogena Corporation is acquired.

1995: Merck and J&J launch Pepcid AC; company acquires the clinical diagnostics unit of Eastman Kodak Company.

1996: J&J acquires Cordis Corporation.

1998: DePuy, Inc. is acquired, and a companywide restructuring is launched.

1999: Centocor, Inc. merges with J&J.

Hofmann, who, much like the General, had started as a shipping clerk and worked his way up the ladder. During Hofmann's ten-year term as chairman, J&J's domestic and overseas affiliates flourished. Hofmann was another firm believer in decentralization and encouraged the training of local experts to supervise operations in their respective countries. Foreign management was organized along product lines rather than geographically, with plant managers reporting to a person with expertise in the field.

1960s–70s: Increased Promotion of Consumer Products

In the early 1960s federal regulation of the healthcare industry was increasing. When James Burke—who had come to J&J from the marketing department of the Procter & Gamble Company—became president of J&J's Domestic Operating Company in 1966, the company was looking for ways to increase profits from its consumer products to offset possible slowdowns in the professional products divisions. By luring top marketing people from Procter & Gamble, Burke was able to put together several highly successful advertising campaigns. The first introduced Carefree and Stayfree sanitary napkins into a market that was dominated by the acknowledged feminine products leader,

Kimberly-Clark. Usually limited to women's magazines, advertisements for feminine hygiene products were low-key and discreet. Under Burke's direction, J&J took a more open approach and advertised Carefree and Stayfree on television. By 1978 J&J had captured half of the market. Meantime, the company expanded its feminine hygiene line through the 1973 acquisition of the German firm Dr. Carl Hahn G.m.b.H., maker of the o.b. brand of tampons.

One of Burke's biggest challenges was Tylenol. Ever since J&J had acquired McNeil Laboratories, maker of Tylenol, the drug had been marketed as a high-priced product. Burke saw other possibilities, and in 1975 he got the chance he was waiting for. Bristol-Myers Company introduced Datril and advertised that it had the same ingredients as Tylenol but was available at a significantly lower price. Burke convinced J&J Chairman Richard Sellars that they should meet this competition head on by dropping Tylenol's price to meet Datril's. With Sellars's approval, Burke took Tylenol into the mass-marketing arena, slashed its price, and ended up beating not only Datril, but number one Anacin as well. This signaled the beginning of an ongoing battle between American Home Products Corporation, maker of Anacin, and McNeil Laboratories.

Sellars, Hofmann's protégé, had become chairman in 1973, and served in that position for three years. Burke succeeded Sellars in 1976 as CEO and chairman of the board, and David R. Clare was appointed president. J&J had always maintained a balance between the many divisions in its operations, particularly between mass consumer products and specialized professional products. No single J&J product accounted for as much as five percent of the company's total sales. With Burke at the helm, consumer products began to be promoted aggressively, and Tylenol pain reliever became J&J's number one seller.

At the same time, Burke did not turn his back on the company's position as a leader in professional healthcare products. In May 1977 Extracorporeal Medical Specialties, a manufacturer of kidney dialysis and intravenous treatment products, became part of the corporation. Three years later, J&J acquired Iolab Corporation, maker of ocular lenses for cataract surgery, and effectively entered the field of eye care and ophthalmic pharmaceuticals. In 1981 the company extended its involvement in eye care through the acquisition of Frontier Contact Lenses. The increased in-house development of critical care products resulted in the creation of Critikon, Inc., in 1979, and in 1983 Johnson & Johnson Hospital Services was created to develop and implement corporate marketing programs.

1980s Tylenol Tampering Tragedy

In September 1982 tragedy struck J&J when seven people died from ingesting Tylenol capsules that had been laced with cyanide. Advertising was canceled immediately, and J&J recalled all Tylenol products from store shelves. After the Food and Drug Administration (FDA) found that the tampering had been done at the retail level rather than during manufacturing, J&J was left with the problem of how to save its number one product and its reputation. In the week after the deaths, J&J's stock dropped 18 percent and its prime competitors' products, Datril and Anacin-3, were in such demand that supplies were back-ordered.

J&J was able to recoup its losses through several marketing strategies. The company ran a one-time ad that explained how to exchange Tylenol capsules for tablets or refunds and worked closely with the press, responding directly to reporters' questions as a means of keeping the public up to date. The company also placed a coupon for $2.50 off any Tylenol product in newspapers across the country to reimburse consumers for Tylenol capsules they may have discarded during the tampering incident and offer an incentive to purchase Tylenol in other forms.

Within weeks of the poisoning incidents, the FDA issued guidelines for tamper-resistant packaging for the entire food and drug industry. To bolster public confidence in its product, J&J used three layers of protection, two more than recommended, when Tylenol was put back on store shelves. Within months of the cyanide poisoning, J&J was gaining back its share of the pain-reliever market, and soon regained more than 90 percent of its former customers. By 1989 Tylenol sales were $500 million annually, and in 1990 the line was expanded into the burgeoning cold remedy market with several Tylenol Cold products; the following year saw the launch of Tylenol P.M., a sleep aid. James Burke's savvy, yet honest, handling of the Tylenol tampering incident earned him a spot in the National Business Hall of Fame, an honor awarded in 1990. Litigation over the incident was finally resolved in 1991, almost a decade after the initial tampering. McNeil Labs settled with over 30 survivors of the poisonings for more than $35 million.

In 1989 Bristol-Myers launched an aggressive advertising campaign that positioned its Nuprin brand ibuprofen pain reliever in direct competition with Tylenol. The move compounded market share erosion from American Home Products' Advil ibuprofen. Both products claimed to work better than Tylenol's acetaminophen formulation.

There were a number of other important developments in the second half of the 1980s. In 1986 J&J acquired LifeScan, Inc., maker of at-home blood-monitoring products for diabetics. That same year, the company expanded its world leading position in baby care products through the acquisition of Penaten G.m.b.H., the market leader in Germany. Following the acquisition of Frontier Contact Lenses, which was renamed Vistakon, J&J introduced the Acuvue brand of disposable contact lenses in the United States in 1988. The popularity of the Acuvue lenses helped propel Vistakon into the number one position in contact lenses worldwide. In 1989 J&J and drug giant Merck & Co., Inc. entered into a joint venture—Johnson & Johnson-Merck Consumer Pharmaceuticals Co.—to develop OTC versions of Merck's prescription medications, initially for the U.S. market, later expanded to Europe and Canada. One of the first product lines developed by this venture was the Mylanta brand of gastrointestinal products.

Burke and Clare retired in 1989 and were succeeded by three executives: CEO and Chairman Ralph S. Larsen, who came from the consumer sector; Vice-Chairman Robert E. Campbell, who had headed the professional sector; and President Robert N. Wilson, who had headed the pharmaceutical sector. The three men were responsible for overseeing the network of 168 companies in 53 countries.

Larsen moved quickly to reduce some of the inefficiencies that a history of decentralization had caused. In 1989 the infant products division was joined with the health and dental units to form a broader consumer products segment, eliminating approximately 300 jobs in the process. Over the next two years, the reorganization was extended to overseas units. The number of professional operating departments in Europe was reduced from 28 to 18 through consolidation under three primary companies: Ethicon, Johnson & Johnson Medical, and Johnson & Johnson Professional Products. In 1990, meantime, J&J formed Ortho Biotech Inc. to consolidate the company's research in the burgeoning biotechnology field, an area J&J had been active in since the 1970s.

Dealmaking in the 1990s and Beyond

J&J was able to counter increasing criticisms of rising healthcare costs in the United States and around the world in the 1990s due in part to the company's longstanding history of social responsibility. The company pioneered several progressive programs including child care, family leave, and "corporate wellness" that were beginning to be recognized as healthcare cost reducers and productivity enhancers. In addition, weighted average compound prices of J&J's healthcare products, including prescription and OTC drugs and hospital and professional products, grew more slowly than the U.S. consumer price index from 1980 through 1992. These practices supported the company's claim that it was part of the solution to the healthcare crisis. In 1992 J&J instituted its "Signature of Quality" program, which urged the corporation's operating companies to focus on three general goals: "Continuously improving customer satisfaction, cost efficiency and the speed of bringing new products to market."

J&J grew at a relatively slow pace in the early 1990s, in part because of the difficult economic climate. Revenues increased from $11.23 billion in 1990 to $14.14 billion in 1993, an increase of just 26 percent. A series of acquisitions in the mid-1990s, however, ushered in a period of more rapid growth, with revenues hitting $21.62 billion by 1996, a leap of 53 percent from the 1993 level. The skin care line had received a boost in 1993 through the purchase of RoC S.A. of France, a maker of hypoallergenic facial, hand, body, and other products under the RoC name. More significant was the acquisition the following year of Neutrogena Corporation for nearly $1 billion. Neutrogena was well-known for its line of dermatologist-recommended skin and hair care products. J&J spent another billion dollars in 1995 for the clinical diagnostics unit of Eastman Kodak Company, which was particularly strong in the areas of clinical chemistry, which involves the analysis of simple compounds in the body, and immuno-diagnostics. In 1997 J&J combined its existing Ortho Diagnostics Systems unit with the operations acquired from Kodak to form Ortho-Clinical Diagnostics, Inc. (LifeScan remained a separately run diagnostics company.)

Another subsidiary that grew through acquisitions in this period was Ethicon Endo-Surgery, Inc., which had been spun off from Ethicon in 1992 to concentrate on endoscopic, or minimally invasive, surgical instruments. J&J acquired Indigo Medical, which specialized in minimally invasive technology in urology and related areas, in 1996, while Biopsys Medical, Inc., specializing in minimally invasive breast biopsies, was purchased in 1997. Another large acquisition occurred in 1996 when J&J spent about $1.8 billion for Cordis Corporation, a world leader in the treatment of cardiovascular diseases through its stents, balloons, and catheters. In 1997, in exchange for several consumer products, J&J acquired the OTC rights to the Motrin brand of ibuprofen pain relievers from Pharmacia & Upjohn. Other important developments during this period included the 1995 introduction of an Acuvue disposable contact lens designed to be worn for just one day but priced at a reasonable level, and the 1995 U.S. approval of the antacid Pepcid AC, an OTC version of Merck's Pepcid that was developed by the Johnson & Johnson-Merck joint venture.

The company's aggressive program of acquisition continued in the late 1990s, beginning with the 1998 purchase of DePuy, Inc. for $3.7 billion in cash, J&J's largest acquisition yet. DePuy was a leader in orthopedic products, such as hip replacement devices. J&J already marketed one of the leading knee replacement devices in the United States, making for a nice fit between the two companies. On the negative side, J&J was forced to initiate a restructuring in 1998 following a number of difficulties. J&J had been a pioneer in the market for coronary stents, devices used to keep arteries open following angioplasty, but its stent sales fell from $700 million in 1996 to just over $200 million in 1998 after competitors introduced second-generation stents and J&J did not. Also troubled was the firm's pharmaceutical operation, which in 1997 and 1998 had seen nine drugs in the development pipeline fail in testing, fail to get government approval, or be delayed. In late 1998 J&J announced that it would reduce its workforce by 4,100 and close 36 plants around the world over the succeeding 18 months. Taking $697 million in restructuring and in-process research and development charges, J&J aimed to save between $250 million and $300 million per year through this effort.

To bolster its drug R&D efforts, J&J completed its first major pharmaceutical deal since the 1961 purchase of Janssen Pharmaceutica. In October 1999 J&J merged with major biotechnology firm Centocor, Inc. in a $4.9 billion stock-for-stock transaction, the largest such deal in company history. With Centocor and Ortho Biotech under its wing, J&J was now one of the world's leading biotech firms. Soon after the merger with Centocor was completed, the FDA approved a key Centocor-developed drug, Remicade, for the treatment of rheumatoid arthritis. Centocor was also developing other pharmaceuticals in the areas of cancer, autoimmune diseases, and cardiology. Also in 1999 J&J acquired the dermatological skin care business of S.C. Johnson & Son, Inc.—which was primarily made up of the Aveeno brand—for an undisclosed amount.

Despite its late 1990s troubles, J&J reported record results for 1999, earning $4.17 billion on revenues of $27.47 billion. Net earnings had nearly quadrupled since 1989, while net sales nearly tripled over the same period. The year 2000 got off to a rough start for the company, however, as it was forced to withdraw from the market a prescription heartburn medication, Propulsid, after the drug had been linked to 100 deaths and hundreds of cases of cardiac irregularity. Propulsid had nearly $1 billion in sales in 1999. Also in early 2000, J&J joined with General Electric Company's GE Medical Systems unit, Baxter International Inc., Abbott Laboratories, and Medtronic, Inc. in a venture to create a global Internet-based purchasing exchange for healthcare providers.

Principal Subsidiaries

Advanced Sterilization Products; Centocor; Cordis Corporation; DePuy; Ethicon, Inc.; Ethicon Endo-Surgery, Inc.; Independence Technology; Indigo Medical, Inc.; Janssen Pharmaceutica Inc.; Johnson & Johnson Consumer Products, Inc.; Johnson & Johnson Development Corporation; Johnson & Johnson Health Care Systems Inc.; Johnson & Johnson Medical; Johnson & Johnson-Merck Consumer Pharmaceuticals Co. (50%); Johnson & Johnson Sales and Logistics Company; Johnson & Johnson Vision Care, Inc.; LifeScan, Inc.; McNeil Consumer Healthcare; McNeil Specialty Products Company; Neutrogena Corporation; Noramco, Inc.; Ortho Biotech Inc.; Ortho-Clinical Diagnostics, Inc.; Ortho Dermatological; Ortho-McNeil Pharmaceutical, Inc.; Personal Products Company; R.W. Johnson Pharmaceutical Research Institute; Therakos, Inc. The company has additional subsidiaries in Canada, Argentina, Brazil, Chile, Colombia, Mexico, Panama, Peru, Uruguay, Venezuela, Austria, Belgium, the Czech Republic, France, Germany, Greece, Hungary, Ireland, Italy, the Netherlands, Poland, Portugal, Russia, Scotland, Slovenia, Spain, Sweden, Switzerland, Turkey, the United Kingdom, Australia, China, Egypt, Hong Kong, India, Indonesia, Israel, Japan, Korea, Malaysia, Morocco, Pakistan, the Philippines, Singapore, South Africa, Taiwan, Thailand, the United Arab Emirates, and Zimbabwe.

Principal Operating Units

Consumer and Personal Care Group; Medical Devices and Diagnostics Group; Pharmaceuticals Group.

Principal Competitors

Abbott Laboratories; Affymetrix, Inc.; Alberto-Culver Company; American Home Products Corporation; Amgen Inc.; Aventis; Bausch & Lomb Incorporated; Baxter International Inc.; Bayer AG; Beckman Coulter, Inc.; Becton, Dickinson & Company; Bristol-Myers Squibb Company; Carter-Wallace, Inc.; Colgate-Palmolive Company; Dade Behring Inc.; The Dial Corporation; Eli Lilly and Company; Genentech, Inc.; The Gillette Company; Glaxo Wellcome plc; Kimberly-Clark Corporation; L'Oréal USA, Inc.; Medtronic, Inc.; Merck & Co., Inc.; Minnesota Mining and Manufacturing Company; Nestlé S.A.; Novartis AG; Perrigo Company; Pfizer Inc.; Pharmacia Corporation; The Procter & Gamble Company; Roche Holding Ltd.; SmithKline Beecham plc; St. Jude Medical, Inc.; Unilever; United States Surgical Corporation.

Further Reading

Alsop, Ronald, "Johnson & Johnson (Think Babies!) Turns Up Tops," *Wall Street Journal,* September 23, 1999, p. B1.

Barker, Robert, "Picture of Health: Johnson & Johnson Seems to Have Cured What Ailed It," *Barron's* March 30, 1987, pp. 15 +.

Barrett, Amy, "J&J Stops Babying Itself," *Business Week,* September 13, 1999, pp. 95–97.

"Changing a Corporate Culture," *Business Week,* May 14, 1984, pp. 130 +.

Dumaine, Brian, "Is Big Still Good?" *Fortune,* April 20, 1992, pp. 50–60.

Easton, Thomas, and Stephan Herrera, "J&J's Dirty Little Secret," *Forbes,* January 12, 1998, pp. 42–44.

Fannin, Rebecca, "The Pain Game," *Marketing and Media Decisions,* February 1989, pp. 34–39.

Foster, Lawrence G., *A Company That Cares: One Hundred Year Illustrated History of Johnson & Johnson,* New Brunswick, N.J.: Johnson & Johnson, 1986, 175 p.

Guzzardi, Walter, "The National Business Hall of Fame," *Fortune,* March 12, 1990, pp. 118–26.

Harris, Roy J., Jr., and Elyse Tanouye, "Johnson & Johnson to Buy Neutrogena in Bid to Boost Consumer-Products Unit," *Wall Street Journal,* August 23, 1994, p. A3.

Hwang, Suein L., "J&J to Acquire Unit of Kodak for $1.01 Billion," *Wall Street Journal,* September 7, 1994, p. A3.

Jacobs, Richard M., "Products Liability: A Technical and Ethical Challenge," *Quality Progress,* December 1988, pp. 27–29.

Johnson & Johnson: Global Expansion in the Face of Intense Competition, Mountain View, Calif.: Frost & Sullivan, 1993.

Kardon, Brian E., "Consumer Schizophrenia: Extremism in the Marketplace," *Planning Review,* July/August 1992, pp. 18–22.

Keaton, Paul N., and Michael J. Semb, "Shaping up That Bottom Line," *HRMagazine,* September 1990, pp. 81–86.

Langreth, Robert, and Ron Winslow, "At J&J, a Venerable Strategy Faces Questions," *Wall Street Journal,* March 5, 1999, p. B1.

Leon, Mitchell, "Tylenol Fights Back," *Public Relations Journal,* March 1983, pp. 10+.

Matthes, Karen, "Companies Can Make It Their Business to Care," *HR Focus,* February 1992, pp. 4–5.

McLeod, Douglas, and Stacy Adler, "Tylenol Death Payout May Top $35 Million," *Business Insurance,* May 20, 1991, pp. 1, 29.

Moore, Thomas, "The Fight to Save Tylenol," *Fortune,* November 29, 1982, pp. 44+.

Murray, Eileen, and Saundra Shohen, "Lessons from the Tylenol Tragedy on Surviving a Corporate Crisis," *Medical Marketing and Media,* February 1992, pp. 14–19.

O'Reilly, Brian, "J&J Is on a Roll," *Fortune,* December 26, 1994, pp. 178–80+.

Rublin, Lauren R., "More Than a Band-Aid: Johnson & Johnson's Has a Strong Prescription for Growth," *Barron's* April 17, 2000, pp. 37–38, 40, 42.

Silverman, Edward R., "J&J Will Slash 4,100 Positions," *Newark Star-Ledger,* December 4, 1998.

——, "More Than Medicine: Johnson & Johnson's CEO Defends the Company's Slow-Growing Divisions," *Newark Star-Ledger,* June 18, 2000.

Smith, Lee, "J&J Comes a Long Way from Baby," *Fortune,* June 1, 1981, pp. 58+.

Waldholz, Michael, "Johnson & Johnson Defends Emphasis on Long-Term Growth As Profit Surges," *Wall Street Journal,* August 8, 1985.

Weber, Joseph, "A Big Company That Works," *Business Week,* May 4, 1992, pp. 124–32.

——, "No Band-Aids for Ralph Larsen," *Business Week,* May 28, 1990, pp. 86–87.

Winslow, Ron, "Head Start: Johnson & Johnson Finds an Elusive Gene and Races to Exploit It," *Wall Street Journal,* May 26, 2000, pp. A1+.

——, "J&J Agrees to Buy DePuy for $3.5 Billion," *Wall Street Journal,* July 22, 1998, p. A3.

Winters, Patricia, "J&J Sets Nighttime Tylenol," *Advertising Age,* February 18, 1991, pp. 1, 46.

——, "Tylenol Expands with Cold Remedies," *Advertising Age,* August 27, 1990, pp. 3, 36.

—Mary F. Sworsky and April S. Dougal
—updated by David E. Salamie

Jordan Industries, Inc.

ArborLake Center, Suite 550
1751 Lake Cook Rd.
Deerfield, Illinois 60015
U.S.A.
Telephone: (847) 945-5591
Fax: (847) 945-5698
Web site: http://www.jordanindustries.com

Wholly Owned Subsidiary of The Jordan Company LLC
Founded: 1988
Employees: 7,000
Sales: $776.9 million (1999)
NAIC: 421450 Medical Supplies Wholesaling; 511130
Book Publishers; 335312 Motor and Generator
Manufacturing; 336399 All Other Motor Vehicle Parts
Manufacturing

Jordan Industries, Inc. (JII) is a vast and varied conglomerate, made up of dozens of companies with overall revenues nearing $780 million. This quiet, unassuming corporation touches the lives of most Americans on a daily basis: from Riverside Bibles to direct mail, from transmission parts to school yearbooks, from elevator motors to home medical supplies, JII is always on the prowl for private companies with a market niche and an itch to expand. There is, however, a crucial difference between a Jordan Industries-style acquisition and those of other firms—at Jordan, the family bond usually lasts for life and new subsidiaries gain access to a strong balance sheet without losing their top executives. Existing management teams are neither stripped nor sent packing; most continue to run their companies with little interference. In JII lingo, buyouts are pursued for long-term growth for both the parent company as well as its subsidiaries.

A Fighting Irish Beginning: Late 1960s

John W. ''Jay'' Jordan II grew up in Kansas City, Kansas, and attended Pembroke Country Day School. After graduating from high school, Jordan traveled to South Bend, Indiana, to attend the University of Notre Dame, home of the legendary Fighting Irish sports teams. There he met his roommate, Thomas H. Quinn, and the two had much in common. Both were bright, ambitious and played football for Notre Dame. Quinn was a defensive back and even played in the famous 10–10 tie with rival Michigan State University.

After college Jordan went on to Carl Marks and Company in New York City as a venture capitalist and then hooked up with David Zalaznick to found The Jordan Company LLC, an investment firm, in 1982. Tom Quinn, meanwhile, had worked in the medical equipment and supplies field for the Deerfield, Illinois-based Baxter International. Quinn's business savvy helped increase sales volume by nearly $1 billion at a Baxter subsidiary, American Hospital Supplies. He later left his position as a group vice-president at Baxter and teamed up with his old college roommate. The two would become famous for an extensive list of LBOs crisscrossing North America, and occasionally overseas, in the 1980s and 1990s.

Buy, Build, and Improve: Late 1980s

Jordan Industries, Inc. was founded in 1988 and was inextricably bound to The Jordan Company, not only by name but by the men running both businesses. The younger company's logo featured ''JII'' and while this was an acronym representing its name, it could just as easily stand for ''Jordan the Second'' since it was founded in the image of its predecessor. Jay Jordan was chairman and CEO of the new holding company, and Tom Quinn was named president and COO. As Quinn explained to a *Chicago Tribune* writer, his partner was ''the financial genius'' in their business ventures and he was ''the operations man.'' Whatever the formula, the team had already made a name for itself with the New York City investment firm, and planned to do the same for the new Chicago-area subsidiary.

Headquartered in Deerfield, a suburb of Chicago, JII was created as a holding company to house a number of independently run subsidiaries in diverse fields of business. Soon after JII's formation, Jordan and Quinn scoured the marketplace for possible acquisitions and one of the earliest was the Kentucky-based Dura-Line Corporation, the leading manufacturer of plastic duct pipes used to install fiber-optic and coaxial cabling in the burgeoning telecommunications industry. Another early acquisition was Dacco, a manufacturer of rebuilt transmission torque converters and other auto aftermarket parts, with headquarters in Tennessee. These two buys were followed by a string of disparate purchases, including Florida-based AIM Electronics, Iowa's Riverside Book & Bible House, and Garden, California's Beemak Plastics.

By the early 1990s more than two dozen family-owned and -operated companies entered the Jordan and Quinn stables, ranging in value from $5 million to upwards of $200 million. Both JII and The Jordan Company maintained healthy stashes of cash for purchases ($100 million for the former and $40 million for the latter in 1991), to complement their established business sectors, though they were not averse to entering new markets if the timing and products were on target. In any given year, Jordan and Quinn analyzed thousands of companies as potential acquisitions, scrutinized under a predetermined set of specifications. These requirements, published in JII corporate materials, formed the bedrock of JII's corporate policy. Any interested party had to meet one or more of the following: 1) Companies that enjoy high margins through proprietary products or services; 2) Historically profitable, well-managed private companies with a consistent track record of sales and earnings; 3) Companies with excellent growth prospects; 4) Synergistic acquisitions of businesses related to its current companies; 5) Subsidiaries and divisions of larger corporate entities, the industry and products of which coincide with JII's strategic objectives.

As JII grew and earned a solid reputation, it was continually mistaken for its New York counterpart. Business and financial writers confused the two, either believing the two companies were in fact one, which operated under either name, or attributing the actions of one to the other and vice versa, since Jordan and Quinn were the executives running both. Yet the most distinct difference was that The Jordan Company, parent to JII, was an investment firm, and the flashier of the two. Another factor was the type of purchases pursued by each company: JII leaned towards products with industrial or business applications, while The Jordan Company acquired some well known consumer brands and franchised food businesses.

''Masters of the Mundane'' (Not): 1990s

Although Jay Jordan considered himself and Tom Quinn ''masters of the mundane,'' their success was anything but. Both The Jordan Company and JII were fostering growth in a myriad of business sectors, allowing mom-and-pop companies

a new lease on life through expansion and increased brand recognition. By early 1990, JII had acquired majority stakes in 17 companies, and the following year sales topped $300 million. Dura-Line Corp. and Dacco were both leading their business segments; Dura-Line had quintupled sales from $8 million to $40 million in just three years, with quadrupled capacity and new plants in Nevada and the United Kingdom. Dacco, too, experienced healthy sales and expanded into California. Yet the biggest splash of the year went to JII's parent company for the purchase of the Archibald Candy Corporation, a name few recognized—except for its subsidiary, Fannie May Candy Shops Inc. Unfortunately, once again, Jordan Industries was credited with the purchase because the 71-year-old Fannie May's headquarters were in Chicago, close to JII headquarters.

Archibald Candy had turned out to be a major coup for The Jordan Company, and it later became North America's largest candy retailer. Jordan Industries, on the other hand, was also reaping the rewards of its newfangled LBO strategies. Two new companies came into its printing and packaging division, the Fremont, California-based Valmark Industries, Inc. and Des Plaines, Illinois's Pamco Printed Tape & Label Company. Both specialized in pressure-sensitive labels and other labeling or printed materials, and joined two Ohio companies bought by JII in the late 1980s. Overall year-end revenues for JII were expected to reach $450 million; its fast-growing subsidiary, Dura-Line Corp., once again bested forecasts by bringing in more than $60 million, with estimates of reaching $100 million before the end of the decade.

Building Up Old & New Markets: 1995–99

At the mid-point of the 1990s, JII was looking to create a healthcare division through several acquisitions. The first of these was Georgia-based Duro-Med Industries, which manufactured and distributed a variety of home healthcare and foot care products under both the Duro-Med name as well as that of a division called Stein's Health Industries. Next came two more Georgia-based healthcare products companies: GAM Industries Inc. (a manufacturer of hot and cold compresses) and TheraBeads (creator and manufacturer of microwaveable heat therapy items) in 1996. Beyond GAM and TheraBeads were many other acquisitions, including two Illinois-based companies (Barber-Coleman Motors and Merkle-Korff Industries) and Minnesota-based Johnson Components, the former two for the Motors & Gears division and the latter for the telecommunications unit.

With the dawn of 1997 came another healthcare buy, Cho-Pat, Inc., a trademarked designer and manufacturer of orthopedic devices sold mostly to the sports-medicine market. Year-end revenues topped $707.1 million (over the previous year's $601.6 million), with JII's assets now worth $930.2 million (well over last year's $682 million). In the later 1990s JII was content to be in its parent company's shadow as The Jordan Company's AmeriKing Corp. had become the second largest Burger King franchisee in the U.S., while Fannie May collaborated on a sweet deal with Hallmark's Golden Crown stores. Yet JII was no slouch; the company had racked up 13 additional acquisitions of its own in the year, which helped fuel 1998 revenues of $943.6 million. In addition, for the first time in its

Key Dates:

1988: Company is formed, buys Dura-Line Corp. and three other companies.
1989: Jordan purchases AIM Electronics and Beemak Plastics.
1990: Sales top $300 million.
1995: Company begins healthcare unit with purchase of Duro-Med Industries.
1996: Revenues pass $600 million.
1998: Assets are valued at more than $1 billion for the first time.
1999: Jordan buys 20 companies in a matter of months; revenues top $776 million.
2000: Company breaks with tradition and sells telecommunications division to Emerson Electronics.

ten-year history, JII's assets were valued at over $1 billion (The Jordan Company's assets were closer to $3 billion).

In 1999, JII conducted business much like it had in the past: by acquiring 15 diversified companies in the first eight months alone. For its direct marketing unit, SourceLink Inc., came a small outfit called DRG (Direct Results Group, Inc.) with offices on both the East and West Coasts. As Phineas Gray, cofounder and CFO of DRG explained in a February 1999 *Adweek* article, being brought into the JII family was "really the best of both worlds. We have a company that is still within our control, but now we have the capital to go out and grow as fast as we want." DRG joined other recent direct mail acquisitions including Illinois-based Paw Print Direct Marketing and Zydeco Direct, located in Ontario.

The scant 15,000-square-foot Deerfield headquarters housed JII's ever-evolving roster of companies, having gone from seven major divisions to 11 in late 1999. Jay Jordan and his other brainchild, The Jordan Company, were set to move into additional digs in the John Hancock Center in New York City during the year. While Jordan was predominantly in New York and Quinn mostly in Illinois, each bounced from one to another of their respective companies' headquarters, scattered throughout the United States and in China, India, Italy, England, Malaysia, Spain, and Sweden.

Change and Refocusing, 2000 and Beyond

In a move contrary to its general philosophy, JII sold off its telecommunications segment (consisting of Dura-Line, LoDan West, inc., Northern Technologies, Inc., and several others) to the St. Louis-based Emerson Electric Company for $440 million (and $540 million in debt) in early 2000. Its ten remaining business units were the Business, Industrial & Consumer Group (graphics, temporary staffing, Riverside bibles, machine parts, and more); Capita Technologies, Inc. (eBusiness services); Internet Services Management Group (Internet networking); Flavor & Fragrance Group (selling to specialty manufacturers using fragrances and flavors in their products); Jordan Specialty Plastics, Inc. (plastic products for industrial and consumer use); Jordan Auto Aftermarket, Inc. (from torque converters to A/C compressors and beyond);

the Healthcare Products Group, Inc. (from asthma and allergy meds to medical devices); Jordan Specialty Printing & Packaging Group (calenders, school yearbooks, paperboard products, and labels); the Motors & Gears, Inc. unit (motors, gears, starters, pumps, electric control panels, and more), and SourceLink, Inc. (marketing services, direct mail and otherwise).

Jordan Industries in 2000 was still researching and seeking out private companies for possible acquisition. In February JII bought Los Angeles-based M/S Database Marketing and was said to be seeking acquisitions in micrographics and document management services. Its Capita Technologies division had successfully revamped Fannie May's web site and online catalogue services, and added healthy Internet sales to the candymaker's revenues. Dealmakers Jay Jordan and Tom Quinn's reputations preceded them and they no longer had to find companies to acquire; scores of middle-range private outfits came to them instead, more than willing to jump into the Jordan corral. While neither The Jordan Company nor Jordan Industries Inc. was a household name, many of their subsidiaries had nevertheless become an integral part in the daily lives of millions.

Principal Operating Units

Business, Industrial & Consumer Group; Capita Technologies, Inc.; Internet Services Management Group; Flavor & Fragrance Group; Jordan Specialty Plastics, Inc.; Jordan Auto Aftermarket, Inc.; Healthcare Products Group, Inc.; Jordan Specialty Printing & Packaging Group; Motors & Gears, Inc.; SourceLink, Inc.

Further Reading

"Candy Land County Has a Mouthful of Sweet Tooths," *Chicago Tribune,* October 25, 1992, p. 1.
"Emerson Electric Acquires Telco Firm for $440 Million," *St. Louis Business Journal,* December 20, 1999, p. 10.
Fraser, Jill Andresky, "Plans to Grow By," *Inc.,* January 1990, p. 111.
Gruber, William, "Firm with Fingers in Many Pies Anticipates Sweet Slice of Profits," *Chicago Tribune,* November 25, 1994, p. 3.
Jones, Sarah, "Sale Gives DRG 'Best of Both Worlds'" *Adweek, New England Advertising Week,* February 8, 1999, p. 3.
"Jordan Co., Officers Buy Fannie May," *Chicago Tribune,* November 5, 1991, p. 1.
Lazarus, George, "AmeriKing's Reign Has Burger King Taking Closer Look," *Chicago Tribune,* February 4, 1999, p. 3.
——, "Archibald Sweetening Its Candy Stable," *Chicago Tribune,* December 2, 1998, p. 3.
——, "Fannie May, Hallmark Alliance Could Be Sweet," *Chicago Tribune,* January 20, 1998, p. 3.
——, "Fannie May's Parent Sinks Teeth into Whopper," *Chicago Tribune,* September 9, 1994, p. 2.
——, "Firm a Whopper Among Burger King Franchisees," *Chicago Tribune,* December 5, 1994, p. 4.
——, "Jordan Co. Hot on Acquisition Trail, Buying Duro-Med," *Chicago Tribune,* November 22, 1995, p. 3.
——, "LBOs Are Forever at Jordan Industries: Growth, Not Fast Payoff, Is Firm's Goal," *Chicago Tribune,* December 1, 1991, p. 3.
Margolies, Dan, "Winning Ways: Jordan Negotiates LBO; Former KC Resident Would Take Control in $245 Million Deal," *Kansas City Business Journal,* November 29, 1996, p. 1.

—Nelson Rhodes

Keebler Foods Company

677 North Larch Avenue
Elmhurst, Illinois 60126
U.S.A.
Telephone: (630) 833-2900
Fax: (630) 530-8773
Web site: http://www.keebler.com

Public Subsidiary (55% Owned by Flowers Industries, Inc.)
Incorporated: 1927 as United Biscuit Company of America
Employees: 11,600
Sales: $2.66 billion (1999)
Stock Exchanges: New York
Ticker Symbol: KBL
NAIC: 311821 Cookie and Cracker Manufacturing; 311919 Other Snack Food Manufacturing (pt)

Keebler Foods Company, majority owned by Flowers Industries, Inc., is the second largest cookie and cracker manufacturer in the United States, marketing its products in more than 75,000 retail locations in the country and in selected international markets. Keebler's brands include Cheez-It, Famous Amos, Plantation, Murray, Ready Crust, and its signature Keebler brand. In addition to manufacturing private label cookies and crackers, the company ranks as the leading manufacturer of Girl Scout Cookies, producing more than 60 percent of such cookies sold.

19th-Century Origins

Keebler took its name from Godfrey Keebler, who in 1853 opened a small bakery in Philadelphia. Godfrey's bakery earned the distinction of becoming the first member of a network of local bakeries that later was amalgamated under the Keebler corporate umbrella. The other constituent bakeries opened up in subsequent generations, neighborhood bakeries that operated under the names Streitmann, Hekman, Supreme, and Bowman. The affiliated bakeries came under the control of a single corporate entity when the United Biscuit Company of America was formed in 1927. By the time of United Biscuit's formation, the

value of geographically separate bakeries operating under a single organization had proven its worth with the advent of the automobile. A fleet of trucks enabled the locally oriented bakeries to develop into regional bakeries, providing the locomotion for a territory-widening distribution system. By 1944, the network of affiliates comprised 16 bakeries whose geographic scope included markets stretching from Salt Lake City, Utah, to Godfrey Keebler's home city of Philadelphia.

More than a century passed from the opening of Godfrey Keebler's bakery to the adoption of the Keebler name as the unifying corporate title for the entire organization. In the decades leading up to that signal decision, the crackers and cookies were marketed under the brand names of their respective bakeries, a sprawling assortment of products and labels as diverse as the number of bakeries that constituted United Biscuit's ranks. Eventually, however, the management of the bakery network tightened the structure of its organization, aping a corporate trend that swept from coast to coast. During the 1960s, countless companies embraced the benefits to be found in centralizing all corporate functions under a single entity. The management of United Biscuit followed suit, realizing that greater corporate efficiency, quality control, and marketing effectiveness could be achieved by operating under one corporate banner. Accordingly, in 1966 Keebler was adopted as the corporate title for the bakery network and the single brand name for all the bakery products.

Although the debut of the Keebler brand name marked the introduction of one of the most recognizable brand names in the country, enviable marketing strength was not enough for the Elmhurst-based company to overcome its fiercest rival, Nabisco, Inc. Nabisco, like Keebler, was formed from a consortium of bakeries, beginning business in 1898. By the latter half of the 20th century, the New Jersey-based cookie and cracker manufacturer had developed into a towering force, its market share representing the yardstick by which Keebler's progress was measured.

1974 United Biscuit Acquisition Proves a Failure

Keebler remained an independent company until 1974, when it was acquired by United Biscuit Company, one of the largest food manufacturers in the United Kingdom. Within the

Company Perspectives:

To be successful in the impulse purchase-driven cookie and cracker category, you need to win customers store by store, day by day, by having the right product in the right place at the right time. At Keebler, we do this by combining great brands and elfin ingenuity with sales and distribution excellence. In our industry, new products and innovative promotions are critical to capturing the all-important impulse purchase. We pair our captivating products and promotions with unparalleled hands-on service, provided by our direct-store-door (DSD) delivery system. Through our company-owned and operated DSD system, we have 3,200 sales and distribution Elves calling on 31,000 supermarkets and mass merchandisers twice weekly. The benefits from this level of close contact with our customers makes the DSD system an invaluable asset to our business, not simply a delivery cost.

corporate folds of United Biscuit, Keebler operated as a unit of UB Investments US Inc., a subsidiary of the British parent company that would preside over Keebler's operations for the next two decades. Organized as such, Keebler continued its perennial battle against Nabisco, but eventually the strategy underpinning the company's war plan proved self-destructive. At United Biscuit behest, Keebler concentrated on developing and marketing salty snacks, such as Zesta Saltines, which, critics contended, diverted the company's attention from its core expertise in cookies and crackers. Further, Keebler drew criticism for trying to directly compete against Nabisco's stalwart brands, such as Frito-Lay, instead of building its market share in product niches where Nabisco's strength was more assailable. Ultimately, the period of United Biscuit's ownership turned Keebler into an unprofitable company, a period, so claimed *ADWEEK Eastern Edition* on October 11, 1999, when Keebler "did almost everything wrong." In 1995, the last year of United Biscuit's control, Keebler registered $93 million in losses. The time had come for profound changes to be made.

1996: New Management Sparks Rapid Growth

Two individuals were credited with Keebler's revival, Sam Reed, who would become the company's president and CEO, and David Vermylen, who would oversee the management of Keebler's brands. Vermylen had spent 14 years working for General Foods, marketing brands such as Stove Top Stuffing, Bird's Eye, and Post cereals. In 1988, he joined his wife in business and for the next three years the pair worked as marketing consultants. In 1991, the Vermylens received a telephone call from Sam Reed, who had worked with Vermylen's wife a decade earlier. Reed, a snack and baking industry veteran of more than 20 years, was about to become the new chief executive officer of Mother's Cookies, and he solicited the Vermylens for help in developing marketing strategies. David Vermylen and Sam Reed ended up working side by side at Mother's Cookies, with Vermylen joining as the company's vice-president of marketing before earning promotion to the post of president.

Reed and Vermylen arrived at Keebler in January 1996. Concurrent with their arrival, a leveraged buyout (LBO) of the company from United Biscuit was begun, restoring, it was

hoped, Keebler's capability to turn a profit. Thomasville, Georgia-based Flowers Industries, a producer of fresh and frozen baked foods, and Artal Luxembourg S.A. acquired Keebler through a joint-venture arrangement, installing Reed and Vermylen as the saviors they would soon prove to be. The company's vice-president of research and development remarked in a November 1999 interview with *Food Processing:* "The leveraged buyout was a catalyst for a huge change in our method of strategic direction. Sam Reed set the tone and standard and provided the permission to change." Reed radically altered the organizational structure of Keebler, placing a great emphasis on research and development, one aspect of the company's operations that had benefited from the era of United Biscuit ownership. In 1996, Keebler opened an 83,000-square-foot technical center in Elmhurst for cookie and cracker development projects. Designed to replicate a functional bakery, including receiving docks, a mixing room, ovens, and manufacturing lines, the technical center enabled Keebler to test all possible scenarios and it enabled Reed to develop products for niches where Nabisco's dominance was less resilient.

New product introductions played a pivotal role in the turnaround campaign begun in 1996. Reed instilled a renewed spirit of freedom and creativity among employees and reorganized the chain of command affecting research and development. New products, more than a dozen a year, were the result. Meanwhile, Vermylen developed a portfolio strategy that emphasized Keebler as the company's signature brand. Toward this end, Reed revived Ernie Keebler, a cartoon character that acted as the company's spokesperson, and his attendant elves. The use of Ernie Keebler and the elves had been discontinued under United Biscuit's ownership, but the fictional figures played a prominent role in the company's advertising and marketing campaigns and as the symbolic centerpiece of the new corporate culture cultivated by Reed and Vermylen.

The most visible aspect of Keebler's progress following the LBO occurred on the acquisition front. Roughly six months after joining Keebler, Reed acquired Sunshine Biscuit Co., the third largest cookie and cracker manufacturer in the country. Sunshine Biscuit was best known to consumers for its Cheez-It brand of snacks, which generated $125 million in annual sales at the time of the Keebler acquisition. Reed hoped to increase the brand's sales volume by distributing Cheez-It through new distribution channels and by relying on his research and development department to develop new varieties of Cheez-It snacks. Under Sunshine Biscuit's ownership, Cheez-It snacks had been sold in supermarkets and convenience stores, a distribution foundation Reed built on by making the brand available in vending machines and mass merchandising outlets. With greater exposure to consumers, Cheez-It sales began to climb, particularly after a flurry of product line extensions. Keebler introduced Hot and Spicy Cheez-It, Nacho Cheez-It, Cheez-It Chip-Its, and Cheez-It Heads and Tales crackers, which were targeted to children. The new product offerings and the additional distribution channels in which Cheez-It snacks were sold boosted sales considerably, more than doubling the brand's sales volume during the late 1990s.

The resounding success of the Sunshine Biscuit purchase convinced Reed of the gains to be made by pursuing growth through acquisitions. To finance further acquisitions, Reed celebrated his second anniversary at Keebler by taking the company

Key Dates:

1853: Godfrey Keebler opens a bakery in Philadelphia.
1927: United Biscuit Company of America is formed.
1966: Keebler is adopted as the corporate title and single brand name for all the company's products.
1974: U.K.-based United Biscuit Company acquires Keebler.
1996: Leveraged buyout of Keebler from United Biscuit is completed; Sunshine Biscuit Co. is subsequently acquired.
1997: Name changes to Keebler Foods Company.
1998: Keebler acquires President Baking Co.; Flowers Industries becomes majority shareholder of Keebler after initial public offering.
2000: Keebler acquires Austin Quality Foods Inc.

public, completing an initial public offering (IPO) of stock in January 1998. Nearly 12 million shares were sold at $24 per share, which gave Reed the financial wherewithal to contemplate his next move on the acquisition front. By September 1998, he had reached an agreement to acquire a private company owned by Taiwan-based President Enterprises Corp., the largest food company in Taiwan. Reed's target was President Baking Co., a nearly $500-million-in-sales cookie manufacturer that ranked as the fourth largest company of its kind in the United States. Headquartered in Atlanta, President Baking manufactured Famous Amos cookies, Plantation brownies, Murray and Murray Sugar Free cookies, and ranked as the leading supplier of Girl Scout Cookies, accounting for 60 percent of total production.

Keebler's acquisition of President Baking was strategically important for several reasons. Keebler enjoyed tremendous national brand recognition, but if the company had a geographic weak point it was in the southeastern United States, where President Baking's Murray brand of cookies was strongest. Aside from providing a core customer base in the Southeast, the Murray brand also steered Keebler, considered a premium brand company, into the value brand category. Equally as important, President Baking possessed a distribution system geared for delivering products to convenience stores, which complemented Keebler's strength in distributing crackers and cookies to supermarkets.

In January 1999, Reed established two new business units to help integrate the distribution of President Baking's brands into Keebler's existing distribution system. Mother's Cookie Co. was formed to oversee the Girl Scout Cookie business and other specialty channels, and Murray Biscuit Co. was organized to manage direct store delivery and direct sales group channels. President Baking Co. Inc. was established as a wholly owned subsidiary of Keebler. As the cumbersome task of incorporating President Baking into the growing Keebler organization progressed, the effect of Reed's influence over the company was tangibly evident. In less than three years, he had added nearly $1 billion in sales while leading a remarkable turnaround in profitability. The $93 million loss posted by Keebler before his

arrival had transformed into a $265 million profit by the end of 1998. Although the company lagged behind Nabisco, controlling approximately 20 percent of the market for cookies and crackers sold to supermarkets, drugstores, and mass merchandisers compared to Nabisco's 40 percent market share, the strides achieved under Reed's leadership were remarkable nonetheless. The announcement that the President Baking purchase was the first of many acquisitions to come promised further advances in the short-term future.

As Keebler entered the 21st century, Reed demonstrated his commitment to further acquisitions by announcing a pending $250 million deal. In January 2000, he agreed to acquire privately held Austin Quality Foods, a $200-million-in-sales manufacturer of cookies and crackers that was best known for its Zoo Animal Crackers brand. On the heels of the Austin Quality Foods deal, speculation arose regarding Keebler's relationship with its parent company. Flowers Industries was expected, at least by some, to sell Keebler or spin it off as a separate company at some point in 2000. As industry pundits offered their various theories regarding the affect of Flowers Industries' future decision on Keebler, one fact remained clear. Keebler, under the vibrant leadership of Reed, was pushing forward impressively, something the company was expected to do in the future regardless of its relationship with Flowers Industries.

Principal Subsidiaries

Bake-Line Products Inc.; Little Brownie Bakers; Denver Bakery Keebler Co.; Chicago Bakery Keebler Co.; President Baking Co. Inc.; Sunshine Biscuit Co.

Principal Competitors

Nabisco Holdings Corp.; Campbell Soup Company; Lance, Inc.

Further Reading

Cohen, Deborah L., "Despite Elves' Efforts, Keebler Stock Price Crumbles: Wall Street Shakes the Hollow Tree," *Crain's Chicago Business,* August 23, 1999, p. 4.
——, "Keebler Spinoff Takes Root for Flowers; Owners Dilemma: Free Keebler or Risk Takeover," *Crain's Chicago Business,* April 24, 2000, p. 1.
Dahn, Lori, "Working Magic," *Food Processing,* November 1999, p. 37.
"Flowers Boosts Keebler Stake to 55 Percent," *Nation's Restaurant News,* February 23, 1998, p. 92.
Gottesman, Alan, "Got Cookies?," *ADWEEK Eastern Edition,* February 9, 1998, p. 16.
"Keebler Starts Two New Business Units," *U.S. Distribution Journal,* January 1999, p. 74.
Lo Bosco, Maryellen, "Keebler Foods in Accord to Buy President Baking," *Supermarket News,* September 21, 1998, p. 43.
Lukas, Paul, "Oreos to Hydrox: Resistance Is Futile," *Fortune,* March 15, 1999, p. 52.
Rewick, C.J., "Keebler Looks to Make First Deal Since IPO," *Crain's Chicago Business,* August 3, 1998, p. 3.
Somasundaram, Meera, "Stronger European Push Seen into U.S. Food Market," *Reuters,* June 26, 2000.

—Jeffrey L. Covell

KINROSS
Gold Corporation

Kinross Gold Corporation

Scotio Plaza, 57th Floor
40 King Street West
Toronto, Ontario
Canada M5H 3Y2
Telephone: (416) 365-5123
Fax: (416) 363-6622
Web site: http://www.kinross.com

Public Company
Incorporated: 1993
Employees: 2,691
Sales: $318.2 million (1999)
Stock Exchanges: Toronto New York
Ticker Symbols: K; KGC
NAIC: 212221 Gold Ore Mining; 212222 Silver Ore
  Mining

In just five years Kinross Gold Corporation went from a newly formed company to North America's fifth largest gold producer. With revenues of $318 million in 1999, the young company considers itself the fastest growing gold producer in the world and its 1998 merger with Amax Gold helped put it there. Among its flagship operations are the aptly named Fort Knox in Alaska, Hoyle Pond in northern Ontario, and the Kubaka property in eastern Russia. Kinross also mines properties in Chile, Zimbabwe, and in the United States' richest gold vein, Nevada. Though gold is its *raison d'être*, Kinross also mines significant quantities of silver.

Birth of Kinross: 1992–93

Gold derived its name from the Latin *aurum* and its luster, malleability, and anticorrosive qualities have made it a prized possession since the earliest civilizations. More than 170 years after the establishment of the gold standard in 1821, several Canadian companies began discussions to unite and create a new company. Two of these companies were publicly held and controlled gold mining interests; the third was the equally-owned offspring of one of the gold industry's titans, Placer

Dome, Inc., and Dundee Bancorp. The discussions concretized in May 1993 when Plexus Resources Corporation, CMP Resources Ltd., and 1021105 Ontario Corp. pooled their interests and became Kinross Gold Corporation. For their contributions, Placer Dome and Dundee Bancorp gained a stake in the new company, with the former owning 17 percent and the latter weighing in with 24 percent (both later sold their shares).

Kinross Gold's key management came from Dundee and Plexus, and all had previous experience in the gold industry. Robert Buchan, Brian Penny, and G.A. (Gord) McCreary came over from Dundee; Art Ditto, from Plexus. Buchan became the upstart's chairman of the board and CEO; Ditto, president and COO; Penny, CFO; and McCreary, vice-president of investor relations and corporate development. By way of a 24 percent interest in Nevada's Denton-Rawhide Mine (formerly owned by Plexus) as well as properties gained from a subsequent deal with Nerco, Kinross had officially joined the gold mining and processing community at a time when gold prices were strong. Next came a 56 percent stake in Falconbridge Gold, which had substantial mining operations in Zimbabwe (the Golden Kopje and Blanket mines), and by the end of the year, the remaining 44 percent for full ownership.

With the Falconbridge deal came the Hoyle Pond mine, in Timmins, Ontario. Not only was this property an extraordinary acquisition, but it later became one of three Kinross flagship operations. By the end of 1993, Hoyle Pond produced 60,000 ounces, the vast majority of the fledgling company's total output of 67,702 ounces of gold, for revenues of $26.3 million. Another $5.9 million came from selling 1.3 million ounces of silver and overall mining revenues topped $32.2 million for its first year of business. From its earliest days Kinross adopted a sound business plan: high yields, low costs, and a modest hedging program as insurance against market downturns. Hedging, used by most precious metals producers, meant arranging to sell future amounts of gold at "forward" or fixed prices, thereby allowing both seller and buyer to circumvent the current gold market.

The practice, though widely accepted, had its detractors; some believed forward sales robbed shareholders of market upswings, forcing producers to fulfill contracts for the earlier agreed-upon prices and losing out on the extra profits when

Company Perspectives:

Kinross Gold Corporation is engaged in the mining and processing of gold and silver ore and the exploration for and acquisition of gold-bearing properties, principally in the Americas, Russia, Australia, and Africa. The company's products are gold and silver produced in the form of doré that is shipped to refineries for final processing.

prices soared. For the bigger companies, this was not a problem—they filled orders at contracted prices and sold additional reserves at the higher prices. Yet bantam producers like Kinross, without massive reserves, could be locked into contracts and lose out on market spikes. Although Kinross's hedging was on a small scale compared to several other gold producers, these forward-sale contracts worked in their favor in 1993 when the average gold spot price was $360 per ounce and Kinross had forward sales locked in for $388 per ounce. Its silver fared nearly as well, with the spot price hitting a low of $4.30 per ounce, while Kinross received $4.47 per ounce.

New Kid on the Block: 1994–96

The next year, 1994, Kinross brought its Hoyle Pond to greater production and annual revenues leapt to $92.1 million, with both gold and silver production up substantially (174,165 ounces of gold at $66.9 million, and 5.2 million ounces of silver for $25.2 million). The soaring revenue represented an almost 186 percent increase over its freshman year. This year also brought the debut of a Kinross mascot, a golden retriever, which appeared on the company's annual report. Now a medium-sized or ''second-tier'' producer, Kinross soon found out how much size really did matter when it went up against industry behemoth Barrick Gold Corporation to acquire the Toronto-based Lac Minerals Ltd. Kinross and another similar-sized Toronto mining company, TVX Gold Inc., planned to merge and split Lac's mining properties. Neither the merger nor the takeover took place; the Toronto-based Barrick's size, reputation, and ready cash reserves to finance the deal were impossible to beat.

With 1995 came a spate of Kinross purchases, including the Macassa Mine of Kirkland Lake, Ontario (ironically, from Barrick); increased ownership of the Denton-Rawhide Mine (for a total of 49 percent); a 25 percent stake in the Aginskoe project in Kamchatka, Russia; and a stake in the Goldbanks Project in Nevada. By year's end, there were eight producing gold mines (three in Canada, three in the United States, and two in Zimbabwe) and three producing silver mines (all U.S.). Year-end revenues climbed to just under $133.3 million, up nearly 45 percent from the previous year. In 1996 came high gold production (hitting 450,000 ounces) and troubles in Zimbabwe with the Golden Kopje mine, due mostly to extreme weather. Yet despite writedowns on Kopje, Kinross finished the year with revenues up by 54 percent, to $208.5 million.

Bouncing Back After a Market Crash: 1997–99

Kinross and competing gold producers had a rude awakening in 1997 when gold prices fell to $295 per ounce. No one, it seemed, was immune to sizeable market shifts regardless of hedging programs. Industry giant Barrick Gold's worth tumbled from $15.4 billion to $8.6 billion, while Kinross suffered its first annual loss. Though Kinross generated $183.5 million in revenues, its loss of $83.7 million came from writedowns on several mines (Kopje, QR, DeLamar, and Macassa) and the realization that the Goldbanks project, in which the company had increased its investment, was going nowhere. Luckily it was the dark before the dawn; a high profile merger was on the horizon.

In April 1998 Kinross bought into the Eastern Goldfields region, covering 533 square kilometers of land in Western Australia. On the heels of this deal the company joined forces with Denver, Colorado-based Amax Gold. Amax, which had been spun off from its parent company in 1987 and was 59 percent owned by Cyprus Amax Minerals Company, was a growing medium-sized mining company much like Kinross. The combination of their assets, however, was a coup for both—Amax brought three major mining operations (Alaska's Fort Knox, a half interest in the Kubaka Mine in Russia, and another half interest in Chile's Refugio Mine) as well as smaller properties while Kinross offered the stability of working capital and cash on hand. The merger gave Kinross reserves totaling 27 million ounces and increased annual gold production to 1.1 million ounces. Though the company was still called Kinross Gold Corporation, Amax was renamed Kinam Gold and operated as the company's largest subsidiary.

Kinross achieved a primary goal in the late 1990s by getting its production costs to under $200 per ounce, only to have them bounce back up by the end of 1999. Unusually harsh climates in Alaska affected Fort Knox's production, while union skirmishes and a tragedy at Hoyle Pond sent per ounce costs soaring from a low of $178 to $243, before coming down to $210 by the end of the year. On the positive side, Hoyle Pond bought out Royal Oak Mines Ltd.'s neighboring interests in Timmins, Ontario, and Kinross upped its ownership of the Kubaka Mine from 50 to 54.7 percent.

Then gold prices crashed again, with the industry suffering its lowest price in two decades. Such leaders as Barrick and Placer Dome came under increasing fire for their hedging practices and were accused of controlling the market with their vast reserves; second-tier producer Kinross took a beating on the stock exchanges but maintained high ratings by analysts. Mike Westcott of Goepel McDermid Securities believed Kinross was ''one of the better management groups out there,'' while the *Toronto Globe and Mail*'s Dave Ebner praised the company's ''strong management and clear vision'' in a June 1999 profile.

In early 1999 Kinross bought out La Teko Resources Ltd., then went on to purchase Newmont Mining Corporation's interest in the True North deposit in Alaska. Kinross finished 1999 with revenues of $318 million, an increase of nearly 15 percent over 1998, though earnings were still at a loss of $231.2 million for the year.

The New Millennium: 2000 and Beyond

In the first quarter of 2000, Kinross bought a 33 percent interest in Dayton Mining Corporation and then announced that quarterly earnings were once again a loss. Production costs,

---

Key Dates:

1993: Company is formed and, after several acquisitions, reaches 25,000 ounces of gold production.
1994: Golden retriever becomes company symbol and appears on annual report.
1995: Kinross purchases Macassa Mine in Ontario.
1996: Company reaches 500,000 ounces of gold production.
1997: Gold prices crash, company closes several mines, and golden retriever is absent from annual report to reflect the darkness of the period.
1998: Company completes merger with Amax Gold; now ranks as fifth largest gold producer in North America.
2000: Production climbs to more than 1.1 million ounces of gold per year, with gold reserves of 27 million ounces.

---

though not as substantial as the previous year ($7.8 million vs. $10 million), were high while yield was down at the Kubaka, Refugio, Denton-Rawhide, and Blanket mines (though up at Fort Knox and Hoyle Pond), and no gold had come from Macassa, since it had been taken out of service. To make matters worse, in May analysts at Goldman Sachs and Lehman Brothers downgraded the stock of several gold companies, including the United States' top producer, Newmont Mining Corporation, and Kinross. Management at Kinross was sure the reverse would be temporary; the company's balance sheet re-

mained healthy and Kinross was considered under-hedged by industry standards. With any upswing in gold spot prices, Kinross was poised to reap the benefits. In addition, ongoing exploration and development at its mining properties was expected to bring annual production levels up to two million ounces in the near future.

Principal Competitors

Lonmin Plc; Phelps Dodge Corporation; Companhia Vale do Rio Doce; Barrick Gold Corporation; Newmont Mining Corporation; Placer Dome, Inc.

Further Reading

Bolland, Pat, "Market in Profile: Q & A with Robert Buchan," *Canada's Business Report,* March 10, 1999.

Daly, John, "Going for the Gold: The Takeover Battle for Lac Minerals Heats Up As Two New Bidders Step into the Ring," *Maclean's,* August 8, 1994, p. 28.

Ebner, Dave, "Kinross Gold Bets on Expansion," *Toronto Globe and Mail,* June 8, 1999, p. B17.

Giese, William, "Wallflower Stocks," *Kiplinger's Personal Finance Magazine,* November 1992, p. 71.

"Goldman Cuts Kinross Gold to Underperform from Market Perform," *Newstraders,* May 25, 2000.

"Lehman Melts Down Four Gold Stocks to Underperform," *Newstraders,* May 3, 2000.

"Setting High Standards," *Mining Magazine,* January 1993, p. 35.

—Nelson Rhodes

Kraus-Anderson, Incorporated

523 South 8th Street
Minneapolis, Minnesota 55404
U.S.A.
Telephone: (612) 332-7281
Fax: (612) 332-0217
Web site: http://www.krausanderson.com

Private Company
Incorporated: 1912 as J.L. Robinson Company
Employees: 1,000
Sales: $710 million (1999 est.)
NAIC: 23331 Manufacturing & Industrial Building
Construction; 23332 Commercial & Institutional
Building Construction

Kraus-Anderson, Incorporated has been in the construction business for over a century. Subsidiary Kraus-Anderson Construction Company ranks as one of the top 50 domestic building contractors in the United States. Serving as general contractor, construction manager, or design/builder, the company completes over 400 projects per year and operates in 15 different market sectors. Another subsidiary, Kraus-Anderson Realty, has operated for over 35 years and grew out of the construction activities. Related endeavors, such as insurance, finance, and advertising concerns also come under the Kraus-Anderson umbrella.

Building a Business: Late 19th Century Through the 1950s

Kraus-Anderson's roots go back to 1897. James L. Robinson operated the business as J.L. Robinson Company through the early 20th century. Robinson built the first of several downtown Minneapolis projects in 1902: a store for George D. Dayton, founder of Dayton-Hudson Corporation. The Tudor-Gothic style YMCA Robinson constructed in 1917 would be converted to apartments nearly 80 years later, a testimony to solid workmanship.

Robinson sold the company to two employees, Matthew N. Kraus and Amos Andersen, in 1929, shortly before the stock market crash. Kraus-Andersen Company concentrated on gas station and sidewalk construction during the Depression years. In 1933, the partners hired Lloyd Engelsma as office manager, estimator, and field supervisor. Engelsma, a Hinckley, Minnesota native, moved to the Twin Cities to study engineering at the University of Minnesota and then attended the Minneapolis College of Law (now William Mitchell College of Law).

Engelsma purchased the business assets in 1937. (The spelling of Andersen was inadvertently changed to Anderson and has been used ever since.) Beginning with little more than a pickup truck, wheelbarrow, and two employees, Engelsma won defense contracts in Minnesota and Wisconsin during World War II and pushed construction volume up to the half million mark. Following the war, Engelsma expanded further; building projects included a church, high school, hospital, and KSTP's radio/television station. Construction volume rose from $1.1 million in 1946 to $2.8 million in 1950.

A second office, opened in 1949, established a foothold across the Mississippi River in St. Paul. The firm operated independently from the Minneapolis-based entity, capitalizing on the rivalry between the neighboring cities, both striving for growth. William Jaeger, Jr., future president of Kraus-Anderson Construction, was hired as project estimator and engineer in 1951. During the mid-1950s, the St. Paul office also worked on county roads in northern Minnesota, built the state's first freeway bridges, and won projects with the U.S. Corps of Engineers.

Industrial and commercial development heated up in the suburban areas during the 1950s and 1960s and provided Kraus-Anderson new opportunities for growth. The company built its first shopping centers and embarked on property ownership and management activities. In 1968, Burton Dahlberg was hired to manage Kraus-Anderson Real Estate, a one person operation in those days.

Expansion Years: 1970s

Construction volume stayed below $10 million into the late 1960s, but change was in store. In 1972, Kraus-Anderson erected its first high-rise, a 32-story apartment building in

Company Perspectives:

All of Kraus-Anderson's construction companies have been built on the philosophy of consistently meeting or exceeding the expectations of our clients. We strive to continually improve the services we deliver by listening to client needs, then constructing effective facilities which actually improve the performance of their operations.

downtown St. Paul. Yet, the company faced a general construction slowdown in the Twin Cities area. In response, Kraus-Anderson pursued industrial construction projects for the first time, building a sugar beet factory in North Dakota.

The company went on to build power plants, electrical transmission stations, grain-handling and flour-milling facilities, and wastewater treatment plants. By 1979, industrial projects comprised 20 to 25 percent of business. Expanding geographically as well, Kraus-Anderson engaged more work in the five-state area of Minnesota, Wisconsin, Iowa, and North and South Dakota, as well as the West and Southwest. The company established Kraus-Anderson of Texas, Inc., in 1974 as part of that expansion drive.

Construction volume for the privately held business rose from $40 million in 1973 to an estimated $220 million in 1979. Kraus-Anderson St. Paul brought in $50 million of the 1979 volume via projects such as condominiums in Hawaii, a theater in Hollywood, and a shopping center in Bismarck, North Dakota.

Kraus-Anderson Building Company, established in 1974 to take on smaller-scale construction projects—in the under $5 million range—contributed more than $25 million to the coffers. Meanwhile, Kraus-Anderson of Minneapolis, Inc. had more than 20 major projects under construction during 1979, including the Northwestern National Life Insurance Co. building. The $42 million project was "one of the most complicated the company has ever tackled and is one of the most unusual buildings under construction in the entire United States," wrote Wayne Christensen for *Corporate Report Minnesota.*

"The 100 Washington Square project is unusual because of the method being used to build its concrete central core. The core, which—along with the four corner columns—will eventually support the weight of the building, is being poured into a 'slipform,' a device usually used in the construction of concrete grain elevators," explained Christensen. Concurrently, the company was involved in the construction of another significant downtown Minneapolis building, the Pillsbury Center, the company's largest project to date.

Jerry R. Svee, Kraus-Anderson executive vice-president and COO, ran both the Minneapolis and the Dallas-based construction operations. Kraus-Anderson of Texas pulled in about ten percent of total construction volume, although Svee was predicting 30 percent of the company's work would be generated by the southern branch within the next five years. Construction projects in Dallas during the 1970s included the Plaza of the Americas Tower and Lincoln Center.

Beyond the construction realm of the business, Kraus-Anderson owned and operated 15 shopping centers, a number of office buildings and apartment complexes, and four bowling alleys. According to the Christensen article, the company had been increasing its real estate holdings at a rate of $15 million a year.

To serve the internal real estate operations and some outside clients, Kraus-Anderson established related businesses during the early 1970s. Kraus-Anderson Insurance Agency, for example, provided property and liability coverage. Kraus-Anderson Mortgage Company was involved in property financing. Key Group Advertising, Inc. produced a full range of advertising services.

By the late 1970s, President and owner Lloyd Engelsma had already handed over the daily operation of the construction end of the business to other company executives, but sons Daniel and Bruce were in line to inherit the family-owned company. Both of the younger men held degrees in business administration and worked for the company their father had built up over the last four decades.

Christensen wrote of Lloyd Engelsma in 1979, "It may well be that his basic decency and honesty have contributed to Kraus-Anderson's getting much of its business over the years, for the conventional wisdom in the construction business, largely dominated by family-owned concerns, holds that many contracts are awarded on the basis of the integrity of the company's principals and not to the lowest bidder."

Stumbling Economy: 1980s

The real estate and construction industries hit some choppy waters in 1980: tight money, inflation, and fluctuating interest rates. Construction contracts in the Minnesota, South Dakota, and North Dakota region fell 24 percent during the year versus a 31 percent increase in 1979, according to a 1981 *Minnesota Business Journal* article by Ken Wakershauser. Despite the difficult economic conditions, Kraus-Anderson lined up a number of significant construction projects, including $25 million worth of construction in Sioux City, Iowa, and a $10 million bank project in Minneapolis.

The company restructured in 1982, combining Kraus-Anderson Minneapolis, Kraus-Anderson St. Paul, and Kraus-Anderson Building Company into a single unit operating as three divisions. The change allowed Kraus-Anderson to work with clients on every step of a project from site selection through financing and construction.

Burton Dahlberg was named president and COO of Kraus-Anderson Incorporated and Kraus-Anderson Realty in 1984 and took responsibility for the related operations while Chairman and CEO Lloyd Engelsma continued to guide the company. Daniel Engelsma succeeded Dahlberg as executive vice-president of the real estate concern, heading up project development and property management.

Back on the construction side, in 1984, Kraus-Anderson was named general contractor for the new Minnesota parimutuel race track Canterbury Downs, a $50 million effort. The Piper Jaffray Tower in downtown Minneapolis and an office building for Cargill in Minnetonka, Minnesota, were also underway.

Key Dates:

1897: Firm is founded as J.L. Robinson Company.
1929: Robinson sells business to employees Matthew N. Kraus and Amos F. Andersen.
1937: Lloyd Engelsma buys company assets from his employers; name changes from Kraus-Andersen to Kraus-Anderson.
1949: Second construction office opens in St. Paul, Minnesota.
1959: Southtown Shopping Center construction signifies period of rapid suburban growth.
1968: Kraus-Anderson Realty Company is established.
1973: Kraus-Anderson achieves listing for first time on *Engineering News Record*'s Top 400 contractors.
1987: Combined sales surpass $370 million.
1997: Company celebrates its 100th anniversary.

Revenues of more than $250 million earned the company 38th place among the largest building contractors in the United States. Additionally, the company ranked among the top 100 shopping center developers in the nation.

By 1987, combined sales had reached $370 million, and the company employed nearly 1,000 people. Kraus-Anderson received some negative press the next year. The city of Minneapolis rejected the construction company's low bid for a parking ramp renovation. "The city's Civil Rights Department is investigating whether the company discriminated against minorities. Until that probe is complete the department is recommending that the company not be allowed to work on any city-assisted project," reported the *Star Tribune* in September 1988.

Overall, Kraus-Anderson fared well during the 1980s, a period when many general contractors folded under market pressures. "We aren't a flying-high company," said Dahlberg in a 1992 *Minneapolis/St. Paul CityBusiness* article by Mark Mensheha. "We do projects that are in our means to do." While other companies built up an already over supplied market, Kraus-Anderson pulled back on real estate development. In the early 1990s, Kraus-Anderson continued "to follow its pattern of restraint," according to Mensheha, focusing on maximizing revenue on existing properties, which numbered more than 80.

Holding Steady Through the Mid-1990s

While the real estate development market continued to slump in the early 1990s, construction stayed steady, producing a volume of $320 million in 1991. Construction at the Mall of America in Bloomington helped a number of contractors, including Kraus-Anderson. The company built R.H. Macy & Co's. $41 million entry in the Mega Mall and worked on about a dozen other improvement projects. About the same period Kraus-Anderson tackled its largest ever hotel project, the $95 million, 816-room Minneapolis Hilton and Towers.

Kraus-Anderson began renovating one of its older properties, Southtown Shopping Center, in 1995. Located in Bloomington, the property survived the 1992 onslaught of the Mall of America and its four million square feet of new retail space.

Built as a "community center" during the late 1950s, Southtown counter-balanced Southdale, a regional shopping center and the county's first indoor mall, Jennifer Waters observed in a 1994 *Minneapolis/St. Paul CityBusiness* article. The $15–$20 million endeavor, the first major upgrade to the property in 15 years, was spurred on in part by the retailing trend toward more big-box offerings and ever increasing competition in the area.

Historically, the company held onto most of the property it developed. Kraus-Anderson, in 1995, owned slightly more than three million square feet of retail space, mainly smaller community or neighborhood centers, and one million square feet of office and warehouse space, according to a *Corporate Report Minnesota* article by Eric J. Wieffering.

Kraus-Anderson's combined revenue climbed to $490 million in 1996: 75 percent from construction and 25 percent from real estate leasing and management, insurance, development, financing, and advertising businesses. The company's annual growth rate had been ten percent over the previous five years.

Endings/Beginnings: Late 1990s into 2000

The company marked its 100th anniversary in 1997, as well as the passing of Lloyd Engelsma. Over a period of six decades, Engelsma built Kraus-Anderson into one of the largest privately held construction firms in the country. His son Bruce Engelsma succeeded him as chairman and CEO of the parent company, Kraus-Anderson, Incorporated.

In 1998, the company added a commercial leasing business, Kraus-Anderson Capital, to the fold. The company was entering a crowded market: leasing companies were among the most common sources of commercial financing. Banks also served the market with low interest loans. Kraus-Anderson Capital, according to a *Minneapolis/St. Paul CityBusiness* article by Tim Huber, planned to concentrate on "small ticket leasing" ($100,000 or less) and target entities such as subcontractors with which it already had formed relationships. Kraus-Anderson's entry into the business was driven by available capital and the desire to retain displaced workers from a discontinued operation.

Kraus-Anderson Construction's affiliation with Anton Construction, Inc. received some favorable ink in 1999. The construction companies worked together under the Construction Partnership Program designed to help small minority-owned firms gain a foothold in the market. Minneapolis-based Anton's revenue was less than $10 million.

By contrast, Kraus-Anderson's revenue climbed from $640 million in 1998 to $710 million in 1999. Its five full-service operating divisions—Minneapolis, St. Paul, Building, Midwest, and North—were all based in Minnesota and handled projects ranging from small remodeling jobs to major new construction. Kraus-Anderson Realty Company owned or managed more than five million square feet of commercial property (office, industrial, medical, multi-unit residential, and shopping centers) in nine states. Other businesses supporting the company's primary operations included: Kraus-Anderson Insurance, which generated sales in excess of $27 million by providing commercial, personal, and cost-containment services;

and Kraus-Anderson Communications Group, a full service advertising agency and special event producer.

Despite these supporting businesses, Kraus-Anderson was first and foremost a construction firm, and with more than a century of experience behind its name would most likely continue to successfully negotiate the challenges of the construction marketplace well into the future.

Principal Subsidiaries

Kraus-Anderson Construction Company; Kraus-Anderson Realty Company; Kraus-Anderson Insurance; Kraus-Anderson Communications.

Principal Divisions

Minneapolis; St. Paul; Building; Midwest; North.

Principal Competitors

M.A. Mortenson Co.; Ryan Cos. U.S. Inc.

Further Reading

Beran, George, "Kraus-Anderson Exec. L. Engelsma Dies," *St. Paul Pioneer Press,* November 22, 1997, p. 5E.

Christensen, Wayne, "Skyline Sculptor," *Corporate Report Minnesota,* July 1979, pp. 48–57.

Forster, Julie, "Building Value," *Corporate Report Minnesota,* May 1997, pp. 44–45.

Hotakainen, Rob, "Affirmative Action Record May Sink Builder's Job Bid," *Star Tribune* (Minneapolis), September 2, 1988, p. 1B.

Huber, Tim, "Kraus-Anderson Enters Leasing Field," *Minneapolis/St. Paul CityBusiness,* May 29, 1998, p. 9.

Jones, Jim, "Kraus-Anderson Gets New Officers," *Star Tribune* (Minneapolis), September 24, 1984, p. 2M.

K-A Quarterly: Special Anniversary Issue, Vol. 5, Number 1, 1987, Kraus-Anderson Inc.

"Kraus-Anderson Bid Rejected," *Star Tribune* (Minneapolis), September 3, 1988, p. 3B.

"Kraus-Anderson, Inc.," *Corporate Report Fact Book 2000,* p. 508.

Levy, Melissa, "Building a Better Future," *Star Tribune* (Minneapolis), July 19, 1999, p. 1D.

Mensheha, Mark, "Kraus-Anderson Thrives by Practicing Restraint," *Minneapolis/St. Paul CityBusiness,* August 14, 1992, pp. 23, 25.

Milton, John W., "How 15 Minnesota Businesses Got Their Start," *CityBusiness 100 Years of Minnesota Business,* December 1999, pp. 94–103.

Neely, Anthony, "Center Cos. Ranks High," *Minneapolis/St. Paul CityBusiness,* April 22, 1987, p. 10.

Wakershauser, Ken, "Forecasting the Future for Real Estate/Construction," *Minnesota Business Journal,* March 1981, pp. 32–34.

Waters, Jennifer, "Southtown Flush with Expansion Plans," *Minneapolis/St. Paul CityBusiness,* November 18, 1994, p. 4.

Wieffering, Eric J., "Kraus-Anderson Updates Dowdy Southtown, Makes Its Own Power Play," *Corporate Report Minnesota,* June 1995, pp. 8–11.

—Kathleen Peippo

KVÆRNER™

Kvaerner ASA

Prof. Kohts vei 15
P.O. Box 169
N-1325 Lysaker
Norway
Telephone: +47 67 51 30 00
Fax: +47 67 51 31 00
Kvaerner House
68 Hammersmith Road
London W14 8YW
England
Telephone: (+44) 20 7339 1000
Fax: (+44) 20 7339 1100
Web site: http://www.kvaerner.com

Public Company
Incorporated: 1853 as Kvaerner Brug
Employees: 50,000
Sales: NOK 70.86 billion (US$9.26 billion)(1999)
Stock Exchanges: London Oslo Stockholm
Ticker Symbol: KVIOa
NAIC: 54133 Engineering Services; 541614 Process, Physical Distribution, and Logistics Consulting Services; 211111 Crude Petroleum and Natural Gas Extraction; 23332 Commercial and Institutional Building Construction; 336611 Ship Building and Repairing

Long known as the largest shipbuilder in Europe, Anglo-Norwegian Kvaerner ASA is redefining itself around three core areas: E&C (engineering and consultancy); oil & gas, and construction. Thus, Kvaerner is selling off its entire shipbuilding division, and although it failed in its goal to divest all 27 of its shipbuilding yards before the end of 1999 (the company sold only seven), it remained committed to a complete withdrawal from that industry. The company also exited the U.S. home construction market, and divested various other concerns, including plastics and pulp and paper operations. The company's restructuring comes in part as a result of its growth-by-acquisition drive in the mid-1990s, which loaded it down with debt at a time when most of its major markets were heading toward collapse. Seeking to reduce its reliance on manufacturing, Kvaerner is orienting itself toward the provision of engineering and other technological services. The leaner, more focused company has shed its diversified conglomerate image to become a major player in the growing market for large-scale engineering and consultancy services. The company's E&C division capitalizes on Kvaerner's strength in the process technologies field, providing services—from design and engineering, to project management and construction, to maintenance services—to the chemicals, pharmaceuticals, power generation, polymers, mining, minerals, iron, steel, and onshore oil and gas industries. Kvaerner's Oil & Gas division concentrates on offshore oil and gas industry, including the design, engineering, and construction of offshore platforms, as well as development of technologies, both above and below the sea surface, to assist that industry. The third Kvaerner division, Construction, concentrates primarily on commercial and infrastructure construction projects, particularly in the United Kingdom, Hong Kong, the Middle East, India, and North America. Led by president and CEO Kjell E. Almskog, the Kvaerner restructuring has been costly for the company, with losses mounting to NKr 5.6 billion (US$732 million) on revenues of NKr 70.86 billion (US$9.26 billion). The company nonetheless expected a return to profitability as early as 2002.

Building Norway's Industrial Giant in the 19th Century

Kvaerner was the result of a series of mergers among several pioneers in Norway's Industrial Revolution in the 19th century. Kvaerner Brug, which was later to give its name to the group of companies, began operations in 1853, establishing its headquarters in Oslo and quickly building a reputation as one of Norway's most prominent shipbuilders. The company's early participation in such key Norwegian industries as power generation and forestry and paper pulp production led to a cooperation agreement with Myrens Verksted. That agreement, made in 1922, divided up the two companies' operations into two key areas, with Kvaerner taking responsibility for the manufacturing of hydroturbine equipment and hydropower generation, and Myrens Verksted concentrating on the pulp industry.

Mryens Verksted quickly boosted its pulping operations when it entered the Kamyr pulp and paper partnership, adding its Norwegian operations to its partners' Swedish and Finnish operations. The Kamyr partnership became the basis for Kvaerner's pulp and paper division, which remained one of the company's key product areas until the end of the 20th century. In the meantime, the Kvaerner-Myrens partnership continued to expand its industrial interests. In 1943 the two companies joined together to take a majority position in another Norwegian company, Thunes Mekaniske Verksted.

Amassing Partnerships in the 1960s

Following World War II, Kvaerner continued to grow and to build new partnerships. By the early 1960s, the diversified operations of Kvaerner and its partner companies were in the process of being restructured into a single entity. The first step of this restructuring began in 1960, when a single president—Kjell Langballe, then president of Kvaerner Brug—was named for the ten member companies in the various Kvaerner partnerships. This Kvaerner ''group'' took on a more formal status in 1967, when the companies were reformed under a single holding company, Kvaerner Industries A/S. The new diversified industrial conglomerate, with ten operating companies, more than 3,200 employees, and annual revenues of NKr 385 million, was listed on the Oslo stock exchange that same year.

By that time, Kvaerner had returned to emphasizing shipbuilding as one of its key industrial areas. The company had acquired a shipyard in Moss in the early 1960s, and by 1965 had unveiled its first Kvaerner-designed gas carrier vessel. The company's early focus on the oil and gas industries was to pay off handsomely, as development of Norway's offshore energy industry began to transform that country into one of Europe's most important oil and gas producers. In the mid-1960s, the company began work on the design and engineering of a new breed of carrier vessel, designed to safely transport liquefied natural gas (LNG) products. By the early 1970s, the company had developed special tanks based on a spherical design, and the company's first LNG-carriers using this design were built in the company's Moss and new Stavanger shipyards beginning in 1973. These carrier designs helped promote Kvaerner's international reputation, as the company built up its own fleet of gas carrier and reefer vessels.

Kvaerner was also strengthening its interests in the offshore oil and gas industry. In the late 1960s, the company introduced a new subsidiary, Kvaerner Engineering, formed to supply engineering and contracting services to Norway's booming offshore industry. Kvaerner Engineering provided the basis of what later became the company's Oil & Gas division. By the late 1970s, the company boosted its oil and gas activities when it began its first offshore construction projects, at Kvaerner Egersund, fol-

lowed by the conversion of the Stavanger shipyard into an offshore platform construction plant. The Moss yard was also converted from shipbuilding during the 1980s. These yards were replaced by the acquisition of the company's first foreign shipbuilding yard, that of the Govan yard in Glasgow, Scotland. That yard, after 30 years of losses, became profitable in 1993 under Kvaerner's ownership.

The success of the Govan acquisition led the company to eye further acquisitions. For this it turned to Erik Tonseth, who had joined the company as a non-executive director in 1988 before being named president and CEO of Kvaerner in 1990. Tonseth, who had begun his career as a judge, had already forged a reputation for himself as something of an empire builder with the Norwegian industrial giant Norsk Hydro. As head of Norsk Hydro's fertilizer division, Tonseth had taken that company on an acquisition drive that was to result in the world's largest fertilizer company in just a few years.

New Leadership Brings Aggressive Expansion

Tonseth quickly turned his empire-building talents to Kvaerner, which, although enjoying a strong reputation for its shipbuilding activity, nonetheless remained highly centered around the Norwegian market. Tonseth took Kvaerner on a buying spree, picking up the Kleven shipyards in Norway, then turning to the international front with the acquisitions of Finland's Masa yards, the Warnow Werft shipyards in Germany, and others, giving the company a portfolio of some 11 yards and establishing itself as Europe's largest shipbuilder. Kvaerner also looked beyond shipbuilding, seeking to build its industrial and engineering expertise in other areas and international markets.

In 1990, the company agreed to split up the Kamyr pulping partnership between itself and Alsthom, forming the core of Kvaerner's Pulp & Paper division. The company also extended its offshore industry activities, turning to the market in the United Kingdom, with investments in Aberdeen and Croydon, as well as expanding its hydroelectric equipment activities into Doncaster. These moves helped to transform the company into an international concern; by the mid-1990s, more than ten percent of the company's workforce resided in the United Kingdom.

That percentage was to change dramatically in 1996. As the company entered into the second half of the decade, it was determined to expand its engineering and shipbuilding and other activities to a worldwide scale. The company's first foray involved the attempted takeover of one of its chief competitors, the United Kingdom's AMEC plc, in 1995. The company's offer of £375 million was rejected, however, amid outcries from the British press against the ''Viking Raider.'' The aborted AMEC takeover sent the company shopping elsewhere, to the Trafalgar House conglomerate, held in large part by Hong Kong-based Keswick. For a purchase price of more than £900 million (US$1.4 billion), Kvaerner leaped onto the international scene, taking over Trafalgar's 34,000-strong workforce, its holdings, including the Cunard cruise line and its U.S.-based housebuilding division, and other interests, including ownership of London's Ritz Hotel.

Trafalgar House had been established in 1956 by British entrepreneur Nigel Broackes. The company's initial focus on property development and real estate led to a listing on the

Key Dates:

1853: Kvaerner Brug is founded to build ships in Norway.

1922: Company forges a cooperation agreement with Myrens Verksted.

1943: Company takes a majority position in Thunes Mekaniske Verksted.

1960: A single president is named for the Kvaerner group of companies.

1965: Production of first Kvaerner-designed carrier vessels begins.

1967: Company is incorporated as Kvaerner Industries and goes public on the Oslo stock exchange.

1973: The LNG carrier vessel is launched.

1978: Kvaerner enters the offshore platform construction business.

1988: Aggressive acquisition program begins.

1995: Company's takeover attempt of U.K. competitor AMEC plc fails.

1999: Kvaerner announces reorganization to exit shipbuilding, and pulp and paper industries.

2000: "New" Kvaerner refocuses on engineering & consultancy, oil & gas, and construction.

London stock exchange in 1963. Broackes quickly expanded his company's focus beyond real estate, acquiring house builder Ideal, and then commercial builder Trollope & Colls. Trafalgar added Cleveland Bridge, one of the world's most famous bridge builders, responsible for the bridge across the Sydney Harbor, in 1970, and then acquired the Cunard Steam-Ship Company in 1971. Other acquisitions brought the company into the offshore energy market. Trafalgar later built up significant positions in the international engineering and construction industries when it purchased John Brown in 1986 and Davy Corporation in 1991. These two companies, both founded in the 1830s, were to form the core of the later Kvaerner E&C division.

The Trafalgar House acquisition made Kvaerner the world's largest engineering and construction firm, and transferred the company's international headquarters to London. The acquisition also loaded the company with a huge debt burden, while Kvaerner inherited Trafalgar's financial troubles. Kvaerner, which was mostly interested in Trafalgar's shipbuilding, engineering, and oil and gas operations, looked to sell off a number of its assets, including the Cunard cruise ship line, which was sold to Carnival Cruises in 1998 for US$500 million, and a number of smaller assets, including the Ritz Hotel. Nonetheless, Kvaerner and CEO Tonseth were criticized for moving too slowly on restructuring after the Trafalgar acquisition, and particularly for seeking the highest possible sale prices.

As such, Kvaerner was caught in a difficult position when the economies of much of the Pacific region collapsed in the late 1990s. With orders slipping and its foreign competitors, particularly the Korean shipbuilding industry, slashing prices, Kvaerner was forced to cut into its margins as well. By 1998, the company had slipped into the red, posting losses of NKr 2 billion on revenues of NKr 82 billion. The company's debt—

which reached US$12 billion by the end of that year, brought on by its ambitious expansion—had come to haunt the company as it approached the new century.

Refocusing in the Late 1990s and Beyond

In October 1998, Kvaerner's board reacted by sacking CEO Tonseth and charting a new course. As a company spokesman told the *Philadelphia Tribune:* Tonseth was "the architect of Kvaerner's transformation from a relatively minor shipbuilding company into a global organization. However the Board decided that the company is no longer moving forward fast enough and a change needed to be made. It was decided that the company needed to stop building and expanding and begin concentrating on management and making what we have more efficient and effective in order to move forward and reduce our current US$12.1 billion debt."

By mid-1999, Kvaerner's course became clear. New CEO Kjell Almskog, formerly of Sweden's ABB Ltd., outlined the company's plans to recreate itself as the "New Kvaerner." The chief component of the company's restructuring involved exiting the shipbuilding industry completely. The company announced its intention to sell all of its shipbuilding yards in 1999, an effort that failed, however, as Kvaerner found takers for only seven of its yards that year. Nonetheless, the company remained committed to exiting that industry as well as another of Kvaerner's former core components, the pulp & paper industry. As Almskog told *Industry Week:* "We need to make Kvaerner half as big but twice as good."

The new Kvaerner was to be centered around three core areas: Engineering and Consultancy (E&C); Oil and Gas; and Construction for the public works sector. By shedding its manufacturing base, Kvaerner placed its future emphasis on its knowledge base capacity, pointing the company, which originated in the Industrial Era, toward a position in the forthcoming Post-Industrial Society.

Principal Divisions

E&C; Oil & Gas; Construction.

Principal Competitors

ABB Ltd.; LASMO plc; AMEC plc; Preussag AG.

Further Reading

Farrelly, Paul, "Pushing the Boat Out," *Independent on Sunday,* March 17, 1996, p. 5.

Harrison, Michael, "Kvaerner Ousts Chief As Debt Pile Grows," *Independent,* October 15, 1998, p. 19.

Knox, Andrea, "A Shipbuilder Changes Industries and Countries," *Industry Week,* June 7, 1999.

Sethov, Inger, "Kvaerner President Resigns," *Philadelphia Tribune,* October 16, 1998, p. 3A.

——, "Kvaerner Swings to Q1 Profit on Core Gains," *Reuters,* May 9, 2000.

——, "Kvaerner Swings to Record Q1 Loss," *Reuters,* May 6, 1999.

—M. L. Cohen

Loews Corporation

667 Madison Avenue
New York, New York 10021-8087
U.S.A.
Telephone: (212) 521-2000
Fax: (212) 521-2525
Web site: http://www.loews.com

Public Company
Incorporated: 1969
Employees: 30,900
Sales: $21.47 billion (1999)
Stock Exchanges: New York
Ticker Symbol: LTR
NAIC: 551112 Offices of Other Holding Companies;
    524126 Direct Property and Casualty Insurance
    Carriers; 524113 Direct Life Insurance Carriers;
    524114 Direct Health and Medical Insurance Carriers;
    524130 Reinsurance Carriers; 312221 Cigarette
    Manufacturing; 721110 Hotels (Except Casino Hotels)
    and Motels; 213111 Drilling Oil and Gas Wells;
    421940 Jewelry, Watch, Precious Stone, and Precious
    Metal Wholesalers

Loews Corporation is a holding company with diversified interests in insurance, tobacco, offshore drilling, hotels, and watches. Run from the post-World War II era to the late 1990s by brothers Preston Robert (Bob) and Laurence (Larry) Tisch, the company was amassed through ''value investing.'' The Tisches earned a reputation for purchasing troubled firms, making them profitable, and selling them at a premium. Bob was known for his operational savvy, while elder brother Larry was considered the financial genius. In the early 21st century, Loews remained in the control of the Tisch families, who held more than 30 percent of the firm's publicly traded stock. Two sons of Larry, James and Andrew Tisch, and a son of Bob, Jonathan Tisch, began running the company in the late 1990s. Among the company's major holdings is an 86.5 percent stake in the publicly traded CNA Financial Corporation, one of the ten largest insurance companies in the United States; CNA contributes

about 75 percent of Loews' revenues. Another 19 percent of revenues is derived from the wholly owned Lorillard, Inc., the oldest and fourth largest U.S. cigarette maker and the producer of such brands as Newport, Kent, and True. Another wholly owned subsidiary, Loews Hotels Holding Corporation, operates 14 hotels and resorts in the United States and Canada. Loews also holds a 52 percent stake in Diamond Offshore Drilling, Inc., one of the world's leading contract drillers of offshore oil and gas wells; and 97 percent of Bulova Corporation, a major distributor of watches and clocks under the Bulova, Accutron, and Sportstime brands.

Early Involvement in Hotels

The Tisch brothers received an early business education from their father, Al, who owned a manufacturing plant in Manhattan. Bob and Larry were given the task of making phone sales to retail stores and wholesale distributors. The two brothers also helped operate a few summer camps their parents owned in New Jersey. This ''hands-on'' experience was coupled with formal training. After a brief hiatus spent in the army, Bob graduated with a degree in economics from the University of Michigan in 1948. Larry graduated cum laude from New York University's School of Commerce at the age of 18, went on to earn an M.B.A. from the Wharton School in Philadelphia, and later enrolled in Harvard's law school.

In 1946, Al and Sadye Tisch sold their summer camps and purchased the Laurel-in-the-Pines Hotel in Lakewood, New Jersey. The hotel business went well, and soon became more than the parents could handle alone. Larry dropped out of Harvard in order to help run the business and Bob soon followed. It was not long before the older couple decided to sign over their share of the hotel (worth about $75,000 at the time) to their sons and give them control of the operation.

The brothers soon began leasing two other small New Jersey hotels and managed to turn a profit. Then, in 1952, they acquired two grand but old hotels in Atlantic City called the Brighton and the Ambassador. They demolished one to build a motel in its place, and quickly resold the other at a profit. Later, the Tisches liquidated some of their New Jersey investments to

Key Dates:

1956: The Tisch brothers erect the Americana Hotel in Bal Harbour, Florida, establishing themselves as major hotel operators.

1960: The Tisch brothers gain control of Loew's Theaters (the apostrophe is later dropped from the corporate name).

1968: The Tisch brothers acquire Lorillard, the oldest U.S. tobacco maker.

1969: The Tisch brothers create a holding company, Loews Corporation, for their diversified interests.

1974: Loews acquires CNA Financial Corporation.

1979: The company purchases a majority stake in Bulova Watch Co.

1985: The movie theaters are divested and a 25 percent stake in CBS is purchased, with Larry Tisch becoming president.

1990: Company acquires Houston drilling firm Diamond M Offshore.

1992: Odeco Drilling is acquired.

1993: Diamond M and Odeco are merged to form Diamond Offshore Drilling, Inc.

1994: CNA acquires Continental Corporation.

1995: Loews engineers the sale of CBS to Westinghouse, with Loews gaining nearly $900 million from the sale; Loews takes Diamond Offshore public through an IPO.

1998: The Tisch brothers step down as co-CEOs; James Tisch is promoted to president and CEO. Lorillard and other tobacco firms reach $206 billion settlement with 46 states over tobacco-related health costs.

2000: A Florida jury awards $144.9 billion in punitive damages in a class-action lawsuit filed against the tobacco industry; Lorillard's share is $16.25 billion.

purchase their first two hotels in New York City. These early transactions established the pattern that would characterize their later business dealings, which grew increasingly diverse and valuable.

In 1956, with only eight years' experience in the business, Bob and Larry erected the $17 million Americana Hotel in Bal Harbour, Florida, and paid for it in cash. Although it was subsequently sold to Sheraton in the 1970s, it represented an important step in the brothers' careers. With the Americana, they firmly established themselves among the major hotel operators, and later acquired such prominent hotels in the United States as the Mark Hopkins, the Drake, the Belmont Plaza, and the Regency.

Adding Theaters and Tobacco in the 1960s

In 1959 a major antitrust ruling forced Metro-Goldwyn-Mayer to relinquish ownership of Loew's Theaters. This decision created an opportunity for the Tisch brothers, allowing them to move into a new business area. Six months before MGM was to divest Loew's, Bob and Larry purchased a large stake in the theater chain; by May 1960 they had gained control of the company.

The brothers did not enter into the theater business because they knew about the motion picture industry. Nor did they purchase Loew's because it was already a profitable operation on its own. On the contrary, Loew's theaters were losing money. They were large, multitiered movie houses with high ceilings and interiors reminiscent of the industry's "golden age," by this time long past. They played only one motion picture at a time and were rarely filled to capacity. Television and the proliferation of films coming out of Hollywood meant that theaters would have to cater to various tastes simultaneously in order to secure larger audiences. The old Loew's theaters were not designed for this purpose.

The reason Bob and Larry Tisch purchased Loew's had to do with real estate. The Loew's theaters, though antiquated, were located on valuable city property. It was the opportunity to acquire this valuable property that prompted the brothers to purchase the company. Almost immediately they began liquidating the theaters, demolishing 50 of them in a matter of months and then selling the vacant lots to developers. This, of course, hastened the demise of the palatial movie house, but it was nonetheless a necessary business tactic. Loew's remained a prominent participant in the movie industry into the early 1980s.

The long-established and well-recognized Loews name became the corporate title under which all Tisch operations (including hotels) were placed. Loews Corporation, a holding company formed in 1969, ran smoothly and efficiently, turning substantial profits every year. By 1968 the brothers again had the capital and the inclination to diversify and invest in a new business sector. This time they acquired Lorillard Industries, America's oldest tobacco manufacturer.

Lorillard, the maker of Kent and Newport cigarettes, had once been a major company with a large share of the tobacco market. Managerial incompetence and discord, however, had paralyzed the company, bringing it near collapse. Upon assuming control of Lorillard, the first thing Larry Tisch did was examine the firm's subsidiaries, particularly its candy and cat food divisions which were consuming a disproportionate amount of resources. The brothers discovered that the top executives spent 75 percent of their time on candy and cat food, which together made up only five percent of Lorillard's total business. Lorillard divested itself of these interests and of the executives who were so fond of them, then redirected the company toward its tobacco operations. Market share slippage was reversed, and Lorillard climbed back to the top ranks of America's tobacco market.

1970s and 1980s: CNA, Bulova, and CBS

A similar scenario took place in 1974, when Loews acquired CNA Financial Corporation, a large insurance firm. The Chicago-based conglomerate had reported a $208 million deficit that year and was expected to lose more. Like Lorillard, its subsidiaries were draining the financial resources of the company. CNA's tangential interests were poorly managed and veritable "money pits." Moreover, there was considerable waste at the top of CNA's corporate structure.

When Loews took charge it divested unprofitable or distractive subsidiaries to concentrate on the worthwhile core businesses. The Tisch brothers then took aim at the wastefulness that plagued CNA's headquarters. Many executives were fired as Tisch austerity measures prevailed over past CNA lavishness. The 3,000-square-foot suite of the former chairman was rented out, as was the corporate dining room. The streamlining had a dramatic and positive effect. In 1975 CNA earned a $110 million profit, and remained financially sound over the next decade, achieving annual revenues of over $3 billion by the late 1980s.

Loews' next major turnaround target was the Bulova Watch Co. In 1979 the Tisch brothers bought 93 percent of the then-troubled firm for $38 million. At the time, Bulova's quality-control problems had contributed to its slip from the top of the watch market to the number two spot. Not only had longtime rival Seiko Corporation won the market share battle, but Bulova was also threatened by Timex Enterprises Inc.'s introduction of competitively priced entries. It looked to some observers as if Bulova had squandered its brand cachet; the name was simply not recognized by a new generation of consumers.

The Tisch brothers applied their proven method of managerial restructuring, but without total success. Bulova's problems went beyond personnel and corporate networks: the product itself needed to be revised. James Tisch, Larry's son, headed the operation and immediately introduced 600 new watch styles, complete with extended warranties. To deal with the image problem, an extensive advertising campaign was launched. The company recovered, albeit slowly. By 1984 it had cut its losses to $8 million (roughly half of its 1980 total), yet it was still not paying for itself. The company did not turn a profit until 1986. That year, Bob Tisch accepted an appointment as U.S. Postmaster General. Despite the concerns of those who felt his absence would weaken the company's performance, most analysts contended that Bob Tisch's move to Washington, D.C., would help Loews, citing the advantages of both political and financial connections.

Late in 1985 Larry Tisch sold the company's namesake movie theaters and purchased a significant amount of CBS Inc. stock to help the company fight a takeover attempt by Ted Turner. Throughout 1986 Tisch increased Loews' holdings in CBS to 24.8 percent and obtained a seat on the board of directors. He was elected president of CBS that September, much to the relief of stockholders and employees, who had grown frustrated and uneasy during the Turner takeover attempt.

Tisch's popularity was short-lived, however. Intending to operate CBS as if it were any other business, he took measures to alleviate waste and make CBS more cost-effective. Wage cuts and spending reductions, along with wholesale firings, caused a serious rift in the huge broadcasting firm. The news division, traditionally given considerable leeway in regard to fiscal accountability, was especially hard hit. Some wondered if Tisch would be able to mend CBS without sacrificing the people and principles that once made it the most respected of the three major American broadcasting networks. Eventually, Loews reduced its investment in CBS to 18 percent through sale of stock back to the company.

Bob Tisch's activities and interests outside Loews garnered attention as well. He was one of New York City's most vocal supporters and had been elected over 15 times to the chairmanship of New York's Convention and Visitors Bureau. In fact it was Bob Tisch and the bureau's president, Charles Grillett, who came up with the idea of using an old jazz expression, the "big apple," to signify New York City. Later, Bob would represent the metropolis as its "official ambassador" (read lobbyist) in Washington, D.C. In 1990, he accepted the chairmanship of that city's chamber of commerce. In 1991, Bob Tisch paid over $75 million to acquire half of the New York Giants professional football team.

Early 1990s: Enter Offshore Drilling, Exit CBS

Over the course of the 1980s, the Tisches had reduced their stake in Loews from 45 percent to 24 percent, prompting some analysts to speculate that they were preparing to dismantle their conglomerate. Instead, the company—which had amassed a $1.75 billion "war chest"—started investing in new ventures, most notably oil. By 1990 Loews had spent $75 million on oil rigs and acquired Diamond M Offshore Inc., a Houston, Texas, drilling company. Loews amassed the world's largest fleet of offshore drilling rigs with the 1992 purchase of Odeco Drilling, Inc., which was merged with Diamond M in 1993 to form Diamond Offshore Drilling, Inc. In spite of that status, Loews' drilling segment lost over $103 million in 1992, 1993, and 1994. The company's annual report for the latter year blamed regional overcapacity and reduced demand for the negative results.

While other large hotel companies struggled in the early 1990s, Loews Hotels thrived under the direction of Jonathan Mark Tisch, son of Bob Tisch. Jonathan Tisch was praised for creative, ambitious, and often philanthropic promotions. His annual "Monopoly Power Breakfasts" featured celebrity contestants who played the famous Parker Brothers game competing on a customized board. Proceeds of the event went to charities. The upscale hotel chain's "Good Neighbor Policy" and its recycling programs earned it industry accolades as well. Following an industry-wide trend, Loews Hotels lost $1.79 million in 1993, then reported a net profit of $17.02 million in 1994.

The Tisches continued to apply their turnaround strategies to Bulova in the early 1990s. In 1995, they completed the divestment of that subsidiary's defense interests in order to concentrate on the core timepiece business. Although sales and profits declined as a result, Bulova was able to stay in the black in the early 1990s.

Loews' two largest investment areas, cigarettes and insurance, were very vulnerable in the early 1990s. Price wars prompted Lorillard to launch a bargain cigarette brand, Style, in 1992, then cut the retail price of its flagship Newport brand by 25 percent in 1994. In the decidedly antismoking climate that predominated, cigarette manufacturers already faced with legislation that banned smoking from virtually all public places also encountered many lawsuits. As of fiscal 1994, Lorillard was a named defendant in 17 individual and class-action suits brought by cigarette smokers, their estates and heirs, and even flight attendants who claimed to be victims of secondhand smoke.

When Loews subsidiary CNA Financial acquired Continental Corporation in December 1994 for $1.1 billion, it became America's third largest property and casualty insurer. It also took on Continental's liabilities regarding Fibreboard Corporation, a company that manufactured asbestos insulation products from 1928 to 1971. In 1993, Continental and its codefendants reached a $2 billion settlement (of which Continental was responsible for $1.44 billion) to cover past and potential liabilities.

Another key divestment came in 1995, when Loews engineered the sale of CBS to Westinghouse Electric Corporation for $5.4 billion. This ended Larry Tisch's controversial reign at CBS, and Loews' share of the proceeds amounted to nearly $900 million, swelling the company's coffers. In late 1995, Loews took Diamond Offshore public, selling about 30 percent of the company in an offering that raised $300 million.

Titular changes in the early 1990s seemed to indicate preparations for a changing of the guard at Loews. In the late 1980s, Bob had occupied the positions of president and chief operating officer, while Larry acted as chairman and CEO. But as the two brothers became septuagenarians, they consolidated their responsibilities, becoming co-chairmen and co-CEOs. James S. Tisch, son of Larry and a likely successor, advanced to president and chief operating officer, while Andrew H. Tisch, another son of Larry, led Lorillard.

Late 1990s and Beyond

In late 1995 Lorillard agreed to buy six discount cigarette brands from B.A.T. Industries PLC for about $33 million, but in April 1996 the Federal Trade Commission rejected the deal on antitrust grounds. Loews Hotel, meantime, entered into a joint venture with MCA Inc. in 1996 to develop three themed luxury hotels in Orlando, Florida, as part of MCA's expansion of its Universal Studios Florida theme park. The first, the Portofino Bay Hotel, opened in the fall of 1999 with 750 rooms. This property aimed to replicate the famous Italian seaside village of Portofino. The Hard Rock Hotel was slated to open in 2000 and the Royal Pacific in 2001. After helping to develop the hotels, Loews Hotels would also manage the properties under a contract arrangement. With the travel industry enjoying a resurgence in the economic boom time of the late 1990s, Loews Hotels moved ahead with other expansion plans as well. The company returned to Miami in 1998 with the opening of the Loews Miami Beach Hotel, an 800-room property in the Art Deco district of Miami Beach. In early 2000 the 590-room Loews Philadelphia Hotel was opened near the downtown convention center, and Loews Hotels also purchased the Coronado Bay Resort hotel in San Diego, California.

In 1997 Loews lost more than $900 million on a pretax basis from its $70 billion securities portfolio as a result of the bearish Larry Tisch's short-selling strategies against the long-running bull market. Net income as a result fell to $793.6 million from the $1.38 billion figure of the previous year. Late in 1998 the succession from one Tisch generation to another came to fruition. The Tisch brothers stepped down from their co-CEO positions but remained co-chairmen. James Tisch was promoted to president and CEO. In addition, an office of the president was formed consisting of James Tisch, Andrew Tisch, who also held the title of chairman of the executive committee, and Jonathan, who also continued to serve as president and CEO of Loews Hotels.

The new leadership at Loews faced many challenges, not the least of which was the increasing level of litigation and regulation facing Lorillard. The settlement costs from tobacco-related suits began to reach significant levels in 1997, when Lorillard paid out $122 million. Payments then escalated to $346.5 million the following year. Late in 1998 Lorillard and the other major tobacco companies reached a $206 billion settlement with 46 states for the reimbursement of public healthcare costs associated with smoking. Settlements with other states totaled another $48 billion. Lorillard took pretax charges of $579 million and $1.07 billion in 1998 and 1999, respectively, in connection with the settlements, the payments for which were to continue into the 2020s. In September 1999 the U.S. Justice Department filed a massive lawsuit against the major tobacco makers, modeled after the state lawsuits, with a potential industry liability well in excess of the state settlement.

Individual and class-action lawsuits continued as well, with Lorillard a defendant in no fewer than 825 cases as of the end of 1999. The most important of these was a class-action lawsuit filed in Florida, *Engle v. R.J. Reynolds Tobacco Co., et al.* The *Engle* trial began in October 1998, with a jury returning a verdict against the defendants in July 1999, finding that cigarette smoking is addictive and causes lung cancer, and that the tobacco companies had engaged in "extreme and outrageous conduct" in concealing the dangers of smoking from the public. The penalty phase of the trial then commenced. In April 2000 the jury awarded $12.7 million in compensatory damages to three sample plaintiffs, but then three months later delivered a potentially huge blow to the industry when it awarded $144.9 billion in punitive damages—by far the largest punitive damage award in U.S. history, dwarfing the $5 billion awarded in a suit against Exxon Corporation in connection with the *Exxon Valdez* oil spill. Lorillard's share was a whopping $16.25 billion. The tobacco companies immediately vowed to appeal, a process that had the potential to last years. In the meantime, Lorillard and the other tobacco firms had been able to manage the increasing litigation payments simply by raising cigarette prices.

Meanwhile, with the insurance market slumping and earnings down, CNA was undergoing a restructuring. In 1998 the company cut its workforce by 2,400, consolidated some processing centers, and exited from certain areas, such as entertainment and agriculture insurance. In October 1999 CNA sold its personal lines insurance business, which included automobile and homeowners insurance, to the Allstate Corporation. In early 2000 CNA put its life insurance and life reinsurance units on the block but in August of that year announced that it would keep them.

Principal Subsidiaries

CNA Financial Corporation (86.5%); Lorillard, Inc.; Loews Hotels Holding Corporation; Diamond Offshore Drilling, Inc. (52%); Bulova Corporation (97%).

Principal Competitors

American International Group, Inc.; The Allstate Corporation; American Financial Group, Inc.; British American Tobacco p.l.c.; Canadian Pacific Limited; The Chubb Corporation; CIGNA Corporation; Citigroup Inc.; Citizen Watch Co., Ltd.; Fossil, Inc.; Four Seasons Hotels Inc.; The Hartford Financial Services Group, Inc.; Hilton Hotels Corporation; Hyatt Corporation; Marriott International, Inc.; Movado Group, Inc.; Philip Morris Companies Inc.; The Prudential Insurance Company of America; R&B Falcon Corporation; The Ritz-Carlton Hotel Company, L.L.C.; SAFECO Corporation; The St. Paul Companies, Inc.; Starwood Hotels & Resorts Worldwide, Inc.; State Farm Insurance Companies; The Swatch Group Ltd.; Timex Corporation; Vector Group Ltd.; Wyndham International, Inc.

Further Reading

Bary, Andrew, "A New Leaf?: Loews' Neglected Stock Could Jump If Tobacco Unit Is Spun Off," *Barron's* November 30, 1998, pp. 23–24.

Browning, E.S., "Tisches Got Stampeded by Bull Run," *Wall Street Journal,* August 15, 1997, p. C1.

Carrns, Ann, "Loews Hotels: The Road Less Traveled," *Wall Street Journal,* May 21, 1997, p. B14.

Dodds, Lynn Strongin, "Nothing to Fear," *Financial World,* September 30, 1986, p. 100.

Fabrikant, Geraldine, "CBS Accepts Bid by Westinghouse," *New York Times,* August 2, 1995, p. A1.

Fairclough, Gordon, and Milo Geyelin, "Tobacco Companies Rail Against Verdict, Plan to Appeal $144.87 Billion Award," *Wall Street Journal,* July 17, 2000, pp. A3, A6.

Geyelin, Milo, and Gordon Fairclough, "Taking a Hit: Yes, $145 Billion Deals Tobacco a Huge Blow, but Not a Killing One," *Wall Street Journal,* July 17, 2000, pp. A1, A8.

Hager, Bruce, "Loews Sees the Future, and It's Oil," *Business Week,* March 19, 1990, pp. 126–27.

——, "Tisch the Younger Takes His Turn," *Business Week,* July 8, 1991, pp. 88–89.

Hamilton, Martha M., "Loews Corp. Hits a Gusher: Firm's Investment in Drilling Rigs Pays Off Big in Newly Thriving Gulf of Mexico," *Washington Post,* November 21, 1996, p. D1.

Jensen, Elizabeth, "Sharp Contrast: Why Did ABC Prosper While CBS Blinked?," *Wall Street Journal,* August 2, 1995, p. A1.

Kadlec, Daniel, "Tisch's Bad Bet," *Time,* November 30, 1998, p. 130.

Lesly, Elizabeth, "Loews Could Be Worth More Dead Than Alive," *Business Week,* December 13, 1993, pp. 104–7.

Lohse, Deborah, "Loews Announces Succession in Tisch Family," *Wall Street Journal,* November 5, 1998, p. A4.

Ozanian, Michael, "America's Most Undervalued Stock," *Financial World,* May 29, 1990, pp. 22–24.

Pesmen, Sandra, "Jonathan Tisch's Road Show," *Business Marketing,* February 1991, pp. 68–70.

Sheridan, Mike, "Rather Than REIT, Tisch Sets Loews Hotels on New-Development Track," *Hotel Strategies,* June 1999, pp. 8–9.

Smith, Randall, "For Tisch Empire, It Looks Like It's Back to the Basics," *Wall Street Journal,* August 2, 1995, p. C1.

Sparks, Debra, "Tisch: The Ultimate Bear," *Business Week,* June 8, 1998, p. 112.

Winans, Christopher, *The King of Cash: The Inside Story of Laurence Tisch,* New York: Wiley, 1995, 288 p.

—April Dougal Gasbarre
—updated by David E. Salamie

Merix Corporation

1521 Poplar Lane
Forest Grove, Oregon 97116
U.S.A.
Telephone: (503) 359-9300
Fax: (503) 357-9755
Web site: http://www.merix.com

Public Company
Incorporated: 1994
Employees: 1,233
Sales: $155.87 million (2000)
Stock Exchanges: NASDAQ
Ticker Symbol: MERX
NAIC: 334418 Printed Circuit Assembly (Electronic
    Assembly) Manufacturing (pt)

Merix Corporation is a leading manufacturer of advanced printed circuit boards that are used in sophisticated electronics equipment. From its manufacturing plant in Forest Grove, Oregon, Merix serves the communications, computer, and test and industrial instrumentation markets, supplying "interconnect" devices that link microprocessors, integrated circuits, and other components. The company derives approximately three-quarters of its annual revenue from sales to the communications and computer markets.

Origins

Merix was born from the corporate structure of Tektronix, Inc., a troubled *Fortune* 500 company that freed itself from several of its divisions as part of a reorganization plan implemented during the early 1990s. Before being beset by the problems that triggered Merix's formation, Tektronix had developed into one of Oregon's most important and largest enterprises. Founded in 1946 and based in Beaverton, Oregon, the company established a lasting presence in the business world by developing a way to accurately measure and display high-speed electrical signals. Tektronix's pioneering developments in the testing, measurement, and calibration of electric signals served it well during the postwar period, creating one of the largest concerns of its kind in the country. The company leveraged its mainstay business to branch out into other businesses, notably the formation of a circuit board operation in 1959.

Tektronix's circuit board business blossomed in the years to follow, eventually earning distinction by occupying a separate facility in 1983 in Forest Grove. From Forest Grove, the circuit board division served a distinguished clientele, supplying products to IBM, NCR, and Rockwell International, among others. Tektronix, meanwhile, was beginning to show its age. Throughout the 1980s, the company was hobbled by declining sales from its core products and, significantly, its strategic focus became blurred by numerous side ventures. Tektronix management took action in the early 1990s, and part of the solution for the company's ills was the creation of Merix.

As Tektronix entered the 1990s, its chief executive officer and chairman, Jerry Meyer, began formulating a plan to rid his company of the unflattering tag of a moribund former powerhouse. An important part of his plan hinged on narrowing the company's focus on its core product lines. Those businesses deemed outside the company's strategic pale were to be either divested or spun off as separate entities. To assist him in his restructuring efforts, Meyer hired John Karalis, a former vice-president and general counsel at Apple Computer, Inc. who joined Tektronix in 1992 as vice-president for corporate development. Karalis was one of the first of a group of former Apple executives who migrated to Tektronix in the early 1990s, a group that included Deborah Coleman, an 11-year Apple veteran who joined Meyer and Karalis in 1992 as vice-president of materials operation.

By the time Coleman joined Tektronix to head the company's circuit board division, she was already a renowned figure in the corporate world. A native of Providence, Rhode Island, Coleman earned a Bachelor of Arts degree in English literature from Brown University in 1974 and an M.B.A. from Stanford Business School four years later. During college, she worked at Texas Instruments, before beginning her post-academic career at Hewlett-Packard as a financial manager. In 1981, in what she later hailed as her best business decision, Coleman joined Apple as part of founder Steve Jobs's Macintosh management team.

At Apple, Coleman established her reputation as an ambitious, indefatigable, and sometimes over-ardent executive. She logged 100-hour work weeks while at Apple, drove a car bearing the personalized license plate "GECEO2B"—proclaiming her goal to be chief executive officer of General Electric Company one day—and struck one of her greatest admirers as being "too bossy, too loud, too rough around the edges, too everything," as quoted in the May 1996 issue of *Oregon Business*. Coleman's supporters acknowledged she had a somewhat abrasive managerial style, but they also applauded her rise within the executive ranks at Apple. She started at Apple developing Macintosh and LaserWriter products, before being selected to manage the Macintosh manufacturing plant. Coleman was named vice-president of operations and later, at the age of 34, she became the youngest chief financial officer of a *Fortune* 500 company in the country.

Merix's 1994 Spinoff

Not long after Coleman joined Tektronix, Meyer and Karalis began implementing their plan to spin off non-strategic internal components operations. The restructuring that ensued included the sale of Tektronix's ceramic packaging operation to VisPro Corp., a combination joint venture and divestiture of its integrated circuits operation, and the spinoff of its Forest Grove circuit board manufacturing plant. Coleman was selected to serve as the chief executive officer and chairperson of the new company created by the March 1994 spinoff, a company named Merix Corporation that began as a $78.5-million-in-sales company. Although Merix was created as a distinct business, its ties to Tektronix remained strong after the spinoff. Tektronix ranked as Merix's largest customer, accounting for nearly half of the circuit board maker's sales immediately following the separation. Further, Tektronix owned a considerable portion of Merix. Merix converted to public ownership in June 1994, with Tektronix retaining a 43 percent interest in its former division.

Despite Merix's financial connections to its former parent company, the Forest Grove-based concern was an independent enterprise capable of standing on its own in its industry. The company was a leading supplier of printed circuit boards, backplanes, and flexible circuits—devices referred to as "interconnect" products because they are used to link microprocessors, integrated circuits, and other components. Armed with approximately $30 million raised from Merix's initial public offering, Coleman was intent on greatly increasing the company's stature, hoping to create a $500-million-in-sales business by the

end of the 1990s. She wasted little time adding to the production capacity and technological expertise of the firm, acquiring a printed circuit board manufacturing facility in Loveland, Colorado, from Hewlett-Packard in 1995. The following year, Coleman acquired the Soladyne division belonging to Rogers Corporation. The acquisition gave Merix a printed circuit board manufacturing facility in San Diego, California. Following the Soladyne acquisition, Merix's sales reached $155.6 million, nearly twice the amount collected two years earlier when Coleman was just beginning to navigate on her own.

Faltering in the Late 1990s

As Coleman prepared for further expansion during the late 1990s, her hopes were dashed for a spurt of explosive growth to catapult the company toward the $500 million mark. Merix, like other companies in its industry, was buffeted by the collapse of markets in the Far East. The impact of the Asian economic crisis was exacerbated by an industrywide oversupply of electronics components, causing scores of electronics firms to adopt defensive postures. Coleman was forced to retreat as well, as Merix's profits plummeted in 1997 and again in 1998. As the industry downturn dragged on, Merix's losses increased, prompting Coleman to scale down the company's operations, lay off workers, and cut costs wherever possible. A $28 million restructuring program was begun in mid-1998 that saw the company shutter its manufacturing facility in Loveland in October 1998. Coleman conceded that the acquisition of the printed circuit board facility was the worst business decision of her career, declaring that she had paid too much for the plant. Coleman also rid Merix of its manufacturing facility in San Diego, selling the former Soladyne business in early 1999 to Tyco Printed Circuit Group Inc., a subsidiary of Tyco International Ltd.

Shortly after Merix's structural changes were complete, the company underwent managerial changes. In the midst of the restructuring process, Mark Hollinger, the company's senior vice-president of operations, was named chief operating officer. In May 1999, Hollinger was promoted to president and promised the chief executive position by September 1999. His ascension was triggered by a decision Coleman made in January 1999 to step down as Merix's chief executive officer, ending her reign five years after it had begun. Coleman professed a desire to devote more time to investing in emerging technology companies, but she was expected to remain Merix's chairperson until at least 2001. Hollinger, meanwhile, inherited a company poised to emerge from a worldwide surfeit of circuit board manufacturing capacity.

As the company waited for conditions to improve, having done what it could to position itself for the market's return to equilibrium, Hollinger declared his intentions to diversify Merix's customer base and to pursue strategic alliances with other concerns in the electronics industry. At the time he took the helm as president in May, there were already signs that recovery was on its way. Merix completed the expansion of its Forest Grove facility, a project that had commenced at the beginning of 1998, and began to hire employees after months of trimming its payroll. By late 1999, when Hollinger added the title of chief executive officer, there were tangible signs of recovery on the company's balance sheet. During Merix's second quarter in fiscal 2000, which represented the last months of calendar 1999, the company recorded $1.2 million in net income, a figure that compared favorably to the $1.9 million loss registered during the same period a year earlier. A significant contributor to the financial results was increased orders from manufacturers of communications equipment, a market segment that grew from 30 percent to approximately 50 percent of Merix's revenue during the previous year. The company's stock recorded an encouraging gain as well, increasing from $5 per share in May 1999 to $14 per share by the end of 1999.

As Merix entered the new century, the company appeared to have put the difficult years of the late 1990s behind it. One positive outcome of the industrywide downturn was the consolidation it triggered, as a form of corporate Darwinism played itself out. Those printed circuit board manufacturers that proved less resilient to the harsh market conditions either exited the business or were acquired by other firms, thereby reducing the number of competitors Merix faced as it plotted its course in the 21st century. Hollinger, who continued to steer the company toward an increased presence in the data communications and wireless communications markets, stood to gain from the return to more favorable market conditions. "The order rate for high-technology printed circuit boards continues to be very strong," he noted in a June 19, 2000 interview with *Electronic News,* "and capacity in the industry is definitely tightening. Demand

from both new and existing customers in the communications market segment is driving much of our sales growth."

As Hollinger formulated his strategy for the future, the judicious expansion underway in mid-2000 buoyed hopes for strident growth in the years ahead. The company's prospects brightened in July 2000 with the announcement of a $65 million investment that was expected to exponentially increase production capacity. Combined with a $25 million expansion of the Forest Grove plant that was announced in May 2000, the additional infusion of capital was expected to double production capacity by mid-2003. With its stature set to increase significantly, Merix pressed forward, intent on remaining an industry leader in the years ahead.

Principal Subsidiaries

Forest Grove Operation.

Principal Competitors

Flextronics International Ltd.; Hadco Corporation; Micron Technology, Inc.; Tyco International Ltd., Viasystems Group, Inc.

Further Reading

"Debi Coleman," *Business Journal-Portland,* February 25, 2000, p. 6.
Dolan, Kerry A., "Fairfield Bound?," *Forbes,* February 27, 1995, p. 142.
Holt, Shirleen, "Business Unusual," *Oregon Business,* May 1996, p. 27.
Keuchle, Jeff, "Good Apples," *Oregon Business,* December 1994, p. S12.
Kosseff, Jeffrey, "Investment Fuels Forest Grove, Ore., Circuit Board Makers Growth," *Knight-Ridder/Tribune Business News,* July 12, 2000, p. ITEM001950BA.
LaBarre, Polly, "The Seamless Enterprise," *Industry Week,* June 19, 1995, p. 22.
Levine, Bernard, "Merix Completes Soladyne Sale to Tyco," *Electronic News,* February 15, 1999, p. 34.
"Merix Moves to Cut Costs," *Electronic News,* August 24, 1998, p. 48.
Williams, Elisa, "CEO of Forest Grove, Ore.-Based Circuit Board Maker Departs," *Knight-Ridder/Tribune Business News,* May 25, 1999, p. OKRB99145147.
Woodward, Steve, "Oregon-Based Circuit Board Maker Credits Restructuring for Sales Rise," *Knight-Ridder/Tribune Business News,* December 24, 1998, p. OKRB98358096.
Zimmerman, Rachel, "Merix CEO Prevails in Male-Dominated Industry," *Business Journal-Portland,* September 30, 1994, p. 16.

—Jeffrey L. Covell

Metro Information Services, Inc.

200 Golden Oak Court
Virginia Beach, Virginia 23452
U.S.A.
Telephone: (757) 486-1900
Fax: (757) 306-0251
Web site: http://www.metrois.com

Public Company
Incorporated: 1979
Employees: 3,148
Sales: $314.6 million (1999)
Stock Exchanges: NASDAQ
Ticker Symbol: MISI
NAIC: 541511 Custom Computer Programming Services;
541512 Computer Systems Design Services

Metro Information Services, Inc. (Metro IS) is an information technology (IT) consulting firm based in Virginia Beach, Virginia. As of mid-2000 it had nearly 40 offices located in metropolitan areas throughout the United States and Puerto Rico. Its services include application systems development and maintenance, IT architecture and engineering, systems consulting, project outsourcing, and general support services. The firm supports all major computer technology platforms, including mainframe, mid-range, client/server, and network environments. As with many other IT consulting firms, Metro IS is shifting toward offering more Internet-related services, as demand for systems to support consumer and business-to-business electronic commerce continues to grow.

Internal Growth of a Private Consulting Firm: 1979–96

Metro Information Services, Inc. was incorporated in 1979 in Virginia as a private company. It was founded by John Fain and Chris Crumley in Virginia Beach, with Fain specializing in the technical side and Crumley the marketing side of the business. They began as a partnership, working out of Crumley's house and hiring out employees to do systems analysis and programming for large banks and manufacturing firms. Within four years the company had opened offices in Norfolk and Richmond, Virginia, and Raleigh, North Carolina. By 1985 they had 125 employees in six cities and $5 million in revenue.

Each new office was set up as a separate, decentralized profit center rather than as a branch office. At each new office, two codirectors—one technical, one a marketing specialist—were responsible for generating business and revenue. The only control exercised by the home office involved personnel and administrative policies.

Metro IS was able to attract customers by generating employee enthusiasm and creating a service mentality toward its clients. The company's employee-motivation techniques stressed teamwork and customer service. Rewards included a profit-sharing plan, an extensive education program for employees, and use of the company's mountain condo. Metro IS was one of six privately owned companies named to the "*Inc.* 500 Honor Roll" by *Inc.* magazine in 1986.

By 1994 Metro IS had 16 offices and 838 full-time consultants. Most of the offices were located in major southern cities. In 1995 the company expanded beyond its regional boundaries and opened offices in Chicago, Cincinnati, Philadelphia, and Phoenix. By the end of the year Metro IS had 20 offices. Revenue was around $85 million a year, and the company had 1,300 employees. Fain was president, CEO, and majority owner of the firm, having bought out Crumley's interest in 1991. Fain wanted to build Metro IS from a strong regional company into a nationwide provider of IT services. Major corporate clients included AT&T, Citicorp, Motorola, and Walt Disney. Its two largest clients, Newport News Shipbuilding and Northern Telecom, accounted for about four percent of the firm's revenue.

Growing Through Acquisitions: 1997–2000

Metro IS went public on January 29, 1997, with an initial public offering of 3.1 million shares of stock at $16 per share. Net proceeds to the company were $33.1 million, which were used to pay off the firm's debt and finance acquisitions. At the time Metro IS had 1,500 employees in 24 offices, the most recent opening in Denver. After going public, Metro IS began

Company Perspectives:

Metro provides a wide range of value-added Information Technology (IT) Consulting and custom software development services through our presence in numerous metropolitan markets in the United States and Puerto Rico. Our experienced Consultants and proprietary systems allow us to deliver high-quality, on-schedule services to our Clients in a cost-effective and efficient manner.

Key Dates:

1979: John Fain and Chris Crumley establish Metro Information Services, Inc. in Virginia.
1986: Company is listed on the "*Inc.* 500 Honor Roll."
1991: Fain purchases Crumley's interest in the company.
1997: Metro goes public.
1999: Company completes several acquisitions to expand nationally.

a series of acquisitions. Its first and second acquisitions took place in July 1997. Metro IS acquired Data Systems Technology, Inc., for $498,000, which gave it offices in Columbia and Greenville, South Carolina. It also acquired J2, Inc., of Kansas City, Missouri, which was doing business as DP Career Associates, for $5.2 million. In December 1998 Metro IS gained an office in the Palo Alto/Silicon Valley area of California, through the acquisition of The Avery Group for about $11.8 million.

From 1997 to 1999 Metro IS's client base grew from less than 400 clients to nearly 800 clients who each generated at least $25,000 in annual revenue. These clients were spread across several different industries, including banking, communications, financial services, healthcare, manufacturing and distribution, government, technology, and transportation.

Further acquisitions in 1999 resulted in new offices in Irvine and San Francisco, California; Camp Hill (Harrisburg), Altoona, and Pittsburgh, Pennsylvania; Charlotte, North Carolina; Hagerstown, Maryland; Kansas City, Missouri; Washington, D.C.; Baltimore, Maryland; and Dallas, Texas. These acquisitions included D.P. Specialists, Inc. for $18.8 million; The Professionals-Computer Management & Consulting, Inc. and Krystal Solutions, Inc. for $18.5 million; Solution Technologies, Inc. for $28.4 million; and Acuity Technology Services, LLC for $40.2 million. At the end of 1999 Metro IS had grown to 45 offices located in 21 states and Puerto Rico and more than 2,700 full-time consultants.

During 1999 Metro IS, along with other IT consulting firms, experienced a slowdown in demand for IT services, mainly affecting mainframe computer systems. Clients were reluctant to start new IT projects in light of potential year 2000 problems. As a result, many mainframe consultants left the company to seek other opportunities. While demand for client/server, network, and Internet-related projects remained high, it was not enough to offset the loss of mainframe consultants. This caused Metro IS to report lower than expected earnings in the second half of 1999, which continued into the first quarter of 2000.

Revenue for 1999 increased 47 percent to $314.6 million, up from $213.9 million in 1998, due largely to acquisitions. Net income was relatively flat, increasing 3.6 percent from $14.6 million in 1998 to $15.1 million in 1999. Net income was affected in part by a net interest expense of $2.9 million in 1999.

As of March 2000 Metro IS had 46 offices in 44 metropolitan markets in the United States and Puerto Rico. Of the firm's 3,148 employees, 2,600 were consultants, approximately 1,600 of which were salaried. Since 1994 the firm had grown at a compound annual rate of 36 percent.

Later in the year, though, Metro IS closed eight of its smaller offices and announced it might release 65 employees, including 40 consultants and 15 office workers. The planned closures were located in Memphis, Milwaukee, Minneapolis, Orlando, Pittsburgh, Portland, Sacramento, and Salt Lake City. Those offices together contributed less than 1.5 percent of Metro IS's revenue in 1999. The closings were not a cost-cutting measure; rather, it was the company's intent to focus on core markets as its business emphasis shifted to electronic commerce.

Metro IS continued to benefit from a strong economy, increased use and reliance on information technology (IT), significant changes in computer technologies, the growth of client/server environments over centralized mainframe computer systems, and a trend among U.S. companies to outsource IT projects. For 2000 Metro IS's strategy was to shift its employees toward Internet, client/server, and network skills that would support an Internet-based economy. The firm wanted to take advantage of the significant shift toward using the Internet for consumer and business transactions and the growth of electronic commerce. The company also planned to open fewer offices in order to concentrate its resources on training its workforce in Internet-related skills and increase its solutions capabilities. It planned to continue to grow through selective acquisitions.

In 1999 and 2000 the company experienced a shortfall in earnings as it missed analyst estimates for three straight quarters. Its stock fell from a high of nearly $28 in January 2000 to less than $10 in mid-year. Revenue shortfall was attributed to training costs and lower revenue caused by the transition from Y2K-related work to e-business solutions. It remained to be seen if Metro IS could recover in 2000 and continue the strong growth it had recorded for much of the 1990s.

Principal Competitors

Andersen Worldwide; Cambridge Technology Partners, Inc.; Computer Horizons Corp.; Computer Sciences Corp.; Keane, Inc.

Further Reading

"Daily Press, Newport, News, Va. Ticker Column," *Knight-Ridder/Tribune Business News,* March 2, 1999.

Hartman, Curtis, "The Inc. 500 Honor Roll," *Inc.,* December 1986, p. 90.

Mayfield, Dave, "Virginia-Based Business Serves As Clearing House of High-Tech Experts," *Knight-Ridder/Tribune Business News,* December 18, 1995.

——, "Virginia-Based Metro Information Services Plans Stock Offering," *Knight-Ridder/Tribune Business News,* January 8, 1997.

Richardson, Vanessa, "Companies to Watch," *Money,* April 1, 1999, p. 56.

"Virginia Beach, Va.-Based Information-Technology Consultants to Close Offices," *Knight-Ridder/Tribune Business News,* May 31, 2000.

Wagner, Lon, "Virginia-Based Metro Information Services Buys Two Firms," *Knight-Ridder/Tribune Business News,* July 2, 1997.

—David P. Bianco

Modern Times Group AB

Skeppsbron 18, Box 2094
S-103 13 Stockholm
Sweden
Telephone: (+46) 8 562 000 50
Fax: +46 820 5074
Web site: http://www.mtg.se

Public Company
Incorporated: 1995
Employees: 1,960
Sales: SKr 4.789 billion (US$541.48 million)(1999)
Stock Exchanges: Stockholm NASDAQ
Ticker Symbols: MTG MTGNY
NAIC: 513120 Television Broadcasting; 513112 Radio
  Stations; 511110 Newspaper Publishers; 511120
  Periodical Publishers

Sweden's Modern Times Group AB (MTG) is one of the Scandinavian market's leading media companies, with interests ranging from television to radio, to electronic retailing and publishing. MTG operates not only in Sweden, Norway, Denmark, and Finland, but also in Estonia and Latvia, as well as in other Eastern European countries. The company is also active in Western Europe, particularly in the Netherlands, Germany, France, the United Kingdom, and Italy. The company's free "subway" daily newspaper, *Metro,* brought the company's activities into the North American and South American markets as well; in May 2000, however, MTG spun off its *Metro* newspaper subsidiary as the independent and publicly listed Metro International SA. With sales of nearly SKr 5 billion (over US$500 million), MTG operates in five primary business areas: Broadcasting, Radio, Publishing, Modern Interactive, SDI Media, and Modern Studios. Broadcasting, grouped under the company's Viasat subsidiary, includes MTG's 17 television stations, including its flagship TV3 group of stations broadcasting to more than 17 million Swedish, Danish, Norwegian, Estonian, Latvian, and Lithuanian viewers, with plans to add a TV3 Finland as well; the company's channels also include the TV8 financial news and documentary channel, acquired in

1999, and Viasat Sport, launched in the same year. In radio, MTG has built a position as one of Sweden's leaders, with its RIX and Power Hit Radio networks. Since the Metro International spinoff, MTG's publishing arm consists of the financial monthly magazine *Kapital,* the business newspaper *Finanstidningen,* and the monthly *Silikon* magazine. The company's Modern Interactive division, led by its TV Shop subsidiary—Europe's leading electronic-based direct-sales company—has operations including television home-shopping and other "infomercial" programming, and programming for radio, Internet, and teletext. The division also oversees the company's Internet-based services, such as its online music store CDON.com and its shareholding in the Everyday Internet services group. The Modern Studios division holds all of the company's production and other content provision activities. Lastly, subsidiary SDI Media is a world-leading provider of subtitling and dubbing for films and television programming. MTG, a former subsidiary of Industriförvaltnings AB Kinnevik, is listed on both the Stockholm and NASDAQ stock exchanges.

Commercial Television Pioneer in the 1980s

MTG began its operations in the mid-1980s when Swedish industrial conglomerate Industriförvaltnings AB Kinnevik moved to enter the newly opening television market in the Scandinavian countries. Up until then, television broadcasting in Sweden, as well as in neighbors Denmark and Norway, had been strictly controlled by the government, and Swedish television audiences were limited to only the state-run television stations. This changed in the late 1980s when the Swedish government opened the country's airwaves for the first time to independent, commercially operated television programmers. The Danish and Norwegian government quickly followed suit.

Kinnevik was among those to be awarded licenses to operate the new commercial stations and became the first commercial television station ever to broadcast to a Swedish audience. Its station, TV3, began broadcasting on New Year's Day 1987 via the Astra satellite system. Its initial potential audience was 1.2 million viewers, but by the end of 1988, the new station could reach as many as 3.4 million viewers. The company soon expanded its broadcasts to reach the Norwegian and Danish television markets, providing programming in all three languages.

Company Perspectives:

The business concept for MTG is to be the best at capitalizing on the daily contact with consumers delivered by the Group's media. This is achieved by packaging products in ways that attract the audiences that advertisers demand and for which consumers are also prepared to pay in the form of subscription fees. In addition, MTG conducts other business related to media to the extent that such businesses either produce services more efficiently than external suppliers or provide extraordinary opportunities for profit or value growth. The business concept is pursued through a dual strategy: to establish MTG's products in geographic advertising markets with growth potential and to position them in segments of these advertising markets that have growth rates above average.

This approach soon gave way to the expansion of the TV3 concept into three separate, country-specific TV3 stations, as commercial broadcasting was allowed in Norway and Denmark. The three TV3 companies now broadcast in the separate languages, offering different programming to each market as well. Because television broadcasting had been a state monopoly in all three countries, TV3 was faced with a paucity of independently produced programming. In order to provide programming for its stations, the company formed its own production company, Strix Television, in 1988. The company also began to compete against the government-run stations for broadcasting rights, winning bids to broadcast such events as the Wimbledon tennis tournament and the ice hockey World Cup in 1989. By the beginning of the next decade, TV3's early entry into commercial television had given it a commanding lead in the race for the Scandinavian market's advertising dollar; at the time, TV3 commanded some 90 percent of all television advertising revenues.

At the start of the 1990s, the Kinnevik media interests—which had already made a foray into publishing—expanded in several new directions. The first was the launch of TV1000, a set-top based pay-TV venture. This station was soon followed by the company's entry into satellite television, when Kinnevik was awarded licenses to operate satellite television stations in Scandinavia. The company launched its Viasat satellite television subsidiary in 1991.

Meanwhile, Kinnevik's media group recognized another growing market and moved to form TV-Shop, providing direct sales marketing via television. TV-Shop would quickly grow to become Europe's largest provider of direct-sales programming, featuring both home shopping programming and the so-called "infomercial" format. Another subsidiary was formed at this time, as Kinnevik moved toward greater vertical integration in its media holdings, with the acquisition of a majority stake in Svensk Text (later renamed SDI), giving the company subtitling and dubbing capacity. SDI later grew to become one of Europe's primary media services operations.

TV3 showed its first profits in 1991, less than four years after its launch. Not all of Kinnevik's media ventures were as successful, and by the end of 1991, the company had exited its pay-TV venture, merging the TV1000 venture with Succé, its chief competitor.

Ruling the Airwaves in the 1990s

Kinnevik continued to develop its portfolio of television assets, including taking a 30 percent share of the new TV4 network, Sweden's first land-based, commercial broadcaster. The company also extended its interests to a different waveband, launching its initial radio station in 1991, marking the Swedish market's first commercial radio broadcasts as the last of the state-run media monopolies were abolished in the early 1990s. Norway, too, was opening its airwaves to commercial radio, and Kinnevik built a position as largest shareholder in P4 Radio Hele Norge. That station won one of Norway's licenses to operate a nationwide, commercial radio network in 1993. By then, Kinnevik's TV & Media division was celebrating the first full year of programming of its new station, the ZTV special interest satellite channel.

Kinnevik's TV & Media division showed its first profits in 1992, despite its continued costly expansion into new areas. Aiding the company's balance sheet were the successful spin-offs of two of its investments, as both TV4—which had quickly grown to become Sweden's most-watched television station—and P4 Radio Hele Norge were taken public as independent companies in 1994. By then, Kinnevik had won several commercial radio licenses for the Swedish market, forming the national radio network RIX and introducing the Power Hit Radio format to the Stockholm and Gothenburg markets. The company also launched its first Text-TV broadcasts, offering news, programming information and other text-based content via the TV3 broadcast network.

The year 1994 proved a turning point for the company. In that year, Kinnevik's TV & Media division adopted the Modern Times Group name. The company also made the decision to migrate its satellite broadcasting from the Astra satellite to the newer Nordic satellite. At the same time, the decision was made to encrypt its broadcasting, requiring access via subscription plans. The company could then generate revenues through both advertisements and viewer subscription fees. Joining the Modern Times' broadcasting family at this time was the newly launched TV6 station. Meanwhile, the company was quick to recognize the potential of the Internet, forming the basis of the Everyday concept, in conjunction with NetCom AB. By 1999, Everyday had matured into a full-grown Internet "portal," providing Internet connection and email, as well as content and access to the World Wide Web.

In 1995, Kinnevik boosted its publishing credits when it launched the free daily newspaper *Metro*. With revenues generated solely through advertisements, Metro was offered free to commuters in Stockholm's subway system. Commuters eagerly greeted the new arrival, and *Metro* quickly beat its own forecasts, turning a profit by the end of its first year. At the same time, MTG expanded its publishing holdings, buying a minority stake in the Finanstidningen business publishing group.

Back on the television front, MTG continued its expansion, introducing the 3+ television channel in Denmark, through a

Key Dates:

Key Dates:

1987: Industrial conglomerate Industriförvaltnings AB Kinnevik forms TV3.
1988: TV3 viewership reaches 3.4 million and expands to Norway and Denmark.
1991: Kinnevik launches the satellite TV venture Viasat.
1993: Kinnevik enters the radio broadcasting business.
1994: Kinnevik's TV & Media division is renamed Modern Times Group (MTG).
1995: Company enters publishing business, launching *Metro*, a free daily newspaper.
1997: Kinnevik spins MTG off as a public company with listings on the Stockholm and NASDAQ exchanges.
1998: MTG is broadcasting on televisions in Estonia, Lithuania, and Latvia.
1999: Internet portal known as Everyday is launched; *Kapital* and *Moderna Tider* magazines are introduced; TV8 is acquired.
2000: MTG's Metro International publishing concern is spun off as separate company.

merger of the TV6 and ZTV formats, before moving outside of Scandinavia to launch the TV3 concept in both Estonia and Lithuania. By early 1997, the Kinnevik concern had gained sufficient size to strike out on its own. In March of that year, the company voted to spin off MTG as a separate, independent company with listings on both the NASDAQ and Stockholm stock exchanges. By then the company's revenues had grown to nearly SKr 3 billion; yet its expansion had come at a price, with the company showing net losses of more than SKr 300 million for the 1997 year.

Independent for the 21st Century

The public offering nevertheless gave MTG the backing to pursue its expansion, not only within its Scandinavian base, but also farther flung on the international front. After the launches of TV3 Estonia and TV3 Lithuania, which were followed by TV3 Latvia, the company turned to its Metro subsidiary for further growth. In 1997, the company launched the *Metro Prague* edition; the success of the Metro format soon brought the company back home, however, as it launched an edition geared specifically toward a Gothenburg commuter readership. *Metro* was to quickly become one of MTG's primary growth vehicles, as the company began introducing still more Metro editions, starting with Budapest in 1998, and then editions in the Netherlands, Helsinki, and Malmö in 1999.

If MTG prided itself on its organic growth—most of its subsidiary operations had been launched by the company itself—it was not averse to expanding through acquisitions. MTG's publishing arm in particular benefited by acquisition, as the company acquired the remaining outstanding shares of subsidiary Finanstidningen in 1998, then added to its publishing holdings that same year with the acquisition of publisher Brombergs Bokörlag. In 1999, MTG launched two new publications, the financial monthly magazine *Kapital* and the monthly general interest magazine *Moderna Tider*. These were followed by

another monthly magazine, *Silikon*, itself based on a popular TV3 television program.

MTG had already returned to profitability by 1998, and by 1999 the company's net profits had grown to SKr 130 million on sales of nearly SKr 4.8 billion. The company's growth reflected a number of strategic moves, not least of which was the continued expansion—and success—of the *Metro* format into new markets, particularly in several cities in the United Kingdom; Zurich, Switzerland; Toronto, Canada; the South American market represented by Santiago, Chile; and the United States as well, with the first *US Metro* appearing in Philadelphia. The success of *Metro* was such that by the end of 1999, the company was said to be in negotiations to introduce the Metro format to another 60 countries worldwide.

Radio, too, was providing strong growth for the company, as MTG began broadcast operations in Latvia and Estonia under the Star FM format, and in Finland under the Groove FM and Star FM brands. The company also took over operation and financing of radio stations in the P4 broadcast network. Meanwhile, the company's TV-Shop subsidiary had grown to become Europe's largest media-based direct-sales company, reaching more than 100 million households in 34 countries. The company's acquisitions of Media Watchers Group in 1998 and Gelula & Co. Inc., of the United States, in 1999, made its SDI Media subsidiary the world's largest dubbing and subtitling services provider in the world.

MTG was also preparing for the advent of digital television; the company held one of Sweden's digital television licenses and was bidding for new licenses at the turn of the century. The company had also acquired a digital television license in 1999 when it purchased small news-and-documentary broadcaster TV8, which held its own digital television license. Yet the lack of reliable digital decoders and the lack of flexibility in the early digital set-top boxes left the company unwilling to pursue investments in the new technology.

The company showed more interest in the booming market for Internet and electronic commerce endeavors. Joining with partner NetCom, MTG expanded its Everyday concept into a full-fledged Internet portal, providing Internet access, content, and other Internet-based services. The Everyday concept was quickly rolled out internationally, with country-specific portals opening in France and the Netherlands, and plans to roll out the Everyday concept throughout Scandinavia and the rest of Europe early in the 21st century. MTG also began to build up a position in the electronic commerce arena, with online sales sites such as CDON.com, selling music over the Internet.

MTG moved into the 21st century with a new structure, reorganizing its holdings into the following divisions: Viasat Broadcasting; Radio; Publishing; Metro International; Modern Interactive; SDI Media; and Modern Studios. The success of the *Metro* newspaper format, however, led the company to spin that division off as a separate, independently listed company, a decision made in May 2000. The spinoff of Metro International returned MTG's focus to its core Nordic countries base, where the company expected to continue to play a major role as a media provider for the 21st century.

Principal Divisions

Viasat Broadcasting; Radio; Publishing; Metro International; Modern Interactive; SDI Media; Modern Studios.

Principal Competitors

Bonnierforetagen; Schibsted ASA; Marieberg.

Further Reading

Goldsmith, Belinda, "Swedish Free Newspaper Eyes the Americas," *Reuters*, July 29, 1999.

Labia, Aisha, "Subway Successes," *Time International*, February 7, 2000, p. 51.

Reece, Damian, "Freesheet Free For All," *Daily Telegraph*, January 23, 2000, p. 9.

Rosenberg, Jim, "Scoop Supports Growing Free Daily," *Editor & Publisher*, May 10, 1997, p. 21.

Short, David, "Metro Makes Tracks Towards Foreign Cities," *European*, May 8, 1998, p. 26.

——, "MTG Breathes New Life into TV8," *Cable Europe*, October 13, 1999.

——, "MTG Goes Digital . . . Almost," *Inside Digital TV*, October 20, 1999.

——, "MTG Wins Swedish DTT Race," *Inside Digital TV*, January 12, 2000.

—M. L. Cohen

Morris Communications Corporation

725 Broad Street
Augusta, Georgia 30903
U.S.A.
Telephone: (706) 724-0851
Toll Free: (800) 622-6358
Fax: (706) 722-7125
Web site: http://www.morris.com

Private Company
Incorporated: 1970
Employees: 6,000
Sales: $540 million (1999 est.)
NAIC: 323110 Commercial Lithographic Printing;
511110 Newspaper Publishers; 511120 Periodical
Publishers; 511130 Book Publishers; 513111 Radio
Networks; 513112 Radio Stations; 541850 Display
Advertising; 541860 Direct Mail Advertising; 561920
Convention and Trade Show Organizers

Morris Communications Corporation (MCC) is a mid-sized media company with holdings in diverse media. Its core business is newspaper publishing, with 45 newspapers including 31 dailies and 14 nondailies in 15 states. Its flagship publication is the *Augusta Chronicle,* and its largest-circulation paper is the *Florida Times-Union* of Jacksonville. MCC also publishes 22 free community papers, or shoppers, in eight states. Its book publishing division includes travel-related titles published and distributed through The Globe Pequot Press, which is one of the top three sources of travel books and maps in the United States. It also publishes several tourist publications, notably the Best Read Guides series and two publications in London, England. Of the company's 20 magazine publications, five are of national interest and the rest are local or regional publications. The five national publications include *Gray's Sporting Journal, Alaska, The Milepost, Quarter Horse News,* and *Barrel Horse News.* The company's nonpublishing properties include 27 radio stations and three radio networks, an outdoor advertising business, direct marketing, commercial printing, event marketing, Internet service providers (ISP), and web hosting services.

Early History

Headquartered in Augusta, Georgia, Morris Communications Corporation (MCC) owns what it calls "The South's Oldest Paper," the *Augusta Chronicle.* The newspaper was established in 1785 as the *Augusta Gazette* and was the town's first newspaper. The Morris family became involved with the *Augusta Chronicle* in 1929, when 26-year-old William S. Morris, Jr., became its bookkeeper. Within a few years he was president of the Chronicle Publishing Co. and publisher of the newspaper. In 1945 Morris and a colleague purchased a controlling interest in the *Chronicle.* In 1955 Morris and his wife acquired the remaining interest in the *Chronicle* and also purchased the *Augusta Herald,* the city's afternoon newspaper. It marked the beginning of the firm's growth.

William S. Morris III, son of William Morris, Jr., joined the firm in 1956, just before turning 22, as assistant to the president. Ten years later he was the publisher of the Augusta newspapers and president of Southeastern Newspapers Corp., successor of the Chronicle Publishing Co.

From 1956 through 1960 the Morris family owned the first licensed radio station in Augusta, WRDW, and its companion television station. The company would not enter radio broadcasting again until 1995, with the acquisition of Stauffer Communications, Inc.

Acquisition of More Newspapers: 1960s–70s

With two Augusta newspapers as its base, MCC began to grow through acquisitions in the 1960s. In 1960 it acquired two daily newspapers in Savannah, Georgia. Two Athens, Georgia daily newspapers were purchased in 1965 and 1967. The company's first Alaskan newspaper was acquired in 1969 in Juneau.

Morris Communications Corporation was established in 1970, with Southeastern Newspapers Corp. as a subsidiary, and descended from a corporate structure dating to the 19th century. Growth and expansion continued in the 1970s. Four Texas dailies were acquired in 1972. In 1979 a commercial printing plant and three nondaily newspapers in northern Georgia were acquired; these were subsequently sold in 1994.

Company Perspectives:

Morris Communications is a privately held media company with diversified holdings that include newspaper and magazine publishing, outdoor advertising, radio broadcasting, book publishing and distribution, computer services, and online services. Newspapers are the foundation and core business of the company owned by the Morris family since 1945. Today the Georgia-based enterprise reaches across the nation, has holdings in Europe, and employs 6,000 people.

Diversification into Other Media: 1980s

During the 1980s MCC made a major technological advance with the development of the Morris Publishing System, an innovative PC-based publishing system. It was used at MCC and later sold to other publishers. MCC had prided itself in being a leader in technology through its newspapers. It was one of the first newspaper publishers to use computerized typesetting, to have completely computerized newsrooms and production departments, and to switch to an offset press. With the advent of the World Wide Web in the 1990s, most of MCC's daily newspapers became available online, offering information over the Internet.

In 1981 MCC acquired *Quarter Horse News.* This biweekly publication was established in 1978 to serve the quarter horse industry in the United States and several other countries. In 1983 the acquisition of Florida Publishing Co. for $200 million gave MCC its largest newspaper, the *Florida Times-Union,* in Jacksonville, Florida, as well as a smaller daily in St. Augustine, Florida.

In 1985 MCC acquired Naegele Outdoor Advertising Inc. Naegele had been founded in 1934 by Robert O. Naegele, Sr., in Minneapolis, Minnesota. According to the *Indianapolis Business Journal,* Naegele Outdoor Advertising was the third largest outdoor advertising company in the United States in 1990 with 18,000 billboards in 15 markets. Several divisions of Naegele were sold in 1991. The remaining divisions were renamed Fairway Outdoor Advertising.

In 1987 MCC established Morris News Service, which became a leading supplier of regional and national news. Bureaus were established in Atlanta, Georgia, and Austin, Texas, but all MCC writers and reporters contributed to the news service. In 1988 two of MCC's afternoon newspapers ceased publication, the *Evening Journal* in Lubbock, Texas, and the *Jacksonville (Fla.) Journal.* In 1989 the company launched *Athens Magazine* and purchased *Gray's Sporting Journal. Gray's* was established in 1975 as a hunting, fishing, and outdoor magazine that featured literary articles and color photo essays.

Continuing Growth Through Acquisitions: 1990s

In 1990 MCC acquired a second Alaskan daily newspaper in Kenai. It also launched *Savannah Magazine.* In August 1992 the National Barrel Horse Association was formed at a meeting at MCC's corporate offices in Augusta. The association became a division of MCC and marketed numerous events related to

barrel horse racing, including world championship and state competitions. MCC would begin publishing *Barrel Horse News* in 1996. In 1993 the company purchased *Spur* magazine, which ceased publication in 1998. The afternoon newspaper *Augusta (Ga.) Herald* ceased publication in 1993. In 1994 MCC acquired *Augusta* magazine, which had been started in 1975. The company sold its North Georgia nondaily newspapers and its commercial printing plant, as well as nondailies in Crescent City, Florida.

MCC acquired Stauffer Communications, Inc. of Topeka, Kansas, in 1994 for $275 million. At the time MCC owned 12 daily newspapers and several magazines. The acquisition boosted MCC from the 24th to the 17th largest newspaper company in the United States. It nearly doubled MCC's gross income from $140 million to an estimated $260 million.

Morris first submitted a bid for Stauffer in July 1994, competing against about 30 other companies. MCC was notified of its winning bid in September 1994 and the purchase was finalized in June 1995. It included 20 daily newspapers, nine nondailies and shoppers, three magazines, seven television stations, eight radio stations and networks, a software company, a computer retail store, an insurance company, and a security alarm company. During 1995 and 1996 MCC sold off the magazines, television stations, insurance company, and security alarm system. Over the next five years MCC would expand its holdings of radio stations, nondaily newspapers, and shoppers, or free community papers. The computer store was closed in 1999.

Of the 20 daily newspapers acquired from Stauffer, the largest was the *Topeka Capital-Journal* with a daily circulation of 63,500, making it the fourth largest MCC daily newspaper. The only other Stauffer daily with more than 10,000 daily circulation was the *Holland (Mich.) Sentinel* with 20,000.

The Stauffer acquisition included four free community papers, or shoppers, in small markets in Florida, Kansas, and Missouri. MCC would expand its free community papers division over the next five years through acquisitions and by establishing new papers. Seven additional free community papers were acquired in 1996 and early 1997 in small markets in Michigan, Nebraska, South Dakota, and Colorado. New papers were launched in small markets in Florida and Nebraska in 1997. Others were purchased in 1999, and three related Nebraska publications were started in December 1999, giving MCC more than 20 free community papers in all.

In 1995 MCC acquired *Alaska* magazine and the *Alaska Journal of Commerce. Alaska* was founded in 1935; published ten times a year, the magazine featured articles about life on America's "last frontier." The *Alaska Journal of Commerce* was established in 1976 and carried general business news covering areas such as tourism, construction, transportation, commercial fishing, and other industries important to Alaska.

In the fall of 1995 MCC entered the Internet business by building an Internet service provider (ISP) and establishing a division of online services to help MCC newspapers develop and execute a World Wide Web publishing strategy. The company's first ISP was built at the *Topeka Capital-Journal,* followed by an ISP in Augusta. By the end of the decade MCC was operating similar services in five other locations, all managed

Key Dates:

1929: William S. Morris, Jr., becomes bookkeeper of the *Augusta (Ga.) Chronicle.*

1945: Morris and a colleague purchase a controlling interest in the *Chronicle.*

1955: Morris and his wife purchase the remaining interest in the *Chronicle* and also buy the *Augusta Herald.*

1967: Williams S. Morris, Jr., dies.

1970: Morris Communications Corporation (MCC) is established, with Southeastern Newspapers Corp. as a subsidiary.

1985: MCC acquires Naegele Outdoor Advertising Inc., the third largest outdoor advertising firm in the United States.

1994: MCC acquires Stauffer Communications Inc. for $275 million.

1997: MCC acquires The Globe Pequot Press and enters the book publishing business; MCC acquires Best Read Guides Franchise Corp.

from Topeka by Morris Digital Works. Within a year of establishing its online division, approximately three-fourths of the company's newspapers had an online presence. In 1997 MCC joined the New York Times Co. as lead investors in Zip2 Corp., a company that would provide MCC with a suite of online products for local content such as restaurants, movies, community events, and other information. By 2000 MCC's online division also operated a web hosting business in Augusta, hosting most of MCC's newspapers' web sites as well as hundreds of those newspapers' customers' own web sites.

MCC's online division also included Stauffer Media Systems, which was established in 1977 to offer business and accounting software designed specifically for the newspaper industry. It later developed leading pre-press software systems. MCC acquired the business in 1995 with its purchase of Stauffer Communications, Inc.

The year 1996 was one of several acquisitions. MCC's purchase of Flashes Publishers, Inc. in Allegan, Michigan, included the monthly *West Michigan Senior Times,* the weekly *Flashes Shopping Guide,* and a commercial printing operation. MCC picked up another commercial printing operation, a weekly newspaper, and two free community papers with the purchase of Broadcaster Press in Vermillion, South Dakota. Other acquisitions that year included *Alaskan Equipment Trader* and two free community papers in Nebraska. The afternoon newspaper *Savannah (Ga.) Evening Press* ceased publication that year. For 1996 MCC's revenues were reported at $360 million.

The two commercial printing operations that MCC acquired in 1996 formed its commercial printing division. Broadcaster Press was a leading centralized web printer in South Dakota that printed 15 weekly newspapers and free community papers along with several monthly publications. The second printing operation came with the purchase of Flashes Publishers of Allegan, Michigan. In addition to owning two nonheat-set web presses, it had its own saddle-stitch binding operation and a full-

service pre-press operation. By the end of the decade the Flashes printing operation was producing about 100 million printed pieces annually.

MCC entered the book publishing business with the acquisition of The Globe Pequot Press in 1997 from AT&T Wireless Services, Inc. Based in Old Saybrook, Connecticut, Globe Pequot published a broad selection of travel-related books, maps, and cassettes. Later in the year MCC purchased Gateway Books and folded it into the Globe Pequot operation. Gateway specialized in travel guides for seniors and retired travelers. ICS Books Inc., based in Merrillville, Indiana, was added to the Globe Pequot operation in 1998; it published outdoor recreation books.

Before the end of 1997 MCC acquired Best Read Guides Franchise Corp., including 17 franchisee tourist guides and related online services. MCC subsequently launched several of its own Best Read Guides, both in print and online-only editions, as part of its tourist publications division. These digest-sized magazines and online-only editions numbered 37 by 2000 and covered resort markets in the United States and Great Britain.

Other 1997 acquisitions included the *Milepost* annual travel guide, which was the oldest continuously published guidebook for Alaska and northwestern Canada. MCC launched three free community papers and purchased two others in 1997. Toward the end of 1997 the *Hilton Head News* was absorbed into the Savannah newspaper operation.

MCC greatly expanded its holdings in radio broadcasting in 1997 and 1998. In late 1997 MCC purchased seven Palm Springs, California, radio stations, which it organized as the Desert Radio Group. In 1998 MCC acquired six stations in Alaska and seven in Washington from Seattle-based Pioneer Broadcasting Co., Inc. MCC added two more Washington stations in 2000. The company's Anchorage Media Group consisted of six radio stations in Alaska. Its nine Washington stations were organized in two groups, the Columbia River Media Group and the Grays Harbor Radio Group. The company also owned an AM-FM duopoly in Amarillo, Texas; an AM-FM combination in Topeka, Kansas; and three Topeka-based radio networks (Kansas Agriculture Network, Kansas Information Network, and Wildcat Sports Network). The Kansas and Texas properties were part of the Stauffer Communications, Inc. purchase of 1995. In 2000 MCC acquired Riviera Radio, an English-language radio station based in the European principality of Monaco that served the international tourist community on the French Riviera.

MCC's first international venture was the acquisition of London-based Cadogan Guides and the establishment of Morris Publications Ltd. in London in 1998. Cadogan published more than 80 travel titles covering popular destinations worldwide. In late 1998 MCC entered the international tourist publication market with the acquisition of *London This Week,* which became *Best Read Guide/London,* and *London in One.* (*London in One* ceased publication in late 1999.) MCC also acquired *Londinium,* a quarterly that listed events and activities for hotel guests in London. The three tourist publications were also published by Morris Communications Ltd. of London.

MCC expanded its outdoor advertising business by purchasing three outdoor advertising companies and absorbing them into Fairway Outdoor Advertising. The acquired companies were Metro Outdoor Advertising in Greenville, South Carolina; Desert Outdoor Advertising in Palm Springs, California; and AAA Outdoor Advertising in Burlington, North Carolina. The Palm Springs purchase gave Fairway sign placement in such cities as Los Angeles and Hollywood. Fairway had five branches: 1) GSA, located in Greenville and Spartanburg, South Carolina, and Asheville, North Carolina; 2) Palm Springs, California; 3) Triad, in Greensboro, High Point, and Winston-Salem, North Carolina; 4) Triangle East, in Raleigh, Durham, and Wilmington, North Carolina; and 5) Twin Cities, in Minneapolis and St. Paul, Minnesota.

MCC entered the direct marketing business in 1998 with the purchase of two Miami-based target marketing firms, The Mailworks and Broadcast Direct Marketing. The companies were renamed Morris Direct Marketing, then became SmarT-Target Marketing. SmarTTarget Marketing provided list services, database systems, creative services, in-depth research, and other target marketing services.

During 1998 MCC launched *Water's Edge* and *Kalamazoo (Mich.) Express,* a specialized publication. *Water's Edge* was a regional magazine aimed at people living on local waterways along the southern East Coast from Hilton Head, South Carolina, to Daytona Beach, Florida.

MCC continued to expand in 1999 with the acquisition of two nondaily newspapers, a free community paper, and a specialized publication, all in South Carolina. It also added two nondaily newspapers and two free community papers in Minnesota and a free community paper in Michigan. During the year three free community papers were launched in Nebraska. MCC's magazine division added two specialized publications, *Coastal Senior* and *Coastal Antiques and Art,* aimed at readers in the Savannah, Georgia area, and one in Ohio, *The Horsetrader.*

In transactions not already covered, MCC added to its Alaskan holdings in 2000 with the purchase of two nondaily newspapers in Alaska, and *Destination Alaska,* a digest-sized port guide for passengers of cruise ships docking in Seattle, Seward, Alaska, and Vancouver, Canada.

Acquisitions in early 2000 also included a specialized publication, *Senior Living,* in Tennessee, as well as start-up of another, *Tennessee Antiques.* For the future, MCC would likely continue to grow by strengthening its divisions through selective acquisitions. The company was owned and managed by the Morris family. Chairman and CEO Williams S. Morris III turned 66 in 2000. His three children, Will, Tyler, and Susie, had all been involved in company management—Will served as president of the corporation. There has been no indication of the company being a takeover target.

Principal Subsidiaries

Fairway Outdoor Advertising, Inc.; Globe Pequot Press; Morris Publications Ltd. (England); SmarTTarget Marketing; Morris Digital Works; Stauffer Media Systems; Southeastern Newspapers Corp.

Principal Divisions

Newspaper Publishing; Outdoor Advertising; Radio Broadcasting; Publishing and Book Distribution; Tourist Publications; Magazines and Specialized Publications; Free Community Papers; Direct Marketing; Commercial Printing; Online and Computer Services; Event Marketing.

Principal Competitors

Cox Enterprises, Inc.; Gannett Co., Inc.; Knight-Ridder, Inc.; McClatchy Newspapers, Inc.

Further Reading

Ascenzi, Joseph, ''Georgia Firm Snaps Up 7 Coachella Valley, Calif., Radio Stations,'' *Knight-Ridder/Tribune Business News,* November 24, 1997.

Badger, T.A., ''Augusta, Ga.-Based Morris Communications Expands in Alaska,'' *Knight-Ridder/Tribune Business News,* August 29, 1998.

Bamberger, Michael, ''Stop the Presses,'' *Sports Illustrated,* April 5, 1999, p. G32.

Davis, Joel, and Lucia Moses, ''Morris Tunes in to Riviera Radio,'' *Editor & Publisher,* May 1, 2000, p. 16.

Fitzgerald, Mark, ''Morris Buys Stauffer,'' *Editor & Publisher,* August 6, 1994, p. 21.

''Georgia's Morris Communications Buys Publisher of Travel Guidebooks,'' *Knight-Ridder/Tribune Business News,* April 17, 1997.

Hopfinger, Tony, ''Augusta, Ga.-Based Communications Firm Broadens Alaska Reach,'' *Knight-Ridder/Tribune Business News,* February 15, 2000.

Ketzenberger, John, ''For Sale: Owner's Decision to Focus on Newspapers Puts Naegele on the Block,'' *Indianapolis Business Journal,* April 2, 1990, p. 1A.

Lehman, Carrie Sloan, ''Morris Communications of Augusta, Ga. to Buy Seattle Firm's Radio Assets,'' *Knight-Ridder/Tribune Business News,* August 17, 1998.

''Morris Communications Becomes Part Owner of Zip2 Corp.,'' *Knight-Ridder/Tribune Business News,* November 14, 1997.

Morris Communications Corp., ''History,'' July 21, 2000, http://www.morris.com/standard/profile/history.html.

''A Quantum Leap for Morris Empire,'' *Georgia Trend,* September 1994, p. 18.

—David P. Bianco

NIKE, Inc.

One Bowerman Drive
Beaverton, Oregon 97005-6453
U.S.A.
Telephone: (503) 671-6453
Fax: (503) 671-6300
Web site: http://www.nike.com

Public Company
Incorporated: 1968 as Blue Ribbon Sports
Employees: 20,700
Sales: $8.78 billion (1999)
Stock Exchanges: New York Pacific
Ticker Symbol: NKE
NAIC: 316219 Other Footwear Manufacturing; 315220
    Men's and Boys' Cut and Sew Apparel
    Manufacturing; 315230 Women's and Girls' Cut and
    Sew Apparel Manufacturing; 339920 Sporting and
    Athletic Goods Manufacturing; 422340 Footwear
    Wholesalers; 448190 Other Clothing Stores; 448210
    Shoe Stores

Founded as an importer of Japanese shoes, NIKE, Inc. (Nike) has grown to be the world's largest marketer of athletic footwear and apparel. In the United States, Nike products are sold through about 20,000 retail accounts; worldwide, the company's products are sold in about 110 countries. Both domestically and overseas Nike operates retail stores, including NikeTowns and factory outlets. Nearly all of the items are manufactured by independent contractors, primarily located overseas, with Nike involved in the design, development, and marketing. In addition to its wide range of core athletic shoes and apparel, the company also sells Nike and Bauer brand athletic equipment, Cole Haan brand dress and casual footwear, and the Sports Specialties line of headwear featuring licensing team logos. The company has relied on consistent innovation in the design of its products and heavy promotion to fuel its growth in both U.S. and foreign markets. The ubiquitous presence of the Nike brand and its Swoosh trademark led to a backlash against the company by the late 20th century, particu-larly in relation to allegations of low wages and poor working conditions at the company's Asian contract manufacturers.

BRS Beginnings

Nike's precursor originated in 1962, a product of the imagination of Philip H. Knight, a Stanford University business graduate who had been a member of the track team as an undergraduate at the University of Oregon. Traveling in Japan after finishing up business school, Knight got in touch with a Japanese firm that made athletic shoes, the Onitsuka Tiger Co., and arranged to import some of its products to the United States on a small scale. Knight was convinced that Japanese running shoes could become significant competitors for the German products that then dominated the American market. In the course of setting up his agreement with Onitsuka Tiger, Knight invented Blue Ribbon Sports to satisfy his Japanese partner's expectations that he represented an actual company, and this hypothetical firm eventually grew to become Nike, Inc.

At the end of 1963, Knight's arrangements in Japan came to fruition when he took delivery of 200 pairs of Tiger athletic shoes, which he stored in his father's basement and peddled at various track meets in the area. Knight's one-man venture became a partnership in the following year, when his former track coach, William Bowerman, chipped in $500 to equal Knight's investment. Bowerman had long been experimenting with modified running shoes for his team, and he worked with runners to improve the designs of prototype Blue Ribbon Sports (BRS) shoes. Innovation in running shoe design eventually would become a cornerstone of the company's continued expansion and success. Bowerman's efforts first paid off in 1968, when a shoe known as the Cortez, which he had designed, became a big seller.

BRS sold 1,300 pairs of Japanese running shoes in 1964, its first year, to gross $8,000. By 1965 the fledgling company had acquired a full-time employee and sales had reached $20,000. The following year, the company rented its first retail space, next to a beauty salon in Santa Monica, California, so that its few employees could stop selling shoes out of their cars. In 1967 with fast-growing sales, BRS expanded operations to the East Coast, opening a distribution office in Wellesley, Massachusetts.

Bowerman's innovations in running shoe technology continued throughout this time. A shoe with the upper portion made of nylon went into development in 1967, and the following year Bowerman and another employee came up with the Boston shoe, which incorporated the first cushioned mid-sole throughout the entire length of an athletic shoe.

Emergence of Nike in 1970s

By the end of the decade, Knight's venture had expanded to include several stores and 20 employees and sales were nearing $300,000. The company was poised for greater growth, but Knight was frustrated by a lack of capital to pay for expansion. In 1971 using financing from the Japanese trading company Nissho Iwai Corporation, BRS was able to manufacture its own line of products overseas, through independent contractors, for import to the United States. At this time, the company introduced its Swoosh trademark and the brand name Nike, the Greek goddess of victory. These new symbols were initially affixed to a soccer shoe, the first Nike product to be sold.

A year later, BRS broke with its old Japanese partner, Onitsuka Tiger, after a disagreement over distribution, and kicked off promotion of its own products at the 1972 U.S. Olympic Trials, the first of many marketing campaigns that would seek to attach Nike's name and fortunes to the careers of well-known athletes. Nike shoes were geared to the serious athlete, and their high performance carried with it a high price.

In their first year of distribution, the company's new products grossed $1.96 million and the corporate staff swelled to 45. In addition, operations were expanded to Canada, the company's first foreign market, which would be followed by Australia, in 1974.

Bowerman continued his innovations in running-shoe design with the introduction of the Moon shoe in 1972, which had a waffle-like sole that had first been formed by molding rubber on a household waffle iron. This sole increased the traction of the shoe without adding weight.

In 1974 BRS opened its first U.S. plant, in Exeter, New Hampshire. The company's payroll swelled to 250, and worldwide sales neared $5 million by the end of 1974. This growth was fueled in part by aggressive promotion of the Nike brand name. The company sought to expand its visibility by having its shoes worn by prominent athletes, including tennis players Ilie Nastase and Jimmy Connors. At the 1976 Olympic Trials these efforts began to pay off as Nike shoes were worn by rising athletic stars.

The company's growth had truly begun to take off by this time, riding the boom in popularity of jogging that took place in the United States in the late 1970s. BRS revenues tripled in two years to $14 million in 1976, and then doubled in just one year

to $28 million in 1977. To keep up with demand, the company opened new factories, adding a stitching plant in Maine and additional overseas production facilities in Taiwan and Korea. International sales were expanded when markets in Asia were opened in 1977 and in South America the following year. European distributorships were lined up in 1978.

Nike continued its promotional activities with the opening of Athletics West, a training club for Olympic hopefuls in track and field, and by signing tennis player John McEnroe to an endorsement contract. In 1978 the company changed its name to Nike, Inc. The company expanded its line of products that year, adding athletic shoes for children.

By 1979 Nike sold almost half the running shoes bought in the United States, and the company moved into a new world headquarters building in Beaverton, Oregon. In addition to its shoe business, the company began to make and market a line of sports clothing, and the Nike Air shoe cushioning device was introduced.

1980s Growth Through International Expansion and Aggressive Marketing

By the start of the 1980s, Nike's combination of groundbreaking design and savvy and aggressive marketing had allowed it to surpass the German athletic shoe company Adidas AG, formerly the leader in U.S. sales. In December 1980, Nike went public, offering two million shares of stock. With the revenues generated by the stock sale, the company planned continued expansion, particularly in the European market. In the United States, plans for a new headquarters on a large, rural campus were inaugurated, and an East Coast distribution center in Greenland, New Hampshire, was brought on line. In addition, the company bought a large plant in Exeter, New Hampshire, to house the Nike Sport Research and Development Lab and also to provide for more domestic manufacturing capacity. The company had shifted its overseas production away from Japan at this point, manufacturing nearly four-fifths of its shoes in South Korea and Taiwan. It established factories in mainland China in 1981.

By the following year, when the jogging craze in the United States had started to wane, half of the running shoes bought in the United States bore the Nike trademark. The company was well insulated from the effects of a stagnating demand for running shoes, however, since it gained a substantial share of its sales from other types of athletic shoes, notably basketball shoes and tennis shoes. In addition, Nike benefited from strong sales of its other product lines, which included apparel, work and leisure shoes, and children's shoes.

Given the slowing of growth in the U.S. market, however, the company turned its attention to growth in foreign markets, inaugurating Nike International, Ltd. in 1981 to spearhead the company's push into Europe and Japan, as well as into Asia, Latin America, and Africa. In Europe, Nike faced stiff competition from Adidas and Puma, which had a strong hold on the soccer market, Europe's largest athletic shoe category. The company opened a factory in Ireland to enable it to distribute its shoes without paying high import tariffs, and in 1981 bought out its distributors in England and Austria, to strengthen its

Key Dates:

1962: Philip H. Knight founds Blue Ribbon Sports (BRS) to import Japanese running shoes.

1963: BRS takes its first delivery of 200 shoes from Onitsuka Tiger Co.

1964: BRS becomes partnership between Knight and William Bowerman.

1966: The company's first retail outlet opens.

1968: Company is incorporated; the Bowerman-designed Cortez shoe becomes a big seller.

1971: BRS begins manufacturing its own products overseas, through subcontractors; the Swoosh trademark and the Nike brand are introduced.

1972: At the 1972 U.S. Olympic Trials, the Nike brand is promoted for the first time; company enters its first foreign market, Canada.

1978: Company changes its name to Nike, Inc.

1979: First line of clothing is launched and the Nike Air shoe cushioning device debuts.

1980: Nike goes public.

1981: Nike International, Ltd. is created to spearhead overseas push.

1985: Company signs Michael Jordan to endorse a version of its Air shoe—the "Air Jordan."

1988: Cole Haan, maker of casual and dress shoes, is acquired; "Just Do It" slogan debuts.

1990: First NikeTown retail outlet opens in Portland, Oregon.

1991: Revenues reach $3 billion.

1994: Company acquires Canstar Sports Inc., the leading maker of skates and hockey equipment in the world, later renamed Bauer Nike Hockey Inc.

1995: Company signs golfer Tiger Woods to a 20-year, $40 million endorsement deal.

1996: The Nike equipment division is created.

1999: Company begins selling its products directly to consumers via its web site.

---

control over marketing and distribution of its products. In 1982 the company outfitted Aston Villa, the winning team in the English and European Cup soccer championships, giving a boost to promotion of its new soccer shoe.

In Japan, Nike allied itself with Nissho Iwai, the sixth largest Japanese trading company, to form Nike-Japan Corporation. Because Nike already held a part of the low-priced athletic shoe market, the company set its sights on the high-priced end of the scale in Japan.

By 1982 the company's line of products included more than 200 different kinds of shoes, including the Air Force I, a basketball shoe, and its companion shoe for racquet sports, the Air Ace, the latest models in the long line of innovative shoe designs that had pushed Nike's earnings to an average annual increase of almost 100 percent. In addition, the company marketed more than 200 different items of clothing. By 1983—when the company posted its first-ever quarterly drop in earnings as the running boom peaked and went into a decline—

Nike's leaders were looking to the apparel division, as well as overseas markets, for further expansion. In foreign sales, the company had mixed results. Its operations in Japan were almost immediately profitable, and the company quickly jumped to second place in the Japanese market, but in Europe, Nike fared less well, losing money on its five European subsidiaries.

Faced with an 11.5 percent drop in domestic sales of its shoes in the 1984 fiscal year, Nike moved away from its traditional marketing strategy of support for sporting events and athlete endorsements to a wider-reaching approach, investing more than $10 million in its first national television and magazine advertising campaign. This followed the "Cities Campaign," which used billboards and murals in nine American cities to publicize Nike products in the period before the 1984 Olympics. Despite the strong showing of athletes wearing Nike shoes in the 1984 Los Angeles Olympic games, Nike profits were down almost 30 percent for the fiscal year ending in May 1984, although international sales were robust and overall sales rose slightly. This decline was a result of aggressive price discounting on Nike products and the increased costs associated with the company's push into foreign markets and attempts to build up its sales of apparel.

Earnings continued to fall in the next three quarters as the company lost market share, posting profits of only $7.8 million at the end of August 1984, a loss of $2.2 million three months later, and another loss of $2.1 million at the end of February 1985. In response, Nike adopted a series of measures to change its sliding course. The company cut back on the number of shoes it had sitting in warehouses and also attempted to fine-tune its corporate mission by cutting back on the number of products it marketed. It made plans to reduce the line of Nike shoes by 30 percent within a year and a half. In addition, leadership at the top of the company was streamlined, as founder Knight resumed the post of president—which he had relinquished in 1983—in addition to his duties as chairman and chief executive officer. Overall administrative costs were also reduced. As part of this effort, Nike also consolidated its research and marketing branches, closing its facility in Exeter, New Hampshire, and cutting 75 of the plant's 125 employees. Overall, the company laid off about 400 workers during 1984.

Faced with shifting consumer interests (i.e., the U.S. market move from jogging to aerobics), the company created a new products division in 1985 to help keep pace. In addition, Nike purchased Pro-form, a small maker of weightlifting equipment, as part of its plan to profit from all aspects of the fitness movement. The company was restructured further at the end of 1985 when its last two U.S. factories were closed and its previous divisions of apparel and athletic shoes were rearranged by sport. In a move that would prove to be the key to the company's recovery, in 1985 the company signed basketball player Michael Jordan to endorse a new version of its Air shoe, introduced four years earlier. The new basketball shoes bore the name "Air Jordan."

In early 1986 Nike announced expansion into a number of new lines, including casual apparel for women, a less expensive line of athletic shoes called Street Socks, golf shoes, and tennis gear marketed under the name "Wimbledon." By mid-1986 Nike was reporting that its earnings had begun to increase again, with sales topping $1 billion for the first time. At that point, the company sold its 51 percent stake in Nike-Japan to its Japanese partner; six months later, Nike laid off ten percent of its U.S. employees at all levels in a major cost-cutting strategy.

Following these moves, Nike announced a drop in revenues and earnings in 1987, and another round of restructuring and budget cuts ensued, as the company attempted to come to grips with the continuing evolution of the U.S. fitness market. Only Nike's innovative Air athletic shoes provided a bright spot in the company's otherwise erratic progress, allowing the company to regain market share from rival Reebok International Ltd. in several areas, including basketball and cross-training.

The following year, Nike branched out from athletic shoes, purchasing Cole Haan, a maker of casual and dress shoes, for $80 million. Advertising heavily, the company took a commanding lead in sales to young people to claim 23 percent of the overall athletic shoe market. Profits rebounded to reach $100 million in 1988, as sales rose 37 percent to $1.2 billion. Later that year, Nike launched a $10 million television campaign around the theme "Just Do It" and announced that its 1989 advertising budget would reach $45 million.

In 1989 Nike marketed several new lines of shoes and led its market with $1.7 billion in sales, yielding profits of $167 million. The company's product innovation continued, including the introduction of a basketball shoe with an inflatable collar around the ankle, sold under the brand name Air Pressure. In addition, Nike continued its aggressive marketing, using ads featuring Michael Jordan and actor-director Spike Lee, the ongoing "Just Do It" campaign, and the "Bo Knows" television spots featuring athlete Bo Jackson. At the end of 1989, the company began relocation to its newly constructed headquarters campus in Beaverton, Oregon.

Market Dominance in the Early to Mid-1990s

In 1990 the company sued two competitors for copying the patented designs of its shoes and found itself engaged in a dispute with the U.S. Customs Service over import duties on its Air Jordan basketball shoes. In 1990 the company's revenues hit $2 billion. The company acquired Tetra Plastics Inc., producers of plastic film for shoe soles. That year, the company opened NikeTown, a prototype store selling the full range of Nike products, in Portland, Oregon.

By 1991 Nike's Visible Air shoes had enabled it to surpass its rival Reebok in the U.S. market. In the fiscal year ending May 31, 1991, Nike sales surpassed the $3 billion mark, fueled by record sales of 41 million pairs of Nike Air shoes and a booming international market. Its efforts to conquer Europe had begun to bear fruit; business there grew by 100 percent that year, producing more than $1 billion in sales and gaining the second place market share behind Adidas. Nike's U.S. shoe market had, in large part, matured, slowing to five percent annual growth, down from 15 percent annual growth from 1980 and 1988. The company began eyeing overseas markets and predicted ample room to grow in Europe. Nike's U.S. rival Reebok, however, also saw potential for growth in Europe, and by 1992 European MTV was glutted with athletic shoe advertisements as the battle for the youth market heated up between Nike, Reebok, and their European competitors, Adidas and Puma.

Nike also saw growth potential in its women's shoe and sports apparel division. In February 1992 Nike began a $13 million print and television advertising pitch for its women's segment, built upon its "Dialogue" print campaign, which had been slowly wooing 18- to 34-year-old women since 1990. Sales of Nike women's apparel lines Fitness Essentials, Elite Aerobics, Physical Elements, and All Condition Gear increased by 25 percent in both 1990 and 1991 and jumped by 68 percent in 1992.

In July 1992 Nike opened its second NikeTown retail store in Chicago, Illinois. Like its predecessor in Portland, the Chicago NikeTown was designed to "combine the fun and excitement of FAO Schwartz, the Smithsonian Institute and Disneyland in a space that will entertain sports and fitness fans from around the world" as well as provide a high-profile retail outlet for Nike's rapidly expanding lines of footwear and clothing.

Nike celebrated its 20th anniversary in 1992, virtually debt free and with company revenues of $3.4 billion. Gross profits jumped $100 million in that year, fueled by soaring sales in its retail division, which expanded to include 30 Nike-owned discount outlets and the two NikeTowns. To celebrate its anniversary, Nike brought out its old slogan "There is no finish line." As if to underscore that sentiment, Nike Chairman Philip Knight announced massive plans to remake the company with the goal of being "the best sports and fitness company in the world." To fulfill that goal, the company set the ground plans for a complicated yet innovative marketing structure seeking to make the Nike brand into a worldwide megabrand along the lines of Coca-Cola, Pepsi, Sony, and Disney.

Nike continued expansion of its high-profile NikeTown chain, opening outlets in Atlanta, Georgia, in the spring of 1993 and Costa Mesa, California, later that year. Also in 1993, as part of its long-term marketing strategy, Nike began an ambitious venture with Mike Ovitz's Creative Artists Agency to organize and package sports events under the Nike name—a move that potentially led the company into competition with sports management giants such as ProServ, IMG, and Advantage International.

Nike also began a more controversial venture into the arena of sports agents, negotiating contracts for basketball's Scottie Pippin, Alonzo Mourning, and others in addition to retaining athletes such as Michael Jordan and Charles Barkley as company spokespersons. Nike's influence in the world of sports grew to such a degree that in 1993 *Sporting News* dubbed Knight the most powerful man in sports.

Critics contended that Nike's influence ran too deep, having its hand in negotiating everything in an athlete's life from investments to the choice of an apartment. But Nike's marketing executives saw it as part of a campaign to create an image of Nike not just as a product line but as a *lifestyle,* a "Nike attitude."

Nearly everyone agreed, however, that Nike was the dominant force in athletic footwear in the early to mid-1990s. The company held about 30 percent of the U.S. market by 1995, far outdistancing the 20 percent of its nearest rival, Reebok. Overseas revenues continued their steady rise, reaching nearly $2 billion by 1995, about 40 percent of the overall total. Not content with its leading position in athletic shoes and its growing sales of athletic apparel—which accounted for more than 30 percent of revenues in 1996—Nike branched out into sports equipment in the mid-1990s. In 1994 the company acquired Canstar Sports Inc., the leading maker of skates and hockey equipment in the world, for $400 million. Canstar was renamed Bauer Nike Hockey Inc., Bauer being Canstar's brand name for its equipment. Two years later Bauer Nike became part of the newly formed Nike equipment division, which aimed to extend the company into the marketing of sport balls, protective gear, eyewear, and watches. Also during this period, Nike signed up its next superstar spokesperson, Tiger Woods. In 1995, at the age of 20, Woods agreed to a 20-year, $40 million endorsement contract. The golf phenom went on to win an inordinate number of tournaments, often shattering course records, and to become only the second golfer in history to win three "majors" within a single year, more than validating the blockbuster contract.

Late 1990s Slippage

For the fiscal year ending in May 1997, Nike earned a record $795.8 million on record revenues of $9.19 billion. Overseas sales played a large role in the 42 percent increase in revenues from 1996 to 1997. Sales in Asia increased by more than $500 million (to $1.24 billion), while European sales surged ahead by $450 million. Back home, Nike's share of the U.S. athletic shoe market neared 50 percent. The picture at Nike soon turned sour, however, as the Asian financial crisis that erupted in the summer of 1997 sent sneaker sales in that region plunging. By fiscal 1999, sales in Asia had dropped to $844.5 million. Compounding the company's troubles was a concurrent stagnation of sales in its domestic market, where the fickle tastes of teenagers began turning away from athletic shoes to hiking boots and other casual "brown shoes." As a result, overall sales for 1999 fell to $8.78 billion. Profits were falling as well—including a net loss of $67.7 million for the fourth quarter of fiscal 1998, the company's first reported loss in more than 13 years. The decline in net income led to a cost-cutting drive that included the layoff of five percent of the workforce, or 1,200 people, in 1998, and the slashing of its budget for sports star endorsements by $100 million that same year.

Nike was also dogged throughout the late 1990s by protests and boycotts over allegations regarding the treatment of workers at the contract factories in Asia that employed nearly 400,000 people and that made the bulk of Nike shoes and much of its apparel. Charges included abuse of workers, poor working conditions, low wages, and use of child labor. Nike's initial reaction—which was highlighted by Knight's insistence that the company had little control over its suppliers—resulted in waves of negative publicity. Protesters included church groups, students at universities that had apparel and footwear contracts with Nike, and socially conscious investment funds. Nike finally announced in mid-1998 a series of changes affecting its contract workforce in Asia, including an increase in the minimum age, a tightening of air quality standards, and a pledge to allow independent inspections of factories. Nike nonetheless remained under pressure from activists into the 21st century. Nike, along with McDonald's Corporation, the Coca-Cola Company, and Starbucks Corporation, among others, also became an object of protest from those who were attacking multinational companies that pushed global brands. This undercurrent of hostility burst into the spotlight in late 1999 when some of the more aggressive protesters against a World Trade Organization meeting in Seattle attempted to storm a NikeTown outlet.

Seeking to recapture the growth of the early to mid-1990s, Nike pursued a number of new initiatives in the late 1990s. Having initially missed out on the trend toward extreme sports (such as skateboarding, mountain biking, and snowboarding), Nike attempted to rectify this miscue by establishing a unit called ACG—short for "all-conditions gear"—in 1998. Two years later, the company created a new division called Techlab to market a line of sports-technology accessories, such as a digital audio player, a high-altitude wrist compass, and a portable heart-rate monitor. Both of these initiatives were aimed at capturing sales from the emerging Generation Y demographic group. In early 1999 Nike began selling its shoes and other products directly to consumers via the company web site. Nike announced in September of that year that it would buy about ten percent of Fogdog Inc., which ran a sporting goods e-commerce site, in exchange for granting Fogdog the exclusive online rights to sell the full Nike line. The company finally earned some good publicity in 1999 when it sponsored the U.S. national women's soccer team that won the Women's World Cup. With its record of innovative product design and savvy promotion and an aggressive approach to containing costs and revitalizing sales, Nike appeared likely to stage an impressive comeback in the early 21st century.

Principal Subsidiaries

Cole Haan Holdings Incorporated; Nike Team Sports, Inc.; Nike IHM, Inc.; Bauer Nike Hockey Inc.

Principal Competitors

adidas-Salomon AG; Callaway Golf Company; Converse Inc.; Deckers Outdoor Corporation; Fila Holding S.p.A.; Fortune Brands, Inc.; Fruit of the Loom, Ltd.; FUBU; HI-TEC Sports USA Inc.; Levi Strauss & Co.; Nautica Enterprises, Inc.; New Balance Athletic Shoe, Inc.; Polo Ralph Lauren Corporation; Puma AG; R. Griggs Group Limited; Rawlings Sporting Goods Company, Inc.; Reebok International Ltd.; Rollerblade, Inc.; Russell Corporation; Sara Lee Corporation; Skechers U.S.A., Inc.; Spalding Holdings Corporation; The Stride Rite Corporation; The Timberland Company; Timex Corporation; Tommy Hilfiger Corporation; VF Corporation; Wolverine World Wide, Inc.

Further Reading

Buell, Barbara, "Nike Catches Up with the Trendy Frontrunner," *Business Week,* October 24, 1988, p. 88.

Collingwood, Harris, "Nike Rushes in Where Reebok Used to Tread," *Business Week,* October 3, 1988, p. 42.

Eales, Roy, "Is Nike a Long Distance Runner?," *Multinational Business,* 1986, pp. 9+.

"Fitting the World in Sport Shoes," *Business Week,* January 25, 1982.

Gallagher, Leigh, "Rebound," *Forbes,* May 3, 1999, p. 60.

Gilley, Bruce, "Sweating It Out," *Far Eastern Economic Review,* December 10, 1998, pp. 66–67.

Gold, Jacqueline S., "The Marathon Man?," *Financial World,* February 16, 1993, p. 32.

Grimm, Matthew, "Nike Vision," *Brandweek,* March 29, 1993, p. 19.

Heins, John, ''Looking for That Strong Finish,'' *Forbes,* May 4, 1987, pp. 74+.

Jenkins, Holman W., Jr., ''The Rise and Stumble of Nike,'' *Wall Street Journal,* June 3, 1998, p. A19.

Katz, Donald R., *Just Do It: The Nike Spirit in the Corporate World,* New York: Random House, 1994.

''Kennel Mates: Nike Bites into Fogdog Ownership,'' *Sporting Goods Business,* October 11, 1999, p. 10.

Klein, Naomi, *No Logo: Taking Aim at the Brand Bullies,* Toronto: Knopf Canada, 2000.

Labich, Kenneth, ''Nike Vs. Reebok: A Battle for Hearts, Minds and Feet,'' *Fortune,* September 18, 1995, pp. 90+.

LaFeber, Walter, *Michael Jordan and the New Global Capitalism,* New York: W.W. Norton, 1999.

Lane, Randall, ''You Are What You Wear,'' *Forbes 400,* October 14, 1996, pp. 42–46.

Lee, Louise, ''Can Nike Still Do It?,'' *Business Week,* February 21, 2000, pp. 120–22+.

Loftus, Margaret, ''A Swoosh Under Siege,'' *U.S. News and World Report,* April 12, 1999, p. 40.

McGill, Douglas C., ''Nike Is Bounding Past Reebok,'' *New York Times,* July 11, 1989, p. D1.

Murphy, Terence, ''Nike on the Rebound,'' *Madison Avenue,* June 1985, pp. 28+.

''Nike Pins Hopes for Growth on Foreign Sales and Apparel,'' *New York Times,* March 24, 1983.

''Nike Sports Shoes: Winged Victory,'' *Economist,* December 2, 1989, pp. 83+.

''Nike Timeline,'' Beaverton, Ore.: Nike, Inc. 1990.

''Nike Versus Reebok: A Foot Race,'' *Newsweek,* October 3, 1988, p. 52.

Richards, Bill, ''Just Doing It: Nike Plans to Swoosh into Sports Equipment But It's a Tough Game,'' *Wall Street Journal,* January 6, 1998, pp. A1+.

——, ''Tripped Up by Too Many Shoes, Nike Regroups,'' *Wall Street Journal,* March 3, 1998, p. B1.

Saporito, Bill, ''Can Nike Get Unstuck?,'' *Time,* March 30, 1998, pp. 48–53.

Sellers, Patricia, ''Four Reasons Nike's Not Cool,'' *Fortune,* March 30, 1998, pp. 26–27.

Steinhauer, Jennifer, ''Nike Is in a League of Its Own: With No Big Rival, It Calls the Shots in Athletic Shoes,'' *New York Times,* June 7, 1997, Sec. 1, p. 31.

Strasser, J.B., and Laurie Becklund, *Swoosh: The Unauthorized Story of Nike, and the Men Who Played There,* San Diego: Harcourt Brace Jovanovich, 1991.

Stroud, Ruth, ''Nike Ready to Run a More Traditional Race,'' *Advertising Age,* June 18, 1984, pp. 4+.

Tharp, Mike, ''Easy-Going Nike Adopts Stricter Controls to Pump Up Its Athletic-Apparel Business,'' *Wall Street Journal,* November 6, 1984.

Thurow, Roger, ''Shtick Ball: In Global Drive, Nike Finds Its Brash Ways Don't Always Pay Off,'' *Wall Street Journal,* May 5, 1997, pp. A1+.

''Where Nike and Reebok Have Plenty of Running Room,'' *Business Week,* March 11, 1991.

Wrighton, Jo, and Fred R. Bleakley, ''Philip Knight of Nike—Just Do It!,'' *Institutional Investor,* January 2000, pp. 22–24.

Wyatt, John, ''Is It Time to Jump on Nike?,'' *Fortune,* May 26, 1997, pp. 185–86.

Yang, Dori Jones, et al., ''Can Nike Just Do It?,'' *Business Week,* April 18, 1994, pp. 86–90.

—Elizabeth Rourke and Maura Troester
—updated by David E. Salamie

NORTEL NETWORKS™

Nortel Networks Corporation

8200 Dixie Road
Suite 100
Brampton, Ontario L6T 5P6
Canada
Telephone: (905) 863-0000
Fax: (905) 863-3408
Web site: http://www.nortelnetworks.com

Public Company
Incorporated: 1914 as Northern Electric Company,
  Limited
Employees: 70,000
Sales: US$22.22 billion (1999)
Stock Exchanges: New York Toronto
Ticker Symbol: NT
NAIC: 334210 Telephone Apparatus Manufacturing;
  334220 Radio and Television Broadcasting and
  Wireless Communications Equipment Manufacturing;
  334290 Other Communications Equipment
  Manufacturing; 334419 Other Electronic Component
  Manufacturing; 511210 Software Publishers; 541512
  Computer Systems Design Services

Nortel Networks Corporation is one of the world's leading providers of networking products and services, with a particular emphasis on the Internet but also active in both public and private voice, data, and video networks. Serving Internet service providers, telecommunications carriers, large to small businesses, and dot-coms, Nortel offers a full range of products and services in several areas of networking: Internet protocol, high-speed access, long distance, optical, and wireless. Nortel was founded as the telephone equipment arm of Bell Canada, and for much of its history it acted in that capacity. During the final decades of the 20th century Nortel gained more and more independence from Bell Canada and its eventual parent, BCE Inc., and by 2000 BCE's interest in Nortel had been reduced to less than four percent. Meantime, Nortel's astonishingly rapid emergence at the forefront of Internet technology by the early

21st century resulted from a more than $30 billion acquisition spree that began in late 1997.

Founded As Arm of Bell Canada in Late 1800s

Nortel's origins can be traced back to 1880, four years after Alexander Graham Bell invented the telephone in 1876. In that year Bell Telephone Company of Canada (Bell Canada) was founded. To develop adequate telephone equipment for the fledgling company, Bell established its mechanical department on July 24, 1882, in Montreal, Canada, with a staff of three that soon expanded to 11. Success came early to the company, and five years later the mechanical department moved to a larger facility to accommodate a staff that had increased to 54.

The growth led to Bell Canada taking out a charter in 1895 for a separate company to take over the mechanical department's work. On December 7 of that year, Northern Electric and Manufacturing Company, Limited was incorporated under the dominion charter. With C.F. Sise as president, the company called its first general meeting of stockholders on March 24, 1896. By 1902 Northern Electric employed 250 people and occupied a 48,000-square-foot plant, which it leased from Bell Canada. That plant had expanded to 241,000 square feet in 1912, the year Northern Electric and Bell Canada worked out a deal whereby Northern would become the storekeeper and purchasing agent for Bell. Meantime, Western Electric Company, the manufacturing arm of National Bell (predecessor of American Telephone and Telegraph [AT&T]), had purchased a stake in Northern in 1906.

In 1895 C.F. Sise had bought a small plant from Alexander Barrie that was involved in manufacturing rubber-coated wire for the fast-growing electrical industry. In turn, Sise offered the company to Bell Canada for what it had cost him. Bell Canada accepted the offer, and on December 19, 1899, the Wire & Cable Company, as the enterprise became known, was granted a province of Quebec charter. Sise was appointed president and Barrie superintendent. In 1901 Western Electric bought a stake in Wire & Cable. A big success, Wire & Cable replaced its provincial charter with a dominion charter in 1911 and changed its name to Imperial Wire & Cable Company.

By then both Northern Electric and Imperial Wire & Cable were playing vital roles as Canada's major suppliers of telephone equipment. In many operational areas, however, their needs and interests overlapped. The management of both companies realized that to increase efficiency and to reduce overhead, the two enterprises should amalgamate. On July 5, 1914, they consolidated under the laws of Canada into Northern Electric Company Limited, which was initially owned primarily by Bell Canada (50 percent) and Western Electric (43.6 percent). Bell Canada increased its stake to 56.3 percent in 1929.

While the general sales division continued to be located in Montreal, the company established supply and repair divisions for western Canada in 1929 and for the Maritime region in 1944. Despite the Great Depression, which forced Northern to cut back production, the company still managed to grow. It established the electronics division in 1931 and expanded its base of operations by purchasing a majority interest in Amalgamated Electric Company Ltd. in 1932 and, in 1935, by launching Dominion Sound Equipment Ltd., a wholly owned subsidiary that supplied Canada with electric sound equipment, acoustic and sound proofing supplies, radio and broadcasting sound equipment, and other lines of electrical equipment.

When the Depression ended, Northern became involved in Canada's World War II effort, converting 95 percent of its operation to war production. By 1944 most of the company's 9,325 employees were engaged in this activity. Soon after the war's end in 1945, Northern immediately began a flurry of construction to meet the expanding communications needs of Canada's growing communities. As a measure of its continuing growth, Northern's workforce expanded to 12,775 by 1948.

Achieving Independence from Western Electric: 1950s–60s

As a result of being partially owned by Western Electric, Northern Electric operated much like a ''branch plant'' of the U.S. firm. Consequently, Northern had a small research and development staff, and its sales efforts were confined to Canada. As its main function was to manufacture Western Electric products for Bell Canada, Northern Electric's product line generally lagged behind Western Electric's by two to three years.

Northern Electric ceased operating like a branch plant in 1956 when Western Electric signed a consent decree with the U.S. Department of Justice in which it agreed to relinquish its interest in Northern Electric. Bell Canada acquired most of Western Electric's interest in Northern Electric in 1957 and the remainder in 1962, at which point Bell Canada held 99.99

percent of Northern's stock. By 1964, Bell Canada had purchased the remaining shares, making Northern Electric 100 percent Bell Canada-owned.

With no product line of its own, and with management knowing that it had to start one to remain competitive, Northern Electric stepped up its research and development efforts, establishing Northern Electric Laboratories—with a staff of 30 to 40 people—in 1958. In 1965 the company made a commitment to develop a switching device known as SP-1, a stored program switch system, which it believed would meet the needs of the Canadian market and spur economic growth. From 12 researchers in 1965, the product development team working on SP-1 grew to more than 100 by the end of the decade. The commitment paid off when Northern put its product on the market. By 1975 not only had every major telephone company in Canada bought the switch, but 25 percent of all sales were being made in the United States.

1970s and Early 1980s: Increasingly Independent, Rolling Out the First Digital Switch

Northern Electric's research and development division had become a conglomerate itself, mushrooming to more than 2,000 employees, and eventually incorporating as a separate entity. On January 1, 1971, Northern Electric's subsidiary, Bell-Northern Research Ltd. (BNR) was formed. In 1973 Bell Canada sold a portion of Northern Electric's shares to the public through an initial public offering, while retaining a majority holding of 90.1 percent. Bell Canada continued to reduce its stake over the remainder of the decade, from 89.9 percent in 1974 to 54.5 percent in 1979. After BCE Inc. was created as the new parent company of Bell Canada in 1983, BCE then held a 53.4 percent stake in Northern.

During the 1970s the company established many new subsidiaries, such as Northern Telecom (International) B.V. in Amsterdam, and Northern Telecom (Asia) Limited in Singapore and Hong Kong, both established in 1974. These subsidiaries reflected its increasingly strong presence in the international marketplace. In 1976 the company's name was changed to Northern Telecom Limited (Northern) to reflect the great advances it had made in manufacturing modern telecommunications equipment.

That same year Northern introduced the first fully digital switch. Although AT&T did not immediately authorize its affiliates to buy the switches, independent U.S. telephone companies quickly did, and by 1978 Northern's sales had jumped by 130 percent from the previous year. The demand for the company's digital switches received a big boost in 1981 when AT&T approved the purchase of the switches for its affiliates. In 1984 the U.S. government broke up AT&T, and sales of Northern's digital switches skyrocketed, with volume increasing 1,200 percent over that of 1976.

Northern had ignored conventional business wisdom and taken chances to rise within the industry. As one company official said, ''When we started to work on the digital central office switches in the 1970s, we were advised to follow AT&T and continue making old analog switches since digital switches would be too expensive.'' Fortunately for Northern, it did not,

Key Dates:

1880: Bell Canada is founded.

1882: Bell Canada establishes its mechanical department.

1895: Bell Canada creates Northern Electric & Manufacturing Company, Limited to take over the mechanical department's work.

1899: The Wire & Cable Company, an electrical wire maker, is incorporated.

1911: Wire & Cable changes its name to Imperial Wire & Cable Company.

1914: Northern Electric and Imperial Wire merge to form Northern Electric Company, Limited, which is primarily owned by Bell Canada and Western Electric.

1956: Under U.S. Justice Department consent decree, Western Electric agrees to divest its interest in Northern.

1958: Company forms Northern Electric Laboratories as an R&D arm.

1962: Bell Canada completes its purchase of shares held by Western Electric, and now owns 99.99 percent of Northern.

1964: Northern Electric becomes 100 percent owned by Bell Canada.

1971: Northern Electric Laboratories is incorporated as a separate entity called Bell-Northern Research Ltd.

1973: Northern Electric goes public through an IPO, with Bell Canada retaining a 90.1 percent stake.

1976: Northern Electric changes its name to Northern Telecom Limited and introduces the first fully digital switch.

1979: Bell Canada's stake in Northern has been reduced to 54.5 percent.

1983: BCE Inc. is created as the new parent of Bell Canada; holds 53.4 percent stake in Northern.

1993: Jean C. Monty takes over as CEO of the company, sparking a company turnaround and moving the company well beyond its phone equipment roots.

1997: John A. Roth succeeds Monty and begins focusing the company on the Internet.

1998: Bay Networks is acquired.

1999: Company changes its name to Nortel Networks Corporation.

2000: Company acquires Qtera Corporation; Clarify, Inc.; Promatory Communications, Inc.; Xros, Inc.; and CoreTek, Inc.; BCE distributes the bulk of its stake in Nortel to its shareholders, reducing its ownership to less than four percent.

and the introduction and marketing of the switch proved to be a major milestone in its history. By 1990 one research firm estimated that the company held close to one-third of the U.S. market for the digital switches.

Mid-1980s to Early 1990s: Declining Fortunes

Northern's fortunes, however, began to change by the mid-1980s. While AT&T was making a comeback with its own switch, Northern made a technological blunder. It began selling new software to provide its phone company subscribers with advanced service capabilities based on new technology. Poor marketing, bugs in the software, and the fact that the processor in Northern's switch could not keep up with all the new tasks the expanded software had to do alienated many company customers. One disgruntled business executive told *Business Week* in 1987, "Their software and capacity problems are still driving us wild. We're giving our orders to AT&T."

Northern launched a public relations campaign to reassure its customers that it had solved the software problems. It also announced the availability of Supercore, a new processor that cost $50 million to develop. "[Supercore] will double the capacity of our switches and eventually increase it to whatever we want," maintained Northern President David G. Vice.

Many in the telecommunications market remained skeptical, however, and rival telecommunications companies such as Japan's NEC Corporation, Sweden's Telefonaktiebolaget LM Ericsson, and Germany's Siemens AG began to make a move for Northern's markets. Despite the setbacks, Northern had become one of the giants in the telecommunications industry. Consolidated revenues for 1989 were US$5.41 billion.

Northern repositioned in 1988 because of concerns that the intense global competition combined with the money it had invested in product and market development had affected its financial performance. Under newly elected Chairman, CEO, and President Paul G. Stern, who took over in March 1989, Northern embarked on a program to restructure the corporation.

Stern's association with Northern began in April 1988 when the company elected him to its board of directors and to membership on the executive committee. He brought to the job a strong background in advanced-technology company management and a reputation for making tough cost-cutting decisions at large corporations. He had previously served as an executive for Burroughs, Unisys, IBM, and Rockwell. Within nine months after Stern assumed the helm, Northern had reshuffled management, cutting 2,500 jobs; closed four of its 41 plants, selling one-fifth of the plants to employees; and changed its bonus system, tying employee incentives in each business unit to company performance.

The dramatic changes caused a stir in Canada. Northern's plans to move its research and development operations from Toronto to Texas and California made Canadians wonder if the company would move its headquarters as well.

Northern, however, quickly saw positive results from the tough measures it took. In 1989 company expenses fell 18.5 percent from the year before, while profits jumped 18 percent on a 13 percent increase in sales. By 1990 Northern was the world's sixth largest telecommunications company, but Stern publicly stated that he was preparing for an even more ambitious goal for Northern—to become the world's leading supplier of telecommunications equipment by the year 2000. Soon after, it took a major step in that direction in January 1991 when it purchased STC PLC, a large British telecommunications company specializing in undersea cable for about US$2.6 billion. The acquisition put Northern in third place behind Alcatel NW of Belgium and U.S.-based AT&T. Northern had already owned 27 percent of STC PLC when it made the deal.

The purchase increased Northern's total debt to C$4.3 billion, 50 percent of its equity, compared to 29 percent before the buyout. Northern said, however, that it planned to help relieve the debt using the C$1.6 billion from the sale of STC's computer's division, ICL Ltd., to Fujitsu Ltd. of Japan.

Behind Northern's seeming turnaround, however, were continuing problems at the company, particularly with its key U.S. customers. While Stern was concentrating on controlling expenses and expanding overseas, several major U.S. phone companies began experiencing problems with the software in Northern's switches. Customers were further irked when Northern was slow in fixing the glitches. Further dissatisfaction, and lost sales, resulted from delays in issuing new versions of the tremendously complicated switch software. With his focus primarily on short-term profitability, Stern had cut R&D spending from 13 percent of revenue to 11 percent, thus jeopardizing the company's longer term viability in the rapidly changing technological environment of telecommunications. In October 1992 the Northern board of directors, growing increasingly aware of these behind-the-scenes problems, installed Jean C. Monty, a longtime Bell Canada executive, as president and chief operating officer, the number two position behind Stern's. Within months, Monty had replaced Stern as CEO, with Stern—who later told *Business Week,* "Nobody is going to shove a president down my throat"—resigning from his position of chairman, the apparent victim of a power struggle. In June 1993 Monty announced that Northern would take a US$1.2 billion pretax restructuring charge covering the cost of fixing the switching software, closing several facilities, and eliminating about nine percent of the workforce. As a result of the sale of STC to Alcatel-Alsthom for US$906 million, the charge also covered a US$500 million writedown in goodwill from the STC acquisition. The charge sparked the company's first quarterly loss in five years, and a 1993 full-year loss of US$884 million. In the wake of the announcement of the charge, Northern's market value was cut nearly in half during one three-week period.

Mid-1990s and Beyond: An Impressive Turnaround and a New Internet Focus

Monty quickly turned Northern Telecom's fortunes around with the help of a man who soon held the number two position, John A. Roth. Roth had joined the company in 1969 as a design engineer, was later instrumental in the establishment of Northern's wireless business, and then served as head of the company's North American operations from 1993 to 1995. He was named chief operating officer in 1995 and then president in February 1997. Monty and Roth were quickly able to mollify the company's angry customers with assurances that the switching software would be rewritten and simplified by the end of 1995, with US$250 million earmarked for this effort. Although the company was unable to meet this timeline, the job was 95 percent complete by mid-1996.

The new leadership also bolstered the R&D budget to nearly 15 percent of revenue, which amounted to US$1.58 billion in 1995. As the digital switching market matured, much of the research dollars went into new specialized areas. With this diversification came a parallel restructuring of the company into four separate businesses, each serving a distinct set of customers and each delivering products tailored for those cus-

tomers. The first business was Northern's traditional switching operations which served old-line phone companies; the others were: a unit focused on broadband networks, which served cable companies and the upstart long-distance companies that were burgeoning in the wake of industry deregulation; one specializing in enterprise networking, which served large organizations—including corporations and government departments—using internal communications networks; and one concentrating on wireless networks, which mainly served the rapidly expanding cellular telephone firms.

The signs of an impressive turnaround were soon unmistakable. Revenue increased smartly, to US$10.67 billion in 1995 to US$12.85 billion in 1996 to US$15.45 billion in 1997. Net income showed a similar upward trajectory, standing at US$473 million, US$623 million, and US$829 million for those three years, respectively. With his job at Northern Telecom complete, Monty moved on to become president and CEO of BCE while maintaining a seat on Northern's board of directors. He turned the Northern reins over to Roth, who was named president and CEO in October 1997.

Roth wasted no time in mapping out the next step in the evolution of Northern Telecom, betting the company's future on the Internet and what he called "web tone." Roth saw that networks were going to increasingly migrate from being telephone-based to being Internet-based. He wanted Northern Telecom to be at the center of the building up of the Internet into a technology as reliable and as instantly accessible as the telephone and its dial tone—thus the concept of web tone. Needing to move quickly to beat out the competition, Roth turned largely to acquisitions rather than attempting to rely only on in-house R&D efforts. The company's soaring stock facilitated the completion of stock-swap acquisitions.

Four major acquisitions were completed in 1998, including Winnipeg-based Broadband Networks Inc., a designer and manufacturer of broadband wireless communications networks (purchased for US$593 million); Chelmsford, Massachusetts-based Aptis Communications, Inc., a start-up firm that concentrated on remote-access data networking (US$290 million); and Kanata, Ontario-based Cambrian Systems Corporation, maker of an innovative technology to speed up Internet traffic (US$300 million). These purchases were dwarfed, however, by the US$9.1 billion stock-swap for Santa Clara, California-based Bay Networks, Inc., which was completed in August 1998. Bay Networks served the corporate market with a host of data networking products and services that meshed well with Northern Telecom's existing corporate operations. The addition of Bay provided Northern with the ability to offer corporate customers integrated networks for sending voice, video, and data over the Internet. With the company focusing increasingly on networking, Northern Telecom was renamed Nortel Networks Corporation in April 1999.

Acquisitions continued in 1999 and 2000; the former year featured three major buyouts but was followed by an accelerating purchasing pace in the latter. Nortel also showed an increasing appetite for optical networking firms. In January the company paid US$3.25 billion in stock for Boca Raton, Florida-based Qtera Corporation, producer of long-distance optical networking systems. Two months later Nortel completed two acquisitions:

the US$2.1 billion purchase of San Jose-based Clarify, Inc., which specialized in customer relationship management software used in Internet communications; and the US$778 million buyout of Fremont, California-based Promontory Communications, Inc., developer of high-speed digital subscriber line (DSL) Internet access platforms. The purchase of optical networking firms took center stage in mid-2000 as Nortel spent US$3.25 billion for Xros, Inc., a Sunnyvale, California-based firm that was developing optical switches; and US$1.43 billion for Wilmington, Massachusetts-based CoreTek, Inc., a start-up that was working to perfect specialized lasers to transmit light beams over fiber-optic lines. Neither Xros nor CoreTek at the time of their acquisition had either revenue or a marketable product but were working on promising optical technologies that Nortel hoped to use to speed up data traffic and increase its volume, while simultaneously reducing costs.

Also in mid-2000 Nortel largely gained its independence from BCE after the latter distributed most of its remaining 40 percent stake to its shareholders. Following the completion of this transaction, BCE held less than four percent of Nortel's stock. In July 2000 Nortel entered into discussions with Corning Inc. about selling its optical components unit to Corning in a stock swap that some observers valued at about US$100 billion and that could have resulted in Nortel owning a significant stake in Corning; the talks faltered, however. One day after the companies confirmed that the negotiations had failed, Nortel announced another blockbuster acquisition. It agreed to acquire San Jose-based Alteon WebSystems, Inc. for more than US$7 billion in stock. Alteon was a leading maker of specialized Internet switches used to speed response times at web sites. In August 2000 Nortel announced that it had agreed to buy Sonoma Systems Inc. for as much as US$540 million in stock. Sonoma, based in Marina del Rey, California, produced integrated access devices for Internet access providers enabling them to simultaneously deliver high-speed video, data, and voice communications over a single connection.

Soon after the announcement of the Sonoma acquisition, Nortel Networks' market capitalization hit US$240 billion, a sixfold increase since Roth had taken over as CEO. Roth planned to continue the breathtaking acquisition pace, vowing to spend ten percent of the company's market cap each year to purchase the new technology it would need to keep pace with the other heavyweights of networking, most notably Cisco Systems, Inc.; Ericsson; and Lucent Technologies Inc. (the equipment arm of AT&T that had been spun off in 1996). Nortel's emphasis on new technology was demonstrated by its generating 60 percent of its revenues from products less than 18 months old. In addition to its clear focus on optical technology, Nortel at the turn of the millennium was also working to establish a more significance presence in the undersea-fiber business and was gaining a reputation as a leader in the area of wireless Internet technologies. The wireless operations were one of the responsibilities of COO Clarence Chandran, who appeared to be in line to succeed Roth.

Principal Subsidiaries

Matra Nortel Communications S.A.S. (France; 50%); Nortel Government Services Inc. (U.S.A.); Nortel Matra Cellular SCA (France); Nortel Networks (Asia) Limited (Hong Kong); Nortel

(CALA) Inc. (U.S.A.); Nortel Networks (Dublin) Limited (Ireland); Nortel Networks (Ireland) Limited; Nortel Networks (Luxembourg) S.A.; Nortel Networks Aptis Inc. (U.S.A.); Nortel Networks Capital Corporation (U.S.A.); Nortel Networks de Colombia S.A.; Nortel Networks Inc. (U.S.A.); Nortel Networks International Finance and Holding B.V. (Netherlands); Nortel Networks NA Inc. (U.S.A.); Nortel Networks plc (U.K.); Northern Telecom do Brasil Comercio e Servicos Ltda. (Brazil).

Principal Competitors

ADC Telecommunications, Inc.; Alcatel; Ascom Holding Ltd.; British Telecommunications plc; Cabletron Systems, Inc.; CIENA Corporation; Cisco Systems, Inc.; Corvis Corporation; Deutsche Telekom AG; Telefonaktiebolaget LM Ericsson; Fujitsu Limited; Harris Corporation; Inter-Tel, Incorporated; InterVoice-Brite Inc.; Juniper Networks, Inc.; Lucent Technologies Inc.; Marconi Communications; Motorola, Inc.; NEC Corporation; Nokia Corporation; Oki Electric Industry Company, Limited; ONI Systems Corp.; PeopleSoft, Inc.; QUALCOMM Incorporated; Redback Networks Inc. Remedy Corporation; Scientific-Atlanta, Inc.; Siebel Systems, Inc.; Siemens AG; Sycamore Networks, Inc.; Tellabs, Inc.

Further Reading

Austen, Ian, "Hooked on the Net," *Canadian Business,* June 26/July 10, 1998, pp. 95+.

Blackwell, Gerry, "Northern Lights," *Canadian Business,* March 1990, pp. 40+.

Campanella, Frank W., "A Switch in Time: Northern Telecom's New Equipment Is Sparking an Earnings Resurgence," *Barron's* October 26, 1981, pp. 43+.

Chisholm, Patricia, and John Daly, "A Giant Cuts Costs," *Maclean's* September 18, 1989, p. 50.

Hardy, Quentin, "Lighting Up Nortel," *Forbes,* August 21, 2000, pp. 52–53.

Hawkins, Chuck, "Is Paul Stern Tough Enough to Toughen Up Northern Telecom?," *Business Week,* August 14, 1989, pp. 84+.

Heinzl, Mark, "Buying into the New Economy: CEO Uses Acquisitions to Turn Nortel into a Huge Player in Technology for the Web," *Wall Street Journal,* July 25, 2000, pp. B1, B4.

——, "Nortel Networks Is Following a Daring Strategy to Recast the Company for Internet Commerce," *Wall Street Journal,* November 1, 1999, p. B13D.

Keller, John J., and Edith Terry, "How Northern Telecom Is Riding Out the Storm," *Business Week,* January 26, 1987, pp. 84+.

Laver, Ross, "Nortel's Driving Force," *Maclean's* August 2, 1999, pp. 13–17+.

McMurdy, Deirdre, "Ringing in a Change: Financial Shocks Hit Northern Telecom," *Maclean's* July 12, 1993, pp. 32+.

Morrison, Scott, "An Engineer Tuned to the Market," *Financial Times,* August 14, 2000, p. 11.

"Northern Telecom's All-Out Attack on Western Electric's Turf," *Business Week,* December 5, 1983, pp. 178+.

Palmer, Jay, "A Comeback Coming?: Until Now, the Telephony Craze Has Bypassed Northern Telecom," *Barron's* February 21, 1994, pp. 12–13.

Reingold, Jennifer, "A Dose of Humility," *Financial World,* October 11, 1994, pp. 56–57.

Stoffman, Daniel, "Mr. Clean," *Canadian Business,* June 1996, pp. 59+.

Symonds, William C., "He Came, He Saw, He Cleaned Up ... He Left," *Business Week,* February 15, 1993, p. 36.

Symonds, William C., et al., ''High-Tech Star: Northern Telecom Is Challenging Even AT&T,'' *Business Week,* July 27, 1992, pp. 54–58.

Weber, Joseph, Andy Reinhardt, and Peter Burrows, ''Racing Ahead at Nortel,'' *Business Week,* November 8, 1999, pp. 93+.

Wickens, Barbara, ''Becoming a Global Giant,'' *Maclean's,* January 14, 1991.

Ziegler, Bart, ''What Really Happened at Northern Telecom,'' *Business Week,* August 9, 1993, pp. 27–28.

—Ron Chepesiuk
—updated by David E. Salamie

Palm, Inc.

5470 Great America Parkway
Santa Clara, California 95052
U.S.A.
Telephone: (408) 326-9000
Fax: (408) 326-7565
Web site: http://www.palm.com

Public Company
Incorporated: 1992 as Palm Computing, Inc.
Employees: 632
Sales: $1.06 billion (2000)
Stock Exchanges: NASDAQ
Ticker Symbol: PALM
NAIC: 334111 Electronic Computer Manufacturing

Since its inception, Palm, Inc. has made personal digital assistants (PDAs) popular as no other company has. The company has sold more than seven million of its devices in 35 countries. Its ingenious PalmPilot has attracted an enthusiastic following, allowing it to protect its controlling market share from rival PDAs powered by Microsoft Corporation's Windows CE operating system.

Silicon Valley Origins

Palm Computing, Inc. was established in January 1992. Its founder, Jeff Hawkins, was formerly vice-president of Grid Systems Corp. and was credited with designing that company's line of pen computers. President and COO Donna Dubinsky was a cofounder of Claris Corp.

Tandy Corporation sponsored Palm Computing's first product: the Zoomer (marketed as the Casio Z-7000 and the Tandy Z-PDA) handheld device that was developed in cooperation with Casio Computing Inc. Three California venture capital firms also backed the company.

Palm soon introduced add-on software for connecting Zoomers to PCs. Other early products were the PalmPrint and PalmOrganizer devices based on the Geos operating system developed by Geoworks of Alameda, California. Sharp used these technologies in its PT-9000 handheld pen tablet machine.

In 1994, Palm began marketing itself as a third-party developer for other makers of handheld computing devices, extending beyond the Geos operating system. Three other platforms were under consideration: Apple's Newton Intelligence, Microsoft's WinPad, and General Magic Inc.'s MagicCap.

In September 1994, Palm debuted its Graffiti handwriting recognition software. Until that time, users of personal digital assistants usually entered information by choosing selections on a tiny screen with a little plastic stylus. Adding any kind of practical keyboard would make the devices too large to carry in one's pocket. Apple's Newton already had a limiting handwriting recognition capability, but Palm's Graffiti could be used for taking notes or sending e-mail. It boasted 100 percent accuracy and a speed to rival typing. Graffiti required users to modify their handwriting somewhat—omitting, for example, the cross bar in the letters "A" and "F" and writing the letter "L" in mirror image. Palm claimed the system could be learned in 20 minutes and mastered in a couple of hours. Palm offered the software for the Newton, Magic Cap, and other PDAs.

Giant modem manufacturer U.S. Robotics, based in Skokie, Illinois, acquired Palm in September 1995 for $44 million. Palm was based in Los Altos, California.

A New Pilot in 1996

Palm introduced its new, simplified PDA, called the Pilot, in the spring of 1996. Rather than attempting to stand alone as a computer, the Pilot was designed to easily and quickly exchange information with a PC. It sat in a cradle that was plugged into the desktop computer.

According to *Time,* venture capitalists in Silicon Valley doubted users would buy a device with as few features as the Pilot offered. However, the very key to the Pilot's success was its Zen-like simplicity. While designing it, Hawkins carried an uncarved block of wood in his shirt pocket for months, tapping on it while deciding the key features the Pilot needed. Eventu-

Company Perspectives:

Design Philosophy: A handheld computer is not a laptop or desktop computer, the focus is on managing and accessing information rather than creating and editing documents. This unique user experience requires a unique set of guiding principles—be simple, wearable and connected. An unwavering commitment to these principles makes Palm products ideal for customers and developers alike.

ally, four functions emerged: a calendar, address book, to-do list, and memo section.

The tiny new device measured just 4.7 inches long, 3.2 inches wide, and 0.7 inches thick. It used ubiquitous miniature flashlight batteries that lasted for months. The basic Pilot 1000 retailed for $299, half the price of a Newton. It could hold 500 addresses and 600 appointments. The Pilot 5000 had four to five times the memory and sold for $369.

It took four months for the Pilots to catch on, but soon they were appearing all over Hollywood. Palm shipped more than a million of them in their first year and a half—a faster launch than Sony Walkmans, pagers, and mobile phones. They certainly outsold all other PDAs. The GridPad that Hawkins had designed nearly ten years earlier was simply too big. The expensive Apple Newton failed in the mass marketplace. The Sharp Wizard and the Hewlett Packard 200LX were limited to tiny niches of gadget enthusiasts.

In the face of Palm's success, Microsoft rushed out its Windows CE 1.0 operating system in its haste to dominate yet another market. The units that used it, equipped with tiny keyboards, offered more features than the Pilot but were difficult to use. They failed to threaten Palm's position; the company controlled two-thirds of the handheld market at the end of 1997.

Microsoft released its updated CE 2.0 software in November 1997 and called its new handhelds ''Palm PCs,'' quickly landing it in court for alleged trademark infringement. Seven companies, including Casio and Philips, allied with Microsoft in developing their own feature-packed handhelds running the CE 2.0 operating system. They generally proved more complex to use than the Pilot. (Palm soon began referring to its devices by company name and model number.)

Palm continuously updated the Pilot's design. It introduced a modem for it in 1997. However, its software was not well received and third party developers moved to quickly fill the void. The Palm III was introduced in March 1998. It could exchange information with other Palm IIIs via a wireless infrared transmission. *Time* magazine documented the phenomenon of strangers swapping video games, contact information, and subway maps by this ''beaming.'' Other new features included refined styling, a protective lid, and more memory.

Palm kept its own offerings relatively simple, leaving 5,000 outside parties to develop software and hardware add-ons. Users could now link with the Internet, corporate networks, and pagers. The Palm III sold for $399. Wireless modems (supplied by Novatel, JP Systems, and Metricom) sold for $350–$400 and doubled the size of the unit.

3Com, based in Santa Clara, California, had acquired U.S. Robotics in June 1997. 3Com manufactured networking adapters and switches. With sales of $570 million Palm accounted for nearly ten percent of 3Com's revenues in the 1998/99 fiscal year. 3Com CEO Eric Benhamou saw the unit as the centerpiece of a revitalized 3Com, according to the *Wall Street Journal*. In fact, although Dubinsky claimed it attracted little interest at the time of the acquisition, Palm Computing emerged as the best part of the merger with U.S. Robotics, which left 3Com with massive excess modem inventories and other difficulties in combining the two product lines.

Dubinsky and Hawkins left 3Com in 1998 because it would not spin off Palm as a separate company. They formed Handspring Inc. and used licensed Palm software in their own, lower-priced device, called the Visor, which was introduced in September 1999. It featured a slot for effortlessly adding a variety of hardware modules, such as digital music players and cameras. (PalmPilots did have a serial port for adding peripherals.)

By this time (September 1999), Palm held an 85 percent market share, and was aggressively licensing its proprietary Palm OS operating system. *Computer Reseller News* reported that Microsoft had turned its attention towards secondary functions beyond organizing data, such as playing music clips and video games.

The new Palm VII arrived in 1999. The handy organizer had morphed into a full-time wireless telecommunications device. It was priced at $599, plus an additional monthly fee ($10–$40) for Palm.net service based on usage. Although its tiny screen could not display all the contents of a typical web page, Palm had lined up more than 1,000 Internet content developers willing to accommodate the Palm VII.

Compaq Computer Corporation unveiled another lower-priced competitor, the Aero 1500, in September 1999. Hewlett-Packard Co.'s Jornada 430, priced the same as the Palm VII, debuted the same month. The Jornada featured a color screen.

3Com picked a new CEO for Palm in December 1999: Carl J. Yankowski, head of the Reebok Brand athletic shoe division of Reebok International Ltd. He also had experience with Sony Corporation, PepsiCo, Inc., Polaroid Corporation, and General Electric Co.

Palm controlled 70 percent of the organizer market; a few progressive corporate network administrators were buying PalmPilots by the hundreds. Sales were growing 65 percent a year. Organizers still accounted for 99 percent of revenues in spite of the emphasis the company was making on licensing its software to other companies, such as America Online Inc. and Motorola Inc.

Qualcomm Inc. and Nokia used Palm OS in their most advanced mobile phones. However, Palm saw smarter mobile phones as the company's second biggest competitive threat after Microsoft. Nokia was also a member of the Symbian consortium, which was developing its own operating system for wireless Internet devices. Handspring and Telefon AB L.M. Ericsson were also members of this effort.

Key Dates:

1992: Palm Computing, Inc. is founded.
1995: U.S. Robotics acquires Palm for $44 million.
1996: New PalmPilots revolutionize handheld computing.
1997: 3Com acquires U.S. Robotics.
2000: Palm goes public in March with a staggering opening day valuation of $53 billion; 3Com distributes all remaining shares in Palm to its stockholders in July.

In this rapidly changing industry, competitors often had to cooperate. For example, Palm's organizers were designed to work with the Windows-based programs running on PCs. Palm's struggles and victories were cited by opposite sides at the Microsoft antitrust trial.

2000 IPO

Palm Inc.'s IPO in March 2000 displayed high-tech speculation at its most febrile. Priced at $38, shares reached $165 each before closing at $95, giving Palm a market valuation of $53 billion—more than that of General Motors and McDonald's, and more than that of its parent company, 3Com, valued at $28 billion. At the time 3Com still owned 94 percent of Palm's stock; however, in July it completed the distribution of its remaining shares to stockholders.

A revamped Microsoft operating system appeared in a series of Pocket PC devices launched by Hewlett-Packard, Compaq, and Casio in April 2000. The Pocket PC enjoyed a sleeker design than the somewhat boxy Pilots. According to the *Wall Street Journal,* independent programmers who developed Palm-based software remained intensely loyal, often refusing to adapt applications for the rival Windows CE systems. Palm claimed to have 70,000 third-party developers registered in the middle of 2000, up from only 3,000 at the beginning of 1999. Many of these had modest operations, some distributing their programs over the Internet as shareware. In contrast, Microsoft had licensed 200 companies to work on Pocket PC programs; many were larger companies.

Revenues in the last quarter of 1999/2000 were more than double those of the previous year. Suppliers of display screens and memory had difficulty keeping up with ever accelerating demand. A few faulty memory chips were allowed into production; Palm offered a software fix.

Boosting its wireless Internet services, Palm bought AnyDay.com, which produced Internet-based calendars, in June 2000 for $80 million in cash and stock options. It had also bought e-mail provider Actual Software Corp. Palm planned to offer expansion slots in its organizers by early 2001, an area where it lagged behind Visor and Pocket PC devices. Personal electronics powerhouse Sony was preparing to introduce its own PDA.

Principal Subsidiaries

Palm Computing Europe SARL (France); Palm Computing K.K. (Japan); Palm do Brasil Limitada; Palm Europe Limited (U.K.);

Palm Europe Limited (Italy); Palm Europe Limited (Switzerland); Palm France; Palm Germany GmbH i.G.; Palm Global Operations, Ltd. (Ireland); Palm Hong Kong Ltd.; Palm Ireland Investment; Palm Latin America, Inc., Argentina Branch; Palm Mexico S.A. de C.V. (Mexico); Palm OS BV (Netherlands); Palm Sales Australia Pty Limited; Palm Sales Canada Inc.; Palm Singapore Sales Pte. Ltd.; Palm Sweden A.B.

Principal Competitors

Casio Computer Co., Ltd.; Microsoft Corporation; Psion; Sybase Inc.

Further Reading

Alsop, Stewart, "Innovative Graffiti Might Actually Make PDAs Useable," *InfoWorld,* September 26, 1994, p. 130.

Bransten, Lisa, and Scott Thurm, "For Palm Computers, an IPO and a Flashy Rival," *Wall Street Journal,* September 14, 1999, p. B1.

Brewin, Bob, "Palm's Mace Is Officially 'Paranoid' About PocketPC," *Computerworld,* April 17, 2000, p. 12.

Buckman, Rebecca, "Microsoft to Unveil Pocket PCs in Big Rematch with Palm Inc.," *Wall Street Journal,* April 18, 2000, p. B6.

Clark, Don, and Ted Bridis, "Palm Is Cited by Both Sides of Microsoft Case," *Wall Street Journal,* May 4, 2000, p. B6.

Croal, N'Gai, "The World in Your Hand," *Newsweek,* May 31, 1999, p. 22.

Gore, Andrew, "Never Say Never Again," *Macworld,* July 2000, p. 23.

Hwang, Diana, "Palm Grasps Handheld Market," *Computer Reseller News,* May 2, 1994, p. 62.

Jackson, David S., "Palm-to-Palm," *Time,* March 16, 1998, pp. 42–44.

Mossberg, Walter S., "The PalmPilot Has Some New Rivals But No Competition," *Wall Street Journal,* July 2, 1998, p. B1.

——, "A Palm-Size Computer That's Easy to Use and Cheap—Finally," *Wall Street Journal,* March 28, 1996, p. B1.

Nakache, Patricia, "Secrets of the New Brand Builders," *Fortune,* June 22, 1998, pp. 167–70.

Nasri, Jennifer, "Investor Frenzy Causes Palm Inc.'s Market Valuation to Soar," *Weekly Corporate Growth Report,* March 13, 2000.

Pui-Wing Tam, "Army of Programmers Helps Palm Keep Its Edge—Loyal Independent Designers Decline to Adapt Software for Rival Microsoft System," *Wall Street Journal,* June 1, 2000, p. B1.

——, "Palm Plans Slot for Hand-Held Devices to Offer Memory Boost, More Functions," *Wall Street Journal,* June 27, 2000, p. B8.

——, "Palm Profit Jumps 82 Percent, Beats Forecasts," *Wall Street Journal,* June 29, 2000, p. B10.

——, "Palm's Founders to Get IPO—At Handspring," *Wall Street Journal,* June 15, 2000, p. B1.

Quittner, Joshua, "PCs? Forget 'Em!" *Time,* May 8, 2000, p. 105.

Sears, Steven M., "Palm IPO Soars, Then Retreats a Bit, Pushing Traders to Unwind Options in Parent 3Com," *Wall Street Journal,* March 3, 2000, p. C26.

Stirpe, Amanda, "Can Palm Hold On?" *Computer Reseller News,* October 18, 1999, pp. 117–18.

Thurm, Scott, "Palm Inc. Gets Ready for New Hands," *Wall Street Journal,* February 28, 2000, p. B1.

——, "3Com Faces Bleaker Future Without Palm," *Wall Street Journal,* March 9, 2000, p. B6.

——, "3Com Names Yankowski to CEO Post at Soon-Independent Palm Computing," *Wall Street Journal,* December 3, 1999, p. B5.

Wildstrom, Stephen H., "The PalmPilot Flies Higher," *Business Week, Industrial/Technology Edition,* March 23, 1998, p. 20.

—Frederick C. Ingram

The Pantry, Inc.

1801 Douglas Drive
Sanford, North Carolina 27331-1410
U.S.A.
Telephone: (919) 774-6700
Fax: (919) 775-5428
Web site: http://www.thepantry.com

Public Company
Incorporated: 1967
Employees: 9,025
Sales: $1.68 billion (1999)
Stock Exchanges: NASDAQ
Ticker Symbol: PTRY
NAIC: 44512 Convenience Stores

With 1,215 convenience stores, The Pantry, Inc. is the second largest convenience store operator in the United States, behind 7-Eleven. Based in Sanford, North Carolina, the company's stores are located in the Southeast near tourist attractions such as Disney Land and Myrtle Beach. Whereas most stores are located in the Carolinas and Florida, others are located in Kentucky, Tennessee, Virginia, Indiana, and Georgia. The company's stores operate under the names The Pantry, Lil' Champ, Quick Stop, Depot, Food Chief, Express Stop, Dash N, Smokers Express, ETNA, and Sprint. Some stores have fast-food outlets such as Subway and Taco Bell. Stores are generally stocked with tobacco products, beer, soft drinks, self-service fast foods, candy, snack foods, newspapers, magazines, dairy products, canned goods, and health and beauty aids. About one-half of the stores' sales stem from fuel, and about one-third of nonfuel sales stem from tobacco products. Investment firm Freeman Spogli & Co. and Chase Manhattan Capital Corporation acquired a controlling interest in the company in 1995. In 1999 The Pantry launched an initial public offering to pay off debt accrued from its many acquisitions.

A Quiet Beginning in 1967

The Pantry was founded in 1967 in North Carolina by businessmen Sam Wornom and Truby Proctor, Jr. The company expanded slowly at first and was described as being "steady and stable," and "a quiet organization niched in the Carolinas, Kentucky, Tennessee, and Indiana." Wornom and Proctor acquired new stores by borrowing against existing stores and paying off debt with new sales. The Pantry was profitable during the 1960s and 1970s and faced few obstacles. Its situation changed in the 1980s, however. Like many other companies, The Pantry was affected by the savings-and-loan bailouts and leveraged buyouts. Its sales dropped. Without cash for renovations, its stores deteriorated. The Pantry had no direction and little hope for the future.

Founder Wornom sold his stake in The Pantry to Montrose Capital in 1987. Montrose was renowned for its famous shareholders, including Dave Thomas, the founder of Wendy's, and Wayne Rogers, the former Trapper John on the TV series M*A*S*H. The company was founded by former Duke University professor Clay Hamner. Montrose gained control of The Pantry in 1990 when it purchased half of cofounder Proctor's shares; Proctor remained CEO.

The Pantry was still struggling in the 1990s. In an effort to get back on track, the company restructured. It closed unprofitable stores and remodeled others. These efforts were futile, however. The Pantry posted losses in 1991 and 1992. It posted a small income in 1993 but another loss in 1994. To make matters worse, The Pantry had too much debt to acquire new stores, which would have helped increase its sales.

Freeman Spogli & Co. in 1995

Tension between cofounder Proctor and Montrose's Hamner led Proctor to sell his remaining shares in The Pantry in 1995 to Freeman Spogli & Co., a Los Angeles-based investment firm specializing in management-led buyouts. Chase Manhattan Capital acquired the rest of the company from Montrose. Freeman Spogli & Co. had tremendous financial resources and the buyout presented great opportunities for The Pantry. Gene Horne, the company's president and CEO, concluded that with Freeman Spogli & Co. The Pantry had "the infrastructure to go to 1,000 to 2,000 stores." Horne was right, but was not destined to be a part of it.

The following year, Peter J. Sodini took Horne's place as president and CEO. Prior to his appointment, Sodini was the CEO of Purity Supreme, Inc., a grocery store chain in New England. Industry analysts credited Sodini with attacking The Pantry's problems head-on and turning the company around.

At the time of his appointment, Sodini described The Pantry as being "in flux." Using resources from Freeman, Spogli & Co. he gave the company direction. Unlike some competitors, Sodini decided against turning its convenience stores into elaborate food stores and decided instead to concentrate on the sale of gas and tobacco. "We like to focus on what we think we do well, which is to run a basic convenience store selling gasoline and the usual amenities you find in the store," he explained.

Sodini was displeased with The Pantry's management, so he replaced many executives with allies from his former employer, the Purity Supreme Grocery Store chain. "Although they didn't have gasoline experience, what they brought in terms of being able to further enhance the merchandise side of their business was significant," Sodini said in *Convenience Store News*.

When it came to gasoline, Sodini himself had no experience. Ironically, this worked to his advantage. According to *Investor's Business Daily,* Sodini quickly realized that most convenience stores selling a lot of gas were not making as much money as they could be, since merchandise brings in higher profits than gasoline. Sodini thought this was also true of The Pantry's stores. "Not much thought was going into the adjoining stores and merchandise," he said. Using his supermarket expertise, he struck deals with suppliers and stocked the company's stores with 25 percent more merchandise than other convenience stores.

Sodini realized, however, that while merchandise helped boost sales, the sale of gasoline was still critical to the company's success. What made him different from competitors was the way he viewed gasoline. Said one analyst in *Investor's Business Daily,* "Most of the top convenience store operators are owned by oil companies, whose focus is to sell more gas. But to Sodini, pumping gas is like selling milk. It's a commodity that has to be competitively priced." The Pantry lowered the price of gas and cigarettes, which helped it compete better with other convenience stores.

Like many other convenience stores in the Southeast, The Pantry was plagued with a high employee turnover and a shortage of employees. To entice employees to sign on and stay, The Pantry paid higher-than-average wages. It also offered many opportunities for advancement and remodeled its stores. "People would rather work in a nice store versus a dump," Sodini commented in *Petrogram*.

Some of the renovations Sodini initiated included increased lighting in its stores, a new logo, and fresh paint. The Pantry painted many of its stores in local college colors. Its efforts proved worthwhile. The company's sales went up, and it further implemented its strategy of cutting prices to increase sales.

Lil' Champ in 1997

In late 1997 The Pantry got word that the 479-store Lil' Champ convenience store chain was for sale. (The Lil' Champ chain was named after founder Julian Jackson, a bantamweight boxing champion in the 1930s.) Analysts believed the Tosco Corporation, the leading independent oil refiner and oil maker in the United States, would buy the chain. Tosco had purchased Circle K, the second largest convenience store operator in the country, two years earlier. The Pantry emerged victorious, however, and acquired the chain for $132.7 million and outstanding debt. Lil' Champ Food Stores, Inc. had 430 stores in northern Florida and 49 in southeastern Georgia.

Although The Pantry was delighted with its new acquisition, Sodini was quick to point out that the situation was not perfect. "Many of the Lil' Champ stores were outdated. Many featured only single-hose product dispensers instead of the more popular multi-product dispensers. About 125 facilities didn't meet federal underground storage tank standards," Sodini said in *Convenience Store News*. "You could say that it was the ugliest mass of stores, but it was still a critical mass," he explained. The Pantry decided to immediately remodel most of the Lil' Champ stores and update them to meet federal standards.

Quick Expansion in the 1990s

The Lil' Champ acquisition was the beginning of a buying spree for The Pantry. It acquired a string of small and mid-sized convenience store chains that it described as "tuck-ins." It also opened some stores in carefully selected markets. "Right now we're like the Statue of Liberty," Sodini told *Convenience Store News*. "Send me your weak and suffering and we'll buy you." In most cases, The Pantry did not change the name of the convenience stores it purchased. Sodini believed that high-quality stores with good sales should be left alone. An exception to this was the Lil' Champ stores, which were run-down and had a poor image. Sodini renamed some of these stores Sprint, suggesting "fast, quick service."

In 1998 The Pantry acquired almost 155 stores through the acquisition of smaller chains. Included in these purchases was the acquisition of Quick Stop, a 75-store chain in the Carolinas, and 41 Zip Mart stores in North Carolina and eastern Virginia.

The following year The Pantry acquired 126 Handy Way stores in central Florida from Miller Enterprises. Many of the Handy Way stores had fast-food outlets such as Hardee's and Subway. The Pantry also purchased 28 stores operating under the Food Chief name from Dilmar Oil Company in South Carolina. The stores were located in high-traffic tourist markets such as Myrtle Beach. Sodini believed the Food Chief acquisitions would significantly enhance the company's already strong presence in South Carolina.

During the same year, The Pantry acquired 49 convenience stores operating under the trade name Kangaroo from Kangaroo, Inc. The purchase helped establish the company's presence in Georgia.

In 1999 The Pantry rose from being ranked the 33rd largest chain in *Convenience Store News* Top 50 Companies to the tenth. Under the direction of Sodini and his new management team, the company had grown from about 400 stores to more than 1,200. Revenues had risen from $427 million to $985 million.

An IPO in 1999

To pay off debt from its many acquisitions, The Pantry went public in June 1999. The company sold 6.25 million shares of common stock to raise $75.6 million in net proceeds. With its debt under control, the company was positioned for further expansion. Some of its many acquisitions included 12 On-the-Way Foods stores from the McKnight Oil Company; ten of the stores were in southwest Virginia and two were in North Carolina. The Pantry also purchased 14 MiniMart stores from Oates Oil Company, located in South Carolina. The MiniMart purchase made The Pantry the largest convenience store operator in South Carolina.

Also in 1999 The Pantry purchased 19 stores from Tip Top Convenience Stores, Inc., operating under the name Big K. Big K stores were located mostly in Mississippi and Alabama. The Pantry also acquired the five-store Market Express convenient store chain in Sumter, South Carolina, and an Amoco station in Hilton Head, South Carolina.

The Pantry's many new stores caused a surge in sales and profits—in 1999 The Pantry posted a net income of $10.4 million on revenues of $160 million. For the second quarter ending in June 2000, The Pantry posted a net income of $6.2 million on revenues of $643 million.

Future Expansions

While The Pantry's aggressive acquisition strategy made it profitable, the convenience store business was highly competitive and vulnerable to rising fuel prices. The Pantry posted a net loss of $2.5 million in the first quarter of 2000; the company attributed the loss to a surge in the price of gasoline. Although the Pantry continued to acquire new stores in 2000, Sodini stressed that he did not have a specific goal in mind. He said the company might or might not continue to expand, depending on whether the right opportunities presented themselves. In 2000 the company's top priority was to remain profitable. "We're not into collecting trophies and we're not in this as a philanthropic venture," said Sodini.

Principal Subsidiaries

Global Communications; Lil' Champ Food Stores, Inc.; Pit Holdings; R & H Maxxon Inc.; Sandhills Inc.

Principal Competitors

7-Eleven, Inc.; RaceTrac Petroleum, Inc.; Swifty Serve Corporation.

Further Reading

Gervickas, Bicki, "Stocking Up the Pantry," *Petrogram,* May/June 1999.
Grugal, Robin M., "Supermarket Guru Revamps Minimart Chain," *Investor's Business Daily,* August 18, 1999.
Morrison, Mitch, "The Pantry Stocks Up On C-Stores," *Convenience Store News,* February 8, 1999.
"The Pantry, Inc.," *Convenience Store News,* August 3, 1988, p. 74.

—Tracey Vasil Biscontini

The Pep Boys—Manny, Moe & Jack

3111 West Allegheny Avenue
Philadelphia, Pennsylvania 19132
U.S.A.
Telephone: (215) 430-9000
Fax: (215) 229-5076
Web site: http://www.pepboys.com

Public Company
Incorporated: 1925 as Pep Auto Supply Co.
Employees: 27,987
Sales: $2.39 billion (1999)
Stock Exchanges: New York
Ticker Symbol: PBY
NAIC: 441310 Automotive Parts and Accessories Stores;
811111 General Automotive Repair

With about 650 company owned and operated automotive aftermarket superstores in 37 states and Puerto Rico, The Pep Boys—Manny, Moe & Jack is a leading auto parts and service chain. The typical Pep Boys supercenter is about 18,200 square feet in size, stocks about 25,000 items, and provides preventive maintenance and repair services at 12 service bays. With its unsurpassed diversity that includes tires, auto parts, accessories, and service, Pep Boys caters to three segments of the automotive aftermarket that it identifies as: "do-it-yourself," "buy-for-resale" (sales to professional mechanics and garages), and "do-it-for-me" (the service side). About 80 percent of company revenue is generated from the sale of merchandise, with the remainder deriving from service. Advertised as "the three best friends your car ever had," the original Pep Boys launched their first auto parts store just as the automobile was coming of age.

Lore-Filled Start in the 1920s

Pep Boys was founded by Emanuel (Manny) Rosenfeld, Maurice (Moe) Strauss, Moe Radavitz, and W. Graham (Jack) Jackson, Philadelphians who met and became friends during their World War I stint in the U.S. Navy. In 1921, less than 15 years after mass production came to the auto industry, the four war buddies put up $200 each to open an auto supplies store in their hometown. Strauss, who had already made two unsuccessful attempts at entrepreneurship, started out as a silent partner—he was already employed at a competing store, and was not ready to give up the steady income.

The partners rented a small storefront in Philadelphia, so small that only the shortest of names would fit on its marquee. Corporate folklore tells of a brainstorming session that adopted the "Pep" from Pep Valve Grinding Compound, one of the shop's first product lines. Pep Auto Supply fit neatly above the shop's front door, but there is more to the chain's christening. The tale goes on to tell of a street cop who, upon issuing equipment citations, would recommend that the motorists go to the "boys" at Pep for replacement parts. The three Pep Boys who remained after Moe Radavitz cashed out in the early 1920s tacked their own names on in 1923.

The corporate caricatures that would later become famous throughout the country were commissioned shortly thereafter and drawn by Harry Moskovitch. Manny, a now-reformed cigar smoker with a Charlie Chaplin mustache, was on the left. Moe, who would be known as "the father of the automotive aftermarket," was in the middle. Jack's grinning caricature made a brief appearance before being replaced with that of Moe's brother, Isaac (Izzy) Strauss, on the right. (The company name stayed the same despite the personnel changes—"Manny, Moe and Izzy" just did not sound right.) As the chain grew, the Pep Boys were rendered in cotton on T-shirts, in ink on match books, and in cement as statues in front of stores. The bizarre but distinctive trademark was later joked about in Johnny Carson's *Tonight Show* monologue, parodied on *Saturday Night Live,* and came to life in Claymation for late 1980s television ads.

In the late 1920s, Manny Rosenfeld brought his brother, Murray, into the business and Izzy Strauss broke away to start his own automotive chain. The sometimes convoluted family ties at Pep Boys remained strong through the 1980s, and the Strauss and Rosenfeld families controlled one-fifth of the chain's stock into the early 1990s.

1930s Through Early 1980s: Expanding into California; Conservative Management

By 1928, Pep Boys had a dozen stores in the Philadelphia area, and Strauss began to feel the pull of the burgeoning Califor-

---

Company Perspectives:

Pep Boys has been a leader in the automotive aftermarket for more than 78 years, always meeting the needs of its customers with dependable automotive parts, supplies and service. Today, the Company remains at the forefront of its industry as the aftermarket continues its rapid technological evolution.

---

nia market. He had lived briefly in the state in the early 1920s, when he became convinced that it was an ideal location for an automotive retail business. In 1932, he sent Murray Rosenfeld, called "perhaps the most astute merchandiser of the Philadelphia group" by *Aftermarket Business* in 1991, out to the West Coast to launch what was commonly known as Pep Boys West. The first two California stores were opened in 1933 in Los Angeles. By that time, the chain had 40 Philadelphia outlets.

Although the founders had planned to operate both segments of the business in concert, the physical distance between them soon forced the division of primary merchandising functions. For example, intense competition compelled Pep Boys West to expand the size of, and selection at, those stores, whereas East Coast outlets concentrated more on service. Manny Rosenfeld stayed in Philadelphia, his brother Murray ran the Los Angeles operation, and Moe Strauss commuted between the two.

During World War II, automotive production was curtailed while car companies focused on war production, and "Murray the merchandiser" stocked Pep Boys West shelves with nonautomotive products such as work clothes, bicycles, and lawn and garden equipment. The West Coast division also experimented with wholesaling and even exporting.

When the retailer went public in 1946, Manny Rosenfeld was named president and Moe Strauss was elected chairman of the board. For the next three decades, the company grew relatively slowly under what was later interpreted as a preponderance of caution—the company insisted on owning, rather than leasing, its stores, and doggedly avoided debt. Under the direction of Moe Strauss, who assumed the additional responsibilities of president in 1960 after Manny Rosenfeld's death, the chain grew by only two new stores over the 20-year period from 1964 to 1984. The fiscally conservative Strauss occupied both posts until 1973, when he relinquished the title of president to son Benjamin; however, he remained chairman through 1977. He was still a member of the board of directors at his death in 1982, over six decades after he helped found the business.

Mid-1980s Through Early 1990s: Rapid Growth and Modernization Under New Management

Ben Strauss advanced to chairman and CEO that year, and Morton (Bud) Krause, son-in-law of Moe Strauss, was named president. When Krause took an early retirement in 1984 at the age of 54, Ben Strauss shouldered the responsibilities of all three offices. In 1986, Strauss called on Mitchell Leibovitz to become Pep Boys' first president from outside the founding families. Leibovitz had joined the company at the age of 33 in 1978 as controller and was promoted to chief financial officer

within a year. He had worked as a teacher and coach before earning an M.B.A. from Temple University by going to night classes. Leibovitz caught Ben Strauss's attention while employed as a CPA for the accounting firm that audited Pep Boys' books. From 1979 to 1984, Leibovitz was in charge of Pep Boys' eastern operations. He closed down 32 "small and stodgy" stores, then opened 60 stores in the ensuing two years. The East Coast expansion was financed with an offering of $50 million in convertible debentures (bonds that can be converted to stock), a debt Moe Strauss would never have taken on.

By 1986, when Leibovitz assumed the presidency, Pep Boys was the second largest chain in the highly fragmented, $100 billion automotive aftermarket industry, after Western Auto Supply Co. Its earnings had increased 18 percent annually from 1982 to 1986, but the new leader had even bigger plans for the retailer. As president, Leibovitz mapped out and executed a five-year plan to consolidate Pep Boys' headquarters and simultaneously expand its geographic reach, in the hopes of its becoming the Home Depot of the retail automotive aftermarket industry. In fact, Leibovitz enjoyed the counsel of Bernie Marcus, the executive who catapulted Home Depot to the upper echelon of the do-it-yourself home repair market. Leibovitz recognized the industrywide changes that could either launch Pep Boys to the top of the heap or see it acquired by a competitor by the end of the century.

During the 1980s, the traditionally fragmented retail automotive aftermarket industry became more competitive as larger chains began to emerge. Many neighborhood service garages were being transformed into convenience stores with gas stations, and some of the larger chains that had provided limited service, such as J.C. Penney and Kmart, also started phasing out auto repairs. All the while, cars were growing increasingly complex and difficult for non-pros to fix.

In the face of these market shifts, Leibovitz set out a five-year plan for Pep Boys that encompassed six goals: store expansion, a refined merchandise mix, increased warehousing and distribution capacity, improved promotion of the service operations, modernization of systems support, and consolidation of the headquarters in Philadelphia. From February 1986 to February 1991, Pep Boys invested $477 million in the plan—almost as much as 1986's sales of $486 million.

During that period, the number of Pep Boys stores doubled to 337, the number of states with Pep Boys locations reached 17, and product offerings tripled from 9,000 items to 24,000. Individual locations were expanded into a "superstore" or "warehouse" format, with an average size of 23,000 square feet, and the company launched an "everyday low price" strategy. These larger stores also featured an increased number of service bays—a fairly unique feature in the industry—and services offered were expanded. Unlike many of its competitors, which would only install tires and batteries (if anything), Pep Boys' mechanics would perform practically any automotive service except body work and engine replacement. Pep Boys' new computerized merchandising and inventory control helped stores tailor their offerings to the local market. For example, rural stores might carry more truck parts, whereas urban stores might stock more foreign car parts. Weekends were added to the retailer's schedule, and hours were extended to 9 p.m. on weeknights.

Key Dates:

1921: Four World War I buddies open an auto supplies store in Philadelphia called Pep Auto Supply, soon renamed Pep Boys.

1923: Official name of business becomes The Pep Boys—Manny, Moe & Jack.

1933: First two California stores are opened in Los Angeles.

1946: Company goes public.

1986: Mitchell Leibovitz becomes the first company president from outside the founding families; the chain includes 159 stores.

1991: Chain has grown to 337 units in 17 states; sales reach $1 billion.

1993: All the company's technicians and mechanics are placed on commission.

1995: A new parts-only store format, PartsUSA, is launched.

1997: PartsUSA outlets are renamed Pep Boys Express; revenues reach $2 billion.

1998: Company sells 100 of its Express outlets to AutoZone and closes an additional nine.

To tout the service bays and increase emphasis on national brands, Leibovitz raised Pep Boys' advertising budget and began to divert funds from traditional, full-page newspaper ads to direct mail, catalogs, and electronic media. He also began phasing the Pep Boys caricature out of advertising and promotional material in an effort to modernize the company's image, even though "the boys" had ranked as one of the automotive aftermarket's five most recognized corporate symbols.

In 1991, as the company concluded its five-year plan and celebrated its 70th anniversary, it also topped $1 billion in annual sales, added eight Sunbelt states to its geographic reach, and more than doubled corporate employment from 5,500 to 14,000. Leibovitz advanced to Pep Boys' chief executive office and the company was added to Standard & Poor's 500 Index in 1990. Although the young leader modestly deflected praise of his transformation of Pep Boys to the management team he had assembled, analysts gave him the lion's share of the credit for modernizing the chain.

Pep Boys is considered a noncyclical business, but its massive expenditures and assumption of debt combined with an early 1990s recession to depress profit growth. Net income declined from $42 million in 1989 to $32 million in 1990, then increased incrementally in 1991 and 1992. Pep Boys was able to begin fueling its continuing expansion and retire debt with cash flow in 1992. The company added 30 stores that year and took advantage of an "early conversion expiration" provision (also known as a "screw clause" to investors) to save $2.3 million in interest on a $75 million convertible debenture.

Pep Boys had long been known for its good working conditions and generous benefits, which helped the company attract and retain some of the industry's best employees for decades. Leibovitz instilled his employees with competitive fervor by staging ritual annihilations of competitors. Whenever competitive pressure from Pep Boys closed down a major rival's store, he added a photo of the closed-down outlet to his collection. Baseball caps bearing the vanquished competitors' corporate logos were incinerated, and Leibovitz videotaped the symbolic destruction for in-house pep rallies.

The year 1993 saw the inauguration of yet another change at Pep Boys that was hailed by *Financial World* as "the final step in transforming the old-fashioned family-owned chain into a nationwide leader." After a year of planning, Leibovitz put all his technicians and mechanics on commission in the hopes of attracting top employees and increasing their productivity. But just three months after he made the shift, consumer fraud inspectors in California, Florida, and New Jersey charged Sears, Roebuck and Co.'s auto service division with systematically overcharging customers for unnecessary repairs. The allegations specifically cited Sears' commission program as the locus of the problem. Although chagrined at the negative publicity surrounding commissioned employees generally, Leibovitz confidently stuck with his plan, which incorporated several safeguards. The cornerstone of Pep Boys' system was an ethics policy that dictated termination of mechanics who made unnecessary repairs. Technicians, who were certified by the Institute for Automotive Service Excellence (ASE), also agreed to have their commission docked if their work had to be redone.

Even with commissions, Pep Boys' service cost 20 to 50 percent less than dealerships and independent garages. Service accounted for 13 percent of the retailer's total revenue in fiscal 1993, and income from that segment was increasing more than ten percent each year in the early 1990s. Sears' subsequent decision to cut back on auto service undoubtedly sent more business to Pep Boys' service bays.

Leibovitz worked to allay customers' ingrained apprehension about gouging in automotive repairs by offering a toll-free "squeal line" and postpaid comment cards addressed to the CEO. Complaints were categorized and tabulated to detect patterns of misconduct, and regional sales managers followed up each complaint with a personal contact. According to the chief, Pep Boys received about 200 complaints and 200 compliments, out of about five million customers, each month. Commendations were reviewed and read on videotape for the firm's "Customer Corner," a video presentation played back in company break rooms across the country.

Pep Boys emerged from the early 1990s recession with strong earnings and stock performance. Even though comparable store sales only increased one percent, profits grew by over 20 percent from 1992 to 1993, to $65.6 million and the share price jumped from less than $20 in early 1992 to over $30 by early 1994. Stock market observers predicted that Pep Boys' stock would increase 20 to 30 percent by the end of 1994. Future expansion was planned for new markets in Chicago, Ohio, Denver, Houston, the San Francisco Bay area, and New England. The chain also planned to increase its grip on existing markets in New York, New Jersey, Baltimore, Washington, D.C., Florida, and its historical strongholds in southern California and Philadelphia.

Mid-1990s and Beyond: Shifting Away from DIY Market

Pep Boys ended 1994 with 432 stores, 4,166 service bays, and revenues of $1.41 billion. Three years later, following the biggest expansion in company history, there were 711 Pep Boys outlets with 6,208 service bays while revenues surpassed the $2 billion mark for the first time. This expansion included the launching in 1995 of a new parts-only store format (with no service bays and no tires) called PartsUSA. By 1997, there were 109 PartsUSA stores, which were rechristened Pep Boys Express that year in an attempt to leverage the name recognition that the Pep Boys brand had gained in its 75-plus-years of existence. The new format was intended to help the company pursue the "buy-for-resale" segment of the automotive aftermarket, which consisted of sales to professional mechanics and garages—as well as traditional do-it-yourself (DIY) customers. The buy-for-resale segment of the market, along with the "do-it-for-me" segment (services), was increasing in importance at the same time that the DIY sector was plateauing. Fewer people were doing their own auto repair in the mid-to-late 1990s because cars were becoming more and more complex. In pursuit of sales to professionals, Pep Boys began rolling out a system for delivering parts to repair shops in 1996. By the end of 1997, about half of the company's units were offering delivery services. At the same time, Pep Boys was pursuing increased service business by signing agreements with fleet customers, such as maintenance agreements with rental car agencies and deals to recondition used cars and make warranty repairs for used car superstores. In 1997 Pep Boys also began testing a service-only format called Pep Boys Service and Tire Center at a location in Moorestown, New Jersey.

With DIY sales continuing to disappoint, Pep Boys decided in October 1998 to refocus on its supercenter format. The company sold 100 of its Express outlets to arch-rival AutoZone, Inc. for $108 million. Pep Boys also closed an additional nine Express units, leaving just 12 in operation. In connection with this contraction, the company recorded pretax charges of $29.5 million, which reduced 1998 net earnings to $5 million. Pep Boys also slowed down its expansion drive, growing by only 24 units in fiscal 1999, and worked to improve the performance of the supercenters by remodeling some of the older units and making other enhancements. At the same time, the rollout of the delivery system continued, culminating by 1999 in 88 percent of the stores participating. Sales for 1999 were flat compared to 1998, but net earnings improved to $29.3 million. In 2000 Pep Boys continued the expansion of its service operations by launching a new program for buyers or sellers of used cars whereby Pep Boys would inspect a vehicle and, assuming the vehicle passed the inspection, provide a certification vouching for the vehicles' mechanical and operational soundness. Pep Boys initially charged between $89.99 and $229.99 for the service.

Principal Subsidiaries

Pep Boys–Manny, Moe & Jack of California; Pep Boys–Manny, Moe & Jack of Delaware, Inc.; Pep Boys–Manny, Moe & Jack of Puerto Rico, Inc.; Colchester Insurance Company; PBY Corporation; Carrus Supply Corporation.

Principal Competitors

AutoZone, Inc.; CARQUEST Corporation; CSK Auto Corporation; Discount Auto Parts, Inc.; General Parts, Inc.; The Goodyear Tire & Rubber Company; Les Schwab Tire Centers; Midas, Inc.; Monro Muffler Brake, Inc.; O'Reilly Automotive, Inc.; Precision Auto Care, Inc.; Rankin Automotive Group, Inc.; Sears, Roebuck and Co.; Wal-Mart Stores, Inc.

Further Reading

Byrne, Harlan S., "Wait 'Til Next Year," *Barron's* January 5, 1998, p. 48.

Halverson, Richard, "Auto Chains Shift Gears to Wholesale As DIY Sales Skid," *Discount Store News,* September 4, 1995, p. 51.

——, "Pep Boys Expanding Bays," *Discount Store News,* June 23, 1997, pp. 1, 126.

——, "Pep Boys to Transition Away from DIY Market," *Discount Store News,* June 22, 1998, pp. 3, 62.

Hass, Nancy, "Truths of Commission," *Financial World,* January 19, 1993, pp. 28–29.

Johnson, Jay L., "Pep Boys on the Fast Track," *Discount Merchandiser,* October 1990, pp. 18–25.

Kharouf, Jim, "Pep Boys Speeding into Area," *Daily Southtown (Chicago),* June 22, 1994, pp. 1–2.

La Monica, Paul R., "Pep Boys: Shifting Gears," *Financial World,* December 5, 1995, p. 24.

Levy, Robert, "Manny, Moe & Jack on the Move," *Dun's Business Month,* July 1986, pp. 28–29.

Lin, Anthony, "Pep Boys Is Revving Up for Its Largest Expansion Drive: Company to Launch Parts-Only Stores and Increase Supercenter Outlets," *Wall Street Journal,* August 10, 1995, p. B4.

Lubove, Seth, "Retail Is Detail," *Forbes,* September 30, 1991, pp. 144, 146.

"Pep Boys: More Than an Industry Leader, an Institution," *Aftermarket Business,* December 1, 1991, pp. 17–39.

"Pep Boys Passes $1 Billion Mark," *Discount Merchandiser,* January 1992, pp. 14–17.

"Pep Boys Tests Service-Only Units," *Discount Store News,* January 26, 1998, pp. 6, 42.

"Pep Boys West, 1933–1983: 50 Years Later, Still Pioneering the Retail Aftermarket," *Home and Auto,* November 15, 1983, pp. 13+.

Rudnitsky, Howard, "Keeping the Family Buggy on the Road," *Forbes,* March 11, 1996, p. 52.

Silverthorne, Sean, "Pep Boys' Mitchell Leibovitz: He Studied Industry Leaders to Recast Auto Parts Store," *Investor's Business Daily,* October 13, 1992, pp. 1–2.

Taylor, Alex III, "How to Murder the Competition," *Fortune,* February 22, 1993, pp. 87, 90.

Wayne, Leslie, "Pep Boys (Manny, Moe, and Jack) See Their Stock Climb," *New York Times,* April 19, 1994.

Weiss, Gary, "Beware the Turn of the Screw," *Business Week,* June 1, 1992, p. 108.

Werner, Thomas, "Seeking No. 1: Pep Boys Expands Auto-Parts Chain by Big Leaps," *Barron's,* July 6, 1987, pp. 34–35.

—April Dougal Gasbarre
—updated by David E. Salamie

PhyCor, Inc.

30 Burton Hills Boulevard, Suite 400
Nashville, Tennessee 37215
U.S.A.
Telephone: (615) 655-9066
Fax: (615) 655-9088
Web site: http://www.phycor.com

Public Company
Incorporated: 1988
Employees: 15,900
Sales: $1.5 billion (1999)
Stock Exchanges: NASDAQ
Ticker Symbol: PHYC
NAIC: 56111 Office Administrative Services

PhyCor, Inc. and its subsidiaries provide administrative management services to physician networks and medical groups. The company manages 40 medical groups with more than 2,500 doctors in 21 states and nearly 26,000 physicians through networks in 29 healthcare markets. Through PhyCor's subsidiary, CareWise, Inc., the company provides support and assistance to more than 3.3 million consumers in making decisions about medical care.

Pioneering New Methods of Management for Physicians

Four former executives of Hospital Corporation of America, Joseph Hutts, Derril Reeves, Thompson Dent, and Richard Wright, founded PhyCor in 1988, pioneering the first physicians practice management (PPM) company. The advent of managed healthcare plans, such as Health Maintenance Organizations (HMOs), led individual physicians and group practitioners to seek outside help in handling complex new issues. In addition to providing physicians with administrative services to meet new demands of financial management, such partnerships reduced physicians' financial risk in working with managed care programs that used a ''capitated'' or fixed-rate reimbursement structure. A large group of physicians or a large company absorbed the risks more easily than an individual doctor or

small medical group and also benefited from the greater clout in negotiating managed care contracts. While multispecialty medical clinics benefited from referrals within the group, physicians also wanted the security of managed care contracts, which provided a stable income as healthcare profits decreased.

From the beginning PhyCor's strategy for helping physicians address changes in the healthcare system involved the acquisition of small to medium-sized clinics that offered primary care and medical specialties. When PhyCor acquired a practice, the company purchased assets in the form of equipment, accounts receivable, and, sometimes, real estate. Under a 40-year contract PhyCor then managed the clinic for approximately 15 percent of revenues from physician fees—after expenses and before physician salaries—and reimbursement of clinic expenses. Some contracts also involved a percentage of profits or interest on capital investment for PhyCor. Doctors received cash, stock, or both, but remained independent and did not become employees of PhyCor. PhyCor left medical decisions to individual doctors, while each clinic's board of directors, consisting of three physicians and three PhyCor administrators, made general decisions, such as the purchase of new equipment.

The company's first acquisitions were located in the South and involved 20 to 100 doctors each. Acquisitions included the Green Clinic of Ruston, Louisiana, in 1988; the Doctors' Clinic of Vero Beach, Florida, in 1989; and the Nalle Clinic of Charlotte, North Carolina, in early 1990. PhyCor sought clinics with the most potential for growth and improvement. After five years of management under PhyCor, the Nalle Clinic reported dramatic changes to its previously unprofitable operations. Revenues rose 30 percent the first year and five percent to ten percent each year afterward. The clinic grew to 106 doctors and 34,000 capitated patients. Some of that growth occurred through the acquisition of 19 family practice physicians, which increased the clinic's primary care doctors to 50 percent of the total. PhyCor also saved the clinic 40 percent on its malpractice insurance premiums.

In addition to lower operating expenses and increased revenues, one of the attractions for physicians in selling their practices to PPMs involved the infusion of capital for equipment and facilities. In 1990 the Greeley Medical Clinic in Colorado approached PhyCor to acquire and manage the clinic's business operations. The physicians there wanted to remain competitive under managed care by adding ten doctors to its staff. PhyCor's acquisition provided funds for expansion beyond the clinic's initial plans. PhyCor added 25 doctors, opened five satellite offices, and planned an ambulatory center and diagnostic imaging center. The Southern Colorado Clinic in Pueblo could not find a lender to finance an ambulatory surgery center; PhyCor bought the clinic in 1992, providing funds for construction of the facility.

PhyCor's expertise in negotiating managed care contracts became a cornerstone of the company's success. On the advice of PhyCor, the executive director of the Greeley Medical Clinic renegotiated a capitated contract with an HMO at a reimbursement rate 28 percent higher than the previous contract. Revenues at that clinic increased 34 percent overall after three years of PhyCor's management, funding a ten percent increase in physician salaries. Another example was the Virginia Physicians Group, where reductions in Medicare reimbursements had deleterious effects. Affiliation with PhyCor facilitated the negotiation of managed care contracts that covered both primary care and specialty care, rather than two, separate contracts, thus reducing financial risks of managed care plans.

PhyCor grew rapidly, especially after it became a public company in January 1992. After three years of operation revenues increased from $1.2 million in 1988 to $90 million by the end of 1991. An initial public offering of 2.5 million shares of stock at $16 per share raised $40 million for the purchase of additional multispecialty medical clinics. With the acquisition of six medical practices, located in Texas, Virginia, New York, and New Hampshire, 1992 revenues reached $136 million through 14 clinics in nine states.

PhyCor lost $13.7 million in 1992, however, as problems at the Miller Medical Clinic led to an $18.6 million write-down. Conflicts between the clinic and the local HMO, from which the clinic received most of its business, preceded PhyCor's ownership of Miller Medical. The clinic lost the contract shortly after PhyCor's acquisition in 1989. PhyCor gracefully exited the problem when it sold Miller Medical to a local, nonprofit hospital for the assumption of debt. From the experience executives at PhyCor learned to look for a mix of payers when buying a medical practice.

The company grew through improvements at existing clinics as well as through acquisition. PhyCor assisted the clinics with the recruitment of physicians, sometimes merging individual medical practices with local clinics. In 1993 same-clinic revenues experienced an average increase of 8.5 percent. With the January offering of $50 million in convertible subordinate debentures, the company acquired four clinics in 1993, in Texas, Alabama, and Illinois. In 1994 the company acquired six physi-

cian practices, including larger clinics such as the Lexington Clinic in Kentucky, the Holt-Krock Clinic in Fort Smith, Arkansas, and the Burns Clinic in Petoskey, Michigan, each with 100 to 175 doctors.

PhyCor also found opportunities to provide practice management services and to develop physician networks. A 1994 agreement with MetLife HealthCare engaged PhyCor to provide medical management and to form physician networks in six markets where MetLife had launched managed care. PhyCor cofounded PhyCor Management Corporation (PMC), investing a minority interest in it as a separate entity. PMC was formed to develop and manage Independent Practice Associations (IPAs), organizational networks by which independent physicians contracted with managed care plans and shared management resources. At the end of 1994 PhyCor operated 25 multispecialty clinics and 11 IPAs while earnings reached $11.7 million.

In February 1995 PhyCor purchased North American Medical Management Company, Inc. (NAMM), a limited service provider for physician practice management. The company did not provide billing, collections, staffing, or scheduling functions, but PhyCor planned to extend those services to NAMM clients. NAMM managed 36 IPAs in seven states, including the Central Florida IPA, a target market for PhyCor. The following September NAMM obtained a contract to manage two IPAs, Tampa Bay Physicians Healthcare, Inc., with more than 260 doctors, and Healthsavers, Inc., with more than 100 doctors, both in Tampa. NAMM immediately found the Tampa IPAs new HMO clients.

Accelerated Growth in Mid-1990s

PhyCor accelerated the number of acquisitions to nine in 1995 and 13 in 1996. These acquisitions were funded by a June 1994 offering of stock, which raised $58.7 million, and a July 1995 offering, which raised $110 million. Notable acquisitions included the Arnett Clinic in Lafayette, Indiana, with more than 100 doctors, and the Guthrie Clinic in Sayre, Pennsylvania, with more than 200 doctors. In September 1995 PhyCor acquired the Casa Blanca Clinic of Mesa, Arizona, one of the largest clinics in Arizona. PhyCor was chosen out of five PPMs for its expertise in negotiating contracts with managed care companies. With 84 doctors, the five-year plan for Casa Blanca involved the addition of three satellite clinics and 80 more doctors. The clinic also chose PhyCor because of the potential opportunities to network with other providers on national contracts. Notable acquisitions in 1996 included the Hattiesburg Clinic in Missouri and the Lewis-Galle Clinic in Roanoke, Virginia, with more than 100 physicians each.

While doctors at some clinics struggled with new managed care guidelines, others, including the PAPP Clinic in Newnan, Georgia, expressed a concern for changing with the trend toward managed care. Acquired by PhyCor in May 1995, the PAPP clinic needed capital and experienced managers to implement information systems and to recruit primary care physicians, as providers of managed care tended to prefer primary care physicians to specialists. The clinic also needed experienced negotiators of managed care contracts to reduce the risk of working with managed care providers.

By the end of 1996 PhyCor owned and operated 43 clinics in 24 states, which provided healthcare in up to 30 specialties each; its IPAs had 8,700 physicians in 15 markets. Revenues reached $766.3 million and garnered $36.4 million in profit. Between 1993 and 1996, managed care as a percentage of revenue almost doubled from 24 percent of revenues to 42 percent in 1996.

PhyCor continued its accelerated growth strategy with 13 acquisitions in 1997, including two management service companies. Of the 11 group practices, Straub Clinic & Hospital in Honolulu was the largest, with nearly 200 physicians. The March 1997 acquisition of the St. Petersburg Medical Clinic and the Suncoast Medical Clinic involved a merger of the two, then renamed St. Petersburg-Suncoast Medical Group. In addition to strengthening PhyCor's presence in Florida and Indiana, the company entered markets in California, Washington, and Maryland for the first time.

PhyCor found ways to create new business and to improve the business of clinics it managed. As the number of multispecialty groups for potential acquisition declined, PhyCor began to combine single-specialty groups to form new multispecialty groups in 1996. In addition to assisting clinic recruitment, PhyCor merged 103 individual practices into clinics in 1997 and assisted in the creation of new group medical practices, which then signed long-term service agreements with PhyCor. By developing physician networks for affiliation with its clinics, PhyCor gained greater leverage in negotiating managed care contracts.

PPMs Suffering Turbulence in the Late 1990s with Increase in Healthcare Costs

In 1997 and 1998, the rising cost of healthcare and related problems at its clinics led to a series of write-offs. After several years of expanding profits, PhyCor realized only a $3.2 million profit on $1.1 billion in revenues in 1997. An asset revaluation charge of $83 million in late 1997 was one of many such write-offs. In 1998 write-offs included a $20 million charge after dissolution of a merger with MedPartners and a $65 million charge to reorganize four unprofitable clinics. Another $120 million restructuring charge was related to duplicate information systems at multispecialty clinics created by PhyCor by merging single-specialty clinics.

As financial difficulties mounted, the company changed direction, preferring management service contracts without the risk of acquiring clinics. In March 1998 NAMM signed a contract with New York and Presbyterian Hospitals Care Network. Services involved the formation of more than 40 small IPAs for physicians in the network. The IPAs were self-governing, risk-sharing physician-organized delivery systems (PODS) with 25 to 50 primary care doctors in each group.

PhyCor acquired only two medical groups early in 1998 as its acquisition strategy shifted to the purchase of other PPMs, including the remaining interest in PCM. PhyCor purchased First Physician Care, Inc., of Atlanta, a physician management company that had contracts for four multispecialty groups, owned a New York IPA with 395 physicians, and provided medical services through three subsidiaries. Morgan Health Group of Atlanta owned an IPA with more than 2,600 physicians. In November 1998 PhyCor acquired Prime Care International, Inc., an Ontario, California-based PPM with more than 2,200 physicians at its IPAs and clinics. PhyCor diversified with the acquisition of CareWise, Inc. of Seattle, which provided demand management services in the form of support to patients making medical decisions.

While executives at PhyCor tried to learn from their difficulties, in 1998 and 1999 the company was plagued with lawsuits from physicians and clinics who wanted to break their agreements with PhyCor. Although a minor percentage of doctors sometimes left a group practice upon acquisition by PhyCor, preferring more autonomy, in 1998 and 1999 doctors resigned from PhyCor-owned clinics in large numbers. Many complained of management practices, but generally steep declines in pay led to the final break. At the Holt-Krock Clinic in Fort Smith, Arkansas, purchased by PhyCor in 1994, physicians cited a ten percent decline in income for primary care physicians and a 17 percent decline for specialists in the second half of 1997 due to the cost of a computer system.

PhyCor hoped to improve doctors' incomes in the future by developing a new model for future acquisitions of medical groups: to charge a lower fee, reduced to 12 percent of revenues after expenses, and to buy fewer assets. This addressed the concerns of younger doctors who faced paying these fees throughout their careers. This issue did not concern older doctors who expected to retire soon. In April 1998, PhyCor already had adopted a policy of 25-year contracts.

The troubles at PhyCor had just begun, however. PhyCor's share value dropped from more than $36 in mid-1997 to less than $10 per share in mid-1998 and the company recorded a loss of $111.4 million on more than $1.1 billion in revenues in 1998. By mid-1999 PhyCor began to negotiate the resale of certain clinics back to the practicing physicians. This included the company's largest clinics—the Holt-Krock Clinic, the Burns Clinic, the Lexington Clinic, and the Guthrie Clinic. In November 1999 PhyCor announced plans to reduce the number of clinics to about 30 during the next year. PhyCor wrote off large losses of value in the clinics, $393.4 million in the third quarter alone. The company ended 1999 with losses of $445 million, though revenues reached $1.5 billion. The company's stock value continued to decline to less than $3.00 per share.

Nationwide PPMs descended from the rapid rise to success as quickly as PhyCor, finding that they were unable to provide appropriate health care at the reimbursement rates that HMOs and managed care insurers wanted to pay. MedPartners, the leading practice management company, founded in 1993, closed its PPM division in late 1998. FPA Medical Management filed for bankruptcy and PhyMatrix quit the business altogether. Some people concerned with health care management viewed PPMs as a failed experiment. Economies of scale did not occur as predicted, many doctors were dissatisfied with the management, and PPMs had overpaid for physician practice assets.

PhyCor reoriented the company's goals toward medical network management and continued management of its core of successful clinics. In late 1999 PhyCor signed a contract with the Rockford Health System to manage the hospital system's clinics, as it separated management of hospital and clinic operations. For a flat service fee PhyCor managed its HMO, Rockford Health Plans.

PhyCor's involvement with physician practice management through ownership continued to be besieged with problems in early 2000 as several doctors resigned their posts because of dissatisfaction with PhyCor management. At Lewis-Gale Clinic 44 doctors quit in six months' time. More than 90 doctors resigned at the Nalle Clinic after they received paychecks for $1,500 each in March. Many paid the $150,000 noncompete penalty in order to continue practicing in the area. A nearby hospital hired several doctors, and others joined or started single-specialty practices. A trend back to single-specialty practices resulted from its efficiency and the lower likelihood of conflicts over reimbursements or equipment purchases. The Casa Blanca clinic closed three clinics in June 2000 because of the resignation of 35 of 100 doctors since January.

Amidst increasing difficulties, two founders of PhyCor resigned from their positions at PhyCor in June 2000—Joseph Hutts, CEO and chairman, and Derril Reeves, vice-chairman, executive vice-president, and chief development officer. Another founder, company President Thompson Dent, replaced Hutts as CEO and chairman. Under new leadership, PhyCor began to initiate contact with each of the 25 clinics left in its ownership to negotiate a repurchase of some or all of their assets and to terminate or restructure management agreements, as appropriate. Whether PhyCor would have any equity after debt had been paid was open to question. PhyCor faced delisting from the NASDAQ stock exchange, but Dent posed a reverse stock split to increase per-share value as an alternative.

PhyCor continued to provide management services in the health care service sector. A new contract for CareWise involved the Great Lakes Health Plan of Southfield, Michigan, and CarePlus Health Plan in New York City, providing 24-hour telephone assistance to nearly 100,000 Medicaid members.

Principal Subsidiaries

CareWise, Inc.; First Physician Care, Inc.; North American Medical Management, Inc.; Prime Care International, Inc.

Principal Competitors

Caremark Rx, Inc.; CONCENTRA Managed Care, Inc.; PhyAmerica Physicians Group, Inc.

Further Reading

Austin, Marsha, "PhyCor Docs Waiting for Prognosis," *Denver Business Journal,* September 3, 1999, p. 3A.

Autry, Ronnie, "Materials Management: Cutting Time and Expense," *Health Management Technology,* February 2000, p. 38.

Baldwin, Gary, "Electronic Commerce Ventures Face Field Tests," *American Medical News,* October 12, 1998, p. 25.

Benson, Don, "Nashville-Based PhyCor Buys Ontario, Calif.-Based Doctors Group," *Knight-Ridder/Tribune Business News,* May 24, 1998, p. KORB9814402C.

Brock, Kathy, "PhyCor Connection to Bankroll Vancouver Clinic's Expansion," *Business Journal-Portland,* February 28, 1997, p. 1.

"CareWise, Inc., Provides a Winning Combination for Medicaid Members of Great Lakes Health Plan and CarePlus Health Plan," *Business Wire,* July 31, 2000, p. 0276.

"CEO Interview-Joseph Hutts, Chairman & CEO, Discusses the Outlook for PhyCor, Inc.," *Wall Street Digest,* February 17, 1997.

De Lafuente, Della, "Medical Group Closes Three Clinics in Mesa, Ariz.," *Knight-Ridder/Tribune Business News,* June 2, 2000, p. ITEM00155003.

Dunbar, John, "Medical-Practice Management Company PhyCor Expands Holdings," *Knight-Ridder/Tribune Business News,* June 21, 1995, p. 6210172.

Freedman, Eric, "Michigan Doctors' Group Enlists Management Firm," *American Medical News,* August 5, 1996, p. 6.

Gonzales, Angela, "Casa Blanca Trims Operations Down to One Facility," *Business Journal—Serving Phoenix & the Valley of the Sun,* July 7, 2000, p. 13.

——, "PhyCor Enters Market," *Business Journal—Serving Phoenix & the Valley of the Sun,* July 21, 1995, p. 1.

Holton, Noel, "Craig County, Va., Clinic Closes After Lone Doctor Resigns," *Knight-Ridder/Tribune Business News,* October 29, 1999, p. OKRB9929314E.

——, "Doctors, Analysts Question Track Record of Physician Management Groups," *Knight-Ridder/Tribune Business News,* January 26, 2000, p. ITEM000270F8.

——, "Nashville-Based Physician Management Company Hopes for Full Recovery," *Knight-Ridder/Tribune Business News,* January 14, 1999, p. OKRB9901418C.

——, "Roanoke, Va., Clinic Cuts 24 Jobs to Reduce Costs," *Knight-Ridder/Tribune Business News,* November 22, 1998, p. OKRB98326095.

Hundley, Kris, "PhyCor Damages Business After Acquiring St. Petersburg, Fla., Practices," *Knight-Ridder/Tribune Business News,* September 16, 1998, p. OKRB98257143.

——, "PhyCor of Nashville, Tenn., Sees Share Price Plummet," *Knight-Ridder/Tribune Business News,* July 24, 1998, p. OKRB98205209.

——, "Two Florida Physicians' Groups Agree to Merge," *Knight-Ridder/Tribune Business News,* March 2, 1997, p. 302B0950.

"Issues in Group Practice Management: An Interview with Craig Faerber," *Healthcare Financial Management,* September 1999, p. 56.

Jaklevic, Mary Chris, "Ark. Docs Want Out of PhyCor Contract," *Modern Healthcare,* April 27, 1998, p. 12.

——, "Irreconcilable Differences Blamed for MedPartners-Phycor Breakup," *Modern Healthcare,* January 12, 1998, p. 2.

——, "Is Less More? PhyCor to Pay Less for Practices' Assets, Lower Its Fees," *Modern Healthcare,* May 4, 1998, p. 17.

——, "PhyCor Pays for Early Mistakes," *Modern Healthcare,* February 2, 1998, p. 21.

——, "PhyCor Rejuvenates N.C. Clinic," *Modern Healthcare,* August 14, 1995, p. 28.

——, "PhyCor to Sell Clinic to Healthshare Group," *Modern Healthcare,* March 1, 1999, p. 17.

——, "PhyCor Will Sell 13 Clinics in 12 Months," *Modern Healthcare,* November 8, 1999, p. 51.

——, "Sparks Flies with PhyCor Docs: Ark. Hospital Hires Almost One-Third of Clinic's Physicians," *Modern Healthcare,* September 21, 1998, p. 30.

Kendall, Melissa, "Acquisition of IPA Manager May Bring Doctors More Biz," *Orlando Business Journal,* February 24, 1995, p. 16.

Larkin, Howard, "The Gold Standard," *American Medical News,* September 9, 1996, p. 32.

Mangan, Doreen, "Are the Doctor Chains a Good Investment?," *Medical Economics,* January 24, 1994, p. 61.

"MetLife HealthCare," *Best's Review—Life Insurance Edition,* August 1994, p. 94.

"News at Deadline," *Modern Healthcare,* June 12, 2000, p. 4.

"Newsmakers," *Modern Healthcare,* October 18, 1999, p. 42.

Nianiatus, George," "Partner of Olean Company Hit with Class-Action Suits," *Business First of Buffalo,* October 12, 1998, p. 20.

Page, Leigh, "N.C. Clinic Abandons Multispecialty Trend," *American Medical News,* April 24, 2000, p. 15.

——, "Payment Dispute Leads to Three-Sided Fight in Texas," *American Medical News,* June 19, 2000, p. 13.

Patton, Janet, "Lexington, Ky. Clinic Will Try to Buy Itself Back from Management Firm," *Knight-Ridder/Tribune Business News,* August 20, 1999, p. OKRB9923208C.

——, "Nashville, Tenn.-Based Clinic Chain PhyCor Buys Half of Advantage Care," *Knight-Ridder/Tribune Business News,* November 5, 1998, p. OKRB983090BB.

"PhyCor, Inc.," *Insider's Chronicle,* July 13, 1992, p. 3.

"PhyCor Planning to Sell Assets of Clinics," *Los Angeles Times,* August 2, 2000, p. C3.

"PhyCor Plans to Cut Clinics," *American Medical News,* November 22, 1999, p. 14.

"PhyCor Reports Record Fourth Quarter and Year-End Results; Announces Probable Acquisition," *Business Wire,* February 17, 1994.

"PhyCor Reports Year-End Results," *Business Wire,* February 18, 1993.

"Physician Transactions," *Modern Healthcare,* September 6, 1999, p. 36.

"PPMs Regroup Through Niche Specialty Care," *Atlanta Business Chronicle,* January 28, 2000, p. B17.

Pitts, Gail, "Pueblo, Colo.-Area Clinic to Open New Facility," *Knight-Ridder/Tribune Business News,* October 26, 1999, p. OKRB99299113.

Schonfeld, Erick, "Doctors Unite: Physician Practice Management Companies Offer Healthy Returns," *Fortune,* March 3, 1997, p. 200.

Shepherd, Gary, "Management Firm Running 2 Bay Area Doctors Groups," *Tampa Bay Business Journal,* September 15, 1995, p. 2.

——, "PhyCor Deal Collapses; Watson to Pursue Bonds," *Tampa Bay Business Journal,* October 23, 1998, p. 1.

——, "PhyCor Inc.," *Tampa Bay Business Journal,* February 18, 2000, p. 13.

——, "St. Pete Doctor Groups to Merge with PhyCor," *Tampa Bay Business Journal,* November 15, 1996, p. 9.

——, "Watson Doctors OK PhyCor Alliance," *Tampa Bay Business Journal,* September 4, 1998, p. 3.

Slomski, Anita J., "Should You Sell Your Practice to Wall Street?," *Medical Economics,* January 24, 1994, p. 52.

Sturgeon, Jeff, "Nine Anesthesiologists Leave Roanoke, Va., Clinic for Nearby Hospital," *Knight-Ridder/Tribune Business News,* March 28, 2000, p. ITEM00890D3.

Tanner, Lisa, "Southwest Physicians Traded Unit for Money to Grow, Office Management," *Dallas Business Journal,* November 22, 1996, p. 1.

Terry, Ken, "PPMs Are Taking Over Hospital Networks," *Medical Economics,* March 23, 1998, p. 54.

Tokarski, Cathy, "Nation's Two Largest Physician Management Firms Become One," *American Medical News,* November 17, 1997, p. 1.

——, "No Way Out," *American Medical News,* November 9, 1998, p. 27.

Volz, David, "Managing Physicians," *Marketing Health Services,* Winter 1998, p. 29.

—Mary Tradii

Power Corporation of Canada

751 Victoria Square
Montreal, Quebec H2Y 2J3
Canada
Telephone: (514) 286-7400
Fax: (514) 286-7424
Web site: http://www.powercorp.ca

Public Company
Incorporated: 1925
Employees: 28,000
Sales: C$14.73 billion (1999)
Stock Exchanges: Toronto
Ticker Symbol: POW
NAIC: 551112 Offices of Other Holding Companies;
    52421 Insurance Agencies and Brokerages; 513210
    Cable Broadcasting Networks; 51111 Newspaper
    Publishers

Power Corporation of Canada controls a variety of companies involved in finance, insurance, and communications. Through subsidiary Power Financial Corporation, the company controls the largest mutual funds company in Canada, Investors Group, and the largest life insurance company in Canada, Great-West Lifeco. The other primary operating subsidiaries include Pargesa Holding, which owns substantial investments in a variety of industries in Europe, and Gesca Ltée, the publisher of Montreal's *La Presse* and three other daily newspapers.

Origins and History of Great-West: 1890s to Mid-1980s

In the early 1890s, Winnipeg was a frontier town of lumbermen and plains traders. As a stop on the slowly growing Canadian Pacific Railway, it was a promising growth point in the western province of Manitoba. The difficulty of transportation combined with drought created hard economic times for the region during the decade, however. An optimistic local businessman, Jeffry Hall Brock, recognized that capital was needed to invest in local farm and retail development. His vision was to collect western Canadians' savings via insurance sales, thereby offering them security and protection, while simultaneously financing development through the proceeds. At this time, only nine of the 40 insurance companies in Canada were Canadian. Not one of these companies was based in western Canada.

The Great-West Life Assurance Company was incorporated in 1891 with a name that reflected the company's regional pride; the hyphen was a typesetter's error. In the first year, 834 life insurance policies were sold, representing more than $2 million worth of protection, by a sales force of three that included Brock. The bold enterprise attracted the involvement of the area's outstanding businessmen, and early shareholders included bakers, farmers, a harnessmaker, and the sheriff. Support came from bustling Toronto as well as from many local rural communities. The mayor of Winnipeg, Alexander Macdonald, became Great-West's first president in 1892. Brock was made managing director.

The company issued its premier manual in 1892, offering six insurance plans. The first claim was received that same year. By the end of 1893, Great-West—competing with five- to 50-year-old companies across Canada—ranked eighth highest in profitability. At this point, the self-confident young company made the remarkable decision to enter the eastern Canadian markets. Its well-established competitors were situated in the East, as were the country's banking, financial, and manufacturing institutions. The West had essentially one industry: agriculture. In Great-West's first three years, it had achieved the financial backing and business volume that had taken other companies up to 15 years to reach.

Great-West's prosperity continued during the next two decades. By the turn of the century, the company was represented in every province and was the country's fastest growing life insurer. As the economy improved when the region's depression lifted, the service industry benefited. In 1896 Great-West gained the largest percentage of new business written, out of 21 Canadian life insurance companies, to make it only $80,000 behind the industry leader in aggregate gain of policies in force. The first shareholder dividends were paid in 1901, and dividends have been paid every year since.

In 1906 the company crossed the border and established U.S. operations in North Dakota. The next year, Great-West topped all Canadian companies in paid-for business. From 50 applications a month in 1893, the company received an average of 375 monthly applications by 1909. However, the growth proved a strain on the founder's health. Brock essentially left the company in 1912 for medical reasons, and he died in 1915. C.C. Ferguson succeeded Brock as CEO in 1915, one year after the onset of World War I.

With the war came a boost to the area's economy, which had declined as the wheat boom receded and freight rates climbed, but the war presented the life insurance industry with the problem of wartime policies. Most firms charged extra premiums for those in the service, but Great-West kept its extra charges at a minimum as part of its war effort. Throughout the war, the company managed to keep up its record, maintained since 1906, for writing more ordinary business in Canada annually than any other company. Nevertheless, the war's impact was felt: claims for wartime deaths totaled $1.5 million. Almost as catastrophic was the flu epidemic that flared up at the war's end from 1918 to 1919, which cost Great-West more than $1 million in death claims.

Canada, like other countries, then contended with conditions following the war, including high rates of inflation and unemployment, labor unrest, and slowed agricultural output. Though the economic situation worsened through the 1920s, Great-West showed a steady increase in business. In 1920, U.S. operations were extended into Michigan and Minnesota. That same year, Great-West became one of the first companies to offer group insurance. The concept took many years to catch on. In 1940 group insurance was still only nine percent of the company's total business. In later years it comprised more than half. In 1926 Macdonald retired as president, succeeded by G.W. Allan, who had been company director for 22 years.

Great-West, which had initially concentrated its investments in farm mortgages, had diversified since the war into government bonds and city mortgages. Because of its diversified investments and the fact that stock holdings were a very small part of the company's portfolio, Great-West was well insulated when the market crash of 1929 occurred.

The Great Depression years of the next decade provided a new challenge. Business declined between 1932 and 1937, but Great-West managed a gradual increase in assets during the period. By the company's 45th anniversary in 1936, it provided coverage for nearly one million people in North America, issu-

ing an average of 60 policies per business day. New insurance plans were introduced during the Depression, including a policy for the professional woman and a family protection policy. By the summer of 1939, Great-West was again enjoying record-breaking figures in applied business.

The decade of depression was ended by the outbreak of World War II, which stimulated employment and industrial activity. The life insurance industry was dramatically revived, and between 1939 and 1945 Great-West enjoyed tremendous growth as well as expansion into Indiana, Missouri, Ohio, Kansas, California, and Pennsylvania. Group insurance and group pension plans steadily increased. Also during the war years, Great-West entered into the individual accident and health insurance fields. The company changed presidents in 1940, when M.F. Christie took the job, and again in 1943, when W.P. Riley assumed the position.

During the postwar boom, the company's business boomed too. In 1946 Great-West's business-in-force reached the $1 billion mark. It would reach its second billion only six years later and its third three years after that. The company continued its expansion in the United States, entering seven more states between 1946 and 1952. In 1958 it started doing business in five more states and the District of Columbia. Also in 1958 Great-West began technological expansion; it purchased the first computer in western Canada.

Growth continued throughout the prosperous 1960s. In 1968 Great-West became the first Canadian company authorized to sell a variable annuity in the United States. More than $1 billion of new business was contracted that year.

Business in the United States grew rapidly. By 1973 Great-West was licensed in 28 states and the District of Columbia, and had opened a marketing office in Denver, Colorado. The company separated its Canadian and U.S. operations, except for investment and corporate operations, in 1979. It also opened the company's U.S. headquarters in Denver that year. By then Great-West Life was operating in 45 states. From 1979 to 1983 U.S. business nearly doubled.

During the next decade, Great-West concentrated on product development, asset management, and developing the two regional operations. The Canadian and U.S. markets developed different needs during the 1980s. One of the company's new products was a universal life policy, first introduced in 1982— the first of its kind designed for the Canadian market. A similar policy was introduced in the United States the following year.

Another Great-West innovation was a system it introduced in Canada that paid agents levelized commissions and offered loan arrangements for agents needing additional income. It was the first insurance company in North America to adopt such a system. This arrangement allowed the sales force to experiment with the sale of new products with less fear of financial repercussion. As a result, universal life business increased from 30 percent in 1983 to almost 60 percent in 1985. Over those three years, career agents enjoyed a 65 percent compound growth rate in average earnings.

In the mid-1980s, the company's structure changed. Great-West had been a joint shareholder-policyholder-owned company from its inception until 1969, when Investors Group acquired controlling interest in the company's common shares. Investors Group was acquired by Power Corporation, a Montreal-based holding company with interests in publishing, pulp and paper, and financial services, in 1969. In 1984 Power Corporation formed Power Financial Corporation to hold Great-West and its other financial service companies.

Origins of Power Corporation

Behind the formation of Power Corporation stood two financiers, A.J. Nesbitt and P.A. Thomson, principal partners in a Montreal investment firm named Nesbitt, Thomson and Company. Shortly after its founding in 1912, the company began underwriting and investing in Canadian hydroelectric utilities, financing the construction of utilities and promoting their development. For nearly 15 years, the investment firm poured its resources into the burgeoning electricity industry, but during the early 1920s the industry was besieged by an unwelcomed intruder, prompting Nesbitt and Thomson to take action. An unnamed speculator from Chicago was marching across the United States, acquiring one utility company after another as he went. Nesbitt and Thomson feared an incursion onto Canadian ground and the probable end to their underwriting and investment activities. To help keep Canada's power sector in Canadian hands the pair resolved to form a holding company that would serve as an umbrella organization for a family of affiliated Canadian utility companies. Consolidation became Nesbitt's and Thomson's mode of defense, and Power Corporation of Canada, formed in April 1925, became the instrument through which the financiers would ward off the hostile threats of foreigners.

Power Corporation started business with an initial capitalization of C$5.5 million, with the majority of the company's shares held by its two founders. Nesbitt was appointed as president of the holding company, but he delegated much of the day-to-day management of Power Corporation to his vice-president, James B. Woodyatt, an electrical engineer and power company executive. With their start-up money, Nesbitt and Thomson did what they did best—invested in utility companies—assembling Power Corporation's first portfolio of properties. They assumed control over three utility companies, Canada Northern Power, Ottawa and Hull Power, and Ottawa-Montreal Power, and made sizable investments in a host of other power companies, including East Kootenay Power, Winnipeg Electric, Dominion Power and Transmission, and Southern Power. By the end of the company's first year, net earnings reached C$246,000.

Nesbitt and Thomson had hoped to profit from an anticipated growth in demand for electricity by industrial and residential customers. Their first five years in business substantiated their hopes, as Power Corporation realized strident growth. To promote the use of electricity, the founders created a department exclusively devoted to encouraging new industries to locate their plants near Power Corporation's utility companies. To spur residential demand, the company opened stores stocked with electrical merchandise, presenting the wonders of the new age to communities near the company's facilities. Most importantly, Nesbitt and Thomson continued to add meaningfully to Power Corporation's utility portfolio, developing a large and diverse collection of assets. Between 1925 and 1930, the founders invested in more than two dozen public utilities operating in a wide geographic area, stretching from the United States to Japan to Brazil. By 1930, Power Corporation's affiliated companies operated 40 power plants, enabling the company to eclipse C$5 million in net earnings for the year.

After a rousing start to its business life, Power Corporation suffered through a tortuous period when the Great Depression brought its strident progress to a halt. Financial stagnation set in, as the company's earnings either fell or remained flat for more than a decade. Further, the company's investments plunged in value. Many were liquidated at substantial losses, striking a deleterious blow to the once-powerful concern. Unlike many other enterprises, however, Power Corporation survived the most severe economic crisis of the 20th century and, after the disruption engendered by World War II, Nesbitt and Thomson could look forward to resuming the progress achieved during their first five years as entrepreneurs.

A Change in Strategy in the 1950s

As Power Corporation celebrated its 25th anniversary in 1950, the company stood poised to reap the rewards of increased energy usage during the postwar industrial expansion set to unfold. Approximately 60 percent of the company's investments were in its six mainstay hydroelectric companies, which supplied electricity or gas to more than two million Canadian customers. At first blush, Power Corporation's enviable foundation in energy suggested great promise for the years ahead, but by the early 1950s the company's future presence in the power sector was already in doubt. Nesbitt and Thomson had taken note of three alarming events. In 1944, Northern Ontario Power, a subsidiary of Canada Northern Power, had been expropriated by the Ontario government's Hydro-Electric Power Commission. Two years later, the French government nationalized the public utility companies controlled by Foreign

Power Securities Corporation, in which Power Corporation had invested heavily not long after its formation. In 1953, the government-controlled Manitoba Hydro-Electric Board assumed control over Winnipeg Electric, underscoring the emergence of a portentous trend for Power Corporation.

Power Corporation continued to invest in power companies as the 1950s progressed, but Nesbitt and Thomson realized the company's future depended on developing a new corporate strategy. Toward this end, the financial settlements obtained from the expropriation of Foreign Power Securities and Winnipeg Electric, coupled with the compensation derived from future government takeovers, provided the capital to diversify the company's portfolio. By 1952, Power Corporation had made substantial investments in other sources of energy and in other industries, most notably in the pulp and paper industry through an investment in Bathurst Power and Paper. Further moves toward diversification followed, as Power Corporation methodically shed its interests in utility companies. The transformation picked up speed following the deaths of Nesbitt in 1954 and Thomson two years later, their mandate for diversification embraced by their sons, A. Deane Nesbitt and Peter N. Thomson, who assumed control over the company.

As Power Corporation entered the 1960s, it prepared to shed the vestiges of its former self. The company began the decade still regarded as a holding company primarily interested in electrical energy, but the percentage of its investment portfolio devoted to hydroelectric power had dropped from 60 to 39 during the previous decade. Its remaining investments were in oil, gas, and pipelines (33 percent); finance (11 percent); pulp and paper (ten percent); and other industries (seven percent). Peter Thomson took over as president and chairman of the company in 1962, marking the beginning of fast-paced changes and the adoption of a new corporate strategy. His efforts were financed by the nationalization of utility companies in which Power Corporation held substantial stakes. In 1961, the government of British Columbia expropriated the principal assets of British Columbia Power, yielding C$8 million in compensation for Power Corporation Two years later, the government of Quebec paid C$19 million for Power Corporation's shares in Shawinigan Water and Power and the Quebec subsidiary belonging to Canada Northern Power. With the proceeds obtained from these expropriations, Thomson altered Power Corporation's investment strategy. Instead of investing in a broad assortment of companies in which Power Corporation maintained little managerial control, Thomson decided to invest in fewer, more diversified companies in which the company could assume a more active managerial posture. Accordingly, the number of companies composing Power Corporation's portfolio dipped from 31 to 18 between 1962 and 1965.

Thomson did not have long to test the merits of his new investment strategy. During the mid- and late 1960s, Power Corporation was beset by a number of problems, as several of its affiliated companies suffered financially. For example, Consolidated-Bathurst, which had been created in 1966 from the merger of Power Corporation's two largest pulp and paper investments, shared in the losses recorded by the rest of the industry as overcapacity and rising operating costs plagued Canadian pulp and paper companies. Canada Steamship Line, another Power Corporation property, was rocked by protracted labor disputes. Other Power Corporation affiliates saw their value plunge as well, with some of the problems attributable to external pressures and some to problems of their own making. For Thomson, the problems were serious enough to warrant a far-reaching response, one that marked a momentous turning point in the history of Power Corporation In 1968, Thomson agreed to merge with Trans-Canada Corporation Fund (TCCF), a C$75-million holding company controlled by legendary entrepreneur Paul Desmarais.

The Desmarais Era Begins in 1968

A native of Sudbury, Ontario, Desmarais was 39 years old when he became chairman and chief executive officer of Power Corporation. Roughly two decades earlier, Desmarais had dropped out of law school to rescue his father's failing bus service. After resurrecting his father's company, Desmarais used it as a foundation for what would become a business empire. He acquired other bus lines in Ottawa, Quebec City, and throughout the province of Quebec, then diversified his interests into life insurance, newspapers, communications, and real estate. By the time of the share-exchange transaction with Power Corporation, Desmarais's core assets included ownership of Provincial Transport, a major inter-urban bus line, majority control of Toronto-based Imperial Life Assurance, a raceway, a radio station, and various real estate properties. Further, Desmarais's TCCF also controlled Gesca Ltée, which controlled *La Presse,* Montreal's largest and most respected daily newspaper, as well as 62 percent of Les Journaux Trans-Canada's three daily newspapers and ten weekly newspapers in Quebec.

Initially, as Power Corporation evolved from an investment holding company into an operating company, Thomson and Desmarais each controlled 30 percent of the voting shares of the newly merged company. By 1970, however, Desmarais had gained sole control. He immediately began stripping away Power Corporation's portfolio in an attempt to consolidate the company's control over a small number of diverse assets. The restructuring process took roughly a decade to complete, which restricted the company's ability to expand in any substantial manner, but by the end of the 1970s Power Corporation was healthy on all fronts and Desmarais could point to robust financial results. In 1979, the company's consolidated net earnings reached C$98 million, more than double the total registered the previous year. In 1980, net earnings swelled to C$121 million, convincing Desmarais that Power Corporation was strong enough to pursue expansion.

Before Desmarais embarked on the acquisition front, he first completed a divestiture—an enormous sale that, for the first time in his business career, left him without a bus service. In 1981, Power Corporation sold its CSL Group, which included Canada Steamship Lines, an operator of oceangoing vessels and Great Lakes freighters, and the bus lines Desmarais had acquired during the 1960s. The C$195 million divestiture allowed Power Corporation, according to federal regulations, to acquire 4.4 percent of the voting shares of Canadian Pacific Limited. A massive rail, shipping, oil, and real estate conglomerate. Also in 1981, Power Corporation invested C$20 million in Pargesa Holding S.A., a Swiss corporation that owned a major interest in Banque de Paris et des Pays-Bas. Subsequently, Power Corporation's major financial holdings in Investor Group, Great-West Life, Montreal Trust, and Pargesa were transferred in 1984 to a new subsidiary, Power Financial Corporation, which completed an initial public offering (IPO) of stock in 1985.

With the proceeds raised from selling a portion of Power Financial to the public, combined with the sale of stock of other Power Corporation subsidiaries, Desmarais eliminated all long-term debt. Once the company was free of debt—a condition Desmarais maintained until the end of his leadership tenure—Power Corporation pursued strategic expansion. In 1986, the company acquired the Quebec and Ontario radio and television stations belonging to Ketenac Holdings Ltd. and Prades Inc., which were later consolidated into a new wholly owned subsidiary, Power Broadcasting. Concurrently, the company, through its Consolidated-Bathurst subsidiary, formed a joint venture with China International Trust and Investment Corporation (CITIC), the international investment arm of the People's Republic of China. Initially, the joint venture constituted the acquisition of a pulp mill in Castlegar, British Columbia, marking the beginning of an enduring business relationship with the Chinese government.

The 1980s ended with the sale of one of Power Corporation's two principal operating companies. Although Desmarais was not looking to sell the company's stake in Consolidated-Bathurst, he could not refuse the unsolicited offer made by Stone Container Acquisition Corporation. In January 1989, Stone Container offered Power Corporation C$25 per share for its interest in the pulp and paper concern, representing one of the largest deals in Canadian business history. Power Corporation received more than C$1 billion from the deal, giving the company the financial means to explore new business opportunities in the 1990s. The company's coffers received another substantial windfall two months after the divestiture of Consolidated-Bathurst. In March, the parent company of Bell Canada offered more than C$500 million for the shares held by Power Financial in Montreal Trust.

Although Power Corporation had a substantial amount of cash to invest as it entered the 1990s, the first half of the decade was bereft of any major transactions equal to the stature of its two 1989 divestitures. By no means, however, did the company retreat from pursuing expansion. Further investment opportunities were developed with CITIC, resulting in the formation of Power Pacific Corporation, which opened offices in Hong Kong in 1994 and Beijing in 1998. In 1996, Compagnie Luxembourgeoisie de Telediffusion, which was indirectly controlled by Pargesa, merged with the broadcasting subsidiaries of Germany-based Bertelsmann, creating CLT-UFA, Europe's largest radio and television group. Another notable event was the C$180 million investment made by Power Corporation in Southam Inc., Canada's largest daily newspaper publisher.

New Leadership for the 1990s

In 1996, Desmarais relinquished his posts as Power Corporation's chairman and chief executive officer, ending an era of remarkable growth for the company. During Desmarais's tenure, Power Corporation's corporate assets had increased from C$165 million to C$2.7 billion, as net earnings swelled from C$3 million to more than C$200 million. The difficult task of equaling this record of leadership fell to Desmarais's two sons, Paul Desmarais, Jr., who was named chairman and co-chief executive officer, and Andre Desmarais, president and co-chief executive officer.

The Desmarais brothers did not shy from imprinting their mark on Power Corporation, as they guided the company toward its 75th anniversary and the beginning of the 21st century. Shortly after they inherited control over the company, Paul, Jr., and Andre sold the company's interests in Southam for C$294 million. The following year the company, through Great-West Lifeco, paid C$3 billion for all of London Insurance Group, which controlled London Life Insurance, a Canadian insurance company with the largest sales force in the country. The acquisition made Great-West Lifeco the largest health and insurance company in Canada, employing more than 7,000 financial representatives.

As the 1990s drew to a close, Power Corporation appeared to have made a seamless transition from one generation of management to the next. The Desmarais brothers proved themselves capable leaders during their first five years in charge, and, after selling Power Broadcasting's Canadian radio and television assets in 1999, possessed the financial resources to galvanize their reputations during the 21st century. The company, during its 75th anniversary year, represented one of Canada's elite business enterprises, supported by stable and diverse holdings in North America, Europe, and Asia. As Power Corporation entered the new century, consolidated assets eclipsed C$57 billion and net earnings exceeded C$500 million.

Principal Subsidiaries

Gesca Ltée; Power Broadcasting Inc.; CITIC Pacific Ltd.; Power Financial Corporation (67.4%); Power Financial Europe B.V. (The Netherlands); Pargesa Holding S.A. (Switzerland); Great-West Lifeco Inc. (76.6%); Great-West Life Assurance Company; Great-West Life & Annuity Insurance; Investors Group Inc. (67.7%); London Insurance Group Inc.; London Life Insurance Company.

Principal Competitors

Berkshire Hathaway Inc.; Brascan Corporation; Loews Corporation.

Further Reading

Fleming, James, *Merchants of Fear*, New York, Viking Press, 1986.
Koselka, Rita, "Cash-Rich and on the Prowl," *Forbes,* April 16, 1990, p. 56.
Leidl, Dave, "Arthur Erickson," *BC Business,* August 1991, p. 56.
McIntosh, Andrew, "Power Shift," *Canadian Business,* August 1996, p. 26.
Power Corporation of Canada, *Power Corporation of Canada: Seventy-Five Years of Growth,* Montreal: Power Corporation of Canada, 2000, 32 p.

—Carol I. Keeley
—updated by Jeffrey L. Covell

Quark, Inc.

1800 Grant Street
Denver, Colorado 80203
U.S.A.
Telephone: (303) 894-8888
Fax: (303) 894-3399
Web site: http://www.quark.com

Private Company
Incorporated: 1981
Employees: 600
Sales: $500 million (1999 est.)
NAIC: 511210 Software Publishers

Quark, Inc. is a privately held company focused on providing software for desktop publishing. Quark claims that more than one million users in more than 100 countries rely on Quark products to create, design, and manage their document production, including newspapers, magazines, books, CD-ROMs, catalogs, brochures, packaging, and online material. The company's flagship product is QuarkXPress, which was first introduced in 1987 when desktop publishing was in its infancy. Originally developed for use on Macintosh computers, Quark-XPress for Windows was introduced in 1992. The program is the market leader among professional users.

Quark, Inc. was founded in 1981 in Denver by Tim Gill, a self-employed computer programmer who wrote the first word-processing program for the Apple III. He named the company after the subatomic particle designated as the building block of all matter. Gill went on to write a variety of text-processing programs for the Apple platform. In 1986 Fred Ebrahimi joined Quark as president and CEO, with Gill continuing as Quark's chairman and chief technology officer. Ebrahimi bought out Gill's original partner for $100,000 and became half-owner of the company, along with Gill.

Introduction of QuarkXPress for Macintosh Users: 1987–92

QuarkXPress was introduced in 1987, at a time when desktop publishing was in its infancy. The program offered precision typography, layout, and color control on a desktop computer. It was initially published only for use on Macintosh computers. QuarkXPress and the coming desktop publishing revolution represented a low-cost alternative to proprietary typesetting systems.

In its reviews of QuarkXPress, *MacUser* said, "Quark-XPress is a superb product that represents a major step forward in the evolution of desktop publishing." Priced at $695, QuarkXPress advanced what Macintosh users could do with presentation text and graphics by incorporating features such as proper kerning, using display-size typefaces, and flowing text and graphics more easily. The program made "true, professional quality page layout easy," according to *MacUser. MacUser* also noted the "extraordinary control" users had over the look of text on the page.

Competing with QuarkXPress was Aldus Corp.'s Page-Maker 2.0, which was priced lower at $495. Aldus had introduced PageMaker in 1986; it was the first full-featured page make-up program to appear. While early desktop publishing (DTP) programs enabled Macintosh users to design professional looking reports, brochures, and other documents, they contained many limitations. Word processing was often clumsy, it was difficult to format text around graphics, and creating lengthy documents was troublesome. To some extent, Page-Maker 2.0 and QuarkXPress addressed these limitations.

Although both programs imitated the way that people accomplished page make-up and publishing, PageMaker and QuarkXPress differed in a fundamental way. PageMaker approached text in terms of columns and galleys, while Quark-XPress asked users to establish blocks or areas on a page into which text or graphics might be placed. The former method imitated book publishing, while the latter copied advertising or display page composition.

In 1988 Quark went international, establishing customer service and technical support offices across Europe and the Far East. In mid-1998 Quark introduced version 2.0 of QuarkXPress. It was the first DTP program capable of performing color separations of four-color line art on the Macintosh. Priced at $795, version 2.0 was aimed at professional graphic artists and others involved in newspaper or magazine publishing. The program was developed jointly with Adobe Systems Inc. and could perform

---

Company Perspectives:

At Quark, our mission is to develop world-class software that keeps you on the leading edge. The Internet has changed everything about the way you do business. Companies that adapt will thrive. Those that rely on outdated tools will be left behind.

To be successful in an increasingly competitive global business environment, you have to know who your customers are, what they want, and the most effective way of delivering enormous amounts of data. How do you cope?

That's where Quark comes in. We're developing an integrated suite of standards-based software solutions that helps you be successful in both print and Internet business, connect you to your customers, collect and analyze data, implement your business decisions, and see the results in real time.

While you've been busy doing your job, we've been busy doing ours. Quark has the tools you need to meet the challenges of the future.

---

color separations on files imported from Adobe's new drawing package, Illustrator '88. Other new features in version 2.0 were style sheets for formatting pages and a "cut, copy, paste" option for moving text or graphic elements. *MacUser* noted that Quark-XPress was showing a steady growth curve and that desktop publishers were choosing it over PageMaker and Ready, Set, Go!. The magazine called version 2.0 "the most professional page-layout package for the Macintosh."

In 1989 Quark introduced QuarkStyle, an inexpensive ($295) and scaled-down version of QuarkXPress. The program came with 72 templates and style sheets and was aimed at the business user who did not need all of the more sophisticated features of QuarkXPress.

At the Scybold Seminars of March 1990, a semi-annual publishing industry conference and exhibition where software companies launched their new publishing products, Quark announced version 3.0 of QuarkXPress for release in April. The upgrade offered a pasteboard feature for manipulating text and graphics. It also added a thumbnail view of documents that let users move and manipulate pages within a document. In addition, the program's color separation features were enhanced.

In its review of version 3.0, *MacUser* said the program "sets a new standard for Macintosh desktop publishing." It noted the program had several "wonderful new features" and that "the interface has been brilliantly redesigned." The program featured three new tools for rotating objects, creating irregularly shaped picture boxes, and zooming the page image. It contained all the major features of PageMaker 4.0, except indexing and table of contents creation.

At the fall 1990 Seybold Computer Publishing Conference, Quark announced it would partner with IBM to develop a version of QuarkXPress for Windows 3.0 and OS/2 and with Steve Jobs's NeXT for its UNIX-based systems. Quark anticipated developing both stand-alone and LAN versions of the

program for IBM. The planned release date for the Windows and OS/2 versions was the third quarter of 1991.

QuarkXPress 3.1 for the Macintosh, scheduled for a fall 1991 release, added color, style-sheet, and trap palettes. The price also increased to $895. During the past year QuarkXPress had gained significant market share on PageMaker, whose 4.0 version was heavily criticized, requiring Aldus to come out with PageMaker 4.01 to fix the bugs in version 4.0.

QuarkXPress for both Windows and Macintosh Platforms: 1992

PageMaker dominated DTP software for Windows with a 61 percent market share in 1990. Ventura Software Inc., a subsidiary of Xerox Corp., was the other major DTP software publisher for Windows. Quark's introduction of QuarkXPress for Windows was delayed beyond its 1991 launch; at the end of 1991 it was still in beta testing. In 1992 the Windows DTP market had an installed PC base of 70 million machines, compared to about five million Macintosh computers. In addition to Quark, Frame Technology Corp. planned to introduce a DTP program for Windows.

By mid-1992 a 12-month delay in the introduction of Quark-XPress 3.1 for Windows was causing doubt about the product among analysts and testers. The delay gave Aldus more time to make improvements in PageMaker, including the development of Aldus Additions, a set of features that could be added on to the basic version of PageMaker. Quark had been first to offer a similar program, called Quark Xtensions, which enabled third-party developers to build add-on products for QuarkXPress.

In the fall of 1992 Quark again delayed the release of QuarkXPress 3.1 for Windows until December. Reviews appearing in *InfoWorld* and *PC Week* in December praised the program for successfully migrating from the Macintosh platform to Windows. The target audience for the program was the professional art director who needed to produce tight layouts quickly and efficiently. Many of the program's production-oriented tools made it easy to transfer documents from the PC to a commercial printing press. Competing programs for Windows included PageMaker 4.0, Ventura Publisher 4.1, and the newly introduced FrameMaker 3.0 from Frame Technology Corp.

In 1993 Aldus released PageMaker 5.0, which offered many improvements in areas where QuarkXPress had been superior. PageMaker 5.0 had more than 100 new features, including support for Windows' Multiple Document Interface, which allowed users to open and work with more than one document.

Quark countered with QuarkXPress 3.2 for Macintosh in mid-1993, with a Windows version scheduled for later in the year. This major upgrade, again priced at $895, featured built-in color separation, faster performance, and support for vertical scaling from 25 to 400 percent of any object's original height.

In 1992 Quark began developing the Quark Publishing System (QPS), a network software package that sold for $100,000 and up. Designed for work groups rather than individual users, the QPS combined QuarkXPress with programs to keep track of assignments, articles, revisions, page layouts, and photographs for large networks of computers used by book, magazine, and newspaper publishers. Quark's strategy was to move beyond its competition with PageMaker for Windows and Macintosh users, which was based primarily on introducing new versions with new features.

From 1991 to 1993 Quark doubled its workforce from 200 to 400 employees. Sales for 1993 reached $120 million, up 50 percent from 1992, with about 60 percent of sales coming from Europe. In 1994 the company announced job opportunities for 100 new employees, including several senior management positions.

At the fall 1993 Seybold San Francisco trade show, Quark announced it would produce QuarkXPress 3.3 for Windows and Macintosh by the end of the year. QuarkXPress 3.2 for Windows remained unreleased, and customers were concerned whether Quark would meet its December 1993 ship date for version 3.3. Quark was planning a simultaneous release of the Windows and Macintosh versions. However, translating the program into different languages for its international version, which supported eight languages, delayed the release of version 3.3 until later in 1994.

In 1994 Quark announced a scaled-down version of its Quark Publishing System editorial management software that would be priced at $7,500, plus an additional $3,000 for six months of technical support and training. Quark also increased the capacity of its full-size QPS with version 1.1, which allowed 100 users per server and could track more than 10,000 individual page files. The company also announced it was exploring the technology to make QuarkXPress a multimedia authoring tool that could incorporate audio and video into text documents.

Meanwhile, the competitive landscape was changing. Ottawa-based Corel Corp. acquired Ventura Publisher from Ventura Software in 1993, and in 1994 rival Aldus Corp. merged with Adobe Systems Inc. The merger of Adobe and Aldus would make it easier for Adobe to bundle its software with PageMaker. Adobe produced an electronic document interchange program called Adobe Acrobat, which became the industry standard, as well as several well-known programs for typesetting and design such as Illustrator, PostScript, and Photoshop.

Competition with Adobe Heating Up: 1995–2000

In 1995 Quark announced plans to launch Xposure, an image editor designed to compete with Adobe's popular Photoshop program. At the time Photoshop had an estimated 90 percent market share on the Macintosh and 50 to 60 percent on

Windows. Quark's multimedia authoring tool, code-named Orion, was also under development. Orion was anticipated to be a new Xtension for QuarkXPress that would let users import audio, video, animation, and hyperlinked text into QuarkXPress documents.

During 1995 reports appeared in the *Denver Business Journal* that Quark was planning to go public, in spite of repeated denials the previous year by company founder Tim Gill. When asked about plans to go public, Gill's response was that Quark had more than $50 million in cash and did not need to go public to raise money. In spite of the firm's explosive growth during the first half of the 1990s, the company experienced high personnel turnover and low morale in 1995. The releases of Xposure and the new QuarkImmedia multimedia authoring software were both delayed. As of April 1996 the development of Xposure had encountered serious technical problems and was not yet in beta testing. QuarkImmedia went into beta testing in February and was due for a mid-1996 release.

In an effort to boost sales of the high-end Quark Publishing System, Quark entered into a strategic partnership with Digital Equipment Corp. that gave it access to Digital's existing relationship with *Fortune* 1000 companies. Introduced in 1992, QPS had an installed base of only 140 sites by 1996, and editorial management systems in general were not being adopted by magazine publishers.

In 1996 Quark purchased a minority interest in Colossal Pictures of San Francisco. Colossal produced and designed films using a wide range of techniques, including live action, cel animation, photo and stop-motion techniques, motion control and clay, and computer and performance animation to produce commercials, cable programming, CD-ROMs, and interactive movies. The investment was seen as part of Quark's strategy to diversify its software offerings. In 1997 Quark acquired mFactory, which made a multimedia authoring package called mTropolis.

DTP Software and Web Authoring Features: 1997–2000

With web site developers becoming dissatisfied with simple HTML to create web pages, desktop publishing and multimedia software companies were working on advanced web authoring software. Among those involved were Quark, Adobe, Corel, Macromedia Inc., Autodesk Inc., and Microsoft. Meanwhile, Adobe released PageMaker versions 6.0 in 1996 and 6.5 in 1997, the latter incorporating new web capabilities that were tempting QuarkXPress users, who had not had a significant update in six years.

QuarkXPress 4.0 was in beta testing during the first half of 1997 and released later in 1997 with a price of $995. The release of version 4.0 returned Quark to the top of its category, although it did not offer the multimedia capabilities found in PageMaker 6.5 and Ventura 7.0. New features in version 4.0 included indexing, automatic list and table-of-contents generation, and a variety of new tools for integrating text and graphics. With their latest versions, PageMaker and QuarkXPress became more directly competitive, with each program including filters that allowed users to import files from the other program. Quark-

XPress remained the market leader over PageMaker among professional desktop publishers.

At the beginning of 1998 Quark acquired Coris Inc., a subsidiary of R.R. Donnelley and Sons that made Coris Publisher 3.0, which had multimedia capabilities. Coris engineers would join Quark to develop content-management software for new applications. Around this time Quark closed the doors on the recently acquired mFactory, saying that its technology appealed to too small of a user base.

Much of 1998 was taken up with Quark's short-lived takeover bid for Adobe Systems. The offer was made in August, just after Adobe announced it would cut 300 jobs, or ten percent of its workforce. Adobe's stock price was also depressed, having lost more than half its value over the past year. Adobe, with 2,700 employees compared to Quark's 500, flatly rejected the offer, and Quark soon announced it would not pursue the acquisition of its larger rival.

The company did acquire a majority interest in Silent GmbH, a German software developer. It also entered into a joint marketing agreement with Sun Microsystems. In another agreement with Corel, the two companies agreed to bundle QuarkXPress 4.0 and CorelDraw 8 into a new product called The Professional Suite, with a suggested list price of $1,095. QuarkImmedia version 1.5 was released toward the end of 1998. The company also announced that sales of QuarkXPress had reached two million units worldwide since its introduction in 1987. Meanwhile the installed base of the company's high-end Quark Publishing System was growing, due in part to new marketing efforts, and would reach an installed base of 500 sites by 2000.

In 1999 Quark was developing a dynamic web publishing system under the code name Troika. Other products under development included a workflow-management and layout application for catalog publishers that was code-named Cypress. Anticipating a new professional-level DTP program from Adobe called InDesign, Quark offered a preview of QuarkXPress version 5. The upgrade would include four new functions: a built-in table editor, document layers, HTML export, and PDF import. Meanwhile, Adobe was offering InDesign to Quark customers and users of other Adobe products for the special price of $299.

Later in 1999 Quark announced a partnership with Vignette Corp. of Austin, Texas, to integrate Vignette's StoryServer with QuarkXPress. The package offered a new web-to-print solution and was put into beta testing in September. The new package, avenue.quark, took a QuarkXPress document and converted it into XML, thus easing the transfer of the document to the web.

As of mid-2000 Quark was circulating demo copies of QuarkXPress 5, but it was unclear whether the upgrade would incorporate Adobe's PDF technology, which was the basis for Adobe Acrobat. PDF made it possible for a document to be retrieved electronically and arrive in a readable format, regardless of software specifics. QuarkXPress 4 included some limited PDF capabilities, and Quark had promised a full-featured PDF engine in version 5. However, its rivalry with Adobe made it unlikely that Adobe's PDF would be built into the new version of QuarkXPress.

Quark remains a company focused on the professional DTP market. Although its new releases have been plagued with delays, they have been well received by customers and reviewers upon their release. Quark has demonstrated its ability to incorporate the new features that its high-end customers want in their professional desktop publishing software. Its challenge will be to maintain its leadership position against traditional competitors Adobe Systems and Corel Corp. as well as new competitors serving the web publishing environment.

Principal Subsidiaries

Quark France S.A.; Quark Scandinavia ApS (Denmark); Quark Deutschland GmbH (Germany); Quark Japan K.K.; Quark Systems Ltd. (U.K.).

Principal Competitors

Adobe Systems Inc.; Corel Corporation; Microsoft Corporation.

Further Reading

Abernathy, Aileen, "Desktop Publishing," *MacUser,* July 1991, p. 179.

Abes, Cathy, "Will Quark Sink or Swim?," *Macworld,* April 1996, p. 48.

Abes, Cathy, and James A. Martin, "Quark Extends Beyond Page Layout," *Macworld,* May 1995, p. 122.

Beale, Stephen, "New Directions for Quark," *Macworld,* May 1999, p. 30.

Borzo, Jeanette, "Quark Sees Staying Power in Letting Customers Choose," *InfoWorld,* May 3, 1993, p. 90.

Bourrie, Sally Ruth, "Quintessentially Quark: Tim Gill," *Colorado Business Magazine,* September 1993, p. 42.

Bowen, Ted Smalley, "QuarkXPress 3.2 for Mac Ships; Windows Version in the Wings," *PC Week,* July 26, 1993, p. 29.

——, "Seybold Wares Run Gamut," *PC Week,* October 18, 1993, p. 37.

Bryer, Amy, "Quark Battles Rumors over Its Latest Version," *Denver Business Journal,* June 9, 2000, p. 5A.

"Bundling Agreement: Quark, Corel Tie Graphics," *InfoWorld,* December 21, 1998, p. 24.

Burns, Diane, and S. Venit, "Change of Xpression," *MacUser,* January 1989, p. 137.

Camp, John S., and Marc Cogan, "A Workout for Two Desktop Publishing Packages," *Electronic Learning,* January 1988, p. 55.

Copeland, Lee, and Lee Pender, "Hostile Takeover?—Quark's Quirky Bid for Adobe," *Computer Reseller News,* August 31, 1998, p. 242.

Cravey, Eric, "InDesign Takes on Quark," *Denver Business Journal,* December 3, 1999, p. 23A.

Degnan, Christa, "Publishing Tools Abound: Vignette, Quark to Team up, Tie StoryServer to XPress," *PC Week,* August 30, 1999, p. 16.

Dzilna, Dzintars, "Quark: Adobe Is a Takeover Target," *Folio: The Magazine for Magazine Management,* September 15, 1998, p. 14.

"Editor's Choice," *PC Magazine (UK),* August 1998, p. 162.

Goldrich, Robert, "Quark Takes Colossal Step," *Shoot,* February 2, 1996, p. 1.

Gruman, Galen, "QuarkXPress Is the Leader in Its Field," *InfoWorld,* December 8, 1997, p. 154.

——, "QuarkXPress Versus PageMaker," *Macworld,* December 1997, p. 86.

Heck, Mike, "QuarkXPress 3.1 Makes Move to Windows," *InfoWorld,* December 14, 1992, p. 79.

Helft, Miguel, "Adobe Rebuffs Quark Takeover Bid," *Knight-Ridder/ Tribune Business News,* August 26, 1998.

——, "Adobe Systems Readies New Desktop-Publishing Software Product," *Knight-Ridder/Tribune Business News,* March 1, 1999.

Horton, Liz, "Quark to Port to IBM, NeXT in 1991," *Folio: The Magazine for Magazine Management,* November 1, 1990, p. 111.

"An Interview with: Tim Gill-Quark," *Computer Reseller News,* March 8, 1999, p. 146.

Jantz, Richard, "QuarkXPress 4.0: Welcome Upgrade," *PC World,* October 1997, p. 118.

Jebian, Wayne, "The New Adobe Takes on Quark," *Folio: The Magazine for Magazine Management,* June 15, 1995, p. 34.

Jensen, Dave, "Popular Desktop Publishing Software for Macs Makes Leap to PCs," *The Business Journal-Milwaukee,* October 10, 1992, p. A10.

Jones, Chris, "Publish or Perish," *InfoWorld,* June 3, 1996, p. 1.

Kang, Cecilla, "Graphic Software Firm Adobe Systems Posts Higher Earnings," *Knight-Ridder/Tribune Business News,* September 17, 1999.

Knibbe, Willem, "Quark Exploring Technology for Multimedia Authoring Tool," *InfoWorld,* March 28, 1994, p. 8.

——, "Quark Shoots for Timely, Concurrent Rollout of Mac, Windows Upgrades," *InfoWorld,* November 22, 1993, p. 19.

Landwehr, Rebecca, "mFactory Shut Down by Quark," *Denver Business Journal,* March 27, 1998, p. 3A.

——, "Quark-Adobe Rivalry Gets Ugly," *Denver Business Journal,* June 2, 2000, p. 3A.

——, "Quark in Hunt for Hires," *Denver Business Journal,* November 7, 1997, p. 1A.

Lemon, Brendan, "The Millionaires Club," *Advocate,* April 28, 1998, p. 28.

Locke, Tom, "Quark Pumps up Management," *Denver Business Journal,* September 30, 1994, p. 3A.

Marsh, Ann, "Pride Goeth Before Destruction," *Forbes,* May 31, 1999, p. 64.

McDougall, Paul, "Quark Lowers Sights, Raises Aim," *Folio: The Magazine for Magazine Management,* March 15, 1994, p. 29.

Moore, Mark, "Quark Pushes Back Release of QuarkXPress 3.3 to March," *PC Week,* January 31, 1994, p. 33.

Nadile, Lisa, "Quark Image Editor to Spar with PhotoShop," *PC Week,* February 27, 1995, p. 13.

Olgeirson, Ian, "Quark Programs for IPO," *Denver Business Journal,* December 1, 1995, p. 1A.

"PageMaker Challenges QuarkXPress," *Folio: The Magazine for Magazine Management,* March 15, 1993, p. 16.

Patz, Debby, "Image-Editing Category Gains XPosure," *Folio: The Magazine for Magazine Management,* April 15, 1995, p. 27.

Pender, Lee, "Quark Draws Questions As It Drops Adobe Bid," *Computer Reseller News,* September 21, 1998, p. 248.

Pepper, Jon, "PageMaker 5.0 Bests QuarkXPress in Heated DTP Race," *PC/Computing,* March 1993, p. 40.

Pfiffner, Pamela, "Quarklmmedia," *MacUser,* January 1997, p. 36.

——, "Quark Takes on New Markets," *MacUser,* April 1995, p. 100.

Picarille, Lisa, "Image Editing, Publishing Tools Debut at Seybold," *PC Week,* March 12, 1990, p. 25.

Pompili, Tony, "Quark, IBM Team up in High-End Desktop Publishing Effort," *PC Week,* October 8, 1990, p. 4.

"Quark," *InfoWorld,* February 23, 1998, p. 31.

"Quark Announces a Barrage of News," *Graphic Arts Monthly,* October 1998, p. 124.

"Quark in a Buying Mood," *Macworld,* August 1997, p. 31.

"QuarkXPress for Power Mac Ships," *Macworld,* October 1994, p. 33.

Robuck, Mike, "Quark Eases Web Route," *Denver Business Journal,* November 5, 1999, p. 12B.

Rooney, Paula, "Delay Turns up Heat on Quark in Windows DTP Market," *PC Week,* June 15, 1992, p. 24.

——, "Quark, Adobe Show Wares at Seybold," *PC Week,* April 19, 1993, p. 20.

——, "Quark Postpones DTP Entry," *PC Week,* October 26, 1992, p. 39.

——, "Quark Prepared to Take on Aldus in Windows Arena," *PC Week,* December 16, 1991, p. 1.

——, "Quark Takes Aim at Aldus with New Mac QuarkXPress," *PC Week,* September 21, 1992, p. 14.

——, "QuarkXPress Headlines at Seybold," *PC Week,* September 14, 1992, p. 33.

——, "Windows Desktop-Publishing Market Heats Up," *PC Week,* February 17, 1992, p. 113.

Rosenberg, Jim, "More Choices," *Editor & Publisher,* January 3, 2000, p. 34.

Roth, Stephen F., "QuarkStyle," *MacUser,* February 1989, p. 269.

Sawyer, Scholle, "Quark Buzz Grows As Upgrade Nears," *MacUser,* May 1997, p. 26.

Simone, Luisa, "The Changing of the Guard?," *PC Magazine,* February 9, 1993, p. 231.

——, "QuarkXPress for Windows Breaks New Ground in DTP," *PC Magazine,* December 8, 1992, p. 37.

"Software Maker Quark Inc. Reports Explosive Growth," *Knight-Ridder/Tribune Business News,* March 2, 1994.

Sucov, Jennifer, "QPS, Others, Battle Industry Ambivalence," *Folio: The Magazine for Magazine Management,* February 1, 1996, p. 43.

Sussman, Ann, "QuarkXPress Attains a Desktop 4-Color Separation Milestone," *PC Week,* July 4, 1988, p. 11.

Svaldi, Aldo, "Will Quark Go Public?," *Denver Business Journal,* July 14, 1995, p. 1A.

Taub, Eric, "QuarkXPress 3.0," *MacUser,* November 1990, p. 52.

Ulanoff, Lance, "Graphics Software," *PC Magazine,* January 10, 1995, p. 147.

Vadlamudi, Pardhu, "Quark Waits for Spring to Launch XPress 4.0, XPosure," *InfoWorld,* September 4, 1995, p. 25.

Walsh, Jeff, "Adobe and Quark Escalate Desktop-Publishing War," *InfoWorld,* October 20, 1997, p. 32.

——, "Adobe Rebuffs Quark's Offer," *InfoWorld,* August 31, 1998, p. 18.

——, "Quark Drops Bid to Buy Adobe," *InfoWorld,* September 21, 1998, p. 48.

Weibel, Bob, "Quark's Big Comeback," *PC/Computing,* September 1997, p. 89.

Wesley, Michael D., "Quark Xpress," *MacUser,* May 1987, p. 73.

Wiggins, Robert R., "On the Xpress Track," *MacUser,* September 1987, p. 92.

Young, Jeffrey, "From Star Trek to Desktop," *Forbes,* July 19, 1993, p. 204.

—David P. Bianco

QuikTrip Corporation

901 N. Mingo Road
Tulsa, Oklahoma 74116
U.S.A.
Telephone: (918) 836-8551
Fax: (918) 834-4117
Web site: http://www.quiktrip.com

Private Company
Founded: 1958
Employees: 4,796
Sales: $1.8 billion (1999 est.)
NAIC: 447110 Gasoline Stations with Convenience
Stores

QuikTrip Corporation operates more than 325 convenience stores in Tulsa, St. Louis, Kansas City, Wichita, Omaha, Des Moines, Atlanta, Phoenix, Dallas, and smaller cities and towns in nine states. Each QuikTrip store features a large soda fountain, a coffee bar, the company's Quick 'n Tasty and HOTZI brands of heat-n-serve sandwiches, as well as QuikTrip's private-label gasoline, Redline.

Exceeding Initial Modest Goals

Chester Cadieux and a college friend opened the first QuikTrip convenience store in a small strip center in Tulsa in 1958. A $5,000 loan from Cadieux's father brought the initial capital investment to $16,000. The store stocked a limited selection of groceries with high prices for the convenience. Cadieux hoped to eventually operate ten stores in the Tulsa area. With the investment by suppliers, Cadieux gathered the capital to open additional stores, quickly exceeding his goal. In 1962 sales reached $1 million and the company recorded net income of $25,000. QuikTrip expanded outside the Tulsa area to Wichita, Kansas City, and Des Moines. One of the secrets of Cadieux's success was that he paid his store managers much higher than the industry standard, attracting quality workers to the company. Also, he reduced overhead by using vendor jobbers for stocking inventory.

In the early 1970s, Cadieux changed the product selection at QuikTrip stores. QuikTrip began to sell gasoline in 1971 as states legalized self-service stations. Cadieux eliminated slow-moving merchandise from his inventory, such as canned vegetables, and stocked a larger quantity of items, priced low for high-volume sales, such as beer, soda, coffee, cigarettes, and candy. QuikTrip introduced a low-priced, private label beer called QT, for "Quittin' Time," finding regular customers among college students and blue collar workers. Cadieux registered the QuikTrip name for federal trademark status in 1975.

QuikTrip expanded its capacity for gasoline sales in 1980, including the introduction of a private label brand of gasoline, Redline. The company added more pumps at existing stations and installed canopies over the pumps to protect customers from the sun and rain. In order to accommodate gasoline sales, QuikTrip relocated over 100 stores between 1982 and 1988. The units closed tended to be small, neighborhood stores or stores located in small towns, whereas new stores served a larger customer base from high traffic locations. QuikTrip experienced some difficulties in relocating stores, having to grapple with zoning ordinances or local resident opposition. In St. Louis, for example, local laws prevented the sale of alcohol at gasoline service stations; in some cases the law was later changed.

In the mid-1980s QuikTrip decided to enter the St. Louis and Atlanta metropolitan areas. QuikTrip considered several markets, but once the decision was made, the company sought saturation in the market. By 1988 QuikTrip had opened ten stores in Atlanta and eight stores in St. Louis. While the company expected to open an additional 100 stores in the St. Louis area over the next decade, in 1988 QuikTrip announced its intention to open 75 QuikTrip stores in the Atlanta area over the next five years. At a cost of $250,000 to build each store, including gasoline pumps, the Atlanta project involved a $50 million investment. QuikTrip usually purchased the land, usually one-acre lots, and then arranged a sale and leaseback of the land after the store had been built.

Stores under construction included large "travel centers." A smaller version of a truck stop, the travel center included a 5,000-square-foot store, 12 gasoline pumps, five diesel fuel pumps with elevated canopy to accommodate large trucks, a truck scale, and a store to serve the needs of truck drivers. Travel centers required a three-acre lot, cost up to $1 million to build, and faced tougher local scrutiny due to concerns about increased traffic and noise.

The company also decided to give QuikTrip stores a new, more vibrant look. QuikTrip replaced the earthtone exterior and interior with a bright red. The interior decor featured red countertops and a red quarry tile floor; almond tile on the walls interspersed with painted red sections of the walls to create contrast. Some gold trim maintained continuity from the previous decor. The company also took more care with landscaping around the store.

Competition from Oil Company Convenience Stores: Late 1980s

While sales exceeded $400 million in the late 1980s, and with half of revenues based on over 200 million gallons of gas, QuikTrip experienced increased competition from oil companies. Oil company service stations started to add convenience stores to their gasoline outlets, such as the Star Markets at Texaco stations. When an oil company gas station and convenience store opened near a QuikTrip store, merchandise sales decreased by $1,000 per week, while gasoline sales decreased 2,000 to 3,000 gallons per week. QuikTrip responded to the situation by adding more gasoline pumps at QuikTrip stores as well as complimentary products, such as motor oil and automobile accessories As QuikTrip accelerated its growth in 1986, with 112 of the company's 290 stores opening between 1986 and 1990, QuikTrip included gasoline pumps at almost all of its new stores. QuikTrip planned to close about 80 stores and reopen twice as many while including more gasoline pumps and seeking better locations for its stores.

Another method used to attract customers to QuikTrip stores, rather than the competition, involved the installation of Automatic Teller Machines (ATMs). The machines did not dispense cash, but dispensed scrip, a paper receipt which the customer exchanged for gasoline and store goods, with the balance of the amount paid to the customer in cash. This type of ATM machine was less expensive to install and provided QuikTrip with the possibility of impulse purchases. QuikTrip did not charge a fee to use the ATM, though individual banks did. QuikTrip tested the QuikTeller machines in Tulsa, later installing them in all of the company's 290 stores by 1990.

QuikTrip began to offer fast foods and fountain beverages at its stores, being the first convenience store to offer a self-serve soda fountain and a self-serve coffee bar. Expensive advertising led the company to phase out the private label beer by this time. In its place the company introduced in 1993 a private label brand of fast food, Quick 'n Tasty and HOTZI sandwiches. Quick 'n Tasty heat-and-serve sandwiches included Texas ham

and Cheese, BarBQ Pork Rib, and the Super Po Boy. QuikTrip sold most of the jumbo-sized sandwiches for one dollar. HOTZI breakfast sandwiches included the sausage, egg, and cheese biscuit and the breakfast burrito.

In its desire to remain competitive and up-to-date, QuikTrip began to build bigger stores, with 4,000 square feet of space, as compared to 3,200 square feet for existing stores. These stores provided customers with larger restrooms, more space to form a line at the cash register, and a larger self-serve beverage area. The stores also added a large storage room for larger quantities of stock. The first such store opened in Wichita and the company planned to use this format for all new stores.

QuikTrip revised its strategy of finding profitable store locations, closing smaller or unprofitable stores and replacing them with stores in more convenient, high-traffic locations. QuikTrip sought locations which customers would find easy to stop into as they returned home from work. High traffic areas drew customers into the stores as long as the traffic was not so high as to prevent customers from attempting to reach the store. The company found that locations with high residential density, such as a nearby apartment complex, and near office parks to be the most successful.

As competition from the oil companies intensified, QuikTrip sought to address the competition "at the pump." The company expanded its service by adding more gasoline pumps, from four to eight, allowing stores to serve up to 16 customers simultaneously. In 1993 QuikTrip decided to begin selling gasoline for a lower price; this strategy reduced the company's profit margin, but garnered volume sales. Competition was particularly high in Atlanta, where no one convenience store or oil company dominated the market. QuikTrip began to test pay-at-the-pump machines at three stores in Atlanta. The new technology allowed customers to use credit cards or ATM debit cards at the gasoline pump, saving customers time from going into the store and waiting in line.

The company initiated a campaign to discourage customers from purchasing high-octane fuels which cost more, but did not provide better quality. Brochures distributed by the company stated that high-octane fuel helped problems with knock, but that most cars ran better on regular unleaded. QuikTrip sought to build trust by taking the stand as well as to increase sales of regular unleaded gasoline.

In 1994 QuikTrip opened its first dual-brand convenience store with a Wendy's Old Fashioned Hamburgers franchise. The store location was a new 9,800-square-foot facility, the company's largest 24-hour travel center, with shower and laundry facilities, and diesel-related products. QuikTrip hoped that dual-branding would generate more traffic at the travel center. QuikTrip began test-marketing the dual-brand concept in St. Louis, Kansas City, Springfield, and Atlanta, where a 3,000-square-foot Wendy's store was attached to each QuikTrip convenience store. In Des Moines QuikTrip planned a new store with a Burger King attached. The Burger King had a separate entry and a drive-through window, but a passageway allowed movement between the convenience store and the restaurant. Cadieux's logic for dual-branding centered on the idea that fast-food restaurants were not the competition, as generally as-

Key Dates:

1958: Company is founded by Chester Cadieux.
1962: Sales reach $1 million.
1971: QuikTrip stores begin selling gasoline.
1984: Company enters Atlanta and St. Louis markets.
1988: Stores are given a new look with QuikTrip's signature bright red decor.
1996: Sales exceed $1 billion.
1999: To compete with oil companies QuikTrip cuts per gallon gross profit to 9.5 cents.

sumed, but the oil company gas stations with their new convenience stores.

QuikTrip's methods of competing worked well for the company. QuikTrip reached a major milestone with the year ending April 28, 1996, exceeding the $1 billion mark in annual sales. The $1.2 billion in revenue marked a 21 percent increase over 1995 revenue of $883 million. While QuikTrip set perhaps an overly ambitious goal of generating $2 billion in sales for fiscal 1997, sales did reach $1.7 billion. In 1997 QuikTrip took the lead in quantity of gasoline sold in the competitive Atlanta market.

QuikTrip launched a web site in 1997, promoting all aspects of the company's business. The company posted its "Guaranteed Gasoline" pledge which promised to pay for automobile repairs if they were caused by use of the company's gasoline. Included on the web site was information on the company's Fleetmaster program for commercial accounts. The program provided detailed reports designed to help transportation companies analyze fuel expenditures. These included an account of expenditures on a weekly and monthly basis, type of product purchased, and odometer readings.

Building on Successful Methods in Late 1990s

QuikTrip initiated another remodeling project in 1998 to improve the external appearance of its stores and to enhance merchandise display. In March QuikTrip started remodeling its 38 stores in the Wichita area. The company also continued to replace older stores with new, larger format stores, selling eight stores in Des Moines in late 1998 with plans for replacement with updated facilities. The age of a QuikTrip store averaged seven years, eliciting references to QuikTrip as an upscale version of the 7-Eleven convenience store.

QuikTrip drew high regard from its competition. In 1998 QuikTrip stores averaged $2 million in merchandise sales and three million gallons of gasoline. This compared to 7-Eleven stores which averaged just under $1 million in merchandise sales and 720,000 gallons for stores that sold gasoline. Oil companies still charged high prices for the convenience of location and speed and for their brands of gasoline, resulting in low volume. Cadieux attributed the success of QuikTrip to store managers whom the company paid $48,000 per year compared to the industry standard of $25,000. At QuikTrip revenues and net income reached $1.9 billion and $32 million, respectively, in 1998, attaining the company a place on *Forbes* Top 100 Privately Held Companies

list. QuikTrip was the largest gas retailer in Tulsa and Kansas City, and third in St. Louis and Atlanta.

Competition with oil company service stations and convenience stores culminated in a reduction in gas prices in January 1999. In order to increase volume sales, Cadieux reduced the company's profit margins by taking a 9.5 cents per gallon cut on gasoline compared to the industry average of 15 cents. Along with reductions in the price of merchandise, QuikTrip's overall gross profit margin dropped to 26 percent, significantly lower than the industry norm of 32 percent.

The company sought to reinvigorate its advertising by hiring an outside advertising agency. After sending questionnaires to 20 agencies, QuikTrip chose Austin Kelly Agency of Atlanta, because it seemed most compatible with QuikTrip's methods and attitudes. While the search progressed, QuikTrip worked with specialty agencies. Sixty Second Airborne in Atlanta created advertisements to promote QuikTrip's private label Select Blend coffee. John O'Hurley, who played J. Determan on the popular television comedy *Seinfeld,* starred in a series of radio ads in which he portrayed the same type of character as he did on Seinfeld, pontificating with pompous amusement. In the ad titled "Humunga Fantastica," O'Hurley's narrative satirized coffeehouse chains, where a small coffee had been renamed tall. In "Stunt Doubles," O'Hurley philosophized about coffee.

Growth for 1999 and 2000 involved expansion into two new markets, Dallas-Fort Worth and Phoenix. The company opened its first QuikTrip store in Phoenix in February 1999 while plans for other stores were held up by local neighborhood groups. Quik Trip entered the Dallas market, the home city of 7-Eleven stores, with plans to open 70 stores in the area. The first store opened in Arlington in December 1999, followed by two stores in Plano in March 2000. At 5,000 square feet, the Dallas area stores were larger than existing stores. QuikTrip included a soda fountain and coffee bar, 12 fuel pumps, and 24-hour service.

Principal Competitors

Hale-Halsell Company; Phillips Petroleum Company; Texaco, Inc.

Further Reading

Allen, James, C., "UMB Using 116 QuikTrip ATMs to Augment Branches in 3 Areas," *American Banker*, May 3, 1995, p. 5.
Bennet, B.L., "Cheap Gas Draws a Crowd," *Atlanta Journal-Constitution*, October 16, 1997, p. Q2.
Carroll, Robert, "Belton Gas Stations Wage High-Octane War," *Kansas City Star*, June 18, 1998, p. 1.
Conkling, Judy, "Three-Phase Remodeling Ahead for Regional QuikTrip Stores," *Wichita Business Journal*, March 6, 1998, p. 6.
Cowles, Anne, "State's 2nd Huge QT Opens," *Atlanta Journal-Constitution*, December 18, 1997, p. K1.
Curtis, Susan K., "Soaring Business Pumps up QuikTrip," *Atlanta Business Chronicle*, July 29, 1994, p. 3A.
Dwyer, Steve. "Settlement Ends Kwik Trip Name Game," *National Petroleum News*, June 1993, p. 15.
Emling, Shirley, "Throwing Away Good Gas Money Many Who Buy Premium Can Use Regular," *Atlanta Constitution*, August 20, 1993, p. S1.

Everly, Steve, "Pumping up Prices: The Cost of Gasoline Headed for the Stratosphere Last Week in the Area," *Kansas City Star,* November 8, 1996, p. A1.

Faust, Fred. "Expanding on the QT . . . Convenience Store Builds State-of-the-Art Units Here," *St. Louis Dispatch,* July 11, 1988, p. 9A.

Fest, Glen, "QuikTrip Is in No Rush to Judgment," *ADWEEK Southwest,* April 26, 1999, p. 8.

Francella, Kevin, P., "C-Store Concept Could Use Fixing: Panel," *U.S. Distribution Journal,* November 15, 1990, p. 4.

Gorham, John, "A Very Smart Retailer," *Forbes,* January 25, 1999, p. 66.

Hartnett, Dwayne, "Oklahoma's QuikTrip Plans to Double Sales, to $2 Billion, Next Year," *Knight-Ridder/Tribune Business News,* June 20, 1995, p. 6200207.

Harty, Cheryl, "Private Labels 'a Proven Success Story,'" *Retail World,* October 11, 1993, p. 10.

Hayes, Jack. "QuikTrip Revs up for Dual-Branding Push in Travel Centers," *Nation's Restaurant News,* October 10, 1994, p. 107.

Kovski, Alan, "Amoco Unveils New Retail Weapon in Gasoline Price War in St. Louis," *Oil Daily,* April 29, 1997, p. 1.

——, "Major Independent Gasoline Retailers Mass for Battle of Atlanta," *Oil Daily,* October 7, 1997, p. 3.

Lameiras, Maria M., "Safe Place: 16 QuikTrips, Children's Shelter Team Up," *Atlanta Journal-Constitution,* February 18, 1998, p. JJ1.

McNichols, Janet, "QuikTrip Faces Resistance to Plans for Page Avenue Site Neighbors Oppose Company's Bid for Gas Station and Restaurant," *St. Louis Dispatch,* January 28, 1999, p. 1.

"QT Sales Top $1 Billion," *Knight-Ridder/Tribune Business News,* p. 6190392.

"QuikTrip Corp," *Convenience Store News,* August 4, 1997, p. 66.

"QuikTrip Corp," *Convenience Store News,* August 3, 1998, p. 96.

"QuikTrip Is Selling Phone Cards, Wireless Phones," *Kansas City Star,* November 2, 1999, p. D14.

"QuikTrip Leaping into D-FW," *Dallas Business Journal,* December 3, 1999, p. 1.

"QuikTrip Planning 75 New Stores," *Atlanta Business Chronicle,* November 28, 1988, p. A1.

"QuikTrip Quikteller Dispenses Quikscrip; C-Store Chain Uses ATMs to Spur Impulse Sales, Enhance Image," *Chain Store Age Executive,* October 1990, p. 86.

"QuikTrip Relies on Radio Humor," *Adweek,* November 15, 1999, p. 6.

"QuikTrip, Wendy's Team Up to Build Facility in West Tulsa," *Tulsa World,* March 22, 1994, p. B1.

Schrodt, Anita, "Innovations on Tap at Latest QuikTrip," *Knight-Ridder/Tribune Business News,* December 4, 1994, p. 12040358.

Silbert, T.W., and J. Dee Hill, "It Was Anything but a QuikTrip," *ADWEEK Southwest,* December 6, 1999, p. 7.

Sowers, Carol, "Neighbors' Battle Far from Over: Convenience Store Invasion Continues," *Arizona Republic,* August 28, 1999, p. 1.

"To Be Kum & Go Stores; 8 Quick Trips Being Acquired," *Des Moines Register,* November 27, 1996, p. S8.

—Mary Tradii

RadioShack Corporation

100 Throckmorton Street
Suite 1800
Fort Worth, Texas 76102
U.S.A.
Telephone: (817) 415-3700
Fax: (817) 415-2647
Web site: http://www.radioshack.com

Public Company
Incorporated: 1960 as Tandy Corporation
Employees: 40,800
Sales: $4.13 billion (1999)
Stock Exchanges: New York
Ticker Symbol: RSH
NAIC: 443112 Radio, Television, and Other Electronics
Stores; 443120 Computer and Software Stores;
454110 Electronic Shopping and Mail-Order Houses;
334210 Telephone Apparatus Manufacturing; 334290
Other Communications Equipment Manufacturing;
334310 Audio and Video Equipment Manufacturing;
335929 Other Communication and Energy Wire
Manufacturing; 811211 Consumer Electronics Repair
and Maintenance; 811212 Computer and Office
Machine Repair and Maintenance; 811213
Communication Equipment Repair and Maintenance

RadioShack Corporation—known as Tandy Corporation from its founding in 1960 until mid-2000—is one of the largest consumer electronics retailers in the United States. Forming the company's core operation are the 7,100 RadioShack stores located throughout the country. The stores feature two main categories of goods and services—electronics parts and accessories, and telephones and telecommunications accessories—as well as audio and video equipment, satellite systems, personal computers, and other electronics products. RadioShack has partnerships with a number of major consumer electronics and computer companies, including Sprint Communications Company in the area of telecommunications; Compaq Computer Corporation, whose Compaq brand is the exclusive computer brand sold at RadioShack; Thomson Multimedia, for a line of RCA-branded digital audio/video products and services; and Microsoft Corporation in the area of Internet access as well as the radioshack.com e-commerce site. RadioShack Corporation also operates eight manufacturing plants in the United States and China that produce electronics products, most of which are sold in company stores; and a network of service centers that repair consumer electronics products and personal computers.

Early History

Founder Charles Tandy's talent for marketing became evident when he took over the leather store his family had operated since 1919. He began to expand into the hobby market. Subsidiary locations had to be found as mail-order and direct sales increased. In 1960, as scouts and campers all over the country made moccasins and coin purses from Tandy leathercraft and hobby kits, the Tandy Corporation was established and began trading on the New York Stock Exchange.

As good as business was, it could not satisfy Tandy's passion for retailing. By the early 1960s, he began looking for a way to diversify. In 1963, Tandy purchased RadioShack, a virtually bankrupt chain of electronics stores in Boston that had been founded in 1921. Within two years, Tandy was making a profit on a company that had nearly $800,000 in uncollectibles when he took over. Ten years after starting with nine Boston outlets, the Tandy Corporation was opening two RadioShack stores every working day.

By all accounts, Charles Tandy was a modest man from Fort Worth, who stayed in his original office and answered his own phone until the day he died. While his CB radio moniker was "Mr. Lucky," Tandy's success was, according to analysts, due to more than just luck. They gave much more credit to three key marketing strategies that Charles Tandy developed and implemented.

First, Tandy stressed the importance of gross profit margins. Popular wisdom said a chain store's profits lay in cutting prices to yield a high sales volume. Tandy thought differently. As far as he was concerned, cutting the profit margin cut the profit. So

Company Perspectives:

Under the brand position, "You've got questions. We've got answers," RadioShack's mission is to demystify technology for the mass market. In extensive research, thousands of Americans cited the patience, knowledge and integrity of RadioShack's 25,000 sales associates making RadioShack America's favorite and most trusted store for electronic products and services.

RadioShack is guided by a vision centered around four key goals: to be the most admired retailer in America; to lead our industry in shareholder return; to be an outstanding corporate citizen, both locally and across the nation; to be the best company to work for in America.

he maintained market prices but reduced RadioShack's 20,000 item inventory to the 2,500 best-selling items.

Second, Tandy kept RadioShack prices competitive. He eliminated a whole spectrum of middleman costs by limiting stock to private label items. At first, the company established exclusive contracts with manufacturers, but as RadioShack grew, more and more items were designed and manufactured by associates or subdivisions of the Tandy Corporation. In the late 1980s, Tandy still manufactured about half of the products sold in its RadioShack stores. Twenty-five North American and six overseas manufacturing plants produced everything from simple wire to sophisticated microchips, and RadioShack's Realistic brand name—which dated back to the 1950s—had achieved nationwide recognition.

Charles Tandy's strategy of pairing high profit margin with high turnover and of in-house marketing and distribution more than proved itself. The gross profit margin on sales for the RadioShack division was consistently above 50 percent.

Even as he consolidated his inventory, Tandy was keenly aware that buyers must be conscious of a company's presence. "If you want to catch a mouse," Tandy was fond of saying, "you have to make a noise like a cheese." So another Tandy strategy was to go all out on advertising. Especially in the early years, as much as nine percent of the corporation's gross profits went straight back into advertising. For years, RadioShack's newspaper ads and flyers were not only frequent but also flamboyant. Bold type and huge letters proclaimed a never-ending series of "super sales."

The third arm of Charles Tandy's strategy was, in the words of one company official, to "institutionalize entrepreneurship." Tandy Corporation and RadioShack employees were living testimony that hard work and impressive sales earn their own rewards. Store managers, division vice-presidents, and Charles Tandy himself regularly earned eight or ten times their relatively modest salaries through bonuses based on a percentage of the profits they had a direct hand in creating; this policy spawned some 60 home-grown millionaires.

As RadioShack's electronics line grew increasingly central to Tandy, the family leather business became more and more of an anomaly. Finally, in 1975, the leather line and a related wall and floor-covering business were spun off into separate companies.

Entering Computer Market in the Late 1970s

When Charles Tandy died suddenly in 1978, at the age of 60, pundits and insiders alike wondered if the corporation could survive without its workaholic director and his individualistic marketing philosophy. Philip North, a director of the company and Tandy's administrative assistant and boyhood friend, stepped in as interim president and CEO of Tandy Corporation.

By his own admission, North knew virtually nothing about the technical side of RadioShack's product line. "All I know about electronics is that the funny end of the battery goes into the flashlight first," he told *Fortune* magazine. However, North knew plenty about his late friend's retailing style. Analysts credited him with keeping the corporation's strong management team together during the adjustment period after Tandy's death.

During these years, North called more and more on the expertise of John Roach, a man whose scientific and computer background had already attracted Charles Tandy's attention. Within a few years of hiring Roach as the manager of Tandy Data Processing, Tandy had made Roach vice-president of distribution for RadioShack. Two years later, in 1975, Roach became vice-president of manufacturing. Roach was then appointed RadioShack's executive vice-president immediately after Tandy died, becoming RadioShack division's president and chief operating officer in 1980, and CEO in 1981. When North retired in July 1982, Roach became chairman as well.

Roach's major contribution was in masterminding Tandy's entry into the computer market. Before Charles Tandy's death, Roach had talked him into venturing into the preassembled computer market. The sale of 100,000 computers between September 1, 1977 and June 1, 1979 kept RadioShack comfortably in the black even as the bottom dropped out of the CB radio market.

As Roach moved up the corporate structure, he intensified investment in computers. In 1982, less than a year after becoming CEO, Roach was singled out as "the best of the best" by *Financial World*, which lauded Roach as "the driving force at the front-running company in the red-hot personal computer race."

Within a short time, however, there were rumblings that the driving force in this hot race might have been burned. By 1984, RadioShack's impressive 19 percent market share had plummeted to under nine percent. According to some critics, one of Tandy's problems resulted from Charles Tandy's policy of limiting RadioShack to private label items, preferably manufactured by one of Tandy's subsidiary divisions. As software and applications software poured out for Apple and IBM-compatible systems, fewer and fewer serious computer users were willing to limit themselves to software designed exclusively for RadioShack's TRS-80, or "Trash-80," as some sneeringly referred to it. In fact, Tandy found that even a superior machine could not overcome the software handicap. Officials at the company were shaken to find their 1983 Model 2000 would not sell, even though it was three times as fast as IBM's own PC, because it was unable to run half of the available IBM software.

In addition, RadioShack's marketing strategies had a vulnerable side. Company policy was to let other retailers test the waters with items such as stereos, CB radios, and "fuzz buster"

Key Dates:

1960: Tandy Corporation is established and begins trading on the New York Stock Exchange.
1963: Tandy buys the RadioShack chain.
1977: Company begins selling personal computers.
1985: Scott-McDuff and Video Concepts are acquired.
1988: GRiD Systems Corporation is acquired.
1991: Computer City chain is launched.
1992: Incredible Universe retail concept debuts.
1993: Company sells most of its manufacturing operations.
1995: Video Concepts is closed down.
1997: McDuff's and Incredible Universe chains are shuttered; RadioShack forms alliance with Sprint.
1998: Computer City chain is sold to CompUSA; RadioShack forms alliance with Compaq.
1999: RadioShack forms alliances with Thomson Multimedia/RCA and Microsoft.
2000: Tandy Corporation changes its name to RadioShack Corporation.

radar detectors. Then Tandy would take over a significant part of the market by introducing a house brand it advertised intensively. It was not always possible, however, to know what would boom and when, and when RadioShack simply did not have stock on hand when the VCR market exploded in the mid-1980s—the same time the computer market was drying up—both sales and revenues fell at an alarming rate.

That crisis led Tandy to modify its policy. In 1984, the company introduced two new computers that were fully IBM-compatible and exchanged the TRS label for Tandy. RadioShack management then set about underselling its Big Blue competitor. Such price competition was a departure from previous marketing strategy, but because Tandy's own in-house manufacturing divisions still produced virtually all the components, from wire to plastic boards to microchips, Tandy was able to keep profits up.

While it never regained its initial share of the PC market, Tandy consistently held first place among IBM-compatibles since it entered the field from 1985 to 1990. Tandy regained its place in the computer market by offering the buyer significant savings over IBM and other compatibles. At the same time, Roach also oversaw a wholesale revamping of the company's image. Ordinary RadioShack stores were given a facelift. To overcome the reluctance of serious business customers to take a computer shelved next to a CB or electronic toy seriously, Roach established a series of specialized RadioShack Computer Centers, providing a level of support and service that earned a "Hall of Fame" award from *Consumer's Digest* in 1985.

Tandy continued to pour money into research and development to assure that they would not be left behind again by new developments in the computer field. In 1988 it acquired GRiD Systems Corporation, an innovator in the burgeoning laptop computer market. GRiD's ability to manufacture and market field automation systems using laptop computers opened a whole new

area of expansion into government and *Fortune* 1000 marketing companies. Sales in GRiD's first year as a Tandy subsidiary exceeded expectations and helped underscore Tandy's image as a leader in personal computer technology by introducing innovations such as handwriting recognition and removable hard disc drive cartridges. In 1989, Tandy acquired the European marketing operations of Victor Microcomputer and Micronic, two respected microcomputer manufacturers. Merged under the name Victor Technologies Group, Tandy used the subsidiary to market GRiD products throughout Europe.

Tandy continued to maintain a high profile in the consumer electronics market outside of computers. In the late 1980s, the company put special emphasis on becoming a major force in both manufacturing and retailing cellular phones and home computers, which it saw as a major consumer product of the 1990s. Extensive efforts also went into the development of more business-oriented technology, including multimedia applications and digital recording. The latter resulted in the development of an erasable and recordable compact disc that commanded a great deal of interest in the electronics industry.

In many ways, during the 1980s, the Tandy Corporation had simply expanded on Charles Tandy's philosophies. The company centered its manufacturing and marketing firmly around computers and consumer electronics which it retailed primarily through its RadioShack outlets. Nonetheless, there were some significant deviations from Charles Tandy's views during the late 1980s. In 1985 the company entered the name brand retail market with the acquisitions of Scott-McDuff and Video Concepts, two electronic equipment chain stores. The 290 stores organized under the Tandy Brand Name Retail Group did not follow the RadioShack policy of selling exclusively private label brands. Other subsidiaries in the Tandy Marketing Companies also began to develop broader distribution channels. Memtek products, which included the Memorex brand of audio and video tapes, became available virtually everywhere such products were sold.

Tandy also made a push to sell its computers outside of RadioShack stores. In 1985, the company edged into broader markets by offering its computers on college campuses, military bases, and through special offers to American Express cardholders. In 1988, Tandy test-marketed its 100SX computer line through 50 Wal-Mart stores. The company also announced plans to develop new computers with Digital Equipment Corporation (reselling the finished product under the DEC name) and to supply personal computers to Panasonic (which would be sold under the Panasonic name).

Some RadioShack dealers saw Tandy's move to broaden its computer distribution as a potentially lethal threat. Many RadioShack dealers depended on their computer business for a significant portion of sales and doubted whether they could survive if customers began to shop around, looking for the same Tandy products for less elsewhere. In August 1988, a small group of dealers formed the RadioShack Dealers Association and began considering a class-action suit against Tandy.

Tandy's foundation at the time was its retail outlets. But beyond remodeling its 7,000 RadioShack stores and refining retail strategies, by the late 1980s, Tandy's own success had left its retail divisions with little room for growth. In 1989, Tandy posted record earnings. Business at RadioShack Stores, however, continued to decline, while sales in Tandy's subsidiaries GRiD, Memtek, Lika, and O'Sullivan Industries grew by over 50 percent.

Focusing on Retail in the Early 1990s

In the early 1990s, with its nonretail segment growing steadily, Tandy turned its attention to boosting its retail division. Leading the way were its McDuff and Video Concept Stores, which experienced an average of 14 percent same-store sales growth in 1989 and 1990. Tandy began a rapid expansion project, more than doubling the number of stores to 380 by the fall of 1991.

RadioShack, however, continued to feel the effects of a soft consumer electronics market. Tandy responded by closing its RadioShack Computer Center chain and by instituting an extensive marketing strategy that emphasized the high quality of both RadioShack products and service. In June 1991, Tandy announced plans to open Computer City, a new chain of computer superstores that was the first to offer IBM, Hewlett-Packard, Apple, Compaq, and Tandy computers, accessories, and software all under one roof. With its new 1000RL, a home computer system developed specifically for family use, Tandy went head-to-head against IBM for the home computer market, betting that this industry segment would grow by ten percent annually in the 1990s.

Also in 1991 Tandy opened the Edge in Electronics, a chain of upscale consumer electronics "boutiques" designed to complement RadioShack's moderately priced goods. Its biggest new foray into consumer electronics retail, however, came with the 1992 launch of Incredible Universe, an elaborate 160,000-square-foot consumer electronics mini-mall, complete with child-care centers, karaoke contests, a recycling center, and a restaurant. According to Tandy literature, Incredible Universe was patterned after "Disney's famous theme-park style of customer service. The store experience is called 'the show,' employees are known as 'cast members' and customers are the 'guests.' " Its $9 million inventory included everything from ten brands of computers to 300 different television sets and over 40,000 music and video titles.

The company took an enormous risk with opening Incredible Universe. Industry analysts predicted that each new store would have to turn over a volume of $100 million annually to remain profitable. Tandy committed itself entirely to the new venture. In 1993, it restructured its entire operations to focus on retailing and, in a bold move, sold most of its manufacturing operations. Victor, Tandy, and GRiD were sold to AST Research, Inc. for $201 million. O'Sullivan Industries, its successful furniture manufacturing arm, was spun off to raise $350 million. Memtek Products was sold to Hanny Magnetics for $128 million, and plans were made to sell Lika's manufacturing facilities for cash and notes.

Tandy then devoted its energies to polishing its image and expanding its base as an electronics retailer. Incredible Universe became a separate division and plans were announced to open 50 units by 2000. Computer City, which posted over $600

million in annual sales in its second year of operation, announced plans to open 20 new stores by the end of 1994. RadioShack improved service in its 6,500 locations and hired the agency Young & Rubicam to design a new advertising campaign that featured the slogan "You've got questions. We've got answers." The chain also changed its merchandise mix, most notably paring back its offerings in the increasingly low-margin personal computer sector and bolstering higher margin lines such as private label batteries and electronics parts. RadioShack also put increased emphasis on such hot areas as cellular telephones and direct satellite systems. For the first time since the early 1980s, RadioShack posted eight straight months of in-store sales growth. The Tandy Brand Name Retail Group's McDuff's and Video Concepts stores grew to become two of the biggest home appliance and electronics appliance retailers in the southeastern and south central United States. In less than two years, Tandy had transformed itself from a longstanding supplier and retailer of consumer electronics into a high-image conglomeration of electronics "superstore" chains.

Late 1990s and Beyond: Refocusing on RadioShack

The "new" Tandy proved to have a short shelf life, however—by decade's end the company would transform itself again. In the brutal environment for consumer electronics retailers in the late 1990s, with fierce competition from arch-rivals such as Best Buy and Circuit City and from general retailers such as Kmart and Wal-Mart, which were increasingly selling basic electronics goods, Tandy was forced to shed one after another of its chains.

Video Concepts was shuttered in 1995, along with 49 McDuff's stores. In late 1996 Tandy announced that it would close the remainder of the McDuff's chain; the entire Incredible Universe chain, which lost an estimated $130 million from 1993 to 1996; and 21 of its 113 Computer City outlets. The latter was operating in the red as well. While the divestments took place in 1997, Tandy took restructuring charges of $230.3 million in 1996, leading to a net loss for the year of $91.6 million on sales of $6.29 billion. The company completed a further retrenching move in mid-1997 when it sold a 20 percent stake in Computer City to a group of computer retailing executives, who took charge of running the chain.

Meanwhile, the RadioShack chain was continuing to be revitalized under the leadership of Leonard Roberts, who took over the presidency in mid-1993, having previously led turnarounds of Arby's and Shoney's Inc. In 1997 RadioShack began forming strategic alliances with key players in the electronics, telecommunications, and computer industries. The first was with Sprint Communications Company, which began operating "Sprint Communications Stores" within RadioShack outlets offering a full range of telecommunications products and services, including long distance and wireless services. The "store within a store" concept was extended to the computer arena the following year through an alliance with Compaq Computer Corporation, which launched "Compaq Creative Learning Centers" featuring personal computers and accessories. The Compaq brand became the exclusive computer brand found in RadioShack stores. A byproduct of these alliances was that entire sections of RadioShack stores were overhauled with the help of outside partners, reducing Tandy's share of the re-modeling costs.

The increasing influence of Roberts was shown by his promotion to president of Tandy Corporation in March 1997. One year later, Roach announced that he would retire at the end of 1998, with Roberts becoming chairman, president, and CEO of Tandy. Also in 1998 Tandy bought back the Computer City stake it had sold, then sold Computer City to CompUSA Inc. for $211 million. It could now be said, as Roberts put it at the 1998 annual meeting, "Tandy is RadioShack, RadioShack is Tandy."

The "store within a store" strategy was clearly paying dividends as RadioShack had already become by 1998 the number one seller of telecommunications products in the country. The chain now had two major categories of business—the longstanding electronics parts and accessories and telecommunications. Further alliances followed. In May 1999 RadioShack entered into a partnership with Thomson Multimedia, owner of the RCA brand, to create a new "store within a store" called the RCA Digital Entertainment Center, where RCA brand televisions, VCRs, camcorders, DVD players, digital cameras, and audio products would be displayed within RadioShack stores. In November of that same year, an alliance with Microsoft Corporation was formed to create the Microsoft Internet Center @ RadioShack, which featured dial-up and broadband Internet access as well as related products and services. Microsoft also agreed to invest $100 million in the e-commerce web site that RadioShack launched in October 1999, radioshack.com.

The newly streamlined and focused Tandy Corporation posted its best results in years in 1999—net income of $297.9 million on sales of $4.13 billion. Tandy Corporation changed its name to RadioShack Corporation in May 2000, the culminating move in its successful refocusing on its RadioShack core.

Principal Subsidiaries

A&A International Limited Partnership; AmeriLink Corporation; RadioShack.com, LLC.

Principal Competitors

Babbage's Etc. LLC; Best Buy Co., Inc.; CDW Computer Centers, Inc.; Circuit City Stores, Inc.; CompUSA Inc.; Creative Computers, Inc.; Dell Computer Corporation; Egghead.com, Inc.; Fry's Electronics, Inc.; Gateway, Inc.; The Good Guys, Inc.; Kmart Corporation; Let's Talk Cellular & Wireless, Inc.; Micro Warehouse, Inc.; Montgomery Ward, LLC; Office Depot, Inc.; OfficeMax, Inc.; PC Connection, Inc.; Sears, Roebuck and Co.; Sharper Image Corporation; Staples, Inc.; The Wiz; Ultimate Electronics, Inc.; Wal-Mart Stores, Inc.

Further Reading

Anderson Forest, Stephanie, "Promises, Promises at Tandy," *Business Week,* January 20, 1997, pp. 28–29.

——, "Radio Shack Looks Like a Palace Now," *Business Week,* May 13, 1996, pp. 153–54.

——, "Thinking Big—Very Big—at Tandy," *Business Week,* July 20, 1992, pg. 85–86.

Biesada, Alexandra, "Incredible Gamble," *Financial World,* June 9, 1992, pp. 49–51.

Clark, Don, and Carlos Tejada, "Microsoft, Tandy Announce Internet Partnership," *Wall Street Journal,* November 12, 1999, p. B5.

Faison, Seth, " 'Incredible Universe' Seeks a Big New York Bang," *New York Times,* November 17, 1994, p. D1.

Farman, Irvin, *Tandy's Money Machine: How Charles Tandy Built Radio Shack into the World's Largest Electronics Chain,* Chicago: Mobium Press, 1992, 464 p.

Goldgaber, Arthur, "Tandy: Out of Juice," *Financial World,* June 17, 1997, p. 26.

Heller, Laura, "Next Wave for RadioShack," *Discount Store News,* April 3, 2000, pp. 1, 44.

——, "RadioShack Provides Foundation for Tandy Turnaround," *Discount Store News,* January 4, 1999, pp. 31–32, 34.

——, "Visionary Offers New Perspective," *Discount Store News,* May 24, 1999, pp. 60, 87.

Hulock, Jim, Todd Mason, and Scott Ticer, "Burned by Superstores, Tandy Is Fighting Fire with Fire," *Business Week,* October 28, 1985, pp. 62+.

Mason, Todd, "Radio Shack Puts on the Pinstripes," *Business Week,* September 1, 1986, p. 66.

——, "Tandy Finds a Cold, Hard World Outside the Radio Shack," *Business Week,* August 31, 1987, p. 68.

Miller, Annetta, "Shufflin' at the Shack," *Newsweek,* June 7, 1993, p. 44.

Palmeri, Christopher, "RadioShack Redux," *Forbes,* March 23, 1998, pp. 54–56.

"Radio Shack's Rough Trip," *Business Week,* May 30, 1977, p. 55.

Ramstad, Evan, "Inside Radio Shack's Surprising Turnaround," *Wall Street Journal,* June 8, 1999, p. B1.

——, "Tandy to Shed Incredible Universe Chain," *Wall Street Journal,* December 31, 1996.

"Tandy Corp. Aims to Get Some Respect," *Business Week,* September 12, 1983, pp. 94+.

"Tandy Plans Huge Store," *New York Times,* February 27, 1995, p. D4.

"Tandy Will Close 233 Stores in Its Revamping," *New York Times,* January 4, 1995, p. D3.

West, James L., *Tandy Corporation: Start on a Shoe String,* New York: Newcomen Society in North America, 1968, 24 p.

"Why Hotshot Tandy Suddenly Sounds So Humble," *Business Week,* May 21, 1984, pp. 45+.

—Maura Troester
—updated by David E. Salamie

RICOH

Ricoh Company, Ltd.

15-5, Minami-Aoyama 1-chome
Minato-ku
Tokyo 107-8544
Japan
Telephone: (03) 3479-3111
Fax: (03) 3403-1578
Web site: http://www.ricoh.co.jp

Public Company
Incorporated: 1936 as Riken Kankoshi Co., Ltd.
Employees: 67,300
Sales: ¥1.45 trillion (US$14.05 billion) (2000)
Stock Exchanges: Tokyo Osaka Nagoya Fukuoka
    Sapporo Kyoto Amsterdam Frankfurt Paris
Ticker Symbol: RICOY (ADRs)
NAIC: 333313 Office Machine Manufacturing; 333315
    Photographic and Photocopying Equipment
    Manufacturing; 334111 Electronic Computer
    Manufacturing; 334112 Computer Storage Device
    Manufacturing; 334119 Other Computer Peripheral
    Equipment Manufacturing; 334210 Telephone
    Apparatus Manufacturing; 334413 Semiconductor and
    Related Device Manufacturing

Ricoh Company, Ltd. is a leading maker of office automation equipment, including copiers, printers, facsimile machines, and related supplies. Other products that the company manufactures and/or markets include personal computers, peripheral devices such as CD-recordable drives, semiconductors, and digital cameras. The company is the world's number one maker of digital copiers and more than 60 percent of Ricoh's revenues are derived from copiers and related supplies. With factories and sales affiliates located throughout Asia, Europe, and North and South America, Ricoh generates about 40 percent of its revenues outside of Japan, with about 18 percent stemming from Europe and 16 percent from the Americas.

Early History: From Photo Equipment to Office Equipment

The company's initial efforts focused on photography, and its ability to win market share was evident as far back as 1936, when Riken Kankoshi Co., Ltd. was formed to produce positive sensitive paper, used to develop film. Under the leadership of Kiyoshi Ichimura the firm instantly took the lead in the Japanese sensitized paper market. In 1938, after deciding to produce cameras as well, Ichimura changed the company's name to Riken Optical Co., Ltd. and introduced the Olympic 4.

The flash bulb and color film invented during the 1930s, and other developments such as new chemicals for film developing and computer-designed lenses originated during World War II, were marketed to the public after the war. In 1950 Riken introduced another camera, the Ricohflex III.

Five years later the company entered the copier market when it developed its first diazo copier, the Ricopy 101. This was followed by the Ricoh Synchrofax in 1959, two micro enlargement copiers in 1960 and 1962, and two duplicators, also introduced in 1960 and 1962.

With a handful of employees and $100,000, the company established its first overseas subsidiary, Ricoh Industries, U.S.A., Inc., in 1962. The subsidiary initially imported cameras, but it soon began marketing copiers when it realized the sales potential in the United States.

In 1963, following the establishment of its successful subsidiary, the Japanese parent company changed its name to Ricoh Company, Ltd. and continued its success in both copier and photographic equipment.

In 1965 Ricoh entered the budding field of office computers with the debut of the Ricoh Typer Standard, a data-processing system. It also introduced the Ricopy BS-1, and electrostatic coated-paper copier.

1970s: Product Expansion and U.S. Growth

The 1970s marked a decade of growth and change for Ricoh and its U.S. subsidiary. During the 1970s Ricoh began to sell

Company Perspectives:

Our Principles: To think as an entrepreneur. To put ourselves in the other person's place. To find personal value in our work.

cameras and other electronic goods on the U.S. market. Ricoh Industries U.S.A., whose annual sales had climbed to $1.3 million by 1970, was renamed Ricoh of America, Inc. In 1973 Ricoh established its second U.S. subsidiary, Ricoh Electronics Co., Ltd., in Irvine, California. Created to assemble copier supplies and parts, the subsidiary made Ricoh the first Japanese company to produce copiers in the United States.

During the mid-1970s Ricoh made advances in three important markets. The Rifax 600S, the world's first high-speed digital facsimile machine, made its debut in 1974 along with the Rinac 1000 System, an information-retrieval system. This was followed by the Ricopy DT1200, the company's first plain-paper copier, in 1975. Also in 1975, Ricoh was honored with Japan's highest award for quality control, the Deming Prize.

In 1976 Ricoh introduced the Ricoh Printer 40, an impact (daisy-wheel) printer, followed by the Ricoh WP-1, a word processor. By this time the company's products covered the field of office automation.

In 1978 Ricoh established Rapicom, formed to develop and market stand-alone, high-speed digital facsimile products, as well as satellite facsimile equipment. Ricoh of America opened a research and development facility in Santa Clara, California, in 1977. In 1979, however, the company assigned U.S. research and development functions to a new entity, Ricoh Systems, Inc.

Early 1980s: Expanding the Ricoh Brand

Despite the fact that it now operated four U.S.-based companies, Ricoh did not have much U.S. visibility, due in part to the company's agreement to sell copy machines in the United States under the labels of Savin and Pitney Bowes, two U.S. manufacturers. Early in the 1980s Ricoh announced its intention to market copiers under its own name and to become a major player in the worldwide office-automation market. Takeshi Ouye, president of Ricoh, planned to move carefully into the office-automation market, predicting in June 1980 in *Modern Office Procedures:* ''We will be in a position to market a total automation system within ten years.'' Ricoh already held the leading position in the international plain-paper copier market, and its additional office products—offset duplicating equipment and systems, diazo copiers, and facsimile, microfilm, word-processing, document, and storage-retrieval equipment—gave the company a boost in its quest for a leading rank in office automation.

In 1981, Ricoh of America began to market Ricoh copiers in the United States. By 1984 the company had achieved a seven percent share of the U.S. market. The firm then decided to venture into more advanced copying machines, moving from the $5,000-and-under price range to the $6,000-to-$13,000

range. This step put Ricoh in direct competition with Xerox Corporation.

Ricoh's four-year-old Rapicom subsidiary landed a major account for Telepress, Ricoh's satellite facsimile product, when it agreed in 1982 to supply the product to Gannett Company, publisher of *USA Today*. Telepress eliminated the practice of physically transporting the newspaper for printing and then again for distribution.

In 1983 Ricoh introduced an ultra-compact hand-held business computer, the Ricoh SP25, in addition to its first personal computer, the Ricoh SP200, and its first laser printer, the Ricoh LP4120. The company also added two more printers to its line the following year: the Ricoh JP5320, an ink-jet model, and the Ricoh TP3220, a thermal printer.

Longtime Ricoh President Takeshi Ouye was elected chairman in 1983, while Hiroshi Hamada became president. Under their leadership, the company continued to globalize. Previously, much of the company's new product research was done overseas, particularly in the United States, and then transferred to Japan, where the products were manufactured. Hamada felt that Ricoh should develop more products domestically and boost production capacity by manufacturing the products both at home and overseas. In the United States, for example, the company made its operation more independent and more responsive to the U.S. economy, merging its U.S. research and development operation, Ricoh Systems, with Ricoh Electronics, the production facility, both of which had reported separately to Ricoh in Japan. In addition, the company established Ricoh UK Products Ltd. in the United Kingdom in 1983, while Ricoh Nederlands opened offices in France and Italy in 1984, as well as a Belgian office in 1985.

In the mid-1980s the company continued aggressive marketing and product development efforts with the introduction of the RINNET System, a local area network; a color copier; an electronic filing system; an electronic whiteboard; and two minicomputers developed in cooperation with AT&T. As a result, sales grew 20 percent annually from 1982 to 1985. Ricoh's alliance with AT&T began with a three-year original-equipment-manufacturing (OEM) contract, in which Ricoh agreed to equip its facsimile machines with AT&T telephones. This was followed, in 1984, by an agreement allowing Ricoh to market AT&T's minicomputers in Japan. In 1985, the two firms created AT&T Ricoh Company, a joint venture to produce and market modified versions of AT&T's compact telephone systems. Ricoh lent its Japanese marketing-and-service network to AT&T, and AT&T helped Ricoh enter the telecommunications field.

In 1984 the company's Atsugi, Japan, plant established a production-technology research center and received the *Nihon Keizai Shimbun* Award for factory automation. Ricoh also established the Ricoh Research Institute of General Electronics Company, and Ricoh Finance. In addition, the company added a thermal paper and toner-production facility to its Fukui plant, while Sindo Ricoh Company began producing zoom plain-paper copiers and toner.

In the United States, Ricoh Electronics opened a fully automated thermal paper manufacturing plant in Irvine, California.

Key Dates:

1936: Riken Kankoshi Co., Ltd. is formed to produce sensitized paper.
1938: After camera production commences, company changes its name to Riken Optical Co., Ltd.
1955: Production of office equipment begins, with the debut of the company's first copier.
1962: First overseas subsidiary is established in the United States.
1963: Company changes its name to Ricoh Company, Ltd.
1973: Ricoh becomes the first Japanese company to make copiers in the United States.
1974: Company produces its first fax machine.
1975: Ricoh is awarded the Deming Prize for excellence in quality control.
1981: Ricoh-brand copiers are marketed for the first time in the United States.
1983: Company introduces its first personal computer and first laser printer.
1987: The Imagio line of digital office automation equipment makes its debut.
1992: Ricoh posts its first-ever operating loss.
1995: Company acquires Savin Corporation and Gestetner Holdings.

In addition, Ricoh began construction of Ricoh Research and Development Center.

Late 1980s: Further Globalizing and Increasing Overseas Production

In 1985 Ricoh Corporation (Canada)—formerly Rapifax of Canada—opened a new facility in NePean, Ontario. Ricoh also established two marketing companies in 1986: Ricoh España S.A., a joint venture with a Spanish distributor of Ricoh products, and Ricoh France S.A., a wholly owned subsidiary. When Ricoh UK Products began production in May, Ricoh became the first Japanese company to manufacture copiers in the United Kingdom. By 1988 the firm had also added facsimile equipment and supplies to its production capabilities.

Under the guidance of President Hiroshi Hamada, Ricoh established its second European manufacturing subsidiary, Ricoh Industrie France S.A., which produced plain-paper copiers and other office-automation equipment and supplies at a new plant in Alsace.

The firm also strengthened its position in the semiconductor arena with the purchase of Panatech Research & Development Corporation's semiconductor division in 1987. In May 1987 Ricoh opened a semiconductor-design center in San Jose, California. The center expanded research and development efforts for Ricoh's semiconductor products, which so far included CMOS, a large-scale integrated device that was incorporated in its copiers, facsimiles, and cameras.

In Japan in 1987 Ricoh introduced Imagio, a new line of office-automation equipment that utilized a digital system that processed images, produced 20 copies a minute, and functioned as an input/output station for electronic filing systems. In addition, the introduction of several new copiers, including a high-speed, multifunctional desktop model, enabled Ricoh to maintain its position as Japan's leading plain-paper-copier company.

In April 1987 Ricoh reorganized and consolidated its U.S. subsidiaries. The move, calculated to create a "separate Ricoh in North America," was another move toward globalization for Ricoh. According to Hamada, in the company's annual report for 1988, the new unit, called Ricoh Corporation, was to "gradually assume greater independence in virtually all aspects of its operations." Hamada also revealed plans to create another independent Ricoh in Europe, a plan that would begin by increasing production capacity.

In 1988 the company released a lightweight, compact eight-millimeter camcorder in the United States and Japan. The company also opened Ricoh Software Research in Santa Clara, California, to develop custom software for three-dimensional computer-aided design and database markets. The software products were designed for existing and future OEM clients. Also that year, Ricoh's overseas sales exceeded domestic sales for the first time—though this proved to be a short-lived development. Ricoh's product line included facsimile machines, data-processing equipment, cameras, and copying machines and supplies. It was one of only a few companies making four different types of copying machines: the diazo, the electrofax, the plain-paper copier, and the duplicator.

While many Japanese companies suffered decreases in their export businesses during the mid- to late 1980s because of the high value of the yen, Ricoh's overseas sales grew. Its success was attributed to substantial gains in sales of facsimile machines and laser printers. In addition, Ricoh's two main office products, copiers and facsimile machines, had earned a major share of the U.S. market. In 1987 Ricoh's share of the laser printer and scanner market was about 24 percent. Ricoh's goal was to double that share by employing more aggressive marketing efforts through an expanded sales force and its American network of dealers, distributors, and OEM arrangements.

Despite the aggressive sales strategy, Ricoh suffered profit declines in 1986 and 1987, due partly to slimmer profit margins caused by appreciation of the yen. To cope with the high yen, the company planned to continue increasing overseas production. In the late 1980s, it began making copiers at its third U.S. manufacturing plant. This, and a fourth plant, which opened in Lawrenceville, Georgia, in 1990, doubled Ricoh's U.S. production. About 20 percent of the products made at these facilities, which included copiers, facsimiles, sorters, automatic document feeders, and supplies, were exported to Japan and Europe.

1990s and Beyond: Weathering Recession and Digitalizing the Product Lines

During the early 1990s Ricoh had to contend with the difficulties of the recessionary Japanese economy, which cut demand for office machinery, as well as the high yen, which made exports from Japan more expensive. Despite its efforts at increasing overseas sales and production, only about 27 percent of revenues were derived outside of Japan at the beginning of the decade, while most of its products were still built in Japan.

The culmination of these trends came in the fiscal year ending in March 1992, when Ricoh posted its first-ever operating loss. Net income for that year was just US$15.4 million on sales of US$7.65 billion, the latter figure a modest seven percent increase over the previous year.

Ricoh embarked on a major cost-cutting initiative in the wake of the disappointing 1992 results. No workers were laid off, but the company no longer replaced every worker who resigned or retired. Ricoh also made major cuts in the products and parts it sold, reducing the number from 5,000 to 3,100. Work was halted on several new products. The company's management was also restructured. Attempting to bolster its overseas operations, Ricoh took a 24 percent stake in Gestetner Holdings PLC, a U.K.-based office equipment firm. Ricoh and Gestetner had worked together since the mid-1960s, and in the early 1990s Ricoh was selling office equipment to Gestetner, which marketed the products in Europe under its own name. Ricoh shifted production of low-end office automation products for the U.S. market from Japan to South Korea. And the company established several subsidiaries and joint ventures in China and Hong Kong for the manufacture of copiers, fax machines, and parts.

On the product development side, Ricoh began revitalizing its product lineup through an increased emphasis on digital products. The company had already introduced its first full-color plain-paper digital copier, the Artage 8000, in 1990, and moved into the burgeoning market for multifunctional digital copiers the following year with the Imagio MF530 (multifunctional copiers were also able to perform other functions, such as sending faxes and/or serving as a computer printer). Ricoh made an early entrance into the CD-recordable (CD-R) device sector, introducing both CD-R discs and CD-R drives in 1992. Making its debut in 1993 was the Preter 500/550, a full-color multifunctional digital copier. The company moved into the scanner market in 1994 with the Ricoh IS20 and into the digital camera field in 1995 with the Ricoh DC-1, which recorded both still and moving images as well as sound.

Ricoh's restructuring and new product development prowess paid off by the mid-1990s as the company posted healthy net income of US$214.8 million on sales of US$11.79 billion for fiscal 1995. Ricoh continued its drive to boost international sales by acquiring Savin Corporation for about US$42 million and taking over Gestetner Holdings for about US$286 million, with both purchases occurring in 1995. Based in Stamford, Connecticut, the financially troubled Savin had been marketing Savin-brand copiers and fax machines made by Ricoh and would continue to do so as a Ricoh subsidiary.

Longtime President Hiroshi Hamada was named chairman and CEO in 1996, while Masamitsu Sakurai was promoted to president and COO. That year, Ricoh helped develop the CD-ReWritable (CD-RW) platform, which enabled users to read, write, and rewrite computer data on compact discs. It introduced the first CD-RW drives and discs in late 1996 and early 1997. Also in 1996 the company began using the Aficio brand for all of its digital copiers sold outside of Japan. In 1997 Ricoh established a new R&D and venture capital financing subsidiary in San Jose, California, called Ricoh Silicon Valley, Inc.

Ricoh was spared the worst effects of the Asian economic crisis of the late 1990s, thanks to its drive to increase overseas sales. By 2000, nearly 40 percent of revenues were derived outside Japan, with the company aiming for a 50–50 split. Sales and net income fell only slightly in fiscal 1998, while the next two years saw Ricoh post solid gains, culminating in net income of US$407 million on sales of US$14.05 billion for fiscal 2000.

Among the company's many product introductions of the late 1990s were the Imagio MF105 Pro, an ultrafast digital copier capable of printing 105 copies per minute (debuting in May 1999); the IPSiO Color 2000, the company's first color laser printer (July 1998); the Ricoh Image Scanner IS450, a flatbed scanner (March 1999); and several increasingly powerful and compact digital cameras. Ricoh was also placing increasing emphasis on semiconductor devices, including application-specific integrated circuits (ASICs), which were used in such areas as central processing units and facsimile engine controllers; and application-specific standard products (ASSPs), which included chip sets for digital cameras and PC card controllers for notebook computers. In mid-2000 Ricoh launched a proactive management restructuring to adopt a U.S.-style separation of executive and operating functions, with the heads of the company's divisions and subsidiaries gaining much more authority and responsibility than before. Ricoh's willingness to embark on major restructurings, along with its respected ability to develop new products and its more balanced stream of revenues, placed the company in a strong position in the early 21st century.

Principal Subsidiaries

Ricoh Optical Industries Co., Ltd.; Tohoku Ricoh Co., Ltd.; Hasama Ricoh, Inc.; Ricoh Unitechno Co., Ltd.; Ricoh Keiki Co., Ltd.; Ricoh Microelectronics Co., Ltd.; Ricoh Elemex Corporation; Ricoh Tottori Technical Development Co., Ltd.; Ricoh System Kaihatsu Co., Ltd.; Ricoh Austria GmbH; Ricoh Australia Pty, Ltd.; Ricoh Canada Inc.; Dong Guan Tailien Optical Co., Ltd. (China); Ricoh Asia Industry (Shenzhen) Ltd. (China); Ricoh Dianzhuang (Shenzhen) Electronics Co., Ltd. (China); Ricoh Electronic Technology (Beijing) Co., Ltd. (China); Ricoh Electronic Technology (China) Co., Ltd.; Ricoh International (Shanghai) Co., Ltd. (China); Shanghai Ricoh Facsimile Co., Ltd. (China); Ricoh France S.A.; Ricoh Industrie France S.A.; Ricoh Deutschland GmbH (Germany); Ricoh Asia Industry Ltd. (Hong Kong); Ricoh Component (H.K.) Ltd. (Hong Kong); Ricoh Hong Kong Ltd.; Ricoh Photo Products (Asia) Ltd. (Hong Kong); Ricoh Hungary Kft.; Ricoh India Limited; Ricoh Italia S.p.A. (Italy); Sindo Ricoh Co., Ltd. (Korea); Ricoh Mexicana, S.A. de C.V. (Mexico); Ricoh Europe B.V. (Netherlands); Ricoh Nederland B.V. (Netherlands); Ricoh Norge A.S. (Norway); Ricoh Polska Sp.zo.o. (Poland); Ricoh Asia Pacific Pte. Ltd. (Singapore); Ricoh España S.A. (Spain); Taiwan Ricoh Co., Ltd.; Gestetner Holdings PLC (U.K.); GR Advanced Materials Ltd. (U.K.); Ricoh UK Ltd.; Ricoh UK Products Ltd.; Ricoh Corporation (U.S.A.); Ricoh Electronics, Inc. (U.S.A.); Ricoh Latin America, Inc. (U.S.A.); Ricoh Silicon Valley, Inc. (U.S.A.); Savin Corporation (U.S.A.).

Principal Competitors

A.B.Dick Company; Canon Inc.; Casio Computer Co., Ltd.; Eastman Kodak Company; Fuji Photo Film Co., Ltd.; Hewlett-

Packard Company; Hitachi, Ltd.; IKON Office Solutions, Inc.; Lanier Worldwide, Inc.; Matsushita Electric Industrial Co., Ltd.; Minnesota Mining and Manufacturing Company; Minolta Co., Ltd.; NEC Corporation; Nikon Corporation; Oki Electric Industry Company, Limited; Pitney Bowes Inc.; SANYO Electric Co., Ltd.; Sharp Corporation; Siemens AG; Toshiba Corporation; Xerox Corporation.

Further Reading

Caplan, Brian, ''When Politics Beats Profits,'' *Asian Business,* March 1990, pp. 55+.

DeTar, Jim, ''Low-Profile Ricoh Gets Aggressive,'' *Electronic News,* May 11, 1998, pp. 1, 70.

Friedland, Jonathan, ''Setting an Example: Japanese Manufacturer Ricoh Slashes Costs,'' *Far Eastern Economic Review,* October 8, 1992, pp. 81–82.

Helm, Leslie, and Rebecca Aikman, ''Office Products: A Japanese Slugfest for U.S. Tuft,'' *Business Week,* May 13, 1985, pp. 98+.

—Kim M. Magon
—updated by David E. Salamie

RPM, Inc.

2628 Pearl Road
P.O. Box 777
Medina, Ohio 44258
U.S.A.
Telephone: (330) 273-5090
Fax: (330) 225-8743
Web site: http://www.rpminc.com

Public Company
Incorporated: 1947 as Republic Powdered Metals, Inc.
Employees: 6,800
Sales: $1.95 billion (2000)
Stock Exchanges: New York
Ticker Symbol: RPM
NAIC: 325510 Paint and Coating Manufacturing; 325520
   Adhesive Manufacturing

RPM, Inc. is one of the world's leading manufacturers of paints and coatings used for maintenance and protection. About 60 percent of sales are generated from the company's industrial division, which makes waterproofing, corrosion control, floor maintenance, and other products under such brands as Alumanation, Day-Glo, Carboline, Mathys, and Tremco. The remainder of sales come from the consumer division, which produces do-it-yourself products for home improvement, automotive repair, marine, and hobby and leisure applications through such brands as Rust-Oleum, Bondex, Bondo, DAP, Wolman, and Zinsser. From its founding through 1999, RPM enjoyed a remarkable 52 consecutive years of increasing sales and earnings; the profit string was broken in 2000, however, although the sales streak remained alive.

Growing Steadily in the Early Years

RPM founder Frank C. Sullivan had built a successful career as a sales executive with a Cleveland paint manufacturer, but decided to move out on his own in 1947. He started Republic Powdered Metals, Inc. in 1947 in a garage on Cleveland's west side with a $20,000 investment. The company manufactured a single product called Alumanation. This heavy-duty protective coating has endured as one of RPM's biggest sellers.

Sullivan's original goal was to create and sell industrial maintenance products—to waterproof, rustproof, and protect existing structures. In order to carry out that goal, he concentrated on attracting talented workers, then provided them with a constructive atmosphere in which to develop their abilities. In addition, financial success during Republic Powdered Metals' first ten years was driven by a management team whose members would spend their entire business lives working at RPM. As late as 1987, eight of the ten men were still active in the management of the company. RPM's leadership was long lauded as one of the most successful and experienced in the coatings industry.

In its first year Republic Powdered Metals achieved $100,000 in revenues, and by 1957 the company had reached the $2 million mark. By 1961 Republic Powdered Metals' sales had outgrown its production capabilities, and a new plant was built in Gilroy, California. That year, Thomas C. Sullivan joined his father's company, advancing to executive vice-president in 1965.

As domestic sales grew year after year, RPM turned its attention to the international marketplace. Success in that arena came quickly, and the effort was rewarded with increasing profits and President Lyndon Johnson's "E" Award for excellence in export expansion in 1964. That year was a turning point for RPM. Frank Sullivan and his management team realized that, to continue to grow and prosper, they had to choose between selling out or going public. In 1964 they chose to go public, and offered 1,000 shares of stock at eight dollars per share, but purchasers were limited to Ohioans until the first national stock offering in 1969. RPM's headquarters were moved to Medina, a small community 25 miles south of Cleveland, that year.

This infusion of capital enabled RPM to make its initial acquisition in 1966. The purchase of the Reardon Company of St. Louis, Missouri, brought RPM into the realm of consumer products with Reardon's well-known brand name, Bondex, the only nationwide line of household patch and repair products.

That first purchase also established many of the criteria for RPM's future acquisitions. The company sought to purchase low-volume, high-margin niche companies that were performing well—as Tom Sullivan pronounced in the *Cleveland Enterprise* in 1992, "We don't do turnarounds." Each product was expected to match RPM's gross profits of 40 percent. A hallmark of the Sullivans' system was that a prospective acquisition have an enthusiastic management team in place, since those leaders would continue the administration that had drawn RPM's attention in the first place. RPM also focused on companies that did not rely on original equipment manufacturers (OEM). That way, RPM and its operating companies were not as sensitive to market fluctuations and economic downturns. Most of RPM's products augmented existing equipment and industrial facilities, avoiding the cyclical nature of companies that rely on new construction or sales of capital goods. Finally, RPM looked for "synergism" with its existing product lines, encouraging the leaders of each operating company to find products or technologies that might compliment the products of their colleagues.

New Leadership and Holding Company in the 1970s

RPM's success was tragically disrupted in 1971 with the unexpected death of Frank C. Sullivan on August 18. The shock precipitated a crisis situation: according to Frank's son and successor, Tom, the elder Sullivan had been "the individual most closely identified with [RPM]." As the new chairman, president, and chief executive officer, Tom feared that the company would lose its credibility along with its leader.

To fend off such speculation RPM, Inc. was incorporated as a holding company under which Republic Powdered Metals, Bondex, and any new acquisitions would operate as wholly owned subsidiaries with a large degree of independence in their daily operations. That "hands-off" approach became a model for all RPM's acquisitions and a strategy envied by other large corporations. Jerry J. Dombick, an industry analyst, praised RPM's "mutual fund of businesses" in a 1993 *Chemical Week* article.

During the years from 1968 to 1977, RPM's sales grew from $7 million to $57 million annually, but the ten-year period was, in the words of the 1987 annual report, "a real test for the RPM management team." The challenge came from outside the company; between 1972 and 1974 the Dow Jones Industrial Average lost almost half of its value. RPM's stock dropped from a high of $23 to $8 per share, in spite of continuously growing sales and earnings.

Despite that brief, but dramatic, downturn, RPM acquired a dozen companies over the course of the 1970s, including Maharam Fabric—later renamed Design/Craft Fabrics—Proko

Industries Inc., and Thibaut Wallcoverings. In 1977, RPM purchased all of Alox Corp.'s stock, thereby acquiring that producer of rust corrosion inhibitors and adding Alox's $5 million annual sales to the balance sheet. The purchase of Maharam Fabric, a Chicago designer and distributor of decorative nonapparel fabrics for the construction industry, added another $10 million in sales to RPM's bottom line.

Later in 1977 RPM announced an offering of 860,000 common shares, which helped to finance the decade's many acquisitions. The stock was issued in November, and sold out the same day. Before the decade was out, RPM acquired Dean & Barry Co., a 77-year-old Columbus-based manufacturer of paints and protective coatings. Before the 1970s' flurry of acquisitions ended, Mohawk products, a well-known brand in the furniture touch-up industry, and Mameco International, a Cleveland manufacturer of urethane sealants, flooring systems, and coatings, were also added. Founded in 1913, Mameco brought sales of $10 million annually to the growing list of RPM subsidiaries.

With all of the acquisitions came increased responsibilities, and in 1978 Tom Sullivan and the board of directors decided to divide his leadership role into two positions: president/chief operating officer and chairman/chief executive. Sullivan recommended his longtime associate and executive vice-president, James A. Karman, for the president's position. The two met at Miami (of Ohio) University and worked together for 16 years before the formation of the holding company. From that point forward, Karman oversaw RPM's daily operations, while Sullivan concentrated on acquisitions and public relations.

In the 1970s and 1980s RPM's exports grew, complemented by overseas licensees and joint ventures that accounted for $50 million in annual sales by 1987. From 1976 to 1985, the company's sales compounded 330 percent, fueled primarily by astute acquisitions. At that time 80 percent of RPM's products fell into the industrial category, while the balance was consumer-oriented. Between 1978 and 1987, RPM divested $50 million in weaker margin operations, and sales grew from $57 million to $300 million. During this period, RPM added several consumer-oriented subsidiaries, and its operating companies concentrated on the development of consumer products in several categories: household, automotive aftermarket, and hobby and leisure.

Continuing to Grow Through Acquisitions in the 1980s

In mid-1983 RPM ventured into the Eurobond markets to finance numerous acquisitions during the decade. "Eurobond" designates securities sold in countries that do not utilize the currency of the bond's denomination. They were attractive to RPM and many other large corporations for several reasons: better rates; less expensive legal, printing, and underwriting costs; and more favorable terms.

In 1980 RPM purchased all assets of Haartz-Mason Inc., a Boston manufacturer of synthetic rubber products, which added sales of about $8 million per year to the list. Euclid Chemical Co., a 1984 acquisition, brought a leading manufacturer of liquid and powder concrete additives into RPM's product lineup. Founded in 1910, Euclid Chemical had about 40 employees and estimated sales of $12 million in 1984. Testor Corporation, a Rockford,

Key Dates:

1947: Frank C. Sullivan founds Republic Powdered Metals, Inc.
1963: Company goes public through an offering limited to residents of Ohio.
1966: Company makes first acquisition, Reardon Company and its Bondex brand.
1969: First national public offering of the company's stock occurs.
1971: Thomas C. Sullivan takes over for his father, who had died unexpectedly. Firm becomes a holding company under the new name RPM, Inc.
1978: James A. Karman is named president.
1985: Carboline Company is acquired.
1987: William Zinsser & Co. is acquired.
1993: Company acquires Dynatron/Bondo Corporation and Stonhard Inc.
1994: Rust-Oleum Corporation is acquired.
1997: Tremco, Inc. is purchased from BFGoodrich Company.
1998: Flecto Company, Inc. is acquired.
1999: DAP Products Inc. and DAP Canada Corp. are acquired; company launches a major restructuring.

Illinois, maker of glue and paints for hobbyists, was purchased from Jupiter Industries Inc. that same year. Founded in 1929, Testor was the world's best-known hobby and craft trademark. The company earned national attention in the mid-1980s when it released a 12-inch plastic replica of the top secret F-19 Stealth fighter jet. Aside from the free publicity, the incident helped to illustrate the high degree of autonomy and responsibility enjoyed by the presidents of RPM's operating companies—Testor's president took all press inquiries, and few news reports mentioned Testor's relationship to RPM.

Westfield Coatings Corp., a manufacturer of specialized high-performance coatings for the paper, wood, and metals industries, was purchased in January 1985. A stock offer of 700,000 shares at $15.50 each was made in connection with the Westfield acquisition. Later that year, RPM acquired Carboline Company from Sun Co. Inc., which put the company at the forefront of specialized corrosion-control products. As RPM's largest acquisition, Carboline expanded RPM's product lines to include specially formulated corrosion-control products used to maintain nuclear reactors. The St. Louis company was one of only a few manufacturers in this exclusive industry, a key factor in its acquisition by RPM. Other Carboline products for the energy, chemical, paper and pulp, and highway industries were manufactured at factories in Ohio, Louisiana, California, and Wisconsin.

RPM returned to the Eurobond market in 1986 for $30 million at just 5.75 percent. The sale helped finance capital investments in manufacturing facilities worldwide and the continued high rate of acquisitions throughout the 1980s. That same year RPM acquired American Emulsions Co. of Dalton, Georgia, a manufacturer of specialty coatings and chemicals for the textile, carpet, and paper industries with annual sales of $10

million. The 1987 addition of William Zinsser & Co. of Somerset, New Jersey, brought more consumer items to RPM's roster of products. The company was the leading U.S. manufacturer of primer-sealers, shellac finishes, and special wallcoverings for the professional and do-it-yourself markets, and its brand of edible glazes for candy and pharmaceutical applications was the leading one in those fields. Craft House Corp., a maker of craft, hobby, and toy products with $20 million in annual sales, further expanded RPM's do-it-yourself business in 1987. Chemical Specialties Manufacturing Corp., Baltimore, was a producer of coatings, cleaners, and additives for the carpet, textile, and floor care market that was added in 1988.

National interest in RPM developed in the mid-1980s. The company had been ranked among *Dun's Business Month*'s top five ''dividend achievers'' for 1983 through 1986 and cited as one of *Fortune*'s ten fastest-growing dividends. But despite this recognition, many institutional investors remained largely unaware of RPM's achievements. When RPM's stock price fell from $17 to $10 after the ''Black Monday'' stock market crash on October 19, 1987, however, analysts noted that the bulk of RPM's 14,000 individual shareholders kept buying, while other individual investors were scared off. Due to this loyalty the stock was able to recover within the same year.

One reason for the neutralization of the crash was related to the U.S. government's national public health advisory regarding the carcinogen radon. On September 12, 1988, the federal government advised all homeowners and renters nationwide to test for radon gas. Later that fall, RPM became one of the first companies to announce the development of a radon barrier system. The Bondex Radon Blocking System, a nontoxic, water-based sealant designed to protect homes and other buildings from radon gas seepage, was produced by Bondex International in 1989. RPM's stock took its sharpest jump in history after the disclosure concerning the five-step radon sealant.

The younger Sullivan's business acumen was not only highlighted by acquisitions, but by divestments as well, especially since 1983. During the ten-year period ending in 1993, RPM sold off businesses accounting for $100 million in sales. Such divestments usually followed a product's move from a niche market to a commodity. For example, when Firestone entered the ethylene propylene diene monomer (EPDM) roofing membrane market in the early 1980s, prices plunged over 75 percent, from 70 cents to 17 cents per square foot. As a result RPM sold off the EPDM operation, even after sinking $10 million into product development.

Expanding into a $2 Billion Company in the 1990s

The recession of the early 1990s did not slow RPM's acquisition or earnings pace. While the economic downturn made many of the 1980s' winners into losers, the worst it did to RPM was to slow its growth rate. Moreover, it was during this time that RPM made its first venture into the high-quality marine paint market with its second largest acquisition. Kop-Coat, Inc., of Pittsburgh, had a diverse line of coatings products under the Wolman, Pettit, Woolsey, and Z-Spar brand names and $55 million in annual sales.

RPM also entered into a joint venture in 1990 with Holderbank Franciere Glaris S.A. of Switzerland, one of the world's largest producers of cement. The arrangement involved the sale of 50 percent of Euclid Chemical Co. to Holderbank's special materials division, Holderchem. The following year saw the expansion of RPM's European influence with the purchase of Rust-Oleum's Netherlands and French operations. The activities complemented RPM's previous forays into Belgium and Luxembourg and gave the company increased access to the world's markets.

In 1991 RPM became the dominant player in fluorescent colorant markets with the purchase of Cleveland's Day-Glo Color Corp. The increased popularity of fluorescent colors in the 1990s saw them applied to plastics, textiles, paints, and inks. Day-Glo constituted about 40 percent of that growing industry. Later that year, RPM acquired Martin Mathys N.V., a Belgian manufacturer of specialty protective coatings for the building maintenance and construction industry. Martin Mathys was founded in 1845, and had distribution throughout the European marketplace by the time it joined RPM's roster.

As the recession gave way to the sustained economic expansion of the mid- to late 1990s, RPM stepped up its acquisition activity. In June 1993 RPM acquired Dynatron/Bondo Corporation of Atlanta, Georgia, which manufactured and marketed products for professional and consumer use in the automotive aftermarket and had annual sales of $45 million. Later that year the company made its largest acquisition yet, that of Stonhard Inc., which boasted sales of $100 million in a new market for RPM—industrial flooring products, including applications for corrosion control and waterproofing. A still larger purchase came in mid-1994 in the culmination of a 15-year courtship of Rust-Oleum Corporation. Having acquired the company's European operations in 1991, RPM was finally able to take over Rust-Oleum itself, its well-known brand name, and its $140 million in sales of protective paints and coatings. The Rust-Oleum acquisition—a $178 million purchase—along with that of hobby paint maker Skilcraft, helped propel RPM's sales past $1 billion for the first time in fiscal 1995. Net income for the year was $61.1 million, more than double the 1990 figure of $27.7 million.

In September 1995 RPM paid $110 million for Providence, Rhode Island-based Dryvit Systems, Inc., maker of exterior insulation finishing systems used in the construction and renovation of homes and commercial buildings. Dryvit had annual sales of about $75 million. As part of a drive to increase international sales, RPM in early 1996 established, through Dryvit, a manufacturing operation in Poland where Dryvit and other RPM products would be produced for sale in eastern and central Europe and in Russia. This and other overseas moves helped increase international sales from $200 million in 1996 (18 percent of overall sales) to $300 million in 1997 (22 percent).

The next major acquisition—and once again the biggest yet—came in February 1997 when RPM purchased Tremco, Inc. from BFGoodrich Company for $236 million in cash. The Tremco business sought by RPM was its roofing systems, sealants, and coatings unit that mainly served the building maintenance sector. Having taken on long-term debt to finance the

Tremco acquisition, RPM later in 1997 reduced its debt load by selling off two noncore Tremco units—an insulating glass business and an auto glass operation, both of which served the original equipment manufacturer market—as well as Craft House, whose line of retail craft products was no longer considered a core area. The purchase of Tremco also led to the merging of two related RPM subsidiaries into the newly acquired firm—Mameco International and the founding RPM firm, Republic Powdered Metals. Meanwhile, in October 1997 RPM and its shareholders celebrated 50 consecutive years of sales and earnings gains at an annual meeting that featured a private concert by the Cleveland Orchestra.

RPM made several acquisitions in 1998 and 1999; these were all on the small side with the exception of two. In March 1998 the company acquired Flecto Company, Inc., the number two North American maker of interior wood stains and finishes through its Varathane and Watco brands. Then in early August 1999 RPM bolstered its do-it-yourself lines with the $290 million cash purchase of DAP Products Inc. and DAP Canada Corp. DAP was the leading maker of caulks, sealants, spackling compounds, and adhesives, selling $250 million in product each year under such brands as DAP, Kwik-Seal, and Durabond.

Within days of completing the DAP acquisition, RPM announced that it would undertake the first major restructuring in its history. Precipitating this initiative was a slackening of sales growth in North America, coupled with the continued downturn in certain overseas markets, most notably in Asia and South America, as well as an increase in service and distribution expenses. The restructuring involved the closing of 23 manufacturing, administrative, and distribution facilities; the elimination of 730 positions from the workforce; and a consolidation of product line distribution and warehousing. Perhaps the most dramatic change was the grouping of operating companies into product-line-centered groups, each of which was responsible for several brands. This had already been successfully carried out with the establishment of the Tremco Group and the merging of Mameco and Republic Powdered Metals into it. Tremco was one of three product line groups within the industrial division, which also included the StonCor Group, which combined Stonhard, Carboline, Plasite Protective Coatings, and Fibergrate Composite Structures, and which concentrated on corrosion protection and polymer technology; and RPM II Group, which was a sort of catch-all grouping that included the remaining industrial product lines and that would specialize in evaluating and acquiring small entrepreneurial companies. RPM's consumer division included three new groups: the Wood Finishes Group, which included Flecto and other wood finishing lines; the Bondo/Pettit, Woolsey/Z-Spar Group, which concentrated on the marine and automotive aftermarket; and the DAP/Bondex Group, which amalgamated the company's household patch and repair products. Other consumer groups included Rust-Oleum, Zinsser, and Testor.

Coincident with the restructuring were a host of management changes, highlighted by the formation of an office of the chairman consisting of Tom Sullivan, chairman and CEO, and Karman, vice-chairman; and the promotion of Sullivan's son, Frank C., to president. RPM also planned to divest within two years several noncore businesses whose combined annual sales were $100 million. The company took a $52 million restructuring charge during the 2000 fiscal year, which brought an end to the streak of consecutive years of increasing net income, at 52 years. Profits fell 57 percent, from $94.5 million in 1999 to $41 million in 2000. Sales, however, increased for the 53rd straight year, rising 14 percent, to almost $2 billion. Despite the profit setback, RPM had posted a remarkable record in the 1990s, with sales increasing more than fourfold from the $444.8 million figure of 1990.

Principal Subsidiaries

American Emulsions Co., Inc.; Bondo Corporation; Carboline Company; Chemical Coatings, Inc.; Chemical Specialties Manufacturing Corporation; DAP, Inc.; Day-Glo Color Corporation; Dryvit Systems, Inc.; Euclid Chemical Company; Fibergrate Composite Structures, Inc.; Flecto Company, Inc.; Guardian Products, Inc.; H. Behlen & Bro., Inc.; Mantrose Bradshaw Zinsser Group; Martin Mathys N.V. (Belgium); Mohawk Finishing Products of Canada; Mohawk Finishing Products, Inc.; Plasite Protective Coatings, Inc.; Radiant Color N.V. (Belgium); RPM Asia Pte. Ltd. (Singapore); RPM/Belgium, N.V.; Rust-Oleum Corporation; Rust-Oleum France S.A.; Rust-Oleum Netherlands B.V.; Star Specialty Coatings; StonCor Group; Stonhard, Inc.; TCI, Inc.; Testor Corporation; Tremco Inc.; Tremco Retail Products of Canada; Westfield Coatings Corporation; William Zinsser & Co.; Wolman Consumer Products; Wood Finishes Group.

Principal Divisions

Industrial Division (including the Tremco Group, the StonCor Group, and RPM II Group); Consumer Division (including the Rust-Oleum Group; the Zinsser Group; the Wood Finishes Group; the Bondo/Pettit, Woolsey/Z-Spar Group; the DAP/Bondex Group; and the Testor Hobby and Leisure Group).

Principal Competitors

Akzo Nobel N.V.; BASF AG; Benjamin Moore & Co.; Dainippon Ink & Chemicals, Incorporated; E.I. du Pont de Nemours and Company; Ferro Corporation; H.B. Fuller Company; Henkel KGaA; Imperial Chemical Industries PLC; Lawter International, Inc.; Lilly Industries, Inc.; Minnesota Mining and Manufacturing Company; NL Industries, Inc.; PPG Industries, Inc.; Rohm and Haas Company; Sherwin-Williams Company; The Valspar Corporation; WD-40 Company.

Further Reading

Batchelor, Bob, "Full RPM," *Inside Business,* October 1999.

Bendix, Jeffrey, "RPM Stirs It Up!" *Cleveland Enterprise,* Summer 1992.

Byrne, Harlan S., "Golden Anniversary," *Barron's* November 3, 1997, p. 49.

——, "RPM Inc.: It's a Good Bet to Extend Its Long String of Earnings Gains," *Barron's,* February 5, 1990, pp. 57–58.

Byrnes, Nanette, "Take the Money and Stay: RPM's Disciplined Management Formula Adds Up to Profits," *Financial World,* April 13, 1993, pp. 54–55.

Cimperman, Jennifer Scott, "RPM Executive Tries to Create Own Legacy at Family Firm," *Cleveland Plain Dealer,* August 29, 1999, p. 1D.

——, "RPM Plans to Slash 730 Jobs," *Cleveland Plain Dealer,* August 10, 1999, p. 1C.

——, "RPM Warns Profits Expected to Dip for 2000," *Cleveland Plain Dealer,* July 12, 2000, p. 2C.

D'Amico, Esther, "The Entrepreneurial Finish," *Paint and Coatings Industry,* April 1999.

Gerdel, Thomas W., "Medina Firm Is Top Corporate Achiever in Dividend Payout," *Cleveland Plain Dealer,* December 10, 1983, p. 2C.

——, "RPM Inc. Agrees on Deal for DAP," *Cleveland Plain Dealer,* July 13, 1999, p. 1C.

Gleisser, Marcus, "RPM Splits Stock, Hikes Dividend for 19th Straight Year," *Cleveland Plain Dealer,* October 10, 1992, p. 1F.

Harrow, Victoria, "Paint by Number," *Small Business News-Akron,* March 1999, p. 31.

Hine, Claudia, "RPM Merges Mameco Line into Newly Acquired Tremco," *Adhesives Age,* June 1997, pp. 37–38.

Karle, Delinda, "Medina Firm's Radon Sealant Excites Investors," *Cleveland Plain Dealer,* October 3, 1988, p. 5B.

Kiesche, Elizabeth S., "The Secret of RPM's Success: Good People and Good Acquisitions," *Chemical Week,* January 27, 1993, p. 51.

Koshar, John Leo, "Burgeoning RPM Reorganizes," *Cleveland Plain Dealer,* September 30, 1978, p. 4D.

Marcial, Gene G., "Has This Outfit Found a Miracle for Oil Spills?" *Business Week,* May 22, 1989, p. 150.

Maturi, Richard J., "Finance: Not Just for Giants," *Industry Week,* October 5, 1987, pp. 34–35.

"Metals Firm Chief Frank Sullivan Dies," *Cleveland Plain Dealer,* August 19, 1971.

"Page from Father's Book Led to Successful Acquisitions," *Cleveland Plain Dealer,* September 18, 1986, p. 15B.

Phillips, Stephen, "RPM Buying Subsidiary of B.F. Goodrich: Tremco Sought for Its Line of Roofing Products," *Cleveland Plain Dealer,* October 23, 1996, p. 1C.

"Profit Protector: RPM's Winning Streak Left Unbroken by Economy's Slump," *Barron's,* August 8, 1983, pp. 42–43.

"Radon Gas Sealant Rings Stock Bells for Medina's RPM," *Cleveland Plain Dealer,* September 24, 1988, p. 10C.

"The Radon Scare Has RPM Glowing," *Business Week,* October 17, 1988, p. 102.

Rehak, Judith, "Sealing the Deal," *Chief Executive,* December 1996, p. 31.

"Revving Up: RPM Inc.'s Sales Speed Ahead with a Boost from Carboline Co." *Barron's,* December 9, 1985, p. 68.

"RPM Becomes Major Player with Purchase of Day-Glo," *Cleveland Plain Dealer,* August 31, 1991, p. 1F.

"RPM Called Safe As Nest Egg; Dividends, Stock Grow Yearly," *Cleveland Plain Dealer,* September 18, 1986, pp. 14B, 15B.

"RPM Chairman Predicts More Good Years," *Cleveland Plain Dealer,* October 31, 1985, p. 6B.

"RPM Inc.'s Power of Persuasion," *Mergers and Acquisitions,* July/August 1994, p. 53.

"A Star Performer That the Pros Have Overlooked," *Business Week,* July 29, 1985, p. 68.

Yerak, Rebecca, "Lessons Learned the Hard Way Give Local Executives Business Savvy," *Cleveland Plain Dealer,* March 1, 1992, pp. 1E, 3E.

——, "RPM Inc. to Sell, Merge Divisions," *Cleveland Plain Dealer,* February 4, 1997, p. 1C.

——, "RPM Sells Third Unit in Month," *Cleveland Plain Dealer,* June 26, 1997, p. 1C.

——, "Staying on Schedule: RPM Inc. Sticks to Five-Year Plans for Growth," *Cleveland Plain Dealer,* October 27, 1993, p. 1F.

—April S. Dougal
—updated by David E. Salamie

SANYO Electric Co., Ltd.

5-5, Keihan-Hondori 2-chome
Moriguchi City
Osaka 570-8677
Japan
Telephone: (06) 6991-1181
Fax: (06) 6991-6566
Web site: http://www.sanyo.co.jp/koho/index_e.html

Public Company
Incorporated: 1950
Employees: 77,071
Sales: ¥1.94 trillion (US$18.31 billion) (2000)
Stock Exchanges: Tokyo Osaka Amsterdam Frankfurt
  Swiss Paris
NAIC: 333311 Automatic Vending Machine Mfg.; 333312
  Commercial Laundry, Drycleaning, & Pressing Machine
  Mfg.; 333313 Office Machinery Mfg.; 333315 Photo-
  graphic & Photocopying Equipment Mfg.; 333319 Other
  Commercial & Service Industry Machinery Mfg.; 333415
  Air-Conditioning & Warm Air Heating Equipment &
  Commercial & Industrial Refrigeration Equipment Mfg.;
  334111 Electronic Computer Mfg.; 334112 Computer
  Storage Device Mfg.; 334119 Other Computer Peripheral
  Equipment Mfg.; 334210 Telephone Apparatus Mfg.;
  334220 Radio & Television Broadcasting & Wireless
  Communications Equipment Mfg.; 334310 Audio &
  Video Equipment Mfg.; 334411 Electron Tube Mfg.;
  334413 Semiconductor & Related Device Mfg.; 334511
  Search, Detection, Navigation, Guidance, Aeronautical, &
  Nautical System & Instrument Mfg.; 335121 Residential
  Electric Lighting Fixture Mfg.; 335122 Commercial, Industrial, & Institutional Electric Lighting Fixture Mfg.;
  335211 Electric Housewares & Household Fan Mfg.;
  335212 Household Vacuum Cleaner Mfg.; 335221 Household Cooking Appliance Mfg.; 335222 Household Refrigerator & Home Freezer Mfg.; 335224 Household Laundry
  Equipment Mfg.; 335228 Other Major Household Appliance Mfg.; 335911 Storage Battery Mfg.; 335912 Primary
  Battery Mfg.; 336991 Motorcycle, Bicycle, & Parts Mfg.;
  336999 All Other Transportation Equipment Mfg.; 339113
  Surgical Appliance & Supplies Mfg.

SANYO Electric Co., Ltd. (Sanyo) is a leading global manufacturer of numerous electronic products. The company produces
video equipment, including televisions, VCRs, and video cameras; audio equipment, including CD players, minidisc players,
and car stereos; home appliances, including refrigerators, vacuum
cleaners, small kitchen appliances, and dehumidifiers; industrial
and commercial equipment, including refrigerator/freezer supermarket showcases, vending machines, incubators, and golf carts;
and information systems and electronic devices, including personal computers, copiers, point-of-sale systems, and semiconductors. A particular area of emphasis is that of environmentally
friendly products, such as rechargeable batteries, solar cells, and
CFC-free compressors for refrigerators and air conditioners. Another growth area is multimedia products, such as digital cameras, LCD projectors, and digital cellular phones. Sanyo has
about 150 subsidiaries and affiliates in 27 countries; about half of
overall sales are generated outside of Japan, with about 20
percent originating elsewhere in Asia, about 17 percent in North
America, and about eight percent in Europe.

Early History: Created Out of Matsushita Electric

Sanyo was born in the shadow of the giant Matsushita Electric
Industrial Co., Ltd., one of Japan's largest industrial institutions.
Sanyo's founder, Toshio Iue, was the brother-in-law of Konosuke
Matsushita and an original partner in Matsushita Electric. Shortly
after World War II, the occupation authority ordered Matsushita
broken up into two smaller companies as part of its industrial
decentralization policy. In 1947 several of Matsushita's operations were turned over to Iue, who set up his own company to
produce and export bicycle lamp generators. Dreaming of one
day having 100 factories around the world, Iue called his company SANYO Electric Works, "Sanyo" being a somewhat generic name that means "three oceans"—referring to the Pacific,
Atlantic, and Indian Oceans. On April 1, 1950, after paying off its
unsecured loans, the company was incorporated as SANYO Electric Co., Ltd. It went public in 1954.

The dynamic economic atmosphere in Japan after the Korean War raised personal incomes and stimulated consumer
demand. Sanyo grew modestly at first, offering only a limited
line of simple electrical appliances. To boost its sales through

Company Perspectives:

Management Philosophy: We are committed to becoming an indispensable element in the lives of people all over the world.

The Basic Meaning: It calls for the company to unite all its business entities as one corporate group that wins the heart and trust of the people all over the world by developing unique technologies and offering superior products and sincere services.

greater name recognition, Iue asked Matsushita for permission to use that company's brand name, National. With only minimal benefit from Matsushita's broad marketing network, Sanyo widened its product line in the early 1950s to include radios, tape recorders, and even televisions. The company later began marketing products under its own name through independent retailers.

Toshio Iue believed in a unique management philosophy called the "white paper" method. Similar to the process by which parliamentary governments announce general policy goals and invite criticism or discussion, the white paper system encouraged a consensus approach to management.

As the Japanese economy began to grow even faster during the mid-1950s, consumers, long deprived of even simple amenities, expressed increasing demand for household appliances. Sanyo was well established in the market and had great success in simple technology items such as washing machines, air conditioners, and improved radios. Iue did not regard other electrical manufacturers as his competition. Instead, he saw consumers—the ones who dictate the market—as competitors. This philosophy generated a very high creative awareness that forced him to anticipate new markets.

Sanyo created a separate affiliate in 1959 called Tokyo Sanyo Electric, which, Iue hoped, would make it easier for the company to respond to market demand and to raise capital. Although Sanyo eventually maintained only a 20 percent interest in Tokyo Sanyo, the two companies frequently engaged in bouts of constructive competition, what Iue himself described as a "friendly rivalry."

International Expansion in the 1960s and 1970s

In pursuit of his goal of running a worldwide company, Iue began to export Sanyo bike lamps to underdeveloped countries. He reasoned that as these countries developed, Sanyo's sales volume would grow accordingly, much as it had done in Japan. Most of these countries, however, lacked fundamental industrial bases, and although Sanyo outsold its European competitors, the growth he expected in these economies never materialized. In 1961 Sanyo established its first overseas factory in Hong Kong. Sanyo also entered into an agreement to market transistor radios in the United States with the American antenna manufacturer Channel Master in the 1950s. This arrangement later was expanded to include Sanyo televisions, tape recorders, and some home appliances.

In 1962 Sanyo marketed a revolutionary new type of battery called the Cadnica. Named for its cadmium and nickel components, the Cadnica was especially durable and also rechargeable. The battery became very popular at the high end of the market and represented a new and profitable product line.

During the mid-1960s Japan maintained such strong price competitiveness in certain market segments—especially textiles and consumer appliances—that these segments became the primary source of the country's exported growth. In 1965 Sanyo became a leading exporter, deriving an ever larger percentage of its profits from the United States.

Two years later, at the end of 1967, Toshio Iue relinquished the company presidency to his younger brother Yuro Iue. While the elder Iue continued to serve as chairman, Yuro made some important changes in the company's direction. He led the development of new divisions outside of the traditional consumer products markets and also placed a greater emphasis on Sanyo's internationalization.

Toshio Iue died in July 1969, leaving Yuro Iue in a dual role as president and chairman. At the end of 1970, he turned over the presidency to another brother, Kaoru Iue. Kaoru introduced a new sales plan to Sanyo, known as the "one-third marketing strategy." Under this scheme, Sanyo would attempt to diversify its manufacturing capacity geographically into three equal sectors: domestic manufacture for the domestic market, domestic manufacture for foreign markets, and foreign manufacture for additional foreign markets. Less a means to Toshio's "100 factories" than a method to reduce risks in the international trade structure, Kaoru's "one-third" plan nevertheless contributed to the balanced growth of the company on a global basis.

In 1973 the American company Emerson Electric asked Sanyo to help revive its subsidiary the Fisher Corporation. Fisher, acquired by Emerson in 1965, had moved its manufacturing operations to Hong Kong due to high labor costs, but continued to suffer from quality problems. The cooperation between Emerson and Sanyo continued until May 1975, when Sanyo, which still had no American manufacturing affiliate, engineered the transfer of several Fisher product lines to Japan and rehabilitated a Fisher speaker plant at Milroy, Pennsylvania. As 50–50 partners, Sanyo and Emerson were unable to resolve numerous differences of opinion in regard to Fisher. Finally, in May 1977 Emerson agreed to sell its share in Fisher to Sanyo. That year the new, profitable Fisher Corporation moved its headquarters from New York to Los Angeles.

Sanyo realized tremendous growth during the 1970s; sales grew from $71.4 million in 1972 to $855 million in 1978. Subsequent growth, particularly in the video sector, was slowed by the ill-fated decision to adopt Sony's Betamax VCR format instead of Matsushita's VHS. Although initially successful, the Betamax eventually became all but obsolete. Sanyo avoided further damage by later switching to the VHS format.

During the same decade it became increasingly evident that to remain competitive in world electronics, Sanyo would have to move more decisively into high-technology markets. This process was begun in the mid-1970s, but pursued in earnest only in the late 1970s, when a variety of products and integrated systems, ranging from LED televisions to home solar energy systems,

Key Dates:

1947: Several operations of Matsushita Electric are turned over to Toshio Iue, who forms Sanyo Electric Works.
1950: Company is incorporated as SANYO Electric Company, Ltd.
1952: Production of radios begins.
1954: Company goes public.
1955: Production of televisions begins.
1959: An affiliate called Tokyo Sanyo Electric is created.
1961: First overseas factory is established in Hong Kong.
1962: The Cadnica rechargeable battery is introduced.
1973: Sanyo begins working with U.S. firm Emerson Electric on reviving Fisher Corporation.
1977: Sanyo takes full control of Fisher.
1986: Sanyo Electric and Tokyo Sanyo merge.
1987: Sanyo's U.S. affiliate merges with Fisher to form Sanyo Fisher (U.S.A.) Corporation.
1988: Sanyo North America Corporation is created as Sanyo's U.S. headquarters.
1990: Nickel-metal hydride batteries are introduced; company develops CFC-free absorption-type chiller/heaters and refrigeration systems.
1992: Company introduces a solar air conditioner.
1994: Lithium ion rechargeable batteries are marketed for the first time.
1995: Company's first digital still camera is introduced.
1999: Major reorganization rearranges operations into five newly created ''truly independent'' companies.

were introduced commercially. Several manufacturing facilities and sales organizations were established in Europe and China.

Mergers: Marking the 1980s

In 1985 a research institute was inaugurated at Tsukuba, the Tsukuba Research Center. By the following year, in light of the increased industrial concentration of competitors and the rising value of the yen, the sibling rivalry between Sanyo Electric and Tokyo Sanyo had become uneconomic. It was decided at that time to merge the two companies to form the ''New Sanyo Electric.'' Similarly, the following year, Sanyo's U.S. affiliate merged with Fisher to become Sanyo Fisher (U.S.A.) Corporation (later renamed Sanyo Fisher Company). The mergers made the entire organization more efficient, but also resulted in the departure of certain key executives, most notably Howard Ladd, a Fisher executive who first introduced the Sanyo name to the United States in the early 1970s.

Kaoru Iue resigned suddenly in 1986 as a demonstration of responsibility for the deaths of customers who died using faulty Sanyo kerosene heaters. He was succeeded by Toshio Iue's son, Satoshi Iue, and subsequently died two years later.

Sanyo's new president promised to expand the company's overseas production capacity. Already the largest Japanese manufacturer outside of Japan, Sanyo built refrigerators in Kenya, portable stereos in Zimbabwe, and air conditioners in Singapore, and operated a television factory in Argentina's desolate Tierra del Fuego. Despite labor problems at a large plant in Arkansas, Sanyo intended to expand in the United States. To that end, in 1988 Sanyo created Sanyo North America Corporation as its U.S. headquarters, with 24 subsidiaries and affiliates.

Roller Coaster 1990s

The bursting of the Japanese economic bubble in 1991 threw the country's economy into a lengthy downturn. Sanyo, like most Japanese electronics firms, was hurt by the difficult economic operating environment at home, where consumer demand—particularly for audio-video equipment—went into a steep decline. Overseas, the electronics firms felt the effects of a high yen, which made Japanese exports more expensive—as did high Japanese labor costs. In late 1992, shortly after the company posted a net loss for the 1992 fiscal year, Satoshi Iue stepped down as president of Sanyo and assumed the mostly ceremonial role of chairman. Yasuaki Takano stepped in as president, having been promoted from the title of vice-president he had held since 1986. Takano assumed responsibility for implementing a sweeping restructuring, which included the shifting of additional production outside of Japan, the adopting of a decentralized management system that focused on discrete profit centers, and an overhaul of the company's audio-video and office automation businesses to cut costs and improve profits. In 1993 Sanyo revamped its research and development activities by consolidating eight R&D facilities into five, creating an overall R&D system that consisted of 13 facilities.

Sanyo also aimed to focus more on value-added products, particularly in those areas in which the company was ahead of the competition. One such area was that of environmentally friendly products, such as rechargeable batteries. In 1990 Sanyo had already extended its offerings to include nickel-metal hydride batteries, which offered 50 percent more energy output than nickel-cadmium batteries, lasted longer, and were free of cadmium, a toxic heavy metal. The even more powerful lithium ion rechargeable battery was introduced in 1994. Meanwhile, in 1990 Sanyo developed new CFC-free absorption-type chiller/heaters and refrigeration systems incorporating hydrogen-absorbing alloys. Such systems were used to heat and cool large buildings, and Sanyo was the clear world leader in such technology in the 1990s. Solar energy continued to be a key area as well, and the company introduced a solar air conditioner in 1992. Three years later Sanyo's solar energy operations were bolstered through the establishment of Sanyo Solar Industries Co., Ltd. Another ''clean energy'' initiative was the development of high-tech waste processors, which Sanyo first introduced in 1994. Available in both home and commercial versions, these devices transformed organic trash—banana peels, coffee grinds, fish bones—into a soil-like substance that could be used as a fertilizer. Sales began to take off in 1997 when the prices of these appliances, which were initially available only in Japan, began to fall.

After posting another loss in 1993, Sanyo returned to the black in 1994 when it reported net income of US$114.5 million on revenue of US$17.12 billion. The following year Sanyo established Sanyo Electric (China) Co., Ltd. to serve as its headquarters subsidiary in China, where by the end of the decade the company had more than 30 subsidiaries and affiliates, 25 of which were manufacturing operations producing air conditioners, consumer electronics, semiconductors, compressors, home appliances, telecommunications equipment, and numerous other products.

Also in 1995 Sanyo introduced its first digital still camera, part of its drive to "enrich people's lives" through multimedia technologies. The company's digital cameras were well received in the market, and by early 1998 Sanyo was making about 30 percent of the world output—more than any other firm—including brands that Sanyo produced for other companies. In the 1990s Sanyo also successfully entered the field of LCD projectors, which were used to make computer-based presentations. By 1998 the company held 15 percent of the world market, placing it in the number two position. Among the company's other key multimedia products in the late 1990s were digital cellular telephones and other personal communications devices.

During the fiscal year ending in March 1999, another management change occurred; Takano was named vice-chairman while Sadao Kondo was promoted to president. Despite Sanyo's continuing innovation, troubles recurred in the late 1990s as a result of the continuing sluggishness of the Japanese economy and the Asian economic crisis that erupted in mid-1997. Profits fell during fiscal 1998, then the company posted a net loss of ¥25.9 billion (US$216 million) for fiscal 1999. In the wake of this result, Sanyo announced in April 1999 a major reorganization that rearranged all of its operations into five newly created "truly independent" companies—Multimedia Company, Home Appliances Company, Commercial Equipment Systems Company, Semiconductor Company, and Soft Energy Company—each with its own president and its own business strategies tied to basic overall objectives of increasing sales, cutting costs, and utilizing human resources in the most effective manner. The company also reformed the role of its board of directors, making the board more action-oriented and giving it greater oversight powers; the membership of the board also was overhauled, most notably with the addition of Corazon C. Aquino, former president of the Philippines. At the same time, Sanyo announced that it would reduce its overall workforce by 6,000 by March 2002, seeking to save about ¥40 billion (US$330 million) annually in labor costs.

Other initiatives that looked toward the new century included several alliances with leading global firms. Sanyo was working with Koninklijke Philips Electronics N.V. of the Netherlands on developing optical sensors used in digital still and digital video cameras. In February 1999 Sanyo entered into an alliance with Eastman Kodak Company to jointly develop next-generation, organic electroluminescent, flat panel displays for use in digital cameras and personal digital assistants. In April 1999 Sanyo diversified into the financial securities industry through the purchase of a 55 percent stake in Osaka-based Yamagen Securities Co., Ltd., an integrated securities company focused on the retail market.

By early 2000 the Japanese economy had not yet fully recovered but other Asian economies were on the upswing and the U.S. and European markets continued to expand. In this environment Sanyo was able to bounce back with solid results

for fiscal 2000: net income of ¥21.7 billion (US$204.6 million) on net sales of ¥1.94 trillion (US$18.31 billion). During the early 21st century, Sanyo planned to continue to focus on multimedia and clean energy. Within these fields, the company had identified three areas that it felt had great potential for growth: products related to a home-based information society, such as "smart" appliances; products related to healthcare, food hygiene control, and an aging society; and environmentally friendly products, such as rechargeable batteries for hybrid vehicles. Sanyo was placing itself on the cutting edge of several potentially explosive areas of 21st-century growth, setting the stage for an exciting if somewhat uncertain future.

Principal Subsidiaries

Tottori Sanyo Electric Co., Ltd.; Sanyo Electric Trading Co., Ltd.; Sanyo Life Electronics Co., Ltd.; Sanyo Electric Credit Co., Ltd.; Sanyo Electric Logistics Co., Ltd.; Sanyo Electric Software Co., Ltd.; Sanyo Electronic Components Co., Ltd.; Sanyo Electric (China) Co., Ltd.; Sanyo North America Corporation (U.S.A.); Sanyo Electric (Hong Kong) Limited; BPL Sanyo Finance Limited; Sanyo Asia Pte., Ltd. (Singapore); Sanyo Europe Ltd. (U.K.).

Principal Divisions

Multimedia Company—TV & Visual Display Products Division; Video Imaging Systems Division; Information Systems Division; Personal Telecommunication Division; Medical Systems Division. Home Appliances Company—Laundry & Cooking Appliances Division; Motor Applied Products Division; Air Conditioning Division; Refrigeration Products Division; Compressor Division. Commercial Equipment Systems Company—Commercial Air Conditioning Division; Vending Machine Division; Food Service Systems Division. Semiconductor Company—TR Division; Thick Film IC Division; BIP-LSI Division; MOS-LSI Division; LCD Division; Domestic Marketing Division; Overseas Marketing Division. Soft Energy Company—New Battery Division; Cadnica Division; Twicell Division; Ion Battery Division; System Battery & Procurement Division; Primary Battery Division; Lighting & Portable Energy Product Division; Battery Sales & Marketing Division.

Principal Divisions

Advanced Micro Devices, Inc.; Apple Computer, Inc.; The Black & Decker Corporation; Canon Inc.; Casio Computer Co., Ltd.; Compaq Computer Corporation; Dell Computer Corporation; Aktiebolaget Electrolux; Fujitsu Limited; General Electric Company; The Gillette Company; Hewlett-Packard Company; Hitachi, Ltd.; Intel Corporation; International Business Machines Corporation; Kyocera Corporation; Lanier Worldwide, Inc.; LG Group; Marconi plc; Matsushita Electric Industrial Co., Ltd.; Maytag Corporation; National Semiconductor Corporation; NCR Corporation; NEC Corporation; Nokia Corporation; Oki Electric Industry Company, Limited; Olivetti S.p.A.; Koninklijke Philips Electronics N.V.; Pioneer Electronic Corporation; Pitney Bowes Inc.; Ralston Purina Company; Ricoh Company, Ltd.; Samsung Group; Seiko Epson Corporation; Sharp Corporation; Siemens AG; Sony Corporation; THOMSON multimedia; Toshiba Corporation; Victor Company of Japan, Limited; Whirlpool Corporation.

Further Reading

Anzai, Tatsuya, ''Making It in China: Sanyo Electric,'' *Tokyo Business Today,* April 1992, p. 51.

Armstrong, Larry, ''Sanyo Tries to Stay One Step Ahead of the Yen,'' *Business Week,* June 9, 1986, p. 46.

''Basic Training, Sanyo Style,'' *U.S. News and World Report,* July 13, 1992, p. 46.

''Consumer Electronics Industry Shows Path of Growth Strategy—into the Abyss,'' *Tokyo Business Today,* October 1992, pp. 38–41.

Eisenstodt, Gale, ''Unidentical Twins,'' *Forbes,* July 5, 1993, p. 42.

Leung, Shirley, ''Sanyo's Chief Departure Is a Loss for Maquiladoras,'' *Wall Street Journal,* April 7, 1999.

Nakamoto, Michiyo, ''The Rising Yen Means Pain for a Supplier,'' *Financial Times,* January 1, 1994, p. 3.

——, ''Tough Times for Sanyo As Electronics Loses Its Spark,'' *Financial Times,* April 6, 1993, p. 24.

Rodger, Ian, ''Waiting for Its Day in the Sun,'' *Financial Times,* January 10, 1991, Sec. I, p. 8.

''Sanyo Sounds Out the Upscale Market,'' *Business Week,* June 11, 1984, p. 154L.

—updated by David E. Salamie

Sapporo Breweries Limited

20-1, Ebisu 4-chome
Shibuya-ku
Tokyo 150-8686
Japan
Telephone: (03) 5423-2111
Fax: (03) 5423-2057
Web site: http://www.sapporobeer.co.jp

Public Company
Incorporated: 1949 as Nippon Breweries, Ltd.
Employees: 5,820
Sales: ¥572.92 billion (US$5.59 billion) (1999)
Stock Exchanges: Tokyo Osaka Nagoya Sapporo
NAIC: 312120 Breweries; 312130 Wineries; 312111 Soft
    Drink Manufacturing; 312112 Bottled Water
    Manufacturing; 422810 Beer and Ale Wholesalers;
    531120 Lessors of Nonresidential Buildings (Except
    Miniwarehouses); 721110 Hotels (Except Casino
    Hotels) and Motels; 722211 Limited-Service
    Restaurants; 722410 Drinking Places (Alcoholic
    Beverages)

Over the course of its more than 120-year history, Sapporo Breweries Limited has evolved from a government-owned beer maker into a multifaceted consumer products concern. In the early 21st century, its interests included the namesake Sapporo beers and a full line of soft drinks, wine, teas, and coffees, as well as real estate, restaurants, and hotels. Sapporo Breweries also imports Guinness Irish stout into Japan. Along with Kirin Brewery Company, Limited, Asahi Breweries, Ltd., and Suntory Ltd., Sapporo ranks among Japan's ''Big Four'' breweries; it holds about 16 percent of the country's beer market, placing it number three behind Kirin and Asahi. Overseas, the Sapporo brand is the best-selling Japanese beer in the United States and is also exported to Taiwan; Sapporo Premium Lager is produced in Ireland on a contract basis by Diageo plc and sold throughout Europe; and a joint venture in China brews Sapporo Premium Lager for the local market.

Late 19th-Century Founding

Beer was introduced to Japan in the mid-1800s. The American primarily responsible for renewing trade relations with Japan, Commodore Matthew Perry, brought several cases of beer to Japan as a gift for the Tokugawa Shogunate. The beverage was so well liked that the Japanese government soon decided to establish a brewing industry. After an extensive search for a suitable area, wild hops were found growing on the island of Hokkaido, the northernmost island in the Japanese archipelago. As a result, in 1876 the Commissioner-General for the development of Hokkaido founded Japan's first brewery in the town of Sapporo. (Coincidentally, the global beer capitols of Munich, Milwaukee, and Sapporo are all located along the 45 degrees north latitude.)

The original government facility was designed by the brewmaster Seibei Nakagawa, who had returned to Japan after studying beer-making techniques in Germany. The first product brewed in the factory was called Sapporo cold beer or German beer, and even some of the early labels were printed in German as well as in Japanese.

In 1886 the brewery was sold by the government to Okura-Gumi, a private trading company. One year later, Okura-Gumi itself was purchased by a group of Japanese businessmen, who then reorganized the brewing operations under the name Sapporo Brewery Ltd. A number of other breweries, which would soon figure prominently in Sapporo's development, also were started during this time, including Nippon Brewing Company Ltd., Osaka Brewery, Kirin Brewery Company, and the Nippon Beer Kosen Brewery.

1906–49: The Dai Nippon Era

In 1906 the Sapporo Brewery, the Nippon Brewing Company, and the Osaka Brewery were amalgamated as the Dai Nippon Brewery Co., Ltd. This process of amalgamation and consolidation continued for 20 years until, in 1933, the Nippon Beer Kosen Brewery also was absorbed by Dai Nippon.

During the 1920s and 1930s Japanese militarists, implementing their plan to make Japan the dominant economic power

404

in Asia, began to centralize the brewing industry. By 1943, the merger of all Japanese breweries was virtually complete: Dai Nippon and Kirin were the only two brewing companies left in Japan. In fact, the militarists were powerful enough to force the Sapporo division of Dai Nippon to establish joint ventures in the occupied territories of Korea and Manchuria.

At this stage, local markets were dominated by particular brands. Dai Nippon sold Sapporo beer in the region north of the Kanto district, primarily in Hokkaido. The company also manufactured Yebisu and Asahi brand beers; the former was popular in the Tokyo area and the latter in the Kansai area. Not surprisingly, because of the increased demand for beer (it was rapidly superseding sake, the traditional drink), its production continued throughout the war.

Postwar Revival of Sapporo

The current structure of Japan's brewing industry originated after World War II during the U.S. occupation. In 1949 the Dai Nippon Brewery, which had cornered nearly 70 percent of the beer market in Japan, was divided into Nippon Breweries, Ltd. and Asahi Breweries, Ltd. Initially, Nippon Breweries marketed beer exclusively under its own brand name; it was not until 1956 that beer displaying the Sapporo label was reintroduced.

Nippon's growth during the postwar period, primarily because of an expanding product line, was impressive; from 1951 to 1981 production at the company's facilities increased by a factor of 15. During that same period, the brewery's sales increased from ¥20 billion to ¥330 billion, and its capitalization from ¥100 million to more than ¥14.1 billion. Supporting this growth was the construction of new breweries, in Osaka, in 1961; in Sendai, in 1971; and in Shizuoka, in 1980.

It was not until 1964 that the Nippon Breweries changed its name to Sapporo Breweries Limited. Shortly thereafter, arrangements were made to merge the Sapporo and Asahi breweries. By this time they had become the second and third largest breweries, respectively, in Japan. (Kirin had captured the largest share of the domestic beer market.) But the merger never materialized.

The formation of a joint venture with Guinness plc, called Sapporo-Guinness, also took place in 1964. This agreement led to the sale of Irish stout in Japan. By 1976 the consumption of stout beer had risen dramatically and a sales war ensued with the Kirin brewery, which had its own version of the beverage. Even though the cost of Guinness's product was twice that of Kirin's, Sapporo managed to maintain about 45 percent of the domestic stout market by relying heavily on Guinness's quality image.

In 1971 Sapporo reintroduced Yebisu Beer to the market as a premium 100 percent barley beer. That same year Sapporo entered the wine market when it formed a joint venture with Mitsui and Company Ltd. to import both wine and liquor. Sapporo Liquor Company Ltd. first began to import Nicolas, Hoch, and Melini wines. The company then started to produce its own wines at the Katsunuma Winery west of Tokyo in 1976; its Polaire brand of wine eventually would include the top five best-sellers in Japan. After the Okayama Winery was established in 1984, a wine cooler, a sparkling wine, and Hyosai, a white brandy, also were added to the growing domestically produced beverage line. In addition, the Sapporo Liquor Company imported Bailey's Irish Cream, Bombay Gin, Green Island Rum, and several scotches, including J&B Rare, Dunhill, Knockando, and Spay Royal.

First established in 1908, Sapporo's research and development division was created to breed varieties of barley and hops especially suited to Japan's climate. In the mid-1970s the Sapporo laboratory developed a technique for the ceramic filtration of beer. Since the introduction of pasteurization in the early part of the 20th century, beer had been sterilized by means of a heating process. This was necessary because the yeast residue in beer rendered it unsuitable for extended storage or long-distance transportation. Yet the problem with heating beer was that the high temperature affected its flavor. Sapporo's unique ceramic filtration method removed the yeast residue from beer without having to heat it. The beer was filtered at a constant temperature of zero to one degree centigrade through a long ceramic cylinder; a thin coating of diatomaceous earth in the tube trapped the yeast residue. The first draft beer made with this new process went on the market in 1977 ("Sapporo Black Label"), and in 1985 the filtration technology was exported to South Korea and to the Miller Brewing Company in the United States. Even so, Sapporo continued to pasteurize many of its products.

Throughout its history, rising prices for raw materials cut into company profits. Sapporo's supply of yeast came from a strain originally developed at the Sapporo laboratory. Although Sapporo brand name beer was brewed exclusively in Japan, much of the barley and hops used in its manufacture was, historically, imported from Canada, Australia, West Germany, and Czechoslovakia. During the 1970s the Japanese government raised the brewery's already high costs by requiring them to purchase domestically grown barley; this accounted for 20 to 25 percent of the barley used in the entire industry. Originally intended to protect farmers who had switched from the cultivation of rice (which was in surplus) to barley, the domestic strain cost brewers 3.7 times as much as imported ones.

In spite of such roadblocks, Sapporo grew consistently. In fact, from 1985 to 1987 the company enjoyed record sales and earnings. Sapporo attributed its success to reduced materials costs, a decreasing interest payment burden, and effective management of surplus funds. Furthermore, the appreciation of the

---

Key Dates:

1876: Japan's first brewery is built in Sapporo by the government.

1886: Government sells the brewery to a private trading company.

1887: Group of Japanese businessmen buy the brewery and reorganize it as Sapporo Brewery Ltd.

1906: The Sapporo Brewery, the Nippon Brewing Company, and the Osaka Brewery are amalgamated as Dai Nippon Brewery Co., Ltd.

1949: Dai Nippon is divided into Nippon Breweries, Ltd. and Asahi Breweries, Ltd.; Nippon Breweries is the successor to Sapporo Brewery but initially markets only Nippon Beer.

1956: Sapporo Beer is reintroduced into the Japanese market.

1964: Nippon Breweries changes its name to Sapporo Breweries Limited; through a joint venture with Guinness plc, the company begins selling Guinness Irish stout in Japan.

1971: Yebisu Beer is reintroduced as a premium, all-barley beer; company enters the wine market as an importer.

1976: Production of wine begins at the Katsunuma Winery, west of Tokyo.

1977: Company introduces the first draft beer, Sapporo Black Label.

1984: The company's first foreign subsidiary is established in the United States.

1994: Sapporo-developed Yebisu Garden Place, a downtown Tokyo office complex featuring retail outlets and condominiums, opens and becomes the company's new headquarters.

1995: Guinness begins contract production of Sapporo Premium Lager for European distribution.

1998: Production of Sapporo Premium Lager begins in China.

---

yen and the consequent lower price of foreign malt also helped boost results.

But as the Japanese beer market fast approached saturation in the mid-1980s, Sapporo sought new markets through geographic and product diversification. Having established distributorships in more than 30 countries around the world, the company founded its first full-fledged foreign subsidiary in the United States in 1984. The Sapporo brand quickly became the number one Japanese beer in the very large U.S. beer market.

Late 1980s and Early 1990s: New Products and Diversification

While striving to maintain a premium image for its flagship beers, Sapporo catered to both ends of the Japanese beer market in the late 1980s and early 1990s. The company introduced the gold-labeled Yebisu Beer and the ultra-dry Kissui ale for the upscale market. Around the same time, it inked a contract with the U.S.-based Stroh Brewing Company to import a bargain-priced beer into the country. After five years of research and development, the company also launched "Drafty," a sparkling alcoholic drink that the company was able to offer at a low price, because of the product's low malt content, which incurred less tax.

In 1988, Sapporo's research and development department expanded into the propagation of rare orchids for sale in the United States, Europe, and domestically. In addition, the Sapporo laboratory conducted research in fields such as soft drinks as well as the application of beer yeast to the development of food seasonings and health food products. Sapporo scientists also investigated the utilization of recent discoveries in biotechnology to develop agricultural chemicals and pharmaceuticals.

The seeds of Sapporo's burgeoning restaurant empire were planted with the establishment of the brewery's first beer hall back in 1899. By 1994, a beer hall division had grown to become Sapporo Lion Limited, a 180-location chain that contributed about five percent of the company's annual revenues and an incalculable amount to Sapporo's brand cachet. Echoing an American trend, the company began to develop several "brew-pubs" featuring boutique beers brewed on site.

Having put its first soft drink, Ribbon Citron, on the market as early as 1909, Sapporo placed ever-increasing emphasis on its nonalcoholic beverage line. By the late 1980s, this product segment included traditional and medicinal teas, Beans brand canned coffees, and a variety of carbonated sodas and mineral waters. The company concentrated on introducing all-natural, wholesome drinks with fruit flavors and light carbonation in the early 1990s.

Although real estate still only contributed 6.5 percent of Sapporo's total annual revenues in the early 1990s, this segment was considered the cornerstone of the company's diversification strategy. Development activities took center stage with the 1994 opening of the Yebisu Garden Place, a downtown Tokyo office complex that featured retail outlets and upscale condominiums that cost the company ¥295 billion and took ten years to complete. The brewer proudly moved its headquarters to the new facility that same year. But far from abandoning its historical birthplace, the company redeveloped its first brewery into what it referred to as a "cultural mall," incorporating public services, retail, and leisure centers.

Late 1990s and Beyond: Seeking Overseas Growth

The second half of the 1990s were marked by expansionary moves overseas. In 1995 the company began exporting the Black Label draft beer to Taiwan. By 1997 sales had exceeded one million cases. In October 1995 the alliance between Sapporo and Guinness expanded. That month, Guinness began contract production in Ireland of a beer called Sapporo Premium Lager. Sapporo contracted with Marubeni Corporation, a Japanese trading firm, to distribute Sapporo Premium in several countries in western Europe. In 1997 distribution was expanded to Russia, Poland, and Sweden. In the U.S. market, the long-successful Sapporo Draft brand was joined by Yebisu and Sapporo Black beer in 1996. The other key country targeted for growth was China. In December 1996 Sapporo established a joint venture with two of the leading breweries in Jiangsu Province, Jiangsu Brewery and Nangton Five Stars Brewery. The joint venture began producing Sapporo Premium Lager for local consumption in May 1998.

Back in Japan, the company's beer lineup underwent some changes. Black Label and Yebisu were steady performers, but Drafty was replaced first in January 1998 by Drafty Special and then in October 1998 by Bräu. The latter, like its predecessors, was part of a rapidly growing category called *Happo-shu,* or sparkling low-malt beverage. Bräu, which sported a low price and was touted for its hops that were grown without the use of chemicals, found more success than either version of Drafty. A fourth brand was added to the product line in 2000: Grand Beer. This beer was targeted at 20- and 30-somethings and according to the company was "characterized by crispness and a refreshing aftertaste."

Sapporo's more aggressive approach to developing new brands could be traced to the heightened competition that characterized the Japanese brewing industry in the late 1990s. The beer market in Japan was maturing, Japanese consumers were developing more diverse beverage tastes, and the appreciation of the yen provided a pricing advantage to what quickly became an onslaught of imported beers from the United States and Europe. Sapporo's revenues declined in both 1996 and 1997; worse yet, in 1997 the company posted its first net loss since its emergence out of Dai Nippon. This development was not tied to the company's struggling beer operations, but rather to an extraordinary loss of ¥29.4 billion from its securities holdings. In September 1998 Sapporo announced that it would reduce its workforce by about 1,000 by the end of 2001, in a cost-cutting and profit-enhancing move. The cuts were slated to be made through attrition, accelerated retirement, and a hiring freeze. Sapporo also planned to close two of its breweries in 2000 and a third in 2002. A further extraordinary loss tied to the slumping Japanese stock market led to a second straight net loss in 1998. Sapporo suffered another decline in sales in 1999, a 5.4 percent drop, but returned to the black, posting net income of ¥4.43 billion (US$43.3 million).

Principal Subsidiaries

Sapporo Lion Limited; Sapporo Wines Limited; Sapporo Beer's Beverage Co., Ltd.; Sapporo Development Co., Ltd.; Yebisu Garden Place Co., Ltd.; Sapporo Hotel Enterprises Limited; Chateau Restaurants Co., Ltd.; Sapporo Logistics System Co., Ltd.; Yebisu Winemart Company Limited; Sapporo Florist Company Limited; Tokyo Energy Service Co., Ltd.; Sapporo Agency Limited; Sapporo U.S.A., Inc.; Sapporo International Europe, B.V. (Netherlands).

Principal Competitors

Adolph Coors Company; Anheuser-Busch Companies, Inc.; Asahi Breweries, Ltd.; Kirin Brewery Company, Limited; Miller Brewing Company; Suntory Ltd.

Further Reading

Harney, Alexandra, "Sapporo to Cut Staff by 30 Percent," *Financial Times,* September 3, 1998, p. 33.

Kanabayashi, Masayoshi, "Top Japan Breweries Expand Quickly to Tap China's Beer Market," *Asian Wall Street Journal,* March 27, 1997, p. 4.

"Sapporo Beer Wants to Set New Challenges," *Yomiuri Report from Japan,* May 19, 1995, p. 3.

Tanaka, Kazuo, *The History of Sapporo Breweries Ltd.*, Sapporo-shi: Hokkaido Shinbunsha, 1993.

—April Dougal Gasbarre
—updated by David E. Salamie

Schlotzsky's, Inc.

203 Colorado Street
Austin, Texas 78701-3922
U.S.A.
Telephone: (512) 236-3600
Toll Free: (800) 846-BUNS; (800) 846-2867
Fax: (512) 236-3601
Web site: http://www.schlotzskys.com

Public Company
Founded: 1971
Employees: 240
Sales: $47.9 million (1999)
Stock Exchanges: NASDAQ
Ticker Symbol: BUNZ
NAIC: 722211 Limited-Service Restaurants; 311919
   Other Snack Food Manufacturing

John C. Wooley, chairman and CEO of the Austin, Texas-based Schlotzsky's, Inc., once stated, "If your name is Schlotzsky's, you can't take yourself too seriously." The award-winning company's trademarked slogan proclaims "Funny Name, Serious Sandwich," yet systemwide sales (corporate plus franchisee sales) of over $400 million for 1999 are no joke. Schlotzsky's is serving up serious competition for sandwich shops such as Subway, Blimpie, and Quizno's by opening an average of 100 new stores for four years in a row. With over two dozen sandwiches and pizzas, salads, soups, and desserts, Schlotzsky's has something for everyone—and to make sure potential new customers know their unusual name, the upscale deli ended the millennium by launching its first major network television ad campaign. With hundreds of restaurants in 38 states and 13 countries (including Argentina, Australia, Bahrain, Canada, China, Japan, Morocco, Turkey, and Venezuela), Schlotzsky's is nibbling its way to the top of the food chain.

"Just One Sandwich . . . It's That *Good!"': 1970s*

When bell bottoms were in (the first time) and not just hippies had long hair, a tiny sandwich shop in Austin, Texas, was opened by local entrepreneur Don Dissman. He sold only one kind of sandwich, and came up with a slogan touting just how delicious his creation was: "Just one sandwich . . . it's *that* good." Austin residents evidently agreed; Dissman's eight-inch round sandwich, served warm, consisted of ham, two kinds of salami, and three cheeses (melted cheddar, mozzarella, and parmesan). Yet the finishing touches of shredded lettuce, tomato, onion, marinated black olives, garlic, and spices made a Schlotzsky's sandwich the talk of the town. The foundation of the sandwich though was its lightly toasted sourdough bun, baked fresh daily from a "secret" recipe. The sandwich soon had a following in Austin and word spread throughout Texas.

Over the next few years, Schlotzsky's grew modestly by about ten percent a year. Dissman began considering expansion plans, and looked into franchising. By 1977 Dissman sold his first franchise, and a new Schlotzsky's opened in the college mecca of Bryan/College Station, home of Texas A & M University. Additional franchises soon popped up outside of Texas, in four neighboring states, and demand continued to grow. Nine years after opening the first Schlotzsky's, as the decade came to a close, Dissman expanded his menu by introducing a six-inch sandwich for lighter appetites, in addition to the original eight-inch classic.

Food for Thought: 1980s

The dawn of the 1980s brought major change: not only did customers continue to rave about Schlotzsky's both in and out of Texas, but by 1981 the chain had entered 13 states and garnered systemwide sales of almost $20 million annually. This year also saw the exit of Dissman, who sold the chain to a group that included John C. Wooley and Gary Bradley. When Wooley and Bradley parted ways the following year and divvied up their business assets, Wooley (along with his brother Jeff) kept the Schlotzsky's interest. The Wooley brothers found the economy slipping and needed to make changes to not only keep Schlotzsky's afloat, but to bolster their bottom line.

Throughout the remainder of the 1980s changes were slowly put into place, despite opposition from the franchisees who had been content to make the same six- and eight-inch sandwiches for over ten years. Yet the Wooleys (with John as CEO and Jeff as a senior vice-president) persevered and in collaboration with the Pillsbury Company came up with a standardized (though still secret) preservative-free bun mix. The brothers also addressed the element of time—Schlotzsky's signature sandwiches were made-to-order, which took time and required patience from customers. Then a new sandwich heating system, called the Marshall Air Conveyor, cut cooking time in half. Increased speed in the kitchen meant faster turnaround and happier customers; happier customers became repeat customers.

Further changes came in 1982 with the debut of the wheat bun, a redesigned logo, and overhauling the restaurant chain's sign. This same year, the first annual Bun Run Race was started in Austin to benefit local charities and improve the community. The idea was welcomed and spread to cities nationwide. Later the Coca-Cola Corporation joined up as co-sponsor of the event, which was rechristened "Run Your Buns Off." The next year, 1983, brought two new Schlotzsky's sandwich selections (roast beef and turkey), followed by the steam-injected baking oven which led to a "two-pass" cheese-melting system in 1986. Another new sandwich, the Philly Cheesesteak, was added in 1987, and the first international restaurant opened in Canada in 1988.

From Sandwich Shop to Upscale Deli: 1990–98

In the early 1990s CEO John Wooley broke the age-old adage "If it ain't broke, don't fix it," by tinkering with Schlotzsky's modestly thriving empire. Both Wooley brothers believed Schlotzsky's had far greater potential than they or their franchisees had tapped, and were convinced the chain could be an international powerhouse. First, Austin restaurant consultant and chef Mike Dyer was hired to spice up Schlotzsky's menu from its six core sandwiches. He added new bread and sandwich varieties, then brought pizzas, soups, salads, and desserts to the menu. John Wooley had decided to offer the latest menu items only at new stores, letting existing franchises determine if and when to adopt the expanded menu (within a year all had come on board). Next came a plan to revise the chain's made-up name (Dissman had liked the old-world charm of the imaginary moniker) since most people did not know what a "Schlotzsky's" was—a Nevada man had once guessed it was a Polish plumbing supply business. The problem was solved by simply adding "Deli" to the name, which took away the guesswork and potential confusion. Then the Schlotzsky's name was parlayed into proprietary brands, beginning with deli-style potato chips, which were soon available in all of the chain's 234 stores by 1992.

By 1994 Schlotzsky's systemwide sales approached $100 million with 353 restaurants in North America, and the follow-

ing year the first international deli stores opened in Japan and Argentina, bringing the total to 463 locations worldwide. At this time the new 2,100-square-foot prototype debuted, as Wooley moved away from strip malls and into stand-alone locations. The newer stores were an immediate hit with weekly sales climbing to $15,000, nearly double those of the existing stores. In mid-December 1995 Schlotzsky's went public, offering shares at $11 each on the NASDAQ under the ticker symbol BUNZ (a second offering raised $29 million two years later). Year-end systemwide sales reached $143 million in 1995, then catapulted to $202 million by the following year with 573 restaurants in North America and beyond.

Within a few years Wooley took his new vision further, by redesigning even larger freestanding locations from 2,700 to 3,200 square feet, with a seating capacity of 70 to 85 patrons. The outside and interiors of all Schlotzsky's outlets were redone, so both old and new stores had a brick facade with green and white awnings on the outside, and warm, inviting wooden furniture and deli cases on the inside. The new decor was hip, fresh, and casual; Schlotzsky's Deli had become a delicious departure from traditional fast food with a menu suitable for the whole family.

The company helped new franchisees build the updated prototypes (with a price tag of more than $1 million each) with interim financing until the concept had proven itself. New stores were, indeed, wildly successful, with weekly sales averaging double that of their existing counterparts. The new design, along with drive-throughs at some units, brought Schlotzsky's increased exposure and skyrocketing sales: while most older outlets had weekly sales in the $10,000 range, newer Schlotzsky's Deli restaurants had brought in weekly sales from $25,000 to $61,000 a week. Technomic, a Chicago-based restaurant industry research firm, named Schlotzsky's as the fastest growing sandwich chain in the United States, with an average of 100 new units yearly between 1995 and 1998. Additionally in 1998, Schlotzsky's became the 37th restaurant chain in U.S. history to have surpassed the 700-unit mark (750 total) with year-end systemwide sales topping $349 million.

Schlotzsky's Kind of "Counter Culture": 1999 and Beyond

In early 1999 Schlotzsky's line of proprietary products had grown from potato chips to more than 100 items (called Schlotzsky's Premium Provisions) and the company inked several agreements with grocery chains. The first retail deal, with Wal-Mart, sold Schlotzsky's potato chips in 480 stores in the central United States. Wal-Mart eventually expanded its agreement to 2,500 of its stores nationwide, and soon other grocers including Brookshire's and Costco signed up as well. While brand sale royalties were not a major priority in Schlotzsky's expansion plans, with four million bags of chips sold in a matter of months, the sales did add up. "We might stand to make a little bit of money off this, but it mostly works as a form of advertising," John Wooley told Andy Battaglia of *Nation's Restaurant News* in October 1999. Further, Wooley explained, "If we make a sliver of profit, that's great. But if we can get stores to stock our products all over the Northeast . . . people will know our name."

Key Dates:

1971: Don Dissman opens first Schlotzsky's restaurant in Austin, Texas.

1977: First franchised Schlotzsky's opens in Bryan/College Station, Texas.

1981: Brothers John and Jeff Wooley acquire Schlotzsky's.

1988: First Schlotzsky's outside the United States opens in Canada.

1991: Deli concept is introduced; store name changes to Schlotzsky's Deli.

1992: Deli Style Potato Chips are launched as first privately branded product.

1995: Company completes its IPO on the NASDAQ, under ticker symbol BUNZ.

1996: Company celebrates its 25th anniversary with 573 restaurants.

1999: Systemwide sales (including franchisee sales) hit $400 million and 759th store is opened.

By spring came another expansion push, and Schlotzsky's became one of less than 15 restaurant chains to appear in nationwide prime-time television advertising. The company debuted its first national advertising campaign during top-rated favorites such as *Dateline, ER, Frasier, Law & Order, West Wing, Will & Grace, Who Wants to Be A Millionaire?,* and the *Today Show.* The $14 million media blitz was funded by franchisees and company-owned stores and was credited with raising brand awareness and propelling weekly sales by as much as 37 percent in noncore markets such as Washington, D.C., and 20 percent in Fresno, California. Systemwide sales had risen 17 percent to $400 million for the year, and Schlotzsky's was booming. The chain was named, for the sixth time, to *Entrepreneur* magazine's annual "Franchise 500" as one of the top franchising opportunities in the sandwich, soup, and salad category.

By 2000 the annual Austin Bun Run race, in its 18th year, had become one of the largest five-kilometer races in the Southwest, attracting 4,000 runners. The other Bun Runs, sprinkled throughout the country, were also thriving and information about upcoming races, finishing times, and running health and fitness in general were available at several Internet sites. Local and national advertising, proprietary brands, giving back to the community, and old-fashioned goodness had brought Schlotzsky's Deli to the upper tiers of its industry. Ranked as the number four sandwich chain in the country (behind Subway, Arby's, and Blimpie), Schlotzsky's was unique among its competitors. Though they were all lumped into the "sandwich" category, (as in no burgers or fried chicken), Schlotzsky's was completely different from Arby's mostly roast beef fare, and its sandwiches were not like the submarines sold by Subway and Blimpie. In a nearly $7 billion market that continued to grow from year to year, there seemed to be ample room for Schlotzsky's unique victuals.

John Wooley believed Schlotzsky's annual sales would be in the $500 million range by 2001 and up to $1 billion by 2006. An estimated 50 new restaurants were slated to open during each of the next two years, then climb to more than 100 units annually again. The only major hurdle in Schlotzsky's future was its stock performance, which had fluctuated from a high of $23 in the first quarter of 1998 to a low of $6 per share in the fourth quarter of 1999. Many investors had sold off Schlotzsky's and other restaurant stocks in favor of hot technology companies. In addition, accounting problems forced the company to restate 1997 earnings and, in 1999, Securities and Exchange Commission accounting charges nearly wiped out profits. Yet some analysts regarded Schlotzsky's stock as an excellent bargain, feeling the company was poised for a upswing. With steadily climbing sales and brand recognition, despite accounting peccadillos, Schlotzsky's was in good shape to lead the sandwich industry's bun race in the coming years.

Principal Subsidiaries

Schlotzsky's Real Estate, Inc.; Schlotzsky's Restaurants, Inc.; Schlotzsky's Brand Product, L.P.; Schlotzsky's Brands I, L.L.C.; Schlotzsky's Brands, Inc.; Schlotzsky's Equipment Corporation; DFW Restaurant Transfer Corp.; 56th and 6th, Inc.; N.A.M.F., Inc., RAD Acquisition Corp.; SREI Turnkey Development, L.L.C.

Principal Competitors

Arby's Inc.; Blimpie International, Inc.; Subway.

Further Reading

Battaglia, Andy, "Schlotzsky's Rolls Out Grocery Line, Eyes 'Premium' Profits," *Nation's Restaurant News,* October 25, 1999, p. 8.

Cebrzynski, Gregg, "Schlotzsky's Plans April Launch for First National TV Ads," *Nation's Restaurant News,* September 28, 1998, p. 14.

Opdyke, Jeff D., "Investors Hungry for a Bargain May Want to Look at Schlotzsky's," *Wall Street Journal,* July 1, 1998, p. T2.

Prewitt, Milford, "GAP Rule Mandates That Schlotzsky's Revise Income Statement," *Nation's Restaurant News,* April 20, 1998, p. 11.

Ruggless, Ron, "Schlotzsky's Goes Upscale Downtown, Modifies Concept for New Urban Units," *Nation's Restaurant News,* March 2, 1998, p. 7.

Sharpe, Patricia, "New Deli," *Texas Monthly,* February 1997, p. 66(3).

Silver, Deborah, "Bread Winner," *Restaurants & Institutions,* June 1, 2000, p. 83.

—Owen James and Nelson Rhodes

Schneider National, Inc.

3101 Packerland
Green Bay, Wisconsin 54313
U.S.A.
Telephone: (920) 592-2000
Toll Free: (800) 558-6767
Fax: (920) 592-2001
Web site: http://www.schneider.com

Private Company
Incorporated: 1938 as Schneider Transfer and Storage
  Co.
Employees: 19,000
Sales: $3 billion (1999 est.)
NAIC: 48411 General Freight Trucking, Local; 484121
  General Freight Trucking, Long-Distance, Truckload

Schneider National, Inc. is the largest trucking firm in the United States. Privately owned by members of the Schneider family, it was a relatively small player until the 1980s, when the trucking industry was deregulated. In that era when many small trucking firms failed, Schneider instead soared to the forefront, chiefly by deploying advanced communications technology. Schneider runs a fleet of approximately 14,000 trucks and 40,000 trailers, distinguished by a signature bright orange color. Its routes encompass the entire United States, and the company also has operations in Canada, Mexico, and Europe. The company also runs a logistics business, which helps other companies determine efficient ways to ship and distribute goods. Schneider is a leader in trucking logistics technology. It uses satellite links and the Internet to monitor aspects of its business, including how much sleep its drivers get and how quickly customers unload Schneider's deliveries. This allows the firm to operate at maximum efficiency. Schneider ships goods by boxed trucks, tanker truck, flatbed truck, in containers, and by rail.

Early Years

Schneider National was founded in 1935 by Al Schneider, known as "A.J.," in Green Bay, Wisconsin. Schneider was raised on a farm in east-central Wisconsin, and his education took him through the eighth grade only. He began with one truck, and took shipments through the Green Bay area. The company grew, as did the Schneider family. Eventually there were five sons and a daughter. One son, Don, worked his way up in the business, becoming president in 1971. Unlike his father, Don had a thorough education to match his home-grown business skills. He graduated from a parochial high school in Green Bay, and then went to St. Norbert College, graduating in 1957. After a period in the Army, Don Schneider entered the University of Pennsylvania's esteemed Wharton School of Finance and Commerce. With this valuable business degree in hand, Don returned to Green Bay in 1961 and became an instrumental Schneider manager. Ten years later, he assumed control of the company. Don Schneider seemed to have brought his father's company an unusual combination of skills. In a profile of the company in the October 31, 1994 *Milwaukee Journal*, an industry analyst proclaimed Schneider "a trucker who thinks like an economist."

Changes After Deregulation in the 1980s

Until 1980, thinking like a *lawyer* might have been the most valuable skill at a trucking company. Trucking was regulated by a web of state and federal statutes that determined minutiae of the industry's routes, rates, and loads. Thus Schneider was licensed to carry cellulose products, for example, but not paper products, and its lawyers had to negotiate for years in order to reclassify disposable diapers as a cellulose product so it could legally ship them. Both government rules and union contracts dictated much of the business. Schneider itself seemed versed in legal finagling. From 1978 to 1981 the company claimed its headquarters were in a facility it used in Illinois, thus getting the company out of a higher licensing fee it would have owed to the state of Wisconsin. The state of Wisconsin sued Schneider for $3.8 million in licensing fees in 1982, and the case was eventually settled on appeal in Schneider's favor. But when the trucking industry underwent deregulation in 1980, such bureaucratic wrangling became much less of a part of the way Schneider and other trucking companies did business. Truckers were freed to compete directly for customers. Around the same time, many large manufacturers and retailers were changing their business

411

Company Perspectives:

Our mission at Schneider is to be the global leader in providing transportation solutions. At Schneider, we're never satisfied with the status quo. Here we apply Schneider's tradition for using technology to solve problems for customers with our transportation service offerings which are by far the broadest in the industry.

pattern, switching to so-called just-in-time delivery. Just-in-time meant that instead of warehousing huge stocks of common items, factories ordered raw materials as needed, and shipped finished goods directly to retailers. This cut costs associated with large inventories, but it put intense pressure on truckers. A truckers' delay of as little as 20 minutes could cause retailers annoying back-ups as they tried to get their goods out to waiting customers.

Don Schneider was quick to realize that his company had to change massively in order to adapt to the new business climate. Two major changes were in employee relations and in new use of technology. In the early 1980s Schneider began giving its drivers bonuses based on performance, while also eliminating perks like reserved parking spaces for upper echelon employees. Deregulation allowed the company to hire non-union drivers, which it did, while pledging to keep its union employees. In 1979, all 1,500 drivers belonged to the Teamsters union. As the company grew, the percentage of unionized drivers became smaller. By the early 1990s, only 500 Teamsters were left, out of a crew of roughly 10,000 drivers. Attrition of the union allowed Schneider more freedom to set its own policies for employees. This gave the company more flexibility, which it needed to adapt to the increased demands of its customers.

Schneider also pioneered the use of satellite technology in trucking. Traditionally, drivers on the road would find a phone at a truck stop and call a company dispatcher for a periodic check-in. This was sometimes a frustrating process, as pay phones were often engaged, or the dispatcher busy and unable to accept the call. Schneider National made a large investment in computer and satellite technology in 1988 to give it a new way to communicate with drivers. The company spent an estimated $50 million initially, and installed a satellite dish and communication console on every truck it owned. Each truck was linked by satellite to the company's home base in Green Bay. Specialized software ran continuous updates on the many variables of the business, not only keeping track of where each truck was, but logging how many hours the driver had slept, fuel use, and average time it took to unload at each customer's facility. Changes in routes could be beamed directly to the driver on the road, and if a customer needed an empty trailer in half an hour, the computer could determine which driver was nearby and eligible for another load. Schneider was the first major trucker to make use of satellite technology, and soon the rest of the industry was scrambling to keep up.

Meanwhile, Schneider prospered financially. The trucking market in the 1980s was characterized by intense competition and recessive prices, yet Schneider managed to grow at around 20 percent annually. Revenue in 1981 was a modest $200 million, but by 1992, revenue exceeded $1 billion. Because the company was privately held, it was able to reinvest freely with an eye to long-term profits, and Schneider continued to put money into technology and new ventures.

Expansion in the 1990s

With its rapid growth, Schneider needed to expand its facilities in the early 1990s in order to accommodate more drivers. The company began work on a huge facility in Memphis in 1990, building a driver service center and operations center and enlarging an existing maintenance center. The driver service center gave drivers a place to relax, rest, and shower while their trucks were being refueled or repaired. Originally planned in the late 1980s as home base for about 600 drivers, by the early 1990s the Memphis site grew into a hub for close to 1,000 truckers. The expansion cost Schneider an estimated $6 million. Schneider also employed its high technology at its new service center. When drivers refueled in Memphis or at any of the company's other major service centers, their mileage was automatically beamed to Schneider's headquarters in Green Bay. If a truck was using an atypical amount of fuel, the computer could note that, and alert personnel of possible maintenance needs on that vehicle. The investment in cutting edge technology let the company save money over the long term, by giving it such tight control over its fleet.

Schneider also began investing in equipment in the early 1990s, specifically truck trailers that could be used on railways. Schneider entered the so-called intermodal transport industry in 1991, working with Southern Pacific railway to serve routes between the Midwest and southern California. Though industrywide far more freight was shipped by road than by rail, being able to combine the two often gave the company more efficient routes. By 1992, Schneider had worked out intermodal shipping agreements with several more railroads, giving it access to most major markets in the United States. Schneider invested some $12 million dollars in the early 1990s, replacing existing truck trailers with trailers that could be stacked on flatbed rail cars. Then the company spent around $600 million over several years to buy a new kind of convertible trailer called a roadrailer. The roadrailer was a modified truck frame that could use steel rail wheels and travel directly on train tracks. Unlike stackable containers, which required special lifting equipment found only in rail yards to place them onto rail cars, the roadrailers could move onto rail tracks anywhere there was a spur. This gave Schneider the kind of flexibility it liked.

Schneider National was an innovative, fast-growing company in the 1990s. It had surpassed much of its competition by embracing change and new technology. In 1993 the company formed a subsidiary, Schneider Logistics, to in effect sell its shipping expertise to clients. Large manufacturers were working to reduce inventory and streamline operations to improve profits, and Schneider was good at seeing how that could be done best. Schneider Logistics garnered large contracts early on, including one with General Motors to improve the delivery of auto parts to its dealers. By 1995, Schneider Logistics had 140 contracts, ranging in size from about $2 million for small companies to $200 million for such large firms as General Motors and auto parts maker PPG Industries. By the mid-1990s,

Key Dates:

1935:   Company is founded in Green Bay.
1971:   Don Schneider, son of founder, becomes president.
1988:   Schneider makes first big investment in satellite technology.
1993:   Valuable subsidiary Schneider Logistics is founded.
2000:   Schneider Logistics is spun off to public.

Schneider was getting 15 percent of its profit from its logistics division, and the subsidiary was the fastest-growing part of the company.

Branching Out in the Late 1990s and After

By the late 1990s, Schneider National was the nation's largest full-load trucking firm, with sales approaching $3 billion. The firm had distinguished itself in the 1980s by moving quickly into advanced communications technology. As the Internet changed the face of business in the United States in the late 1990s, Schneider found a way to adapt. In June 1999, the company launched a new subsidiary, Schneider Brokerage, which handled a web-based service. Schneider Brokerage operated a web site called the Schneider Connection, which posted trucking jobs online and let shippers find available loads. Schneider also found other ways to work with the Internet. In June 2000 Schneider Logistics formed an alliance with an online construction service business, ContractorHub.com. ContractorHub.com brought together businesses looking for construction contractors and contractors looking for jobs. Schneider Logistics provided the new company with its expertise in shipping, order fulfillment and tracking, and gained exposure through ContractorHub.com's wide marketing.

By the year 2000, Schneider's logistics subsidiary had grown so rapidly and profitably that the parent decided to spin it off to the public. Schneider wanted cash to help pay for more technological development at Schneider Logistics, and to allow the subsidiary to expand into international markets. This was the first time the closely held Schneider had let any piece of it fall to investors. However, the company announced it would sell off only a minority share in Schneider Logistics. The majority would still be held by Donald Schneider and other shareholders of the private parent firm.

Principal Subsidiaries

Schneider Logistics; Schneider Brokerage.

Principal Competitors

J.B. Hunt Transport Services; Covenant Transport Inc.

Further Reading

Bigness, Jon, "Driving Force," *Wall Street Journal*, September 6, 1995, pp. A1, A11.

Booker, Ellis, "Schneider Looks for 'Deep Visibility'" *InformationWeek*, October 25, 1999, p. 76.

Cohen, Warren, "Taking to the Highway," *U.S. News & World Report*, September 18, 1995, pp. 84–87.

Kenyon, Richard L., "A Long-Distance Mover and Shaker," *Milwaukee Journal*, October 31, 1994, 00. 13–16, 22.

Levenson, Marc, "Riding the Data Highway," *Newsweek*, March 21, 1994, pp. 54–55.

Machalaba, Daniel, "An Industry's Direction Rides on Schneider National," *Wall Street Journal*, May 24, 1993, p. B4.

——, "Truckers Lift Rates for the Long Haul, Citing Surging Traffic and Rising Costs," *Wall Street Journal*, March 31, 1994, p. A4.

——, "Trucking Firms, Amid Heavy Demand, Seek Rate Rise," *Wall Street Journal*, December 9, 1999, p. B6.

Magnet, Myron, "Meet the New Revolutionaries," *Fortune*, February 24, 1992, pp. 94–101.

Mayo, Virginia, "Wisconsin Sues Trucking Firm," *Capital Times* (Madison, Wis.), February 2, 1982, p. 26.

Muller, E.J., "Don Schneider: A Humble Leader," *Distribution*, November 1993, pp. 32–36.

Provost, Richard, "Schneider Expands Facility to Serve As Home Base to 1,000 Truckers," *Memphis Business Journal*, March 5, 1990, pp. 44–46.

"Schneider Launches Nationwide Intermodal Service," *American Shipper*, December 1992, p. 67.

—A. Woodward

Seaboard Corporation

9000 West 67th St.
Shawnee Mission, Kansas 66202
U.S.A.
Telephone: (913) 676-8800
Fax: (913) 676-8872
Web site: http://www.seaboardcorp.com

Public Subsidiary of Seaboard Flour Company
Incorporated: 1928 as Rodney Milling
Employees: 9,763
Sales: $1.26 billion (1999)
Stock Exchanges: American
Ticker Symbol: SEB
NAIC: 311611 Animal (Except Poultry) Slaughtering;
11221 Hog and Pig Farming; 483111 Deep Sea Freight
Transportation; 52313 Commodity Contracts Dealing;
311211 Flour Milling; 311119 Other Animal Food
Manufacturing; 311812 Commercial Bakeries; 111219
Other Vegetable (Except Potato) and Melon Farming;
322223 Plastics, Foil, and Coated Paper Bag
Manufacturing; 49313 Farm Product Warehousing and
Storage; 221112 Fossil Fuel Electric Power Generation

Seaboard Corporation is a diversified company whose largest business consists of pork production for domestic and foreign consumption. Seaboard and its subsidiaries also sell commodities such as grains and seeds, process citrus fruit and seafood, grow sugar cane, make wine, generate electrical power, mill flour and animal feed, and ship cargo between the United States and points south. The company was a leading poultry producer until January 2000, when it sold this operation to ConAgra for $375 million. Seaboard is publicly traded, but 75 percent of its shares are held by the Seaboard Flour Company, which is owned by heirs of founder Otto Bresky.

Origins

Seaboard traces its roots to the early part of the 20th century. Company founder Otto Bresky started out in 1916 as a flour broker, buying his own mill in Atchison, Kansas, two years later. In 1919 he purchased the Imperial Brewing Company of Kansas City and converted it to a milling operation. Bresky's company became known as Rodney Milling in 1928 when he purchased a company of that name, which he then incorporated under. Gradual growth continued over the next three decades, with purchases of Ismert-Hinke Milling in 1938 and Consolidated Flour Mills in 1950.

In 1959 Rodney Milling merged with Hathaway Industries, Inc. and became a publicly traded company. The newly united firms took the name of Seaboard Allied Milling Corporation. Seaboard soon began expanding, following a strategy of building flour mills near populous areas in the East and Southeast. The first of these was completed in 1962 in Chattanooga, Tennessee, with another built in 1966 in Jacksonville, Florida. Also in 1966, the company initiated its first overseas venture, investing in a flour mill in Guayaquil, Ecuador, in conjunction with Continental Grain Company. Shortly after this more moves were made abroad, with mills built in Freetown, Sierra Leone, in 1968 and Georgetown, Guyana, a year later.

Back in the United States, Seaboard built a mill in Culpepper, Virginia, in 1970 and enlarged it just two years later. The year 1973 saw founder and patriarch Otto Bresky step down from a leadership role after more than half a century with the company. His son, Seaboard President Harry Bresky, took the reins of the still largely family-owned concern and kept it on its course of expansion. The 1970s saw more mills built in New York, Louisiana, Liberia, and Nigeria, and the expansion of businesses in Ecuador and Liberia. The company also purchased a mill in Tennessee and an Ecuadorian animal feed company, and opened another feed plant in Nigeria. Seaboard capped the decade with construction of a new corporate headquarters in Merriam, Kansas.

In the face of increasing competition, the company made a dramatic strategic shift in early 1982 when it sold its American flour mills to Cargill, Inc. for $40 million. Its name was also shortened during the year, to Seaboard Corporation. The company was now preparing to move in new directions, and soon founded a subsidiary, Seaboard Marine, Ltd., to ship goods between the United States and Central and South America. Two baking companies in Puerto Rico were also purchased at this time.

414

Company Perspectives:

Seaboard Corporation is a diversified and vertically integrated agribusiness and ocean transportation company. Our goal across all of our business lines is to provide exceptional value to our customers.

Through diversity in geographic regions and business segments, we are well positioned to take advantage of a robust U.S. economy and the dynamic changes taking place overseas.

Moving into Poultry

At the beginning of 1984 Seaboard entered the poultry business with the purchase of Central Soya's poultry division, which consisted of three facilities located in the southern United States. The processing plants, in Athens and Canton, Georgia, and Chattanooga, Tennessee, had a combined capacity of 400 million pounds of broiler chicken per year. A year later Seaboard added more by acquiring Elberton Poultry of Georgia. The company continued to grow overseas during the mid-1980s as well, building a new polypropylene bag factory in Nigeria and a shrimp farm in Honduras.

Seaboard also was taking advantage of the capacity of its Marine division by shipping produce from Central and South America to the United States. To expand this operation, the company purchased a Miami-based produce distributor and several farming operations in Central America.

During the latter half of the 1980s the company expanded several of its poultry processing facilities and constructed a new plant in Mayfield, Kentucky. Seaboard also moved into other areas at this time, forming a joint venture to raise Atlantic salmon near Maine and starting a Bermuda-based subsidiary to run a power-generating barge near the Dominican Republic. In 1990 the company purchased a recently closed pork and lamb processing facility owned by Cornbelt Meat, Inc. The 650,000-square-foot Albert Lea, Minnesota plant utilized a workforce of more than 750. Seaboard received financial assistance from the city to reopen the plant, and union workers also accepted lower wages in order to return to their jobs.

Focusing on Pork

As it had done with poultry, Seaboard quickly began to invest in the business of processing pork. The company built a feed milling and pig feeding operation in Colorado in 1991, and the following year broke ground on a pork processing facility in Oklahoma. Seaboard would also soon build a feed mill and facilities for production of some two million hogs per year in that state. As had been the case in Minnesota, the company received numerous financial incentives to locate its operations there. Overseas, the company also bought additional flour mills in Puerto Rico and Zaire in 1992.

In 1994 Seaboard announced the closing of its Minnesota pork plant, which it later would sell to Farmland Foods. The company also settled a four-year-old shareholder lawsuit which charged that majority stockholder Seaboard Flour had profited unfairly from certain business dealings with Seaboard Corporation. The settlement stipulated that the Bresky family-owned company pay Seaboard $10.8 million, plus $2 million in legal fees.

After months of delays, Seaboard's new state-of-the-art pork processing facility in Guymon, Oklahoma, was opened on January 6, 1996. The $110 million plant was capable of processing four million hogs annually when it was in full operation. At least 1,160 workers would be utilized, spread over two shifts. The plant was so large that it required expansion of hog production capacity throughout the region. Hogs were to be grown in Kansas, Colorado, and Texas, as well as in Oklahoma. Half were produced by Seaboard, with a quarter from farms under contract to the company and the rest from outside suppliers. The company also secured a $9.5 million tax-exempt loan from the state of Kansas to build 26 hog waste lagoons. The loan, which had been obtained through a loophole in a law that banned state assistance of corporate hog farming, caused an uproar among state legislators.

Seaboard was doing well with pork, and the following year announced plans to set up a second large facility in Kansas, one which could also process four million hogs per year. Unlike many of its competitors, Seaboard sold a significant amount of pork abroad, more than triple the industry average of seven percent. The company was the leading supplier to Japan, which purchased almost half of all U.S pork exports.

Continuing Foreign Expansion

Seaboard continued to seek other opportunities overseas, and purchased an interest in Ingenio y Refineria San Martin del Tabacal S.A. of Argentina, a grower and processor of sugar cane and a grower of citrus fruit. Investments were also made in a flour, cookie, and pasta company in Mozambique and flour mills in Haiti, Lesotho, and Angola. Other international moves in the mid- and late-1990s included the acquisition of controlling interest in Bulgaria's leading wine producer, which had formerly been nationalized, and the purchase of a Zambian milling company. Seaboard also sold its flour milling and baking businesses in Puerto Rico and, in the United States, bought a stake in a seafood processing venture in Maine in partnership with Continental Grain Co.

In November 1998 the notoriously publicity-shy Seaboard was the subject of a lengthy article in *Time* magazine that claimed the company had received $150 million in ''corporate welfare'' during the 1990s. *Time* alleged that Seaboard actively sought the biggest handouts, and had abandoned the Albert Lea, Minnesota pork plant, which devastated that city financially, when it found a sweeter offer in Oklahoma. Rick Hoffman, CEO of the company's Seaboard Farms subsidiary, responded by telling the Associated Press that, ''There were no programs that Seaboard solicited by the state that did not already exist for other new businesses.'' He also declared that much of the money *Time* claimed was earmarked for Seaboard did not in fact benefit the company.

Seaboard and other large animal processors were also being criticized by organizations such as the National Audubon Society and the Sierra Club for causing pollution, making the areas

Key Dates:

1918: Flour broker Otto Bresky purchases a mill in Atchison, Kansas.
1928: Bresky purchases Rodney Milling and incorporates his business under that name.
1938: Ismert-Hinke Milling is acquired.
1950: Company purchases Consolidated Flour Mills.
1959: Company merges with Hathaway Industries, Inc.; name changes to Seaboard Allied Milling.
1960s–70s: Company builds flour mills in eastern and southeastern United States.
1966: First foreign investment is made in Ecuadorian flour mill.
1982: Company sells U.S. milling operations to Cargill, Inc.; name shortened to Seaboard Corporation.
1984: Seaboard purchases Central Soya's poultry division.
1990: Seaboard buys pork processing facility from Cornbelt Meats, Inc.
1996: New pork processing operation opens in Oklahoma.
2000: Company sells poultry interests to ConAgra, Inc.

surrounding their facilities unpleasant to inhabit, and reducing the size of important wetlands in the plains states. The company's foes cited an $88,000 fine Seaboard had paid to Oklahoma for improper disposal of hog carcasses as evidence of its wrongdoing.

In 1999 Seaboard announced it was spending $144.5 million to buy 50 percent of Dominican Republic power-generating company Haina, which owned five electrical plants. Annual revenues topped $1.25 billion, up from $715 million just four years earlier. Income from pork accounted for nearly half that amount, with marine operations responsible for another quarter.

In January 2000 the company made its biggest divestment ever, selling its poultry operations to ConAgra, Inc. for $375 million in cash and debt assumption. Other activity for the year included the purchase of another hog processing company and investment in a flour and feed milling business in Kenya. In Texas, Seaboard made a deal to acquire the Jacintoport Marine Terminal of Houston. The company would own the buildings on the site and lease the land from the city's port authority. Seaboard Marine already used the facility, which featured a high speed bagged-cargo loading system.

At the start of the new century, Seaboard Corporation was going strong, strengthening its hog production operations and continuing to diversify overseas by expanding its milling, power generating, and food production businesses. The company was now ranked among the top five U.S. pork producers.

Principal Subsidiaries

A & W Interlining Services Corp.; Agencia Maritima del Istmo, S.A. (Costa Rica); Agencias Generales Conaven, C.A. (Venezuela); Cape Fear Railways, Inc.; Chestnut Hill Farms Honduras, S.A. de C.V. (Honduras); Chestnut Hill Farms, Inc.; Consorcio Naviero de Occidente, C.A. (Venezuela); Cultivos Marinos, S.A. de C.V. (Honduras); Empacadora Litoral, S.A. de C.V. (Honduras); H&O Shipping Limited (Liberia); Ingenio y Refineria San Martin del Tabacal (Argentina); National Milling Company of Guyana, Ltd. (Guyana); National Milling Company Limited (Zambia); Port of Miami Cold Storage, Inc.; Representaciones Maritimas y Aereas, S.A. (Guatemala); S.B.D., LLC; Samovar International Finance, Inc. (Puerto Rico); SASCO Engineering Co./ Seaboard Sales Corporation Ltd. (Bermuda); Sea Cargo, S.A. (Panama); Seaboard de Colombia, S.A. (Colombia); Seaboard de Honduras, S.A. de C.V. (Honduras); Seaboard del Peru, S.A. (Peru); Seaboard Farms, Inc.; Seaboard Freight & Shipping Jamaica Limited (Jamaica); Seaboard Guyana, Ltd. (Bermuda); Seaboard Holdings Ltd. (British Virgin Islands); Seaboard Marine Bahamas, Ltd. (Bahamas); Seaboard Marine Ltd. (Liberia); Seaboard Marine of Florida, Inc.; Seaboard Overseas Limited (Bahamas); Seaboard Ship Management Inc.; Seaboard Shipping Services (PTY) Ltd. (South Africa); Seaboard Trading and Shipping Ltd.; Seaboard Transport Inc.; Secuador Limited (Bermuda); Shilton Limited (Cayman Islands); Transcontinental Capital Corp. (Bermuda) Ltd. (Bermuda); Vinprom Rousse AD (Bulgaria).

Principal Competitors

Alico, Inc.; Baltek Corp.; Cargill, Inc.; ConAgra, Inc.; CSX Corp.; Dole Food Company, Inc.; Farmland Industries, Inc.; Hormel Foods Corp.; IBP, Inc.; Nicor, Inc.; Premium Standard Farms, Inc.; Smithfield Foods, Inc.; Tate & Lyle PLC.

Further Reading

Barlett, Donald, and Steele, James B., "The Empire of the Pigs," *Time*, November 30, 1998.
Hardy, Eric S., "Wall Street's Dark Corners," *Forbes*, February 28, 1994, p. 126.
Hendricks, Mike, "Hog Farms Slip Through Tax Loophole," *Kansas City Star*, January 13, 1996, p. A1.
Mansur, Michael, "Proposal Called Wetlands Threat," *Kansas City Star*, March 14, 1998, p. C3.
Nicolova, Rossitsa, "Seaboard Hoping to Uncork Bulgarian Winery's Potential," *Kansas City Business Journal*, August 27, 1999, p. 4.
Palmer, Eric, "Something to Squeal About—Seaboard Makes Plans to Hog the Market," *Kansas City Star*, June 23, 1998, p. D1.
"Seaboard Catalyst in Hog Fight," *The Topeka Capital-Journal*, August 31, 1999.
"Seaboard Disputes Magazine Report," *Associated Press Newswires*, November 27, 1998.

—Frank Uhle

The Seiyu, Ltd.

1-1, Akabane 2-Chome
Kita-ku
Tokyo 115-0045
Japan
Telephone: (03) 3598-7000
Fax: (03) 3982-5094
Web site: http://www.seiyu.co.jp

Public Company
Incorporated: 1956 as Seibu Stores
Employees: 18,080
Sales: ¥875.37 billion (US$8.04 billion) (2000)
Stock Exchanges: Tokyo Paris Frankfurt Düsseldorf
NAIC: 445110 Supermarkets and Other Grocery (Except
    Convenience) Stores; 452110 Department Stores

The Seiyu, Ltd. (Seiyu) leads the Seiyu Group, a subgroup of the Saison Group, a diversified conglomerate with interests in retail, food, finance, real estate, entertainment, and other areas. Saison Group is one of Japan's largest retail concerns. The Seiyu Group consists of 22 main companies, within which The Seiyu, Ltd. represents the group's main business of superstore retailing and operates about 200 stores throughout Japan. Seiyu maintains a wide range of store formats, including large general merchandise stores, which are centrally operated and predominantly self-service department stores; supermarkets; and specialty stores. Among other activities, Seiyu also develops and operates shopping centers. Seiyu was originally founded in 1956 to become the supermarket arm of the privately owned Seibu Distribution Companies—now the Saison Group. At the time, the company took the name of its parent, Seibu Stores, and is the oldest of Japan's major superstore chains by one year, although its competitor Ito-Yokado Co. Ltd. had been operating in another form since the early 20th century.

Early History

The key personality in the history of Seiyu is Seiji Tsutsumi. Until 1991 Tsutsumi was the head of the then Seibu Saison Group before stepping down to become chairman of the Saison Corporation within the same group. Over several decades, he was the driving force behind Seibu's successful retailing operations. His half-brother, Yoshiaki Tsutsumi, was head of the independent Seibu Railways Group. Competition between the brothers contributed to the respective buildup of their companies after the original Seibu companies were split between the two brothers by their father. The early years were difficult for the company. Seiyu was established as a three-store chain with supermarkets in Odawara, Taira, and Shizuoka; however, all three original stores soon failed. The first successful store opened in Tsuchiura in 1958. Others followed but the pace of store openings remained slow, and by 1962 there were only five stores with less than 5,000 square meters in sales space. The main reason for the slow opening of new stores was Seiyu's dependence on its parent company, Seibu Distribution. At the time, Seibu was conducting an ill-fated and costly experiment with a department store in Los Angeles. With Tsutsumi's tight overall control of the group's operations and a lack of funds due to losses from department stores, growth was restricted. In many respects, Seibu stores operated as small department stores. Each store sourced and sold goods independently and did not practice self-service selling.

In November 1962 Tsutsumi decided that it was time to extend the supermarket side of the business. This was a period when Tokyo was growing rapidly, and large housing developments were springing up around the city. Following Tsutsumi's directive, the company began to search for new store sites close to this new housing. These estates represented a totally new market for Japanese retailers, with younger families from all over Japan beginning to move to the capital.

In addition, the company made a positive move toward becoming a chain store business and developed the retail strategy of self-service discount department stores whereby the company would open self-service outlets similar to department stores offering household and food items at a discount. This was the first step in the development of Seiyu's modern superstores.

Five months later, in April 1963, the company changed its name to Seiyu Stores Ltd., a move that emphasized the distinction between Seiyu and Seibu, and indicated a move to greater independence from the Seibu Group. The decision was not

---

Company Perspectives:

Founded in 1963, Seiyu has grown into one of Japan's largest retailers by maintaining a clear understanding of market trends and tailoring its business to meet the needs of consumers. Seiyu strives to maintain the highest standards of quality in every aspect of its operations, from appealing original-brand merchandise to store development to strict freshness checks for food.

---

entirely voluntary. Complaints from small businesses led the Ministry of International Trade and Industry (MITI) to instruct the company not to operate under the same name as its sister department stores.

Following this change Seiyu rapidly expanded its chain of stores. To achieve this it took advantage of its connection with the Seibu Railway Company, locating stores along major rail arteries to the west of Tokyo. This land was not only cheap, but the sites had several other advantages. Stores at railway terminals provided a guaranteed flow of customers by catching commuters as well as local residents. In urban Japan, unlike most Western nations, shopping by car was seriously restricted because of road congestion and even in the early 1990s railway terminals were employed as prime retail sales.

Throughout the 1960s, Seiyu expanded first along the two main Seibu railway lines, and after 1965 stores were opened along lines operated by Japan National Railways and Keio Railways to the west of Tokyo, and along Sobu railway lines to the north. Store sizes ranged between 900 and 3,000 square meters depending on the site. On the whole, medium-sized stores of slightly more than 1,000 square meters of sales space were employed, with the emphasis on food and household products. The larger superstore outlets also carried a few clothing lines.

In 1969 Seiyu opened its first major distribution depot at Fuchu. In the same year production capacity for private brands was expanded with the founding of the Seiyu Stockbreeding Company and the Seiyu Meat Company. Seiyu Shoes Ltd. and Seiyu Marine Products Ltd. were established in 1970.

Expansion and Diversification in the 1970s

By this time the Seiyu chain had grown to more than 80 stores, all within Tokyo and neighboring regions. The early 1970s saw further expansion and diversification. Through the takeover of Koma Stores Ltd., a Kyoto chain of 12 outlets, Seiyu Stores Kansai Ltd. was founded. At the center of the Kansai region is Osaka, Japan's second largest city and the country's second largest market. It was also the home base for the major superstore chains of Daiei Inc., Nichii, and Izumiya. Seiyu's entry in 1970 was part of a strategy to open stores throughout the country. The Kansai company acted as a gateway to Nagoya and the southern island of Kyushu, leaving the Tokyo headquarters responsible for the north of Japan.

In 1971 Seiyu acquired a majority shareholding in the regional Uoriki chain in the Central Japan Alps. Unlike the takeover of Koma in Kyoto, this was not simply a market entry strategy. Although Uoriki was a small local chain, it dominated food retailing in the area, and Seiyu maintained this strong position, becoming highly successful in the region. The company was renamed Seiyu Stores Nagano Ltd. in 1971.

In 1972 the Seibu Group established links with Sears, Roebuck & Co., giving Seibu access to the Sears catalog. Catalog corners were set up in some large Seiyu stores as well as in department stores, and Seiyu gained access to Sears's retail experience. Sears maintained a 2.24 percent stake in Seiyu into the 1990s, selling the stake in 1992.

Also in 1972, experiments were set up in small store retailing. This was the beginning of the highly successful Family Mart convenience store chain. Seiyu opened a small number of experimental stores during the mid-1970s, eventually establishing Family Mart Company as a viable chain in 1978. Family Mart eventually became the third largest convenience store chain in Japan and in 1981 was made independent from Seiyu Group, with the Family Mart Group becoming a separate, autonomous part of the Saison Group, partially owned by Seiyu.

Throughout the mid-1970s Seiyu continued a strategy of store expansion and business diversification and in 1974 expanded production of its own name brands to more than 500 items. These early brands were designed chiefly as discount goods to attract price-conscious consumers. In 1976 Seiyu went public with a listing on the first section of the Tokyo Stock Exchange.

Ties with Sears, Roebuck were strengthened when the companies exchanged research teams between 1974 and 1978. Sears's chief objective was to gather information on the Japanese market, while Seiyu was interested in learning more about the Sears system of retailing. In 1978 Seiyu established an office in Chicago for the purpose of gathering information and sourcing new products suitable for its business in Japan. Further offices were established in Peking in 1979 and in Paris in 1982.

Although the implementation of a new Large Store Law in 1974, restricting the opening of large stores, did not hinder the opening of stores of less than 1,500 square meters, problems with small local retailers made new large store developments increasingly difficult toward the end of the 1970s. In 1979 MITI tightened the law further, making all new stores of more than 500 square meters subject to official approval. The consequence of this new legislation was that large companies such as Seiyu found it no easier to open medium-sized stores than to open large ones. A new strategy of opening large stores, usually more than 5,000 square meters, emerged and many stores exceeded 10,000 square meters in sales space. Small and medium supermarkets were opened only in rare cases.

In 1979, Seiyu moved its headquarters to Tokyo's tallest building, the Sunshine 60 in Ikebukuro. The building was constructed to let, and the Saison Group was the main tenant. The building's spectacular size was similar to that of Sears, Roebuck headquarters in Chicago. The complex included a Seiyu superstore, one of the few in central Tokyo.

Further Diversification in the 1980s

By the beginning of the 1980s Seiyu was operating retail outlets that ranged from small convenience stores and medium-sized supermarkets to large-scale department stores. The company was also involved in producing a wide range of own-name brands, notably fresh and processed food products and household goods. The type of low-price, low-quality own-name brands previously available were no longer acceptable to Japanese consumers, and Seiyu responded to this problem in two ways, improving the quality of its supermarket brands and introducing the Shoku no Sachi own-name foodstuffs brand in 1984. In 1980 Seiyu had introduced the Mujirushi Ryohin brand. Mujirushi Ryohin means "good unbranded products"; these high-quality basic goods soon became very popular and Mujirushi Ryohin became a famous brand. Sold initially in special areas of Seiyu stores, against a background of plain stone floors and unpolished wooden shelving, goods were packaged in plain wrappers and sold without the elaborate designs found on much Japanese packing. In doing this, Seiyu created a unique brand image. Large sales within larger Seiyu stores and Seibu department stores led to the opening of independently sited specialty stores under the Mujirushi Ryohin name, including in 1983 the opening of a store in the highly fashionable Aoyama district of Tokyo. Eventually, Daiei, Jusco Co., Ltd., and Uny Co., Ltd. all created their own versions of Mujirushi Ryohin. By 1991 there were 217 Mujirushi Ryohin specialty stores in Japan, stocking a range of more than 1,800 items. In 1991 Seiyu opened a Mujirushi Ryohin store in London.

By 1983 the Seiyu name was widely known in all parts of Japan and the group responded by changing the name of its main subsidiaries. Seiyu Stores Ltd. became The Seiyu, Ltd., and the main regional companies also simplified their names to Kansai Seiyu Ltd. and Nagano Seiyu Ltd. Kansai Seiyu was merged with the head company in 1988.

Building on the success of the Mujirushi Ryohin specialty stores, Seiyu continued to expand beyond its traditional core of food retailing. In 1983 links were formalized with Time Ltd. in the United States, and Seibu Time Ltd. was established. Seibu

Time Ltd. began producing a number of magazines, including *Money Japan,* launched in 1985; *Lettuce Club,* launched in 1987; and *any,* launched in 1989.

In the areas of information and culture marketing, further developments included the production and distribution of films. The group's chairman and founder, Seiji Tsutsumi, had always encouraged all forms of art, and his retail stores were the venue for art exhibitions and performances. Cine Saison Ltd. was established in 1984 within the main Seiyu Group structure, and in 1985 began producing one Japanese movie a year. Within a few years, 12 Seiyu stores and shopping centers were operating cinemas, and eight more had facilities to run regular drive-in movies.

Beginning in 1987, Seiyu also operated the 774-seat Ginza Saison Theater in central Tokyo and was responsible for organizing a large number of cultural events throughout the latter half of the 1980s. In 1988 the Soviet Ballet Institute School was opened in Tokyo, and in the same year a cultural exchange agreement was established with Robert Redford's Sundance Institute, a film school in the United States.

To strengthen the company's image at the upper end of the retail market, Seiyu began to remodel its larger stores as department stores in the 1980s, increasing the ratio of nonfood products and introducing more concessions within stores. The company also began to use the Seibu name on these larger stores to emphasize the department store image. Kasugai Seibu, Koriyama Seibu, and Maebashi Seibu were all examples of department stores run by Seiyu, with sales that were among the highest for individual outlets in Japan.

Seiyu also opened and began operating two large shopping complexes. The Hikari-ga-Oka complex in northwest Tokyo was completed in 1987. Part of a major housing development, it included a Seiyu-operated Seibu department store, a separate supermarket, many specialty stores, restaurants, and a cinema. Seiyu aimed to operate the complex as a community center, providing evening classes and various family events on weekends. The Hikari-ga-Oka complex was one of Seiyu's most successful projects of the late 1980s.

In 1988, Seiyu opened the Rakuichi complex at Nagahama in Shiga prefecture, its second and more ambitious shopping center development. Rakuichi was a shopping center and entertainment complex that included a superstore, specialty stores, a conference center, and an amusement park. It was designed to cater to a wide geographical area. This kind of development was emulated by other Japanese retailers and represented the desire to offer complete one-stop shopping and entertainment.

Toward the end of the 1980s Seiyu consolidated various arms of its business. Seiyu Finance Ltd., originally established in 1982, was merged with Tokyo City Finance (TCF) in 1989. The new company offered a wide range of financial services to Seiyu customers, including consumer credit, mortgages, life and other insurance, securities, and some business finance services. These services were offered both independently and at special counters within major stores. Meanwhile, in 1988, Seiyu purchased the Inter-Continental Hotels and Resorts hospitality chain for ¥280 billion.

Seiyu expanded its international operations during the latter half of the 1980s, establishing links with companies in South Korea, Indonesia, Thailand, and Hong Kong. These links were formed to promote contract production in the poorer Southeast Asian countries of cheap consumer goods. In addition, food products were imported from the western United States. By the early 1990s, Seiyu had five buying and representative offices in southeast Asia and three more in the United States. In 1990 the company opened its first large overseas store, a Seiyu department store, in Hong Kong.

1990s: The Mall, Food Plus, and Post-Bubble Restructuring

Seiyu continued to pursue new ventures in the 1990s, a decade marked by sustained economic sluggishness in Japan following the bursting of the country's economic bubble in 1991. Seiyu entered into a joint venture with L.L. Bean Inc., a U.S. retailer of outdoor clothing and equipment, and Matsushita Electric Industrial Co., Ltd. of Japan in 1992. That year, the joint venture opened the first L.L. Bean store in Japan. By 1996 there were seven such units in the country. Seiyu also developed a new store concept in this period called Food Plus, which combined the food offerings of a typical supermarket with a large drugstore, and sometimes a home center as well. Two Food Plus stores were opened in 1996, with the second one encompassing about 4,800 square meters of selling space and offering about 55,000 items. Seiyu also developed a new concept for its shopping malls, which it called simply ''The Mall,'' and which was designed to be community-oriented, was anchored by a Seiyu store, and included numerous specialty stores as well as eating and drinking establishments. The first such shopping center was opened in Kasugai in 1992, and there were six by 1997. The Mall and Food Plus concepts were the main vehicles for the domestic expansion of Seiyu's core business in the mid- to late 1990s.

Following up on the opening of the Seiyu store in Hong Kong in 1990, Seiyu pursued a modest overseas expansion in the mid-1990s, focusing on the emerging markets of east Asia. In April 1995 a Seiyu department store was opened in Singapore, followed by a second unit in November 1996. The first Seiyu store in China debuted in June 1996, while Indonesia entered the company orbit in October of that year through a new Seibu outlet. Two Seiyu supermarkets opened in Bangkok, Thailand, in late 1996. All of these ventures were initiated through partnerships with local companies.

The mid-1990s also saw Seiyu begin to feel the full effects of the economic difficulties in Japan. In addition to an ongoing slump in consumer spending and increased competition in the retail sector—in part due to government deregulatory measures that spurred the opening of new stores—the company's finance subsidiary, Tokyo City Finance, was suffering from mounting losses resulting from the plunge in the Japanese property market that left TCF burdened with bad loans. The troubles at TCF led Seiyu to post extraordinary losses of ¥18.7 billion in the year ending in February 1995 (fiscal 1994) and ¥45.3 billion the following year. As a result, Seiyu posted a net loss of ¥6.32 billion (US$60.3 million) in fiscal 1995. Fiscal 1996 brought an additional ¥47.2 billion in extraordinary losses and a net loss of ¥2.99 billion (US$24.8 million). This latest loss would have

been even worse had Seiyu not sold a large block of shares in Family Mart, reducing its shareholding from 33 percent to 22 percent and posting an extraordinary gain of ¥44.52 billion in the process. In March 1997 two Seiyu Group companies—drugstore operator Asahi Medico, Ltd. and photoprocessor Seiyu Photo Service Co., Ltd.—were merged to form Asahi Medix Co., Ltd. The new company ran a chain of 67 drugstores and 233 photoprocessing shops.

In October 1997 Seiyu initiated a far-reaching restructuring program aimed at sparking a company turnaround. First, the management was revamped with five new corporate directors being appointed, the overall number of directors being reduced from 31 to 14, and Noriyuki Watanabe, a former stockbroker who had been vice-president at Family Mart, replacing Katsuhiro Fujiseki as president of Seiyu. Watanabe chose as his vice-president, Masao Kiuchi, the head of Ryohin Keikaku Co., Ltd., the publicly traded subsidiary of Seiyu that operated the extremely successful Mujirushi Ryohin. Having somewhat neglected its core retailing businesses while foraying into its various nonretailing ventures, Seiyu had a fair number of outdated and underperforming stores. The company began closing some of these, with 13 shuttered in 1997 and another six the following year, and overhauling others. Seiyu also began jettisoning numerous group companies, aiming to reduce the number of subsidiaries from 101 to 25 by 2002. In February 1998 its ownership of Inter-Continental Hotels and Resorts was sold to Bass PLC of the United Kingdom for ¥370 billion (US$2.9 billion). That same month, Seiyu sold its remaining 21.6 percent stake in Family Mart to ITOCHU Corporation, a Japanese trading firm, for ¥135 billion (US$957 million). Other transactions that affected fiscal 1997 results included the sale of shares in Ryohin Keikaku, which reduced the company's stake from 53.6 percent to 46.2 percent, and an initial public offering of stock in S.S.V. Inc., which decreased Seiyu's interest from 55.7 percent to 45.7 percent. S.S.V. operated supermarkets, mainly in the Nagano, Aichi, and Gifu prefectures. With another write-off, mostly related to TCF, of ¥166.2 billion (US$1.3 billion), Seiyu posted a net loss of ¥59.5 billion (US$468 million) for fiscal 1997. The company returned to the black in 1998, but only because additional asset sales—including the further reduction of its stake in Ryohin Keikaku to 21.6 percent—offset more restructuring charges.

Seiyu remained a troubled firm at the dawn of the millennium, burdened by a debt load in excess of ¥911.5 billion (US$7.46 billion), a figure that was equivalent to 52 times the total shareholders' equity of ¥17.28 billion (US$144 million). In August 1999, with the company's capital having fallen further to ¥11.71 billion, Seiyu allocated ¥20 billion (US$175 million) in new shares to six companies in the Saison Group. This increased Seiyu's capital to ¥21.71 billion. Later that year the company sold another 15 percent of its stake in Ryohin Keikaku. In January 2000 Seiyu sold Asahi Medix to Sumitomo Corporation. Soon thereafter Seiyu reported a net loss for the 1999 fiscal year. The outlook for Seiyu appeared bleak, especially as some prominent Japanese retailers were at this same time declaring bankruptcy. The company also could not expect any more financial assistance from the Saison Group, as Saison was facing its own crisis from the failure of Seiyo Corp., a Japanese property developer and a Saison Group firm. This forced Seiyu to look for outside financing, and in April 2000 the company raised another ¥15.62 billion through the sale of additional shares. About half of this offering was purchased by Sumitomo, giving the trading company a nearly 12 percent stake in Seiyu. Observers speculated that the new alliance between Seiyu and Sumitomo might very well lead to the dissolution of the Saison Group. In any event, Seiyu was eager to resume a more aggressive program of store openings to regain momentum in its core businesses, and it needed to fund this expansion.

Principal Subsidiaries

S.S.V. Inc.; The Endo Chain Co., Ltd.; Hayashibe Co., Ltd.; Seiyu Foods Co., Ltd.; Smile Corp.; The SCC, Ltd.; L.L. Bean Japan, Inc.; Wakana Co., Ltd.; Pacific Tour Systems Corp.; Libro Co., Ltd.; S.S. Communications, Inc.; Smis Co., Ltd.; Hospitality Network Corp.; Nicoh Inc.; Tokyo City Finance Co., Ltd.; Seiyu (Thailand) Co., Ltd.; Beijing Zhong Shang Seiyu Co., Ltd. (China); Seiyu (Singapore) Private Limited; Seiyu (Shatin) Co., Ltd. (Hong Kong); Seiyu Pacific Pte., Ltd.

Principal Competitors

The Daiei, Inc.; The Daimaru, Inc.; Isetan Company Limited; Ito-Yokado Co., Ltd.; JUSCO Co., Ltd.; Marui Co., Ltd.; Matsuzakaya Co., Ltd.; Mitsukoshi, Ltd.; Mycal Corporation; Takashimaya Company, Limited; Tokyu Department Store Co., Ltd.; Uny Co., Ltd.

Further Reading

Amaha, Eriko, "Into the Unknown: Investing in Restructures Takes Courage," *Far Eastern Economic Review,* July 9, 1998, p. 44.

Asao, Kunio, *Seibu Sezon Gurupu,* Tokyo: Nihon Jitsugyo Shuppansha, 1985.

"The Emporia Strike Back," *Economist,* October 29, 1994, pp. 83–84.

"Look Out," *Economist,* October 24, 1998, pp. 108+.

Sakamaki, Sachiko, "Simple Success: Japanese Chain's Anti-Brand Chic Is a Consumer Hit," *Far Eastern Economic Review,* August 21, 1997, p. 75.

Shirouzu, Norihiko, "Seiyu's Move to Restructure Impresses One Contrarian," *Asian Wall Street Journal,* September 22, 1998, p. 17.

Tominaga, Masabumi, *Seiyu Sutoa no Keiei,* Tokyo: Nihon Jitsugyo Shuppansha, 1978.

—Roy Larke and Kenji Arima
—updated by David E. Salamie

SFX Entertainment, Inc.

650 Madison Avenue, 16th Floor
New York, New York 10022
U.S.A.
Telephone: (212) 838-3100
Fax: (212) 750-6692
Web site: http://www.sfx.com

Wholly Owned Subsidiary of Clear Channel
  Communications, Inc.
Incorporated: 1997
Employees: 2,700
Sales: $1.68 billion (1999)
Stock Exchanges: New York
Ticker Symbol: SFX
NAIC: 71131 Promoters of Performing Arts, Sports, and
  Similar Events with Facilities; 71141 Agents and
  Managers for Artists, Athletes, Entertainers, and Other
  Public Figures

SFX Entertainment, Inc. is the largest owner and operator of venues for live entertainment in the United States. Since its founding in 1997 the company has acquired many of the largest concert promotion companies in the United States and has begun doing the same in Canada and Europe. Two-thirds of its revenues come from this area. SFX companies also manage sports celebrities, promote monster truck shows, and put together touring theatrical productions. To boost revenues, SFX has signed corporate sponsorship contracts, expanded its venues' premium-priced seating, and increased the number of events each venue schedules. The acquisition of the company by media giant Clear Channel Communications could further strengthen its dominance, giving it access to that corporation's network of radio and television stations.

Origins

SFX founder Robert F.X. Sillerman was born in 1948 and grew up in the world of entrepreneurship and entertainment. His father, Michael McKinley Sillerman, had founded the Keystone Radio Network, which ended up going bankrupt when Robert was 13. The younger Sillerman took to the world of business from an early age, founding a greeting card company while still in his teens and a marketing consultation firm while an undergraduate at Brandeis University. Following graduation he worked in the field of marketing, founding National Discount Marketers, Inc. in 1974. In 1978 he formed a business partnership with legendary New York radio personality Bruce ''Cousin Brucie'' Morrow. Sillerman-Morrow Broadcasting Group bought eight radio stations and a TV station before selling out in 1985. Sillerman continued investing in radio and founded SFX Broadcasting, Inc. with Steven Hicks in 1992 to acquire the stations owned by Command Communications and Capstar Communications. The company's name was created by scrambling Sillerman's middle and last initials. In 1993, SFX Broadcasting went public.

Sillerman was ahead of the curve in radio consolidation, buying up stations at a time when they were relatively cheap. In the early 1990s the Federal Communications Commission loosened rules forbidding ownership of multiple stations in the same market, which helped make owning a string of stations more profitable. SFX acquired additional stations over the next several years, and when the 1996 Federal Telecommunications Act further lifted ownership restrictions, the company went on a buying spree. Purchases of Multi-Market Radio, Inc., ABS Communications, Prism Radio Partners, Liberty Broadcasting, and Secret Communications soon increased the company's portfolio to more than 70 stations in 20 markets.

In late 1996 SFX made its first foray into the world of concert promotion with the acquisition of Delsener/Slater of New York, one of the top concert promoters in the northeastern United States. The $20 million deal gave SFX a company that staged concerts at a number of different venues and also operated an 11,000-seat amphitheater on Long Island. Within a few months this new line of business was expanded through the $55 million acquisition of Sunshine Promotions, Inc. of Indiana. Sunshine owned two amphitheaters and an indoor theater and held leases on several others. A new division, SFX Concerts, was formed to operate the two companies. SFX's goal was to utilize its chain of radio stations to advertise the events promoted by this division.

Company Perspectives:

SFX has established a new model for live entertainment, one built on providing an unparalleled standard of global service and creativity in the industry. SFX's whole is greater than the sum of its parts. Never before has the live entertainment industry been packaged in a manner that makes it so accessible to fans, marketers, and talent. Through synergy and cross-pollination of all aspects of the industry, from venues to content, we have created new strategic business opportunities for our varied constituencies, including marketers who now have unmatched opportunities to showcase their products and services in the most creative, interactive and impacting way.

In August 1997 SFX announced that it would be acquired by the Capstar unit of Dallas-based Hicks, Muse, Tate & Furst, led by former Sillerman partner Steven Hicks. The deal was put on hold, however, because of scrutiny by the Justice Department's antitrust division. Meanwhile, SFX was expanding its concert promotions division dramatically. In mid-December four major companies were acquired, including top promoters Bill Graham Presents of San Francisco, Contemporary Group of St. Louis, and Concert/Southern Promotions of Atlanta, as well as Network Magazine Group and SJS Entertainment, a radio and concert industry publishing, research, and production firm. The combined cost was more than $230 million. Just two weeks later a $155 million deal to buy PACE Entertainment Corp. and subsidiary Pavilion Partners was announced. The Houston-based PACE was the largest producer of touring theatrical productions outside New York City and also promoted concerts and motorsport events, while Pavilion owned 11 amphitheaters around the country. To support the buying spree, SFX sold $350 million in bonds and made arrangements for $300 million in credit.

SFX Going Solo; Acquisitions Coming Fast and Furious in 1998

In the spring of 1998 SFX Broadcasting received clearance for its acquisition by Hicks, Muse, Tate & Furst, with newly christened SFX Entertainment, Inc. to be spun off as a separate entity. Shortly thereafter, five more major acquisitions were announced. SFX Entertainment would spend $227 million to purchase concert promoters Avalon Attractions of Los Angeles and Don Law's Blackstone Entertainment of New England, souvenir company Event Merchandising, Inc., the Oakdale Theater of Wallingford, Connecticut, and Falk Associates Management Enterprises (FAME), an agency that represented basketball stars such as Michael Jordan and Patrick Ewing. After this batch of acquisitions, SFX asserted that it had gained control of more than 40 percent of the concert market nationwide.

SFX's national buying binge was causing much consternation within both the investment community and the traditionally fragmented, regionally based concert touring business. Some questioned the premium prices being paid for promotion companies, whose take on a typical event was usually only three to four percent of the gross. Others wondered about Sillerman's agenda, insisting that he was merely repeating his radio game

plan of consolidating a fragmented industry so that he could drive up prices and sell out when the market peaked. He denied this charge, insisting that he expected his then six-year-old daughter to take over the company from him when she grew up. Entertainment business insiders predicted a negative impact on up-and-coming acts, who would not have the name recognition to be booked into SFX's nationwide circuit of venues. Some talent agents also feared that performers would book tours directly with SFX, eliminating the need for their services in dealing with multiple promoters across the country. Most observers predicted that SFX would ultimately have to raise ticket prices in order to turn a profit, possibly causing a backlash among audiences in the process. The company denied this, too, stating that the best seats would likely become more expensive, but that others in the rear could be reduced in price and the overall balance would remain the same.

In July 1998 SFX purchased sports marketing firm Marquee Group for $100 million. Sillerman had helped launch it in 1994 and owned nine percent of its stock. A month later Magicworks Entertainment, Inc. was acquired, also for $100 million. This Miami-based company promoted concerts and managed touring events such as magician David Copperfield and musicals *Jekyll & Hyde* and *Evita*. It had been a partner of PACE unit PACE Theatricals for some time. Also acquired was production company American Artists, which controlled several theaters in the Boston area.

A big coup for SFX came in August, when it made a deal to buy Cellar Door Companies for $105 million. Cellar Door promoted concerts in the Midwest and South, and had been one of the last major holdouts against the SFX onslaught. Jack Boyle, Cellar Door's head, was placed in charge of SFX's music division. The company also formed a new unit, SFX Live, which was to market entertainment events on a national basis.

Controversy Following SFX's Rapid Growth: 1998–99

In late summer the U.S. Justice Department launched an informal inquiry into whether the company was attempting to monopolize the concert promotions business. Several major entertainment industry figures also were criticizing SFX in the press, including top Creative Artists Agency agent Tom Ross and USA Networks CEO Barry Diller, whose company owned Ticketmaster. Each of these sparks soon fizzled, however. The Justice probe was dropped by the end of the year, Ross left CAA in part because of his comments about SFX, and the company suddenly signed a deal with Ticketmaster giving the latter exclusive ticketing rights to all SFX events for seven years. SFX-owned companies Next Ticketing and Capital Ticketing were to be folded into Ticketmaster as part of the arrangement.

In January 1999, SFX spent $18 million for talent agency Integrated Sports International and quickly followed this up with a $100 million deal to acquire interest in seven concert venues. April saw the announcement of a plan to buy TourVen, Inc., a promoter of traveling shows such as "Barney's Big Surprise." In the summer SFX stock moved from the NASDAQ to the New York Stock Exchange, and the company acquired Hendricks Management Co., a baseball player representation firm. SFX also launched an online ticketing site, SFX.com, in conjunction with Ticketmaster.

The summer of 1999 saw court approval granted for the $96 million purchase of the bankrupt Livent, a deal that had been initiated a year earlier. Livent, once one of the premier theatrical production companies, owned such touring shows as *Ragtime* and *Fosse,* as well as a number of venues in Canada and the United States. Its bankruptcy had been attributed to widespread accounting fraud.

More acquisitions followed, including the purchase of figure skating promoter Candid Productions and SFX's first European company, Apollo Leisure Group of the United Kingdom. The $254 million Apollo deal gave SFX control over more than 25 theaters in the United Kingdom as well as Tickets Direct, a ticketing agency. To keep the ball rolling, SFX arranged for another $1.1 billion in credit and offered 8.6 million new shares of stock at $41 each. A deal with American Express to become SFX's official card also was signed, one of a string of relationships with corporate sponsors such as Levi's, VH1, and Ford that the company had negotiated. One of SFX's goals was to increase the amount of national advertising at each venue it controlled, with the company now running commercials on giant video screens before some performances.

In the face of SFX's increasingly firm grip on the market, 11 of its competitors formed the Independent Promoters Organization (IPO) to collectively bid for the services of major acts. Members of IPO would include number two U.S. concert promoter Universal Concerts, Metropolitan Entertainment, Belkin Productions, and others. Some performers, including Eric Clapton, Celine Dion, and Shania Twain, had avoided SFX venues during the recent summer season at their agents' insistence. The company produced successful tours of its own, however, including those of 'N Sync, Cher, and the Backstreet Boys. Ticket sales in general were up, and SFX claimed $750 million worth had been sold during the year compared with $600 million for 1998.

Entering the 21st Century: A Growing Presence in Europe

European expansion was now on SFX's agenda, and in September Midland Concert Promotions Group Ltd. was acquired. The British company produced concerts, wrestling, and motorsport events and had sizable real estate holdings. SFX also had bought Barry Clayman Corp. of the United Kingdom in

August, and EMA Telstar Group of Stockholm in September. A month later SFX acquired 80 percent of Mojo Works of the Netherlands, the leading promoter in that country.

The company also was building its sports business. New purchases included SME Power Branding, a sports brand identity firm whose clients included Major League Baseball, and Tellem and Associates, a baseball talent agency. At year's end SFX consolidated the 14 sports companies it owned into SFX Sports Group, which would be headed by FAME CEO David Falk. The company also was concentrating on building its own brand identity, and over the next few months began to add the initials SFX to the names of its subsidiaries.

SFX was adding to its online presence as well, making a minority investment in David Bowie's Ultra-Star Internet Services LLC, which hosted official web sites for entertainers and sports teams. The company also formed a joint venture in Europe with World Online to create a music, sports, and theater Internet portal.

Early March 2000 saw the predictions of some of Sillerman's detractors come true when it was announced that SFX would be sold to radio giant Clear Channel Communications of Texas. The deal would give SFX stockholders $3 billion, with Clear Channel also taking on $1.1 billion in debt. Clear Channel owned 867 radio stations and 19 television stations in the United States, as well as 550,000 outdoor advertising displays. SFX now owned or operated 120 entertainment venues in 31 markets, offered touring Broadway shows in 55, and was the largest promoter of monster truck shows in the country. SFX Sports represented 650 athletes and sports broadcasters.

While the deal was being finalized, SFX continued its buying spree, picking up Electric Factory Concerts of Philadelphia and Jujamcyn Productions of Minneapolis, a touring theatrical production company. SFX already owned half of Jujamcyn, acquired through PACE Entertainment. Sports Management Group also was purchased by the company in May 2000 and was promptly folded into SFX Sports Group. Shortly thereafter, Canada's second largest concert promoter, Core Audience Entertainment, was acquired.

With the details of its purchase by Clear Channel still being worked out, SFX, Inc. stood unchallenged as the leader of the U.S. live entertainment field. The changes its frenetic buying activity had wrought in the marketplace were still being assessed, however, and SFX was still developing its own identity as a company rather than as merely the sum of many parts. Acquisition by the nation's largest radio conglomerate would create further opportunities for expansion and new marketing synergies, but it would take time before the full impact of this relationship became known.

Principal Subsidiaries

American Artists Limited, Inc.; Apollo Leisure Group Limited (U.K.); Atlanta Concerts, Inc.; Avalon Acquisition Corp.; Barry Clayman Corporation Limited (U.K.); Bill Graham Presents, Inc.; Cellar Door Holding Company; Concert Southern Chastain Promotions; Contemporary Group, Inc.; Core Audience Entertainment (Canada); Delsener/Slater Enterprises, Ltd.; DLC Corp.; Electric Factory Concerts, Inc.; EMA Telstar Gruppen AB (Sweden); Event Merchandising Inc.; Irving Plaza Concerts, Inc.; Jujamcyn Productions Company, LLC; Magicworks Concerts, Inc.; Magicworks Theatricals, Inc.; Midland Concert Promotions Group Limited (U.K.); Mojo Works b.v. (The Netherlands; 80%); NEXT Ticketing, LLC; Oakdale Theater Concerts, Inc.; PACE Entertainment Corporation; Rainbow Concert Productions, Inc.; SFX Broadway, Inc.; SFX Family Entertainment, Inc.; SFX Marketing, Inc.; SFX Rights, Inc.; SFX Sports Group, Inc.; SFX Theatrical Group, Inc.; Sunshine Concerts, LLC; Westbury Music Fair, LLC. The company also owns directly, or through its subsidiaries, several hundred other companies in the United States and Europe.

Principal Competitors

Feld Entertainment, Inc.; HOB Entertainment, Inc.; IMG; Independent Promoters Organization; Jujamcyn Theaters; Manhattan Theatre Club; Nederlander Organization, Inc.; Ogden Corp.; On Stage Entertainment, Inc.; Shubert Organization, Inc.; TBA Entertainment Corporation; The Walt Disney Company; Westwood One, Inc.; William Morris Agency, Inc.; Worldwide Entertainment & Sports Corp.

Further Reading

Brownlee, Lisa, "Texas Titan's Big Corral—Radio Cowboy's New SFX Deal Jacks Up His Entertainment Clout," *New York Post,* March 5, 2000, p. 62.

Cavazos, Nick, "The New America: SFX Broadcasting, Inc. Riding a Strong Rebound in Radio Industry," *Investor's Business Daily,* January 24, 1995, p. A4.

Furman, Phyllis, "SFX Marks the New Spot: Radio's Sillerman Ready to Go Live from New York," *New York Daily News,* March 9, 1998, p. 20.

Gosselin, Peter G., "SFX Chief Spends $1B to Become Concert King," *Boston Globe,* November 15, 1998, p. A1.

Harrington, Richard, "A Concert Promoter Out to Steal the Show?," *Washington Post,* August 28, 1998, p. B1.

Milner, Brian, "Courts Approve Livent Sale to SFX," *Globe and Mail,* July 9, 1999, p. B3.

Morse, Steve, "SFX Deal Is Part of Industry Trend: Fallout for Concertgoers and Musicians Unclear," *Boston Globe,* May 5, 1998, p. C1.

Newman, Melinda, "Indie Concert Promo Biz Reshaped by SFX's Rise," *Billboard,* September 4, 1999, p. 1.

Petrozzello, Donna, "Robert F.X. Sillerman," *Broadcasting & Cable,* July 11, 1994, p. 69.

Sandler, Adam, "Sea Change—SFX Rewrites Rules of Concert Game," *Daily Variety,* July 30, 1998, p. A1.

Stieghorst, Tom, "SFX Broadcasting Goes on Buying Spree in Concert-Promotion Business," *Knight-Ridder Tribune Business News,* February 15, 1998.

Sullivan, Jim, "When It Comes to Pop Concerts, He Is the Player," *Boston Globe,* May 16, 1999, p. N1.

Waddell, Ray, "Giant SFX Makes $750M in '99 Grosses," *Billboard,* January 8, 2000, p. 106.

——, "Giant SFX, Ticketmaster Strike Deal," *Amusement Business,* November 23, 1998.

——, "Radio's SFX Buys Delsener/Slater," *Amusement Business,* October 21, 1996, p. 6.

——, "SFX Buys Three Concert Promoters," *Billboard,* December 27, 1997, p. 98.

—Frank Uhle

Shannon Aerospace Ltd.

Shannon Airport
County Clare
Ireland
Telephone: 353 (61) 370010
Fax: 353 (61) 370020
Web site: http://www.shannonaerospace.com

Private Company
Incorporated: 1992
Employees: 800
Sales: IR £50 million (1999 est.)
NAIC: 48819 Other Support Activities for Air
Transportation

Shannon Aerospace Ltd. specializes in heavy maintenance and overhauls of narrow-body airliners. A joint venture of Lufthansa and Swissair, its clients include SAS, Aerolineas Argentinas, and Malév Hungarian Airlines. In spite of its technical pedigree and continued growth, profits have been elusive, largely due to overcapacity in the maintenance and overhaul business.

Origins

In the late 1980s, Guinness Peat Aviation (GPA) had 100 client airlines around the world and was predicting the world's jet fleet would grow 60 percent by the end of the century.

GPA was the wildly successful leasing venture started by Dr. Tony A. Ryan. In July 1989, GPA Group Ltd., the holding company, announced plans for a new subsidiary, Shannon Aerospace Ltd., to manage GPA's non-airline businesses, including its 50 percent investments in aircraft painting company GPA Expressair Ltd. and Shannon Engine Support Ltd.

GPA also announced plans for a joint venture with Lufthansa and Swissair for a major maintenance and overhaul facility for civil airliners. In fact, it was this joint venture that became known as Shannon Aerospace.

Both Lufthansa and Swissair were recognized for their technical expertise. Lufthansa's existing technical unit employed 10,500 people, while that of Swissair employed 3,000. The two airlines each held 35 percent of the new company, with GPA holding the remaining 30 percent.

The lower costs of doing business in Ireland attracted Lufthansa and Swissair to the project. Dr. Tony Ryan was credited with bringing them on board. Like GPA itself, Shannon Aerospace was based on the west coast of Ireland, an area with particularly high unemployment. The Irish government was promoting the area as a center for high-tech business development. It was offering a tax rate of just ten percent for service industries through 2005.

TEAM Aer Lingus (TAM), a unit of Ireland's state airline, already conducted third-party maintenance operations on the opposite side of the country in Dublin. However, 18 percent of the Irish workforce was jobless, not counting the many who had left the country to find work.

A 110-acre aviation park opened at Shannon Airport in October 1991. The Shannon Aerospace facility cost IR £80 million (US$113 million) and opened for business in September 1992. The building, which consisted of a maintenance hangar and adjacent painting hangar, was the largest in Ireland under one roof, measuring 240 meters by 92 meters (788 feet by 302 feet). It eclipsed the US$60 million facility Team Air Lingus had built just two years earlier in Dublin.

The new venture targeted markets in Europe, Africa, and the Middle East. Its three owners were expected to supply at least a quarter of its business. However, Shannon Aerospace purported to be independent in its business decisions, particularly regarding pricing and scheduling. It announced US$10 million worth of contracts at the time of its opening, though some of these were canceled. Shannon Aerospace also served as GPA's line maintenance base in the beginning, while GPA agreed to send its Boeing 747s and MD-80s to Swissair for overhauls.

A Lufthansa Boeing 737-200 was first into the service bay. Shannon Aerospace initially specialized in Boeing 737s and the

Company Perspectives:

Shannon Aerospace specialises in performing heavy maintenance checks on Boeing 737, 757, 767, McDonnell Douglas MD-80 and Airbus A320 family aircraft, as well as offering a comprehensive range of specialist services.

Its FAA and JAA Approved Shannon-based facility includes five maintenance lines, two painting bays and workshops. It also includes in-house training facilities which incorporate some of the industry's most advanced training methods.

During the past decade, the facility has attracted an enviable reputation for its reliable turn-around times and consistent record of releasing aircraft back to commercial service on time. Our approach represents a unique blend of experience, accountability and productivity, coupled with open and transparent customer relationships.

MD-80/DC-9 family of aircraft. It planned to soon add Boeing 757 and 767 aircraft to its repertoire.

Shannon Aerospace started off with 600 employees, with plans to eventually employ 1,075 workers. This made the company the second largest employer in the midwest region of Ireland after the De Beers diamond mining operation. Training was started in Ireland and completed on the continent, at Swissair, Lufthansa, and Austrian Airlines, a close partner to Swissair. Lufthansa and Swissair supplied most of the 50 managers in the beginning. Dr. Herbert Groeger from Lufthansa was chief executive.

Employment rose ten percent by 1993. Eighty percent of the employees were less than 25 years old; fewer than five percent were female. Irish girls generally could not take technical subjects in high school and were still a rarity in the blue collar workforce. However, a new program called New Opportunities for Women, funded by Shannon Aerospace and the European Social Fund, prepared women for further training as mechanics. Shannon Aerospace was still on target to meet its projected staffing levels. Its IR £20 million training scheme was the largest the country had ever seen.

Lufthansa subsidiary Condor Flugdienst operated many Boeing 757s, and Shannon Aerospace began servicing these in 1993. Other customers apart from its founders included Air Sweden and Ghana Airways. It entered a long-term relationship with the Italian operator Eurofly in 1994. In October of the same year, Shannon Aerospace beat out TAP Air Portugal to win a IR £5 million contract from KLM. The order provided for 10 D-checks on Boeing 737s.

D-checks were performed every ten years and took 28 days to complete, including paint. I-checks were done every five years. C4-checks were also considered heavy maintenance. According to *Air Transport World,* Shannon offered clients "full transparency" regarding work in progress via a state-of-the-art data processing system.

Rescued in 1995

Even as the first planes were rolling into Shannon Aerospace's hangars, conditions were developing in the world market that would nearly lead to the company's collapse in the mid-1990s. The world's airlines lost billions of dollars in the wake of the Gulf War and the hesitancy of many travelers to book international flights. The latest generation of commercial jet aircraft also required less maintenance. Finally, oversupply in the market, including new facilities in low-wage regions, kept considerable pricing pressure on the company.

By 1994, Shannon Aerospace's Irish owner, GPA, was suffering serious financial trouble in the wake of its failed 1992 flotation. GPA's fleet accounted for more than a third of Shannon Aerospace's contract work. Swissair's profits were also falling.

Shannon Aerospace had hoped to break even by 1995. While the company was still growing, with a client base of two dozen airlines, it needed still more business to reduce unit costs. It had more than 700 employees and 150 trainees; by then, 40 percent of the workforce was female.

In 1995, Shannon Aerospace asked the Irish government for IR £12 million as part of a restructuring plan. The government, which had already given the company IR £23 million through the Shannon Development Authority, asked for its continental partners to invest more cash as well. Instead, Lufthansa would have preferred to transfer its Boeing 737 maintenance work to Shannon instead—a prospect which angered German labor unions.

Under a rescue plan announced in late April, the government did decide to invest another IR £12 million in Shannon Aerospace. It had already rescued its rival, TEAM Aer Lingus, putting it in the curious position of subsidizing two competitors. Not surprisingly, both British aerospace companies and German trade unions objected to the rescue package.

Lufthansa and Swissair required GPA to also pay IR £12 million as well as give up its 30 percent shareholding. GPA would have had to pay a similar amount had Shannon Aerospace been liquidated. Neither airline invested any more of its own cash, but assumed GPA's share of liabilities.

Lufthansa finally agreed to transfer its Boeing 737 aircraft work to Shannon Aerospace beginning in 1998. Lufthansa Technik Aktiengessellschaft was then obliged to lay off half of its 380 maintenance staff at Berlin's Schonefeld Airport.

In August 1995, after a detailed audit, Lufthansa and Swissair agreed to each acquire half of GPA's interest in Shannon Aerospace. Lufthansa Technik's Wolfgang Godhe was then named CEO, with Swissair's Martin Kaiser as his deputy.

Both Lufthansa and Swissair planned to transfer their narrow-body overhauls to Shannon through 1999. At the end of 1995, Lufthansa Technik also bought out Shannon Turbine Technologies, a joint venture between GPA and Sulzer, the Swiss engineering firm.

Although Shannon Aerospace focused on narrow-body aircraft, it added the Boeing 767 in December 1995 since it was so closely related to the Boeing 757. The company had also decided to add the Airbus A319/320/321 family as MD-80 work began to taper off.

Key Dates:

1989: GPA Group plans maintenance venture with Lufthansa and Swissair.
1992: Shannon Aerospace opens for business.
1995: GPA bails out and the state gives IR £12 million to rescue the company.
1998: FLS buys rival TEAM Aer Lingus.
2000: Shannon Aerospace accelerates recruitment due to two-year backlog.

New Techniques in Late 1990s

Swissair and Lufthansa decided to exit the narrow-body heavy maintenance field in the late 1990s. By this time, Swissair's SR Technics AG subsidiary (formed from its Technical Services Division in 1997) and Austrian Airlines had also stopped working on MD-80s.

The Danish Group FLS bought TEAM Aer Lingus in late 1998. Shannon Aerospace had 750 Irish workers at the time, with plans to increase employment to 900 within a year. It was also investing IR £5.5 million in extending its workshops and upgrading its information technology infrastructure. It planned to add another production line or two to accommodate a new contract to overhaul 100 Airbus aircraft for Lufthansa. Revenues for the year reached IR £38 million (US$52 million). In February 1999, Lufthansa Technik announced plans to open a commercial airliner painting facility (Lufthansa Aircraft Painting Shannon Limited) at Shannon Airport within a year.

A new area of expertise was that of non-destructive testing. Airbus Industries designated a quarter of each operator's Airbus fleet as "sample" aircraft requiring four times the number of inspections during their D-checks. Shannon Aerospace also began conducting transit checks for transatlantic operators flying into Shannon, beginning with Continental Airlines.

Martin Kaiser was appointed managing director (chief executive) at the end of 1999 as Shannon Aerospace continued to expand. Some new clients added late in the decade were Aeroflot, the Dutch airline Transavia, and North American Airlines. In May 2000, Shannon Aerospace announced ambitious plans to recruit 300 more workers in the next three years. A two-year order backlog certainly justified the move.

Principal Competitors

Air France Industries; Braathens Technical Division; Cargolux Airlines International S.A.; FLS Aerospace Holding Group A/S; Heavylift Aircraft Engineering; Icelandair Technical Operations; Jet Aviation; KLM Engineering & Maintenance; Monarch Aircraft Engineering Ltd; Sabena Technics NV/SA; Shannon MRO Ltd.

Further Reading

Cleary, Catherine, "Burton in Emergency Talks About Aircraft Firm," *Irish Times,* Business This Week, March 31, 1995, p. 2.
——, "Objections to Rescue Plan for Shannon," *Irish Times,* June 7, 1995, p. 14.
——, "Shannon Aerospace Completes £24 Million Refinancing Package," *Irish Times,* Bus. Sec., August 5, 1995, p. 15.
Dalby, Douglas, "Aircraft Mechanics Break Gender Barrier," *Irish Times,* Business This Week, October 1, 1993, p. 4.
Donoghue, J.A., "Shaping Up in Shannon," *Air Transport World,* November 1992, p. 91.
Duffy, Paul, "The One You Call First," *Air Transport World,* March 1998, pp. 97–103.
Dunne, Jim, "Taxpayers Subsidize Competing Losers," *Irish Times,* Business This Week, April 28, 1995, p. 3.
Fitzgerald, Gerry, "Shannon Venture Bolsters GPA Development Plan," *Aviation Week & Space Technology,* February 15, 1993, pp. 35+.
Hogan, Dick, "Aerospace Order Books Are Full," *Irish Times,* Business This Week, May 14, 1993, p. 2.
Maguire, Kevin, "Shannon Reaps Benefit of Stability," *Daily Telegraph,* May 13, 1991, p. 25.
Murdoch, Bill, "Aircraft Leaser to Trim Losses," *Irish Times,* March 16, 1995, p. 16.
O'Kane, Paul, "Lufthansa Transfers Work to Shannon Aerospace," *Irish Times,* May 20, 1995, p. 12.
——, "Shannon Aerospace Secures £5 Million KLM Contract," *Irish Times,* October 22, 1994, p. 16.
"Order on Evidence Overruled," *Irish Times,* Business This Week, July 2, 1999, p. 51.
Taylor, Cliff, "Industrial Policy Bound to Create Headaches," *Irish Times,* Business This Week, April 28, 1995, p. 2.

—Frederick C. Ingram

Sigma-Aldrich Corporation

3050 Spruce Street
St. Louis, Missouri 63103
U.S.A.
Telephone: (314) 771-5765
Toll Free: (800) 521-8956
Fax: (314) 286-7874
Web site: http://www.sigma-aldrich.com

Public Company
Incorporated: 1975
Employees: 7,332
Sales: $1.04 billion (1999)
Stock Exchanges: NASDAQ
Ticker Symbol: SIAL
NAIC: 325188 All Other Inorganic Chemical
   Manufacturing; 325199 All Other Basic Organic
   Chemical Manufacturing; 325413 In-Vitro Diagnostic
   Substance Manufacturing; 325414 Biological Product
   (Except Diagnostic) Manufacturing; 422210 Drugs
   and Druggist' Sundries Wholesalers; 422690 Other
   Chemical and Allied Products Wholesalers

Sigma-Aldrich Corporation is a developer, manufacturer, and distributor of a wide range of biochemicals, organic chemicals, chromatography products, and diagnostic reagents. The company is the world's leading seller of chemicals to research laboratories, pharmaceutical companies, and hospitals, with a product line that includes 85,000 substances sold under five well-known chemical brands: Sigma, Aldrich, Fluka, Supelco, and Riedel-de Haën. Sigma-Aldrich has more than 150,000 customers in more than 160 countries; the majority of its sales to these customers are on the small side, averaging about $300. About 55 percent of sales are generated outside the United States. The company maintains manufacturing facilities in Missouri, Pennsylvania, Texas, Wisconsin, Germany, Israel, Switzerland, and the United Kingdom. Approximately 46 percent of sales are derived from company-manufactured products.

Born Through a 1975 Merger

Sigma-Aldrich Corporation is the result of a 1975 merger between two specialty chemical companies, one that manufactured biochemicals (Sigma Chemical Company) and another that manufactured organic chemicals (Aldrich Chemical Company). While offering divergent products, both companies regarded high-quality products and customer service a priority. The merger, therefore, represented a convergence of business strategy as well as the creation of a diversified product line that ranked Sigma-Aldrich at the top of the specialty chemical industry. In particular, because of the scientific community's involvement in the growing field of biomedical research, Sigma-Aldrich's product catalog became standard issue in pharmaceutical laboratories around the world.

Sigma Chemical Company was started in 1945 in St. Louis. At a time when sugar was scarce Dan Broida, a biochemist, began a storefront business to manufacture saccharin. The company later went on to produce biochemicals and diagnostic products. Sigma's customers ranged from hospitals to university laboratories. Scientific fields concerned with the study of life sciences as well as disease diagnostics use biochemicals as the basic substances to develop pharmaceuticals and diagnostic tests.

Aldrich Chemical Company, founded by the Harvard-educated chemist Dr. Alfred R. Bader, began manufacturing organic chemicals in a Milwaukee garage six years after Broida established Sigma. Aldrich's first products were those chemicals not offered by Eastman Kodak, a leader in the chemical industry. Bader soon decided that his company could engage in direct competition with larger companies, and he began offering a broad line of organics sold to research laboratories of pharmaceutical companies. The company did excedingly well and its customer list soon included the likes of Abbott Laboratories and Ciba-Geigy.

The 1975 merger between the two companies matched skill for skill and talent for talent. Broida assumed the role of chairman and Bader took the position of company president. While the combined company interests still remained small compared to those of the larger industry firms, the business acumen of Sigma-Aldrich's management went a long way in securing an impressive

---

Company Perspectives:

Sigma-Aldrich is a financially sound company with unequaled broad scientific knowledge. Our customers are in Life Science and High Technology areas that will make enormous progress toward benefiting mankind in the new millennium. We intend to play our part.

---

percentage of the specialty chemical research market. By 1979 the company laid claim to between 30 and 40 percent of the $100 million research market. Sales climbed to $68 million, representing an annual increase of 15 percent. Earnings jumped 24 percent to $9.2 million, causing Wall Street analysts to predict continued growth of 20 percent a year.

Sigma-Aldrich's marketing success, achieved by neither a large sales force nor expensive advertising outlays, relied on the distribution of catalogs. In addition to advertising products available on a phone-order basis, the catalog offered detailed information about the physical properties of the marketed chemicals. The value of the catalog as a reference source as well as an advertising tool was evident, and it soon became a company trademark. Initially compiled by Bader in the early 1950s as a one-page, one-chemical listing, the catalog grew to include 40,000 chemicals by the late 1970s. Sigma-Aldrich's small sales force distributed 300,000 free copies of the catalog in 1979.

The company's reputation among chemists as a manufacturer of quality products matched a distribution network that ensured most orders would be filled in 24 hours. Interestingly enough, in the early years of Sigma-Aldrich's business an average order amounted to less than $100. This indicated a customer profile of academicians or laboratory researchers experimenting with relatively small quantities of chemicals. Although this profile was altered somewhat in the ensuing years due to the increasing pressure to supply bulk commercial chemicals, Sigma-Aldrich fiercely defended its business as first and foremost a service to the research community.

Overseas expansion in the late 1970s found 125 countries purchasing Sigma-Aldrich's products with company subsidiaries operating in Canada, the United Kingdom, Japan, Germany, and Israel. Nearly 40 percent of sales in 1979 resulted from overseas business.

1980s: Growing Alongside the Exploding Biomedical Industry

In the 1980s the company's growth matched the explosion in the U.S. biomedical research market. Despite such gains Sigma-Aldrich's management, much to the chagrin of some industry analysts, refused to alter the strategy that laid the framework for previous company growth. Rather than set long-term goals or exploit the bulk chemical market as some observers suggested, Broida defended his company's straightforward "opportunistic" policy of keeping pace with state-of-the-art developments in the scientific fields of immunology, microbiology, and endocrinology. By supplying chemicals in small quantities to research centers, Sigma-Aldrich's growth and profits corre-

sponded to breakthrough research in the development of pharmaceuticals from recombinant DNA.

Wall Street analysts also criticized the company's B-Line Systems, Inc. subsidiary, which had been inherited from the Sigma side of the company lineage. Manufacturing metal frameworks for industrial plants, the subsidiary was criticized for competing in the business of specialty chemicals on the one hand, and for contributing small profit margins on the other. Despite such criticism, however, the company's lack of long-term debt, its sparkling earnings record, and its annual profit increase of 20 to 25 percent mitigated the seriousness of such complaints.

Upon Dan Broida's death in 1981 several changes in policy and management affected the company structure. Tom Cori, a nine-year Sigma veteran, became company president. Common stock, formerly controlled by a 50 percent insiders interest, now became more widely held. In 1985, 2.2 million of the 8.68 million outstanding shares were sold for $129.5 million. Most of this stock had been held by relatives of Broida and the sale reduced their holdings to 1.3 million shares. This new figure represented approximately the same interest held by the Bader family.

Of the 2.2 million shares sold the company purchased 500,000. Apparently Bader had been opposed to the company purchase partially on the grounds that $13 million was borrowed to finance the transaction. Company indebtedness now totaled $32.4 million in short-term loans due in part to a $16 million expansion program started in 1980. Some five million shares, on the other hand, were now estimated to be available for trade in the over-the-counter market. Price per share between July and September 1985 ranged from $60.50 to $71, well over the company's $14 per share book value. A three-for-one stock split was soon in order.

By 1986 some 1.5 million company catalogs circulated yearly. Sigma-Aldrich's orders continued to average less than $150 each; on the other hand company profits totaled $29 million on volume of $215 million. Although president of a company with such impressive achievements, Cori did not rest on his laurels. Limited governmental funds for scientific research as well as the effect of the strong dollar on overseas sales offered some cause for concern. To facilitate expansion by broadening Sigma-Aldrich's product line, the company purchased Pathfinder Laboratories. The new subsidiary, costing $1.5 million in stock during 1984, manufactured radioactive chemicals. A much larger acquisition came in 1989 when Sigma-Aldrich purchased one of its main European competitors, Switzerland-based Fluka Chemie AG, from Ciba-Geigy and Hoffmann-La Roche. Fluka, maker of biochemicals and organic chemicals for the laboratory market, had annual sales of about $55 million.

1990s: Slower Growth and Restructuring

In 1991 Sigma-Aldrich took a significant step toward filling more bulk orders through the establishment of a fine chemicals division, which was charged with large-scale manufacturing of chemicals for the pharmaceutical and biopharmaceutical industries. That same year, Bader retired from his position as chairman and was named chairman emeritus. Cori took on the additional

Key Dates:

1945: Sigma Chemical Company is founded in St. Louis by Dan Broida to manufacture saccharin.
1951: Alfred R. Bader launches Aldrich Chemical Company as a Milwaukee-based manufacturer of organic chemicals.
1975: Sigma Chemical and Aldrich Chemical merge to form Sigma-Aldrich Corporation, which is based in St. Louis.
1981: Broida dies; Tom Cori takes over as company president.
1989: Fluka Chemie AG is acquired.
1991: Company establishes its fine chemicals division to handle bulk sales.
1993: Supelco, Inc. is acquired.
1997: Company purchases 75 percent interest in Riedel-de Haën.
1998: Genosys Biotechnologies, Inc. is acquired.
1999: The remaining 25 percent of Riedel-de Haën is acquired; major restructuring is launched, reorganizing the company into four business divisions: diagnostics, fine chemicals, laboratory products, and life sciences.
2000: Company divests B-Line Systems and is now focused fully on life sciences chemicals.

title of chairman. Bader's new role was short-lived, however, as in early 1992 he was voted off the board of directors and stripped of his chairman emeritus title. The reason for the board's action was never made public, although it was speculated to involve either an allegation that Bader had made a bet against the company's stock through a call option, a charge Bader denied, or the fact that Bader had failed to report his exercising of the option to the Securities and Exchange Commission in a timely manner, an action that Bader said had been "an honest mistake." In any event, Bader, who was held in high esteem by numerous Sigma-Aldrich customers on six continents, continued to be one of the largest holders of the company's stock into the early 21st century, when he held about six percent.

While sales and earnings growth slowed in the early and mid-1990s to 15 percent or less per year, Sigma-Aldrich continued to expand aggressively through such internal growth initiatives as the adding of manufacturing and distribution capacity as well as through acquisitions. In May 1993 the company acquired Supelco, Inc. from Rohm and Haas Company for $54.7 million. Based in Bellefonte, Pennsylvania, Supelco was a worldwide supplier of chromatography products used to analyze and purify drugs and had annual sales of $48 million. In 1994 David R. Harvey was named president and chief operating officer, with Cori remaining chairman and CEO. In the area of plant expansion, Sigma-Aldrich by 1997 had three new manufacturing facilities up and running: the first in St. Louis specializing in industrial tissue culture products, the second in the United Kingdom for pharmaceutical intermediates, and the third in Israel for immunochemicals. Meantime, in 1996, the company was fined $480,000 by the federal government for illegally exporting toxic substances that could be used to make chemical weapons; Sigma-Aldrich said that it had "inadvertently violated" U.S. export laws and that there was no evidence that the substances had actually been used to make such weapons.

Acquisitions returned to the fore in the late 1990s. In June 1997 the company purchased a 75 percent interest in Riedel-de Haën, a German maker of laboratory chemicals. In March 1999 Sigma-Aldrich purchased the remaining 25 percent. In December 1998 the company stepped up its presence in the biotechnology sector with the $39.5 million purchase of Texas-based Genosys Biotechnologies, Inc., one of the world's leading suppliers of custom synthetic DNA products—essential components of gene research.

In spite of the company's acquisition drive, growth slowed to a trickle by 1998, when sales increased by just six percent and net income barely edged ahead, increasing by only 0.1 percent. During 1999, a year in which the company was proceeding in a similar direction, significant changes took place at Sigma-Aldrich. In October, Harvey was promoted to president and CEO, with Cori remaining chairman. One month later, Harvey announced that the company would launch a major restructuring and would sell off its noncore B-Line Systems subsidiary. Through the restructuring, Sigma-Aldrich was reorganized into four main business units: laboratory products, which focused on chemicals used for research conducted in academia and industry and which accounted for about 55 percent of the company's revenues; life sciences, which concentrated on specific areas of research, including molecular biology, immunochemistry, cell biology, and chromatography (20 percent of sales); fine chemicals, which was retooled to include both large-scale manufacturing of chemicals and custom manufacturing (15 percent of sales); and diagnostics, which focused on products used to help diagnose and treat diseases, with a particular emphasis on tests in the areas of coagulation and immunoassay (ten percent). Sigma-Aldrich also hoped to drive growth through e-commerce, having successfully launched an award-winning web site in September 1998 through which five percent of U.S. orders were being placed by the end of 1999. With the completion in May 2000 of the sale of B-Line Systems to Cooper Industries, Inc. for $425 million, Sigma-Aldrich could, for the first time in its history, plan for the future as a company with a single focus—supplying chemicals to the life science industries.

Principal Subsidiaries

Sigma-Aldrich Co.; Sigma-Aldrich, Inc.; Sigma-Aldrich & Subs Foreign Sales Corporation (Barbados); Fluka Holding AG (Switzerland); Sigma-Aldrich Company, Ltd. (U.K.); Sigma-Aldrich Foreign Holding Co.; Sigma-Aldrich Finance Co.

Principal Divisions

Diagnostics; Fine Chemicals; Laboratory Products; Life Sciences.

Principal Competitors

Aceto Corporation; Albright & Wilson plc; Beckman & Coulter, Inc.; Becton, Dickinson & Company; Bio-Rad Laboratories, Inc.; Ciba Specialty Chemicals Corporation; DEKALB Genetics Corporation; Great Lakes Chemical Corporation;

Holliday Chemical Holdings PLC; ICN Pharmaceuticals, Inc.; TECHNE Corporation.

Further Reading

Bader, Alfred, *Adventures of a Chemist Collector,* London: Weidenfeld and Nicolson, 1995, 288 p.

Boswell, Clay, "Sigma-Aldrich Set for Global Growth in Pharmaceuticals and Fine Chemicals," *Chemical Market Reporter,* August 3, 1998, p. 17.

Byrne, Harlan S., "Sigma-Aldrich: The Right Chemistry for Strong Performance," *Barron's* May 17, 1993, pp. 47–48.

Corey, Andrea, "Sigma-Aldrich Restructuring, Selling Metals Division," *St. Louis Business Journal,* February 21, 2000, p. 8.

——, "Web Site Eases Ordering for Sigma-Aldrich Clients," *St. Louis Business Journal,* February 14, 2000, p. 40.

Flannery, William, "Sigma-Aldrich Meeting Erupts over Dispute," *St. Louis Post-Dispatch,* May 6, 1992, p. 1B.

Lerner, Matthew, "Sigma-Aldrich Strengthens Role As Pharma Supplier," *Chemical Market Reporter,* July 7, 1997, p. 14.

Manor, Robert, "Bad Bet?: Sigma-Aldrich Founder Bader Decries Dismissal," *St. Louis Post-Dispatch,* April 16, 1992, p. 1B.

Montgomery, Leland, "Betting on Biotech with Sigma Aldrich," *Financial World,* June 11, 1991, pp. 21–22.

Moore, Samuel K., "Sigma-Aldrich Reorganizes Chemicals, Sells Metals Operation," *Chemical Week,* December 1, 1999, p. 16.

Papanikolaw, Jim, "Sigma-Aldrich Sells Its B-Line Systems to Cooper Industries," *Chemical Market Reporter,* April 3, 2000, p. 3.

Rothenberg, Eric, "Consistent Chemistry," *Financial World,* August 9, 1988, p. 42.

Stamborski, Al, "Sigma Announces It Will Sell Its Only Non-Life Sciences Business," *St. Louis Post-Dispatch,* March 28, 2000, p. C7.

Van Arnum, Patricia, "Sigma-Aldrich Builds Its Position in the Life Sciences Arena," *Chemical Market Reporter,* June 19, 2000, p. 15.

—updated by David E. Salamie

Sime Darby Berhad

21st Floor, Wisma Sime Darby
Jalan Raja Laut
50350 Kuala Lumpur
Malaysia
Telephone: (3) 291 4122
Fax: (3) 298 7398
Web site: http://www.simenet.com

Public Company
Incorporated: 1958 as Sime Darby Holdings Ltd.
Employees: 29,000
Sales: M$9.91 billion (US$2.61 billion) (1999)
Stock Exchanges: Kuala Lumpur
NAIC: 551112 Offices of Other Holdings Companies;
113210 Forest Nurseries and Gathering of Forest
Products; 221112 Fossil Fuel Electric Power
Generation; 233110 Land Subdivision and Land
Development; 234930 Industrial Nonbuilding
Structure Construction; 311223 Other Oilseed
Processing; 325510 Paint and Coating Manufacturing;
326211 Tire Manufacturing (Except Retreading);
333415 Air-Conditioning and Warm Air Heating
Equipment and Commercial and Industrial
Refrigeration Equipment Manufacturing; 335222
Household Refrigerator and Home Freezer
Manufacturing; 421110 Automobile and Other Motor
Vehicle Wholesalers; 421810 Construction and
Mining (Except Petroleum) Machinery and Equipment
Wholesalers; 421830 Industrial Machinery and
Equipment Wholesalers; 541330 Engineering
Services; 561510 Travel Agencies; 561520 Tour
Operators; 622110 General Medical and Surgical
Hospitals; 713910 Golf Courses and Country Clubs

Sime Darby Berhad is the largest conglomerate in Malaysia and one of the largest in southeast Asia. Within its orbit are more than 270 operating companies in 23 countries, with its most extensive foreign operations in Hong Kong (which accounts for 25 percent of revenues), Singapore (14 percent), and Australia (11 percent). (The company generates 38 percent of its revenues domestically.) Its broadly diversified activities include a wide range of industries, with the core businesses being plantations (including oil palm and the company's original business, rubber), tire manufacturing, heavy equipment and motor vehicle distribution, property development, power generation, and engineering services. Other business operations include paint manufacturing, refrigeration product manufacturing, travel and tourism services, hospitals, and golf courses.

Focus on Rubber in the Early Years

The moniker "Sime Darby" was contrived in 1910 from the names of two European business partners: William Sime and Henry Darby. William Sime, a traveler and adventurer from Scotland, ventured to Malaysia when he was in his late 30s. Natural rubber—synthetic rubber was still being developed—had just been introduced to that country from Brazil. Sime and other entrepreneurs at the time recognized that the climate of Malaysia's jungle region was similar to that of Brazil's. Therefore, rubber could just as easily be grown in that country and sold not only in Malaysia but throughout southeast Asia and the world. Sime suggested to his friend Henry Darby, an English banker, that they start a rubber plantation there. Darby agreed to help fund the effort and together they formed Sime, Darby & Co., Ltd.

Sime Darby initially encountered stiff opposition to its venture from locals, who were wary of outsiders coming in to operate a plantation in Malacca. To quell their contempt, Sime and Darby forged friendships with several members of the Chinese business community. The most notable of those business leaders was Tun Tan Cheng Lock. Lock would later lead the Malaya independence movement—in the 1990s, the Malay Peninsula was made up of parts of Burma, Thailand, and Malaysia. Among other distinctions, Lock ultimately was crowned a Knight Commander of the British Empire and also received Malaysia's highest award, which is called "Tun." With the help of Lock and other business leaders, Sime and Darby were able to procure about 500 acres of rubber plantations in the dense jungles of Malacca.

Rubber markets surged during the 1910s and Sime Darby enjoyed healthy sales. The company expanded, becoming a

---

Company Perspectives:

Sime Darby is fully committed to the development and progress of the Asia-Pacific region, dedicated to the pursuit of excellence, and the realisation of its corporate objectives, while consistently upholding its longstanding values of integrity and professionalism.

---

manager for owners of other plantations and then moving into the trading end of the industry. Sime set up a branch office in Singapore in 1915 and shortly thereafter established a marketing office in London. Demand for rubber eventually outstripped Sime Darby's production capacity, and by the late 1920s the company found it necessary to clear more jungle. To do so, Sime Darby purchased Sarawak Trading Company in 1929. Sarawak (later renamed Tractors Malaysia) held the franchise for Caterpillar heavy earthmoving equipment. That important purchase signaled Sime Darby's expansion into the heavy equipment business, which would eventually become a major component of its expansive network. In 1936 the company's head office was relocated from Malacca to Singapore.

Sime Darby made a fortune in the global rubber industry during the 1920s and 1930s. Growth in that industry began to fade, however, as natural rubber was gradually supplanted by synthetic rubber. Sales of natural rubber boomed during World War II as warring nations purchased all available supplies. The war, however, also led to significant advancements in synthetic rubber technology.

Diversification and Malaysianization in the 1960s and 1970s

By the 1960s, then, Sime Darby Holdings—the company was incorporated in the founders' home country of England in 1958 and its name was changed to Sime Darby Holdings Ltd.—was forced to begin looking elsewhere for revenues. To that end, Sime Darby became one of the first rubber plantations in the region to convert to the production of palm oil and cocoa oil.

Sime Darby's diversification turned out to be a smart move. Demand for its oils and other agricultural products surged during the late 1960s and 1970s, and the company began to accumulate excess cash. A good deal of it was used to acquire other companies, thereby expanding Sime Darby's reach into several other industries. Much of Sime Darby's success during that period was attributable to its acquisition of the giant Seafield Estate in 1971 and the establishment of Consolidated Plantations Berhad that same year. Through Consolidated Plantations, which became the company's main plantation subsidiary, Sime Darby became a leading force in the region's thriving agricultural sector. In addition to growing the oil palms and cocoa, the company began processing the crops into finished products for sale throughout the world.

As its sales and profits spiraled upward during the early and mid-1970s, Sime Darby became a shiny feather in Britain's cap. To the surprise and chagrin of the British stockholders, however, the company was wrested from their control by the Malaysian government late in 1976. The intriguing events leading up to the takeover began in the early 1970s. During that time, Sime Darby's chief executive, Denis Pinder, began investing the company's cash in new subsidiaries throughout the world. The company's stock price soared as Sime Darby's sales spiraled upward. At the same time, some observers charged that Sime Darby was engaged in corrupt business practices (with critics coining the phrase "Slime Darby").

Allegations of corruption were confirmed in the eyes of some detractors when, in 1973, Darby's outside auditor was found stabbed to death in his bathtub. The Singapore police ruled the death a suicide, but Pinder still ended up in prison on misdemeanor charges. Pinder's successor took up where he left off, investing in numerous ventures, most of which were located in Europe. Unfortunately, many of those investments quickly soured. Some Malaysians felt that Sime Darby was taking profits from its successful domestic operations and investing them unwisely overseas. So, in 1976 the Malaysian government trading office bought up Sime Darby shares on the London stock exchange. It effectively gained control of the company and installed a board made up mostly of Asians.

Also in 1976, Asian and British board members were able to agree that Tun Tan Chen Lock's son, Tun Tan Siew Sin, would be an acceptable replacement as chairman of Sime Darby's board. In 1978 Sime Darby was reincorporated in Malaysia as Sime Darby Berhad. Its headquarters was moved to Kuala Lumpur the following year.

Staggering in the Early 1980s; Rebounding in the Late 1980s and Early 1990s

Sime Darby jettisoned some of its poorly performing assets during the late 1970s and early 1980s under Lock's leadership. But it also continued investing in new ventures. It purchased the tiremaking operations of B.F. Goodrich Philippines in 1981, for example, and secured the franchise rights to sell Apple Computers in southeast Asia in 1982. The addition of B.F. Goodrich Philippines marked the company's entrance into the tire manufacturing sector; also in 1981 came the establishment of Sime Darby International Tire Company, which in 1988 was renamed Sime Darby Pilipinas, Inc. In 1984 the company purchased a large stake in a Malaysian real estate development company, United Estates Berhad, and used it to begin developing plantation lands. This company later was renamed Sime UEP Properties Berhad. In Malaysia, Sime Darby acquired the franchises for BMW, Ford, and Land Rover vehicles.

By the early 1980s Sime Darby's push to diversify had given it a place in almost every industry, from agricultural and manufacturing to finance and real estate. Although it did diversify into heavy equipment, real estate, and insurance businesses, new management also plowed significant amounts of cash into the company's traditional commodity and plantation operations. Sime Darby became a favorite of investors looking for a safe bet. Indeed, the mammoth enterprise tended to minimize risks after the investment mistakes of the early 1970s and seemed content to operate as a slow-growth multinational behemoth that could withstand any market downturns. Even if something did go wrong, the company had a war chest of nearly a half billion U.S. dollars from which it could draw.

Unfortunately, Sime Darby's staid strategy negatively impacted its bottom line. Sales dipped to M $2.78 billion in 1992

Key Dates:

1910: William Sime and Henry Darby found Sime, Darby & Co., Ltd. to start a rubber plantation in Malaysia.
1915: Branch office is opened in Singapore.
1929: Acquisition of Sarawak Trading Company propels the company into heavy equipment business.
1936: Company's head office is moved to Singapore.
1958: Company is incorporated in the United Kingdom as Sime Darby Holdings Ltd.
1971: Company takes over Seafield Estate and incorporates Consolidated Plantations Berhad.
1976: Malaysian government gains control of the company.
1979: The headquarters is moved to Kuala Lumpur.
1981: B.F. Goodrich Philippines is acquired, marking the beginning of tire manufacturing for the group.
1984: Company moves into property development through the purchase of a large stake in United Estates Berhad.
1993: Sime Darby merges with the formerly publicly traded Consolidated Plantations.
1994: Company acquires 40 percent interest in Port Dickson Power, a Malaysian power generation firm.
1995: Company purchases controlling stake in United Malayan Banking Corporation; the unit is reorganized as Sime Bank and SimeSecurities.
1998: Asian financial crisis leads Sime Darby to record the first full-year net loss in its history.
1999: Sime Bank and SimeSecurities are divested.
2000: Interest in Port Dickson Power is increased to 60 percent; the company's interest in insurance firm Sime AXA is divested.

full-service resort with condominiums in Florida (Sandestin Resorts) and a hotel in Australia, among other enterprises. As the company dumped its cash into expansion and diversification, sales and profits bolted. Revenues climbed from M$2.53 billion in 1987 to M$4.98 billion in 1990 to M$6.20 billion in 1992. During the same period, net income soared from M$85 million to M$353 million.

Sime Darby realized a stunning 65 percent average annual growth in earnings during the late 1980s and early 1990s. Despite its gains, though, critics charged that the company had concentrated too heavily on traditional commodity industries and had failed to move into the 1990s with the rest of Malaysia. In fact, Sime Darby continued to garner about 43 percent of its sales from commodity trading activities in 1993 and only 18 percent from manufacturing. The rest came from heavy equipment distribution, insurance, and its property/tourism holdings. Although building strength in those businesses had added to the company's sales and profits during the late 1980s and early 1990s, the strategy had caused Sime Darby to fall behind more progressive holding companies in the region that were participating in booming high-tech, gaming, brokering, and manufacturing sectors. Many company insiders believed that Sime Darby would have to eliminate its heavy reliance on commodity industries if it wanted to sustain long-term growth.

Mid-1990s and Beyond: Aggressively Expanding, Then Retrenching Following Financial Crisis

Ahmad, the successful chief executive, also recognized the need for change at Sime Darby. The company's stock price began to fall in 1993 and its rapid revenue and profit growth began to subside in comparison with late 1980s levels. In 1993 Ahmad stepped back from control of the company when he named Nik Mohamed Nik Yaacob to serve under him as chief executive. Among Mohamed's first moves was to initiate the merger of the company's plantation assets, organized as Consolidated Plantations, and the parent company, Sime Darby (Sime Darby had owned 51 percent of Consolidated, which was publicly traded). The company also bolstered its regional insurance business in 1993 by joining forces with AXA of France for its insurance operations in Malaysia and Singapore. These efforts signaled an end to the company's historical emphasis on commodities and reflected Mohamed's desires to increase activity in manufacturing, high-tech, financial services, and other fast-growth businesses and reduce Sime Darby's bureaucracy.

To that end, Sime Darby began increasing investments in businesses such as power generation, oil and gas, and heavy equipment exporting. In heavy equipment, Sime Darby bought the Australian distributor of Caterpillar equipment, Hastings Deering (Australia) Ltd., in 1993. In power generation, a key move came in 1994 when Sime Darby took a 40 percent interest in Port Dickson Power Sdn. Bhd., an independent power producer in Malaysia. That same year, the company acquired U.K.-based Lec Refrigeration plc, which was involved in the manufacturing, marketing, and servicing of refrigeration equipment and related products. At the same time, Mohamed worked to absorb the flurry of acquisitions conducted during the previous several years and streamline the company into some sort of cohesive whole. Despite restructuring activities, Sime Darby managed to boost sales to US$3.15 billion in 1994, about US$186 million of which was netted as income.

before plunging to M$2.17 billion in 1983. Sime Darby lumbered through the mid-1980s with annual sales of less than M$2.5 billion, and net income skidded from about M$100 million in the early 1980s to a low M$59 million in 1987. To turn things around, Sime Darby's board promoted Tunku Ahmad Yahaya to chief executive. Ahmad was a veteran of the company's executive ranks and was a favorite nephew of Malaysia's first prime minister, Tunku Abdul Rahman. Under Ahmad's direction, the giant corporation began a slow turnaround. Significantly, Ahmad was instrumental in luring Tun Ismail to Sime Darby's board. Ismail was a highly influential central bank governor and the chairman of Sime Darby's biggest shareholder. Ismail became nonexecutive chairman of the company following the death of Tun Tan Siew Sin in 1988.

During the late 1980s and early 1990s Ahmad invested much of Sime Darby's cash horde into a bevy of new companies and ventures. Sime became a relatively big player in the global reinsurance business, for example, and tried to boost its activities related to heavy equipment and vehicle manufacturing. Most notably, Sime began pouring millions of dollars into property and tourism in key growth areas of Malaysia in an effort to get in on the development and tourism boom that began in that nation in the late 1980s. The success of that division prompted the company to invest as well in tourism overseas. Through its UEP subsidiary, for instance, Sime Darby bought a

In 1995 Sime Darby stepped up its acquisition drive through the purchase of a controlling 60.4 percent interest in United Malayan Banking Corporation from Datuk Keramat Holdings Berhad. The US$520 million purchase deepened the company's involvement in the country's fast-growing financial services sector. United Malayan, which was the fourth largest bank in Malaysia in terms of assets, soon was reorganized as Sime Bank Berhad, with the company's brokerage arm becoming a subsidiary of Sime Bank under the name SimeSecurities Sdn. Bhd.

For the fiscal year ending in June 1997 Sime Darby posted record net income of M$835.8 million (US$322.9 million) on record revenues of M$13.24 billion (US$4.35 billion). Sime Bank and SimeSecurities played a key role in these stellar results (accounting for 30 percent of pretax earnings), but the eruption of the Asian financial crisis in July 1997 quickly proved that the acquisition of United Malayan had been ill-timed, if not also ill-advised. The severity of the crisis in Malaysia, which included a steep decline in the Malaysian stock market and a sharp depreciation of the ringgit (the nation's currency), led Sime Bank to post the largest loss in Malaysian banking history—M$1.6 billion (US$431 million) for the six months to December 1997. In turn, Sime Darby posted its first loss in decades for the same six-month period, a loss of M$676.2 million ($172.7 million). With other Sime Darby units being hit hard by the crisis as well, the company posted the first full-year loss in its close to 90-year history in the 1998 fiscal year, a net loss of M$540.9 million (US$131 million).

Sime Darby subsequently beat a hasty retreat from its aggressive expansion, determining that the prudent course would be a return to the company's core areas: plantations, property development, tire manufacturing, heavy equipment and motor vehicle distribution, and power generation. In June 1999 Sime Darby sold Sime Bank and its SimeSecurities subsidiary to Rashid Hussain, who merged it with RHB Bank to form the second largest commercial bank in Malaysia. During the 1999 fiscal year, the company also sold Sandestin Resorts for US$131 million. Sime Darby returned to the black in 1999, with net earnings of M$821.8 million (US$216.3 million) on revenues of M$9.91 billion (US$2.61 billion). A further pull-back from the financial services sector came in March 2000 when Sime Darby sold its interest in Sime AXA, its insurance joint venture with AXA of France.

Meantime, an area of growing interest was emerging at the turn of the millennium as Sime Darby increased its interest in Port Dickson Power to 60 percent, giving it majority control and turning Port Dickson into a company subsidiary. Flush with cash from the sale of its financial services units, Sime Darby appeared poised to make additional forays into the power generation sector. Given the near disaster of its aggressive moves into financial services, however, the company was likely to proceed with much caution in all of its future expansionary endeavors in a return to its traditional style of conservative management.

Principal Subsidiaries

Consolidated Plantations Berhad; SD Holdings Berhad; Sime UEP Properties Berhad (51.2%); Tractors Malaysia Holdings Berhad (71.7%); DMIB Berhad (51%); Sime Tyres International (M) Sdn. Bhd.; Kuala Lumpur Golf & Country Club Berhad; Subang Jaya Medical Centre Sdn. Bhd.; Sime Engineering Sdn. Bhd.; Sime Coatings Sdn. Bhd.; Mecomb Malaysia Sdn. Berhad; Puchong Quarry Sdn. Bhd. (85.4%); Sime Inax Sdn. Bhd. (80%); Chubb Malaysia Sendirian Berhad (70%); Sime Rengo Packaging (M) Sdn. Bhd. (70%); Sime SembCorp Engineering Sdn. Bhd. (70%); Port Dickson Power Berhad (60%); Sime Darby Hong Kong Limited (74.9%); Sime Singapore Limited (69.1%); Sime Darby Pilipinas, Inc. (Philippines; 97.2%); Lec Refrigeration plc (U.K.; 98.5%); Sime Darby Australia Limited; Hastings Deering (Australia) Ltd.

Principal Divisions

Plantations & Commodity Trading Division; Insurance Services Division; Tyre Manufacturing Division; Heavy Equipment & Motor Vehicle Distribution Division; Property Development Division.

Principal Competitors

Bridgestone Corporation; The Goodyear Tire & Rubber Company; Harnischfeger Industries, Inc.; HSBC Holdings plc; Hutchison Whampoa Ltd.; Jardine Matheson Holdings Limited; Komatsu Ltd.; Marubeni Corporation; Pacific Dunlop Limited; Sumitomo Corporation; Swire Pacific Ltd.

Further Reading

Appell, Douglas, "Analysts Spy Signs of Vigor at Once-Dozy Sime Darby," *Asian Wall Street Journal,* June 20, 1996, p. 13.
"Blue-Chip Company Shows Its Edge," *Malaysian Business,* March 16, 2000.
Brown, Tom, "Big Firm Moves Here," *Seattle Times,* June 18, 1991, p. 1F.
Cooke, Kieran, "Sime Darby Looks Outside Asia to Spread Its Wings," *Financial Times,* May 2, 1995, p. 17.
Jayasankaran, S., "Blue Chip in the Red: Trouble at Sime Darby's Banking and Stockbroking Arms Has Triggered a Large Loss at the Malaysian Firm," *Far Eastern Economic Review,* March 19, 1998, pp. 51–53.
——, "First Blood," *Far Eastern Economic Review,* March 12, 1998, p. 56.
Lopez, Leslie, "Earnings at Sime Darby Imperiled by Unit's Loss," *Asian Wall Street Journal,* March 4, 1998, p. 1.
——, "Malaysia's Troubles Reach Sime Darby," *Asian Wall Street Journal,* November 10, 1997, p. 1.
Pura, Raphael, "Malaysian Giant Sime Darby Plots a Cautious Expansion," *Wall Street Journal,* May 10, 1995, p. B4.
"Reality Hits Sime Darby," *Malaysian Business,* May 1, 1999.
"Seeking Opportunities," *Far Eastern Economic Review,* March 3, 1994, p. 50.
"Temptations of Power," *Malaysian Business,* December 1, 1999.
Tsuruoka, Doug, "Through the Wringer," *Far Eastern Economic Review,* March 3, 1994, p. 52.
——, "Wake-Up Call," *Far Eastern Economic Review,* March 3, 1994, pp. 48–52.
Yee, Chen May, "Sime Darby Moves to Restore Stature," *Asian Wall Street Journal,* March 9, 1998, p. 3.

—Dave Mote
—updated by David E. Salamie

Sodiaal S.A.

170 bis
Boulevard du Montparnasse
75014 Paris
France
Telephone: (+33) 1 44 10 90 10
Fax: (+33) 1 43 21 62 99
Web site: http://www.sodiaal.fr

Cooperative
Incorporated: 1964 as Sodima
Employees: 8,004
Sales: EUR 2.71 billion (US$2.5 billion) (1999)
NAIC: 311511 Fluid Milk Manufacturing; 311514 Dry,
   Condensed, and Evaporated Dairy; 311513 Cheese
   Manufacturing

Sodiaal S.A. is France's leading dairy cooperative, owned by more than 15,000 dairy farmers located throughout France. Sodiaal processes more than ten percent of the country's milk supply, placing it second behind former Besnier dairy processing subsidiary Lactalis, which processes some 20 percent of all French fresh milk. Sodiaal is best known for its Yoplait brand of yogurts and other fresh dairy products; through a worldwide network of licensees, subsidiaries, and joint-venture partnerships, such as those created with General Mills in the United States and Dairy Crest in the United Kingdom, Yoplait has captured the leading share in many of the world's markets. Sodiaal also produces fresh milk products under the Candia brand name, including milk drinks, fortified and vitamin-rich milks for the children's market, and sterilized milks, among others. Sodiaal's Les Fromageries Riche Mont manufactures cheese products, including camemberts, bries, and other cheese specialties. Sodiaal also produces milk and dairy products for the industrial sector, through subsidiary Sodiaal Industrie. Despite the cooperative's brand successes, Sodiaal has struggled to remain profitable since the late 1990s, posting losses of more than EUR 15 million on sales of EUR 2.7 billion in 1999. In mid-2000, after examining the possibility of shedding its money-losing industrial and cheese production units—which

raised an outcry among its members—the company instead shed its CEO, Nicolas Le Chatelier, naming Jean-Claude Dorbec in his place.

Building a Dairy Cooperative Leader in the 1960s

Dairy cooperatives came into existence in France in the 1800s, but it was not until the 1960s that local organizations began to organize their production and sales operations on a regional level. At that time, several cooperatives became dissatisfied with the limitations of the regional structure and wanted to organize on a national level. In 1964, six cooperative unions joined forces to create SODIMA (Société de Diffusion de Marques). The cooperatives pooled their resources and knowledge to develop a wide range of fresh dairy products and open the national market in France.

In 1965, SODIMA launched the first national and comprehensive line of dairy products under the Yoplait brand. Through Yoplait's success, SODIMA was able to grow rapidly. Just four years later, Yoplait was introduced outside of France; SODIMA drew up a franchise agreement to give foreign companies the right to use the Yoplait brand name while the union continued to provide marketing, technical, and sales assistance.

In 1971, several member cooperatives also began to market Candia, the first national brand of fluid milk in France. Candia was an attempt to stimulate the milk market by changing milk's image from common household staple to something far more appealing. Advertisements depicted milk as more of a luxury beverage, and Candia milk was packaged in brightly colored wrappers instead of the usual white. Like Yoplait, Candia was a success; a year later, the cooperatives introduced Candia skimmed fresh milk.

In 1974, in order to reflect the company's changing interests, SODIMA changed the words behind its acronym to "Société de Développements et d'Innovations des Marchés Agricoles et Alimentaires" (Association for Development and Innovation in the Agricultural and Food Markets).

In 1975, Candia launched Viva, milk with a guaranteed vitamin content, and in 1976, it introduced Candy, a variety of flavored milks. By 1977, Yoplait was being marketed in 22 foreign countries, and the American General Mills Company had acquired the Yoplait franchise to produce and market its yogurt products in the United States. Yoplait soon became a major contender in the U.S. yogurt market. A year later, SODIMA's annual worldwide yogurt sales topped one billion cups.

In 1982, SODIMA created the Yoplait International Institute, an organization to define the guidelines for innovation and research of Yoplait products. Half of the institute's members were from SODIMA member cooperatives and half were from Yoplait's international franchisers. Its chairman, André Gaillard, was also SODIMA's honorary president. SODIMA also organized the André Gaillard International Research Center, to be overseen by the Yoplait International Institute. Located in a suburb of Paris, the center was to coordinate SODIMA's research policies, focusing on biotechnology and the development of new products.

In 1985, SODIMA International S.A. was founded as a subsidiary responsible for Yoplait business outside of France; it is especially concerned with marketing, technical, and sales activities.

Throughout the 1970s and 1980s Candia continued strengthening its position as a leader in the French milk market: pasteurized fresh milk was successfully repositioned and a liquid, ready-to-drink breakfast was introduced. Candia continued to grow in popularity with French consumers; by now, it handled about a third of all packaged milk produced in France.

In 1988, Yoplait began to market Ofilus, a variety of fermented milks with bifidus and acidophilus bacteria, two strains that help balance the digestive and intestinal flora. Ofilus comes in two varieties, one called Ofilus Nature, aimed at health-conscious, regular yogurt eaters, and one called Ofilus Double Douceur, aimed at those who prefer creamy foods. Yoplait had also become a leader in the fresh-cream market, introducing Silhouette, a cream with only a 12 percent fat content.

In 1988 SODIMA created two more subsidiaries: SODIMA CLB, in Lyons, responsible for Candia marketing and sales; and SODIMA Frais, in Paris, responsible for Yoplait marketing and sales. The sales staff of cooperatives producing Candia and Yoplait were transferred to these two main branches so that each brand would have a single sales force and delivery system.

In 1988, ULPAC, one of the founding cooperatives of SODIMA, and Centre Lait, another union member, merged into the Alliance Agro-Alimentaires 3A, to collect milk from the central and southwest regions of France and produce both Yoplait and Candia products. The union of these two cooperatives signaled the cooperatives' desire to strengthen the agricultural sector in their regions in preparation for the upcoming single European market in 1992.

Name Change in the 1990s

In July 1989 SODIMA announced the creation of SODIAAL (Société de Diffusion Internationale Agro-Alimentaire). Headquartered in Paris, this group economically united six SODIMA-member cooperatives. Each cooperative was responsible for managing one aspect of SODIAAL, such as milk intake or investments. SODIAAL—which took over as the cooperative's name in the 1990s—was formed in anticipation of the unification of the European market in 1992 and the expected increase in business opportunities. The cooperative actively sought expansion into new international markets, forming partnerships with local dairy groups. One such partnership was created in 1990, when Sodiaal and former British milk monopoly Dairy Crest created the joint-venture Yoplait Dairy Crest Ltd., with Sodiaal's share of the partnership at 51 percent. Yoplait Dairy Crest quickly achieved success in the United Kingdom, introducing new products such as the best-selling Petit Filous line.

By then, Sodiaal had also begun to look beyond Europe. In 1989, Yoplait opened a plant in Tianjin, China, with the larger ambition of developing the modern Chinese dairy industry. International Trust and Investment Corporation, working through Tianjin Agricultural Industry and Commerce Corporation, was SODIMA's main partner in the venture. The cooperative also reached agreement with U.S.-based General Mills to form the partnership Yoplait/General Mills Inc. in order to market the Yoplait name to the American consumer. The combination of the Yoplait formula with the marketing and distribution clout of General Mills all but assured the brand of success—by 1999, Yoplait had overtaken Dannon as the number one-selling brand of yogurt in the United States.

By the mid-1990s, Sodiaal had seen its annual sales grow to more than FFr 17 billion. While the Yoplait brand accounted for nearly 29 percent, and Candia sales added an additional 23 percent, the company's industrial sales, through Sodiaal Industrie remained its chief revenue generator, with 30 percent of the company's sales. Yet in 1996, after weathering the extended economic crisis, the cooperative was faced with a new industry-specific crisis, as prices for industrial dairy products, including for butter and powdered milk, collapsed worldwide. By the end of 1996, Sodiaal watched as its profits slipped—down to just FFr 6 million, from more than FFr 76 million the year before.

Sodiaal moved to enter new markets in order to increase its sales, launching Yoplait Polska as a first step in entering the countries of eastern Europe as well as two subsidiaries for marketing Yoplait and Candia in Tunisia. These moves helped Sodiaal return to profitability in 1997. Yet the cooperative was unable to sustain this tendency—by the end of 1998, the company's losses had reached FFr 62 million, a figure which rose to FFr 100 one year later, while revenues remained largely stable.

Sodiaal began to eye the necessity of restructuring its operations. In 1998, the cooperative's cheese division underwent a name change, from the industrial-sounding Idéval to the more evocative Les Fromageries Riches Monts. The cooperative, which had limited its new product development largely to the

Key Dates:

1964: Six regional dairy cooperatives establish national marketing cooperative SODIMA.
1965: Sodima introduces Yoplait brand.
1969: First international franchise agreement is signed for Yoplait brand.
1971: Company introduces Candia fresh milk brand.
1990: Sodima is reformed as Sodiaal; forms U.K. joint-venture Yoplait Dairy Crest.
1997: Yoplait Polska subsidiary is opened.
1998: Company changes name of Idéval cheese division to Les Fromageries Riches Monts.
1999: Yoplait becomes number one yogurt brand in United States.
2000: Jean-Claude Dorbec is named CEO.

introduction of new flavors for existing products, also sought to recapture growth through new product innovations, such as the introduction of its drinkable yogurt Zap in 1998. By 1999, however, Sodiaal was rumored to be considering a more drastic reorganization, including the sale of its cheese and industrial products subsidiaries—with one potential buyer being former Besnier dairy processor Lactalis, the largest private dairy processor in France—in order to refocus the group on its more profitable Yoplait and Candia lines. These proposals, favored by CEO Nicolas Le Chatelier, raised an outcry among much of the French dairy industry and Sodiaal's own members, who feared pricing pressures should these divisions fall into private hands. In July 2000, Sodiaal removed Le Chatelier from his position, replacing him with former head of the Cedilac-Candia division Jean-Claude Dorbec.

Sodiaal entered the new century seeking partnerships—rather than outright sales—for its troubled divisions. At the same time, the cooperative expected to continue its highly successful formula of spreading the Yoplait and Candia names through a system of franchises, partnerships, and licenses. These efforts had already paid off for the company—in 1999, Yoplait topped rival Dannon in yogurt sales for the first time. In that year, the company announced a new joint-venture partnership, with Finnish dairy cooperative Valio, to form the joint ventures Yoplait Valio Nord OY in Finland, and Yoplait Valio Nord AB in Sweden.

Principal Subsidiaries

SODIMA International S.A.; Les Fromageries Riches Monts S.A.; Yoplait S.A.; Cedilac-Candia S.A.; Sodiaal Industrie; Yoplait Dairy Crest Ltd. (U.K.; 51%); Yoplait/General Mills Inc. (U.S.A.; 50%); Yoplait Polska (Poland; 65%), Yoplait Valio Nord OY (Finland; 50%); Yoplait Valio Nord AB (Sweden; 50%).

Principal Competitors

Lactalis S.A.; Bongrain S.A.; Nestlé S.A.

Further Reading

Denis, Anne, "Sodiaal appelle de ses voeux de nouveaux mécanismes de fixation du prix du lait," *Les Echos*, June 2, 1997, p. 17.
Grandi, Michel de, "Sodiaal mise sur l'innovation en 1998," May 28, 1998, p. 12.
Le Masson, Thomas, "Changement de direction chez Sodiaal," *Les Echos*, July 27, 2000, p. 14.
——, *Memoires du lait*, Paris: Albin Michel, 1994.

—updated by M.L. Cohen

SOUTHERN STATES

Southern States Cooperative Incorporated

6606 W. Broad Street
Richmond, Virginia 23260
U.S.A.
Telephone: (804) 281-1000
Fax: (804) 281-1381
Web site: http://www.southernstates-coop.com

Cooperative
Incorporated: 1933
Employees: 6,000
Sales: $1.36 billion (2000)
NAIC: 42291 Farm Supplies Wholesalers

Southern States Cooperative Incorporated is one of the largest farmer cooperatives in the United States and operates the largest livestock exchange in the country. Owned by 307,000 farmers, the cooperative offers its farmer-members high-quality products at discounted prices and also sells its products to the general public through its own retail stores and through independent dealers. Southern States manufactures, sells, and processes seed, fertilizer, and fuel. It also sells farm, lawn, garden, and animal health supplies. The company gins cotton and markets livestock, corn, peanuts, soybeans, and grains. Through its Turf Division, it offers turf management products and services. Other services include specialty catalogs, sales financing, and an aquaculture program. Based in Richmond, Virginia, Southern States was founded by agronomist W.G. Wysor to provide quality seed to Virginia farmers at an affordable price. Southern States has stores in 17 states from Michigan to Florida and west to Texas. In 2000 the company entered into a joint venture with Agway, a cooperative of 71,000 farmers in 12 northeastern states. Its partnership with Agway will extend its reach into the northern United States. In its fiscal year ending June 30, 2000, Southern States had sales nearing $1.5 billion.

A Need for Good Seed in 1923

Southern States Cooperative Incorporated began in 1923 when Virginia farmers tried to fill the need for good quality, disease-resistant clover and alfalfa seed that would grow in Virginia's soil and climate. About 150 farmers gathered in Richmond, pledged $11,000 in capital, and called themselves the Virginia Seed Service. The farmers hired W.G. Wysor, the man who had called the meeting, as general manager. Wysor, called "Bud Wysor" by friends, was an extension agronomist (field crop specialist) at Virginia Tech. Friends and colleagues described Wysor as being "sharp and shrewd" and "a visionary." Wysor's vision for the Virginia Seed Service was to turn it into a multi-state, full-service cooperative. With the help of his fellow farmer-members, Wysor's vision became a reality.

The Virginia Seed Service grew slowly at first—its first order for a few pounds of clover seed totaled less than $10. The company struggled through the Depression, droughts, world wars, and "wide swings in the farm economy." The Virginia Seed Service gradually added to its product line. In 1926 it began selling its first farm supply item: binder twine, and a decade later purchased its first fertilizer plant. In 1933 the company changed its name to Southern States Cooperative Incorporated. A year later, Southern States expanded outside of Virginia into Delaware and Maryland.

Fuel in the Mid-1930s

In 1938 Southern States' board of directors approved a proposal to add the sale of petroleum to the company's list of products. The move was significant for Southern States. In the late 1930s and early 1940s only very large farms had storage sites that could store petroleum products, which were used to fuel farming equipment. The vast majority of farmers had to lug fuel drums to gas stations and pay retail or only slightly discounted prices for fuel. Southern States offered its members petroleum at wholesale prices. The company also moved aggressively into farm delivery. Its aim was to deliver fuel and other products to its members. By the end of World War II Southern States had established a fuel delivery system.

The first Southern States cooperative opened in West Virginia in 1941, and in 1945 the company established a cooperative in Kentucky. Southern States operated in five states—Virginia, Delaware, Maryland, West Virginia, and Kentucky—for the next four decades. However, while it had stopped extending its territo-

Company Perspectives:

"Analysts come and analysts go. When times are good in agriculture, there are analysts who predict that population growth has overtaken our ability to produce, and thus agriculture will always be good.

Then when favorable weather in the major producing regions results in two or three bin-busting crops at the same time that export demand slows and prices drop, analysts have a tendency toward doomsday predictions for farming.

The fact of the matter is that neither analysis is true. The demand for food globally is growing at about the same rate as productivity. This means that in years of good weather and slow demand growth, prices will be low and stocks will build. During periods of lower yields and stronger demand, prices will be high.

In this regard, agriculture has not changed over the years; it's still a volatile industry. We at Southern States continue to look for ways to help farmers through the peaks and valleys."   *—Wayne Boutwell, president and CEO*

ries, Southern States continued to expand and diversify its product line.

During this time, Southern States' focus was on fuel. Terry Ragsdale explained in *Foodstuffs* that fuel has always been critical to Southern States' success: "Petroleum is important from the standpoint of off-season business," explained Ragsdale, executive vice-president and COO of Southern States. "We're heavily into farm supplies and, therefore, the spring and fall are big times for us. But we need business in winter months, and that's where products like propane and heating oil fit in."

Southern States purchased the Kentucky Oil Marketers at Owensboro in 1946. Two years later Southern States entered into a joint venture with GLF, later renamed Agway Inc. Together the two cooperatives purchased a 75 percent interest in Petrol Refining Company, based in Texas City, Texas. Southern States and Agway eventually gained 100 percent control of Petrol Refining and renamed it Texas City Refining. While the new company was profitable in the 1960s and 1970s, it floundered in the 1980s. Southern States sold Texas City Refining in 1988.

New Direction in the 1980s and 1990s

In February 1997 Southern States President and CEO Gene A. James formally retired and Wayne Boutwell took his place. Boutwell was the first president and CEO of Southern States hired from outside of the company. Southern States believed Boutwell's shrewd business sense and extensive farming experience would take Southern States in a new direction. Having grown up on his family's farm, Boutwell knew all about the trials of agriculture. He had served as a staff member for the U.S. Department of Economic Research Services and received his Ph.D. in agricultural economics. Boutwell had also served as Mississippi Republican Senator Thad Cochran's legislative assistant for agriculture and natural resources.

At the beginning of his tenure with Southern States, Boutwell noted that the company surpassed other farming cooperatives in terms of its product diversity and geographic location. Southern States offered more products than other cooperatives and its retail stores were located close to high-income suburbs, which Boutwell felt gave the cooperative a competitive advantage. In an article on *Insidebiz.com,* Boutwell said, "Every morning we wake up, there's a new subdivision that used to be a farm. We understand that," he said. "We don't fight it, we just simply say 'As the customer base changes, we're going to change.'"

While Boutwell was impressed with Southern States, he realized the company lagged behind other cooperatives in the area of meats. Boutwell met with Michigan Livestock Exchange in 1997 with the hopes of acquiring the company. Michigan Livestock Exchange was a livestock cooperative that helped farmers raise and sell cattle, hogs, and sheep. Michigan also helped form alliances between farmers and beef processors and cattle feedlots. On April 1, 1998, Boutwell reached his goal and Southern States acquired Michigan Livestock Exchange. The acquisition made Southern States the largest livestock exchange in the United States. Once the deal was final, Michigan Livestock Exchange moved its headquarters from Lansing to Richmond and became the livestock division of Southern States.

In 1997 Southern States purchased the retail stores and other assets of FCX, a Raleigh-based cooperative formerly called the Central Carolina Farmers, and expanded into North Carolina. With the purchase of the farming supply assets of Gold Kist, Inc. in 1998, the company moved into South Carolina, Georgia, Florida, Alabama, Mississippi, Arkansas, Louisiana, and Texas. Under the terms of the acquisition, Southern States assumed Gold Kist's 100 retail farm supply stores in addition to the company's peanut and grain buying stations, cotton gins, fertilizer plants and terminals, crop protection product distribution centers, feed mills, and other operations. The acquisition was amicable on both sides: with Southern States taking over the farming sector of its business, Gold Kist was free to concentrate on poultry processing. As of 2000 Gold Kist processed 14.5 million chickens per week, making it the second largest poultry processor in the United States, behind Tyson Foods. Southern States hoped the new territories it gained through the Gold Kist acquisition would boost its sales.

Heading North in 1999 and 2000

Near the turn of the century Southern States became part owner of a new soybean research company "dedicated to the development of elite soybean varieties." The company, called Soygenetics LLC, was owned by FFR Cooperative (a cooperative in which Southern States had a stake), Limagrain Genetics, and Land O'Lakes. Soygenetics was the third largest soybean company in North America. "We must offer our soybean growers products that compete both in cost of production and value to the world market. We are now in a much stronger position to provide new opportunities while protecting the interest of our soybean producers," said Greg Adlich, vice-president of Southern States Crops Division and acting chairman of the board for FFR Cooperative.

Southern States also continued to expand its territories. In 1990 the company purchased Wetsel Seed Co., a horticultural supplier. In addition to serving much of Southern States' territory, Wetsel served businesses in Indiana, New York, Ohio, and Pennsylvania. As of 2000 Wetsel operated as a subsidiary of Southern States.

In July 2000 Southern States finalized an agreement with Agway, Inc. in which the two cooperatives pooled their resources in product marketing, distribution, and retailing. According to a Southern States company press release, "Southern States would supply farm, lawn, home and garden, vegetable seed and bird food products for 500-plus Agway consumer dealers in Ohio, Maryland, Delaware, Pennsylvania, New York, New Jersey, New Hampshire, Rhode Island, Connecticut, Vermont, Massachusetts, and Maine." By combining their resources, the cooperatives were able to offer dealers more products at lower prices and to better compete in a marketplace undergoing a trend toward consolidation. Together, Southern States and Agway serviced 1,300 dealers in 26 states, including many states in the northeastern United States, an area of potential growth for Southern States. "We are very excited about this relationship and very comfortable serving this type of dealer base and their product lines," said Carl Cromwell, vice-president of the farm and home business unit, in a Southern States company press release. "At Southern States, we are excited about the growth opportunities this presents for us and for the Agway dealers."

The partnership was not the first between Southern States and Agway. The two companies co-owned a bulk and bagged feed plant in Gettysburg, Pennsylvania, and were also co-manufacturers of Legends, a popular line of horse feed. In addition, Southern States and Agway, along with four other companies, manufactured Pro-Pet LLC pet food.

Around the time it finalized the Agway deal, the Farmer's Catch Division of Southern States received a $10 million loan for aquaculture development from the National Marines Fisheries Service (NMSF), an agency of the Department of Commerce's National Oceanic and Atmospheric Administration. Aquaculture is the cultivation of finfish, shellfish, and aquatic plants. NMFS estimates that about 30 percent of the seafood the world consumes is produced through aquaculture. However, since many fish are over-harvested, this percentage is expected to rise significantly in the future to meet the demand for seafood.

According to a company press release, Southern States planned to use the loan to help farmers finance state-of-the-art closed systems for tilapia fish production, a fingerling nursery, and a processing plant.

A Vulnerable Future

While Southern States' sales continued to rise throughout the late 1990s, the company posted a net loss of $2.1 million in 1999, as compared with net incomes of $10.7 million in 1998 and $27.5 million in 1997. In its 1999 annual report, the company attributed much of the loss to "badly depressed crop and livestock prices" and "the most damaging drought since the dust-bowl days." The company also cited the cost of integrating and relocating the headquarters of the Michigan Livestock Exchange as contributing to the loss.

While Southern States would always remain vulnerable to forces of nature such as drought, with 307,000 farmer-members, (up from about 215,000 in 1999), and its new partnership with Agway, Inc., analysts believed in 2000 that Southern States would continue to be a valuable and viable cooperative for its farmer-members in the years to come.

Principal Competitors

Archer Daniels Midland Company; Cenex Harvest States Cooperatives; The Scoular Company.

Further Reading

Abcede, Angel, "This Co-op's Cash Crop Needs No Watering." *National Petroleum News,* March 1994, p. 43.

"Agway and Southern States Announce Retail Relationship." *PR Newswire,* May 17, 2000.

Roop, Jason, "The New Statesman," *Insidebiz.com,* July 22, 1998, http://www.insidebiz.com/richmond/cover/cover072298.htm.

"Southern States Gets Livestock Unit." *Richmond Times-Dispatch,* March 17, 1998.

—Tracey Vasil Biscontini

The Sportsman's Guide, Inc.

411 Farwell Avenue
South St. Paul, Minnesota 55075
U.S.A.
Telephone: (651) 451-3030
Toll Free: (800) 882-2962
Fax: (651) 450-6130
Web site: http://www.sportmansguide.com

Public Company
Incorporated: 1977 as Olen Company, Inc.
Employees: 875
Sales: $162.5 million (1999)
Stock Exchanges: NASDAQ
Ticker Symbol: SGDE
NAIC: 45411 Electronic Shopping and Mail-Order
  Houses

The Sportsman's Guide, Inc. is a leading marketer of value-priced outdoor gear and general merchandise through catalogs and the Internet. Over its history the company has transformed itself from a home-based business selling specialty deer-hunting items to a catalog merchant pitching the outdoors lifestyle and, more recently, an up-and-coming e-tailer seeking to broaden its market appeal.

Hunting for Customers: 1970–85

Gary Olejnik—hunter, angler, and outdoorsman—founded a home-based, mail-order business in 1970 and operated it as a sole proprietorship under the name Olen Company. Targeting other deer hunters, Olejnik first sold decals, and later belt buckles, shirts, deer patches, and wildlife art. Initially, Olejnik sold his wares through magazine ads. He introduced a 16-page catalog in 1975. Olejnik and Leonard Paletz, his boss at Fidelity Products, an office equipment mail-order business, joined forces in 1977 and incorporated as Olen Company, Inc.

Olejnik selected and tested products for the retail mail-order business, and Paletz, former COO at Fidelity, headed up the operation. The men mailed the company's first catalog, a 52-page offering, to 347,000 prospective customers.

Mail-order sales in general rose 44 percent from 1980 to 1984. The sporting goods niche jumped 73 percent during the period, rising from $860 million to $1.5 billion. By 1985, Sportsman's Guide sales reached $8.4 million.

Sportsman's Guide sent out nine million catalogs in 1986, primarily to middle-income, blue collar men interested in hunting and the outdoors. Among the 16,000 items in the 88-page catalog were dart and stun guns, ninja stars and other martial arts weapons, inflatable beds and boats, and clothing. Sales to women generated about 18 percent of business. In 1986, the catalog merchandiser bagged sales of $14 million. Pre-tax earnings were $1 million.

The sales jump during 1986 was generated by increased catalog mailings—up three million from 1985. Equally important, the average order size rose thanks to purchase incentives and a single-rate shipping fee. Amid the soaring sales, Olejnik and Paletz planned for an expansion.

Rising, Falling Fortunes: 1986–90

In May 1986, the company completed its initial public offering (IPO), raising $2.31 million. The capital funded a move into a 55,000-square-foot office and warehouse space. The previous facility had measured only 18,000 square feet. The company also changed its name to The Sportsman's Guide, Inc. during that pivotal year.

By this time, the industry was cranking out significantly more than ten billion catalogs a year. Holiday season wish books from Sears, Roebuck or Montgomery Ward had been overrun by specialty catalogs enticing Yuppies with everything from gourmet foods and trendy fashions to sophisticated electronic equipment. Sportsman's Guide continued to serve "Mr. Average Guy, otherwise known as 'Joe Six-Pack,' and his family," according to Al Mosko in the *Penny Stock Journal* in 1987.

"A few smart catalog merchandisers still remember Joe and cater to his needs. The Sportsman's Guide, Inc., is one such organization. Ever since its first catalog came out 10 years ago, the company's customer always has been the middle-income, no-nonsense outdoorsman,'' continued Mosko. Many outdoors-oriented catalog companies had shifted from the functional to the fashionable, but not Sportsman's Guide. Furthermore, the company took pride in its ''Buy America'' policy.

The Sportsman's Guide, like any other catalog retailer, needed to provide good service and quality products to keep customers. The company offered speedy delivery and a liberal return policy. Guns, knives, boots, camping equipment, and other hard goods produced the bulk of sales volume; about one-quarter of the fall/winter catalog offerings were private label apparel such as shirts and jackets.

As he had since the early days, Gary Olejnik continued to field test products—the company's return rate fell below the industry's three to ten percent range. Olejnik's endorsements, under the name ''Gary Olen,'' provided entertaining reading for catalog customers. ''Considering the number of 'Dear Gary' letters that the company receives, customers closely identify with the Sportsman's Guide spokesman,'' observed Mosko.

In an effort to move the business to a year-round operation, Sportsman's Guide mailed out 2.6 million copies of its first spring/summer catalog in 1987. The company historically depended on the fourth quarter—October through December—for the bulk of revenues. The new publication featured low-priced fishing, camping, and backpacking products plus some year-round items from the fall/winter catalog. Sportsman's Guide upped its mailings for the original catalog to 14.4 million.

In another move, Sportsman's Guide acquired the assets of P&S Sales, Inc. of Chapel Hill, North Carolina, during 1987. The 29-year-old catalog retailer carried more clothing than Sportsman's Guide and served a slightly older and more affluent market. Its customers participated in outdoor action/adventures like mountain climbing or safaris in addition to hunting, shooting, and camping. The two companies had been exchanging their mailing lists for some time: Paletz compiled Sportsman's Guide's customer list from names purchased from other outdoor publications.

Sportsman's Guide reported losses of $2.1 million in 1988 on sales of $18.1 million, an 18.4 percent decline in revenue from 1987. The spring/summer catalog failed to take off, forcing the company to liquidate excess inventories. Start-up costs had contributed to losses in excess of half a million dollars a year earlier.

''What we should have done is test the concept before going into it full bore,'' Paletz said in a July 1989 *Star Tribune* article by Jim Jones. A cutback on spring catalog mailings in 1988

resulted in even fewer sales, and Sportsman's Guide dropped the offering in 1989.

The misstep turned Sportsman's Guide's optimistic outlook into a dire one. Three creditors had filed an involuntary bankruptcy petition in April 1989. Florida investor Vincent W. Shiel bailed out Sportsman's Guide with an offer to buy controlling interest and extend loans. The court granted Sportsman's Guide's request to convert the involuntary bankruptcy into a Chapter 11 reorganization.

''Shiel learned about the Sportsman's Guide's liquidity problems when an employee of the firm who formerly worked for Shiel at Gander Mountain called and asked if he'd be interested,'' explained Jones. Shiel had turned around the Wisconsin-based cataloger in the early 1980s and held controlling interest in hunting and fishing equipment distributors in Massachusetts, Texas, and Ohio.

Shift in Strategy: Early to Mid-1990s

By 1991 Sportsman's Guide recovered the ground it had lost. Then in the fall of 1992, the company introduced value-priced marketing, a move that spiked sales but produced thin margins. Sales climbed from $38.2 million in fiscal 1992 to $60.2 million in 1993, but the company fell into the red for the first time since the reorganization. In response, Sportsman's Guide introduced wider margin products: military surplus in late 1993 and manufacturers' closeout merchandise the following year.

Sales climbed to $96.1 million in 1994, and the company produced its first significant net earnings in history: $2.7 million. The 60 percent increase in sales was driven primarily by an increase in catalog editions and mailings. In 1994, Sportman's Guide sent out one catalog each month and introduced its first specialty catalog, military gear. About 39 million catalogs were mailed to existing and prospective customers. New customers, gained mainly from rented mailing lists, made up about 30 percent of 1994 sales. Ammunition and shooting accessory sales, boosted by talk of increased government regulation, also contributed to the record volume.

To help support the growth, Sportsman's Guide brought in managers with solid direct marketing experience and upgraded facilities as well as telephone and computer systems. Cofounder Gary Olen (Olejnik) served as president and CEO. Investor Vincent Shiel acted as chairman of the board.

Sales rose to $101.8 million in 1995, but the company lost $1.7 million due to soft consumer demand and sharply rising postage and paper costs. Paper prices jumped 60 percent and third class postage 14 percent during the year. Consumer mail-order company profits fell nationwide.

Sportsman's Guide had added ten new specialty catalogs and increased mailings in 1995, but the customer response rate was slow. To boost sales the company introduced a membership program offering discounts and a payment plan.

Early in 1996, a $6.2 million buyout deal with Atlanta, Georgia-based Vista 2000, Inc. fell apart. The financial and operational condition of the home security and personal safety

Key Dates:

1970: Gary Olejnik begins selling items aimed at deer hunters.
1977: Business incorporates as Olen Company, Inc.
1986: Public stock offering is completed; name changes to The Sportsman's Guide, Inc.
1987: First spring/summer catalog leads to near disaster.
1992: Value-pricing strategy is introduced.
1998: Online retail store is launched.

product manufacturer proved to be unfavorable. As its direct-mail subsidiary, Sportsman's Guide would have produced Vista's catalogs and handled orders and, in turn, would have sold its own products wholesale to Vista's customers.

With the Vista deal dead, business proceeded as usual, or at least as usual for this cataloger. "Sportsman's Guide has few, if any exact competitors," wrote Jennifer Waters in a 1996 *Minneapolis/St. Paul CityBusiness* article. "Think about it. Where else would you find in one catalog everything from hand grenades to traveling urinals, bullets to camouflage bikinis?"

Through the "Fun-to-Read" catalog Olen continued to speak directly to his customers, and the language, as Waters illustrated, was down to earth. "Example: 'No more pulling up anchor, unscheduled plane landings, crossing your legs or hoping for open gas stations,' reads the copy accompanying the Little John traveling urinal."

Although Sportsman's Guide was unique in product mix, the company had competition. Other catalog retailers serving the hunting and fishing market included Cabela's Inc., Bass Pro Shops Inc., and The Orvis Company, Inc. Sportsman's Guide competed for value-oriented consumers with such discounters as Wal-Mart Stores, Inc. and Kmart Corporation.

Plan Paying Off: Late 1990s

Sales climbed more than ten percent in 1996 to $112.3 million but, more importantly, Sportsman's Guide earned $2.3 million. Military surplus and closeouts produced 40 percent of sales. The company began to aggressively pursue closeouts of name brand shoes, boots, clothing, watches, and other items during the year. Sportsman's Guide sold the items at 25 to 60 percent of original retail prices.

Despite their upswing, Sportsman's Guide, along with other catalog retailers, remembered the downturn in 1995 and continued to fine-tune its operations to survive in an ever-changing environment. During 1997, Sportsman's Guide opened a second retail outlet to help move excess product. The company's first outlet was located at the main warehouse and distribution facility. The company also introduced a more sophisticated analysis of its 3.5 million-name file in an effort to improve customer response.

Sportsman's Guide netted $2.5 million in earnings in 1997 from sales of $128.1 million. The company posted record sales despite a UPS strike during the third quarter: many consumers

assumed that mail-order businesses were dependent on UPS for receipt and delivery of products and put off purchases.

Back in July 1997, Sportsman's Guide announced plans for an additional stock offering to repay stockholders who supported the company during the reorganization period, but the offer was delayed due to the UPS strike. Finally, in early 1998, Sportsman's Guide raised $9.6 million for the company and $1.2 million for selling shareholders. The stock sold at $6.50 per share, bringing in proceeds 27 percent below the projected take. The company planned to use the capital to buy more brand name closeouts, military surplus, and direct imports. To heat up sluggish trading, Sportsman's Guide moved from the local over-the-counter market to the NASDAQ and changed its symbol from GIDE to SGDE.

Sportsman's Guide told prospective shareholders that the market it served constituted an underserved and growing segment of the catalog industry. The number of men 45 years of age and older was expected to increase almost three times faster than the overall U.S. population through the first decade of the 21st century. The number of lower- and middle-income families was also rising.

The company sent out more than 61 million catalogs to about 3.7 million customers in all 50 states during 1997. Excerpts from the catalogs, which were created and designed inhouse, had been featured in Jay Leno's "Headlines" segment on *The Tonight Show* on more than one occasion. In addition to creative writing, the company enticed buyers with markdowns on brand names such as Timberland, Ray-Ban, Remington, and Rocky.

Positioning for the Future: Late 1990s–2000

Sportsman's Guide began taking orders from customers via its web site in April 1998, offering 1,000 items and capitalizing on the infrastructure already in place to process and ship the web orders. As its Internet sales increased, the company anticipated significant savings in catalog preparation, paper, printing, and postage costs; the largest cost for catalog companies was advertising, an estimated 20 percent of sales. Furthermore, phone order processing expense ran about four percent of sales compared with one-half of one percent for Internet-based orders.

Recognition of the fledgling effort came quickly. The Center for Internet Commerce took notice of Sportsman's Guide in December 1998, and the next month *Internet Stock Review* included Sportsman's Guide among the top 20 companies to watch in 2000.

Unseasonably warm winter weather slowed demand for cold weather products, reducing fourth quarter sales in 1998. However, increased catalog circulation combined with a larger number of higher margin products helped Sportsman's Guide maintain its profitability. Sales in 1998 were $142.9 million and net income $1.4 million.

Closeouts, military surplus, and private-label direct imports accounted for about 60 percent of Sportsman's Guide's sales volume. Olen told the *Wall Street Transcript* early in 1999, "We make our profit on the buy, not on the sell." By buying an entire allotment of manufacturer's closeouts, for example, Sportsman's Guide was assured of a unique offering at the lowest possible price. Military surplus purchased from around the world served as low-cost alternatives for items ranging from wool coats and snowshoes to underwear and sleeping bags. Direct imports allowed the company to offer key products made to its own specifications.

During the first quarter of 1999, Sportsman's Guide began posting all of its catalogs on the Internet, thus becoming one of the first catalogers to make the move. The company introduced its first specialty catalogs developed exclusively for the web in September. Overall in 1999, Sportsman's Guide invested about $1.2 million to establish and advertise www.sportmansguide .com, the e-commerce site launched in April 1998, and www .bargainoutfitters.com., launched in November 1999 as an online liquidation outlet. The company also established strategic alliances with other Internet sites and online service providers.

Internet sales for 1999 approached $13 million, a big leap over 1998 sales of $1.1 million. Total sales climbed to $162.5 million, but earnings fell to nearly the break-even point at $12,000.

A strategy for 2000 was to improve profitability by reducing the number of mailings. Unprofitable specialty catalogs and lifeless customer segments were eliminated. The decrease in mailings produced a corresponding reduction in sales during the first quarter of 2000. Sportsman's Guide also experienced a lower-than-expected customer response rate from its catalog offerings, though Internet sales figures continued to grow.

Sportsman's Guide's community/destination web site www.guideoutdoors.com was activated in June 1999. The company said, "The site is one of the most comprehensive electronic destinations for outdoor lifestyle and recreation enthusiasts and is designed to be a preeminent portal for people with a passion for 'everything outdoors.' " The content aspect of the site ranged from forecasts of weather conditions to features by nationally known outdoor experts. A section of the site was dedicated to women, a segment of outdoor enthusiasts the company was trying to cultivate as customers.

Late in June, Gary Olen announced his retirement as CEO; he remained as chairman of the company he cofounded. Gregory R. Binkley, the company's president and COO, succeeded Olen. Binkley joined Sportsman's Guide in 1994 as vice-president of operations and was named president and COO in April 1998. He also led the Internet subsidiary Guideoutdoors.com Inc. as president and CEO.

Over its 30-year history, Sportsman's Guide had mined a unique niche in the general merchandise catalog market. From all appearances, the company seemed poised to do the same in the ever-expanding cyberspace market. Business-to-consumer online transactions were predicted to exceed $60 billion by 2003, and Sportsman's Guide already was stalking its share.

Principal Subsidiaries

Guideoutdoors.com Inc.

Principal Competitors

Cabela's Inc.; Bass Pro Shops Inc.

Further Reading

Barshay, Jill J., "Sportsman's Guide Catalog Has Would-Be Investors in Its Sights," *Star Tribune* (Minneapolis), July 15, 1997, p. 1D.
——, "Sportsman's Guide Offering Falls Short," *Star Tribune* (Minneapolis), February 6, 1998, p. 1D.
Beran, George, "St. Paul's Sportsman's Guide Takes Second Look at Vista Buyout Offer," *Knight-Ridder/Tribune Business News*, April 24, 1996.
Cho, Joshua, "Subscribing to Success," *Catalog Age*, November 1997.
Fink, Laurie, "The Sportsman's Guide Hopes to Find Way Out of Chapter 11," *Minneapolis/St. Paul CityBusiness*, July 10, 1989, p. 10.
"Georgia Firm to Buy Sportsman's Guide, a Minnesota Catalog Firm," *Knight-Ridder/Tribune Business News*, January 27, 1996.
Huber, Tim, "Sportsman's Guide Shoots for Growth," *Minneapolis/St. Paul CityBusiness*, May 1, 1998, p. 13.
——, "Sportsman's Guide Suffers Bad News," *Minneapolis/St. Paul CityBusiness*, June 19, 1998, p. 11.
Jones, Jim, "Investor Draws a Bead on Sportsman's Guide," *Star Tribune* (Minneapolis), July 7, 1989, p. 1D.
Kafka, Peter, "Catalog Industry Is on Hold," *Minneapolis/St. Paul CityBusiness*, June 1997.
Mosko, Al, "High-Fashion Catalogs May Be In, But Sportsman's Guide Goes After Mr. Six-Pack," *Penny Stock Journal*, 1987.
Oslund, John J., and Dan Freeborn, "The 8th Annual Star Tribune 100: Business Prepares for the E-Economy," *Star Tribune* (Minneapolis), March 29, 1999, p. 1D.
Pokela, Barbara, "Company News," *Star Tribune* (Minneapolis), November 1, 1989, p. 2D.
——, "Company News," *Star Tribune* (Minneapolis), January 18, 1990, p. 2D.
"Public Offerings Popular in 1986," *Minneapolis/St. Paul CityBusiness*, January 28, 1987, pp. 1, 20.
Regan, Shawn, "The Right Stuff," *Ventures*, November 1998, pp. 36–39.
Riggs, Larry, "Getting It Online," *Direct*, May 15, 1998, pp. 63 + .
"The Sportsman's Guide, Inc.," *Corporate Report Fact Book 2000*, p. 382.
"The Sportsman's Guide, Inc.," *Cruttenden Roth Incorporated*, 1989.
"Sportsman's Guide Lost $2.1 Million in '88," *Star Tribune* (Minneapolis), March 24, 1989, p. 2D.
"Sportsman's Guide Makes 'Model' Gains," *Catalog Age*, November 1997.
"The Sportsman's Guide (SGDE)," *Wall Street Transcript*, March 1, 1999.
Stavig, Vicki, "Stun Guns and Splatball Pistols," *Corporate Report Minnesota*, February 1987, pp. 45–48.
Waters, Jennifer, "Sportsman's Is on Hunt to Regain Profitability," *Minneapolis/St. Paul CityBusiness*, May 17–23, 1996, pp. 1, 36.

—Kathleen Peippo

Stora Enso Oyj

Kanavaranta One
P.O. Box 309
FIN-00101 Helsinki
Finland
Telephone: (20) 46 131
Fax: (20) 46 21471
Web site: http://www.storaenso.com

Public Company
Incorporated: 1896 as Aktiebolaget W. Gutzeit & Co.
Employees: 40,226
Sales: EUR 10.64 billion (US$11.33 billion) (1999)
Stock Exchanges: Helsinki Stockholm
NAIC: 113110 Timber Tract Operations; 113310
    Logging; 115310 Support Activities for Forestry;
    321113 Sawmills; 322110 Pulp Mills; 322121 Paper
    (Except Newsprint) Mills; 322122 Newsprint Mills;
    322130 Paperboard Mills; 322211 Corrugated and
    Solid Fiber Box Manufacturing; 322222 Coated and
    Laminated Paper Manufacturing; 422110 Printing and
    Writing Paper Wholesalers

Stora Enso Oyj, which was formed in late 1998 from the merger of Sweden's Stora Kopparbergs Bergslag AB and Finland's Enso Oyj, is one of the leading global forest products groups. In 1999 world rankings of producers, it held the number two positions in magazine paper, newsprint, consumer packaging board, and sawn softwood, and the number three position in fine paper. Following the completion of its February 2000-announced acquisition of Consolidated Papers, Inc., a U.S. maker of coated papers for magazines, annual reports, and labels, Stora Enso would bolster these positions and gain a significant presence in the important U.S. paper market. Pre-Consolidated Papers, Stora Enso derived more than three-quarters of its revenues from countries in the European Union (with 17 percent from Germany alone), about six percent from other European countries, another six percent from North America, about seven percent from the Asia-Pacific region, and the remaining four percent elsewhere. In addition to its production operations, Stora Enso through its Papyrus unit distributes fine papers and other products to printers, graphic design studios, and other customers in 13 European countries. The company owns 2.1 million hectares (5.2 million acres) of Nordic forestland. Among Stora Enso's shareholders, the Finnish state and the Swedish investment group Investor AB each own 24.1 percent of the voting rights.

Stora's Copper Mining Origins: 13th–18th Centuries

Of the two firms that joined to form Stora Enso, Stora had by far the longer history. In fact, the company claimed to be the world's oldest existing joint-stock company. It went through several transformations during its 700-plus-year history. Throughout most of its life, Stora was one of Europe's largest copper producers as its official name, Stora Kopparbergs Bergslags (The Great Copper Mountain Mining Company), indicated. It was Sweden's first, and for a considerable period only, major enterprise of international significance. As copper output declined in the 19th century, Stora diversified into iron and steel production as well as forestry products. It remained active in these sectors until the 1970s, when it decided to concentrate on the pulp and paper industry. As a result of a series of acquisitions in the 1980s, Stora became Europe's largest forestry company, a position it held into the mid-1990s when a handful of rivals surpassed it through a series of mergers and acquisitions.

Peasant farmers began mining the copper mountain near Falun in central Sweden around the year 1000. The first documentary evidence of the mine appears in a letter from 1288 giving the Bishop of Västerås a one-eighth share in the mine in exchange for landholdings. The document shows that a cooperative organization by this time was managing the mine, with shares being bought and sold.

The mine was controlled by Swedish nobles and German merchants, who were responsible for selling the copper in the European market. Mine operations were conducted by master miners, who excavated the ore on a rotation basis. They were supervised by a royal bailiff after King Magnus Eriksson granted a charter, bestowing a series of privileges on the mine, in 1347.

The decree of 1347 acknowledged that the mine played a decisive role in the national economy and its importance grew over the next few centuries. The improvement of production techniques boosted the annual output of the mine from 80 tons of copper in the late 15th century to 750 tons 100 years later.

This was occurring as copper output in central Europe was declining. The mine soon became a prime source of national wealth, accounting for 60 percent of the gross national product, as foreign demand grew for Swedish copper. ''Sweden stands or falls with the Copper Mountain,'' read one proclamation from the royal government, which viewed the mine as a means to improve its poor financial position and support its series of military campaigns in the Baltic region and central Europe during the 17th century.

Having declared that the crown had regal rights to the copper deposits, the Swedish kings demanded taxes on the mined ore and tried to monopolize the mining and trading of copper.

Their success in this demand was limited, however. By 1650, when annual copper production from the mine hit a peak of 3,000 tons, the metal had become the country's most important export product and Sweden dominated the European copper market, supplying two-thirds of the continent's copper needs.

The highest authority over mine operations was the Royal Mine Board in Stockholm and the king's local representative was the mine master. The mine master was in charge of allocating mining rights to the master miners, who paid one-tenth of their ore production to the crown as rent, plus one-fourth of the crude copper they produced from smelters as tax. The total number of mining shares was fixed at 1,200, an arrangement that lasted until Stora became an *aktiebolag*—public limited company—in 1888.

The decline of Stora's mine was signaled by two giant cave-ins in 1655 and 1687, after which production never exceeded 1,500 tons a year and output gradually sank to an annual level of 900 tons by the late 18th century. During this period, copper was still Sweden's second largest export item after iron, but its importance declined sharply in the early 19th century.

Diversifying into Iron, Steel, and Forest Products, 19th Century

The mine owners then decided to develop the forest and iron-ore resources in the region to replace the falling copper production. They had considerable experience of both products since they had harvested and transported wood to fuel the copper smelters, while they manufactured mining tools out of iron ore.

In the early 1800s Stora began producing pig iron and bar iron as a new business venture, becoming one of the country's leading manufacturers in this sector by mid-century. It bought or leased tracts of forest to supply the iron furnaces and forges with charcoal fuel.

In conjunction with the change in its activity, Stora also underwent an organizational reform in 1862 that transformed its legal status and administrative rules. The crown's influence over operations was ended with the abolition of the master miner's office. Supervision of the company's mining operations and its manufacturing activity in iron and wood products, which had been managed separately, were merged under a three-member collective leadership—this marked the official establishment of Stora Kopparbergs Bergslag.

By the 1870s, Stora Kopparbergs had begun to assume its modern profile. It used its ownership of forest lands to become one of the country's largest wood product companies. Its Domnarvet sawmill was the largest water-powered mill in the nation and the sawn timber it produced accounted for more than half of the company's sales. A large iron works was also built at Domnarvet during the decade to replace the company's dozen scattered and inefficient small works.

Mining operations, meanwhile, contributed a decreasing share of corporate revenues. The mine accounted for one-quarter of sales in 1870, but its output of copper and recently discovered gold and silver amounted to only a tenth of sales by 1890. The mine also generated income from the production of sulfur pyrites as well as the distinctive Falun red paint that adorns many houses in the Swedish countryside; the production of Falun red paint dated back to the mid-18th century.

Erik Johan Ljungberg, who became general manager of Stora Kopparbergs in 1875, emphasized the strategy of making a limited number of basic products in a few large plants to achieve economies of scale. A sawmill at Skutskär on the mouth of the Dalälven River was acquired in 1885 and expanded to become one of the world's largest, with two pulp mills added in the 1890s. A giant paper mill for newsprint was also established at Kvarnsveden, near Domnarvet, in 1897.

Additional forests and the ore mines at Grängesberg were purchased as well as other ironworks, including the Söderfors facility that was later developed into the company's specialty steelworks. These facilities were powered by hydroelectric stations built by Stora along the Dalälven River in the early 20th century.

When Stora Kopparbergs Bergslag became a limited share company in 1888, with Ljungberg appointed managing director and chairman of the board, it was the largest concern in Sweden in terms of sales and number of employees. It had an initial share capital of SKr 9.6 million, with eight shares being exchanged for each old share dating from the 17th century. During Ljungberg's time, corporate sales grew from SKr 4.5 million to more than SKr 30 million.

Expanding on the Stora Core: 1900–75

By the time of Ljungberg's death in 1915, the foundations of the modern Stora Kopparbergs were clearly laid with the saw and pulp mills at Skutskär, the paper mill at Kvarnsveden, and the iron and steel works at Domnarvet, all of them concentrated

Key Dates:

1288: First documentary evidence of mining at the copper mountain near Falun, Sweden.

1347: King Magnus Eriksson of Sweden grants a royal charter, bestowing a series of privileges on the mine.

1650: Annual copper production hits peaks of 3,000 tons.

1687: Second of two giant cave-ins marks the beginning of a gradual decline in mine output.

Mid-18th century: Production of Falun red paint commences.

Early 19th century: Stora begins producing pig iron and bar iron, and later moves into forest products.

1862: Mining, iron, and wood activities are combined within a single company, Stora Kopparbergs Bergslag.

1872: Norway-based W. Gutzeit & Co. erects the first steam-powered sawmill in Finland, on the island of Kotka.

1885: Stora acquires a sawmill at Skutskär.

1888: Stora Kopparbergs Bergslag becomes a limited share company; Enso Träsliperi Aktiebolaget is born through the building of the first groundwood mill on the Vuoksi River.

1896: W. Gutzeit & Co. is reincorporated in Finland as Aktiebolaget W. Gutzeit & Co.

1897: A paper mill for newsprint is established by Stora at Kvarnsveden.

Early 20th century: Stora builds hydroelectric stations to power its plants.

1907: Enso adds a paper machine to its mill.

1909: Gutzeit acquires Aktiebolaget Pankakoski and its groundwood mill.

1910: Enso builds large hydroelectric power station on the Vuoksi River.

1912: Gutzeit acquires the financially troubled Enso.

1916: Stora becomes part of the Wallenberg empire with the appointment of Marcus Wallenberg, Sr., as chairman.

1918: The Finnish government becomes majority shareholder in Gutzeit.

1927: Gutzeit is renamed Enso-Gutzeit Osakeyhtiö.

1931: Enso-Gutzeit acquires Tornator Osakeyhtiö.

1939–40: Enso-Gutzeit suffers heavy damage in Soviet attacks on Finland; 1940 territorial concessions lead to loss of significant facilities and forestland.

1961: Stora begins overseas expansion with the building of a pulp mill in Nova Scotia, Canada.

1963: Enso-Gutzeit begins international expansion.

1976: Stora begins focusing on forest products through divestment of specialty steel unit.

1977: Stora's commercial steel operations are divested.

1984: Purchase of Billerud makes Stora the largest forestry company in Europe.

1986: Enso-Gutzeit acquires Varkaus; Stora acquires Papyrus.

1988: Stora acquires Swedish Match.

1990: Stora acquires Feldmühle Nobel, based in Germany.

1992: Mining operations in Falun come to an end.

1996: Enso-Gutzeit acquires Veitsiluoto; E-G adopts new name, Enso Oyj.

1997: Enso acquires majority control of the German firm E. Holtzmann & Cie AG.

1998: Stora purchases majority control of a Chinese fine paper mill, Suzhou Papyrus Paper; Stora and Enso merge to form Stora Enso Oyj.

2000: Stora Enso announces that it will acquire Consolidated Papers, Inc. of the United States.

---

along the Dalälven River Basin. The company would spend the next 60 years developing and expanding these core facilities. The sectors in which Stora operated formed the backbone of the country's industrial breakthrough in the late 19th century, enhancing the company's importance to the nation.

In 1916, Stora Kopparbergs became one of the crown jewels of the extensive Swedish industrial empire controlled by the Wallenberg family with the appointment of Marcus Wallenberg, Sr., the head of the dynasty, as chairman.

Emil Lundqvist, one of the top executives in the Wallenberg sphere, was named managing director of Stora Kopparbergs in 1923 and he oversaw the company's steady growth over the next two decades. Under Lundqvist, sales increased threefold to SKr 131 million, while profits grew from SKr 2 million to SKr 11 million.

Lundqvist was succeeded by Ejnar Rodling and Håkan Abenius, who presided over an almost uninterrupted expansion with sales approaching SKr 1 billion by the early 1960s. Annual capital investment rose from SKr 20 million in 1945 to more than SKr 150 million in 1960, with the construction of five new power stations and expansion of existing industrial facilities.

But the 1960s proved to be a period of growing difficulties for Stora Kopparbergs. Increased international competition depressed prices for the bulk commodities that were the company's primary products. It introduced rationalization measures to boost production capacity, while developing special grades of standard products to reduce its heavy dependence on goods particularly vulnerable to economic cycles. These included new types of pulp and high quality iron and steel. In 1961, Stora Kopparbergs also established its first overseas venture with the building of a pulp mill in the Canadian province of Nova Scotia.

The recession that followed the oil shock of the early 1970s posed a new challenge for the company's next president, Erik Sundblad. Mounting losses in both commercial steel and specialty steel operations placed a heavy burden on the company. It was clear that what was needed was the creation of larger units that could operate at lower cost through economies of scale.

Focusing on Forest Products: 1976–89

Instead of expanding the steel business through acquisitions, however, Stora Kopparbergs decided to sell it. The first step occurred in 1976 with the sale of its specialty steel unit to Uddeholm, another Swedish specialty steel company. This was followed a year later with the transfer of its commercial steel operations, mainly consisting of the Domnarvet Steelworks and iron mines, to Svenskt Stål AB, a new company created by the government to concentrate the country's ailing steel industry under one umbrella group.

With these moves, Stora Kopparbergs became primarily a pulp and paper company with substantial resources in forests and hydroelectric power. Its new strategy of concentrating on this sector was inaugurated with the purchase of Bergvik & Ala, a Swedish forestry company, in 1976.

The early 1980s were marked by a power struggle between the Wallenbergs and the Swedish automaker Volvo, which had been permitted to buy a stake in the company, over ownership control of Stora Kopparbergs, with the family eventually emerging victorious.

Following the sudden death of Sundblad in 1984, Bo Berggren, a former deputy managing director, became the new company head. Within months, Stora Kopparbergs, which had been Sweden's second biggest forestry company after Svenska Cellulosa AB, suddenly emerged as Europe's largest, with sales of SKr 13 billion, after the SKr 3.6 billion purchase of Billerud, Sweden's fifth largest forestry company.

The deal was significant for other reasons besides size. It broadened the company's product range from its traditional areas of newsprint and fine paper to Billerud's specialized area of packaging, including sack paper and liquid packaging board. It also obtained its first main production facility within the European Community (EC) with Billerud's eucalyptus pulp mill in Portugal. The company marked this milestone by shortening its name for general usage to Stora, the Swedish word for ''great'' or ''large.''

Pulp- and papermaking is one of the world's most capital-intensive industries. Stora realized that only the largest companies would be able to survive and compete in international markets against huge U.S. rivals. The company's size was further enlarged with the decision by the Wallenbergs to concentrate their forestry holdings under Stora. This phase began in 1986 when Stora acquired Papyrus, then the country's fifth largest pulp and paper company. The SKr 5.8 billion deal boosted Stora's annual sales to SKr 18 billion.

In 1988, Stora paid SKr 5.9 billion for Swedish Match, another Wallenberg-controlled company. The deal underscored Stora's strategy of becoming a forest products group that spanned the entire manufacturing process from raw materials to finished consumer products. Although Swedish Match was best known for matches and lighters, it also produced a range of timber-based building products, including flooring, doors, and kitchen furnishings. The acquisition boosted Stora's sales to almost SKr 40 billion.

Expanding Outside Sweden: 1990–98

Having consolidated its position at home, Stora then decided to expand its international operations, especially in the EC, which accounted for almost half of its sales. One worry was that its production of paper and pulp remained largely concentrated

in Sweden, which could be a handicap as competition intensified in the EC single market after 1992.

In 1990, it first bought the French paper concern Les Paperteies de la Chapelle-Darblay in partnership with the Finnish forestry company Kymmene. But it then pulled out of the deal when it saw a more attractive target. This was the DM4 billion takeover of Feldmühle Nobel, the German forest products and engineering group. Stora had cooperated with Feldmühle Nobel for more than 20 years, with the two companies jointly operating pulp and newsprint mills in Sweden. Ownership of Feldmühle Nobel made Stora the largest producer of lightweight coated magazine paper and newsprint in Europe, while increasing its sales to SKr 62 billion in 1990.

Stora had to rein in some of its other ambitions in order to finance the purchase of the German firm, one of the largest ever transactions in Europe. It decided to sell some of the Swedish Match units as well as the engineering operations of Feldmühle Nobel; the latter were sold to Germany's Metallgesellschaft AG in June 1991 for US$706 million. This still left Stora as the dominant power in the European pulp and paper industry and one of the world's largest forest products companies.

Stora suffered from the effects of the global recession in pulp and paper products in the early 1990s, leading the firm to initiate restructuring efforts. Stora announced in 1990 that it would cut 3,500 jobs from its workforce, then in late 1991 said that a further 2,500 would be eliminated. The company took restructuring charges totaling SKr 400 million in 1991 and SKr 847 million in 1992, leading to a net loss for the latter year of SKr 1.36 billion. Also in 1992 came the historic ending of mining operations in Falun.

Stora's financial performance trailed the overall industry in the mid-1990s, a period marked by industrywide overcapacity and an increasing pressure for global consolidation. A spate of mergers left Stora as the fourth largest forestry company in Europe by early 1998, trailing UPM-Kymmene Corporation and Enso Oyj, both based in Finland, and Svenska Cellulosa AB of Sweden. In one of its last initiatives before joining the merger wave itself through the late 1998 linkup with Enso, Stora acquired majority control of Suzhou Papyrus Paper, the largest producer of coated fine paper in China, earlier in 1998.

Enso's Roots, Late 19th Century

Enso Oyj, which was known as Enso-Gutzeit Osakeyhtiö from 1924 to 1996, was a typical Finnish forest-based company in that it developed through acquisitions. Its origin lies in the founding of a sawmill in 1872 on the island of Kotka, off the southern coastline of Finland at the estuary of the Kymi River. Previously sawmills were small and water-powered, as steam-powered sawmills were forbidden by the government. A new policy was adopted in 1861, however, enabling steam-driven sawmills to be erected throughout Finland. This change in policy led industrialists to build sawmills at suitable points on the coast at places where timber could be floated and sawn goods shipped abroad. One such location was the island of Kotka. Here the Norwegian industrialist Hans Gutzeit erected a sawmill, which was opened on November 16, 1872. Hans

Gutzeit came from Norway, where the company W. Gutzeit & Co. had built Norway's first steam-powered sawmill in 1858.

The new mill at Kotka had six frame saws and two circular saws as well as auxiliary machinery of the most modern design at that time. The machinery was powered by a steam engine of about 100 horsepower. To operate the new mill, Gutzeit imported skilled operators from Norway. It was popularly known as the Norway Mill. In 1880 Hans Gutzeit returned to Norway, where the board had its seat. In Kotka, management was given to a residential manager, the Norwegian Christian Holt.

Kotka Island was a favorite place for new sawmills. Soon there were many mills, all of whose logs were floated from the large Päijänne lake system. The competition for the most favorable forest resources was fierce, however, and resulted in ever increasing prices. The Gutzeit mill began to look for new sources for its raw material. Eventually it found that it could build a mechanical transport facility from Finland's largest lake system, the Saimaa Lakes, over an isthmus to a small lake, connected to the Kymi River. Large volume, however, was needed to justify this investment, and so Gutzeit started buying forestland in the Saimaa basin. To eliminate a potentially dangerous competitor—Egerton Hubbard & Co., an English-owned St. Petersburg-based company that owned AB Utra Wood Co., a sawmill in the Saimaa basin—Gutzeit purchased the latter company, together with the sawmill, receiving a forest area of 100,000 hectares (247,000 acres).

During this time, Alexander Gullichsen, another Norwegian, had entered the company as a clerk. He was a very able man and rose steadily through the ranks of the company. He was the first to recognize the possibility of obtaining raw material from the Saimaa basin and it was he who negotiated the Utra Wood deal. Eventually he was nominated managing director of Aktiebolaget W. Gutzeit & Co., the name given to the owner of the Kotka mill when it was incorporated as a Finnish company in 1896 (hereafter called Gutzeit). Although the ownership of the company was still mainly Norwegian, Holt and Gullichsen were considered to be Finns, having become naturalized citizens of Finland.

As a new step in the development of the company, Gullichsen in 1908 built a sulfate pulp mill at the Kotka sawmill to make use of the waste wood, which up until that time was burned. More important for the diversification of the company was the range of acquisitions generated by Gullichsen's initiative.

In northern Karelia, not far from the Russian border, was an old iron ore refinery. In 1902 this had been converted into a mechanical wood pulp mill when the old iron works had to be closed. This groundwood mill was incorporated as a company in 1904 under the name of Aktiebolaget Pankakoski. This company was purchased in 1909 by Gutzeit and a board mill was added.

Of greater significance, however, was the acquisition of Enso. This took Gutzeit further into the field of chemical pulp making and eventually into paper. It also led to a change in the company's name. Enso was built in 1888 as the first groundwood mill on the huge Vuoksi River, which drains the Saimaa basin into Lake Ladoga through a series of mighty falls, and was considered too large to be harnessed for industrial purposes. Nevertheless, Baron Adi Standertskjöld, a Finnish industrialist who had sold his groundwood mills at Inkeroinen on the Kymi River, came to the Räikkölä Falls in 1887 to buy a site on which to build a new groundwood mill. The founder gave the name Enso to the falls and the mill; eventually the name was extended to the township that grew up around them. "Enso" is derived from the Finnish word *ensi,* meaning "first," as the mill was the first on the Vuoksi River. The new company was named Enso Träsliperi Aktiebolaget (hereafter called Enso). The mill was designed by the Swedish engineer Hedbäck. In order to use the falls as a source of power, a small channel with sluices was excavated beside the main rapids, which were left to flow freely. Nine turbines generated 2,000 horsepower. When the first shipment of groundwood pulp left the mill in February 1889, it had to be transported by horse and sledge to Viipuri where it could be loaded on to a train for transportation to St. Petersburg.

The area was a wilderness. To accommodate the workers, the company had to build houses, for which purpose they constructed a small brick manufacturing unit. The office staff was minimal, consisting of the residential manager, a cashier-bookkeeper, a correspondent-dispatcher, and a messenger boy.

Emergence of Enso-Gutzeit, Early 20th Century

In 1907 a "yankee-type" paper machine—that is, a machine equipped with a large drying cylinder of several meters' diameter called a yankee cylinder—was added. At the same time the company decided to build a dam across the river to obtain more power. The Swedish engineering company commissioned for the work failed, however, and the project had to be discontinued after more than a year's futile labor. The Finnish engineer A. Sandsund, who took on the work soon afterward, was successful and in 1910 the new dam, the largest of its kind at the time, was completed. The work was extremely expensive and was such a strain on finances that the owners decided to sell the company to Gutzeit in 1912. The latter was well aware of the value of its purchase. Gutzeit now owned a mill that could make use of all the small wood that came from the company's forests when logs were cut for the sawmills. It also had an ample supply of hydraulic power at its disposal. As its first project, the new owner planned a new board machine. New forestry holdings were added by the purchase in 1913 of over 70,000 hectares (173,000 acres) from the Finland Wood Co.

In 1917 Gutzeit's driving force, Alexander Gullichsen, died. Another Norwegian, Herman Heiberg, was nominated managing director. Major changes in ownership soon occurred, however. In October 1918 the Finnish government purchased 4,400 Gutzeit shares from the Norwegian owners, becoming the majority shareholder with more than half of the company's 7,200 shares. Enso's residential manager, Sölve Thunström, was nominated managing director of the group.

Since the Saimaa Lake basin was the most important area for wood purchasing and transport, the company developed a lake transport fleet, assisted by a shipyard and machine shop, Laitaatsillan Konepaja, founded by the company near the town of Savonlinna. It was considered, however, that other shipping companies or shipowners would suffer from Gutzeit's monopoly on service shops in the district, and a rival machine shop was started in 1917 in Savonlinna, only six kilometers (3.7

miles) from Laitaatsalmi. The rival company was later named Oy Lypsyniemen Konepaja. It had problems from the start, and was heading for bankruptcy in 1919 when it was saved by Gutzeit, which had become a majority shareholder. Lypsyniemen Konepaja entered a phase of rapid growth and later specialized in machinery for the pulp industry.

The rapid development of the Gutzeit group in the early 1920s, as well as the decrease in the value of the Finnish markka, compelled the company to increase its capital. In 1923 the Finnish government subscribed for Gutzeit's new shares, raising government ownership of the company to 87 percent.

Thunström left the company in 1924 and V.A. Kotilainen was nominated managing director and chief executive officer of the group. The new manager found that the finances of the company were excessively dependent on short-term loans and he concentrated his efforts upon the strengthening of the company's balance sheet. In a few years he managed to get rid of the short-term debt, and to reduce total borrowings to only 46 percent of annual sales. The head office was transferred to Enso and in 1927 the company was renamed Enso-Gutzeit Osakeyhtiö (Enso-Gutzeit Ltd.).

Another industrial unit was soon added to the company. In 1877 Wolter Ramsay founded a small company in Lahti, south of Lake Päijänne, for the manufacturing of bobbins for English textile mills. The company derived the name Tornator Osakeyhtiö from the Latin word *tornare*, meaning "to turn." When Ramsay died suddenly in 1890, the ownership of Tornator was transferred to the Wolff family. Gradually Eugen Wolff took the leading role in the company. His ambition was to establish a large mill on the Vuoksi River and when he heard that the owner of Tainionkoski Manor at the eponymous falls on the Vuoksi River, G. Törnudd, had died in 1894, he convinced his brother, Reguel Wolff, that Tornator should buy Tainionkoski Manor. This led to the purchase of the manor in 1895. During the years 1896–97 Eugen Wolff erected a bobbin production unit at Tainionkoski, as well as a paper mill and a groundwood mill. He later began to build a sulfate pulp mill at Tainionkoski, and started to manufacture grease-proof paper. This new product proved successful, securing a good market for the company in western Europe, especially in England. By 1918, however, Eugen Wolff had tired of his pioneering work and sold his shares to the Finnish government.

Enso-Gutzeit (E-G) had long been interested in Tornator, its neighbor on the Vuoksi River. In 1931 Enso-Gutzeit purchased the privately owned shares of the company. Thus E-G became the owner of all forest-based interests in the Vuoksi Valley and also of the valuable lakeshore at the beginning of the river. The chief executive, V.A. Kotilainen, now had the resources to turn the company into the leading timber, pulp, board, and paper enterprise in Finland. He also had a team of talented specialists at his disposal. A sulfate pulp mill was built at Enso in 1930, but Kotilainen wanted to increase further the share of sulfate pulp in the company's product line. In the 1930s Enso-Gutzeit built the large Kaukopää sulfate mill, a gigantic unit for its time, on the southern shore of Lake Saimaa. The company had acquired the valuable area through the Tornator merger. Previously sulfate pulp had been of minor interest, but with the development of paper and paperboard packing the process had become more

promising. The mill was designed to produce 80,000 tons a year but by 1937 production had increased to 120,000 tons a year.

E-G was always eager to purchase forestland. In 1913 the total area of Gutzeit forests was 400,000 hectares (990,000 acres). The acquisition of Tornator brought another 79,000 hectares (195,000 acres) and the purchase of a timber company in easternmost Karelia in 1937 brought still more. When World War II began in 1939, E-G owned 523,000 hectares (1.3 million acres) of forestland.

With the addition of new mills and machinery, the company wanted to increase its power facilities. By 1936 Enso had already become the largest paperboard mill in Finland. In 1938 the company decided to make full use of the Enso falls for power production. It planned to increase the height of the Enso falls by adding a dam, raising the water level above the falls so that the Vallinkoski rapids, four kilometers (2.5 miles) upstream from Enso, were combined with Enso, making the Enso falls 16 meters (52 feet) high. At this time, most industrial power plants were built in rapids or falls of six to ten meters (20–33 feet). When war broke out in 1939 this gigantic construction project was still unfinished.

World War II Damage, Concessions, and Rebuilding

In 1941 E-G acquired all the shares of the Insulite Company of Finland from its founder, an American company wishing to withdraw from Finland. This factory, near Kotka, added another new line of business to E-G. Its product, insulite, was a board made of aspen fibers and well suited to the needs of the new owners. In Helsinki in 1940 E-G erected a factory to make packaging boxes for special requirements in Finland.

Finland was attacked by the Soviet Union on November 30, 1939. Damage was inevitable as most of E-G's facilities were in Karelia, near the border with the Soviet Union. Soviet bombs caused some damage to the mills and the raw material woodpiles at Enso and Kaukopää were burned. The total amount of wood lost was 650,000 cubic meters (23 million cubic feet). The Norway Sawmill in Kotka was completely destroyed by Soviet bombs, but the worst was still to come. In the 1940 armistice Finland had to cede a large part of Karelia to the Soviet Union. Among the cessions was the Enso mill town with its large power plant still under construction. E-G also lost the easternmost sawmills and hydraulic power stations as well as almost 100,000 hectares (247,000 acres) of forestland.

Politics also affected E-G at the top management level. CEO Kotilainen had taken part in organizing services to civilians, such as food supply, education, and medical care, in the Russian area occupied by Finland in 1941–44, and he had to step down from all public offices at the demand of the Soviets. A new managing director and chief executive officer, William Lehtinen, was nominated on October 1, 1945. He had previously been a member of the board, responsible for sales and marketing.

E-G now had to compensate for the loss of Enso. All of the Enso employees were guaranteed employment at the other mills in the vicinity, mainly at Tornator and Kaukopää. This led to temporary overstaffing. At the Tainionkoski falls a new hydraulic power station was built in 1945 to compensate for the loss of the Enso station that had been nearing completion. At the end of

1946 E-G purchased the Joh. Parviaisen Tehtaat Oy, an industrial company in central Finland specializing in plywood and mechanical wood processing. In addition to providing an entry into the plywood business, the new acquisition brought a factory for prefabricated houses, a product in strong demand after the war. To domestic demand were added the Soviet war-reparation claims, which included large quantities of prefabricated housing. The Soviet demand for many kinds of machinery as war reparation led to a heavy workload for E-G's subsidiary, the Lypsyniemen Konepaja machine shop. In 1945, E-G purchased the former metallurgical works in the Vuoksi River Valley of Outokumpu Oy, the well-known copper company, which transferred its activities to western Finland. E-G concentrated its chemical plants in these facilities, specializing in processing the byproducts of the pulp mills. The central laboratories of the company were also transferred there. In 1947, to facilitate international shipment of its products, E-G established a ship-owning company, Merivienti Oy, and a shipping company, Oy Finnlines Ltd., which was Merivienti's subsidiary.

Postwar Expansion and International Ventures

The company needed new paper mills to realize its strategic growth plans, however. A new newsprint paper mill was completed by 1955 at Summa on the southern coastline, east of Kotka. Production of kraft paper was started at the Kotka mills. At the factories in Lahti, the production of textile bobbins was discontinued and replaced by a paper-converting and box-making plant. The joinery at the Lahti factories was developed. At Kaukopää a bleaching plant was built and a linerboard machine was erected. The production of white linerboard, used as packaging for consumer goods, began. In 1959 the company began building another large sulfate pulp mill near the old Tornator Tainionkoski mills. This new pulp mill with a capacity of 150,000 tons, initially named Kaukopää II, was renamed Tainionkoski mills after the old Tornator mills ceased operation in 1963. A new mill with production capacity for 100,000 tons of bleached sulfate pulp was built in northern Karelia at Uimaharju between 1962 and 1967.

In 1962 Pentti Halle was nominated chief executive officer after the retirement of William Lehtinen. In the same year, the company moved headquarters into a new building in central Helsinki, designed by architect Alvar Aalto.

The internationalization of E-G began in 1963 when the company became a shareholder in the Dutch Roermond paper mill company. Two years later E-G acquired all the shares of this company, but in 1972 Roermond was sold back to the Dutch. Even though this first experiment in internationalization proved futile, E-G continued in other directions. In order to procure linerboard for international markets, E-G formed a joint venture, together with the Finnish company Oy Tampella Ab and with American interests to establish a U.S. pulp and linerboard mill, Pineville Kraft Corporation, in Louisiana. This mill went into operation in 1968. Later, however, the two Finnish minority partners sold their shares to their U.S. partners. A more lasting investment abroad was the formation of a Canadian venture, Eurocan Pulp & Paper Co. Ltd. (Eurocan) in British Columbia. At first E-G had 50 percent of the shares, the other 50 percent being divided between the Finnish companies Tampella and Kymmene. Eurocan went into operation in 1970. It had a

sawmill and a sulfate pulp mill plus a kraftliner machine and a kraft paper machine in Kitimat. For years the Canadian company had financial problems and Tampella sold its shares to Kymmene. In 1979 Kymmene sold its shares to E-G. The latter replaced the partnership by an agreement with the Canadian company West Fraser Timber Co. Ltd. in 1980. It took years of negotiations and new agreements, however, before Eurocan became a viable business and a profitable investment.

Later E-G continued its expansion abroad. In addition to sales offices in many locations in different parts of the world, the company owned production facilities—in addition to Eurocan—in Barbados, France, the United Kingdom, the Netherlands, and Indonesia.

Pentti Halle was to retire as chief executive officer in 1972. The board of administration, the highest authority below the general meeting of shareholders, had already employed Aarne Hildén as executive vice-president. He had gained international business experience in the service of Esso, the large oil company. It seemed obvious that Hilden should be nominated chief executive officer, which in Enso's case also included becoming chairman of the board. Intrigues took place within the company, however, influenced by politicians at high levels, and eventually the post of chief executive officer was awarded instead to Olavi J. Mattila, chief executive officer of Valmet Oy. Pentti Salmi, from within the company, was nominated managing director. This period resulted in a troubled decade for the company, before Mattila retired in 1983. Pentti Salmi was then nominated chief executive officer. Under his command E-G's business developed steadily.

Growth Through Acquisition: 1986–98

In the late 1980s major changes took place in the Finnish business world. Mergers, takeovers, and the selling off of divisions were common. E-G and the largest Finnish family-owned industry, A. Ahlström Oy, were involved in one such deal. Gutzeit's managing director in the days before the Enso acquisition, Alex Gullichsen, had already been interested in acquiring the Varkaus mills and factories in the northern Saimaa area when the owner, the Viipuri merchant Paul Wahl & Co., was willing to sell at the beginning of the 1900s. Although details of the deal had already been discussed, A. Ahlström Oy managed to buy the Varkaus mills and factories before Gullichsen had reached a decision. Thus Varkaus became one of Ahlström's most attractive assets. At Varkaus, Ahlström built a large pulp mill, a paper mill, a sawmill, a plywood factory, and machine shops. During the reshuffle of the 1980s, however, Ahlström found a need to shed some of its financial burdens so that it could afford to remain a family-controlled business. In 1986 the Varkaus pulp and paper mills and sawmills were sold to E-G. Part of the price paid by E-G was the transfer of its machine shops in Savonlinna, Lypsyniemen Konepaja, to A. Ahlström Oy. E-G had finally achieved its aim of taking over the Varkaus mills, 80 years after the intention was first announced.

Other changes took place in the structure of E-G; the company sold its interests in fiberboards and plywood in 1990 to Schauman Wood Oy, a subsidiary of the Kymmene group. Political changes in the Soviet Union resulted in new ventures involving E-G. Because part of the company's forest resources had to be ceded to the Soviet Union after the war, E-G regularly purchased timber from behind the frontier. The Soviet era of *perestroika* and *glasnost* led to new ideas for joint ventures. In October 1989 E-G agreed with the authorities of the Soviet Union to form a jointly owned Finnish company, Enocell Oy, with 80 percent of the shares held by E-G. Enocell was to take over the activities of the Uimaharju sulfate pulp mill, where a replacement pulp mill was being constructed, from the beginning of 1992. Most of the raw materials were to be supplied by the Soviet partner. Another joint venture, Ladenso, was formed in Soviet Karelia to concentrate on forest development and related activities, while E-G expanded further in eastern Europe with the 1994 opening of a new plant in eastern Germany at Eilenburg through a new unit called Sachsen Papier. The Eilenburg plant produced newsprint using wastepaper as a raw material; this contrasted with the company's other papermaking, all of which was based completely on wood.

Enso-Gutzeit played a prominent role in the global consolidation of the forest products sector in the mid-to-late 1990s that was triggered by industrywide overcapacity. In 1996 E-G acquired fellow state-controlled Finnish papermaker Veitsiluoto, temporarily becoming the largest forest industry firm in Finland (the merger-created UPM-Kymmene Corporation soon leaped ahead). Out of the merger also came a new name for the company, Enso Oyj. The Finnish state maintained control of more than 60 percent of the voting rights in Enso. In 1997 Enso took a majority 50.4 percent stake in E. Holtzmann & Cie AG, a German maker of newsprint and magazine paper. Enso was now the second largest maker of forest products in Europe, trailing only UPM-Kymmene. Within two years, Enso had increased its interest in Holtzmann to 100 percent.

Formation and Early Development of Stora Enso: 1998 and Beyond

In June 1998 the boards of directors of Stora Kopparbergs Bergslag AB and Enso Oyj approved a merger valued at about US$8.5 billion. In November the competition authorities of the European Union approved the deal, and the following month it was consummated. Although it was billed as a merger of equals—Stora had 1997 sales of US$5.69 billion, and Enso, US$5.51 billion—technically, Enso Oyj changed its name to Stora Enso Oyj, and took over Stora Kopparbergs Bergslag, which became a subsidiary of Stora Enso. Investor AB and the Finnish state each emerged with 24.1 percent of the voting rights in Stora Enso, which was headquartered in Helsinki but had exchange listings in both Helsinki and Stockholm. Named to the CEO position of Stora Enso was Jukka Härmälä, who had headed Enso, while the leader of Stora, Björn Hägglund, became deputy CEO. The new company immediately took over the top spot among European forest products firms, while worldwide it ranked among the top five in revenues and the top two in production capacity, trailing only the U.S. giant International Paper Company. The main areas of focus for Stora Enso were identified as publication papers (newsprint and magazine paper), fine paper, and packaging boards—in each of these sectors, the company was one of the top three players in the world.

As with most mergers of this magnitude, integration issues were in the forefront in the months following the creation of Stora Enso. Through synergies and cost-cutting, savings of

EUR 700 million (US$662 million) were anticipated through 2002. Among the integration measures taken in 1999 and early 2000 were the divestment of fine paper mills in Denmark and Finland; the sale of stakes in noncore assets, such as a Finnish shipping company; and the sale of the former Stora head office in Stockholm. It was also announced that the integration would include the elimination of 2,000 jobs—about five percent of the workforce—in the years 1999 through 2002. In May 2000 Stora Enso sold the bulk of its electricity power generation assets to Fortum Corporation, a Finnish energy group, for SKr 15.85 billion (EUR 1.9 billion).

The year 2000 was filled with global paper industry acquisitions, and in February Stora Enso announced one of the largest, a proposed EUR 4.9 billion (US$4.7 billion) takeover of Consolidated Papers, Inc. This purchase would be a key step toward the achievement of a main company goal: gaining a significant presence in the North American market, the largest paper market in the world. Based in Wisconsin Rapids, Wisconsin, Consolidated Papers was among the North American leaders in the production of coated paper and super calendered printing paper (a type of uncoated paper used in periodicals and advertising materials), making for a neat fit with core areas of Stora Enso. Consolidated Papers also held a leading North American position in specialty papers, and owned and managed almost 700,000 acres of forestland in Wisconsin, Michigan, Minnesota, and Ontario, Canada. Stora Enso began planning for a listing of its stock on the New York Stock Exchange, for the integration of Consolidated Papers with the goal of producing annual cost savings of US$110 million by 2002, and for additional acquisitions, particularly in the other region it had targeted for growth: southeast Asia.

Principal Subsidiaries

Stora Kopparbergs Bergslag AB (Sweden; 98.7%); STORA ENSO NEWSPRINT & MAGAZINE PAPER: Stora Enso Publication Papers Oy Ltd; Kymenso Oy; Varenso Oy; Stora Enso Sachsen GmbH (Germany); Stora Enso Maxau GmbH & Co KG (Germany); Stora Enso Langerbrugge NV (Belgium); Stora Enso Corbehem SA (France); Stora Enso Kabel GmbH (Germany); Stora Enso Reisholz GmbH (Germany); Stora Enso Hylte AB (Sweden); Stora Enso Kvarnsveden AB (Sweden); Stora Enso Port Hawkesbury Ltd (Canada). STORA ENSO FINE PAPER: Stora Enso Fine Paper Oy; Berghuizer Papierfabriek NV (Netherlands); Stora Enso Fine Paper AB (Sweden); Stora Enso Nymölla AB (Sweden); Stora Enso Grycksbo AB (Sweden); Stora Enso Mölndal AB (Sweden); Stora Enso Uetersen GmbH (Germany); Stora Enso Suzhou Paper Co Ltd (China; 60.7%). STORA ENSO PACKAGING BOARDS: Corenso United Oy Ltd (71%); Stora Enso Ingerois Oy; Stora Enso Pankakoski Oy Ltd; Laminating Papers Oy; Stora Enso Barcelona S.A. (Spain); Stora Enso Packaging Oy; ZAO Pakenso (Russia); Stora Enso Packaging AB (Sweden); Pakenso Baltica SIA (Latvia); Stora Enso Paperboard AB (Sweden); Stora Enso Fors AB (Sweden); Stora Enso Newton Kyme Ltd (U.K.). STORA ENSO TIMBER: Stora Enso Timber Oy Ltd (73.5%); Holzindustrie Schweighofer AG (Australia); Puumerkki Oy; Stora Enso Timber AB (Sweden). STORA ENSO PULP: Kemijärven Sellu Oy; Enocell Oy (98.4%); Stora Enso Pulp AB (Sweden); Celulose Beira Industrial SA (Portugal). STORA ENSO MERCHANTS: Papyrus Merchants AB (Sweden); Papyrus AB (Sweden). STORA ENSO ENERGY: Pamilo Oy (51%); Stora Enso Energy AB (Sweden); Kopparkraft AB (Sweden; 99.9%). STORA ENSO FOREST: AS Stora Enso Metsä; Stora Enso Skog AB (Sweden).

Principal Divisions

Stora Enso Magazine Paper; Stora Enso Newsprint; Stora Enso Fine Paper; Stora Enso Packaging Boards; Stora Enso Timber; Stora Enso Pulp; Stora Enso Merchants; Stora Enso Asia Pacific.

Principal Competitors

Abitibi-Consolidated Inc.; Asia Pulp & Paper Company Ltd.; Bowater Inc.; Cartiere Burgo S.p.A.; Georgia-Pacific Corporation; International Paper Company; Riverwood International Corporation; Sappi Limited; Smurfit-Stone Container Corporation; UPM-Kymmene Corporation; Weyerhaeuser Company.

Further Reading

Baxter, Andrew, "Enso Hopes London Listing Will Draw Foreign Investors," *Financial Times*, June 20, 1989, p. 33.

Carnegy, Hugh, "Paper Profits Clear Space for Restructuring: Enso-Veitsiluoto Merger Highlights Concentration of Finnish Industry," *Financial Times*, June 7, 1995, p. 32.

"Four Major Mergers: Two Trans-Atlantic Blockbusters," *Pulp and Paper*, April 2000, pp. 13–15.

Hallvarsson, Mats, "The Jewel of the Kingdom," in *Sweden Works: Industry in Transition*, Stockholm, New Sweden 1988 Committee, 1987.

Hoving, Victor, *Enso-Gutzeit Osakeyhtiö, 1872–1958*, Helsinki: Frenckhellin Kijapaino Osakeyhtiö, 1961.

Jewitt, Caroline, "Stora Enso Sets Off on a Global Crusade," *Pulp and Paper International*, June 2000, pp. 29–31.

Karonen, Petri, *Enso-Gutzeit Oy laivanvarustajana: Oy Finnlines Ltd ja Merivienti Oy vuosina, 1947–1982*, Imatra: Enso-Gutzeit, 1992, 240 p.

Kenny, Jim, "Stora Enso Aims for a Smooth Transition," *Pulp and Paper International*, June 1999, pp. 20–21, 25.

Korpijaakko, O., "Gutzeit-yhtmän vaiheet 1872–1947," *Enso-Cutzeit Personnel Magazine, 75th Anniversary Issue*, 1947.

Kylmala, Timo, *Kutsetin Mies*, Helsinki: Kirjayhtyma, 1986.

Latour, Almar, "Paper Firms Join in Europe, Creating Giant," *Wall Street Journal*, June 3, 1998, p. A11.

McIvor, Greg, "Big Is Beautiful, but Not Automatically," *Financial Times*, June 18, 1998.

McIvor, Greg, and Tim Burt, "Paper Giants Open a New Chapter: The Stora-Enso Merger Could Be the First of Many," *Financial Times*, June 3, 1998, p. 26.

Moore, Stephen D., "Scandinavian Paper Firms Wrestle with Price Declines," *Wall Street Journal*, September 5, 1996, p. B8.

Rydberg, Sven, *En man föör sig: Emil Lundqvist och Stora Kopparberg under mellankrigstiden*, Stockholm: Atlantis, 1985, 154 p.

——, *The Great Copper Mountain: The Stora Story*, Falun, Sweden: Stora Kopparbergs Bergslags AB, 1988, 244 p.

——, *Stora Kopparberg: 1,000 Years of an Industrial Activity*, Stockholm: Gullers International, 1979, 93 p.

Salonen, O., "Piirteita Parviaisen Tehtaiden synnysta ja kehityksesta," *Enso-Gutzeit Personnel Magazine, 75th Anniversary Issue*, 1947.

Starkman, Dean, "Stora Enso to Buy Consolidated Papers," *Wall Street Journal*, February 23, 2000, p. A3.

"Stora's Homespun Remedies Go Against the Industry Grain," *Financial Times*, March 17, 1998, p. 36.

Sullivan, Aline, "Stora's Story: A Company As Old As the Millennium Puts on a New Face," *International Herald Tribune*, November 27, 1999, p. 17.

Taylor, Robert, "Stora Builds Its Muscle in the Community," *Financial Times*, April 30, 1990, p. 27.

Urry, Maggie, "Stora Stays with Go-Ahead Strategy After 700 Years," *Financial Times*, June 16, 1988, p. 32.

Verespej, Michael A., "Who Owns Whose Trees?," *Industry Week*, March 20, 2000, pp. 58+.

Wyman, Vic, "Enso Powers into Newsprint in Eastern Germany," *Pulp and Paper International*, December 1994, p. 28.

—Nils G. Björklund and John Burton
—updated by David E. Salamie

Suez Lyonnaise des Eaux

1, rue d'Astorg
75008 Paris
France
Telephone: (+33) 1 40 06 67 89
Fax: (+33) 1 40 06 67 33
Web site: http://www.suez-lyonnaise-eaux.fr

Public Company
Incorporated: 1858 as Compagnie Universelle du Canal
  Maritime de Suez
Employees: 333,132
Sales: EUR 31.46 billion (US$30.53 billion) (1999)
Stock Exchanges: Paris
NAIC: 221310 Water Supply and Irrigation Systems;
  2211 Electric Power Generation, Transmission and
  Distribution; 221210 Natural Gas Distribution; 5131
  Radio and Television Broadcasting

Suez Lyonnaise des Eaux has transformed itself into one of the world's leading multi-utility powerhouses, offering private water, gas, electricity and waste-management services in more than 120 countries. The result of a 1997 merger between Compagnie de Suez—the company that constructed the Suez Canal—and Lyonnaise des Eaux-Dumez, and joined with the holdings of Société Générale de Belgique (SGB), Suez Lyonnaise des Eaux is the world's leading water treatment and services group (vying with fellow French company Vivendi) through its subsidiaries Degrémont, Lyonnaise des Eaux, and two new U.S. subsidiaries, Nalco Chemical and United Water Resources, acquired in 1999. Through its Tractebel subsidiary, based in Belgium, Suez is also the world's fifth largest independent energy producer, with a capacity of more than 42,000 megawatts per year. In 2000, the company regrouped its waste management, under its Tractebel and SITA subsidiaries. While power generation remains Suez Lyonnaise des Eaux's main revenue source, the company has also launched itself into France's communications market, with shareholdings in cable television, internet and mobile telephony (NOOS), satellite television (TPS), and broadcast television (M6). These activities

represent only slightly more than one percent of Suez Lyonnaise des Eaux's annual sales of nearly EUR 31.5 billion. Until 2000, the company was also active in construction, through subsidiary Groupe GTM; this subsidiary was merged into a joint venture with French construction and services giant Vinci. The company is led by President and CEO Gerard Mestrallet, who is credited with guiding the merger between Suez and Lyonnaise des Eaux and transforming the company from a sprawling conglomerate into a streamlined, coherent power utilities group.

Constructing History in the 19th Century

Compagnie Universelle du Canal Maritime de Suez was the brainchild of Ferdinand de Lesseps, formed in the 1850s in order to dig and then operate the Suez Canal. De Lesseps, an engineer and diplomat, was acting under the proposal of Napoleon, who sought to link the Mediterranean and the Gulf of Suez, thereby establishing shorter sea and trade routes between Europe and India. Construction on the canal, one of the first great modern engineering triumphs, began in 1858 and ended in 1869. The canal, operated by Compagnie de Suez, was 44 percent owned by the Egyptian government, which at the time was engaged in a massive modernization program that landed the country in debt—primarily to the British government, which had established itself as the leading colonial power throughout much of North Africa and the Middle East. In order to reduce its debt, the Egyptian government agreed to transfer its 44 percent stake in the Suez Canal to the British government in 1875. The canal, which remained partly owned by Compagnie de Suez, nonetheless came under the de facto control of the British. Even so, the Suez concession proved highly lucrative to its French builder and operator, and Compagnie Universelle du Canal Maritime de Suez grew to become one of France's richest corporations.

Meanwhile, another French powerhouse was being conceived. The advent of electricity and the steady increases in outfitting France's cities and towns with running water and sewer services led to the creation of a new group based in Lyon and called Lyonnaise des Eaux et de l'Eclairage. The company, which started with water services, quickly added other utilities services, including electricity generation and distribution and gas production and distribution, which at the time also served to provide public lighting networks. By the outbreak of World War I, Lyonnaise des Eaux et de l'Eclairage had established itself as one of France's leading utilities companies. The company next began to expand internationally, building up a network of international operations located primarily among France's colonial holdings, including Morocco and Algeria in North Africa, Togo and Congo in Central Africa, and various island possessions in the Pacific.

In the middle of the 20th century, however, both Lyonnaise des Eaux et de l'Eclairage and Compagnie Universelle du Canal Maritime de Suez were to see their businesses altered by government intervention. Lyonnaise des Eaux et de l'Eclairage's turn came following World War II, when the French government, faced with the task of reconstructing the country after the long German occupation, nationalized the gas and electricity industries in 1946. Refocused on its water services, the now-named Lyonnaise des Eaux began building its network of water customers, topping the 300,000 mark by the end of the 1950s.

At that time, Compagnie Universelle du Canal Maritime de Suez itself was in the process of changing its identity—literally at gunpoint. With the rise to power of Gamal Abdel-Nasser in 1956, the British army abandoned its military protection of the Suez Canal. One month later, in July 1956, Nasser nationalized the Suez Canal. An attempt to retake the canal by force—in a campaign mounted by French, British, and Israeli troops in December of that same year—ended under pressure from the United Nations.

Deprived of the activity that had provided its name for nearly a century, Compagnie Universelle du Canal Maritime de Suez renamed itself Compagnie Financière de Suez in 1958 and began a new life as one of France's major financial powers. Taking the form of a holding company, Compagnie Financière de Suez quickly began amassing a variety of investments in

different sectors, not least of which was the banking sector, when the company created its own bank in 1959. The Suez bank, taking on the name Banque de Suez et de l'Union des Mines (BSUM) in 1966, became one of the company's most important and most profitable holdings. This was particularly the case after the takeover of the Bank of Indochina, forming the Banque Indosuez in 1974.

The mid-1960s had already seen Suez take on another significant holding: that of Lyonnaise des Eaux, when Suez purchased the majority shareholder's position in the growing water utility. Despite Suez's financial position in Lyonnaise des Eaux, the two companies' operations were to remain separate for the next 30 years. Nonetheless, the powerful financial backing of Suez and other shareholders enabled Lyonnaise des Eaux to begin an expansion drive that was to make it not only one of the world's top water services and treatment companies before the end of the century, but a diversified conglomerate in its own right.

One of Lyonnaise des Eaux's earliest expansion moves came in 1972 with the acquisition of Degrémont, boosting the company to the leading ranks of water treatment and distribution services providers. Diversification followed throughout the rest of the decade. In 1975, the company acquired a position in Cofreth, taking it into heating equipment and services. Waste management followed with the acquisition of a major stake in SITA, while the company moved beyond utility services and into mortuary services with the acquisition of PFG in 1979.

Powering into the 21st Century

Lyonnaise des Eaux continued to pursue its international expansion, moving into the water distribution and wastewater treatment markets in Spain, the United Kingdom, the United States, and into other foreign markets. Lyonnaise des Eaux also added to its diversified portfolio in 1986 when it launched its own cable television subsidiary, Lyonnaise Communications, later renamed Lyonnaise Câble before joining with the cable television operations of France Telecom to become NOOS. The following year, Lyonnaise des Eaux boosted its French communications position when it took a stake in the new French independent television start-up, M6 Television.

By then, Compagnie Financière de Suez—which had undergone a brief period as a nationalized entity between 1982 and 1987, when it was once again privatized—was also preparing a major international move. In 1988, Compagnie Financière de Suez took over control of the diversified holding group Société Générale de Belgique (SGB). One of Belgium's oldest and most prominent holding companies—its interests included Générale de Banque as well as a major holding in Belgian energy provider Tractebel—SGB launched Compagnie Financière de Suez onto a new level of diversified operations, described by one *International Herald Tribune* observer as: "a sprawling, unprofitable mess."

Vowing to build itself into a two-headed industrial and financial giant, Compagnie Financière de Suez added to its debt load, already heavy after the SGB acquisition, by acquiring Groupe Victoire in 1989. The following year, the company changed its name to Compagnie de Suez. But the heavy debt load and the inability to turn around its new and unprofitable

Key Dates:

1858: Compagnie Universelle du Canal Maritime de Suez is formed.
1880: Lyonnaise des Eaux et de l'Eclairage is founded.
1914: Lyonnaise des Eaux begins international expansion.
1946: French gas and electricity industries are nationalized.
1956: Egypt seizes control of Suez Canal.
1958: Suez changes name to Compagnie Financière de Suez.
1959: Suez bank is created.
1966: Banque de Suez et de l'Union des Mines (BSUM) is formed.
1967: Suez becomes majority shareholder of Lyonnaise des Eaux.
1972: Lyonnaise des Eaux acquires Degrémont.
1974: Banque Indosuez is created.
1975: Lyonnaise des Eaux acquires Cofreth and SITA.
1979: Lyonnaise des Eaux acquires PFG.
1982: Compagnie Financière de Suez is nationalized by French government.
1986: Lyonnaise des Eaux enters cable television industry.
1987: Compagnie Financière de Suez undergoes privatization; Lyonnaise des Eaux takes share in M6 television.
1988: Compagnie Financière de Suez takes over Société Générale de Belgique.
1989: Compagnie Financière de Suez takes over Groupe Victoire.
1990: Lyonnaise des Eaux merges with Dumez construction group.
1994: Compagnie Financière de Suez sells off Groupe Victoire.
1996: Compagnie Financière de Suez sells off Banque Indosuez, acquires majority position in Tractebel.
1997: Merger of Compagnie Financière de Suez and Lyonnaise des Eaux-Dumez forms Suez Lyonnaise des Eaux.
1998: Suez Lyonnaise des Eaux sells Générale de Banque; acquires non-North American operations of Browning Ferris Industries.
1999: Company acquires Nalco Chemical; increases holding to full control of Tractebel, Calgon, and United Water Resources.
2000: Company acquires full control of SITA, Trigen Energy.

holdings caused the former canal builder to take on water. With its losses mounting, Compagnie de Suez named Gerard Mestrallet, who had headed the SGB holdings since the early 1990s, as CEO and president of the entire company in 1995. Charged with restructuring the company, Mestrallet made a series of moves that surprised the investment community, starting with the sell-off of Groupe Victoire in 1994, then taking the still more radical step of divesting what many considered Suez's chief asset, the Banque Indosuez, in 1996. The com-

pany's exit from banking continued with the sale of Générale de Banque in 1998.

In the meantime, Lyonnaise des Eaux itself had grown through its merger with construction giant Dumez in 1990, forming as Lyonnaise des Eaux-Dumez SA. The new company was now centered around its water distribution and other diversified services, and its construction operations, which included the GTM-Entrepose construction group, acquired by Dumez in 1987. The company's construction subsidiaries were reformed as Dumez-GTM in 1994, and then as GTM, before being spun off into a merger with the Vinci Group in 2000. At the same time, Lyonnaise des Eaux exited the mortuary services sector, selling off what was by then named OFG-PFG group.

As Lyonnaise des Eaux increased its communications operations—buying up 16 additional cable television concessions, making it France's largest cable television provider in 1995, and then taking part in the launch of French satellite television venture TPS—Compagnie de Suez, via its SGB share position, was moving closer toward energy services and building up a majority stake in Tractebel.

This set the stage for the merger of Lyonnaise des Eaux with its longtime majority shareholder Compagnie de Suez, an operation completed in 1997. The merger of the two companies created a French giant with annual revenues of FFr 190 billion (approximately US$35 billion) per year. At the time of the merger, the company outlined its plans for what was to become Suez Lyonnaise des Eaux, calling for an increased concentration on four principal markets: water, energy, waste treatment, and communications. While shedding operations outside of its new focus, the company began building its international positions, notably with the acquisition of SGB, and the raising of its stake in Tractebel to more than 99 percent.

Suez Lyonnaise des Eaux also began a series of significant acquisitions, such as the purchase of the non-North American activities of waste management company Brown-Ferris Industries, but also by adopting the policy of friendly takeovers of companies in which it already held shareholder positions. As such the company acquired water-treatment firms Calgon and United Water Resources in the United States in 1999. In that same year, the company paid more than US$4 billion to acquire Nalco Chemicals, the world's number one producer of chemicals for water treatment. The Nalco acquisition enabled Suez Lyonnaise des Eaux to edge out longtime rival Vivendi (formerly Société Générale des Eaux, and itself undergoing a transformation into a media and communications giant) as the world's number one water services provider.

Suez Lyonnaise des Eaux continued its transformation in 2000, buying up the remaining shares in SITA, before joining that company's waste treatment operations with those of Tractebel. The company also bought out the remaining stock in Trigen Energy, based in the United States, boosting its position in that crucial market. By mid-year 2000, the company was rumored to be in merger talks with German utility group Veba/Viag. With more than EUR 31 billion in revenues at the close of the 1999 year, Suez Lyonnaise des Eaux was prepared to defend its powerhouse position into the next century.

Principal Subsidiaries

ELYO; Tractebel (Belgium; 98%); Trigen Energy Inc.; Aquazur; Degrémont; Calgon; Lyonnaise des Eaux; Nalco Chemical (USA); United Water Resources Inc. (U.S.A.); SITA; NOOS (50%); M6 (34%); TPS (50%).

Principal Competitors

American Water Works Company; National Grid; Azurix; Ogden Corporation; Bouygues S.A.; Severn Trent PLC; Brambles Industries; United Utilities; CANAL+; VINCI; Electricité de France; Vivendi; France Telecom Group; Waste Management, Inc.

Further Reading

Balmer, Crispian, ''Suez Lyonnaise to Buy United Water,'' *Reuters Business Report*, August 23, 1999.

Barkin, Noah, ''Suez Vows to Create Global Energy Force,'' *Reuters*, August 20, 1999.

Duez, Valérie, and de Kerdel, Yves, ''Interview: Gérard Mestrallet,'' *Journal des Finances*, August 27, 1999.

Patton, Susannah, ''Big Challenge Ahead for Suez Lyonnaise Chief,'' *International Herald Tribune*, February 25, 1998.

Sullivan, Anne, ''Pure and Simple, Water Offers a Sea of Investing Opportunities,'' *International Herald Tribune*, April 22, 2000.

——, ''Tractebel the Intractable,'' *Economist*, February 27, 1999.

—M. L. Cohen

Sweetheart Cup Company, Inc.

10100 Reisterstown Road
Owings Mills, Maryland 21117
U.S.A.
Telephone: (410) 363-1111
Toll Free: (800) 800-0300
Fax: (410) 998-1828
Web site: http://www.sweetheart.com

Private Company
Incorporated: 1926 as Maryland Baking Company
Employees: 8,050
Sales: $1.2 billion (1999 est.)
NAIC: 322215 Paper Dishes Made from Purchased Paper
or Paperboard; 326199 Other Plastics Product
Manufacturing

Sweetheart Cup Company, Inc. manufactures disposable paper, plastic, and foam products for the foodservice and dairy industries as well as for consumer use. Customers of the Foodservice Division include schools, entertainment and recreation facilities, and independent and national restaurant chains, especially fast-food restaurants. Sweetheart's Packaging Division produces containers for ice cream, sour cream, yogurt, and other dairy products and provides packaging equipment designed for the containers. The Consumer Division produces disposable cups, plates, bowls, and eating utensils for retail distribution. The company's brands include Sweetheart; Trophy; Lily; Preference; Jazz; Simple Elegance; Silent Service; Guildware; and private-label brands.

From Ice Cream Cones to Paper Cups

Sweetheart Cup Company began in 1911 as an ice cream cone bakery operated by four Russian immigrants, the Shapiro brothers, led by Joseph Shapiro. With a bakery outside Boston, the Shapiros decided to move the business to a warmer area where people consumed more ice cream. In 1919 Joseph and another brother took the train from Boston to the first stop south of the Mason-Dixon line and Baltimore became home base for the company, renamed the Maryland Baking Company. One brother managed the existing bakery, while Joe Shapiro opened a bakery in Owings Mills, Maryland. The fresh-baked cones were too delicate to ship long distance, so other family members established a network of ice cream cone bakeries in other cities. This method of expansion placed the company close to its customers, mostly candy and tobacco stores, for better service.

During the 1930s Maryland Baking Company used the network of family businesses as support for production and sales of related products, including drinking straws, matchbooks, and other paper products. The first Sweetheart brand product was the drinking straw. The brand derived from the image of two children sharing a milkshake, each drinking from a straw and their heads forming the two curved arcs of a heart. The Shapiro family expanded the facilities at Owings Mills for the production and distribution of new products.

The company began to produce paper cups after World War II. Actually, a family vote of 14-to-1 decided against expansion into production of paper cups, but Joseph Shapiro proclaimed a majority of one in favor. The Maryland Baking Company made its first paper cup product, a seven ounce cup with wax coating and adopted the name Maryland Cup Corporation. The decision proved to be lucrative. As the mobility of Americans increased, vending machines which used paper cups began to appear in offices, gasoline stations, ballparks, and schools. Maryland Cup found customers among all of these businesses, as well as hospitals and nursing homes. Also, highway expansion led to the proliferation of fast-food restaurants which also used paper products and McDonald's became an important customer from the mid-1950s.

Innovation, Customer Service, Good Timing Spur Growth: 1960s–70s

The company continually developed new disposable products, including foam and plastic products, to address the growing market for convenience foods. In 1957 Maryland Cup began to produce plastic containers which dairy product manufacturers purchased for packaged items, such as cottage cheese, sour cream, and yogurt. In 1961 the company introduced a heavy-

460

weight paper cup for over-the-counter hot drinks. Maryland Cup expanded its production capacity to support growing sales. The company opened a plant in Cambridge, Massachusetts, for the new paper cup; consolidated paper cup manufacturing and warehousing in Baltimore; and opened a plant in Wilmington, Massachusetts, to produce throwaway plastic products.

In 1961 the Shapiro family combined their 32 business operations to form one company in preparation for an initial public offering of stock. Merrill Bank, Joseph Shapiro's son-in-law, became president and two nephews took the lead of the company's major divisions; Samuel Shapiro headed the plastics division and Henry Shapiro headed the McDonald's Hamburgers division.

In 1962 Maryland Cup started a new division to cultivate the Sweetheart brand of disposable cups, plates, and eating utensils for the consumer market. Disposable products came into everyday use with more casual lifestyles and higher incomes. Previously seen as summertime products, used for picnics and outdoor activities, disposable paper and plastic tableware began to sell in supermarkets year-round. The company developed new consumer products, such as the Tumblet brand of clear, plastic glasses, and the Casual Cups brand of cone-shaped plastic, hot drink cups which inserted into reusable holders. Sales of the company's consumer products more than doubled between 1964 and 1969.

Another dimension of the casual lifestyle involved the expansion of fast-food restaurants. Maryland Cup found customers in such chains as Dairy Queen and A&W Root Beer as well as independent restaurants. With product development an essential ingredient in customer service, the company developed clamshell foam containers for McDonald's hamburgers and the flat yellow banana split dish. New customers also included entertainment complexes such as Disneyland, and sports arenas, such as the Orange Bowl.

Institutional sales also increased during the 1960s as a labor shortage in foodservice and increases in the minimum wage made disposable dinnerware an attractive option to hiring a dishwasher. The disposable products proved to be a cost saver, reducing payroll and payroll tax expense as well as the expense of soap, hot water, and replacement of ceramic dinnerware. By 1970 the company sold disposable products to 500 institutional users.

Product development was also instrumental in the growth of sales to hospitals, plant cafeterias, and airlines. In 1969 Maryland Cup introduced a stronger, dual-ply plastic plate which looked like china and provided a rigid support. The company addressed the problem of waste disposal by working on the biodegradability of the molecular structure with plastic producers and on the development of better after-burners which reburned the ash left when a hospital burned the plastic plates.

To support its growing sales, Maryland Cup initiated a capital investment program to expand production capacity in the late 1960s, spending approximately $20 million a year from 1967 through 1970. The company added a drinking straw factory, through the acquisition of Flex Straw Company International in 1969, and two new paper cup manufacturing facilities. Through a joint venture with General Industrial Plastics Ltd., Maryland Cup opened a plant in the United Kingdom to produce disposable plastic containers for ice cream and other dairy products. The company opened a 65,000-square-foot plastic plant in Manchester, New York, in 1970 for the production of injection-molded plastic containers for the food and dairy customers as well as for plastic cups. At this time Maryland Cup operated 27 plants in major metropolitan areas throughout the United States, including Los Angeles, Chicago, Dallas, St. Louis, Atlanta, and Pittsburgh.

Maryland Cup took a total system approach to customer service and customers did not mind paying a premium for the company's products. Maryland Cup produced high-speed packaging equipment designed for filling the company's plastic containers and then loaned the equipment to its customers without a fee. The Flex-E-Fill filled various size containers with ice cream or sherbet. Hospitals, which served fruit juice up to five times per day, used the Liquid-Fill machine to fill and seal plastic cups of juice. The company also produced the Twin-Filler, which filled ice cream cones and wrapped them in paper packaging. Customer service included assistance with packaging design, promotional programs, and ideas for new products.

Maryland Cup experienced two decades of steady growth as the demand for convenient disposable products continued to grow. During the 1960s sales increased steadily, from $39.2 million in 1960 to $170 million in 1970. Annual revenue increases ranged from ten percent to 20 percent, while earnings grew steadily. During the 1970s the demand for vending cups decreased, but soda fountains at convenience stores generated new business. The popularity of yogurt as a health food increased demand for plastic dairy containers. New consumer products involved usability in microwave or conventional ovens.

By 1980 sales at Maryland Cup reached $580 million with 14 disposable products factories, ten 'Eat-it-All ice cream cone bakeries, and international joint ventures in the United Kingdom, the Netherlands, Japan, and Canada. The company became more efficient, installing a semi-automated, 231,000-square-foot distribution center in Owings Mills. In the Netherlands, new manufacturing equipment for the production of paper cups helped the company meet increased demand from fast-food restaurants there. A new distribution center opened in Gosport, England. Maryland Cup continued to produce equipment for the foodservice industry and improved its Liqui-Fill machine for the institutional market.

Winstead, the company's research subsidiary, focused on improvement of resource materials and lowering production costs. In 1980 Winstead installed new equipment for thermoforming plastic products by a more energy- and resource-efficient process. The technology used a new hydraulic and electromagnetic method to form plastic. Winstead also developed a new material for coating paper products, making them more durable and less expensive to produce.

Key Dates:

1911: Four Russian immigrants start an ice cream cone bakery firm.

1919: The business relocates to Baltimore and becomes Maryland Baking Company, incorporating seven years later.

1957: Company begins making paper cups; changes name to Maryland Cup Company.

1957: Company begins production of plastic containers.

1961: Shapiro family combines their businesses into one company, in preparation for initial public offering.

1969: New dual-ply plastic plate increases sales to institutional market.

1980: Sales reach $580 million after two decades of steady growth.

1983: Company is acquired by Fort Howard Paper Company.

1989: Business is spun off as Sweetheart Holdings, Inc. with Sweetheart Cup as a subsidiary.

1993: Sweetheart Holdings is acquired by American Industrial Partners.

1997: Company sells ice cream cone operations.

1999: Sweetheart merges with Fonda Group.

Maryland Cup adapted to new consumer demands with new products. The company worked with fast-food chains to create packaging, such as a domed-lid salad container and "ovenable" containers for carryout pizza. In the early 1980s the fast-food industry accounted for about 30 percent of the company's sales, with McDonald's accounting for approximately ten percent of sales. As convenience stores added foodservice to compete with fast-food chains, Maryland Cup assisted in the development of display materials. Maryland Cup generated demand for plastic containers by helping dairy customers to formulate desserts for distribution to the consumer market.

Deterioration of Values, Revenues: 1980s

The Shapiro family still held a majority of company stock, but as members of the Shapiro family neared retirement, they had to decide the future of the company. After the death of Samuel in 1982, the family decided to sell the company. In 1983 Fort Howard Paper Company purchased Maryland Cup for $536 million in cash and stock. Fort Howard found Maryland Cup an attractive acquisition due to its excellent marketing and sales skills, presence in Europe, and complementary line of products. Fort Howard planned to bring its expertise in material cost management to Maryland Cup.

The merger between Fort Howard and Maryland Cup proved to be a fiasco as the company cultures clashed from the first executive meeting. Fort Howard replaced Maryland Cup's values of service and quality with an emphasis on profit and more profit. Fort Howard's methods of reducing overhead conflicted with Maryland Cup's emphasis on employee and customer relations. Maryland Cup treated employees as family, Fort Howard treated them as an expense, reducing the number of employees by over 2,000 people. Many high level employees

quit and Fort Howard fired several high level managers. At the time of the acquisition, the top five executives had been with the company an average of 45 years. By 1986, key employees had become employees of major competitors, selling disposable products to customers of Maryland Cup. Fort Howard's purportedly contentious approach to sales alienated many customers, losing their trust as well as their willingness to pay a premium for Sweetheart products. While Fort Howard invested over $250 million in factory improvements, especially the large Owings Mills facilities, and cut costs drastically, the reduction in sales made factory efficiency an irrelevant achievement.

Fort Howard sought to boost revenues and fill unused factory capacity with the acquisition of the Lily Cup Company in 1986. Lily Cup added its popular Trophy brand of thin-walled, foam cups, however, the strategy failed to achieve its purpose as many of Lily Cup's products were obsolete. Also, the acquisition of Lily Cup resulted in further decreases in revenues, as customers who had used Lily Cup as a secondary supply source began to use James River Corporation, the maker of Dixie cups, as a secondary source. In 1988 sales of the combined companies should have reached close to $2 billion, adjusted for inflation, but Fort Howard Cup realized only $858 million in sales.

Employee morale also suffered. Fort Howard had already damaged morale by firing employees and cutting funds for employee picnics and sports leagues. Morale suffered further as Fort Howard cut medical benefits for retirees and liquidated the employee pension fund. In 1986 the pension fund maintained a surplus value of $6 million, but by 1991 had been reduced to a $17 million deficit.

Morgan Stanley Group, Inc., which had taken Fort Howard private through a leveraged buyout in 1988, decided to spin off Fort Howard Cup in 1989. R.P. Silver and D.G. Horrigan, executives at Continental Can Company, formed Sweetheart Holdings, Inc., which then purchased the company from Morgan Stanley for $532.5 million. They renamed the disposable products company the Sweetheart Cup Company and relocated from Green Bay, Wisconsin, to Chicago. In reality Morgan Stanley's Leveraged Equity Fund II owned Sweetheart Holdings.

CEO Silver tried to renew Sweetheart's sales and quality service by hiring new salespeople and providing them with better incentive and benefits packages. Sweetheart continued to founder, however, with annual losses in the millions of dollars. As debt hampered the company, Sweetheart lost a large regular sale in 1990 when McDonald's stopped using the styrofoam clamshell container due to environmental concerns. In 1991 Sweetheart generated gross revenues of $105 million, compared to $210 million by Maryland Cup in 1983.

In 1993 Morgan Stanley sold Sweetheart Holdings to American Industrial Partners, Inc., (AIP) a private investment group, for $441 million. AIP owned 66.3 percent of the company and General Motors Corporation employee benefits plan owned 33.7 percent. Funds from the acquisition relieved the company of nearly half of its debt, bringing the net worth of the company to $100.5 million, but annual interest payments still amounted to $37.5 million. AIP planned to spend more than $40 million annually to update Sweetheart's manufacturing facilities and hoped to take the company public when finances stabilized.

Sweetheart Cup posted its first annual profit in five years for fiscal 1994, with sales at $845.5 million and net earnings of $9.2 million.

In May 1994, AIP named William F. McLaughlin, formerly of Nestlé, as the new president and CEO of Sweetheart Cup Company. McLaughlin immediately began to reduce overhead as he cut salaried staff by ten percent and closed outdated manufacturing facilities or laid off factory workers. He planned to reduce total employee count from 8,500 to 7,000, telling workers that 7,000 jobs were better than no jobs if the company did not rebound. He also instituted a training program to reestablish the service skills and commitment to quality for which Maryland Cup was renowned. Toward that end McLaughlin found new business in the designing and printing display advertising for the company's customers, focusing on promotions with a short lifecycle and requiring small batches of materials.

McLaughlin restructured company operations to focus on its six categories of customers: foodservice distributors, such as Kraft and Sysco; national fast-food chains, including Wendy's and Taco Bell; ice cream cone customers; customers for dairy and ice cream containers; Canadian customers; and McDonald's restaurants, which accounted for 13 percent of annual sales. Sweetheart Cup no longer used a linear work-flow, from scheduling to manufacturing to shipping, but utilized central coordinating offices to bring interdepartmental efficiency into the company. The coordinating offices operated at each of the company's 14 locations. McLaughlin opened a satellite office in Baltimore for the customer relations, data processing, research and development, and engineering departments. The Owings Mills plant had grown to 1.5 million square feet with 13 facilities by this time.

McLaughlin's goals for 1995 involved finding new customers in the foodservice industry; expanding the market for Lily Cup brands; and expanding the ice cream cone business. He confronted difficult challenges as rising costs of the company's major resources, plastic resin and paper, led to a 20 percent increase in the price of paper products and a 27 percent increase in the price of plastic products. Sweetheart continued to close and consolidate facilities for more efficient operations. In October 1997 Sweetheart Cup sold Eat-It-All ice cream cones and reinvested funds into improved efficiency. The company restructured again, creating the Foodservice, Packaging, and Consumer Products Divisions.

In 1998 AIP sold 48 percent of the voting stock of Sweetheart Holdings to Fonda Group, a manufacturer of paper plates, napkins, trays, and tray covers. Through a stock swap the Fonda Group and Sweetheart Holdings formed SF Holdings Group, the new parent of Sweetheart Cup. Dennis Mehiel was named CEO and chairman of the board.

Entering a New Century, Returning to Old Values

In a return to Maryland Cup's innovation to serve customer needs, Sweetheart became involved in the development of environmentally sound packaging, which came to fruition in late 1999. The company had been working with Ben & Jerry's Ice Cream since 1996 to design a container which did not use the environmentally destructive bleached paperboard. The new container used a clay-coated, unbleached brownkraft paperboard, which Ben & Jerry's began using for its quart containers of vanilla ice cream.

With McDonald's, Sweetheart formed the EarthShell Corporation to produce environmentally friendly foodservice packaging. EarthShell created hinged-lid containers with a "new-to-the-world" material, a composite of limestone, potato starch, water, and a protective coating. The material was produced with clean, energy efficient methods and resulted in a biodegradable material which disintegrated in water and decomposed quickly. EarthShell installed additional production lines in April 2000 to produce the containers for McDonald's. EarthShell planned to make bowls, plates, and cups from the material as well.

Sweetheart continued to develop new products to meet current foodservice needs. New products included a chicken bucket, a Trophy brand 24-ounce foam cup for hot drinks, a frozen dessert cup with dome lid, and an award-winning wax-coated paper French fry cup.

In February 2000 Sweetheart began construction on a one million-square-foot distribution center 15 miles from the Owings Mills site. The $23 million project consolidated distribution operations in Maryland and Massachusetts. With 80 to 125 trucks per day transferring stock from Owings Mills manufacturing facilities, Sweetheart planned to use the center to serve the mid-Atlantic and northeastern United States. Sweetheart also relocated its company headquarters to Owings Mills.

Principal Divisions

Foodservice; Packaging; Consumer Products.

Principal Competitors

Dart Container Corporation; Fort James Corporation; Solo Cup Company.

Further Reading

Berman, Phyllis, and Khalaf, Roula, "A Sweetheart of a Deal," *Forbes*, September 3, 1990, p. 39.

Crider, Jeff, "Sweetheart Cup Closes Riverside, RI, Plant," *Knight-Ridder/Tribune Business News*, September 3, 1997, p. 903B0951.

"Cup Maker Sweet on Chicago, Moving from Green Bay," *Chicago Sun Times*, November 16, 1989, p. 81.

Drummer, Randyl, "Ontario, Calif., Business Park Lands Two Deals," *Knight-Ridder/Tribune Business News*, November 10, 1997, p. 1110B1050.

"EarthShell Corporation and Sweetheart Cup Company Agree to Expanded Production," *Business Wire*, April 19, 2000, p. 1679.

"EarthShell Corporation Reports on Installation of New Conveyor System at Sweetheart Facility and Other Relevant Progress," *PR Newswire*, November 12, 1999, p. 3495.

Easton, Thomas, "Crushing Maryland Cup," *Baltimore Morning Sun*, November 22, 1992, p. 1A.

——, "For Morgan Stanley & Co., Cup Maker Is Just Another Investment," *Baltimore Morning Sun*, November 22, 1992, p. 23A.

"Environmentally Conscious Carton: Kraft Paperboard Eliminates Bleaching in Process," *Dairy Foods*, May 1999, p. 48.

"Fort Howard: New Marketing Muscle from Maryland Cup," *Business Week*, July 18, 1983, p. 132.

Haddad, Anne, "Sweetheart Cup Building Leaves Neighbors Cold; Distribution Center Near Hampstead Will Be Size of 23 Football Fields," *Baltimore Sun*, November 2, 1999, p. 6B.

Harris, William, "Packaging," *Forbes*, January 3, 1983, pp. 200–01.

Johnson, Ian, "Sweetheart's New Suitor AIP Brings Its Back-to-Basics Approach to Deal," *Baltimore Morning Sun*, June 13, 1993, p. 1H.

Katz-Stone, Adam, "Sweetheart Cup Co.," *Baltimore Business Journal*, February 25, 2000, p. 19.

Kennedy, Julie, "Fast Food, Fast Growth: Now Maryland Cup Looks Beyond Chains for Further Sales Gains," *Barron's* September 7, 1981, p. 33.

MacDonald, Michelle E., "Why Sweetheart Cup Loves Intermodal," *Traffic Management,* April 1994, p. 47.

Mans, Jack, "Tamper-Evident Packaging; an Industry Requirement," *Dairy Foods*, February 1994, p. 69.

"Marketing Made Easy," *Food Management,* September 1999, p. 93.

"McLaughlin to Become Sweetheart Prexy," *Nation's Restaurant News*, May 2, 1994, p. 76.

"Morgan Stanley to Sell Sweetheart," *Pulp & Paper*, August 1993, p. 25.

"Rising Costs Cut Profit at Sweetheart: Sales Increase Doesn't Offset Material Prices," *Baltimore Sun*, May 26, 1995, p. C12.

Rogers, Donna, W., "Giant Cup Landmark in Augusta, Ga, Celebrates 50 Years," *Knight-Ridder/Tribune Business News*, January 3, 1998, p. 103B0927.

Smith, Sarah, "Sweetheart Merges with Fonda," *Plastic News*, January 12, 1998, p. 3.

Sullivan, Joanna, "Sweetheart Restructuring; Layoffs Expected," *Baltimore Business Journal*, February 17, 1995, p. 1.

—Mary Tradii

Taylor Corporation

1725 Roe Crest Drive
North Mankato, Minnesota 56003
U.S.A.
Telephone: (507)625-2828
Fax: (507)625-2988

Private Company
Incorporated: 1975
Employees: 12,000
Sales: $1 billion (1999 est.)
NAIC: 323110 Commercial Lithographic Printing

Taylor Corporation, a leading North American commercial printer, claims to hold 90 percent of the formal wedding invitation market. As a holding company, Taylor Corporation owns more than 70 businesses located in 19 states, three Canadian provinces, the United Kingdom, Australia, the Netherlands, Sweden, and Mexico. In addition to wedding invitations, subsidiaries produce items such as business cards and forms, and graduation announcements. The parent company holds a number of non-printing businesses as well. Chairman and CEO Glen A. Taylor owns 89 percent of the business and is majority stakeholder in the National Basketball Association franchise the Minnesota Timberwolves.

Humble Beginnings: 1950s to Mid-1970s

Glen Taylor, the second of seven children, grew up on a farm outside a small southern Minnesota town and took on adult responsibilities early in life. As a teenager, he worked for his father or for neighboring farmers. He married while still in high school. When his father became a feed distributor, Glen took over operation of the farm and spent his first year out of high school as a full-time farmer as well as new husband and father.

In 1959, the Taylors moved to Mankato, Minnesota, where Glen attended college and worked part-time at Carlson Wedding Service. Established after World War II by Bill Carlson, the 18-person operation started out as a mimeograph service and then moved to custom printed wedding invitations and specialty products.

Taylor's first job, the least desirable position in the company, was napkin stamping. When another student took some time off, Carlson placed Taylor in the stockroom. Taylor promptly overhauled the inventory system. Carlson rewarded his young employee's initiative by making what had been a fill-in position permanent. A go-getter in college as well, Taylor graduated a year earlier than his peers. He applied for and was offered teaching positions but decided to stay instead with Carlson, who wanted him to help manage the growing business.

Carlson's firm grew rapidly during the 1960s thanks in part to innovations in the printing industry. Furthermore, UPS broadened Midwest service and opened the door to a larger marketplace for small rural businesses. Carlson would build a new plant in North Mankato and expand the operation three times.

Taylor played a pivotal role in the growth as well. He encouraged Carlson to deviate from tradition and add colored paper and inks, updated texts, and new designs, a move which proved fruitful for the company. With an eye toward his own future as well as the company's, Taylor negotiated for a cut of the profits when he devised a way to improve efficiency of the napkin stamping operation.

Preparing for retirement, Carlson sold shares of the business to three employees, including Taylor, in 1967. Seven years later, Taylor, who had been in charge of inventories, purchasing, and marketing, bought majority interest from Carlson and part of the holdings of the other two managers. The printing business was producing $6 million in revenues at the time.

Taylor Taking Over: 1970s–80s

In January 1975, Taylor formed a holding company with Carlson Craft as its first subsidiary. He then purchased an Indiana-based wedding stationery company in August of that year. After turning the struggling operation around, Taylor proceeded to purchase other businesses and effectively establish printing companies from the ground up. As he added subsidiaries during the late 1970s, Taylor groomed future managers from the ranks of younger employees, many of them starting out as part-time student workers, just as he had done.

With a strong management team in place and business booming, Taylor turned to other challenges: he ran for the Minnesota Senate in 1980. Although he had been active in community affairs, Taylor's only previous political involvement had been as treasurer of a senator's election campaign. Taylor ran for that seat himself when the incumbent retired.

Once in office, Taylor was elected assistant minority leader in 1983 and majority leader in 1985. As assistant minority leader the Independent-Republican senator drew on his business experience to reorganize the caucus office. Later on the Senate floor he worked to find common ground between the opposing parties. Taylor concentrated on workers and employment compensation and education issues during his time in office.

Few fellow senators knew the scope of Taylor's business concerns, but via a steady stream of acquisitions, start-up operations, and new product lines, Taylor had built up a business amassing revenues of $200 million by 1985.

According to a 1987 *Corporate Report Minnesota* article, Taylor Corporation was the country's largest printer of wedding stationery, producing invitations, response and reception cards, thank you notes, and church programs. The company's subsidiaries held 50 percent of the U.S. market and 80 percent of the Minnesota, North Dakota, South Dakota, and Iowa markets in these niche areas. Taylor Corporation's 20 wholly owned subsidiaries were located in 11 states as well as one in Canada. North Mankato-based Carlson Craft, the largest concern, had 1,500 employees. Overall, Taylor employed about 4,000 people.

In addition to wedding-related products, Taylor Corporation subsidiaries produced items such as personal stationery, business cards and letterhead, graduation announcements, and prom and homecoming decorations. Glen Taylor also held partial ownership in a North Mankato bank, a Post-It notes (3M) printing operation, and an engineering company.

In addition to his business and legislative accomplishments, Taylor was a committed member of community service organizations such as the Mankato area Chamber of Commerce, Jaycees, YMCA, and the United Way. He was also attuned to the well-being of people in his employ, offering higher wages and broader benefits than typical of rural Minnesota. Taylor Corporation was among the first companies in the state to establish onsite child care.

Furthermore, Taylor Corporation had produced profits each year since its inception and strove to internally fund its growth. "We've had the seller carry us for a while a few times," Taylor

said in a January 1987 *Corporate Report Minnesota* article by Jay Novak, "but we've never had to get money from a bank." Fiscally conservative Taylor also kept a cash reserve fund of more than $5 million.

Taylor attributed his company's success to quality products and commitment to customer service. Moreover, the structure of the company played a role in winning business. Since subsidiary companies were quite small and frequently competed against each other, customers, in general, were unaware of the magnitude of the umbrella company, Taylor Corporation. "There's a perception that if you're a little smaller, you care about your customers more—or your suppliers, or employees. We'd hate to have someone say, 'Well, they're so big they don't need our business,' " Taylor told Novak.

Taylor Corporation depended on the small order customers and the independent vendors who sold the majority of their products. Orders of $30 to $40 were Taylor's bread and butter, and the company promised rapid turnaround and a no-fault reprint policy.

Something Old, Something New: 1990s

Taylor left the Senate in 1989 and set aside thoughts of running for governor. "Part of it had to do with a divorce, another part had to do with his rejection by the right wing of the Republican party because he wasn't partisan enough. A lot of it had to do with his devotion to his companies, to the thrill of victory," Jay Weiner reported for the *Star Tribune*.

By the early 1990s, Taylor had grown his enterprise to some 35 companies. The number of employees exceeded 7,000, roughly half located in Minnesota. Much of the company's new growth had come from expanded North Mankato-based businesses and new product lines.

Taylor Corporation revenues passed the half-billion-dollar mark in 1993. In its September 1994 issue, *Twin Cities Business Monthly* reported the company had compiled an annual compound growth rate of almost 13 percent over the past ten years and nearly 25 percent over the past 20 years, while maintaining a solid financial position and enviable profitability record.

Although printing remained the core business concern, Taylor continued to delve into other business areas. Non-printing businesses included a direct mail marketing company, an office supply retailer, and a water-temperature control and hydraulic brake part manufacturer. Taylor owned at least six community banks in Minnesota with combined assets of more than $275 million through Taylor Bancshares of Mankato.

Taylor moved into yet another new arena in 1994 and succeeded where others had failed when he executed an $88 million deal to keep the Timberwolves NBA franchise in Minnesota. Carrying over business practices from his other endeavors, Taylor and a group of limited partners put down over 50 percent of the total purchase price in order to limit borrowing. Then the veteran of business buyouts completely restructured the franchise, hired good managers, provided vision and direction for the organization, and backed it all up with the resources to achieve their goals.

Key Dates:

1975: Glen A. Taylor establishes Taylor Corporation with former employer's business as first subsidiary.
1980: Taylor enters political arena.
1985: Company revenues reach $200 million, up from $6 million a decade earlier.
1993: Revenues exceed $500 million.
1994: Taylor enters professional sports market.
1999: Taylor Corporation nears $1 billion in sales.

Some aspects of the high profile sports/entertainment concern fell outside his realm of experience, such as the astronomical salaries demanded by star players and negotiated by agents, but as in his primary business of printing, Taylor strove to satisfy the customer. Taylor succeeded in upping the numbers of both season ticket holders and corporate sponsors.

Meanwhile, printing, like many other industries, faced the challenges of rapidly changing technologies and pricing pressures during the 1990s. Costly capital expenditures and a corresponding jump in capacity prompted a move toward increased consolidation according to a 1997 *Minneapolis/St. Paul City-Business* article by Jennifer Ehrlich. Yet rising stock prices had become a prohibitive factor. "Because the market has risen so fast, the value being placed on companies is too high, and it doesn't make as much sense as it did in the past to buy them," Taylor told *Minnesota Business & Opportunities* in 1998. Thus, the company turned its focus to internally generated growth.

Taylor did make another purchase in the professional sports segment of his businesses. He bought a Women's National Basketball Association franchise, the Minnesota Lynx, in 1998. A deal to buy the Minnesota Twins baseball team was also briefly on the table. Taylor had to set aside all his activities for a time in early 1999 when he underwent triple bypass surgery.

Even though his purchase of the Timberwolves had thrust Taylor into the public spotlight—Taylor's health concerns were covered by Minneapolis/St. Paul area sportswriters—Taylor Corporation continued to fly "below radar." Tina Lassen wrote in a November 1999 *Northwest Airlines World Traveler* article, "Only those who live in the Mankato area or happen to run their own printing companies have heard of the Taylor Corporation—maybe. Taylor Corporation maintains an exceptionally low profile, mostly because it operates its facilities under a variety of names, many of them acquisitions. Taylor Corporation companies come with names like Web Graphics Midwest, Litho Tech, Ad Graphics, LabelWorks, Precision Press—not exactly the stuff that grabs the attention of *Forbes*." Nonethe-

less, self-made billionaire Taylor did find a place among *Forbes* list of 400 most wealthy Americans.

Not unexpectedly, Taylor had over his lifetime sought victory in all he endeavored to do. The Timberwolves franchise prospects, both on the floor and in the front office, improved under his leadership. Likewise, Taylor Corporation flourished: estimated annual revenues were pushing the billion dollar mark.

Yet Taylor maintained an air of humility, according to Lassen's November 1999 article. "Taylor is an enigma, a Wall Street mind who yearns for a weekend of farm chores. A man who explains his leadership skills as 'a God-given gift. It's not one of those things you take credit for.'"

Principal Competitors

Hallmark Cards, Inc.; Quebecor Inc.

Further Reading

"American Pad & Paper Announces Definitive Agreement to Sell Its Creative Division to Taylor Corporation," *Business Wire,* April 19, 2000.

Aschburner, Steve, "Wolves Owner Has Successful Triple-Bypass Surgery," *Star Tribune* (Minneapolis), January 13, 1999, p. 1C.

"Colorado Firm Buys Minnesota's St. Paul Book & Stationery," *St. Paul Pioneer Press,* November 21, 1996.

Ehrlich, Jennifer, "Printers Pressed," *Minneapolis/St. Paul CityBusiness,* September 5, 1997, p. 1, 36.

Geisler, Karen Padley, "Growing in Place," *Minnesota Real Estate Journal,* January 4, 1993, p. 10.

Giombetti, Anthony F., "The Right Moves," *Minnesota Business & Opportunities,* January 1998, pp. 44–49.

Houle, Dennis, "Where Are They Now?" *Corporate Report* (Minnesota), January 1999, pp. 44–53.

Kennedy, Tony, "Taylor Has Scored Big in Arenas of Business and Politics," *Star Tribune* (Minneapolis), August 6, 1994, p. 1A.

Lassen, Tina, "Taylor Made," *Northwest Airlines World Traveler,* November 1999.

Novak, Jay, "Executive of the Year: Glen Taylor," *Corporate Report Minnesota,* January 1987, pp. 53–63.

Novak, Jay, et al., "Best of Business," *Twin Cities Business Monthly,* September 1994, 42–53.

Parry, Kate, "Legislator Hopes His Firm's Day Care Will Inspire Others," *Star Tribune* (Minneapolis), May 26, 1987, p. B3.

Solberg, Carla, "Minnesota's Richest Get Richer," *Corporate Report* (Minnesota), February 2000, pp. 26–47.

Stand, Phil, "Taylor-Made for Politics," *Minnesota Business Journal,* March 1985, p. 77.

Vance, Daniel J., "Glen Taylor," *Connect Business Magazine,* 1997.

Weiner, Jay, "A Flair for the Dramatic," *Star Tribune* (Minneapolis), November 4, 1994, p. 7S.

—Kathleen Peippo

Taylor Publishing Company

1550 W. Mockingbird Lane
Dallas, Texas 75235
U.S.A.
Telephone: (214) 819-8100
Toll Free: (800) 677-2800
Fax: (214) 819-8131
Web site: http://www.taylorpub.com

Wholly Owned Subsidiary of Castle Harlan Partners III
Incorporated: 1943
Employees: 1,500
Sales: $100 million (1999 est.)
NAIC: 51113 Book Publishers; 323117 Books Printing;
   511199 All Other Publishers

Taylor Publishing Company is one of the leading publishers of yearbooks in the United States, producing them for more than 9,000 middle and high schools and 500 colleges and universities. Taylor also offers a range of specialty publications, including several popular series on the subjects of sports and gardening. Another Taylor business is reunion services, in which the company offers a complete package for high schools that includes planning the event and notifying alumni. Taylor recently was purchased by Castle Harlan Investment Partners III of New York for $93.5 million.

Beginnings

Founded in 1938, Taylor Publishing was built on the combined experiences of the three Taylor brothers, Herbert C. (known as H.C.), Edgar M. (E. M.), and J.W., Jr. (Bill). Working on his high school yearbook, H.C. had learned about book production and become intrigued with engraving. In 1923, he and E.M., who had been working as a salesman, joined with engraving salesman Roy Beard to buy a Houston company called Star Engraving. Star was restructured to produce diplomas, invitations, and announcements, and to sell class rings. Business thrived, and Bill, the youngest Taylor brother, joined Star as a traveling salesman in 1929, just before the Depression pulled the rug out from under the American economy. Luckily

the Taylors' business stayed afloat, for even in hard times people valued school memorabilia.

While his brothers insisted on producing their goods using the costly photoengraving process, Bill began experimenting with a more affordable process called photo-offset lithography. Meanwhile, differences had caused the brothers to dissolve their partnership with Roy Beard. The Taylors sold their shares of the company and, in 1938, launched Taylor Engraving Company in Houston. Along with several lines of school jewelry, the company offered steel and copper plate engraving for diplomas and invitations. They had no equipment of their own, relying on Caudle Engraving in Dallas for production. The arrangement proved a good marriage.

In 1939, Taylor Engraving moved to Dallas and reorganized as a partnership of H.C. and E.M. The brothers opened a tiny 12- by 12-foot office and all three hit the road to woo customers. Soon E.M. tried peddling one of Bill's lithography yearbooks and was stunned at the positive response. All three brothers saw a new future for the business. Taylor Engraving slowly withdrew from announcements and jewelry and focused on lithographed yearbooks. Their first year in business, the company produced small cardboard-cover yearbooks and sold them to 35 schools. It was a modest but admirable beginning.

Buoyed by the success of their new product, the brothers took out a $1,500 loan, made a down payment on a Davidson press, rented a new office, and hired their first employee. The new employee labored as hard over the press as the brothers did at selling. The coming of World War II war brought hard times again, plus the rationing of paper and ink. Then E.M. had a brainstorm. If the company pitched memory books to the military, they could requisition paper and ink for military projects. These yearbooks for graduating cadets became a huge hit. By 1943, the company was prosperous enough to require another move. That same year, the brothers filed incorporation papers and became Taylor Publishing Company. They had ten busy employees.

By the end of the war, Taylor was selling $500,000 in cadet books a year. But peacetime meant shifting their focus again. As a transition they launched county military books, collecting the

468

photos and military stories of servicemen within a given county radius, and publishing them. The books were popular and the blooming postwar economy gave them a push. At the same time, Taylor concentrated on building its school yearbook business. To this end, a full-time salesman was dispatched to the Southeast.

Bill Taylor returned home from the Air Corps and joined Taylor full-time in 1945. He hired and trained the growing sales force and, in 1946, hatched the company's next great innovation, called the "Blue Book." The Blue Book was simply a step-by-step storyboard that walked customers through the production of a yearbook. This powerful sales tool proved so useful that by 1959 it was the centerpiece of Taylor's new business of conducting seminars for student yearbook staffs. These seminars eventually became the core of an entire division of the company, the Seminar Division, and were still used in the 1990s.

Postwar Growth

Taylor grew quickly—sometimes too quickly—in the late 1940s and into the 1950s. By 1947 plant expansion had eaten up all the space at the company's existing location, so it bought land for a new plant. The operation was under one roof again by October 1948, but two years later facilities had more than doubled again. Despite the expanding production facilities, Taylor struggled to keep up with demand. Spring was invariably demanding for the company, as graduation day deadlines pushed production. Eventually, Taylor devised a summer delivery that helped take pressure off of production and allowed the yearbooks to include year-end pictures such as proms, athletics, and graduation. Naturally, this idea was popular all around.

By the 1950s, growth necessitated innovation. In 1952, Taylor linked with L.G. Balfour Company, then a leader in the class jewelry business. Balfour began pitching Taylor yearbooks along with its product line, using its national sales force to introduce Taylor from New England to California. In 1953, typesetting replaced hand-lettering and freed up the art staff, who had been laboriously setting every ad by hand.

By its third decade, Taylor was ready to go public. Its first shareholders meeting as a publicly held company took place in the summer of 1960. Response was as strong as the company's sales, for Taylor was the leader in U.S. yearbook publishing. Capital infusions allowed acquisitions, including that of Joe Alexander Press of Austin, Texas; Newsfoto Publishing Company of San Angelo, Texas; and Yearbooks Inc. of Monrovia, California. Newsfoto was an especially important acquisition, for it had been a fierce competitor, known for quality and affordability.

Joe Alexander Press and Newsfoto operated as separate companies under Taylor's management. Yearbooks Inc. was made a branch of the parent company and provided a bridge into California's market. Yearbooks Inc. was renamed and struggled through peaks and busts until operations were shut down in 1982. In 1962, Taylor acquired American Beauty Cover Company (ABC) of Dallas, which had long supplied Taylor with yearbook covers. Sales volumes climbed to an all-time high in 1963, but Taylor was creaking from its own sudden growth. The order backlog was daunting and plant equipment and staff were severely taxed. Spring production in 1965 broke more records, and a new plant was slated for a 1967 opening.

Changes and Challenges: 1960s–80s

The mid-1960s saw crucial changes in the company's leadership and direction: Herbert C. Taylor stepped down as company chairman in 1965, though he remained on the board; E.M. moved from president to chairman; and Bill became president. At this time, the bulk of Taylor's business was school yearbooks, and the remaining ten percent of sales came from reprinting rare books and cattle sale catalogs, and miscellaneous commercial printing jobs such as specialty advertising brochures. By the late 1960s, Taylor had all the requisite charms of a prime acquisition target and had been approached by corporate giants such as RCA and Times-Mirror. Then the Connecticut-based International Silver Company—later Insilco—approached Taylor and proved compatible. The merger agreement went through in 1967. Randy Marston, a financial wizard with Insilco who helped hammer out the deal, went on to form a bond with Bill Taylor so close that Taylor named Marston his executive heir. Marston and his family moved to Dallas in 1969.

After the boom of the mid-1960s, Taylor was startled by sagging profits in 1968 and 1969. By 1970, Taylor had hit a low point. The company's problems were widespread and long-standing, a result of growth without modernization. One dominating crisis was in typesetting, where the company employed antiquated hot metal linotype machines. When the head of this production walked out one day, unable to bear the hard work and his chronically revolving staff, the company was forced to switch to the still-revolutionary cold type process within five months in order to make production. To cope with the backlog, Taylor brought in outside management consultants who worked for more than eight months to overhaul the production system. By 1972, Taylor's efforts were paying off and the company celebrated its best production season ever.

Business boomed between 1972 and 1976, and annual profits passed the $2 million mark for the first time in the early 1970s. The yearbook field had changed enough that Taylor's association with Balfour's sales force needed revising. Yearbooks had become a specialty, sufficiently complex that they needed a sales force of their own. In 1970, 80 percent of Taylor's yearbook sales came from combined sales offices. By 1989, it was less than 20 percent. Both delivery and sales were stable enough for Bill Taylor to retire in 1976. The baby boom had peaked, though, and student enrollments were already declining, a trend that would continue through the 1980s. Fifteen of Taylor's yearbook competitors went under. Taylor revved up its sales team and moved to even more high-tech solutions to production problems, to save on labor and time. The company managed to hang on to its market share and increase profits even though school enrollment declined 26 percent. In 1977, Taylor opened the doors of its first manufacturing venture in the north, a plant based in Pennsylvania. A Fine Books Division and a Publishing Division were created, growing by 1989 to account for 12 percent of Taylor's annual sales.

With the 1980s, technology brought its own revolutions. The company was offering videotaped "yearbooks" as supplements to printed volumes and employing four-color scanners, continuous tone processors, and other new technologies. Taylor had broken ground in the mid-1970s by paginating its yearbooks with a computerized copy preparations system, which had yet to become the new wave in publishing. New online laser color scanners improved the quality of photos and Taylor also led the pack by using lithographed hard covers, broadening customers' creative choices. Taylor was well-poised, therefore, to take advantage of the almost daily innovations in computer-assisted publishing.

Diversification and Computerization in the 1990s

Taylor was also honing its specialty publications and began to focus on four topics: gardening, sports, cooking, and self-help/health books. This division produced such titles as *Spirits of the Sky: The Airplanes of World War II* and *Antique Roses of the South* in the fall of 1990. Taylor also was donating a portion of net proceeds from some of its self-help titles to relevant organizations, such as the National Coalition Against Domestic Violence, which received money from sales of *The Battered Woman's Survival Guide*. At the same time, Taylor was moving aggressively into distribution, representing 17 different presses and publishers in 1990, including Cybourg Communications, Story Line Press, and Mississippi River Publishing Company.

While Taylor was trotting to keep up with the technological advancements in publishing, Insilco—which had changed its name in 1969—had continued a buying blaze through the 1970s and 1980s, acquiring Rolodex Corporation, Signal Transformer, ESCOD Industries, and General Thermodynamics, among others. Its interests ranged from publishing to cable and wire assemblies, specialized connector systems, power transformers, and the metal tubing used in heat transfer applications and radiators. Insilco was growing at a speed that might have stunned the Taylor brothers.

The growth proved too much to manage, however, and in January 1991, Insilco filed for Chapter 11 bankruptcy. The company's troubles seemed not to impact Taylor Publishing too much. By April 1993, Insilco emerged from Chapter 11; by November of that same year, it was trading stock on the NASDAQ. During that same period, Taylor was implementing a new system for scanning photos and line graphics, printing more than ten million pictures a year in its yearbooks, and paginating more than 150,000 pages a week. Automated pagination and other new technologies that saved labor without sacrificing quality were key to Taylor's lead in the industry. The scanning system cut pagination costs by roughly half, improved image quality, reduced the annual consumption of film, and nearly eliminated the need for a copy camera and stripping department. The new system hit a few bumps before running smoothly, but the benefits were immense.

In 1993, Insilco's balance sheet was much improved, it had a new board of directors, and its net sales had increased from $578.5 million in 1992, to $615.1 million. Just more than a quarter of those sales were in Insilco's Technologies Group, mostly serving the telecommunications and electronic components end markets; another quarter was due to the Metal Parts Group, which included the two operating units Thermal Components and Steel Parts; and nearly 33 percent of its sales were in Office Products/Publishing Group. Taylor alone contributed about 16 percent of 1993 sales. In the summer of 1994, Taylor was awarded a patent for its Electronic Yearbook Publication System, which covered the digital processing of pictures for yearbooks. It had best-selling books about the Dallas Cowboys, Green Bay Packers, and Detroit Lions. Seeing that commemorative sports books were so popular, Taylor began negotiations with other teams. The digital picture publishing gave Taylor an edge over competitors and the company reported an increase in yearbook orders in 1994.

Insilco had maintained market position even during its bankruptcy and reorganization. Taylor did likewise, throughout its parent company's troubles. By 1994, it was marketing its yearbooks through 250 exclusive, commissioned sales representatives and producing about 30 percent of the country's yearbooks annually. The following year Taylor debuted its Positively For Kids book series. The 40-page hardcovers, which primarily consisted of photographs, profiled athletes who had overcome obstacles to rise to the top. The concept was a hit, with sales of 150,000 copies for the debut offering, a profile of Dallas Cowboys quarterback Troy Aikman.

The company filed suit against top competitor Jostens, Inc. in 1997, alleging that the country's dominant yearbook company was trying to monopolize the market. Although a jury found for Taylor and awarded it $25.3 million, the verdict was later overturned by a Federal District Court judge, a ruling that was upheld in the Fifth U.S. Circuit Court of Appeals.

In 1998 Taylor unveiled another technical innovation, Net Chek, which gave yearbook staffs online access to their book's galleys and allowed them to do instant markup and correction, saving much time and money in the process. By now an estimated 80 percent of the company's yearbooks were being created using desktop publishing software, three-fourths of which utilized Taylor's own proprietary UltraVision product.

A year later Taylor came up with another first for the industry, an online ordering system offered in conjunction with American School Directory, a web-based information service that covered the entire United States. Orders continued to be taken by the traditional methods of collecting money at schools or via mail, as well.

In December 1999, Insilco announced that it was selling Taylor Publishing to New York-based Castle Harlan Partners III, a unit of merchant bank Castle Harlan, Inc. The $93.5 million deal was completed the following year. Castle Harlan also owned Commemorative Brands, Inc. of Texas, a class ring manufacturer, and expected the two companies to complement each other.

After more than 60 years in business, Taylor continued to be a leader in the field of yearbook publishing, and it was still recognized as a technological innovator. The company also was finding success with specialty publications and reunion planning, but yearbooks remained its bread and butter, with more than 90 percent of its income derived from this area.

Principal Divisions

Reunion Services; Yearbooks; Fine Books; Trade Books.

Principal Competitors

Jostens, Inc.; Herff Jones, Inc.; Walsworth Publishing Co.

Further Reading

Aucoin, Patsi, ''Feeling at Home at Work: Taylor Publishing's 450 'In-Homes' Enjoy Answering to Themselves,'' *Dallas Business Journal,* January 23, 1989, p. 16.

Chism, Olin, ''Books Aren't Publisher's Whole Story,'' *Dallas Morning News,* January 23, 1994, p. 8J.

Lodge, Sally, ''Taylor Spotlights Sports Superstars: A Texas Publisher Signs Up Athletes to Tell Their Stories,'' *Publishers Weekly,* October 21, 1996, p. 43.

''Pagination Costs Cut in Half,'' *Graphics Arts Monthly,* September 1993, p. 84.

Raley Borda, Laura, ''Largest Dallas-Fort Worth Area Commercial Printing Companies,'' *Dallas Business Journal,* December 17, 1993, p. 10.

Seago, Kate, ''Yearbook Publisher Works Nonstop to Meet Deadlines,'' *Dallas Morning News,* May 12, 1998, p. 18A.

Solis, Sianne, ''Investor Group to Buy Taylor Publishing,'' *Dallas Morning News,* December 21, 1999, p. 1D.

Steinberg, Don, ''Publisher Installs DECnet,'' *PC Week,* July 28, 1987, p. C8.

Summer, Bob, ''Sleuthing Around,'' *Publishers Weekly,* September 20, 1993, p. 22.

——, ''Taylor Publishing: Building Identity,'' *Publishers Weekly,* October 19, 1990, p. 39.

Wasowksi, Andy, *Never an Easy Spring: A History of Taylor Publishing Company, The First 50 Years: 1930–1989,* Dallas: Taylor Publishing Company, 1989.

—Carol I. Keeley
—updated by Frank Uhle

Texas Pacific Group Inc.

301 Commerce Street, Suite 3300
Fort Worth, Texas 76102
U.S.A.
Telephone: (817) 871-4000
Fax: (817) 871-4010
Web site: http://www.texpac.com

Partnership
Incorporated: 1993 as Air Partners L.P.
Employees: 20
Sales: $75 million (1999 est.)
NAIC: 523910 Venture Capital Companies

Texas Pacific Group Inc. (TPG) is a private investment partnership involved in leveraged buyouts, joint ventures, and large-stake purchases of companies. The investment group focuses primarily on buying financially troubled companies with brand-name recognition. Typically, TPG does not involve itself in the day-to-day operations of the companies it controls, but it does provide strategic direction. TPG's holdings include Del Monte Foods Company, J. Crew Group, Ducati Motorcycles, Beringer Wine Estates, On Semiconductor, ZiLOG, Bally International, Oxford Health Plans, and Piaggio S.p.A.

Founder's Background

The central figure behind Texas Pacific's formation and growth is David Bonderman, a Los Angeles native whose renowned deal-making talents arose from an eclectic professional background. He was a Phi Beta Kappa graduate of the University of Washington in 1963, a distinction that helped him earn admittance to Harvard Law School, where he was awarded his postgraduate degree magna cum laude in 1966. After a year studying Islamic law at the American University of Cairo, Bonderman moved to New Orleans and taught law at Tulane University for a year. Next, he moved to Washington, D.C., and spent a year working as an assistant in the Justice Department's civil rights division, before joining the prestigious Washington, D.C., law firm Arnold & Porter. At Arnold & Porter, Bonderman quickly distinguished himself, becoming known for

his work on high-profile and controversial cases, notably the complex 1982 bankruptcy reorganization of Braniff International Airlines. Bonderman also provided legal assistance on historical preservation cases as part of his pro bono work, particularly litigation involving Washington, D.C.'s Union Station and the city's storied Willard Hotel. Bonderman's pro bono work also took him outside the nation's capital. One such case ultimately led to his decision to create TPG.

During the early 1980s, a citizens' group in Fort Worth, Texas, pitted itself against the federal government. The Fort Worth residents were fighting against a proposed federal highway that they claimed would despoil the city's historic district. Significantly, the group was led by Robert Bass, one of four Fort Worth brothers whose inheritance from a wildcatter great-uncle had been built into a multibillion-dollar family fortune. Bonderman was hired to argue against the proposed highway and prevailed, impressing Bass a great deal and, unwittingly, steering his professional career in an entirely new direction.

Bass was immensely wealthy, but the 35-year-old was itching to aggrandize his already considerable fortune and to establish a name for himself. His eldest brother, Sid, had been responsible for the Bass brothers' fame and fortune, parlaying their $50 million inheritance into $4 billion through a series of spectacular business deals he concluded with the help of his advisor, Richard Rainwater, one of the country's celebrated investors. Robert Bass spent more than a decade watching the headline-grabbing maneuvers of his brother and he pined for his time in the limelight. He wanted to emulate his elder brother and distance himself from him at the same time. He wanted to make his own fortune and he asked the 41-year-old Bonderman to lead the investment team he was gathering. Bonderman immediately agreed. On the day he finished his last case for Arnold & Porter in 1983—winning a dismissal from the Supreme Court—Bonderman packed his bags and moved to Fort Worth to spearhead the growth of the leveraged buyout (LBO) company Robert M. Bass Group.

LBO firms, which use the asset value of a target company in order to finance the debt incurred in acquiring the company, were few in number when Bass and Bonderman entered the fray in 1983. During the 1980s, Kohlberg Kravis Roberts & Co.

1993: Founder, Bonderman, acquires bankrupt Continental airlines; forms Texas Pacific later in the year.
1996: Texas Pacific invests in AT&T Paradyne, Beringer Wine, Ducati Motorcycles, and Del Monte Foods.
1997: Firm invests in J, Crew Group.
1998: Firm invests in ZiLOG and Oxford Health Plans.
1999: Texas Pacific invests in Piaggio S.p.A, Bally International, and Motorola's SCG Holding.
2000: Texas Pacific invests in Gemplus S.A., Seagate Technology, and Petco Animal Supplies.

(KKR), one of the industry's pioneers, attracted national attention from its massive and shrewd takeovers, but aside from KKR there were few LBO firms of note. Most of those involved in the industry acquired established companies in industries characterized by consistent cash flows, targeting companies they perceived as undervalued. Bonderman, in his new role as Bass's investment lieutenant, adopted a different approach, targeting financially troubled companies, those with labyrinthine financial structures, and companies facing an uncertain regulatory future.

Bonderman Builds His Reputation in the 1980s

Initially, The Bass Group moved into cable television, purchasing stocks soon after the federal government deregulated cable-television pricing in 1984. Bonderman completed his first deal in cable television two years later, acquiring Wometco Cable TV. Like most of Bonderman's deals to follow, the $645 million purchase of Wometco was highly leveraged, with Bonderman offering only $62 million in equity. By the early 1990s, the cable television market had matured as Bonderman had anticipated, fueling a sixfold increase in Bass Group's initial investment. Bonderman's first success was followed by a string of others, galvanizing his reputation as a savvy dealmaker. Among the transactions that earned Bonderman praise was his $250 million acquisition—entirely debt financed—of the Plaza Hotel in New York City, which was sold seven months later to Donald Trump for $410 million. Also in 1988, Bonderman pushed for the $400 million acquisition of American Savings & Loan not long after the California savings and loan concern had been seized by the government. Bonderman presided over the liquidation of billions of dollars of assets and orchestrated the thrift's recovery. By 1997, Bass Group's $400 million investment was worth $2 billion. Bonderman's record of success continued into the 1990s, highlighted by the $388 million he used to gain control of National Reinsurance Corp. His strategy paid off two years later when National completed an initial public offering, giving the Bass Group a sevenfold increase on its initial investment.

The pivotal deal in Bonderman's career and the catalyst for the formation of TPG occurred in 1993. It was a moment that demonstrated the contrarian inclinations of the country's up-and-coming investor. Continental Airlines, mired in its second bankruptcy within a decade, became the object of Bonderman's attention in 1993, Aside from its own profound financial prob-

lems, Continental was embroiled in protracted labor disputes and ensconced in an industry rocked by the recessive economic conditions that pocked the early 1990s—additional aspects of the airline's misfortune that made the most speculative investors keep their distance. Bonderman disregarded the consensus and wanted to push ahead with the deal, but Bass balked at the proposal. Bonderman responded by submitting his resignation. He was certain the Continental deal had lucrative potential.

To move forward with his buyout of Continental, Bonderman formed Air Partners, the predecessor venture to TPG. To aid in his bid, Bonderman enlisted the help of James Coulter, who had been part of the investment team at Bass Group, serving as Bonderman's closest advisor. The pair soon raised $66 million, enough to acquire a 42 percent controlling interest in Continental in April 1993. Bonderman brought the airliner out of bankruptcy—a $9 billion reorganization—and reversed the company's fortunes considerably. Ultimately, the investors in the Continental buyout recorded a 1,000 percent return on their investment, as Continental's operating income surged to $716 million in 1997 from a loss of $108 million during the year preceding the buyout. More important for the future capital raising efforts of TPG, Bonderman was hailed as Continental's savior.

TPG's 1993 Formation Triggers Spending Spree

TPG was formed in 1993, not long after the creation of Air Partners. Air Partners had been created to facilitate the acquisition of Continental, an impromptu partnership that brought investors together for a specific purpose. Bonderman and Coulter wanted a more lasting organization, however, and formed TPG, a private investment partnership, as a permanent vehicle for their deal-making in all types of industries. Bonderman established his office in Fort Worth and Coulter set up the main office in San Francisco, which represented the rationale behind the name the two partners chose: Texas Pacific Group. In San Francisco, Coulter was joined by a third partner, William Price. Previously, Price had been in charge of strategic planning and development at General Electric Capital Corp. His experience as a consultant was tapped by Bonderman and Coulter to help recruit the managers who would run TPG's companies. Bonderman and Coulter carried on the same type of professional relationship they had forged at Bass Group. Bonderman, the visionary, was responsible for creating the ideas, Counter's task was to turn Bonderman's ideas into reality, and Price was charged with ensuring that the reality worked smoothly.

As TPG got underway, the partnership's greatest asset was the esteemed investment record of Bonderman. Based largely on his reputation, the venture was able to raise $720 million for its first investment fund in 1993, $220 million more than the partners had expected. With this capital, TPG announced in its prospectus to investors that it would be "pursuing complex transactions, focusing on industries undergoing change, and applying cautious contrarianism." A flurry of investment deals followed, as TPG became arguably the most prominent investment company in the 1990s.

TPG's least successful deals occurred early in the private equity company's history. In 1995, the group acquired 45 percent of Newscope Resources Ltd. for $40 million and, in partnership with another investment group, acquired the caramel and marshmallow businesses belonging to Kraft General Foods Inc. Newscope, a Calgary-based energy and production company with operations in Louisiana, Mississippi, and Texas, was renamed Denbury Resources Inc. In the years following the name change, the company struggled to withstand falling energy prices and its profits plunged. Kraft's $150-million-in-sales caramel and marshmallow businesses were combined after TPG's investment and renamed Favorite Brands International. The company's stature swelled after an acquisition spree made it the fourth largest candy firm in the United States, but the expansion came at a price. By the end of the 1990s, Favorite Brands had proven itself to be one of TPG's more troublesome investments, as the candy maker's interest expenses exceeded its cash flow.

TPG recorded more encouraging results with its investments in 1996. The year included four memorable investments that demonstrated the wide scope of Bonderman's acquisitive eye. In a $175 million deal, TPG acquired AT&T Paradyne, a modem manufacturer that pioneered digital compression technology. Bonderman also demonstrated his willingness to invest in foreign companies, completing the intricate buyout of Italian motorcycle manufacturer Ducati Motorcycles. The other notable acquisition in 1996 reflected TPG's interest in growth industries. The company paid $395 million for Nestlé S.A.'s Wine World Estates (renamed Beringer Wine Estates Holdings), which gave Bonderman's investors a stake in the California wine industry before the expansion of distribution channels brought domestic wines to the mass market. By the end of 1996, TPG's influence as a strategic agitator had produced enviable results. The group recorded a return rate on its investments of 105 percent.

After its success with its first investment fund, TPG had little problem raising the capital for its second, the TPG Partners II fund. The group raised $2.5 billion in 1997, which it immediately wanted to put to use. A rapidly growing stock market, however, forced TPG to restrain its acquisitive activities, but the year featured two massive deals nonetheless. First, TPG completed the $800 million buyout of Del Monte Foods Company, the largest branded canner and distributor of fruits and vegetables in the country. In October, the investment group completed a $560 million deal for J. Crew Group, a clothing company struggling to add retail stores to its foundation of catalogue sales. In 1998, two more significant investments were made, as TPG gambled heavily on troubled health maintenance organization (HMO) Oxford Health Plan through a $350 million investment. The investment group also completed a $416 million buyout of semiconductor manufacturer ZiLOG, an acquisition that signaled TPG's newly reached decision to invest in the technology sector.

As TPG entered 1999, it was in the final stages of investing the capital raised for the TPG Partners II fund. No longer hesitant, the investment group threw itself headlong into the LBO market, completing a series of investments. Internationally, the company acquired Piaggio S.p.A, the Italian manufacturer of Vespa motor scooters; Bally International Ltd., the Swiss luxury shoe designer; and Great Britain's Punch Taverns,

the operator of approximately 1,500 pubs in England, Wales, and Scotland. TPG added to its HMO holdings by investing $75 million in Magellan Health Services Inc., the nation's largest behavioral healthcare company. In the technology sector, the investment group increased its presence by investing $337 million in the semiconductor components group of Motorola Inc., which was renamed On Semiconductor.

By the beginning of the new century, TPG was ready for its third round of investments, having concluded the 1990s as perhaps the most high-profile investment group in the country. Bonderman and his team were able to raise $4 billion in early 2000 to ensure that TPG would remain at the forefront of its industry in the coming years. For the immediate future, TPG was expected to increase its investments overseas, particularly in Europe, and deepen its involvement in the technology sector by buying into semiconductor and telecommunications companies. The company's progress during the first half of 2000 indicated as much, as Bonderman spent more than $740 million on technology-related acquisitions during the first six months of 2000. The largest of these acquisitions occurred in March 2000, when TPG completed the biggest tech-related private equity transaction in European history, investing $450 million in Gemenos, France-based Gemplus S.A., a leader in smart cards and software for wireless applications. With considerably more capital at its disposal, TPG promised to attract further attention as it pressed forward with its LBO activities, intent on exponentially recouping its investments in the global marketplace.

Principal Subsidiaries

Bally Management Ltd.; Beringer Wine Estates Holdings, Inc.; Del Monte Foods Company; Denbury Resources Inc.; Ducati Motor Holding S.p.A.; J. Crew Group, Inc.; ON Semiconductor Corp.; Punch Taverns Group Ltd.; ZiLOG, Inc.

Principal Competitors

Kohlberg Kravis Roberts & Co.; Hicks, Muse, Tate & Furst Incorporated; Clayton, Dubilier & Rice, Inc.

Further Reading

Atlas, Riva, "Thrills! Chills! Hondo Bondo Spills?," *Institutional Investor,* January 1999, p. 32.

Carlsen, Clifford, "Bigger in Texas: New Buyout Fund Hits $2.3 Million," *San Francisco Business Times,* April 4, 1997, p. 21.

Elliot, Heidi, "Finding Value in Maturity," *Electronic News,* August 31, 1998, p. 42.

Grover, Mary Beth, "Technoleverage," *Forbes,* May 29, 2000, p. 202.

Harbert, Tam, "Texas Pacific Group Continues High-Tech Investing Spree," *Electronic Business,* June 2000, p. 30.

Rutberg, Sidney, "J. Crew Founders Get Big Bucks in Texas Pacific Deal," *Daily News Record,* December 12, 1997, p. 12.

Trigaux, Robert, "Texas Group Pays $175 Million for Modem Maker AT&T Paradyne," *Knight-Ridder/Tribune Business News,* June 20, 1996, p. 6200229

Werner, Ben, "Texas Investor Ropes 20% of Magellan," *Baltimore Business Journal,* July 23, 1999, p. 1.

—Jeffrey L. Covell

The Titan Corporation

3033 Science Park Road
San Diego, California 92121-1199
U.S.A.
Telephone: (858) 552-9500
Fax: (858) 552-9645
Web site: http://www.titan.com

Public Company
Incorporated: 1981 as Titan Systems Inc.
Employees: 7,600
Sales: $406.6 million (1999)
Stock Exchanges: New York
Ticker Symbol: TTN
NAIC: 334511 Search, Detection, Navigation, Guidance,
    Aeronautical, and Nautical System and Instrument
    Manufacturing; 334517 Irradiation Apparatus
    Manufacturing; 513322 Cellular and Other Wireless
    Telecommunications; 513340 Satellite
    Telecommunications; 541512 Computer Systems
    Design Services

Historically, The Titan Corporation was a defense department contractor involved in areas such as wireless communications, navigational systems, information systems, and other high-technology projects. Following a reduction in defense spending in the early 1990s, Titan redefined itself by seeking commercial applications for new technologies it had developed. At the end of the decade its most highly publicized venture was its SureBeam electron beam technology for the irradiation of ground beef, which went online in 2000 following approval by the Food and Drug Administration (FDA) and the U.S. Department of Agriculture. In 1999 the company's stock rose 760 percent and was named the top performer on the New York Stock Exchange.

As of mid-2000 Titan had four core businesses: Titan Systems Corp., Cayenta, Titan Wireless, and SureBeam. It also had an Emerging Technologies group that developed commercial applications for new technologies. The company planned to develop new start-up companies based around these technologies and spin off minority interests in them as a way of raising capital. Titan also continued to be an active defense contractor as well. Its subsidiary Titan Systems itself had some 16 business subsidiaries involved in such fields as communication services, information systems, signal and imaging systems, electronic systems, and more.

Primarily a Defense Contractor: 1980s

Dr. Gene W. Ray cofounded Titan Systems Inc. in 1981 as a defense contractor. Prior to 1981 Ray worked for defense contractor Science Applications International Corp., where he was a member of the board of directors and held managerial positions, including executive vice-president and general manager of the systems group.

In 1985 La Jolla, California-based Titan Systems acquired Electronic Memories & Magnetics Corp., a maker of military microcomputers and memory systems, for about $26 million. At the time, Titan was operating as a systems engineering contractor for defense programs and had revenue of $24.3 million for fiscal 1984. Titan's president and CEO, Gene W. Ray, became head of the combined operation, renamed The Titan Corporation.

In 1987 Titan's revenue was $92.8 million and net income was $1.5 million. The company's stock was listed on the New York Stock Exchange. Titan specialized in providing high-technology solutions to the U.S. government and international customers in systems development and integration. Its technical specialties included electro-optics, pulsed power sciences and applied mechanics and computational fluid dynamics, systems software development, space and surveillance systems, and advanced defense systems.

Titan was organized into three business groups: Titan Technologies, Titan Systems, and Titan Electronics. Titan Technologies included electro-optics, pulsed power, computational fluid dynamics, and applied mechanics. Titan Systems designed, developed, deployed, and tested highly advanced communications, aerospace, and weapons systems for defense. Titan Electronics provided militarized computers, electronic subsystems, and meteor-burst communications equipment.

Company Perspectives:

The Titan Corporation creates, builds and launches technology-based businesses and offers innovative global technology solutions. Three of Titan's four core businesses develop and deploy communications and information technology solutions and services. In addition, Titan markets the leading technology for the electronic pasteurization of food products and is continually identifying promising technologies suitable for commercialization.

For 1988 Titan reported a loss of $11.2 million on revenue of $96.7 million. Losses were attributed to one-time charges from internal restructuring and changes in the industry. At year-end Titan divested a number of its operations in an attempt to remain competitive in a cost-conscious defense market. In January 1989 it sold off its advanced materials division, which manufactured ferrite powders and related products, to Nippon Iron Powder Co., a subsidiary of Mitsui Mining & Smelting Co. It also sold its 87 percent interest in Computing Applications Software Technology Inc. Its simulator trainer line of business, Severe Environment Systems Co., was discontinued in October 1988. After selling 80 percent of its interest in its Canadian operations in 1987, it sold the remaining 20 percent in 1988. The company was also pursuing new commercial opportunities in radiation processing and explosive detection.

For 1989 Titan reported a profit of $2.3 million on slightly higher revenue of $97.7 million. During the year the company restructured, selling all of the outstanding stock in its subsidiary, Meteor Communications Corp., to MCC's former owners and employees.

Diversifying into Commercial Markets: 1990s

In 1990 Titan acquired Government Systems Inc., formerly Linkabit, a division of Boston-based M/A-Com Inc. Government Systems, which was located in San Diego and had about 500 employees, supplied surveillance products for use in intelligence collection.

For 1991 Titan reported a growing business in education and training products. Its revenue increased 18 percent to $146.5 million, while net income rose 49 percent to $3.4 million. The acquisition of Linkabit contributed to the increase in revenue, as did growth in the commercial and international areas of all of Titan's business segments. Revenue from the electronics segment decreased.

Shrinking defense budgets were causing the company to diversify into other areas, and about 30 percent of revenue came from non-defense sales. More than 60 percent of the firm's 1991 revenue came from the sale of high-tech software and hardware products. It was producing more satellite communications products for both defense and commercial applications. In June 1991 Titan announced a joint venture with Motorola to produce a portable satellite terminal. Titan was also producing the next generation of satellite terminals for the U.S. Navy. The company was also developing laser communication technology, and during 1991 it had a full-scale demonstration of simultaneous,

two-way laser communication between an aircraft and a submerged submarine. Titan had about 1,500 employees in 1991.

By 1992 it was clear that U.S. defense spending would be cut drastically in the coming years. That was motivating defense contractors to convert their technology into commercial applications. Three areas that Titan was working on were a satellite scrambling system for satellite TV, medical instrument sterilization, and a pay-per-use retrieval system using CD-ROM data-storage disks.

In 1992 Titan acquired the Satcom product line from Gamma Microwave Inc. of Santa Clara, California. Gamma Satcom, which would be renamed Titan Gamma Satcom, produced commercial radios for high data rate earth stations and sold them to satellite equipment manufacturers in the United States as well as to other U.S. and international users. The acquisition was part of Titan's overall strategy to expand into commercial markets.

Titan Satellite Systems Corp. was formed in mid-1992 as a joint venture of The Titan Corp. and Houston Satellite Systems, a Denver-based home satellite equipment manufacturer that was owned in part by EchoSphere, the largest U.S. home satellite distributor. The venture was formed to enter the satellite television descrambler business. Titan and competitor General Instrument Corporation jointly owned patents on a satellite descrambler system. Titan had acquired the technology from M/A-Com Inc. in 1990, but M/A-Com had already sold the commercial application of the scrambling system to General Instrument and signed a five-year non-compete agreement. The venture involving Titan and Houston Satellite Systems was formed after the non-compete agreement expired in 1992. GI's system was called VideoCipher, while Titan's would be marketed as the Link-A-Bit system. However, by March 1993 Titan Satellite Systems had shut down operations after major providers of satellite programming decided against using the system for technical reasons. Titan also reported that programmers were not interested in developing the necessary encryption for the system. Later in the year Titan Corp. provided the technology for International Cargo Management Systems to introduce a cargo tracking device that utilized a network of U.S. Department of Defense satellites.

In September 1992 Titan broke ground in Denver on a 28,000-plus square-foot facility for medical products sterilization. The facility would use electron beams to kill bacteria on medical devices. The Titan division was called Titan Scan, and a second facility was planned for San Diego.

For 1992 Titan's revenue increased slightly to $149 million, while net income rose to $3.6 million. During the year Titan experienced an $11 million reduction in revenue from the U.S. Department of Defense, although defense revenue accounted for about 70 percent of overall sales in 1992. During the year Titan invested heavily in commercial business areas. Earnings were negatively affected by losses in new commercial software and satellite communication businesses as well as by investments in research and development and start-up costs for Titan Satellite Systems Corp. and Titan Scan.

For 1993 revenue remained relatively flat, increasing slightly to $149.4 million. However, the company reported a net loss of

$7.9 million. During the year it received $10 million from the U.S. Navy after a defense contract dispute was resolved. Commercial applications under development included satellite communications, broadcast systems, medical and food sterilization, and environmental systems and solutions. During the year Titan sold off its Applications Group for about $19 million.

Titan was focused on two areas, information systems and applied technologies. In information systems Titan developed software, manufactured secure satellite television communications, defense communications, and government information systems. Applied technologies included the manufacture of medical sterilization systems and utilizing technology in other niche markets.

For 1994 Titan reported lower revenue of $136.2 million, due largely to the earlier sale of the firm's Applications Group. During the year government revenue remained fairly constant, with commercial revenue accounting for 32 percent of sales. The company returned to profitability with net income of $5.95 million.

Enjoying Record Growth: 1998–2000

The year 1998 was one of record growth for Titan. Revenue rose 75 percent to $303 million, and the company's workforce increased from 1,400 at the end of 1997 to 2,500 at the end of 1998. During the year Titan acquired six companies: VisiCom Laboratories, Inc., of San Diego; Transnational Partners II, LLC of San Diego; Horizons Technology, Inc. of San Diego; Validity Corp. of San Diego; Delfin Systems of Santa Clara; and Florida-based DBA Systems, Inc. Through its subsidiary, Titan Software Systems, Titan and Cap Gemini America LLC were awarded a contract from the state of Wyoming to provide Y2K services for the state's computer systems.

In February 1999 the U.S. Department of Agriculture (USDA) approved the irradiation of red meat as a way to eliminate food-borne illnesses, with final regulations due at the end of the year. The FDA had approved the process for red meat in 1998. Titan announced it would build the first electronic pasteurization system specifically designed to pasteurize ground beef in Sioux City,

Iowa. The system, patented by Titan under the name SureBeam and utilizing electron beam technology, would eliminate such bacteria as E. coli, Listeria monocytogenes, salmonella, and campylobacter. The SureBeam system utilized electricity and did not use gamma radiation or radioactive isotopes. It was the same technology that Titan had been using since 1992 to sterilize medical instruments. A number of large ground beef producers had signed up to use the system.

Titan would later provide a similar system utilizing X-rays to Hawaii Pride LLC in Hilo, Hawaii, to address the state's fruit fly problem regarding local fruit and flower products.

The USDA's final regulations governing irradiation were issued in December 1999 and included labeling requirements. Following a 60-day waiting period, Titan's Sioux City facility began operating. Titan had multi-year contracts with food producers Cargill Inc., IBP Inc., and Tyson Foods, Inc., among others. Kraft Foods, Inc. signed an agreement with Titan to research the process in early 2000. By March 2000 it was estimated that 75 percent of the U.S. ground beef industry and nearly 50 percent of the poultry processors had signed agreements with Titan to use the SureBeam technology. The first food products to be treated with the SureBeam electron pasteurization technology were rolled out in May 2000. Later in 2000 Titan registered an initial public offering to spin off 16 percent of SureBeam Corp.'s stock to the public.

For the year 1999, Titan's stock increased 760 percent and was noted as the best performer on the New York Stock Exchange. Titan was one of the first companies to set up an in-house incubator to create start-up companies for the commercialization of new technologies. Titan developed two such start-ups in 1999: Wave Systems, which provided specialized electronic product distribution and metering systems for Internet access devices, and IPivot, which was sold to Intel for $500 million. Titan's eight percent ownership in IPivot netted it $41 million in cash. Overall revenue for 1999 was about $407 million, and net income rose to $21 million.

At the end of 1999 Titan filed for a proposed public offering of stock in its business-to-business e-commerce subsidiary, Cayenta. During 1999 Cayenta evolved from a commercial software integration business to a services provider offering a full line of Internet-based management systems. Titan planned to spin off 20 percent of Cayenta.

At the beginning of 2000 Titan acquired Advanced Communications Systems, which was founded in 1987. ACS was primarily a government contractor supplying communications, information systems, and aerospace services to U.S. government agencies. It was a major provider of satellite communications to the U.S. Navy.

Titan Wireless was seen as another strong growth area for the company. It had been providing wireless services for defense for 20 years; now it was building a global wireless communications service business. Titan's wireless segment tripled during 1999, accounting for $27 million in revenue. Using its satellite communications technology, Titan reached an agreement with companies in 16 countries to provide long-distance telephone service. Service in ten of those countries was up and running by mid-2000. It appeared that Titan would also become an Internet service provider in developing nations.

While Titan's commercial businesses seemed to be firing on all cylinders, the company continued to have a very active defense business. In early 2000 it obtained a $29 million contract from the U.S. Navy's Space and Naval Warfare Systems Center.

Titan continued with its acquisitions in 2000. Among the companies it acquired were AverStar, Inc., a private company headquartered in Burlington, Massachusetts, that supplied information systems and products. On the horizon were plans for more spinoffs from the company's Emerging Technologies group. Among the areas it was involved in were fingerprint and card scanning systems; motion-tracking technology to create three-dimensional views of trajectory speed and movement of objects; Internet transaction metering systems; and wireless broadband multimedia modem technology and wireless LAN technology.

Principal Subsidiaries

Titan Systems Corporation; Cayenta, Inc.; Titan Wireless, Inc.; SureBeam Corporation; Advanced Communications Systems; Atlantic Aerospace Electronics Corporation; AverStar, Inc.; Intermetrics, Inc.; Pacer Infotec, Inc.; Computer Based Systems, Inc.; MJR Associates, Inc.; DBA Systems, Inc.; Delfin Systems; Eldyne, Inc.; Horizons Technology, Inc.; LinCom Corporation; Titan Linkabit; Pulse Engineering, Inc.; SenCom Corporation; System Resources Corporation; Unidyne Corporation; Validity Division; VisiCom Laboratories, Inc.

Principal Competitors

Booz-Allen & Hamilton Inc.; Computer Sciences Corporation; SAIC (Science Applications International Corporation); Sapient Corporation; Flow International Corporation; Steris Corporation.

Further Reading

"Aloha Fruit Flies," *Progressive Grocer,* August 2000, p. 66.

"AverStar Agrees to Buyout," *Washington Business Journal,* March 31, 2000, p. 36.

Brydolf, Libby, "Economic Conversion: Technology's Not the Problem," *San Diego Business Journal,* December 21, 1992, p. 13.

"EM&M Agrees to Be Bought by Titan Systems for $26M," *Electronic News,* March 11, 1985, p. 39.

Epstein, Victor J., "San Diego-Based Irradiation Spin-Off to Offer Stock," *Knight-Ridder/Tribune Business News,* August 24, 2000.

"Giant Technology Performer on NYSE," *San Diego Business Journal,* March 27, 2000, p. B10.

Hill, Martin, "Titan Corp. Signs with Kraft Foods," *San Diego Business Journal,* February 28, 2000, p. 13.

"Irradiated Hamburgers Hit the Grill," *Prepared Foods,* June 2000, p. 90.

King, Angela G., and Tsukasa Furukawa, "Nippon Iron Acquires Titan's Advanced Materials Division," *American Metal Market,* January 11, 1989, p. 4.

Lambert, Peter D., "Titan Scrambles for Piece of Descrambler Market," *Broadcasting,* June 22, 1992, p. 34.

"M/A-COM, Inc.," *Boston Business Journal,* August 13, 1990, p. 30.

Rothstein, Linda, "Ready, Set, Irradiate," *Bulletin of the Atomic Scientists,* March 2000, p. 9.

Salkin, Stephanie, "Alliance to Offer Irradiated Meat," *ID: The Voice of Foodservice Distribution,* August 1999, p. 16.

Sculley, Sean, "Clash of the Titans," *Broadcasting & Cable,* April 19, 1993, p. 68.

Seavy, Mark, "Satellite Broadcast Battle," *HFD-The Weekly Home Furnishings Newspaper,* August 3, 1992, p. 66.

Siedsma, Andrea, "Going Global," *San Diego Business Journal,* May 8, 2000, p. 35.

——, "Titan Corp. Enjoys Titanic Growth," *San Diego Business Journal,* April 26, 1999, p. 1.

——, "Titan Soars Toward the Billion Dollar Club," *San Diego Business Journal,* March 27, 2000, p. 1.

Taylor, John, "Meatpackers Will Test Irradiated Beef," *Knight-Ridder/Tribune Business News,* April 14, 1999.

——, "San Diego-Based Firm Plans to Implement Irradiation in Iowa Meat Plant," *Knight-Ridder/Tribune Business News,* December 17, 1999.

Tetzeli, Rick, "Cargo That Phones Home," *Fortune,* November 15, 1993, p. 143.

"Titan Buys Product Line of Santa Clara Company," *San Diego Business Journal,* January 27, 1992, p. 19.

"The Titan Corp.," *San Diego Business Journal,* October 16, 1995, p. 35.

"The Titan Corp.," *San Diego Business Journal,* September 6, 1999, p. 41.

"Titan, Houston Satellite Joint Venture Ends," *HFD-The Weekly Home Furnishings Newspaper,* March 15, 1993, p. 104.

"Titan Wins Wyoming Project," *PC Week,* October 5, 1998, p. 82.

Wood, Christopher, "Denver Romances Titan Corp.," *Denver Business Journal,* September 25, 1992, p. 1.

—David P. Bianco

UNISYS

Unisys Corporation

Unisys Way
Blue Bell, Pennsylvania 19424
U.S.A.
Telephone: (215) 986-4011
Fax: (215) 986-2312
Web site: http://www.unisys.com

Public Company
Incorporated: 1886 as American Arithmometer Company
Employees: 35,800
Sales: $7.54 billion (1999)
Stock Exchanges: New York Amsterdam Brussels
  London Switzerland
Ticker Symbol: UIS
NAIC: 334111 Electronic Computer Manufacturing;
  334112 Computer Storage Device Manufacturing;
  334113 Computer Terminal Manufacturing; 334119
  Other Computer Peripheral Equipment Manufacturing;
  511210 Software Publishers; 541512 Computer
  Systems Design Services; 541519 Other Computer
  Related Services

Unisys Corporation is a major provider of computer-related services and technologies to customers in the financial services, communications, transportation, publishing, commercial, and government sectors, in more than 100 countries. The company offers an integrated suite of products and services known as Unisys e-@ction Solutions designed to help its customers meet the challenges and seize upon the opportunities of the Internet economy. Unisys provides consulting, systems integration, and outsourcing services; designs, implements, and maintains computer networks and multivendor information systems; and manufactures high-end, mission-critical servers for such organizations as the NASDAQ and the New York Clearinghouse.

Adding Machine Origins

Unisys, formed from the 1986 merger of the Burroughs Corporation with Sperry Corporation, traces its origins to over 100 years before that; in 1885, William Seward Burroughs invented the first recording adding machine. Burroughs called his device an arithmometer and the next year he and three partners founded the American Arithmometer Company in St. Louis, Missouri. Creating a commercially viable version proved difficult; Burroughs was unable to patent a salable model until 1892. Once on the market though, the adding machine became a success—in 1897 Burroughs was awarded the Franklin Institute's John Scott Medal in honor of his invention. Burroughs died of tuberculosis the next year, however, sadly before realizing much profit from his invention. The company, which moved to Detroit in 1905, was renamed the Burroughs Adding Machine Company in his memory.

During the early years of the 20th century, Burroughs consolidated a position in the adding machine business by acquiring both Universal Adding Machine and Pike Adding Machine in 1908, and Moon-Hopkins Billing Machine in 1921. By 1914 the company offered 90 different types of data-processing machines which, with the help of interchangeable parts, could be modified into 600 different configurations. Accountants formed the core customer base, and in 1917 Burroughs increased courtship of those customers with the debut of a magazine devoted to accounting called *Burroughs Clearing House*. By the 1920s Burroughs was an established mainstay of the office-machine industry and remained so for the next three decades, with adding machines still at the heart of the product line.

1950s: Expanding into Computers

All of that changed, however, as a result of J. Presper Eckert and John W. Mauchly's invention of ENIAC, the first electronic computer, in 1946. At first the market for computers appeared to be limited to a handful of government agencies that used them for large-scale number crunching. The only companies to commit themselves to computer research and development were large electronics and office-machine firms for whom the computer was a natural extension. When the Defense Department awarded the design contract for the new SAGE early-warning computer system in 1952, Burroughs, IBM, RCA, Remington Rand, and Sylvania were all prime choices. IBM won, giving that company an advantage competitors struggled to overcome.

Company Perspectives:

What makes Unisys unique in its ability to serve tens of thousands of customers worldwide?

Our people.

Unisys people have the creativity, technical excellence, tenacity, and can-do spirit to help our clients solve their business problems. In more than 100 countries around the world, leading financial services institutions, airlines, communications providers, commercial market leaders, and government agencies rely on Unisys. We help them apply information technology to streamline operations . . . anticipate and adapt to change . . . attract and retain new clients . . . enable executives to make informed decisions . . . support front-line employees responding to customer needs . . . and achieve new levels of competitiveness and success.

Burroughs did not immediately plunge wholeheartedly into computer technology, preferring, along with Sperry Rand's UNIVAC unit, NCR, Control Data, and Honeywell, to keep up with IBM during the 1950s. At the end of the decade Burroughs's reputation was still, in the words of a *Time* magazine correspondent, that of "a stodgy old-line adding machine maker." Even so, in 1952 the company developed an add-on memory for Eckert and Mauchly's ENIAC. The following year the company name was shortened to Burroughs Corporation, in recognition of its diversification. In 1956 Burroughs introduced its first commercial electronic computer and acquired ElectroData Corporation, a leading maker of high-speed computers. Burroughs also entered the field of automated office machines, introducing the Sensitronic electronic bank bookkeeping machine in 1958.

Burroughs entered the computer field during the tenure of John Coleman, whose last major act as president was to negotiate a partnership agreement between his company's computer operations and those of RCA, which was also looking for a way to catch up to IBM through a pooling of financial resources. RCA approved the agreement in 1959, but Coleman died before he could sway Burroughs's board of directors and the plan was never realized. Business historian Robert Sobel wrote that the Burroughs-RCA partnership might have produced "the best possible challenger for IBM."

1960s Through Early 1980s: Struggling to Compete with IBM

Coleman was succeeded by executive vice-president Ray Eppert. Under Eppert, Burroughs expanded its place in the rapidly growing bank-automation market in 1960, as the company began selling magnetic inks and automatic check-sorting equipment. In 1961 the company introduced the B5000 computer, which was less expensive and simpler to operate than other commercial mainframes. Expansion and diversification during the early years of the computer age led to a fourfold increase in sales between 1948 and 1960, from $94 million to $389 million. At the same time, however, increased research and development costs cut profit margins, a problem the company struggled with until the late 1960s.

Despite this surge in earnings, Burroughs remained among the smallest of IBM's main competitors in the early 1960s. Although the B5000's distinctive design had earned a solid following, Burroughs's computer product line remained narrow and the company was still too dependent on accounting machines. Research and development costs continued hacking away at profit margins, leaving the company's future clouded.

In 1964 Ray Macdonald became executive vice-president and began overseeing the company's day-to-day operations. With the help of several like-minded executives, he took control of Burroughs from Eppert and committed the company to a course of steady profit growth through cost cutting. Macdonald succeeded Eppert as CEO in 1967. Burroughs's financial performance continued improving and the company became a Wall Street favorite before the decade was out.

The Defense Department awarded Burroughs a contract in 1967 to build the Illiac IV supercomputer which had been designed by a team at the University of Illinois—a major coup for the company. The Illiac IV was ten to 20 times faster than any existing supercomputer in 1972 and was delivered to NASA's Ames Research Center in California. The sudden lag in research and development created by Macdonald's policy of cutting costs also contributed to two significant technical failures around this time. The B8500 mainframe, which had been scheduled for delivery in 1967, had to be scrapped altogether in 1968, after Burroughs engineers realized they could not produce reliable components at a reasonable price. The B6500 was riddled with breakdowns caused by the development team's strategy for bringing the project in on time and under budget—namely, cutting corners in the high-speed circuitry design and neglecting to test the completed machines properly before delivery.

An interesting aspect of Macdonald's stewardship was his reemphasis on accounting machines as an integral part of Burroughs's product line. Foremost among his talents was a genius for salesmanship; the company won a considerable chunk of the high-speed accounting machines market from rival NCR. In 1974 Burroughs entered the facsimile equipment business, acquiring Graphic Services for $30 million. The next year the company paid $8.8 million for Redactron, a maker of automatic typewriters and computer-related equipment.

Ray Macdonald retired in 1977 and was replaced by Paul Mirabito, his hand-picked successor. During Mirabito's brief tenure, the consequences of Macdonald's fiscal policies began manifesting themselves in earnest. In 1979 IBM announced a powerful new generation of computer systems. Burroughs countered by announcing its own new series of systems. Unfortunately, although Burroughs's design ideas were good, the company did not have the development or manufacturing resources to translate them into actual computers. Burroughs's inability to deliver finished products resulted in an embarrassing stream of canceled orders. Years of salary cuts and other forms of budget-tightening had engendered low morale among field engineers and a reputation for poor service among clients. Customer complaints came to a head in 1981, when 129 Burroughs users sued the company over product unreliability and difficulty in getting their machines fixed.

Mirabito had retired in 1979 and was replaced by W. Michael Blumenthal, the former chairman of Bendix and secretary

Blumenthal concentrated on Burroughs's computer business in an effort to secure the position of the largest of IBM's U.S. competitors. In 1981 the company covered one weak spot by acquiring System Development Corporation, a software development firm, for $9.6 million. Burroughs also procured Memorex that year, maker of disc drives and other data-storage equipment, for $85.2 million, despite Memorex's shaky financial condition. These moves added $1 billion to the company's annual sales.

Mid-1980s: Burroughs + Sperry = Unisys

Blumenthal eventually decided that economies of scale were necessary to compete with IBM. In 1985 Burroughs launched a $65-per-share takeover bid, worth $3.7 billion, for Sperry Corporation. Sperry had been a takeover candidate since holding unsuccessful merger talks with ITT in March 1984. The Sperry board of directors and investors, from whom Burroughs hoped to obtain shares, balked at the offer, though, and the deal fell through. Burroughs came back with a $70-per-share bid, worth $4.1 billion, in May 1986, and a four-week battle ensued. Sperry executives, anxious to preserve the company's independence, argued against selling out. The board put up a defense that included an $80-per-share stock buyback offer while casting about for a white knight. Sperry eventually agreed to a $76.50-per-share deal worth $4.8 billion—at the time, by far the largest merger in the history of the computer industry and one of the largest in U.S. corporate history. The resulting company was the second largest computer firm in the nation, leapfrogging over Digital Equipment Corporation.

Sperry, which was founded in 1933 but traced its roots back to the 1910-formed Sperry Gyroscope Co., originally made aircraft instruments. In 1955 the manufacturer jumped into the computer business, merging with Remington Rand, whose history dated back farther than Burroughs or Sperry. In 1873 E. Remington & Sons, forerunner of Remington Typewriter Co., introduced the first commercially successful typewriter. After producing the first ''noiseless'' typewriter in 1909, Remington introduced the first electric typewriter in the United States in 1925. Two years later, Remington Typewriter merged with Rand Kardex to form Remington Rand. The latter introduced the world's first business computer, the 409, in 1949. The following year, Remington Rand acquired Eckert-Mauchly Corporation, the company founded by the developers of the ENIAC and the UNIVAC. The 1955 merger of Sperry and Remington Rand resulted in Sperry Rand, which quickly became one of the industry's leading companies due to its technical prowess and by the 1960s had gained a reputation for wonderful products. At the same time Sperry had inherited a legacy of poor management and marketing from Remington Rand. By the time Burroughs showed interest, the renamed Sperry Corporation had profitable defense-electronics operations, but a struggling computer business.

Six months after the acquisition, the combined company adopted the name Unisys Corporation. The moniker was selected from suggestions submitted by Burroughs and Sperry employees and was conceived as a synthesis of the words ''United Information Systems.'' But the real work of fusing the two companies still remained. Over the next two years the Unisys workforce was reduced by 20 percent—24,000 of the 121,000 positions were

---

Key Dates:

1873: E. Remington & Sons, forerunner of Remington Typewriter Co., introduces the first commercially successful typewriter.

1885: William Seward Burroughs invents the first recording adding machine, the arithmometer.

1886: Burroughs and partners found the American Arithmometer Company.

1905: American Arithmometer is renamed the Burroughs Adding Machine Company.

1910: Sperry Gyroscope Co. is formed as a maker of aircraft instruments.

1925: Remington introduces the first electric typewriter in the United States.

1927: Remington merges with Rand Kardex to form Remington Rand.

1933: Sperry Corporation is formed.

1946: J. Presper Eckert and John W. Mauchly invent ENIAC, the first electronic computer.

1949: Remington Rand introduces the world's first business computer, the 409.

1950: Eckert and Mauchly found Eckert-Mauchly Corporation, which is acquired later in the year by Remington Rand.

1953: Burroughs Adding Machine is renamed Burroughs Corporation.

1955: Sperry merges with Remington Rand to form Sperry Rand.

1956: Burroughs introduces its first commercial electronic computer and acquires high-speed computer maker ElectroData.

1961: Burroughs introduces the B5000 computer.

1986: Burroughs and Sperry merge to form Unisys Corporation.

1987: Unisys acquires Convergent Technologies, maker of office workstations.

1991: Company settles its role in a Pentagon procurement scandal by pleading guilty to fraud and bribery and agreeing to pay $190 million in damages, penalties, and fines.

1992: Company forms a unit dedicated to providing information technology services.

1996: ClearPath line of computers is introduced.

1999: The Unisys e-@ction Solutions suite of integrated hardware and services is unveiled.

---

of treasury in the Carter administration—a move that surprised many industry observers. Blumenthal took over a company that was deceptively profitable, chalking up record sales of $2.8 billion in 1979. He immediately set about shaking up Burroughs's corporate culture, firing veteran executives and replacing them with his own appointees, phasing out the adding machine and calculator businesses, implementing a plan to improve repair service, and discontinuing accounting practices that tended to inflate earnings. Blumenthal's reforms did not come without cost, however; in July 1980, the company reported its first drop in quarterly profits in 17 years.

eliminated—while unwanted and redundant businesses were placed on the market in order to generate cash. In December 1986, Unisys sold Sperry Aerospace to Honeywell and later sold off Memorex's marketing arm.

Late 1980s and Early 1990s: Sinking Fortunes and a Turnaround

Meanwhile Unisys stepped up diversification of its product line. In 1987 Unisys obtained Timeplex, a high-tech communications equipment company, for $300 million, and Convergent Technologies, a maker of office workstations, for $351 million. By 1989 the company had begun to move into the small and mid-sized computer market, adopting AT&T's popular Unix operating system as the standard configuration for Unisys machines. In 1989 Unisys also began manufacturing its own personal computers for the first time.

Unisys was not entirely successful in the late 1980s, however. Despite strong earnings growth from the time of the Sperry deal through 1988, the company posted a loss of nearly $100 million in the first quarter of 1989. Management shakeups in 1987 had resulted in the departure of two key executives— vice-chairman Joseph Kroger, the former president of Sperry who commanded intense loyalty from former Sperry employees, and Paul G. Stern, a physicist whom Blumenthal had brought into the company from IBM and made president and chief operating officer in 1982. Sluggish sales, manufacturing cost overruns, and fierce price competition among the many companies using the Unix system all cut into revenues.

Unisys also found itself caught up in the Pentagon procurement scandal of 1988. Federal prosecutors brought charges against some Unisys executives—including former vice-president Charles Gaines, who headed the Washington, D.C., office of one of the company's defense units—with fraud, bribing Defense Department officials into yielding classified procurement documents, and making illegal campaign contributions to members of Congress; these activities allegedly occurred at Sperry prior to the merger. Unisys had already begun an internal investigation when the government made the accusations public. According to Paul Mann of *Aviation Week & Space Technology,* the company settled its part in the Operation Ill Wind court case in September 1991, pleading guilty to fraud and bribery and agreeing to pay a record of up to $190 million in damages, penalties, and fines. In the same article, James A. Unruh, who succeeded Blumenthal in 1990, was quoted as saying, "we as a company must accept responsibility for the past actions of a few people, even though today we have a completely different management team and different shareholders."

Unisys's difficulties continued and deepened in the early 1990s, with much of the troubles easily traced back to the merger of Burroughs and Sperry. The operations of the two companies had never been properly integrated, leaving duplicate R&D, marketing, and accounting departments. Already saddled with a huge debt load from the 1986 merger, Unisys was forced to take on an additional $1.4 billion in debt to cover negative cash flow, as the company's mainframe computers were quickly losing market share to IBM and Amdahl. The company's stock, which sold for about $50 in 1987, collapsed to a low of $1.75 during 1990. Unisys posted successive net losses of $639 million in 1989, $436 million in 1990, and $1.39 billion in 1991. Bankruptcy neared.

Amid a depressed global economy, Unruh managed to turn Unisys's fortunes around by 1992 through a draconian restructuring, the success of which surprised many observers. Unisys exacted additional drastic employee reductions, eliminating some 23,000 people from 1989 through 1991. At the end of 1991, the remaining Unisys workforce was roughly half the size of that at the time of the merger. An additional 6,000 jobs were cut in 1992, leaving a workforce of 54,300. Other major restructuring costs led Unisys to take massive charges of $1.2 billion in 1991, directly contributing to overall unprofitability for the year. These measures, however, were expected to reduce costs on an annual basis by approximately $800 million. In its aggressive drive to cut costs, Unisys reduced its 50,000-product line by 15,000 items, having determined that ten percent of its products were bringing in 90 percent of the revenue. Its mainframe computer lines were reduced from four to two (Sperry's 2200 series and Burroughs's A series). The Timeplex subsidiary, responsible for only a small fraction of overall revenues, was divested. The company shuttered seven of its 15 manufacturing facilities, and Unisys began concentrating on those market sectors where it was traditionally the strongest: banking, airlines, government, and communications. Debt was brought down to a more manageable $1.4 billion, from its peak of $3.5 billion.

This massive reengineering effort not only pulled Unisys from the brink of disaster, it also resulted in two solid years of financial performance: for 1992, net income of $361.2 million on sales of $8.7 billion, and for the following year, net income of $565.4 million on $7.74 billion in revenues. Unisys was much smaller—revenues had totaled $10.11 billion in 1990— but much more profitable.

Mid-1990s and Beyond: Shift to Services and Continued Restructuring

As the turnaround was taking shape, Unruh pushed the company in a new direction. With a clear shift taking place from mainframes to networked computing, Unruh moved to deemphasize the former through an expansion into computer services. Beginning in 1992 with the formation of a unit dedicated to providing information technology services, Unisys became active in the areas of systems consulting and design and systems integration services. One rationale behind the shift to services was that as computer systems grew ever more complex, in-house personnel were less and less able to cope, leading to a growing market for outside information technology expertise. Building on its existing mainframe maintenance activities, Unisys was able to generate $1.3 billion from services in 1992, then $2 billion the following year. By 1994 the company's "services and solutions" unit was generating more revenue than the mainstay mainframe hardware operations.

Unfortunately, Unisys's comeback proved short-lived. Services revenues were growing about 30 percent per year but the company had failed to make a profit from its new activities, losing about $54 million during 1995 alone. Part of a 1994 profit decline was attributed to a delay in getting the company's latest servers, the 550 and 580, to market. Another factor was a $186 million charge for a further restructuring of the mainframe operations, including a workforce reduction of 4,000 and the long overdue merging of the 2200 series and the A series into a single mainframe line. After the depressed profit figure of $100.5 million for 1994, Unisys posted a net loss of $624.6 million in 1995 thanks to a $717.6 million charge for another restructuring (the fifth in seven years). This time the company reorganized itself into three units: hardware and software, which included mainframes, servers, and a recent foray into PCs; maintenance and networking, which concentrated on servicing and connecting computers; and services, which involved consulting and outsourcing in integrated systems design. This restructuring also involved the paring of a few thousand more workers from the payroll and the consolidating of facilities and manufacturing, as well as the 1995 sale of its defense contracting unit to Loral for $862 million.

The following year Unisys introduced to positive market reaction the ClearPath line of computers, which combined proprietary mainframes with open systems capable of running standard Unix and Windows NT software and applications in a single system. In April 1996 Unruh managed to defeat Greenway Partners' proposal to shareholders for a breakup of Unisys into three parts. (Greenway held nearly a five percent stake in Unisys.) A similar breakup proposal one year later failed as well. In September 1997 Unruh stepped aside from his leadership position at Unisys, having kept the company alive but having never fully turned it around. The financial ups and downs and the frequent restructurings had left the remaining workforce demoralized. Nevertheless, most observers praised Unruh's shift into services, and during 1997 that unit finally turned its first profit.

Unruh helped select his successor, Lawrence A. Weinbach, former head of accounting and consulting giant Andersen Worldwide. The new chairman, CEO, and president immediately began working to improve employee morale, meeting with more than one-third of the workforce and revoking unpopular policies from recent austerity programs, such as the elimination of the company match on 401(k) contributions. Weinbach also initiated $1.04 billion in fourth-quarter 1997 charges, which resulted in a net loss for the year of $853.6 million. Some $900 million of the charges were to write down the value of goodwill left from the acquisition of Sperry, with the remainder going toward reducing debt. At year-end 1997 debt stood at $1.4 billion but was reduced to less than $1 billion by the end of 1999.

In addition to focusing on debt reduction, Weinbach moved Unisys out of the manufacturing of PCs and smaller servers. The company began outsourcing the manufacture of such hardware to Hewlett-Packard in 1998. He also jettisoned the company's three unit structure in favor of a simpler division between hardware, which would now focus on high-end servers and mainframes, and services, which included maintenance as well as consulting and systems design. On the hardware side, Unisys worked to upgrade its existing mainframe line, while also introducing in 1999 a mainframe-class server called the Unisys e-@ction ClearPath Enterprise Server, which was Intel microprocessor-based and ran Windows NT (later Windows 2000) software. This server was part of a comprehensive and integrated portfolio of hardware and services—known as Unisys e-@ction Solutions—that Unisys unveiled in 1999 to support the burgeoning e-business market. On the services side,

Unisys became more selective in the type of projects it took on, concentrating on key markets where it had the most expertise—including financial services, government, communications, transportation, and publishing.

By 1999, 70 percent of the company's revenues were being generated by the services operations. For the year, Unisys posted net income of $510.7 million on sales of $7.54 billion, its best year since 1993. It was difficult to predict whether this turnaround would last longer than that of the early 1990s. As Unisys's services side grew, profit increases were likely to be harder won, as its services business was markedly less profitable than its hardware side. Nevertheless, one possible avenue for early 21st-century growth was in international markets, and Unisys was seeking acquisitions to fuel an overseas push in services. In 1999 the company made several acquisitions, including Datamec, a Brazilian application outsourcing company, and City Lifeline Systems Limited, a U.K.-based provider of services and solutions for firms trading in fixed-income securities.

Principal Subsidiaries

Unisys Canada, Inc.; Unisys Australia Limited; Unisys New Zealand Limited; Unisys España S.A. (Spain); Unisys (Schweiz) A.G. (Switzerland); Unisys Osterreich Ges.m.b.H. (Austria); Unisys Belgium; Unisys Deutschland G.m.b.H. (Germany); Unisys Sudamericana S.A. (Argentina); Unisys Electronica Ltda. (Brazil); Datamec, S.A. (Brazil); Unisys France; Unisys Italia S.p.A. (Italy); Unisys Limited (U.K.); Unisys Nederland N.V. (Netherlands); Unisys de Mexico, S.A. de C.V.; Unisys Korea Limited; Unisys South Africa, Inc.; Unisys de Colombia, S.A.; Unisys World Trade, Inc.

Principal Competitors

Amdahl Corporation; American Management Systems, Incorporated; Andersen Consulting; AT&T Corp.; British Telecommunications plc; Bull; Cap Gemini Ernst & Young; Compaq Computer Corporation; Computer Sciences Corporation; DecisionOne Holdings Corp.; Dell Computer Corporation; Electronic Data Systems Corporation; Ernst & Young International; Fujitsu Limited; Getronics NV; Hewlett-Packard Company; Hitachi, Ltd.; InaCom Corp.; International Business Machines Corporation; International Computers Limited; NCR Corporation; Perot Systems Corporation; PricewaterhouseCoopers; Sabre Inc.; Siemens AG; Silicon Graphics, Inc.; Sun Microsystems, Inc.

Further Reading

"At Last, Sperry Leaps into the Office," *Business Week,* November 8, 1982, pp. 124+.

Barrett, Amy, "Unisys Aims for the Top of the Tree: Will Weinbach's New Push Erase Its Second-Tier Status?," *Business Week,* November 9, 1998, p. 138.

——, "Unisys—Has It Hit Bottom?," *Financial World,* November 28, 1989, p. 16.

Benoit, Ellen, "All Dressed Up," *Forbes,* March 24, 1986, pp. 106+.

Bock, Gordon, and Russell Mitchell, "How Burroughs Finally Won Sperry," *Business Week,* June 9, 1986, pp. 28+.

Bulkeley, William M., "Unisys, Back from the Edge, Stresses Service, Comfort," *Wall Street Journal,* April 22, 1999, p. B4.

——, "Unisys Expects Profit to Trail Forecasts," *Wall Street Journal,* June 30, 2000, p. B6.

Byrne, John A., "Univacuum," *Forbes,* June 6, 1983, pp. 156+.

"Can Burroughs Catch Up Again?," *Forbes,* March 28, 1983, pp. 78+.

Carey, David, "Once Is Not Enough," *Financial World,* July 12, 1988, pp. 22+.

England, Robert Stowe, "A Bet Against: Whither Mainframes? At Unisys, James Unruh Is Betting the Company That Their Future Is Bleak," *Financial World,* August 1, 1995, pp. 46–48.

——, "Ugly Duckling," *Financial World,* October 12, 1993, pp. 36–37.

Hooper, Laurence, "Unruh Saves Unisys, Now Aims to Put It on Cutting Edge," *Wall Street Journal,* September 25, 1992, p. B4.

Linden, Dana Wechsler, "The Bean Counter As Hero," *Forbes,* October 11, 1993, pp. 46+.

"The Long Road Back for Burroughs," *Business Week,* May 18, 1981, pp. 119+.

Macdonald, Ray W., *Strategy for Growth: The Story of Burroughs Corporation,* New York: Newcomen Society in North America, 1978, 28 p.

Mann, Paul, "Unisys Admits Bribery and Fraud, Will Pay Record $190 Million Fine," *Aviation Week & Space Technology,* September 16, 1991.

Mitchell, Russell, "Unisys: So Far, So Good—but the Real Test Is Yet to Come," *Business Week,* March 2, 1987, pp. 84+.

Mitchell, Russell, and Gordon Bock, "Can Burroughs Break Out of the Bunch in the Mainframe Race?," *Business Week,* December 9, 1985, pp. 78+.

Narisetti, Raju, "Campaign at Unisys Emphasizes Firm's Vigor in Bid for New Image," *Wall Street Journal,* September 24, 1998, p. B12.

——, "Unisys's New Chairman Is Bullish Despite Slow Sales: Weinbach's Plan Calls for Paring Debt and Relying on New Technologies," *Wall Street Journal,* January 7, 1998, p. B12.

Narisetti, Raju, Joann S. Lublin, and Elizabeth Macdonald, "Unisys Bets on Weinbach, Top Manager, Names Him As Chief to Turn It Around," *Wall Street Journal,* September 24, 1997, p. B5.

Petre, Peter, "The Struggle over Sperry's Future," *Fortune,* December 9, 1985, pp. 78+.

Reingold, Jennifer, "Unisys: Nobody Said Diversifying Was Easy," *Business Week,* July 15, 1996, p. 32.

Reingold, Jennifer, and Phillip L. Zweig, "Can He Stop the Unisys Slide?," *Business Week,* June 3, 1996, pp. 64–67.

"Sperry: Pouring Its Resources into High-Growth Products," *Business Week,* February 15, 1982, pp. 80+.

"Unisys Posts $48M Net," *Electronic News,* April 27, 1992.

Unisys Profile, Blue Bell, Penn.: Unisys Corporation, 1989.

Uttal, Bro., "The Blumenthal Revival at Burroughs," *Fortune,* October 5, 1981, pp. 128+.

——, "How Ray Macdonald's Growth Theory Created IBM's Toughest Competitor," *Fortune,* January 1977.

——, "A Surprisingly Sexy Computer Marriage," *Fortune,* November 24, 1986, pp. 46+.

Verity, John W., and Joseph Weber, "So Far, Married Life Seems to Agree with Unisys," *Business Week,* October 3, 1988, p. 123.

Weber, Joseph, "This Is Hardly the Turning Point Unisys Had in Mind," *Business Week,* August 28, 1989, pp. 82+.

——, "Unisys: Out of the Bleak and into the Black," *Business Week,* June 8, 1992.

Ziegler, Bart, and Joann S. Lublin, "Task at Unisys Isn't for 'Faint of Heart' As Unruh Confirms Plans to Step Down," *Wall Street Journal,* June 20, 1997, p. B6.

—Douglas Sun and Jay P. Pederson
—updated by David E. Salamie

United Way
of America

United Way of America

701 North Fairfax Street
Alexandria, Virginia 22314-1045
U.S.A.
Telephone: (703) 836-7100
Toll Free: (800) 411-UWAY; (800) 411-8829
Fax: (703) 836-5276
Web site: http://www.unitedway.org

Nonprofit Company
Founded: 1887 as Charity Organizations Society
Employees: 10,000
Contributions: $3.77 billion (1999)
NAIC: 813212 Voluntary Health Organizations; 813211
    Charitable Trusts, Awarding Grants

United Way of America (UWA) is a charitable organization with the simple goal of enabling people to help one another in any and all circumstances. Operating over 1,400 individual United Way chapters throughout the United States, UWA also works with more than 45,000 humanitarian groups, setting standards for fund collection, coordinating activities, and making recommendations for disbursal of donations. Through its innovative use of corporate payroll deductions (collected by the local chapters), United Way keeps operating expenses to a minimum, well below the usual administrative costs allowed for charitable organizations. Though plagued by a management scandal in 1992, UWA has remained at the forefront of emergency relief services for more than 100 years.

In the Beginning: 1887–1949

Charity has always begun in the hearts of the well-intentioned; the origins of the United Way of America chapters throughout the United States were no exception. This particular organization can be traced back to several disparate societies, the earliest of which was the Charity Organizations Society, founded in Denver, Colorado, in 1887. Several related groups began distributing goodwill both nearby and in other cities and states, operating under various names yet with the same goals. By 1888 the Denver outfit had organized its first campaign and raised $21,700 for its causes, an impressive amount of money at the time.

In 1894 when a federal act decreed that for-profit companies must pay taxes, charitable groups or nonprofit agencies received a major coup—tax exemption. With relief from any tax burden, nonprofit groups flourished; however, the tax-free status attracted a number of unsavory characters, who had no intentions of dispersing their funds for altruistic purposes. These imitators led to the creation of the Committee on Benevolent Associations, formed by the Chamber of Commerce in Cleveland, Ohio, in 1900. This committee was the earliest attempt to regulate charitable and philanthropic endeavors, to set clear guidelines, and to safeguard the interests of both those contributing and those receiving funds.

Over the next several years, after the reelection and assassination of President McKinley and into the Teddy Roosevelt years, charitable organizations grew rapidly around the country. In Chicago alone, there were over 3,000 registered charities by 1905; in 1913 the first Community Chest was formed, a name brought to instant fame by the wildly popular Parker Bros. *Monopoly* game, in which players were given a yellow card for landing on the "Community Chest" space. The cards either rewarded players with cash gifts or sought "a donation" for various community-related projects.

As nonprofit agencies blossomed, so did efforts at self-regulation. Through a number of committees and associations, including the Associated Charities (founded 1908), the National Association of Societies for Organizing Charity (1911), the National Information Bureau (1918), and the American Association for Community Organizations (1918), standards and policies continued to evolve. The American Association for Community Organizations (AACO), created by the leaders of 12 charitable groups in Chicago to gain a clearer focus into community planning and the role of social work, was considered the breeding ground of what led to the formation of the United Way of America. Those involved with the AACO set in motion the critical tenets and goals of what a charitable organization should be, and how such goals should be met.

If World War I and its aftermath gave humanitarian groups a sobering glimpse into the depths of human suffering, the onset of the Great Depression was a panoramic view of despair. Charity was in high demand and those who freely contributed in the past found themselves hard put to donate much of anything.

Company Perspectives:

The mission of the United Way movement is to increase the organized capacity of people to care for one another.

Even after the United States recovered, and a majority of Americans were back on their feet, sharper, deeper lines had been drawn between the haves and the have-nots. United Way chapters struggled to provide for their constituents, and relief was ironically provided by another declaration of war. World War II production fueled the nation's economy in the 1940s; in the postwar years, with the Baby Boom and widespread financial security, the urgent need for charity itself declined while donations from both corporations and individuals increased.

A Larger Focus: 1950–89

As the 1950s ended and the 1960s began, charitable agencies continued to evolve on local, state, and national levels. More service organizations were created to safeguard the altruistic from the malevolent, including the National Council on Community Foundations (later renamed the Council on Foundations in 1964), the Institute of Community Studies (which evolved into the Management and Community Studies Institute), the Commerce and Industry Combined Health Appeal, and the National Budget and Consultation Committee (made up from combining the American Way Community Services and the Joint Budget Committee of the Community Chests and Councils). From this conjoined council came the 1963 publication *Standards for National Voluntary Health, Welfare, and Recreations Agencies,* a much needed procedural for the ever-growing nonprofit societies popping up across the country. In the same year the procedural came out, more than two dozen Community Chests and United Fund chapters in Los Angeles, California, joined forces and officially began using the name United Way, Inc.

Two presidential proclamations—the first in 1957 from President Eisenhower and the second in 1963 from President Kennedy—allowed charitable groups to receive contributions from federal employees. The earliest executive order created the Uniform Federal Fund-Raising Program, permitting federal employee gift-giving to local accredited groups; the second presidential edict broadened the network of health and welfare agencies eligible to receive gifts from federal employees. In 1964 United Way chapters declared a "War on Poverty" and instituted various programs to combat hunger in the United States. Help for the crusade came from the newly initiated federal employee payroll deduction plan, while the charitable groups eligible for these deductions (those originally instituted under Presidents Eisenhower and Kennedy) merged to form the Combined Federal Campaign (CFC).

By the mid-1960s United Way was a well known organization with more than 30,000 affiliated agencies nationwide, and sought consolidation and cooperation from the federal government and national groups. To promote these goals, the *Statement of Consensus on Government and Voluntary Sector in Health and Welfare* was issued. By 1967 the population of the United States totaled more than 195.8 million people, with an entire generation in turmoil over the Vietnam War. War supporters marched down Fifth Avenue in New York City, antiwar demonstrators gathered at the Lincoln Memorial, and United Way agencies managed to collect more than $700 million through its 31,300 individual agencies across the country. Funds were distributed to more than 27 million families in need.

The onset of the next decade found United Way's national governing body, the United Community Funds and Council of America (UCFCA), reorganizing itself into the streamlined and more simply named United Way of America (UWA) in 1970. At the same time, William Aramony was appointed to head the group, and he brought forth the "Thirteen Point Program for Rebirth and Renewal of United Way." The new program's purpose included attracting more volunteers on local, regional, and national levels, as well as raising public awareness of just what the United Way chapters did and for whom. Additionally, in an effort to bring uniformity to its many chapters, UWA leaders passed a resolution to discontinue use of names other than "United Way," and the national headquarters moved from New York City to Alexandria, Virginia.

In 1973, two years after relocating from New York to Virginia, UWA scored a major coup in public promotion of its goals by partnering with the National Football League (NFL). Players and coaches made public service announcements about their involvement with United Way chapters, and these associations brought widespread attention to UWA's programs. The NFL exposure helped UWA garner support and initiate the "Program for the Future," in which national goals were transcribed for use at local levels in 1976. A year later, the Program for the Future's success led to annual contributions of more than $1 billion for the first time. Leaders of the UWA agencies continued to plan for the future and identified five areas in which to concentrate their efforts: inclusiveness, area-wide services, volunteers and public policies, agency relations, and personalization of services.

Always Ready to Help: 1980s–1993

With the emergence of another decade came diversified goals within the charity sector. Programs to deal with newer issues affecting the country, including environmental concerns and societal pressures on women and minorities, were instituted. As UWA's focus became more all-encompassing, its member agencies' money-raising abilities increased as well; nationally more than $1.68 billion was raised in 1981, amounting to the highest single-year increase in funds (more than ten percent over 1980). In 1982 the organization opened its new National Service and Training Center in Alexandria, with all costs covered by a $4 million fundraiser sponsored by John V. James, chairman of Dresser Industries, and John R. Opel, chairman and CEO of IBM. At the same time, a Volunteer Leadership Development Program was established to educate and train group leaders to maximize their skills.

Both new programs came in handy when the government established FEMA (Federal Emergency Management Agency) in 1983 with an initial $50 million grant, followed by a subsequent grant of $40 million a few months later. Charged with the responsibility of managing FEMA funds, UWA created a national board with its own representatives as well as those from

Key Dates:

1887: The Charity Organizations Society is formed in Denver, Colorado.

1888: First money-raising campaign, United Way, raises over $21,000.

1894: Federal act exempts charitable organizations from taxes.

1957: Uniform Federal Fund-Raising Program initiated by President Eisenhower.

1963: Several Los Angeles, California-based organizations come together under the name United Way, Inc.

1977: United Way agencies top the billion-dollar mark in donations.

1970: William Aramony becomes president; national agencies reorganize and become the United Way of America (UWA).

1971: Headquarters moves from New York City to Alexandria, Virginia.

1973: United Way alliance with the NFL begins.

1983: FEMA (Federal Emergency Management Agency) is founded and overseen by United Way and five other charitable groups.

1984: Nationwide donations top $2 billion.

1990: Donations top $3 billion.

1992: Aramony resigns and is indicted for fraud and mismanagement of funds; Elaine L. Chao is installed as first female president and CEO.

1996: Chao resigns and Aramony files a lawsuit.

1997: Betty Stanley Beene is installed as president and CEO.

1999: Annual contributions exceed $3.7 billion.

five other nonprofit groups, so funds could be administered on an as-needed basis to local agencies throughout the United States.

By the middle of the 1980s UWA had come a long way from its humble origins in Colorado. What had begun as a handful of like-minded charitable agencies had become a multifaceted alliance of thousands, united in purpose and achievement. In 1985 contributors anted up an amazing $2.33 billion, up some nine percent from the previous year and just eight years from first topping the billion-dollar mark. As the organization approached its 100-year anniversary in 1987, it published a treatise called *Rethinking the Future and Beyond.* The tome discussed UWA's current focus as well as thoughts for its second hundred years and beyond. During its centennial year, the U.S. Postal Service honored UWA with a commemorative stamp as more than 3,000 gathered in the nation's capital for the Centennial Volunteer Leaders Conference. In addition, UWA established a program for young people called the Young Leaders Conference.

Continuing its focus on America's youth, UWA gave gifts totaling more than $100,000 to youth volunteer programs in four cities across the United States (Galesburg, Illinois; Tucson, Arizona; Tulsa, Oklahoma; and West Palm Beach, Florida) in 1987. Two years later, northern and central California were devastated by an earthquake, and UWA led the emergency

services. Local chapters not only coordinated operations with FEMA teams but brought in major contributions from the NFL ($1.25 million), Sony Corporation ($1 million), and scores of concerned Americans.

With the debut of the 1990s, UWA was again putting its ideals and beliefs on paper, this time in a publication entitled *Mobilizing a Caring America: Principles for the 1990s.* The 103-year-old organization was definitely doing something right: Americans donated more $3 billion dollars to UWA chapters in 1990, just in time for the next imbroglio, the outbreak of the Gulf War in 1991. UWA set up an Operations Center and coordinated services with the U.S. military, as well as other groups such as the American Red Cross and USO.

The early 1990s, however, also brought controversy to the UWA. In 1992, William Aramony resigned as president, and the post was temporarily filled by Kenneth W. Dam. Aramony was under investigation for fraud and mismanagement of funds, and the organization underwent intense scrutiny for its overall policies and dealings, as well as specific transactions with seven agencies that had been spun off in recent times. After soliciting suggestions from some 6,000 UWA volunteers throughout the country and outside counsel, UWA's Board of Governors voted for sweeping changes and reformed much of the organization's financial operations. The Board itself was expanded to 45 members, 15 of whom were United Way representatives, and a new president and CEO was installed: Elaine L. Chao, a former director of the Peace Corps. Chao was UWA's first woman president, as well as its first Asian American director.

Next came the trial of Aramony and two codefendants. All were found guilty in 1995, with Aramony convicted on 25 counts of fraud, filing false tax returns, conspiracy, and money laundering. Sentenced to seven years in prison, three years probation, and a fine of over $550,000, Aramony vowed to appeal (which he did, unsuccessfully). Though UWA suffered a black eye from the extensive publicity, the organization was soon back doing what it did best when much of the Midwest was ravaged by floods, though with noticeably less in donations. After the Aramony scandal, contributions fell to their lowest point since World War II, and many United Way chapters withdrew from the national organization, though most would later return. To boost its public image, UWA initiated several new programs, including ''SkyWish'' with Delta Airlines, wherein travelers donated frequent flyer mileage to critically ill patients in need of life-saving transportation.

1994 and Beyond

The middle and late years of the decade found UWA investing in technological advances and promoting the organization through its first major advertising campaign. Temerlin McCain of Irving, Texas, donated the time and effort necessary to create UWA's latest ''helping hands'' logo, as well as the catchphrase ''Reaching those who need help. Touching us all.'' Fortunately for UWA, Aramony's trial and sentencing had faded from the memory of most Americans, and by 1994 the organization was named as *Financial World*'s leading charity. The following year, 1995, UWA was involved in the torch relays for the Atlanta Olympics and published *Strategic Direction for United Way: Charting the Path for Building Better Communities,* outlining plans for the future. Then came another catastrophic event requiring the expertise of UWA's many dedicated volunteers: the Oklahoma City bombing. UWA agencies not only helped survivors and the families of victims, but sent a technology team to the premises as well.

The national UWA organization received a jolt in 1996 when Aramony filed a $5 million lawsuit for earnings and retirement benefits he claimed were due to him. Moreover, Elaine Chao resigned as president and CEO. Chao was replaced by Betty Stanley Beene, formerly the chief executive of Tri-State (New York) United Ways chapters. As Beene took the reigns in 1997, there were 4,400 UWA chapters across the United States, and the organization had gone global with a UWA web site (www.unitedway.org) and United Way Online for use by its local agencies. The next year, 1998, UWA and the NFL celebrated 25 years of collaboration, an alliance that had brought recognition to both parties. The cost of the commercial air time—donated by the NFL before, during, and after televised games—was worth upwards of $1 billion; the exposure had been priceless. Additionally, another humanitarian-themed postage stamp was unveiled by the U.S. Postal Service, with the words "Giving & Sharing: An American Tradition" printed on the stamp.

As the century came to a close, UWA was stronger than ever, with leadership programs for all ages and agencies working to conquer need on all levels of society. For its efforts on behalf of children UWA was given two remarkable gifts from the Bank of America Foundation, the first for $10 million, followed by a second grant for $40 million, with the latter being one of the largest corporate grants ever. Annual contributions also hit another all-time high, with donations totaling more than $3.5 billion for 1998 and $3.77 billion for 1999, due in large part to support from individuals (Bill Gates, Infoseek's Steve Kirsch, and Alexis de Tocqueville Society members) and such corporations as Bank of America, Boeing Company, General Motors Corporation, IBM, J.C. Penney Company, Pfizer, United Parcel Service, and Wal-Mart Stores. In 2000, Beene announced that she would step down from her leadership role at UWA in 2001. The organization's Board of Governors announced, in turn, that it would begin looking for a replacement and would also perform its own extensive review of the organization's structure and governance system. Specifically, UWA hoped to study ways in which the concept of community in the United States was changing, and sought, according to a press release, "to evolve from community fundraiser for health and human services to catalyst for achieving real change in the quality of life in communities."

Principal Competitors

American Red Cross; Goodwill Industries International, Inc.; The Salvation Army USA.

Further Reading

"Aramony Trial Date Set for February," *Fund Raising Management*, November 1994, p. 8.

"Best Buy and United Way to Launch After-School Music Program," *Business Wire,* June 1, 2000.

Clifford, Sarah, "Charity: When Big Is Better," *Inc.*, Feb 1987, p. 11.

Gabor, Andrea, "Fundraising in Trying Times; James Robinson of American Express on Marketing United Way," *U.S. News & World Report*, May 4, 1987, p. 53.

Galper, Joseph, "Generosity By the Numbers," *American Demographics*, August 1998, p. 24.

Gattuso, Greg, "How Much Is Too Much?," *Fund Raising Management*, October 1996, p. 3.

——, "1992 Giving to United Way Dips 4.1 Percent," *Fund Raising Management*, October 1993, p. 10.

——, "UWA Names New President," *Fund Raising Management*, October 1996, p. 7.

"Giving Through United Way Soars to $3.58 Billion," *Fund Raising Management*, October 1999, p. 7.

McLaughlin, Thomas, "Lessons from United Way," *Association Management*, August 1995, p. 24.

Olcott, William, "UWA Head Steps Down, Gets Reward," *Fund Raising Management*, July 1996, p. 7.

"Planning the United Way," *American Demographics*, November 1986, p. 24.

Santoro, Elaine, "Salvation Army Breaks United Way Ties," *Fund Raising Management*, September 1996, p. 6.

Sanz, Cynthia, "A Little Help for His Friends: William Aramony Faces Prison for Diverting the United Way His Way," *People Weekly*, April 17, 1995, p. 89.

—Nelson Rhodes

U.S. Bancorp

U.S. Bank Place
601 Second Avenue South
Minneapolis, Minnesota 55402-4302
U.S.A.
Telephone: (612) 973-1111
Fax: (612) 973-2446
Web site: http://www.usbank.com

Public Company
Incorporated: 1929 as First Bank Stock Investment
    Company
Employees: 26,891
Total Assets: $81.53 billion (1999)
Stock Exchanges: New York
Ticker Symbol: USB
NAIC: 551111 Offices of Bank Holding Companies;
    52211 Commercial Banking (pt); 52221 Credit Card
    Issuing (pt); 52232 Financial Transactions Processing;
    52239 Other Activities Related to Credit
    Intermediation (pt)

U.S. Bancorp, headquartered in Minneapolis, is the nation's 11th largest financial services holding company, operating in 16 states in the West and Midwest, through more than 1,000 banking locations. U.S. Bancorp is a leading provider of corporate trust services and is the leading supplier worldwide of Visa corporate and purchasing cards. The company also offers investment, payment systems, asset management, insurance, and banking services to consumers and businesses. Subsidiary U.S. Bancorp Piper Jaffray provides brokerage and investment banking services through some 100 offices.

History of First Bank System Inc.

In April 1929, just one-half year before the great stock market crash, 85 banks located in the Ninth Federal Reserve district joined together in a loose confederation called First Bank Stock Investment Corporation. Since the Federal Deposit Insurance Company (FDIC) had not yet been created, the pur-

pose of the confederation was to provide mutual financial support during difficult economic times. Although there was a great deal of speculation going on during this time in Wall Street brokerage houses, most banks throughout the country remained financially conservative and extremely cautious about using their assets for anything except the most stable investments.

Despite their fiscal conservatism, a number of banks were forced to close their doors during the 1920s. With the stock market crash of October 1929 and the onset of the Great Depression, conditions for the banking industry grew harsher and harsher. Many banks were forced to close during the years between 1929 and 1932. As the depression grew worse during the first few months of Franklin Roosevelt's presidency, he decided in early 1933 to close all the nation's banks for ten days. The purpose of this dramatic decision was to make certain that only those banks with stable financial ledgers would be permitted to reopen their doors to the public. When the ten-day period was over, all First Bank Stock Investment Corporation subsidiaries were allowed by the federal government to reopen without any mandated reorganization. The conservative policies adhered to by First Bank management were so sound, in fact, that the holding company was able to start an acquisitions campaign that lasted through much of the 1930s.

During the 1940s, banks that belonged to the First Bank confederation largely operated independently of one another. Managers at the individual banks were fiercely loyal to their own self-interests, and never hesitated to engage in extensive price cuts if they thought it might take a profitable customer away from another bank within the confederation. In fact, the competition among confederation banks was most intense in the Twin Cities of Minneapolis and St. Paul, Minnesota, where the largest individual banks in the First Bank system fought one another for customers. One cause of this counterproductive competition among the banks was the restrictive and antiquated branching legislation in Minnesota and other states in the region.

In 1954, the Bank Holding Company Act was passed by the U.S. Congress. This legislation gave the First Bank confederation and other bank holding companies throughout the nation the approval for already existing multi-state banking operations. Banks within the First Bank confederation were spread across a

489

Company Perspectives:

We strive to create superior value for our shareholders by fulfilling our customer promise.

We simplify our customers' lives by delivering anytime, anywhere access to a comprehensive range of financial solutions. This is the essence of the U.S. Bancorp brand. ''Simplify'' means satisfying customer expectations for quality, convenience and execution, while meeting the need for confidence and security. ''Access'' is providing a wide range of choices for doing business with us. ''Solutions'' result from our knowledge of the customer, the superior performance of our products and services, and the expertise of our people.

---

four-state area during this time, including Montana, South Dakota, North Dakota, and Minnesota. For the remainder of the 1950s, and throughout the decade of the 1960s, the banks of the confederation expanded their presence in these states by engaging in an aggressive acquisitions policy. By the 1970s, however, member banks of the confederation were operating so independently of one another that there was not only a lack of uniformity in services, but an overall lack of direction and centralized decision making.

During the late 1970s and early 1980s, the economy in the United States went into a tailspin, and the First Bank confederation was faced with the challenges of high inflation, uncertain interest rates, and growing competition from nonbank financial service companies. Confederation management recognized the need for more centralized control and in 1982 began to prepare a comprehensive strategy for this purpose. In 1985, First Bank management made its first significant decision by selling 28 smaller, rural banks with little prospect for future growth. This decision resulted in the sale of 45 offices over a four-state region. Another major decision involved the 1988 merger of the large Minneapolis and St. Paul banks, and additional suburban banks in the Twin Cities area, into First Bank National Association. The increase in operational efficiency and reduction in service costs provided the bank with a greater opportunity to compete effectively in the entire Twin Cities metropolitan area. Management at First Bank also purchased banks in the states of Washington and Colorado during this time, taking advantage of recent federal legislation that weakened many barriers to national banking.

More than the recession of the early 1980s led First Bank to reassess the adequacy and effectiveness of a loose confederation and hands-off management style. The farm crisis of the early to mid-1980s created credit quality problems for the regional banks affiliated with First Bank which were outside of the greater Twin Cities metropolitan area. Under the bank's own credit examination, its credit losses amounted to $424 million by 1986. This loss was compensated for by the $397 million in realized gains when the investment securities were sold. Yet when rising interest rates led to a substantial unrealized loss estimated at $640 million in the long-term bonds which had been bought to replace the securities recently sold, the company decided upon a hedging strategy to minimize the

loss. Unfortunately, the hedging strategy failed, and the bonds were finally sold at a pre-tax loss of $506 million in 1988.

First Bank's emphasis on merchant banking, capital markets, and lending specializations proved disastrous during the mid-1980s. With decreasing capital levels resulting from the securities and bond losses, rising noninterest costs, an increasing amount of nonperforming assets, and weakening profitability, the company announced a comprehensive reorganization strategy in late 1989. The strategy included a withdrawal from merchant banking and lending specializations and a concentration on more basic banking services, such as merchant processing, credit cards, automated teller machines, and cash management. The company also began to capitalize upon and extend its geographic franchise. In 1989, First Bank recorded a restructuring expense of $37.5 million, while also reporting a $175 million provision for credit losses.

After a four-month search, in January 1990 the First Bank board of directors hired John F. (Jack) Grundhofer to act as chairman, president, and chief executive officer. Grundhofer, a former vice-chairman and senior executive officer at Wells Fargo, immediately initiated a massive cost-cutting strategy designed to bring the bank back to profitability. Grundhofer and his hand-chosen management team examined each line of the bank's business to determine whether or not it could remain competitive in the market. Grundhofer's first move was to stop lending to large corporations and concentrate more on retail banking, trusts and investments, and small and middle-range businesses. As a result, First Bank's portfolio of loans was drastically reduced. All the bank's national lending programs and its indirect auto loan programs were entirely eliminated, thus allowing the company to concentrate on expanding its regional commercial lending program and its direct consumer loan program. In general, First Bank's loan portfolio was gradually restructured to emphasize a larger number and more diverse mix of consumer loans.

The most important move that Grundhofer made, however, was to commit $150 million in First Bank funds to a cost-cutting technology program. When he arrived on the scene in the beginning of 1990, Grundhofer discovered that First Bank was mired in 1950s and 1960s technology. Over 45 banks under First Bank's umbrella had 47 different data processing centers, 715 different kinds of basic consumer deposit accounts, 16 loan processing centers, eight consumer loan centers, and 20 item processing centers. The bank also was without any centralized pricing structure for its products or services, and each bank within the system offered various kinds of products and services. The company's installment loan system was initially brought in during 1959 and was still in use. First Bank's customer information system dated back to 1964, without the benefit of any update since that time. In addition, its online savings system was more than 20 years old.

Within two years Grundhofer consolidated the bank's 47 data processing centers into one, and drastically reduced or eliminated all the other loan and processing centers. He implemented a fixed price structure for the bank's products and services, and standardized the products and services each of the banks offered within the First Bank system. As First Bank's efficiency ratio improved, more customers were attracted to the

Key Dates:

1891: United States National Bank of Portland is founded.

1902: United States National and Ainsworth National merge.

1925: United States National merges with Ladd and Tilton, Oregon's oldest bank.

1929: First Bank Stock Investment Corporation is formed.

1964: United States National Bank of Portland is renamed United States National Bank of Oregon.

1968: First Bank Stock Investment Corporation is renamed First Bank System, Inc.; United States National Bank reorganizes as a holding company called U.S. Bancorp.

1988: First Bank National Association is formed through the merger of large banks in Minneapolis, St. Paul, and the greater Twin Cities region.

1990: First Bank hires John (Jack) Grundhofer as CEO, chairman, and president.

1993: First Bank acquires U.S. Bancorp's corporate trust operations in Oregon and Washington.

1995: U.S. Bancorp acquires West One Bancorp of Idaho.

1997: In its largest acquisition, First Bank purchases U.S. Bancorp and adopts the U.S. Bancorp name; company also acquires Piper Jaffray Companies Inc.

services provided by the bank. By 1992, a customer could walk into any of First Bank's affiliates in the Twin Cities area and get a cashier's check or automobile loan within ten minutes. The bank also developed an extremely useful and very popular 48-hour turnaround on small business loans; for a $250,000 loan, the customer was asked to fill out a brief two-page application. Other processing capabilities that were improved by the bank's emphasis on technological development included a customer's ability to access account information from a remote site. Finally, all of the bank's numerous customer service phone centers were consolidated into two locations.

When the cost-cutting technology program began to show financial rewards, Grundhofer decided to increase First Bank's asset base through an aggressive acquisitions program. First Bank purchased U.S. Bancorp's Oregon and Washington corporate trust operations in early 1993. Prior to this, it had purchased the California corporate trust subsidiary of Bankers Trust New York Corporation in 1992. The company acquired Colorado National Bank with over $3 billion in assets, and Boulevard Bancorp in Chicago with over $1.5 billion in assets. Perhaps the most important acquisition involved the purchase of the domestic corporate trust of J.P. Morgan & Company, one of the largest and most prestigious banks in the United States. In May 1994, the company confirmed its acquisition of Metropolitan Financial Corporation for approximately $800 million. Metropolitan Financial, a Minneapolis, Minnesota-based bank with $5.7 billion in assets, operated a multi-state banking office network located in Minnesota, North Dakota, Iowa, Nebraska, Kansas, and Wyoming. The purchase of Metropolitan helped push First Bank's assets to $34.5 billion, ahead of the assets at First Fidelity Bancorp, the nation's 25th largest bank holding company.

In 1990 and 1991, the bank's capital restoration program involved a private placement of new common stock, which raised some $145 million from an investment partnership headed by Lazard Freres, and $30 million from the State Board of Administration of Florida. The bank also initiated a public offering of $114.5 million of preferred stock. These moves placed First Bank's capital ratio in the top percentile of regional banks in the United States.

Under Grundhofer's leadership, by the beginning of 1995 First Bank had grown into one of the largest and most successful of the regional banks. With its financial condition clearly improved, First Bank began to develop a community initiatives program that became a model for regional banks. First Bank's extensive community outreach program involved volunteerism, youth-employment projects, event sponsorships, and grants to nonprofit organizations. The company offered a comprehensive line of mortgage products and services to help low and moderate income families purchase their own homes. The bank also tailored loans for people with disabilities, provided customer assistance for non-English speaking peoples, and offered free accounts and services to individuals with low-income jobs. First Bank also extended credit to small businesses that fostered community development and rehabilitation by working closely with the Small Business Administration.

First Bank continued to focus its efforts on growth through acquisitions, and in March 1995 the company completed its acquisition of holding company First Western Corporation, which owned Western Bank in Sioux Falls, South Dakota. The sale included Western Bank's 12 branches in South Dakota. Also that year First Bank bought Southwest Bank, First Bank of Omaha, and FirsTier Financial Inc., greatly furthering its presence in Nebraska. The acquisitions made First Bank the largest banking firm in Nebraska, with a leading market share in Lincoln and the number two spot in Omaha. The FirsTier purchase was the largest bank acquisition in Nebraska history. Continuing with its flurry of acquisitions in 1995, First Bank bought the corporate trust operations of BankAmerica Corporation, making First Bank the nation's largest corporate trust company in terms of revenues. The following year First Bank added to its corporate trust operations by purchasing the municipal and corporate bond trustee division of Comerica Inc., a banking company based in Detroit.

Though acquisitions were a primary concern of First Bank, the company also focused on streamlining operations. The company's trust and investment division implemented a cost-cutting plan, which included personnel cuts and technology enhancements, to decrease expenses and boost revenues. First Bank also made the decision to depart the mortgage banking industry by selling its FBS Mortgage and Colorado National Mortgage operations. The bank planned to continue offering mortgage loans through its bank branches.

In the mid-1990s First Bank also spent a great deal of time, money, and energy in its attempt to acquire First Interstate Bancorp. First Bank lost out to Wells Fargo & Co., which had made several hostile takeover bids for First Interstate before succeeding. The battle was the largest hostile takeover attempt in the history of U.S. banking and, while it left First Bank without the First Interstate empire, the company gained a $200 million termination fee. First Bank hoped to use these funds to finance a significant acquisition, one that would enhance its operations and make it a strong contender in the rapidly consolidating and highly competitive U.S. banking industry.

History of U.S. Bancorp

U.S. Bancorp was organized as a holding company by the United States Bank of Oregon in the late 1960s, a time when many large banks across the country acknowledged and fostered their transformation into diversified financial services organizations by forming bank holding companies. The company's historical roots, however, stretch back nearly a century before the descriptive phrase ''diversified financial services organizations'' became part of banking nomenclature, reaching back into the late 19th century to a simpler age when the business of banking comprised the rudimentary tasks of receiving deposits, cashing checks, and extending and collecting loans. Banking would develop into a much more sophisticated business by the time U.S. Bancorp first emerged in the late 1960s, but the company's true origins stemmed from the efforts of a handful of wealthy and influential businessmen during the early 1890s and their organization of The United States National Bank of Portland.

From out of the uncharted Portland wilderness, Oregon developed into a bustling commercial and industrial hub during the 19th century, its growth propelled by successive waves of settlers into the Pacific Northwest and the subsequent establishment of a spectrum of businesses and industries. As the community evolved from a secluded settlement into a burgeoning town and finally into one of the principal cities underpinning the Pacific Northwest's economy, banks were there to promote and support its growth, serving as a crucial source of capital in a region far removed from the established financial centers in the eastern United States. Starting in 1859, when the first national bank in Portland, the Ladd and Tilton, was organized, Portland's business operators began to utilize bank loans to develop their enterprises. As the town grew, requiring more and more capital to fund its development, the number of banks increased, totaling five in the state of Oregon by 1872, then jumping to 16 by 1880. Roughly a decade later, when more than 40 national banks were operating in Oregon, United States National Bank of Portland (U.S. National) was organized by nine businessmen.

Led by Donald MacLeay, an immigrant from Scotland who made his fortune in the grocery and shipping business, and George Washington Ewing Griffith, a wealthy Kansas businessman, the founding directors, all of whom were born outside of Oregon, organized U.S. National on February 5, 1891, then opened the bank four days later in rented offices in downtown Portland. Although U.S. National operated without a vault during its inaugural year, the apparent lack of security did not dissuade customers from bringing their banking business to the city's newest bank. During the bank's first day 15 customers opened new accounts, depositing a total of $21,886.30. By the end of its first year, fledgling U.S. National had become a thriving enterprise, holding $450,000 in deposits and capital stock and administering more than $350,000 in loans. It was an encouraging start for U.S. National, but before there was much chance for celebration, economic conditions in Oregon and throughout the nation soured, providing the bank with its first great test of resiliency while still in its infancy.

In 1893, two years after U.S. National began operating, a severe economic depression gripped the country, devastating more than 500 of the nation's banks and more than 16,000 businesses by the end of the year. Among the victims of the harsh economic conditions were a number of stable and respected Portland banks, but despite its status as a neophyte in the area's banking community U.S. National beat back the debilitating effects of the economic downturn. The bank's deposits slipped from a high of more than $400,000 in 1892 to less than $340,000 in 1896, but when the discovery of gold in the late 1890s swept away any lingering effects of the economic depression in the Pacific Northwest, U.S. National emerged stronger than ever before. For this strength the bank was indebted to the financial malaise of the early and mid-1890s, a deleterious period for many banks that left U.S. National occupying a more powerful position. Of Oregon's 41 national banks operating in 1892, only 27 remained after the depression, creating a more consolidated banking industry that buoyed U.S. National's position considerably. Of these 27 national banks, only four would survive to compete during the 20th century: Ainsworth National, Merchants National, First National, and the upstart U.S. National.

Less than a decade old in 1900, U.S. National had already passed Ainsworth National in volume of business to rank as the third largest bank and was gaining ground on Merchants National to secure the industry's second position. Growth would come quickly during the first decades of the new century as bankers recouped their losses from the 1890s and shared in the prosperity of the times. During the first decade of the century, the number of national banks in Oregon increased from 27 to 75, and deposits quadrupled as the city of Portland, with 200,000 residents by 1910, flourished economically. As one of the city's stalwart banks, U.S. National benefited greatly from the more robust economic conditions and was able to conclude several pivotal transactions that secured its inclusion among the region's leading banks. In 1902 U.S. National and Ainsworth National, the fourth largest bank, agreed to merge, creating a banking entity that kept the U.S. National corporate title and controlled resources valued at more than $2 million. Three years later U.S. National merged with Wells Fargo Company's Portland bank as growth and prosperity reigned, then in 1917 the bank merged with another large Portland bank, Lumbermens National. The merger with Lumbermens National increased U.S. National's deposits by $6.5 million and made it the second largest bank in the Pacific Northwest.

By the beginning of the 1920s U.S. National had deposits of more than $36 million, having grown considerably during its first 30 years of operation. In 1925 the bank set the tone for the magnitude of growth ahead when it merged with the venerable Ladd and Tilton. Aside from being the region's oldest bank, Ladd and Tilton represented a potent banking competitor with more than $20 million in deposits and 30,000 depositors. Once Ladd and Tilton was merged into U.S. National, U.S. National received a substantial boost to its stature, becoming the largest bank north of San Francisco and west of Minneapolis, with resources totaling $64.6 million, deposits reaching $60 million, and a large base of 75,000 depositors.

The 1920s were heady years for U.S. National, but as the events of the next decade unfolded, the bank faced economic conditions far more menacing than those surmounted during the 1890s. During the Great Depression more than half of the country's banks were financially ruined, thousands of businesses were devastated, and the ranks of the unemployed swelled beyond precedent. Like the economic depression touched off in 1893, however, U.S. National withstood the pernicious effects of financial collapse all around it, although deposits once again shrank during the period. Deposits reached a high of $71 million in September 1931, then over the next eight months fell by $10 million; however, by the late 1930s business began to recover and the bank's deposits eclipsed $100 million. Perhaps the most important occurrence during the otherwise crippling 1930s was the enactment of legislation enabling banks to establish branches, which U.S. National began doing in 1933 and would continue to do thereafter.

During the 1940s U.S. National expanded its presence geographically by acquiring existing banks and converting them to U.S. National branches, such as the bank's 1940 purchase of the Medford National Bank, First National of Corvallis, and the Ladd and Bush Bank of Salem. Although the number of banking units comprising U.S. National's growing branch network rose only modestly during World War II, climbing from 26 to 29, deposits nearly tripled during the war years, leaping to $581 million by the end of 1945. Following the war, when an era of widespread prosperity gave large segments of the American population substantially more disposable income than ever before, the national banking industry underwent a dramatic shift as banks across the country began focusing on the consumer with concerted intensity. Loans for consumer purchases proliferated, and U.S. National responded by augmenting its consumer credit department with a branch consumer credit department in 1949. Bank advertising during the era reflected the significant shift in focus, as advertisements began to emphasize the availability of loans for individuals and the use of bank credit, rather than encouraging thrift as they had done since U.S. National's inception.

Between 1945 and 1955, 35 banking units were added to U.S. National's branch system, the bulk of which—29—were acquired through mergers and acquisitions as the bank swallowed smaller competitors and outpaced larger competitors with its aggressive expansion across the state of Oregon. Aside from ranking as one of the larger state banks in the nation, U.S. National also began to distinguish itself as an industry pioneer during the 1950s by offering such innovative services as drive-up banking, erecting the first motor banking facility in Oregon in 1956, and leading the way with a computerized system to post checks in 1957.

In contrast to the 1950s, U.S. National expanded its branch network through internal means during the 1960s, creating new banking facilities rather than absorbing existing banking units through mergers or acquisitions. By 1965 the bank operated 100 branches across the state, a considerable presence that the bank's directors had acknowledged the previous year by changing the bank's name from United States National Bank of Portland to United States National Bank of Oregon. Other, more significant changes were in the offing as the bank entered the late 1960s and began to formulate a plan for the future, in search of a way to contend with the mounting pressures affecting banks during the period.

The business of banking had become a complex and highly competitive endeavor by the 1960s, substantially more sophisticated than when U.S. National first opened its doors in 1891. In addition to a much broader range of financial services offered by commercial banks, the market for these services had become more competitive since World War II. Between 1945 and 1960, savings in commercial banks such as U.S. National had doubled, whereas the amount in savings and loan associations had sextupled and the amount in credit unions had increased an enormous tenfold, absorbing business that would traditionally have gone to commercial banks.

In response, commercial banks began to form one-bank holding companies during the late 1960s, enabling them to acquire and organize other subsidiaries that could legally offer a broader range of services. In so doing, banks hoped to beat back the competition and keep noncommercial banks from entering into financial activities that historically had been under the exclusive purview of commercial banks. On September 9, 1968, U.S. National followed the nationwide trend by forming U.S. Bancorp as a one-bank holding company, heralding the development of a vast financial services network and the extension of U.S. Bancorp beyond Oregon's borders.

Once able to delve into new businesses, U.S. Bancorp did so with fervor, organizing a host of financial services subsidiaries during the 1970s: Bancorp Leasing, Inc., which was organized to enhance service to business customers through lease financing; U.S. Bancorp Financial, Inc., a subsidiary formed to specialize in asset-based commercial financing; and Mount Hood Credit Life Insurance Agency, which was created to centralize and streamline credit-related insurance activities throughout the U.S. National system. Numerous other subsidiaries were formed in the wake of U.S. Bancorp's founding, transforming the U.S. National-U.S. Bancorp network into a genuine regional financial services organization.

By the beginning of the 1980s, U.S. Bancorp was well on its way to becoming one of the preeminent regional financial services organizations in the country. Decidedly acquisitive throughout the 1980s, the holding company started the decade by establishing The Bank of Milwaukee, a state-chartered bank, in 1980, making U.S. Bancorp a multi-bank holding company. During the year, the company also acquired State Finance and Thrift Company of Logan, Utah, and established Citizen's Industrial Bank in Littleton, Colorado, further bolstering its out-of-state presence in regions where U.S. National was not allowed to operate. By the end of the year U.S. Bancorp's territory included California, Texas, Washington, Utah, Idaho, Colorado, Montana, and its home state of Oregon, giving the company ample room to grow as the decade progressed.

With the acquisition of Spokane-based Old National Bancorp and Seattle-based Peoples Bancorp in 1987, U.S. Bancorp became the largest bank holding company based in the Northwest. During the late 1980s, the company continued to aggressively pursue smaller rival banks, hoping to achieve a dominant position in markets opened up earlier in the decade. Other large banking organizations followed a similar strategy, creating a nationwide trend toward consolidation that left U.S. Bancorp as the last major independent bank in the Pacific Northwest by the early 1990s. With $19 billion in assets in 1992, the company ranked as the 32nd largest bank in the United States.

During the next two years, U.S. Bancorp's management began to focus its efforts on achieving greater efficiency by streamlining the company's operations and eliminating nearly a quarter of its workforce through layoffs and the divestiture of noncore subsidiaries. After two years of implementing severe downsizing measures, the company announced a momentous acquisition in 1995 that added substantially to U.S. Bancorp's already sizable holdings. Intent on strengthening its position in Idaho, where the company maintained only a token presence, U.S. Bancorp officials announced the $1.6 billion acquisition of West One Bancorp of Idaho in May, which the shareholders of both banking organizations agreed to in October. Completed at the end of 1995, the deal made U.S. Bancorp one of the 30 largest banking organizations in the country, with $30 billion in assets and $21 billion in deposits.

Buoyed by its purchase of West One, U.S. Bancorp continued its quest for growth in 1996. In an age of industry consolidation, U.S. Bancorp hoped to expand and grow to stave off takeover attempts, and acquisitions proved an optimal way to grow quickly. The company bought Northern California-based California Bancshares Inc. for about $327 million, boosting its presence there from 57 branches to 93 and expanding its area of operations from 22 counties to 27. In December 1996 U.S. Bancorp grew its presence in northern California further with the acquisition of Sacramento-based Business & Professional Bank. The small bank had four offices in the Sacramento region. U.S. Bancorp picked up another small bank with the purchase of Sun Capital Bancorp of Utah. The fast-growing Sun Capital had three branches in St. George, in the southern portion of Utah. U.S. Bancorp also hoped to capitalize on the growth of in-store banking and made plans to open about 200 supermarket branches from 1996 to 2000. The company inked a deal with Albertson's Inc. to provide exclusive banking services to about 170 Albertson's stores in Oregon, Washington, Idaho, and Nevada.

Though U.S. Bancorp continued to strengthen operations and grow, industry analysts believed the bank was not immune to takeover attempts. U.S. Bancorp's strategy of acquiring small companies, some analysts felt, was insufficient and would not protect the bank from larger adversaries. In addition, small to mid-sized banks were growing more scarce, leaving U.S. Bancorp with few potential acquisitions, and competition was growing. The bank ran into a small obstacle when its attempt to buy 61 branches in California from Wells Fargo & Co. in 1996 failed. Still, U.S. Bancorp remained confident and hopeful that it would be able to continue functioning independently.

First Bank System Acquires U.S. Bancorp: Late 1990s

In early 1997 First Bank System announced it would acquire U.S. Bancorp for about $8.8 billion, extending First Bank's reach to the Pacific Ocean. The deal, which was one of the largest in U.S. banking history, nearly doubled First Bank's asset size and created a mega-bank serving about 17 states in the Midwest and West. The merged entity took the name U.S. Bancorp, with headquarters remaining in Minneapolis. First Bank's Grundhofer served as president and CEO, while U.S.

Bancorp's Gerry Cameron continued as chairman until his retirement in 1998. According to the *Star-Tribune,* Grundhofer commented on the merger at a press conference and said, "Our regions are contiguous, compatible and are in attractive growth markets. Our banks both have strong market presence. Our business strategies are virtually identical."

As part of the consolidation efforts, nearly 4,000 staff members were laid off, the bulk of them from among U.S. Bancorp's 14,000 workers, including about 2,000 positions in the Portland region. Loan servicing operations in Portland were moved to Minneapolis, and credit card processing operations were moved to Fargo, North Dakota, where First Bank's credit card division was based.

In late 1997 the new U.S. Bancorp announced it would buy Minneapolis-based Piper Jaffray Companies Inc. for about $730 million. The acquisition greatly enhanced U.S. Bancorp's ability to provide investment banking and securities brokerage services to customers and created the 11th largest brokerage in the nation. U.S. Bancorp continued to grow in 1998 and bought Northwest National Bank, a small, family-owned bank in Vancouver, Washington, near Portland, Oregon. In the summer of 1998 U.S. Bancorp gained an exclusive contract to provide the Department of Defense with purchasing cards and electronic commerce systems. The bank beat out several competitors to gain the lucrative contract.

In 1999 U.S. Bancorp exited the retail banking scene in Kansas when it sold its 20 branches to INTRUST Bank of Wichita, Kansas' largest bank. The company also sold eight branches in Iowa. Though U.S. Bancorp left Kansas, it strove to increase its presence in southern California in 1999 by acquiring several banks. The bank purchased Bank of Commerce, based in San Diego, for $314 million in stock. Bank of Commerce operated ten branches. U.S. Bancorp also bought Western Bancorp of Newport Beach for about $958 million in stock. Western Bancorp operated Santa Monica Bank and Southern California Bank and had 31 branches. The bank was known for its commercial lending operations. In the fall of 1999 U.S. Bancorp announced it would buy Peninsula Bank of San Diego for about $104 million in stock. Prior to the three acquisitions, U.S. Bancorp had 88 branches in southern California.

U.S. Bancorp grew its U.S. Bancorp Piper Jaffray division with the acquisition of Libra Investments, Inc., in early 1999 and the investment banking operations of John Nuveen Co. in September. The following year the company bought specialty leasing company Oliver-Allen Corporation. Also in 2000 the bank continued its acquisition streak in southern California when it purchased Scripps Financial Corp. of San Diego. The buy included nine branches of Scripps Bank, primarily a commercial bank.

Though U.S. Bancorp appeared to be on the fast track of growth in the late 1990s, its consumer banking operations, which accounted for about one-third of U.S. Bancorp's earnings, struggled, and retail revenue grew a mere four percent in 1999. U.S Bancorp's 1999 net income was $1.51 billion, up from 1998 net income of $1.33 billion, but the company failed to meet its growth goals. To stoke up its consumer banking division, U.S. Bancorp hired hundreds of new branch tellers, customer service representatives for its telephone operations, and small business bankers. The bank also added new electronic banking services and began to overhaul more than 1,000 branches. Still, the company's stock continued to sag, and during the first half of 2000 its stock price fell 11 percent. U.S. Bancorp's Grundhofer remained optimistic and confident about the bank's future, stating in his letter to shareholders in the company's 1999 annual report that U.S. Bancorp hoped to meet its growth goal of 12 to 15 percent by the end of 2001.

Principal Subsidiaries

U.S. Bank National Association; U.S. Bank National Association MT; U.S. Bank National Association ND; U.S. Bank National Association OR; U.S. Bank Trust Company, National Association; U.S. Bank Trust National Association; U.S. Bank Trust National Association MT; U.S. Bancorp Investments, Inc.; FBS Capital I; U.S. Bancorp Venture Capital Corporation; U.S. Bancorp Community Development Corporation; U.S. Bancorp Information Services, Inc.; U.S. Bancorp Equity Capital, Inc.; USB Trade Services Limited; U.S. Trade Services, Inc.; U.S. Bancorp Capital I; U.S. Bancorp Piper Jaffray Companies Inc.; First Building Corporation; First Group Royalties, Inc.; First System Services, Inc.; U.S. Bancorp Card Services, Inc.; U.S. Bancorp Insurance Services, Inc.

Principal Competitors

Citigroup Inc.; Wells Fargo & Company; KeyCorp.

Further Reading

Anderson, Michael A., "U.S. Bancorp's Interstate Bid Begins Anew," *Business Journal-Portland,* May 19, 1986, p. 1.

Bennett, Robert A., "Roger Faces Goliath," *United States Banker,* June 1992, p. 20.

Condon, Bernard, "Brother, Can You Spare a Bank?", *Forbes,* April 3, 2000.

Crockett, Barton, "U.S. Bancorp to Ax 52 Branches After Merger," *American Banker,* October 27, 1995, p. 4.

DePass, Dee, "FBS Reaches West," *Star-Tribune Newspaper of the Twin Cities Minneapolis-St.Paul,* March 21, 1997, p. D1.

Fitch, Mike, "Mother Lode's Buyer Got Good Deal, Say Observers," *Puget Sound Business Journal,* November 6, 1989, p. 22.

Heind, John, "Buy or Be Bought," *Forbes,* May 18, 1987, p. 48.

Jaffe, Thomas, "Cheap Bank," *Forbes,* June 29, 1987, p. 122.

Jordon, Steve, "First Bank Is Poised to Grow in Nebraska," *Omaha World-Herald,* June 9, 1995, p. 14.

——, "U.S. Bancorp Chairman Is Building for Long Haul," *Omaha World-Herald,* June 21, 2000, p. 18.

Kapiloff, Howard, "Fourth-of-July Merger Fireworks," *American Banker,* July 5, 1994, p. 1.

Klinkerman, Steve, and Karen Gullo, "First Bank System to Purchase Morgan's Corporate Trust Unit," *American Banker,* January 5, 1993, p. 5.

Manning, Jeff, "Bankruptcies May Be Lever for U.S. Bank," *Business Journal-Portland,* December 9, 1991, p. 1.

Milligan, John W., "Making First Bank Work," *US Banker,* March 1, 1997, p. 32.

Ota, Alan K., "First Bank Begins to Issue Pink Slips at U.S. Bancorp," *Portland Oregonian,* June 4, 1997, p. C1.

——, "U.S. Bancorp: Hunter or Prey?", *Portland Oregonian,* September 12, 1996, p. B1.

——, "U.S. Bancorp on Guard Duty," *Portland Oregonian,* May 8, 1996, p. B1.

Ota, Alan K., and Steve Woodward, "First Bank Wooed U.S. Bank in Polite but Insistent Romance," *Portland Oregonian,* March 26, 1997.

"Purchase by U.S. Bancorp to Create Northwest Giant," *New York Times,* May 9, 1995, p. D2.

Rhoads, Christopher, "First Bank System Buying U.S. Bancorp Pricey $8.4B Deal Is Banking Industry's Fourth Largest Ever," *American Banker,* March 21, 1997, p. 1.

"Shareholders Approve Merger of U.S. Bancorp & West One, Bancorp," *PR Newswire,* October 3, 1995, p. 1.

Silvestri, Scott, and Laura Mandaro, "U.S. Bancorp CEO Talks Like a Buyer," *American Banker,* June 19, 2000, p. 1.

Talley, Karen, "U.S. Bancorp's Piper Deal an Integration Success," *American Banker,* November 10, 1999, p. 1.

Taylor, John H., "No Chest-Beater," *Forbes,* May 11, 1992, p. 172.

"U.S. Bancorp Will Acquire Piper Jaffray," *Portland Oregonian,* December 16, 1997, p. B1.

Zack, Jeffrey, "Technology Gives First Bank's Grundhofer a Cost-Cutting Edge," *American Banker,* May 9, 1994, p. 1.

Zimmerman, Rachel, "Branch Closures Likely in U.S. Bank-West One Deal," *Puget Sound Business Journal,* August 25, 1995, p. 7.

—Jeffrey L. Covell and Thomas Derdak
—updated by Mariko Fujinaka

Utah Medical Products, Inc.

7043 South 300 West
Midvale, Utah 84047
U.S.A.
Telephone: (801) 566-1200
Toll Free: (800) 533-4984
Fax: (801) 566-2062
Web site: http://www.utahmed.com

Public Company
Incorporated: 1978
Employees: 275
Sales: $29.4 million (1999)
Stock Exchanges: NASDAQ
Ticker Symbol: UTMD
NAIC: 33911 Medical Equipment and Supplies
    Manufacturing; 339112 Surgical and Medical
    Instrument Manufacturing

Utah Medical Products, Inc. designs, manufactures, and distributes disposable and reusable products mainly for women and babies. It sells fetal monitoring devices that allow physicians to track the condition of the fetus as well as products to assess the mother's health status. The company also provides tools for electrosurgery, an innovation that first began in the early 1990s that allowed physicians in small clinics or their offices to take biopsy samples from the cervix. Its third main line includes breathing accessories, feeding tubes, and several other items for premature or critically ill babies. With facilities in Midvale, Utah; Athlone, Ireland; and Redmond, Oregon, that have a total of about 200,000 square feet, Utah Medical Products successfully competes in selected niche markets. It is one of the many companies that comprise Utah's growing biomedical products industry.

Origin and Early History

On April 21, 1978, James Young, Ralph Walker, and Reed Chidester incorporated Utah Medical Products, Inc. under Utah law "to develop, manufacture and market medical devices and supplies, with principal interest directed toward disposable, unique and high volume products,'' according to the firm's 1982 annual report.

The firm's initial product was the Delta-Flow Flush device, first sold in March 1979 for maintaining "catheter patency during invasive arterial pressure monitoring procedures.'' In February 1980 it began producing and marketing its Dispiro Disposable Spirometer, a disposable device used by respiratory therapists to measure pulmonary function. The Disposa-Hood for giving oxygen to babies was first made and sold in May 1980. Two years later the company began making and selling its Arthroscopy Drainage Cannula Set for draining and collecting fluid discharges resulting from inserting an arthroscope into the knee joint.

In April 1982 Utah Medical Products reached an out-of-court settlement with Sorenson Research Company over a lawsuit filed by Sorenson in January 1980. Sorenson charged Utah Medical Products with violating patent rights because the defendant's Delta-Flow product closely resembled Sorenson's Intra-Flow device. In February 1982 a jury in the U.S. District Court in Salt Lake City found Utah Medical Products guilty of patent violations, but during the appeal process the two firms settled. Utah Medical Products paid Sorenson $175,000 and dropped its appeal. In turn, Sorenson granted Utah Medical Products a nonexclusive license to continue making and selling Delta-Flow and also to pay Sorenson six percent of Delta-Flow net sales until the Sorenson patent expired in 1989.

More Developments in the 1980s

On July 21, 1983 UMED, Inc., Utah Medical Products' wholly owned subsidiary, merged with Salt Lake City's Medicor, with Medicor being the surviving entity. In September 1983 Utah Medical Products gained a new president when Fred P. Lampropoulos resigned as Medicor's chairman to assume his new duties. By this time the original founders and officers had departed. In addition to Lampropoulos, who had become a company director in 1981, the other directors included Dr. William Dean Wallace, who had served as Medicor's founding president before becoming the executive vice-president and a director of Utah Medical Products in 1983. Christopher A.

Company Perspectives:

With a particular interest in healthcare for women and their babies, Utah Medical develops, manufactures, and markets a broad range of disposable and reusable specialty medical devices designed for better health outcomes for patients and their care-providers.

Cutler, Ph.D., another Medicor founder and officer, became a director of Utah Medical Products in 1984 and vice-president of engineering a year later.

In 1984 Utah Medical Products sold Medicor's Salt Lake City facility and also began leasing 32,000 square feet in a building in Midvale, a Salt Lake City suburb, where it set up its corporate offices, warehouse, and manufacturing facilities. In 1986 it still owned a Lehi building with a tool and die shop and injection molding capabilities but eventually sold that facility.

Utah Medical Products suffered through a bad financial year in 1983. According to its 1983 annual report, its net sales declined from $935,344 in 1982 to $701,257 in 1983, and its net income of $106,612 in 1982 slipped to a 1983 net loss of $1.1 million.

In 1984 the company's net sales rebounded to $1.98 million and then in 1985 reached $3.3 million. The company remained unprofitable in both years, however, with net losses of $455,000 and $269,000, respectively.

In 1986 the company did much better, with net sales increasing to $5.7 million and a net income of $440,953. At the end of the year the firm employed 120 individuals. Two customers accounted for the majority of 1986 sales. Hewlett-Packard purchased $2.7 million worth of company products, mainly flush devices, transducer kits, and the firm's disposable transducer; that brought in 47 percent of sales. Deseret Medical, another Utah medical products firm, bought products worth nine percent of 1986 sales.

Several key developments occurred in 1987. The company in June introduced its Intran device to monitor intrauterine pressure during difficult deliveries. In 1987 Fred Lampropoulos left the firm to start Merit Medical Systems, a move that would result in litigation. He was replaced as company president by Dr. William Dean Wallace.

In December 1987 the firm signed an important agreement with Baxter Healthcare in which Baxter invested $1.15 million in the company and loaned it another $1.15 million. Baxter also made a six-year supply agreement to buy Utah Medical Product devices, which the company estimated would bring in $40 million in revenue. Since Baxter supplied hospitals globally, this contract in effect represented Utah Medical Products' entry into international markets. Later these agreements were amended and expanded. For example, in 1990 the company signed a three-year contract with Baxter's Japanese Division to have exclusive distribution rights to UMP's Deltran disposable blood pressure transducer.

The company at the end of 1989 reached $17.9 million in net sales and $2.6 million in net income. That solid financial performance, also seen in other indicators such as increasing total assets and decreasing long-term debt, continued into the 1990s.

Growth and Challenges in the 1990s and Beyond

In 1990 Utah Medical Products enjoyed a ''successful year,'' according to Chairman/President Dr. William Dean Wallace in the firm's annual report. The company completed purchasing its property and building in Midvale. *Business Week* in its May 21, 1990 issue ranked the Midvale firm as number 33 in its list of ''Hot Growth Companies.'' *Forbes* on November 12, 1990 honored the company by ranking it as number 57 in the list of its ''200 Best Small Companies in America.'' In its November 1991 issue *Forbes* ranked Utah Medical number 26 in the same list, based on its average five-year annual return on equity of 29.4 percent.

Baxter Healthcare remained Utah Medical Products' main customer as the new decade began, accounting for 41 percent of sales in 1991 and 37 percent in 1992. The agreement between the two firms was extended and amended in January 1993 for another three years. Utah Medical employed 393 individuals at the end of 1992, and its annual sales for that year increased to $36.1 million, while its 1992 net income was $6.9 million.

On December 31, 1992 Kevin L. Cornwell became Utah Medical Products' president and CEO. With a B.S. in chemical engineering, an M.S. in engineering-economic systems, and an M.B.A., all from Stanford University, Cornwell had worked 21 years in management and investment positions before joining Utah Medical Products.

The departure of Dr. William Dean Wallace resulted in litigation. After a federal grand jury had charged him with 18 separate offenses, including five counts of tax evasion, he had resigned as the president of Utah Medical Products but remained on its board of directors. On December 23, 1992 U.S. District Judge David Sam ruled that Wallace was not guilty of insider trading and falsifying documents, and he dismissed Wallace's five tax evasion charges.

In December 1992 Utah Medical Products said that it expected Wallace to continue working for the firm, mainly on research and development projects, but in April 1993 the company fired Wallace. In June 1993 Wallace filed a civil lawsuit against Utah Medical Products. In March 1994 seven of Wallace's nine claims against Utah Medical Products were dismissed by Third District Judge David S. Young.

In 1992 Utah Medical Products and Merit Medical Systems settled patent litigation concerning Merit's IntelliSystem and Monarch angioplasty inflation products. Utah Medical granted Merit a nonexclusive license to its angioplasty patents for a single licensing fee of $600,000. Merit committed to pay 5.75 percent annual royalties, not exceeding $450,000, to Utah Medical for annual sales of its products using the angioplasty patents.

In 1994 another lawsuit was filed concerning the relationship between the two Utah medical devices firms. Merit Medical stockholder David D. Bennett claimed that Merit and its founder Fred Lampropoulos committed fraud in the company's initial stock prospectus by claiming that Merit had no products that competed with Utah Medical products. Bennett also charged that the 1992 patent litigation settlement between the two firms proved that Merit "owed its entire corporate existence to cannibalizing Utah Medical personnel, customers and technology." In 1998 the Third District Court granted Merit a summary judgment that ended Bennett's claim.

Although Utah Medical Products and Merit Medical Systems initially had a serious legal contest, the reality was that the two firms in the 1990s specialized in different kinds of medical devices. Merit continued to develop products for diagnosing and treating cardiovascular disease. Utah Medical specialized in items mostly for women and babies. Its winter/spring fact sheet listed three product lines for use in 1) neonatal intensive care, 2) labor and delivery, and 3) gynecology, urology, and electrosurgery.

Utah Medical began offering its third product line in 1991 when it entered the market for minimally invasive surgery (MIS). It started selling its trademarked Finesse electrical generators and disposable Prendiville Loops for a gynecological procedure to cut out precancerous tissues on the cervix. Done in doctors' offices or clinics, this form of electrosurgery was less expensive than laser surgery and quicker and safer than traditional scalpel methods used in hospitals. In 1991 its generators and Loops brought in only three percent of total revenues but increased to 15 percent the following year.

Utah Medical's electrosurgery products for office or clinical use was part of a general trend in medical care as high-tech items based on microelectronics and computers allowed many procedures to be done in decentralized settings. This was obvious from the decline in hospital occupancy rates that began in the 1980s and the increasing use of smaller surgical centers, clinics, and even more home healthcare.

Most hospitals had been started as centralized institutions, a key feature of the Industrial Revolution that began initially around 1750 in Great Britain. Hospitals gradually replaced home healthcare, just as factories replaced home or small shop production. By the 1960s, however, the United States had entered the early phases of the so-called Postindustrial Society or Information Age characterized by decentralization. Alvin Toffler's 1980 book *The Third Wave* described this ongoing transformation.

Starting in 1992, biomedical products companies like Utah Medical Products faced increased regulatory demands from the U.S. Food and Drug Administration (FDA). The time needed for initial product approvals by the FDA increased significantly. Established firms simply passed on higher FDA fees to the consumers, but smaller companies sometimes struggled to meet the tougher requirements.

Utah Medical Products was just one of Utah's 145 biomedical companies that employed 7,891 workers and produced estimated revenues of $865.5 million, according to a study by the University of Utah's Bureau of Economic and Business Research reported in the May/June 1994 *Utah Business*. The industry was aided by the state's well educated workforce, research universities like the University of Utah and Brigham Young University, and low wages influenced by Utah's right-to-work law, which made unions optional.

In May 1995 Utah Medical Products announced its plans to build a manufacturing plant in Athlone, Ireland. In 1995 the company enjoyed its best financial performance of the decade, with annual net sales reaching $42 million and a net income of $8.4 million.

When the firm's Irish plant was completed in 1997, the new facility allowed the firm to save on distribution costs to European Community customers and take advantage of Europe's less demanding government regulations, compared with the U.S. Food and Drug Administration.

The new Irish plant was important because 25 percent of Utah Medical Products' revenues came from foreign sales. Only 25,000 square feet of the planned 75,000-square-foot plant were finished, however, because the company's important contract with Baxter was collapsing in 1997. Thus Paul Richins, the company's chief administrative officer, said in the November 11, 1998 *Deseret News*, "I wouldn't call (the Ireland plant) a smashing success, because the volumes have been much lower, and we've had to work to try to get enough business there to keep that plant at a level where it can be profitable. But we've been able to do that."

In 1997 Utah Medical Products' financial performance declined after several years of expansion. Its net sales declined to $24.3 million from $38.7 million in 1996. In addition, the firm's net income fell from $8.8 million in 1996 to $4.3 million in 1997. Sales and income increased over the next two years, with 1999 bringing in $29.4 million in net sales and net income of $5.5 million. It was clear that after the Baxter Healthcare agreements ended, Utah Medical Products in the late 1990s had to rely on other options to strengthen its market position.

In 1999 Utah Medical Products received 47 percent of its revenues from its labor and delivery products, including devices for monitoring both the fetus and the mother, vacuum systems that replaced forceps in difficult deliveries, and other products for umbilical cord management.

The company's blood pressure monitoring and other miscellaneous products brought in 25 percent of its 1999 revenues. These items for adult use included erectile dysfunction pumps. Subcontracting injection molding for other companies was also in this category.

Gynecology, electrosurgery, and urology products accounted for 15 percent of 1999 annual revenues. This third category included generators and tools for using electrosurgery to take biopsy samples from the cervix and also endoscopic irrigation devices used in urology.

The firm's neonatal products, responsible for 13 percent of 1999 revenues, were designed to help premature and critically ill babies survive. Products in this line included disposable hoods to help babies get enough oxygen, blood filtering systems, spinal fluid sampling devices, feeding tubes, and several other items.

To face strong competitors in 2000, Utah Medical Products continued to be led by a strong management team headed by Kevin Cornwall, president, CEO, and chairman of the board. It seemed that the company finally had found a long-term leader, unlike its two former presidents who each had stayed about five years and then left under clouds of litigation.

Principal Subsidiaries

Utah Medical Products Ltd. (Ireland); Columbia Medical, Inc.

Principal Competitors

Abbott Laboratories; Argon Medical; Baxter Cardiovascular Group; Becton, Dickinson & Company; Clinical Innovations; Corometrics; GE Medical; Kendall International, Inc.; Marquette Electronics, Inc.; Medex; Prism Enterprises; Quest Medical; Spectramed; Tyco International Ltd.

Further Reading

Kratz, Gregory P., "Exporting Utah," *Deseret News,* November 11, 1998, p. A1.

"7 of 9 Claims Against Firm Dismissed," *Deseret News,* March 26, 1994, p. B4.

Sorensen, Daniel P., "Biomedical Bottle-Up," *Utah Business,* May/June 1994, pp. 104–06+.

"Utah Medical Among '200 Best,' " *Deseret News,* November 19, 1991, p. D8.

"Utah Medical Products Approves New International Distribution Pact," *Deseret News,* July 5, 1990, p. B5.

"Utah Medical Products Grows with New Chief," *Salt Lake Tribune,* December 13, 1987, p. F3.

"Utah Medical Products' New Chief Named As Predecessor Is Cleared," *Deseret News,* December 30, 1992, p. D7.

"Utah Medical Products to Build Plant in Ireland," *Deseret News,* May 5, 1995, p. D9.

"Utah Medical Wraps Up Deal to Buy Most Assets of OB Tech," *Deseret News,* January 4, 1994, p. D6.

—David M. Walden

The Vermont Teddy Bear Co., Inc.

6655 Shelburne Road
Shelburne, Vermont 05482
U.S.A.
Telephone: (802) 985-3001
Toll Free: (800) 829-BEAR; (800) 829-2327
Fax: (802) 985-1304
Web site: http://www.vermontteddybear.com

Public Company
Incorporated: 1984
Employees: 274
Sales: $21.6 million (1999)
Stock Exchanges: NASDAQ
Ticker Symbol: BEAR
NAIC: 45112 Hobby, Toy & Game Shops; 339931 Doll and Stuffed Toy Manufacturing

The Vermont Teddy Bear Co., Inc. (doing business as The Vermont Teddy Bear Company) provides a new twist on the classic plush toy that originated in 1903 and was named after President Theodore Roosevelt. It is the leading manufacturer of hand-crafted teddy bears in the United States. Its Vermont-made ''Bear-Gram'' gift service, pioneered in 1990, delivers personalized teddy bears dressed in one of more than 100 different costumes. Bears are shipped in boxes with airholes and accompanying hand-written notes from ''Bear Counselors.'' The company has positioned its products as a gift alternative to flowers and candy and advertises its Bear-Grams through live reads with radio personalities in all 50 states.

Launching a One-Man Business: 1981

The Vermont Teddy Bear Company was created in 1981 when 30-year-old John Sortino began sewing cloth bears on his wife's sewing machine for his newborn son. His first creation was named Bearcho because its thick black eyebrows and mustache resembled those of Groucho Marx. Later bears were machine washable and dryable with movable arms and legs and were cuddly and safe for children. They had, according to Sortino, personality.

Teddy bear lore is fuzzy on the question of who made the first stuffed bear. The Steiff Co. of Germany displayed its stuffed toy at a fair in Leipzig in 1903, but credit generally goes to Thomas Michtom of Brooklyn, New York, for naming his creation after President Theodore Roosevelt, who had refused to shoot a bear cub on a hunting expedition in Mississippi. Sortino, whose son's many stuffed animals were manufactured in countries other than the United States, was determined that ''there should be a teddy bear made in America.'' He saw himself and his company as ''stewards of a uniquely American tradition based on the best American virtues: compassion, generosity, friendship and a zesty sense of whimsy and fun,'' according to a 1996 article in the *Daily Telegraph*.

Sortino had moved to Vermont from New York state, where he held a series of jobs after graduation from Plattsburgh College with a degree in mathematics: He was a scrimshaw artist, a United Parcel Service driver, and worked for the Boy Scouts of America. In 1981, Sortino sold 50 bears. That number increased to about 200 in 1982. In 1983, Sortino gave up his two part-time jobs to start peddling his bears on Burlington's Church Street Mall. ''Everyone thought I completely lost my mind,'' Sortino was later quoted in a 1992 *Montreal Gazette* article, but while standing behind his pushcart, he dreamed of ''getting big.'' With a small network of home workers, he began buying equipment and finding U.S. suppliers for materials. He recycled plastic from the wholesale ice cream tubs used by Ben & Jerry's, a Waterbury, Vermont. ice cream maker, for his teddy bears' joints. ''I wanted to be part of the re-industrialization of America,'' he explained to the *Washington Post* in 1994.

Sortino's company lumbered along for its first six years. In 1987, a private investor put $1 million into the fledgling company, most of which the company had lost by 1989. At this point, the bears were marketed principally through wholesalers and the company's own retail outlets in several northeastern locations. In 1989, with sales of $351,000, Sortino was faced with either going out of business or making a drastic change in operations. The company's own president and chief operating officer, Spencer Putnam, recommended declaring bankruptcy. Instead, Sortino chose to break out of the Burlington area and begin promoting his bears directly in the New York market.

"I took what was practically the last of our money and went to New York and began a radio campaign two weeks before Valentine's Day of 1990," Sortino recalled in the *Washington Post*. Well-known radio personalities, such as Don Imus, Rush Limbaugh, and Howard Stern, were enlisted to ad-lib pitches to sell the teddies. A toll free number in New York City was set up to receive calls.

Sudden and Spectacular Growth in the Early 1990s

Immediately the sales started rolling in. In two weeks, the company payroll increased from ten employees to 50. By the end of 1990, sales were up fivefold to $1.75 million as a result of the "Bear-Gram," the company's new telephone gift service. By 1993, sales had reached $17 million (91 percent of which were due to phone orders), and the company was named national winner of the "Best of America" awards sponsored by Dunn & Bradstreet Small Business Services and the National Federation of Independent Businesses Foundation. *Inc. Magazine* ranked it 21st among America's fastest-growing public companies. The company went public in December 1993, reaping $10 million in paper profits. With its old-fashioned-looking bears, complete with movable limbs and lifetime warrantee, The Vermont Teddy Bear Company had made its mark in a market dominated by Gund, Dakin, and more established bear makers. In 1994, the Smithsonian offered two Vermont mohair teddies, Smithson T. and Alice R. Bear, for sale in its catalogue. According to the Smithsonian's spokeswoman, in a 1994 article in the *Washington Post*, the Vermont teddy bears recalled one of the original bears in the museum's collection.

At The Vermont Teddy Bear complex, business was moving right along. In a maze-like building whose departments were separated by picket fences, workers sewed and stuffed new teddies. There was a one-of-a-kind department with bears dressed in custom-made clothing—Charlie Chaplin garb, a Vermont state trooper's uniform, a scuba diving outfit—and a bear hospital, where bears sporting casts, crutches, and arm slings sat side by side customers' ailing bears waiting to be repaired. On the other side of the building, "Bear Counselors" answered telephones and took orders—Bear-Grams—from customers who, absent this alternative, might have sent flowers. The atmosphere was laid back, with Frank Sinatra music pumped in through loudspeakers, an employee pinball machine, and mobile massage service. The company's factory and retail store became one of the hottest tourist spots in the state, attracting 80,000 visitors in 1994.

In fact, while the teddy bear remained a staple childhood companion, about 80 percent of all Bear-Gram recipients were adults. According to Putnam, in a 1994 *Washington Post*, the success of The Vermont Teddy Bear Company occurred because the company redefined the teddy bear as a gift item appropriate to all ages and occasions. "We married a cuddly, appealing creature with the concept of an impulse purchase," he was quoted as saying. Where once a husband might have sent flowers or chocolates to his wife for Valentine's Day, he now sent a teddy bear. Women, who were by far the company's greatest repeat customers, sent teddy bears to friends and family to commemorate personal occasions throughout the year.

The success of the Bear-Gram stimulated another growth period for the company. In 1994, bears, which sold for $60 to $250, began to be marketed in high-end retail outlets such as FAO Schwarz, Bloomingdale's, Henri Bendel's, and 250 smaller gift stores across the country, as well as in catalogues such as Spiegel. Television and billboard advertisements complemented the company's own catalogue, which went out to a mailing list of one million and featured other Vermont-made products such as children's books and toys to accompany specific bears. Down the road from the original factory, the company began construction on its new 62,000-square-foot, $7.5 million headquarters on a 57-acre parcel of land, complete with giant beanie hat and whirring propeller atop garishly painted farm-style buildings. Sortino, projecting a continued rise in sales, stockpiled somewhere between $3.5 and $4 million worth of bears and accessories. In 1995, the company moved into its new complex, set up a warehouse and fulfilment center in Livingston, England, and was on its way toward launching a manufacturing plant in the United Kingdom.

Losses Lead to New Leadership in the Mid-1990s

However, all did not follow happily ever after for the fairy tale-like business. While the company had grown more than expected in 1994, expansion was at times chaotic and even precipitous. Marketing by radio to the New York, Boston, and Chicago markets was expensive—30 percent of the company's revenue in 1994—and resulted in a $54,000 loss for that year, despite sales of $20.6 million. The attempt to break into the overseas market was aborted shortly after Vermont Teddy Bear began marketing its bears in Britain in 1995. The company was left with a huge excess of bears. In August 1995, the company's board of directors, disturbed about losses of $330,000 per month and the company's $2 million debt, asked John Sortino to step down as chief executive officer. R. Patrick Burns, who had been a marketing executive at L.L. Bean and Disney Direct Marketing, took over the company.

Burns's agenda focused on reducing advertising and manufacturing costs, while relying more heavily on catalogue sales and sales at company stores, which he planned to open in New England and New York. At his initiative, the company signed a licensing agreement with Tyco Toys Inc. to make lower-priced miniature replicas of the company's hand-made toy bears to be sold at Wal-Mart and Toys 'R' Us stores. Under his stewardship, Vermont Teddy Bear also fired 16 percent of its 200-employee workforce to offset continued losses in 1995 of more than $2 million.

Key Dates:

1981: John Sortino sews his first teddy bear.
1983: Sortino founds The Vermont Teddy Bear Co., Inc. (The Vermont Teddy Bear Company).
1990: Vermont Teddy Bear introduces the ''Bear-Gram.''
1993: The company holds its initial public offering.
1994: The company builds a $6 million factory which doubles as a tourist attraction.
1995: R. Patrick Burns replaces John Sortino as chief executive officer.
1996: The company opens its first store on Madison Avenue in New York City.
1997: Elisabeth B. Robert becomes the company's chief executive officer.
1998: The company closes all retail outlets.
1999: The company partners with Zany Brainy, Inc. to place Make-A-Friend-For-Life kiosks in toy stores.

In 1996, the $17 million company opened its first outlet on Madison Avenue. A second store followed in Freeport, Maine. Neither of these stores proved very successful, however, and after losses of $2 million in 1997, both stores closed in 1998. The company also put more of its marketing dollars into its catalog operations, increasing circulation and expanding its offerings beyond teddy bears to everything from snowglobes to t-shirts and knapsacks.

However, the improvement in sales was only slight, and Elisabeth B. Robert, the company's chief financial officer since 1995, who replaced Burns as chief executive officer after he resigned in 1997, redirected The Vermont Teddy Bear Company to focus its efforts once again on Bear-Grams and radio advertising. Robert had prior experience in finance, manufacturing, legal affairs, and systems management. Since earning a graduate degree in business from the University of Vermont in 1984, she had worked as an executive for Vermont Gas, as a campaign manager, and for a fledgling high-tech firm. ''Radio ads are great for encouraging impulse buys,'' Robert told the *Boston Globe* in a May 2000 article. Complementing the company's decision to return to its roots was its web site, where potential customers could view what they would get for their $85 Bear-Gram. By 1998, although stock prices were still at a low of 31 cents, Vermont Teddy Bear produced 195,000 stuffed bears and tallied sales of $17.2 million. To keep up with growing demand, the company added a second sewing shift and, in 1999, a second manufacturing facility in Newport, Vermont.

The company sewed 260,000 bears to produce revenues of $21.6 million in 1999, surpassing its prior peak in sales of $20.5

million set in 1994. Driving the expansion, according to Roberts in her annual letter to stockholders, was the company's radio advertising campaign in new markets across the country, backed by the company's web site, which received 25 percent of total orders by June 1999. The company also closed its remaining satellite stores in 1999 and entered into its first wholesale partnership with leading toy retailer Zany Brainy, Inc. to market its Make-A-Friend-For-Life concept via kiosks in toy stores nationally. The plan called for Vermont Teddy Bear to supply Zany Brainy with the necessary bear components, outfits, and accessories so that customers might construct customized teddy bears onsite.

By 2000, Vermont Teddy Bear was well on its ways to implementing the five-year plan it established in 1999, expanding and diversifying its markets, distribution channels, and product lines. In April, it reported 50 to 60 percent growth for the year to date and announced plans to lease a new 60,000-square-foot facility next to its Shelburne factory. In 1999, it had expanded its product line to include lower cost, imported teddy bears designed and manufactured for corporate customers. It also debuted its PreFUR'd Member service, offering discounts to repeat customers to coincide with slower business periods. The strategy seemed to be successful. While Valentine's Day (followed by Christmas and Mother's Day) remained the company's busiest holiday, online purchases, boosted by Yahoo's decision to feature the Bear-Gram on its new Internet mall, began to account for about 30 percent of total Vermont Teddy Bear sales. The company was now advertising on more than 500 radio stations and was aiming for a ''hipper, edgier'' product.

Principal Competitors

Gund, Inc.; 1-800-FLOWERS.COM; Applause Enterprises; North American Bear Company.

Further Reading

Auerbach, Jon, ''Struggling in a Bear Market,'' *Boston Globe*, November 26, 1995, p. 81.

Calta, Marialisa, ''The Place the Teddy Bears Have Their Christmas,'' *Washington Post*, December 22, 1994, p. T6.

Pedley, Brian, ''Travel,'' *Daily Telegraph*, May 20, 1996, p. 28.

Reidy, Chris, ''Vermont Company Repositions Teddy Bear,'' *Boston Globe*, May 12, 2000, p. E4.

Sabo, Sandra R., ''Teddy Bears, Vermont Style,'' *Beans & Bears!*, November 1999, p. 51.

Smith, Geoffrey, ''Can Teddy Bears Come Out of the Woods?,'' *Business Week*, March 18, 1996, p. 12.

Sneyd, Ross, ''It's a Bear Market,'' *Los Angeles Times*, September 19, 1995, p. D8.

—Carrie Rothburd

Vodafone Group PLC

The Courtyard
2 - 4 London Rd
Newbury
Berkshire RG 14 1JX
United Kingdom
Telephone: +44-1635-33-251
Fax: +44-1635-45-713
Web site: http://www.vodafone-airtouch-plc.com

Public Company
Incorporated: 1985 as Racal Telecommunications Group
   Ltd.
Employees: 35,150
Sales £7.87 billion (US$12.55 billion) (2000)
Stock Exchanges: London New York
Ticker Symbols: VOD.L; VOD
NAIC: 513322 Cellular and Other Wireless
   Telecommunications

Since its landmark merger with Mannesmann AG, Vodafone Group PLC has become the first truly global wireless phone company. The largest company in Great Britain, where it pioneered cellular service, it has poised itself to become the largest in the world within a few years. Vodafone has 59 million subscribers around the world and has been focusing its future on bringing the Internet to consumers in Europe and beyond via wireless—not land-based—networks.

Origins

Vodafone was the brainchild of Racal Electronics Ltd., a modestly prosperous U.K. electronics firm, and Millicom, a U.S. communications company. Developed as a joint venture during the early 1980s, Vodafone was granted a license to develop a cellular network in the United Kingdom and was introduced under the auspices of Racal in January 1985. The new subsidiary's success was stunning. The corporate sector was quick to appreciate the advantages of mobile telecommunications, and individuals were equally quick to spot the status symbol potential of the new technology; fueled by business need and Yuppie culture, the demand for mobile phones skyrocketed.

Vodafone found itself one of only two entrants in the United Kingdom in a virtually unregulated new industry; the other member of the duopoly was Cellnet, which remained Vodafone's principal competitor into the 1990s. Throughout the 1980s the company created much of the technology—and enjoyed most of the profits—of this rapidly expanding field. Racal Telecommunications' profit and loss history from 1985 to 1989 succinctly describes the matter: in the year of its creation, Vodafone was operating at a loss of £10 million; by the end of the decade pretax profits were over £84 million. Racal soon developed allied divisions, including Vodac, Vodata, and Vodapage, to expand the number and type of services the company offered.

By 1988 Racal Telecommunications Group Ltd., as Vodafone and the related subsidiaries were officially known, was by far the most successful player on the Racal Electronics team. The parent company, fearing that the Telecommunications Group was hampered on the stock market by its subsidiary status, and wishing, in addition, to enhance other aspects of its business with profit from Vodafone stocks, proposed a partial flotation of the subsidiary. Millicom, the second largest shareholder, who lobbied for a complete sell-off, opposed the move; in the end, only 20 percent of the share capital of Racal Telecom was offered on the market. Three years later, however, Racal Electronics reconsidered, and Racal Telecom was separated from its parent company in 1991, at which time the name was changed to Vodafone Group Ltd.

Dominant in the 1990s

Vodafone was a market leader in the United Kingdom since its inception. Its main competitor, Cellnet, jointly owned by British Telecom and Securicor, was also granted its license in 1985 and grew as steadily as Vodafone. However, it always remained a step or two behind, with Vodafone generally enjoying some 56 percent of the market. The two remained the only companies on the scene for approximately eight years. Although an industry regulator, Oftel, existed, frequent rumors

Company Perspectives:

We aim to be the world's leading wireless telecommunications and information provider bringing more customers more services and more value than any other of its competitors.

that the duopoly would be subjected to some sort of price regulation never materialized—on the grounds, it is thought, that further competition in such an obviously lucrative industry was bound to eventually appear. As the *Daily Mail* commented in early 1993, ''Profits from mobile phones have been mouthwatering.'' Such competition did appear when Mercury, in a joint venture between Cable & Wireless and the telephone company U S West, issued its challenge in 1993.

Amid much publicity and a flurry of marketing, Mercury's Personal Communications Network, called One-2-One, was launched. Mercury's advertising campaign hammered home a message of lower costs. By offering low prices and even free off-peak local calls, Mercury forced the two telecommunications giants into a price war—but only in the London area, where Mercury's operations began.

One-2-One was seen primarily as a bid for the private market of mobile telephone users, whereas the majority of Vodafone's customer base was in the corporate sector, where demand and the tariffs charged were historically higher. Despite this, the company was clearly not unmindful of the competitors' interest in the vast untapped private market. It first responded to the threat of Mercury's introduction with its own countermarketing. After One-2-One was operating, Vodafone introduced new options such as Low Call, which, with its lower rental costs but higher call charges, was targeted at individuals who used their phones less frequently than business customers. Another new initiative, MetroDigital, a service begun in 1993 that allowed subscribers low rates when calling from an urban ''home cell,'' was aimed at least in part at the personal user market.

Mercury's One-2-One employed the new digital technology rather than the analog systems used until then by Vodafone and Cellnet. Digital technology represented a significant advance in the industry, as its use allowed for higher quality, better security, and lower costs. Not to be outdone, Vodafone too was expanding its digital network, and the company expected operations to be fully digital by the end of the 1990s.

As of the mid-1990s it was too soon to assess the ramifications of Mercury's entry into the market, or indeed that of newcomer Hutchison Microtel, which began operating its Orange network in 1994. Most financial analysts predicted, however, that there was room for all in a market so ripe for expansion; increased competition would thus have little effect on profit margins.

Although Vodafone Ltd. was clearly its flagship company, the Vodafone Group as a whole comprised several wholly owned subsidiaries that supported or complemented the activities of Vodafone Ltd. Vodac was the group's service provider, buying cellular airtime wholesale from Vodafone and selling it, equipment, and services to customers via service centers, retail outlets, dealers, mail order, and special corporate accounts. Another subsidiary, Vodapage, operated a nationwide radio-paging network; among the services it offered were Healthcall Medical Answerline Service; Neighbourhood Watch Information Line, a crime prevention service; and even the Rare Bird Alert News Service. Paknet, a radio-based national public data communications network, had a client base of banks, retailers, utilities, alarm companies, and others, and has a variety of applications. Country councils have used it to handle traffic measurements; British Rail uses it for credit card authorization.

Vodafone has been involved as well in a number of other specialized applications of its capabilities. ''SafeLink,'' introduced in 1992 in conjunction with the West Yorkshire Police, gave individuals fast access to the police via the Vodafone network. The ''Callsafe'' service, developed the same year, allowed stranded motorists to contact the Automobile Association. Perhaps the company's highest profile special application, however, came in 1993 when it provided the emergency mobile phone service to environmental rescue workers following the wreck of the tanker *Braer* in the Shetland Islands.

Vodata, another crucial subsidiary, developed and marketed new products and services for Vodafone and Vodapage customers. The company pioneered information services for users such as the Automobile Association's ''Roadwatch'' and the *Financial Times*' ''CityLine.'' ''Recall,'' the world's largest voice messaging service, was introduced in 1992. ''Vodastream'' fax allowed customers access to up-to-date macroeconomic statistics compiled by the Central Statistical Office; ''Met fax'' gave the latest weather bulletins; and ''Vodafax Broadcast'' allowed the facsimile transmission of information to several different destinations simultaneously.

Vodafone Group International was a rapidly growing component of the group. Active in seeking opportunities and implementing projects abroad, Vodafone International looked likely to one day be as important to the group as Vodafone Ltd. itself. In 1993 the company was awarded a license in Australia to operate that country's third digital mobile telephone network. In the same year consortia of which Vodafone was a member received similar licenses to operate in Greece and Germany. Vodafone also had substantial interests in France, Scandinavia, Hong Kong, Fiji, Malta, and Mexico. Although start-up costs for foreign ventures were obviously high, the field was very lucrative, and Vodafone was continually on the lookout for new possibilities. Analysts predicted that Vodafone would increase its investments with the aim of acquiring more foreign associates and, eventually, subsidiaries.

A digital system that allowed international calls between participating countries was introduced in the early 1990s. Called the Global System for Mobile Communications (GSM), it was first used by Vodafone, whose introduction of EuroDigital in 1991 allowed customers to ''roam'' throughout Europe and Scandinavia. In 1994 the company acquired a ten percent stake in Globalstar, an international consortium formed to develop a satellite-based network that would allow mobile telecommunications to operate everywhere in the world (except the polar ice caps) by 1998.

Key Dates:

1985: Racal Electronics and Millicom launch joint venture to develop a cellular telephone network.
1991: Vodafone Group Ltd. is floated as an independent company.
1997: The six cellular subsidiaries are reorganized under the Vodafone brand.
1999: Vodafone merges with AirTouch, a large cellular operator on the U.S. West Coast.
2000: Mannesmann AG is acquired in the world's largest merger to date.

As of 1994, Vodafone operated one of the world's largest cellular networks, with over one million subscribers. This, combined with the company's increasingly high international profile, made it a safe bet that Vodafone would continue its prominent role in the expanding mobile telecommunications industry. The *Mail on Sunday* confidently predicted in 1993: "We're on the verge of a communications explosion. By 2000, nearly all of us will have a phone in our pocket." It was highly likely that for many, that phone would be a Vodafone.

Digital phones took some time to catch on due to a limited service range and reliability problems; they accounted for only 13 percent of mobile phones in Britain in 1995. However, the new wave of digital entrants did force Vodafone and other analog providers like Cellnet to trim their pricing somewhat. Earnings for the fiscal year ending March 1996 fell four percent in the face of stiff competition from Orange and One-2-One. However, Vodafone's foreign operations soon began to post positive results.

Thanks to its profitable operations at home, the concept of credit remained foreign to Vodafone until July 1996, when it sought European capital to increase its stake in France's number two mobile phone provider, SFR. It paid FFr 1.8 billion (US$346 million) to raise its shareholding from ten percent to 16.5 percent. Vodafone also had equity positions in a number of other European and Asian cellular companies.

Chris Gent, who had sat on Vodafone's board for a dozen years, was appointed CEO in January 1997. He had never attended college but won a reputation as a shrewd businessman in the banking and computing industries. The company introduced a new corporate identity in the summer of 1997, uniting the six cellular providers it had acquired (Vodac, Talkland, Vodacom, Vodacall, Astec, and People's Phone) under the Vodafone brand. Vodafone began to restructure its network, laying off 250 employees. Its 300 retail outlets dropped competitors' products after the change. The success of One-2-One and Orange prompted regulators to allow Vodafone and top rival Cellnet relative freedom. All four providers promoted heavily during the Christmas 1997 season, each hoping to ensure its fair share of the widening market. The fastest growing segment—low-income clients—was being accommodated through pre-payment plans.

The Merger of the Millennium

Beginning January 1, 1999, subscribers became able to retain their phone numbers after switching providers. On the same date, 11 European countries introduced the Euro currency unit, making cross-border acquisitions theoretically more attractive. However, Telecom Italia's shareholders still chose the hostile offer Italian typewriter manufacturer Olivetti tendered in February 1999 over the friendly one of Deutsche Telekom largely due to nationalistic sentiment.

It would be a few months before Vodafone exploited the possibilities of the redefined European financial environment. Meanwhile, it merged with U.S. West Coast cellular company AirTouch in the summer of 1999, paying US$68 million. Although this merger thwarted Bell Atlantic from its plans for coast-to-coast wireless coverage, Gent was soon planning a huge new venture with this East Coast company as well.

German telecommunications giant Mannesmann AG bought Orange for US$33 billion in October 1999. Some saw the expensive purchase as a move to dissuade potential corporate raiders. However, the teaming of Orange and Mannesmann scuttled plans Vodafone had with Mannesmann's German and Italian mobile phone units and Vodafone launched its own takeover bid on November 16.

Before the takeover was closed, Vodafone had formed a joint venture (Multi Access Portal or MAP) with Vivendi, the French media and telecom group, shutting off a potential white knight from Mannesmann. The German company was also constrained by a lack of poison pill and other takeover defenses in its home country.

After a spirited campaign played out in the media, in February 2000 Vodafone AirTouch acquired Mannesmann AG in the largest corporate takeover ever, surpassing even the merger of AOL and Time Warner in the preceding month. At US$180 billion, the final price was nearly twice the original offer. Vodafone shareholders owned 50.5 percent of the new company, Mannesmann shareholders 49.5 percent. Its market value of US$314 billion made it the largest British company and the world's sixth largest, according to *Barron's*.

It also entered the millennium as the only truly global wireless phone company. The post-merger Vodafone claimed more than 42 million mobile telephone subscribers in 25 countries. (*Business Week* reckoned Vodafone was paying US$9,000 per customer.) However, the real prize was Mannesmann's position in the European Internet market. Gent hoped to use the German company's established ground-based Internet service to grow Vodafone's own new wireless-based Internet service. Although relatively untried at the time, the fusion of mobile telephone and e-commerce technologies offered unprecedented marketing opportunities.

In April 2000, the Verizon Wireless joint venture with Bell Atlantic was launched. The European Commission approved the Vodafone-Mannesmann merger in the same month, stipulating that the combined company sell off its Orange unit and allow competitors access to its international network for three years. Vodafone also planned to sell Mannesmann's old automotive and engineering businesses.

Vodafone was showing strong customer growth in all areas. Its stock had doubled in the previous six months as investors caught on to the group's potential. In May 2000, France Telecom SA announced it was buying Orange for £25.1 billion (US$37.4 billion), creating Europe's second largest mobile phone group with 21 million subscribers. Aggressive competition surely lay ahead. The Globalstar communications satellite, in which Vodafone had an interest, was launched in the same month, and the Vizzavi Internet portal developed with Vivendi debuted.

Ever looking forward, Vodafone was developing new devices offering faster mobile connections than most Americans had on their home PCs. Its control of the tiny screen on millions of such units across Europe and beyond placed it at the center of a telecommunications revolution. More than one analyst expected Vodafone to become the world's largest company.

Principal Subsidiaries

Airtel Movil SA (21.7%); Belgacom Mobile (Belgium; 25%); Europolitan AB (71.1%); Globalstar L.P. (U.S.A.; 6.5%); Japan Telecom (27%); Libertel (Netherlands; 70%); Mannesmann Mobilfunk GmbH (Germany; 99.1%); MisrFone Telecommunications Co. (Egypt; 60%); Mobilfon SA (Romania; 20.1%); Omnitel Pronto Italia S.p.A. (Italy; 76%); Panafon SA (Greece; 55%); Polkomtel SA (19.6%); RPG Cellcom Ltd. (India; 20.6–49.0%); Safaricom (Kenya; 40%); SFR (France; 20%); Shinsegi Telecom Inc. (South Korea; 11.7%); tele.ring Telekom (Austria; 53.8%); Telecel Comunicacoes Pessoias SA (Portugal; 50.9%); Verizon Wireless (U.S.A.; 45%); Vodacom Pty. Ltd. (South Africa; 31.5%); Vodafone Australia (91%); Vodafone Fiji Ltd. (49%); Vodafone Hungary (50.1%); Vodafone Malta Ltd. (80%); Vodafone New Zealand.

Principal Competitors

British Telecommunications PLC; Deutsche Telekom; France Telecom Group; AT&T Corp.

Further Reading

Baker, Stephen, and Kerry Capell, "Chris Gent, King of the Web?" *Business Week,* February 14, 2000, pp. 60–61.

Brewis, Janine, "Vodafone More Than a Match for Mannesmann," *Corporate Finance,* March 2000, pp. 22–26.

Brown, Malcolm, "Slow March of the Mobiles," *Management Today,* December 1993, pp. 54–57.

"Calling the Masses," *Sunday Times,* June 20, 1993.

"Crossed Lines over Survey," *Sunday Times,* March 28, 1993.

Evans, Richard, "The New Microsoft," *Communications International,* April 2000, pp. 29–32.

——, "Tomorrow, the World," *Barron's* March 6, 2000, p. 28.

Ferguson, Anne, "Securing Racal's Future," *Management Today,* August 1988, pp. 30–31.

Guyon, Janet, "What Does This Gent Really Want?" *Fortune,* March 6, 2000, pp. 163–166.

"Harrison's Happy Ending," *Daily Telegraph,* June 9, 1993.

"The Lex Column: Mobile Market," *Financial Times,* June 8, 1994.

"A Line to the Future," *Mail on Sunday,* February 7, 1993.

"Mobile Telephones: London Calling," *The Economist,* August 5, 1995, p. 60.

Naik, Gautam, and Anita Raghavan, "France Telecom Confirms Plan to Buy Vodafone Unit; Purchase of Orange for $37.4 Billion Intensifies a Battle," *Wall Street Journal,* May 31, 2000, p. A21.

O'Sullivan, Tom, "Mobile Phone Rivals Plan Marketing Blitz," *Marketing Week,* December 11, 1997, p. 22.

——, "Vodafone Cuts Lines to Challenge Rivals," *Marketing Week,* July 10, 1997, p. 23.

Palmer, Jay, "Loud and Clear," *Barron's* December 16, 1996, p. 15.

Reed, Stanley, Kerry Capell, Heidi Dawley, and Stephen Baker, "Ready to Take on the World," *Business Week,* June 12, 2000, pp. 70–71.

Ryan, Vincent, "Vodafone AirTouch's Shock to the System," *Telephony,* February 14, 2000, pp. 35–36.

Schneiderman, Ron, *Future Talk: The Changing Wireless Game,* New York: IEEE Press, 1997.

Shishkin, Philip, and William Boston, "Vodafone Wins EU Clearance to Acquire Mannesmann in Record $180 Billion Deal—Competitors to Get Access to Network for Three Years; Orange Must Be Shed," *Wall Street Journal,* April 13, 2000, p. A14.

"Stay Well Connected for the Phoney War," *Daily Mail,* February 3, 1993.

"Upwardly Mobile," *Economist,* August 13, 1988, pp. 62–64.

"Vodafone: Casting a Worldwide Network," *Investors' Chronicle,* January 7, 1994.

"Vodafone Finds the Right Response," *Corporate Finance,* July 1996, p. 9.

"Vodafone Move Fuels Price War," *Financial Times,* June 17, 1993.

"Vodafone: On Line for a Breakthrough," *Investors' Chronicle,* October 22, 1993.

"Vodafone Signs up for $1.8 Billion Satellite Telecoms Venture," *Independent,* March 25, 1994.

Wallace, Charles P., "A Vodacious Deal," *Time,* February 14, 2000, p. 63

Wonacott, Peter, and Silvia Ascarelli, "Hutchison Whampoa Sells Stake in Vodafone, Raising $5.03 Billion," *Wall Street Journal,* March 23, 2000, p. A19.

—Robin DuBlanc
—updated by Frederick C. Ingram

Wallace Computer Services, Inc.

2275 Cabot Drive
Lisle, Illinois 60532-3630
U.S.A.
Telephone: (630) 588-5000
Fax: (630) 588-5115
Web site: http://www.wallace.com

Public Company
Incorporated: 1908 as Wallace Press, Inc.
Employees: 8,464
Sales: $1.53 billion (1999)
Stock Exchanges: New York
Ticker Symbol: WCS
NAIC: 323110 Commercial Lithographic Printing;
      323113 Commercial Screen Printing; 323115 Digital
      Printing; 323116 Manifold Business Forms Printing

Wallace Computer Services, Inc. is a commercial printer and printer of business forms and labels with a history dating back to 1908. In addition, the company offers print management services to its corporate customers through its Total Print Management (TPM) program. Wallace operates more than 40 manufacturing facilities, nine distribution and warehousing hubs, and 150 sales locations. It has won numerous awards for excellence, both from customers such as American Airlines, Federal Express, and Sears, Roebuck & Co., and from industry associations such as Printing Industries of America and the National Association for Printing Leadership, among others.

Operating As a Private Company: 1908–60

In 1908 the company was established as an Illinois commercial printer under the name Wallace Press, Inc. Its founder, Walter Franklin Wallace, Sr., was born in Chicago in 1881. He graduated from Yale University in 1903 and became a trade publication editor. Around this time he inherited a farm in suburban Chicago. In 1908 he sold the farm to buy a printing press and started Wallace Press, Inc. as a one-person commercial printer. One of his first customers was Sears, Roebuck &

Co., for which he printed catalogs and manuals. By 1923 sales surpassed $1 million. In 1928 the company moved to a larger facility in downtown Chicago. Wallace received its first order for a business form in 1930. For the next several decades Wallace operated as a printer of business forms and labels as well as a commercial printer of brochures, catalogs, and other materials for business.

In 1952 the founder's son, Walter F. "Bob" Wallace, Jr., took over as president of the company. He had attended Northwestern University and learned the printing business as a plant worker. In 1957 the company expanded and opened a second manufacturing location in Clinton, Illinois. The plant's first order was shipped in early 1958, and overall the company's sales reached more than $12 million.

Period of Expansion: 1960s–70s

In 1960 Wallace created a direct sales force to service forms users in all parts of the United States. In 1961 Wallace became a publicly held company, with its shares trading on the New York Stock Exchange. The company was reorganized in June 1963 as Wallace Business Forms, Inc., a Delaware corporation.

In 1966 Wallace expanded through acquisitions in the East and Southeast. It began construction of a new corporate headquarters and press division in Hillsdale, Illinois. The company also expanded into Virginia with its new plant in Luray. The plant broke even in its first year of operation.

In 1978 Wallace initiated a new strategy to become a single-source supplier and distributor of business forms, labels, and commercial and direct response printing. The company began to implement an aggressive acquisitions strategy that continued through the end of the century.

New Name Better Reflection of Company's Business: 1980s

In 1981 the company changed its name to Wallace Computer Services, Inc., to better reflect the wide range of products it sold to computer users, especially forms and labels. Toward the end of 1985 the Occupational Safety and Health

Administration (OSHA) began requiring that drums of motor oil and other hazardous chemicals be specially labeled. This created a boon for label printers such as Wallace, which developed Printware, a computer program to generate labels on a personal computer. Printware saved customers the trouble of stocking large quantities of labels that would have to be discarded whenever a formula changed. With Printware, they could create a generic label, then print and create label variations as needed.

At the end of the 1980s, Wallace was the fifth largest producer of business forms in the United States. It had 27 consecutive years of increased sales and earnings and raised its dividend every year since 1973.

Innovations and Acquisitions Fueling Growth: 1990s

In 1990 Wallace completed a 300,000-square-foot distribution center in St. Charles, Illinois. It was the central point for ordering all stock items from Wallace. Wallace's revenues for fiscal 1991 ending July 31 were hurt by a nationwide recession that affected the business forms industry. In 1992 Wallace introduced W.I.N., the Wallace Information Network, which was the first Windows-based information management system in the printing industry. During the coming decade this system would attract customers and allow Wallace to expand into print management services for its customers.

In 1995 Wallace entered into an alliance with distributor United Stationers to improve its position in the contract stationers market, selling office supplies wholesale to large companies. It planned to use a variation of W.I.N. to offer one-stop shopping for office supplies. That same year Wallace also acquired Forms Engineering, a Los Angeles-based direct mail printer with about $38 million in annual sales, to complement its own direct mail division, Colorforms.

Also in 1995 rival Canadian printer Moore Corp. launched a $1.3 billion hostile takeover bid for Wallace. Based on an analysis by investment banker Goldman, Sachs & Co., Wallace rejected the bid. Later, minority shareholder Wyser-Pratte, a New York arbitrage firm, challenged Goldman's valuation of the company, claiming that Goldman inflated Wallace's value by as much as 18 percent. Wyser-Pratte owned about 2.7 percent of Wallace's stock.

Following Moore's announced bid, Wallace's stock rose 33 percent. Wallace subsequently rejected a second, higher bid

from Moore, which was the largest business forms printer in North America. Moore was losing U.S. market share to Wallace, in part because of Wallace's innovative W.I.N. system, which allowed customers to design and produce standard business documents, labels, and other forms on the computer, as well as manage inventory for both paper and electronic forms. Wallace would often run the systems onsite for its customers. Although Moore had a similar technology, Wallace's was more advanced. For fiscal 1995 ending July 31, Wallace's revenues were $713 million, compared with Moore's revenues of $2.6 billion. Moore withdrew its bid for Wallace at the end of 1995.

Responding to increased growth, Wallace constructed a new 100,000-square-foot corporate headquarters in Lisle, Illinois, in 1996. During the year Wallace acquired Post Printing Inc., of West Bend, Wisconsin, which had about 80 employees and annual revenues around $8 million. For fiscal 1996, Wallace reported sales of $862.3 million, an increase of 21 percent over 1995. Earnings rose 32 percent to $73 million. Wallace's growth came at a time when the business forms printing industry was shrinking at the rate of about two percent a year; it was attributed in part to the success of the Wallace Information Network (W.I.N.). Newly acquired customers included large firms such as BankAmerica Corp. and Rubbermaid Inc. During the year Wallace expanded its capacity at existing plants. It opened a new distribution center in Los Angeles, added 100,000 square feet to a plant in Georgia, and increased its Tennessee plant by 75,000 square feet.

Wallace's strategy for growth was to become a business partner to its customers, not just a vendor. Among its alliances and partnerships, Wallace provided American Express Travel Management Services with a cost-effective solution to automate the travel expense reporting process. American Express characterized the partnership as ''a breakthrough in the development of electronic form applications.'' Wallace considered itself part of a network of relationships and alliances, many of which were based on five-year contracts. Wallace's emphasis had evolved from a pure product orientation to more of a service orientation. It had moved into forms management to manage the whole process of storage, distribution, and procurement. In many cases Wallace employees would run that business segment onsite at its customer's location. The W.I.N. system gave Wallace's customers access to the company's internal operating systems, so customers could track inventory and orders. At the same time Wallace was building closer relationships with its own suppliers, in some cases outsourcing some aspects of its manufacturing. In the contract stationers market, Wallace's alliance with United Stationers allowed it to combine product categories and offer customers a broader range of office supplies.

With the acquisition of Graphic Industries, Inc. in 1997 and the creation of the Wallace Integrated Graphics commercial press group, Wallace became one of the largest printers in North America. Graphic Industries owned the largest network of sheet-fed commercial printing plants in the United States. The Atlanta-based company focused on high-quality, short-to-medium run collateral and high color marketing materials and annual reports for *Fortune* 2000 customers. It had 20 manufacturing plants and $450 million in annual sales. The acquisition reduced Wallace's reliance on business forms, which accounted for 34 percent of Wallace's revenues before the acquisition and

Key Dates:

1908: Company is established as an Illinois commercial printer under the name Wallace Press, Inc.
1923: Sales surpass $1 million for the first time.
1930: Wallace receives its first order for a business form.
1960: Wallace creates a national direct sales force.
1961: Wallace becomes a publicly held company on the New York Stock Exchange.
1963: Company is reorganized as Wallace Business Forms, Inc.
1981: Company changes its name to Wallace Computer Services, Inc.
1992: Wallace introduces the Wallace Information Network (W.I.N.), the first Windows-based information management system in the printing industry.
1995: Wallace rejects a hostile takeover bid from rival Canadian printer Moore Corporation Ltd.
1997: Wallace acquires Graphics Industries, Inc.
1998: Sales surpass $1 billion for the first time; company introduces Total Print Management service.

would contribute only 22 percent of Wallace's revenues after the combination. Overall, the $8 billion business forms industry was shrinking nearly four percent annually as companies replaced many forms applications with electronic systems. The $24 billion commercial printing market, on the other hand, was growing at two to three percent a year.

Wallace initially offered $18.50 a share for Graphic Industries, or about $260 million, in September 1997. When another firm, envelope maker Mail-Well Inc., said it was prepared to offer $20 a share or more, Wallace raised its bid to $21.75 a share, or about $438 million in all, including the assumption of $130 million of Graphic Industries' debt.

For fiscal 1997 ending July 31, Wallace reported a five percent increase in revenues to $906.3 million, although sales on a unit basis increased 12 percent. Earnings increased 11 percent to $81.3 million. In addition to the Graphic Industries acquisition, Wallace purchased Moran Printing Co. of Orlando, Florida, during the year. It also opened a label design center to assist customers in creating labels on demand with its Printware software package.

For fiscal 1998 ending July 31, sales surpassed $1 billion for the first time, increasing 50 percent to $1.36 billion due in large part to the acquisition of Graphic Industries. Net income, however, declined nine percent to $74.2 million. During the year Wallace entered into a joint marketing arrangement with Boise Cascade Office Products (BCOP), a subsidiary of Boise Cascade Corporation. Known as the BW Single Source Program, the agreement allowed each company to introduce the other company to its top 200 customers and allowed each company to market its products and services to those customers. Under the agreement, Wallace would provide custom printed products and central management services, while BCOP would supply stock office products and related supplies. In addition, both companies would provide customers with value-added services. In December 1998 Wallace sold its contract stationers business, Visible Computer Supply, to BCOP to increase the two companies' joint marketing efforts.

It was in 1998 that Wallace created a new service called Total Print Management (TPM). Based on Wallace's enterprise-wide information system W.I.N., TPM provided greater control and efficiencies for buyers of commercial printing. This and other Wallace services were highly dependent on the company's Wallace Information Network (W.I.N.), which was introduced in 1992. The W.I.N. system included a suite of management tools applicable to customer processes, including inventory management, end-user ordering, version control, tracking, and follow-up. Nearly 500 Wallace customers were using the W.I.N. system by mid-1999.

In June 1998 Wallace acquired Good Decal Co., an Englewood, Colorado-based maker of pressure sensitive labels, decals, and screen printed graphic overlays, for $13.3 million. In February 1999 it sold Mercury Printing of Memphis, Tennessee, which was part of the Graphic Industries acquisition, for $7 million. Mercury's and Visible Computer Supply's product lines were not compatible with Wallace's strategic direction.

In May 1999 Wallace acquired Commercial Press, Inc., a San Diego-based commercial printer, for about $25 million. The acquisition brought Wallace up to 27 commercial print facilities across the United States. The same month Wallace acquired Denver Graphic, Inc., a small prime label company, for about $3 million. The acquisitions were part of Wallace's strategy to expand its commercial printing business.

At the beginning of 2000 CEO Robert Cronin retired. President and Chief Operating Officer Michael Duffield succeeded him as interim CEO. Duffield had served as president and COO of Wallace since August 1998, when CEO Cronin succeeded retiring Theodore Dimitriou as chairman of the company.

In February 2000 Wallace acquired Metro Printing, Inc., a commercial printer serving the Minneapolis-St. Paul, Minnesota market. The company had 125 employees and annual sales of $12 million. The acquisition was Wallace's 24th purchase of high-quality commercial printers that were being networked by Wallace as part of its Total Print Management (TPM) program. For fiscal 1999, TPM generated about 40 percent of Wallace's revenues, or more than $600 million.

Also in February Wallace announced several cost-cutting measures in an effort to improve earnings and cash flow. It closed unprofitable printing plants in Cleveland, Tampa, and Miami and began phasing out a multiple-use plant in Lebanon, Kentucky. In addition, about 300 jobs were eliminated, and certain underutilized assets were written off.

In June 2000 Wallace was ranked 29th in *American Printers'* annual list of the "Top 50 Fastest Growing Printers." It was the second consecutive year that Wallace appeared on the list. The company's sales had grown nearly 70 percent from 1997 to 1999, due in large part to its acquisition strategy. Since acquiring Graphic Industries in 1997, Wallace had expanded its commercial printing capabilities by acquiring commercial printers, which were organized under the company's Integrated Graphics division, to take advantage of the growth in the commercial printing market. At the same time, Wallace continued to decrease its reliance on printing business forms and labels, which were organized under the Forms and Labels division.

Principal Divisions

Integrated Graphics; Forms and Labels.

Principal Competitors

Moore Corp. Ltd. (Canada); Quebecor Inc. (Canada); R.R. Donnelley & Sons Co.; Consolidated Graphics Inc.

Further Reading

"Amexco Pact," *Travel Weekly,* February 5, 1996, p. 66.

Avery, Susan, "Boise Aligns with Wallace for Integrated Supply," *Purchasing,* March 26, 1998, p. 84.

Denny, Sharon, "OSHA Regulations Bring Windfall to Label Makers," *Oil Daily,* March 17, 1986, p. B11.

Duschene, Stephanie, "Solving Problems with Someone Else's Solution," *Graphic Arts Monthly,* May 1999, p. S18.

Ezell, Hank, "Founder of Atlanta-Based Industries to Step Aside, Assume Role as Consultant," *Knight-Ridder/Tribune Business News,* October 14, 1997.

"Gerard's Cross," *Economist (US),* August 5, 1995, p. 5.

Giese, William, "10 Good Stocks the Bulls Missed," *Changing Times,* June 1991, p. 51.

Gramig, Mickey H., "Atlanta-Based Graphic Industries to Be Bought by Chicago-Based Company," *Knight-Ridder/Tribune Business News,* September 29, 1997.

Hajewski, Doris, "Wisconsin Printing Company Sold to Illinois-Based Computer Firm," *Knight-Ridder/Tribune Business News,* October 25, 1996.

Hapaaniemi, Peter, "The Best of Both Worlds," *Chief Executive,* June 1997, p. S12.

LaMonica, Paul R., "Hard to Get," *Financial World,* May 20, 1996, p. 44.

Leibowitz, David S., "This Time Won't Be Different," *Financial World,* May 30, 1989, p. 50.

Murphy, H. Lee, "Expansion into Printing Holds Promise for Biz Forms Maker, But Wallace Faces Heavy Debt Load from Purchase," *Crain's Chicago Business,* November 16, 1998, p. 49.

——, "Major Acquisition Will Take Wallace Beyond Biz Forms," *Crain's Chicago Business,* October 6, 1997, p. 24.

——, "Wallace Diversified with Printing Buy," *Crain's Chicago Business,* November 17, 1997, p. 26.

——, "Wallace Regains Its Balance After Navigating Hostile Waters," *Crain's Chicago Business,* January 13, 1997, p. 24.

Osterland, Andrew, "Popping Pills," *Financial World,* October 21, 1996, p. 36.

Picker, Ida, "Robert Cronin of Wallace Computer Services: Double Trouble," *Institutional Investor,* February 1997, p. 29.

Rodrigues, Tanya, "Local Pressroom Bought by Illinois-Based Firm," *San Diego Business Journal,* June 14, 1999, p. 30.

"Second Opinion," *Forbes,* March 11, 1996, p. 18.

"Wallace Completes Buy," *Graphic Arts Monthly,* February 2000, p. 28.

—David P. Bianco

Wells' Dairy, Inc.

1 Blue Bunny Drive
Le Mars, Iowa 51031
U.S.A.
Telephone: (712) 546-4000
Fax: (712) 546-1782
Web site: http://www.bluebunny.com

Private Company
Incorporated: 1917
Employees: 2,200
Sales: $530 million (1999 est.)
NAIC: 311520 Ice Cream and Frozen Dessert
   Manufacturing

Wells' Dairy, Inc. is the nation's largest family-owned dairy and ice cream company. Purchased at supermarkets, convenience stores, and vending machines, products with the Wells Blue Bunny logo include milk, ice cream, sherbert, frozen and fresh yogurt, sour cream, juice, cottage cheese, drumsticks, ice cream sandwiches, and treats such as Mickey Mouse bars, Mississippi Mud, Health Smart, The Champ, Bomb Pops, Pink Panther, and Cyberbyte. The company's milk and other dairy products are sold in Iowa, Nebraska, South Dakota, Minnesota, Missouri, Arkansas, Kansas, Oklahoma, Wisconsin, Illinois, and Indiana. Wells Blue Bunny Ice Cream and related items are sold in all 50 states and 30 foreign countries. The company makes not only its brand-name products but also produces ice cream and other items for Con-Agra, Pillsbury's Haagen-Dazs line, General Mills, Weight Watchers, and Walt Disney Company.

Origins As an Iowa Family Business

Though not incorporated until 1977, Wells' Dairy traces its origins back much further. The Wells family left Chicago at the turn of the 20th century to take advantage of federal homesteading laws allowing a person to own 160 acres of federal land after living on it, or "proving it up," for five years. In 1905 the family moved to South Dakota, where they were instrumental in founding the community of Wellsburg. In 1911 a terrible drought prompted the family to move again.

Fred Hooker Wells, Jr., one of the sons who had left Chicago with his parents, and his wife Miriam, decided to head back to Chicago. However, they ran out of adequate funds in Le Mars, Iowa, and decided to stay in that small northwestern Iowa town. Fred Wells, Jr., began raising hogs, an operation facilitated by a railroad line from Le Mars to the packing yards in Chicago. When cholera killed the hogs, Wells turned to another option.

Wells had gained some dairy experience back in Chicago, and he next decided to start a business delivering milk. On October 24, 1913, he signed a contract with Ray Bowers, who sold Wells a horse, a milk wagon, and a few milk cans and bottles. Bowers also agreed to sell Wells the milk he produced and not deliver milk himself in the same territory for five years.

All Wells family members helped in the dairy. Miriam Wells, for example, bottled the milk, and her sons helped their father deliver it to Le Mars residents. In 1918 they were able to construct a small building for business use, next to their home. The business continued to grow in the booming 1920s. During this time, the family also began making its own ice cream that was pasteurized before being frozen.

In the late 1920s the family established a plant in Sioux City, Iowa, with the help of Robert Harris and A. Paige, two employees who each invested $5,000 in the new facility. Harry Cole Wells, the brother of Fred Wells, Jr., moved from Doland, South Dakota, to manage the Sioux City business. In 1929 Fairmont Creamery bought the Wells Dairy plant in Sioux City, and the Le Mars firm agreed not to sell its products in the Sioux City region for the next five years.

Challenging the Competitors in the 1930s

In 1934 Wells Dairy resumed its Sioux City sales after the Fairmont agreement ended. The firm also expanded to smaller communities in northwest Iowa, including Remsen, Cherokee, Akron, Craig, Rock Valley, Brunsville, and Maurice. The growing firm not only challenged Fairmont but also upset members of the Farm Holiday Association. Wells Dairy continued to buy milk as prices declined to less than 25 cents a gallon, while the Association tried to get everyone to dump their milk to protest such low prices. In one episode in 1932 Association members threw rocks at a Wells Dairy vehicle carrying cans of milk. The

Company Perspectives:

Part of our success at Wells' Dairy is that we take into account the work/life balance of our employees; that is, we give consideration to issues that affect men and women with family responsibilities. In addition, we put a premium on innovation and results rather than formal processes. This kind of focus on people and innovation has given us dynamic, productive employees. We continually benefit from the successful pioneering of the people at Wells'.

Wells truck broke through an Association roadblock in what the family later called its historic ''midnight ride.''

During the Great Depression, Wells Dairy sponsored a contest for a new logo and name for its increasingly popular ice cream. Inspired by his son's love of a blue bunny he had seen at Easter in a department store window, a *Sioux City Journal* artist named George Vanden Brink won $25 for the original Blue Bunny logo.

In 1936 the dairy added its first continuous ice cream freezer that produced 150 gallons per hour. The company also hired a few new employees as its business slowly expanded. By this time, a second generation of the Wells family began making major contributions to the business. For example, Roy Wells began serving as the Wells Dairy general and production manager, while Harry Lee ''Mike'' Wells started a route to deliver milk in Sioux City.

During both good and bad times, the Wells family and its small business paid cash and refused to incur debt. Later generations would maintain that this fiscal conservatism helped provide the foundation for a successful long-term operation.

During World War II, the Wells family continued to run the dairy, with some of the sons exempt from military duty because they worked in the essential food industry. The family also worked to improve the dairy industry as a whole. For example, in January 1944 the Association of Ice Cream Manufacturers of Iowa elected Roy Wells to serve as its new president.

Postwar Developments

After Fred H. Wells, Jr., died in 1954, his sons Harold, Mike, Roy, and Fay, and their cousin Fred D. Wells, son of Harry Cole Wells, ran the family business as a partnership. Meanwhile, new facilities were added in the postwar period. For example, the main part of what the company would call the North Plant was built in Le Mars in the 1950s for the manufacture of ice cream products. In 1963 the company constructed its Le Mars Milk Plant. The family retained ownership and management of the business when it was incorporated under Iowa law in 1977 as Wells' Dairy, Inc.

The newly incorporated business expanded in the 1980s, a decade marked by phenomenal growth of the American economy and the addition of millions of new jobs. New corporate offices were added in 1980, and Wells' Dairy built new facilities for its growing fleet of trucks used to deliver milk around Iowa and nearby states. In 1983 Wells' Dairy purchased an Omaha plant. After being remodeled, the Omaha plant processed milk, yogurt, and fruit juice.

In the mid-1980s the firm's North Plant in Le Mars was enlarged through the purchase of five adjacent lots. New production lines, a mix department, and a high-rise freezer helped the company double the North Plant's capability. When completed, the expanded plant covered the equivalent of one city block, with its first floor taking up 109,000 square feet and its second floor comprising 44,000 square feet. Meanwhile, under the supervision of Doug Wells, a grandson of founder Fred Wells, Jr., a new quality control department was organized to monitor the firm's plants in both Le Mars and Omaha. The company in the late 1980s also added a Central Receiving Warehouse and a Technical Center.

The 1990s and Beyond

When the 1990s began, the company distributed its products in 27 states and employed over 1,000 individuals. Even more growth was on the horizon. In 1991 competitor Merritt Foods went out of business, and Wells' Dairy bought its assets and the rights to sell its products, including the frozen confection known as the Bomb Pop, originated by James S. Merritt and Doc Abernathy back in 1955. Wells' Dairy through its acquisition of Merritt Foods entered the vending business for the first time.

In 1991, with its business expanding, Wells' Dairy purchased 112 acres south of Le Mars where it built its new South Plant. The facility was described as ''A duplication of the North Plant, but larger, faster,'' by David Wells, grandson of founder Fred Wells, Jr., in the company history *The Wells Spring*. ''Basically we do the same thing at both plants, except for a few items,'' he added.

The South Plant was designed to produce a new low-fat, low-sodium dessert created jointly by Wells' Dairy and Omaha's ConAgra, as well as to expand Wells ice cream production by some 20 million gallons annually. The new plant was built with the aid of a $600,000 forgivable loan to Wells' Dairy from the Iowa Department of Economic Development. Since the new plant planned to employ some 245 new workers, government officials offered the incentive to promote Iowa's economic health. However, some critics referred to the loan derisively as a form of corporate welfare.

South Plant production crews made their first ice cream bars on July 2, 1992, using a state-of-the-art Glacier Omni 3000 ice cream machine. In the 1990s that plant was expanded to include 21 production lines. The company also built an automated storage and retrieval system that stored up to 2.8 million cubic feet of ice cream products.

Legal entanglements cropped up for Wells' Dairy in the late 1990s. In 1997 the company pled guilty to federal charges of fixing milk prices in contracts with Minnesota, South Dakota, and Iowa school districts from 1986 to 1992. In this case, heard in the U.S. District Court in St. Paul, the dairy accepted a $1 million criminal fine and agreed to cooperate with investigations into price fixing in the dairy industry. The company also agreed to negotiate restitution settlements with the school districts, while prosecutors agreed not to bring criminal charges against any company leaders.

Key Dates:

1913: Fred Hooker Wells, Jr., starts delivering milk in Le Mars, Iowa.
1920s: Family begins delivering ice cream in Sioux City, Iowa.
1935: The business adopts the ''Blue Bunny'' name for its ice cream.
1950s: Main ice cream plant is constructed in Le Mars.
1963: The company builds its Le Mars Milk Plant.
1977: Wells' Dairy, Inc. is incorporated.
1980: New corporate office is built in Le Mars.
1991: Wells' Dairy acquires Merritt Foods.
1994: The Iowa legislature declares Le Mars to be the Ice Cream Capital of the World.
2000: Company opens a new museum/visitor center in Le Mars.

Based on its 1999 revenues of $530 million, Wells' Dairy was ranked as number 465 in *Forbes* magazine's July 6, 2000 listing of the top 500 private companies. New products and marketing methods were a priority. The company replaced its ''funny bunny'' logo, prominent on the Blue Bunny ice cream label, with a classic rabbit image. Pursuing a more sophisticated image, the company recruited television actor Kelsey Grammar to perform in eight radio spots. Grammar, best known for his role as psychiatrist Frasier Crane on the television show ''Frasier,'' projected an epicurean persona and had a distinct voice immediately recognizable to many Americans.

Associations with large food conglomerates continued in the late 1990s as well. In January 1999 Pillsbury closed a Woodbridge, New Jersey, plant that made Haagen-Dazs ice cream and then in February contracted with Wells' Dairy to manufacture Haagen-Dazs pint and bulk products, as well as that brand's ice cream, sorbet, and chocolate-coated ice cream bars. Prompted by the lucrative Haagen-Dazs contract, Wells Dairy began a 120,000-square-foot addition to its South Plant in Le Mars. When completed, the plant would comprise some 550,000 square feet. However, on March 27, 1999, an explosion shut down the South Plant for two months.

Wells Dairy also faced the challenge of acquiring enough milk to meet demand for its growing product line and sales. Although it did ship in milk from as far away as California, the company preferred to purchase its perishable milk supplies within 150 miles of Le Mars. ''The closer to Le Mars, the better,'' said Dan Wells, senior vice-president and treasurer of Wells' Dairy, in the January 13, 1999 *Omaha World-Herald*.

In 1999 dairy farmers near Le Mars had about 65,000 dairy cattle that supplied Wells' Dairy with its main raw material, but the company estimated that in two or three years it would need milk from another 30,000 to 60,000 dairy cattle. Thus Wells' Dairy did all it could to promote the local dairy industry, including working with accountants to develop a business plan to show prospective dairy farmers. Still, Dan Wells maintained that his family was not interested in owning dairy farms.

The company in 1999 operated various facilities in Le Mars, Omaha, El Paso, Phoenix, and Kansas City, Missouri. Through co-packer agreements, Wells' Dairy products were sold in all 50 states and in 30 nations, including Indonesia, Mexico, Russia, Japan, Singapore, and Saudi Arabia. About 2,200 individuals worked for Wells' Dairy; some drove and maintained the company's 200 semitrailer trucks, while others produced milk, sour cream, cottage cheese, and over 2,000 ice cream products.

In 2000, Wells' Dairy remained a family-owned and operated business. Fay Wells served as the chief executive officer, with Gary Wells as the executive vice-president, Dan Wells as senior vice-president and treasurer, David Wells as vice-president of engineering, and Mike Wells as vice-president of sales and transportation. To share its history and promote its business, Wells' Dairy in March 2000 opened the new Ice Cream Capital of the World Visitor Center also sponsored by the Le Mars Chamber of Commerce and local businesses. In 1994 the Iowa legislature had proclaimed Le Mars to be the Ice Cream Capital of the World because it produced the most ice cream in one location. The Visitor Center presented videos of the company's history and the history of ice cream, first made in the 16th century. A restored delivery truck used by many dairies in the 1930s sat in the museum's parking lot. After viewing interactive computer programs and a mock-up of an ice cream plant, visitors were invited to eat ice cream at an old-fashioned soda fountain and were given the chance to buy souvenirs. By June 2000 over 13,000 persons had visited this unique museum to learn of the legacy of the Wells family and its role in making ice cream the quintessential American treat.

Principal Competitors

Prairie Farms Dairy Inc.; Dreyer's Grand Ice Cream, Inc.; Schwan's Sales Enterprises, Inc.; Ben & Jerry's Homemade, Inc.; Nestlé S.A.

Further Reading

Bergstrom, Kathy, ''Actor Hops on With Blue Bunny,'' *Des Moines Register*, April 15, 1999, p. 10.
Bowman, Judy, ''Former Journalist Scoops Up History of Le Mars' Wells Dairy,'' *Sioux City Journal*, June 30, 2000, p. A9.
Clark, Gerry, ''Energizing the Bunny,'' *Dairy Foods*, April 1999, p. 70.
''Fire Puts Wells' Plant Out of Commission,'' *Dairy Foods*, May 1999, p. 14.
Gustafson, Paul, ''Two Milk Producers Fined for Price Fixing,'' *Star Tribune* (Minneapolis), May 21, 1997, p. 3B.
King, Jackie, ''Corporate Welfare,'' *Business Record* (Des Moines), December 5, 1994, p. 10.
''Le Mars Firm Sees Need for More Local Dairy Farmers,'' *Omaha World-Herald*, January 13, 1999, p. 24.
Palmer, Jane, ''The Scoop in Le Mars,'' *Omaha World-Herald*, June 28, 2000, p. 39.
Sandrock, Fran, *The Wells Spring: A Family Story of Survival and Success,* Le Mars, Iowa: Wells' Dairy, Inc., 2000.
''Wells Dairy Is Awarded $600,000 to Build Plant,'' *Omaha World-Herald*, May 9, 1991, p. 22.
''Wells Dairy to Add 120,000 Square Feet,'' *Omaha World-Herald*, February 20, 1999, p. 22.
''Wells' Dairy Unveils New Brand Identity,'' *Frozen Food Age*, May 1997, p. 50.

—David M. Walden

Western Wireless Corporation

3650 131st Avenue Southeast, Suite 400
Bellevue, Washington 98006
U.S.A.
Telephone: (425) 586-8700
Fax: (425) 586-8666
Web site: http://www.wwireless.com

Public Company
Incorporated: 1994
Employees: 3,971
Sales: $567.34 million (1999)
Stock Exchanges: NASDAQ
Ticker Symbol: WWCA
NAIC: 513322 Cellular and Other Wireless
Telecommunications (pt); 551112 Offices of Other
Holding Companies

Western Wireless Corporation is a leading operator of wireless cellular telephone systems, marketing its service under the Cellular One brand name. Western Wireless operates in 19 states west of the Mississippi River, primarily serving rural areas. The company's cellular systems provide service to approximately 875,000 customers through licenses covering 83 Rural Service Areas and 18 Metropolitan Statistical Areas. Through its subsidiary Western Wireless International, the company owns interests in mobile telephone joint ventures in Iceland, Ireland, Ghana, Haiti, Croatia, Georgia, Latvia, Bolivia, and Côte d'Ivoire, serving approximately 320,000 customers.

Origins

John W. Stanton's professional career was steeped in cellular communications, as were the careers of many of the executives who joined him in developing Western Wireless. A graduate of Whitman College, Stanton continued his education at Harvard Business School, finishing his studies in 1979. Professionally, Stanton earned a name for himself at McCaw Cellular Communications, a Seattle-based company headed by John McCaw. Stanton joined McCaw in 1983 when the company was involved primarily in the cable television business. McCaw saw a brighter future for his company in cellular communications, however, and selected Stanton to execute his vision. Stanton, who served in various capacities under McCaw, ultimately becoming vice-chairman, led the charge into the new and unknown field of cellular communications. He persuaded British Telecom to help finance McCaw Cellular's aggressive expansion, snatched the highly prized New York cellular market from a host of rival suitors, and guided the company through its initial public offering (IPO) of stock—the largest IPO in the state's history. Stanton spent eight years building McCaw Cellular into a formidable cellular heavyweight. The value of his contributions was evident when the company completed the largest merger in the history of the telecommunications industry. With assets exceeding $9 billion, McCaw Cellular merged with AT&T Corp. in 1994, a transaction valued at $11.5 billion that created AT&T Wireless Services.

For Stanton, news of the historic merger arrived while he was busily involved creating a new force in the fast-growing cellular communications industry. He left McCaw in 1991, but before his departure he already had begun his career as an entrepreneur. In 1988, he founded Pacific Northwest Cellular and a predecessor company. Subsequently, he and his wife, Theresa Gillespie, who served as Pacific Northwest Cellular's chief financial officer, acquired another cellular concern. Fairfield, California-based General Cellular Corporation, which had filed for bankruptcy in 1992 after accumulating more than $100 million in losses, was Stanton's target. He joined investment bankers Goldman Sachs and San Francisco-based Hellman & Friedman in buying the senior debt of General Cellular, which then was converted to equity to bring the company out of bankruptcy. In July 1994, Stanton doubled the size of Pacific Northwest Cellular by combining it with General Cellular, at the time valued between $240 million and $275 million, according to documents filed with the Securities and Exchange Commission. The merger created Stanton's new vehicle for expansion, Western Wireless Corporation.

Western Wireless, which operated under the banner Cellular One, began with a coverage area that included 89 markets in 16 western states. The demographics of the company's markets revealed its distinctive quality and the essence of Stanton's strategy. The markets were in rural areas, so-called second- and third-tier communities that had been passed by, or in some cases shunned by, the rapidly growing list of cellular operators. The fierce battles, as Stanton had experienced in his fight for the New York cellular market years earlier, were being contested in the nation's largest metropolitan markets. The vast expanses of territory in between the heavily populated cities were, in large part, ignored. Although cities such as Los Angeles and New York contained millions of potential cellular subscribers, Stanton's supporters pointed out that there were far more small, rural markets than there were major cities. Further, as Stanton set his sights on communities such as Poplar Bluff, Missouri, and Aberdeen, South Dakota, the capital needed for licensing fees would be far less than the funds required to secure licenses in large markets. "The rural business is a better place to be than in the urban business," Stanton explained in a May 31, 1999 interview with *Wireless Review*. "Not because of the number of competitors, but because of the fundamental utility of the product. A rural customer is someone who is always a long way from a pay phone and spends more time in their car than an urban customer ever does."

As Stanton established a name for Western Wireless in rural markets, he also steered the company in another direction, one that demonstrated the talent of the management team he had assembled. Many of the executives working with Stanton had arrived from McCaw Cellular, where, under Stanton's tutelage, their abilities were borne out in the execution of Craig McCaw's vision. The same expertise would be shown in Stanton's new venture, a Western Wireless subsidiary named VoiceStream that was formed in 1994. While Stanton pursued rural markets with his Cellular One service, he also tapped into urban markets with VoiceStream to utilize a new piece of the wireless spectrum dedicated to personal communications services, more commonly known as PCS. Stanton decided to pursue urban PCS licenses because the technology represented an advancement over the analog technology used by most cellular carriers. PCS, a completely digital service, offered better operating capacity for cellular carriers as well as features such as paging, text messaging, and caller identification (caller ID).

Beginning with Western Wireless's first year of business, the expansion of Cellular One's rural cellular business and VoiceStream's urban PCS business occurred simultaneously. In 1994, Stanton pursued rural licenses, continuing with the $38 million acquisition spree he had conducted under General Cellular earlier in the year, when the company secured markets in South Dakota, Nebraska, Texas, Kansas, and Missouri. He also prepared for the multimillion-dollar bidding on PCS licenses, scheduled for auction by the Federal Communications Commission (FCC) in November 1994. Stanton applied to bid in 12 markets, including Seattle, Phoenix, Portland, San Antonio, and Des Moines, Iowa.

As Stanton earmarked millions of dollars for purchasing PCS licenses, he built one of the largest cellular operators in the country. Sales by the end of 1995—the company's first full year in business—reached $146 million. The cost of obtaining rural cellular and PCS licenses, however, was quickly taking its toll on the company, leading to a $56 million loss for the year, half of which was attributable to high interest costs and financing expenses. Debt was a consequence of Stanton's strategy, but not long after announcing the company's loss in 1995, Stanton could point to tangible results that justified the millions in investment dollars. In the spring of 1996, Western Wireless surged past many of the companies scrambling to deploy PCS by becoming operational in two major trading areas: Honolulu and Salt Lake City. Stanton had become one of the first operators to deploy PCS, and with licenses in hand for five other major trading areas, he would soon add to Western Wireless's network. First, he sought to reduce some of the company's mounting debt.

1996 Debut on NASDAQ

In May 1996, Stanton turned to the public securities market as a means to pay down debt and to inject his company with a fresh supply of capital. He sold 16.2 percent of the company for $23.50 per share, raising $258 million. The IPO ranked as the second largest in the state's history, trailing McCaw Cellular's 1987 IPO by $27 million. Stanton also sold $200 million in publicly traded debt, however, giving the company a total of $458 million, which ranked as the largest debut into the public securities market in Washington's history.

During the months immediately following the IPO, Western Wireless unveiled VoiceStream PCS in Albuquerque, New Mexico, and in Portland, Oregon. The company concluded the year by deploying service to two more trading areas, for a total of six by the end of 1996, before deploying the last of its initial seven networks in early 1997. Because of this expansion, the company's PCS operations extended to Des Moines, Iowa, Oklahoma City, and Seattle. Not only did Stanton win praise for his speed to market, but he also earned applause from industry pundits for an astute technological gamble. He built VoiceStream's system around a wireless communications standard different from what a majority of his U.S. competitors used, choosing the European standard called GSM, which was destined to become the most widely used standard in the world. One industry analyst noted as much in the December 24, 1999 issue of the *Puget Sound Business Journal*. "They moved into GSM when others weren't," the analyst explained, "and it's really paying off for them. They've ended up with the largest GSM footprint in the United States."

Key Dates:

1988: Stanton forms Pacific Northwest Cellular.
1992: General Cellular Corporation files for bankruptcy and subsequently is acquired by Stanton.
1994: Pacific Northwest Cellular and General Cellular are combined to form Western Wireless Corporation.
1996: VoiceStream PCS service becomes operational in six markets.
1999: VoiceStream is spun off from Western Wireless.

Late 1990s and VoiceStream's Spinoff

Western Wireless's success with VoiceStream stole the limelight as the company entered the late 1990s, but meaningful progress was achieved in the company's cellular operations as well. The company began developing a presence internationally through its subsidiary Western Wireless International Corporation (WWI). Beginning in 1996, the subsidiary commenced building and launching wireless networks abroad, aided by a number of mobile telephone joint ventures. Over the course of the next three years, WWI began operating cellular networks in Latvia, Georgia, Iceland, Croatia, Ghana, and Haiti. In January 2000, WWI, through a joint venture with the Modern Africa Growth and Investment Company, completed the acquisition of Comstar in Côte d'Ivoire. Concurrently, an operating joint venture of WWI was in the midst of constructing a cellular network in Bolivia. WWI also held a 67 percent interest in a company that was granted a cellular license in Ireland.

Domestically, Western Wireless's cellular operations continued to follow the strategy embraced at the company's formation. Licenses to provide service to rural areas were acquired by the handful, fueling the company's expansion. In 1996, Western Wireless maintained 74 properties with combined territory that included 6.1 million potential customers. By 1999, the company offered service in 101 properties with licensed coverage of 9.1 million people.

As Western Wireless prepared to exit the 1990s, it did so without the fast-growing business developed by its VoiceStream subsidiary. By 1999, VoiceStream had acquired PCS licenses for an additional 23 markets in 13 states, enabling

it to increase its number of subscribers to 1.7 million. Stanton had immediate plans to rapidly expand VoiceStream's subscriber ranks, but he did not believe VoiceStream could attract the attention it deserved while operating under Western Wireless's corporate umbrella. He decided to spin off the subsidiary to Western Wireless shareholders, thereby creating two separate companies. Although entirely distinct entities, Western Wireless and VoiceStream Wireless Corp. shared one common characteristic. Stanton served as chairman and chief executive officer of both companies. Whether he would continue to serve in these dual capacities remained to be answered as Western Wireless and VoiceStream Wireless pursued their development in the 21st century.

Principal Subsidiaries

WWC Holding Co., Inc.; Western Wireless International Corporation; Meteor Mobile Communications (67%).

Principal Competitors

Rural Cellular Corporation; Verizon Wireless; ALLTEL Corporation; SBC Communications Inc.

Further Reading

Baker, Sharon M., "Flying High with Wireless," *Puget Sound Business Journal,* December 24, 1999, p. 8.
——, "Three Cellular Pioneers Plan Own PCS Bids," *Puget Sound Business Journal,* November 11, 1994, p. 1.
——, "Western Wireless Completes Huge Initial Offering," *Puget Sound Business Journal,* May 31, 1996, p. 3.
Beach, Tarre, "On-Line; Western Wireless Poised to Serve Crow Reservation," *Wireless Review,* September 30, 1999, p. 16.
Locke, Tom, "Telecom Firms Escalate Competing Wireless Services in Boulder," *Knight-Ridder/Tribune Business News,* August 28, 1996, p. 8280340.
Mayfield, Dave, "Sprint, Omnipoint, Western Wireless Join Virginia Telephone," *Knight-Ridder/Tribune Business News,* January 15, 1997, p. 115B1120.
Meyers, Jason, "Eyes on the Prize," *Telephony,* November 4, 1996, p. S28.
Todd, Karissa, "The Titans of Wireless," *Wireless Review,* June 1, 1999, p. 3.

—Jeffrey L. Covell

White Castle System, Inc.

555 West Goodale Street
Columbus, Ohio 43215-1171
U.S.A.
Telephone: (614) 228-5781
Toll Free: (800) 843-2728
Fax: (614) 464-0596
Web site: http://www.whitecastle.com

Private Company
Incorporated: 1924 as White Castle System of Eating
   Houses Corporation
Employees: 12,000
Sales: $438 million (1999 est.)
NAIC: 722211 Limited-Service Restaurants

Considered the first fast-food hamburger chain and known for its unique steam-grilled patties, White Castle System, Inc. has long since been surpassed by the burger giants—McDonald's Corporation, Burger King Corporation, and Wendy's International, Inc. White Castle operates 345 restaurants located primarily in urban areas in the Midwestern and eastern United States. Unlike most hamburger chains, White Castle's restaurants, with the exception of a small number located outside the United States, are not franchised; all U.S. units are owned and operated by White Castle System, of which the E.W. Ingram family has been sole proprietor since 1933. In the early 21st century, E.W. Ingram III—grandson of founder E.W. Ingram—directed the company as chairperson, president, and CEO, while his father, E.W. Ingram, Jr., held the position of chairman emeritus.

White Castle System also owns and operates three bakeries, two meat processing plants, and two frozen sandwich plants. Its subsidiary, PSB Company, manufactures White Castle restaurant equipment. Another subsidiary, White Castle Distributing, Inc., markets and distributes frozen White Castle hamburgers to supermarkets nationwide. The company prides itself on its generous employee benefit plans and a turnover rate that is unusually low for the fast-food industry.

Although primarily known for its square hamburgers, White Castle also offers cheeseburgers, chicken sandwiches, french fries, onion rings, breakfast meals, and dessert pastries. Through a cobranding deal with AFC Enterprises, Inc., several dozen White Castle units also sell menu items from the Churchs Chicken chain. In their 75-plus years of existence, White Castle hamburgers have developed an image that sets them apart from other fast-food burgers. The pop music group The Beastie Boys sang an ode to the sandwiches in the 1980s, and the Canadian pop group The Smithereens wrote "White Castle Blues" several years later. According to a *Columbus Monthly* story on the 70th anniversary of the company, "Public opinion about the hamburgers [which sell at a rate of 480 million a year] seems to fall into three categories: Those who swear by the things, those who detest them, and those who haven't tried them out of fear or lack of opportunity and are waiting to be included in the first two categories."

White Castle hamburgers have such nicknames as Sliders, Gut Bombs, Castles, Whitey-One-Bites, and Belly Busters, and in recent years, the company's marketing team has capitalized on this image. Company publicity refers to the hamburgers as "Sliders" and has even stated that "the full impact of eating White Castle hamburgers normally isn't felt until the day after." The company also sponsors contests for recipes incorporating White Castle hamburgers and sells clothing emblazoned with the White Castle logo or its "Slider" nickname.

Fast-food Pioneer in the 1920s

The distinctive taste of White Castle hamburgers is attributed to one of the restaurant's cofounders, Walter Anderson. Anderson worked in a Wichita, Kansas restaurant and had perfected a unique way of cooking hamburger patties, adding shredded onions and placing both halves of the bun over the sizzling meat. In 1916, he rented a remodeled streetcar, bought a griddle plate and refrigerator, and opened his own hamburger stand. Using the slogan "buy 'em by the sack," Anderson sold a good number of hamburgers.

By 1921, he had three hamburger stands in operation and was looking to finance the opening of a fourth. That year, he met E.W. "Billy" Ingram, a real estate and insurance broker. With a $700 loan, the two founded the first White Castle restaurant, an

11- by 16-foot cement block structure that resembled a small castle, complete with turrets and battlements.

At that time, hamburgers were a relatively novel food item, sold at fairs, amusement parks, carnivals, and some restaurants. Very few hamburger stands were in operation, and the ones that were had reputations as unclean purveyors of products that were less than 100 percent pure beef. According to a speech by Ingram at a 1964 Newcomen Society meeting in Columbus, Ohio, his and Anderson's goal was to "break down a deep-rooted prejudice against the hamburger by constantly improving its quality and serving it in clean and sanitary surroundings." He added that the two chose the name White Castle, because " 'White' signifies purity and cleanliness and 'Castle' represents strength, permanence and stability."

The two established a motto: "Serve the finest products, for the least cost, in the cleanest surroundings, with the most courteous personnel." The two also had another motto: "He who owes no money will never go broke." Within 90 days of opening its first restaurant, the firm of Anderson and Ingram repaid its debt. Profits were fueled back into the organization, and more restaurants were opened. In 1924, Anderson and Ingram incorporated their company as White Castle System of Eating Houses Corporation. Competing hamburger stands inspired by the success of White Castle popped up all over Wichita, run by theater operators, real estate brokers, and even Ingram's own dentist.

Between 1923 and 1931, White Castle System established 100 restaurants in cities across the Midwest. In his speech to the Newcomen Society, Ingram claimed that in each city where they opened a restaurant, "We searched carefully but did not find any places specializing in the sales of hamburger sandwiches." He went on to add that White Castle created its own competition.

In its early years, White Castle also focused on the quality of its coffee. "We try to serve the best coffee in town" signs were hung in each restaurant, earnestly stating a company goal during the first 30 years of business. Indeed, White Castle took this statement seriously, setting uniform standards throughout its restaurant system. Adherence was maintained using a hydrometer created especially for White Castle coffee.

In keeping with trends in the burgeoning foodservice industry, White Castle was also concerned about the nutritional value of its hamburgers. The company hired the head of the physiological chemistry department at a Big 10 university to spend a summer studying the food value of its burgers. The chemist hired a student as test subject, asking him to eat nothing but White Castle hamburgers for the entire summer. At the end of the period, the student was found to be in good health, despite the fact that he was "eating 20 to 24 hamburgers a day during the last few weeks." The professor recommended that calcium be added to the flour used in the buns and suggested a specific weight ratio of

meat to bun to provide a more nutritious balance of proteins, carbohydrates, and fat. White Castle complied, and altered its recipe only slightly since that time.

1930s and 1940s: Fast-food Innovator

In 1931 White Castle became the first fast-food restaurant to advertise in a newspaper. Ingram and Anderson chose to concentrate on generating new carryout business, as counter space inside the restaurant was limited to less than 20 seats. Using Anderson's "buy 'em by the sack" slogan, White Castle ran a quarter-page ad in two St. Louis evening newspapers. Included in the advertisement was a coupon offering five hamburgers for a dime between two p.m. and midnight on the following Saturday. The advertisement was a success. By two p.m. that Saturday, most White Castles had lines forming outside their takeout windows. Within an hour, some operations had run out of buns. Supply houses had to work overtime to produce buns and burgers to meet the demand. Buoyed by the achievements of their original advertisement, Ingram and Anderson continued the practice, making coupons valid for 24-hour periods, to prevent the flood of customers they experienced the first time.

The year 1931 was one of innovations for the company. Although there was no doubt that Anderson's "buy 'em by the sack" slogan was successful, a problem arose in that the burgers at the bottom of a sack full of hamburgers would often be crushed by the time a customer arrived at his destination. To prevent this from happening, White Castle developed cardboard cartons with heat-resistant linings—the first paper cartons used in the food industry. The company then expanded this concept to include cardboard containers for hot and cold drinks, french fries, and pie.

Other innovations introduced during this time included improving the quality and safety of beef through the use of frozen hamburger patties (another 1931 initiative), as well as a patented coffee mug design and exhaust systems and specially designed griddles in the restaurants. In 1932 White Castle incorporated its first subsidiary, the Paperlynen Company, to manufacture paper hats worn by White Castle employees. Company engineers had developed a machine that manufactured paper hats so quickly that one machine could make enough hats in two weeks to supply the entire White Castle chain for a year. Realizing they had a potentially profitable business on their hands, the company began marketing the paper caps to other foodservice establishments. By 1964, Paperlynen was selling more than 54 million caps worldwide a year.

As part of its marketing drive in the early 1930s, White Castle also began a campaign "to upgrade the image of the hamburger" in the minds of housewives. In each city where White Castles were located, the company hired hostesses who went by the name of "Julia Joyce." Julia Joyce would guide housewives on tours of their local White Castle, allowing them to examine the cleanliness of White Castle kitchens and the sanitary manner in which hamburgers were cooked. After the housewives finished their tour, the hostess presented each with a coupon offering five carryout hamburgers for ten cents redeemable immediately, as well as a coupon for children, valid the following Saturday. Julia Joyce also set up meetings with local women's clubs where she served hamburgers, coffee, soft drinks, and pie in carryout containers and then went on to

Key Dates:

1916: Walter Anderson opens a hamburger stand in Wichita, Kansas.

1921: Anderson and E.W. Ingram open the first White Castle restaurant, also in Wichita.

1924: Anderson and Ingram incorporate their firm as White Castle System of Eating Houses Corporation.

1931: Company innovations include newspaper ads, coupons, paper cartons for the burgers, and the use of frozen hamburger patties.

1932: Paperlynen Company is formed to make paper hats worn by White Castle workers.

1933: Anderson sells his interest in the company to Ingram.

1934: The company is relocated to Columbus, Ohio; Porcelain Steel Building Company is established as a manufacturing subsidiary.

1949: The use of a five-holed hamburger patty begins, speeding the cooking time and eliminating flipping.

1965: Chain begins using all-vegetable oil for fried foods.

1966: The founding Ingram dies; his son E.W. Ingram, Jr., takes over as president.

1977: E.W. Ingram III is named president of the company.

1979: The first drive-through unit is opened in Indianapolis.

1981: The "Hamburgers to Fly" home delivery program is launched.

1986: First overseas foray, with the granting of franchise rights to a Japanese firm.

1987: "Hamburgers to Fly" is replaced by the marketing of frozen burgers in supermarkets through a newly established subsidiary, White Castle Distributing, Inc.

1996: Through a franchising deal, expansion into Mexico begins; Churchs Chicken items are added to the menu of selected units through a cobranding arrangement.

explain how White Castle's carryout service could be used for families or club outings.

Perhaps one of White Castle's most unusual innovations was the design and construction of semipermanent restaurants that could be easily transported from one location to another. Because White Castles were relatively small (15 feet by 11 feet), many landlords refused to lease such a scant parcel of land for more than 30 days. Ingram came up with the idea of developing a building that could be moved, thus preventing the loss of a building when landlords refused to renew the restaurant's lease. In 1928 Ingram hired L.W. Ray to patent a movable restaurant unit. Modeled after Chicago's Water Tower landmark, the restaurant consisted of a metal frame with siding, battlements, and turrets made of white porcelain. In 1934 White Castle incorporated another subsidiary, the Porcelain Steel Building Company, to manufacture Ray's unique White Castle buildings as well as most of the company's kitchen equipment. Porcelain Steel constructed 55 of these restaurants, although only two ultimately had to be moved.

Ingram bought out his partner's interest in the operation in 1933 and the following year moved to Columbus, Ohio, pur-

chasing a ten-acre tract of land on which the company set up corporate headquarters and its Porcelain Steel manufacturing operations. Despite the severe economic effects of the Great Depression, White Castle's business grew steadily during the 1930s, from 59 million burgers sold during its first decade of operation to 294 million by the end of its second.

World War II, however, had a somewhat negative impact on White Castle's growth. Due to shortages of beef caused by rationing, the number of restaurant units shrunk from 100 to 70. White Castle's subsidiaries stopped making restaurant equipment and devoted their efforts to supporting the war. At the close of the war, when the restaurant business remained in a slump, Porcelain Steel began supplying fertilizer spreaders to O.M. Scott & Sons Company.

1950s Through 1980s: Steady, Modest Growth

In 1949, a White Castle employee made the discovery that broken hamburger patties cooked faster. This led to the development of White Castle's signature five-holed hamburger, a process that allowed the burger to cook more quickly and eliminated the time-consuming task of flipping the burger. The economy resumed its growth in the 1950s, and White Castle expanded into high-traffic urban areas in the Midwest and Northeast, such as Detroit, Minneapolis/St. Paul, Cleveland, and New York City. During that time, the company began the practice of selling frozen burger patties to customers who wanted to cook them at home. In 1957 the company hired Simpson Marketing of Chicago to handle advertising, and the number of hamburgers sold reached 846 million.

By 1963, White Castle was operating 100 restaurants in 11 metropolitan areas and owned 34 prime properties and two manufacturing subsidiaries. Growth continued steadily throughout the 1960s with little change in menu—with the exception of its 1965 decision to use all-vegetable oil for french fries, onion rings, and other fried foods (another industry first). When founder Billy Ingram died in 1966, his son E.W. (Edgar) Ingram, Jr., subsequently assumed the post of president.

White Castle's expansion remained conservative and modest, supported by internal funding and very few loans. Growth of the fast-food industry exploded in the 1970s and 1980s, led by the expansion of the McDonald's, Burger King, and Wendy's restaurant chains. From 1970 to the late 1980s, however, White Castle grew slowly but steadily, collecting stories about customers who "would do anything to get their hands on [White Castle] hamburgers." These included tales of a man who rented a silver Rolls Royce to take his wife to dine at White Castle in honor of their 50th wedding anniversary, as well as the story of a family who moved to a western state and missed White Castle hamburgers so much they had another family member drop bags of burgers down by parachute as he flew his plane over their farm.

In 1977 E.W. (Bill) Ingram III took over as president of the company, the third generation of Ingrams to hold that post. Two years later, in response to changes in the fast-food industry, the company opened its first drive-through establishment, in Indianapolis. The number of White Castle hamburgers sold topped 2.3 billion.

From 1977 to 1987, the number of restaurants grew by more than 100, and White Castle entered the second most productive period of its history. In 1981 the company instituted its innovative "Hamburgers to Fly" program, a service that provided a toll free number through which people could order frozen White Castle burgers and have them delivered anywhere in the United States within 24 hours. The service, according to company officials, was "an overnight success." During the 1980s, frozen White Castle hamburgers virtually created their own supermarket niche as private entrepreneurs purchased frozen burgers from restaurants and resold them to grocery stores at a profit. In 1987, White Castle decided to get in on its own game. The company discontinued its "Hamburgers to Fly" program, incorporated White Castle Distributing, Inc., and began an intensive campaign to market its frozen burgers at supermarkets across the United States. Sales grew by an average of 15 to 20 percent annually. By 1990, White Castle frozen hamburgers had captured the number three position in the frozen sandwich category, with annual sales of $27.2 million.

Gross sales exceeded $268.5 million in 1986, with per unit sales averaging $1.3 million, near the best in the industry. In 1987 White Castle ended its 30-year relationship with Simpson Marketing of Chicago and hired Gunder & Associates, a Columbus agency, to handle its $5 million advertising account. Shortly thereafter, the company instituted several new marketing strategies, including breakfast meals, children's meals, and a chicken sandwich.

While new store openings in the United States continued at a rate of 25 units a year, the company also expanded overseas in the 1980s, granting its first franchise rights to a Japanese firm in 1986. Soon, four White Castle units were operating in Kyoto, and other franchises were established in Thailand, Malaysia, Indonesia, and Singapore. By 1989, White Castle had 243 restaurants in operation, with an average volume per store second only to McDonald's.

1990s and Beyond

In 1991 White Castle celebrated its 70th anniversary with the slogan, "After 70 years, it's like nothing else. Nothing." The company took out a full-page color advertisement in *USA Today,* detailing the history of White Castles and previewing its coupons for 70 cent value meals. Sales that year hit $305 million. In 1993 the company launched a new advertising campaign featuring the theme "White Castle, What You Crave"; it was created by the firm's new ad agency, the Detroit unit of J. Walter Thompson. The following year, E.W. Ingram III added the chairmanship to his title of president and CEO, with E.W. Ingram, Jr., being named chairman emeritus.

By the mid-1990s, the company was selling 500 million burgers per year, and the number of U.S. units had reached 300. In 1995 White Castle Distributing began marketing frozen hamburgers and cheeseburgers through convenience stores and vending machines. White Castle's franchise-led expansion into the Pacific Rim had proved less than successful, but the company launched another attempt at overseas growth in 1996 with its first unit in Mexico City. This, too, was a franchised operation. Also in 1996 White Castle entered into a cobranding

arrangement with Churchs Chicken, a unit of AFC Enterprises, Inc. and a fast-food chain similar to White Castle in its simple menu, value pricing, and demographics. Through the deal, selected White Castle units began adding Churchs Chicken food items to their menus. White Castle had been looking for ways to expand its menu, and this arrangement provided an efficient method for doing so. By early 1999, more than 87 units were selling Churchs Chicken products. The menu in selected markets also was expanded through the addition of Early Start Omelet sandwiches and jalapeño cheeseburgers in 1997.

By 1999 gross restaurant sales had reached $438 million. Plans for the early 21st century included the opening of 20 to 25 new stores each year. After nearly 80 years in business, White Castle System continued to grow in much the same manner it had throughout its history: conservatively, thoughtfully, and with a good dose of Billy Ingram's homespun wisdom.

Principal Subsidiaries

PSB Company; White Castle Distributing, Inc.

Principal Competitors

Burger King Corporation; Checkers Drive-In Restaurants, Inc.; CKE Restaurants, Inc.; McDonald's Corporation; Sonic Corp.; TRICON Global Restaurants, Inc.; Wendy's International, Inc.; Whataburger, Inc.

Further Reading

Bacha, Sarah Mills, "Leading White Castle Continues to Be Domain of Ingram Family Lineage," *Columbus Dispatch,* August 22, 1994.

Chenoweth, Doral, "Change Comes Slowly, Surely at White Castle," *Columbus Dispatch,* September 11, 1995.

Harden, Mike, "Fast-Food Fortress," *Columbus Dispatch,* June 9, 1996, p. 1C.

——, "White Castle Finally Getting Its Due from Academia," *Columbus Dispatch,* November 12, 1997, p. 1C.

Hogan, David Gerard, *Selling 'em by the Sack: White Castle and the Creation of American Food,* New York: New York University Press, 1997.

Ingram, E.W., Sr., *All This from a 5-Cent Hamburger!: The Story of the White Castle System,* New York: Newcomen Society in North America, 1975.

Kapner, Suzanne, "White Castle: Fast Food's Most Consistent Player Turns 75," *Nation's Restaurant News,* August 5, 1996, pp. 19, 152.

Kramer, Louise, "White Castle Leaps into Co-Branding with Churchs," *Nation's Restaurant News,* November 11, 1996, p. 3.

Mehta, Stephanie, "White Castle's Successful Recipe: Burger, Burger, Burger, Fries," *Wall Street Journal,* July 25, 1995, p. B1.

Meinhold, Nancy M., "From 'Doggy Bag' to Shopping Bag," *Food Processing,* October 1991, p. 14.

Oliphant, Jim, "White Castle: 70 Years of Sliders," *Columbus Monthly,* February 1991, p. 26.

Walkup, Carolyn, "E. W. Ingram," *Nation's Restaurant News,* February 1996, p. 81.

Wiedrich, Bob, "Every Worker's King at White Castle," *Chicago Tribune,* November 30, 1987, p. C1.

Williams, Brian, "Passing Family Business to the Next Generation Requires Give and Take," *Columbus Dispatch,* March 1, 1999.

—Maura Troester
—updated by David E. Salamie

Ziff Davis Media Inc.

28 East 28th Street
New York, New York 10016-7930
U.S.A.
Telephone: (212) 503-3500
Fax: (212) 503-5661
Web site: http://www.ziffdavis.com

Private Company
Incorporated: 2000
Employees: 3,397
Sales: $598.3 million (1999)
NAIC: 511120 Periodical Publishers; 514191 Online
Information Services

Ziff Davis Media Inc. is the leading U.S. publisher of technology and Internet magazines and also ranks as the sixth largest U.S. magazine publisher. Among the company's key publications are the consumer-oriented *PC Magazine, Ziff Davis SMART BUSINESS for the New Economy, Yahoo! Internet Life, FamilyPC, Expedia Travels,* and *eshopper;* the business-focused *eWEEK, Inter@ctive Week, Sm@rt Partner,* and *The Net Economy;* and in the gaming world, *Electronic Gaming Monthly, Official U.S. PlayStation Magazine, Computer Gaming World,* and *Expert Gamer.* One other U.S. title, *Macworld,* is produced through a joint venture with International Data Group. The company licenses its content and brands to licensees who produce some 50 additional titles in 30 international markets. The company also publishes four magazines in China through joint ventures.

The history of Ziff Davis Media is unusually complex, highlighted by three major events—a huge asset sale (1985) and two breakups of the company into several separate pieces (1994 and 2000). The company also evolved significantly over the years. It started out publishing specialty consumer magazines and then branched out into business niche publications, before refocusing on the computer magazine niche following the 1985 divestments. It then branched out again, into such related areas as trade shows and exhibitions, database and CD-ROM publishing, and online publishing. Following the 1994 breakup, it focused on its technol-

ogy publications and the ZDNet online content site. The company soon regained a presence in the trade show field and launched a cable television channel, ZDTV. But then in 2000, the company was broken apart yet again, with the technology publications gaining independence within Ziff Davis Media Inc., and the other Ziff units going their separate ways.

Niche Magazine Pioneer

The ultimate predecessor of the company was effectively formed in 1927—initially as Popular Aviation Company, becoming Ziff-Davis Publishing Company shortly thereafter. Founded by majority partner William B. Ziff, World War I flyer, author, and lecturer, and minority partner Bernard Davis, the company launched a line of hobby and leisure magazines with *Popular Aviation* (still published today as *Aviation*). During the early years, the company grew at a tremendous rate (expanding to 32 times its initial size in its first ten years), publishing a combination of reference, trade, and juvenile books; "pulp" magazines such as *Amazing Stories, Air Adventures, Mammoth Detective, Mammoth Mystery,* and *Mammoth Western;* and specialty consumer magazines such as *Modern Bride, Popular Aviation, Popular Electronics,* and *Radio News.* Although the company was successful with most of its various publishing ventures, William Ziff never devoted his full attention to the business, preferring to focus on his writing, flying, and other interests, so Davis effectively handled day-to-day operations. By the early 1950s, the company was losing money.

When Ziff died of a heart attack in 1953, his share in the company passed to his son, William B. Ziff, Jr., then 24 and a student of philosophy. He surprised his family by deciding to give up his promising academic career to run Ziff-Davis. Unlike his father, he immediately immersed himself in the business, buying out Davis in 1956. He concentrated on expanding the company's specialty consumer line by aggressively acquiring additional niche magazines. His timing was perfect in that the arrival of television as *the* medium for mass communication spelled the downturn for general interest magazines such as *Life* and the *Saturday Evening Post.* Ziff's response to television was to focus on publications that were tightly focused on narrow topics, giving readers specialized information they

Company Perspectives:

Ziff Davis Media Inc. is the leading information authority for buying, using and experiencing technology and the Internet.

could obtain nowhere else and providing advertisers an audience tailored for their products. Over the next 30 years, Ziff-Davis acquired such titles as *Car and Driver, Popular Mechanics, Psychology Today,* and *Stereo Review,* identifying each as the market leader in its particular field or one that Ziff-Davis could move into that position.

Meanwhile Ziff recognized another lucrative area for growth through the acquisition of what *Newsweek* called "obscure but highly profitable trade publications." Similar to Ziff's consumer titles, these business journals were each targeted at a narrow audience, primarily people in the travel and aviation industries for whom the titles became "must" reading. The titles included *Business & Commercial Aviation, Hotel & Travel Index, Travel Weekly, World Aviation Directory,* and the flagship of the group, *Meetings & Conventions,* which by 1983 generated $12 million in annual revenues.

In 1969 Ziff formed the Ziff Communications Company and made Ziff-Davis one of its divisions. At this time, he transferred ownership through trust funds to his three sons, who held a 90 percent interest, and three nephews, who held the remaining ten percent. Ziff himself remained in firm control of the company throughout this period as chairman, with a hands-on management style criticized by some insiders and outside observers as autocratic but difficult to question given the company's continued profitability.

Besides innovation in developing special interest magazines, Ziff Communications also pioneered in its approaches to market research and advertising. Through heavy expenditures on market research, the company gathered detailed profiles of who was reading each magazine, the content they sought, and the advertising to which they might respond. This data helped each editor tailor his or her magazine to the readership and enabled the advertising salespeople to precisely target potential clients. The market research data was also shared with the advertisers themselves to design campaigns in what was known as "consultative selling." Another advertising innovation was offering clients discounts for placing the same ad in a group of related magazines. By 1984, these strategies had fueled the company's continuing growth, with the group of Ziff consumer magazines alone posting estimated annual revenues of $140 million.

Early 1980s: Expanding into Computer Magazines and Databases

According to many observers, Ziff had become bored with the business and with his success when in the early 1980s he began to take Ziff Communications into new territory. In 1979 he spent $89 million to purchase Rust Craft Greeting Cards Incorporated for its six television stations, but within a few years he sold them for $100 million, saying that television was not the "turn-on" he had hoped for. A longer-lasting and eventually more successful foray was into a new area of specialty publishing: computer magazines. The initial titles in this line, such as *PCjr,* were developed in-house beginning in 1981, but Ziff Communications soon returned to its acquisition strategy, most notably through the purchase of *PC Magazine* in 1982. The beginning years for these magazines were difficult, however, as the boom in the computer industry spawned a boom in the publication of specialty computer magazines. Although most of these titles were losing money in the early 1980s, the losses eventually represented an investment that was recouped many times over. Similarly, another new Ziff venture at this time was the 1980 acquisition of Information Access Company (IAC), a pioneer in electronic publishing and one of the first companies to produce databases on CD-ROM, including *Magazine Index, National Newspaper Index,* and *Trade and Industry Index.* IAC designed its InfoTrac workstations that accessed these databases to be user-friendly and offered full text on some of them, providing a competitive advantage over other indexes that offered only article abstracts.

Meanwhile, Ziff's consumer and business publications were reaching their peak of success. By 1984, many of these magazines were the circulation and/or revenue leaders in their respective markets. *Car & Driver* outpaced *Road & Track, Popular Photography* was the top choice for photographers, and *Cycle* led *Cycle World* for motorcyclists. Annual revenue for the most part was increasing. For example, *Car & Driver* posted $33 million in revenue in 1983, a gain of 18.6 percent over the previous year. The business publications were in similarly strong positions as market leaders—with $12 million in 1983 revenue for *Meetings & Conventions,* an increase of 20.5 percent—and enjoyed particularly high margins. Many in the industry were surprised, then, by the October 1984 announcement that Ziff was placing 24 magazines up for sale, 12 in its consumer group and 12 in its business group. Rumors soon began to circulate that William Ziff, Jr., was becoming progressively more ill with prostate cancer and wished to simplify his estate and protect his family's future. His three sons were 14, 18, and 20.

Mid-1980s Through Early 1990s: Focusing on Computer Magazines, Expanding into Trade Shows, Internet

After much speculation about possible purchasers, receipt of a variety of bids (for the whole lot, for one group or the other, and for individual magazines), and estimates that Ziff would receive between $300 million and $750 million for all 24 titles, CBS Inc. announced on November 20, 1984, that it had reached an agreement with Ziff to purchase the complete consumer group for $362.5 million, thought to be a record at the time for the sale of a group of magazines. The very next day, Rupert Murdoch announced that he had bought the entire business group for $350 million. Following these sales, Ziff Communications was essentially reduced to its computer magazines and IAC—none of which were offered in the auction, in part because their financial situations were less robust.

William Ziff, Jr., reduced his role in the operation of Ziff Communications for the next few years as he successfully battled against cancer. How closely the fortunes of the company were tied to his involvement is evident from the company's

Key Dates:

1927: William B. Ziff and Bernard Davis found Popular Aviation Company, publisher of *Popular Aviation* magazine; the company is soon renamed Ziff-Davis Publishing Company.

1953: Ziff dies and is succeeded by his son, William B. Ziff, Jr.

1956: Ziff, Jr., buys out Davis.

1969: Ziff Communications Company is formed, with Ziff-Davis becoming one of its divisions.

1980: Database publisher Information Access Company (IAC) is acquired.

1981: Ziff completes its first foray into computer magazines, with launch of *PCjr*.

1982: Company acquires *PC Magazine*.

1984: Company sells consumer and business magazines to focus on computer magazines and IAC.

1991: Line of European computer magazines is launched.

1993: Ziff, Jr., retires; Eric Hippeau takes over as chairman.

1994: First consumer computing magazines debut, including *FamilyPC*. Ziff family places the company up for sale; Ziff-Davis Publishing is sold to Forstmann Little & Co., IAC is sold to The Thomson Corporation, and Ziff-Davis Exhibitors is sold to Softbank Corporation; Ziff-Davis Publishing launches online news service ZDNet.

1996: Ziff-Davis Publishing is sold to Softbank.

1998: Softbank takes company public as Ziff-Davis Inc.; ZDTV cable channel is launched.

2000: Ziff-Davis sells its publishing arm to private investors, who rename the unit Ziff Davis Media Inc.

struggles during these years: 1985 saw the company post a loss of $10 million on $100 million in revenue. With his cancer in remission, he returned to full-time leadership of the company in 1987 and oversaw a second application of the Ziff formula for special interest publishing, this time fueling a growth spurt through the computer magazines left out of the 1984 sale. Like the business niche publications so recently sold, the computing publications developed and acquired by Ziff targeted a specific audience needing help with their purchase decisions—buyers of personal computers in the business world. Such magazines as *PC Magazine* and *MacUser* thus focused tightly on product specifications, evaluations, and recommendations from the editors. Using similar market research and advertising techniques honed through the company's decades of innovative magazine publishing, Ziff's line of computer magazines soon began to dominate the industry. By 1991, *PC Magazine* boasted a circulation of more than 800,000, more than $160 million in advertising revenue, and a ranking as the tenth largest U.S. magazine.

There were some failures along the way as well. Contributing to them was the development of significant competitors in the computer magazine industry, notably International Data Group (IDG), publisher of *InfoWorld* and *PC World*, and CMP Publications, publisher of *VAR Business* and *Windows Magazine*. Ziff had acquired *Government Computer News* in 1986

and invested heavily in it, but finally surrendered to IDG and its competitive title when it sold the magazine to Cahners Publishing. Among Ziff's start-ups that failed were *PCjr*—one of the first Ziff computer magazines—and *Corporate Computing*. The latter was launched with great fanfare early in 1992 and positioned as the one magazine for executives needing to make computer purchases. To meet its objective, it had to cover all bases from personal computers to networks to mainframes. At the time, however, the business market was shifting toward personal computers and thus right back to the strength of Ziff's other magazines. Feeling that *Corporate Computing* was beginning to compete with the flagship *PC Magazine*, as well as *PC Week*, the company folded the title just over one year after launch, having invested $10 million in it.

With increasing competition leading to slowing growth in advertising revenue, Ziff Communications reacted with three strategies. First, to lessen reliance on the U.S. market, Ziff launched an ambitious line of European computer magazines early in 1991. The second response was to move beyond the corporate computing world, said by some observers to be maturing, into home computing, which was viewed as the next big growth area. In another combination of organic and acquired growth, the company purchased *Computer Gaming World* and launched two new titles in 1994—*Computer Life* and *FamilyPC*, the latter in a joint venture with Walt Disney Company. The third area was a recommitment to electronic publishing through IAC and the development of online systems.

From the mid-1980s IAC had continued to expand, and by 1992 the company was the leader in full text with more than two million articles culled from more than 1,000 sources. The sheer amount of information offered through the products spun out of its databases began about this time to run up against the limits of CD-ROM technology. One option—almost a stopgap measure—offered to large libraries having large enough mainframes was to mount the database directly on it for patrons to access via the terminals used to access the library's catalog. The longer-term solution that IAC began to implement in 1993 was dubbed InfoTrac Central 2000 and allowed libraries to have their patrons access the IAC databases directly via the Internet.

IAC, whose strength had traditionally rested in the library market, now sought ways to achieve a longstanding goal of lessening the company's dependence on its main market. It formed a new consumer/educational division to target the home market, and it increased its presence in the corporate market through acquisitions. In 1991 it acquired Predicasts Inc., whose databases included *PROMT*—a competitor of IAC's *Trade and Industry Index*. In 1994 IAC acquired Sandpoint, which had developed a software application called Hoover designed to run on Lotus Notes, a groupware application that was becoming increasing popular with corporations. Hoover was an interface like InfoTrac, but a much more powerful one since it allowed a user to access information from many different types of platforms, from CD-ROMs to online systems to broadcast news sources (the name was derived from its being like a vacuum cleaner for information). Users of Hoover would also find a system more flexible in the different ways it allowed users to access information. By 1994, there were 16,000 users of Hoover at 70 companies.

Further electronic publishing initiatives in the early 1990s were highlighted by the development of the Interchange Online Network. The company had successfully tested the online services market over several years with Ziffnet, which was an online extension of its computer magazines offered through such services as CompuServe and Prodigy. Interchange was designed as an online service of its own and promised to be the first one to fully implement a graphical-user interface (GUI). True to Ziff tradition, it was designed to be a special interest service as opposed to the existing general-interest services. The first interest area to be developed was, predictably, computers, but plans were made to develop other areas including sports, health, and personal finance. Interchange would offer more than simply electronic text of magazines, adding such features as discussion groups, product information, and reference sources. As the Internet and the ''information superhighway'' became household names in the early 1990s, Interchange represented Ziff's claim to its piece of the multibillion-dollar digital information market.

1994: Breakup of Ziff Communications

Late in 1993, as revenue for Ziff Communications approached $1 billion, William Ziff, Jr., announced that he was retiring as chairman of the company and would have only an advisory role in the future as chairman emeritus. Eric Hippeau, who had already been in charge of all operations except corporate finance as chairman and CEO of Ziff-Davis Publishing, now assumed full control of Ziff Communications as chairman. That an outsider was placed in charge of what had always been a family-run business was telling to some observers who predicted that the company would either be sold or go public, but such rumors were denied for several months, with Ziff pointing out that two of his sons and one nephew were vice-presidents at the company. Nevertheless, within months, in June 1994, the company announced that it had hired Lazard Freres & Company to handle the sale of the company, seeking $2 billion or more. The decision to sell stemmed from William Ziff's sons' wishes not to make running the company their career. The two brothers who had been vice-presidents at the company, Dirk and Robert, wished to invest the proceeds from the sale in their investment company, Ziff Brothers Investments. The third brother, Daniel, was a college student at this time (he later joined Ziff Brothers Investments).

At the time of the sale, the company was the unquestioned leader in computer magazine publishing and a leading electronic information provider through IAC. In 1994 the company expected a profit of $160 million on $950 million in revenue. Still, some observers thought that William Ziff was again selling out at a time when the company's most prized possessions—the computer publications—were past their peak. Others, however, pointed to numbers showing that the business magazine group (all the U.S. computer magazines except those aimed at consumers) alone was expecting revenues of $505 million and $146 million in operating income in 1994. The figures did show that Ziff's other units were either marginally profitable or losing money, in many cases from heavy investing in new ventures, such as the new consumer magazines and the Interchange system. In the end, these variances in the divisions, perhaps coupled with the enormity of the company, forced the

sellers to accept a piecemeal sale rather than a sale of the whole company as they had hoped for. In October 1994 the New York investment firm of Forstmann Little & Co. purchased Ziff-Davis Publishing Co.—the business and consumer computer magazines, the international magazine group, a market research division, and the Ziffnet online service—for $1.4 billion. Ziff-Davis Exhibitors, a unit that managed computer trade shows, was bought by Softbank Corporation of Japan for $202 million, and The Thomson Corporation, a huge Canadian publisher, purchased Information Access Company for $465 million. Finally, in December 1994 AT&T purchased the Interchange Online Network, at the time still undergoing final testing, for $50 million. All told, the sales exceeded $2.1 billion.

1994–96: The Forstmann Little Interregnum

Ziff-Davis Publishing remained largely intact following its purchase by Forstmann Little, with Hippeau continuing as chairman and the editorial contact remaining unaltered. Revenues for 1994 were an estimated $852 million. Ziff-Davis continued to thrive under its new ownership, with the company producing three of the top four publications in high-tech ad dollars in the first nine months of 1995: *PC Magazine, PC Week,* and *Computer Shopper.* Operating earnings increased to $190 million in 1995 from the $140 million figure of the previous year. Seeking to benefit from the burgeoning Internet, Ziff-Davis in late 1994 launched ZDNet, a web site featuring online versions of a number of Ziff-Davis publications. ZDNet almost immediately faced stiff competition from a competing online news service, CNET. ZDNet, however, was one of the first web sites to make its content free to all users and rely on advertising as its primary revenue stream; it also was a pioneer in e-commerce through its 1996 launch of a web site spinoff of *Computer Shopper* magazine, computershopper.com. In 1995 Ziff-Davis entered into a joint venture with Internet portal Yahoo! Inc. to launch the consumer-oriented *Yahoo! Internet Life,* envisioned as the ''*TV Guide* of the Internet.'' This title faced formidable competition as numerous Internet magazines were hitting the newsstands at this time, but by 1996 its advertising rate base had risen to 200,000.

The Forstmann Little era proved short-lived. Softbank, which had purchased Ziff-Davis Exhibitors after having lost out to Forstmann Little in the bidding for Ziff-Davis Publishing, came forward in late 1995 with an offer that was too rich for Forstmann Little to pass up. The purchase price was $2.1 billion, with the deal, which was completed in February 1996, providing Forstmann Little with a hefty profit on a less-than-18-month investment. Softbank was the leading distributor of computer software in Japan and had augmented its computer trade show unit with the purchase earlier in 1995 of Comdex, the industry's largest. It now also owned the number one U.S. publisher of computer and high-tech magazines.

1996–99: Ownership by Softbank

Under Softbank's ownership, as well as the continued leadership of Hippeau, Ziff-Davis rapidly expanded its publication line, particularly with new overseas titles in Europe and China. By 1998 the company was publishing 26 titles worldwide by itself or through joint ventures. Ziff-Davis also licensed its name or the name of a publication to other companies for more than 50 additional titles. In April 1998 Softbank took the company public under the name Ziff-Davis Inc., selling 26 percent of the common stock through an IPO that raised nearly $400 million. At the same time, Ziff-Davis restructured its debt, resulting in a reduction in its debt load from $2.5 billion to $1.6 billion. Interest payments had led the company to post net losses during both 1996 and 1997.

A public company for the first time in its long and convoluted history, Ziff-Davis Inc. began with three main operations: magazine publishing; tradeshows and conferences, including the former Ziff-Davis Exhibitors and Comdex, which were combined into ZD Events Inc.; and the Internet activities of ZDNet. A fourth segment was added in May 1998, a 24-hour cable television channel called ZDTV, which was launched despite the failures of previous ventures by the company into cable, two computer TV shows. Although Ziff-Davis helped launch ZDTV, it was initially owned by another subsidiary of Softbank. Ziff-Davis then purchased ZDTV in February 1999.

During 1998 Ziff-Davis's magazine operations suffered from a combination of factors that cut into ad revenues: fewer new computer product introductions, computer industry consolidation, and the Asian economic crisis which dampened computer sales in that region. Late in the year the company announced that it would cut its workforce by ten percent, or about 350 employees, and shutter three niche technology publications. A $46 million charge was taken in connection with these moves, leading to another net loss for the year.

While revenue was declining in the publishing sector, ZDNet's sales were on the rise, increasing from $32.2 million in 1997 to $56.1 million in 1998. Like most early Internet ventures, ZDNet was in the red, but its net loss narrowed in 1998 to $7.8 million, compared to $21.2 million the previous year. In April 1999 Ziff-Davis created a tracking stock for ZDNet and sold 16 percent of the unit to the public through an IPO. In the topsy-turvy world of what might be considered the 1999 Internet stock bubble, by mid-1999 ZDNet had a market capitalization greater than that of Ziff-Davis, despite Ziff-Davis's 84 percent stake in ZDNet. Also by this time, Softbank had invested heavily in Internet companies, including such stalwarts as Yahoo! and E*Trade, gaining billions in the process. With Softbank wishing to shift its focus completely to the Internet, Ziff-Davis announced in July 1999 that it was exploring strategic options, including a possible sale of the company.

Turn of the Millennium: Breakup of Ziff-Davis, with Ziff Davis Media Emerging

Eventually, Softbank settled on a plan to retain only ZDNet, and began selling off the other parts of Ziff-Davis piecemeal. In January 2000 ZDTV was sold to Vulcan Ventures, Inc. In April 2000 the magazine unit was sold for $780 million to Willis Stein & Partners, L.P. and James D. Dunning, Jr., a U.S. magazine industry veteran. The ZD Events unit was to be spun off to shareholders as a new company called Key3Media Group, Inc. Then ZDNet would emerge as a stand-alone publicly traded company, in which Softbank would hold about a 45 percent stake. But in July 2000 Ziff-Davis—which in essence at that point consisted only of ZDNet—agreed to be purchased by ZDNet's arch-rival, CNET Networks Inc., for $1.6 billion in stock.

As a result of this maze of transactions it was the publishing unit that emerged as the most direct successor to the publishing company founded more than 70 years earlier by a Ziff and a Davis. Fittingly, the unit's new owners—who were granted the exclusive use of the Ziff Davis name—created a holding company called Ziff Davis Media Inc., with its main subsidiary called Ziff Davis Publishing Inc. Dunning was named chairman, president, and CEO of both Ziff Davis Media and Ziff Davis Publishing. The sale of the publishing unit—which did not include *Computer Shopper,* retained by ZDNet because of its related e-commerce web site—included a licensing agreement with ZDNet, whereby Ziff Davis Media would not be allowed to use the content of its existing magazines on the Internet for a three-year period and would then have to share the content with ZDNet for another two years. In return, Ziff Davis Media would receive a royalty of up to five percent of ZDNet's revenues during the first three years.

Under Dunning's leadership, a more aggressive and savvier strategy quickly became evident at Ziff Davis Media. Titles were revamped and renamed to reflect the increasing importance of the Internet and the so-called New Economy—*PC Computing* became *Ziff Davis SMART BUSINESS for the New Economy* and *PC Week* was redubbed *eWeek*—as well as to deemphasize the somewhat passé term ''PC.'' In June 2000 the company began publication of *The Net Economy* magazine, which was aimed at business and technical managers, Internet service providers, telecommunications firms, cable and wireless service providers, and other companies that provided network-based services. Ziff Davis also began developing new titles in areas outside of technology but with a focus on what was assumed to be the Internet-centered economy of the 21st century. With e-commerce revolutionizing shopping, the company launched *eShopper.* Similarly, Ziff Davis saw the need for a new travel magazine that would inform consumers about how to use the Internet to enhance their travel planning and experiences. The company joined with Expedia, Inc., operator of a leading online travel service, to launch *Expedia Travels* in the fall of 2000, with an initial circulation of 200,000. This title in some ways brought the company full circle, returning it to its travel magazine roots. In addition, Ziff Davis Media had plans for still more launches, having concluded that in the Net-centric world of the 21st century it could develop a new title in nearly every magazine category. Meantime, in July 2000 Ziff Davis Media agreed to sell its publishing subsidiaries in the United Kingdom, France, and Germany, along with the ten titles they produced, to VNU, a Dutch publishing group. The move meant that Ziff Davis Media would directly own only U.S. publications. All international titles, with the exception of those in China, would be produced through licensing arrangements with third parties; the company continued to publish four magazines in China through joint ventures.

Principal Subsidiaries

Ziff Davis Publishing Inc.; Ziff Davis Internet Inc.; Ziff Davis Development Inc.

Principal Competitors

Freedom Technology Media Group; Imagine Media, Inc.; International Data Group; United News & Media plc; Upside Media Inc.

Further Reading

Auerbach, Jon G., and Joseph Pereira, "With PC Ads on Hold, Ziff-Davis Takes a Hit," *Wall Street Journal,* October 9, 1998, p. B1.

Block, Valerie, "Investors Hope to Reboot Ziff-Davis," *Crain's New York Business,* December 13, 1999, p. 3.

Bulkeley, William M., "Ziff-Davis to Explore Its Options, Including a Sale," *Wall Street Journal,* July 15, 1999, p. B4.

Callahan, Sean, "Ziff-Davis Faces Uncertain Future," *Advertising Age's Business Marketing,* August 1999, pp. 2, 50.

Carmody, Deirdre, "Forstmann to Acquire Ziff-Davis," *New York Times,* October 28, 1994, pp. D1–D2.

Churbuck, David C., "Motivated Seller," *Forbes 400,* October 17, 1994, pp. 350–54.

Doan, Amy, "Geek TV," *Forbes,* July 5, 1999, pp. 150–51.

Dugan, I. Jeanne, " 'I Live, Breathe, Sleep Computer,' " *Business Week,* December 1, 1997, p. 126.

Fabrikant, Geraldine, "For a Ziff Sale, Spit and Polish and Good Timing," *New York Times,* September 9, 1994, pp. D1–D2.

——, "For Ziffs, Sale Is a Family Affair," *New York Times,* June 10, 1994, pp. 37, 46.

Furman, Phyllis, "Ziff's Favorite Son," *Crain's New York Business,* August 5, 1996, p. 3.

Garigliano, Jeff, "Ziff-Davis' Intriguing IPO," *Folio,* April 1, 1998, p. 13.

Harvey, Mary, "Is 'PC' Passé?: Defining the New Ziff Davis," *Folio,* May 2000, pp. 15+.

Johnson, Bradley, "Wm. Ziff Retires, but His Company Stays in Family," *Advertising Age,* November 23, 1993, p. 22.

——, "ZDTV Marries Computers, Cable, but Who Will See It?," *Advertising Age,* April 13, 1998, p. S20.

——, "Ziff-Davis Goes Public," *Advertising Age's Business Marketing,* May 1998, pp. 3, 48.

Kleinfield, N.R., "The Big Magazine Auction," *New York Times,* November 16, 1994, pp. D1, D3.

——, "CBS to Buy 12 of Ziff's Magazines," *New York Times,* November 21, 1984, pp. D1, D3. Landler, Mark, "Auctioning Off an Empire," *Business Week,* June 27, 1994, p. 27.

Levison, Andrew, "Ziff-Davis: For Sale," *Online,* September/October 1994, pp. 31–38.

Lipin, Steven, "Persistence Pays Off in Second Sale of Ziff-Davis," *Wall Street Journal,* December 29, 1995, p. C1.

——, "Ziff-Davis Unit of Forstmann Set to Be Sold," *Wall Street Journal,* November 9, 1995, p. A3.

Mangalindan, Mylene, and Jennifer L. Rewick, *Wall Street Journal,* July 20, 2000, p. B14.

Manly, Lorne, "Ziff Re-Boots," *Folio,* April 15, 1995, pp. 36–38, 57.

Palmeri, Christopher, " 'The Idea That Print Is Dead Is Preposterous' " *Forbes,* June 10, 1991, pp. 42–44.

Prior, Teri Lammers, "CMP, IDG, and Ziff-Davis: Can They Still Fly High?," *Upside,* October 1996, pp. 100–02+.

Rose, Matthew, "Ziff-Davis to Sell Its Magazine Unit for $780 Million," *Wall Street Journal,* December 7, 1999, p. B15.

——, "Ziff-Davis to Spin Off Events Business, Merge What Is Left of Firm into ZDNet," *Wall Street Journal,* March 7, 2000, p. B8.

Wayne, Leslie, "Murdoch Buys 12 Ziff Publications," *New York Times,* November 22, 1984, pp. D1, D13.

Weber, Jonathan, "Mogul for a New Age: Bill Ziff's Media Empire Is Built on High Tech—and High Standards," *Los Angeles Times,* October 10, 1993, p. D1.

Weinberg, Neil, and Amy Feldman, "Bubble, Bubble . . .," *Forbes,* March 11, 1996, p. 42.

—updated by **David E. Salamie**

Zodiac S.A.

2 rue Maurice Mallet
92137 lssy-les-Moulineaux
Cedex
France
Telephone: (+33) 1 41 23 23 23
Fax: (+33) 1 46 48 83 87
Web site: http://www.zodiac.fr

Public Company
Incorporated: 1897 as Société Mallet, Mélandri et de
    Pitray
Employees: 6,500
Sales: FFr 5.49 billion (US$891.1 million) (1999)
Stock Exchanges: Paris
Ticker Symbol: ZODFF (OTC)
NAIC: 33641 Aerospace Product and Parts
    Manufacturing; 326199 All Other Plastics Product
    Manufacturing

Zodiac S.A. of France is a world-leading manufacturer of parts and equipment for the aeronautics, airline equipment, and marine-leisure industries. The company's inflatable boats represent more than 40 percent of the worldwide market, a segment the company itself pioneered as early as the 1930s. Through a long list of acquisitions, Zodiac has built itself into a diversified operation with leadership status in such niche product areas as aircraft escape slides, parachute systems, helicopter floats, and flexible fuel tanks (Aeronautics Equipment division); passenger seats and on-board toilets and sanitation systems (Airline Equipment); inflatable boats and rescue rafts, above-ground swimming pools, and related equipment; and inflatable toys (Marine-Leisure). Zodiac's customers include Airbus, Boeing, various departments of defense, and most of the world's civil airlines. The company generates the majority of its sales (64 percent) through the civil aviation sector, including some 28 percent of sales from its aircraft seating operations alone. Zodiac's inflatable boats continue to provide some 13 percent of sales, however, and have made the Zodiac brand name known throughout the boating world. That world has increasingly leaned toward North America, which accounted for 54 percent of Zodiac's sales in 1999. French sales accounted for 17 percent of the company's revenues. The chief architect of Zodiac's growth from a small single-product company in the late 1970s to a diversified manufacturer and distributor with nearly FFr 5.5 billion in annual sales is Chairman and President Jean-Louis Gerondeau. A public company that helped initiate Paris's secondary market in the early 1980s, Zodiac continues to be controlled by its founding families, which hold 30 percent of the company's shares and some 40 percent of voting rights. This position helps to protect the company from the possibility of a hostile takeover.

Aviation Pioneer in the 19th Century

Zodiac was born out of the pioneering efforts of the world's earliest aviators, as the dream of flying became a reality toward the end of the 19th century. Hot-air ballooning, first developed early in the century, remained primarily an adventurer's pastime in France in the late 1870s, when Maurice Mallet took his first balloon flight. Mallet became friends with one of the country's most well-known balloonists, Paul Jovis, and together Mallet and Jovis founded the Union Aéronautique de France to develop new ballooning and aeronautics techniques and equipment. Mallet took over the flying of the association's balloons after Jovis's death in 1891 and became world-renowned when he broke the record for the longest balloon flight, flying from Paris to Walhen, Germany, over three days in 1892.

These and other ballooning triumphs helped spark a surge of popular interest in ballooning at the end of the century, and Mallet and two friends formed the partnership Société Mallet, Mélandri et de Pitray to open a "ballooning park" in Paris's Bois de Boulogne in 1897. The company quickly turned to manufacturing balloons for others and was renamed Ateliers de Constructions Aeronautiques Maurice Mallet to emphasize its new direction in 1899.

Mallet's company grew along with the interest in aviation then sweeping France. While others pursued developments of so-called "heavier-than-air" craft, Mallet continued to research designs in lighter-than-air craft, developing new fabrics and technologies and then turning to the construction of dirigibles as well. For this, Mallet formed a new company, the partnership Société Française des Ballons Dirigeables in 1908.

Mallet introduced the prototype for a new type of foldable, dirigible balloon that was easy to transport and set up. Targeted not simply to private ballooning enthusiasts, but also to the business sector—for use as an advertising medium—Mallet introduced the first Zodiac collapsible balloon in 1909. At the same time, Mallet also put into place an international sales network, through a system of agents located in the United States, Japan, Canada, and the former Austro-Hungarian empire. In that year, Mallet changed his company's name again, now to Société Française des Ballons Dirigeables et d'Aviation Zodiac.

The addition of "Aviation" to the company's name signaled its growing interest in heavier-than-air craft, and in 1909 Mallet built its first biplane, for French aviator Maurice Farman. By the outbreak of World War I, Mallet's original workshops had been transformed into full-fledged manufacturing facilities. The company was called to support the war effort, focusing its attention wholly on balloon and dirigible craft for the French war effort. When balloons proved impractical as bombing craft, Mallet opened a second facility for airplane manufacturing, turning out more than eight airplanes each month by the end of the war.

Yet the end of the war meant the sudden loss in defense contracts, leaving the company in a precarious financial position. The company began to branch out from aeronautics for the first time, adding its first marine products—patrol boats for the French navy—in the 1920s. Meanwhile, the company continued to develop its lighter-than-air craft, introducing a semi-rigid dirigible in 1930.

Soon after, Zodiac's expertise in inflatable fabrics, techniques, and materials led one of its engineers, Pierre Debroutelle, to begin work on developing other types of craft. In 1934, Debroutelle finished a small inflatable kayak. The prototype caught the attention of the French navy, which commissioned Zodiac to build an inflatable boat capable of carrying torpedos and other bombs.

Zodiac's participation in the French war effort sent the company underground during the Nazi occupation of France during World War II. Nonetheless, Debroutelle continued experimenting in secret on his inflatable boat concept using scrap materials.

Meanwhile, the invention of outboard motors during the war years gave new possibilities to Debroutelle's designs. In 1946, Zodiac debuted the first of its U-shaped Zodiac boats.

Postwar Leisure Leader

The appearance of the jet engine during the war years turned public attention away from dirigible craft. Zodiac continued to manufacture balloons and other craft, primarily for advertising uses. To generate revenues, the company diversified into the manufacture of other products, including a line of office furniture and manure spreaders. Although the company continued development of its inflatable boat designs, its sole market for this craft came from the defense industry, which adopted Zodiac's inflatable for life rafts. Doubts about the Zodiac designs' seaworthiness were dispelled by several voyages made by Alain Bombard in the Zodiac Mark III. The company quickly gained the leading position as a supplier of life boats and other rescue craft in France.

The postwar economic boom, and the rise of an entirely new phenomenon—the so-called leisure market—were to transform Zodiac. With both time and money on their hands, French consumers turned toward new leisure activities, and boating became a popular past time. The Zodiac boats quickly captured a leading share of the new market for inflatable leisure craft. The company also gained new recognition when famed sea explorer Jacques Cousteau commissioned the company to build the *Amphritrite*. Meanwhile, the company was branching out into the burgeoning aerospace industry, designing special measuring balloons for the French CNES space research center. The company, which simplified its name to Zodiac S.A. in 1965, also moved to establish itself on the international market, launching the partnership Zodiac Española S.A. in Spain. The company took full control of this subsidiary in 1968, before forming a subsidiary in the United States, in Annapolis, Maryland, two years later. By then, Zodiac had captured the leading position in the inflatables market in France and had taken a place among the world's leading manufacturers of inflatable boats. The company's growing participation in the aerospace industry led to the creation of a dedicated subsidiary, Zodiac Space. Yet the company's primary product remained its leisure boating range.

The downturn of the world economy, following the Oil Embargo of 1973, nearly brought Zodiac to bankruptcy. As the company's focus had increasingly narrowed around its boating products, the company was especially hard hit by the collapse of the leisure market, as consumers weathered a new inflationary period. Recognizing the need to take the company into new directions, Zodiac brought in a new management team, led by Jean-Louis Gerondeau as chairman, in 1973.

Gerondeau initially sought to diversify the company into other sports leisure categories, building on the Zodiac brand name, while protecting itself from the seasonal nature of its core boating market. The company proved unable to find a suitable acquisition target, however, and instead placed its efforts into enhancing its international network. In 1977, the company established a Greek subsidiary, Zodiac Hellas, following that with an implantation in Italy in 1978, through Zodiac Italia, and then Germany, with the opening of its Zodiac Deutschland subsidiary in 1979.

Key Dates:

1879: Maurice Mallet and Paul Jovis establish the Union Aéronautique de France.
1897: Mallet forms the Société Mallet, Mélandri et de Pitray in Paris.
1899: Company is renamed Ateliers de Constructions Aeronautiques Maurice Mallet.
1908: Mallet establishes the Société Française des Ballons Dirigeables; introduces collapsible dirigible.
1909: Company changes name to Société Française des Ballons Dirigeables et d'Aviation Zodiac; builds first biplane.
1930: Company introduces V10 semi-rigid airship.
1934: Prototype for first inflatable boat is developed.
1946: Company introduces U-shaped Zodiac inflatable boat.
1953: Begins manufacturing lifeboats.
1964: Opens first foreign subsidiary, Zodiac Espanola S.A. in Spain.
1965: Company simplifies name to Zodiac S.A.
1970: New subsidiary Zodiac Space is formed; company launches Zodiac of North America.
1973: Jean-Louis Gerondeau takes over as company chairman.
1983: Zodiac is listed on Paris's secondary market.
1991: Company establishes Zodiac Hurricane Technologies Inc.
2000: Zodiac reorganizes aeronautics operations into Zodiac Aerospace.

Diversifying for the 21st Century

That same year brought Zodiac a new opportunity for diversifying its operations. Yet the company's acquisition of Aérazur, which had been a rival dirigible maker between the world wars, took Zodiac away from its sports leisure base. Whereas Zodiac had concentrated on inflatable boats after World War II, Aérazur had turned to the manufacture of aeronautic fabrics. The merger of Aérazur into Zodiac proved more than complementary, since the two companies were able to take advantage of each other's expertise and technology. With Aérazur, Zodiac turned toward the aerospace market—a segment that later accounted for two-thirds of the company's sales.

Zodiac quickly moved to boost its new aeronautics division, acquiring two more French companies—EFA, Bombard-L'Angevinière in 1980, as well as a major share in Sicma, a leading maker of airplane seats. The company also bought up Sevylor, then Europe's leading inflatable products manufacturer, in 1981, adding that company's range of inflatable toys, rafts, and boats. The following year, Zodiac once again strengthened its international presence, opening subsidiaries in Holland and the United Kingdom. By 1983, eager to continue its acquisition drive, Zodiac went public, becoming the first company to receive a listing on the new secondary market (the French version of the OTC) launched by the Paris bourse. In that year the company posted annual sales of FFr 709 million.

By the middle of the 1980s, Zodiac, which had risen to the leading ranks in the French domestic market, was prepared to raise its international profile. The company began a series of foreign acquisitions that were to transform the company from a small French corporation to one of the leaders in its markets—with the bulk of its sales coming from North America. The first step toward this transformation came in 1987, when the company acquired Air Cruisers of Belmar, New Jersey. The following year the company took the still bigger step of acquiring Pioneer Aerospace Corporation, based in South Windsor, Connecticut. Zodiac also had been enhancing its operations in Canada. After establishing its own distribution subsidiary, Zodiac Inflatable Technologies, in Toronto, the company moved to take over all of its Canadian distribution activities, acquiring the formerly independent company Zodiac Marine Ltd. in 1987, before taking majority control of chief Canadian competitor Hurricane Rescue Craft Inc. These three Canadian operations were merged into a new Zodiac subsidiary, Zodiac Hurricane Technologies Inc. in 1991.

The following year, Zodiac's acquisition of Weber Aircraft Inc., with operations in Texas and California producing airplane seating, helped consolidate the company's newest division, that of Airline Equipment, firmly establishing the company's presence in that market. Raising its stake in Sicma Aero Seat to 100 percent that same year also boosted the Airline Equipment division and made the company one of the world's leaders in that sector.

Zodiac's diversification as well as its growth on the international front helped protect it from the crisis that rocked the aerospace industry in the early 1990s. The worldwide recession, the end of the Cold War, shrinking defense budgets, and a collapse of the airline passenger market due to hostilities surrounding the Persian Gulf War had combined to cripple the aerospace industry. The company's sales and profits continued to grow, and by the mid-1990s, when the aerospace sector rebounded, the company showed double-digit growth, reaching annual sales of FFr 3.4 billion and net profits of FFr 201.7 million in 1995.

By then, the company's leisure-marine operations, which received a boost with the acquisition of swimming pool equipment manufacturer Fountainhead Technologies, accounted for only about 40 percent of its sales. Aerospace and airline equipment had reached 68 percent of sales, in time for a new boom in the industry, as passengers once again returned to the skies and airlines returned to enhancing their fleets. In 1998, Zodiac turned its interest to a new area of the airplane, when it acquired MAG Aerospace, a leading maker of toilets and sanitation systems for airplanes. That same year, the company acquired longtime rival Avon Inflatables Ltd., giving the company a commanding position in the United Kingdom's inflatable marine products category.

In the mid-1990s, Zodiac made its first moves to diversify beyond the aerospace and marine markets and into the automobile market. The rising demand for airbag systems for automobiles represented an opportunity for Zodiac, with its longstanding expertise in inflatable products. As such, the company set up its own air bag manufacturing operations under its Aérazur subsidiary. By the end of the decade, Zodiac's air bag operations had already reached sales of more than FFr 350 million.

Zodiac continued to make new acquisitions at the century's close. In 1999, the company acquired Nautive, the leisure life raft division of Germany's Autoflug, further strengthening Zodiac's worldwide leadership position in inflatable boats. Later in 1999, Zodiac added to its aeronautics operations when it acquired France's Intertechnique SA.

The Intertechnique acquisition prompted the company to reorganize its aeronautics operations into the newly named Zodiac Aerospace subsidiary. Formed in June 2000, Zodiac Aerospace was composed of three divisions: Aero Safety Systems; Airline Equipment; and Aircraft Systems. The Intertechnique acquisition helped raise the company's revenues to nearly FFr 5.5 billion and solidified Zodiac's transformation from a pioneer in air transport to one of the 21st century's major aeronautics manufacturers.

Principal Subsidiaries

Aérazur; Air Cruisers Company (U.S.A.); Amfuel (U.S.A.); Avon Inflatables Ltd. (U.K.); Barracuda South Africa; DBC (Canada); Mongram Sanitation (U.S.A.); Muskin Leisure Products Inc. (U.S.A.); Plastriemo; Parachutes de France; Pioneer Aerospace Corporation (U.S.A.); Sevylor International; Sicma Aero Seat; Sicma Aero Seat Services Inc. (U.S.A.); Weber Aircraft Inc. (U.S.A.); Zodiac Espanola SA (Spain); Zodiac Group Australia Pty Ltd.; Zodiac Hurricane Technologies (Canada); Zodiac International; Zodiac Italia; Zodiac-Kern GmbH (Germany); Zodiac Pool Care, Inc.

Principal Competitors

K & F Industries, Inc.; B/E Aerospace, Inc.; Buderus.

Further Reading

Fainsilber, Denis, ''Après le rachat d'Intertechnique, Zodiac prévoit un nouveau bond de ses bénéfices,'' *Les Echos,* March 12, 1999, p. 20.

——, ''Zodiac porté par la reprise des commandes d'avions,'' *Les Echos,* December 16, 1996, p. 11.

Fay, Pierrick, ''Interview: Jean-Louis Gerondeau,'' *Journal des Finances,* October 2, 1999.

Levi, Catherine, ''Jean-Louis Gerondeau: Nos diversifications doivent rester cohérentes,'' *Les Echos,* November 3, 1998, p. 50.

—M. L. Cohen

INDEX TO COMPANIES

Index to Companies

Listings in this index are arranged in alphabetical order under the company name. Company names beginning with a letter or proper name such as Eli Lilly & Co. will be found under the first letter of the company name. Definite articles (The, Le, La) are ignored for alphabetical purposes as are forms of incorporation that precede the company name (AB, NV). Company names printed in bold type have full, historical essays on the page numbers appearing in bold. Updates to entries that appeared in earlier volumes are signified by the notation **(upd.)**. Company names in light type are references within an essay to that company, not full historical essays. This index is cumulative with volume numbers printed in bold type.

533

Chesapeake and Ohio Railroad, **II** 329; **V** 438–40; **10** 43; **13** 372. *See also* CSX Corporation.

Chesapeake Corporation, 8 102–04; 10 540; **25** 44; **30 117–20 (upd.)**

Chesapeake Microwave Technologies, Inc., **32** 41

Chesebrough-Pond's USA, Inc., II 590; **7** 544; **8 105–07; 9** 319; **17** 224–25; **22** 123; **32** 475

Cheshire Wholefoods, **II** 528

Chester Engineers, **10** 412

Chester G. Luby, **I** 183

Chester Oil Co., **IV** 368

Cheung Kong (Holdings) Limited, I 470; **IV 693–95; 18** 252; **20 131–34 (upd.);** **23** 278, 280. *See also* Hutchison Whampoa Ltd.

Chevrolet, **V** 494; **9** 17; **19** 221, 223; **21** 153; **26** 500

Chevron Corporation, II 143; **IV** 367, **385–87**, 452, 464, 466, 479, 484, 490, 523, 531, 536, 539, 563, 721; **9** 391; **10** 119; **12** 20; **17** 121–22; **18** 365, 367; **19** 73, 75, **82–85 (upd.); 25** 444; **29** 385

Chevron U.K. Ltd., **15** 352

Chevy Chase Savings Bank, **13** 439

Chevy's, Inc., **33** 140

Chevy's Mexican Restaurants, **27** 226

ChexSystems, **22** 181

Cheyenne Software, Inc., 12 60–62; 25 348–49

CHF. *See* Chase, Harris, Forbes.

Chi-Chi's Inc., 13 151–53; 14 195; **25** 181

Chiat/Day Inc. Advertising, 9 438; **11 49–52**

Chiba Riverment and Cement, **III** 760

Chibu Electric Power Company, Incorporated, V 571–73

Chic by H.I.S, Inc., 20 135–37

Chicago & Calumet Terminal Railroad, **IV** 368

Chicago and Alton Railroad, **I** 456

Chicago and North Western Holdings Corporation, I 440; **6 376–78**

Chicago and Southern Airlines Inc., **I** 100; **6** 81

Chicago Bears Football Club, Inc., IV 703 **33 95–97**

Chicago Bridge & Iron Company, **7** 74–77

Chicago Burlington and Quincy Railroad, **III** 282; **V** 425–28

Chicago Chemical Co., **I** 373; **12** 346

Chicago Corp., **I** 526

Chicago Cubs, **IV** 682–83

Chicago Cutlery, **16** 234

Chicago Directory Co., **IV** 660–61

Chicago Edison, **IV** 169

Chicago Flexible Shaft Company, **9** 484

Chicago Heater Company, Inc., **8** 135

Chicago Magnet Wire Corp., **13** 397

Chicago Medical Equipment Co., **31** 255

Chicago Motor Club, **10** 126

Chicago Musical Instrument Company, **16** 238

Chicago Pacific Corp., **I** 530; **III** 573; **12** 251; **22** 349; **23** 244; **34** 432

Chicago Pneumatic Tool Co., **III** 427, 452; **7** 480; **21** 502; **26** 41; **28** 40

Chicago Radio Laboratory, **II** 123

Chicago Rawhide Manufacturing Company, **8** 462–63

Chicago Rock Island and Peoria Railway Co., **I** 558

Chicago Rollerskate, **15** 395

Chicago Screw Co., **12** 344

Chicago Shipbuilding Company, **18** 318

Chicago Steel Works, **IV** 113

Chicago Sun-Times Distribution Systems, **6** 14

Chicago Times, **11** 251

Chicago Title and Trust Co., **III** 276; **10** 43–45

Chicago Tribune. *See* Tribune Company.

Chick-fil-A Inc., 23 115–18

Chicken of the Sea International, 24 114–16 (upd.)

Chicopee Manufacturing Corp., **III** 35

Chief Auto Parts, **II** 661; **32** 416

Chieftain Development Company, Ltd., **16** 11

Chiers-Chatillon-Neuves Maisons, **IV** 227

Chilcott Laboratories Inc., **I** 710–11

Child World Inc., **13** 166; **18** 524

Childers Products Co., **21** 108

Children's Book-of-the-Month Club, **13** 105

Children's Palace, **13** 166

Children's Record Guild, **13** 105

Children's Television Workshop, **12** 495; **13** 560; **35** 75

Children's World Learning Centers, **II** 608; **V** 17, 19; **13** 48; **24** 75

Childtime Learning Centers, Inc., 34 103–06

Chiles Offshore Corporation, 9 111–13

Chili's Grill & Bar, **10** 331; **12** 373–74; **19** 258; **20** 159

Chillicothe Co., **IV** 310; **19** 266

Chilton Corp., **III** 440; **25** 239; **27** 361

Chiminter, **III** 48

Chimio, **I** 669–70; **8** 451–52

China Airlines, 6 71; **34 107–10**

China Borneo Co., **III** 698

China Canada Investment and Development Co., **II** 457

China Coast, **10** 322, 324; **16** 156, 158

China Communications System Company, Inc. (Chinacom), **18** 34

China Development Corporation, **16** 4

China Eastern Airlines Co. Ltd., 31 102–04

China Electric, **II** 67

China Foreign Transportation Corporation, **6** 386

China Industries Co., **II** 325

China International Capital Corp., **16** 377

China International Trade and Investment Corporation, **II** 442; **IV** 695; **6** 80; **18** 113, 253; **19** 156; **25** 101; **34** 100. *See also* CITIC Pacific Ltd.

China Light & Power, **6** 499; **23** 278–80

China Mutual Steam Navigation Company Ltd., **6** 416

China National Automotive Industry Import and Export Corp., **III** 581

China National Aviation Corp., **I** 96; **18** 115; **21** 140

China National Cereals, Oils & Foodstuffs Import and Export Corporation, **24** 359

China National Chemicals Import and Export Corp., **IV** 395; **31** 120

China National Heavy Duty Truck Corporation, **21** 274

China National Machinery Import and Export Corporation, **8** 279

China National Petroleum Corp. (SINOPEC), **18** 483

China Navigation Co., **I** 521; **16** 479–80

China Orient Leasing Co., **II** 442

China Resources (Shenyang) Snowflake Brewery Co., **21** 320

China Southern Airlines Company Ltd., 31 102; **33 98–100**

China Zhouyang Fishery Co. Ltd., **II** 578

Chinese Electronics Import and Export Corp., **I** 535

Chinese Metallurgical Import and Export Corp., **IV** 61

Chinese Petroleum Corporation, IV 388–90, 493, 519; **31 105–108 (upd.)**

Chinese Steel Corp., **IV** 184

The Chinet Company, **30** 397

Chino Mines Co., **IV** 179

Chinon Industries, **III** 477; **7** 163

Chipcom, **16** 392

Chippewa Shoe, **19** 232

CHIPS and Technologies, Inc., 6 217; **9 114–17**

Chiquita Brands International, Inc., II 595–96; **III** 28; **7 84–86; 21 110–13 (upd.)**

Chiro Tool Manufacturing Corp., **III** 629

Chiron Corporation, 7 427; **10 213–14; 36 117–20 (upd.)**

Chisso Chemical, **II** 301

Chiswick Products, **II** 566

Chita Oil Co., **IV** 476

Chitaka Foods International, **24** 365

Chivers, **II** 477

Chiyoda Bank, **I** 503; **II** 321

Chiyoda Chemical, **I** 433

Chiyoda Fire and Marine, **III** 404

Chiyoda Kogaku Seiko Kabushiki Kaisha, **III** 574–75

Chiyoda Konpo Kogyo Co. Ltd., **V** 536

Chiyoda Mutual, **II** 374

Chloé Chimie, **I** 303

Chloride S.A., **I** 423

Choay, **I** 676–77

Chock Full o'Nuts Corp., 17 97–100; 20 83

Chocoladefabriken Lindt & Sprüngli AG, 27 102–05; 30 220

Chocolat Ibled S.A., **II** 569

Chocolat-Menier S.A., **II** 569

Chocolat Poulait, **II** 478

Chogoku Kogyo, **II** 325

Choice Hotels International Inc., 6 187, 189; **14 105–07; 25** 309–10; **26** 460

ChoiceCare Corporation, **24** 231

ChoicePoint Services, Inc., **31** 358

Chorlton Metal Co., **I** 531

Chorus Line Corporation, 25 247; **30 121–23**

Chosen Sekiyu, **IV** 554

Chotin Transportation Co., **6** 487

Chouinard Equipment. *See* Lost Arrow Inc.

Chow Tai Fook Jewellery Co., **IV** 717

Chris-Craft Industries, Inc., II 176, 403; **III** 599–600; **9 118–19; 26** 32; **31 109–112 (upd.)**

Christal Radio, **6** 33

Christensen Boyles Corporation, 19 247; **26 68–71**

Christensen Company, **8** 397

Christiaensen, **26** 160

Christian Bourgois, **IV** 614–15

Christian Broadcasting Network, **13** 279

German Cargo Service GmbH., **I** 111
German Mills American Oatmeal Factory, **II** 558; **12** 409
Germania Refining Co., **IV** 488–89
Germplasm Resource Management, **III** 740
Gerrity Oil & Gas Corporation, **11** 28; **24** 379–80
Gervais Danone, **II** 474
GESA. *See* General Europea S.A.
Gesbancaya, **II** 196
Gesellschaft für Chemische Industrie im Basel, **I** 632
Gesellschaft für den Bau von Untergrundbahnen, **I** 410
Gesellschaft für Linde's Eisenmachinen, **I** 581
Gesellschaft für Markt- und Kühlhallen, **I** 581
Gesparal, **III** 47; **8** 342
Gestettner, **II** 159
Gestione Pubblicitaria Editoriale, **IV** 586
GET Manufacturing Inc., **36** 300
Getty Images, Inc., 31 216–18
Getty Oil Co., **II** 448; **IV** 367, 423, 429, 461, 479, 488, 490, 551, 553; **6** 457; **8** 526; **11** 27; **13** 448; **17** 501; **18** 488; **27** 216
Getz Corp., **IV** 137
Geyser Peak Winery, **I** 291
Geysers Geothermal Co., **IV** 84, 523; **7** 188
GFS. *See* Gordon Food Service Inc.
GFS Realty Inc., **II** 633
GHH, **II** 257
GHI, **28** 155, 157
Ghirardelli Chocolate Company, 24 480; **27** 105; **30 218–20**
GI Communications, **10** 321
GI Export Corp. *See* Johnston Industries, Inc.
GIAG, **16** 122
Gianni Versace SpA, 22 238–40
Giant Bicycle Inc., **19** 384
Giant Cement Holding, Inc., 23 224–26
Giant Eagle, Inc., **12** 390–91; **13** 237
Giant Food Inc., II 633–35, 656; **13** 282, 284; **15** 532; **16** 313; **22 241–44 (upd.)**; **24** 462
Giant Industries, Inc., 19 175–77
Giant Resources, **III** 729
Giant Stores, Inc., **7** 113; **25** 124
Giant TC, Inc. *See* Campo Electronics, Appliances & Computers, Inc.
Giant Tire & Rubber Company, **8** 126
Giant Video Corporation, **29** 503
Giant Wholesale, **II** 625
GIB Group, V 63–66; **22** 478; **23** 231; **26 158–62 (upd.)**
Gibbons, Green, van Amerongen Ltd., **II** 605; **9** 94; **12** 28; **19** 360
Gibbs Automatic Molding Co., **III** 569; **20** 360
Gibbs Construction, **25** 404
GIBCO Corp., **I** 321; **17** 287, 289
Gibraltar Casualty Co., **III** 340
Gibraltar Financial Corp., **III** 270–71
Gibson, Dunn & Crutcher LLP, 36 249–52
Gibson Greetings, Inc., 7 24; **12 207–10**; **16** 256; **21** 426–28; **22** 34–35
Gibson Guitar Corp., 16 237–40
Gibson McDonald Furniture Co., **14** 236

GIC. *See* The Goodyear Tire & Rubber Company.
Giddings & Lewis, Inc., 8 545–46; **10 328–30**; **23** 299; **28** 455
Giftmaster Inc., **26** 439–40
Gil-Wel Manufacturing Company, **17** 440
Gilbane, Inc., 34 191–93
Gilbert & John Greenall Limited, **21** 246
Gilbert-Ash Ltd., **I** 588
Gilbert Lane Personnel, Inc., **9** 326
Gilde-Verlag, **IV** 590
Gilde-Versicherung AG, **III** 400
Gildon Metal Enterprises, **7** 96
Gilkey Bros. *See* Puget Sound Tug and Barge Company.
Gill and Duffus, **II** 500
Gill Industries, **II** 161
Gill Interprovincial Lines, **27** 473
Gillett Holdings, Inc., 7 199–201; **11** 543, 545
The Gillette Company, III 27–30, 114, 215; **IV** 722; **8** 59–60; **9** 381, 413; **17** 104–05; **18** 60, 62, 215, 228; **20 249–53 (upd.)**; **23** 54–57; **26** 334; **28** 247
Gilliam Furniture Inc., **12** 475
Gilliam Manufacturing Co., **8** 530
Gilman & Co., **III** 523
Gilman Fanfold Corp., Ltd., **IV** 644
Gilmore Brother's, **I** 707
Gilmore Steel Corporation. *See* Oregon Steel Mills, Inc.
Gilroy Foods, **27** 299
Giltspur, **II** 587
Gimbel Brothers, Inc. *See* Saks Holdings, Inc.
Gimbel's Department Store, **I** 426–27; **8** 59; **22** 72
Gindick Productions, **6** 28
Ginn & Co., **IV** 672; **19** 405
Ginnie Mae. *See* Government National Mortgage Association.
Gino's, **III** 103
Gino's East, **21** 362
Ginsber Beer Group, **15** 47
Giorgio Beverly Hills, Inc., **26** 384
Giorgio, Inc., **III** 16; **19** 28
Girard Bank, **II** 315–16
Girbaud, **17** 513; **31** 261
Girl Scouts of the USA, 35 193–96
Girling, **III** 556
Giro Sport Designs, **16** 53
Girod, **19** 50
Girsa S.A., **23** 170
Girvin, Inc., **16** 297
Gist-Brocades Co., **III** 53; **26** 384
The Gitano Group, Inc., 8 219–21; **20** 136 **25** 167
GJM International Ltd., **25** 121–22
GK Technologies Incorporated, **10** 547
GKH Partners, **29** 295
GKN plc, III 493–96, 554, 556
Glaceries de Saint-Roch, **III** 677; **16** 121
Glaces de Boussois, **II** 474–75
Glacier Bancorp, Inc., 35 197–200
Glacier Park Co., **10** 191
Gladieux Corp., **III** 103
Glamar Group plc, **14** 224
Glamor Shops, Inc., **14** 93
Glasrock Home Health Care, **I** 316; **25** 81
Glass Containers Corp., **I** 609–10
Glass Fibres Ltd., **III** 726
Glasstite, Inc., **33** 360–61
GlasTec, **II** 420
Glatfelter Wood Pulp Company, **8** 413

Glaverbel, **III** 667
Glaxo Holdings plc, I 639–41, 643, 668, 675, 693; **III** 66; **6** 346; **9 263–65 (upd.)**; **10** 551; **11** 173; **20** 39; **26** 31; **34** 284
Gleason Corporation, 24 184–87
Glen & Co, **I** 453
Glen Alden Corp., **15** 247
Glen Cove Mutual Insurance Co., **III** 269
Glen-Gery Corporation, **14** 249
Glen Iris Bricks, **III** 673
Glen Line, **6** 416
Glencairn Ltd., **25** 418
Glendale Federal Savings, **IV** 29
The Glenlyte Group, **29** 469
Glenlyte Thomas Group LLC, **29** 466
Glenn Advertising Agency, **25** 90
Glenn Pleass Holdings Pty. Ltd., **21** 339
Glens Falls Insurance Co., **III** 242
GLF-Eastern States Association, **7** 17
The Glidden Company, I 353; **8 222–24**; **21** 545
Glimcher Co., **26** 262
Glitsch International, Inc., **6** 146; **23** 206, 208
Global Access, **31** 469
Global Apparel Sourcing Ltd., **22** 223
Global Crossing Ltd., 32 216–19
Global Energy Group, **II** 345
Global Engineering Company, **9** 266
Global Information Solutions, **34** 257
Global Interactive Communications Corporation, **28** 242
Global Marine Inc., 9 266–67; **11** 87
Global Natural Resources, **II** 401; **10** 145
Global Telesystems Ltd. *See* Global Crossing Ltd.
Global Transport Organization, **6** 383
GlobalCom Telecommunications, Inc., **24** 122
GlobaLex, **28** 141
Globe & Rutgers Insurance Co., **III** 195–96
Globe Co. **I** 201
Globe Electric Co., **III** 536
Globe Feather & Down, **19** 304
Globe Files Co., **I** 201
Globe Grain and Milling Co., **II** 555
Globe Industries, **I** 540
Globe Insurance Co., **III** 350
Globe Life Insurance Co., **III** 187; **10** 28
Globe National Bank, **II** 261
Globe Newspaper Co., **7** 15
Globe Pequot Press, **36** 339, 341
Globe Petroleum Ltd., **IV** 401
Globe Steel Abrasive Co., **17** 371
Globe Telegraph and Trust Company, **25** 99
Globe-Union, **III** 536; **26** 229
Globe-Wernicke Co., **I** 201
Globetrotter Communications, **7** 199
Globo, **18** 211
Gloria Jean's Gourmet Coffees, **20** 83
La Gloria Oil and Gas Company, **7** 102
Gloria Separator GmbH Berlin, **III** 418
Glosser Brothers, **13** 394
Gloster Aircraft, **I** 50; **III** 508; **24** 85
Gloucester Cold Storage and Warehouse Company, **13** 243
Glovatorium, **III** 152; **6** 266; **30** 339
Glycomed Inc., **13** 241
Glyn, Mills and Co., **II** 308; **12** 422
GM. *See* General Motors Corp.

341–42, 344; **33** 47–48; **34 296–302** **(upd.)**
Motown Records Company L.P., **II** 145; **22** 194; **23** 389, 391; **26 312–14**
Moulinex S.A., **22 362–65**
Mound Metalcraft. *See* Tonka Corporation.
Mount. *See also* Mt.
Mount Hood Credit Life Insurance Agency, **14** 529
Mount Isa Mines, **IV** 61
Mount Vernon Group, **8** 14
Mountain Fuel Supply Company. *See* Questar Corporation.
Mountain Fuel Supply Company, **6** 568–69
Mountain Pass Canning Co., **7** 429
Mountain Safety Research, **18** 445–46
Mountain State Telephone Company, **6** 300
Mountain States Mortgage Centers, Inc., **29 335–37**
Mountain States Power Company. *See* PacifiCorp.
Mountain States Telephone & Telegraph Co., **V** 341; **25** 495
Mountain States Wholesale, **II** 602; **30** 25
Mountain West Bank, **35** 197
Mountleigh PLC, **16** 465
Mounts Wire Industries, **III** 673
Mountsorrel Granite Co., **III** 734
Movado Group, Inc., **28 291–94**
Movado-Zenith-Mondia Holding, **II** 124
Movie Gallery, Inc., **31 339–41**
Movie Star Inc., **17 337–39**
Movies To Go, Inc., **9** 74; **31** 57
Moving Co. Ltd., **V** 127
The Moving Picture Company, **15** 83
The Mowry Co., **23** 102
MPB Corporation, **8** 529, 531
MPM, **III** 735
Mr. Coffee, Inc., **14** 229–31; **15 307–09**; **17** 215; **27** 275
Mr. D's Food Centers, **12** 112
Mr. Donut, **21** 323
Mr. Gasket Inc., **11** 84; **15 310–12**
Mr. Gatti's, **15** 345
Mr. Goodbuys, **13** 545
Mr. How, **V** 191–92
Mr. M Food Stores, **7** 373
Mr. Maintenance, **25** 15
Mr. Payroll Corp., **20** 113
MRC Bearings, **III** 624
MRN Radio Network, **19** 223
Mrs. Baird's Bakeries, **29 338–41**
Mrs. Fields' Original Cookies, Inc., **27 331–35**
Mrs. Paul's Kitchens, **II** 480; **26** 57–58
Mrs. Smith's Frozen Foods, **II** 525; **13** 293–94; **35** 181
MS-Relais GmbH, **III** 710; **7** 302–03
MSAS Cargo International, **6** 415, 417
MSE Corporation, **33** 44
MSI Data Corp., **10** 523; **15** 482
M6. *See* Métropole Télévision.
MSL Industries, **10** 44
MSNBC, **28** 301
MSR. *See* Mountain Safety Research.
MSU. *See* Middle South Utilities.
Mt. *See also* Mount.
Mt. Beacon Insurance Co., **26** 486
Mt. Carmel Public Utility Company, **6** 506
Mt. Goldsworthy Mining Associates, **IV** 47
Mt. Lyell Investments, **III** 672–73
Mt. Summit Rural Telephone Company, **14** 258
Mt. Vernon Iron Works, **II** 14

MTC. *See* Management and Training Corporation.
MTC Pharmaceuticals, **II** 483
MTel. *See* Mobile Telecommunications Technologies Corp.
MTG. *See* Modern Times Group AB.
MTM Entertainment Inc., **13** 279, 281
MTV, **31** 239
MTV Asia, **23** 390
Mueller Co., **III** 645; **28** 485
Mueller Furniture Company, **8** 252
Mueller Industries, Inc., **7 359–61**
Mujirushi Ryohin, **V** 188
Mukluk Freight Lines, **6** 383
Mule Battery Manufacturing Co., **III** 643
Mule-Hide Products Co., **22** 15
Mülheimer Bergwerksverein, **I** 542
Mullen Advertising, **13** 513
Mullens & Co., **14** 419
Multex Systems, **21** 70
Multi Restaurants, **II** 664
Multibank Inc., **11** 281
Multicom Publishing Inc., **11** 294
Multilink, Inc., **27** 364–65
MultiMed, **11** 379
Multimedia, Inc., **IV** 591; **11 330–32**; **30** 217
Multimedia Security Services, Inc., **32** 374
Multiple Access Systems Corp., **III** 109
Multiple Properties, **I** 588
MultiScope Inc., **10** 508
Multitech International. *See* Acer Inc.
Multiview Cable, **24** 121
Münchener Rückversicherungs-Gesellschaft. *See* Munich Re.
Munford, Inc., **17** 499
Mungana Mines, **I** 438
Munich Re, **II** 239; **III** 183–84, 202, **299–301**, 400–01, 747; **35** 34, 37
Municipal Assistance Corp., **II** 448
Munising Paper Co., **III** 40; **13** 156; **16** 303
Munising Woodenware Company, **13** 156
Munksjö, **19** 227
Munksund, **IV** 338
Munsingwear, Inc., **22** 427; **25** 90; **27** 443, 445. *See also* PremiumWear, Inc.
Munson Transportation Inc., **18** 227
Munster and Leinster Bank Ltd., **16** 13
Mura Corporation, **23** 209
Murdock Madaus Schwabe, **26 315–19**, 470
Murfin Inc., **8** 360
Murmic, Inc., **9** 120
Murphey Favre, Inc., **17** 528, 530
Murphy Family Farms Inc., **7** 477; **21** 503; **22 366–68**
Murphy Oil Corporation, **7 362–64**; **32 338–41 (upd.)**
Murphy-Phoenix Company, **14** 122
Murray Bay Paper Co., **IV** 246; **25** 10
Murray Corp. of America, **III** 443
Murray Goulburn Snow, **II** 575
Murray Inc., **19** 383
Murrayfield, **IV** 696
Murtaugh Light & Power Company, **12** 265
Musashino Railway Company, **V** 510
Muscatine Journal, **11** 251
Muscocho Explorations Ltd., **IV** 76
Muse Air Corporation, **6** 120; **24** 454
Music and Video Club, **24** 266, 270
Music-Appreciation Records, **13** 105

Music Corporation of America. *See* MCA Inc.
Music Go Round, **18** 207–09
Music Man, Inc., **16** 202
Music Plus, **9** 75
Musical America Publishing, Inc., **22** 441
Musician's Friend, **29** 221, 223
Musicland Stores Corporation, **9 360–62**; **11** 558; **19** 417
Musitek, **16** 202
Muskegon Gas Company. *See* MCN Corporation.
Musotte & Girard, **I** 553
Mutoh Industries, Ltd., **6** 247; **24** 234
Mutual Benefit Life Insurance Company, **III** 243, **302–04**
Mutual Broadcasting System, **23** 509
Mutual Gaslight Company. *See* MCN Corporation.
Mutual Life Insurance Co. of the State of Wisconsin, **III** 321
Mutual Life Insurance Company of New York, **II** 331; **III** 247, 290, **305–07**, 316, 321, 380
Mutual Medical Aid and Accident Insurance Co., **III** 331
Mutual of Omaha, **III** 365; **25** 89–90; **27** 47
Mutual Oil Co., **IV** 399
Mutual Papers Co., **14** 522
Mutual Safety Insurance Co., **III** 305
Mutual Savings & Loan Association, **III** 215; **18** 60
Mutualité Générale, **III** 210
Mutuelle d'Orléans, **III** 210
Mutuelle de l'Ouest, **III** 211
Mutuelle Vie, **III** 210
Mutuelles Unies, **III** 211
Muzak, Inc., **7 90–91**; **18 353–56**; **35** 19–20
Muzzy-Lyon Company. *See* Federal-Mogul Corporation.
MVC. *See* Music and Video Club.
Mwinilunga Canneries Ltd., **IV** 241
MXL Industries, **13** 367
MY Holdings, **IV** 92
Myanmar Oil and Gas Enterprise, **IV** 519
MYCAL Group, **V** 154
Myco-Sci, Inc. *See* Sylvan, Inc.
Mycogen Corporation, **21 385–87**
Mycrom, **14** 36
Myer Emporium Ltd., **20** 156
Myers Industries, Inc., **19 277–79**
Mygind International, **8** 477
Mylan Laboratories Inc., **I 656–57**; **20 380–82 (upd.)**
Myllykoski Träsliperi AB, **IV** 347–48
Myokenya, **III** 757
Myrna Knitwear, Inc., **16** 231
Myson Group PLC, **III** 671
Mysore State Iron Works, **IV** 205

N.A. Otto & Cie., **III** 541
N.A. Woodworth, **III** 519; **22** 282
N. Boynton & Co., **16** 534
N.C. Cameron & Sons, Ltd., **11** 95
N.C. Monroe Construction Company, **14** 112
N.E.M., **23** 228
N.H. Geotech. *See* New Holland N.V.
N.K. Fairbank Co., **II** 497
N.L. Industries, **19** 212
N M Electronics, **II** 44

INDEX TO INDUSTRIES

Index to Industries

ACCOUNTING

Andersen Worldwide, 29 (upd.)
Deloitte & Touche, 9
Deloitte Touche Tohmatsu International, 29 (upd.)
Ernst & Young, 9; 29 (upd.)
KPMG International, 33 (upd.)
L.S. Starrett Co., 13
McLane Company, Inc., 13
Price Waterhouse, 9
PricewaterhouseCoopers, 29 (upd.)
Robert Wood Johnson Foundation, 35
Univision Communications Inc., 24

ADVERTISING & OTHER BUSINESS SERVICES

A.C. Nielsen Company, 13
ABM Industries Incorporated, 25 (upd.)
Ackerley Communications, Inc., 9
Adecco S.A., 36 (upd.)
Adia S.A., 6
Advo, Inc., 6
Aegis Group plc, 6
AHL Services, Inc., 27
American Building Maintenance Industries, Inc., 6
The American Society of Composers, Authors and Publishers (ASCAP), 29
Analysts International Corporation, 36
Armor Holdings, Inc., 27
Ashtead Group plc, 34
The Associated Press, 13
Barrett Business Services, Inc., 16
Bates Worldwide, Inc., 14; 33 (upd.)
Bearings, Inc., 13
Berlitz International, Inc., 13
Big Flower Press Holdings, Inc., 21
Bozell Worldwide Inc., 25
Bright Horizons Family Solutions, Inc., 31
Broadcast Music Inc., 23
Burns International Security Services, 13
Cambridge Technology Partners, Inc., 36
Campbell-Mithun-Esty, Inc., 16
Carmichael Lynch Inc., 28
Central Parking Corporation, 18
Chiat/Day Inc. Advertising, 11
Christie's International plc, 15
Cintas Corporation, 21
Computer Learning Centers, Inc., 26
CORT Business Services Corporation, 26
Cox Enterprises, Inc., 22 (upd.)
Cyrk Inc., 19
Dale Carnegie Training, Inc., 28
D'Arcy Masius Benton & Bowles, Inc., 6; 32 (upd.)
DDB Needham Worldwide, 14
Deluxe Corporation, 22 (upd.)
Dentsu Inc., I; 16 (upd.)
Deutsche Post AG, 29
Earl Scheib, Inc., 32
EBSCO Industries, Inc., 17
Education Management Corporation, 35
Employee Solutions, Inc., 18
Ennis Business Forms, Inc., 21

Equifax Inc., 6; 28 (upd.)
Equity Marketing, Inc., 26
ERLY Industries Inc., 17
Euro RSCG Worldwide S.A., 13
Fallon McElligott Inc., 22
Fiserv, Inc., 33 (upd.)
FlightSafety International, Inc., 29 (upd.)
Florists' Transworld Delivery, Inc., 28
Foote, Cone & Belding Communications, Inc., I
Gage Marketing Group, 26
Grey Advertising, Inc., 6
Gwathmey Siegel & Associates Architects LLC, 26
Ha-Lo Industries, Inc., 27
Hakuhodo, Inc., 6
Handleman Company, 15
Havas SA, 33 (upd.)
Hays Plc, 27
Heidrick & Struggles International, Inc., 28
Hildebrandt International, 29
Interep National Radio Sales Inc., 35
International Management Group, 18
Interpublic Group Inc., I
The Interpublic Group of Companies, Inc., 22 (upd.)
Iron Mountain, Inc., 33
ITT Educational Services, Inc., 33
J.D. Power and Associates, 32
Japan Leasing Corporation, 8
Jostens, Inc., 25 (upd.)
JWT Group Inc., I
Katz Communications, Inc., 6
Katz Media Group, Inc., 35
Kelly Services Inc., 6; 26 (upd.)
Ketchum Communications Inc., 6
Kinko's Inc., 16
Korn/Ferry International, 34
Labor Ready, Inc., 29
Lamar Advertising Company, 27
Learning Tree International Inc., 24
Leo Burnett Company Inc., I; 20 (upd.)
Lintas: Worldwide, 14
Mail Boxes Etc., 18
Manpower, Inc., 30 (upd.)
marchFIRST, Inc., 34
National Media Corporation, 27
New England Business Services, Inc., 18
New Valley Corporation, 17
NFO Worldwide, Inc., 24
Norrell Corporation, 25
Norwood Promotional Products, Inc., 26
The Ogilvy Group, Inc., I
Olsten Corporation, 6; 29 (upd.)
Omnicom Group, I; 22 (upd.)
On Assignment, Inc., 20
1-800-FLOWERS, Inc., 26
Outdoor Systems, Inc., 25
Paris Corporation, 22
Paychex, Inc., 15
Pierce Leahy Corporation, 24
Pinkerton's Inc., 9
PMT Services, Inc., 24
Publicis S.A., 19
Publishers Clearing House, 23

Randstad Holding n.v., 16
RemedyTemp, Inc., 20
Rental Service Corporation, 28
Robert Half International Inc., 18
Ronco, Inc., 15
Saatchi & Saatchi PLC, I
ServiceMaster Limited Partnership, 6
Shared Medical Systems Corporation, 14
Sir Speedy, Inc., 16
Skidmore, Owings & Merrill, 13
SOS Staffing Services, 25
Sotheby's Holdings, Inc., 11; 29 (upd.)
Spencer Stuart and Associates, Inc., 14
Superior Uniform Group, Inc., 30
Sylvan Learning Systems, Inc., 35
Taylor Nelson Sofres plc, 34
TBWA Advertising, Inc., 6
Thomas Cook Travel Inc., 33 (upd.)
Ticketmaster Corp., 13
TMP Worldwide Inc., 30
TNT Post Group N.V., 30
Towers Perrin, 32
Transmedia Network Inc., 20
Treasure Chest Advertising Company, Inc., 32
TRM Copy Centers Corporation, 18
True North Communications Inc., 23
Tyler Corporation, 23
U.S. Office Products Company, 25
UniFirst Corporation, 21
United News & Media plc, 28 (upd.)
Unitog Co., 19
Vedior NV, 35
The Wackenhut Corporation, 14
Wells Rich Greene BDDP, 6
Westaff Inc., 33
William Morris Agency, Inc., 23
WPP Group plc, 6
Young & Rubicam, Inc., I; 22 (upd.)

AEROSPACE

A.S. Yakovlev Design Bureau, 15
The Aerospatiale Group, 7; 21 (upd.)
Alliant Techsystems Inc., 30 (upd.)
Aviacionny Nauchno-Tehnicheskii Komplek im. A.N. Tupoleva, 24
Avions Marcel Dassault-Breguet Aviation, I
B/E Aerospace, Inc., 30
Banner Aerospace, Inc., 14
Beech Aircraft Corporation, 8
The Boeing Company, I; 10 (upd.); 32 (upd.)
British Aerospace plc, I; 24 (upd.)
Canadair, Inc., 16
Cessna Aircraft Company, 8
Cobham plc, 30
Daimler-Benz Aerospace AG, 16
DeCrane Aircraft Holdings Inc., 36
Ducommun Incorporated, 30
Empresa Brasileira de Aeronáutica S.A. (Embraer), 36
Fairchild Aircraft, Inc., 9
G.I.E. Airbus Industrie, I; 12 (upd.)

ENGINEERING & MANAGEMENT SERVICES

Speedway Motorsports, Inc., 32
Spelling Entertainment Group, Inc., 14
The Sports Club Company, 25
Station Casinos Inc., 25
Stoll-Moss Theatres Ltd., 34
Stuart Entertainment Inc., 16
Tele-Communications, Inc., II
Television Española, S.A., 7
Thomas Cook Travel Inc., 9
The Thomson Corporation, 8
Thousand Trails, Inc., 33
Ticketmaster Corp., 13
The Todd-AO Corporation, 33
Toho Co., Ltd., 28
The Topps Company, Inc., 34 (upd.)
Touristik Union International GmbH. and
   Company K.G., II
Toy Biz, Inc., 18
Trans World Entertainment Corporation, 24
Turner Broadcasting System, Inc., II; 6
   (upd.)
Twentieth Century Fox Film Corporation,
   II; 25 (upd.)
Universal Studios, Inc., 33
Univision Communications Inc., 24
Vail Associates, Inc., 11
Viacom Inc., 7; 23 (upd.)
Walt Disney Company, II; 6 (upd.); 30
   (upd.)
Warner Communications Inc., II
Washington Football, Inc., 35
West Coast Entertainment Corporation, 29
Wherehouse Entertainment Incorporated,
   11
Wildlife Conservation Society, 31
Wilson Sporting Goods Company, 24
Wizards of the Coast Inc., 24
World Wrestling Federation Entertainment,
   Inc., 32
YankeeNets LLC, 35
YES! Entertainment Corporation, 26
YMCA of the USA, 31

FINANCIAL SERVICES: BANKS

Abbey National PLC, 10
Abigail Adams National Bancorp, Inc., 23
Algemene Bank Nederland N.V., II
Allied Irish Banks, plc, 16
American Residential Mortgage
   Corporation, 8
AmSouth Bancorporation, 12
Amsterdam-Rotterdam Bank N.V., II
Anchor Bancorp, Inc., 10
Australia and New Zealand Banking Group
   Ltd., II
Banc One Corporation, 10
Banca Commerciale Italiana SpA, II
Banco Bilbao Vizcaya, S.A., II
Banco Bradesco S.A., 13
Banco Central, II
Banco do Brasil S.A., II
Banco Espírito Santo e Comercial de
   Lisboa S.A., 15
Banco Itaú S.A., 19
Banco Santander Central Hispano S.A., 36
   (upd.)
Bank Austria AG, 23
Bank Brussels Lambert, II
Bank Hapoalim B.M., II
Bank of Boston Corporation, II
Bank of Mississippi, Inc., 14
Bank of Montreal, II
Bank of New England Corporation, II
The Bank of New York Company, Inc., II
The Bank of Nova Scotia, II
Bank of Tokyo, Ltd., II
Bank of Tokyo-Mitsubishi Ltd., 15 (upd.)

Bank One Corporation, 36 (upd.)
BankAmerica Corporation, II; 8 (upd.)
Bankers Trust New York Corporation, II
Banque Nationale de Paris S.A., II
Barclays PLC, II; 20 (upd.)
BarclaysAmerican Mortgage Corporation,
   11
Barings PLC, 14
Barnett Banks, Inc., 9
BayBanks, Inc., 12
Bayerische Hypotheken- und Wechsel-
   Bank AG, II
Bayerische Vereinsbank A.G., II
Beneficial Corporation, 8
BNP Paribas Group, 36 (upd.)
Boatmen's Bancshares Inc., 15
Canadian Imperial Bank of Commerce, II
Carolina First Corporation, 31
Casco Northern Bank, 14
The Chase Manhattan Corporation, II; 13
   (upd.)
Chemical Banking Corporation, II; 14
   (upd.)
Citicorp, II; 9 (upd.)
Citigroup Inc., 30 (upd.)
Commercial Credit Company, 8
Commercial Federal Corporation, 12
Commerzbank A.G., II
Compagnie Financiere de Paribas, II
Continental Bank Corporation, II
CoreStates Financial Corp, 17
Countrywide Credit Industries, Inc., 16
Crédit Agricole, II
Crédit Lyonnais, 9; 33 (upd.)
Crédit National S.A., 9
Credit Suisse Group, II; 21 (upd.)
Credito Italiano, II
Cullen/Frost Bankers, Inc., 25
The Dai-Ichi Kangyo Bank Ltd., II
The Daiwa Bank, Ltd., II
Dauphin Deposit Corporation, 14
Deposit Guaranty Corporation, 17
Deutsche Bank A.G., II; 14 (upd.)
Dime Savings Bank of New York, F.S.B.,
   9
Donaldson, Lufkin & Jenrette, Inc., 22
Dresdner Bank A.G., II
Fifth Third Bancorp, 13; 31 (upd.)
First Bank System Inc., 12
First Chicago Corporation, II
First Commerce Bancshares, Inc., 15
First Commerce Corporation, 11
First Empire State Corporation, 11
First Fidelity Bank, N.A., New Jersey, 9
First Hawaiian, Inc., 11
First Interstate Bancorp, II
First Nationwide Bank, 14
First of America Bank Corporation, 8
First Security Corporation, 11
First Tennessee National Corporation, 11
First Union Corporation, 10
First Virginia Banks, Inc., 11
Firstar Corporation, 11; 33 (upd.)
Fleet Financial Group, Inc., 9
FleetBoston Financial Corporation, 36
   (upd.)
Fourth Financial Corporation, 11
The Fuji Bank, Ltd., II
Generale Bank, II
Glacier Bancorp, Inc., 35
The Governor and Company of the Bank
   of Scotland, 10
Grameen Bank, 31
Great Lakes Bancorp, 8
Great Western Financial Corporation, 10
GreenPoint Financial Corp., 28
Grupo Financiero Serfin, S.A., 19
H.F. Ahmanson & Company, II; 10 (upd.)

Habersham Bancorp, 25
Hancock Holding Company, 15
The Hongkong and Shanghai Banking
   Corporation Limited, II
HSBC Holdings plc, 12; 26 (upd.)
Huntington Bancshares Inc., 11
The Industrial Bank of Japan, Ltd., II
J.P. Morgan & Co. Incorporated, II; 30
   (upd.)
Japan Leasing Corporation, 8
Kansallis-Osake-Pankki, II
KeyCorp, 8
Kredietbank N.V., II
Kreditanstalt für Wiederaufbau, 29
Lloyds Bank PLC, II
Long Island Bancorp, Inc., 16
Long-Term Credit Bank of Japan, Ltd., II
Manufacturers Hanover Corporation, II
MBNA Corporation, 12
Mellon Bank Corporation, II
Mercantile Bankshares Corp., 11
Meridian Bancorp, Inc., 11
Metropolitan Financial Corporation, 13
Michigan National Corporation, 11
Midland Bank PLC, II; 17 (upd.)
The Mitsubishi Bank, Ltd., II
The Mitsubishi Trust & Banking
   Corporation, II
The Mitsui Bank, Ltd., II
The Mitsui Trust & Banking Company,
   Ltd., II
National City Corp., 15
National Westminster Bank PLC, II
NationsBank Corporation, 10
NBD Bancorp, Inc., 11
NCNB Corporation, II
Nippon Credit Bank, II
Norinchukin Bank, II
Northern Rock plc, 33
Northern Trust Company, 9
NVR L.P., 8
Old Kent Financial Corp., 11
Old National Bancorp, 15
PNC Bank Corp., 13 (upd.)
PNC Financial Corporation, II
Pulte Corporation, 8
Rabobank Group, 33
Republic New York Corporation, 11
Riggs National Corporation, 13
The Royal Bank of Canada, II; 21 (upd.)
The Royal Bank of Scotland Group plc, 12
The Ryland Group, Inc., 8
St. Paul Bank for Cooperatives, 8
The Sanwa Bank, Ltd., II; 15 (upd.)
SBC Warburg, 14
Seattle First National Bank Inc., 8
Security Capital Corporation, 17
Security Pacific Corporation, II
Shawmut National Corporation, 13
Signet Banking Corporation, 11
Skandinaviska Enskilda Banken, II
Société Générale, II
Society Corporation, 9
Southtrust Corporation, 11
Standard Chartered PLC, II
Standard Federal Bank, 9
Star Banc Corporation, 11
State Street Boston Corporation, 8
The Sumitomo Bank, Limited, II; 26 (upd.)
The Sumitomo Trust & Banking Company,
   Ltd., II
The Summit Bancorporation, 14
SunTrust Banks Inc., 23
Svenska Handelsbanken, II
Swiss Bank Corporation, II
Synovus Financial Corp., 12
The Taiyo Kobe Bank, Ltd., II
The Tokai Bank, Limited, II; 15 (upd.)

FOOD SERVICES & RETAILERS

HEALTH & PERSONAL CARE PRODUCTS

HEALTH CARE SERVICES

HOTELS

INFORMATION TECHNOLOGY

INSURANCE

LEGAL SERVICES

MATERIALS

MINING & METALS

PUBLISHING & PRINTING

RUBBER & TIRE

WASTE SERVICES

NOTES ON CONTRIBUTORS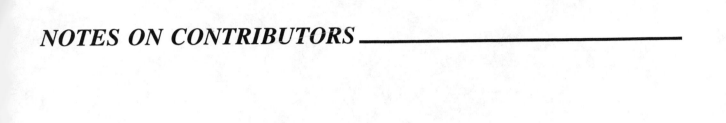

Notes on Contributors

BIANCO, David P. Freelance writer.

BISCONTINI, Tracey Vasil. Pennsylvania-based freelance writer, editor, and columnist.

COHEN, M. L. Novelist and freelance writer living in Paris.

COVELL, Jeffrey L. Freelance writer and corporate history contractor.

FUJINAKA, Mariko. Freelance writer and editor living in Paso Robles, California.

HALASZ, Robert. Former editor in chief of *World Progress* and *Funk & Wagnalls New Encyclopedia Yearbook*; author, *The U.S. Marines* (Millbrook Press, 1993).

INGRAM, Frederick C. South Carolina-based business writer who has contributed to *GSA Business, Appalachian Trailway News,* the *Encyclopedia of Business,* the *Encyclopedia of Global Industries,* the *Encyclopedia of Consumer Brands,* and other regional and trade publications.

JAMES, Owen. Freelance writer.

PEIPPO, Kathleen. Minneapolis-based freelance writer.

RHODES, Nelson. Freelance editor, writer, and consultant in the Chicago area.

ROTHBURD, Carrie. Freelance writer and editor specializing in corporate profiles, academic texts, and academic journal articles.

SALAMIE, David E. Part-owner of InfoWorks Development Group, a reference publication development and editorial services company.

TRADII, Mary. Freelance writer based in Denver, Colorado.

UHLE, Frank. Ann Arbor-based freelance writer; movie projectionist, disc jockey, and staff member of *Psychotronic Video* magazine.

WALDEN, David M. Freelance writer and historian in Salt Lake City; adjunct history instructor at Salt Lake City Community College.

WERNICK, Ellen D. Freelance writer and editor.

WOODWARD, A. Freelance writer.